D1114938

Theory and Practice in Clinical Social Work

Edited by

Jerrold R. Brandell, Ph.D.

THE FREE PRESS

New York London Toronto Sydney Singapore

THE FREE PRESS
A Division of Simon & Schuster Inc.
1230 Avenue of the Americas
New York, NY 10020

Designed by Carla Bolte

Manufactured in the United States of America

10 9 8 7 6 5 4

Library of Congress Cataloging-in-Publication Data
Theory and practice in clinical social work/edited by Jerrold R.
Brandell.
p. cm.
Includes bibliographical references and index.
1. Psychiatric social work. 2. Social case work. I. Brandell,
Jerrold R.
HV689.T48 1997
362.2′0425—dc20 96-43919
CIP

ISBN 0-684-82765-4

This book is dedicated to three gifted teachers of clinical practice

ERIKA FROMM, PHD

JOSEPH G. KEPECS, MD

DEAN SCHNECK, MSSW

Contributors

Maryann Amodeo, MSW, PhD, is director of the Alcohol and Drug Institute for Policy, Training and Research and associate professor, Boston University School of Social Work, Boston.

Steven Barlam, MSW, LCSW, is the director of Senior Care Management, Beverly Hills, California.

Roxanne Barzone, MSW, ACSW, is a lecturer and faculty field instructor, Wayne State University School of Social Work, and the project coordinator of the Wayne State University Collaborative Project between Social Work and Education, Detroit.

Jerrold R. Brandell, PhD, BCD, is associate professor and chairperson of the Graduate Concentration in Mental Health, Wayne State University School of Social Work, Detroit, and maintains a part-time clinical practice in the Ann Arbor area.

Margaret O'Kane Brunhofer, PhD, BCD, is a lecturer at the Wayne State University School of Social Work, Detroit, and maintains a clinical practice in Birmingham, Michigan.

Kay Martel Connors, MSW, LCSW-C, is senior clinician, group clinic coordinator, at the Kennedy Krieger Family Center, Baltimore.

Carlton Cornett, LCSW, is engaged in the full-time private practice of clinical social work in Nashville, Tennessee.

Margaret G. Frank, MSSW, BCD, is coordinator, Postgraduate Certificate Program in Advanced Child and Adolescent Psychotherapy, Boston University School of Social Work, and maintains a private practice in in psychoanalysis and psychoanalytic psychotherapy in Newton, Massachusetts.

Bruce D. Friedman, PhD, ACSW, is an associate professor and BSW program coordinator at the Wayne State University School of Social Work, Detroit.

Charles D. Garvin, AM, PhD, is professor of social work, University of Michigan, Ann Arbor, Michigan.

Eda G. Goldstein, DSW, is professor and chairperson of the Social Work Practice Curriculum Area, New York University Shirley M. Ehrenkranz School of Social Work, and maintains a private practice in New York City.

Donald K. Granvold, PhD, is professor of social work, University of Texas at Arlington, and maintains a private clinical practice in individual, couples, and marital treatment.

Roberta Graziano, DSW, is associate professor, Hunter College School of Social Work, and maintains a private practice in New York City.

Sidney H. Grossberg, PhD, MSW, BCD, is executive director of Counseling Associates, Southfield, Michigan, and also maintains a private clinical social work practice.

Karen Kayser, MSW, PhD, is an associate professor, Graduate School of Social Work, Boston College, Chestnut Hill, Massachusetts.

Louise R. Kerlin, ACSW, is an adjunct faculty member, Wayne State University School of Social Work, and clinical social worker in full-time practice in the Detroit area.

Judith Mishne, DSW, is professor, PhD program coordinator of the Specialization in Children and Adolescents, and coordinator of the Advanced Certificate Post Master's Program, New York University Shirley M. Ehrenkranz School of Social Work, and maintains a private practice in New York City.

David P. Moxley, PhD, is associate professor, Wayne State University School of Social Work, Detroit.

Laura L. Myers, MSW, is a doctoral candidate in social work at the University of Georgia and is employed as a social worker and evaluation research consultant at Athens Family Counseling Center, Athens, Georgia.

Fredric Perlman, PhD, a faculty member at IPTAR (Institute for Psychoanalytic Training and Research), maintains a private practice of psychoanalytic psychotherapy and psychoanalysis in New York City, and is a member of the International Psychoanalytic Association.

Ramona Rukstele, ACSW, BCD, is a clinical social worker in the Departments of Psychiatry and Obstetrics/Gynaecology, Sinai Hospital (Detroit, Michigan), and adjunct faculty member in the Wayne State University School of Social Work, Detroit.

Gerald Schamess, MSS, LICSW, is professor, Smith College School for Social Work, Northampton, Massachusetts.

Roberta Ann Shechter, DSW, BCD, is an adjunct faculty member of the New York University Shirley M. Ehrenkranz School of Social Work and at the Hunter College

School of Social Work, City University of New York, and engaged in the private practice of psychoanalytic psychotherapy and psychoanalysis in New York City.

Harriet Hailparn Soares, MSW, LCSW, is a clinical social worker and consultant at Senior Care Management, Beverly Hills, California.

Lenora Stanfield, MSW, MPH, is an adjunct faculty member, Wayne State University School of Social Work, and maintains a private practice in Detroit.

Frederick H. Strieder, PhD, is director, Treatment Program, Kennedy Krieger Family Center, Baltimore.

Bruce A. Thyer, PhD, LCSW, is professor of social work and adjunct professor of Psychology (Clinical) at the University of Georgia, and associate clinical professor of psychiatry and health behavior at the Medical College of Georgia, Augusta, Georgia.

Phyllis I. Vroom, PhD, is associate professor and associate Dean, Wayne State University School of Social Work, Detroit, and project director, Wayne State University Collaborative Project between Social Work and Education.

Froma Walsh, MSW, PhD, is professor, School of Social Service Administration and Department of Psychiatry, the University of Chicago, and codirector of the university-affiliated Center for Family Health, Chicago.

Barbara Halin Willinger, CSW, BCD, is a clinical social work supervisor at St. Luke's/Roosevelt Hospital Center (New York), and maintains a private practice in New York City.

Contents

Foreword

Although it is now over twenty-five years since the founding of the National Federation of Societies for Clinical Social Work, the practice of clinical social work, vigorous and creative, remains difficult to define. Is it psychotherapy, and, if so, is it any different from the treatment practiced by other mental health professionals such as psychiatrists and psychologists? Or is clinical social work a unique form of therapeutic intervention buttressed by traditional social work values? Is clinical social work, with its concern for the client's social functioning, more involved than are other disciplines with social contexts, environmental deficits, and societal dysfunctions?

Clinical social work has meant and still means many things to many different people. It has been argued that clinical social work has no *unique* function and therefore can have no *unique* operational definition. Yet it has to be separated from other fields and occupations, if for no other reason, by its discrete reality.

Almost every time clinical social work is distinguished from other perspectives and dissected, theoreticians and practitioners end up acknowledging that not only does it seem to defy a definition with which most of us can agree, but its major concepts, constructs, and hypotheses also seem difficult to define and locate. In the 1200-page *Handbook of Clinical Social Work* edited by Diana Waldfogel and Aaron Rosenblatt in the early 1980s, the editors concluded that the definition of clinical social work "is still unresolved."

There are many reasons why clinical social work is not easy to define. Most of its theoretical underpinnings are borrowed from other disciplines; consequently, it is most difficult to assert what belongs exclusively within its scope. Clinical social workers also serve more clients and work in more diverse settings than do any other mental health professionals. Thus their responsibilities and job functions are extremely diverse, and what they have in common is difficult to discern. The fields of practice in clinical social work (addictions, mental health, and school social work, to name but a few) are so numerous that at times it appears overwhelming simply to list them, let alone ascertain how they relate to each other. In addition, there are many factions and conflicting ideologies in clinical social work; when proponents discuss their respective points of view, often more heat than light is generated.

For those of us in clinical social work who seek a clearer focus in our activities and wish to have more theoretical underpinnings as we help our clients, Dr. Jerrold Brandell has made a splendid contribution. In convening many of the field's best, bravest, and most knowledgeable writers, Brandell has achieved much of significance. First, he and his colleagues have moved us a long way in determining just what clinical social work is. As we travel from chapter to chapter, we begin to realize that clinical social workers are *always* socially conscious mental health professionals who amass whatever skills and concepts are necessary to genuinely enhance the well-being of an individual, family, group, or community suffering from psychosocial distress. Second, as we examine the diverse aspects of practice, we note that clinical social workers, more than any other professional group, are almost always at the forefront of diagnostic thinking and therapeutic skills. Third, recognizing always that individuals can never be isolated from their social milieus if they are going to be helped to feel and function at maturer levels, Brandell and his colleagues demonstrate when and how to intervene in the social environment, as well as what may make this form of intervention contraindicated. Finally, this book demonstrates selectively and with precision which theoretical concepts may be well utilized for specific clients and for specific fields of practice.

Brandell and his collaborators have provided another valuable service for us by producing this book. They have helped to make us feel much prouder to be clinical social workers. Over the years, many of us have at times felt apologetic when we introduced ourselves to colleagues and friends in other mental health disciplines. In reading *Theory and Practice in Clinical Social Work*, one notes over and over that as clinical social workers not only do we bring the finest in clinical understanding and clinical intervention as we work with children, teenagers, adults, and the aged, but we have now established a solid research base to undergird our practices. We can move from one treatment modality to another with genuine expertise. The clinical social worker not only works well with individuals but he or she is equally at home with marital treatment, family therapy, group therapy, and more.

I am confident that *Theory and Practice in Clinical Social Work* will be utilized as a constant reference by social work students at all levels, by both inexperienced and seasoned practitioners, and by supervisors, educators, and administrators. In addition, many members of other mental health professions will be able to enrich their therapeutic role-sets as they journey with Dr. Brandell and his able colleagues.

HERBERT S. STREAN, DSW

Distinguished Professor Emeritus, Rutgers University
Director Emeritus, New York Center for Psychoanalytic Training

Acknowledgments

A number of people provided much-appreciated assistance and support during the preparation of this book. I am grateful to Susan Arellano, senior editor at the Free Press, through whose encouragement and guidance this project was initially conceived; to my editor, Philip Rappaport, for his expert help in bringing it to fruition; and to Loretta Denner, my production editor, for her professionalism and meticulous attention to detail. I thank Dean Leon W. Chestang of the Wayne State University School of Social Work for his generosity and support. I am indebted to a number of colleagues at my school and wish to make special mention of those who participated in the discussion group on advanced clinical social work theory and practice during the 1994–95 academic year: Peggy Brunhofer, Bruce Friedman, Louise Kerlin, David Moxley, Mel Raider, Ramona Rukstele, Phyllis Vroom, and Bob Wills. I thank my secretaries, Kathy Clevenger and Giselle Smith, for their professional competence and responsiveness, particularly as deadlines approached. My good friend and associate, Roberta Shechter, showed unwavering interest and lent expert counsel, and Rick Perlman offered penetrating insight and enthusiastic participation. Finally, I owe a great debt to my wife, Esther, and to my children, Andrea and Joe, whose love and tolerance throughout the duration of this project place them in a very special category.

Introduction

In 1922 Mary Richmond, a pioneer in the charity organization movement, first identified the dual focus on person and environment as the defining characteristic of social casework. The person-in-environment configuration has proved to be an especially durable framework and arguably remains as distinctive a feature of clinical social work practice today as it was for social casework seventy-five years ago. It emphasizes the need to understand clients as operating within multiple environmental milieux or systems that both influence their behavior and reactions and are reciprocally influenced by them.

Recent definitions of clinical social work have continued to emphasize the transactions between person and environment, although interest has gradually shifted to the provision of specific clinical services. The National Federation of Societies for Clinical Social Work proposed the following definition for clinical social work in 1977:*

> Clinical social work integrates significant social work concepts with knowledge of human behavior and needs within an environmental context. The clinical social worker is a health care provider for individuals alone, in families and in groups where there are problems in biopsychosocial functioning. The objectives of the clinical social worker are both preventive and remedial and the methods used are varied, including any combination of clinical psychotherapy, group psychotherapy, family therapy, and concrete services and interventions on behalf of clients with social systems and the environment. (Pinkus et al., 1977, p. 255)

More recently, several influential social work professional organizations (the boards of the National Association of Social Workers and the National Registry of Health Care Providers, and the American Board of Examiners in Clinical Social Work) achieved consensus around the following definition:

---

*For a more detailed discussion of the evolution of the term *clinical social work* and the controversies surrounding its use, see Waldfogel and Rosenblatt, 1983; Dorfman, 1988; and Northen, 1995.

> Clinical social work practice is the professional application of social work theory and methods to the treatment and prevention of psychosocial dysfunction, disability, or impairment, including emotional and mental disorders. It is based on knowledge and theory of psychosocial development, behavior, psychopathology, unconscious motivation, interpersonal relations, environmental stress, social systems, and cultural diversity with particular attention to person-in-environment. It shares with all social work practice the goal of enhancement and maintenance of psychosocial functioning of individuals, families, and small groups.
>
> Clinical social work encompasses interventions directed to interpersonal interactions, intrapsychic dynamics, and life-support and management issues. It includes but is not limited to individual, marital, family and group psychotherapy. Clinical social work services consist of assessment; diagnosis; treatment, including psychotherapy and counseling; client-centered advocacy; consultation; and evaluation. (NASW, 1989)

The contemporary practice of clinical social work, while preserving the historical emphasis on person-in-environment (as the foregoing definitions suggest), has been transformed by an ever-widening clinical domain and by substantially altered contexts for practice. A hallmark of contemporary clinical social work practice is the nature and scope of the social problems that clinicians must confront, which vary in perhaps all other respects with the possible exception of their severity and complexity. The understanding and treatment of posttraumatic stress, violence in homes and in communities, chronic mental disorders, alcoholism and substance abuse, and the psychosocial sequelae of life-threatening illness are just a few of the daunting clinical challenges that social workers face in today's practice landscape. The settings or practice contexts have also changed. Clinical social workers today are as likely to find themselves providing time-sensitive therapy in health maintenance organizations as they are supportive casework in traditional family service agencies; those who several generations ago might have worked with psychotic children in long-term child psychiatric facilities may instead be employed in elementary and middle schools, leading children's groups for trauma survivors; and increasing numbers of social workers who are attracted by the prospect of autonomous practice are pursuing part-time or full-time careers in the private practice of clinical social work.

Clinical social work practice has been shaped by a number of significant, if not transformative, changes in society. Some have held responsible such influences as the erosion of the traditional nuclear family, the pervasive presence of violence, and the insidious ubiquity of alcohol and drugs, which they believe have combined to magnify existing social issues and create new ones. Others identify changing patterns of child care, the overall contraction of leisure time, the invasive impact of technologies, inter alia, as salient factors. The psychological, social, and economic sequelae of racism, ageism, sexism, and other forms of discrimination and oppression against vulnerable individuals, groups, or communities must be considered as well. While there is no question of the value of such discussions for social workers, clinical or otherwise, they are for the most part beyond the scope of a clinical anthology such as this one.

It is, of course, true that good clinical practice has always required the provision of a spectrum of psychosocial, psychotherapeutic, psychoeducational, and developmental services to individuals, couples, families, and small groups. Likewise, social work clinicians have always been expected to develop competencies in diagnosis, direct intervention, and preventive services and to be able to identify and treat a variety of biopsychosocial dysfunctions (including, but not limited to, individual intrapsychic conflicts, interpersonal issues, environmentally generated stressors, mental and emotional disorders, and developmental challenges). What makes today's practice climate unique, however, is a combination of need for increasingly specialized substantive knowledge of specific clinical issues and their treatment, and the appearance of both government and agency mandates for documenting treatment outcomes and effectiveness, often in the face of scarce resources. Furthermore, the reality of clinical practice in a service delivery system that is increasingly guided by the philosophy of managed care can all too easily translate into a strategy of accommodation for the social work clinician.

The principal objective of this collection is to provide the advanced clinical social work student and beginning-level postgraduate clinician with a guide to the contemporary practice of clinical social work: to the theories that inform practice, the treatment modalities themselves, and selected clinical themes and issues. Accordingly, the book is organized into three parts, addressing: frameworks for clinical practice, specific treatment modalities, and specialized clinical issues, themes, and dilemmas. The contributors are clinical scholars and master practitioners from across the United States who are well known in their respective fields of expertise. They represent a variety of clinical orientations and specializations. Some identify with the cognitive-behavioral end of the clinical spectrum, others adhere to a family systems or a contemporary psychoanalytic approach, and still others consider themselves eclectic in orientation. Collectively, these authors have treated nearly every conceivable clinical population, in virtually every practice context, using the entire spectrum of treatment modalities. Such diversity is of obvious importance, for it accurately reflects the state of clinical social work practice in the United States.

The process of selecting which particular theoretical frameworks, therapeutic modalities, and specialized practice issues to include was a particularly difficult task. Although we believe that this book faithfully mirrors the world of contemporary social work practice, it is not, nor was it ever intended to be, encyclopedic in scope. It is a guide, a handbook for clinicians, but should by no means be considered an exhaustive or comprehensive collection. More specifically, the decision to focus on those theoretical frameworks and clinical issues that comprise the first and third parts of the book, respectively, was based on current trends and the collective judgment of a number of the contributors. Unquestionably, other theoretical frameworks exist, as do a variety of clinical issues and themes that have not been addressed. Again, although there was perhaps a subjective component in the process of determining exactly what to include, we believe that this was minimized by adhering to a criterion of general relevance.

It may be useful to explain why it is that this collection is entitled "Theory and Practice *in* Clinical Social Work" rather than "*The* Theory and Practice *of* Clinical

Social Work." Although the difference may ostensibly be a minor one, this is somewhat misleading. In fact, clinical social work does not have a unified theory, nor does it conform to a particular model of practice. Clinical social work draws from a number of theories and models of practice, and for many, this represents the discipline's greatest strength. This book is a guide for the understanding and integration of this rich and diverse framework of clinical theories and practice models, and the particular ways in which this knowledge may be applied.

REFERENCES

Dorfman, R. (Ed.). (1988). *Paradigms of clinical social work.* New York: Brunner/Mazel.

National Association of Social Workers. (1989). *NASW standards for the practice of clinical social work.* Washington, DC: NASW Press.

Northen, H. (1995). *Clinical social work knowledge and skills.* New York: Columbia University Press.

Pinkus, H., et al. (1977). Education for the practice of clinical social work at the master's level: A position paper. *Clinical Social Work Journal,* 5, 251–268.

Richmond, M. (1922). *What is social casework?* New York: Russell Sage.

Waldfogel, D., & Rosenblatt, A. (Eds.). (1983). *Handbook of clinical social work.* San Francisco: Jossey-Bass.

Part I

Frameworks for Clinical Practice

1

Systems Theory

Bruce D. Friedman

Because of the complex nature of the clinical enterprise, a number of social work theorists have worked assiduously to develop explanatory models for clinical practice. One such model is the ecosystems perspective, more usefully understood as a perspective or a paradigm rather than a theory because it provides a framework for organizing other theories to explain events. With its roots in Bertalanffy's systems theory and Bronfenbrenner's ecological environment, the ecosystems perspective provides a framework that permits users to draw on theories from different disciplines to analyze the complex nature of human interactions.

SYSTEMS THEORY

Ludwig von Bertalanffy (1901–1972) is credited with being the originator of systems theory. Bertalanffy, a theoretical biologist born and educated in Austria, became dissatisfied with the way that linear, cause-and-effect theories explained growth and change in living organisms. He felt that change might occur because of the interactions between the parts of the organism, a point of view that represented a dramatic change from the theories of his day. Existing theories had tended to be reductionistic, understanding the whole by breaking it into parts. Bertalanffy's introduction of systems theory changed that framework to look at the system as a whole with its relationships and interactions with other systems as a mechanism of growth and change. This changed the way people looked at systems and led to a new language, popularizing terms such as *open and closed systems, entropy, boundary, homeostasis, inputs, outputs,* and *feedback.*

General systems theory is likened to a science of wholeness. Bertalanffy (1968) advocated for "an organismic conception in biology that emphasized consideration of the organism as a whole or a system" (p. 12). He saw the main objective of the biological sciences as the discovery of organizational properties that could be applied to organisms at various levels for analysis. This led to the basic assumption that "the whole is more than the sum of its parts" (Bertalanffy, 1968, p. 18). Bertalanffy's approach is derived from a basic concept that relies heavily on linear-based, cause-and-effect properties to explain growth and change in living organisms. There are two conditions on which these properties depend: that an interaction occurs between parts and that the condition describing the relationship between the parts is linear. When these two conditions are present, Bertalanffy felt that the interaction was measurable and was subject to scientific inquiry.

In order to measure the interaction, Bertalanffy applied basic scientific principles to various types of organisms that explain and measure behavior. It is important to understand that Bertalanffy's original conception of systems theory was one of organization. He saw it as a method of organizing the interaction between component parts of a larger organism. Since it was a way of organizing information rather than explaining observations, it was easily adaptable to many different scientific fields, including psychology, psychiatry, sociology, and social work. The important distinction among the various fields adopting these principles was how they used other theories to explain the interaction within the organism. Thus, systems theory is an organizational theory that looks at interactions between systems: how a field defines the system determines the nature of the interaction.

In clinical social work, the most elemental social unit is the person. The interaction between social units creates a social organization, which is defined as "any social entity comprised of two or more persons/social units who share purpose, who show functionally interdependent and reciprocal relationships, and where the social organization itself has functional and reciprocal relationships with its social environment" (Chess & Norlin, 1991, p. 31). The social organization can then be defined as a social group, family, formal organization, or community. The functional properties are the same in all of these contexts. All are entities of two or more units having some type of functional and reciprocal relationship within the social environment; thus, systems are interactional. To understand more fully the interactional properties of systems theory, it may be useful to define certain concepts Bertalanffy used.

SYSTEMS TERMINOLOGY IN RELATIONSHIP TO SOCIAL WORK PRACTICE

Bertalanffy believed that all things, living and nonliving, could be regarded as systems and that systems have properties that are capable of being studied.

Each system is a unit of wholeness that has a distinct property or structural limitation that delineates it from other systems, a property he termed the system's *boundary.* The boundary is what makes each system unique and gives it definition.

Some boundaries are clearly defined; others may be permeable. In defining a person as a system, one may literally identify the person's skin as the boundary. Access to the person beyond the boundary is through various forms of communication, the five sensory modalities, or through microorganisms that find ways of permeating the outer shell, or skin, of the person. However, the structure of the person is clearly defined by her or his physical being.

Social organizations also have boundaries, which may be defined by different norms. For example, a family is a system that defines its boundaries through sociological and legal definitions; groups are social organizations that define their boundary through group membership; communities are social organizations that define their boundaries through either geographic definitions of community or an ethnic boundary definition, as in ethnic communities. Through this process, it is possible to see that each system has a characteristic boundary and way of defining itself.

Systems grow through an exchange of energy between the system and its environment, a process that is possible only if the boundary possesses permeability. The amount of information or energy that is permitted to pass through a given system's boundary determines the permeability of that boundary. The more permeable the boundary, the greater the extent of interaction that the system has with its environment, leading to greater openness.

Bertalanffy differentiated between open and closed systems, observing that "living organisms are essentially *open systems*" (1968, p. 32). An open system, unlike a closed system, exchanges matter with its environment; *closed systems* "are isolated from their environment" (ibid., p. 39). An example of a closed system that may serve adaptive purposes could be an ethnic minority community that limits access to the majority cultural institutions due to active discrimination directed against its members.

Recognizing that system growth derives from the ability of the system to import energy or system inputs from other systems, openness is a critical quality for system functioning, and possibly even survival. However, there are other times when systems do close as a perceived means of protecting the system. In these instances the system is exporting (system outputs) more energy than it is able to import. Since systems rely on a flow of energy, with outputs relying on fresh inputs, too much exporting can lead to a state of disorder, referred to as *entropy*. When the system is importing more than it is exporting, it is termed *negative entropy* or *negentropy*, a state of system growth.

The exchange of information between the system and its environment is regulated by a process called *feedback*, a method of evaluation used to determine whether the system's outputs are consonant with the perceived *outcomes* (goals) that the system has established for itself. In addition to this internal feedback, the system also has a method of measuring responses from the external environment. In both situations, if the system perceives a variance between output and outcome, it can alter the process by varying the level of inputs.

This modifying of levels of inputs and outputs is the form of control that all systems have in their interactions with their environment. In social work terms, an open system would generally (though not invariably) be considered a functional system, while a closed system would be classified as dysfunctional. A functional system interacts dynamically with the larger environment, a need that supports the survival of the system. Because there is a cause-and-effect relationship between the system and the environment, both are constantly changing in consequence of this interaction, so that the open nature of the system is one of constant change. Change does not always relate to disorder. Bertalanffy felt that if a system was working properly, it would achieve a form of dynamic equilibrium with the environment that he called *steady state.* Steady state is achieved through a process of ordering and growth that Bertalanffy referred to as *negative entropy* (Chess & Norlin, 1991).

The concept of steady state is a little misleading; *steady* here means not "constant" but a sense of balance between the system and the larger social environment (Anderson & Carter, 1990). To put it slightly differently, the ability of the system to adapt to its environment through changes in its structure leads to states of *equilibrium* and *homeostasis,* both of which relate to differing types of balance. Equilibrium is the sense of being in balance. When something is in balance, there is little variability in movement before the state of balance is disrupted. On the other hand, homeostasis is a state of variable balance where the limits to maintain balance are more flexible (Anderson & Carter, 1990). These limits are determined by the system and may be likened to the idea of something bending without breaking.

ECOLOGICAL ENVIRONMENT

The concept of ecological environment is credited to Uri Bronfenbrenner (1917–). Bronfenbrenner grew up in a state institution for the "feebleminded," where his father was the neuropathologist. Prior to any formal teaching in psychology, Bronfenbrenner lived on three thousand acres where the patients spent their time working on the farm or in the shops of the institution. Through these early life experiences, combined with his extensive study of the work of theorists such as Kurt Lewin, Bronfenbrenner developed a strong belief in the resilient nature of human beings. He regarded this resiliency as embedded in a cultural context that helped to form and shape the individual.

Bertalanffy's model assumed a linear cause-and-effect relationship between social units within the system. Bronfenbrenner, however, had some difficulty with the linear relationship and felt that systems theory did not fully capture the complex dynamics that occur within social systems. In pure scientific situations, all aspects of systems can be carefully controlled from environmental effects. However, Bronfenbrenner (1979) observed that there are a number of additional environmental factors in human social systems, which he referred to collectively as the *ecological environment:*

> The ecological environment is conceived as a set of nested structures, each inside the next, like a set of Russian dolls. At the innermost level is the immediate setting containing the developing person. . . . The next step, however, already leads us off the beaten track for it requires looking beyond single settings to the relations between them. (p. 3)

In essence, this view states that human development cannot be seen in isolation but must be viewed within the context of the individual's relationship with the environment. In addition, each individual's environment is unique. The "person's development is profoundly affected by events occurring in settings in which the person is not even present" (Bronfenbrenner, 1979, p. 3). For example, within the context of a family, there may be forces affecting the parental subsystem that trickle down to affect the children without the children even being aware of them. If a parent is experiencing stress at work and displaces his or her frustration at home by yelling at the children, one may see how events outside the child's immediate environment may exert a pronounced effect on the child's development.

When the concept of ecological environment is introduced into the formula of human development, the result is a complex matrix for defining behavior. System theory, as an organizational theory, can begin to introduce order to this complexity by lending it conceptual clarity.

ECOLOGICAL SYSTEMS THEORY AND PERSPECTIVE

The juxtaposition of Bronfenbrenner's ecological environment with Bertalanffy's systems theory leads to the ecological systems perspective, which examines transactional relationships between systems. Since Bertalanffy and Bronfenbrenner developed their theoretical concepts for other disciplines, the connection to social work was not readily apparent. Germain has made strides in applying these concepts to the social work profession.

C. B. Germain has been instrumental in adapting these two theoretical models into an ecological systems perspective with specific applicability to social work. Germain strongly advocated looking at the biopsychosocial development of individuals and families within cultural, historical, communal, and societal contexts, a perspective that requires us to look as well at all events within the person's life. Social workers need to go beyond the scope of looking at the individual and to rely on public policy, practice, and research to gain the information needed to make an adequate assessment.

Germain characterized the nature of relationships between systems as transactional and "reciprocal exchanges between entities, or between their elements, in which each changes or otherwise influences the other over time" (Germain, 1991, p. 16). Such relationships are no longer linear but are circular, both systems in the interaction affecting each other.

The idea of behavior as a function is adapted from Lewin's field theory, which asserts that an individual can be studied by examining that person in the context of his or her environment. This may be symbolically represented through the equation $B = f(PE)$ where B is the individual's behavior, a function of the interplay between person (P) and environment (E) (Lewin, 1935). Field theory adumbrates aspects of both Bronfenbrenner's theory and Germain's ideas regarding the person-in-environment.

Early social science practice focused on either the behavior of the person or the environment, not the complex interaction between the two (Bronfenbrenner, 1979). The ecological systems perspective, in contrast, is specifically concerned with the nature of such interactions between the individual (or group, family, community) and the greater environment. A case vignette may help illustrate the dual nature of person and environment interactions. Valerie was a sixteen-year-old African American high school student, who was involved in a program entitled Career Beginnings, designed to identify at-risk high school students who had the potential for graduating from high school and then continuing their education at the college level. Valerie showed much promise and was academically successful. Her goal was to pursue a career in medicine.

Everything seemed to be progressing well for Valerie in the program. She had a good job, was responsible, had a good mentor, and maintained a 3.8 grade point average. Shortly before her seventeenth birthday, she appeared to be gaining weight. When asked, Valerie admitted that she was pregnant. Upon further exploration, Valerie said that she was the first generation in her family to be close to graduating from high school. She also revealed that she was feeling pressured by her mother and her grandmother to have a baby. Valerie was a first-born child, as was Valerie's mother. Both Valerie and her mother were born when their respective mothers were sixteen. As Valerie approached her seventeenth birthday, both her mother and her grandmother (who lived with them) began pressuring her to have a child since they viewed motherhood as Valerie's primary role and sixteen as being the appropriate age to begin to have children. In effect, the family environment did not place the same emphasis on completing high school as did the program.

This case demonstrates the interplay of familial values on the individual. There may be times when the individual's goals are at variance with environmental forces that are acting on the individual and dictate a different path.

This example raises the importance of understanding the interactional quality of relationships between person-in-environment. Shulman refers to this as "client-system interaction" (1992, p. 5) and describes the need for understanding the context surrounding the individual. In such a process, the worker begins by looking at the client's strengths rather than trying to identify the causes of the problem.

The nature of transactional relationships in the matrix of person-in-environment leads to the following six assumptions of the ecosystems perspective:

Assumption 1, there is an underlying intelligible general order in the world to which all matter relates.

Assumption 2, the whole is greater than the sum of its parts, also referred to as *non-summativity*.

Assumption 3, all forms of human social organization exhibit key features of general order as well as those distinctive to humans and to several classes of human social organization.

Assumption 4, the individual is both the cause and the effect of all forms of human social organization.

Assumption 5, social organization is characterized by varying degrees of functional interdependence both in the relationships among the member units of the organization and in the relationship between the organization and its environmental setting.

Assumption 6, when fully developed, all forms of social organizations display self-maintaining and development characteristics. (Chess & Norlin, 1991, pp. 33–36)

Germain's (1991) position is that all organisms exist in a particular order in the world. A reductionist approach necessitates the need to understand that order. However, through the ecosystems perspective, it is not necessary to know the order to facilitate systemic change or adaptation; change becomes possible through the identification of the system's strengths.

The ecosystem perspective views individuals as both the cause and effect of their situation. Since the person is in a *dynamic* situation, each change he or she makes causes a reactive change in the larger system. Germain (1991) identifies adaptation, life stress, coping, power, and human relatedness as important concepts for understanding the nature of the interactions of person-in-environment.

Adaptation

Given the dynamic nature of interaction between person-in-environment relationships, adaptation is the central ecological concept. Adaptation relates to the cause-and-effect relationship between the person and the environment, with change as the inevitable outcome of the interaction. "Adaptation may be directed to changing oneself in order to meet environmental opportunities or demands, or it may be directed to changing the environment so that physical and social settings will be more responsive to human needs, rights, goals, and capacities" (Germain, 1991, p. 17). Adaptation as it relates to equilibrium would provide a short list of choices, whereas in achieving homeostasis, the system would have a more extensive range of options from which to choose. The following example illustrates the process of adaptation.

Sarah, who was eighty years old, had suffered from polio since the age of two. Throughout her life, she constantly fought both her own body and her inability to access the larger systems that society had to offer. Sarah had undergone a number of spinal fusion procedures that temporarily alleviated some of her more distressing polio symptoms, helping her to adapt somewhat more successfully to the environment. But Sarah did not stop there. As an early activist, she became involved in bringing awareness to the plight of disabled individuals. She served on her local town's disabilities committee and when the Americans with Disabilities Act was passed in 1990, she became the director of the town's commission on disabilities.

Although confined to a wheelchair because of her polio, Sarah continued to be an active leader in helping businesses in the town become more accessible to the disabled. When Sarah's husband died, she might have become reclusive, since in many respects he was her link to the outside world, chauffeuring her to meetings and otherwise helping her to remain connected to the world outside their home. However, because she was able to identify and develop strengths and to adapt to her environmental milieu by utilizing the resources she had helped to create, Sarah remained active and involved.

Life Stress

Person-in-environment interaction leads to a normal tension, also referred to as *life stress.* Whenever different entities interact with each other, the ebb and flow between them creates some friction. The system's need to continue to adapt and achieve a state of homeostasis is itself a source of stress: "Life stress encompasses both the external demand and the internal (conscious and unconscious) experience of stress, including both emotional and physiological elements. What is perceived as stressful varies across age, gender, culture, physical and emotional states, past experience, and the perceived and actual nature of the environment" (Germain, 1991, p. 20). In other words, two people in exactly the same environmental situation may have different experiences owing to their differing perceptions of that situation. For one it may be comparatively stressful, while for a second, comparatively stress free.

Irrespective of the unit of analysis—individual, couple, family, group, or community—the ecosystem perspective is applied in essentially the same fashion, as the following example will illustrate.

A group of previously married individuals, Center Singles, consisting of persons in their mid-thirties to mid-fifties, provided a variety of functions for its members. For some the group symbolized a social outlet, for others it was purely educational, and for still others the group was a means of social support. This was possible since the group's goals were global, with a central focus on the problem of being newly single following a divorce or the death of the member's spouse. The global nature of the group's goal was an attraction, since in all likelihood, more specific goals would have limited its membership. As a consequence, there were significant differences among group members that represented each person's capacity to cope with that particular life stress.

Two group members will be used as further illustration of this concept. Susan was in her mid-forties and had three children ranging in age from fourteen to eighteen. Susan's husband had recently told her that he wanted a divorce, to which Susan reacted with surprise and anger. She felt unable to function and had problems concentrating on such simple tasks as addressing envelopes. She was constantly on the verge of tears.

Elaine was also in her mid-forties. She had four children ranging in age from thirteen to twenty-one. When her husband told her that he wanted a divorce, the first thing she did was to look at the want ads and find a job. Both Susan and Elaine were motivated to join the group for similar reasons, yet each dealt with this life stress differently.

Coping

The ability to cope requires both problem solving—what needs to be done to manage stress—and the ability to regulate negative feelings. The outcome of these factors leads to increased self-esteem, which helps to diminish the negative feelings caused by a particular stressor.

For a person to cope successfully with stress, the individual must partially block out negative feelings "so that hope is maintained and some problem solving can begin. As problem solving proceeds, self-esteem is elevated, hope is strengthened, and the defenses that were needed at the outset begin to relax" (Germain, 1991,

p. 22). Each individual deals with life stress along a continuum in which adaptive coping and maladaptive defenses constitute the extremes.

The locus of the stress is an external source; however, the need to cope and to develop defenses arises from the internal anxiety created by an external stressor. Each person relies on her or his own strengths in order to cope with stressful situations. When people feel as though their resources have been tapped, then their coping ability is reduced, and maladaptive defenses may predominate.

Power

Power has its derivation from a source extrinsic to the individual. Dominant groups in society use their position of power to influence subordinate groups through transactions in which resources are either provided or withheld. Germain observes, "The abuse of power by dominant groups creates both social and technological pollutions" (1991, p. 24).

The abuse of power by a dominant group can also be a source of tension in person-environment interactions. These tensions affect whole segments of the population, not just one individual. How the individual experiences this tension and is able to adapt to the tension-producing situation determines that individual's capacity for negotiating power inequities and imbalances.

Human Relatedness

Paramount in the concept of person-in-environment is the individual's ability to develop relationships and attachments. Three important relational aspects of person-in-environment interactions have been identified: (1) the attributes of human relatedness, competence, self-direction, and self-esteem, which are all outcomes of the person-in-environment gestalt; (2) the interdependence of such attributes, each deriving from and contributing to the development of the others; and (3) the apparent absence of cultural bias in such attributes. In other words, every human society, apparently irrespective of culture, values relatedness. Kinship structures and the rules for relating may vary by culture, but the attributes of human relatedness, competence, self-direction, and self-esteem are predictable outcomes of the person-in-environment relationship (Germain, 1991, p. 27).

Since these attributes—human relatedness, competence, self-direction, and self-esteem—exist in all cultures regardless of how the particular culture defines them, it underscores our need to understand the cultural values that contribute to the makeup of each client system.

Joe was a forty-year-old Jewish professional who had recently gone through a messy divorce. In this case, the divorce meant that he had minimal contact with his two sons. This proved especially difficult for Joe since much of his identity as a Jew was linked to culturally prescribed responsibilities as a husband and a father. His lack of contact with his sons was dissonant with his cultural value of fatherhood.

CLINICAL TOOLS FOR INFORMATION GATHERING

Certain assessment tools can be helpful in gathering information about the client and his or her environment. Three such tools—the genogram, ecomap, and the social network map—permit a graphic depiction of some aspect of the client's ecological environment, providing important interactional data that can aid the social worker in the assessment process. Such tools can also significantly shorten the traditional case recording process (Sheafor, Horejsi, & Horejsi, 1994).

Genogram

The genogram is similar to a family tree. It can describe family relationships in as many generations as the worker and the client wish, but is typically limited to three generations. The genogram provides a historical overview of the family and is a useful way of obtaining a sense of the client's historical milieu. By involving the client in helping to identify each generation and the characteristics of the people within it, visual pieces of data are created that can be used to great advantage in the assessment process. Such data provide a picture that can often be used by the client to identify previously hidden patterns. Once these historical patterns emerge, the client is much better equipped to develop strategies for behavioral change.

Karen, forty-two years old, had been married and divorced three times and was involved in a relationship with a man addicted to drugs and alcohol. A genogram helped Karen and her worker understand that all the men in Karen's life—her grandfather, father, and previous husbands—had been substance abusers with depressive personalities just like the man in her current relationship (Figure 1.1).

Ecomap

Whereas the genogram identified the historical ecology of the client, the ecomap identifies the client's current social context. The ecomap works by using circles to represent different factors affecting the client and by identifying other systems that have an interface with the client system. An ecomap of a family can also identify the exosystems, or those systems that affect other family members but do not have a direct impact on the identified client. The ecomap is constructed by having the client identify all the organizations that have some impact on his or her life. Each organization is depicted by a circle. The client then identifies the nature and direction of the flow of energy between the organization and self. Because this process meaningfully involves the client in identifying the current situation and pictorially expressing it through the ecomap, the client may develop a better understanding of her or his situation and ultimately reveal strategies for resolving the dilemma.

Helen was a thirty-nine-year-old single mother who had recently moved into the community but continued to have strong ties to her former residence. Her eight-year-old daughter was experiencing problems resulting from the girl's father's decision to move out of the country. An ecomap helped the mother identify resources and supports in her new community (Figure 1.2).

FIGURE 1.1

A Genogram of a Client's Relationship

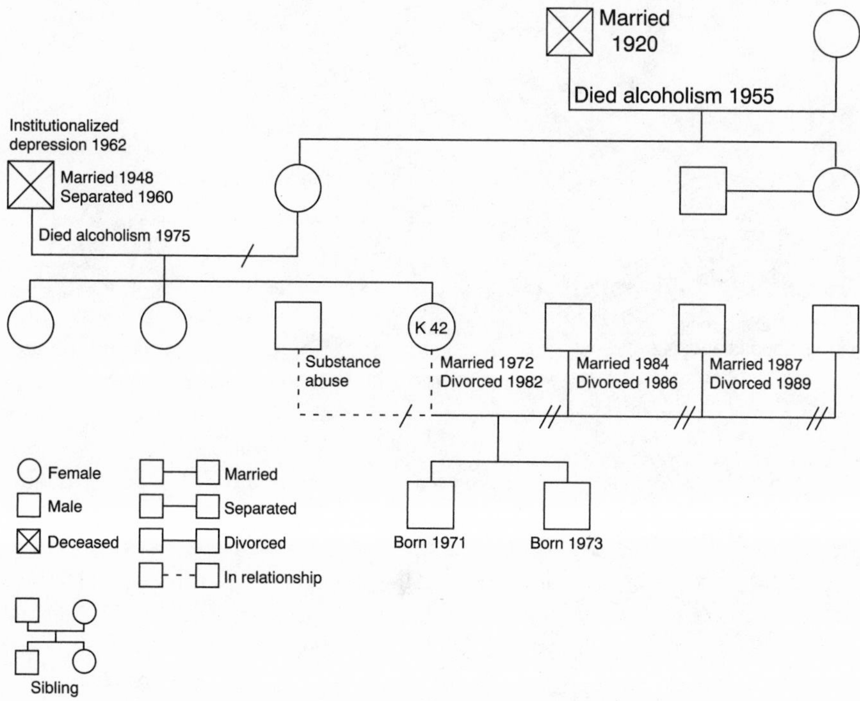

Social Network Map

A social network map is "a tangible aid that is proffered by social intimates or inferred by their presence and has beneficial emotional or behavioral effects on the recipient" (Gottlieb, 1983, p. 28). The social network map is used in tandem with the social network grid to identify and engage the client in defining his or her social supports. Social supports are important and can be classified into five interaction systems necessary for an individual's well-being—emotional integration, social integration, opportunity for nurturance, reassurance of worth, and assistance (Friedman, 1993, p. 16)—and enable the individual to negotiate problematic situations and sustain well-being.

The social network map consists of concentric rings, with the client identified as the innermost ring. The client is then asked to identify supports and place them on the map, quantifying the amount of support received through placement in closer proximity to the center of the map. The closer to the center, the greater the amount of support provided to the client. The tandem social network grid is used as a means of quantifying the level of support that the client receives from his or her network. This is not an objective measure but is based on the client's subjective perceptions in identifying the valence of the support.

Mark, forty years old and homeless, had bounced around from shelter to shelter

FIGURE 1.2
Ecomap

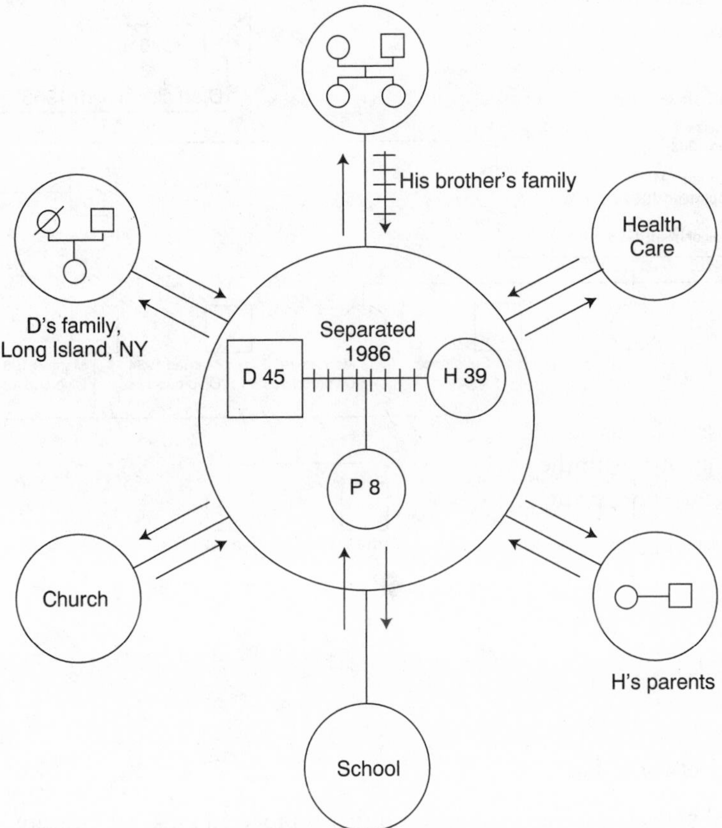

and was linked to the formal support system. However, he had no informal support system, as a network map revealed. This became a tool in building positive informal supports that helped him sustain a job and independent housing (Figure 1.3).

SUMMARY

Social work has been defined recently as "the professional activity of helping individuals, groups, or communities enhance or restore their capacity for social functioning and creating societal conditions favorable to this goal" (Barker, 1995, p. 357). This definition emphasizes the role of the professional in understanding the client system within its ecological environment in order to build on client strengths. Social work clinicians need a theoretical framework that will enhance their understanding of person-in-environment interactions, which the ecosystems perspective can provide.

Regardless of the system's size (individual, family, group, or community), an ecosystems perspective provides an interactional view of any system within the context of its environment. The environmental context includes the interplay among multiple influences—biological, psychological, and social. The role of the worker is to support the growth of the client system, a perspective that enables the clinician to work on multiple levels, incorporating other theories to develop strategies that address the person-in-environment change process. An ecosystems perspective places the focus on the interaction between person and environment rather than on one or the other. Since this perspective is not a theory but a method for organizing information, the worker uses other substantive theories, such as psychoanalytic and/or cognitive and behavioral theories, to help in the analysis of a particular person-in-environment interaction.

Germain, who was an influential social work theorist, adapted Bertalanffy's and Bronfenbrenner's frameworks and created a social work model to describe person-in-environment interaction. She believed that the best method of analysis was to break down this interaction into its component parts—adaptation, life stress, coping, power, and human relatedness—to gain a clearer picture of client strengths. All systems interact with the environment as both causes and effects of a given situation, and it is important for the worker to understand fully the dynamic nature of

FIGURE 1.3
Social Network Map for a Homeless Man

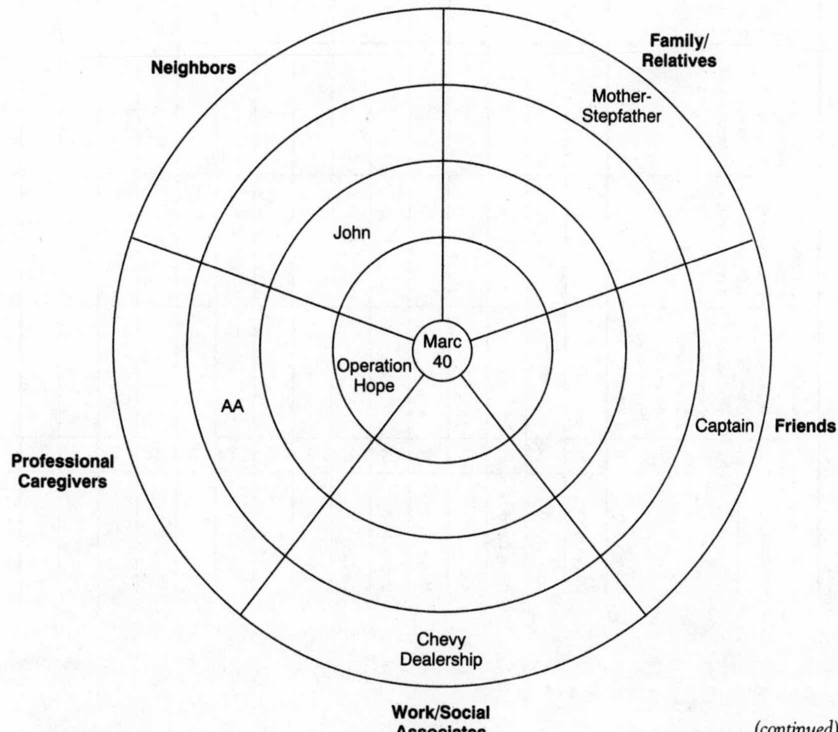

(continued)

FIGURE 1.3 *(continued)*

ID______ Respondent: ______ Name	#	Area of Life 1. Household 2. Other Family 3. Work/School 4. Organizations 5. Other Friends 6. Neighbors 7. Professionals 8. Other	Concrete support 1. Hardly ever 2. Sometimes 3. Almost always	Emotional Support 1. Hardly ever 2. Sometimes 3. Almost always	Information/ Advice 1. Hardly ever 2. Sometimes 3. Almost always	Critical 1. Hardly ever 2. Sometimes 3. Almost always	Direction of help 1. Goes both ways 2. You to them 3. Them to you	Closeness 1. Not very close 2. Sort of close 3. Very close	How often seen 1. Few times/yr. 2. Monthly 3. Weekly 4. Daily 0. Does not see	How long known 1. Less than 1 yr. 2. 1–5 yr. 3. More than 5 yr.
Operation Hope	01	7	3	3	3	2	3	3	4	1
John	02	5/6	2	3	3	2	1	3	4	1
Chevy Dealer	03	3	3	1	1	1	2	1	4	1
AA	04	7	1	2	2	2	1	2	3	3
Mother	05	2	1	1	1	3	2	1	1	3
Stepfather	06	2	1	1	1	3	2	1	1	3
Captain	07	5	1	1	1	2	2	2	4	2
	08									
	09									
	10									
	11									
	12									
	13									
	14									
	15									
1-6		7	8	9	10	11	12	13	14	15

this interaction. Just how the social worker chooses to gain that knowledge is left up to the worker, since the ecosystems perspective does not dictate which tools to use but relies on the creativity of each worker to assess fully the dynamics of person-in-environment interaction.

Three specific tools—the genogram, the ecomap, and the social network map—were presented as methods for acquiring that knowledge. These tools demonstrate the variety of techniques useful in gaining information about different aspects of systemic interaction. The more knowledge that the worker has about person-in-environment interaction, the better informed he or she is, and the better able to identify system strengths that will strengthen or restore the client's social functioning.

REFERENCES

Anderson, R. E., & Carter, I. (1990). *Human behavior in the social environment: A social systems approach, 4th ed.* New York: Aline De Gruyter.

Barker, R. L. (1995). *The social work dictionary.* Washington, DC: NASW Press.

Bertalanffy, L. V. (1968). *General system theory: Foundation, development, application.* New York: George Braziller.

Bronfenbrenner, U. (1979). *The ecology of human development: Experiments by nature and design.* Cambridge, MA: Harvard University Press.

Chess, W. A., & Norlin, J. M. (1991). *Human behavior in the social environment: A social systems model.* Boston: Allyn & Bacon.

Friedman, B. D. (1994). *No place like home: A study of two homeless shelters.* Ann Arbor, MI: University Microfilms International.

Germain, C. B. (1991). *Human behavior in the social environment: An ecological view.* New York: Columbia University Press.

Gottlieb, B. (1983). *Social support strategies: Guidelines for mental health practice.* Newbury Park, CA: Sage.

Holman, A. M. (1983). *Family assessment: Tools for understanding and intervention.* Newbury Park, CA: Sage.

Lewin, K. (1935). *A dynamic theory of personality.* New York: McGraw-Hill.

Lewin, K. (1976). *Field theory as human science.* New York: Gardner Press.

McMahon, M. O. (1996). *The general method of social work practice: A generalist perspective* (3rd ed.). Boston: Allyn & Bacon.

Rauch, J. B. (Ed.). (1993). *Assessment: A sourcebook for social work practice.* Milwaukee, WI: Families International.

Rodway, M. R. (1986). Systems theory. In F. Turner (Ed.), *Social work treatment: Interlocking theoretical approaches* (3rd ed.) (pp. 514–539). New York: Free Press.

Sheafor, B. W., Horejsi, C. R., & Horejsi, G. A. (1994). *Techniques and guidelines for social work practice* (3rd ed.). Boston: Allyn & Bacon.

Shulman, L. (1992). *The skills of helping: Individuals, families, and groups.* Itasca, IL: F. E. Peacock Publishers.

2

Behavioral and Cognitive Theories

Bruce A. Thyer and Laura L. Myers

Initially introduced into the social work literature in the mid-1960s, behavioral (Thomas, 1967) and cognitive theories (Werner, 1965) can now be considered mainstream perspectives for clinical social work. In a survey of social workers published in 1978, Jayaratne found behavioral approaches to be a preferred theoretical orientation by over one-third of the respondents. More recently, Strom (1994) surveyed a random sample of practicing clinical social workers and found that 67 percent used a cognitive-behavioral orientation in their work and that 32 percent employed a behavioral orientation (respondents could report using more than one theoretical orientation). The behavioral/cognitive–behavioral perspective was employed by more social workers than such respected models as systems (reportedly used by 53 percent of the respondents), ecological (11 percent), task centered (48 percent), and ego psychology (53 percent), being exceeded in usage only by the psychodynamic (83 percent) orientation.

Most schools of social work now provide some level of training in behavioral theory and practice (Thyer & Maddox, 1988), and the majority of the controlled outcome studies on the effectiveness of social work practice that yielded positive results have been based on behavioral social work methods (Reid & Hanrahan, 1982; MacDonald, Sheldon, & Gillespie, 1992). Most general social work practice textbooks contain content on social learning theory, and a large literature exclusively devoted to behavioral social work now exists (Thyer, 1981a, 1985).

Behavioral and cognitive-behavioral perspectives are sufficiently encompassing as to have applicability to virtually all areas of social work practice, from clinical work with individuals (Thyer, 1988), couples, families, and groups, to community practice (Rothman & Thyer, 1984), and to the formulation of social welfare policies (Thyer, 1996). Indeed, the entire M.S.W. curriculum could be centered around contemporary social learning theory and behavioral-cognitive methods of practice (Thyer & Wodarski, 1990), in a manner similar to that of the singular orientations found at the schools of social work at Smith College (psychodynamic) and the University of Pennsylvania (functionalist) in earlier days.

BEHAVIORAL THEORY AND CLINICAL SOCIAL WORK

A behavioral approach to clinical social work rests on a conceptual foundation known as social learning theory (SLT), that is, learning theories used to explain social behavior. The empirically supported learning theories that comprise SLT involve the processes of respondent conditioning, operant conditioning, and observational learning. Together, these three ways in which human beings learn form a theory of normative human growth and development (Bijou, 1993; Schlinger, 1995; Thyer, 1992a), a framework for conceptualizing so-called psychopathology (Ullman & Krasner, 1969), a comprehensive theory of human personality (Lundin, 1974), and a widely applicable approach to clinical practice (Thyer, 1983).

The basic principles of SLT are relatively simple and uncontroversial:

1. Human behavior consists of what we do—both observable behavior and unobservable behavior. Overt acts, covert speech, thoughts and cognition, feelings, dreams: all those phenomena people engage in are considered behavior.
2. To a large extent, much (but not all) human behavior is learned through life experiences. This learning occurs throughout the life span.
3. It seems very likely that similar fundamental learning processes give rise to individual human behavior across cultures and life circumstances and account for both normative and many so-called dysfunctional actions, feelings, and thoughts.
4. Interpersonal behavior is also a function of these learning processes, giving rise to dyadic, group, organizational, community, and societal phenomena. These larger-scale activities are, to a great extent, a more complex operation of fundamental learning mechanisms.
5. There are at least three major learning processes well supported empirically that collectively comprise social learning theory: respondent conditioning, operant conditioning, and observational learning.

Note that behavior is defined as what a person does—whether it can be observed or not. Thoughts and feelings are seen as much a part of the body's behavior as is publicly observable action. Moreover, all aspects of behavior, overt action, thoughts, and feelings are seen as strongly influenced by respondent, operant, and observational learning and can potentially be therapeutically modified through the informed, professional use of such learning mechanisms. While it is true that early behaviorist John Watson defined psychology as the study of overt behavior only, in the 1930s and 1940s B. F. Skinner attempted to apply learning theory principles to the analysis of private events—phenomena such as thoughts and feelings occurring beneath the skin. It is not true that behavioral practice is concerned only with the client's observable activities. Many aspects of client problems involve affective states (feelings) and thoughts and are a central focus of behavioral assessment and intervention. Also, it is not true that behaviorists claim that all behavior is learned. They do claim that much is learned, and what is learned or not learned through SLT is an empirical question to be answered through data-based experimentation and naturalistic observation, not by theoretical argumentation.

Behavioral theorists are modest in their claims, quite content that the processes on which they focus are an important part of understanding clinical phenomena, but not inherently denying the potential role of other variables (e.g., biology, genetics). It is up to the advocates of other approaches to demonstrate both the validity of their theory and the effectiveness of the clinical social work treatments derived from that theory. To the extent that they do so, in accordance with the empirical, scientific, and analytical approach on which clinical social work is based, well and good. The profession is well served, as are clients, which is more important than theoretical squabbles.

Behaviorally oriented clinical social workers do take justifiable pride in noting the close match between SLT and the traditional person-in-environment approach of social work practice. Examine the following quotations. The first is from the behavioral perspective:

> Men act upon the world and change it, and are changed in turn by the consequences of their action. Certain processes which the human organism shares with other species, alter behavior so that it achieves a safer and more useful interchange with a particular environment. When appropriate behavior has been established, its consequences work through similar processes to keep it in force. If by chance the environment changes, new forms of behavior disappear, while new consequences build new forms. (Skinner, 1957, p. 1)

Here are three quotations from the social work perspective:

> The human being and the environment reciprocally shape each other. People mold their environments in many ways and, in turn, they must then adapt to the changes they created. (Germain, in Bloom, 1992, p. 407)

> The ecosystems perspective is about ". . . building more supportive, helpful and nurturing environments for clients through environmental helping, and increasing their competence in dealing with the environment by teaching basic life skills. (Whittaker & Garbarino, 1983, p. 34)

> The ecological perspective makes clear the need to view people and environments as a unitary system within a particular cultural and historic context. Both person and environment can be fully understood in terms of their relationship, in which each continually influences the other within a particular context. . . . Ecological thinking examines exchanges between A and B, for example, that shape, influence, or change

> both over time. A acts, which leads to a change in B, whereupon the change in B elicits a change in A that in turn changes B, which then changes or otherwise influences A, and so on. (Germain & Gitterman, 1995, p. 816)

The parallels between the two are striking, so much so that it would seem that contemporary social workers are reinventing the wheel, woefully ignorant of the social learning theory antecedents of current models or are simply choosing to ignore the similarities between the two approaches.

The social learning theorist cites with approval the view of John Howard Griffin, author of *Black Like Me:*

> You place the white man in the ghetto, deprive him of educational advantages, arrange it so he has to struggle hard to fulfill his instinct for self-respect, give him little physical privacy and less leisure, and he would after a time assume the same characteristics you attach to the negro. These characteristics don't spring from whiteness or blackness, but from a man's *conditioning.* (Griffin, 1960, p. 89, italics added)

We will next turn to a review of the basic principles of SLT. Each type of learning that is described will be followed by an example of its operation in everyday life, then by an illustration of a clinical phenomenon, and concluding with one or more brief practice vignettes.

Respondent Learning

The wounded body shrinks even from a gentle touch.
—Ovid

Everyday Examples of Respondent Learning

After the birth of her son John, Laura decided to breast-feed him. When John cried, she would place him at her breast, and he would nurse. After a few moments, her milk would let down and begin to flow. After a week or so, Laura noticed that she would experience milk flow when she picked up the baby as he was crying; it was no longer necessary for him to nurse before she let down. In respondent learning terms, John's nursing at the breast is an unconditioned stimulus, producing the unconditioned response of the release of milk. John's crying (and Laura's picking him up preparatory to nursing) was initially neutral; it had no effect on milk flow. However, after being repeatedly paired in time with the (preceding) physical unconditioned stimulus of nursing, his crying became a conditioned stimulus, which produced the conditioned response of milk flow.

During the winter months, as the air became less humid, Bruce received a shock from static electricity when he touched the car door handle. After this happened a few times, he began hesitating to touch the car door and sometimes had to force himself to do so. Initially, the door handle is a neutral stimulus. After being mildly painfully shocked (an unconditioned stimulus) a few times and snatching his hand away (avoidance, an unconditioned response to the shock), Bruce began avoiding (the conditioned response) touching the door handle (which had now become a conditioned stimulus). As spring approached, Bruce stopped getting shocked when he touched the car door. With repeated touches in the absence of shock, his hesitancy in touching it declined and eventually vanished (until next winter!). This illustrates the process of respondent extinction.

Clinical Examples of Respondent Learning

Some patients undergoing cancer chemotherapy experience severe nausea after the drugs are intravenously administered. Initially, clinic stimuli (sights, sounds, smells, staff, etc.) are neutral events. The chemotherapy is an unconditioned stimulus for the unconditioned response of nausea and emesis, with the latter being natural or unlearned responses. After a number of episodes of entering the clinic, receiving the medication, and becoming nauseated, some patients become ill prior to receiving the medication, often on entering the clinic itself. In this case, previously neutral aspects of the clinic, paired with the unconditioned stimulus of the medication, become a conditioned stimulus, eliciting the conditioned response of nausea in the absence of the chemotherapy.

In a case report by a clinical social worker (Shorkey & Taylor, 1973), a child who was hospitalized for the treatment of severe burns was receiving debridement therapy, a very painful procedure. After a number of treatment sessions, which took place in the child's hospital room, the child began screaming and thrashing about when the nurses providing debridement treatments merely entered the room. His severe reaction threatened the healing process and made it very difficult to treat him. The debridement therapy can be viewed as an unconditioned stimulus (he did not "learn" to feel pain as his severe burns were being treated), and the pain and thrashing about during these treatments can be seen as an unconditioned response (almost everyone withdraws and cries out in response to severe pain). In time, the sight of the nursing staff in their distinctive uniforms became a conditioned stimulus, producing the conditioned response of crying and thrashing.

Clinical Treatment Using Respondent Conditioning

At the age of sixty-seven years, a retired professor was attacked and severely bitten by a large dog, and required emergency room treatment and painful stitches. Subsequently she developed a severe fear of dogs, meeting the criteria for a specific phobia. Her life became dominated by her fear of dogs, being preoccupied with anticipating encountering dogs even when the dreaded beasts were not around. Treatment consisted of social worker–assisted gradual exposure to small dogs in the controlled setting of the consulting room. Using conventional clinical skills (support, encouragement, humor, reinforcement for successive approximations, etc.), the social worker helped her to become much less fearful, and she was able to resume her life unimpaired by her morbid fears. (See Thyer, 1981b for a fuller clinical description of this client's treatment.)

In this true example, the dog was initially a neutral stimulus, and being bitten was an unconditioned stimulus. The unconditioned response is the emotional reaction of fear and avoidance behavior. After the attack, dogs in general had become a conditioned stimulus, evoking the conditioned responses of fear and avoidance, even if they were nonthreatening. Gradual real-life exposure therapy has such an impressive degree of empirical support that it can be considered a first-choice treatment for phobic disorders (Wilson, 1989).

Patients experiencing pretreatment nausea following cancer chemotherapy have been taught progressive relaxation (PR) training skills. Relaxation inherently inhibits nausea, and by first learning PR techniques with the social worker outside the chemotherapy clinic, patients can then practice them in the clinic itself. Pairing relaxation with the clinic stimuli can reduce or eliminate respondently learned pretreatment nausea (see Boynton & Thyer, 1994).

Operant Learning

Verily there is a reward for the righteous.
—Psalms, 58:11

The concept of positive reinforcement has entered our everyday lexicon, but even well-trained clinicians are sometimes confused by the distinctions among positive and negative reinforcement, positive and negative punishment, and extinction. Inasmuch as these are conceptually and practically different learning processes, it is worth distinguishing them.

Colloquially, positive reinforcement can be labeled rewarding. It occurs when a consequence is presented (hence the word *positive*) and the behavior rewarded subsequently increases (becomes stronger, more frequent, or is maintained) in the future (with such strengthening giving rise to the word *reinforcement*). Negative reinforcement can be familiarly construed as relief. If a behavior's consequence consists of removing something unpleasant and the behavior is subsequently strengthened, then negative reinforcement is involved.

Positive punishment occurs when a behavior's consequence consists of presenting something aversive, which results in a decrease in the likelihood of that behavior. Because something is presented, the term *positive* is used. Because the result is a decrease in behavior, the operation is called punishment. As you might suspect, negative punishment involves the removal (hence *negative*) of something pleasant, resulting in a decrease (hence *punishment*) in the future probability of that behavior. Colloquially, think of negative punishment as operating similar to a fine. Figure 2.1 presents these distinctions conceptually, and the following illustrations describe their operation more concretely. It is common for social workers to think that the terms *punishment* and *negative reinforcement* mean the same thing. They do not. Negative reinforcement is good. People like getting reinforced, whereas virtually no one likes being punished.

Operant extinction can occur with behaviors being maintained through reinforcement. If reinforcers are discontinued, the behavior may strengthen temporarily (this is called an *extinction burst*), but will then decline and ultimately cease entirely. Interestingly, behaviors maintained with a continuous schedule of reinforcement (every time a behavior occurs, reinforcement follows) are easier to extinguish than behavior with a history of being reinforced only every now and then. Behaviors that occasionally yield reinforcing consequences are sometimes very durable and quite

FIGURE 2.1
The Four Types of Operant Learning

		Behavior Subsequently (its effects)	
		Increases	Decreases
A consequence is:	presented	Positive reinforcement (reward)	Positive punishment
	removed	Negative reinforcement (relief)	Negative punishment (fine)

resistant to extinction. People will persist in repeating a particular behavior for long periods of time if in their past this sometimes resulted in reinforcement (particularly if the reinforcers are particularly powerful ones).

Examples of Positive Reinforcement

A child volunteers to answer in class and is praised by her teacher for answering. Volunteering is strengthened. Here praise and social approbation are functioning as a reinforcing consequence.

A youth desirous of being accepted by a street gang must pass an initiation test—perhaps stealing something from a local shopping mall. He commits the crime and is lavishly praised by the established members of the gang. Here, social praise is serving to positively reinforce dysfunctional (in the long run) behavior.

Smoking crack produces an immediate and intense rush, a highly pleasurable sensation that lasts for a few minutes and then subsides. Almost anything that enables one to gain access to crack will be strengthened by this positive reinforcer. Burglary, prostitution, and robbery are examples of behaviors that are maintained in part by the positive consequences of smoking crack.

Clinical Practice Using Positive Reinforcement

In a group home for chronically mentally ill individuals, the activity therapist provided the clients with an exercise bicycle, hoping they would voluntarily ride it. Instead it gathered dust, despite its strategic location in the TV room. After one week, she arranged to positively reinforce riding short distances on the exercise bike with contingent low-calorie snacks. The miles ridden by the residents soared. This was continued for a week, and then discontinued for seven days to see if maybe they would now ride on their own. Instead, bike riding plummeted. During the fourth week, contingent snacks were once again made available for riding the exercise bike, and mileage once again dramatically increased. The contingent snack program was thereafter left in place as a regular part of the group home's programming to encourage the clients to get some aerobic exercise (see Thyer, Irvine, & Santa, 1984, for additional data and details).

Examples of Negative Reinforcement

You step out into the bright sunlight, and your eyes hurt. Putting on sunglasses alleviates the pain. In the future, you are more likely to put on your sunglasses in bright light.

A crack addict has gone for a prolonged period without using the drug. A profound dysphoric mood and unpleasant physical sensations occur, caused by the drug's withdrawal symptoms. Reusing crack temporarily produces relief from these noxious sensations and moods. Using crack is thus also negatively reinforcing (producing relief) of drug-seeking behavior in the established addict who is experiencing withdrawal.

Clinical Practice Using Negative Reinforcement

Barth (1986, p. 155) describes a practice vignette where brief periods of time-out or social isolation are used with a disruptive boy in a group work setting. If he sits still and is quiet for a brief period, he is allowed to rejoin the group. In this illustration, if it is assumed that being in time-out is aversive, then being released from time-out contingent on appropriate behavior is used to negatively reinforce such behavior.

Examples of Positive Punishment

A child uses a curse word in front of a parent and is slapped hard across the mouth. In the future, the child uses that curse word less often in front of that parent. In this case, an aversive stimulus (the slap) is presented, and the subsequent effect on behavior is a reduction.

A husband carefully prepares a gourmet meal and serves it to his wife when she returns home from a hard day at the office. Instead of praising his efforts, she throws the meal at him, heats up a microwave dinner, and pops open a beer, while criticizing his culinary efforts. If gourmet cooking for his wife declines in frequency, it can be said that his spouse positively punished such behavior through her contingent aversive criticism and by her throwing the hot food at him.

Clinical Practice Using Positive Punishment

An eleven-year-old-boy, Mark, who lived in a Salvation Army group home, swore profusely at the dinner table. Despite the efforts of the cottage parents, coaxing and other forms of verbal persuasion had no effect on reducing Mark's profanity. After consultation with a social worker, the cottage parents took an unobtrusive baseline of the frequency of Mark's swearing during the thirty-minute dinner period. After five days, Mark was informed that he would have to wash cottage windows for ten minutes each time he swore. Failure to complete his window washing assignments satisfactorily could result in a curtailment of other privileges. After one day of the window washing contingency, he virtually stopped swearing. After two weeks with little profanity, the contingent chore was discontinued, and regrettably, swearing quickly increased, so after five days window washing was reinstated. Swearing dropped to near zero again, and remained very low for the rest of the year. Because the aversive chore of window washing was presented to Mark, contingent on swearing, and the result was a decrease in the frequency of profanity, this procedure is appropriately labeled positive punishment (see Fischer & Nehs, 1978, for data and further details).

Examples of Negative Punishment

You are speeding along the highway, en route to the monthly meeting of the local clinical social work society, and you are pulled over by a policewoman because you were going too fast. The net result is that you lose a large sum of money (the fine). If you exceed the speed limit less often in the future, then speeding can be said to have been negatively punished.

A clinical social worker accurately records a client's diagnosis on insurance forms. Because of her truthfulness in revealing a marital problem as the focus of treatment, in lieu of a formal clinical disorder, the insurance company demands that the honest social worker repay some reimbursements already provided. If in the future the social worker becomes less truthful in completing insurance forms, telling the truth can be said to have been negatively punished.

Clinical Practice Using Negative Punishment

Young children meeting criteria for attention deficit disorder with hyperactivity were given academic assignments to work on in class. If they stayed focused on their tasks, they had access to twenty minutes of play time at the end of the work period. If their attention wandered and they were seen to not be completing their assignments, the teacher flipped over a card on a stand, indicating that one minute of free time was deducted from their recess. Additional episodes of off-task behavior resulted in additional minutes being deducted from play time. Compared to baseline levels of work and time on task during medication treatment (Ritalin), the response cost contingency (or fine) greatly promoted the children's attention to academic work, as well as accuracy. In this instance, something pleasant (play time) was reduced contingent on undesirable behavior. While such contingencies were in effect, the undesirable behavior was greatly reduced; hence this is an illustration of negative punishment. (see Rapport, Murphy, & Bailey, 1982, for a complete description of this program).

Examples of Operant Extinction

Every time in your life that you have turned on a light switch in your bathroom, the light turns on. One night you go into the bathroom and flip the switch, but nothing happens. You will perhaps flip it a few more times but will eventually give up (and engage in some other more reinforcing behavior, like changing the light bulb).

If you were so fortunate to have won a large prize in your state's lottery, you might persist for many months or years in buying lottery tickets, particularly if sometimes you won another $5, $10, or $20. If you never won and never knew anyone else who ever won, it is likely that your lottery participation would drop off and stop completely (which is why states so cleverly arrange schedules of reinforcement of lottery winnings, and widely advertise them, to induce people to continue playing). There is a large literature on the power of various types of schedules of reinforcement; Ferster and Skinner (1957) is a good place to begin learning about these principles in detail.

Clinical Practice Using Operant Extinction

Anthony, an eleven-year-old black child, was severely retarded and lived in a residential facility because of his history of severe aggression. Anytime anyone got within a few feet of Anthony, he would hit, kick, bite, scratch, or spit in an effort to get the person to move away. This behavior made it impossible for his parents to keep him in their home. To make a complex story very brief, assessment determined that Anthony found the close proximity of others to be aversive, and his aggression was speculated to be a negatively reinforced operant response. When he aggressed, he got what he wanted: people moved back and left him alone.

A trial treatment program was devised whereby the social worker (Bruce, wearing heavy clothes and gloves) would enter the playroom, which was well stocked with toys, and attempt to engage Anthony in play, all the while remaining within a couple of feet of him. No matter what aggressions Anthony performed (and they were many), Bruce did not move away or indicate pain. This treatment was construed as involving the principle of operant extinction. The reinforcers maintaining maladaptive behavior (aggression) were tentatively identified (people backing away, other reactions by Anthony's victims), and it was hypothesized that stopping this pattern of negative reinforcement would lead to a reduction in aggression. Detailed records were made of the frequency of Anthony's aggression, and over the forty-five-minute experimental treatment session, aggression dramatically declined. This result also occurred during a second forty-five-minute treatment session and justified several subsequent day-long treatments involving multiple staff. Similar results were obtained during these lengthier sessions, and after several such programs, Anthony's aggression was greatly reduced. Facility records of his aggression in nontreatment settings (e.g., school, dorm) revealed reductions in aggression following this treatment program. No punishment was ever employed in Anthony's treatment. (See Figueroa, Thyer, & Thyer 1992, for details on this case)

Observational Learning

For behaviour, men learn it, as they take diseases, one of another.
—Francis Bacon

The use of observational learning, also known as learning via imitation, is a widespread method in behavioral social work. Modeling can be used to help a client acquire a new behavior through observing someone else perform the behavior, as opposed to instructing the client verbally without an actual demonstration of what is expected. Modeling and its associated practices of role playing and behavioral rehearsal can be used to help clients acquire social skills, assertiveness, daily living skills, and other adaptive behavior. A well-articulated theory of observational learning has lagged behind the development of some well-established empirical principles regarding effective models. For example, people are more likely to imitate models who resemble them; imitating real-life models is more effective in producing behavior change than imitating written descriptions of behavior to be modeled; models who are seen by clients being rewarded for displaying certain behaviors will likely be more effective in inducing the client to display the desired actions; models who are seen to display imperfect performance initially and gradually become more competent are more effective than models who exhibit perfect behavior on the first attempt (see Rosenthal & Bandura, 1978).

Observational learning was a major component in the assertiveness training approach developed by social workers Eileen Gambrill and Cheryl Richey (1976) and Sandra and Martin Sundel (1980). Modeling was also used by Butterfield and Parsons (1973) to help parents teach their mentally disabled child to develop skills in chewing solid food. Sheldon Rose has published a series of outcome studies on social work with groups, with the group work serving as the context in which members role-play, model, rehearse, and practice new interpersonal skills (see Gammon & Rose, 1991, for one such example). Modeling is widely used as a component of behavioral marital and family therapy, social skills training in a variety of clinical contexts, and helping clients overcome pathological fears (e.g., Kornhaber & Schroeder, 1975).

There does remain controversy whether observational learning is a distinct method of acquiring new behavior, or if it is a special form of operant learning (Baer & Deguchi, 1985). Certainly it is a fundamental method of acquiring behavior. It appears that humans have the capacity of learning through imitation virtually from birth, and observational learning is well documented among animals (see Thyer, 1992a). It makes sense that if modeled behavior is reinforced, both the new behavior and the likelihood of imitation are strengthened. Beginning this process as infants, it would seem that generalized skills in observational learning would become well established by the time one reaches adulthood (which is typically the case). Many experiments with humans have shown that if imitated behavior is reinforced, the likelihood of imitation is greatly strengthened. If imitated behavior never produced reinforcing consequences, would imitation continue? It seems unlikely.

Keep in mind that it is not people who are reinforced, punished, or extinguished, it is behavior. It is not correct to state, "I reinforced the client"; the correct statement is, "I reinforced the client's self-disclosure" (or some other action).

Summary on Social Learning Theory

The illustrations and case presentations discussed so far represent extremely simple examples of behavioral phenomena influenced by social learning theory and their practical applications to clinical social work. However, by building on these elementary principles, researchers have developed sophisticated theoretical accounts for some very complex clinical phenomena. For example, social worker Richard Stuart (1980) has put forth a conceptual model of marital discord and an extensive model of marital therapy based almost exclusively on operant principles, and Gerald Patterson (1982) has similarly employed this approach in conceptualizing and intervening in dysfunctional families.

Using social learning theory, Ivar Lovaas developed and tested a psychosocial intervention for autistic youth, which, when applied early and intensively enough, resulted in normative emotional and intellectual functioning for about 50 percent of the clients when followed up some years later (Lovaas, 1987; McEachin, Smith, & Lovaas, 1993). Gordon Paul devised and rigorously evaluated a psychosocial treatment for persons with chronic mental illness (schizophrenia), which resulted in earlier discharge from the hospital, less recidivism, less aberrant behavior, and virtually no use of psychotropic medications, compared to standard treatment (Paul & Lentz, 1977; Paul & Menditto, 1992). Nathan Azrin has tested a community-reinforcement approach to helping alcoholics, with dramatic positive results in terms of long-term abstinence (Azrin, 1976). Clearly it would be a mistake to discount behavioral methods as appropriate only for developing theoretical models about simple problems like enuresis or phobia. Some of the most difficult and recalcitrant issues social workers deal with are being effectively addressed using behavioral methods, and this conceptual framework has much to offer the field.

COGNITIVE THEORY

People are disturbed not by things, but by the views they take of them.
—Epictetus

Cognitive theory has been a viable model of clinical social work practice for over three decades, beginning with Harold Werner's early work describing the applications of Albert Ellis's rational emotive therapy (RET) approach to the field (Werner, 1965). Most practice textbooks that address behavioral social work practice either subsume cognitive therapy in the behavioral chapter or deal with it as a separate chapter in its own right (e.g., Werner, 1979). What exactly distinguishes cognitive therapy from mainstream behavior therapy is sometimes a confusing issue, because almost all cognitive theory is an expansion or extension of social learning theory rather than its repudiation. Cognitive therapists do not disavow the validity of the principles of respondent, operant, and observational learning. Rather they claim that there are additional elements that need to be considered in arriving at an etiological understanding of clients, in assessment, and in devising treatments. A number of these elements follow (Scott, 1995, p. 123):

1. Individuals respond to cognitive representations of environmental events rather than to the events per se.
2. Learning is cognitively mediated.
3. Cognition mediates emotional and behavioral dysfunction.
4. At least some forms of cognition can be monitored.
5. At least some forms of cognition can be altered.
6. As a corollary to assumptions 3, 4, and 5, altering cognition can change dysfunctional patterns of emotion and behavior.
7. Both cognitive and behavioral therapeutic change methods are desirable and can be integrated.

There are four major types of interventions in cognitive therapy (Fischer, 1978, pp. 177–187):

1. Changing misconceptions, unrealistic expectations, and other faulty ideas.

2. Modifying irrational statements to oneself.
3. Enhancing problem-solving and decision-making abilities.
4. Enhancing self-control and self-management.

Wodarski and Bagarozzi (1979) note that "all models assume that cognitive behaviors comply with the same laws that influence the control of overt behaviors" (p. 200), while Werner (1982) states that "the cognitive therapist fully supports the use of a learning theory (behavior modification) approach" (p. 61). Albert Ellis, the founder of the widely popular rational emotive therapy, recently altered the name of his model to *rational emotive behavior therapy,* which he says more accurately reflects his views on the relationship between cognitive and behavioral therapy (Ellis, 1994), and Aaron Beck's seminal work on cognitive therapy for clinically anxious clients describes mainstream behavior therapy procedures such as assertiveness training, breathing exercises, exposure therapy, modeling, and homework exercises (Beck & Emery, 1985).

The difference between behavior therapy and cognitive therapy has been succinctly stated by Werner (1982, p. 3): "The cognitivist says that the primary determinant of emotion and behavior is thinking." Accordingly, much of cognitive therapy consists of carefully listening to clients, asking them to describe significant events in their lives and what happened both externally and internally, in an attempt to isolate possible irrational or other dysfunctional ways of thinking that purportedly mediate maladaptive overt actions and covert emotions.

The cognitive theory of RET postulates the following:

> People usually create self-defeating feelings and behaviors by constructing irrational or self-defeating beliefs. . . . RET holds that when people take their strong preferences or desires for success, love or comfort, and define them as musts and commands, they tend to make themselves grandiosely anxious, depressed, hostile, and self-pitying. (Kendall et al., 1995, p. 170)

Originally, in the 1950s and 1960s, Ellis developed a listing of eleven or so major categories of irrational beliefs derived from his clinical experience, a list that rapidly grew to several hundred specific types. More recently he has been refining these into a far fewer number of central core irrational cognitions, which are maintained to be etiologically related to certain emotional, cognitive, and behavioral disorders—for example:

1. I must be thoroughly competent, adequate, achieving, and lovable at all times, or else I am an incompetent worthless person.
2. Other significant people in my life must treat me kindly and fairly at all times, or else I can't stand it and they are bad, rotten, evil persons who should be severely blamed, damned, and vindictively punished for their horrible treatment of me.
3. Things and conditions absolutely must be the way I want them to be and must never be too difficult or frustrating. Otherwise, life is awful, terrible, horrible, catastrophic, and unbearable. (Kendall et al., 1995, p. 172).

Treatment in Ellis's model consists of listening to the clients describe events in their lives wherein they became angry, fearful, depressed, and so forth, and in inquiring as to the thoughts that occurred following these ostensibly upsetting events. RET uses an *ABC* model of cognitive theory, with *A* being the activating event (what happened in the client's life), *B* being the irrational beliefs the client said to herself, and *C* being the consequence—the emotions, other thoughts, and behaviors following the reiteration of the irrational belief(s). In most cases the therapist can elicit the client's having made one or more irrational self-statements of the type described. The social worker can then educate clients to the effect that it was not environmental events that upset them, but rather what they had covertly told themselves regarding those events that produced distress. Further work involves teaching the client to construct more rational self-statements and to practice these during daily life when encountering troubling events. The theory is that as rational self-talk replaces irrational beliefs, pathological behavior, affect, and thoughts will be eliminated. To a large extent, RET consists of a deliberate psychoeducational effort at producing a profound philosophical reorientation on the part of the client, aligning the person with new, more rational core beliefs to replace the irrational ones causing distress. This approach is not without controversy, of course. Who decides what constitutes a "rational" belief? The usual collection of dead European men? Albert Ellis? The social worker? The client?

Cognitive theory (CT) as developed by Aaron Beck has produced another well-developed model of practice that, like RET, enjoys a strong tradition of empirical research support as highly effective for a growing number of clinical disorders. Originally developed for work with seriously depressed clients, Beck's version of CT is being applied to nearly the entire spectrum of DSM-defined conditions, among them, affective disorders, anxiety disorders, and personality disorders. Rather than postulating irrational beliefs as the etiological source of pathology, Beck claims the existence of a construct he calls cognitive sets (the distinctions between Beck's and Ellis's views continue to elude the finest brains in psychotherapy). As in RET, clinicians using Beck's CT help patients in an educational and instructional process to identify covert faulty thinking using a variety of verbal tools. Among these are "counting automatic thoughts" (e.g., "There's another fearful thought. I'll just count it and let it go"), asking questions (e.g., "Where is the logic?" "Are you thinking in all-or-none terms?"), generating alternative interpretations, and normalizing anxiety (or depression, or something else), among quite literally dozens of specific techniques (see Beck & Emery, 1985, for a review).

Other specific approaches to therapy that rely on some variation of cognitive theory include Meichenbaum's stress inoculation training, D'Zurilla and Goldfried's problem-solving training, Rehm's self-control therapy, Barlow's panic control treatment, and Linehan's dialectical behavior therapy for persons meeting the criteria for borderline personality disorder (see Hollon & Beck, 1994, for a review).

There are a large number of clinical assessment instruments designed to measure clients' reports of irrational cognitions (there is no way to measure cognitions directly, of course), and considerable correlational research has demonstrated associations between reported irrational beliefs and client problems (e.g. Himle, Thyer, & Papsdorf, 1982). Such studies corroborate (but do not prove) the hypothesis that irrational beliefs cause pathological states.

Cognitive theory (and its associated therapies) has spawned a number of professional organizations and journals. Both Ellis and Beck have established official training programs for their versions of cognitive therapy, with various levels of qualifications available. Most large cities now have some type of specialty clinic offering cognitive therapy, whose practitioners may or may not be affiliated with one of the training institutes. The journal *Cognitive Therapy and Research* was founded in 1976 and was followed by outlets such as the *Journal of Cognitive Psychotherapy.* In 1994 the Association for Advancement of Behavior Therapy (AABT), which had published the journal *Behavior Therapy* since 1970, founded *Cognitive and Behavioral Practice.* In 1990 *Behavior Therapy* added the subtitle *An International Journal Devoted to the Application of Behavioral and Cognitive Sciences to Clinical Problems,* with these developments reflecting the increasing emphasis within AABT of cognitive research and practice on its original behavioral orientation. And of course there have long been theoretical journals (as opposed to practice ones) devoted to cognitive phenomena (e.g. *Cognitive Development, Cognitive Psychology,* and *Cognitive Science*).

A LOOK TOWARD THE FUTURE

Is social learning theory "going cognitive"? Cognition is sometimes erroneously differentiated from behavior, with cognitive therapy said to deal with changing cognitions and behavior therapy said to be limited to changing overt behavior, but ignores a client's thinking processes and feelings. Recall from the definition of behavior that cognition *is* behavior, itself to be explained by the principles of social learning theory. The current *Social Work Dictionary* reflects this perspective:

> *Behavior:* Any action or response by an individual, including observable activity, measurable physiological changes, cognitive images, fantasies, and emotions. Some scientists consider even subjective experiences to be behaviors. . . .
>
> *Behavior therapy:* Application of *behavior modification* principles in clinical settings to assess and alter undesired behaviors . . . using techniques based on empirical research. . . .
>
> *Cognitive theory:* A group of concepts pertaining to the way individuals develop the intellectual capacity for receiving, processing, and acting on information. . . .
>
> *Cognitive therapy:* Clinical *intervention* using *cognitive theory* concepts that focus on the client's conscious thinking processes, motivations, and reasons for certain behavior. (Barker, 1995, pp. 33, 34, 65)

For the behavior analyst, cognition (and feelings) are behaviors of the body that require explanation in the same manner that overt, publicly observable actions are accounted for. Rather than postulating, as does cognitive theory, that environmental events happen, that these are cognitively processed, and, based on this cognition, overt behavior and affect result, the behaviorist hypothesizes that environmental events occur and that this results in overt behavior, affect, and cognition. These results may not be concurrent—some may occur before others—but regardless of this temporal ordering, all are seen as largely a function of environmental experiences.

Recall the client who was bitten by a dog. Later in life, when she avoided dogs, feared them, and could narrate negative thoughts about them, the cause of the overt behavior, the fear, and the cognitions was the experience of being bitten. Her later negative thoughts are not held to *cause* her to fear and flee dogs. Rather, being bitten caused all three behavioral phenomena. Thus mainstream behavior analysis postulates a thorough environmental determinism, whereas the cognitive theorist maintains a largely mental determinism, influenced to some extent by the environmental factors favored by the behaviorist. This issue is not moot, however. If one believes in largely environmental determinants, then social work intervention will be more likely to have an environmental focus: alleviating aversive conditions and deprivations, reinforcing adaptive abilities, teaching, shaping, and coaching functional life skills, working with the client in real-life contexts, and so forth. If one subscribes to a cognitive account, then social work practice is more likely to take the form of office-based Socratic argumentation, uncovering irrational self-statements, repeating affirmations, and other verbally oriented mechanisms of changing clients' mentation. The reader may make her own appraisal about which approach seems most consistent with social work's person-in-environment perspective.

The causal role of cognition has been an important topic of philosophical debate for several millennia, and social workers will not likely resolve the issue to the satisfaction of everyone. As a practical matter, Bandura (1977) has long noted that the most effective method of changing cognitions is through engaging in overt behavior. If you want to help a phobic think more rationally about dogs, and to be less fearful, helping the client experience a series of harmless (perhaps even pleasant) encounters with dogs may be more effective in improving affect and cognition and in reducing avoidance than would be verbal cognitive therapy conducted in an office. And cognitive therapy is eclectic: "RET also employs many behavioral methods, most commonly reinforcement, response cost, assertiveness and skill training, and in vivo extinction and implosion to fearful stimuli" (Kendall et al., 1995, p. 180). Thus for the clinical social worker using these theories, it is not a question of doing cognitive therapy *or* behavior therapy; most employ both approaches. Even the behavior analyst may employ so-called cognitive therapy techniques, but she would likely (privately!) construe them in social learning theory terms rather than accept mentalistic accounts of their mechanism of action.

To a large extent, behavior theory has always been concerned with explaining cognitive phenomena. Throughout his career, B. F. Skinner wrote incisive works theorizing about private events such as thinking, self-control, self-talk, and emotions (see Thyer, 1992b, for references). In one of his last books Skinner (1989) wrote chapters with titles such as "The Place of Feeling in the Analysis of Behavior," "The Origins of Cognitive Thought," "The Initiating Self," and "The Listener."

In addition to explaining cognitive processes, behaviorists have always focused on treating cognitive and affective disorders with behavior analysis and therapy. Behavior therapy never was exclusively focused on changing overt actions. For example, the earliest behavior therapy method ever rigorously tested was Wolpe's technique of systematic desensitization (SD; see review by Fischer, 1978). SD was developed in the 1950s, the dawn of formal behavior therapy. It was explicitly designed to treat pathological affective states, originally those related to clinical anxiety, and was eventually applied to most so-called neurotic conditions.

Part of the error, of course, lies in the very terms *behavior therapy* and *cognitive therapy*, inasmuch as we are not accustomed to the technical term *behavior* subsuming cognition and affect. But such has been the case for decades, and it is time to stop perpetuating the myth that these are two different fields (Thyer, 1992c). Behavior theory *is* cognitive theory. Behavior therapy *is* cognitive therapy.

As a further practical matter, both behavior therapy and cognitive therapy have impressive track records of empirical support for a wide variety of formal disorders and problems in living. For example, cognitive therapy, as developed by Aaron Beck, seems very effective in the treatment of major depression, perhaps as effective as conventional antidepressant medications. Panic disorder, generalized anxiety disorder, phobias, anorexia and bulimia, delusional behavior and other clinically important aspects of schizophrenia, posttraumatic stress disorder, obsessive-compulsive disorder, alcoholism, and sexual dysfunctions are but a few of the formal disorders for which cognitive and/or behavior therapy have considerable research support in the form of numerous well-controlled outcome studies (see reviews by Hollon & Beck, 1994; Emmelkamp, 1994).

These developments have profoundly influenced social work theory and intervention models. During the past two decades, a large number of methodologically sound outcome studies have been conducted on clinical social work practice. Here are some of the conclusions of review articles summarizing this body of evidence:

> Turning now to the vital question of which methods are most strongly correlated with positive outcome we see that behavioural and cognitive-behavioural methods (whether deployed in groups or with individuals) sweep the board. . . . The majority of positive results within research of an experimental and quasi-experimental kinds are accounted for by behavioural and cognitive-behavioural approaches. (MacDonald, Sheldon, & Gillespie, 1992, p. 635)

> Social workers are generating an empirical basis that supports claims to effectiveness for a broad range of problems. . . . The influence of the behavior modification movement is apparent and pervasive. The majority of the experiments involve evaluation of skills training or contingency contracting within the frame of reference of learning theory. (Reid & Hanrahan, 1982, pp. 338, 329)

> Most of the studies with unequivocally positive outcomes test forms of practice that relied heavily on problem-solving and task centered methods, usually in conjunction with behavioral methods. (Rubin, 1985, p. 474)

Behavioral and cognitive interventions are closely linked to their underlying theoretical conceptualizations. It would be a mistake in logical reasoning to assume that the effectiveness of the interventions proves the validity of the theory (cf. Thyer, 1992d), but a greater danger is for the profession to ignore or misrepresent social learning theory, which often happens (Thyer, 1992c). Respondent, operant, and observational learning elements are a significant component to many of the psychosocial and interpersonal problems encountered in practice. Knowledge of these elements is essential to effective clinical social work.

REFERENCES

Azrin, N. H. (1976). Improvements in the community-reinforcement approach to alcoholism. *Behaviour Research and Therapy, 14,* 339–348.

Baer, D. M., & Deguchi, H. (1985). Generalized imitation from a radical-behavioral viewpoint. In S. Reiss & R. R. Bootzin (Eds.), *Theoretical issues in behavior therapy* (pp. 179–217). New York: Academic Press.

Bandura, A. (1977). Self-efficacy: Toward a unifying theory of behavioral change. *Psychological Review, 84,* 191–215.

Barker, R. L. (1995). *The social work dictionary* (3rd ed.). Washington, DC: NASW Press.

Barth, R. P. (1986). *Social and cognitive treatment of children and adolescents.* San Francisco: Jossey-Bass.

Beck, A. T., & Emery, G. (1985). *Anxiety disorders and phobias: A cognitive perspective.* New York: Basic Books.

Bijou, S. W. (1993). *Behavior analysis of child development* (2nd ed.). Reno, NE: Context Press.

Bloom, M. (1992). A conversation with Carel Germain. In M. Bloom (Ed.), *Changing lives: Studies in human development and professional helping* (pp. 406–409). Columbia, SC: University of South Carolina Press.

Boynton, K. E., & Thyer, B. A. (1994). Behavioral social work in the field of oncology. *Journal of Applied Social Sciences, 18,* 189–197.

Butterfield, W. H., & Parson, R. (1973). Modeling and shaping by parents to develop chewing behavior in their retarded child. *Journal of Behavior Therapy and Experimental Psychiatry, 4,* 285–287.

Ellis, A. (1994). Radical behavioral treatment of private events. *Behavior Therapist, 17,* 219–221.

Emmelkamp, P. (1994). Behavior therapy with adults. In A. E. Bergin & S. L. Garfield (Eds.), *Handbook of psychotherapy and behavior change* (pp. 379–427). New York: Wiley.

Ferster, C. B., & Skinner, B. F. (1957). *Schedules of reinforcement.* New York: Appleton-Century-Crofts.

Figueroa, R. G., Thyer, B. A., & Thyer, B. A. (1992). Extinction and DRO in the treatment of aggression in a boy with severe mental retardation. *Journal of Behavior Therapy and Experimental Psychiatry, 23,* 133–140.

Fischer, J. (1978). *Effective casework practice: An eclectic approach.* New York: McGraw-Hill.

Fischer, J., & Nehs, R. (1978). Use of a commonly available chore to reduce a boy's rate of swearing. *Journal of Behavior Therapy and Experimental Psychiatry, 9,* 81–83.

Gambrill, E. D., & Richey, C. A. (1976). *It's up to you: Developing assertive social skills.* Millbrae, CA: Les Femmes.

Gammon, E. A., & Rose, S. D. (1991). The coping skills training program for parents of children with developmental disabilities: An experimental evaluation. *Research on Social Work Practice, 1,* 244–256.

Germain, C. B., & Gitterman, A. (1995). Ecological perspective. In R. L. Edwards (Ed.), *Encyclopedia of social work* (pp. 816–824). Washington, DC: NASW Press.

Griffin, J. H. (1960). *Black like me.* New York: Signet.

Himle, D. P., Thyer, B. A., & Papsdorf, J. D. (1982). Relationship between irrational beliefs and anxiety. *Cognitive Therapy and Research, 6,* 219–223.

Hollon, S. D., & Beck, A. T. (1994). Cognitive and cognitive-behavioral therapies. In A. E.

Bergin & S. L. Garfield (Eds.), *Handbook of psychotherapy and behavior change* (pp. 428–466). New York: Wiley.

Jayaratne, S. (1978). A study of clinical eclecticism. *Social Service Review, 52,* 621–631.

Kendall, P. C., Haaga, D. A. F., Ellis, A., Bernard, M., DiGiuseppe, R., & Kassinove, H. (1995). Rational-emotive therapy in the 1990s and beyond: Current status, recent revisions, and research questions. *Clinical Psychology Review, 15,* 169–185.

Kornhaber, R. C., & Schroeder, H. E. (1975). Importance of model similarity on extinction of avoidance behavior in children. *Journal of Consulting and Clinical Psychology, 43,* 601–607.

Lovaas, O. I. (1987). Behavioral treatment and normal educational and intellectual functioning in young autistic children. *Journal of Consulting and Clinical Psychology, 55,* 3–9.

Lundin, R. W. (1974). *Personality: A behavioral analysis.* New York: Macmillan.

MacDonald, G., Sheldon, B., & Gillespie, J. (1992). Contemporary studies of the effectiveness of social work. *British Journal of Social Work, 22,* 615–643.

McEachin, J. J., Smith, T., & Lovaas, O. I. (1993). Long-term outcome for children with autism who received early intensive behavioral treatment. *American Journal of Mental Retardation, 97,* 359–372.

Patterson, G. R. (1982). *Coercive family process.* Eugene, OR: Castalia.

Paul, G. L., & Lentz, R. J. (1977). *Psychosocial treatment of chronic mental patients: Milieu versus social-learning programs.* Cambridge, MA: Harvard University Press.

Paul, G. L., & Menditto, A. A. (1992). Effectiveness of inpatient treatment programs for mentally ill adults in public psychiatric facilities. *Applied and Preventive Psychology, 1,* 41–63.

Rapport, M. D., Murphy, H. A., & Bailey, J. S. (1982). Ritalin vs. response cost in the control of hyperactive children. *Journal of Applied Behavior Analysis, 15,* 205–216.

Reid, W. J., & Hanrahan, P. (1982). Recent evaluations of social work practice: Grounds for optimism. *Social Work, 27,* 328–340.

Rosenthal, T., & Bandura, A. (1978). Psychological modeling: Theory and practice. In S. L. Garfield & A. E. Bergin (Eds.), *Handbook of psychotherapy and behavior change* (pp. 621–658). New York: Wiley.

Rothman, J., & Thyer, B. A. (1984). Behavioral social work in community and organizational settings. *Journal of Sociology and Social Welfare, 11,* 294–326.

Rubin, A. (1985). Practice effectiveness: More grounds for optimism. *Social Work, 30,* 469–476.

Schlinger, H. D. (1995). *A behavior analytic view of child development.* New York: Plenum.

Scott, W. D. (1995). Cognitive behavior therapy: Two basic cognitive research programs and a theoretically based definition. *Behavior Therapist, 18,* 122–124.

Shorkey, C. T., & Taylor, J. E. (1973). Management of maladaptive behavior of a severely burned child. *Child Welfare, 52,* 543–547.

Skinner, B. F. (1957). *Verbal behavior.* Englewood Cliffs, NJ: Prentice Hall.

Skinner, B. F. (1989). *Recent issues in the analysis of behavior.* Columbus, OH: Merrill.

Strom, K. (1994). Social workers in private practice: An update. *Clinical Social Work Journal, 22,* 73–89.

Stuart, R. B. (1980). *Helping couples change: A social learning approach to marital therapy.* New York: Guilford.

Sundel, S. S., & Sundel, M. (1980). *Be assertive: A practical guide for human service workers.* Beverly Hills, CA: Sage.

Thomas, E. J. (1967). *The socio-behavioral approach and applications to social work.* New York: Council on Social Work Education.

Thyer, B. A. (1981a). Behavioural social work: A bibliography. *International Journal of Behavioural Social Work and Abstracts, 1,* 229–251.

Thyer, B. A. (1981b). Prolonged in-vivo exposure therapy with a 70-year-old woman. *Journal of Behavior Therapy and Experimental Psychiatry, 12,* 69–71.

Thyer, B. A. (1983). Behavior modification in social work practice. In M. Hersen, P. Miller, & R. Eisler (Eds.), *Progress in behavior modification* (pp. 173–226). New York: Plenum.

Thyer, B. A. (1985). Textbooks in behavioral social work: A bibliography. *Behavior Therapist, 8,* 161–162.

Thyer, B. A. (1988). Radical behaviorism and clinical social work. In R. Dorfman (Ed.), *Paradigms of clinical social work* (pp. 123–148). New York: Guilford.

Thyer, B. A. (1992a). A behavioral perspective on human development. In M. Bloom (Ed.), *Changing lives: Studies in human development and professional helping* (pp. 410–418). Columbia, SC: University of South Carolina Press.

Thyer, B. A. (1992b). The term "cognitive-behavior therapy" is redundant (letter). *Behavior Therapist, 15,* 112, 128.

Thyer, B. A. (1992c). Behavioral social work: It is not what you think. *Arete, 16*(2), 1–9.

Thyer, B. A. (1992d). Social work theory and practice research: The approach of logical positivism. *Social Work and Social Sciences Review, 4*(1), 5–6.

Thyer, B. A. (1996). Behavior analysis and social welfare policy. In M. A. Mattaini & B. A. Thyer (Eds.), *Finding solutions to social problems: Behavioral strategies for change* (pp. 41–60). Washington, DC: American Psychological Association.

Thyer, B. A., Irvine, S., & Santa, C. (1984). Contingency management of aerobic exercise by chronic schizophrenics. *Perceptual and Motor Skills, 58,* 419–425.

Thyer, B. A., & Maddox, K. (1988). Behavioral social work: Results of a national survey on graduate curricula. *Psychological Reports, 63,* 239–242.

Thyer, B. A., & Wodarski, J. S. (1990). Social learning theory: Towards a comprehensive conceptual framework for social work education. *Social Service Review, 64,* 144–152.

Ullman, L. P., & Krasner, L. (1969). *A psychological approach to abnormal behavior.* New York: Prentice-Hall.

Werner, H. D. (1965). *A rational approach to social casework.* New York: Association Press.

Werner, H. D. (1979). Cognitive therapy. In F. J. Turner (Ed.). *Social work treatment* (2nd ed.) (pp. 243–272). New York: Free Press.

Werner, H. D. (1982). *Cognitive therapy.* New York: Free Press.

Whittaker, J., & Garbarino, J. (1983). *Social support networks: Informal helping in the human services.* New York: Aldine.

Wilson, G. T. (1989). Behavior therapy. In American Psychiatric Association, *Treatments of psychiatric disorders* (pp. 2026–2036). Washington, DC: Author.

Wodarski, J. S., & Bagarozzi, D. A. (1979). *Behavioral social work.* New York: Human Sciences Press.

3

Psychoanalytic Theory

Jerrold R. Brandell and Fredric T. Perlman

The historical relationship between clinical social work and psychoanalysis is both fascinating and extremely complex. Classical psychoanalytic theory and, later, ego psychology stand in relation to social work theory and practice in much the same way that the theory of relativity stands in relation to modern theoretical physics. In each case, the introduction of a new and radical theory has had far-reaching ramifications for the existing framework of knowledge.

In this chapter, psychoanalytic ideas and their unique contributions and adaptations to the practice of clinical social work will be discussed and explored in depth. Psychoanalytic theory, of course, is not a unified body of knowledge; rather, it is composed of multiple theories, models, and schemata pertaining to development, psychopathology, and clinical method and technique. It is a literature of vast scope whose evolution spans an entire century.

PSYCHOANALYSIS AND CLINICAL SOCIAL WORK: A CONCISE HISTORY

The earliest historical influence of psychoanalytic ideas on the social work field seems to have occurred in the late 1920s. Strean (1993) observes that the professional climate in social work favored the introduction of psychoanalytic ideas at this time, inasmuch as caseworkers had begun to recognize the limitations of advice giving, moral suasion, and manipulation of the environment in their work with clients.[1] Beginning in the early 1920s, with the advent of the child guidance movement and work with clinical populations such as the shellshock victims of World War I, the context for social work practice shifted dramatically. Many social workers began to work in hospitals and clinics, thereby extending their exposure to psychiatrists and psychiatric thinking (Goldstein, 1995). The influence of psychiatric thinking so dominated social work during this period that it led one historian to describe it as the "Psychiatric Deluge" (Woodroofe, 1971; Goldstein, 1995). Freud's theories, in particular, stimulated great interest among many social workers.

Psychoanalytic theory placed emphasis on the individual and imputed meaning to pathological symptoms. It presumed the existence of an unconscious and of universal experiences in early childhood development (such as the Oedipus complex) that, failing adaptive resolution, might persist into later development and serve as a basis for psychopathology. It also provided a model for understanding the tendency of individuals to translocate and to repeat early childhood conflicts in adult relationships, even extending to the relationship between client and worker (Goldstein, 1995).

Annette Garrett, in a publication that appeared in 1940, became one of the first social work authors to comment on the transformative impact of Freud's work on social work theory and practice. She observed that the concepts of *social diagnosis* and *social treatment,* originally derived from the pioneering work of Mary Richmond, had gradually evolved into *psychosocial diagnosis* and *psychosocial treatment.* The incorporation of Freudian ideas into social work practice thus enabled social workers to individualize the person-in-environment configuration; each client was regarded as having a unique set of personal experiences, specific strengths and weaknesses peculiar to him or her, and highly individualized, idiosyncratic ways of operating in the world (Strean, 1993).

During the past seventy years, psychoanalysis has exerted a powerful and at times revolutionary influence on the field of clinical social work, a phenomenon paralleled in other social and behavioral sciences. Although it can be argued that the impact of psychoanalytic thinking has pervaded a variety of clinical social work approaches, three classical approaches to social casework may illustrate this influence most clearly: the diagnostic or psychosocial school, the functional school, and the problem-solving approach.

The Diagnostic or Psychosocial School

Although Mary Richmond is often credited with having originated the diagnostic or psychosocial approach to casework, there were a number of other early contributors.

---

[1]Psychoanalysis offered a radically new perspective, one that augmented and complemented the caseworker's understanding of how social forces contribute to the client's maladjustment with a unique emphasis on the client's motives, conflicts, disturbing wishes, defensive adaptations, and personal history (Strean, 1993, pp. 6–7).

Gordon Hamilton, Bertha Reynolds, Charlotte Towle, Fern Lowry, Marion Kenworthy, Betsey Libbey, Annette Garrett, and Florence Hollis are among those whose teaching and scholarship helped to shape this approach to casework (Hollis, 1970).

An important link between psychoanalysis and the psychosocial approach is in the latter's use of Freudian personality theory as a basic organizing framework. According to Hollis (1970, p. 36), dynamic personality theory, augmented by ego psychological principles, provided the most useful approach to an understanding of the individual and his or her relative success or failure in adaptive functioning.

Sigmund Freud, Karl Abraham, Anna Freud, Thomas French, Franz Alexander, August Aichorn, Ernst Federn, Abram Kardiner, Erik Erikson, Heinz Hartmann, Ernest Kris, Rudolf Loewenstein, René Spitz, Margaret Mahler, W. R. D. Fairbairn, Donald Winnicott, Harry Guntrip, Edith Jacobson, Robert White, Otto Kernberg, and Heinz Kohut (Hollis, 1970, p. 39; Woods & Hollis, 1990, pp. 31–32) are psychoanalytic theorists whose work has had particular influence on the psychosocial school.

The influence of psychoanalytic theory is especially evident in the psychosocial school's view of diagnosis. Diagnosis is conceived of as having three equally important facets: *dynamic diagnosis,* in which the individual's interplay with others in his or her environment is examined; *etiological diagnosis,* where the focus is on both current and historically remote features of the person-environment matrix; and *classificatory diagnosis,* in which an effort is made to classify various aspects of the individual's functioning, typically including a clinical diagnosis (Hollis, 1970, p. 52). Other psychoanalytic ideas, such as resistance, transference, and countertransference, have also been integrated into the psychosocial perspective.

The Functional School

The functional theory of casework, developed by Virginia Robinson and Jessie Taft at the Pennsylvania School of Social Work in the 1930s, was also linked to psychoanalysis. The functionalists, however, rejected the classical psychoanalytic ideas that the psychosocial school had embraced, characterizing them as "mechanistic, deterministic view(s) of man . . . [who is seen as] . . . prey to the dark forces of an unconscious and . . . the harsh restrictive influences of internalized parental dicta in the early years" of development (Smalley, 1970, pp. 82–83). Freud's disciple, Otto Rank, whose theories emphasized human growth, the development of the self, and the will as a controlling and organizing force, became an important force in functional theory as a member of the teaching faculty at the University of Pennsylvania. Rank's work also emphasized such ideas as the use of relationship to facilitate growth and the significance of time as a factor in the helping process, ideas that Taft and others used as the basis for the functional model.

One of Rank's unique contributions, according to Smalley, was his theory of birth trauma.[2] "Rank emphasized the development of life fear and death fear out of the

---

[2]Rank's book, *The Trauma of Birth,* first published in 1924, was at first favorably received by Freud (Jones, 1957). Within two years, however, with the publication of *Inhibitions, Symptoms, and Anxiety* (Freud, 1926), Freud had completely reversed himself, rejecting Rank's thesis in toto.

birth experience and saw all individuals as experiencing and expressing these two fears throughout life . . . the fear of not living, not experiencing, not realizing potential which may be thought of as the death fear; and the fear of separation, of independent existence outside of the womb" (Smalley, 1970, pp. 92–93).

Functional theory has also drawn from Erik Erikson's model of psychosocial and psychosexual development, and to some extent, from the work of Karen Horney and Erich Fromm. Although such fundamental tenets of the functional approach as the function of agency and the use of time as a dimension in the casework relationship are not especially psychoanalytic, the emphases on separation and individuation and on developmental crises and adaptations appear to have an unmistakable psychoanalytic cast.

The Problem-Solving Model

The problem-solving model was developed by Helen Harris Perlman in the 1950s at the University of Chicago. Perlman's model has been described by one author as an effort to traverse the often contentious debate that had erupted between the functional school and the diagnostic school by the 1950s, although she was largely unsuccessful in achieving this objective (Goldstein, 1995, p. 37). Perlman's model of casework is very closely tied to ego psychological theory, and she views the casework process itself as a "parallel to the normal problem-solving efforts of the ego" (1953, pp. 308–15). With the use of such concepts as *partializing* (breaking down large problems into smaller, more manageable tasks), Perlman attempted to "translate ego psychology into action principles" (Perlman, 1970, p. 135).

The problem-solving model also emphasized the significance of relationship, and Perlman did write of such relational phenomena as transference and countertransference. However, she was always careful to make clear distinctions between casework and depth psychology. Casework always aimed to "maintain the relationship on the basis of reality," to keep client and caseworker firmly anchored in their joint purpose, aware of "their separate and realistic identities," and their goal of achieving "a better adaptation between the client and his current problem-situation" (1957, p. 78). Such goals stand in marked contrast to those of psychoanalysis and psychoanalytic psychotherapy, where there is considerably greater emphasis and attention given to remote or distal causes of intercurrent symptoms and failures in adaptation, and to the intrapsychic basis of conflict in general. Furthermore, whereas the transference relationship is promoted in psychoanalysis and in certain psychoanalytic psychotherapies, the effort in the problem-solving approach is "to so manage the relationship and the problem-solving work so as to give minimum excitation to transference" (Perlman, 1957).

FOUNDATIONS OF THEORETICAL PSYCHOANALYSIS

Psychoanalysis is the creation of Sigmund Freud (1856–1939), a Viennese neurologist whose pioneering studies of hysteria, obsessional illness, and other obscure disorders of unknown etiology led him from the practice of neurology to the creation of a new form of treatment based on the investigation of the individual sufferer's mental life. Freud discovered that certain mental illnesses occurred when the sufferer's personality was permeated by the intrusion of powerful and mysterious impulses from deep within the psyche. At one time, Freud thought these mysterious impulses were delayed reations to traumas, especially sexual traumas that had been experienced in early childhood and then dissociated. He soon discovered, however, that these mysterious impulses were not merely the reactions to untoward events of childhood; rather, they were expressions of instinctual drives at the core of the psyche. Normally these instinctual forces are repressed, Freud wrote, but in neurosis they rise up like demonic forces from the deep. Neurotic symptoms such as the hysterical paralyses, amnesias, obsessions, and phobias could be seen as the battleground where the forces of the invading instinctual drives were locked in combat with the defending forces of the embattled personality.

Freud devoted his life to the study of these invading instinctual forces—of their origins in the mind and their influence on mental life. He came to think of the mind as an organization of hierarchically ordered mental systems, in which higher systems, which are associated with mature development, regulate the activity of lower systems, which are more primitive. Instinctual forces, he believed, emanated from the great darkness at the center of psychic life, which he called the unconscious or, later, the id. He endeavored to identify the elemental instinctual forces, to trace their development, and to discern their influence, not only on the individual but on the cultural life of humankind. During the course of his career, Freud continually modified his investigative-therapeutic techniques, and wrote extensively about his discoveries, applying them not only to the problems of psychopathology and pathogenesis but also to the psychology of dreams, mythology, creativity, and love and to critical issues in anthropology, developmental psychology, religion, and political science.

The structure of Freud's psychoanalytic enterprise was exceedingly complex. Freud conceived of psychoanalysis as a research method, a therapeutic technique, a theory of mental functioning, a theory of psychopathology, and a theory of human development. Each of these theories was intimately connected with each of the others. As a result of clinical discoveries, the entire network of theories was continually modified. In the course of his lifetime, Freud propounded three theories of the instincts (1905, 1914b, 1920), two theories of anxiety (1895a, 1926), and two different models of the mind (1900, 1923).

One of the most important trends in the development of Freudian theory was the progressive expansion of his focus from the study of instinctual drives and of the unconscious to the investigation of higher strata of the mind responsible for processing and regulating the instincts in accordance with realistic and moral considerations. Freud initially was little interested in the higher functions of the mind, which he thought were easily understood through introspection. His expanding clinical experience, however, yielded new data that dramatically disconfirmed this naive assumption. Many patients, he learned, suffered from feelings of guilt of which they were utterly unaware and over which they could exert no control. He also discovered that defensive functioning was largely unconscious. These discoveries revealed that the higher stratum of the mind was largely unconscious and far more complex in its functioning than he had originally recognized. Freud's early work may be characterized as a *psychology of the id* or *depth psychology*, while the later work is usually summarized by the term *ego psychology*.

One of the extraordinary features of Freud's scientific style was that he never systematized his ideas or categorically renounced any of his earlier points of view, even when he propounded new ideas that contradicted the old. As a result, his students could hold different "Freudian" positions, each the product of a different phase of Freud's theoretical development.

In the years since Freud's death, psychoanalysts around the world have reshaped Freud's theory in accordance with their own views and empirical data.[3] The result has been a proliferation of psychoanalytic theories, a process paralleled by efforts to identify their most salient common characteristics. Some have paid special attention to the problem of object relations,[4] characterizing these theories as having either a drive/structure or relational-structure basis (Greenberg & Mitchell, 1983). Others have grouped psychoanalytic theories into several dominant psychologies or orientations of psychoanalytic thought, which collectively have been referred to as the *four psychologies of psychoanalysis* (Pine, 1988). Although each of these psychological systems or orientations—drive theory, ego psychology, object relations theory, and the psychology of the self—has certain distinctive features, it is arguable as to whether any of the four can be thought of as an essentially separate psychological system (Pine, 1990).

We have based the following discussion on somewhat different premises. It is our understanding that the impetus for the development of each major school of psychoanalytic thought has typically involved certain fundamental questions thought to be irreconcilable within the framework of existing theory. Each of these schools has retained certain features of traditional or mainstream psychoanalytic theory, so that in most instances, the differences among these major schools reflect processes that are both qualitative and evolutionary. We therefore prefer to speak of the continuities and discontinuities of the respective schools. Because the discontinuities between traditional psychoanalytic theory and later developments in ego psychology are somewhat less pronounced than are, for example, those between traditional psychoanalytic theory and psychology of the self, traditional psychoanalytic theory and later ego psychology are presented in the same discussion. This same rationale permits us to separate the discussion of the various object relations theories, both British and American, from self psychology.

CLASSICAL PSYCHOANALYTIC THEORY

Classical psychoanalytic theory derives from the *structural model* or viewpoint of psychoanalysis (Freud, 1923).[5] It represents an integration of Freud's theories of instinctual life with his later understanding of the ego and ego development. Classical psychoanalytic treatment techniques emphasize self-knowledge or insight as the

---

[3]Psychoanalysis is properly regarded as an empirical science, although it is also a naturalistic one; it is most usefully thought of as postdictive—seeking to explain behavior and its antecedents—rather than making any attempt to predict behavior (Holzman, 1970, p. 5).

[4]Defined as the "individual's interactions with external and internal (real and imagined) other people, and to the relationship between their internal and external object worlds" (Greenberg & Mitchell, 1983).

[5]Explained in the section on metapsychological viewpoints.

essential curative factor in psychotherapy. Classical psychoanalytic theory has been refined in each generation of Freud's followers. The most influential proponents of the classical position have included theorists like Otto Fenichel, Anna Freud, Annie Reich, Bertram Lewin, Leo Rangell, Jacob Arlow, and Charles Brenner. Much of the following exposition of classical theory derives directly from Freud. The more contemporary views discussed here derive largely from the views of Charles Brenner and his collaborators. Because Brenner's thinking includes a number of significant modifications, it is often characterized as *contemporary classical* or *contemporary structural theory*.

Psychoanalytic theory posits that the mind is a product of evolutionary development, which functions to ensure adaptation and survival. Mental activity is governed by a fundamental propensity to seek pleasure and avoid pain. Freud called this the *pleasure-unpleasure principle,* or sometimes simply the *pleasure principle.* It is likely that the pleasure principle is favored by natural selection because pain is associated with injury, which threatens survival, while pleasure is associated with the satisfaction of needs, which promotes survival. Organisms failing to seek pleasure and avoid pain would probably be prone to extinction.

Freud held that the mind is moved to activity by the pressure of genically determined motivations, or instinctual drives, whose satisfaction is pleasurable. The automatic pursuit of pleasurable satisfactions is modified by successive developmental experiences in which pleasure seeking is paired with aversive contingencies that provoke affects of unpleasure. This is exemplified by the normal experiences of socialization in which primitive infantile pleasures are disrupted by parental discipline. Socialization challenges the pleasure principle by creating situations in which the child learns that the pursuit of instinctual pleasures will be met by aversive contingencies such as punishment or the withdrawal of affection. As a result, urges to pursue those instinctual pleasures trigger contradictory affective signals motivating contradictory tendencies toward both approach and avoidance. This approach-avoidance dilemma may be characterized as a condition of psychic conflict.

Psychoanalytic research reveals that mental life is characterized by the pervasive presence of psychic conflict. This is a consequence of the prolonged dependency of the child on his or her parents and, later, the extended family and wider social environment. As a result of this extensive dependency, a child undergoes a protracted process of development and socialization during which many innate desires for pleasurable activity and human relatedness are subject to the idiosyncratic responsiveness and disciplinary reactions of the child's significant caretakers. When these responses to the child's behavior are repetitive and painful, they eventually precipitate psychic conflict in the child who both wants to gratify her pleasurable inclinations yet avoid the painful consequences she expects her behavior to elicit. Psychic conflict challenges the mind to produce new patterns of pleasure seeking that will gratify desires while avoiding or minimizing expected aversive consequences.

Freud discovered that psychological symptoms and character pathologies are complex structures, unconsciously produced by the mind in order to avoid or minimize unpleasure. He characterized these structures as *compromise formations.* The concept of compromise conveys the discovery that psychological symptoms and character problems, however painful or crippling, are intended to achieve a measure of pleasure while averting a measure of pain.

At one time, psychoanalysts believed that psychic conflict and compromise formation were features of mental illness, while mental health was characterized by the absence of psychic conflict. Psychoanalytic data, however, have revealed this to be an inaccurate view of mental health. Analysis of the healthy aspects of any individual's mental functioning, such as a happy vocational choice or the pursuit of a pleasurable hobby, regularly reveals the influence of the same desires and conflicts that determine the patient's symptoms and character pathology (Brenner, 1982).

Conflicts, Compromise Formations, and Their Aftermath

The analysis of compromise formations requires a familiarity with their basic anatomy. Psychoanalytic data reveal that compromise formations regularly include wishes of childhood origin that are associated with, and therefore arouse, aversive affects, such as anxiety and guilt, and psychological defenses that function to reduce the unpleasure of these aversive affects. This section will provide a more detailed description of these components.

Wishes of Childhood

Childhood wishes are formed by the interaction of biological and social-experiential factors. In the first days of infancy, biologically rooted needs produce tension states that are devoid of psychological content. These diffuse tensions acquire structure when caretakers provide "experiences of satisfaction" appropriate to the infant's actual need. As a result, diffuse tensions are gradually transformed into wishes to repeat these experiences of satisfaction (Freud, 1900). Because these experiences entail specific activities with specific persons, wishes always include representations of these activities and persons. These aspects of the wishes are called their *aims* and *objects.* Every individual's wishes are unique and personal, because they are formed by unique personal experiences.

Psychoanalysts have traditionally employed a theory of drives (or instinctual drives) to conceptualize the biological sources of mental life. The psychoanalytic concept of instinctual drives differs from the ethological concept of instincts. In lower animals, instincts are "specific action potentials" with genically determined, prestructured patterns of action (Thorpe, 1956). The evolution of higher vertebrates, however, includes the progressive substitution of learned behavior for these preprogrammed action patterns (Lorenz, 1937). In psychoanalytic theory, instinctual drives give rise to tensions, but not to specific programs for action. Wishes, which arise when these tensions are structured by experiences of satisfaction, are specific schemata for action. Because they represent the motivational pressure of drives, wishes are also referred to as *drive derivatives.* Drives themselves, however, are not observable and must be regarded as hypothetical constructs (Brenner, 1982). Psychoanalytic theory has traditionally employed the related idea of drive energy to conceptualize the driving force of wishes in mental life. Although some contemporary theorists reject these energetic ideas (Greenberg & Mitchell, 1983; Mitchell,

1988; Klein, 1976), many analysts find them useful because they provide a means for conceptualizing the fluctuating intensities with which wishes are invested.

Psychoanalytic theorists since Freud have wrestled with the challenge of identifying and classifying the basic drives. Many different drives have been suggested over the years. Freud himself posited basic drives for sex and self-preservation (Freud, 1905), and later, for life and for death (1920). Other theorists hypothesized drives for power and masculinity (Adler, 1927), individuation (Jung, 1916, 1917), aggression (Hartmann, Kris, & Lowenstein, 1949), mastery (Hendricks, 1942), attachment (Bowlby, 1969), effectance (White, 1963), safety (Sandler, 1960), empathy (Kohut, 1971, 1977), and so on. Are all of these drives primary motivations, or may some be better understood as derivative expressions of more basic drives? Most theorists believe that science is best served if primary drives can be identified. To date, no scientific consensus about primary motivations has been achieved. Most traditional analysts, however, recognize the existence of two primary drives: the sexual and the aggressive. This classification is based on clinical findings that regularly reveal the prominent role of sexual and aggressive wishes in the psychodynamics of symptoms and other pathology.

The Sexual Drive

In psychoanalytic thought, sex has a broader meaning than it does in everyday discourse. In psychoanalysis, the word *sexual* connotes a broad range of pleasures that are not necessarily connected with sexual intercourse or even with overtly sexual conduct. The semantic extension of the terms *sex* and *sexuality* highlights the plasticity of the sexual drive and the continuity of sexual development from childhood to adulthood. Human sexuality does not arise in adulthood or even in adolescence, but in early childhood. Although the sexual wishes of childhood differ from those of adulthood, they are predecessors of adult sexuality, and their motivational influence is discernible when the sexual wishes of adulthood are studied. Although adult sexuality supersedes childhood sexuality, it does not entirely replace it. Childhood sexual wishes are absorbed into the larger network of adult desires and in some cases may substitute for adult desires. Because some childhood sexual wishes are inevitably conflictual, their role in adult sexuality often results in disturbances of sexuality and love life. Adult sexuality, then, cannot be adequately understood without an appreciation of its roots in the sensual desires of childhood.

Childhood sexuality (or *infantile sexuality*) is composed of numerous sensual pleasures, experienced in relation to sensitive parts of the body, such as the skin, the mouth, the anus, and the genitals (the *erogenous zones*). Freud believed that these pleasures are initially stimulated by the activities of baby care, such as holding, feeding, touching, and bathing, and then subsequently pursued as ends in their own right. He also believed that the maturation of the sexual drive through childhood entailed a sequenced intensification of oral, anal, and phallic (clitoral) sexual wishes (Freud, 1905). Between the ages of about three and six, these sexual wishes give rise to the formation of the *Oedipus complex*.

The Oedipus complex is a configuration of psychological forces characterized by the concentration of sexual wishes on one parent, usually of the opposite sex, and the emergence of hostile feelings for the remaining parent, who is now the child's rival in love. Numerous variations in this typical pattern occur under different familial conditions. Siblings, for example, may become objects of oedipal desire, through early displacement away from a loved parent, or when a child's relations with parents thwart typical oedipal development (Abend, 1984; Sharpe & Rosenblatt, 1994). The Oedipus complex typically entails feelings of inadequacy, fears of the rival parent's retaliation, and usually feelings of defeat. These painful consequences normally motivate a retreat from oedipal strivings and efforts to limit awareness of persisting oedipal desires, a process that initiates the latency phase, during which sexual wishes are relatively dormant. The Oedipus complex actually consists of both positive oedipal and negative oedipal strivings. The positive Oedipus complex reflects the child's wish for a sexual relationship with the opposite-sex parent and a concomitant wish for the demise of the same-sex parent. Due to the child's sense of vulnerability and fundamental ambivalence, however, negative oedipal strivings coexist with the positive ones. In effect, the child also desires a sexual union with the parent of the same sex, a wish that gives rise to feelings of rivalry with the opposite-sex parent for the former's affections. In most instances, the positive Oedipus complex supersedes the negative Oedipus complex, a condition that traditional psychoanalytic theory stipulates is necessary for the emergence of a heterosexual orientation and cohesive identity in adulthood (Moore & Fine, 1990). Sexual desire reemerges as a prominent motivation under the hormonal impetus of adolescence, which introduces the genital pleasure of orgasm. The sexual wishes of adulthood provide a context for the gratification of childhood sexual wishes as well. These are normally evident in the activities of foreplay, which typically include kissing, touching, anal stimulation, and other such features that derive from childhood sensual experience. The influence of infantile sexual wishes is also evident when the person chosen as a partner in adulthood *(object choice)* resembles a primary object of childhood sexuality.

The Aggressive Drive

Most psychoanalysts recognize that destructive wishes play an important role in mental life. Although there is little dispute about the centrality of aggression, there is widespread disagreement about how best to understand it. Analysts differ on whether the aggressive drive exerts a continuous pressure for discharge, as does the sexual drive, or, whether aggression is a "reactive instinct" (Fine, 1975), triggered by frustration, perceived threats, or other noxious conditions. Freud and many of his followers believed that the aggressive drive generates a more or less continuous flow of destructive impulses (Freud, 1920; Hartmann, Kris, & Loewenstein, 1949). Friedman and Downey (1995) have recently argued that aggression is related to the organizing influence of male hormones on the fetal brain and is thus a typical feature of male psychology, evidenced by rough-and-tumble play among boys. They suggest that aggression in males may express genically determined strivings for dominance over other males. Other important theorists conceptualize aggression as a reaction to threats or injuries to self-esteem (Kohut, 1972; Rochlin, 1973), for example, or to physical or mental pain (Grossman, 1991), to the experience of "ego weakness" (Guntrip, 1968), to the frustration of dependency needs (Fairbairn, 1952; Saul, 1976), to "the internally felt experience of excessive unpleasure" (Parens, 1979), and others.

Psychological data support the view that hostile aggression is a reaction to pain, frustration, and feelings of endangerment. These mental states can be episodic and situational, but they may also be chronic features of mental life. Traumatic events, for example, often leave emotional "lesions," which give rise to a continuous stream of aggressive wishes. Captain Ahab's unrelenting hatred for Moby Dick, the great whale that bit off his leg, is a good example. All children experience frustrations and disappointments and are prone to feel small, powerless, damaged, or unloved, at least at times. Oedipal strivings, for instance, normally entail feelings of anxiety and guilt, which may persist as feelings of doom or endangerment. The ultimate failure of oedipal ambitions often leaves a feeling of inferiority. In this view, aggression is an inevitable aspect of mental life since everybody suffers to some extent from the painful residue of childhood conflicts. It is likely that aggression may become a central motivation of mental life in accordance with the degree to which such painful states dominate subjective experience. It may also be observed that people who endure a great deal of pain or frustration as a result of maladaptive compromise formations are also prone to be aggressive as a consequence of their unhappiness. Aggression is not only a component of psychic conflict; it may also be a consequence of it.

Unpleasures

Psychic conflict occurs when wishes become associated with painful affects of *unpleasures* in the course of development. Freud (1926) discovered that childhood wishes were regularly associated with anxiety (i.e., fear). He found that these fears fall into one of four basic categories, each representing a specific danger: loss of the object (mother or primary caretaker), loss of the love of the object, punishment, especially by genital mutilation (castration), and fear of being a "bad" child who deserves to be punished (fear of conscience, or *superego*). When a wish is associated with any of these dangers, the impulse to enact it triggers mounting anxiety. This may reach traumatic levels if not alleviated by the reassurance of protective caretakers or by independent measures. Over time, the child gradually learns various ways to reduce anxiety, called *defenses*. One important defense is repression, which entails a shifting of attention away from tempting but dangerous wishes. As awareness of the wish diminishes, the associated fear is also reduced. Eventually the child learns to recognize the onset of anxiety and to employ defenses to curtail its development. When anxiety is employed as a signal of danger, it is called *signal anxiety*.

Contemporary psychoanalysts have offered many additions and refinements to Freud's 1926 theory. Many theorists have proposed additions to the classification of psychological dangers and anxieties: fear of loss of the personality or "aphanisis" (Jones, 1911), fear of being eaten (Fenichel, 1929), fear of ego disintegration (A. Freud, 1936), engulfment by persecutory objects (Klein, 1946), ego dissolution (Bak, 1943), narcissistic injuries, such as humiliation or disillusionment with an ideal object (Kohut, 1966), dissolution of self (Frosch, 1970) or fragmentation anxiety (Kohut, 1971), separation anxiety (Mahler, 1968, 1972), and annihilation anxiety (Hurvich, 1989, 1991), to name a few. There is no arbitrary limit to the number of childhood fears that may be identified, although any proposal should conform to childhood psychology. Fears of one's own death, for example, is not regarded as a fear of early childhood since young children have no concept of death. In children's thought, death signifies known dangers, such as bodily damage or separation from loved ones. The study of childhood fears is complicated by the fact that some fears are disguised expressions of more basic anxieties. The theoretical desideratum is to identify the elemental fears. At present, this remains an unsettled issue.

An important theoretical innovation follows from the discovery that anxiety is not the only painful affect with which childhood wishes are associated. Brenner (1974) has demonstrated that *depressive affects* (or *miseries*) also instigate psychic conflict. He has proposed an important revision in the psychoanalytic theory of affects and their relation to psychic conflict (Brenner, 1975, 1982). In his view, all affects are composed of two components, sensations of pleasure and unpleasure, which are innate potentials, and ideas of gratification and calamity, which derive from experience. Pleasurable affects include sensations of pleasure in conjunction with ideas of gratification. Unpleasurable affects include sensations of unpleasure in conjunction with ideas of misfortune or calamity. The ideational component also entails a temporal dimension: gratification or calamity may occur in the future, in the present, or in the past. Happy reminiscences, for example, pertain to the past gratifications, while excited anticipation pertains to future expectations. Similarly, anxiety includes the anticipation of future calamities, while depressive affect includes calamities that have occurred. In Brenner's view, the ideational components of anxiety and depressive affect are identical. These are the four dangers Freud described, conceptually reformatted as the calamities of childhood (Brenner, 1982).

Brenner's revised theory expands the explanatory range of dynamic thinking and better explains certain clinical data. In Brenner's view, both anxiety and depressive affect are regularly occurring components of psychic conflict. Psychic conflict occurs when wishes are associated with depressive affect, just as when they are associated with anxiety (Brenner, 1982). This is a normal aspect of the mourning process, during which every wish for reunion with the lost object elicits a wave of misery. It is also typical of many pathological conditions, especially depressive conditions, in which psychic conflict is characterized by prominent feelings of loss, of being unloved, of being punished or morally condemned, and of being inferior (Brenner, 1982). Both anxiety and depressive affect typically include ideas pertaining to more than one calamity. A child who fears that he will be viciously attacked by a punitive parent, for example, is also likely to feel either anxious or miserable about the loss of the parent's love. Insofar as depressive affect is a motivational factor in psychic conflict, the term *signal anxiety* should be replaced by the term *signal affect* (Jacobson, 1994).

Defense

The third component of psychic conflict is defense. The theory of defense is a cornerstone of psychoanalytic theory (Freud, 1894). The theory of defense has undergone numerous changes and revisions, and like the other aspects of psychoanalytic theory, it is subject to numerous controversies. Defenses may be defined as psychological activities that reduce the unpleasure of psychic conflict by blocking, inhibiting, or distorting awareness of disturbing mental contents. Defenses are traditionally conceptualized as methods for blocking or disguising the expression of the drive derivatives that arouse unpleasure. Contemporary theorists, however, recognize that the unpleasure associated with drive derivatives may be warded off independent of the drive (Abend, 1981; Brenner, 1981, 1982). This is particularly important in clinical work with impulsive patients who habitually "forget" about the consequences of their conduct. Of course, defenses against negative affects may also be adaptive, for example, in situations where anxieties are unrealistic and unduly inhibiting, or in circumstances that require courage or fortitude in the face of unpleasure.

The traditional concept of defense mechanisms entails the assumption that defenses are discrete mental functions that can be observed and classified. In the course of his career, Freud described at least ten different defenses. In her pioneering study of the ego, Anna Freud (1936) listed nine different defenses: regression, repression, reaction formation, isolation, undoing, projection, introjection, turning against the self, and reversal. She later (1936/46) added intellectualization and identification. In the years that followed, this list grew to include twenty-two major and twenty-six minor defenses (Laughlin, 1979). Contemporary structural theory explains this proliferation as a consequence of the idea that defense requires special mechanisms. In fact, what are cited as defense mechanisms are simply ego functions that are deployed in situations of psychic conflict to reduce unpleasure. "Whatever ensues in mental life that results in diminution of unpleasurable affects—ideally in their disappearance—belongs under the heading of defense . . . the ego can use for defense whatever lies at hand that is useful for the purpose" (Brenner, 1981, p. 558). Affects, ideas, attitudes, alterations of attention, and even wishes (drive derivatives) may serve as defenses. Brenner thus concludes: "Modes of defense are as diverse as psychic life itself" (p. 561).

The Genesis of Psychic Conflicts and Compromise Formations

The analysis of psychological conflicts and compromise formations also requires a knowledge of the genesis of psychic conflict. Psychic conflict comes into existence during the course of individual development as a result of childhood experiences and the way that they are interpreted by the child. Childhood normally entails many pleasurable experiences, which give rise to wishes for an expanding variety of pleasures. These are often felt as desires of great urgency and power and are often irresistible to the immature child. Even as these wishes reach new levels of intensity, however, every child must undergo a succession of socialization experiences, such as weaning and toilet training, in which their expression is limited, restricted to special circumstances, or utterly forbidden. Discipline often entails punishment and temporary withdrawals of the parent's loving attentiveness, interactions that are threatening to the child. The character of the child's subjective perception may be quite distorted because of the child's emotional reactions to discipline and as a result of his or her immature cognitive functioning. Whenever a parent punishes a child or restricts a child's pleasure, especially a pleasure in which the child is highly invested, the child is prone to become frustrated and angry. The angrier the child becomes, the more likely he or she is likely to believe that the parent is equally angry. Parents who discipline, even lovingly, may thus come to be perceived as fantastical figures of devastating power. These distorted representations of the parent's aggressive intentions are an aspect of the child's *psychic reality.*

Psychic reality is the true context of existence from the child's point of view (Freud, 1900). Psychic reality is only partially determined by objective events. Wishes, affects, and related cognitive distortions result in the formation of a privately constructed universe in which highly unrealistic wishes, such as the wish to be both sexes or the wish to marry the parent, may appear quite reasonable. Accompanying these wishes, fears of horrendous dangers, such as abandonment or castration, may appear equally real and imminent. Sometimes aspects of psychic reality may be recognized as fantastical in nature, an insight that dissipates their compelling quality. The situation is more complicated when the construction of psychic reality includes memories, however fragmentary, disguised, or elaborated, of seduction and incest, or of other threatening or horrifying events. When psychic reality has been shaped by such objective events, fantastically exaggerated elaborations of these memories tend to exert a persistent influence over the person, based on an enduring sense of actuality. Psychic conflicts are thus bound to be particularly damaging and intractable when parents are actually abusive or when childhood is characterized by the occurrence of unusual traumas, such as a death in the family, an accident, an illness, or surgery.

No matter how entangled in psychic conflict a child's wishes may be, they exert a persistent pressure toward gratification, thus motivating an unending succession of efforts to achieve fulfillment, in both fantasy (imaginary action) and action. In the course of these efforts, childhood wishes are shaped and reshaped by the impact of aversive contingencies on the one hand and by the discovery of pleasurable substitutes on the other. Repetitive trials eventually produce compromise solutions. The best compromises confer a maximum of pleasure with a minimum of unpleasure. These compromises are valued and retained as preferred schemata or blueprints for future gratifications of the wish. They may be repeated with numerous variations whenever the wish arises, in both fantasy and action. Of course, the inexorable process of socialization soon imposes new restrictions and unpleasures, which in turn necessitate the formation for new compromise formations.

Pine (1970) illustrates this developmental process in regard to the transformation of anality (pleasure related to bowel functioning) and scopophilia (pleasure in looking at others). He describes the compromise formations of two eight year olds who are intensely invested in anal wishes. One talks incessantly about bathroom odors and the need to avoid them, a pattern that keeps these thoughts in mind. A second vigorously sprays the toilet with aerosol spray, thus creating a potent new odor to enjoy. Two other eight year olds desire to look at their mother's naked body, but are frightened of the sight of her penisless genital. Each takes every opportunity to look, but each allays anxiety differently. One simply "looks through" his mother; the other gleefully points at his mother's fat. In each case, the scopophilic wish may be enjoyed while the desire to look is disguised or denied. In each of these cases, the primary wish of childhood has given rise to derivative forms, new editions that minimize their aversive emotional consequences. The continuing development of each childhood wish thus entails the creation of successive compromise formations, each represented by particular patterns of conduct and corresponding anthologies of private fantasies (Arlow, 1969). By the time adulthood is reached, mental life will include numerous layers of developmentally stratified compromise formations. All are rooted in the primary wishes and conflicts of childhood. These are the hidden organizers of psychic life.

The Metapsychological Perspectives

What is referred to as the Freudian *metapsychology* is actually a collection of six axiomatic principles that serves as the explanatory basis for Freud's most important formulations about human behavior and psychopathology. The term *metapsychology* came to be used to refer to this framework because it emphasized phenomena that went beyond the extant psychological systems of Freud's time. The six viewpoints or perspectives are the topographical, structural, dynamic, economic, genetic, and adaptive. Some authors have suggested that the genetic and adaptive perspectives, unlike the first four perspectives, were not as clearly explicated by Freud as by later theorists, although there is a general consensus that these two perspectives are nevertheless implicitly represented in Freud's writings (Moore & Fine, 1990).

The Topographical Perspective

According to the topographic model (Freud, 1900) the mind is composed of three systems: the system unconscious, the system preconscious, and the system conscious. The system unconscious, which represents the primitive core of instinctual strivings, functions entirely according to the pleasure principle and is incapable of delaying or inhibiting pleasure seeking. It generates desires for which it seeks representation in conscious thought and fulfillment in action. The unconscious is developmentally superseded by a higher system, the preconscious, which functions in tandem with the system conscious. The preconscious is composed of contents and thought activities that are readily identifiable and accessible to consciousness, and it is therefore also referred to as the preconscious-conscious. The preconscious is capable of realistic thought, moral self-evaluation, and conscious regulation of pleasure seeking according to the reality principle. Most important, the preconscious inhibits the primitive impulsivity of the unconscious by blocking the mental representations of unconscious desires through repression and other defenses. The preconscious performs this function because certain primitive impulses, which are pleasurable in the system unconscious, are experienced as unpleasurable in the (more realistic) system preconscious. Finally, the system conscious is conceptualized as a sense organ, capable of perceiving outer stimuli, bodily sensations (including emotions), and the mental contents of the preconscious. In this early formulation, Freud conceptualized psychic conflict as occurring between the unconscious and the preconscious-conscious.

The Structural Perspective

Freud employed the topographic model until it became clear that it did not accurately match the clinical data. The topographic model predicts that the anti-instinctual activities of the preconscious should be accessible to conscious awareness. Clinical data revealed, however, that some aspects of defensive and moral functioning (unconscious defenses and unconscious guilt), both anti-instinctual features of the preconscious, are in fact inaccessible to consciousness. Accordingly, Freud developed a revised model, which has come to be known as the structural model (Freud, 1923). According to the structural model, the mind is constituted by three agencies—the id, the superego, and the ego—each of which serves a different set of functions. The id is a new term for the older system unconscious, which continuously generates primitive impulses that press for satisfaction. The superego, a mental system composed of internalized representations of parental authorities, functions as an inner supervisor, providing love and approval for moral behavior, as well as condemnation and criticism for immoral desires and conduct. The ego is the executive system of the mind, responsible for the organization of mental life and the management of social conduct. The ego functions to integrate the demands of the id and the superego with the conditions and contingencies of external social reality. The ego is the seat of consciousness, although aspects of ego functioning (unconscious thoughts, ego defenses) are unconscious. The structural model permits the conceptualization of psychic conflict between the three systems, each of which pursues potentially contradictory aims. In accordance with the structural model, the terms *unconscious, preconscious,* and *conscious* may be used as adjectives to describe the accessibility to consciousness of specific mental contents rather than as nouns to denote mental systems.

The Dynamic Perspective

The dynamic perspective, which can be traced to *Studies on Hysteria* (Breuer & Freud, 1893–1895), postulates that behavior is motivated; it is lawful, has an identifiable cause, and is purposive (Holzman, 1970). The dynamic perspective is necessary to understand not only neurotic symptoms and other forms of psychopathology, but also the neurotic meaning of ostensibly insignificant behavioral acts associated with everyday living (also termed *parapraxes*),[6] such as slips of the tongue, the forgetting of names, misreadings, and bungled actions (Freud, 1901; Holzman, 1970). It is an especially important and facilitative viewpoint in psychoanalytic efforts to understand the latent meaning of dreams.

In *The Psychopathology of Everyday Life* (Freud, 1901), the dynamic perspective is brought to life by literally hundreds of examples of parapraxes. A representative vignette follows:

> I forbade a patient to telephone to the girl he was in love with—but with whom he himself wanted to break off relations—since each conversation served only to renew the struggle about giving her up. He was to write his final decision to her, though there were difficulties about delivering letters to her. He called on me at one o'clock to tell me he had found a way of getting round these difficulties, and amongst other things asked if he might quote my authority as a physician. At two o'clock he was occupied in composing the letter that was to end the relationship, when he suddenly broke off and said to his mother who was with him: "Oh! I've forgotten to ask the professor if I may mention his name in the letter." He rushed to the telephone, put through his call and

[6]From the Greek, literally translated as "abnormal or faulty actions."

said into the instrument: "May I speak to the professor, please, if he's finished dinner?" In answer, he got an astonished: "Adolph, have you gone mad?" It was the same voice which by my orders he should not have heard again. He had simply "made an error," and instead of the physician's number he had given the girl's. (p. 222)

The Economic Perspective

It is not possible to explain mental life solely on the basis of qualitative variables. All the motivations already described vary in their intensities at different times, resulting in an endless shifting in the balance of psychological forces within the mind. The economic perspective is an outgrowth of Freud's observations concerning the strength of the drives and other mental phenomena that seemed to require a quantitative explanation. In his early clinical work, Freud had been impressed by the power of intrusive ideas and the compelling character of rituals in obsessive-compulsive neurosis, the refractory nature of conversion symptoms to even the most aggressive medical interventions, and the potency of paranoid delusions. These forms of psychopathology, as well as his experience with the resistance of his neurotic patients, convinced him that a quantitative factor underlies much of behavior, pathological or otherwise (Holzman, 1970). The mechanisms of displacement and condensation, both of which Freud had originally discussed in connection with the concepts of primary and secondary process and dream analysis (Freud, 1895b; 1900), were also conceived of quantitatively. Displacement is the intrapsychic operation whereby the intensity or interest of an idea that is anxiety generating is shifted onto a second idea that has an associative connection to the first but is less anxiety arousing. Condensation is an unconscious defensive operation through which a single image, as in a dream, actually serves to represent multiple ideas or meanings.

The Genetic Perspective

The genetic point of view, like the topographical, economic, and dynamic viewpoints, is anchored in Freud's earliest papers and several lengthier works, for example, *Studies on Hysteria* (1893–1895) and *The Interpretation of Dreams* (1900). The genetic viewpoint asserts that a meaningful psychological understanding of the adult is of necessity predicated on a thorough comprehension of that person's childhood experiences. Stated in slightly different terms, the genetic perspective postulates that the past persists into the present (Holzman, 1970). This particular viewpoint, which has been expropriated by popular culture to a greater degree than perhaps any other, has given rise to the somewhat simplistic notion that dysfunctional behavior and psychopathology in adulthood are almost invariably linked to unhappy childhood experiences.

Freud actually never regarded past experiences as the sole criterion for the development of later psychopathology. He did propose that the historical legacy of experiences acquired meaning as a consequence of a "mutual interaction between and integration of constitutional factors and environmental events" (Holzman, 1970, p. 56). In other words, such constitutional factors as the strength of the drives and various individual endowments and capabilities exert influence and are, in turn, influenced by the nature of the individual's experiences in his or her environmental milieu.

The Adaptive Perspective

The adaptive perspective, chiefly concerned with the relationship of the individual to the surrounding environment, highlights the influence of both interpersonal and societal forces. This has been termed the individual's "commerce with the real world" (Holzman, 1970, p. 58). Although the adaptive perspective was present in a nascent form in Freud's early formulations of drive theory (1900, 1905), it was not until his publication of *The Ego and the Id* (1923) that the importance of the extramural environment was emphasized. The development of Freud's concept of the ego and its relationship to the environment opened the way for dramatic developments in psychoanalytic theory.

EGO PSYCHOLOGY

In a sense, our exploration of ego psychology has already begun with the discussion of compromise formations, defense theory, and the metapsychological perspectives. In the early stages of his career, Freud was primarily concerned with exploring the depths of the mind in an effort to discover its primordial origins. He saw mental life as the refracted expression of primitive strivings. His first view of the curative process in psychoanalysis rested on the assumption that bringing these strivings to life (i.e., making the unconscious conscious) would permit them to be dealt with in a more adaptive way. Accordingly, he had little interest in studies of consciousness, which he regarded as superficial. With the introduction of structural theory in 1923, the importance of the preconscious was expanded, and the psyche was depicted as having greater complexity.

The 1923 formulation of structural theory was epochal, permitting various problems in normal development as well as the influence of environmental variables and the character of the infant's earliest relationships to caregivers to be studied in entirely new ways. At the same time, ego psychological theorists have managed to preserve more or less intact Freudian drive theory, which may differentiate this school from either object relational or self psychological theories (Mitchell & Black, 1995). The more prominent architects of ego psychology are Anna Freud, Heinz Hartmann, Rene Spitz, Margaret Mahler, Erik Erikson, and Edith Jacobson. It is to certain of their contributions that we now turn.

Anna Freud and Defense Theory

Perhaps Anna Freud's most significant contribution to ego psychology was her clarification of defense theory and specification of the principal mechanisms of defense. She was also considered a pioneer in the field of child psychoanalysis and devoted much energy to studying the psychoanalytic treatment process and to developing research instruments such as the Hampstead Profile, a comprehensive, developmentally based instrument for assessing a patient's ego functioning and object relations. Anna Freud's efforts to explicate the structural model and Sigmund Freud's revised theory of anxiety (Freud, 1926), and to make these consonant with a superordinate focus on the ego and its functions, led her to consider such problems as the "choice of neurosis" and "motives" for defense. In fact, she distinguished four principal motives for defense against the drives: superego anxiety (or guilt), objective anxiety (in children), anxiety about the strength of drives, and anxiety stemming from conflicts between mutually incompatible aims (A. Freud, 1936). On the basis of her extensive observations of and psychoanalytic work with young children, Anna Freud later developed the concept of developmental lines (A. Freud, 1963), a variegated developmental schedule that permitted the clinician-researcher to follow important changes in sexual, aggressive, and social developmental "lines" from infancy to adolescence.

The Ego and Adaptation

Heinz Hartmann's contributions were designed to enhance and expand the scope of psychoanalytic theory, with the objective of transforming it into a system of general psychology (Goldstein, 1995; Mitchell & Black, 1995). A central argument of Hartmann's most important work, *Ego Psychology and the Problem of Adaptation* (1939), was that the human infant was born with innate "conflict-free ego capacities" that would be activated in an "average expectable environment," thereby ensuring the infant's survival and adaptation. The capacities to which Hartmann referred included language, perception, memory, intention, motor activity, object comprehension, and thinking (Hartmann, 1939). Hartmann's notion of conflict-free ego capacities contrasted with more traditional psychoanalytic ideas, where adaptation is achieved only as an outcome of frustration and conflict. Hartmann also proposed the twin concepts of *alloplastic adaptation,* the individual's efforts to alter external realities to meet various human needs, and *autoplastic adaptation,* which refers to the individual's efforts to accommodate to external realities.

The Developmentalists: René Spitz, Margaret Mahler, and Erik Erikson

Spitz and Mahler, both of whom began their professional careers as pediatricians, are well recognized for their important contributions to developmental ego psychology. Working as a consultant in a foundling home during World War II, Spitz first described the dramatic sequelae of a syndrome that exacted a profound developmental toll on the infants he studied. Although the nutritional needs of these infants were met quite adequately and care was provided for them in hygienic environments, they were deprived of interaction with maternal caregivers. Seemingly as a direct consequence of the absence of mother-infant interaction, they became withdrawn, failed to achieve developmental milestones, and had very high morbidity and mortality rates (Spitz, 1945).[7] Spitz characterized this syndrome as *anaclitic depression* (depression associated with thwarted dependency needs). Spitz later identified what he termed the three psychic organizers: the baby's social response at approximately three months, the emergence of stranger anxiety at eight months, and the child's "no" response, first observed at about fifteen months (Spitz, 1965). Spitz's greatest contribution may have been his systematic effort to identify the particular facilita-

---

[7]If the infant's mother was able to resume her maternal functions during the first three months, the downward spiral that otherwise often led to retardation, marasmus, and death could be reversed.

tive environmental conditions that spur the development of the "innate adaptive capabilities" Hartmann had previously described (Mitchell & Black, 1995).

Mahler's work was also principally with young children, although the original focus of her clinical research was psychotic youngsters. Mahler believed that the nature of the ego pathology she observed in psychotic children was inadequately addressed within the traditional framework of drive theory. She proposed that these children suffered from defects or failures in the organization of internalized self and object representations and experienced a corresponding difficulty in differentiating self from not self; in consequence, such children were largely incapable of acquiring an enduring sense of self that is distinct and separable from others. This, in turn, suggested to Mahler that the infant's "mediating human partner," as Spitz had also maintained, had a highly significant role in the evolution of the infantile ego. Ultimately Mahler turned to the study of normal infant development. Mahler's theory of the separation-individuation process, recent criticisms notwithstanding (Horner, 1985; Stern, 1986), introduced a schema that transformed not only the study of infant pathology but has also served as the theoretical basis for a psychoanalytic approach to the psychotherapy of adults with borderline personality disorder (Masterson & Rinsley, 1975).[8] On the basis of her longitudinal investigations of maternal-infant pairs in a nursery setting, Mahler portrayed a process that begins at birth and continues into the child's fourth year (Mahler, Pine, & Bergmann, 1975). Characterizing infants as essentially nonrelated or objectless at birth (the autistic phase), she described their gradual emergence via a period of maternal-infant symbiosis into four relatively discrete stages of separation and individuation: differentiation (five to nine months), practicing (nine to fifteen months), rapprochement (fifteen to twenty-four months), and the development of the object constancy (twenty-four to thirty-six months and beyond).

Erikson's greatest contributions to ego psychology involved his theory of psychosocial and psychosexual epigenesis[9] and the detailed attention he gave to the concept of ego identity. Whereas Spitz and Mahler had focused their attentions on the earliest developmental processes of the infant's emerging ego, Erikson's psychosocial epigentic theory examined ego development across the entire life span and highlighted social-environmental factors to a greater degree than any existing ego psychological model. In Erikson's view, healthy ego development was contingent on the mastery of specific developmental tasks and normative crises associated with each of eight life cycle stages he identified:

---

[8]Masterson and others have hypothesized that adolescents and adults with borderline pathology have experienced a derailment in the normal separation-individuation process during the critical rapprochement phase; this leads to what has been described as the core dilemma of the borderline character: fear of loss of self versus fear of loss of the other.

[9]*Epigenesis* is a term that Erikson expropriated from the field of embryology. It is defined as "the predetermined sequential development of the parts of an organism," (Holzman, 1970, p. 160). Each part follows an internal organismic timetable, permitting it to emerge and then to become successfully integrated with the rest of the organism. In such a developmental schema, the earliest stages of growth have an inherently greater vulnerability to disruption than the later ones, since the effect of such disruption on early stages will thereby influence all subsequent ones.

1. *Basic trust versus basic mistrust.* Coterminous with Freud's oral phase, the principal experiential mode in this stage is oral-receptive. In optimal circumstances, there is a preponderance of positively valenced experiences with one's mother, which culminate in basic trust.
2. *Autonomy versus shame and doubt.* Coincides with the anal stage in Freud's model of the libidinal stages; emphasis on the child's newly emerging autonomy, coextensive with increased radius of locomotor activity and maturation of the muscle systems. Success in this phase results in the child's pleasure in independent actions and self-expression, failure to shame and self-doubt.
3. *Initiative versus guilt.* Corresponds to Freud's phallic stage. Sexual curiosity and oedipal issues are common, competitiveness reaches new heights, and the child's efforts to reach and attain goals acquires importance. Danger arises when the child's aggression or manipulation of the environment triggers an abiding sense of guilt.
4. *Industry versus inferiority.* Occurs during the latency period in Freud's model; associated with the child's beginning efforts to use tools, his sense of being productive, and of developing the capability to complete tasks.
5. *Identity versus identity diffusion.* Ushered in by adolescence. This stage is perhaps the most extensively developed in the Eriksonian model; stable identity requires an integration of formative experiences "that give the child the sense that he is a person with a history, a stability, and a continuity that is recognizable by others" (Holzman, 1970, p. 163). Erikson also enumerated seven aspects of identity consolidation (Erikson, 1959) that are critical codeterminants of success or failure in this stage: (1) a time perspective; (2) self-certainty; (3) role experimentation; (4) anticipation of achievement; (5) sexual identity; (6) acceptance of leadership; and (7) commitment to basic values.
6. *Intimacy and distantiation versus self-absorption.* The major developmental task of this phase, which occurs during early adulthood, is the individual's capacity for healthy sexual and nonsexual intimacy while still retaining a firm sense of personal identity. Should such intimacy be impossible, there is a "regressive retreat to exclusive concern with oneself," (Holzman, 1970).
7. *Generativity versus stagnation.* This penultimate phase of the adult life cycle involves the adult in the critical tasks and responsibilities of parenting. Parenthood is not inextricably tied to generativity, however; just as there are adults who relinquish or are otherwise unable to fulfill parental responsibilities, so too are there childless adults whose generativity involves the pursuit of creative or artistic initiatives;
8. *Integrity versus despair and disgust.* Ego integrity is the culmination of ego identity (Erikson, 1959; Goldstein, 1995). It reflects a level of maturity signaling the individual's acceptance of the past, particularly past disappointments and mistakes.

Jacobson: The Self and the Object World

The daunting task of summarizing the considerable scope of Edith Jacobson's contributions to the psychoanalytic literature has been previously discussed (Greenberg &

Mitchell, 1983). Jacobson attempted to integrate the Freudian emphasis on constitutional factors in development (including instinctual drives) with the growing recognition of the potent imprint of life experience. In a series of papers that culminated in the publication of *The Self and the Object World* (1964), Jacobson revised and reformulated Freud's theory of psychosexual development and various aspects of classical metapsychology, particularly the economic principle. Although she never actually disputed the primacy of the drives, she theorized that the mother-infant relationship had complementarity with innate maturational forces and, furthermore, that the distinctive features of the infant's instinctual drives acquire meaning only within the milieu of the caregiving relationship. In Jacobson's model of early development, a complex reciprocal interchange between the infant's ongoing experience with caregivers and the maturational unfolding of the drives leads to the formation of self images and object images. These images have different hedonic valences, and it is the infant's gradual capacity for integrating good and bad experiences of objects and of self that is finally necessary for mature affectivity. The phenomenology of affective disorders was also of considerable interest to Jacobson, whose book *Depression: Comparative Studies of Normal, Neurotic, and Psychotic Conditions* (1971) continued her exploration of the complex relationship between affectivity and the inner representational world.

OBJECT RELATIONS THEORY

None of the psychoanalytic theory groups discussed in this chapter actually constitutes a fully separate psychoanalytic psychology. This is perhaps especially true of object relations theory, a general heading under which is subsumed several distinct groups of theories, each possessing distinctive theoretical premises and complementary approaches to psychoanalytic treatment.

Grotstein (1996) traces the psychoanalytic use of the term *object* to a series of six papers written by Freud: "Three Essays on the Theory of Sexuality" (1905), "Family Romances" (1909), "On Narcissism: An Introduction" (1914a), "Mourning and Melancholia" (1917), "A Child Is Being Beaten" (1919), and "The Ego and the Id (1923). In the original use of this term (1905), Freud had sought to minimize the importance of the infant's caretakers, who were viewed more so with respect to their inhibition or facilitation of the child's instinctual wishes rather than as human beings in their own right. Gradually, however, Freud demonstrated increasing interest in the role of objects, which we can glean from "his conception of the ego-ideal, the superego, and the Oedipus Complex itself . . . contributions [where the object is conceived] as being incorporated into the psychic structure" (Grotstein, 1996, p. 91). In Freud's essay on the mourning process (1917), there was further exploration of the relationship between external object loss and the internal process through which the object is established as an identification in the mourner's ego. Freud also made use of object relations ideas in his examination of the role that sadism and masochism played in pathological narcissism.

A number of theorists have shaped object relations thinking since Freud: Karl Abraham (1924a), whose model of object relations was embedded in an eloquent paper on the development of the libido; Sandor Ferenczi (1913), whose postulation of an infantile desire to return to a prenatal symbiotic state anticipates the work of Maragaret Mahler; Ian Suttie (1935), who wrote that the infant comes into the world with an innate need for companionship, nonsexual love, and security, all of which evolve in the mother-infant relational matrix (Mishne, 1993); Imre Hermann (1933, 1936), who hypothesized that there was a human instinct to cling that paralleled the instinctual behavior of other primates;[10] and Michael Balint and Alice Balint, among whose theoretical contributions were the instinct of "primary object love" (1939)[11] and "the basic fault" (1937), a concept that designated a primary breach in the ego arising during the preoedipal period.

Contemporary object relations theories, however, have been especially influenced by several major theorists: Harry Stack Sullivan, Melanie Klein, and Donald Winnicott.

Interpersonal Psychoanalysis: The Work of Harry Stack Sullivan

Interpersonal psychoanalysis derives from the clinical work and theoretical formulations of Harry Stack Sullivan (1892–1949), an American psychiatrist who pioneered the psychotherapeutic treatment of severely disturbed individuals. Sullivan, who studied medicine in Chicago, was greatly impressed by the exciting intellectual developments in philosophy and the social sciences at the University of Chicago. He was particularly influenced by the work of such social thinkers as George Herbert Meade, Edward Sapir, John Dewey, and other proponents of the American pragmatist school of philosophical thought. Sullivan's distinctive approach to psychotherapy and psychiatry reflected his profound immersion in this intellectual milieu (Chapman, 1976; Mullahy, 1970; Perry, 1982).

Sullivan was deeply dissatisfied with existing psychoanalytic theory. He distrusted the abstract, metaphorical concepts of Freudian theory which, in his view, pertained to mental systems and structures that are not observable and, hence, only hypothetical in nature. In contrast to Freudian theorists, Sullivan, who was greatly influenced by Bridgman's "operationalism" (Bridgman, 1945; Sullivan, 1953), believed that psychiatric theories should, to the greatest extent possible, employ "operational" terms with definable and empirical referents. Sullivan also found that Freudian theory (as it existed during his formative years of psychiatric practice) was inadequate to the understanding and treatment of the severely mentally ill patients with whom he worked. As a result, Harry Stack Sullivan's clinical and theoretical contributions to psychiatric and psychoanalytic thought are strikingly original, and couched in his own highly idiosyncratic terminology.

Over the years, Sullivan came to reject basic features of Freudian theory. Most important, Sullivan repudiated Freud's belief that human motivations are determined by

---

[10]Grotstein (1996, p. 95) observes that Hermann's work seems to have adumbrated the well-known experiments of H. F. Harlow (1959) in this regard.

[11]In their assertion of such an instinct, the Balints repudiated Freud's concept of primary narcissism and the idea that infants only gradually develop attachments to objects (Grotstein, 1996).

instinctual drives. In opposition to Freud's classical drive theory, Sullivan posited that human motivations are primarily interpersonal in nature, determined by interpersonal relationships, especially the relationships of childhood and adolescence, and understandable only in terms of such relationships. Sullivan believed that human beings respond to two sets of motivations. One set is characterized as the satisfaction of bodily and emotional needs, including sexuality and intimacy. A second set of motivations is related to the experience of anxiety and related strivings for security. Both the satisfaction of needs and the achievement of security are interpersonal events occurring in relation to other persons. In contrast to the Freudian conception of personality as the characteristic way that the individual organizes the competing claims of id, ego, and superego, Sullivan conceptualized personality as the characteristic ways that the individual interacts with other people in the the pursuit of satisfactions and security. Mental illness, he argued, can best be understood as a disturbance of interpersonal relations. Sullivan's efforts to employ operational concepts and his concomitant emphasis upon interpersonal relations gradually gave rise to a new psychoanalytic orientation in which the primary focus was on interpersonal relations rather than intrapsychic events.

Sullivan's approach to treatment reflected this shift of emphasis. If mental illness and other malformations of personality are the consequence of pathogenic interpersonal relationships, he reasoned, mental health may best be promoted by the creation of healthy interpersonal relationships. In the late 1920s, Sullivan implemented this idea at Sheppard and Enoch Pratt Hospital in Baltimore, where he developed an unusual inpatient psychiatric unit for male schizophrenics in which ward staff were specially trained to interact with patients and to foster comfortable and emotionally rewarding interpersonal relationships with them in order to help correct their unhealthy relationship patterns. Sullivan also developed a distinctive method of conducting individual therapy with patients. Abandoning the free association method of classical psychoanalysis, Sullivan employed a conversational approach to patients, conceptualizing his role as that of a participant-observer in the relationship with the patient. His goal was to engage the patient in a collaborative study of the patient's interpersonal relationships so that the patient's unhealthy patterns of relating to others could be discovered and understood. Most important, Sullivan stressed the importance of establishing a healthy relationship with the patient in order to correct habitual maladaptive interpersonal patterns. Employing these techniques, Sullivan achieved unparalleled therapeutic gains with patients that had previously been regarded as hopeless and untreatable. As his work became known, Sullivan became one of America's most respected and admired psychiatrists. He acquired a growing circle of collaborators that included some of the leading thinkers in psychoanalysis, such as Clara Thompson, Erich Fromm, and Frieda-Fromm Reichman, all of whom contributed to the development of the interpersonal school of psychoanalysis.

Sullivan never attempted to establish a comprehensive theoretical system, and contemporary therapists working within the interpersonal tradition have introduced their own technical and theoretical innovations (Arieti, 1974; Chrzanowski, 1977; Fromm-Reichman, 1950; Havens, 1976, 1986; Levenson, 1972; Thompson, 1964; Witenberg, 1973). Interpersonal psychoanalysis is best described as "a set of different approaches to theory and clinical practice . . . with shared underlying assumptions and premises" (Greenberg & Mitchell, 1983, p. 79). These include Sullivan's rejection of Freudian instinct theory, his basic view of psychopathology as a disturbance of interpersonal relationships, his belief in the interpersonal roots of mental illness, and his emphasis upon the curative importance of healthy interpersonal relationships. Interpersonal psychoanalysis has often been criticized by exponents of traditional psychoanalysis as being superficial or lacking in depth because of its focus on the interpersonal field and its rejection of drive concepts. However, Sullivan's ideas are now believed to have exerted a profound and far-reaching influence on contemporary psychoanalytic thinking (Havens & Frank, 1971).

An overarching theme in Sullivan's writings is that the human infant is born into a relational milieu; relational configurations in his theoretical model evolve out of actual experience with others. Sullivan repeatedly underscored the assertion that human beings can be understood only within the "organism-environment complex"[12] and consequently are incapable of "definitive description in isolation" (Sullivan, 1930, p. 258). In Sullivan's developmental model, a superordinate importance is placed on the interpersonal field together with the efforts that children devise to maintain relatedness with significant others.

Needs for satisfaction are "integrating tendencies" that impel the individual to seek physical and emotional contact with others. The integration of relationships in the pursuit of satisfactions is complicated, however, by the arousal of painful affective states which Sullivan characterizes as anxiety. Sullivan's notion of anxiety differs from Freud's view of anxiety in two principal ways. In his mature formulation (Freud, 1926), Freud conceptualized anxiety as a form of fear related to specific typical danger situations of childhood (loss of the mother, loss of the mother's love, castration, and guilt). Sullivan used the term anxiety to include any form of mental suffering, distress, or anguish aroused in an interpersonal situation. A second difference pertains to the manner in which anxiety is generated. In Freudian theory, anxiety is a signal of danger, typically aroused by the mobilization of repressed wishes associated with specific danger situations. Accordingly, "drives and reality are inextricably linked as sources of danger to the ego" (Holzman, 1970, p. 143). In Sullivan's theory, the infant's experience of anxiety is aroused by anxiety (in its more narrowly defined sense) or by other strong affects of distress in the caregiver. Babies are exquisitely sensitive to the moods of others, and, through a phenomenon Sullivan termed empathic linkage, experience the caregiver's anxiety as if it were their own. While needs for satisfaction are integrating tendencies that foster relatedness, anxiety and other forms of emotional suffering are aversive experiences that impair interpersonal relations. Excessive anxiety in infancy and childhood predispose the affected individual to experience anxiety in the context of his or her adult relationships. This vulnerability to anxiety contributes to disturbances of interpersonal relationships that are usually referred to as psychopathology or mental illness.

Sullivan believed that the most basic differentiation for the infant was "not be-

---

[12]It is not difficult to see a clear parallel between Sullivan's use of this term and the social work emphasis on the person-in-environment matrix; interestingly, however, Sullivan is not often cited by social work historians as having had a significant influence on the development of social work theory.

tween light and dark, or between mother and father, but between anxious states and non-anxious states" (Mitchell & Black, 1995, p. 68). During development, the child forms schematic impressions or "personifications" of himself and of his mother. Pleasurable experiences give rise to impressions of the "good mother" and the "good me," while experiences of anxiety produce impressions of the "bad mother" and the "bad me." Extremely painful or terrifying interpersonal situations elicit representations of the "evil mother" and the "not me." The memory of such experiences are vigorously avoided and may be terrifying when they are aroused. "Evil mother" and "not me" experiences are associated with severe mental illness.

Sullivan introduced the term self-system to collectively characterize the myriad psychological activities which the individual employs to avoid anxiety ("bad me" and "not me") and to insure feelings of security ("good me"). In Sullivan's writing, security is defined as the absence of anxiety. The self-system is an expansive system of mental states, symbols, and coordinated activities which function to promote feelings of security by assessing the safety of interpersonal situations, anticipating the arousal of anxiety, and minimizing anxiety through the activation of security operations. Security operations roughly parallel the concept of defense in the traditional Freudian system: they operate covertly, out of the individual's awareness, serving to diminish anxiety and other feelings of emotional distress associated with the "bad me" or "not me," and to restore feelings of security and well-being that are the affective concomitants of the "good me." The concept of security operations also differs from the traditional Freudian concept of defenses, however, in significant ways. In classical Freudian theory, defenses are mental activities designed to reduce anxiety arising from intrapsychic conflict (i.e., conflict between id, ego, and superego). In Sullivan's theory, security operations are intended to diminish the anxiety and emotional distress that arise from disturbances in interpersonal relationships. While defenses are best understood as intrapsychic phenomena, security operations entail an interpersonal dimension. Security operations promote relatedness and facilitate the satisfaction of emotional needs by preserving security in interpersonal situations.

Security operations develop and become increasingly sophisticated as the child matures. Typical security operations of early childhood include apathy and somnolent detachment, both of which reflect a process of disengagement from an anxiety-arousing interpersonal situation, such as an anxious or anguished mother. As the child develops progressive cognitive capabilities, other security operations become possible. A typical security operation of later development is selective inattention, a tactical redeployment of focal attention from disturbing aspects of interpersonal experience to aspects which enhance the individual's feelings of self-esteem or security. As a result of selective inattention, disturbing aspects of interpersonal phenomena are excluded from experience and memory. An individual's security operations include complex patterns of interpersonal activity that manifest as typical aspects of the individual's interpersonal relationships. For example, habitual compliance or placating behavior, aggressive bullying or dominating, emotional withdrawal or constriction, pomposity and self-centeredness, may be conceptualized as complex security operations intended to avoid anxiety in interpersonal situations, that is, to maintain the vulnerable individual's sense of comfort and security. Sullivan summarizes such patterns of interpersonal conduct as the dramatization of roles, or the repetitive enactment of emotionally safe relational configurations, interpersonal patterns which Sullivan calls *me–you patterns* (Sullivan, 1953).

In sum, Sullivan's interpersonal approach to psychoanalysis is prototypical of psychoanalytic schools of thought which diverge from classical Freudian theory by positing that human motivations and personality structure derive from the interpersonal experiences of development, rather than from the unfolding influence of instinctual drives. Other psychoanalytic theorists who shared this point of view are Fairbairn (1952) and Guntrip (1968, 1971). Greenberg and Mitchell (1983) group these schools of thought together as the relational theories of psychoanalysis.

In addition to his enduring impact on psychoanalytic theory, Sullivan's contributions have had a major impact on the understanding and treatment of schizophrenia (Sullivan, 1962). Sullivan was passionate in his arguments against professional "objectivity" and "detachment" in the psychotherapy of schizophrenic clients, since he believed that the distorted interpersonal relations of the schizophrenic originally developed from a matrix of disordered relationships between the client and members of the client's family. Although a relational approach to the psychotherapy of schizophrenia has enjoyed less popularity since the recent ascendancy of biological psychiatry, Sullivan's emphasis upon the social context of psychopathology remains a viable theoretical premise.

The Work of Melanie Klein

Some have asserted that Melanie Klein (1882–1960) and her theory of object relations have exerted an influence on the contemporary world of psychoanalysis second only to that of Freud (Mitchell & Black, 1995). Though this claim is arguable, most would concede that Klein's theoretical positions were at the center of a protracted debate in the British psychoanalytic establishment that ultimately led to the creation of three separate schools of psychoanalysis in that country. Klein was also the first psychoanalyst to treat children with the psychoanalytic method, "a project . . . long overdue . . . [that] aroused considerable interest in the psychoanalytic community" when her first paper was published in 1919 (Greenberg & Mitchell, 1983). Although the history of psychoanalysis is replete with controversies over theory and technique, perhaps none has attained the notoriety and divisiveness or equaled the profound ramifications of the prolonged disagreement between Melanie Klein and Anna Freud.

The schism that developed between Klein and Anna Freud began in the mid- to late 1920s over issues of technique in child analysis. A fundamental premise of Klein was that the play of young children was equivalent to the free associations of adult clients; so long as the meaning of their play was interpreted to them, children, like adults, were suitable subjects for psychoanalytic treatment. Anna Freud's position, however, was that small children could not be analyzed owing to an inherently weak and rudimentary ego that would be incapable of managing deep interpretations of instinctual conflict (Mitchell & Black, 1995). Klein published a number of theoretical and clinical papers and several books over a period of some forty years. Although she steadfastly maintained that her observations and psychoanalytic work with children were intended as confirmations and extensions of Freud's hypotheses, her discoveries led to her to portray the mind "as a continually shifting, kaleidoscopic stream of primitive, phantasmagoric images, fantasies, and terrors," a vision that seemed very unlike that of Freud (Mitchell & Black, 1995, p. 87). In Freud's model of the mind, the oedipus complex has a developmentally profound, transformative impact on the psyche that yields the creation of new conflict-mediating structures (the mature ego and superego), which have stability and coherence. An almost inexorable progression of the libido culminates in the six year old's genital sexuality and the accompanying oedipal dilemma; this, for Freud, constitutes the core conflict or nuclear complex of the neuroses. In fact, Klein never questioned the primacy of the Oedipus complex, but located it at a much earlier point in development than did traditional psychoanalytic theory. Klein's fundamental view of the nature of oedipal phenomena also differed from the traditional perspective. For Klein, "the very nature of the Oedipus complex changed from a struggle over illicit pleasures and the fear of punishment, to a struggle for power and destruction and the fear of retaliation" (Greenberg & Mitchell, 1983, p. 123).

Sigmund Freud had theorized that infants proceed from a state of primary narcissism to object love via autoerotism; in effect, true object love is not possible until the libido progresses to the oedipal stage. The Kleinian infant, by contrast, is both psychologically separate and object seeking from the moment of birth (Klein, 1964; Grotstein, 1996). Klein went further, however, proposing that infants as young as three weeks of age are subject to a primitive anxiety state, which she called *persecutory anxiety*. She believed this configuration of anxiety was linked to schizoid mechanisms (e.g., splitting, projective identification, idealization, and magic omnipotent denial) and that such intrapsychic experience resulted in the infant's first developmental organizer, the paranoid-schizoid position (Klein, 1964). In the paranoid-schizoid position, "*paranoid* refers to the central persecutory anxiety, the fear of invasive malevolence, coming from the outside. . . . *Schizoid* refers to the central organizing defense: splitting, the vigilant separation of the loving and good breast from the hating and hated bad breast (Mitchell & Black, 1995, p. 93). The infant who is operating out of the paranoid-schizoid position has a bifurcated and fragmented experience of objects; "the child attempts to ward off the dangers of bad objects, both external and internal, largely by keeping images of them separate and isolated from the self and the good objects" (Greenberg & Mitchell, 1983, p. 125). Relations with objects are, by definition, always partial and either all good or all bad, but never composed of both good and bad parts. According to Klein, however, the infant gradually begins to integrate the experiences of good and bad breast–other, so that whole object relations ultimately become possible (Klein, 1935). Klein has termed this important shift in intrapsychic experience, which begins at approximately three to four months, the *depressive position.*

The depressive position (the second developmental organizer of infancy) is initiated by the infant's growing concern for the welfare of the libidinal object who has been the recipient of hateful fantasies of vengeance and annihilation characteristic of the paranoid-schizoid position.[13] Concomitant with the infant's newly emerging

---

[13]In Kleinian theory, the regulation and containment of aggression has the quality of a leitmotif, though with specific meanings at various developmental stages.

capacity for whole object relations is an ability to experience ambivalence or both good (loving) and bad (hateful) feelings toward the same object. Although this represents a critical developmental achievement for the infant, it simultaneously creates new dangers since

> the whole mother who disappoints or fails the infant, generating the pain of longing, frustration, desperation, is destroyed in the infant's hateful fantasies, not just the purely evil bad breast (with the good breast remaining untouched and protected). The whole object (both the external mother and the corresponding internal whole object) now destroyed in the infant's rageful fantasies is the singular provider of goodness as well as frustration. In destroying the whole object, the infant eliminates her as a protector and refuge . . . [which leads to] . . . intense terror and guilt. (Mitchell & Black, 1995, p. 95)

The target of the infant's destructive urges is also a deeply loved figure toward whom the infant feels profound gratitude (Klein, 1964). These feelings, coupled with the child's regret and sorrow over her or his destructiveness, serve as the basis for fantasies of reparation. Such fantasies are intended to repair the damage and transform the annihilated object into a whole object once again.

The concept of projective identification, which some believe to be a sine qua non for the understanding and treatment of borderline and other severe personality disorders, is also attributed to Klein (1946, 1952). Projective identification represents not simply a strategy of defense but is a significant though developmentally primitive mode of interaction. In projective identification, the subject projects unwanted parts of the self into others for "safekeeping." Ogden, a contemporary Kleinian, has defined the concept in the following manner: "Projective-identification is a concept that addresses the way in which feeling states corresponding to the unconscious fantasies of one person (projector) are engendered in and processed by another person (the recipient), that is, the way in which one person makes use of another person to experience and contain an aspect of himself" (Ogden, 1982, p. 1).

Klein and her theories have been criticized for a number of reasons. A basic premise of Klein is that the infant is capable of a complex fantasy life from birth, a contention that receives little support from either cognitive psychology or the neurosciences (Tyson & Tyson, 1990). Others have noted that in Klein's framework, where mental life is viewed as fragmented and chaotic, there is "considerable fuzziness concerning the relationship between fantasy and the establishment of character or psychic structure" (Fairbairn, 1952; Kernberg, 1980; Mishne, 1993). At the same time, the magnitude of Klein's influence is indisputable and of particular importance for our discussion of the theorist whose work we now consider, D. W. Winnicott.

The Middle Tradition and D. W. Winnicott

There was considerable divisiveness within the British psychoanalytic community by the early 1940s, principally due to theoretical differences between Anna Freud and Melanie Klein, which had given rise to an increasingly contentious and acrimonious professional environment. At the time, Ernest Jones was the official head of the psychoanalytic movement in Britain, and he had worked diligently to foster a professional climate of "creative exploration, inclusiveness, and openness to emerging ideas," an ambience that had made possible relative quiescence, if not harmony, between Melanie Klein and adherents of mainstream psychoanalysis—at least until the arrival of the Freuds from Vienna in 1938 (Borden, 1995).[14] As relations between those faithful to Anna Freud's views and those who pledged loyalty to Melanie Klein began to deteriorate, Jones worked to uphold the integrity of the British Psycho-Analytic Society. In 1943 and 1944, he organized what have come to be known as the "Controversial Discussions," a series of formal theoretical debates, the original intent of which were to provide Melanie Klein with an opportunity to clarify her position on Sigmund Freud's metapsychology (Kohon, 1986; Mishne, 1993; Borden, 1995) and to explore the nature of theoretical differences between the Kleinians and (Anna) Freudians. The result of these discussions,[15] which failed to remedy deep theoretical differences between the two camps, was the organization of the British psychoanalytic community into three distinct groups: the Kleinians, the Freudians, and a middle or independent group.

The independent group consisted of a number of seminal thinkers, among them D. W. Winnicott, W. R. D. Fairbairn, John Bowlby, Michael Balint, and Harry Guntrip. Each of these theorists developed object relations theories based on Klein's basic postulate of an infant who is object seeking from the moment of birth. At the same time "they also all broke with Klein's premise of constitutional aggression . . . proposing instead an infant wired for harmonious interaction and nontraumatic development but thwarted by inadequate parenting" (Mitchell & Black, 1995, pp. 114–15). D. W. Winnicott (1896–1971) is regarded by many as the best-known representative of the independent group (Grotstein, 1996; Borden, 1995). Winnicott, like Spitz and Mahler, was originally trained as a pediatrician and spent over forty years working with infants and mothers. His careful observations of infants and their mothers led him to assert that "there is no such thing as an infant. There is only the infant and its mother" (Winnicott, 1960, p. 39). This declaration, which is truly axiomatic for Winnicott, underscores the critical importance that he attributed to the earliest object relations between infant and caregiver.

Winnicott is especially well known for his ideas about primary maternal preoccupation, good-enough mothering, and the holding environment, his formulation of the true self and the false self, and the concept of the transitional object.

Primary Maternal Preoccupation, Good-Enough Mothering, and the Holding Environment

Winnicott believed that the emergence of a health-promoting psychological milieu for each human infant depends on her or his mother's capacity for what Winnicott termed *primary maternal preoccupation.* The state of primary maternal preoccupation,

---

[14]Ernest Jones (1879–1958), a pioneer in the early psychoanalytic movement, was a close friend and disciple of Freud. The contribution for which he is most often remembered is his three-volume biography of Freud (Jones, 1953, 1955, 1957).

[15]See King & Steiner (1991) for a detailed account of these meetings.

which gathers considerable momentum in the last trimester of pregnancy, reflects each mother's natural absorption with the baby growing inside her. The expectant mother becomes "increasingly withdrawn from her own subjectivity . . . and more and more focused on the baby's movements, on the baby's vitality. . . . The mother finds her own personal interests, her own rhythms and concerns fading into the background" (Mitchell & Black, 1995, p. 125). Winnicott has also characterized this as mother's identification with the infant (Winnicott, 1965).

Good-enough mothering, which commences with the mother's primary maternal preoccupation, initially requires that mother meet the symbiotic needs of her newborn. If she is well attuned with her baby, whatever she offers the baby is provided at the "right time" for her baby rather than being timed to meet her own needs. As her baby faces experiences that evoke frustration, aggression, or loss, the good-enough mother is able to provide empathically attuned support, or *holding.* Winnicott stresses that good-enough mothering is a natural and spontaneous process that evolves out of each mother's intuitions and leads to the creation of a facilitative or holding environment on which each infant depends. He also observed that the extensive adaptations and accommodations that a mother makes to her infant gradually diminish; the result is brief lapses that teach baby that mother is not omnipotent (Moore & Fine, 1990). Such maternal failures in empathy are coterminous with significant advances in the infant's psychomotor development; while infantile omnipotence is lost, there is new-found delight in the infant's exciting forays into the object world outside the infant-mother matrix (Winnnicott, 1958a, 1965).

True Self and False Self

Winnicott wrote that all individuals begin life with a true self, an "inherited potential" that represents the infant's core self or essence. In a facilitative environment, the true self, which has been equated with the spontaneous expression of the id, continues to develop and becomes firmly established. The false self, on the other hand, is a facade that the infant-child erects so as to achieve compliance with mother's inadequate adaptations, whether these maternal failures are in the form of deprivations or impingements on the child's growth (Goldstein, 1995). Infants exposed to such repeated deprivations or impingements are able to survive, but in Winnicott's estimation they are able to do so only at the cost of "living falsely" (Winnicott, 1960, 1965; Mishne, 1993). Although Winnicott emphasized that the partition or distribution of self experience into "true" and "false" is always present in varying degrees (even in normal infants), the false self has an almost palpable presence in various forms of child and adult psychopathology. Winnicott treated a number of patients with basic pathology of the self, individuals who might have been diagnosed with schizoid or borderline disorders. What impressed him most about such patients was their profound inner alienation. In such patients, "subjectivity itself, the quality of personhood, is somehow disordered" (Mitchell & Black, 1995, p. 124). Winnicott gradually came to understand that these adult patients suffered from "false self disorders," and the bridge he "constructed between the quality and the nuances of adult subjectivity and the subtleties of mother-infant interactions provided a powerful new perspective for viewing both the development of the self" and the process of treatment (Mitchell & Black, 1995, p. 125).

The Transitional Object

Winnicott's concept of the transitional object is perhaps the best known of his theoretical ideas, though its popularization may have contributed to a blurring of its original meaning (Mitchell & Black, 1995). The transitional object is typically a blanket, teddy bear, or other inanimate but nevertheless cherished possession of the infant. The soothing and calming qualities with which it is endowed are especially evident during stressful separations from caregivers and at bedtime (Winnicott, 1951). Its odor and tactile characteristics hold a special significance, in that they are believed to be reminiscent of mother. In mother's absence, it is the transitional object that enables the infant to sustain the illusion of a calming, comforting mother. Because the transitional object is a creation of the infant and, unlike mother, remains under her control, it serves to promote the infant's increased autonomy and independence (Moore & Fine, 1990). The blanket or teddy bear, however, is not simply a symbolic re–creation of mother, designed to facilitate the infant's transition from symbiotic merger to relative autonomy; it is rather a "developmental way station,"

> a special extension of the child's self, halfway between the mother that the child creates in subjective omnipotence and the mother that the child finds operating on her own behalf in the objective world. The transitional object . . . cushions the fall from a world where the child's desires omnipotently actualize their objects to one where desires require accommodation to and collaboration of others to be fulfilled. (Mitchell & Black, 1995, p. 129)

Although Winnicott originally presented the concept of the transitional objects and transitional experience in the context of early infant development (1951), he later broadened this framework to include aspects of adult experience. The transitional experience for the child is embedded in a capacity for play, whereas for the adult, transitional experience is a "protected realm" where there exist opportunities to "play with" new ideas and fantasies and cultivate one's own creative impulses (Greenberg & Mitchell, 1983).

Winnicott's theories, unlike those of Freud, Klein, or Sullivan, have never attained the status of a school of thought, nor did Winnicott ever make the claim that his theories, taken together, represented "a comprehensive theory of object relations" (Bacal & Newman, 1990, p. 185). His papers, many of which were originally presented as talks (Greenberg & Mitchell, 1983), have a stylistic informality and poetic quality that at times can be almost seductive to the reader; at other times, however, these same inherent ambiguities and his idiosyncratic, discursive style make Winnicott difficult, even frustrating, to read. Despite this, and despite recent criticisms of Winnicott's distortion of traditional psychoanalytic ideas (Greenberg & Mitchell, 1983), his influence has remained strong. Winnicott's vision has enriched our understanding not only of infant development but of the significant relationship between environmental failures in early life and the phenomenology of certain disorders of adulthood.

THE PSYCHOLOGY OF THE SELF

The psychology of the self, introduced by Heinz Kohut, has only recently emerged from a vigorous and at times rancorous debate within psychoanalytic circles. The evolution of Kohut's self psychology is represented in a series of books and papers published between 1959 and 1984. Kohut originally introduced "his theoretical and technical innovations *within* the framework of classical drive theory" (Greenberg & Mitchell, 1983, p. 357), but subsequently presented a significantly expanded and revised framework (Kohut, 1977, 1984) that has become the basis for an important and distinctive theory of psychoanalytic psychology.

Heinz Kohut (1913–1981) received a traditional psychoanalytic education and worked for many years in the classical tradition with his analytic clients. The original impetus for the development of his theory came from his clinical experiences with clients, particularly those who seemed unable to make use of interpretations that followed the classical formulas. Kohut had noted that despite his most concerted efforts, these clients frequently evinced no benefit from his interpretive work, and in many cases, their symptoms actually became worse (Leider, 1996). After repeated efforts to revise and refine his formulations proved unsuccessful, Kohut surmised that the essential difficulty was not that he had timed his interpretations poorly or that the focus was either too narrow or too global, but that the fault lay with the fundamental theoretical assumptions of classical theory. These theoretical premises, Kohut argued, were useful in the treatment of the classical neuroses (e.g., hysterical, obsessive-compulsive, and phobic disorders), but by the latter part of the twentieth century, such cases were no longer seen with the same frequency as they had been in Freud's day. If classical neurotic cases were modal in the 1920s, clients with borderline and narcissistic personality disorders, in particular, seemed to be diagnosed with increasing frequency by the 1960s and 1970s.

Kohut's vision of the human condition gradually evolved into something quite different from that of Freud. The Freudian view of humankind can be characterized as an ongoing battle between primitive desires and civilized precepts for behavior, a struggle that is repeated anew with each succeeding generation. In such a perspective, guilt represents a supreme accomplishment, a painful though essential ingredient for the renunciation of instinct, which is a sine qua non for civilized behavior. Kohut, on the other hand, addressed himself not to battles but to

> isolation . . . painful feelings of personal isolation. . . . Kohut's man in trouble was not riddled with guilt over forbidden impulses; he was moving through a life without meaning. . . . He looked and acted like a human being, but experienced life as drudgery, accomplishments as empty. Or he was held captive on an emotional roller coaster, where exuberant bursts of creative energy alternated with painful feelings of inadequacy in response to disrupting perceptions of failure. The creative process was short-circuited. . . . Relationships, eagerly, even desperately pursued, were repeatedly abandoned with an increasing feeling of pessimism at ever getting what one really "needs" from another. (Mitchell & Black, 1995, p. 149)

Kohut asserted that one of the most fundamental distinctions between self psychology and classical psychoanalytic theory concerned human nature. Kohut believed that classical psychoanalysis was chiefly concerned with Guilty Man, "whose aims are directed toward the activity of his drives . . . and who lives within the pleasure principle," attempting "to satisfy his pleasure-seeking drives to lessen the tensions that arise in his erogenous zones" (Kohut, 1977, p. 132). Kohut's concept of Tragic Man, however, illuminates "the essence of fractured, enfeebled, discontinuous human existence" (Kohut, 1977, p. 238). It represents Kohut's effort to explain such clinical phenomena as the schizophrenic's fragmentation, the pathological narcissist's efforts to cope with diffuse and painful vulnerabilities, and the despair of those approaching old age with recognition that important ambitions and ideals remain unrealized.[16]

Kohut and his adherents have introduced several terms and concepts that are associated with psychoanalytic self psychology, each of which we shall explore in some detail: mirroring, idealizing, and partnering selfobjects; the tripolar self; the self types; empathy and transmuting internalization; cohesion, fragmentation, and disintegration anxiety; and compensatory structures.

Mirroring, Idealizing, and Partnering Selfobjects

Kohut used the term selfobject to refer to a particular kind of object relationship in which the object is actually experienced as an extension of the self, without psychological differentiation. He observed that "the expected control over such [selfobjects] . . . is then closer to the concept of control which a grownup expects to have over his own body and mind than to the . . . control which he expects to have over others" (Kohut, 1971, pp. 26–27). Kohut believed that infants are born into an interpersonal milieu that optimally provides them with three distinctly different though equally necessary kinds of selfobject experiences. One kind of experience calls for mirroring selfobjects, "who respond to and confirm the child's innate sense of vigor, greatness and perfection." A second variety of selfobject experience requires the powerful and reassuring presence of caregivers "to whom the child can look up and with whom he can merge as an image of calmness, infallibility, and omnipotence" (Kohut & Wolf, 1978, p. 414). Kohut later introduced a third selfobject realm, referred to as alter ego or partnering selfobjects. This third variety provides a range of experiences through which children acquire a sense of belonging and of essential alikeness within a community of others.

The Tripolar Self

The tripolar self is the intrapsychic structure over which are superimposed the three specific selfobject experiences we have described. The first pole, that of grandiose-exhibitionistic needs, is associated with the need for approval, interest, and affirmation (mirroring). The second pole, the idealizing pole, is associated with developmental needs for

---

[16]Erikson had, of course, addressed this particular phenomenon (though from an ego psychological perspective) in his description of "ego integrity versus despair," the eighth and final normative crisis in the human life cycle.

closeness and support from an (omnipotent) idealized other (Leider, 1996).[17] The third pole is that of the alter ego, and it involves the ongoing need for contact with others who are felt to bear likeness to the self. These three poles are "structures that crystallize as a result of the interaction between the needs of the self and the responses of those important persons in the environment who function as selfobjects" (Leider, 1966, p. 141).

The Self Types

Kohut and other exponents of psychoanalytic self psychology believe that the self is most usefully understood within the intersecting matrices of developmental level and structural state. Four principal self types that have been identified are: (1) the *virtual self,* an image of the newborn's self that originally exists within the parent's mind and evolves in particular ways as the parental "selfobjects emphatically respond to certain potentialities of the child" (Kohut, 1977, p. 100); (2) the *nuclear self,* a core self that emerges in the infant's second year, serving as the basis for the child's "sense of being an independent center of initiative and perception" (Kohut, 1977, p. 177); (3) the *cohesive self,* the basic self structure of a well-adapted, healthily functioning individual, characterized by the harmonious "interplay of ambitions, ideals, and talents with the opportunities of everyday reality" (Leider, 1996, p. 143); and (4) the *grandiose self,* a normal self structure of infancy and early childhood that develops originally in response to the selfobject's attunement with the child's sense of himself or herself as the center of the universe.

Empathy and Transmuting Internalization

Kohut, whose theoretical contributions have focused on development of the personality, psychopathology, and psychoanalytic technique, placed a great deal of emphasis on the role of empathy in human development.[18] Self psychology defines empathy as "vicarious introspection," the feeling of oneself into the experience of an other; the capacity for empathic attunement in the child's selfobject milieu is considered to be of the utmost importance. At the same time, a critical impetus for healthy self-development involves what are described as minor, relatively nontraumatic lapses in parental empathy. Such lapses, because they are optimally frustrating, serve as a catalyst for the child's development of transmuting internalizations. Transmuting internalization is an intrapsychic process whereby the child gradually "takes in" functions associated with the selfobject, which may range from self-calming and self-soothing to pride, humor, and stoicism in the face of adversity. In other words, through an almost imperceptible, bit-by-bit process of translocation, these functions gradually become enduring parts of the child's own self-structure, though they are transformed to "fit" the child's unique self.[19]

---

[17]Kohut has referred to this as the need for "uplifting care," both literally and figuratively speaking, from the idealized selfobjects.

[18]Akhtar (1988) also notes that self psychology has made contributions to the study of sociopolitical processes and the philosophy of human nature.

[19]The key elements in the sequence of transmuting internalization are, in order, optimal frustration, increased tension, selfobject response, reduced tension, memory trace, and development of internal regulating structure.

Cohesion, Fragmentation, and Disintegration Anxiety

Cohesion is the term used in self psychology to refer to a self state that serves as the basis for robust, synchronous, and integrated psychological functioning. Self cohesion makes possible the harmonious interplay of ambitions, ideals, and talents in the context of everyday realities. It also protects the individual from regressive fragmentation in the face of adversity or obstacles that may interfere with the satisfaction of object or selfobject needs (Leider, 1996). Individuals who are fragmentation prone (who tend, under stress, to develop such symptoms as hypochondriasis, hypomanic excitement, or disturbances in bodily sensation and self perception) have been unable to acquire stable, consolidated, and enduring self-structures. Whether this is a consequence of parental pathology, environmental vicissitudes, or a combination of the two, it is invariably associated with the unavailability of parental selfobjects to perform important selfobject functions. Such developmental deficiencies are associated with self or selfobject disorders (e.g., narcissistic pathology, borderline states, depression, and psychosis). Disintegration anxiety is defined as the fear of the breaking up of the self, which, according to Kohut, is the most profound anxiety a human being is capable of experiencing. A related term, *disintegration products,* refers to various symptoms produced by an enfeebled, disharmonious self (e.g., paranoia, narcissistic rage, exhibitionism, and other paraphilias).

Compensatory Structures

When in the course of early development, the parental selfobjects fail to respond adequately to a particular constellation of selfobject needs (whether for mirroring, idealizing, or partnering) it is sometimes possible to compensate for these deficiencies through more intensive structuralization of a second set of selfobject needs. As an example, an individual who has experienced developmental arrest in the area of ambitions (perhaps due to chronic disappointments in his or her efforts to evoke mirroring responses from a parent) may find the same selfobject to be far more accessible for the fulfillment of idealizing or partnering needs. The evolution of compensatory structures is motivated by the individual's need to rise above developmental obstacles and to repair defects in self-structure (Leider, 1996). Compensatory structures, however, are regarded as normative, and as Kohut observes, "there is not one kind of healthy self—there are many kinds" (Kohut, 1984, p. 44).[20]

RECENT DEVELOPMENTS IN SELF PSYCHOLOGY

Self psychology is no longer the unitary theory it was during Kohut's lifetime, though most who are identified with his theories continue to subscribe to two basic features of his work: the central importance of the therapist's sustained, empathic immersion in the subjective experience of the client, and the concept of selfobjects and the

---

[20]*Defensive structures,* another term Kohut used, are differentiated from compensatory structures in that the former "cover over" the primary defects in the self; compensatory structures actually compensate for the defect rather than simply disguise it.

selfobject transference (Mitchell & Black, 1995). There has been considerable divergence and ferment within self psychology in recent years, a situation that has prompted one well-known theorist to observe that "self psychologists no longer have a common language" (J. Palombo, personal communication).

The analyst and infant researcher Joseph Lichtenberg has addressed himself to Kohut's developmental concepts and their particular meaning in the light of important new developments in the field of infant research (Lichtenberg, 1983, 1989). Infant research has also been of interest to Lachmann and Beebe, who have paid special attention to self psychological notions of self-regulation and transmuting internalization, expanding and extending Kohut's original formulations (Lachmann & Beebe, 1992, 1994). Stolorow's intersubjectivity theory (Stolorow, Brandschaft, & Atwood, 1987), while based on the organizing framework of Kohut's system, represents a more revolutionary paradigm. "Rather than the individual, isolated self, Stolorow's emphasis is on the fully contextual interaction of subjectivities with reciprocal, mutual influence" (Mitchell & Black, 1995, p. 167). Bacal (1995) and Basch (1986, 1988), and others too numerous to mention, have also shaped the burgeoning literature of psychoanalytic self psychology.

CONCLUSION

This chapter began by exploring the relationship between clinical social work and psychoanalysis in some depth, examining particular social work treatment theories and their incorporation of various psychoanalytic concepts. We also summarized a range of psychoanalytic systems, from traditional Freudian theory to Kohut's psychology of the self. Various models of development have also been included, principally because psychoanalytic developmental theories are typically closely linked to psychoanalytic theories of psychopathology. Finally, we have labored to explicate major theoretical disagreements in order to reveal the richness and complexity of this vast body of literature. We hope that this chapter has provided a useful overview of important psychoanalytic theories and controversies and the unique relationship between them and clinical social work.

REFERENCES

Abend, S. (1981). Psychic conflict and the concept of defense. *Psychoanalytic Quarterly, 50,* 67–76.

Abend, S. (1984). Sibling love and object choice. *Psychoanalytic Quarterly, 53,* 425–430.

Abraham, K. (1921). Contributions to the theory of the anal character. In *Selected papers of Karl Abraham* (pp. 370–92). London: Hogarth, 1973.

Abraham, K. (1924a). A short study of the development of the libido. In *Selected papers on psycho-analysis* (pp. 418–450). London: Hogarth, 1948.

Abraham, K. (1924b). The influence of oral eroticism on character formation. In *Selected papers on psycho-analysis* (pp. 393–406). London: Hogarth, 1948.

Abraham, K. (1925). Character formation and the genital level of libido development. In *Selected papers on psycho-analysis* (pp. 407–17). London: Hogarth, 1948.

Adler, A. (1927). The practice and theory of individual psychology. New York: Harcourt.

Akhtar, S. (1988). Some reflections on the theory of psychopathology and personality development in Kohut's self psychology. In J. Ross & W. Myers (Eds.), *New Concepts in psychoanalytic psychotherapy* (pp. 227–252). Washington, DC: American Psychiatric Press.

Arieti, S. (1974). *Interpretation of schizophrenia.* New York: Basic Books.

Arlow, J. (1969). Unconscious fantasy and disturbances of conscious experience. *Psychoanalytic Quarterly, 38,* 1–27.

Arlow, J., & C. Brenner. (1964). *Psychoanalytic concepts and the structural theory.* New York: International Universities Press.

Bacal, H. (1995). The essence of Kohut's work and the progress of self psychology. *Psychoanalytic Dialogues, 5,* 353–356.

Bacal, H., & K. Newman. (1990). *Theories of object relations: Bridge to self psychology.* New York: Columbia University Press.

Bak, R. (1943). Dissolution of the ego: Mannerism and delusions of grandeur. *Journal of Nervous and Mental Diseases, 98,* 457–464.

Balint, A. (1949). Love for the mother and mother-love. *International Journal of Psychoanalysis, 30,* 251–259.

Balint, M. (1937). Early development states of the ego. Primary object love. *International Journal of Psychoanalysis, 30,* 265–273, 1949.

Basch, M. (1986). "How does analysis cure?" An appreciation. *Psychoanalytic Inquiry, 6,* 403–428.

Basch, M. (1988). *Doing psychotherapy.* New York: Basic Books.

Benjamin, J. (1988). *The bonds of love: Psychoanalysis, feminism, and the problem of domination.* New York: Pantheon.

Borden, W. (1995). Making use of theory in practice: Legacies of the independent tradition. Unpublished manuscript.

Bowlby, J. (1969). *Attachment and loss:* Vol. I. *Attachment.* New York: Basic Books.

Brenner, C. (1975). Affects and psychic conflict. *Psychoanalytic Quarterly, 44*: 5–28.

Brenner, C. (1981). Defense and defense mechanisms. *Psychoanalytic Quarterly, 50,* 557–569.

Brenner, C. (1982). *The mind in conflict.* New York: International Universities Press.

Breuer, J., & Freud, S. (1893–95). *Studies on hysteria.* (J. Strachey, Trans.). London: Hogarth, Vol. 2.

Bridgman, P.W. (1945). Some general principles of operational analysis. *Psychological Review, 52*: 246–249.

Brown, D., & E. Fromm. (1986). *Hypnotherapy and hypnoanalysis.* Hillsdale, NJ: Lawrence Erlbaum Associates.

Chapman, A.H. (1976). *Harry Stack Sullivan: The man and his work.* New York: Putnam.

Chodorow, N. (1989). *Feminism and psychoanalytic theory.* New Haven, CT: Yale University Press.

Chrzanowski, G. (1977). *Interpersonal approach to psychoanalysis.* New York: Gardner Press.

Erikson, E. (1959). *Identity and the life cycle: Vol. 1. Selected papers, Psychological issues.* New York: International Universities Press.

Fairbairn, W. (1952). *An object relations theory of the personality.* New York: Basic Books.

Fenichel, O. (1929). Dread of being eaten. In H. Fenichel & D. Rapaport (Eds.), *The collected works of Otto Fenichel, First Series* (pp. 158–159). New York: Norton.

Fenichel, O. (1945). *The psychoanalytic theory of neurosis.* New York: Norton.

Ferenczi, S. (1913). Stages in the development of the sense of reality. In *Sex in psychoanalysis* (E. Jones, Trans.). New York: Basic Books, 1950.

Fine, R. (1975). *Psychoanalytic psychology.* New York: Jason Aronson.

Fischer, C. (1954). Dreams and perception: The role of unconscious and primary modes of perception in dream formation. *Journal of the American Psychoanalytic Association, 2,* 389–445.

Freud, A. (1936). *The ego and the mechanisms of defense.* London: Hogarth Press.

Freud, A. (1963). The concept of developmental lines. *Psychoanalytic Study of the Child, 18,* 245–265.

Freud, S. (1894). The neuropsychoses of defense. *The standard edition of the complete psychological works of Sigmund Freud* (J. Strachey, Trans.). London: Hogarth, Vol. *SE,* 3, 45–61.

Freud, S. (1895a). On the grounds for detaching a particular syndrome from neurasthenia under the description "anxiety neurosis." *SE, 3,* 87–113.

Freud, S. (1895b). Project for a scientific psychology. *SE,* 1, pp. 283–387.

Freud, S. (1900). *The interpretation of dreams. SE,* 4 and 5.

Freud, S. (1901). *The psychopathology of everyday life. SE,* 6.

Freud, S. (1905). *Three essays on the theory of sexuality. SE,* 7, 125–245.

Freud, S. (1908). Character and anal eroticism. *SE,* 9, 169–175.

Freud, S. (1909). Family romances. *SE,* 9, 235–241.

Freud, S. (1911a). Psycho-analytic notes on an autobiographical account of a case of paranoia (dementia paranoides). *SE,* 12, 1–82.

Freud, S. (1911b). The handling of dream interpretation in psycho-analysis. *SE,* 12, 89–96.

Freud, S. (1912a). The dynamics of transference. *SE,* 12, 99–108.

Freud, S. (1912b). Recommendations to physicians practicing psycho-analysis. *SE,* 12, 111–120.

Freud, S. (1913). On beginning the treatment. *SE,* 12, 123–144.

Freud, S. (1914a). On narcissism: an introduction. *SE,* 14, 67–102.

Freud, S. (1914b). Remembering, repeating, and working-through. *SE,* 12, 147–156.

Freud, S. (1915). Observations on transference-love. *SE,* 12, 159–171.

Freud, S. (1916). Some character types met with in psycho-analytic work. *SE,* 14, 159–171.

Freud, S. (1917). Mourning and melancholia. *SE,* 14, 237–260.

Freud, S. (1919). "A child is being beaten": A contribution to the study of the origin of sexual perversions. *SE,* 17, 175–204.

Freud, S. (1920). Beyond the pleasure principle. *SE,* 18, 7–64.

Freud, S. (1923). *The ego and the id. SE,* 19, 12–66.

Freud, S. (1925). Some psychical consequences of the anatomical distinction between the sexes. *SE,* 19, 241–258.

Freud, S. (1926). *Inhibitions, symptoms, and anxiety. SE,* 20, pp. 75–175.

Friedman, R., & Downey, J. (1995). Biology and the oedipus complex. *Psychoanalytic Quarterly, 64,* 234–264.

Fromm-Reichman, F. (1950). *Principles of intensive psychotherapy.* Chicago: University of Chicago Press.

Frosch, J. (1970). Psychoanalytic considerations of the psychotic character. *Journal of the American Psychoanalytic Association, 18,* 24–50.

Gill, M., & Brenman, M. (1959). *Hypnosis and related states: Psychoanalytic studies and regression.* New York: International Universities Press.

Glover, O. (1941). *Problems of psychoanalytic technique.* New York: Psychoanalytic Quarterly.

Goldstein, E. (1995). *Ego psychology and social work practice.* New York: Free Press.

Greenberg, J., & Mitchell, S. (1983). *Object relations in psychoanalytic theory.* Cambridge: Harvard University Press.

Greenson, R. (1967). *The technique and practice of psychoanalysis.* New York: International Universities Press.

Grossman, W. (1991). Pain, aggression, fantasy, and concepts of sadomasochism. *Psychoanalytic Quarterly, 60,* 22–52.

Grotstein, J. (1996). Object relations theory. In E. Nersessian & R. Kopffv (Eds.), *Textbook of psychoanalysis* (pp. 89–125). Washington, DC: American Psychiatric Press.

Guntrip, H. (1968). *Schizoid phenomena, object relations, and the self.* New York: International Universities Press.

Guntrip, H. (1971). *Psychoanalytic theory, therapy and the self.* New York: Basic Books.

Harlow, H. (1959). Love in infant monkeys. *Scientific American, 200,* 68–74.

Hartman, H. (1939). *Ego psychology and the problem of adaptation.* New York: International Universities Press.

Hartman, H., Kris, E., & Lowenstein, R. (1949). Notes on the theory of aggression. *Psychoanalytic Study of the Child, 3–4,* 9–36.

Havens, L. (1976). *Participant observation.* New York: Jason Aronson.

Havens, L. (1986). Making contact. Cambridge: Harvard University Press.

Havens, L., & Frank, J., Jr. (1971). Review of P. Mullahy, *Psychoanalysis and Interpersonal Psychiatry, 127,* 1704–1705.

Hendricks, I. (1942). Instinct and the ego during infancy. *Psychoanalytic Quarterly, 11,* 33–58.

Hermann, I. (1933). *Zum Triebleben der Primaten. Imago,* 19, 113.

Hermann, I. (1936). *Sich-Anklammern-Auf-Suche-Gehen. International Zeitschrift Psychoanalyse, 22,* 349–370.

Hollis, F. (1970). The psychosocial approach to the practice of social casework. In Robert W. Roberts & Robert H. Nee (Eds.), *Theories of social casework* (pp. 33–75). Chicago: University of Chicago Press.

Holzman, P. (1970). *Psychoanalysis and psychopathology.* New York: McGraw-Hill.

Horner, T. (1985). The psychic life of the young infant: Review and critique of the psychoanalytic concepts of symbiosis and infantile omnipotence. *American Journal of Orthopsychiatry, 55,* 324–344.

Hurvich, M. (1989). Traumatic moment, basic dangers, and annihilation anxiety. *Psychoanalytic Psychology,* 6, 309–323.

Hurvich, M. (1991). Annihilation anxiety: An introduction. In Siegel, H., Barbanel, L., Hirsch, I., Lasky, J., Silverman, H., & Warshaw, S. (Eds.), *Psychoanalytic reflections on current issues* (pp. 135–154). New York: New York University Press.

Jacobson, E. (1964). *The self and the object world.* New York: International Universities Press.

Jacobson, E. (1971). *Depression: Comparative studies of normal, neurotic, and psychotic conditions.* New York: International Universities Press.

Jacobson, J. (1994). Signal affect and our psychoanalytic confusion of tongues. *Journal of the American Psychoanalytic Association, 42,* 15–42.

Jones, E. (1911). The psychology of morbid anxiety. In: *Papers in psychoanalysis,* 4th Edition. London: Bailliare, Tindall, and Cox.

Jones, E. (1953). *The life and work of Sigmund Freud, 1856–1900, The formative years and the great discoveries* (Vol. 1). New York: Basic Books.

Jones, E. (1955). *The life and work of Sigmund Freud, 1901–1919, Years of maturity* (Vol. 2). New York: Basic Books.

Jones, E. (1957). *The life and work of Sigmund Freud, 1919–1939, The last phase* (Vol. 3). New York: Basic Books.

Jung, C. G. (1916). *Collected works of C. G. Jung, The relations between the ego and the unconscious* (Vol. 7, pp. 1–201). Princeton, NJ: Princeton University Press.

Jung, C. G. (1917), *Collected Works of C. G. Jung, On the psychology of the unconscious* (Vol. 7, pp. 202–406). Princeton, NJ: Princeton University Press.

Kernberg, O. (1980). *Internal world and external reality.* Northvale, NJ: Jason Aronson.

King, P., & Stiner, R. (Eds.) (1991). *The Freud-Klein controversies, 1941–1945.* London: Routledge.

Klein, G. (1976). *Psychoanalytic theory: An exploration of essentials.* New York: International Universities Press.

Klein, M. (1932). *The psychoanalysis of children.* London: Hogarth Press.

Klein, M. (1935). A contribution to the psychogenesis of manic-depressive states. In *Contributions to psychoanalysis, 1921–1945.* New York: McGraw-Hill, 1964.

Klein, M. (1946). Notes on some schizoid mechanisms. In *Envy and gratitude and other works, 1946–1963.* New York: Delacorte Press, 1975.

Klein, M. (1952). Some theoretical conclusions regarding the emotional life of the infant. In *Envy and gratitude and other works, 1946–1963,* New York: Delacorte Press, 1975.

Klein, M. (1964). *Contributions to psychoanalysis, 1921–1945.* New York: McGraw-Hill.

Kohon, G. (Ed.). (1986). *The British school of psychoanalysis: The independent tradition.* London: Free Association Books.

Kohut, H. (1966). Forms and transformations of narcissism. *Journal of the American Psychoanalytic Association, 14,* 243–272.

Kohut, H. (1971). *The analysis of the self.* New York: International Universities Press.

Kohut, H. (1972). Thoughts on narcissism and narcissistic rage. *Psychoanalytic Study of the Child, 27,* 360–400.

Kohut, H. (1977). *The restoration of the self.* New York: International Universities Press.

Kohut, H. (1984). *How does analysis cure?* Chicago: University of Chicago Press.

Kohut, H., & Wolf, E. (1978). The disorders of the self and their treatment: An outline. *International Journal of Psychoanalysis, 59,* 413–425.

Lachmann, F., & Beebe, B. (1992). Representational and selfobject transferences: A developmental perspective. In *New therapeutic visions: Progress in self psychology* (Vol. 8, pp. 3–15). Hillsdale, NJ: Analytic Press.

Lachmann, F., & Beebe, B. (1994). Representation and internalization in infancy: 3 principles of salience. *Psychoanalytic Psychology, 11*(2), 127–166.

Laughlin, H. (1979). *The ego and its defenses.* Northvale, NJ: Jason Aronson.

Leider, R. (1996). The Psychology of the self. In E. Nersessian & R. Kopff (Eds.), *Textbook of psychoanalysis* (pp. 127–164). Washington, DC: American Psychiatric Press.

Levenson, E. (1972). *The Fallacy of understanding.* New York: Basic Books.

Lichtenberg, J. (1983). *Psychoanalysis and infant research.* Hillsdale, NJ: Analytic Press.

Lichtenberg, J. (1989). *Psychoanalysis and motivation.* Hillsdale, NJ: Analytic Press.

Lorenz, K. (1937). The nature of instincts. In C. Schiller (Ed.), *Instinctive behavior.* New York: International Universities Press, 1957.

Mahler, M. (1968). *On human symbiosis and the vicissitudes of individuation.* New York: International Universities Press.

Mahler, M. (1972). The rapprochement subphase. *Psychoanalytic Quarterly, 41,* 487–506.

Mahler, M., Pine, F., & Bergmann, A. (1975). *The psychological birth of the human infant.* New York: Basic Books.

Masterson, J., & Rinsley, D. (1975). The borderline syndrome: The role of the mother in the genesis and psychic structure of the borderline personality. *International Journal of Psychoanalysis, 56,* 163–177.

McDevitt, J. (1996). The continuity of conflict and compromise formation: A 25 year follow-up. *Journal of the Amnerican Psychoanalytic Association* (in press).

Mishne, J. (1993). *The evolution and application of clinical theory.* New York: Free Press.

Mitchell, J. (1975). *Psychoanalysis and feminism.* New York: Vintage.

Mitchell, S. (1983). Aggression and the endangered self. *Psychoanalytic Quarterly, 62,* 351–382.

Mitchell, S. (1988). *Relational concepts in psychoanalysis.* Cambridge, MA: Harvard University Press.

Mitchell, S., & Black, M. (1995). *Freud and beyond: A history of modern psychoanalytic thought.* New York: Basic Books.

Moore, B., & Fine, B. (1990). *Psychoanalytic terms and concepts.* New Haven, CT: Yale University Press.

Mullahy, P. (1970). *Psychoanalysis and interpersonal psychiatry.* N.Y.: Science House.

Ogden, T. (1982). *Projective identification and psychoanalytic technique.* Northvale, NJ: Jason Aronson.

Parens, H. (1979). *The development of aggression in early childhood.* Northvale, NJ: Jason Aronson.

Perlman, H. (1953). The social components of casework practice. In *The social welfare forum.* New York: Columbia University Press.

Perlman, H. (1957). *Social casework: A problem-solving process.* Chicago: University of Chicago Press.

Perlman, H. (1970). The problem-solving model in social casework. In Robert W. Roberts & Robert H. Nee (Eds.), *Theories of social casework* (pp. 129–179). Chicago: University of Chicago Press.

Perry, H. S. (1982). *Psychiatrist of America: The life of Harry Stack Sullivan.* Cambridge, MA: Harvard University Press.

Pine, F. (1970). On the structuralization of drive-defense relationships. *Psychoanalytic Quarterly, 39,* 17–37.

Pine, F. (1985). *Developmental theory and clinical process.* New Haven, CT: Yale University Press.

Pine, F. (1988). The four psychologies of psychoanalysis and their place in clinical work. *Journal of the American Psychoanalytic Association, 36,* 571–596.

Pine, F. (1990). *Drive, ego, object, and self.* New York: Basic Books.

Rank, O. (1924). *The trauma of birth.* New York: Harper & Row, 1973.

Rapaport, D. (1960). *The structure of psychoanalytic theory.* New York: International Universities Press.

Rapaport, D. (1967). *Collected papers of David Rapaport.* Merton Gill (Ed.). New York: Basic Books.

Reich, W. (1933). *Character analysis.* New York: Pocket Books, 1976.

Reiser, M. (1990). *Memory in mind and brain: What dream imagery reveals.* New York: Basic Books.

Rochlin, G. (1973). *Man's aggression: The defense of the self.* Boston: Gambit.

Sandler, J. (1960). The background of safety. *International Journal of Psychoanalysis, 41,* 352–365.

Saul, I. (1976). *The psychodynamics of hostility.* Northvale, NJ: Jason Aronson.

Schafer, R. (1992). *Retelling a life.* New York: Basic Books.

Searles, H. (1965). *Collected papers on schizophrenia and related subjects.* New York: International Universities Press.

Shapiro, D. (1965). *Neurotic styles.* New York: Basic Books.

Sharpe, S., & Rosenblatt, A. (1994). Oedipal sibling triangles. *Journal of the American Psychoanalytic Association, 42,* 491–523.

Smalley, R. (1970). The functional approach to casework practice. In Robert W. Roberts & Robert H. Nee (Eds.), *Theories of social casework* (pp. 77–128). Chicago: University of Chicago Press.

Spence, D. (1982). *Narrative truth and historical truth.* New York: Norton.

Spitz, R. (1945). Hospitalism: An inquiry into the genesis of psychiatric conditions in early childhood. *Psychoanalytic Study of the Child, 1,* 53–73.

Spitz, R. (1965). *The first year of life.* New York: International Universities Press.

Stern, D. (1986). *The interpersonal world of the infant.* New York: Basic Books.

Stolorow, R., Brandschaft, B., & Atwood, G. (1987). *Psychoanalytic treatment: An intersubjective approach.* Hillsdale, NJ: Analytic Press.

Strean, H. (1993). Clinical social work: An evaluative review. *Journal of Analytic Social Work, 1*, 5–23.

Sullivan, H. (1930). Socio-psychiatric research. In *Schizophrenia as a human process*. New York: Norton, 1962.

Sullivan, H. (1940). *Conceptions of modern psychiatry*. New York: Norton.

Sullivan, H. (1953). *The Interpersonal theory of psychiatry*. New York: Norton.

Sullivan, H. (1956). *Clinical studies in psychiatry*. New York: Norton.

Sullivan, H. (1962). *Schizophrenia as a human process*. New York: Norton.

Suttie, I. (1935). *The origins of love and hate*. New York: Matrix House, 1952.

Thompson, C. (1964). *Interpersonal psychoanalysis: The selected papers of Clara Thompson*. New York: Basic Books.

Thorpe, W. (1949). *Learning and instinct in animals*. Cambridge, MA: Harvard University Press.

Tyson, P., & Tyson, R. (1990). *Psychoanalytic theories of development*. New Haven, CT: Yale University Press.

Wallerstein, R. (1985). Defense mechanisms and the structure of the mind. *Journal of the American Psychoanalytic Association, 31* (Supplement), 201–225.

White, R. (1963). *The ego and reality in psychoanalytic theory*. New York: International Universities Press.

Willick, M. (1985). The concept of primitive defenses. *Journal of the American Psychoanalytic Association, 31* (Supplement), 175–200.

Winnicott, D. (1951). Transitional objects and transitional phenomena. *Through paediatrics to psycho-analysis*. London: Hogarth Press, 1958.

Winnicott, D. (1958a). The capacity to be alone. *The maturational process and the facilitating environment*. New York: International Universities Press, 1965.

Winnicott, D. W. (1958b). *Through paediatrics to psychoanalysis*. London: Hogarth Press.

Winnicott, D. (1960). The theory of the parent-infant relationship. In *The maturational process and the facilitating environment*. New York: International Universities Press, 1965.

Winnicott, D. (1965). *The maturational process and the facilitating environment*. New York: International Universities Press.

Witenberg, E. (ed.). (1973). *Interpersonal explorations in psychoanalysis: New directions in theory and practice*. New York: Basic Books.

Woodroofe, K. (1971). *From charity to social work in England and the United States*. Toronto: University of Toronto Press.

Woods, M. & Hollis, F. (1990). *Casework: A psychosocial therapy*. New York: McGraw-Hill.

Part II

Specific Treatment Modalities

4

Clinical Practice with Children

Margaret G. Frank

The dimensions of clinical work with children have changed markedly in the past two decades. Clinicians, including those in private practice, face new challenges emanating from the political and economic scene that impinge on mental health service settings. Changes in the form of family structure have prompted major shifts in attitudes toward parents and parenting, evoking new dimensions in countertransference. Finally, the expansion of theories that can inform and guide clinical work with children, although exciting, may leave us questioning, "What is in the best interest of the child?"

This chapter addresses clinical practice with children in the context of today's world, with specific attention to these current pressures. (A detailed discussion of theories, as represented in the words of Melanie Klein, D. W. Winnicott, and Harry Stack Sullivan, among others, may be found in Chapter 3.) The underlying premise of this chapter is that treatment informed by psychoanalytic developmental object relations theory may help the practitioner to navigate the rapids of contemporary pressures. The combined impact of time pressures, social attitudes, and new laws impinging on social work often works against the establishment of a truly therapeutic focus. Knowledge of the ways in which life events can shape development and produce adaptations enables clinicians to maintain and sharpen the therapeutic focus on the child. Furthermore, informed clinical work with children helps to prevent burnout.

THEORY

This brief review of psychoanalytic developmental object relations theory begins with the perspective that clinicians must have an intimate knowledge of the child's development in the physical, cognitive, social, and psychological realms. Such knowledge must begin with some vision of normal development, as difficult as this may be to define. The process of growth itself is equally critical to understand.

The formulations of Margaret Mahler et al. (1975) emphasized the growth process as one in which the child moves from "oneness to separateness." Her observations and formulations focused on the intricate interplay of the growth of the body, neurological maturation, and cognitive development, which collectively propel the child in the direction of becoming an autonomous and independent being. The early work and observations of Daniel Stern (1985) had a somewhat different emphasis. He and his colleagues viewed growth as a process of acquiring the ability to attach.

Although these positions seem to be in conflict, they have nevertheless contributed to our more intimate knowledge of development. Development can be seen as a navigation between a lesser differentiated state toward greater and greater differentiation. The process is then one of a constant redefining of how to attach and how to acquire autonomy. This is indeed a lifelong process. One might say that the best form of adulthood is one in which the individual is able to be intimate and relate to another without fear of loss of self and at the same time is capable of relative autonomy without fearing the loss of the other.

Anyone who has had close acquaintance with toddlers knows that in early toddlerhood, they require assistance from adults in putting on their clothes. This need springs from less developed physical dexterity and immature cognitive functions, which join together to create a dependency. Sometime later, they eagerly express their interest in being able to zip their *own* jackets despite offers and, all too often, the caregiver's impatience. We see in this the toddler's delight in the acquisition of new skills, a stepping-stone to autonomy. Even when the skill has been reliably acquired and help has been recently rebuffed, the toddler may turn about, frequently requesting help despite ability. This can be seen as "checking in" to test the availability of an earlier form of attachment. In addition there may be the question in their minds: "What do I lose if I gain this new skill?" a question that is present at all ages to some degree.

While I do not share her perspective, Judith Viorst, in her book *Necessary Losses*, views the entire life process from the perspective of loss. I believe she underestimates the pleasures gained by mastery. Furthermore, she does not give sufficient consideration to Jacobson's (1964) concept of the child's incorporation of and identification with the caregiving person's functions as a way of holding on to her.

Today, all theories of development despite their differences reveal a common interest in the representational world (Sandler & Rosenblatt, 1962). Each believes that the formation of self and other (object) is derived from a complicated matrix of forces composed of the child's innate endowment in combination with the qualities and aptitudes of the caretaking environment. In addition, there is recognition that development itself has a potentially defining quality. We observe this in the toddler who at the height of mastery is having "a love affair with the world" (Greenacre, 1953). At this stage of development, it is expected that such a child will have what would in later life be viewed as strong grandiose features. However, as cognitive development proceeds, the illusion of expansive capacity begins to break down. Children nearing the rapprochement period (Mahler, Pine, & Bergmann, 1975) are increasingly able to compare and observe. These abilities prompt a state of disillusionment about themselves and the object; if all goes well, it brings them into greater contact with the reality principle. If I were to try to speak for a well-put-together rapprochement phase child, the words for his experience might be, "Gee, I'm not as fantastic as I thought I was, but then I am able to do lots of things and I will learn more." This child's affect might include a combination of sadness and pleasure. Speaking about the object, the child might say, "I thought you were perfect, powerful, and omniscient. I am disappointed that you are not. But I am also relieved, because if *you* have limitations, then I don't have to be distressed about *my own*—which I'm just discovering." I am not attempting to do justice to Mahler's concept of the rapprochement crisis, but rather to give a flavor to the transmuting definitions of self and object that are formed across the phases of development.

Concomitant with the formation of self and object representations, inner and outer experiences influence the structure of object relations. The structures of self and object are always accompanied by affect. Object relations are the myriad formulations subjectively formed by the child that involve expectations of the object as well as views of how the self must be in relation to the object (other).

The concept of object relations has greatly expanded our understanding of transference. Over twenty years ago, we viewed transference as binoculars that gave us insight into the character of mothers and fathers. Today we learn from the transference about the nature of the subjective experiences drawn by the child from early life experiences. While parents may well have been involved in the formation of the self and object definitions, the full dimensions of object relations cannot be placed solely at their feet. The easiest way of understanding this is to look at a child who has had some painful physical condition over a long period in his young life. The mother may do her best to bring comfort to her infant, but pain will inevitably be associated with his experience of himself and the object. The definition of self may include being the recipient of pain. Similarly, that object may well be viewed as an inflicter of pain or at the very least incapable of relieving his suffering. Let us envisage pain becoming a part of the toddler's experience. This child might conclude that had he not tried to explore and master various tasks associated with a particular developmental phase(s), he would have been protected from his painful condition.

The death of an important family member, should it occur in the period of oedipal or triadic object relations (Blanck & Blanck, 1986), might well lead the child to conclude that he was being punished for his newly unfolded gender ambition. This could even cause a retreat from the world of competition and ambition. These brief what-ifs are intended to underscore the importance of events beyond the parent-child interaction that may be influential in the formation of self and object definitions. In addition I have tried to show how the phases of development have an "editorial" influence.

Object relations are scenarios reenacted in the world at large and, most important for the clinician, within the treatment situation. In their simplest form we can imagine the opening scenes in the treatment of several different children.

Sally, age eight, comes into her therapist's office and immediately starts to admire the room. She moves carefully. When she touches the different play things, she replaces them neatly. The therapist has not given any clues, verbally or nonverbally, that this is desirable behavior. We can infer that Sally brings to this session her unconscious conclusions derived from we-know-not-what-yet, that this is the way she must be with the object. Putting aside the caution one expects in early settings, we may ponder whether she is keeping order as a response to her own inner turmoil (conflict) or beginning the process of telling her object relations story.

Sally's behavior is in contrast to another child, who maintains a belligerent and distant stance. In response to a few opening words from the therapist, this child is immediately angry, dubious that anyone can do anything for her, and openly challenging. The process of starting to decipher the object relations scenario brings us to question whether this child's life experiences have prompted the view that there is no one out there for her. Is this belligerent stance a protection against hurt and disappointment or a life view?

The purpose of treatment is to view the object relations scenarios in their most complex forms and help the child client to understand them. Concomitant with such understanding, it is of equal importance that therapists seek to provide children with new object experiences. Treatment aims to shift the child's object relations scenarios.

I have emphasized the importance of the therapist's understanding the ways in which developmental experiences are woven into the fabric of self and object definitions and their scenarios. The level of this understanding must be so profound that our theory can be put into words that the client is able to grasp. In addition, the therapist must know herself and be able to endure being seen in a way that does not agree with her self-perception.

BEGINNING TREATMENT

There are guiding principles covering the many ways one might start the treatment process, and they can be translated into different approaches. It is important for the therapist to think about who he or she intends to be for the client. Therapists are not friends, although friendships may occur. A therapist is a "story decipherer." The therapist has an extraordinary interest (that gives rise to a new object experience) and enjoys puzzles despite the fact that some puzzle pieces may be sad, hard to imagine, or even repulsive. It is important to engage the child in unraveling his own story and becoming a co-investigator insofar as this is possible.

Therapeutic alliance

Some years ago I saw an eight-year-old boy for treatment. His parents pursued the referral under pressure from his school. He was known as a "liar," appeared defiant, and never seemed to be in synch with adults and other children. He came to his first session somewhat breathless and bubbling with a story that intended to explain his tardiness for our meeting. He told me that he had been assigned the task of being garbage monitor for the day. As he was emptying the trash down the shoot, he fell in.

He reported that his classroom was on the third floor, and he fell toward the second floor with garbage all around him. He described how he managed to catch the second floor trash door, open it, and get out.

One could certainly be caught by the unreality of this story. I responded that I thought maybe he was telling me that he had been through some scary and dangerous situations. I noted that it certainly was not easy to get to my office and that I was impressed that he had made it. There are so many metaphors in this communication that describing them all might fill the chapter. I chose to stay with the affect. He allowed a beguiling smile to appear and asked me if I believed what he told me. I replied that I believed he told me a story about his feelings about coming to my office. I added that these were just my thoughts, and I wondered what he thought of them. I thus avoided the expected object position. Focusing on his feelings rather than the veracity of his story provided an opportunity for a new object experience. Inviting his thoughts about my reading of his story was a beginning approach to the working alliance.

Let us look at the beginning work with a belligerent child who does not come to treatment willingly. He may challenge the therapist in many ways. "What am I here for? I'm not going to talk to you. You'll just spill everything I say to my parents. You'll get me in more trouble." The therapist who sees the reflection of the object definition in these words might say, "Wow, you sound as if you are talking to the enemy! If I were that kind of person, I wouldn't want to talk to me either." Clinicians are often moved in early sessions to try to tell children that they are friendly, understanding, and can be trusted. Although all these qualities may be true, they need to be demonstrated over time—not discussed. No one can believe another person's words about such qualities, particularly if they are qualities not known in that person's object repertoire. In this vignette the therapist highlights the object definition and casts a shadow of doubt about the reality of it. She too would not want to talk to such a person. The therapist proceeds to address the child's anxieties quite directly. "You ought to know that I can never promise to keep all that we might talk about confidential. I can promise to talk with you first and tell you my reasons if I think something should be told to your parents or the school. I can also promise to give you a chance to tell me the reasons for your objections if you have them. You may not believe me about this, so we'll have to see in time." This therapist recognizes that she is providing a sharply different object experience, so this is acknowledged to the child along with the fact that the therapist may not seem believable, at least for the time being.

There is another important point to underscore in this intervention: the ability of the therapist to take the lead and put things into words. Principles of child treatment in the early days derived from the old analytic stance of waiting for the client to expose herself and her anxieties. We are aware that this can be experienced by the client as the therapist's withholding and possibly even as a kind of entrapment rather than the intended neutral space in which the client can allow her story to unfold. Children with well-developed ego capacities may make good use of such space. However, we see increasing numbers of ego-impaired children. The therapist who puts matters into words is demonstrating that all feelings, including the child's mistrust, can be talked about. The child client is exposed to the clinician's comfort with thoughts and feelings that others in the child's world may find unacceptable. The therapist can follow these interventions with an awareness that the child does not even want to be there. She might then pursue the question of why he is being seen. Most children respond to this line of inquiry with, "I don't know," even if there has been extensive preparation. In the name of open exchange, it is important for the therapist to respond with what she knows from the referral sources: "I know that the school is concerned about you. They tell me you often disrupt classes." "So, you are going to try to make me the way the school wants me to be?" responds the child with considerable challenge. "No," replies the therapist. "I just figure that there are reasons for what you do. You could be trying to tell the school something that you don't even know you're trying to tell. I also figure that a boy of ten years should be having more fun than you seem to have. It can't be fun having people mad at you all the time." The therapist is again direct (about the school complaints) and at the same time allies herself with the child, his feelings, and his future potential. This young man asked, quite skeptically, what kind of message he might be attempting to convey. The therapist responded somewhat deliberately, attempting to cultivate the early working alliance: "I don't know for sure. You and I have to figure that out together. You might be trying to tell them that you are angry. You might be asking for punishment for some reason we don't know about yet. [Here the therapist is referring to the possibility of a not-as-yet understood conflict]. You might be asking for attention and not know the other ways to ask and get it. From what I know of you and your family, you seem quite used to angry adults." This last observation, of course, is specifically about the child's object relationships.

A third child, age seven, begins her treatment by being very occupied by the toys and games. Anna barely looks at the therapist and there are few spontaneous words. She is active and seemingly quite interested in the room and its contents. The few comments she makes have to do with things that she likes to play with that are not in the room. In reporting about the session later, the therapist commented that she felt as though she did not exist for this child. She attempted to have a verbal exchange with her by asking her if she knew why she was seeing the therapist. The child did not answer or even appear to hear. "Well, when you would like me to tell you what I know about why we will be seeing each other, would you let me know?" The girl's activity increased. The therapist remarked that she knew the child had seen another therapist and had not liked her. She wondered what it was that Anna did not like. Anna responded, "Too many questions."

An important question facing the clinician as the diagnosis (which includes an assessment of object relations) begins to evolve is which of various different approaches to use in beginning the treatment. If the child has a narcissistic disorder and has placed herself behind a "force field," the therapist is going to have to wait it out and try to gain her attention. If Anna is trying to control the situation, the therapist will have to allow this (within bounds) and ultimately search out the reasons for such a need for control. As the therapist's dilemma acquires both consciousness and greater clarity, she may then share it with the child. This therapist, using the clues given to her, remarked, "You know, I have a problem. I think privacy is very important, and questions make people uncomfortable. I hope when you feel like letting me know a little about you that you will tell me how I might learn about you."

Such an intervention covers a number of dimensions. The client is left with the control and is encouraged to use it to resolve the therapeutic dilemma. The therapist allies herself with Anna's dislike of intrusiveness and at the same time sets the goal for the beginning of treatment. The therapist wonders if Anna could simply tell her anything about herself that she wished to tell and in that way obviate the therapist's need to ask questions. Anna responds positively. Again, the child is left in charge and is enabled to pursue the task at hand. At the end of her first session, Anna announced to her mother, who had been waiting for her, "I told her a lot about me, and she never asked one question."

The guiding principles for beginning treatment involve setting the stage (and each child patient may need a different stage) for telling the story of that child's experience and unique point of view. The therapist by her very presence inaugurates a unique process that provides a different object experience. Her interest and her responses to the child's words, affects, and actions shapes this evolving therapeutic process.

TREATMENT SETTING

Clinical social workers intend to create a holding environment (Winnicott, 1958), a space that has physical, psychological, and affective dimensions designed to facilitate development. These dimensions are, in fact, not separate. Much of what has just been discussed belongs to the dimension of psychological space. It is important to view the physical setting from an object relations perspective. To put this simply, we must be consciously aware of the messages that we give children through our physical setting, our "child supplies," and our demeanor.

Years ago, before I really understood what I was hearing from my young client, Dan, a ten year old, asked if we could walk down the corridor of the clinic we were in. He peered into each of the rooms when the door was open. I focused in my own mind on the meaning of his curiosity. It was years later that I recognized the importance of his comments about each room. Dan remarked on viewing the first room, which had posters of large smiles on the wall, that the social worker in that office did not like anger. A room brimming with toys prompted him to say that children who went in there did not use words the way we did. He wondered if the worker was uncomfortable with children. A third room was very neat and orderly and prompted an observation from Dan that it would be hard to be at ease in that space if you felt like being messy. With hindsight, that trip down the hall felt like accompanying Goldilocks as she searched in the home of the three bears for the right porridge. It is my view that as one's experience in child treatment increases, the amount of play materials can decrease to a bare minimum. If a child needs to tell about himself through a displacement in play, he will create ways to do this. One boy I saw used to sit up on the top of my couch and call down to me, "Space to earth." This form of positioning and communication was part of his story about how little understood he felt. He did not feel he was a member of his family, but rather as though he were from another galaxy where they have feelings and bad thoughts they do not have on earth—or at least in his earthly family.

A six year old in therapy recently made faces with a ballpoint pen on her therapist's and her own fingers. She subsequently directed a finger family drama that told aspects of her story.

A holding environment provides the safety and space necessary for the emergence of the child's scenarios. Therapists need to observe and know themselves well enough to see if they are imprinting the situation too strongly with their own interests or needs. In the beginning of my career, I saw a young girl who behaved like a dog at home. Her family was frantic about her. In a toy store, I found a small rubber dog that hopped about when a rubber bulb was pressed. The "puppy" became her tool for talking about herself, her fears, and her view of her own development. The dog play continued in the therapy sessions even as it abated at home. When I brought my work to consultation, I was asked if I had tried to connect the play with her real life or if I had possibly become enamored of our mode of communication. Some sessions later, I asked my client if she thought that we were using the rubber puppy to tell her own story. She enthusiastically agreed and added that she was not sure I had known this. Although for many months this symbolic play had been both necessary and quite therapeutic for her, it seemed that she was now able to explore meaning of her behavior more directly. It became clear that I was prompting a mode of communication to which I had become attached far beyond the child's need.

DIAGNOSTIC PROCESS

The discussion of beginning treatment and even the treatment setting addresses some aspects of child assessment. I am not referring to labels, although they have their place in clinical communication. Rather, from the moment of meeting the child, we are assessing her development. We ask and attempt to observe how development has been blocked or skewed. As noted earlier, assessment covers how the self and object are defined. In addition, we need to observe whether the child's sense of separateness is developing adaptively. Separation refers to a view of the self as a separate and unique being, not to physical distance or proximity. A toddler might hit his mother and call out, "Ouch." The toddler's mother might reply, "Not you ouch—me ouch." Here she would be promoting the separateness between the two of them.

It is somewhat easier to assess psychological separateness in adults. The adult client who proceeds to talk as if you know the characters she is referring to in her session or seems to assume that you know what has happened during the week is demonstrating more of a sense of oneness than separateness. It is as if the therapist is part of her and thus has somehow been there in her "nonsession" life. The diagnostic process is ongoing and if the treatment goes well, there will be changes in what we see. In the beginning of the chapter I noted that a grasp of "normal" or expectable development is important. If we are working with a five year old, we are less concerned when we observe a fair amount of magical thinking, developmentally within the normal range for five year olds. The same quality of thought in an older child prompts us to explore what has interfered with an acceptance and recognition of reality. The child of two or three who strikes out physically when angered demonstrates that language has not yet become a tool of the ego. This is expected for phases of early development. While physical expressions of feelings remain with most people for life, the balance tips toward greater use of language as development proceeds. The diagnostic questions that arise if a child tells the therapist that he cannot talk about something are: Does he have the ability but some reservations, or are we seeing a state of lesser ego development? Finally, we might conjecture that his feelings come from a preverbal time and he has never tried to use words for early felt affects. One young client told his therapist that when he gets mad, he feels hot and as if the feelings go right out to his toes and fingertips. Such a description prompts the vision of babies whose "feelings" are visceral and involve a whole body experience. Affect is not differentiated in an infant. The boy who was helped to find the words to provide this description was at least able to describe the undifferentiated affective state. Much of his treatment focused on affect differentiation, which enables the ego to manage feelings better.

The diagnostic process is inextricably related to the direction of treatment. I know of no child treatment that does not involve therapeutic work on how feelings are managed, as well as definitions of self and object and their concomitant self-object scenarios. If these are the universal diagnostic dimensions, then with each child client, we attempt to see how their unique life experience has affected their functioning.

In today's world of shortened time for therapy and multiple family and environmental issues to which the clinician must attend, the objection is often raised that there is not enough time to think diagnostically. My response may seem harsh, but this is nonsense. The capacity of the clinician to look at clinical work through the special lens of object relations must be developed. It can then be put to use for a single encounter or ten or one hundred. It is true that we learn more with time and that the variable of time enables us to affirm or discard hypotheses. Clearly treatment is affected by limited time, though it is possible for one to provide a new object experience even in a single encounter. Whether a single meeting is sufficient to challenge the client's view of the object is the question.

THE HEART OF TREATMENT

I am reluctant to approach treatment with stage divisions. Such a view runs counter to our awareness that many themes are present throughout the course of our work. This perspective can be seen in the recent rejection of developmental theories that emphasize stages rather than phases (Tyson, 1986; Tyson & Tyson, 1990). A phase approach emphasizes the timelessness of the past, that it is never lost. Developmental experiences can always be seen in the fabric of the personality of the growing child. Likewise, treatment themes are always present over the full course of treatment. They are never totally settled.

Trust is a state of being that emerges most prominently in the beginning of treatment. It is never attained. There is no fixed point of trust. As a new issue emerges, a child's anxiety and mistrust of the process or the therapist, or both, can arise anew.

Andrew, a boy of eleven, came from a physically and verbally abusive home. Work was being done with his parents. In time he was able to tell his therapist stories of the abuse, though initially he did not trust that his exposure of his parents would not cause his loss of them. For all the psychological inferences that can be made from this fear, most poor, urban youths are quite familiar with the social service system. He was very fearful that he would become a foster child and be separated from his parents and siblings. The therapist was forthright with him and acknowledged that they both knew this had happened to a lot of children whom Andrew knew. The therapist noted that his situation was different since both his parents were willing to try to find out why they were so hard on Andrew. She made no promises, but did note that his family had a good chance of staying together. A degree of trust was established in these early exchanges.

Somewhat later, in the heart of treatment, Andrew seemed to close down and become removed from the therapist. He played with some toy soldiers who shot each other in the back even though they were supposed to be on the same side. One soldier who was the main perpetrator of ill deeds begged the others not to tell the captain what he had done. He was fearful that he would be dishonorably discharged. The therapist entered the arena of communication through play. She focused on the fears of the soldier, and Andrew responded with elaborations. Then she turned her attention to questioning why anyone would tell on him. In this inquiry, she recognized that the issue of trust was appearing again in response to new material. When staying with the soldier play did not seem to yield enough elaboration, she remarked, "You know, sometimes I imagine your home life is like living in a war zone. You are all supposed to be on the same side but it doesn't feel that way." She continued by suggesting that maybe she was the captain, and he was fearful of her knowing something more about him. He thought that this was silly and shut down completely, offering neither words nor play. The therapist took this response as a signal that she was on the right track. She surmised that he was getting close to his own sadistic and angry feelings. She continued, offering her thoughts in a way that allowed him escape. "You know, Andrew, I've been having some thoughts that may not be right. I'd like to hear your views on them. We have spent a lot of time talking about how angry your parents are. Neither of us like it. I want to tell you that it is not their anger that I think is wrong but what they do with it. So, if by chance you felt like the angry soldier who wanted to shoot people in the back, I would say that of course you are angry. But you don't hurt people with your feelings (except yourself); you just spend a lot of time in fantasies. [Andrew's symptoms included intense daydreaming at school, which had a deleterious effect on his school performance.] You think I would disapprove of your anger and your mean wishes. What you don't know is that I can't imagine how anyone would not be angry and scared by what goes on in your home." [The case anecdotes in this chapter telescope the therapists' interventions for teaching purposes. In reality the above approach would be spread over time].

In the face of Andrew's nascent exposure of his own anger, a new level of trust will have to be established. The therapist seems to have read his anxiety in the play correctly and has taken the lead in working on the issue of trust. It will not come right away; while there is comfort in knowing that you can complain about the external world safely, it is harder to believe that one can safely reveal one's internal world. The therapist's acceptance of Andrew's feelings and her ability to put thoughts and feelings into words are all new object experiences.

A major part of therapeutic work involves attempting to dislodge the early object scenario. This is not easy to accomplish, since despite all of its known limitations and pitfalls, it is a familiar work. It contains the child's definition of self and object. There is order even in the disorder. Last year, an adult client who was making considerable progress remarked to me that if her days are no longer so painful, she may not know who she is.

In the heart of the treatment process following a considerable accumulation of new object experiences, the therapist may have to tackle the child's attachment to his own self-object scenario. This work was done with Andrew.

Andrew repeatedly came in with feelings, thoughts, or events in which he continued to view the therapist as untrustworthy. One day she challenged him by asking him, despite his expressed worries, what he thought her reaction would be. He smiled and responded that she was never as harsh as he feared. She wondered what would happen to him if he let himself trust her. He responded that he might get hurt and disappointed, and besides it just was not the way things work. Here we see the defensive function of retaining the scenario and a hint that his inner world would have to be reordered. The therapist labeled his negative thoughts as "pessimism" and then said that she and he would have to replace pessimism with guarded optimism. She suggested a strategy for Andrew that he might find useful the next time he feels doubtful about her. The first step was to recognize the feelings and tell her; then he could try believing her but be ready for disappointment. He was intrigued and amused with the strategy and quite impressed that she wanted to hear each time he doubted her. He wondered if she would feel insulted. She replied that she would rather hear his truthful feelings. Finally, she told him that when he was little, he did not have the option of thinking about strategies. All he could do to protect himself was to anticipate the worst, and although he now has greater abilities to protect himself, he takes those old attitudes with him everywhere.

One might view this as a cognitive approach, and perhaps it is, since cognition is greatly affected by our object relations. It is, however, an approach that emerged in the context of many new relational experiences. Andrew's first attempt to use the strategy came, seemingly, outside of the transference. He was considering going to a class party (his social skills had improved greatly). He was struggling to fight off his pessimistic view. If it prevailed, he would not go. He was able to talk about his fears of being ignored or insulted by one of the other children. The therapist remarked that he was going to a class party and not home. Andrew laughed. They planned what he might do if the party was not great, one option being his freedom to leave (a freedom that he did not have as a young child when things were bad at home). They talked about the way he might present himself to the other children. The therapist role-played a child who did not expect to have fun. In her drama she included an invitation to play a game that came from his classmates. Then she replied in a sullen way that the game they suggested was no fun. Andrew, a bright child, again laughed and said to her that no one would want to play with her, that she was spoiling their fun.

The class outing was moderately successful, sufficient at least for Andrew to want to continue practicing this approach. The working alliance has enabled Andrew to develop his observing ego and to identify with the therapist's benign attitudes so that he is able to laugh at himself.

COUNTERTRANSFERENCE

For the purposes of this discussion, the term *countertransference* will cover all the reactive feelings of the therapist. A more totalistic understanding of countertransference has enabled us to leave behind the notion that countertransference is toxic. It is no longer a subject for shame, nor does it necessarily imply pathology in the therapist. It can now be seen as a tool of great value, and its value is enhanced when the therapist is able to separate the foundations of his own reactions from those of the client. It is both too neat and unreal to posit that some countertransference reactions do come from the personality of the therapist, and others are prompted by the client. A blend of the two is more likely the case. What is essential is the ongoing process of the therapist's knowing herself.

Recently I picked up a newborn infant who was fussing. I managed to soothe him for a short while, and then his crying began in earnest. When I handed him back to his mother, I commented that I had failed. She replied that I now knew what her days were like. She did not have much peace and had to work hard to hold onto the feeling that she is a good mother. Both of us clearly have an investment in being soothing and comforting. No apologies needed. The infant, at this time, for whatever reason, was not affirming these self views.

There is no question in my mind that people who enter the field of child therapy are prompted in part by a wish to repair some of their own early life experiences. There may well be a competition with our own mothers to do a better job. Sometimes this is displaced onto the natural mother of the child client.

When I teach child therapy, I often ask the students to write a list of how they wish to be experienced by their clients. Their lists reveal that they wish to be experienced as warm, understanding, helpful, pleasant, and safe. Our knowledge of object relations tells us that it is impossible to be experienced in the ways we might wish. The issue then becomes how much disappointment and sense of failure is experienced by the therapist, and in addition, what the therapist does with such feelings. Earlier in the chapter I presented the idea that disappointments, which can become toxic when they accumulate beyond a certain level, can be reduced or prevented by a knowledge of object relations theory.

CASE EXAMPLE 1

Theresa is a clinical social worker in pediatric oncology. She works with parents of children who have cancer and often directly with the child patients themselves. Her particular work setting has excellent resources for family and child psychological support. The medical teams are by and large respectful of the mental health staff, with whom they are actively involved. It is a given that all the patients, parents and children, face extreme psychological pain as well as the inevitable physical pain associated with the cancer itself and various procedures used in the treatment of the disease.

Emma, one of Theresa's clients, is seven years old and has recently been diagnosed as having a rare brain tumor. She is the middle child in a family of three. Her parents have histories in which loss is all too familiar. They came to parenting with only "ghostly" models for raising children, both having lost their own parents prior to adoles-

cence. They met and were married while they were in their teens. They lost two children through miscarriages prior to Emma's birth. Emma's parents have raised her and their other children in a strict way, with little ability to be flexible or playful. Although they are loving in their own fashion, they are uncomfortable with feelings and, one might add, ignorant as to how to handle them. Thus they do not and cannot accept the feelings of their children. At the time of Emma's diagnosis, they were inundated with their own feelings and paralyzed by the task of helping Emma and her siblings with their fears. The parents have been amenable to treatment, which has focused on their own neediness, the emotional stress that they are barely able to handle, and the management and care of their children, particularly Emma.

When Theresa started her work with Emma, she introduced herself as the person who would help Emma with her questions about her cancer, the medical treatments, and her worries. (In such a description, we note that she tentatively approaches the realm of feeling.) In discussions of her work, Theresa wondered if her hesitation about getting into feelings is related to the fact that she is aware that the prognosis for Emma is guarded, or in response to her awareness that feelings have typically been avoided in this family. In this question, she is checking to see if her countertransference is guiding her work more than the needs of her client. Emma is an attractive and quite verbal child. The entire team responded to her with positive feelings. In the beginning phase of their work, Emma was full of questions about the chemotherapy and the location of her tumor. She approached herself somewhat like a science project for school. Theresa honored her intellectual curiosity, knowing that it enabled her to achieve some mastery even while it helped to defend against powerful affects. Again she pondered whether her approach was guided by her own greater comfort with the intellectual frame. The first sign of feelings emerged as Emma began to lose her hair. She focused on life at school, worrying that the other children would tease her. There were discussions about whether she would want to wear a wig or brightly colored scarves. As Emma and Theresa navigated through these concerns, Theresa used the exchange to move more deeply into the realm of Emma's feelings. She told her that it was good that Emma had been able to express these worries. She added that most children with cancer had many more worries and she hoped that if Emma did, she would bring them up. This was an important intervention in that it supported Emma's first attempts to get into her feelings, endorsed the reality that there were more, and put the control in Emma's hands. Another clinician might have asked the child if she had more worries. While not intended, this kind of question corners the child into having to admit or deny, and it is usually the latter. It also makes the clinician seem unaware of the reality that, of course, there are more worries and feelings. The therapist's ability to inquire and listen provides a new object experience. Theresa was able in her consultation to discuss her own fears about handling Emma's worries. The ultimate anxiety, we can all anticipate, was her fear that Emma would ask about her own death. Theresa did not want Emma to die, but she knew it was a real possibility.

Theresa did not wish to inflict any more pain and anxiety on this child. Discussions in consultation centered around the therapist's feelings, and the varying needs that clients and therapists have for denial. Theresa even discussed her feelings about losses in her life. These discussions yielded an awareness that if Emma asked questions about her death, she would want to know. She could be helped with her fears while she is alive. It was stressed that Emma is bright and can read the cues in her environment. Recently she had been observed with a medical technician and overheard saying to her, "Don't tell me it won't hurt if it will. Tell me how long it will hurt and how big the hurt will feel." She had also told Theresa that her family was always cheerful when they were with her during her treatments and she knew that was not how they felt. She wished they could all be sad together.

The ultimate question raised in consultation was the therapist's temporary inability to see the usefulness of her work with such a young child who was going to die. This question is important. If left unstated, it becomes a contributing force to burnout. The reader must surely see the parallel between what consultation can offer a skilled therapist when space is given for her countertransference and the space the therapist tries to provide the child client. Through discussions in consultation, the therapist was able to underscore the importance of the quality of Emma's emotional experience as long as she was alive. While never disregarding the cancer, she was able to concentrate on Emma's object relations. She knew from her experience that Emma needed to be afforded space for anger as well as for grief. Her own sense of purpose was restored.

In the months that followed, Emma asked questions about her treatment. These were addressed in the company of the medical staff, her parents, and her therapist. Alone with her therapist, she asked if she was going to die. Theresa spoke to her about the ability of her doctors. She was aware that she was answering out of her own wishes to be reassured. Soon Emma asked the question again, and Theresa was able to answer that they would do their best, but that she had a serious tumor from which she would die. She went on relating that they did not know when, and not knowing was the hardest thing to face. Emma chimed in that she hated not knowing. Anger began to emerge. Did she get this cancer from her father or her mother? Maybe they didn't take good enough care of her when she was younger. [The need to find a source of blame helps with the ambiguity.] She wondered if she got the cancer because she was bad. Not uncommonly, she saw the cancer as an evil growing within her. She expressed feelings that it was unfair. Why her? She thought that the angrier she got, the faster the cancer would grow.

These questions and beliefs emerged over a period of time. Theresa was able to hear them and discuss them with Emma. They talked about how hard it is when you cannot see a reason for things that happen. They discussed her wish to blame her parents. Theresa helped her to see that we look to our parents to take care of everything. She told her that everyone experiences profound disappointment when they realize that their parents cannot protect them from fear and pain. The therapist was aware that she was speaking to developmental work that is done in the rapprochement phase. Emma's disillusionment predated the onset of her cancer and was reactivated by everyone's helplessness regarding her disease. (The therapist spoke in her consultation meetings about her own fantasies that she was endowed with magic, which she could use for her clients and herself.) Emma and Theresa talked together about her wish to blame her parents and how that blame often shifted to herself. They explored her "badness." Her anger, jealousy, and competitiveness began to unfold. Emma remarked that she never even knew she had words for these feelings. In addition she was nervous about telling them to someone else. She went through a period in which she was sure that Theresa did not like her.

(This response contained elements of her object expectations and a projection of her self view.) The therapeutic relationship opened the way for Emma to acquire the ability to explore feelings (ego development) and it also provided new object experiences.

Emma's parents, while not keeping pace with their daughter, were increasingly able to deal with their own feelings and those of their children. Emma lived with greater enthusiasm and interaction with her friends, teachers, family, and the medical staff. Her bright sense of humor carried her through many difficult situations. The quality of her life experience was enriched even as the end of her short life was inevitable.

CASE EXAMPLE 2

Mark was the chief clinical social worker in a residential treatment setting for "antisocial" boys. Tim, his client, aged ten years, was referred to the residence after outpatient individual treatment could not stem the tide of belligerent behavior, stealing, and precocious sexual behavior. His mother was simply unable to manage him. Her emotional resources were drained, leaving her barely able to cope with earning a living and tending to four other children. His father was more absent than present, which had been the case all of Tim's life. Diagnostic assessment of Tim revealed a picture of a child who was pressured to act. He had a poor repertoire for handling his feelings and impulses, and his pervasive anxiety drove him into action. His developmental history revealed a seeming absence of guidance. His overwhelmed mother (coupled with an absent father) provided him with few caretaking functions with which to identify.

Mark, his therapist, carried only a few treatment cases. He had the responsibility of administering the treatment services in this setting. Working in a residence is somewhat like working in a fishbowl. Mark's investment in his success with any of his clients had the added countertransferential element of Mark's wanting to look competent to his staff. Tim was assigned to Mark because of the therapist's skill and experience and because Tim was such a disruptive child.

Treatment began with Tim's presenting in a skeptical and angry way. Foul language punctuated the early sessions as he declared that he had been put in jail. The residence stank, the food would poison him, the other kids were rotten, and he could spit on them all. It did, however, appeal to his narcissism to be seen by the chief social worker. He alternated between using it to assert that he did not have to answer to any staff member but the chief and in challenging Mark that he, Tim, must be too difficult for the other therapists. He was sure that he was too difficult for Mark too. Tim kept goading Mark into admitting that he was frightened of Tim.

Mark was worried that he would become angry at Tim and join the ranks of an object world that Tim knew all too well. An awareness of his own fear and potential anger led him to recognize that he was also learning about Tim's inner experience. Mark questioned how he might use this awareness. Tim had rapidly alienated himself from other children and most of the staff. He came to Mark's office one day (not a scheduled appointment) to request that he be allowed to go home. No one liked him in this place. Mark saw an entrée into Tim's inner experience. He remarked that he had also noticed that Tim had no friends and wondered if Tim preferred it that way. "Maybe this is all you know, Tim." (This intervention was aimed at beginning to disclose the object relations scenario.) Tim was furious and challenged his therapist, calling him stupid and ignorant about kids. He should be a garbage man. "Is that how you see yourself, Tim, as a piece of garbage? I think you are telling me that you have never been valued and that you don't value yourself." (Such remarks are intended to resonate with Tim's self representations.) The therapist continued that he did not really think that Tim wanted everyone to be angry with him, but that was all he had known in his life. "I'm not sure you would know that you were you if people weren't yelling at you all the time."

In a later session when Tim was again asserting that he frightened his therapist, Mark responded, "Tim, I can't say that I am not worried about our work." (It is noteworthy that the therapist uses a word that is milder than frightened. *This is done to differentiate himself from Tim and to enable Tim to begin the task of differentiating affects.) Mark continues, "I think you are frightened because you have a tornado [a word chosen to highlight the enormity of Tim's feelings] of feelings inside of you." Tim's body appeared less tense even as he remarked, "Yuck, all that shrink talk!"*

Soon after, Tim approached another child in residence with an invitation to have sex. Although the setting contained several willing partners, he chose a child whom he must have intuited would be terrified. The boy screamed and was psychologically overwhelmed by the assault. The staff was furious with Tim. Tim came to an emergency session rather subdued and low-keyed in affect. Mark was aware of his own anger. He had hoped that he would see improvement in Tim but felt distressed by the major disruption that Tim had caused in the residence. He recalled wanting to say to Tim, "That's it! Out you go." At the same time he was aware that he would be falling into a transference trap—a repetition of Tim's object expectations.

Mark started the session by saying, "Tim, you are telling us a story in your behavior, and you and I have to find words for it." Uncharacteristically, Tim listened quietly. His eyes glistened as though tears might emerge. "The other day I told you I was worried about our work, but I am not giving up! I think you are testing me. You broke a major rule here by approaching that boy sexually, and you chose a boy who would be terrified the way you are. You created a major upset against yourself. That couldn't have been fun."

Tim's response was quietly spoken while he asked if he was going to have to leave. Mark replied, "Absolutely not! You are going to stay until you and I manage the whirlwind inside of you." The therapist then asked Tim what he had been feeling about Mark after the last meeting. Tim stammered and had a hard time saying that he was beginning to like Mark. He even had a bad daydream in which Mark put his arms around him. Mark questioned why that was bad but did not wait for answer. This was not a true question but rather the therapist's way of communicating his disagreement with the designation of "bad."

He continued that Tim had never had a father who was around steadily, so he missed out on fathers' hugging their sons. He proposed that he was telling everybody that he wished for physical contact with a man when he approached the boy on his floor. He was also telling everybody that he thought that this was such a bad wish that they should be furious with him and punish him for it. He did indeed get everyone to beat up on him. The therapist left out, for the time being, Tim's wish for physical closeness with himself. He wanted to concentrate on the use of words rather than actions. In addition he did not wish to risk a homosexual panic. The therapist had to grapple with his own feelings, which vacillated between being angry and discouraged with his own work (self-blame) and his desire to become a replacement father for Tim, thus bypassing the painful material of Tim's self views drawn from his father's desertion and his mother's overwhelmed state. He revealed in consultation how hard it was for him to face his own feelings toward a different but similarly absent father. The temptation to try to be a replacement figure is not unlike the magical wishes observed in the first case discussion. Awareness and discussion defused the positive countertransference. This enabled the therapist to be clear about the child's wishes and needs and yet steer the treatment in a therapeutic direction.

The two cases illustrate the very complicated linkage between the therapist's awareness of self and his or her fantasies and feelings, as they mesh with those of the child client. No aspect of treatment can be discussed without keeping an eye on the countertransference, which can enter even the process of diagnostic assessment. Therapists informed by psychoanalytic object relations theory are far better equipped to observe the ways in which they may be replicating the child's object expectations. It is important to be aware that such replications are unavoidable. They become a different object experience when the therapist is willing and able to discuss the here and now in the transference and link it to the child's object relations scenarios. Mark acknowledged his worries and distress to Tim. He acknowledged that for the moment he was like all the other caretakers Tim had known. He pursued Tim's need for such reactions and challenged him to see if he could feel comfortable with people feeling fondness for him.

TERMINATION

It has become rare to end treatment in a timely way as a response to therapeutic progress. Termination, even under the best of circumstances, activates for all clients (and their therapists) a range of feelings about loss. Untimely endings of treatment evoke strong feelings of desertion, the all-too-well-known failure of the object. Negative self representations are also activated: "This wouldn't be happening if I weren't so bad." Too often therapists, who experience guilt about an inappropriate termination, wish to shield themselves from anger, which in reality they do not deserve. They will blame agency policy, shortage of money, or their own need to search for another position. The intensity of their countertransference interferes with the importance of receiving and containing the client's feelings. There are, of course, no acceptable reasons for the child. Essentially it boils down to the conviction that "if you really loved me, you would not let this happen." The child feels helpless, and this is mirrored in the therapist's own reactions. But the therapist has much to offer the child. By eliciting fantasies and feelings associated with this loss, the entire experience of parting may offer something previously unknown in the child's object scenarios.

Mark and Tim worked together for over two years. Their's was a planned termination. Tim was to return to his home and school and to begin outpatient therapy with a therapist in the community. They had several months to work on his departure. Tim started a session in this period by saying, "So, you are going to throw me out!" This was supposed to be a joke. Mark smiled but responded that Tim would probably feel that way in the months to come, and it was important for them to talk about it each time it came up. Tim kept wondering why he could not continue seeing Mark even if he was going home. Mark did not protect himself by explaining administrative constraints. He created space for all of Tim's feelings of self-doubt, which had been reactivated. Tim fantasized that his treatment would end by his showing up for his session and Mark not being there. Mark responded that this was how it was with his father. He and Tim could do it differently. They could have a session and lunch out. They could check in with each other on the telephone. In time, they might even plan a reunion. "No one is going to disappear!" The therapeutic effort continued to emphasize new object experiences and to uncover all of the conflictual, object-representational ties to the old scenario.

Treating children is not unlike attempting to repair a complicated design in a handmade oriental carpet. Each design is different even if there are expected patterns. Both child and therapist become weavers. The life story, the endowment of the child, and factors in the child's environment create the pattern. How the threads are arranged and where they interfere with each other is part of the process of assessment. This chapter has attempted to demonstrate that therapeutic work is greatly enhanced when guided by psychoanalytic developmental object relations theory. Readers will note the equal importance of the therapist's awareness of herself, her own history and feelings. Treating children stirs the psyche of the therapist. Comfort with this phenomenon enriches the creativity of the therapy.

REFERENCES

Blanck, G., & Blanck, R. (1986). *Beyond ego psychology: Developmental object relations theory.* New York: Columbia University Press.

Greenacre, P. (1953). *Trauma, growth, and personality.* London: Hogarth Press.

Greenson, R. (1965). The working alliance and the transference neurosis. *Psychoanalytic Quarterly, 34,* 155–181.

Jacobson, E. (1964). *The self and the object world.* New York: International Universities Press.

Mahler, M., Pine, F., & Bergmann, A. (1975). *The psychological birth of the human infant.* New York: Basic Books.

Sandler, J., & Rosenblatt, B. (1962). The concept of a representational world. *Psychoanalytic Study of the Child, 17,* 128–145.

Stern, D. N. (1985). *The Interpersonal World of the Infant.* New York: Basic Books.

Tyson, R. (1986). The roots of psychopathology and our theories of development. *Journal of the American Academy of Child Psychiatry, 25,* 12–22.

Tyson, P., & Tyson, R. (1990). *Psychoanalytic theories of development.* New Haven, CT: Yale University Press.

Winnicott, D. W. (1985). *Collected Papers.* London: Tavistock.

Winnicott, D. W. (1989). *Psychoanalytic explorations.* Cambridge, MA: Harvard University Press.

Viorst, J. (1986). *Necessary losses.* New York: Simon & Schuster.

5

Clinical Social Work with Adolescents

Judith Mishne

INDIVIDUAL TREATMENT

Psychotherapy

The term *psychotherapy* was used by Freud, and the theory and techniques of individual psychotherapy have been enriched by the use of classical and newer psychoanalytic theories of mental functioning and psychopathology. These theories reflect the evolving conceptions of psychoanalytic foci: drive theory, ego psychology, object relations theory, self psychology, and the amplifications, modifications, and extensions of self psychology that are represented by inclusion of data that are, in turn, derived from infant research, neurophysiology, and communication theory, philosophy of science, and the intersubjective interplay between the two differently organized subjective worlds of clinician and patient.

Alexander (1953) reminds us that psychotherapy is older than psychoanalysis and originally was the traditional domain of psychiatrists, which is now shared with other clinicians, notably social workers, psychologists, and psychoanalysts: "While it is customary to divide individual psychotherapeutic procedures into two categories, the *supportive* and *insight-oriented* psychotherapies, it must be borne in mind that supportive measures are knowingly or inadvertently used in all forms of psychotherapy; and conversely, some degree of insight is rarely absent from any sound psychotherapeutic approach" (p. 270).

Intensive Insight-Oriented Individual Therapy and Supportive Individual Therapy

Intensive uncovering insight-oriented individual treatment seeks to increase the ego's capacity to tolerate emotionally conflictual situations that are partially or completely repressed. These situations commonly originate in early childhood, and their later reverberations are precipitated by subsequent actual life situations and relationships. The principal therapeutic tool is transference. Transference occurs when the client relives early personal relationships in the treatment because old patterns and reactions are transferred, or displaced, onto the therapist, and then repeated through the regression that is commonly characteristic in intensive, uncovering therapy. By contrast, supportive individual treatment is indicated

> whenever the functional impairment of the ego is of temporary nature caused by acute emotional stress. In such cases the therapeutic task consists, first of all, in gratifying dependent needs during the stress situation, thus reducing anxiety. Another important therapeutic device consists of reducing emotional stress by giving the patient an opportunity for emotional abreaction. (Alexander, 1953, p. 281)

Commonly support involves a review and examination of the client's stress situation and offering advice and clarification to assist in judgment and clearer assessment of stressors. If the continual involvement in external life situations proves beyond a client's coping capacities, environment manipulation might well be required and necessary.

Supportive treatment goals are the improvement of ego functions to promote better adaptation to the inner and outer world and the provision of symptom reduction and relief and overt behavioral change without attempts to modify the personality or greatly reduce unconscious conflict. Repression can be maintained because the therapy focuses on preconscious and conscious elements of mental life. "It is always the ego in its various functions that is supported in psychodynamically-oriented individual supportive therapy. Support can be accomplished directly by focusing on problematic ego functions, or indirectly, by decreasing the pressure or strain on the ego from drives, superego prohibitions and external reality" (Rockland, 1989, p. 8). The concept of adaption is crucial in supportive therapy. Some authors base recovery on the empowerment of the client and the creation of new connections (Herman, 1992; Kardiner & Spiegel, 1947; Symonds, 1982), whereby there is a re-formation of faculties such as capacity for trust, autonomy, initiative, competence, identity, and intimacy (Erikson, 1963).

By comparison, the goals of insight-directed intensive psychotherapy are more ambitious than in the case of supportive treatment. In intensive therapy the clinician attempts to help the client achieve greater self-awareness and some degree of underlying personality change. The immediate relief of symptoms is secondary and should not be used as a guideline to consider termination of therapy. The goal is to make the underlying conflict conscious, thereby permanently staving off later or subsequent symptom formation or symptom substitution. The techniques of uncovering insight-oriented psychotherapy bring unconscious and preconscious focus into consciousness; this includes conscious comprehension of drives and drive derivatives, as well as the preconscious and unconscious superego and ego functions, especially the ego's defenses.

The distinction between supportive and insight-oriented psychotherapy can be blurred. Generally, the frequency of appointments—two and three times a week versus once a week—is a recognized criterion of distinction. Individual supportive treatment is a mode of therapy focused less on unconscious intrapsychic conflicts and generally more on interpersonal and environmental conflicts. It is a therapeutic intervention in which less regression is encouraged than in insight-oriented uncovering treatment. The focus on the here-and-now rather than on early infantile conflicts generally dictates that the clinician assume a more active stance than the nongratifying, nondirective neutral clinician, providing uncovering insight-oriented treatment. "'Neutral' means that the therapist does not take sides in the client's inner conflicts or try to direct the client's life decisions. . . . The . . . neutral stance is an ideal to be striven for, never perfectly attained" (Herman, 1992, p. 135). In supportive treatment, the clinician's stance of neutrality is less than in insight-oriented therapy. In the context of a frequently needed, reflective, educative, advising therapeutic role, active support is provided. Basic character change is not a goal; rather, supportive treatment aims to increase the client's capacity for reality testing, strengthen object relations, and loosen fixations. Supportive individual treatment is the most appropriate intervention for many adolescents and other clients living amid considerable chaos; in some situations outreach, collaborative contacts with family members, teachers, and others and even environmental manipulations are necessary, in conjunction with direct work with the client. Generally supportive treatment is of shorter duration than uncovering insight-directed psychotherapy. The therapist who is providing supportive treatment will comment and reflect on apparent behavior patterns, reactions, and relationships, leaving some areas deliberately untouched and unexplored, so as not to assault needed defenses.

Insight-oriented uncovering individual treatment is the optimal intervention for clients suffering internal conflict—conflict that is not with an environment, that is producing chaos and traumata. The conflict, commonly originating in the past, is not accessible to conscious awareness and problem-solving efforts. The client's problems are intrapsychic; if interpersonal conflicts or academic or work problems are apparent and to be treated by analytic uncovering techniques, they must be transformed into intrapsychic problems. Complaints about interpersonal, intrafamilial, and work-related difficulties are common presenting problems. These stresses must be due to circumscribed basic intrapsychic conflicts, in contrast to those caused by constitutional or environmental failures. This method of therapy is best suited for suffering individuals who nevertheless possess a fairly intact psychic structure. Clients who present basic ego weakness or deficits commonly manifest poor frustration tolerance, poor impulse control, meager capacity for drive modulation, inadequate self/other distinctions, inadequate reality testing, and impaired object relations, all of which interfere with a capacity to develop transference and contain acting out. Individuals who have suffered greater injury are best treated in supportive individual therapy, in contrast to the more intact client, who possesses the ego strengths to tolerate and profit from uncovering treatment through more complete working through of basic conflict. Generally working through evolves out of reenactment in the transference of repetitive object choices, and comprehension of the repetition compulsion (repeated self-injurious behaviors), via insight and introspection.

Treatment technique in insight-oriented therapy is predicated on abstinence—an absence of advice and active support. In a climate of empathic attunement, the principal tool is interpretation, reflection, and demonstration of the connection of the early traumas with the current presenting problems. Some clinicians tend to minimize the significance of genetic interpretations, believing that they divert attention from the immediacy of transference feelings. In many instances, "pushing the present back into the past, can serve as a defense for the analyst against painful countertransference feelings" (Giovacchini, 1987, p. 253). In sum, the degree of needed abstinence or emotional holding and support the client is provided is determined by the original assessment, which emphasizes ego assessment, and the nature of transference manifestations. "A careful diagnostic assessment and appraisal of the patient's strengths, life circumstances, psychological mindedness, and intrapsychic structure determine which level of intervention is appropriate. A misappraisal may have serious consequences if too much regression is encouraged and the patient becomes overwhelmed and despairing, feeling that hopes for 'cures' have been betrayed" (Mishne, 1993, p. 89). Dewald (1964) reflects on complications when clinicians confuse methods, goals, and the readiness of patients to handle material that is unconscious, and he cites massive inappropriate regression, therapeutic stalemates, and severe, dangerous acting out when abstinence and insight uncovering approaches are misapplied to clients who need more active direction and support. The importance of skilled assessment cannot be overemphasized.

Assessment

The evaluation and diagnostic label is not meant as a pejorative depreciation or stigmatizing effort. Diagnoses, rather, are shorthand descriptions of presenting problem(s), underlying character structure, physical state, and nature of milieu and environmental stressors. Diagnosis should offer information about the client's and family's strengths and weaknesses, thereby to provide guidelines for optimal treatment planning. The distinction between evaluation and treatment is not merely a semantic one. A basic confusion is introduced when initial contacts are regarded as "treatment" before any insight is gained about the structure, nature, and history of the problems. Clients cannot genuinely engage in contracting and mutual goal setting before they have a better understanding of their presenting problems and the reasons they have been offered a particular therapeutic modality. They need to comprehend the nature of the prescribed therapy, including an estimate of the time and cost involved:

> Beginning treatment before formulating a diagnosis is analogous to prescribing antibiotics indiscriminately for any undiagnosed physical disease. There are various modalities of ongoing intervention, but few agencies and clinics provide the full range.

> Without a diagnostic assessment, clients may simply be forced into whatever modality a given agency offers, with no differentiation of case need. The reality that an agency cannot be all things to all people, and rather should, on appropriate occasions, refer clients elsewhere, underscores the need for assessment as a separate and distinct phase. (Mishne, 1983, p. 27)

Buxbaum (1954) emphasizes that "diagnostic and dynamic considerations, rather than philosophies, should be introduced in order to select the best therapeutic procedure for specific cases" (pp. 299–300). Anna Freud (1962) believes that the diagnostic approach provides data to determine a decision for or against treatment, the choice of therapeutic model, and treatment aims and goals, based on distinguishing transitory from permanent pathology:

> When diagnosing the mental disturbances of children, the child analyst is confronted with difficulties which are due to the shifting, internal scene in a developing individual, and which are not met in adult psychiatry. One of these difficulties concerns the fact that, during development, symptoms, inhibitions and anxieties do not necessarily carry the same significance which they assume at a later date. Although in some cases they may be lasting, and the first signs of permanent pathology, in other cases, they need be no more than transient appearances of stress which emerge whenever a particular phase of development makes specially high demands on a child's personality. . . .
>
> Another difficulty for the diagnostician is bound up with the well-known fact that there are no childhood alternatives to the adult's efficiency or failure in sex and work, vital factors which are used in adult psychiatry as indications of intactness or disturbance. . . .
>
> Since, thus, neither symptomatology nor life tasks can be taken as reliable guides to the assessment of mental health or illness in childhood, we are left with the alternative idea that capacities for growth are the most significant factors in determining a child's mental health. Accordingly, it becomes the diagnostician's task to ascertain where a given child stands on the developmental scale, whether his position is age-adequate, retarded or precocious, and in what respect; and to what extent the observable internal and external circumstances and existent symptoms are interfering with the possibilities of future growth. (A. Freud, 1962, pp. 149–150)

In determining what holds individuals back, consideration must be given to fixation and regression. In situations of fixation, we note the tendency in psychic development for residuals of earlier phases to acquire and retain strong "charges" of psychic energy. Arrests or fixations of development occur in instinctual, superego, and ego organization, and this causes various degrees of persistence of primitive, often childlike ways of thinking, reasoning, and relating to people, to attempt to derive satisfaction or retain an old sense of danger and fear. In addition to insufficiently understood constitutional reasons for fixation, there are early experiences in which the child's developing immature ego was overwhelmed by too much stress. These traumatic experiences, such as parent loss, separations, and critical illness, usually involve an unfortunate combination of excessive frustration and excessive gratification. (A bereaved young mother, suffering from her spouse's untimely death, allows their three-year-old son to sleep with her; thus the child suffers the pain and frustration due to loss of the father and excessive gratification from inordinate closeness and overstimulation from mother.) With disturbances of development and conflict over current functioning, regression to earlier behavior and functioning occurs. (Thus, the boy, arrested and too tied to mother, may seek overindulgence and inappropriate closeness with mother when facing adolescent stressors.)

Regression presents itself in two forms: libidinal and ego regression. Libidinal regression is a retreat to an earlier phase of instinctual organization, especially of the infantile period. Such a retreat or falling back occurs when a predetermined maturation step presents the individual with difficulty he or she is unable to master. A simple example of libidinal regression is evident at instances of serious emotional stress; for example, a twelve-year-old child resumes thumb sucking, a habit previously abandoned. In ego regression, the mind may revert to modes of functioning typical of an earlier period of life. The concept of regression is intimately related to the hypothesis that in the course of attaining adulthood, an individual passes through a series of maturational phases, each with a phase-appropriate mental organization. The makeup of each such organization is inferred from the way instinctual drives discharge, ego functions operate, and conscience and ideals guide. Under stress or trouble with successful management of age-appropriate maturational stages, there is disruption of mental functioning, and regression occurs. A college senior who is achieving well in school fears graduation and career choices, and regresses into earlier dysfunctional patterns and academic poor performances, the original presenting problems that necessitated therapy. Despite enormous therapeutic and academic gains for three years, the demands of adult life after college pose a threat sufficient to cause substantial regression.

Other factors are also important in the evaluation of children and adolescents. Kessler (1966) suggests scrutiny of (1) the age of discrepancy (i.e., the difference between the child's chronological age and behavioral age), (2) the frequency and duration of the symptom(s), (3) the number of symptoms, (4) the degree of social disadvantage, (5) the intractability of the behavior, (6) the child's personality or general adjustment, and (7) the degree of the child's inner suffering (often overlooked). These criteria inform the clinician of areas of strength and weakness in the child and family (e.g., areas where fixation or regression appears), and how and in what respects the child handles age-appropriate tasks despite symptoms. Such issues also suggest hypotheses about possible contaminating factors, be they past, present, constitutional, or family induced. Simultaneous assessment of the child's parents permits the clinician to ascertain not only to what extent they contribute to the maintenance of the child's problems but also to what extent they support healthy aspects of the child's personality.

McDonald (1965) notes other criteria and issues to explore, and she includes constitutional and organic impairment, "major psychological traumas and the child's and parent's external world" (p. 601). Assessment of the child's parents permits the clinician to ascertain a clear grasp of family life, which includes information about the structure of the family, the familial and extended family interpersonal relationships, parents' employment and financial base, lifestyle, and values.

Psychological testing may be another assessment tool but generally is not a standard diagnostic procedure. Academic problems and developmental delay may be better understood by means of intelligence and projective testing. Suspicions of learning disability suggest a need for extensive psychological testing and evaluation of academic work, commonly executed by psychologists and trained special education instructors. An appraisal of an adolescent's physical condition is essential during the assessment process, and this may or may not require the attention of physicians for a physical or neurological exam, or both. Organic pathology must be considered, and attention must be given to chronic physical diseases and disabilities that exact some emotional stress and adjustment. Concerns about child abuse and substance abuse commonly require assessment efforts by psychologically and medically trained clinicians.

Throughout the evaluation processes, it is crucial to note how parents and adolescents share material. The importance is far beyond factual data, such as the child's developmental history, accounts of illness and separation, or the adolescent's articulation of presenting problems. The child's and parent's emotional attitudes, feelings, and style of relating to each other and to the clinician are often more telling than hard data and facts. The clinician must be alert to affects of depression, anger, anxiety, aloofness, and indifference. Do the members of the family present apathy, anger, helplessness, enthusiasm, or empathy? Parental style, the nature of parenting provided, and parental motivation are probably key prognostic issues that serve as guidelines for the ongoing planning for therapy (Mishne, 1983).

The process of the assessment phase involves listening, exploration, and efforts to begin to form an alliance with family members. Clinicians must be alert to becoming overidentified with the teenager or the parents, becoming infected by parental anxieties, or feeling pressed to provide premature advice and recommendations before the depth and true nature of the presenting problems are understood. The process of the diagnostic study stresses the importance of observation and verbal communication in therapeutic work, diminishes any aura of mystery or magic about such procedures, and enables the parents and adolescent to feel actively involved and to focus their attention on the work ahead. Often an assessment affords relief for parents' guilt and anxiety as they secure help for their child and themselves. In collecting information, the diagnostician must recognize and respect parental resistance or the adolescent's resistance. Parents may object to a necessary school inquiry, questions about their marriage, and explicit expectation that they remain actively involved on behalf of their child. Adolescents may and often do displace any and all problems onto their parents or teachers, feel stigmatized about needing help, and thereby oppose any idea of ongoing contact. If there is not a working through of the parents' and adolescent's resistances, it frequently increases, resulting in a disinclination to complete the assessment phase or to begin treatment. In many situations, strong parental resistance offers a clear diagnostic message of where treatment interventions should begin: with them. In other situations, a child's resistance reflects parental uncertainty, covert resistance, or ineffective parenting, that is, the parent is afraid or otherwise unable to set limits and expectations. A young child cannot be permitted to make decisions about the need for treatment, and in some instances this may be equally true for the adolescent client. Ideally the adolescent is allowed considerable input into the decision to seek help. This is obviously not the case, however, when the teenager is a nonvoluntary client, perhaps referred by the juvenile court, school, or some other such agency of power.

It is unrealistic for a clinician to expect resistances and such defenses as denial or projection to be surrendered quickly or easily. Parents and adolescents may project all difficulties onto teachers and the school; time is needed for them to arrive at a more realistic understanding of what are legitimate reasons for insistent referrals by school personnel. Teenagers are not allowed autonomy regarding attendance at school or in regard to medical or dental needs. Similarly, they are often not able to make wise decisions regarding psychotherapy contact. In such situations, where the clinician faces intense resistances, ambivalence, or parental ineffectiveness, it is wise to remain firm and patient, clarifying the situation rather than allying with the regressive infantile stance of the parents or teenager or identifying with parents' covert rejection and helplessness. Firm limits, outreach, and persistence often constitute a form of caring that overwhelmed parents have not been able to provide their child. When the referral is nonvoluntary, the clinician is well advised to inform the adolescent about expectations and reality and take a therapeutic stance that will not permit collusion; for example, if the teenager misses appointments, this reality will not be kept in confidence and withheld from parents, school, the juvenile court, probation department, or other relevant authority (Mishne, 1986).

During the early portion of the assessment process, parents may require assistance in preparing their adolescent for the diagnostic study, and at the conclusion, children as well as parents need a follow-up or "informing interview." This is necessary to communicate the diagnosis and recommendations, to cope with any anxiety and resistances, and to motivate family members to act on the recommendations. Sharing findings and recommendations requires skill and sensitivity on the part of the clinician. Parents and adolescents should receive the clinician's explanation of the conflicts confronting the child and where and why the child seems stuck developmentally. The significance of the adolescent's conflict and its potential impact on the teenager's long-range development and future adjustment often must be estimated. Recommendations and findings need to be presented simply and clearly, minus the jargon of the profession. Parents, adolescent, and clinician frequently need time and several appointments to consider the emotional significance of recommendations. Professionals often lose sight of the impact of therapy on a child and parents, minimizing the investment of time and energy and the effect on the family (Mishne, 1983). In cases involving adolescents, there are a number of situations where a therapist surmises that although a child presents some problems, the child's problems serve as entrée for parents with either marital or individual problems. A recommendation for marital or individual treatment of the parent may indeed be the outcome, accompanied by no recommendation of any therapy for the teenager. There are instances where an adolescent who is not seen directly benefits greatly by improvement of the family milieu or by improvements in parents, through the provision of parent guidance or individual therapy to a parent.

The informing interview with the adolescent should generally be done with the child alone, and after the interview with the parents. In general, the approach used with the parents is also appropriate for the adolescent. The clinician should share with the teenager the assessment observations, impressions, and recommendations and should help the adolescent deal with anxiety and resistance. The recommendations should be presented as logically fitting with the presenting problems and in age-appropriate language. Adolescents should always be seen for a follow-up interview. Often children want to know about their parents' reactions and responses, which frequently can be shared openly. However, if the parents have been very resistive to the recommendations, the clinician must not reveal all, since it is not useful to create dissension between adolescent and parent(s). When the clinician and parents differ, this fact can be recognized with the teenager while careful attention and respect is given to the parents' opinions.

The Recommendation for Individual Treatment

The criteria for determining indications and contraindications for individual or family or group therapy are many and varied. There are a number of fundamental theoretical struggles in the clinical field, and in some cases, decisions are made on the basis of clinician bias, philosophy, orientation, and training. Some clinicians, trained in several methods of intervention, are more open to issues of diagnosis and considerations of criteria for determining the optimal modality. Offer and Vanderstoep (1975) reflect on the struggles regarding treatment recommendations and cite the psychoanalytic and systems analysis perspectives. The psychoanalytically oriented practitioner considers several interventions, in contrast to family systems analysts, who generally believe "that the question of indications and contraindications is a 'non-question'" (p. 145). The psychoanalytically oriented practitioner uses a nosological classification and views individuals and families from a psychodynamic point of view; according to this view, certain problems are suitable for treatment by family therapy, and others are not. Systems analysts in the field of family therapy make no distinctions and strongly object to considerations of indication and contraindication; some believe assessment is merely a device to deal with the therapist's anxiety and advocate an action-oriented point of view. Such a view leads therapists to engage in rearranging the family system, since the unit of attention is not the individual but the family system.

My psychoanalytic perspective and affirmation of a diagnostic process requires distinctions and cautions regarding indications and contraindications. The presence of severe psychotic-like depression; severe masochistic character pathology; hard-core psychopathology, child abuse, and/or domestic violence; perversion; criminality; a firm decision for divorce; and the existence of unyielding prejudice against family or group therapy point to a clear recommendation for individual treatment. Similarly, highly narcissistic individuals who lack empathy and are fixated in struggles regarding self-esteem or self-regard are inappropriate candidates for group therapy. Adolescents with deficient controls generally cannot be effectively treated in group or family therapy. Suggestive clients who are easily led become stimulated to excessive acting out in group treatment (Heacock, 1966). Ginnott (1961) enumerates several other criteria to exclude specific children and teenagers from group therapy, among them, those experiencing intense sibling rivalry who require one-to-one attention; sociopathic adolescents who present shallowness, cruelty, persistent stealing, intense selfishness, impulsivity, or lack of empathy; those with accelerated drive expressions; highly sexualized or extremely aggressive children; children eroticized due to their exposure to perverse sexual activities or as the result of sexual victimization; and children traumatized by overt catastrophes. All such adolescents need supportive individualized treatment.

In sum, individualized insight-oriented therapy is optimal for teenagers with discrete areas of internal conflict, strong basic ego structure, psychological mindedness, and a capacity for insight. More damaged adolescents who suffer from constitutional, perceptual, and cognitive deficits or whose families present severe pathology need active and supportive treatment. Supportive treatment is appropriate for severely disturbed adolescents who present habit disorders in eating, discipline, and sleeping, related to a lack of appropriate parental direction or environmental structure, limits, and boundaries. Some adolescents with adequate personality development can be helped by a brief course of supportive treatment following trauma due to surgery, divorce, or death of a parent. In supportive work, the attention should focus on the present, with efforts toward improving rational control, diminishing anxiety and depression, and reinforcing secondary ego processes. Adolescents who are considered "less than neurotic," with diagnoses of borderline or narcissistic personality disorder, often can be engaged only by individual supportive interventions; sometimes they can move into a more uncovering insight-oriented treatment.

The Treatment Relationship

Individual treatment can be behavioral, supportive, uncovering, reconstructive, or interpretive and reflective. Mistakes, failures to assess the client properly, or the inflexible provision of one modality or form of treatment to all clients can cause a teenager to become more disturbed. Some clinics offer short-term treatment exclusively; others provide only individual treatment and in cases of adolescent clients omit necessary family work with parents; still others provide only a family or group form of intervention. Too frequently slogans, panaceas, agency bias, or dictates from third parties via insurance companies control practice, with the result that there is little demonstrated respect for the individual. The genuine nature of the problems and, in many instances, severely rationed care results in the client's remaining unmet actual needs, crisis, or a revolving door, with patients continually returning for needed ongoing attention. The treatment process and the nature of the treatment recommended (supportive or insight oriented) are nevertheless regulated to varying degrees by these outside forces today. This is true in both private and agency-based practice and thus cannot be ignored. These outside forces, in dictating the length of the care provided, determine in fact whether an actual therapeutic relationship can or cannot be established.

The Therapeutic Alliance

In a genuine treatment process (one that is not merely an extended diagnostic evaluation concluding with directions about behaviors), the therapeutic alliance is most important in the treatment relationship. The therapeutic alliance is seen as emanating out of the client's "conscious or unconscious wish to cooperate and his readiness to accept the therapist's aid in overcoming intense difficulties and resistances" (Sandler, Kennedy, & Tyson, 1980, p. 45). The alliance does not arise solely out of the adolescent's wish for pleasure in the treatment situation but rather involves a genuine comprehension of problems and the need to deal with them. The alliance is not an end unto itself but rather a means to an end, a way of facilitating the treatment process. According to Basch (1980) it is based on a new and correct relationship, "a fund of trust" (p. 133), whereby the client views the therapist as an important person with whom to work. Along with a rapport and positive feeling for the therapist, the alliance is based on an accurate appraisal of a need for understanding and gratification in being understood. Adolescent clients will look to therapy for relief only if they have the capacity for self-observation and some awareness that there are significant problems.

Not all teenagers have sufficient inner ego structure for self-observation and self-awareness. More disturbed clients, who are often the most defended, also tend to have difficulties in self/other distinctions, and they may merge with the clinician to form a quasi-symbiotic relationship. This merging of the therapist's and patient's egos can result in a "pseudoalliance" since it does not represent a true therapeutic splitting (into self-observing and self-experiencing functions) of the ego. The therapist consistently and repeatedly interjects his own secondary process and rational behavior into the treatment situation (Keith, 1968, p. 38). Often clients do not experience their symptoms as painful. This is especially true with adolescents, who might project blame onto parents or experience their self-injurious behaviors as ego syntonic. Thus they often do not experience anguish or anxiety. Rather, parents and other concerned adults suffer and worry, and they must insist on the teenager's involvement in treatment. In such cases the parents usually make the initial alliance, which supports and sustains the treatment.

> The alliance of therapy cannot be taken for granted; it must be painstakingly built by the efforts of both patient and therapist. Therapy requires a collaborative working relationship in which both partners act on the basis of their implicit confidence in the value and efficacy of persuasion rather than coercion, ideas rather than force, mutuality rather than authoritarian control. (Herman, 1992, p. 136)

Herman (1992) notes that traumatic experiences have shattered these beliefs and, in consequence, damage the client's ability to enter into a trusting relationship and form an alliance. Thus, there are predictable difficulties in forming a working alliance if the patient has suffered severe traumata, especially in the context of family relationships. The treatment relationship is an unequal relationship in which the therapist has superior status and power. "Feelings related to the universal childhood experience of dependence on a parent are inevitably aroused. These feelings, known as transference, further exaggerate the power imbalance in the therapeutic relationship" (Herman, 1992, pp. 134–135).

Transference

In his early considerations of transference, Freud (1912, 1915, 1916–1917) stated that all people unconsciously displace and transfer the libidinal aspects of their primary object relationships to current object relationships. The term *transference,* derived from adult psychoanalytic therapy, refers to the views and relations the client presents about significant early childhood objects: parents, siblings, and significant caretakers. Transference phenomena are expressed in the patient's current perceptions, thoughts, fantasies, feelings, attitudes, and behavior in regard to the analyst (Sandler, Kennedy, & Tyson, 1980). Self psychology posits different transference phenomena for patients with structural deficits, who suffer faulty self-esteem, and who are incapable of making clear self/other distinctions. They develop a "selfobject transference" that must be distinguished from the classic definition and understanding of transference. Selfobject transference (merger and mirror transference) is not the displacement phenomenon of classic transferences but rather a use of the therapist to provide a missing part of the self for the client. Because children and adolescents typically continue to reside with the significant early objects, they generally do not displace feelings and defenses and perceptions from their past. More generally they demonstrate what have been called subtypes of transference:

> 1. Habitual modes of relating (revealing in treatment various aspects of character and behavior as they would to any person);
> 2. Transference of current relationships (whereby in treatment the child's and adolescent's mode of relating is an extension of, or defensive displacement from, the relationship with primary objects);
> 3. Transference which is predominantly that of past experiences (i.e., when past experiences, conflicts, defenses, and wishes are revived in treatment, as a consequence of analytic work and are displaced onto the therapist in the manifest or latent preconscious content);
> 4. Transference neurosis (meaning the concentration of the conflicts, repressed infantile wishes, fantasies, etc.), on the person of the therapist with the relative diminution of their manifestations elsewhere. (Sandler, Kennedy & Tyson, 1980, pp. 78–104)

Another transference phenomenon commonly demonstrated by children and adolescents is that of externalization in the transference. Children and adolescents often do battle with their environments and use the therapist to represent a part of their personality structure. During the adolescent upheaval, externalization and projections are common defenses with which the teenager wards off inner conflict; the superego function is relegated to outside authority figures whom the teenager defies but also invites to control or punish him or her for disobedience and defiance (Furman, 1980):

> However, the externalization not only changes an inner battle into an outer one; it also supplants a very hard inner threat into a usually milder punishment from the outside. The visible misbehavior is seen as less of a violation than the inner forbidden activity or wish, e.g., masturbatory activity or sexual or aggressive feelings towards forbidden objects. (p. 27)

In addition to these subtypes of transference manifest by adolescents and children, many have noted specific types of adolescent transference patterns related to the adolescent's habitual style of relating. These patterns can tax or disrupt the therapeutic alliance and also obstruct ego growth, thus requiring identification and active management (Meeks, 1971). Meeks has noted four patterns: (1) the erotic transference, (2) the omnipotent transference, (3) the negative transference, and (4) the superego transference—the therapist as superego. Management of these varied transference phenomena includes acceptance of the adolescent's feelings, avoidance of counterattack, and a firm refusal to accept unrealistic blame and excessive criticism. As the adolescent is helped to explore and comprehend his or her anger, the empathic therapist tries to reflect a recognition of how things appear and feel from the client's perspective. The therapist does not try to force his or her views on patients, but "neither does he attempt to avoid his responsibility as an adult to offer his ethical conclusion. . . . Such openness in discussions also encourages the adolescent to think about his own assumptions and to use his own powers of logic to the best possible advantage" (Meeks, 1971, p. 135).

Self psychology views these transference patterns more as narcissistic transference, common in adolescence, which is a time of heightened narcissism and self-regard. Idealization and deidealization of the therapist are common, and Goldberg (1972) recommends that the therapist not confront but "accept the narcissistic disorder of the adolescent patient as existing alongside a relative paucity of object love and not try to change narcissistic investment into object love. Treatment consists of a gradual undermining of the grandiosity and exhibitionism of the patient as well as a diminution of his search for unattainable ideals" (Goldberg, 1972, p. 5). In all, the therapy focuses on recognition and acceptance of the adolescent's narcissism in a nonjudgmental fashion, utilizing the transference to demonstrate the use of the clinician as a regulator and modulator of self-esteem.

Transference phenomena can be particularly intense in individual psychotherapy. In group and family therapy, there can be considerable dilution or diminution because of the presence of other family or group members. When others are present, patients commonly conceal more private feelings, hopes, and fantasies. Some adolescents, struggling for age-appropriate self-presentation, tend to be less open in the presence of others about any productions in treatment in the realm of play, poetry, or painting; they may be similarly disinclined to reveal feelings of anger, omnipotence, grandiosity, or dependency longings. Such feelings are generally most easily shared by adolescents in the privacy of individual psychotherapy.

Countertransference

Countertransference, like *transference,* is an overused term that commonly covers any and all feelings and reactions from the therapist in response to the patient. In fact, there are varied and conflicting definitions that reflect differing perspectives regarding the legitimate domain of this term. Dewald (1964), for example, states that countertransference arises not out of a client's behavior alone but from unconscious and preconscious forces within the therapist that cause the therapist to react to the client in ways that are inappropriate to the current reality of the therapeutic relationship. Such unrealistic, unprovoked reactions are viewed as displacements from significant early relationships with the therapist's siblings and parents. Giovacchini (1985b) differs with this formulation and offers a broader definition:

> I believe countertransference is ubiquitous; it is found in every analytic interaction in the same way transference is. Everything a therapist or a patient thinks, feels or does can be viewed as being on a hierarchal spectrum, one end dominated by unconscious, primary process elements, and the other end dominated by reality-oriented, secondary process factors. When a patient directs his feelings toward the therapist, the primary process elements of the spectrum represent transference, and in a similar fashion that part of the analyst's responses that stems primarily from the more primitive levels of his psyche can be viewed as countertransference. (Giovacchini, 1985, p. 45)

Some clinicians make distinctions along Giovacchini's spectrum, designating reality-oriented factors as counterreactions and those that emanate out of unconscious primary process variables as countertransference. Marcus (1980) defined countertransference as a reaction to a specific client, to the client's transference response, or to other components of the client's material. When used defensively it can interrupt or disrupt the therapist's analyzing function because it "activates a developmental residue and creates or revives unconscious conflict, anxiety and defensiveness" (Marcus, 1980, p. 286). When not used defensively, it can be a valuable diagnostic tool and effective treatment response in which a clinician is led to reflect and undertake a frank examination of his or her aroused feelings to avoid or resolve various therapeutic impasses or stalemates.

There are appropriate and all but universal countertransferences or counterreactions (according to one's definition of therapist's responses) to specific clients—those who are very impulsive, acting out, highly narcissistic, extremely aggressive, unmotivated and resistive, or suicidal. Such adolescents arouse understandable anxiety, fears, and frustration in all therapists. Furthermore, there is a wide variation in the client-therapist fit. One cannot work with equal effectiveness with all of one's clients. "Rather than viewing treatability only in terms of the patient's limitations, it is more realistic to consider the patient/therapist relationship as the axis that determines treatability. A patient may not be treatable by a particular therapist, but that does not make that patient untreatable" (Giovacchini, 1985, p. 450).

Some adolescent clients provoke anger, rejection, and hostile demands for compliance; others cause therapists, like parents, to feel anxious, overwhelmed and helpless, or ashamed and professionally mortified. Clients who are productive and promising may please and gratify the therapist, who unconsciously uses the client as a narcissistic extension, as a source of pride and praise. Signs of countertransference problems are the therapist's lateness, boredom, overinvolvement, fear, anger, mistakes about scheduling, and so on. The therapist must be self-observing and self-aware and seek appropriate sources of help and support in order to minimize the potentially negative impact such countertransference reactions may otherwise have. Supervision, consultation, and personal treatment help the therapist to stay in touch with and control his or her unconscious and preconscious early conflicts, and properly modulate conscious behaviors and responses. The goal is to provide a safe holding environment, one that is characterized by restraint, appropriate containment of drive expression, attunement, an absence of nihilistic pessimism, and a continuous sense of concern and compassion, based on the clinician's ability to remember the adolescent's history. This enables the therapist to see that earlier injuries and pain have in fact produced unpleasant defenses such as denial, projection, and externalization.

Empathy is crucial in all treatment relationships. Kohut, founder of self psychology, included it as a central concept in his seminal psychoanalytic papers on psychoanalytic therapy. In 1975, Kohut pronounced psychoanalysis as the science of empathy par excellence. Earlier, Kohut discussed introspection as the process of self-observation of the inner world of fantasies, feelings, and wishes and empathy as the process in which others were similarly understood. He used the phrase *vicarious introspection* to denote that through empathy one observes vicariously the inner world of another. Empathy is a central concept in self psychology, and Kohut conceived of it as curative in the treatment process. He called it "a value neutral method of observation attuned to the inner life of man" (1984, p. 395).

Clearly empathy is a critical ingredient in countertransference, and accurate empathy is composed of affective and cognitive components. Empathy is not used to satisfy or gratify patients' needs, nor is it the same as sympathy or support. "Rather, empathy informs the individual as to what is needed or yearned for by the other" (Lynn, 1991, p. 16). Ornstein (1978) notes that Kohut summarized his understanding of empathy with the following propositions:

> 1) Empathy, the recognition of the self in the other, is an indispensable tool of observation without which vast areas of human life, including man's behavior in the social field, remains unintelligible. 2) Empathy, the expansion of the self to include the other, constitutes a powerful psychological bond between individuals which, more perhaps than love, the expression and sublimation of the sexual drive, counteracts man's destructiveness against his fellows; and 3) Empathy, the accepting, confirming and understanding human echo evoked by the self, is a cherished nutriment without which human life as we know it and cherish it could not be sustained. (p. 84)

In the context of the treatment relationship utilizing a self psychology perspective, efforts by the therapist must evoke efforts at empathic immersion, in order to gain understanding of each client's demands, hopes, fears, ambitions, and symptomatic behavior. "The theory of self psychology removes the focus from the patient's faulty functioning in favor of learning to understand the underlying structure responsible for the faulty functioning" (Basch, 1980, p. 409). Interpretations are offered following the achievement of understanding, to assist in structure building, that is, "compensatory structures where development was earlier interrupted and thwarted by traumatic empathic failure" (Basch, 1986, p. 404). While better cognition and insight might occur, a goal of treatment is to open a path of empathy between self and selfobject and deepen the client's capacity for self-acceptance. A further treatment goal is the development of a cohesive self, through a process

Kohut called *transmuting internalization.* Transmuting internalization occurs as clients develop a capacity "to accept the hurts that are caused by failures of optimal responses by important others" (Solomon, 1991, p. 132). Kohut (1984) views treatment as a correctional emotional experience, and it is generally agreed that the expanded theoretical constructs of self psychology have been particularly useful in consideration of countertransference and for working with the more fragile populations. It is especially productive in clinical work with adolescents.

The Real Relationship

Alexander (1963) was one of the first to challenge the concept of analytic neutrality. He stated emphatically that the analyst's values are subtly learned by the client through verbal and nonverbal communications and by the experience of genuineness, warmth, and respect in a corrective emotional experience with a real person. Marmor (1982) emphasized the values of empathic warmth, attentive listening, and active participation in the treatment process. More recently, some have recommended self-disclosure, particularly in work with adolescent clients who clearly respond to their therapist's gender, age, appearance, style, humor, and other characteristics. Psychoanalysis is an intensive, in-depth process of uncovering that requires the client to lie on a couch, whereas psychotherapy is conducted face to face and aims instead for symptom reduction, behavioral and personality changes, and a return to, or resumption of, normal progressive development. In psychotherapy, the emphasis is primarily on the here-and-now and the manifestations of transference, which may or may not be addressed in any depth. Thus, the real relationship may well dominate over the transference relationship. The relative infrequency of psychotherapy contacts (when compared to analysis) stimulates the real relationship rather than a transference relationship.

Self psychology's approach, based on Kohut's expanded views of empathy, is predicated on the therapist's greater emotional availability and spontaneity, resulting in a "generally calmer and friendlier atmosphere." In individual psychotherapy with adolescents, support, reflections, enhancement of self-esteem, education, and guidance in a talkative and responsive interchange are more frequent interventions than interpretations of the transference or of defenses, or the elaboration of fantasies and unconscious primary process material, as is the case in analysis. In psychotherapy, the focus of therapy is not on interpretations but rather on the provision of empathic support, acceptance, soothing, and admiration from a trusted and private real person who clearly demonstrates warmth, regard, and respect.

Resistance and Working Through: Foci in the Middle Phase of Treatment

The beginning phase of treatment consists of assessment, selection of appropriate intervention, initial engagement, and contracting, hopefully culminating in the development of a working alliance that is based on the growing treatment relationship between the adolescent client and the therapist. Resistance, commonly dealt with in the middle phase of treatment, is defined as any obstruction that evolves in the process of treatment, and in the treatment relationship. It should be distinguished from a lack of motivation for change or a lack of interest in entering therapy and forming a relationship with a professional person. Some resistances are present from the beginning of treatment and are characteristic of the emotional structure of the client. These are called *character resistances,* which are distinguished from the opposition that arises in the course of therapy. Such opposition arises because internal conflict is defended, and there is always some degree of resistance to removing these defenses.

Dewald (1984) noted that resistances emerge during the treatment process at varying levels of consciousness. They are caused by the patient's fear of change or gratification arising from regressive infantile drives, early patterns, or infantile relationships, and the need to maintain repression of the unconscious conflicts that produce anxiety and guilt. Resistances should not be viewed pejoratively, because they operate through the ego and demonstrate ego development. A complete lack of defenses and resistance is an ominous sign, suggesting lack of psychic structure, possible decompensation, or a propensity for merger and indiscriminate compliance. It is important to understand why, what, and how the client is avoiding. Therefore, resistances and defenses should not be assaulted with confrontational or intellectualized reflections and interpretations.

Anna Freud (1958, 1978) discussed the inability or unwillingness of children and adolescents to maintain a stable therapeutic alliance, tolerate frustrations, and translate feelings into words rather than actions. There is a "type of juvenile patient who does not allow anxiety to find expression in thought or words but constantly negates it" (Sandler, Kennedy, & Tyson, 1980, p. 58). Adolescents often demonstrate resistance before and during the course of therapy; this may be stimulated by their own lack of motivation or fear of stigma and/or parental resistances about the need for treatment. Many teenagers resist their parents' referral because of their wish for autonomy and their fear that the therapist—the agent of the parents—will attempt to transform them in accord with the parents' needs and not the adolescent's preferences. Silences, broken appointments, tardiness, action rather than verbalization, passive-aggressive behavior, impatience, boredom, and resentment are standard adolescent manifestations of resistance.

Defenses are commonly used in the service of resistance. *Defense* is a term used to describe struggles of the ego, unconsciously employed, to protect the self from perceived danger. The threat of recognition or conscious awareness of repressed wishes or impulses causes anxiety and guilt and must be avoided. Assessment and diagnosis determine whether the defenses demonstrated are age adequate, primitive, or precocious, and whether they prove to be effective in binding impulses and anxiety to promote coping and adaptation. Defenses employed shape the individual's personality and style of coping with reality. Some patient's defenses are ineffectual and create secondary interference with reality functioning and consequent disequilibrium. Among the defenses are these:

- *Denial* and *projection,* primitive defense mechanisms employed when the ego attempts to avoid painful reality.

- *Identification with the aggressor,* primitive defense, often employed to avoid feeling fear of one's own helplessness.
- *Splitting,* a primitive defense that reflects defective object relations and a lack of self and object constancy; thus, people and the self are perceived as all good or all bad.
- *Reaction formation,* a more advanced defense, entailing replacement in conscious awareness of a painful idea or feeling by its opposite.
- *Isolation of affect,* demonstrated through a division or compartmentalization of thinking, that is, separating a powerful emotional experience from the affects aroused.
- *Intellectualization* and *rationalization,* which may provide emotional distance from overwhelming affects, moods, stimuli, and feelings.
- *Withdrawal* into solitude, often an attempt to ward off painful acknowledgments of personal or familial problems and inadequacies.
- *Acting out,* a displacement of behavioral response from one situation to another. It is the partial discharge of drive tension that is achieved by responding to the present situation as if it were the situation that originally gave rise to the drive demand. It is more than a single thought or expression; it is real acting and action and can constitute character structure in a chronic and habitual pattern of reaction (e.g., explosiveness and impatience at the slightest correction or criticism).
- *Sublimation,* a high-level defense involving the neutralization and transformation of drives, ego energies, and sense of self into activities that promote cohesion via immersion in, for example, academics, athletics, artistic, or musical activities, which are conflict-free efforts and interests.

The defenses must be recognized, understood, and accepted as the patient's needed protection against anxiety. Many adolescent clients are often objectionable, assaultive, draining, and provocative, yet despite this reality, a nonpunitive therapeutic stance must be maintained. The discussion of countertransference and counterreactions suggested ways to maintain therapeutic calm, objectivity, and ongoing commitment to the adolescent client.

Working Through

The term *working through* was originally used by Freud to describe the continuing application of analytic work to overcome resistances that persisted after interpretation of repressed instinctual impulses. The goal of working through is to make insight effective in order to bring about significant and lasting change. The client's intellectual understanding of various life experiences or even the effects of trauma may lead to initial improvements. However, unless there is a working through, therapeutic gains and changes commonly will not be maintained.

Agency-based practice and rationed insurance coverage for clinics and private therapy often preclude the lengthy treatment necessary to effect a genuine working through. However, when longer-term therapy is possible, it can strengthen the working-through process, after the client's attainment of earlier treatment gains (e.g., mastery of reality, the enactment of age-appropriate life roles and tasks). Introspection and insight are linked with working through, which occurs when the client's ego identifies with the therapist, sharing in the therapist's understanding, and taking part in the therapeutic effort.

Anna Freud (1965) stated that insight and introspection, normal in the adult, are not present in the child. Children and many adolescents are not self-observant; rather, they are preoccupied with action and the outer world. Adolescent efforts are not typically directed toward understanding the past, because of their intense preoccupation with current real difficulties and apprehensions about the future. It is usually not until late adolescence that young clients internalize the analyzing, observing, and reflecting function of their therapists, and they begin to acquire and retain an understanding of the genesis of their difficulties. Thus, children and teenagers who are provided treatment may require additional therapy later in adulthood, when more genuine working through is possible.

It is critical to bear in mind that even insight has limitations. Self-understanding produces neither magical change nor relief. Working through and resolution of both internalized and externalized conflicts require considerable time and repeated encounters with and recognition of newly learned truths. Many clinicians believe that "sufficient working through has taken place when the [young patient] has moved to the next level of development and established himself there" (Sandler, Kennedy, & Tyson, 1980, p. 184). This progression would involve an alteration of balance among the defenses, neutralization of resistances, formation of new identifications, and reconstruction of the ego ideal (Campell, 1981).

Termination

The topic of termination has received relatively scant attention in the clinical literature. Some believe this is due to the fact that the concluding phase of treatment produces the greatest amount of stress and difficulty. Related transference reactions, counterreactions, and countertransference problems, though common, have received little attention as a consequence. How the therapeutic process is brought to a conclusion may in fact be the most important aspect of the entire treatment process, solidifying gains or, if unsuccessful, weakening and undoing the therapeutic work. Ferenczi (1927) was the first to focus specifically on the concluding phase of treatment and noted that completion is attainable "only if unlimited time is at one's disposal" (p. 82). The next significant examination was Freud's seminal paper, "Analysis Terminable and Interminable" (1937), in which he offered guidelines and criteria for concluding analytic work. He emphasized relief of the patient's suffering, the conquering of anxieties and inhibitions, and the therapist's conviction that treatment be successful enough to ensure against relapse and repetition of the patient's symptoms and pathology. He emphasized sufficient intrapsychic structural change to permit optimal functioning.

Under optimal conditions, when individual psychotherapy has been of sufficient duration to effect a meaningful treatment relationship and corrective emotional experience, the termination phase is of utmost significance. It entails loss and separation, emancipation and growth, and it always reactivates earlier losses and separations that the client has endured. Ideally, the client will conclude treatment feeling strengthened and fortified by the experience of mastering the current loss. Termination can offer an opportunity to rework and modify earlier separation problems; it can evoke panic and rage, guilt and grief, or a sense of accomplishment and mastery.

The classic criteria for termination generally exclude decisions based solely on symptom relief; rather, there is an emphasis on movement beyond points of arrest or fixation and demonstration of the capability to handle ongoing and predictable future developmental and environmental problems. Psychotherapy, in contrast to psychoanalysis, focuses primarily on the here-and-now and on the interaction and interpersonal relationship of client and clinician. Less attention is given to early conflicts, and instead, the focus is on capacity for reality testing, stronger, more age-appropriate object relationships, and loosened fixations. Particularly with children and adolescents, the young person's failure to develop progressively (or damage that interferes with such growth) is the most significant feature in undermining future mental health (A. Freud, 1962).

Dewald (1964) suggested that for clients treated in insight therapy, indications for termination are some structural change in the personality, the lessening or elimination of symptoms, or evidence of improved capacity to tolerate specific symptoms and conflicts. Other indicators are improvements in relationships, work life, academics, and, more generally, self-awareness and self-control. For those seen in supportive therapy, indications for appropriate termination would be the reduction of symptoms, better management of drive expression, improved self-esteem, and cessation of the prior regressive pull. Decisions about termination may be determined by external factors, such as the family's or therapist's change of locale, change of jobs, or the conclusion of the internship for a clinician who has been in training.

Clients' reactions to termination are many and varied. With some, conflicts intensify during the conclusion of therapy due to resistance to facing old losses, sadness, and grief. Mourning is often masked by a facade of anger and denial, which may break down, revealing intense grief, sadness, and anxiety. Some clients try to stave off the date of scheduled termination with denial, regression, and resumption of old symptoms.

Countertransference dilemmas are frequent during this phase of treatment. A therapist's overly intense attachment, dislike of a client, therapeutic overambition, or overidentification will interfere with an effective termination. Therapist and client are both affected by the termination phase, the reasons for conclusion of treatment, and the nature of therapeutic gains achieved and maintained. The real relationship is usually more evident at the conclusion of treatment, since termination connotes a separation between two individuals whose relationship has been in the nature of a collaboration on a precious enterprise (Hurn, 1971). This real relationship must have professional parameters in accord with the prior treatment relationship.

A CASE EXAMPLE OF LATE ADOLESCENCE

Late adolescence is viewed as a stage of consolidation and stabilization. We anticipate and expect clarity and purposeful actions, productivity, constancy of emotions, stable self-esteem, and more mature functioning. Narcissism has lessened, and there is a greater tolerance for frustration, compromise, and delay. In his seminal work on adolescence, Blos (1962) noted that the adolescent strives for:

1. a highly idiosyncratic and stable arrangement of ego functions and interests;
2. an extension of the conflict-free sphere of the ego (secondary autonomy);
3. an irreversible sexual position (identity constancy);
4. the stabilization of mental apparatuses (p. 129).

Current social realities and the enhanced awareness of the length of time involved in preadult personality consolidation, plus adolescents' extended financial dependency and their lengthier academic preparation, have expanded our concept of adolescence and the coextensive mastery of age-appropriate tasks beyond the teenage and even college years. This expanded perspective of adolescence, including Erikson's concept of "moratorium" (a time for contemplation, role experimentation, or work or travel), has redefined the adolescent stage of life in contemporary Western society.

Based on this expanded contemporary view of adolescence, Beth, a twenty-one-year-old college graduate from an upper-middle-class, midwestern Jewish family, may be viewed as an older adolescent. She had not resolved what Anna Freud (1958) noted as the central issues of adolescence: (1) impulses—acceptances versus rebellion, (2) love versus hate of parents, (3) revolt versus dependency, (4) idealism versus narcissism, and (5) generosity versus narcissism:

Beth was referred for treatment by her father's previous therapist, following her father's request. She agreed with her father's concerns and seemed motivated for therapy at the onset of contact. She expressed an immediate sense of relief to "be doing something positive now" and was clearly pleased by the natural fit between herself and this clinician. Beth had just moved into the city following college graduation. She was employed at her first job in the fashion industry and, subsidized by her father, resides in a comfortable semiluxury apartment that she shares with a roommate. She presented as a wholesome and very attractive young woman, with athletic interests and abilities. She described a wide circle of friends from college to whom she is devoted. Much of her time and energy involves friends and shared activities, such as health club daily workouts, jogging, rollerblading, skiing, charity fund raisers, group gatherings, group summer and ski houses, and going to dinner and clubs with these friends. Beth is devoted to her family and communicates with them constantly, which involves daily calls with her father at his office, frequent evening calls to Dad and his second wife, as well as calls to her older sister and stormy weekly conversations with her mother.

A combative and conflictual relationship with her mother was a major presenting problem. Weight management and control of her eating was also of real concern. Beth acknowledged a long-standing reading disability, struggles with some academic work, and well-concealed poor self-esteem, secondary to her history of academic problems. This made her uncertain about whether to pursue graduate studies in business, an area of interest and one in which she had achieved notable mastery, given her competence with figures and numbers. Because of her reading disability, Beth shamefully revealed that she was completely unable to engage in many intellectual pursuits and could not even peruse the newspaper by herself at home. She knows she is an attractive and engaging young person but often feels empty and too eager to keep "busy busy," to distract herself.

Beth dates these feelings back to elementary school. Her academic difficulties surfaced in the fourth grade, at the time of her parents' divorce. Both Beth and her sister were provided psychotherapy as children, and Beth took responsibility to have reports and summaries of her childhood treatment forwarded to me. Following an assessment, she committed herself to biweekly individual psychotherapy, which her father agreed to underwrite. She wanted to work on the problems she had with her mother, weight management, her history of romantic problems with boyfriends, and feeling better about herself. She easily entered into a treatment contract and soon developed a therapeutic alliance.

The process of treatment was a mix—initially supportive, then, insight-oriented psychotherapy, as Beth became less concerned about her present circumstances and future, and could reflect on her earlier experiences and observe their later reverberations. Beth was able to move from a posture of rage, disregard, and contempt for her mother, to a position whereby she felt and demonstrated greater empathy and compassion for her mother and for herself. As her controls improved, there was a decided improvement in her transactions with her mother and diminution of the longstanding guilt that had always followed her explosions and rebelliousness. Beth's mother, who was self-employed, was described as a warm and intelligent woman who was very attractive despite her being grossly overweight. She was overly dependent on her own parents and seemed to be stuck in self-defeating patterns that had prevented her from remarrying or becoming romantically connected with a genuinely available partner since her divorce.

Beth's anger and shame about her mother's life appear to be a natural outcome of her mother's long-term involvement with a married man and her inability to sever this connection. Beth's mother was unable to break off this relationship despite her supposed personal aspirations and years of promises to Beth that she would do so. Beth's greater enjoyment of time with her father and stepmother generated eternal conflicts between Beth and her mother. It also gave rise to demands and accusations from her mother, followed by Beth's explosive verbal abuse, and finally Beth's reactive guilt. As she reflected on the longstanding nature of their conflict, Beth came to recognize her lack of complete and genuine separation-individuation from her mother; furthermore she seemed to mirror her mother in weight management problems and in her unwise romantic choices of boyfriends who did not treat her well.

The manifest transference was one of idealization, with the therapist perceived as the all-good, empathic idealized maternal object. The corresponding counterreaction or countertransference (Marcus, 1980) is best described as a positive maternal one, with the therapist taking care and attention not to impose her personal values or goals (e.g., enrollment in graduate school) on Beth. Utilizing a self psychology perspective, interpretations were offered to assist in structure building. In addition to better cognition and insight, goals of Beth's treatment involved the opening of pathways of empathy between Beth and her mother and the deepening of Beth's capacity for self-acceptance and em-

pathy for herself and her mother. A further objective was the development of greater self-cohesion, which evolved through transmuting internalizations, that is, the internal changes that occur as patients develop a "capacity to accept the hurts that are caused by failures of optimal responses by important others" (Solomon, 1991, p. 132).

After two years of therapy, Beth appeared to demonstrate a significant degree of working through. As a consequence, it seems unlikely that she will regress to the earlier mother-daughter rageful battles or food management difficulties. Out of identification with the therapist and the therapeutic work, she has made substantial gains. She has become less impulsive and less erratic with food management, has resolved love versus hate of her mother, is more realistic and less worshipful of father, and has assumed greater responsibility for her finances. She has been able to increase her earnings and savings, is more independent of father (save for therapy bills), and is idealistic and generous about giving, emotionally, to all in her family, as well as friends. She has made additional gains in romantic relationships, and although she is not involved in an exclusive attachment, she has enjoyed far better relationships with boyfriends of late.

Termination was decided on by Beth, based on her feeling strengthened and fortified by the treatment experience. She felt ready "to graduate" because of the elimination of symptoms and presenting problems, and improvements in her relationships, work performance, self-esteem, and self-control. The real relationship was more evident during the planned termination phase, with Beth's commenting on the closeness and support she felt she had received. She indicated comfort at the thought that she could and would return at any point if she found it necessary. Beth appeared to have resolved the tasks of late adolescence at the conclusion of therapy. Accordingly, no objections or questions were raised about her decision, since it is crucial to effect an appropriate letting go of adolescent clients based on the therapist's surrender of omnipotent hopes of safeguarding the adolescent patient against future dangers, life vicissitudes, and regression. One must allow the adolescent opportunity to take the chance of independent passage (Ekstein, 1983).

Reflections on the Treatment Process

Work with Beth was supportive and empathic, and the self psychology perspective was employed. In a warm and friendly ambience, the therapist permitted and encouraged emotional availability and spontaneity, and the treatment process focused on techniques of understanding, explanations, and interpretations of Beth's demands, hopes, ambitions, struggles, and symptomatic behaviors. Beth's lack of separation and individuation from mother was viewed not from the perspective of oedipal anxiety or fears of oedipal victory but rather out of the fear of disintegration anxiety, the effects of mild learning disability, and the mortification inherent in lack of early mastery of academics. Beth's aggression and adhesive negative attachment to her mother were redefined, not ignored, and the therapist, through interpretive linkages and genetic reflection, enabled Beth to understand her bond of anger as the result of her shame over her mother's overweight, poor self-control, and long involvement with a married man. Interpretations, when offered, focused on Beth's low self-esteem and embarrassment about herself and her mother, rather than her overadmiration and idealization of her father, the more competent and effective parent. There was no focus on Beth's faulty functioning but rather effort to understand the underlying structure responsible for the faulty functioning. By providing "experience near" explanations of Beth's self-experiences, she was aided in being able to develop self-soothing techniques and to understand more accurately her retaliatory responses to her mother's repeated traumatizing empathic failures. The self psychology approach avoided critical confrontation with Beth's evasions, demands, and excitability; the therapist's reflections instead focused on providing explanations and origins of her actions and behavior.

The goal of enhancement of Beth's self-perceptions was achieved, as evident in her growing capacity to empathize with herself and her mother and better understand the shortcomings in their selfobject bond. She demonstrated insight into her mother's relationship with Beth's maternal grandparents and was thereby able to experience greater tolerance and compassion toward her mother. Additional educational interventions addressed her learning disability and its short-term and long-term effects on her self-esteem. Greater understanding enabled Beth to exert better self-control and tone down her affective exchanges with her mother and her boyfriends. In addition, she began to consider the possibility of graduate school courses. She also demonstrated improved performance at her job, evident from the promotions and increased responsibility that she had been given.

In the transference Beth idealized the therapist as the good mother who is consistently patient, calm, and empathic. Through identification and transmuting internalization, Beth felt less frantic or overwhelmed and increasingly could engage in well-modulated and controlled deliberations and problem solving. With better self-control and self-understanding she was also able to surrender a "tough" demeanor, which she came to understand as her defensive facade in disagreements. When disappointed by mother or a boyfriend, Beth learned to relate in a more benign and less reactive manner; imperfections and small slights from others now could be experienced as manageable. With better self/other distinctions, learned in treatment, Beth felt less provoked and personally diminished by the inconsiderate behavior of others. She came to see herself and the other more realistically, and with this enhanced self-acceptance, better able to accept her "imperfect" mother and the shortcomings of her friends. Beth's mother was able to respond positively to Beth's improved mode of relating to her, and this was vividly demonstrated when Beth required surgery. Beth's mother as well as her father came to be with her, and her mother functioned in a considerate parental fashion, with a noticeable absence of the explosive arguments, accusations, and childish demands that Beth's mother typically made of her.

Beth's treatment was initially supportive and then shifted to an insighted-oriented focus. Beth seemed to benefit and grow from the curative effect of the "correctional emotional experience" (Kohut, 1984, p. 78). The improvements seemingly evolved out of a therapeutic dialogue that provided understanding and explanations of what went wrong in Beth's early childhood and throughout her adolescence.

CASE EXAMPLE OF EARLY ADOLESCENCE

Blos (1962) states that the distinctive character of early adolescence resides in the disengagement from one's parents, which causes the young person to search, at times frantically, for new attachments and love objects. The efforts at separating from the parents coincide with a period of diminished coping skills and high vulnerability. The challenge of dealing with all the biological and psychosocial changes is enormous. Normally, parental values and standards have already been deeply embedded in the young person, but during early adolescence, shifts of varying intensity are made toward separation and independence. The search for new attachments is an effort to escape loneliness, isolation, and depressed moods. In this search for new interests and attachments, friends are often idealized, and the peer group becomes an all-important bridge away from the security of the nuclear family to increasing autonomy. The lonely, more isolated young adolescent who lacks friendships suffers greatly, as will the youngster who experiences slowness or lags behind in pubertal development. Rebellious and acting-out behavior are not uncommon for the junior high school population. Turbulence, unruliness, belligerence, and defiance can markedly interfere with ordered learning and study patterns, as young adolescents struggle to integrate the perceptions of others with self-perceptions of their dramatic bodily changes. Not uncommonly, the young adolescent feels compelled to assume a position of exaggerated independence that leads to rebellious attitudes toward adults in general and parents in particular.

Billy displayed many of the characteristic psychological features of early adolescence, by late latency (age ten and a half) when he was originally referred for therapy by the social worker at his school. He was described as a bright child who read far above grade level but refused to produce in school. He would not participate in class discussions or interact with peers, and the school planned to fail him on the basis of his refusal to work. In previous years he had been passed solely on the basis of his obvious intellect. Billy's parents also described problems at home, including his isolation from the family, stubbornness, passive resistance, and egocentrism. The oldest of five children in a lower-middle-class intact black family, Billy's isolation, passivity, and femininity, and his tendency to discharge aggression via passive-aggressive sadomasochistic means, had the effect of provoking peers, parents, and teachers to act out aggressively toward him.

He was treated for almost four years, his treatment commencing shortly before he entered middle adolescence and continuing as he generally adjusted to this phase of development. Billy brought material into treatment in various ways. Despite being verbal and articulate, for a protracted period he was relatively silent, preferring to draw endlessly; ultimately, after a year or so, he began to share fantasies and associations. Initially however, he resisted discussion or even the therapist's references to his problems at home or in school. His reactions consisted of rationalizations, intellectualizations, and projections in response to the therapist's gentle attempts to focus on the maladaptive patterns and self-defeating behaviors that were the basis for his referral for treatment. He resisted any comment, reflection, or interpretation, keeping up an endless barrage of defenses, or silence, ostensibly to ensure control and to defend against his fear of expressing aggression. It also became apparent that he needed to keep the therapist at a safe distance. In recognition of Billy's anxiety, the therapist backed off and engaged in more active listening, observation, and mirroring; it became increasingly obvious that Billy was struggling with his wish for and fear of closeness, sibling rivalry, and a fear of failure. After almost two years of treatment, as Billy entered puberty, he acknowledged that he wished to be the best and favorite child the therapist had ever treated.

In the context of a slowly evolving but eventually close relationship with his therapist, Billy demonstrated insight about fear of his own angry impulses; he also came to accept the therapist's explanations of how he had externalized these angry impulses into elaborate fears of tornados, floods, fires, storms, and a plane crashing into the clinic. While increasingly more verbal, Billy continued with his artistic productions, compulsively drawing airplanes, racing cars, and ships. Gradually he shared omnipotent, megalomaniacal fantasies through the epics and stories he spun, which were associated with either his drawings or with the toy soldiers he often brought into treatment sessions.

After two years of treatment following his entry into adolescence, he had made significant gains. His school work reflected vast improvement, and he achieved superior grades. He was less provocative at home and at school and slowly began to participate in swimming classes and a Little League baseball team. He still lagged in physical development and in social relationships with peers. In his search for a new love object, he fastened onto the therapist, preferring her company to that of all others. The transference appeared to have a selfobject basis, initially for mirroring and merger, and later for idealization. He articulated a wish for daily sessions, and ultimately, with some degree of resentful resignation, accepted an increase from biweekly to three-times-weekly appointments. Gradually Billy demonstrated increased capacity for self-observation, and he was able to verbalize feelings and fantasies; this development contrasted sharply with his former need to keep them confined to his solitary daydreams and obsessive drawings at home and in each treatment hour. He could articulate his belief that the therapist's reflections and explanations had helped him to figure things out, "like my imagination baby games and heroes, full of monsters, racing cars, stars and pilots. I used to like to lose myself thinking about these make-believe people because I'm the opposite and want to feel good and forget I'm the shortest in my class, not popular, not a big shot, not a good athlete, and too frightened to fight and defend myself. I'm now an excellent student and it's the only thing in my control. I guess I'm just brains and no brawn."

In his increased early adolescent identification with his therapist, Billy spoke of becoming a therapist and often read about psychological matters, consulting encyclopedias and library books. With a twinkle in his eye, Billy often spoke of reading a book about Freud, in which there was a story about a grown man afraid of the dark because he was locked in a closet as a child. The man was also afraid of dogs, and the book, according to Billy, stated that the fear of dogs was really a substitute, or displacement. Billy would then ponder the meaning of his own fears of bugs, a ball coming at him, contact team sports, or other unexpected events, and their significance as displacements from his earlier fears of his dad. Billy's father used to spank him before therapy, at which time his therapist changed his parents' handling of him.

Billy had now resumed a progressive line of development and slowly but surely worked through his long-standing anger, feelings of displacement, and sibling rivalry caused by the births of four younger siblings in rapid succession. Most significant was his ability to work through the original trauma that had led to his developmental arrest and fixations.

Billy's grandmother was his surrogate mother throughout his preschool years. She cared for him daily because of the parents' respective work schedules and chronic financial pressures. Though she was not elderly and had enjoyed good health, Billy's grandmother died suddenly from an aneurysm; shortly after, Billy's depression, withdrawal, and school problems became apparent. Although he could share memories of his happiness and closeness with his grandmother, as well as the memory of her funeral, it took over a year for him to establish an emotional connection with his shock, despair, and sense of loss after her death. He could recount details and fragments about her. He had vivid memories of his grandmother's teaching him to read, taking him to the Natural History Museum, and telling him about dinosaurs. He recalled their play, games and the obvious pleasure and approval she had for his artwork, and he speculated that perhaps this is why he still has such a passion for drawing. Unresolved mourning was apparent, and at first, Billy showed no abreaction or breakthrough of his unshed tears for grandmother. He used his excellent intellect and emerging insight to conjecture that his fear of floods and tornadoes was tied to his fear of all forms of unexpected and uncontrolled destructive phenomena—not just father's spankings but also grandmother's sudden death. By age twelve and a half, mourning and grief work were well under way.

Despite the evident gains, becoming a teenager produced considerable stress and regression. There was a short-lived decline in his superior academic achievements, and his argumentativeness with teachers resurfaced. Billy would engage the teacher in power struggles over the curriculum, deprecate black studies content, and refuse to do homework and simple assignments. He was aware of his conflictual feelings regarding his own racial identity, which were manifested in both fantasies about his actual American Indian ancestors and his wish to be white or Indian rather than black. Billy reverted to obsessive drawings and ruminations, and was generally ambivalent about active-passive conflicts and masculine-feminine issues. He demonstrated the heightened narcissism of adolescence and was preoccupied with his short stature and his new interest in guitar playing. He drew endless pictures of guitars, session after session. He was also preoccupied with his independent intellectual pursuits and his astounding, superior scores on academic achievement tests. Though not compliant with all academic expectations and assignments, he soon regained his excellent level of academic success and was chosen to give a series of science lectures. His test scores enabled him to change school districts and enter a more demanding, prestigious high school. Peer relationships, while improved, were somewhat meager, due to Billy's self-absorption and wary distant stance with classmates.

Billy planned his termination well ahead, based on his own assessment of his progress and his pending entry into high school, which he viewed, appropriately, as a developmental milestone. At termination it was gratifying to learn that he had voluntarily joined his high school swim team (not because of father's pressure for masculine activities), choosing to risk himself in the area he used to fear the most: athletics and competition with peers. Billy concluded his treatment in his own way, insistent on the autonomy of setting a date a few weeks earlier than the therapist considered ideal. The therapist honored Billy's wish for autonomy in regard to his termination and graduation from therapy out of respect and also to applaud his age-appropriate self-assertion, a major treatment gain. It was viewed as essential to conclude the therapy relationship on a positive note.

Reflections on the Treatment Process

Work with Billy began on a supportive basis and in the middle phase shifted to insight-oriented psychotherapy. A self psychology perspective was employed. Initially, Billy could tolerate little warmth and rapport, keeping his distance and shutting out any of the therapist's reflections or interpretations. He seemed to demand mirroring. No confrontation or interpretations about character defenses or resistances were offered, since it was apparent that Billy would experience the therapist's "correct" genetic interpretations as "forced feedings" (i.e., as critical or assaultive). Efforts were made to listen and observe, and to mirror Billy actively. Admiring his drawings seemed to be useful and more appropriate than attempts to interpret them. Empathic and accepting commentary was offered, and no attempt was made to push Billy toward insight or self-observation. As he demonstrated a symbiotic merger or pseudoalliance, a selfobject merger and mirroring transference were revealed, eventually followed by an idealizing selfobject transference.

Following extensive assessment sessions with Billy's parents, there was a brief period of parental guidance and education about more effective parental responses to Billy's withholding and provocative behavior. Billy's father was able to curtail physical punishments completely, and both the mother and the father formed a solid parental alliance with the clinician. The parents were not seen regularly, but only when they felt the need for some sort of a progress report about their son's therapy. Their commitment to transporting Billy two and three times weekly for sessions was noteworthy; over nearly four years of treatment, Billy arrived punctually at 8:00 A.M. and was then transported to school.

Well into the middle phase of the treatment, Billy developed more trust and became ready for explanations and reflections. Demonstrating identification and transmuting internalizations, Billy evidenced growing insight and self-awareness; he could be self-reflective and was more effective in soothing himself. His aggression was not ignored, but reframed in terms of his defiant use of anger when anxious or depressed. Affirmation, soothing, pacification, and praise for artistic and verbal productions calmed Billy and strengthened his self-esteem. His surrender of shame paralleled his diminished grandiosity and earlier sense of entitlement.

During the almost four years of treatment, the therapist's efforts were directed at providing nonjudgmental acceptance and understanding of Billy. Such a therapeutic milieu provided Billy with an "experience near" interchange that asked no more of him than he was able to give. In the narcissistic transference, the therapist often feels ignored or reduced to little more than a mirror. This "thankless role" ebbed in the face of Billy's discernable gains and growth, as it became apparent that the therapeutic process had enabled this boy to fill deficits and begin to replace selfobject functions with self-functions. Billy's improved level of functioning, working through of grief and trauma, and enhanced self-regard enabled him to enter adolescence with a better-developed self-structure characterized by a firm racial and gender identity, cohesion, and a genuine, age-appropriate level of functioning.

CONCLUSIONS

Adolescents are generally recognized as one of the most difficult age groups to treat. Some clinicians and researchers do not believe that adolescents can actually engage in and maintain a therapeutic alliance. Others believe that only short-term periods of therapy are possible, with adolescents coming for help periodically when stress becomes overwhelming. A number of writers recommend the setting of only moderate goals, specifically to increase the ego's tolerance for conflicts and to improve reality testing. Since teenagers are attempting to disengage from their parents, many resist any dependent relationship with an adult parental figure. The decathexis from parental love objects often results in impoverishment of the ego because of the pain and mourning associated with the loss of the close and loving parent-child ties. This mourning process may leave little ego energy for attachment to an individual therapist. Frequently encountered treatment obstacles in work with adolescent clients have consisted of a lowered threshold for frustration, a preference for action rather than verbalization of feelings, and new weaknesses and immaturities of ego structure. Because of the adolescent narcissistic withdrawal, many teenagers have little if any libidinal energy available with which to explore their past or relate in the present. Due to all of the realities and the specific vulnerabilities of adolescents, supportive, empathic treatment is the best beginning intervention. Insight-oriented psychotherapy may later be possible if the alliance is positive and when the teenager is motivated to seek greater self-understanding and mastery of age-appropriate tasks.

The adolescent therapist is cautioned regarding the use of confrontation to avoid the possibility of regressive fragmentation. Many adolescents are not candidates for group or family therapy, because of the stressors in the family or because some are unable to empathize with peers or tolerate public self-exposure due to their shaky self-esteem or self-regard. Group and family interventions can be threatening to many adolescents who are very sensitive to criticism and self-conscious with peers. Individual psychotherapy is appropriate for the widest range of adolescents: the severely disturbed, the teenager in a traumatic home situation, or one who presents a habit disorder, ego deficits, or developmental disability.

Specialization in adolescent therapy can begin only during formal clinical education. Adolescents present special demands; their communications are frequently unclear, and they are reticent, resistance prone, and rebellious, with a propensity for action rather than words and the sharing of feelings. Work with this population requires lengthy, ongoing training, experience, and supervision.

In addition, to be able to do intensive psychotherapy with adolescents, any aspiring therapist, regardless of discipline, will require some personal treatment in order to develop a therapeutic, objective, empathic response that both embodies self-awareness and self-observation and also controls against regression and countertransferential acting out with adolescent clients. We may or may not have encountered, struggled with, or lived through the identical pain and stresses that our clients experience, but as adolescents, we once all engaged in the same developmental struggles for autonomy, separation, and individuation. We have also suffered the same fears of narcissistic injury and failure as our teenage clients. We once encountered with alarm, anxiety, and excitement our first love, erotic arousal, and sexual and emotional intimacy. Thus, clinical work with adolescents strikes continuous, responsive chords in all therapists in a unique, though stressful manner, which must be recognized and contained.

REFERENCES

Alexander, F. (1963). The dynamics of psychotherapy in the league of learning theory. *American Journal of Psychiatry, 120,* 440–448.

Alexander, F. (1953). Current views on psychotherapy. In *The scope of psychoanalysis: Selected papers of Franz Alexander, 1921–1961* (pp. 276–289). New York: Basic Books.

Basch, M. (1980). *Doing psychotherapy.* New York: Basic Books.

Blos, P. (1962). *On adolescence.* New York: Free Press.

Buxbaum, E. (1954). Technique of child therapy: A critical evaluation. *The Psychoanalytic Study of the Child, 9,* 297–333.

Campbell, R. J. (1981). *Psychiatric dictionary* (5th ed.). New York: Oxford University Press.

Dewald, P. (1964). *Psychotherapy: A dynamic approach.* New York: Basic Books.

Ekstein, R. (1983). The adolescent self during the process of termination of treatment: Termination, interruption or intermission. In M. Sugar, S. Feinstein, J. Looney, A. Swartzberg, & A. Sorosky (Eds.), *Adolescent psychiatry: Vol. 9. Developmental and clinical studies* (pp. 125–146). Chicago: University of Chicago Press.

Erikson, E. (1963). *Childhood and society* (2nd ed.). New York: Norton.

Ferenczi, S. (1927; 1955). The problem of the termination of the analysis. In M. Balint (Ed.), *Final contributions to the problems and methods of psychoanalysis.* New York: Basic Books.

Freud, A. (1958). Adolescence. *The Psychoanalytic Study of the Child, 13,* 255–278.

Freud, A. (1962). Assessment of childhood disturbances. *The Psychoanalytic Study of the Child, 17,* 149–158.

Freud, A. (1965). *The writings of Anna Freud: Vol. 6. Normality and pathology in childhood: Assessment of development* (pp. 3–7). New York: International Universities Press.

Freud, A. (1978). The role of insight in psychoanalysis and psychotherapy: Introduction to the Anna Freud Hampstead Center Symposium, held at the Michigan Psychoanalytic Society, March. In H. P. Blum (Ed.), *Psychoanalytic explorations of technique: Discourse on the theory of therapy.* New York: International Universities Press.

Freud, S. (1912). The dynamics of transference. In *The standard edition of the complete psychological works of Sigmund Freud: Vol. 12* (pp. 97–108). London: Hogarth Press.

Freud, S. (1915). Observations on transference love. In *The standard edition of the complete psychological works of Sigmund Freud: Vol. 12* (pp. 157–171). London: Hogarth Press.

Freud, S. (1916, 1917). Introductory lectures on psychoanalysis. In *The standard edition of the complete psychological works of Sigmund Freud: Vol. 12* (pp. 15–16). London: Hogarth Press.

Freud, S. (1937, 1950). Analysis terminable and interminable. In *Collected papers: Vol. 5* (pp. 316–357). London: Hogarth Press.

Furman, E. (1980). Transference and externalization in latency. *The Psychoanalytic Study of the Child, 35,* 267–284.

Ginott, H. (1961). *Group psychotherapy with children.* New York: McGraw-Hill.

Giovacchini, P. (1987). *A narrative textbook of psychoanalysis.* Northvale, NJ: Jason Aronson.

Giovacchini, P. (1985a). Introduction: Countertransference responses to adolescents. In M. Sugar, S. Feinstein, J. Looney, A. Swartzberg, & A. Sorosky (Eds.), *Adolescent psychiatry: Vol. 12. Developmental and clinical studies* (pp. 447–448). Chicago: University of Chicago Press.

Giovacchini, P. (1985b). Countertransference and the severely disturbed adolescent. In M. Sugar, S. Feinstein, J. Looney, A. Swartzberg, & A. Sorosky (Eds.), *Adolescent psychiatry: Vol. 12. Developmental and clinical studies* (pp. 449–467). Chicago: University of Chicago Press.

Goldberg, A. (1972). On the incapacity to love: A psychotherapeutic approach to the problem in adolescence. *Archives of General Psychiatry, 26,* 3–7.

Heacock, D. R. (1966). Modification of the standard techniques for out-patient group psychotherapy with delinquent boys. *Journal of the National Medical Association, 58,* 41–47.

Herman, J. L. (1992). *Trauma and recovery*. New York: Basic Books.

Hurn, H. T. (1971). Toward a paradigm of the terminal phase. *Journal of the American Psychoanalytic Association, 19*, 332–348.

Kardiner, A., & Spiegel, A. (1947). *War, stress and neurotic illness* (Rev. ed., *The traumatic neuroses of war*). New York: Hoeber.

Keith, C. R. (1968). The therapeutic alliance in child psychiatry. *Journal of Child Psychiatry, 7*, 31–53.

Kessler, J. (1966). *Psychopathology of childhood.* Englewood Cliffs, NJ: Prentice Hall.

Kohut, H. (1971). *The analysis of the self.* New York: International Universities Press.

Kohut, H. (1978). Introspection, empathy and psychoanalysis: An examination of the relationship between mode of observation and theory. In P.H. Ornstein (Ed.), *The search for the self: Selected writings of Heinz Kohut, 1950–1978: Vol. 2* (pp. 205–232). New York: International Universities Press.

Kohut, H. (1978). The psychoanalyst in the community of scholars. In *The search for the self: Vol. 2* (pp. 685–721). New York: International Universities Press.

Kohut, H. (1984). *How does analysis cure?* A. Goldberg & P. Stepansky (Eds.). Chicago: University of Chicago Press.

Lynch, V. J. (1991). Basic concepts. In H. Jackson (Ed.), *Using self psychology in psychotherapy* (pp. 15–25). Northvale, NJ: Jason Aronson.

McDonald, M. (1965). The psychiatric evaluation of children. *Journal of the Academy of Child Psychiatry, 4*, 569–612.

Marcus, I. (1980). Countertransference and the psychoanalytic process in children and adolescents. *The Psychoanalytic Study of the Child, 35*, pp. 285–298.

Marmor, J. (1982). Changes in psychoanalytic treatment. In S. Slipp (Ed.), *Curative factors in dynamic psychotherapy* (pp. 60–70). New York: McGraw-Hill.

Meeks, J. (1971). *The fragile alliance: An orientation to the out-patient psychotherapy of adolescents.* Baltimore: Williams & Wilkins.

Mishne, J. (1983). *Clinical work with children.* New York: Free Press.

Mishne, J. (1986). *Clinical work with adolescents.* New York: Free Press.

Mishne, J. (1993). *The evolution and application of clinical theory: Perspectives from four psychologies.* New York: Free Press.

Offer, D., & Vanderstoep, E. (1975). Indications and contraindications for family therapy. In M. Sugar (Ed.), *The adolescent in group and family therapy* (pp. 145–160). New York: Brunner/Mazel.

Ornstein, P. (1978). *The search for the self: Selected writings of Heinz Kohut 1950–1978: Vol. 1.* New York: International Universities Press.

Rockland, L. H. (1989). *Supportive psychotherapy: A psychodynamic approach.* New York: Basic Books.

Sandler, J., Kennedy, H., & Tyson, P. L. (1980). *The technique of child psychotherapy: Discussions with Anna Freud.* Cambridge, MA: Harvard University Press.

Solomon, M. F. (1991). Adults. In H. Jackson (Ed.), *Using self psychology in psychotherapy* (pp.117–133). Northvale, NJ: Jason Aronson.

Symonds, M. (1982). Victim responses to terror: Understanding and treatment. In F. Ochberg & D. Soskis (Eds.), *Victims of terrorism.* Boulder, CO: Western University.

6

Family Therapy:

Systems Approaches to Clinical Practice

Froma Walsh

Over the past three decades, systems theory and family therapy have emerged as a major approach to understanding human functioning and to the treatment of dysfunction. This chapter provides an overview of family systems approaches to practice, beginning with a description of basic principles and key processes in family functioning that guide assessment and intervention. A survey of the foundational models and more recent developments is presented. Guidelines are offered for family and couples therapy, with application to diverse client populations and problem situations.

HISTORICAL EVOLUTION

The crucial influence of the family and larger social forces in individual development has been recognized in social work from its earliest focus on the concept of person-in-environment. With the ascendancy of the psychoanalytic model, attention became focused on the impact of the mother-child dyadic relationship in early childhood. Based on a linear-causal model of influence, deficiencies in the mother's personality and mothering style were assumed to be responsible for any disturbance in an offspring. Clinicians generally saw family members, mostly mothers, apart from and collateral to the primary treatment of an individual.

A paradigm shift occurred in the late 1950s with the development of general sys-

I thank my daughter, Claire Whitney, for her assistance in the preparation of this chapter.

tem theory, communications theory, and cybernetics (Watzlawick, Beavin, & Jackson, 1967). Direct observation of whole families in studies of schizophrenia led to a breakthrough in thinking about the family context of human problems and therapeutic intervention to change dysfunctional patterns of interaction. Apart from questions of origin of presenting problems, these investigations attended to ongoing transactional processes, noting recursive cycles that reinforced disturbed behavior or symptoms. From these observations, it was a natural step to conceive of therapeutic intervention to alter dysfunctional processes in sessions with whole families.

The 1960s was a period of rapid expansion of theory and experimentation with different family approaches to treat a wide range of problems. The emergence of distinct schools or models of family therapy in the 1970s brought a refinement of therapeutic strategies and techniques, based on particular views of problem formation and the process of change. Over the past decade, more recent developments in the field have integrated and expanded that foundation with newer approaches that reflect advances in clinical theory, practice, and research, as well as greater attention to issues concerning gender and cultural diversity. A shift has also taken place from a focus on family deficits to an emphasis on building family strengths. Various models differ somewhat in focus and in particular beliefs about therapeutic objectives and how they can be reached most effectively. Yet within this diversity, family therapy approaches share a common conceptual base in systems theory.

FAMILY SYSTEMS ORIENTATION

The practice of family therapy is grounded in a set of basic assumptions about the interplay of individual, family, and social processes. The assessment and treatment of dysfunction are guided by these principles of systems theory. Family therapy is not simply a therapeutic modality in which all members are treated conjointly; in fact, individuals may be seen separately or brought together in different combinations. A family systems approach is distinguished less by who is in the room and more by how the clinician attends to the relationship system in problem formulation and intervention planning. Interventions may focus on a couple relationship or combine individual work and direct work with the whole family or part of a system, such as parents, siblings, or key extended family members. Multisystem interventions may involve schools, the workplace, or a health care delivery system. Therapy is aimed at modifying dysfunctional patterns—structures, interactions, and beliefs—in which symptomatic behavior is embedded in order to enable healthy individual, couple, and family functioning.

Interactional View: Process and Context

Foremost, family systems theory emphasizes interaction and context. A systemic orientation attends to the family and social context of human problems and change processes. A basic premise is that dysfunction cannot be adequately understood or changed apart from its psychosocial context.

From a biopsychosocial perspective, interactions involve the interplay among the multiple influences of biological, psychological, and social factors. A systems-oriented assessment may lead to a variety of interventions, depending on the relevance of various system levels to problem resolution. The level of family is most often the interactive focal point for assessment purposes—a kind of clearinghouse for this multiplicity of forces. The family is viewed as an open system that functions in relation to its broader sociocultural context and evolves over the life cycle (Minuchin, 1974). This ecological view recognizes the importance of larger systems influences, especially cultural and socioeconomic factors. Families are composed of subsystems (e.g. adult couple, parental, sibling), and they interact with other systems, such as workplace, religious, health care, and educational institutions. The family operates according to certain rules and principles that apply to all human systems (Bertalanffy, 1968).

Moreover, systems approaches attend to processes over time, from ongoing interactions to multigenerational and life cycle influences on current functioning. Transactional patterns within the family are viewed as central to shaping and reinforcing individual behavior and personality. Therefore, family or relationship processes are given at least equal emphasis with the content of a problem. The interactional patterns that surround, ameliorate, or exacerbate a symptom are as clinically significant as the description of a disorder. Here systems theory resonates with early social work theory: the psychosocial unit becomes the individual in social context. Systems-based therapies offer the principles and methods for direct interventions, with the system as a powerful means to bring about individual change.

Because problems are viewed in context, conceptualizations of what is normal or pathological become less based on invariant objective criteria; rather they are seen as dependent on the particular situation or context. In essence, function and dysfunction—or normality versus pathology—must be defined relative to the fit between the individual, family, and context and the psychosocial demands of the situation. For instance, in a low cohesion family where members tend to function separately, each fending alone, a crisis requiring close teamwork and mutual support can elicit dysfunction because the family's style conflicts with immediate demands. Inherent in this view is the assumption that all families have strengths as well as vulnerabilities. When dysfunction emerges in stressful situations, family resources can be mobilized to meet those challenges. Family therapy aims to strengthen and empower distressed families to function more effectively.

Symptoms of family dysfunction may be generated by an overload of external stressors, such as job loss, economic strain, or racism. Symptoms may be triggered by a crisis within the family, such as traumatic loss or by persistent stresses of coping with a chronic illness. We must be cautious not to equate family distress with family pathology. A biopsychosocial systems perspective is necessary to be mindful of the multiple, recursive influences on individual and family functioning.

Circular Causality

In family systems theory, individuals are seen as interrelated so that a change in any one member affects other individuals and the group as a whole; this in turn affects the first individual in a circular chain of influence. Every action in this sequence is also a reaction. It is critical to understand the recursive patterns of interaction between symptoms and other parts of the system that maintain or exacerbate the problem or resources that could be mobilized in problem resolution. This viewpoint is useful even for conditions that are partially or in large part biologically determined. In tracking this sequence of interactions around the symptoms, one might find a repetitive pattern, perhaps involving other family members, that eventually circles back to a starting point, exacerbating the situation. This circular tracking process is one of the key elements of a systems-oriented assessment, providing a more wholistic view of the biological and interactive influences surrounding a presenting problem. Skilled intervention seeks to interrupt a dysfunctional sequence to promote problem resolution.

Although circular process can reinforce problems, not all participants have equal influence over others. We have become increasingly aware of the culturally shaped and reinforced gender differential that operates in the family, granting husbands greater power, resources, and privilege over their wives (McGoldrick, Anderson, & Walsh, 1989). Clinicians must be particularly cautious not to take a neutral stance or a no-fault position in cases of wife abuse where an abusive husband must be held accountable for his destructive behavior regardless of his wife's part in the interaction sequence.

Nonsummativity

From a systems perspective, the family as a whole is greater than the sum of its parts, and it cannot be described simply by summing up characteristics of individual members or even of various dyads. It is necessary to attend to the gestalt: the family as a functional unit, its organization and interaction patterns involving the interlocking of behavior among members.

Equifinality

According to this principle, it would be an error, or genetic fallacy, to confuse origin with significance in determining outcome (Watzlawick, Beavin, & Jackson, 1967). The same origin may lead to different outcomes, just as the same outcome may result from different origins. The impact of initial conditions or events, such as early childhood trauma, may be outweighed by the mediating influence of the family organization and ongoing interactional patterns. Family processes in response to a traumatic event are crucial for coping and adaptation. Thus, one family may be disabled, while another family rallies in response to similar life challenges.

With multiple influences, there is no one-to-one correlation between an individual's presenting problem or psychiatric diagnosis and a single pattern of family dysfunction. Therefore, it is erroneous to type a family by the diagnosis of a dysfunctional member (Walsh & Anderson, 1988). For example, just as no single pattern has been found to distinguish all families—or all mothers—with a schizophrenic offspring (Walsh & Anderson, 1988), labels such as "schizophrenic families" or "schizophrenogenic mother" carry faulty attributions of parental blame and fail to recognize the diversity of family styles and levels of functioning. Problems may be primarily biologically based, as in schizophrenia, or largely resulting from social or economic pressures. Family distress may result from unsuccessful attempts to cope with an overwhelming situation. Therefore, the interaction of influences involving the individual, the family, and larger social systems must always be carefully assessed.

ASSESSMENT OF FAMILY FUNCTIONING

What Is a Normal Family?

Recent perspectives from constructivism and social constructionism (Hoffman, 1990), have brought greater awareness that clinical views of normality, health, and pathology are socially constructed. Clinicians co-construct the pathologies and patterns they "discover" in clients' lives. Moreover, therapeutic objectives are influenced by both family and therapist beliefs about healthy functioning. Clinicians need to be aware of their own implicit assumptions, values, and biases embedded in cultural norms, professional orientations, and personal experience. With clinical theory, training, and nomenclature so pathology based, I have remarked, only half-jokingly, that a normal family might be defined as one that has not yet been clinically assessed (Walsh, 1993).

The very concept of the family has been undergoing redefinition in recent decades, in the midst of major social changes and economic uncertainties. The idealized 1950s norm of the intact nuclear family, headed by a breadwinner father and supported by a homemaker mother, now accounts for less than 7 percent of households. Changing gender roles and a multiplicity of diverse family arrangements have broadened our view of the normal family (Walsh, 1993). Nearly 70 percent of mothers of school-age children are in the workforce, primarily out of financial necessity, as dual-earner families have become the norm (Piotrkowski & Hughes, 1993), and with the rise of single-parent households (most undersupported by noncustodial parents, Walsh, 1991). Despite a high divorce rate of 50 percent of current marriages, most individuals continue to seek loving, committed relationships. Three-quarters of divorced men and two-thirds of women go on to remarry. Stepfamilies are expected to become the most common family form by the year 2000 (Visher & Visher, 1993). Increasingly, gay and lesbian couples and families are gaining visibility and legal status (Laird, 1993). Adoption by single parents as well as by couples is on the rise (Anderson et al., 1993).

The myth that one family form is essential for family functioning and the healthy development of children nevertheless has continued to stigmatize and pathologize those who do not conform to the standard. In reifying one particular model, prevalent only in the affluent post–World War II era, it is forgotten that historically and cross-culturally, family diversity has always been the norm (Walsh, 1993). A growing body of research on variant family forms is showing that well-functioning families and healthy children, as well as dysfunctional ones, can be found in a variety of family arrangements. What matters more than form are family processes, involving the quality of family relationships.

Research and conceptualization of normal family processes over the past two decades has important clinical utility in providing empirical grounding for assessment to identify components of healthy family functioning that can be fostered in family intervention (Walsh, 1993). It should be kept in mind that any assessment must consider functioning in context: relative to each family's structure, values, resources and constraints, and life challenges. We can nonetheless identify key processes that tend to distinguish well-functioning from dysfunctional families in the domains of organization, communication and problem solving, life cycle development, and belief systems (Walsh, in press).

Organizational Patterns

The functioning of any family must be considered in terms of how effectively it organizes its structure and available resources to master challenges through the life cycle. At the outset, the family constellation needs to be determined, including all members of the current household, the extended family system, (including noncustodial parents and relatives after separation or divorce), and other key relationships that could serve as potential resources.

Family adaptability is one of the core requisites for well-functioning families (Olson, 1993). Stability (homeostasis) and flexibility (morphogenesis) are counterbalancing forces in family systems. To function well, a family needs clear leadership, continuity, and predictable and consistent rules, roles, and patterns of interaction. This stability must be balanced by an ability to adapt to changing circumstances or life cycle developmental demands. Lacking adaptability or a flexible structure, families at the dysfunctional extreme tend to be either overly rigid and autocratic or chaotically disorganized and leaderless.

Family rules, or norms, are delimited and enforced to maintain a steady, stable state in the ongoing interactional system. All family members contribute to the homeostatic balance, as in forming or shifting an alliance, rescuing a family member in distress, and through silence or distance. A child may misbehave when parental conflict escalates beyond tolerable limits, thereby deflecting attention from the marital conflict and easing family tension. In other cases, the devilish behavior of an acting-out adolescent may be offset by the angelic behavior of a sibling, who contributes in this complementary way to the overall family balance. The reciprocal interplay of such behavioral patterns may become obvious only when the devilish child leaves home and the angel starts to misbehave in response to similar interactional cues. An individual treatment that succeeds for a child (e.g., to leave home) may have no impact on the system, which may substitute another sibling into the symptomatic position.

At the same time, *flexibility* is required for a family to adapt to change. A fundamental shift of rules, or "second-order change," may be required, as in transition from one developmental stage to the next to fit new phase-appropriate demands

(Carter & McGoldrick, 1989; Olson, 1993). Crisis events, such as significant losses, may require major adaptational shifts of family rules and roles in order to ensure the continuity of family life. When a husband is laid off from work, a traditional couple's gender-based rules and roles must be altered as his wife takes a job outside the home and he assumes the bulk of homemaking responsibilities.

Cohesion is the other central dimension of family organization. Families must balance needs for closeness and connectedness with a respect for separateness and individual differences. Dysfunctional families tend to be characterized by extremes of enmeshment or disengagement. An *enmeshed* pattern limits or sacrifices individual differences to maintain a sense of unity. Members are expected to think and feel alike; differences, privacy, and separation are regarded as threats to the survival of the family. Identity formation may be blocked, with little sense of self, or a distorted, rigid role assumed, based on parental needs and projections. A *disengaged* pattern of too low cohesion reinforces individual differences, separateness, and distance at the expense of family relatedness, at the extreme fragmenting the family unit and isolating individual members.

The functional balance of connectedness shifts as families move through the life cycle. For instance, the high cohesion that is functional in families with small children shifts at adolescence to support differentiation and autonomy of adolescent members. Cultural norms vary considerably regarding the balance of family and individual priorities. Clinicians must be cautious not to presume that a highly cohesive family style is necessarily dysfunctional. Research on lesbian couples found, for instance, that although they scored at the high extreme on cohesion, the relationships were not pathologically fused but were mutually satisfying and functioned to fortify the relationship in a homophobic social environment (Zaks, Green, & Marrow, 1988).

Boundaries, the rules determining who does what, where, and when, are crucial structural requisites. Boundaries need to be clear and firm yet permeable. *Interpersonal boundaries* define and separate individual members and promote their differentiation and autonomous functioning. *Generational boundaries,* the rules differentiating parent and child roles, rights, and obligations, maintain hierarchical organization in families. They are established by the parental-marital subsystem and in turn reinforce the leadership and authority of the parental unit, as well as the exclusivity of the marital relationship. The complexity of divorced and stepfamily configurations poses challenges in sustaining workable parenting coalitions across households and involving biological and steprelations (Walsh, 1991). Generational boundaries are breached when a parent abdicates leadership, assuming a childlike position, or when a child functions as a parental child, in place of, or taking care of, a parent. While it may be functional and necessary for older children to assist parents with responsibilities, especially in single-parent or large families, it can become dysfunctional if rigid role expectations block age-appropriate developmental needs. In the most destructive breaching of generational boundaries, a parent turns inappropriately to a child to fill a matelike role for a parent, to the extreme of sexual abuse.

Family-community boundaries are also important. Well-functioning families maintain a clear sense of the family unit with permeable boundaries connecting members with the community. Social networks are vital for support and resilience, especially in times of stress. In a closed system, family isolation contributes to dysfunction and interferes with socialization and emancipation of offspring.

The concept of the triangle and the dysfunctional process of triangulation have been central to the clinical application of systems theory (Haley, 1976; Bowen, 1978). This refers to the tendency of two-person systems, especially in couple relationships, to draw in or scapegoat a third person when tension develops between the two. Dysfunctional triangles are often formed by breaching generational boundaries in a parent-child coalition against the other parent, as commonly occurs in high-conflict divorce. A grandparent-child coalition may be formed against a single parent. In other cases, a triangulated child may assume the role of go-between for parents, thereby balancing loyalties and regulating tension and intimacy. In a united front pattern, a couple may avoid conflict to rally together in mutual concern about a symptomatic child. All three members of a triangle are active participants, reinforcing the pattern. In more dysfunctional families, these patterns are more rigid and likely to be replicated in multiple interlocking triangles throughout the family system.

Gender has come to be seen as a fundamental structural axis in families (Goldner, 1988), with a gendered power differential and role division reflecting and reinforced by the larger patriarchal society. An equal sharing of power—in authority, responsibility, and privilege—in the couple-parental unit fosters healthy couple intimacy and optimal family functioning (Beavers & Hampson, 1993; Walsh, 1989).

No structural form is inherently normal or abnormal. Any evaluation should assess the fit of a family's organization with its functional demands in developmental and social contexts (Aponte, 1994). Family resilience requires clear yet flexible leadership, mutual support, and teamwork in order to meet life challenges effectively.

Communication Processes

Communication is vital in facilitating the organization and functioning of a family system and each member's development. Every communication has two functions: a content (report) aspect, conveying factual information, opinions, or feelings, and a relationship (command) aspect, which defines the nature of the relationship (Ruesch & Bateson, 1951). The statement "Eat your vegetables" conveys an order with expectation of compliance and implies a hierarchical differentiation of status or authority in the relationship, as between parent and child. All verbal and nonverbal behavior, including silence (or spitting out the vegetables), conveys interpersonal messages (e.g., "I won't obey you!"). In an ongoing relationship, communication regularly left unclear or unresolved risks dysfunctional consequences.

In a family evaluation, clinicians assess family members' ability to communicate openly about both pragmatic (instrumental) and emotional issues. Clarity and congruence of communication in verbal and nonverbal messages are important for healthy functioning (Epstein et al., 1993), although cultures vary considerably in norms regarding directness and degree of expression (McGoldrick, Pearce, & Giordano, 1996). Specific patterns to note include toxic or sensitive subjects where communication is blocked, gender constraints (e.g., males are good at instrumental problem solving but constricted at emotional expression), and specific relationships where communication is conflictual.

Functional families tend to establish a climate of mutual trust that encourages the open expression of a wide range of feelings and empathic responses, with tolerance for differences. Dysfunctional families, in contrast, tend to perpetuate a climate of mistrust, with repeated criticism, blaming, and scapegoating. Highly reactive emotional expression can fuel destructive cycles of conflict and despair, escalating to violence and family dissolution.

Problem solving is perhaps the most crucial family process. Well-functioning families are characterized not by the absence of problems but by the ability for joint problem solving and conflict resolution. Families can have difficulties solving instrumental problems, such as juggling job and child care responsibilities, and more affective aspects of problems, such as nurturance and comforting a sick child. Families can falter at various steps in the problem-solving process (Epstein et al., 1993): identifying the problem, communicating with appropriate people about it, developing a set of possible solutions, deciding on one alternative, carrying it out, monitoring to ensure it is carried out, and evaluating the effectiveness of the problem-solving process. A systemic assessment attends to the process of collaborative problem solving: how decisions are made can be as crucial as the decision itself. Negotiation and compromise are important and can be hindered by rivalry or power struggles. Mutual accommodation, respect for each member's needs and contribution, and reciprocity over time are crucial for long-term relationship harmony and balance (Walsh, 1989).

Multigenerational Patterns and the Family Cycle

Family functioning is assessed in the context of the multigenerational system moving forward over time (Carter & McGoldrick, 1989). A genogram and family time line (McGoldrick & Gerson, 1985), used to schematize relationship information and track system patterns, guide the formulation of treatment objectives and focal points for intervention. It is useful to note linkages between the timing of symptoms and critical events that have disrupted or threaten the family (Walsh, 1983). Healthy families are better able to balance intergenerational continuity and change, and maintain links between their past, present, and future direction (Beavers & Hampson, 1993).

In a systemic model of human development, the individual life cycle is seen to coevolve with the family and culture over time. Each can be represented schematically along two time dimensions—one historical and intergenerational (the vertical axis) and the other developmental and unfolding into the future (the horizontal axis) (Carter & McGoldrick, 1989). The vertical axis includes the family history and patterns of relation and functioning that are transmitted down the generations. It encompasses family attitudes and beliefs, legacies and myths, taboos, rituals and traditions, and loaded issues, all of which influence future expectations, hopes, and dreams, as well as catastrophic fears. The horizontal axis describes the stresses impinging on a family as it moves forward through time, coping with stressful events and transitions posed by individual and family development. These include both the predictable, normative stresses and unpredictable, disruptive circumstances, such as untimely death, birth of a child with disabilities, job loss, or social and political unrest. Families may lose perspective on time when a problem arises, as members become overwhelmed by an immediate crisis or catastrophic fears. They may confound immediate situations with past events, become stuck in the past, or be cut off emotionally from painful memories and contacts.

Relationships evolve through stages as the family unit and each member moves through the life cycle. Boundaries shift, psychological distance among members changes, and roles within and between subsystems are redefined. Family life cycle models identify stages of family development, each with particular developmental tasks and transitional stresses (Carter & McGoldrick, 1989). Divorce, single parenting, and remarriage pose additional life cycle challenges for many families. The increasing diversity of family forms, lifestyle options, and timing of nodal events makes it imperative that no single model or life trajectory be deemed as the normal or essential course for proper development (Walsh, 1993).

Frequently symptoms and dysfunction coincide with transitions from one stage to another or in the context of stressful events. Carter and McGoldrick suggest that a family's coping ability depends on the convergence of developmental and multigenerational strains. Although all change is to some degree inherently stressful, strain on the family system increases exponentially when current stressors intersect with vulnerable multigenerational issues. Because the legacies of past experiences and myths surrounding them can extend over many generations, family life cycle transitions are especially likely to reactivate past unresolved conflicts and losses, particularly when similar developmental challenges are confronted. For instance, a man whose mother died in childbirth may avoid intimacy leading to marital conflict when his wife expresses a desire to become pregnant. Serious unresolved issues for one or both parents predict high risk for a normative transition. However, vulnerability in one partner can be offset by a spouse's successful family-of-origin experience or resolution of past issues, in the context of a trusting couples relationship.

Many families function well until they reach a critical point in the life cycle at which complications arose a generation earlier (Walsh, 1983). A mother may become anxiously preoccupied that her teenage daughter will become pregnant when the daughter approaches the same age that the mother became pregnant out of wedlock. A father may begin to have serious conflict with his teenage son despite a good prior relationship when that son reaches the age at which he had lost his own father. Therapy might make such covert linkages overt and then help clients make a difference in their current relationships.

Family Belief Systems

Family therapists have become increasingly interested in the constructions or meaning systems that family members develop and share. A family's approach and responses to a stressful event are strongly influenced by their belief system, with both immediate and long-term ramifications. Reiss (1981) has described the family paradigm as an enduring structure of shared beliefs, convictions, and assumptions about the social world that are shaped by pivotal family experiences and, in turn, influence basic problem-solving styles and meanings attached to current and future life challenges. These beliefs contribute to the family's perception of events, the meanings ascribed, and expectations about their likely consequences.

A family's beliefs about their competence to face and master life challenges are particularly important for family resilience (Walsh, in press). In this regard, personal and culturally based beliefs about what is normal are important to explore with clients (Walsh, 1993). The myth that a healthy family is problem free leads families to feel deficient for having a problem when actually problems are inevitable in all families. The myth that for healthy development one must marry and conform to the idealized intact nuclear family model with traditional gender roles contributes to a sense of deficiency for unmarried individuals, working mothers, and remarried, adoptive, and gay or lesbian and other family arrangements.

Relationship rules, both explicit and implicit, serve as norms, providing a set of expectations about roles, actions, and consequences that guide family life and limit members' behaviors. In a marital quid pro quo, an implicit bargain is formed as to how partners define themselves and their expectations of each other in the relationship. A culturally influenced gender-based power differential operates in overt or covert expectations that a wife subordinate her needs in deference to the priorities of her husband (Walsh, 1989).

Family belief systems are derived from a number of sources. Culture, class, race, ethnicity, and religion contribute greatly to family beliefs and practices (McGoldrick, Giordano, & Pearce, 1996). Optimally functioning families tend to be bolstered by a transcendent moral or spiritual value orientation, a sense of cultural roots, and belief in success through shared efforts (Beavers & Hampson, 1993). However, racism and classism and other forms of social and institutionalized discrimination disempower poor minority families and other marginalized groups, and they generate a sense of shame and stigma. Aponte (1994) writes that it is not only "bread," or financial security, but also spirit that has become impoverished in families in minority communities, where hope for a better future has been lost.

Within families, stories or legends become encoded into family scripts that provide a conscious or covert blueprint, guiding behavior when a family is facing a dilemma or crisis (Byng-Hall, 1988). Such legends and scripts lay the foundation for family myths, secrets, and taboos. Stories and myths can be empowering or debilitating, depending on their underlying themes and responsiveness to changing circumstances.

Family identity and beliefs are stored and conveyed through family rituals, including celebrations of holidays, rites of passage (e.g. bar/bat mitzvah), family traditions (e.g., annual gatherings) and routine family interactions (e.g., dinner and bedtime routines). Rituals provide stabilization and continuity over time and also facilitate transitions, as in the inclusion of children in a remarriage ceremony. Family therapists often use rituals in therapeutic intervention to foster change or healing (Imber-Black et al., 1988). Rituals are very useful in cases where a loss or life cycle transition has not been adequately marked, such as a suicide or stillbirth. Clinicians should routinely inquire about family beliefs and be especially mindful where there is a difference in background between partners or between the family and therapist.

MAJOR APPROACHES TO FAMILY THERAPY

Over the past three decades, a number of approaches to family therapy have been developed. They are all grounded in a systems orientation but differ somewhat in focus on various aspects of family functioning and in views about the process of change. This overview will focus on the major foundational models of family therapy that have been most influential in this evolving practice field. The models can be usefully categorized as problem-solving approaches, which are brief, pragmatic interventions, focused on immediate situations and their resolution, and intergenerational approaches, which are more exploratory, growth oriented, and historically focused.

Problem-Solving Approaches

Structural Model

Structural family therapy, as developed by Salvador Minuchin (1974) and colleagues at the Philadelphia Child Guidance Center, has emphasized the importance of family organization for the functioning of the family unit and the well-being of its members. The model focuses on the patterning of transactions in which symptoms are embedded. Problems are viewed as an indication of imbalance in the family's organization, particularly a malfunctioning hierarchical arrangement with unclear parent and child subsystem boundaries. Most commonly, symptoms are a sign of a maladaptive reaction to changing environmental or developmental requirements, such as an inappropriate accommodation to a life cycle transition. Child-focused problems are seen as symptoms of system problems and are thought to detour conflict between parents or, particularly in single-parent families, between parent and grandparent.

The structural model is based on the view of the family as a social system, operating within specific social contexts. Three components are emphasized. First, the family structure is that of an open sociocultural system in transformation. Second, the family undergoes development over time, progressing through successive stages requiring reorganization. Third, the family adapts to changed circumstances in ways that allow it to maintain continuity and to further the psychosocial growth of its members.

The therapeutic approach centers on strengthening the structural foundation for family functioning (the organizational domain): in particular, a generationally appropriate hierarchy, with parents maintaining a strong leadership unit and with clear boundaries that are neither too diffuse (as in enmeshment) nor too rigid (as in disengagement). The aim of therapy is to repair or modify dysfunctional organizational patterns so that the family can better perform basic functional tasks and cope with life stresses. It is expected that presenting problems, a symptom of family distress, will be resolved as this reorganization is accomplished.

Structural family therapy is short term and involves three processes: joining, enactment, and restructuring:

1. The therapist joins the family system in a position of leadership to form the therapeutic system. Joining operations are actions aimed at relating to and blending with the family to gain entry into the system in order to gain influence to bring about change.
2. The therapist assesses the family experientially by getting the family to enact its presenting problem interactionally in the interview. The therapist confronts and pushes members to test out their interactional flexibility and limits.
3. Based on the interactional diagnosis and a structural mapping of the immediate family field, the therapist employs tasks and directives designed to restructure the family around its handling of the presenting problem. The therapist is active in shifting triangular patterns in sessions by blocking dysfunctional coalitions while promoting more functional alliances. Particular attention is directed to strengthening the parental subsystem and reinforcing appropriate generational boundaries.

Structural family therapy is action oriented, based on the conviction that change in behavior occurs independent of insight on the part of members. Live consultation is used to facilitate the training and implementation of direct, active, therapeutic intervention in sessions. Therapists may be telephoned or called out of sessions for consultation by the supervisor or team of trainees or colleagues who are observing the interview through a one-way mirror.

The structural approach grew out of attempts to develop a therapeutic approach first with delinquent youths and then with poor, inner-city multiproblem families; later it was applied successfully to a broad array of problems ranging from psychosomatic disorders to anorexia nervosa. It is most often used in cases of child-focused symptoms (Minuchin & Fishman, 1981). Structural problems involving the extended family may also be addressed, such as struggles between a single-parent mother and grandmother over the proper care and loyalty of a child. Here the treatment focus would not be on exploring the origins of conflict but rather on restructuring the family hierarchical arrangement so that symptoms are no longer reinforced.

Strategic and Systemic Approaches

In the early development of the field of family therapy, among the most innovative and influential approaches were the strategic and systemic models of the MRI (Mental Research Institute) group in Palo Alto, the problem-solving approach of Haley and Madanes, and the systemic model of the Milan team. More recently, solution-focused and constructionist-narrative approaches have been advanced. These systems-oriented problem-solving approaches focus on the immediate social situation of the identified patient. Assuming that all problems have multiple origins, a presenting problem is viewed as both a symptom and a response to current dysfunction in family interaction. It is considered important to understand how a family has attempted to resolve its problems, since a misguided attempted solution may exacerbate the problem or itself become a serious problem. Strategic therapists contend that most families do what they do because they believe it is the right or best way to approach a problem or because it is the only tack they know to take. The therapeutic task is to interrupt ways of handling the problem that do not work, that is, patterns that are dysfunctional. It requires learning a family's language and beliefs in order to see the problem through various members' eyes, taking into account the values and expectations that determine their approach to handling the problem and their inability to change (Selvini Palazzoli, Boscolo, Cecchin, & Prata, 1980).

Proponents of these approaches view normal families as highly flexible, using a large repertoire of behaviors to cope with problems. In contrast, a pathological family demonstrates a rigidity and a paucity of alternatives. Beyond this generalization, they believe that each family must define what is normal or healthy for itself. The responsibility of the therapist is limited to initiating change that will get a family "unstuck" from unworkable interactional patterns that maintain symptoms.

Strategic therapists have generally been more concerned with developing a theory of therapeutic change than with developing a model of the family. Haley (1976) has made a careful distinction between the two, believing that clinicians have been hampered by theory that attempts to explain human experience and pathology but does not lead to problem solution. He therefore selectively focused on key family variables involving power and organization that he considered relevant to therapeutic change.

The goal of therapy is limited to solving the particular problem that is presented. The symptom is regarded as a communicative act that is part of a repetitious sequence of behaviors among family members, serving a function in the interactional network. Therapy focuses on problem resolution by altering the feedback loop that maintains the symptomatic behavior. The therapist's task is to formulate the problem in solvable, behavioral terms and to design an intervention plan to change the dysfunctional family pattern.

The early strategic approaches, while sharing with experiential and behavioral approaches a grounding in communications theory, were distinct in assuming that change depends more on indirect means of influence than on insight or simply improved communications. The therapist's stance was highly intellectual and remote from personal involvement, yet at the same time active and pragmatic, planning and carrying out a strategy to achieve specific behaviorally defined objectives. Techniques of relabeling, reframing, directives, and indirect interventions were developed and employed to this end.

Relabeling and reframing refer to the strategic redefinition of a problem or a situation in order to cast it in a new light. It can be particularly useful in shifting a family's rigid view or stereotypic response, in altering an unproductive blaming or scapegoating process, or in overcoming resistance to change. For example, a problem presented as "inside" an individual, as a character trait, is redefined behaviorally in interactional context. A label of "hysteric" or a diagnosis of "depression" might be defined as a wife's futile attempt to get attention from her unresponsive husband. In a vicious cycle, the more she complains, the more he withdraws; the more he withdraws, the more upset she becomes. In the reformulation of a problem or set, new solutions can become apparent.

Directives are carefully designed behavioral tasks assigned to families to be carried out either in a session or between sessions. They have several purposes. They are used to gather direct information about the ways family members interact and how they will respond to and resist change. They are also useful in intensifying the therapist's relationship and influence with the family by involvement in action outside of sessions. Well-formulated and well-timed directives are considered a highly effective way of bringing about a structural modification as well as a behavioral change.

Indirect techniques are a type of directive that might seem to be in opposition to objectives but actually serve to move the family toward them. Relabeling and reframing are commonly used to redefine what has been viewed as resistance as a well-intentioned attempt to be protective of other family members. In paradoxical instructions, a therapist might prescribe the symptom, or direct clients to do the opposite of their intended goal, along with a rationale for doing so. One woman who was obsessed with finding a meaningful relationship was offered the recommendation that she should begin with a meaningless relationship in order to enjoy it without the worry of a serious commitment. While such injunctions can be quite effective, their use requires careful planning, timing, and skill and is contraindicated in potentially violent or life-threatening situations.

There are some distinctions among the various strategic and systemic approaches. The MRI approach centers on the issue of how families attempt to handle or resolve normal problems in living (Weakland, Fisch, Watzlawick, & Bodin, 1974). Based on the assumption that all families confront problems, the therapy focuses on how families maintain a problem by precisely the means they are using to handle the problem. The attempted solution thus becomes the problem requiring therapeutic change.

The strategic problem-solving approach developed by Haley and Madanes combines an interactional view with basic structural principles (Haley, 1976; Madanes, 1981). Like Minuchin, Haley considers family functioning in the context of its current ecosystem and passage through the life cycle, with individual symptoms and family crises arising when families are unable to adjust to transitions and become stuck, particularly at launching in young adulthood (Haley, 1973).

The Milan approach has emphasized three principles for conducting family interviews and obtaining useful information for change (Selvini Palazzoli, Boscolo, Cecchin, & Prata, 1980). First, working hypotheses are formed about the connection of symptoms with family relationships, to test out and confirm or reject. Second is the use of circular questioning, to elicit feedback from various family members about relationship patterns, such as who is more connected or concerned about an issue. Paradoxical instruction in prescriptions linking the symptom with the system, once seen as the most powerful aspect of the intervention approach, has come to be viewed as less important than the conversational process generated by circular questioning. The third principle of neutrality concerns the therapist's avoidance of judgment, criticism, or moral alignment with any part of the system. In response to criticism that a therapist can never be neutral, the emphasis has shifted to the importance of a therapeutic stance of respectful curiosity (Boscolo, Cecchin, Hoffman, & Penn, 1987; Cecchin, 1987). A widely used intervention is positive connotation, which involves reframing the symptom's adaptive function for the family and the good intentions of members, thereby joining the family in order to facilitate change.

Solution-Focused and Narrative Approaches

More recent developments of solution-focused (deShazer, 1988; O'Hanlon & Weiner-Davis, 1989) and narrative approaches (Anderson & Goolishian, 1988; White & Epston, 1990; Freedman & Combs, 1996) are based in constructivist and social constructionist views of reality (Hoffman, 1990). These approaches refocus therapeutic attention from problems and the patterns that maintain them to solutions and the processes that enable them. With this shift, less concern is given to the nature of problems or how they have developed, and more is directed to future possibilities (Penn, 1985). Therapists search for exceptions—solutions that have worked in the past in other situations and might work now and in the future. Like the MRI model, people are thought to be constrained by their narrow, pessimistic views of problems, which limit the range of alternatives for resolution. However, these newer approaches oppose the view that symptoms necessarily serve ulterior functions for the family, and they assume that clients really do want to change. The therapeutic relationship eschews the hierarchical power-based position of earlier structural-strategic approaches. Instead, it is built on trust and respect of clients and oriented toward recognizing and amplifying the positive strengths and resources that clients bring and the potentials they may have lost sight of. Therapeutic rituals are used to facilitate both continuity and change (Imber-Black, Roberts, & Whiting, 1988).

Solution-focused approaches avoid complex formulations when simple assumptions will lead more quickly to change. It is believed that complicated problems do not necessarily require complicated solutions. A risk here lies in too narrow a focus that fails to address the broader web of influences in the social context of a problem situation.

In narrative approaches, the therapeutic conversation and process of "restorying" a problematic experience are emphasized. White's technique of externalizing problems serves as a means through language to reframe problem situations toward more enabling and empowering constructions that encourage problem resolution. An external force is defined as responsible for wreaking havoc on the lives of clients. The therapist then aligns with the symptomatic child (or with a couple or family), as a therapeutic team who together will gain control over and defeat this negative force. The goal is to leave clients feeling successful and victorious, shifting a vicious cycle to a virtuous cycle.

Behavioral Approaches

Behavioral approaches to family therapy have developed chiefly from behavior modification and social learning traditions in clinical psychology, and they have increasingly incorporated a cognitive component (see Chapter 2 in this book). They emphasize the importance of family rules and communication processes, as well as a functional approach to outcome. Therapy attends to the interactional behaviors and conditions under which social behavior is learned, influenced, and changed. Cognitive-behavioral approaches have been used most successfully with marital conflict (Baucom, Epstein, & Rankin, 1995; Christensen, Jacobson, & Babcock, 1995), sexual difficulties (Heiman, Epps, & Ellis, 1995), and families of conduct-disordered adolescents (Barton & Alexander, 1981; Patterson et al., 1975).

Families are viewed as critical learning contexts, which are simultaneously created and responded to by members. According to social exchange principles, the exchange of benefits outweighs costs in well-functioning families. Since family relationships involve behavioral exchange over a wide range of possibilities, there are many opportunities for rewarding exchanges likely to maintain the relationship. The importance of positive reward for desired behavior is stressed. In well-functioning families, not only is maladaptive behavior not reinforced, but, more important, adaptive behavior is rewarded through attention, acknowledgment, and approval.

Relationship failure is explained by deficient reward exchanges, as when exchanges shift from positive rewards to coercive control (Patterson et al., 1975). Symptoms or maladaptive behavior, regardless of origin, are seen as reinforced or rewarded by the family. Relationships may also become distressed due to communication deficits when there is a discrepancy between the intended communication and the impact of the message on the receiver.

Treatment problems and goals are specified in concrete and observable behavioral terms, as in the strategic models described above. However, the emphasis of behavioral learning approaches is on guiding family members in a straightforward way to learn more effective modes of dealing with one another by changing the interpersonal consequences of behavior or contingencies of reinforcement. The therapist teaches the couple or family more effective and benign ways of influencing behavior by reinforcing it in a positive manner (Jacobson, 1981). Family members learn to give each other approval and acknowledgment for desired behavior instead of rewarding and reinforcing maladaptive behavior with attention and concern.

The therapist analyzes communication processes, including both the informational content and the relational components (relationship rules implicit in how messages are conveyed). Building skills in negotiation and problem-solving processes is a central focus of interventions. Reciprocity and equitability are especially encouraged in the marital relationship. Adaptability, the capability of using diverse behaviors in different situations, is also stressed as an aim of therapy (Weiss, 1978).

In sum, the basic learning principle underlying the behavioral approaches is that social reinforcement is made contingent on adaptive behavior rather than maladaptive or symptomatic behavior. Imitative behavior, or modeling, is also an important part of the process. The therapist, within a positive therapeutic alliance, serves as both a social reinforcer and model, defining his or her role as an educator.

Psychoeducational Approaches

The development of the psychoeducational model has been the most promising advance in family intervention with schizophrenia and other serious and chronic mental illnesses. It has also been increasingly utilized with a range of chronic physical disorders and with life cycle challenges, such as divorce and remarriage, or stressful transitions, such as job loss. These approaches draw on elements of behavioral and structural family models but eschew the more indirect interventions of strategic approaches. They provide family education to foster coping with a serious disorder or stressful life challenge and offer concrete guidelines and support for crisis management, problem solving, and stress reduction.

Psychoeducational family interventions have been adapted to a number of formats, including one-time or periodic family consultations, brief time-limited groups, or ongoing family or multifamily groups. Interventions are often timed with stressful transitions. Brief psychoeducational "modules" timed for critical phases of an illness or life challenge encourage families to accept and digest manageable portions of a long-term coping process. Examples include postdiagnosis or hospital discharge; the initial crisis, chronic, terminal, or bereavement phases of a chronic or life-threatening illness (Rolland, 1994); or early separation and divorce, single parenting, and planned remarriage. Such a cost-effective, preventive intervention is especially useful with families at high risk of maladaptation or relapse of a mental or physical illness.

With major mental illness, in contrast to more traditional psychiatric treatment approaches that have presumed families to be pathogenic influences, the psychoeducational approach engages the family as valued and essential collaborators in the treatment process. The rationale for family intervention is explicitly based on the importance of support to the family as caregiver, practical information, and problem-solving assistance through the predictably stressful periods that can be anticipated in the future course of a chronic illness or life transition. This approach does much to correct the blame-laden causal attributions and unhelpful treatment experience of many families of the mentally ill (Walsh, in press).

Goldstein and his colleagues (Goldstein, 1981) conducted the first controlled studies that demonstrated the combined effectiveness of family therapy and drug maintenance over either intervention alone in helping schizophrenic patients maintain functioning in the community in the high-risk months following hospitalization. The family therapy model was brief (six weeks), problem focused, and concrete. The aims of the program were to identify specific stress events of current concern to the family and then to help them develop coping strategies to prevent the recurrence of such events or to mitigate their destructive impact. Interactional conflicts and stresses viewed as potential precipitants of a psychotic episode were emphasized.

The psychoeducational model developed by Anderson and her colleagues (Anderson, Reiss, & Hogarty, 1986) has impressively demonstrated effectiveness in the treatment of chronic schizophrenia and reduction of family distress. In a controlled study, family intervention, combined with drug maintenance and social skills training, produced the best results, dramatically reducing relapse rates and improving functioning.

The intervention model is based on the assumption that environmental sources of stress interact negatively with a core biological vulnerability to produce disturbed cognitions and behaviors. Families are viewed as caregiving resources for the long-term management of schizophrenia, assisted by concrete support and information. A highly structured family-oriented program was designed to avoid treatment dropout, decrease relapse rates, sustain functioning in the community, and decrease family stress. Basic program goals are twofold: (1) decreased vulnerability to environmental stimulation through maintenance chemtherapy and (2) increased stability and predictability of the family environment by lowering family anxiety, increasing their knowledge about the illness and their confidence about their ability to manage it. As these aims are achieved, reciprocal pressures between the patient and family are reduced.

The intervention program is operationalized in five phases. Phase I, connecting with the family, establishes an alliance with families by attending, in a noncritical manner, to family needs and experiences and to specific areas of stress in their lives. Phase II, a day-long survival skills workshop, provides a group of families with current empirically based knowledge about schizophrenia and its treatment, emphasizing the importance of medication compliance in avoiding relapse. Concrete principles and techniques for managing the illness are outlined, with information about what families can realistically expect. Families are encouraged to set clear limits on disruptive behavior and to shift attention and time to their own and other family members' needs and pursuits. Phase III involves ongoing supportive sessions, every two to three weeks for a year or more, to sustain functional gains, gradually resume responsibilities, avert crises, and reinforce family boundaries. Phases IV and V offer families two options once basic contract goals have been reached with stabilization at what appears to be an optimal level of functioning: either periodic supportive maintenance sessions or more intensive family therapy to resolve long-standing conflicts. With chronic illness, some ongoing supportive contact, however minimal, is recommended rather than complete termination, since periodic exacerbations of symptoms are likely.

The psychoeducational model developed by Falloon (Falloon, Boyd, & McGill, 1984) is a cost-effective home-based family intervention approach, emphasizing behavioral problem-solving techniques. Like the other psychoeducational approaches, there is an emphasis on lowering expectations to the level of solving daily problems one at a time, measuring success in small increments, and maintaining the morale of the treatment team, the most important members of which are the family.

Intergenerational Growth-Oriented Approaches

Psychodynamically Oriented Approaches

Several pioneers in the field of family therapy developed growth-oriented intergenerational approaches to family therapy that bridge psychodynamic, object relations, and family systems theories. Whereas early psychoanalytic theory was focused primarily on maternal influences in early childhood as determining normal or pathological individual development, family systems therapists shifted attention to the ongoing dynamic processes of the family as a social unit across the generations and over the course of the life cycle.

Psychodynamically oriented approaches conceptualize family interaction in terms of object relations, related internalizations, and introjection and projection processes (Meissner, 1978). The parents, individually and in the marital and parental relationships they construct, are regarded as crucial determinants of healthy or pathological family functioning and the processes of separation and individuation necessary for the healthy development of offspring. It is assumed that the capacity to function as a spouse and as a parent is largely influenced by each individual's family of origin experiences. The relative success or failure in accomplishing developmental tasks is thought to be determined largely by residues of internalized objects and the organization of introjects contributing to identity integration. Spouses are successful in forming a productive shared marital experience to the extent that their relationship is organized in terms of a successfully differentiated and individuated sense of self rather than being contaminated by pathogenic introjects (Scharff & Scharff, 1986).

The interlocking of projection and introjection processes forms a shared projection process based on complementarity of needs. Complementary need patterns are thought to influence mate choice as well as marital and parent-child relationship patterns (Boszormenyi-Nagy & Spark, 1973). Reciprocal relationship bargains involve implicit agreements among family members to relate on the basis of unfulfilled needs. Dysfunctional families are blocked by a greater degree of unconscious unresolved conflict or loss that interferes with realistic appraisal of and response to other family members (Paul & Paul, 1975). Accordingly, Framo (1970) has viewed symptoms as resulting primarily from unconscious attempts by spouses or parents to reenact, externalize, or master through current relationships the intrapsychic conflicts originating in the family of origin. Current life situations are interpreted in the light of the parents' inner object world and role models.

The symptomatic member may serve as a scapegoat for unresolved family conflicts (Ackerman, 1958). In some cases, the loss of a significant relationship in the family of origin may disrupt the entire family system, with emotional upheaval and unresolved grief expressed in symptoms by a family member (Paul & Paul, 1975). In other cases, symptoms may express an irrational role assignment or projective transference distortion, which is reinforced by family myths and ritualized into the family's structural pattern. For example, Stierlin (1974) described the ways in which adolescent separation problems can result from centripetal and centrifugal family patterns (similar to concepts of enmeshment and disengagement), with intense family pressures either to bind or to expel members.

Assessment and treatment involve exploration of the complex multigenerational family patterns over time and their connection to resulting disturbances in current functioning and relationships. Extended family members may be included in family sessions, or individual members may be encouraged to work on changing relationships with the family of origin outside of sessions (Framo, 1980). Either way, the aim of therapy is for family members to confront and deal with one another directly in order to work through unresolved conflicts. Negative introjects from the past are tested out in reality and altered or brought up to date in direct contact with their sources in the family of origin rather than by analysis of the transference patterns with the therapist (Framo, 1970). Where unresolved loss affects current functioning and blocks relationships, resolution of the lost relationship becomes the central task (Paul & Grosser, 1991). The role of the therapist is that of a catalyst, actively encouraging the family's awareness of intense conflictual emotions, interpreting their sources and consequences, as well as identifying shared defense mechanisms. The therapist takes charge in preparing, guiding, and processing such highly charged work. In direct confrontation, the therapist makes covert family processes overt and accessible to resolution through insight and action for emotional working through. The conjoint process builds empathy and mutuality, strengthening the marital and family unit.

The contextual approach of Boszormenyi-Nagy (1987) emphasizes the importance of covert but powerful family-of-origin loyalty patterns. The therapeutic aim is toward the reconstruction and reunion of relationships in the resolution of grievances. Therapy focuses on the ethical dimension of family relationships, examining the multigenerational legacies of parental accountability and filial loyalty that guide members over the course of the life cycle. Families are thought to be strengthened by moves toward trustworthiness, based on consideration of members' welfare interests for survival, growth, and relatedness. Trustworthiness functions to increase autonomy in problem solving. In well-functioning families, autonomy is encouraged by the family legacy, and members are not bound by any real or imagined "ledger" of unpaid debts. Autonomy is attained through efforts toward relational equitability. While imbalances of fairness are seen as inevitable, flexibility and reciprocity over time are crucial requisites. Ideally, the family life cycle is characterized by open negotiation of transitions and changing loyalty commitments, with awareness of legacy expectations. Understanding and resolution of loyalty and legacy issues require active concern for the extended family, yet intergenerational relationships must neither prevent other contacts nor create pressure for escape.

Bowen Model

In Bowen's (1978) theory of the family emotional system and method of therapy, functioning is thought to be impaired by poorly differentiated relationship patterns characterized by high anxiety and emotional reactivity. This anxiety commonly results in triangulation or cutoffs of highly charged relationships. Stresses on the family system, especially by death, can decrease differentiation and heighten reactivity. Underfunctioning, or symptoms, may be linked with and reinforced by overfunctioning in other parts of the system in a compensatory cycle. Improved functioning is believed to result when emotional reactivity no longer blocks intellectual processes. It is assumed that current marital or family problems or symptoms in a child will be resolved with the increased differentiation of the spouses or parents from their extended families.

The goal of therapy is to assist adult individuals to modify troubled relationships with their families of origin, achieving a higher level of differentiation and reduced anxiety in direct contact. This process differs from other intergenerational approaches that promote direct confrontation and sharing of feelings among family members in conjoint therapy sessions. Through a coaching process (Carter & [McGoldrick] Orfanidis, 1976; Herz, 1991), a client may be seen individually and coached to change himself or herself in relation to other family members in contacts between sessions. In couples therapy, each partner is encouraged to work separately on his or her own extended family relationships that are blocking or intruding into their relationship.

The therapist assumes a role as consultant or coach, guiding each individual through carefully planned stages of intervention. The therapist takes a somewhat cognitive stance, toning down emotional reactivity, discouraging transference reactions, and guarding against his or her own triangulation in the family emotional system.

Therapy begins with a family evaluation process that surveys the entire nuclear and extended family field. A genogram (McGoldrick & Gerson, 1985) is sketched to diagram the network of relationships, important facts and nodal events (e.g. births, deaths, illnesses, ethnicity and religion), and complex relationship information (e.g. alliances, conflicts, triangles, and cutoffs). A time line is constructed to note patterns in the timing, sequence, concurrence, or replication of symptoms and critical events. The aim is to obtain a working knowledge of the entire family system before undertaking work with any individual or part of the family. A client may be asked to contact extended family members to clarify obscured or missing information and to gain new perspectives on the family.

The process of change typically requires a commitment to long-term work in stages (Carter & [McGoldrick] Orfanidis, 1976). First, in engagement, the client is helped to gain perspective of an overview of self-with-others. It is crucial not to set out to change others but rather to change oneself in relation to them. The genogram is used to plan steps of intervention. Next, in the reentry phase, the client begins the process of differentiation by redeveloping personal relationships with key family members, repairing cutoffs, detriangling from conflicts, and changing the part played in emotionally charged vicious cycles. The therapist encourages the client to take an "I position," a clear statement asserting one's own thoughts and feelings without attacking, defending, or withdrawal. Humor is used to detoxify emotional situations. Techniques of detriangling and reversals expressing the unacknowledged other side of an issue are two of many means employed to break up rigid communication patterns and open up a closed system. Follow-through of the work is essential, given the anxiety generated and the need to handle self-correcting reactions by others in the system that can undermine change. Sessions may start at weekly or biweekly intervals and be spaced out as work proceeds. The approach requires strong motivation and persistence to be effective.

Experiential Approaches

Experiential approaches to family therapy were developed by two leading pioneers in the field: Virginia Satir (1964, 1972), who blended a communication approach with a humanistic frame of reference, and Carl Whitaker (Napier & Whitaker, 1978), who practiced a highly idiosyncratic style of intervention. Experiential approaches are highly intuitive and a relatively nontheoretical form of therapy. Current behavior and feelings are seen as the natural consequence of one's life experience. Regardless of awareness or intent, old pains are propagated and made stronger by current interaction around them. To explain and change behavior, several important aspects of family process and their mutual influence are taken into account. These ingredients—individual self-worth, communication, system operations, and rules—are all believed to be changeable and correctable (Satir, 1972).

The goal of these growth-oriented approaches is a fuller awareness and appreciation of oneself in relation to others through providing an intense, affective experience in the open communication of feelings and differences. Focused on the immediate experience, important information is elicited in current behavior with others, emphasizing the wholistic nature of human interaction in relational systems. The therapist takes a phenomenological approach to assessment and treatment of the individual in the family context. The approach is characterized by exploration, experimentation, and encouragement of spontaneity of members' responses to one another. Experiential exercises, such as family sculpting and role play, are used to facilitate this process. The therapist's role is facilitative, following and reflecting the family interaction process and stimulating genuine and nondefensive relating through the clinician's own experience with the family.

THE PRACTICE OF FAMILY THERAPY

Table 6.1 provides a summary of the major approaches to family therapy. For each model, the view of symptoms or pathology, the goals of therapy, and strategies and techniques for processes of change are delineated. Despite differences in particular strategies and techniques employed in various approaches, all focus on direct assessment and change of significant relationships. Currently most clinicians with a family systems orientation combine or integrate elements from the various approaches and incorporate multidimensional views of family functioning (Breunlin, Schwartz, & Karrer, 1992). All family therapy training approaches value live observation of sessions by a team of consultants, including supervisors and other trainees. Observation through a one-way mirror, and the reflecting team approach, offer a metaperspective of the therapeutic system and the opportunity for new and varied feedback and recommendations between the therapist and family (Papp, 1980; Andersen, 1987).

The field of family therapy, with its rich diversity, continues to flourish and find broad application. Family systems approaches are being used effectively with problems ranging from child or adolescent behavior disorders, and individual, couple, or family relationship problems, to more recent application with illness, disability, and loss (McDaniel, Hepworth, & Dougherty, 1992; Rolland, 1994; Walsh & McGoldrick, 1991). It is useful in combination with other therapeutic approaches, including psychotropic interventions, for substance abuse (Stanton & Todd, 1982; Steinglass, 1987) and serious mental disorders (Anderson et al., 1986; McFarlane, 1983). The Internal Family Systems Model, developed by Schwartz (1995), bridges interest in the person and the system, attending to the system of relationships within the individual, with particular application to clients with eating disorders and adult survivors of childhood trauma. Multisystemic approaches have been developed to work effectively with sexual abuse (Trepper & Barrett, 1989) and with a range of children and families at risk (Combrinck-Graham, 1996). (For reviews of application and efficacy see Lebow & Gurman, 1995, and the special edition of the *Journal of Marital and Family Therapy*, edited by Pinsof & Wynne, 1995.)

The often asked question "When is family therapy indicated?" requires reframing from a systems perspective. When problems are conceptualized systemically, an individual's problems cannot be understood or changed apart from the context in which they occur and the functions they may serve. Thus, the question of indications becomes one of appropriate context for change: "What is the symptom-maintaining, solution-promoting context of a problem situation? How can impasses to change most effectively be dealt with? Who is needed to collaborate in the change process?"

CLINICAL EXAMPLE 1

Mrs. Ramirez came to a child guidance clinic requesting help with her daughter's school problems. The therapist learned that problems had been noted by the school for some time but had worsened in recent weeks. A critical question involves temporal context: "Why now?" It was important to inquire about other recent stress events in the family system. Seven weeks earlier, the eldest son, age eighteen, had been killed, caught in the cross-fire of a gang shooting. The bullet had also shattered the family unit. Mr. Ramirez turned to alcohol to drown his pain, isolating himself from the family. The sixteen-year-old son carried the family rage out into the streets, seeking revenge for the senseless killing. Two other sons showed no reaction, keeping to themselves so as not to burden their parents further. Mrs. Ramirez, alone in her grief, turned her attention onto her daughter's preexisting school problems, which took her mind off her unbearable loss. Family therapy provided the context for shared griefwork, where members could be helped to express a whole range of intense emotions and to respond empathically and comfort one another. Family resilience was fostered by repairing the family fragmentation, promoting a more cohesive network for mutual support and healing. On follow-up, the daughter was doing well in school and the sharing of the loss experience had brought family members closer and enabled them to deal more effectively with other problems in their lives.

It is important for clinicians to appreciate the value of a systemic approach in general practice as distinct from the use of family, couples, or multifamily group therapy modalities. All forms of intervention, from biomedical to psychoanalytic, are enriched by a systems lens, regardless of how many people are in the room, as in the following individual therapy case.

CLINICAL EXAMPLE 2

Dave entered therapy because he had become despondent by his unsuccessful quest to find and marry the "perfect woman," resorting to ever more desperate blind dates and newspaper ads as he found a fatal flaw in each prospect. He expressed a need for help

TABLE 6.1

Major Approaches to Family Therapy

Model of Family Therapy	*View of Symptoms or Pathology*	*Goals of Therapy*	*Process of Change Strategies and Techniques*
Problem-solving approaches			
Structural			
Minuchin Philadelphia Child Guidance Center	Symptoms result from current family structural imbalance: • Malfunctioning hierarchical arrangement and boundaries • Maladaptive reaction to changing requirements (developmental, environmental)	Reorganize family structure: • Shift members' relative positions • Create clear, flexible subsystems and boundaries • Promote more adaptive coping	Therapist uses power and action to shift interaction patterns: • Joining family • Enactment of problem • Map structure, plan stages of restructuring • Task assignments and paradoxical intervention
Strategic/systemic			
Palo Alto group Haley & Madanes Milan approach Ackerman team Solution focused Narrative	Multiple origins of problems; symptoms maintained by family's • unsuccessful problem-solving attempts • problem-saturated narratives	Solve presenting problem; specific behaviorally defined objectives Search for exceptions and unique outcomes Envision new possibilities; generate new stories	Pragmatic, focused, future oriented: • Change symptom-maintaining sequence to new outcome • Substitute new behavior patterns to interrupt feedback cycles • Relabeling, reframing, circular questions • Externalize problems
Behavioral			
Patterson Alexander Jacobson	Maladaptive, symptomatic behavior reinforced by family attention and reward	Concrete, observable behavioral goals, social reinforcement (acknowledgment, approval) of adaptive behavior	Therapist as social reinforcer, model, educator Change contingencies of reinforcement; interpersonal consequences of behavior Guide family to reward desired behavior

Psychoeducational Anderson Goldstein Falloon	Biologically based disorders; stress/diathesis Normative and nonnormative adaptational challenges (e.g., remarriage; chronic illness)	Family management of chronic illness; Reduction of stress and stigma Mastery of family adaptational changes	Information Management guidelines/adaptational tasks Social support Respectful collaboration
Intergenerational/ Growth-oriented approaches			
Psychodynamic Ackerman Boszormenyi-Nagy Framo Paul Stierlin	Symptoms due to shared family projection process stemming from unresolved past conflicts or losses in family of origin	Resolution of family-of-origin conflict and losses: Family projection processes Relationship reconstruction and reunion Individual and family growth	Insight-oriented, linking past and present dynamics Assist in resolution of conflicts, losses Facilitate healthier modes of relating
Bowen approach Bowen Georgetown Group Carter McGoldrick	Functioning impaired by relationships with family of origin: • Poor differentiation • Anxiety (reactivity) • Triangulation • Cutoffs	Differentiation Cognitive functioning Emotional reactivity Modification of relationships in family system: • Detriangulation • Repair cutoffs	Coach individual action outside sessions: • Survey multigenerational field (use of genogram) • Plan-focused interventions to change self directly with family Therapist takes cognitive stance, minimizing transference reaction
Experiential Satir Whitaker	Symptoms are nonverbal messages in reaction to current communication dysfunction in system	Direct, clear communication Individual and family growth	Change here-and-now interaction in conjoint session: • Share feelings about relationships —Self-disclosure —Direct communication —Experiential techniques: sculpture • Uses therapist experience with family to model, catalyze process

with his own fears of losing his freedom and autonomy if he ever did marry a woman like his mother. In Dave's prior individual therapy, he had come to view his mother's "domineering, controlling personality" as the source of his problems with intimacy and commitment. In systems-based therapy, it was important for Dave to gain a view of the interactional context of his mother's problematic behavior. Over the years, his father had repeatedly complained that she robbed him of his zest for life by always stopping him from doing what he had loved to do, from active sports to travel adventures. To expand his view of the situation and better understand how this interactional pattern came about and was reinforced, Dave was coached to have conversations with his older sister about their childhood family experience. He learned that after his father had suffered a heart attack (when Dave was five), he had refused to comply with medical advice to avoid risky behavior, instead keeping up a macho stance. His denial and failure to take responsibility for his own health triggered his wife's anxiety and reinforced her overresponsible position: as he impulsively took dangerous risks, she became hypervigilant and continually monitored him to stop him from life-threatening behavior. Her nagging and control functioned (for the whole family) to keep him healthy and alive, allowing him to keep up his bravado.

This new perspective shifted Dave's belief system. From viewing the problem locus as within his mother—and generalized to "controlling women"—he came to see the problem as an interactional cycle involving both parents. His mother's intentions and actions, when more fully understood in context, lost their negative charge and could be seen as crucial efforts that saved his father's life and his pride. He also came to see his father in a less idealized but more human light. Viewed as an active (albeit covert) participant in the shared dilemma, paradoxically, he was seen both less a cardboard macho character and less a passive, controlled victim. Dave gained new compassion for his father, in context, by awareness of constraints to acknowledging his own vulnerability by social expectations to fit cultural images of masculinity. A systemic perspective freed Dave to differentiate his own position, with confidence that he could hold his own in a relationship and actively participate in shaping its course. He was also helped to develop a closer, less anxious relationship with his mother (now widowed), whom he had kept at distance. Offered the option of bringing his mother in for a few focused conjoint sessions or initiating contacts between sessions on his own, he chose the latter, with the visits prepared for and processed in session. The changes that occurred fostered his greater sense of ease in a budding intimate relationship, which eventually led to his own satisfying marriage.

As a basic worldview, a systems perspective is distinguished by attention to individuals and problems in context; interactions between individuals, families, and larger systems; circular versus linear processes; and patterns that connect over time. For any presenting problem the context can be punctuated in a more broadly inclusive or focused way. A systemic assessment includes inquiry about the family and social context of a problem, interactional processes surrounding it, timing in the family life cycle, and multigenerational and cultural influences that may be relevant. The inclusion of other family members yields more information, through different perspectives and direct observation of transactions.

In systemic intervention models, therapeutic transference plays a diminished role, because the therapist can observe patterns and promote change directly among key family members. Transference reactions do occur in family therapy but are redirected for expression and change back into the natural relationship network. Also, systemic models have reconceptualized transference from dyadic to triangular or whole systems terms and examined how these complex relationship patterns are replicated in current systems in the patient's life. Countertransference issues are stimulated as well in family therapy. In fact, the emotional power of a family and the likelihood that some member or relationship in the family may feel too close to home for a therapist requires awareness of the interface issues between clinicians' own family experiences and the families they are working with.

A clinician's ethical stance needs to be carefully considered in every situation. We need to be careful not to impose our values on clients with a differing cultural orientation or family style. Yet we cannot remain silent when harmful abuses are taking place. Just as we cannot not communicate, it is not possible to be neutral: silence and inaction reinforce existing social structures and interactions. We must be particularly mindful of family and social patterns that maintain gender bias, racism, heterosexism, and other forms of discrimination. Family therapists have become increasingly attentive to issues of social justice in theory and practice, and view their responsibility as not limited to intrafamilial processes in the therapy room, but also in addressing larger system patterns that affect the well-being of children and families.

An integrative strength-promoting approach to family therapy involves a crucial shift in emphasis from family damage to family challenge. A family resilience model for research and practice (Walsh, 1996 & in press) seeks to understand how families can survive and rebound through stressful crisis or persistent adversity and to foster key processes for resilience with clients in distress. As family therapy has evolved from a focus on family deficits to family strengths and resources, the therapeutic relationship has become more collaborative and empowering of clients' potentials. Successful interventions rest as much on tapping into resources of the family as on change techniques by the therapist (Karpel, 1986). In the wake of social and economic upheaval, the need to strengthen families has never been more urgent. While no single model of family health fits all, family therapists share a deep conviction in the potential for family resilience and repair.

REFERENCES

Ackerman, N. (1958). *The psychodynamics of family life.* New York: Basic Books.

Ahrons, C., & Rogers, R. H. (1989). *Divorced families: Meeting the challenges of divorce and remarriage.* New York: J. Wiley.

Andersen, T. (1987). The reflecting team: Dialogue and metadialogue in clinical work. *Family Process, 26,* 415–428.

Anderson, C. M. (1982). The community connection: Impact of social networks on family and individual functioning. In F. Walsh (Ed.), *Normal family processes* (1st ed.). New York: Guilford.

Anderson, C. M., Reiss, D., & Hogarty, G. (1986). *Schizophrenia and the family.* New York: Guilford.

Anderson, H., & Goolishian, H. (1988). Human systems as linguistic systems: Preliminary and evolving ideas about the implications for clinical theory. *Family Process, 27*: 371–393.

Anderson, S., Piantanida, M., & Anderson, C. (1993). Normal processes in adoptive families. In F. Walsh (Ed.), *Normal family processes* (2nd ed.). New York: Guilford.

Aponte, H. (1994). *Bread and spirit: Therapy with the new poor.* New York: Norton.

Barton, C., & Alexander, J. (1981). Functional family therapy. In A. Gurman & D. Kniskern, *Handbook of family therapy.* New York: Brunner/Mazel.

Bateson, G. (1979). *Mind and nature: A necessary unity.* New York: Dutton.

Baucom, D., Epstein, N., & Rankin, L. (1995). Cognitive aspects of cognitive-behavioral marital therapy. In N. Jacobson & A. Gurman (Eds.), *Clinical handbook of couple therapy.* New York: Guilford.

Beavers, W. R., & Hampson, R. (1993). Measuring family competence: The Beavers Systems Model. In F. Walsh (Ed.), *Normal family processes* (2nd ed.). New York: Guilford.

Bertalanffy, L. (1968). *General system theory and psychiatry: Foundation, developments, applications.* New York: Braziller.

Boscolo, L., Cecchin, G., Hoffman, L., & Penn, P. (1987). *Milan systemic family therapy: Conversations in theory and practice.* New York: Basic Books.

Boszormenyi-Nagy, I. (1987). *Foundations of contextual family therapy.* New York: Brunner/Mazel.

Boszormenyi-Nagy, I., and Spark, G. (1973). *Invisible loyalties.* New York: Harper & Row.

Bowen, M. (1978). *Family therapy in clinical practice.* New York: Jason Aronson.

Boyd-Franklin, N. (1989). *Black families in therapy: A multi-systems approach.* New York: Guilford.

Breunlin, D., Schwartz, R., & Karrer, B. (1992). *Metaframeworks: Transcending the models of family therapy.* San Francisco: Jossey-Bass.

Byng-Hall, J. (1988). Family scripts and loss. In F. Walsh & M. McGoldrick (Eds.), *Living beyond loss: Death in the family.* New York: Norton.

Carter, B., & McGoldrick, M. (1989). *The changing family life cycle: Framework for family therapy* (2nd ed.). Boston: Allyn & Bacon.

Carter, E., and (McGoldrick) Orfanidis, M. (1976). Family therapy with one person and the family therapist's own family. In P. Guerin (Ed.), *Family therapy: Theory and practice.* New York: Gardner Press.

Cecchin, G. (1987). Hypothesizing, circularity, and neutrality revisited: An invitation to curiosity. *Family Process, 26,* 405–414.

Christensen, A., Jacobson, N., & Babcock, J. (1995). Integrative behavioral couple therapy. In N. Jacobson & A. Gurman (Eds.), *Clinical handbook of couple therapy.* New York: Guilford.

Combrinck-Graham, L. (1996). *Children in families at risk.* New York: Guilford.

de Shazer, S. (1988). *Clues: Investigating solutions in brief therapy.* New York: Norton.

Epstein, N., Bishop, D., Ryan, C., Miller, I., & Keitnor, G. (1993). The McMaster model: View of healthy family functioning. In F. Walsh (Ed.), *Normal family processes* (2nd. ed.). New York: Guilford.

Falicov, C. (1996). Thinking culturally in family therapy. *Family Process.*

Falloon, I., Boyd, J., & McGill, C. (1984). *Family care of schizophrenia: A problem solving approach to the treatment of mental illness.* New York: Guilford.

Framo, J. (1970). Symptoms from a family transactional viewpoint. In N. Ackerman (Ed.), *Family therapy in transition.* Boston: Little, Brown.

Framo, J. (1980). Family of origin as a therapeutic resource for adults in marital and family therapy: You can and should go home again. *Family Process, 15*:193–210.

Freedman, J., & Combs, G. (1996). *Narrative therapy.* New York: Norton.

Goldner, V. (1988). Generation and gender: Normative and covert hierarchies. *Family Process, 27,* 17–21.

Goldstein, M. (Ed.). (1981). *New developments in interventions with families of schizophrenics.* San Francisco: Jossey-Bass.

Haley, J. (1973). *Uncommon therapy: The psychiatric techniques of Milton Erikson.* New York: Norton.

Haley, J. (1976). *Problem-solving therapy.* San Francisco: Jossey-Bass.

Hatfield, A., & Lefley, H. (1990). *Families of the mentally ill: Coping and adaptation.* New York: Guilford.

Heiman, J., Epps, P., & Ellis, B. (1995). Treating sexual desire disorders in couples. In N. Jacobson & A. Gurman (Eds.), *Clinical handbook of couple therapy.* New York: Guilford.

Herz, F. (1991). *The family tapestry.* New York: Norton.

Hetherington, M., Law, T., & O'Connor, T. (1993). Divorce: Challenges, changes, and new chances. In F. Walsh (Ed.), *Normal family processes* (2nd ed.). New York: Guilford.

Hoffman, L. (1981). *Foundations of family therapy.* New York: Basic Books.

Hoffman, L. (1990). Constructing realities: An art of lenses. *Family Process, 29,* 1–13.

Imber-Black, E., Roberts, J., & Whiting, R. (Eds.). (1988). *Rituals in families and family therapy.* New York: Norton.

Jackson, D. (1965). Family rules: Marital quid pro quo. *Archives of General Psychiatry, 12,* 589–594.

Jacobson, N. (1981). Behavioral marital therapy. In A. Gurman & D. Kniskern (Eds.), *Handbook of family therapy.* New York: Brunner/Mazel.

Karpel, M. (1986). *Family resources.* New York: Guilford.

Laird, J. (1993). Lesbian and gay families. In F. Walsh (Ed.), *Normal family processes* (2nd ed.). New York: Guilford.

Lebow, J., & Gurman, A. (1995). Research assessing couple and family therapy. *Annual Review of Psychology, 46,* 27–57.

Madanes, C. (1981). *Strategic family therapy.* San Francisco: Jossey-Bass.

McDaniel, S., Hepworth, J., & Doherty, H. (1992). *Medical family therapy: Psychosocial treatment of families with health problems.* New York: Basic Books.

McFarlane, W. (Ed.). (1983). *Family therapy in schizophrenia.* New York: Guilford.

McGoldrick, M., Anderson, C., & Walsh, F. (1989). *Women in families: Framework for family therapy.* New York: Norton.

McGoldrick, M., and Gerson, R. (1985). *Genograms in family assessment.* New York: Norton.

McGoldrick, M., Giordano, J. & Pearce, J., (Eds.). (1996). *Ethnicity and family therapy* (2nd Ed.). New York: Guilford.

Meissner, W. W. (1978). The conceptualization of marital and family dynamics from a psychoanalytic perspective. In T. Paolino & B. McCrady (Eds.), *Marriage and marital therapy.* New York: Brunner/Mazel.

Minuchin, S. (1974). *Families and family therapy.* Cambridge, MA: Harvard University Press.

Minuchin, S., and Fishman, C. (1981). *Family therapy techniques.* Cambridge, MA: Harvard University Press.

Napier, A. Y., & Whitaker, C. (1978). *The family crucible.* New York: Harper & Row.

O'Hanlon, W., & Weiner-Davis, M. (1989). *In search of solutions in brief therapy.* New York: Norton.

Olson, D. (1993). Circumplex model of marital and family systems: Assessing family functioning. In F. Walsh (Ed.), *Normal family processes* (2nd ed.). New York: Guilford.

Papp, P. (1980). The Greek chorus and other techniques of paradoxical therapy. *Family Process, 19,* 45–57.

Patterson, G. R., et al. (1975). *A social learning approach to family intervention.* Eugene, OR: Castalia Publishers.

Paul, N., & Grosser, P. (1991) Operational mourning and its role in conjoint family therapy. In F. Walsh & M. McGoldrick (Eds.), *Living beyond loss.* New York: Norton.

Paul, N., and Paul, B. (1975). *A marital puzzle: Transgenerational analysis in marriage.* New York: Norton.

Penn, P. (1985). Feed forward: Future questions, future maps. *Family Process, 24,* 299–310.

Pinsof, W., & Wynne, L. (Eds.). (1995). Special edition, The Effectiveness of marital and family therapy. *Journal of Marital and Family Therapy, 21* (4).

Piotrkowski, C. S., & Hughes, D. (1993). Dual earner families in context: Managing family and work systems. In F. Walsh (Ed.) *Normal family processes* (2nd ed.). New York: Guilford.

Reiss, D. (1981). *The family's construction of reality.* Cambridge, MA: Harvard University Press.

Rolland, J. S. (1994). *Families, illness and disabilities: An integrative treatment model.* New York: Basic Books.

Ruesch, J., and Bateson, G. (1951). *Communication: The social matrix of psychiatry.* New York: Norton.

Satir, V. (1964). *Conjoint family therapy.* Palo Alto, CA: Science and Behavior Books.

Satir, V. (1972). *Peoplemaking.* Palo Alto, CA: Science and Behavior Books.

Scharff, D. & Scharff, J. (1986). *Object relations family therapy.* New York: Jason Aronson.

Schwartz, R. (1995). *The internal family systems model.* New York: Guilford.

Selvini Palazzoli, M., Boscolo, L., Cecchin, G., & Prata, J. (1980). Hypothesizing—circularity—neutrality: Three guidelines for the conductor of the session. *Family Process, 19,* 3–12.

Skolnick, A. (1991). *Embattled paradise: The American family in an age of uncertainty.* New York: Basic.

Slipp, S. (1988). *The technique and practice of object relations family therapy.* New York: Jason Aronson.

Speck, R., and Attneave, C. (1973). *Family networks.* New York: Pantheon.

Stanton, M., and Todd, T. (1982). *The family therapy of drug abuse and addiction.* New York: Guilford.

Steinglass, P. (1987). *The alcoholic family.* New York: Basic Books.

Stierlin, H. (1974). *Separating parents and adolescents.* New York: Jason Aronson.

Trepper, T., & Barrett, M. J. (1989). *Systemic treatment of incest: A therapeutic handbook.* New York: Brunner/Mazel.

Visher, E. B. & Visher, J. S. (1993). Remarriage families and stepparenting. In F. Walsh (Ed.), *Normal family processes* (2nd ed.). New York: Guilford.

Walsh, F. (1981). Family therapy: A systemic orientation to treatment. In A. Rosenblatt & D. Waldfogel (Eds.), *Handbook of clinical social work.* San Francisco: Jossey-Bass.

Walsh, F. (1983). The timing of symptoms and critical events in the family life cycle. In H. Liddle (Ed.), *The family life cycle: Implications for clinicians.* Rockville, MD: Aspen.

Walsh, F. (1989). Reconsidering gender in the marital "quid pro quo." In M. McGoldrick, C. Anderson, & F. Walsh (Eds.), *Women in families: Framework for family therapy.* New York: Norton.

Walsh, F. (1991). Promoting healthy functioning in divorced and remarried families. In A. Gurman & D. Kniskern (Eds.), *Handbook of family therapy* (2nd ed.). New York: Brunner/Mazel.

Walsh, F. (1993). Conceptualizations of normal family processes." In F. Walsh (Ed.), *Normal family processes.* New York: Guilford.

Walsh, F. (Ed.). (1993). *Normal family processes* (2nd ed.). New York: Guilford.

Walsh, F. (1996) The concept of family resilience. *Family Process, 35* (3), 261–281.

Walsh, F. (in press). *Strengthening family resilience: Crisis and challenge.* New York: Guilford.

Walsh, F., & Anderson, C. (1988). *Chronic disorders and the family.* New York: Haworth.

Walsh, F., and McGoldrick, M. (Eds.). (1991). *Living beyond loss: Death in the family.* New York: Norton.

Walsh, F., & Scheinkman, M. (1993). The family context of adolescence. In P. Tolan & B. J. Cohler (Eds.), *Handbook of clinical research and practice with adolescents.* New York: Wiley.

Walsh, F., & Scheinkman, M. (1989). (Fe)male: The hidden gender dimension in models of family therapy. In M. McGoldrick, C. Anderson, & F. Walsh (Eds.), *Women in families.* New York: Norton.

Watzlawick, P., Beavin, J., and Jackson, D. (1967). *Pragmatics of human communication.* New York: Norton.

Weakland, J., Fisch, R., Watzlawick, P., & Bodin, A. (1974). Brief therapy: Focused problem resolution. *Family Process, 13,* 141–168.

Weiss, R. L. (1978). The conceptualization of marriage from a behavioral perspective. In T. Paolino & B. McCrady (Eds.), *Marriage and marital therapy.* New York: Brunner/Mazel.

White, M., & Epston, D. (1990). *Narrative means to therapeutic ends.* New York: Norton.

Wynne, L., McDaniel, S., & Weber, T. (1986). *Systems consultation: A new perspective for family therapy.* New York: Guilford.

Zacks, E., Green, R. J., & Marrow, J. (1988). Comparing lesbian and heterosexual couples on the circumplex model: An initial investigation. *Family Process, 27,* 471–484.

7

Cognitive-Behavioral Therapy with Adults

Donald K. Granvold

Cognitivism emerged during the late 1950s when behaviorism was strongly challenging psychoanalytic theory. So profound has been the cognitive movement that it has been described as revolutionary in its impact on both the conceptualization of human functioning and human change interventions (Baars, 1986; Dember, 1974; Mahoney, 1977). Professionals with backgrounds in psychoanalytic theory and many who were trained in behaviorism have actively participated in this movement, and the influence of both schools of thought can be discerned in various cognitive-behavioral methods. This movement has had a discernible influence on social work theory and practice (Berlin, 1980, 1985; Berlin & Marsh, 1993; Brower & Nurius, 1993; Franklin, 1995; Granvold, 1988, 1989, 1994a, 1996; Nurius, 1991; Nurius & Berlin, 1994; Nurius & Majerus, 1988; Richey, 1994; Saleebey, 1992; Schinke, Blythe, & Gilchrist, 1981; Schinke & Singer, 1994; Shorkey, 1994). To date, more than twenty distinct varieties of cognitive therapy can be identified (see Table 7.1) (Mahoney & Lyddon, 1988). The focus of all cognitive methods is on the private, inner experience of the individual. These phenomena are ascribed a central role in the etiology, maintenance, and treatment of various emotional disorders, maladaptive behaviors, and psychosocial conditions.

While cognition is recognized as being highly viable for intervention, most cognitivists believe in reciprocal determinism (Bandura, 1978)—the view that cognitions, behavior, personal factors (emotions, motivation, physiology, and physical factors), and social-environmental factors are interactive. Consistent with this view, early in the cognitivist movement, behavioral factors were specified for incorporation in the

TABLE 7.1
Current Cognitive Therapies

Personal construct therapy (Kelly, 1955)
Logotherapy (Frankl, 1959)
Rational-emotive therapy (Ellis, 1962)
Cognitive therapy (Beck, 1970, 1976)
Multimodal therapy (Lazarus, 1971, 1976)
Problem-solving therapies (D'Zurilla, 1988; D'Zurilla & Goldfried, 1971, Spivack & Shure, 1974)
Rational behavior training (Goodman & Maultsby, 1974; Maultsby, 1984)
Rational stage-directed therapy (Tosi & Eshbaugh, 1980)
Cognitive behavior modification (Meichenbaum, 1977)
Integrated cognitive behavior therapy (Wessler, 1984)
Motor-evolutionary psychotherapy (Burrell, 1987)
Constructivist cognitive therapy (Guidano, 1984, 1987; Guidano & Liotti, 1983, 1985)
Cognitive developmental therapy (Mahoney, 1980, 1985, 1991)
Lay epistemic therapy (Kruglanski & Jaffe, 1983)
Neocognitive psychotherapy (Suarez, 1985)
Piagetian therapy (Leva, 1984; Rosen, 1985; Weiner, 1975)
Cognitive-experiential therapy (Weiner, 1985)
Developmental therapy (Ivey, 1986)
Humanistic cognitive therapy (Werner, 1984)
Characterological transformation (Johnson, 1985)

Source: "Recent Developments in Cognitive Approaches to Counseling and Psychotherapy" by M. J. Mahoney & W. J. Lyddon, *The Counseling Psychologist,* Vol. 16, No. 2, April 1988. Reprinted by permission of Sage Publications.

design of assessment and treatment methodologies. Cognitive intervention thus evolved to cognitive-behavioral intervention, a more accurate descriptor for the interventions practiced by most cognitivists.

The two original cognitive interventions, Albert Ellis's rational-emotive therapy (RET) (Ellis, 1962) and Beck's cognitive therapy (CT) (Beck, 1976), focused specifically on the examination of existing beliefs on the basis of rationality and validity. While both included behavioral assignments, the primary objective was cognitive restructuring, and, in essence, the behavioral assignments were to support the cognitive change or to evoke emotion for the purpose of desensitization. The cognitive-behavioral interventions developed by behaviorally trained theorists took a markedly difference approach. The intention with these methods was the development of strategies to teach specific cognitive skills rather than to restructure existing cognition (Hollon & Beck, 1994). Self-instruction training and stress inoculation training (Meichenbaum, 1977) and problem-solving training (D'Zurilla & Goldfried, 1971) represent these latter behaviorally oriented cognitive-behavioral approaches. Thus, although both approaches incorporate cognitive and behavioral methods, they go about it differently. As the methods have evolved, the distinctions between them have become increasingly fuzzy. Furthermore, many more cognitive-behavioral approaches have been developed, often designed to treat specific disorders (Barlow & Cerny, 1988; Bourne, 1990; Linehan, 1993; Marlatt & Gordon, 1985; Rehm, 1977). Hollon and Beck (1994) significantly state that "although it is clear that differences in process and procedure do exist [among all cognitive-behavioral approaches], it is still not known whether these variations have implications for efficacy" (p. 430).

EFFECTIVENESS OF COGNITIVE-BEHAVIORAL INTERVENTIONS

Cognitive-behaviorists have emerged as a driving force in the multidisciplinary field of psychotherapy. Cognitive-behavioral approaches are among the most frequently used intervention procedures. This distinction is well deserved given the established efficacy of the methods. In this age of empirical practice bias, social workers and other mental health professionals have sought "proven" procedures, those on which they can rely to produce both rapidly effective and resilient (long-lasting and relapse resistant) change. A mass of findings supports the efficacy of cognitive and cognitive-behavioral methods in the treatment of a broad range of emotional disorders and behavioral problems (Beck, 1995; Brower & Nurius, 1993; Craighead, Craighead, Kazdin, & Mahoney, 1994; Dattilio & Freeman, 1994; Freeman & Dattilio, 1992; Freeman, Pretzer, Fleming, & Simon, 1990; Freeman, Simon, Beutler, & Arkowitz, 1989; Granvold, 1994a; Hollon & Beck, 1986, 1994; Kuehlwein & Rosen, 1993; Scott, Williams, & Beck, 1989; Vallis, Howes, & Miller, 1991).[1]

---

[1]Treatment efficacy has been demonstrated in the treatment of *affective disorders* (Beutler et al., 1987; Blackburn, 1988; Bowers, 1990; Dobson, 1989; Hollon & Najavits, 1989; Michelson & Ascher, 1987; Perris, 1989), *anxiety and panic disorders* (Barlow, 1988; Barlow, Craske, Cerney, & Klosko, 1989; Beck & Emery, 1985; Beck, Sokol, Clark, Berchick, & Wright, 1992; Butler, Fennell, Robson, & Gelder, 1991; Clark, Salkovskis, Hackmann, Middleton, Anastasiades, & Gelder, 1994; Dattilio & Kendall, 1994; Michelson & Ascher, 1987), *social phobia* (Becker, 1992; Emmelkamp, Mersch, Vissia, & van der Helm, 1985; Gelernter et al., 1991; Heimberg, 1990; Mattick, Peters, & Clarke, 1989), *personality disorders* (Beck, Freeman, and associates, 1990; Freeman & Leaf, 1989; Layden, Newman, Freeman, & Morse, 1993; Linehan, Armstrong, Suarez, Allmon, & Heard, 1991; Linehan, 1993; Rothstein & Vallis, 1991; Turner, Becker, & DeLoach, 1994), *posttraumatic stress disorder* (Dancu & Foa, 1992; Foa, Rothbaum, Riggs, & Murdock, 1991; Meichenbaum, 1994; Parrott & Howes, 1991), *schizophrenia* (Chadwick & Lowe, 1990; Kingdon & Turkington, 1991, 1994; Perris, 1989; Perris, Ingelson, & Johnson, 1993; Perris & Skagerlind, 1994), *child sexual abuse* (Deblinger, 1992; Duehn, 1994; Laws, 1989; Sgroi, 1989), *impulse control disorders* (Hazeleus & Deffenbacher, 1986; Lochman, Burch, Curry, & Lampron, 1984; Novaco, 1975, 1977a, 1977b), *chronic pain* (Corey, 1988; Eimer, 1989; Keefe et al., 1990; Kerns, Turk, Holzman, & Rudy, 1986; Linton, Bradley, Jensen, Spangfort, & Sundell, 1989; Miller, 1991; Salkovskis, 1989; Sanders et al., 1989; Turk, Meichenbaum, & Genest, 1983), *eating disorders* (Agras et al., 1992; Craighead & Agras; 1991; Cooper & Fairburn, 1984; Edgette & Prout, 1989; Fairburn, 1981; Fairburn et al., 1991; Garner, 1992; Garner et al., 1993; Mitchell et al., 1990; Smith, Markus, & Kaye, 1992; Telch, Agras, Rossiter, Wilfley, & Kenardy, 1990; Wilson & Fairburn, 1993), *medical disorders* (Dahlquist, Gil, Armstrong, Ginsberg, & Jones, 1985; Getka & Glass, 1992; Jay, Elliott, Katz, & Siegel, 1987; Kaplan, Atkins, & Lenhard, 1982; Kendall et al., 1979; Meichenbaum, 1993; Perry, Fishman, Jacobsberg, Young, & Frances, 1991; Telch & Telch, 1986), *substance abuse* (Beck, Wright, & Newman, 1992; Beck, Wright, Newman, & Liese, 1993; Chaney, O'Leary, & Marlatt, 1978; Sanchez-Craig, Annis, Bornet, & MacDonald, 1984; Schinke & Singer, 1994; Shorkey, 1994; Woody et al., 1983), *couple problems* (Baucom & Epstein, 1990; Baucom, Sayers, & Scher, 1990; Dattilio & Padesky, 1990; Ellis, Sichel, Yeager, DiMattia, & DiGiuseppe, 1989; Granvold & Jordon, 1994), and *family problems* (Bedrosian & Bozicas, 1994; Epstein, Schlesinger, & Dryden, 1988; Huber & Baruth, 1989; Munson, 1994).

The broad base of support for cognitive-behavioral treatment methods extends to applications across diverse populations. Clients from various socioeconomic backgrounds and educational levels have been effectively treated. Procedures have been designed and modified for application to all ages, from preschoolers to the elderly. Treatment formats have included individual, group, couple, and family interventions. Although clinicians have enjoyed remarkable success in applying cognitive-behavioral procedures to an array of populations and problems, applications to at-risk populations with which social workers so often come into contact are ripe for further development.

THEORETICAL DEVELOPMENTS IN COGNITIVE PSYCHOTHERAPIES AND PRACTICE IMPLICATIONS

Mahoney (1993) notes an evolution within the cognitive therapy revolution resulting in a philosophical bifurcation among cognitivists. He goes on to state that constructivism is the source of "the first major conceptual debate in the field" (Mahoney, 1993, p. 189). Constructive metatheory or constructivism has emerged in contrast to traditional or orthodox cognitive therapy. Constructivism represents a philosophic departure from the ontological realist stance of most early cognitivists and carries with it an array of practice implications. (Ontology is the study of the nature of reality and existence.)

Constructivist metatheory was spawned in an intellectual environment significantly shaped by the influence of postmodernism (Neimeyer, 1995). The postmodern perspective rejects the view of an objective reality in favor of the intersubjectivity of all human experience. The human condition is complex and its meaning relative. Science is considered to be essentially interpretive rather than computational (Neimeyer & Mahoney, 1995). The cardinal assertion of constructivism is that human knowing is proactive. People are active participants in the creation of their own reality. As noted above, constructivism stands in contrast to realism ontologically. According to realism, there is a singular, stable, external reality that can be known. "Truth" objectively exists, and cognitions can be "checked" against this reality. Such a correspondence theory of truth (validity) is rejected by constructivists in favor of a conceptualized personal reality, unique unto the individual, which can be appraised on the basis of viability. Here, viability is a function of consequences for the individual adopting the conceptualization and the "overall coherence with the larger system of personally or socially held beliefs into which it is incorporated" (R. Neimeyer, 1993a). Epistemologically, constructivism is based on a motor theory of the mind in which "the mind appears as an active, constructive system, capable of producing not only its output but also to a large extent the input it receives, including sensations that lie at the base of its own constructions" (Guidano, 1988, p. 309). Knowledge is an evolutionary result and an interactive process. This view is in contrast to the sensory theories, which hold that information flows inward through the senses to the mind, where it is maintained, a view Popper (1972) referred to as "the bucket theory of the mind."

On the basis of these philosophic differences, constructivists approach clinical practice in a markedly different way from traditional cognitivists:

1. Individual life span development is explored. Particular attention is paid to attachment processes across the life cycle.
2. Individuals are viewed from a systems perspective in which a client's experience produces a series of perturbations to the equilibrium of the self-system. These perturbations are viewed as inherent to the process of change and development. Thus, rather than framing client concerns as problems, a process orientation is adopted. The goal of therapy based on a problem view is corrective—to modify, minimize, or eliminate the problem. The process orientation goal is to explore clients' personal meanings and guide the transformation of these meanings into more highly viable meaning constructs (Lyddon, 1990). A problem is conceptualized as a discrepancy between a client's current capacity and the developmental challenges being experienced.
3. Emotional expressions are considered by constructivists to be integral to the personal meaning and personal development processes of the individual. Rather than exercising efforts to control, diminish, or terminate emotional expressiveness (considered to be counterproductive), clients are encouraged to explore, experience, and express their emotions.
4. While both constructivist and traditional cognitive therapists promote a collaborative relationship with the client, seeking an understanding of the idiosyncratic meanings the client brings to therapy, constructive therapists tend to be far less active-directive in the disputation of distorted, "unrealistic," or "irrational" beliefs and opt rather to invite the client to construct an alternative view or they challenge the viability of views held. Constructivists tend to be more metaphoric, approximate, exploratory, and intuitive (R. Neimeyer, 1993b). See the following sources for a more comprehensive and in-depth exposure to constructivist psychotherapies: Granvold, 1996; Kuehlwein & Rosen, 1993; Mahoney, 1991, 1995, in press; G. Neimeyer, 1993; R. Neimeyer, 1993b; Neimeyer & Mahoney, 1995.

The constructivist movement is strong within the cognitivist ranks. Most cognitivists are philosophical constructivists, and although constructive psychotherapy approaches may be evident in their clinical procedures, many continue to practice predominantly traditional cognitive-behavioral treatment. The remainder of this chapter is devoted to the explication of traditional cognitive-behavioral treatment procedures. It should be emphasized, however, that the boundaries between constructivism and traditional cognitivism are fuzzy. The content that follows may be representative of the actual practice behaviors of both persuasions at various points.

COMMON FEATURES OF COGNITIVE-BEHAVIORAL TREATMENT

Although there is great variability in the way that cognitive-behavioral treatment is practiced, there are distinguishing features that set cognitive-behavioral intervention apart from other approaches. The following features are generally agreed on by cognitive-behaviorists and are reflected in the ways clinical practice is performed.

Idiosyncratic Subjective Experience

The unique private meanings the client holds in relation to the problem and its context are the focus of the collaborative treatment experience. The therapist seeks to understand (1) the specific meanings of life events and corresponding emotional responses, (2) the perceptual patterns, information-processing patterns, beliefs, and belief structures that are operative in organizing reality, and (3) the causal connections the client makes between stimuli in his or her world and responses either experienced by oneself or observed in others (attributional thinking). Attention to these phenomena validates the client and provides the shared awareness and meaning base from which the client and the therapist collaboratively proceed. Self-report data are relied on heavily in establishing the client's problems and their etiology.

Collaborative Effort

Resolution of the client's problem is a collaborative effort of the client and the therapist. The client provides specific content related to views of self, others, and the world; implements the strategies developed in a session; and reports outcomes of the efforts. The therapist provides structure, assessment measures and guidelines, characteristic information related to the client's problem and its treatment, alternative intervention strategies for selection and implementation, and evaluation tools and procedures for measuring the outcomes. The generation of a treatment strategy is a team effort in which the client and the therapist join forces against the problem. Trust, an important ingredient in the therapeutic alliance, is built through the collaborative approach. The objective is not only for the client to trust the therapist (and his or her honesty, caring, and expertise) but for the client to develop and expand trust in self. The collaborative effort may also focus on the client's motivation to change; this is a requirement with involuntary clients and those who are receiving treatment for problems such as addictions (Beck et al., 1993).

Unconditional Regard for Self and Others

The therapist represents the view that all humans are worthy as a given and acts to promote the adoption of this philosophy by the client (Ellis, 1977a; Granvold, 1994b). Unconditional regard for oneself and others is based on self-acceptance—acknowledgment that each of us has strengths and limitations, skills and talents offset by ineptness and error proneness, knowledge and ignorance, exceptional traits and flaws, and fallibilities. Self-esteem (which is all too often conditionally founded) is discarded in favor of self-acceptance. It is in the context of accepting oneself with one's flaws and shortcomings as inherently human that the assumption of worthiness can be reconciled as unconditional. To make worthiness anything but unconditional is a formula for failure given the imperfect nature of human beings. This standard of acceptance is applied across the board to all humankind in the form of unconditional regard for others. All are worthwhile *with* their imperfections. Rating one's own traits and behavior and that of others is considered to be acceptable if the rating is not generalized to represent worth, value, or dignity. Nor does this stance promote a disappreciation for excellence, a lack of interest in competence, or a lack of enthusiasm for achievement and developing of skills. It is healthy to work toward goals and objectives, to cultivate and hone skills, to limit ignorance through study, and to unleash creativity through experimentation and practice. These activities, however, are in no way measures of self-worth or personal value.

Structured and Directive Approach

Traditional cognitive therapy is focused on a specific problem that may be cognitive, emotional, behavioral, physical-physiological, social-environmental, or a combination of these areas. In whatever way it is conceptualized, the therapist and the client specifically define the problem or problems they have targeted for change. Treatment has direction and prescribed procedures for resolving the problem. The therapist acts to maintain control of the treatment by setting treatment guidelines and limits, maintaining a strategic focus on targeted problems, and managing such issues as noncompliance, power struggles, and preparation to end treatment. Although a pervasive spirit of collaboration is sought with the client, the ultimate responsibility for the conduct of treatment resides with the therapist.

Active Approach

The client is expected to take an active role both within and outside the treatment setting. Freeman and Dattilio (1992) noted that the client does not come in to be "therapized" but instead actively participates in resolving the problem. After the strategy for change is formulated collaboratively, the client puts the change effort into effect and gathers outcome data. Homework assignments are used to promote the transfer of gains from the treatment setting to the client's natural environment and to produce more resilient change (Granvold & Wodarski, 1994). Homework is graduated in level of demand and is structured to facilitate generalization across populations, settings, and circumstances within given settings. The assessment and outcome data that the client gathers are brought to the therapist for collaborative consideration in evaluating the effectiveness of the treatment strategy and the modification of the change effort.

Education Model

Cognitive therapy involves didactic instruction, along with such techniques as bibliotherapy, written assignments, the use of audiotapes and videotapes, and attendance at lectures and seminars. Early in treatment, it is necessary to present the cognitive-behavioral model to the client. The interactive nature of cognitive, emotional, behavioral, physical-physiological, and social-environmental factors and their contribution to emotional disturbance and maladaptive behavior are explained and discussed. The antecedent-behavior-consequence (ABC) approach to assessment and intervention is identified and applied. The client's misconceptions about the problem and its treatment are addressed early in treatment. The nature of the therapeutic relationship is discussed, with attention focused on the expected collaboration between the therapist and the client. Empirical practice procedures are delineated. Throughout treatment, the therapist educates the client with problem-specific information and content relevant to the treatment process. For example, the concept of relapse prevention is introduced early in treatment, and procedures for the prevention of relapse are presented and discussed at strategic intervals. The development of the client's knowledge of the problem and conceptual grasp of cognitive-behavioral treatment are critical to the collaborative enterprise between the client and the therapist.

Socratic Methods

The use of Socratic questioning or guided discovery is one of the key features of cognitive-behavioral treatment. Far greater results can be expected through the use of the Socratic method than through direct suggestions, explanations, or directives. Skillful questioning facilitates the disclosure of critical cognitive phenomena and leads the client through a process of self-discovery and reasoning. The Socratic method (1) stimulates the client's development of self-awareness and self-observation; (2) facilitates the shift from vague, ill-defined concerns to focused definitions of the problem; (3) gives the therapist access to the client's characteristic patterns of perceiving, reasoning, information processing, and problem solving; (4) exposes the client's belief system; (5) exposes the client's coping mechanisms and tolerance of stress; and (6) is effective in the therapist's modeling of reasoning, the challenging of irrational beliefs, and problem solving (Granvold, 1994b). Questioning also facilitates the client's active participation in the treatment experience, fosters the collaborative effort, and limits the therapist's authoritarian role that is typical of some treatment approaches.

Empirical Focus

The client and the therapist embark on an empirical investigation of the client's cognitive functioning as it relates to his or her emotional and behavioral responses. Once precepts, ideas, beliefs, attitudes, and expectations are identified, an attempt is made to validate them in a systematic way. The process involves the generation of hypotheses that, when tested, will "prove" that targeted cognitions are either valid, rational, and adaptive or lack support. These experiments may be in-session exercises in logic, reasoning, or recall of life experiences or may involve homework. Disproved hypotheses are revised on the basis of evidence and then retested. Outcome measures are used to document the cognitive, emotional, and behavioral changes that the client experiences as a result of the process. These measures not only are meaningful in evaluating specific cognitive restructuring and behavior change, but serve to document the success of treatment and the efficacy of the methods that are used.

Time-Limited Treatment

The therapist's provision of structure to the treatment experience and the active participation of the client shorten the length of time required for effective results. Cognitive-behavioral treatment is an efficient approach, and the inherent generalizability of cognitive change combined with behavior change promotes lasting effects. The comparative brevity of cognitive-behavioral treatment methods makes for a comfortable fit with the time limits set by managed care and third-party payer systems.

Relapse Prevention

For treatment to be considered successful, the results must be sustained long after treatment is terminated. In the past, change efforts that showed convincing signs of success at the point of termination often failed to be sustained for a significant period after termination. In short, the methods showed short-term efficacy but were not resilient against posttreatment challenges. Rather than discard the proved methods, a series of strategies to prevent relapse were developed and incorporated in treatment along with the original procedures.

Marlatt (1985) described relapse prevention as "a self-management program designed to enhance the maintenance stage of the habit-change process" (p. 3). Relapse-prevention strategies are integral parts of cognitive treatment for all categories of problems. Procedures aimed at maintenance and relapse prevention include self-efficacy development, coping skills training, knowledge of and inoculation against relapse, environmental planning (stimulus control procedures), self-monitoring, lifestyle change, social system support, fading, early detection of relapse cues, and follow-up contacts and booster sessions (Granvold & Wodarski, 1994). These and other procedures promote clients' sustained mastery of the cognitive, emotional, and behavioral skills developed in treatment and better prepare clients to cope with future challenges to their well-being.

ASSESSMENT

Assessment and intervention have been described as flowing imperceptibly into one another (Weiss & Margolin, 1977). Among the meanings one can draw from this caveat is that assessment itself may effect change (unless it is accomplished totally unobtrusively) and assessment drives intervention. Ethical treatment is bound to a designed assessment strategy.

Cognitive-behavioral intervention relies on assessment that is comprehensive and specific, historic and contemporary, and initial and ongoing. Furthermore, assessment should focus on the therapeutic relationship and the process of therapy.

Seeking an understanding of the client requires an exploration of cognitive functioning, behavior in the context of antecedents and consequences, emotional functioning, physical and physiological data (including medical and medication/drug information), and social-environmental functioning. Such an assessment is based on the view that these factors are reciprocally influential (Bandura, 1978), and thus the "cause" of the client's condition is multiply and interactionally determined. It is out of a global understanding of the client that specific treatment goals can be identified. Treatment goals may be defined in terms of problem or process; individual, social, or environmental; or cognitive, emotional, behavioral, or physical/physiological. In whatever terms they are stated, treatment goals are to derive from a comprehensive yet specific understanding of the client.

Assessment is both historic and contemporary. Family-of-origin content, developmental events, remarkable life events (e.g., trauma, successes), and factors that have prompted counseling at this time are viable explorations. This content often serves to elucidate the client's current concerns, coping capacity, and change potential. Traditional cognitive-behavioral therapists tend to be highly here-and-now focused (with the exception of issues such as posttraumatic stress disorder of a historic nature), and thus the time spent on history is far less than the time devoted to current functioning. Furthermore, historic determinations are integrated with the meanings derived from presenting problems and current behavior.

Assessment is initial and ongoing. Initial assessment findings shape the early phase of intervention. It is necessary to continue to assess the client over time both to gain more comprehensive or in-depth understanding of the client in his or her social and environmental context and to track ongoing change throughout treatment and at points beyond termination. Berlin and Marsh (1993) provide an excellent description of the range of considerations to guide the therapist in the process of continuous assessment.

Assessment of the therapeutic relationship and therapy process provides valuable feedback regarding the client's assessment of the therapist as a collaborator in the change effort and the client's appraisals of the methods being implemented and outcomes achieved. Both client and therapist are involved in constructing and reconstructing an understanding (Berlin & Marsh, 1993; Sundel & Sundel, 1993), a process that may remain at a highly inferential level if it is not made explicit.

Assessment serves to guide the selection of appropriate interventions and to provide evaluative criteria to determine the efficacy of the therapeutic intervention implemented (Jacobson & Margolin, 1979). As clinical problems are specified, client and therapist collaborate in the assessment process. Although comprehensive assessment relies on exploration in various domains, the utility and relevance of these different domains vary among clinical problems specified for change (Craighead et al., 1994). Thus, for example, some targeted problems may be more environmentally influenced, while others are more specifically cognitive-emotional-behavioral.

Cognitive functioning is recognized as only one ingredient in the dynamic puzzle of human functioning. Cognitive-behavioral treatment, however, relies heavily on the assessment of cognitive functioning and the influence of social learning factors on the clinical problem. In the material that follows, the process of cognitive assessment will be presented in detail. (For information on behavioral assessment refer to Barlow, 1981; Berlin & Marsh, 1993; Ciminero, Calhoun, & Adams, 1986; Corcoran & Fischer, 1987; Craighead et al., 1994; Haynes, 1978; Hersen & Bellack, 1976; Hudson, 1990; Mash & Terdal, 1976; Nay, 1979; and Sundel & Sundel, 1993.)

Cognition is not a single phenomenon. Its meaning is variable, and therefore different assessment devices and formats are used depending on the component of cognitive functioning under scrutiny. Cognitive targets of assessment can be subclassified into three categories:

1. *Cognitive content* (also referred to as *cognitive products*), which includes thoughts, self-verbalizations, decisions, accessible beliefs, values, attributions, images, and recognition-detection meanings attached to stimuli (Ingram & Kendall, 1986).
2. *Cognitive process,* the mechanism by which information is selected (input), transformed, and delivered (output). Included are such functions as selective attention, perception, encoding, storage, and retrieval.
3. *Schema,* a term used to represent two aspects of cognition. First, it denotes cognitive structure—the way in which information is organized and internally represented (Ingram & Kendall, 1986); structure is the mechanism that serves to store information (iconic-sensory phenomena and beliefs) and comprises associative linkages and networks of meaning and memory nodes. Information processing is guided by these activities. Second, schema represents cognitive propositions stored in cognitive structures. Schemas are inflexible, general rules, or silent assumptions (beliefs, attitudes, concepts) that develop as enduring concepts from past (early) experiences; form the basis for screening, discriminating, weighing, and coding stimuli; and form the basis for categorizing, evaluating experiences, and making judgments and distorting reality situations (Rush & Beck, 1978). The individual's perceptual filters, views of self, others, and the world, and cohesive factors that form the bases of appraising and judging are all based on schemas.

Cognitive Content

The assessment of cognitive content (products) is typically conducted through an interview, with paper and pencil or a computer. An extensive array of standardized measures have been developed for problem areas in which clients' self-statements, thoughts, satisfaction, expectations, and beliefs are sought. In addition to standardized measures, forms for monitoring and recording faulty cognitions and associated responses have also been developed (for example, the Daily Record of Dysfunctional Thoughts by Beck et al., 1979, and the Rational-Emotive Therapy Self-Help Form by Ellis & Dryden, 1987). These forms may be used as homework, thereby producing individualized data that may not be exposed by standardized measures. (For additional information on the assessment of cognitive content, see Kendall & Hollon, 1981; Kendall & Korgeski, 1979; Merluzzi & Boltwood, 1989; Merluzzi, Glass, &

Genest, 1981; Michelson & Ascher, 1987; Schwartz & Garamoni, 1986; and Segal & Shaw 1988.)

Cognitive Process

The assessment of cognitive-process functions is more difficult to accomplish than is the assessment of cognitive content. The assessment of information processing is most frequently accomplished through interview procedures. Beck et al. (1979) described faulty information processing, such as arbitrary inference, selective abstraction, and overgeneralization, that is characteristic of depressed clients. They detailed the use of Socratic questioning to expose the process and to validate or invalidate the thinking and thus to arrive at specific information-processing errors. The assessment of cognitive process functions through this interview format has been applied to an array of problems, including anxiety (Beck & Emery, 1985; Freeman & Simon, 1989; Guidano & Liotti, 1983), agoraphobia (Michelson, 1987; Thorpe & Burns, 1983), depression (Beck et al., 1979; Freeman, 1990), personality disorders (Beck et al., 1990; Rothstein & Vallis, 1991), anorexia nervosa (Garner & Bemis, 1985), and substance abuse (Beck et al., 1993).

Another cognitive-process assessment procedure, developed by Mahoney (1991), is stream of consciousness, "an exercise in which the client is invited to attend to and, as best one can, report ongoing thoughts, sensation, images, memories, and feelings" (p. 295).

Schemas

Assessment of schemas is conducted through probing and Socratic exploration, questionnaires, and personal journals. The objective is vertical exploration, the accessing of core meanings—views about self, others, the world, and the future. Examples of structured assessment methods for use in the interview include *downward arrow technique* (Burns, 1980), in which a chain of meanings is derived from a triggering event or a cognition considered possibly to stem from a maladaptive schema; *laddering* (Neimeyer, 1993c), in which a personal construct ladder is elicited to explore meanings surrounding identity and core constructs; and *repertory grid* (Kelly, 1955), a means of eliciting a client's significant constructs through the development of a matrix of elements important in his or her domain (personal meaning networks and interpersonal relationships).

Access to schematic functioning may be done through the use of paper-and-pencil methods, which allow more open-ended or subject-directed reporting of cognitions. Useful questionnaires for this purpose are Dysfunctional Thought Record (Beck et al., 1979), Thought Listing (Cacioppo & Petty, 1981), and Think-Aloud techniques (Genest & Turk, 1981).

The personal journal can be a useful assessment technique for various aspects of cognitive functioning. Mahoney (1991) suggests alternative formats, including current events, memories, a structured "life review project," dreams and fantasies, and reflective "notes to myself." Content recorded can produce insights into the client's "web of associations" and expose core meaning structures. Neimeyer and Neimeyer (1993) suggest bringing the journal into treatment to be read aloud by the client or therapist. Journal content, in addition to being highly meaningful itself, may stimulate therapeutic discussions producing highly salient content.

INTERVENTIONS

Cognitive-behavioral therapists use an array of techniques in their treatment strategies and target cognition, behavior, and, to a lesser degree, emotions as entry points in the change process. The ways in which cognitive and behavioral elements are integrated and the process believed to mediate change differ across approaches (Hollon & Beck, 1994). Some approaches are more strongly cognitive with a focus on the cognitive restructuring of peripheral cognitions and uncovering and restructuring core meaning structures and self-schemas. Others are oriented toward cognitive development: the teaching of new cognitive skills. Cognitive-behaviorists also consider physical and physiological factors and social and environmental influences on client functioning. While not specifically addressed here, treatment strategies may well include intervention in these components of human functioning as well. The following is a presentation of several major cognitive-behavioral treatment approaches.

Cognitive Restructuring

Cognitive restructuring encompasses a set of procedures with the common goal to challenge, dispute, modify, and change existing cognitions (peripheral beliefs, schemas) or cognitive processes (perception, information processing). Typically, the rationality or validity of cognitive constructs (or processing) is examined. That is, does logical or empirical evidence exist to support the client's belief or cognitive processing? The two major interventions with a cognitive restructuring focus are Ellis's rational-emotive behavior therapy and Beck's cognitive therapy.

Rational-Emotive Behavior Therapy

Rational-emotive therapy (RET) was founded in 1955 by Albert Ellis. Disenchanted with the ineffectiveness and inefficiency of psychoanalytic methods (in which he was trained), Ellis turned to philosophy, an early love, from which to derive his pioneering cognitive treatment method. The bedrock of RET lies in the works of early philosophers (e.g., Epictetus, Aurelius, Socrates) through twentieth-century philosophers, (e.g. Heidegger, Tillich) and many in between (e.g. Kierkegaard, Kant, Spinoza, Schopenhauer) whose common set of beliefs "hold that emotional upsetness largely originates in illogical, unrealistic, and irrational thinking and that humans have the distinct ability to monitor this kind of thinking, to reflect on it, and to change it, so that they significantly help themselves solve their everyday problems and their fairly severe disturbances" (Ellis, 1989, p. 7).

In addition to drawing on philosophy, Ellis also turned to behavior therapy methods, which he had used to treat himself for severe fears of public speaking and social anxiety about dating. Thus, behavior rehearsal procedures have come to be incorporated in RET from its early beginnings, prompting Ellis to proclaim himself to be the first cognitive-behavioral therapist (Ellis, 1989). RET was renamed rational-emotive behavior therapy (REBT) in 1993 on the grounds that RET has always stressed and made use of behavioral components (Ellis, 1993).

REBT is a logico-empirical method of psychotherapy in which human disturbance is viewed as largely the product of faulty beliefs as outlined in Ellis's early work, *Reason and Emotion in Psychotherapy* (1962). Ellis clearly stated the integral interrelationship of thinking and emotion and professed that sensing, moving, emoting, and thinking are not experienced in isolation. While stressing the interactive view of human psychological processes, Ellis has accorded cognition a special role in human psychological processes and points to, in particular, the evaluative role thought plays in psychological health and disturbance (Ellis & Dryden, 1987).

Rationality and Irrationality. The concept of rationality is central to REBT. Humans are viewed as being biologically predisposed to think irrationally, and this tendency has a notable bearing on psychological disturbance. Ellis defines "rational" as "that which aids and abets people achieving their basic goals and purposes" (Dryden & Ellis, 1988, p. 217). These goals and purposes are products of long-term hedonism instead of short-term hedonism in the psychologically healthy human being. In other words, those who delay the immediate satisfaction of their desires in favor of the promotion of ultimate valued and physically healthy consequences are viewed as functioning rationally. "Irrational" means that which prevents people from achieving these ultimate goals. Ellis notes that "even if everybody had had the most rational upbringing, virtually all humans would often irrationally escalate their individual and social preferences into absolutistic demands on a) themselves, b) other people, and c) the universe around them" (Ellis, 1984, p. 20). Hence, Ellis concludes that there is a human tendency toward irrationality. To elucidate further the issue of rational versus irrational thinking, Ellis posits that rational beliefs "are evaluative cognitions of personal significance that are preferential (i.e., nonabsolute) in nature. They are expressed in the form of 'desires,' 'preferences,' 'wishes,' 'likes,' and 'dislikes'" (Ellis & Dryden, 1987, p. 5). Irrational beliefs differ in two respects from rational beliefs: "First they are absolute (or dogmatic) in nature and are expressed in the form of 'musts,' 'shoulds,' 'oughts,' 'have-to's,' etc. Second, as such they lead to negative emotions that largely interfere with goal pursuit and attainment (e.g., depression, anxiety, guilt, anger)" (Ellis & Dryden, 1987, pp. 5–6).

The ABCs of REBT. REBT is known for its ABC model of human disturbance, a model that has more recently been labeled the expanded ABC theory (Ellis, 1991; Ellis & Bernard, 1986). A stands for activating event, B represents the individual's belief(s) about the event, and C denotes the person's emotional and behavioral responses or consequences, which derive from B. Ellis's model posits that restructuring the belief(s) at B, which means changing from irrational to rational thinking through disputation—D—will produce greater emotional well-being—E. According to REBT theory, A is not merely an external reality but the individual's perception of A. While A appears to "cause" emotional and behavioral consequences directly, the contention is that B's serve as mediators between A and C. The client, through Socratic dialogue, is taught to challenge his or her irrational thinking and to replace it with rationality.

To illustrate this model, consider the family member of a hospitalized patient who is upset (angry, frustrated, agitated) when a physician fails to meet with the patient and family at an agreed-upon time.

A. The failure of the physician to appear for the consultation.
B. "The doctor *must* honor his or her commitments in a timely fashion."
"I can't stand it when people make idle commitments."
"Doctors have no feelings for their patients or their patients' families and should be punished for their lack of caring."
"My sick family member and I must not matter to the doctor."
C. Emotions: anger, hostility, frustration, resentment.
Behavior: client angrily confronts the social worker and nursing staff regarding the doctor's "irresponsibility," swears and threatens to change doctors or hospitals or call an attorney.
D. "Why must the doctor keep the appointment?"
"Where is it written that doctors *must* be on time?"
"Even though I am upset, where is the evidence that I can't stand it?"
"How does the physician's failure to keep the appointment make him or her an uncaring person?"

Disputation of the beliefs is accomplished through Socratic dialogue.

Derivatives of Irrational Beliefs. Irrational beliefs tend to be rigid, absolutistic, demanding, expectations, and judgments: "Things must be a certain, fixed way" or "Things must go my way." Three major derivatives flow from irrational beliefs: that something is awful (catastrophization), "can't stand it" (demandingness and low frustration tolerance), and damnation ("What a no-goodnik *you* are and *I* must be for such treatment!"), which constitutes rating self and others as subhuman.

Ellis (1962, 1994) has identified eleven major illogical, irrational and self-defeating ideas with which most people in our society have been directly or indirectly indoctrinated. The list is acknowledged as being neither inclusively definitive nor nonoverlapping:

1. It is a dire necessity for adult humans to be loved or approved by virtually every significant other person in their community.
2. One absolutely must be competent, adequate, and achieving in all important respects, or else one is an inadequate, worthless person.
3. People absolutely must act considerately and fairly, and they are damnable villains if they do not. They are their bad acts.

4. The idea that it is awful and terrible when things are not the way one would very much like them to be.
5. The idea that emotional disturbance is mainly externally caused, and people have little or no ability to increase or decrease their dysfunctional feelings and behaviors.
6. The idea that if something is or may be dangerous or fearsome, one should be constantly and excessively concerned about it and should keep dwelling on the possibility of its occurring.
7. The idea that one cannot and must not face life's responsibilities and difficulties, and that it is easier to avoid them.
8. The idea that you must be quite dependent on others and need them and cannot mainly run your own life.
9. The idea that one's history is an all-important determiner of one's present behavior, and that because something once strongly affected one's life, it should indefinitely have a similar effect.
10. The idea that other people's disturbances are horrible, and that one must feel very upset about them.
11. The idea that there is invariably a right, precise, and perfect solution to human problems, and that it is awful if this perfect solution is not found.

While receiving extensive confirmation from clients and colleagues that these self-defeating beliefs are often operative when an individual is emotionally distressed, Ellis (1994) does not consider them to be a panacea against human disturbances and states that with some people they actually may have limited applicability.

Unconditional Regard for Self and Others. Another salient component of REBT is unconditional regard for self and others (Ellis, 1962, 1973, 1977a). Ellis contends that negative self-rating is a major cause of human disturbance and presents innumerable problems that result when people fail to value themselves very highly (Ellis, 1977a). Among the consequences are their diminished appraisal of their successes, a strong demand to prove themselves, intense seeking of approval, self-sabotage of their potential achievements, obsessive comparisons with others, intense performance anxiety, short-range hedonism, a lack of self-discipline, defensiveness, hostility, depression, withdrawal, lack of self-confidence, and self-berating. Ellis makes a profound distinction between self-esteem and self-acceptance when he writes that self-esteem "means that the individual values himself because he has behaved intelligently, correctly, or competently" (1977a, p. 101). Hence, conditions are placed on self-esteem that evolve from an appraisal of performance. Obvious flaws in this process result from such characteristics as the imperfect nature of human functioning, changes in skill level over time, extreme, unrealistic performance standards, and the unrealistic expectation that one can exert control over uncontrollable factors.

In addressing the unconditional acceptance of self, Ellis and Dryden (1987) write that "the person accepts herself and others as fallible human beings who do not have to act other than they do and as too complex and fluid to be given any legitimate or global rating" (p. 18). Self-acceptance, or unconditional self-regard, involves the acknowledgment and acceptance of one's strengths and limitations. One's knowledge, talent, skills, and aptitudes are counterbalanced by one's ignorance, incompetence, ineptness, and lack of potential in specific areas. Inasmuch as all humans possess a ledger of strengths and limitations, it is unrealistic to expect to perform with exceeding competence in all areas of life. In short, accepting oneself with one's flaws and limitations is tantamount to the psychologically healthy acceptance of self as human.

Detecting and Disputing Irrational Beliefs. The key to detecting irrational beliefs is in looking for "shoulds," "musts," and "ought to's." Although not all irrational beliefs include *should, must,* or *ought to,* most do. Others may be merely unrealistic or unempirical statements (Ellis, 1977b). By asking, "What is it about A that is causing you C?" the client's unique view (e.g., evaluation, expectation, judgment) of the activating event is uncovered. The likely consequence of this process is the discovery of an irrational thought. A client who is upset (angry, frustrated, hurt, resentful, jealous) over his failure to receive a raise at work could be queried as follows:

Therapist: What is it about not getting a raise that is upsetting to you?
Client: I believe that I deserve a raise.
Therapist: Let's assume that you do. Why must you get what you deserve?
Client: Because if you do what you're supposed to do, you should get what you have coming.
Therapist: It sounds as if you are saying that you should be treated fairly.
Client: Yes, that's it.
Therapist: Why must you be treated fairly?
Client: I guess, because I just should . . . that's what's right.
Therapist: I agree with your desire to be treated fairly, but what evidence do you have that people, you included, are always treated fairly?
Client: None really, I guess. Unfairness seems to be more typical, or at least real common.

In this way the therapist guides the client in reaching the awareness that his emotional distress is the product of an expectation of fairness and, furthermore, the client articulates an acknowledgment that unfairness is somewhat common:

Therapist: A desire for fairness is a reasonable expectation. But given the commonplace occurrence of unfair treatment in our world, do you think you can legitimately expect to always be treated fairly?
Client: No, not really.
Therapist: What could you tell yourself about being treated unfairly that would allow you to feel less upset?
Client: I guess I could say that I'd *like* to always be treated fairly, but it's not reasonable to *expect* to always be treated fairly.
Therapist: Excellent. You've shifted from a demand statement to a preference. Now when you make this shift, how do you feel about not getting a raise?
Client: Upset . . . but less upset, I guess. I still don't like it.

This client has gained an initial awareness of the irrational thought (demand for fairness). The ABCDE model of REBT could be taught at this time and, in many cases, bibliotherapy recommended for more effective knowledge development. It takes repeated bombardment of irrational thoughts with logico-empirical disputation to promote effective change. Furthermore, it is likely that a given client functions with a range of irrational beliefs under an array of circumstances. Therefore, it is necessary in treatment sessions to apply REBT methods repetitively to various activating events.

Cognitive Homework. Clients are assigned various forms of cognitive homework. Alternative methods, formal and informal, may be employed to facilitate disputing irrational beliefs. Written disputing forms, audiotape disputing and unstructured in vivo rehearsal are all useful options. Bibliotherapy and prerecorded audiotapes are used to expand the client's understanding and to reinforce rational thinking. A number of imagery techniques, including rational-emotive imagery (Ellis, 1979; Maultsby, 1977; Maultsby & Ellis, 1974), are taught in-session and practiced as homework. Clients gain experience in modifying emotional responses through changing their beliefs while vividly imaging the activating event.

After a brief period during which the therapist instructs the client in relaxation, the client is asked to: re-create the activating event in his or her mind (or to imagine the worst thing that could happen to him or her), implode his or her extreme emotional responses, and shift feelings from unhealthy extreme emotions to more appropriate emotive responses such as disappointment and frustration through altering the belief(s) underlying the emotions. The therapist may verbally instruct the client to shift his or her thoughts from irrational to rational beliefs while imaging: "Rather than thinking that it's terrible to be laid off your job, think that it's only unfortunate." After the client is given time to achieve the shift, the therapist asks the client to report any changes in emotional intensity or in the actual emotions being experienced.

Emotive Techniques. REBT is known for its use of emotive evocative methods, particularly "shame attacking" exercises in which clients publicly act "shameful" (e.g., walk in public with a banana on a string to draw negative attention as a means of developing a tolerance for judgmental and negative feedback and a reduction in approval needs), feel the associated feelings, and become desensitized (tolerate and reduce the discomfort) (Ellis, 1969; Ellis & Becker, 1982, Ellis & Dryden, 1987). Clients are encouraged to evoke their emotions creatively for the purpose of in vivo disputing of associated irrational beliefs or to "prove" that actual consequences are less negative than expected.

Behavioral Techniques. Behavioral assignments have been used in REBT since its inception in recognition of the effect behavior change can have on cognitive change (Emmelkamp, Kuipers, & Eggeraat, 1978). Clients are consistently encouraged to revisit the activating event for the purpose of in vivo desensitization and to do so floodingly if it is therapeutically appropriate (Ellis, 1979; Ellis & Dryden, 1987).

Ellis uses various behavioral methods to overcome resistance and to reinforce the practice of cognitive change. Rewards and penalties are employed to promote the performance of challenging, emotionally discomforting assignments. Clients are taught to use the Premack Principle (Premack, 1965, 1971) in which the performance of homework is a contingency for doing high-reward activities such as watching television, pleasure reading, or talking on the telephone.

Skill training is often used in REBT when a client evidences deficiencies in skills central to or in support of a change effort. Verbal and communication skills, assertiveness, parenting, and behavioral skills to enhance sexual functioning (e.g., noncoital sensate pleasuring techniques) are examples of skills areas that may be taught in therapy (or assigned for development outside therapy) to meet performance deficiencies.

To illustrate skill training, consider Martha, a recently divorced woman, whose former husband, Roger, often told her of his recent dating activities when returning the children to her care after visitation. Martha felt deeply hurt when he made these disclosures (since she continued to feel love and attachment to him). In a role play, the therapist played Martha while Martha took the role of Roger. The therapist assertively stated: "Roger, I have no desire to hear about your dating activities. When you pick up or return the children, the only information we need to discuss is that related to the children. I would appreciate your cooperation in honoring this request."

After several iterations during which Martha (role playing Roger) became increasingly argumentative, the roles were reversed. Similarly, the therapist (role playing Roger) began with an accepting response to the assertive stance taken by Martha. With each subsequent rehearsal, however, Martha's assertiveness was met with greater resistance from the therapist. Martha was given the homework assignment to assert herself with Roger consistent with the rehearsal in session.

Cognitive Therapy

Cognitive therapy (CT) (Beck, 1976; Beck et al., 1979) posits that the treatment of an emotional disturbance or behavioral problem is achieved through accessing and modifying "the cognitive content of one's reaction to the upsetting event or stream of thought" (DeRubeis & Beck, 1988, p. 273). The cognitive content includes peripheral thoughts, beliefs, attitudes, appraisals, values, causal attributions, and meanings that may be accessed relatively easily through client self-report. Schemas comprise a second component of cognitive content.

First, consider the peripheral beliefs comprising the content of the cognitive reaction to an upsetting event. Beck and his colleagues (Beck et al., 1979; Beck, J. 1995; DeRubeis & Beck, 1988) encourage the client to view this cognitive content as a hypothesis (rather than a fact) and to scrutinize and appraise the belief carefully. This process tends to produce a different view, which strengthens over time. For example, the belief that "husbands and wives should agree" may commonly operate to prompt emotional upset in a marital partner when there is disagreement between mates. This belief may be modified under scrutiny to "it's okay for husbands and wives to disagree," followed by repeated application of the alternative view when disagreement occurs. Over time, the strength of the latter belief is expected to increase along with a reduction in the degree of emotional and behavioral reactivity when disagreement is experienced.

The second component of cognitive content comprises core beliefs or schemas (underlying meaning structures) that form the basis for categorizing, evaluating, judging, and distorting reality situations (Rush & Beck, 1978) and are considered to be the core of the cognitive disturbance. Core beliefs are not readily accessible and are identified through the common themes that run through the individual instances of disturbance (DeRubeis & Beck, 1988). These themes are then evaluated on the bases of their utility (the consequences of holding them, both positive and negative) and validity (their fit with logic or concrete evidence). This process is done through Socratic dialogue and produces client awareness of the core meanings implicitly underlying the client's cognitive, emotional, and behavioral responses to life events. Thus, a causal connection is made between these schemas and emotional disturbance and maladaptive behaviors. Through this process, the therapist guides the client in considering an alternative view, one of far greater utility and validity. Repetitive challenge of faulty core beliefs and replacement with alternative views is achieved to promote the client's shift in commitment to core meanings that produce greater emotional well-being and adaptive functioning. Many related and unrelated life events that have historically stimulated episodes of emotional distress are considered in order to promote generalization, and the therapist provides verbal reinforcement for effective cognitive restructuring.

In addition to addressing cognitive content factors as they relate to human disturbance, Beck and his colleagues also address the process of cognitive functioning. Various types of thinking errors (information processing errors) are identified, and their contributions to clients' distortions and ultimate disturbance and dysfunction are explicated. These errors, along with peripheral and core beliefs, are targeted for intervention. The following definitions, taken from Beck's work (Beck et al., 1979), comprise common information-processing errors:

1. *Absolutistic/dichotomous thinking* is evidenced in the tendency to view experiences, objects, and situations in a polarized manner: good/bad, right/wrong, or strong/weak ("I am a total failure." "Life's a bitch.").

2. *Overgeneralization* "refers to the pattern of drawing a general rule or conclusion on the basis of one or more isolated incidents and applying the concept across the board to related and unrelated situations" (Beck et al., 1979, p. 14). ("I am a poor tennis player. I'm just no good at sports." "I didn't meet anyone or enjoy singles Sunday school. Singles groups just don't work for me.")

3. *Selective abstraction* involves focusing on the negative in a situation, ignoring other positive (sometimes more salient) features, and viewing the entire experience as negative based on the selective view. ("My work performance evaluation was terrible," stated by one whose evaluation included a few average or below-average ratings but, comparative to the work group, was an overall high rating.)

4. *Arbitrary inference* refers to the process of reaching a specific conclusion when there is no evidence to support it, when the evidence is circumstantial, vague or unclear, or when there is evidence to the contrary. Freeman (1983) describes two

forms of arbitrary influence: *mind reading*—"She thinks I'm weak, I know it." "They think I'm great!"—and *negative prediction,* which involves imagining or anticipating that something bad or unpleasant is going to happen without adequate or realistic support for the prediction ("I'm going to do terribly at this job interview." "I'll never have a love relationship again," stated by a recently divorced person.)

5. *Magnification and minimization* involve errors in evaluating the significance or extent of a behavior, condition, or event that are so extreme as to constitute a distortion. For example, a husband finds out that his wife forgot to take the dog to the veterinarian for a routine visit and becomes extremely upset and chastises her (magnification). After twelve years with her law firm, Mary Ann becomes one of the 15 percent to be promoted to partner. She believes and says that "anyone could have done it" (minimization).

6. *Personalization* is the act of relating a negative event or situation to oneself without the adequate causal evidence to make the connection. People may take the view that they are the cause or object of a negative event. "If I had been home with Dad, he wouldn't have had the heart attack" (cause). "They made the college degree requirements more stringent just because I'm enrolling" (object).

Learning these common errors allows the client to label his or her problematic cognitive processing and in so doing to become more sensitive to flawed thinking even as it is happening. Clients quickly learn to discount their initial thinking (when an error in information processing is recognized) and rapidly replace it with sounder conclusions.

Behavioral methods are used both to enhance and support cognitive change, and to produce change in beliefs. Among many behavioral methods used in CT, the two most central to the approach will be covered: self-monitoring and scheduling activities.

Self-monitoring is assigned to the client in which an hour-to-hour record of activities, associated mood and other pertinent data are completed for at least one week, and often much longer (DeRubeis & Beck, 1988). The record is useful in hypothesis testing, becoming a repository of evidence to judge hypotheses more accurately than mere memory. It provides content for in-session exploration and facilitates acknowledgement of the relationship between mood and activities.

DeRubeis and Beck (1988) identify the purpose of scheduling activities in CT as twofold: "1) to increase the probability that the client will engage in activities that he or she has been avoiding, and 2) to remove decision-making as an obstacle in the initiation of an activity" (p. 279). For example, mastery and pleasure activities are assigned to the depressed client to interfere behaviorally with depressive symptomatology, or the anxious client may be given "graded task" assignments, which expose him or her to low-demand, anxiety-provoking situations in vivo. The success of CT lies, in part, in the creative use of the extensive time between treatment sessions.

To summarize, in CT the client is guided in the identification of information-processing functions (errors), causal attributions, (exaggerated) expectations, and beliefs (peripheral or core) associated with the disturbance. The therapist prompts the client in stating these cognitions as hypotheses, and together client and therapist seek evidence (logical or empirical) to support the hypotheses. In the light of little or no evidence to support the hypotheses, new meanings are generated. These new meanings undergird and reinforce a more positive view of self, enhanced self-efficacy, greater emotional self-control, a more realistic view of available life opportunities, and a greater sense of hope for the future. Behavioral procedures are used to test out, enhance, and promote change in cognitive functioning, to stimulate emotional change, to effect behavior change, and to achieve the transfer of change from the therapeutic environment into the client's natural environment.

To illustrate the cognitive restructuring of a negative causal attribution, consider Joe, a client whose fifteen-year-old stepdaughter, Linda, is in residential treatment for extreme acting-out behavior (incorrigibility, fighting with peers, truancy, and promiscuity). Joe has been highly critical of Linda throughout the ten years he has known her and has tended to interpret her motives as negative and manipulative. One of his goals in therapy is to learn to see the positive in Linda and to "give her the benefit of the doubt." Joe, Linda, and May, Linda's mother, have all been taught the cognitive model; thus Joe has initial awareness that his thoughts, beliefs, and ways of processing information are highly influential in shaping meanings, eliciting emotions, and prompting behavioral responses to given stimulus conditions. The following is a family therapy excerpt:

Joe: Linda was home for visitation last weekend, and she was up to her usual tricks. I asked her to mow the yard, which she did—except that she left the parking strip unmowed. I know that she skipped mowing at the curb just to spite me.

Linda: I did *not,* Dad! I just forgot. It was the first time I've ever mowed the yard!

Therapist: Linda, while you sound angry, what *are* you feeling right now?

Linda: I *am* angry. He's always putting me down. I can never do anything right in his eyes.

Therapist: You feel as if you can't measure up to his expectations?

Linda: No, I *can't!*

Therapist: And you feel criticized by your dad much of the time?

Linda: Yes, I do.

Therapist: Besides anger, what other emotions are you experiencing? Anything else?

Linda: Yes, I guess I feel hurt, too . . . and disappointment . . . because I do try [stated with marked sadness].

Therapist: I think that I understand your feelings here, Linda, and what you're thinking. [Turning to Joe.] Joe, what is your reaction to what Linda has just said?

Joe: Well, right now I'm feeling a little sad for her because I can be a difficult person to work for. Even the men at the plant tell me so. . . . I have a reputation as a hard driver. [After a brief interchange in which Linda and Joe are guided by the therapist in clarifying their respective intentions, sharing their feelings, and expressing their mutual caring and desires to get along better, the focus shifts to Joe.]

Therapist: Joe, how do you feel when you think of Linda as acting spitefully toward you?

Joe: Angry and disgusted. I feel as if she's never going to behave responsibly.

Therapist: Do you like these feelings?

Joe: No, not at all. I have been hoping that my relationship with Linda would improve, but my anger and resentment toward her just seem to make it worse.

Therapist: This may seem obvious, but do you want to change your feelings toward Linda?

Joe: Certainly . . . yes. I really do.

Therapist: And, as we've discussed before, you're willing to do the work to change the mental habits that may be operating to hurt your relationship?

Joe: Yes, I really am.

Therapist: That's great, Joe. I'm pleased, too, that you are willing to put time and effort into the process. Joe, suppose that we test out your statement that Linda failed to mow the parking strip just to spite you?

Joe: Okay.

Therapist: Where's the evidence to support that view?

Joe: I guess there really isn't any hard evidence. It is what I think.

Therapist: Can you think of any other explanation for Linda's behavior besides being spiteful?

Joe: Yes. Perhaps she just forgot, or maybe she didn't see it. The parking strip is on the other side of the sidewalk—a little removed.

Therapist: These *are* plausible explanations, Joe. Now how do you feel toward Linda when you attribute her behavior to these factors rather than her being spiteful?

Joe: I don't really feel so angry or resentful—more just frustrated with her that she couldn't complete the job right.

Therapist: So you have identified alternative, plausible explanations for Linda's failing to mow the parking strip, views that compete with the thought that she acted out of spite for you.

Joe: That's right.

Therapist: Now, which views serve you better in achieving the goals you have for your relationship with Linda?

Joe: That she's not acting out of spite. Rather she just made a mistake—human error, I guess you could call it.

Therapist: That's a great way to put it, Joe. We humans are all error prone, even you and me!

Cognitive Skills Training Methods

Behaviorally trained theorists developed cognitive-behavioral interventions designed to teach specific cognitive skills in contrast to those whose focus is to restructure existing cognitions. Most of these methodologies have been developed to treat specific disorders rather than as general treatment methodologies for broad application. Two notable exceptions are Meichenbaum's self-instruction training (Meichenbaum, 1977) and problem-solving training (D'Zurilla, 1988; D'Zurilla & Goldfried, 1971).

Self-Instruction Training

Self-instruction involves the use of self-verbalizations to guide the performance of a task, skill, or problem-solving process. Drawing on the work of Luria (1959, 1961) and Vygotsky (1962), Meichenbaum and Goodman (1971) developed a method to treat hyperactive, impulsive children. Before performing tasks automatically, young children verbalize instructions. As they develop skill and begin to act automatically, the verbalizations become subvocalized.

Meichenbaum (1975) recognized that verbal mediation could be inserted between a stimulus and response to prevent maladaptive behavior and performance deficiency. In this manner, the stimulus-response chain can be interrupted, and the maladaptive response can be inhibited. The anticipated result is an increased likelihood that an adaptive response will follow a given stimulus.

Self-instruction training provides the client with step-by-step self-statements (including verbal self-reinforcement and coping statements) for the development of competency in the performance of targeted tasks and skills. A five-step procedure is used to instruct the client (Meichenbaum, 1977):

1. The therapist models performance of the task while talking to himself or herself out loud (*cognitive modeling*).
2. Clients perform the same task while receiving verbal guidance from the therapist (*overt, external guidance*).
3. Clients perform the task while instructing themselves out loud (*overt self-guidance*).
4. Clients perform the task while whispering instructions to themselves (*faded, overt self-guidance*).
5. Clients perform the task while instructing themselves privately (*covert self-instruction*).

The self-statements modeled by the therapist and rehearsed by the client may incorporate error correction, self-praise, and coping statements. Initial self-instruction training should begin with simple tasks, followed by more complex skills such as problem solving. Complex tasks should be broken down into manageable incremental steps to allow for response chaining and successive approximation. Homework may be assigned in which the client practices the rehearsal of self-instruction while performing tasks.

The verbalizations modeled by the therapist and rehearsed by the client include several performance-relevant skills:

- *Statements regarding task completion:* "I'm going to ask her for a date."
- *Guidance of performance by self-instruction:* "Relax, approach her comfortably, and make the invitation."

- *Coping self-statements and error-correcting options:* "I can still approach her even if I feel some anxiety. That's okay."
- *Self-reinforcement:* "There, I did it!"

Self-instruction has been used to treat a wide range of academic and clinical problems in various populations. Effective results have been reported in improving the self-control of hyperactive, impulsive children; reducing children's aggressiveness; developing social skill in social isolates; enhancing memory recall in children; improving creativity in college students; reducing test anxiety; improving problem-solving skills in the elderly; and reducing psychotic speech in adult schizophrenics. It has been modified to include such components as operant procedures (for example, social and token reinforcement), relaxation training, stimulus-modeling films and tapes, and covert modeling procedures.

To illustrate self-instruction, consider Abe, a thirty-year-old man, who sought treatment for social inhibition. His desire was to learn to approach women and, ultimately, to date. The outline noted above was implemented in Abe's treatment. The therapist asked Abe, "What might you actually think to yourself or say to yourself if you were to approach a woman and ask her for a date?" Abe's soliloquy of inner debate consisted of the following: (1) "I want to go out with her"; (2) "I'm afraid that she'll turn me down"; (3) "Maybe I should just blow it off and forget it. No, I've got to try. I'll never get anywhere if I don't ask her or someone else out. The worst that she could say is no, and I can take it. I wouldn't like it, and I'd feel awkward, but I can take it" (self-debate); *(4) "I am going to ask Mary out for a date"* (the decision); *(5) "Hi, Mary, I'm happy to see you here today [singles Sunday school]"* (the approach); *(6) "Would you like to go to lunch with me after church?"* (the request). *Abe repeatedly rehearsed this sequence out loud with the therapist and then silently to himself. Abe was instructed to self-instruct relaxation statements and coping statements during the approach and throughout the interaction and to make statements of self-reinforcement for his performance (including occasions when he experienced rejection—emphasizing process rather than outcome).*

The possibility of rejection was discussed, and a range of possible responses was generated and role played:

- *"I understand, Mary, perhaps another time."*
- *"I have really enjoyed getting to know you, and I look forward to seeing you next week."*
- *"You'd rather just remain friends and not go out. That's fine by me. I enjoy our friendship."*
- *"That's unfortunate. I was looking forward to getting to know you better. Perhaps another time."*

The therapist taught behavioral skills, such as eye contact, body posturing, and verbal expressions, to promote effective social approaching, engaging, and requesting. These skills were also repeatedly rehearsed through the step-wise procedures of therapist modeling, behavior rehearsal with coaching, and role playing.

Abe was assigned in vivo assignments to approach women and engage them in conversation (e.g., store clerks, coworkers) while entertaining the thought, "I'm going to ask you out," that is, acting as if this is an actual dating approach, whether or not he had a genuine desire to date those he approached. The ultimate test of self-instruction procedures was accomplished when Abe asked a woman for a date. His initial attempt was met with rejection. After two sessions in which the rejection was addressed and further rehearsal of self-instruction undertaken, Abe was prepared to try again. It took four subsequent approaches before Abe received an acceptance.

Problem Solving

Problem solving has been classified alternatively as a behavioral procedure and a cognitive-behavioral procedure. D'Zurilla and Goldfried (1971) define problem solving as "a behavioral process, whether overt or covert in nature, which (a) makes available a variety of potentially effective response alternatives for dealing with the problematic situation and (b) increases the probability of selecting the most effective response from among these various alternatives" (p. 108). D'Zurilla (1988) has modified this definition, specifying problem solving as "a cognitive-affective-behavioral process through which an individual (or group) attempts to identify, discover, or invent effective or adaptive means of coping with problems encountered in everyday living" (p. 86). Problem-solving deficiencies have been found to be associated with a variety of personal and interpersonal problems (Dobson & Dobson, 1981; Jacob, Ritchey, Cvitkovic, & Blane, 1981; Kazdin, Esveldt-Dawson, French, & Unis, 1987; Nezu & Carnevale, 1987; Vincent, Weiss, & Birchler, 1976; Weisz, Weiss, Wasserman, & Rintoul, 1987), and training in problem solving has been found to improve the functioning of various clinical populations (Bedell, Archer, & Marlow, 1980; Chaney, O'Leary, & Marlatt, 1978; Ewart, Burnett, & Taylor, 1983; Jannoun, Munby, Catalan, & Gelder, 1980; Nezu, 1986; Nezu, Nezu, & Houts, 1993).

Problem-solving training has been used effectively with both children and adults, and it can be used alone or in conjunction with other methods. There are several approaches to problem solving, but the most widely accepted is the five-step model of D'Zurilla and Goldfried (1971): (1) problem orientation, (2) problem definition and formulation, (3) generation of alternative solutions, (4) decision making, and (5) implementation and verification of solutions. Problem orientation relates to the cognitive "set" of the individual in relation to problem solving and coping with life situations. D'Zurilla (1988) identifies the significant problem-orientation factors as follows: "problem perception, causal attributions, problem appraisals, beliefs about personal control, and values concerning the commitment of time and effort to problem solving" (p. 89). Step 2, problem definition and formulation, involves an assessment of the problem and the establishment of an achievable goal. The third step involves "brainstorming" to generate alternative solutions to the problem. At step 4 the alternatives are evaluated, and a solution is selected for implementation. The final component of the process is designed to determine the effectiveness of the problem-solving effort and, if the solution is found to be lacking, to promote modification of the original solution or a return to step 3 to select another promising alternative solution.

The goal of problem solving is to treat life problems that are antecedents of maladaptive responses and are considered to be causally related to these responses. Only when these antecedent problems are difficult to define or change is the approach to be applied to the maladaptive responses (D'Zurilla, 1988). Examples of problem-solving issues are as follows:

- How can I make better use of my time?
- How can my husband and I do more novel activities?
- How can I reduce the disruptive behavior of my children at the table?
- How can I get my aging father to take better care of himself?
- How can I reduce the stress of my job?

The effectiveness of problem solving can be extended through the use of such adjuncts as cognitive restructuring and training in social skills, assertiveness, self-control techniques, and coping skills.

CONCLUSION

The principles and practice of cognitive-behavioral therapy have been subject to misunderstanding and misinterpretation. This chapter has focused on the elucidation of features common to the methodology and to the specification of assessment and treatment procedures. The presentation has been heavily weighted on the cognitive component of cognitive-behavioral treatment given the more recent development of cognitive procedures. The procedures presented are highly applicable to the clinical challenges confronting social work practitioners and are worthy of strong consideration for implementation across clinical populations, problems, and settings.

Cognitive-behavioral intervention appears to be effective in the treatment of a broad range of adult and child disorders. Empirical support continues to build for the application of various cognitive-behavioral approaches to treatment. It is in the context of this rich empirical support that a formidable challenge is being posed to infuse constructivist methods into the existing fabric of cognitive-behavioral treatment. Those cognitive-behaviorists whose behavioral orientations have been stretched to encompass cognitive components in their treatments may well experience constructive methods to be unacceptable for their "empiricist" blood. Those with psychodynamic backgrounds or "leanings" may warmly embrace the infusion of postmodernism and view this as an opportunity to take cognitivism into the twenty-first century. Just when we thought that the behaviorists and dynamicists had largely reached a summit, it's back to the future! The stage is set for the next series of debates.

Despite the impending dissension (system perturbation), it is of some solace that traditional cognitive-behavioral interventions appear to have surpassed simply "promising" and are considered to have come of age (Hollon & Beck, 1994). It is on this basis that cognitive-behaviorists can proceed with confidence in applying and refining their methods.

REFERENCES

Agras, W. S., Rossiter, E. M., Arnow, B., Schneider, J. A., Telch, C. F., Raeburn, S. D., Bruse, B., Perl, M., & Koran, L. M. (1992). Pharmacological and cognitive-behavioral treatment for bulimia nervosa: A controlled comparison. *American Journal of Psychiatry, 149*, 82–87.

Baars, B. J. (1986). *The cognitive revolution in psychology*. New York: Guilford.

Bandura, A. (1978). The self system in reciprocal determinism. *American Psychologist, 33,* 344–358.

Barlow, D. H., & Cerny, J. A. (1988). *Psychological treatment of panic.* New York: Guilford.

Barlow, D. H. (1981). *Behavioral assessment of adult disorders.* New York: Guilford.

Barlow, D. H. (1988). *Anxiety and its disorders: The nature and treatment of anxiety and panic.* New York: Guilford.

Barlow, D. H., Craske, M., Cerny, J. A., & Klosko, J. S. (1989). Behavioral treatment of panic disorder. *Behavior Therapy, 20,* 261–268.

Baucom, D. H., & Epstein, N. (1990). *Cognitive-behavioral marital therapy.* New York: Brunner/Mazel.

Baucom, D. H., Sayers, S., & Scher, T. G. (1990). Supplementary behavioral marital therapy with cognitive restructuring and emotional expressiveness training: An outcome investigation. *Journal of Consulting and Clinical Psychology, 58,* 636–645.

Beck, A. T. (1970). Cognitive therapy: Nature and relation to behavior therapy. *Behavior Therapy, 1,* 184–200.

Beck, A. T. (1976). *Cognitive therapy and the emotional disorders.* New York: International Universities Press.

Beck, A. T., Rush, A. J., Shaw, B. F., & Emery, G. (1979). *Cognitive therapy of depression.* New York: Guilford.

Beck, A. T., & Emery, G. (1985). *Anxiety disorders and phobias: A cognitive perspective.* New York: Basic Books.

Beck, A. T., Freeman, A., & associates (1990). *Cognitive therapy of personality disorders.* New York: Guilford.

Beck, A. T., Sokol, L., Clark, D. A., Berchick, R. J., & Wright, F. D. (1992). A crossover study of focused cognitive therapy for panic disorder. *American Journal of Psychiatry, 149*(6), 778–783.

Beck, A. T., Wright, F. D., Newman, C. F. (1992). Cocaine abuse. In A. Freeman & F. M. Dattilio (Eds.), *Comprehensive casebook of cognitive therapy* (pp. 185–192). New York: Plenum.

Beck, A. T., Wright, F. D., Newman, C. F., & Liese, B. S. (1993). *Cognitive therapy of substance abuse.* New York: Guilford.

Beck, J. S. (1995). *Cognitive therapy: Basics and beyond.* New York: Guilford.

Becker, J. S. (1992). Social phobia. In A. Freeman & F. M. Dattilio (Eds.), *Comprehensive casebook of cognitive therapy.* New York: Plenum.

Bedell, J. R., Archer, R. P., & Marlow, H. A., Jr. (1980). A description and evaluation of a problem solving skills training program. In D. Upper & S. M. Ross (Eds.), *Behavioral group therapy: An annual review.* Champaign, IL: Research Press.

Bedrosian, R. C., & Bozicas, G. D. (1994). *Treating family of origin problems: A cognitive approach.* New York: Guilford.

Berlin, S. B. (1980). Cognitive-behavior intervention for problems of self-criticism among women. *Social Work Research and Abstracts, 16,* 19–28.

Berlin, S. B. (1985). Maintaining reduced levels of self-criticism through relapse prevention treatment. *Social Work Research and Abstracts, 21,* 21–33.

Berlin, S. B., & Marsh, J. C. (1993). *Informing practice decisions.* New York: Macmillan.

Beutler, L. E., Scogin, F., Kirkish, P., Schretlen, D., Corbishley, A., Hamblin, D., Meredith, K., Potter, R., Bamford, C. R., & Levenson, A. I. (1987). Group cognitive therapy and Alprazolan in the treatment of depression in older adults. *Journal of Consulting and Clinical Psychology, 55,* 550–556.

Blackburn, I. M. (1988). An appraisal of cognitive trials of cognitive therapy for depression. In C. Perris, I. M. Blackburn, & H. Perris (Eds.), *Cognitive psychotherapy* (pp. 329–364). New York: Springer.

Bourne, E. J. (1990). *The anxiety and phobia workbook.* Oakland, CA: New Harbinger.

Bowers, W. A. (1990). Treatment of depressed in-patients: Cognitive therapy plus medication, relaxation plus medication, and medication alone. *British Journal of Psychiatry, 156,* 73–78.

Brower, A. M., & Nurius, P. S. (1993). *Social cognition and individual change: Current theory and counseling guidelines.* Newbury Park, CA: Sage.

Burns, D. D. (1980). *Feeling good: The new mood therapy.* New York: Signet.

Burrell, M. J. (1987). Cognitive psychology, epistemology, and psychotherapy: A motor-evolutionary perspective. *Psychotherapy, 24,* 225–232.

Butler, G., Fennell, M., Robson, P., & Gelder, M. (1991). Comparison of behavior therapy and cognitive behavior therapy in the treatment of generalized anxiety disorder. *Journal of Consulting and Clinical Psychology, 59,* 167–175.

Cacioppo, J. T., & Petty, R. E. (1981). Social psychological procedures for cognition response assessment. In T. Merluzzi, C. Glass, & M. Genest (Eds.), *Cognitive assessment* (pp. 309–342). New York: Guilford.

Chadwick, P. D. J., & Lowe, C. F. (1990). Measurement and modification of delusional beliefs. *Journal of Consulting and Clinical Psychology, 58,* 225–232.

Chaney, E. F., O'Leary, M. R., & Marlatt, G. A. (1978). Skill training with alcoholics. *Journal of Consulting and Clinical Psychology, 46,* 1092–1104.

Ciminero, A. R., Calhoun, K. S., & Adams, H. E. (Eds.). (1986). *Handbook of behavioral assessment* (2d ed.). New York: Wiley.

Clark, D. M., Salkovskis, P. M., Hackmann, A., Middleton, H., Anastasiades, P., & Gelder, M. (1994). A comparison of cognitive therapy, applied relaxation and imipramine in the treatment of panic disorder. *British Journal of Psychiatry, 164,* 759–769.

Cooper, P. J., & Fairburn, C. G. (1984). Cognitive behaviour therapy for anorexia nervosa. Some preliminary findings. *Journal of Psychosomatic Research, 28,* 493–499.

Corcoran, K., & Fischer, J. (1987). *Measures for clinical practice: A sourcebook.* New York: Free Press.

Corey, D. (1988). *Pain: Learning to live without it.* New York: Macmillan.

Craighead, L. W., & Agras, W. S. (1991). Mechanisms of action in cognitive-behavioral and pharmacological interventions for obesity and bulimia nervosa. *Journal of Consulting and Clinical Psychology, 59,* 115–125.

Craighead, L. W., Craighead, W. E., Kazdin, A. E., & Mahoney, M. J. (Eds.). (1994). *Cognitive and behavioral interventions: An empirical approach to mental health problems.* Needham Heights, MA: Allyn & Bacon.

Dahlquist, L. M., Gil, K. M., Armstrong, F. D., Ginsberg, A., & Jones, B. (1985). Behavioral management of children's distress during chemotherapy. *Journal of Behavior Therapy and Experimental Psychiatry, 16,* 325–329.

Dancu, C. F., & Foa, E. G. (1992). Posttraumatic stress disorder. In A. Freeman & F. M. Dattilio (Eds.), *Comprehensive casebook of cognitive therapy* (pp. 79–88). New York: Plenum.

Dattilio, F. M., & Freeman, A. (Eds.). (1994). *Cognitive-behavioral strategies in crisis intervention.* New York: Guilford.

Dattilio, F. M., & Kendall, P. C. (1994). Panic disorder. In F. M. Dattilio & A. Freeman (Eds.), *Cognitive-behavioral strategies in crisis intervention.* New York: Guilford.

Dattilio, F. M., & Padesky, C. A. (1990). *Cognitive therapy with couples.* Sarasota, FL: Professional Resource Exchange.

Deblinger, E. (1992). Child sexual abuse. In A. Freeman & F. M. Dattilio (Eds.), *Comprehensive casebook of cognitive therapy* (pp. 159–167). New York: Plenum.

Dember, W. N. (1974). Motivation and the cognitive revolution. *American Psychologist, 29,* 161–168.

DeRubeis, R. J., & Beck, A. T. (1988). Cognitive therapy. In K. S. Dobson (Ed.), *Handbook of cognitive-behavioral therapies* (pp. 273–306). New York: Guilford.

Dobson, D. J., & Dobson, K. S. (1981). Problem-solving strategies in depressed and nondepressed college students. *Cognitive Therapy and Research, 5*, 237–249.

Dobson, K. S. (1989). A meta-analysis of the efficacy of cognitive therapy for depression. *Journal of Consulting and Clinical Psychology, 57*, 414–419.

Dryden, W., & Ellis, A. (1988). Rational-emotive therapy. In K. S. Dobson (Ed.), *Handbook of cognitive-behavioral therapies*. New York: Guilford.

Duehn, W. D. (1994). Cognitive-behavioral approaches in the treatment of the child sex offender. In D. K. Granvold (Ed.), *Cognitive and behavioral treatment: Methods and applications* (pp. 125–134). Pacific Grove, CA: Brooks/Cole.

D'Zurilla, T. J. (1988). Problem-solving therapy. In K. S. Dobson (Ed.), *Handbook of cognitive-behavioral therapies*. New York: Guilford.

D'Zurilla, T. J., & Goldfried, M. R. (1971). Problem solving and behavior modification. *Journal of Abnormal Psychology, 78*, 107–126.

Edgette, J. S., & Prout, M. F. (1989). Cognitive and behavioral approaches to the treatment of anorexia nervosa. In A. Freeman, K. M. Simon, L. E. Beutler, & H. Arkowitz (Eds.), *Comprehensive handbook of cognitive therapy* (pp. 367–383). New York: Plenum.

Ellis, A. (1962). *Reason and emotion in psychotherapy*. New York: Lyle Stuart.

Ellis, A. (1969). A weekend of rational encounter. *Rational Living, 4*, 1–8.

Ellis, A. (1973). *Humanistic psychotherapy: The rational-emotive approach*. New York: McGraw-Hill.

Ellis, A. (1977a). Psychotherapy and the value of a human being. In A. Ellis & R. Grieger (Eds.), *Handbook of rational-emotive therapy*. New York: Springer.

Ellis, A. (1977b). The basic clinical theory of rational-emotive therapy. In A. Ellis & R. Grieger (Eds.), *Handbook of rational-emotive therapy*. New York: Springer.

Ellis, A. (1979). The practice of rational-emotive therapy. In A. Ellis & J. M. Whitely (Eds.), *Theoretical and empirical foundations of rational-emotive therapy* (pp. 61–100). Monterey, CA: Brooks/Cole.

Ellis, A. (1984). The essence of RET—1984. *Journal of Rational-Emotive Therapy, 2*(1), 19–25.

Ellis, A. (1989). The history of cognition in psychotherapy. In A. Freeman, K. M. Simon, L. E. Beutler, & H. Arkowitz (Eds.), *Comprehensive handbook of cognitive therapy* (pp. 5–19). New York: Plenum.

Ellis, A. (1991). The revised ABC's of rational-emotive therapy (RET). *Journal of Rational-Emotive and Cognitive-Behavior Therapy, 9*(3), 139–172.

Ellis, A. (1993). Changing rational-emotive therapy (RET) to rational emotive behavior therapy (REBT). *Behavior Therapist, 16*, 257–258.

Ellis, A. (1994). *Reason and emotion in psychotherapy: A comprehensive method of treating human disturbances* (Rev. and updated). Secaucus, NJ: Birch Lane Press.

Ellis, A., & Becker, I. (1982). *A guide to personal happiness*. North Hollywood, CA: Wilshire.

Ellis, A., & Bernard, M. E. (1986). What is rational-emotive therapy (RET)? In A. Ellis & M. E. Bernard (Eds.), *Clinical applications of rational-emotive therapy*. New York: Plenum.

Ellis, A., & Dryden, W. (1987). *The practice of rational-emotive therapy*. New York: Springer.

Ellis, A., Sichel, J. L., Yeager, R. J., DiMattia, D. J., & DiGiuseppe, R. (1989). *Rational-emotive couples therapy*. New York: Pergamon.

Eimer, B. N. (1989). Psychotherapy for chronic pain: A cognitive approach. In A. Freeman, K. M. Simon, L. E. Beutler, & H. Arkowitz (Eds.), *Comprehensive handbook of cognitive therapy* (pp. 449–465). New York: Plenum.

Emmelkamp, P. M. G., Kuipers, A. C. M., & Eggeraat, J. B. (1978). Cognitive modification versus prolonged exposure *in vivo:* A comparison with agoraphobics as subjects. *Behavior Research and Therapy, 16,* 33–41.

Emmelkamp, P. M. G., Mersch, P. P., Vissia, E., & van der Helm, M. (1985). Social phobia: A comparative evaluation of cognitive and behavioral interventions. *Behaviour, Research and Therapy, 23,* 365–369.

Epstein, N., Schlesinger, S. E., & Dryden, W. (Eds.). (1988). *Cognitive-behavioral therapy with families.* New York: Brunner/Mazel.

Ewart, C. K., Burnett, K. F., & Taylor, C. B. (1983). Communication behaviors that affect blood pressure: An A-B-A-B analysis of marital interaction. *Behavior Modification, 7,* 331–344.

Fairburn, C. G. (1981). A cognitive behavioral approach to the treatment of bulimia. *Psychological Medicine, 11,* 707–711.

Fairburn, C. G., Jones, R., Peveler, R. C., Carr, S. J., Solomon, R. A., O'Connor, M. E., Burton, J., & Hope, R. A. (1991). Three psychological treatments for bulimia nervosa: A comparative trial. *Archives of General Psychiatry, 48,* 463–469.

Foa, E. B., Rothbaum, B. O., Riggs, D., & Murdock, T. (1991). Treatment of PTSD in rape victims: A comparison between cognitive-behavioral procedures and counseling. *Journal of Consulting and Clinical Psychology, 59,* 715–723.

Frankl, V. E. (1959). *Man's search for meaning: An introduction to logotherapy.* New York: Washington Square Press.

Franklin, C. (1995). Expanding the vision of the social constructionist debates: Creating relevance for practitioners. *Families in Society, 76,* 395–406.

Freeman, A. (1983). Cognitive therapy: An overview. In A. Freeman (Ed.), *Cognitive therapy with couples and groups.* New York: Plenum.

Freeman, A. (1990). Cognitive therapy. In A. S. Bellack & M. Hersen (Eds.), *Handbook of comparative treatments for adult disorders* (pp. 64–87). New York: Wiley.

Freeman, A., & Dattilio, F. M. (Eds.). (1992). *Comprehensive casebook of cognitive therapy.* New York: Plenum.

Freeman, A., & Leaf, R. C. (1989). Cognitive therapy applied to personality disorders. In A. Freeman, K. M. Simon, L. E. Beutler, & H. Arkowitz (Eds.), *Comprehensive handbook of cognitive therapy* (pp. 403–433). New York: Plenum.

Freeman, A., Pretzer, J., Fleming, B., & Simon, K. M. (1990). *Clinical applications of cognitive therapy.* New York: Plenum.

Freeman, A., & Simon, K. M. (1989). Cognitive therapy of anxiety. In A. Freeman, K. M. Simon, L. E. Beutler, & H. Arkowitz (Eds.), *Comprehensive handbook of cognitive therapy* (pp. 347–365). New York: Plenum.

Freeman, A., Simon, K. M., Beutler, L. E., & Arkowitz, H. (Eds.). (1989). *Comprehensive handbook of cognitive therapy.* New York: Plenum.

Garner, D. M. (1992). Bulimia nervosa. In A. Freeman & F. M. Dattilio (Eds.), *Comprehensive casebook of cognitive therapy* (pp. 169–176). New York: Plenum.

Garner, D. M., & Bemis, K. M. (1985). Cognitive therapy for anorexia nervosa. In D. M. Garner & P. E. Garfinkel (Eds.), *Handbook of psychotherapy for anorexia nervosa and bulimia* (pp. 107–146). New York: Guilford.

Garner, D. M., Rockert, W., Davis, R., Garner, M. V., Olmstead, M. P., & Eagle, M. (1993). Comparison of cognitive-behavioral and supportive-expressive therapy for bulimia nervosa. *American Journal of Psychiatry, 150,* 37–46.

Gelernter, C. S., Uhde, T. W., Cimbolic, P., Arnkoff, D. B., Vittone, B. J., Taneer, M. E., & Bartko, J. J. (1991). Cognitive-behavioral and pharmacological treatments of social phobia: A controlled study. *Archives of General Psychiatry, 48,* 938–945.

Genest, M., & Turk, D. C. (1981). Think aloud approaches to cognitive assessment. In T.

Merluzzi, C. Glass, & M. Genest (Eds.), *Cognitive assessment* (pp. 233–269). New York: Guilford.

Getka, E. J., & Glass, C. R. (1992). Behavioral and cognitive-behavioral approaches to the reduction of dental anxiety. *Behavior Therapy, 23,* 433–448.

Goodman, D. S., & Maultsby, M. C. (1974). *Emotional well-being through rational behavior training.* Springfield, IL: Charles C. Thomas.

Granvold, D. K. (1988). Treating marital couples in conflict and transition. In J. S. McNeil & S. E. Weinstein (Eds.), *Innovations in health care practice.* Silver Spring, MD: National Association of Social Workers.

Granvold, D. K. (1989). Postdivorce treatment. In M. R. Textor (Ed.), *The divorce and divorce therapy handbook.* Northvale, NJ: Jason Aronson.

Granvold, D. K. (Ed.). (1994a). *Cognitive and behavioral treatment: Methods and applications.* Pacific Grove, CA: Brooks/Cole.

Granvold, D. K. (1994b). Concepts and methods of cognitive treatment. In D. K. Granvold (Ed.), *Cognitive and behavioral treatment: Methods and applications.* Pacific Grove, CA: Brooks/Cole.

Granvold, D. K. (1996). Constructivist psychotherapy. *Families in Society: The Journal of Contemporary Human Services, 77*(6), 345–357.

Granvold, D.K., & Jordan, C. (1994). The cognitive-behavioral treatment of marital distress. In D. K. Granvold (Ed.), *Cognitive and behavioral treatment: Methods and applications* (pp. 174–201). Pacific Grove, CA: Brooks/Cole.

Granvold, D. K., & Wodarski, J. S. (1994). Cognitive and behavioral treatment: Clinical issues, transfer of training, and relapse prevention. In D. K. Granvold (Ed.), *Cognitive and behavioral treatment: Methods and applications* (pp. 353–375). Pacific Grove, CA: Brooks/Cole.

Guidano, V. F. (1984). A constructivist outline of cognitive processes. In M. A. Reda & M. J. Mahoney (Eds.), *Cognitive psychotherapies: Recent developments in theory, research, and practice* (pp. 31–45). Cambridge, MA: Ballinger.

Guidano, V. F. (1987). *Complexity of the self: A developmental approach to psychopathology and therapy.* New York: Guilford.

Guidano, V. F. (1988). A systems, process-oriented approach to cognitive therapy. In K. S. Dobson (Ed.), *Handbook of cognitive-behavioral therapies.* New York: Guilford.

Guidano, V. F., & Liotti, G. A. (1983). *Cognitive processes and emotional disorders.* New York: Guilford.

Guidano, V. F., & Liotti, G. A. (1985). A constructivist foundation for cognitive therapy. In M. J. Mahoney & A. Freeman (Eds.), *Cognition and psychotherapy* (pp. 101–142). New York: Plenum.

Haynes, S. N. (1978). *Principles of behavioral assessment.* New York: Gardner.

Hazaleus, S. L., & Deffenbacher, J. L. (1986). Relaxation and cognitive treatments of anger. *Journal of Consulting and Clinical Psychology, 54,* 222–226.

Heimberg, R. G. (1990). Social phobia: Cognitive behavior therapy. In A. S. Bellack & M. Hersen (Eds.), *Handbook of comparative treatments for adult disorders.* New York: Wiley.

Hersen, M., & Bellack, A. S. (Eds.). (1976). *Behavioral assessment: A practical handbook.* New York: Pergamon.

Hollon, S. D., & Beck, A. T. (1986). Cognitive and cognitive-behavioral therapies. In S. L. Garfield & A. E. Bergin (Eds.), *Handbook of psychotherapy and behavior change* (3rd ed.). New York: Wiley.

Hollon, S. D., & Beck, A. T. (1994). Cognitive and cognitive-behavioral therapies. In A. E. Bergin & S. L. Garfield (Eds.), *Handbook of psychotherapy and behavior change: An empirical analysis* (4th ed.) (pp. 428–466). New York: Wiley.

Hollon, S. D., & Najavits, L. (1989). Review of empirical studies on cognitive therapy. In A. Frances & R. Hales (Eds.), *Review of psychiatry* (Vol. 7, pp. 643–667). New York: American Psychiatric Press.

Huber, C. H., & Baruth, L. G. (1989). *Rational-emotive family therapy: A systems perspective.* New York: Springer.

Hudson, W. W. (1990). *The multi-problem screening inventory.* Tempe, AZ: Walmyr.

Ingram, R. E., & Kendall, P. C. (1986). Cognitive clinical psychology: Implications of an information processing perspective. In R. E. Ingram (Ed.), *Information processing approaches to clinical psychology* (pp. 4–21). New York: Academic Press.

Ivey, A. E. (1986). *Developmental therapy: Theory into practice.* San Francisco: Jossey-Bass.

Jacob, T., Ritchey, D., Cvitkovic, J., & Blane, H. (1981). Communication styles of alcoholic and nonalcoholic families when drinking and not drinking. *Journal of Studies on Alcohol, 42,* 466–482.

Jacobson, N. S., & Margolin, G. (1979). *Marital therapy.* New York: Brunner/Mazel.

Jannoun, L., Munby, M., Catalan, J., & Gelder, M. (1980). A home-based treatment program for agoraphobia: Replication and controlled evaluation. *Behavior Therapy, 11,* 294–305.

Jay, S. M., Elliott, C. H., Katz, E., & Siegel, S. E. (1987). Cognitive behavioral and pharmacological interventions for children's distress during painful medical procedures. *Journal of Consulting and Clinical Psychology, 55,* 860–865.

Johnson, S. M. (1985). *Characterological transformation: The hard work miracle.* New York: Norton.

Kaplan, R. M., Atkins, C. J., & Lenhard, L. (1982). Coping with a stressful sigmoidoscopy: Evaluation of cognitive and relaxation preparations. *Journal of Behavioral Medicine, 5,* 67–82.

Kazdin, A. E., Esveldt-Dawson, K., French, N. H., & Unis, A. S. (1987). Problem-solving skills training and relationship therapy in the treatment of antisocial child behavior. *Journal of Consulting and Clinical Psychology, 55,* 76–85.

Keefe, F. J., Caldwell, D. S., Williams, D. A., Gil, K. M., Mitchell, D., Robertson, C., Martinez, S., Nunley, J., Beckham, J. C., Crisson, J. E., & Helms, M. (1990). Pain coping skills training in the management of osteoarthritic knee pain: A comparative study. *Behavior Therapy, 21,* 49–62.

Kelly, G. A. (1955). *The psychology of personal constructs* (Vols. 1 & 2). New York: Norton.

Kendall, P. C., & Hollon, S. D. (1981). *Assessment strategies for cognitive-behavioral interventions.* New York: Academic Press.

Kendall, P. C., & Korgeski, G. P. (1979). Assessment and cognitive-behavioral interventions. *Cognitive Therapy and Research, 3,* 1–21.

Kendall, P. C., Williams, L., Pechacek, T. F., Graham, L. E., Shissalak, C., & Herzoff, N. (1979). Cognitive-behavioral and patient education interventions in cardiac catheterization procedures. *Journal of Consulting and Clinical Psychology, 47,* 49–58.

Kerns, R. D., Turk, D. C., Holzman, A. D., & Rudy, T. E. (1986). Comparison of cognitive-behavioral and behavioral approaches for the treatment of chronic pain. *Clinical Journal of Pain, 1,* 195–203.

Kingdon, D. G., & Turkington, D. (1991). The use of cognitive behavior therapy with a normalizing rationale in schizophrenia: Preliminary report. *Journal of Nervous and Mental Disease, 179,* 207–211.

Kingdon, D. G., & Turkington, D. (1994). *Cognitive-behavioral therapy of schizophrenia.* New York: Guilford.

Kruglanski, A. W., & Jaffe, Y. (1983). The lay epistemic model in cognitive therapy. In M. Rosenbaum, C. M. Franks, & Y. Jaffe (Eds.), *Perspectives on behavior therapy in the eighties.* New York: Springer.

Kuehlwein, K. T., & Rosen, H. (Eds.). (1993). *Cognitive therapies in action: Evolving innovative practice.* San Francisco, CA: Jossey-Bass.

Laws, D. R. (Ed.). (1989). *Relapse prevention with sex offenders.* New York: Guilford.

Layden, M. A., Newman, C. F., Freeman, A., & Morse, S. B. (1993). *Cognitive therapy of borderline personality disorder.* Needham Heights, MA: Allyn & Bacon.

Lazarus, A. A. (1971). *Behavior therapy and beyond.* New York: McGraw-Hill.

Lazarus, A. A. (1976). *Multimodal behavior therapy.* New York: McGraw-Hill.

Leva, L. M. (1984). Cognitive behavioral therapy in the light of Piagetian theory. In M. A. Reda & M. J. Mahoney (Eds.), *Cognitive psychotherapies: Recent developments in theory, research, and practice* (pp. 233–250). Cambridge, MA: Ballinger.

Linehan, M. M. (1993). *Cognitive-behavioral treatment of borderline personality disorder.* New York: Guilford.

Linehan, M. M., Armstrong, H. E., Suarez, A., Allman, D., & Heard, H. L. (1991). Cognitive-behavioral treatment of chronically parasuicidal borderline patients. *Archives of General Psychiatry, 48,* 1060–1064.

Linton, S. J., Bradley, L. A., Jensen, I., Spangfort, E., & Sundell, L. (1989). The secondary prevention of low back pain: A controlled study with follow-up. *Pain, 36,* 197–207.

Lochman, J. E., Burch, P. R., Curry, J. F., & Lampron, L. B. (1984). Treatment and generalization effects of cognitive behavioral and goal setting interventions with aggressive boys. *Journal of Consulting and Clinical Psychology, 52,* 915–916.

Luria, A. (1959). The directive function of speech in development. *Word, 18,* 341–352.

Luria, A. (1961). *The role of speech in the regulation of normal and abnormal behaviors.* New York: Liveright.

Lyddon, W. J. (1990). First-and-second-order change: Implications for rationalist and constructivist cognitive therapies. *Journal of Counseling and Development, 69,* 122–127.

Mahoney, M. J. (1977). Reflection on the cognitive-learning trend in psychotherapy. *American Psychologist, 32,* 5–13.

Mahoney, M. J. (1980). Psychotherapy and the structure of personal revolutions. In M. J. Mahoney (Ed.), *Psychotherapy process: Current issues and future directions* (pp. 157–180). New York: Plenum.

Mahoney, M. J. (1985). Psychotherapy and human change process. In M. J. Mahoney and A. Freeman (Eds.), *Cognition of psychotherapy* (pp. 3–48). New York: Plenum.

Mahoney, M. J. (1991). *Human change processes: The scientific foundations of psychotherapy.* New York: Basic Books.

Mahoney, M. J. (1993). Introduction to special section: Theoretical developments in the cognitive psychotherapies. *Journal of Consulting and Clinical Psychology, 61,* 187–193.

Mahoney, M. J. (Ed.). (1995). *Cognitive and constructive psychotherapies.* New York: Springer.

Mahoney, M. J. (in press). *Constructive psychotherapy techniques.* New York: Guilford.

Mahoney, M. J., & Lyddon, W. J. (1988). Recent developments in cognitive approaches to counseling and psychotherapy. *Counseling Psychologist, 16,* 190–234.

Marlatt, G. A. (1985). Relapse prevention: Theoretical rationale and overview of the model. In G. A. Marlatt & J. R. Gordon (Eds.), *Relapse prevention* (pp. 3–70). New York: Guilford.

Marlatt, G. A., & Gordon, J. R. (Eds.). (1985). *Relapse prevention.* New York: Guilford.

Mash, E. J., & Terdal, L. G. (Eds.). (1976). *Behavior therapy assessment: Diagnosis, design and evaluation.* New York: Springer.

Mattick, R. P., Peters, L., & Clarke, J. C. (1989). Exposure and cognitive restructuring for social phobia: A controlled study. *Behavior Therapy, 20,* 3–23.

Maultsby, M. C. (1977). Rational-emotive imagery. In A. Ellis & R. Grieger (Eds.), *Handbook of rational-emotive therapy.* New York: Springer.

Maultsby, M. C. (1984). *Rational behavior therapy.* Englewood Cliffs, NJ: Prentice Hall.

Maultsby, M. C., & Ellis, A. (1974). *Techniques for using rational-emotive imagery.* New York: Institute for Rational-Emotive Therapy.

Meichenbaum, D. (1975). Theoretical and treatment implications of developmental research on verbal control of behavior. *Canadian Psychological Review, 16,* 22–27.

Meichenbaum, D. (1977). *Cognitive-behavior modification.* New York: Plenum.

Meichenbaum, D. (1993). The "potential" contributions of cognitive behavior modification to the rehabilitation of individuals and traumatic brain injury. In M. Ylvisaker (Ed.), *Seminars in speech and language* (pp. 18–38). New York: Thieme Medical Publishers.

Meichenbaum, D. (1994). *A clinical handbook/practical therapist manual: For assessing and treating adults with PTSD.* Waterloo, Ontario, Canada: Institute Press.

Meichenbaum, D., & Goodman, J. (1971). Training impulsive children to talk to themselves: A means of developing self-control. *Journal of Abnormal Psychology, 77,* 115–126.

Merluzzi, T. V., & Boltwood, M. D. (1989). Cognitive assessment. In A. Freeman, K. M. Simon, L. E. Beutler, & H. Arkowitz (Eds.), *Comprehensive handbook of cognitive therapy* (pp. 249–266). New York: Plenum.

Merluzzi, T. V., Glass, C. R., & Genest, M. (Eds.). (1981). *Cognitive assessment.* New York: Guilford.

Michelson, L. (1987). Cognitive-behavioral assessment and treatment of agoraphobia. In L. Michelson & L. M. Ascher (Eds.), *Anxiety and stress disorders: Cognitive-behavioral assessment and treatment* (pp. 213–279). New York: Guilford.

Michelson, L., & Ascher, L. M. (Eds.). (1987). *Anxiety and stress disorders: Cognitive-behavioral assessment and treatment.* New York: Guilford.

Miller, P. C. (1991). The application of cognitive therapy to chronic pain. In T. M. Vallis, J. L. Howes, & P. C. Miller (Eds.), *The challenge of cognitive therapy: Applications to nontraditional populations* (pp. 159–182). New York: Plenum.

Mitchell, J. E., Pyle, R. L., Eckert, E. D., Hatsukami, D., Pomeroy, C., & Zimmerman, R. (1990). A comparison study of antidepressants and structural intensive group psychotherapy in the treatment of bulimia nervosa. *Archives of General Psychiatry, 47,* 149–157.

Munson, C. E. (1994). Cognitive family therapy. In D. K. Granvold (Ed.), *Cognitive and behavioral treatment: Methods and applications* (pp. 202–221). Pacific Grove, CA: Brooks/Cole.

Nay, W. R. (1979). *Multimethod clinical assessment.* New York: Gardner.

Neimeyer, G. J. (Ed.). (1993). *Constructivist assessment: A casebook.* Newbury Park, CA: Sage.

Neimeyer, R. A. (1993a). An appraisal of constructivist psychotherapies. *Journal of Consulting and Clinical Psychology, 61,* 221–234.

Neimeyer, R. A. (1993b). Constructivism and the cognitive psychotherapies: Some conceptual and strategic contrasts. *Journal of Cognitive Psychotherapy: An International Quarterly, 7,* 159–171.

Neimeyer, R. A. (1993c). Constructivist approaches to the measurement of meaning. In G. J. Neimeyer (Ed.), *Constructivist assessment: A casebook* (pp. 188–232). Newbury Park, CA: Sage.

Neimeyer, R. A. (1995). Constructivist psychotherapies: Features, foundations, and future directions. In R. A. Neimeyer & M. J. Mahoney (Eds.), *Constructivism in psychotherapy* (pp. 11–38). Washington, DC: American Psychological Association.

Neimeyer, R. A., & Mahoney, M. J. (Eds.). (1995). *Constructivism in psychotherapy.* Washington, DC: American Psychological Association.

Neimeyer, R. A., & Neimeyer, G. J. (1993). Constructivist assessment: What and when. In G. J. Neimeyer (Ed.), *Constructivist assessment: A casebook.* Newbury Park, CA: Sage.

Nezu, A. M. (1986). Efficacy of a social problem solving therapy approach for unipolar depression. *Journal of Consulting and Clinical Psychology, 54,* 196–202.

Nezu, A. M., & Carnevale, G. J. (1987). Interpersonal problem solving and coping reactions of Vietnam veterans with posttraumatic stress syndrome. *Journal of Abnormal Psychology, 96,* 155–157.

Nezu, C. M., Nezu, A. M., & Houts, P. S. (1993). Multiple applications of problem-solving principles in clinical practice. In K. T. Kuehlwein & H. Rosen (Eds.), *Cognitive therapies in action: Evolving innovative practice.* San Francisco, CA: Jossey-Bass.

Novaco, R. W. (1975). *Anger control: The development and evaluation of an experimental treatment.* Lexington, MA: D. C. Heath.

Novaco, R. W. (1977a). Stress-inoculation: A cognitive therapy for anger and its application to a case of depression. *Journal of Consulting and Clinical Psychology, 45,* 600–608.

Novaco, R. W. (1977b). A stress-inoculation approach to anger management in the training of law enforcement officers. *American Journal of Community Psychology, 5,* 327–346.

Nurius, P. S. (1991). Possible selves and social support: Social cognitive resources for coping and striving. In J. Howard & P. Collero (Eds.), *The self-society dynamic: Cognition, emotion, and action.* New York: Cambridge University Press.

Nurius, P. S., & Berlin, S. S. (1994). Treatment of negative self-concept and depression. In D. K. Granvold (Ed.), *Cognitive and behavioral treatment: Methods and applications.* Pacific Grove, CA: Brooks/Cole.

Nurius, P. S., & Majerus, D. (1988). Rethinking the self in self-talk: A theoretical note and case example. *Journal of Social and Clinical Psychology, 6,* 335–345.

Parrott, C. A., & Howes, J. L. (1991). The application of cognitive therapy to posttraumatic stress disorder. In T. M. Vallis, J. L. Howes, & P. C. Miller (Eds.), *The challenge of cognitive therapy: Applications to nontraditional populations* (pp. 85–109). New York: Plenum.

Perris, C. (1989). *Cognitive therapy with schizophrenic patients.* New York: Guilford.

Perris, C., Ingelson, U., & Johnson, D. (1993). Cognitive therapy as a general framework in the treatment of psychotic patients. In K. T. Kuehlwein & H. Rosen (Eds.), *Cognitive therapy in action: Evolving innovative practice* (pp. 379–402). San Francisco: Jossey-Bass.

Perris, C., & Skagerlind, L. (1994). Schizophrenia. In F. M. Dattilio & A. Freeman (Eds.), *Cognitive-behavioral strategies in crisis intervention.* New York: Guilford.

Perry, S., Fishman, B., Jacobsberg, L., Young, J., & Frances, A. (1991). Effectiveness of psychoeducational interventions in reducing emotional distress after human immunodeficiency virus antibody testing. *Archives of General Psychiatry, 48,* 143–147.

Popper, K. R. (1972). *Objective knowledge: An evolutionary approach.* London: Oxford University Press.

Premack, D. (1965). Reinforcement theory. In D. Levine (Ed.), *Nebraska Symposium on Motivation.* Lincoln, NE: University of Nebraska Press.

Premack, D. (1971). Catching up with common sense or two sides of a generalization: Reinforcement and punishment. In R. Glaser (Ed.), *The nature of reinforcement.* New York: Academic Press.

Rehm, L. P. (1977). A self-control model of depression. *Behavior Therapy, 8,* 787–804.

Richey, C. A. (1994). Social support skill training. In D. K. Granvold (Ed.), *Cognitive and behavioral treatment: Methods and applications.* Pacific Grove, CA: Brooks/Cole.

Rosen, H. (1985). *Piagetian dimensions of clinical relevance.* New York: Columbia University Press.

Rothstein, M. M., & Vallis, T. M. (1991). The application of cognitive therapy to patients with personality disorders. In T. M. Vallis, J. L. Howes, & P. C. Miller (Eds.), *The challenge of cognitive therapy: Applications to non-traditional populations* (pp. 59–84). New York: Plenum.

Rush, A. J., & Beck, A. T. (1978). Adults with affective disorders. In M. Hersen & A. S. Bellack (Eds.), *Behavioral therapy in the psychiatric setting.* Baltimore, MD: Williams & Wilkins.

Saleebey, D. (Ed.). (1992). *The strengths perspective in social work practice.* New York: Longman.

Salkovskis, P. (1989). Somatic problems. In P. Hawton, P. Salkovskis, J. Kirk, & D. Clark (Eds.), *Cognitive behavior therapy for psychiatric problems* (pp. 235–276). New York: Oxford University Press.

Sanchez-Craig, M., Annis, H. M., Bornet, A. R., & MacDonald, K. R. (1984). Random assignment to abstinence and controlled drinking: Evaluation of a cognitive-behavioral program for problem disorders. *Journal of Consulting and Clinical Psychology, 52,* 390–403.

Sanders, M. R., Rebgetz, M., Morrison, M., Bor, W., Gordon, A., Dadds, M., & Shepherd, J. R. (1989). Cognitive-behavioral treatment of recurrent nonspecific abdominal pain in children: An analysis of generalization, maintenance, and side effects. *Journal of consulting and Clinical Psychology, 57,* 294–300.

Schinke, S. P., & Blythe, B. J., & Gilchrist, L. D. (1981). Cognitive-behavioral prevention of adolescent pregnancy. *Journal of Counseling Psychology, 33,* 5–9.

Schinke, S. P., & Singer, B. R. (1994). Prevention of health care problems. In D. K. Granvold (Ed.), *Cognitive and behavioral treatment: Methods and applications* (pp. 285–298). Pacific Grove, CA: Brooks/Cole.

Schwartz, R. M., & Garamoni, G. L. (1986). A structural model of positive and negative states of mind: Asymmetry in the internal dialogue. In P. C. Kendall (Ed.), *Advances in cognitive behavioral research therapy* (Vol. 5, pp. 1–62). New York: Academic Press.

Scott, J., Williams, J. M. G., & Beck, A. T. (Eds.). (1989). *Cognitive therapy in clinical practice: An illustrative casebook.* New York: Routledge.

Segal, Z. V., & Shaw, B. F. (1988). Cognitive assessment: Issues and methods. In K. S. Dobson (Ed.), *Handbook of cognitive-behavioral therapies* (pp. 39–81). New York: Guilford.

Sgroi, S. M. (1989). *Sexual abuse treatment for children, adult survivors, offenders and persons with mental retardation: Vol. 2. Vulnerable populations.* Lexington, MA: Lexington Books.

Shorkey, C. T. (1994). Use of behavioral methods with individuals recovering from substance dependence. In D. K. Granvold (Ed.), *Cognitive and behavioral treatment: Methods and applications* (pp. 135–158). Pacific Grove, CA: Brooks/Cole.

Smith, D., Marcus, M. D., & Kaye, W. (1992). Cognitive-behavioral treatment of obese binge eaters. *International Journal of Eating Disorders, 12,* 711–716.

Spivack, G., & Shure, M. B. (1974). *Social adjustment of young children: A cognitive approach to solving real-life problems.* San Francisco: Jossey-Bass.

Suarez, E. M. (1985). *Neo-cognitive psychotherapy. Manuscript in preparation.* Coral Gables, FL: Advanced Human Studies Institute.

Sundel, S. S., & Sundel, M. (1993). *Behavior modification in the human services* (3rd ed.). Newbury Park, CA: Sage.

Telch, C. F., Agras, W. S., Rossiter, E. M., Wilfley, D., & Kenardy, J. (1990). Group cognitive-behavioral treatment for the nonpurging bulimic: An initial evaluation. *Journal of Consulting and Clinical Psychology, 58,* 629–635.

Telch, C. F., & Telch, M. J. (1986). Group coping skills instruction and supportive group therapy for cancer patients: A comparison of strategies. *Journal of Consulting and Clinical Psychology, 54,* 802–808.

Thorpe, G., & Burns, L. (1983). *The agoraphobia syndrome.* New York: Wiley.

Tosi, D. J., & Eshbaugh, D. M. (1980). Rational stage-directed therapy and crisis intervention. In R. Herink (Ed.), *The psychotherapy handbook* (pp. 550–553). New York: New American Library.

Tosi, D. J., & Salovey, P. (1985). Rational stage-directed therapy and crisis intervention. In R. Herink (Ed.), *The psychotherapy handbook* (pp. 550–553). New York: New American Library.

Turk, D., Meichenbaum, D., & Genest, M. (1983). *Pain and behavioral medicine: A cognitive-behavioral perspective.* New York: Guilford.

Turner, R. M., Becker, L., & DeLoach, C. (1994). Borderline personality. In F. M. Dattilio & A. Freeman (Eds.), *Cognitive-behavioral strategies in crisis intervention.* New York: Guilford.

Vallis, T. M., Howes, J. L., & Miller, P. C. (Eds.). (1991). *The challenge of cognitive therapy: Applications to nontraditional populations.* New York: Plenum.

Vincent, J., Weiss, R., & Birchler, G. (1976). A behavioral analysis of problem solving in distressed and nondistressed married and stranger dyads. *Behavior Therapy,* 6, 475–487.

Vygotsky, L. (1962). *Thought and language.* New York: Wiley.

Weiner, M. L. (1975). *The cognitive unconscious: A Piagetian approach to psychotherapy.* Davis, CA: International Psychological Press.

Weiner, M. L. (1985). *Cognitive-experiential therapy: An integrative ego psychotherapy.* New York: Brunner/Mazel.

Weiss, R. L., & Margolin, G. (1977). Assessment of marital conflict and accord. In A. R. Ciminero, K. S. Calhoun, & H. E. Adams (Eds.), *Handbook of behavioral assessment.* New York: Wiley.

Weisz, J. R., Weiss, B., Wasserman, A. A., & Rintoul, B. (1987). Control-related beliefs and depression among clinic-referred children and adolescents. *Journal of Abnormal Psychology,* 96, 58–63.

Werner, H. (1984). *Cognitive therapy: A humanistic approach.* New York: Free Press.

Wessler, R. L. (1984). Alternative conceptions of rational-emotive therapy: Toward a philosophically neutral psychotherapy. In M. A. Reda & M. J. Mahoney (Eds.), *The cognitive psychotherapies: Recent developments in theory, research, and practice* (pp. 65–79). Cambridge, MA: Ballinger.

Wilson, G. T., & Fairburn, C. G. (1993). Cognitive treatments for eating disorders. *Journal of Consulting and Clinical Psychology,* 61, 261–269.

Woody, G. E., Luborsky, L., McLellan, A. T., O'Brien, C. P., Beck, A. T., Baline, J., Herman, I., & Hole, A. (1983). Psychotherapy for opiate addiction? Does it help? *Archives of General Psychiatry,* 40, 639–645.

8

Psychoanalytic Psychotherapy with Adults

Fredric T. Perlman

Psychoanalytic psychotherapy is a method for the treatment of mental and emotional disorders through verbal means that promote their understanding. By *mental and emotional disorders,* I mean patterns of thought, feeling, and behavior that restrict the pursuit of life's pleasures and impose objectively unnecessary suffering. By *understanding,* I refer to understanding in the conventional sense, as well as understanding in the psychoanalytic sense. In conventional usage, understanding refers to an attitude of acceptance and empathy based on the fundamental commonalities of human nature. In the psychoanalytic sense, understanding refers to a discernment of the motivations and mental processes that determine subjective experience and behavior. Understanding in the first sense, that is, in the sense of human understanding, is a basic feature of most psychotherapies, including psychoanalytic therapy, and it is a powerful agent of therapeutic change. This type of understanding engenders feelings of being a person like other persons, of being coherent, understandable, and acceptable to others (Rogers, 1957, 1961; Truax, 1963; Truax & Carkhuff, 1967). In psychoanalytic therapy, however, while human understanding is very important, it is only part of the interpersonal context within which psychoanalytic understanding is pursued. Psychoanalytic therapy is predicated on the observation that mental and emotional disorders are the expression of conflicts between unconscious contradictory motivations and that these disorders can be ameliorated when unconscious motivations are brought to light.

Psychoanalytic psychotherapy derives from the theory and technical procedures of psychoanalysis. Psychoanalysis originated with the work of Sigmund Freud

(1856–1939), a Viennese physician whose pioneering efforts to help patients suffering from obscure mental disorders led him from the practice of neurology to the field of psychology. Freud discovered that when these patients speak freely about the thoughts that pass through their minds, they regularly express hitherto unconscious wishes, fears, and other painful affects, which illuminate the motivational basis of their pathologies. Moreover, he found that when these unconscious motivations were uncovered and exposed to conscious reflection, his patients acquired increased control over their pathological functioning. The investigation of a patient's mental life, Freud learned, was thus tantamount to the treatment of that patient's mental or emotional problems. The optimal therapeutic process is thus an individualized investigative procedure that produces self-knowledge, or insight. Insight may be defined as the recognition (or re-cognition) of hitherto unconscious motivations and of their influence on thought, feeling, and behavior. Psychoanalytic therapy aims to modify maladaptive patterns by enabling the client to apprehend, understand, and regulate the psychological forces responsible for their existence.

THEORETICAL FOUNDATIONS

The practice of psychoanalytic therapy requires a knowledge of psychoanalytic theory. Psychoanalytic theory has undergone many modifications since its inception. In his own lifetime, Freud repeatedly revised his views in accordance with accumulating clinical data. In the years since his death, psychoanalysts around the world have shaped and reshaped psychoanalytic theory in accordance with their own evolving views and clinical experiences. This has resulted in a proliferation of psychoanalytic schools, each championing its own points of view. Although I refer to psychoanalysis as a singular entity, the reality is that there are many psychoanalyses and therefore many versions of psychoanalytic therapy. In this chapter, I discuss psychoanalytic therapy from the vantage point of traditional Freudian thought, especially (though not exclusively) from the perspective of contemporary structural theory (Arlow & Brenner, 1964; Brenner 1976, 1982, 1994; Dowling, 1991). (For a concise review of traditional and contemporary structural theory, see Chapter 3 in this book.)

Briefly restated, psychoanalytic theory posits that mental activity is governed by a fundamental propensity to seek pleasure and avoid pain, termed the *pleasure principle.* Mental activity is motivated by instinctual drives, which acquire psychological representation in the form of specific wishes as a result of "experiences of satisfaction" during development. Since they derive from drives, these wishes are also called *drive derivatives.* Because the gratification of wishes is inherently pleasurable, wishes motivate mental activity. Wishful mental activity becomes complicated as a result of experiences through which the developing child comes to believe that the pursuit of specific wishes will entail calamitous consequences. As a result of such experiences, the arousal of certain wishes elicits contradictory affective signals: affects of pleasure, linked to fantasies of wish-fulfillment, and affects of unpleasure, linked to the aversive contingencies with which these are associated. These contradictory affective signals instigate an approach-avoidance dilemma characterized as *psychic conflict.*

Wishes are shaped by experiences of satisfaction with human caretakers and bear the imprint of these experiences. Wishes feature mental representations of the specific activities that have been pleasurable and of the persons with whom they were enjoyed. They may be classified as being predominantly sexual or aggressive, according to the character of their aims. In practice, most wishes contain a mixture of sexual and aggressive strivings. (The terms *sexual* and *aggressive* have a broader meaning in psychoanalytic terminology than they do in common parlance.) Affects of unpleasure are shaped by the hurtful experiences of childhood, both real and imagined. These affects are composed of two aspects: bodily sensations of unpleasure and accompanying mental representations of calamities. These representations of calamity constitute the ideational content of unpleasurable affects. The typical calamities of childhood pertain to loss, especially the loss of parental figures or the loss of their love, and to punishment, including genital mutilation, and harsh parental attitudes that induce feelings of shame or guilt When calamities are anticipated, however unrealistically, the result is anxiety. When calamities are experienced as having already occurred, they produce depressive affect. Most unpleasurable affects contain a mixture of anxiety and depressive affect, and they pertain to a mixture of calamities (Brenner, 1982).

In conditions of psychic conflict, mental activity naturally produces an array of alternative compromise solutions, or compromise formations, each of which permits a limited measure of gratification at a limited cost of unpleasure. Compromise formations are effected through the use of defenses. Defenses are mental activities of any kind that serve to reduce unpleasure. Defenses are deployed in complex ways to alter, disguise, or otherwise distort the experience of wishes and of the unpleasures they arouse. As a result of defenses, childhood wishes and associated affects of unpleasure are typically inaccessible to conscious apprehension as such, and can be perceived only through derivative manifestations (Brenner, 1982).

Compromises are not all equally adaptive, however, since each results in a different balance of pleasure and unpleasure. In any condition of psychic conflict, the compromise promoting the best balance of pleasure and unpleasure is naturally preferred over alternatives. This compromise will be repeated whenever the conflictual wish arises. With repetition, compromise formations become enduring programs for the organization of mental activity. Mental activity is construed as a sequence of mental events, instigated by the arousal of specific wishes that trigger associated affects of unpleasure which, in turn, mobilize the deployment of defenses to reproduce a favored compromise formation. Such sequences of wish-unpleasure-defense are repeated automatically and without conscious deliberation. We are rarely aware that our preferred patterns of living are the end products of such complex activity and often mistakenly regard them as expressions of basic unitary motives. Such programs of mental activity are called *structures,* because they are "processes with a slow rate of change" (Rapaport, 1960). These programs are the structures explained by contemporary structural theory and illuminated by psychoanalytic therapy.

One of the most remarkable discoveries of psychoanalytic research is that the wishes of childhood, coupled with the unpleasures and defenses with which they are associated, persist as motivations shaping the mental life of the adult. While the lives of adults differ from those of children in significant ways, adult patterns of thinking, feeling, and behaving derive from those of childhood. Adult patterns are formed as the habitual compromise formations of childhood are progressively reshaped to fit the changing circumstances of life. New compromise formations may be conceptualized as alternative pathways in the sequence of mental events described in the preceding paragraph. All adult compromise formations are developmentally linked to their predecessors, however, and tend to reflect their continuing influence. The extraordinary continuity of psychic conflict and compromise formation in mental life, from childhood through adulthood, is responsible for the fact that we have more or less the same personalities throughout our lives (for an exceptional longitudinal study, see McDevitt, 1996).

At one time, psychoanalysts believed that psychic conflict was a feature of mental illness, while mental health was a state of freedom from psychic conflicts. Psychoanalytic research, however, has demonstrated that mental activity is always characterized by psychic conflicts and compromise formations. Mental health and mental illness are not distinguishable, then, by the absence or presence of psychic conflicts. The difference between normality and pathology lies in the character of the compromise formations to which they give rise. Healthy compromise formations promote adaptive functioning, characterized by a favorable balance of pleasure over unpleasure, while pathological compromise formations promote maladaptive functioning, with an unfavorable balance of pleasure and unpleasure. Analysis of the healthy aspects of any individual's mental functioning, such as a happy vocational choice or the pursuit of a pleasurable hobby, regularly reveals the influence of the same desires and conflicts that determine their psychopathology. This may be illustrated by the following examples.

> Mr. A *is an actor who sought help with crippling bouts of stage fright that had caused him to miss several performances. Although he had always been nervous about performing, he had never before been so paralyzed that he could not go on stage. He was frustrated and furious at himself, especially since his stage fright appeared just when he was playing a leading role in a play that could make him a star. His stage fright felt like some "cosmic punishment" for a crime he could not remember committing.*
>
> Mr. A *had grown up in an inner-city slum, one of many children in a marginally intact family, headed by an alcoholic father who was chronically aloof and contemptuous. As a child,* Mr. A *secretly nurtured fantasies of great wealth and fame. He imagined that he would use his success to inspire others. He began to act in plays at school, and studied acting at a teen center. Later, he attended a professional acting school. He experienced intense feelings of "personal triumph" whenever he performed well, and had pursued his career with intense zeal, despite the many painful "sacrifices," including years of menial work and professional insignificance.*
>
> *In the course of a lengthy therapy, we discovered that* Mr. A*'s ambitions were motivated, in part, by unconscious wishes to hurt his father, to make him burn with envy at his son's prestige and status. These vengeful wishes triggered little recognizable anxiety or guilt, because they were disguised as artistic dreams, and masked by altruistic concerns for others. If he felt any residual guilt, his "sacrifices" were ample atonement.*

When Mr. A landed a leading role in a Broadway play, however, his long-simmering desire to torment his father was stimulated by the prospect of his imminent stardom. At the same time, the chronic deprivation that permitted him to atone through "sacrifices for his art" was about to be ameliorated. As a result, he became increasingly panicked and guilt ridden. Consciously, he was terrified that the audience would hate him and that the critics would ridicule him as a pompous fraud. His stage fright and his missed performances were a pathological compromise formation, fueled by vengeful wishes to hurt his father (by being a star), fear of his father's retaliation (the audience and critics despise and ridicule him), and guilt (his stage fright is a "cosmic punishment"). Mr. A kept his panic within limits by periodically missing performances, a symptom that undermined his success (i.e., inhibited his aggression) and thereby diminished his feelings of anxiety and guilt.

Similar motivations are apparent in a healthy aspect of Mr. A's life. Mr. A volunteered to teach acting to inner-city youths at the teen center where he first took acting lessons. He took great pleasure in this work, which won him praise from other actors, as well as gratitude from community center staff, and enabled him to enjoy the admiration of the boys he taught. All of these experiences gratified unconscious desires to supersede his father in social importance and success. The fulfillment of these wishes was highly disguised, and any guilt he may have experienced was balanced by the obvious generosity and social virtue of his efforts. These activities are clearly a successful compromise formation, forged of the same psychic conflicts which gave rise to his painfully disrupted career.

Ms. B was a twenty-nine-year-old nurse who entered therapy complaining of failed relationships, feelings of inadequacy, and a painful sexual inhibition. She was inclined to become romantically "enchanted" by sophisticated and worldly men. She enjoyed being wined and dined, and could be coaxed into bed if the man were sufficiently aggressive. Once lovemaking commenced, however, she typically became nauseated and disgusted by any further thoughts of sex. She believed that her inhibition was due to "guilt over sex," for which she blamed her strict Catholic upbringing.

Ms. B was the first of four children. Her mother was a cold and bitter woman who offered little warmth or nurturance. Ms. B was always her father's favorite. Her father was an "enchanting" man, who was always loving, kind, and nurturing to her. Analytic treatment revealed that her sexual problems were caused by the persistent influence of unconscious sexual desires for her father. Although she was aware of loving her father a great deal, she was not aware of her sexual desires for him, nor was she aware that she chose her sexual partners on the basis of their similarities to him. Her lovemaking with "enchanting" men thus represented the fulfillment of unconscious incestuous desires, as a result of which sex had become morally abhorrent and disgusting. Her sexual relationships were a compromise formation, in which her incestuous sexuality was partially gratified in a disguised form at the cost of anxiety, guilt, and disgust, which she minimized by attributing them to her Catholic upbringing. Her nausea was the somatic equivalent of moral disgust.

While Ms. B suffered in her love life, she derived great pleasure from her work as a nurse. She was devoted to her clients and enjoyed the feeling of intimacy she experienced from caring for their bodily needs. She was especially moved by feelings of tenderness to-

ward her elderly male clients and felt "privileged" to care for them. These professional activities were highly pleasurable because they permitted her to gratify her wishes for greater intimacy with her father without arousing the feelings of guilt and disgust associated with sexual desires. Her professional life was a successful compromise formation.

Compromise formations are fueled by psychological forces of which we have only partial awareness. Mr. A, for example, knew that he was ambitious and fearful of the audience's criticism, but he did not know that his theatrical ambitions were intended to achieve a triumphant revenge against his father or that he feared his father's retaliatory attack. Ms. B knew she was "enchanted" by men of a certain type and that she felt guilty and disgusted when trying to make love to them. She did not know that she yearned for a sexual union with her father or that she felt frightened, guilty, and disgusted by this fantasy. Although Mr. A and Ms. B are intelligent and reasonable persons, neither could exercise control over the pathological aspects of their lives. Both were encouraged by their friends to "straighten up and fly right," but neither could. Both felt they were "in the grip of something," something alien to themselves that they could neither understand nor control. In each case, what was experienced as alien was nothing other than disowned aspects of themselves, which had acquired the status of being "alien" as a result of defensive activities, exercised over a lifetime. Because these clients had little understanding or sense of ownership in relation to their own unconscious wishes, their ability to regulate their mental functioning was severely handicapped.

The therapist who treats clients like Mr. A or Ms. B may endeavor to change their maladaptive patterns of thought or behavior through guidance, advice, or other prescriptive measures. Psychoanalytic psychotherapy differs from other therapies, because it does not attempt to modify maladaptive patterns by any direct means. It is a "radical" (from *radex,* Latin for "root") form of treatment because it attempts to illuminate the motivational roots of the client's problems. While other therapists modify pathological patterns by direct means, the psychoanalytic therapist seeks only to understand his or her clients and to help them to understand themselves.

With increased understanding of the emotional forces by which they are motivated, clients are able to forge new and more adaptive solutions for their psychic conflicts, and to replace habitual pathological compromise formations with healthier and more gratifying ones. As the client becomes familiar with his or her inner conflicts, the client is able to think about them with the most mature aspects of his or her personality. This process of reflection enables the client to appreciate the childhood character of his or her wishes and unpleasures, to contemplate the circumstances in which they formed, and to weigh their present significance and importance—in brief, to reconsider them from the vantage point of mature judgment (Loewald, 1971). This process facilitates their gradual transformation. Mr. A, for instance, recognized that his wish for vengeance was a plan he had made as a child, when he had no better means to cope with the suffering he experienced on a daily basis at his father's hands. Although his vengeful fantasies enabled him to endure the pain of his father's contemptuous attitudes, he recognized that he was no longer subject to these indignities. Of course, he still felt the sting of these childhood injuries, such as feelings of helpless indignation and humiliation. On reflection, however, these feelings became less painful as he reviewed them from his adult perspective. His father was, after all, an unhappy and frustrated man. He should not have taken out his frustration on his son, but his nasty and denigrating attitudes carried less weight when viewed from this present vantage point. Mr. A's feelings of helplessness and inadequacy were recontextualized as the "psychic reality" of a small boy that no longer applies to Mr. A, the man. Other significant aspects of Mr. A's conflicts, such as his fear of punishment and his feelings of guilt, were also progressively modified as they became accessible to his mature reflection and judgment. Similar observations can be made about Ms. B, who eventually came to accept her incestuous desires as an aspect of her fantasy life, to recognize the wish-fulfilling confusion that enabled her to identify her "enchanting" lovers with her father, and finally, to differentiate consciously between her lovers and her father.

With progressive understanding, clients can alter their maladaptive patterns of living and replace them with more adaptive patterns. This process occurs spontaneously as a result of shifts in the organization of wishes, unpleasures, and defenses brought about by the client's understanding and reflection. The new patterns are also compromise formations, and they too are subject to continuing analysis and reorganization, a process that permits the creation of ever more adaptive compromises. Therapeutic change in psychoanalytic psychotherapy may be understood as a beneficial reorganization of compromise formations.

> Mr. A *began approaching his theatrical career more realistically. He felt less exalted and triumphant when the audience applauded, and his stage fright gradually dissipated. He took greater pleasure in the perfection of his craft and eventually began directing theatrical productions, activities that permitted the satisfaction of other desires he had previously ignored. As he reflected on his vengeful fantasies,* Mr. A *sought a more mature resolution of his problems with his father, which prompted him to initiate a "dialogue" in which he aggressively confronted his father for his myriad failings. As his persistent wish to humiliate his father was repeatedly observed and explored,* Mr. A *slowly adopted a more realistic attitude, which permitted him to establish a limited but happier relationship with his father.*

> *As* Ms. B *came to recognize the incestuous fantasies that motivated her love life, she was able to better discriminate between reality and fantasy and began enjoying full sexual relations without nausea or other impairments. As a result, she was able to form more lasting relationships. Her behavior in these relationships, however, reflected an attitude of dependency and entitlement, which had characterized her relationship to her father. As these features of her continuing yearning for her father's love were analyzed,* Ms. B *slowly came to recognize both the power and the futility of her wishes to relive her childhood relationship with her father, and through this, to compensate herself for the painful feelings of rejection she experienced in relation to her mother. Her emerging desire for a partner with whom she could feel more adult and competent gradually superseded her desire for a father figure. Her new relationships were less enchanting (she was not refinding Daddy), but permitted her to experience new forms of intimacy, which eventually included marriage and motherhood.*

As the client's compromise formations become healthier, permitting greater pleasure at less psychic cost, they cease to attract the client's attention, and the focus of the therapeutic work shifts. When the client has achieved sufficient mastery over his or her conflicts, the motivation for treatment often gradually dissipates, and therapy comes to a natural conclusion. Many clients who are excited by their emotional growth wish to continue in therapy to achieve further self-knowledge, often to pursue more ambitious therapeutic goals. Since self-knowledge is never total, every therapy is in a sense incomplete. There is no fixed point at which psychoanalytic therapy should come to an end. Termination never implies perfect health or the absence of conflicts.

THE PROCESS OF PSYCHOANALYTIC PSYCHOTHERAPY

Psychoanalytic psychotherapy is a collaborative undertaking. It cannot be administered to a passive or uninvolved client. The therapist cannot directly observe the client's inner life. Only the client has access to a knowledge of his or her inner world. The therapist cannot reliably infer the nature of the client's psychic conflicts from a knowledge of the client's symptoms, psychiatric diagnosis, lifestyle, social relations, work history, culture, socioeconomic status, family background, or any source other than the client's most private thoughts and musings. Psychoanalytic therapy, then, must be a collaborative undertaking, or it cannot be undertaken at all.

Psychoanalytic psychotherapy is a difficult and demanding form of therapy. It requires a sustained effort over a protracted period of time, often many years. The client must be willing to expose his or her innermost thoughts and feelings to another person, a stranger, about whose attitudes and feelings he or she can have little knowledge. The client must be willing to tolerate the emotional discomforts this exposure evokes and to persist in the process even when it is painful. The therapist must have the skills, confidence, and emotional fortitude to accept the responsibilities this entails. The therapist presides over the entire therapeutic process. He or she is responsible for providing a safe and supportive context in which to explore buried feelings and for offering the client a coherent understanding of those feelings. The therapist is also responsible for protecting the client and the therapy from the emotional turbulence the process unleashes.

It is sometimes said that therapy begins with the first contact between the therapist and the client. While the first contact ought to be therapeutic, in a general sense, psychoanalytic therapy per se can be initiated only after both parties have met and come to a mutual understanding and agreement about the nature of the treatment and the procedures to be employed. This agreement or *therapeutic contract* (Menninger, 1958) is the rational basis of all further interactions between client and therapist. In psychoanalytic therapy, the roles of client and therapist are clearly defined. The client's task is to communicate his or her thoughts to the therapist. Most psychoanalytic therapists invite the client to free associate—to say aloud all the thoughts that come to mind, without censorship or conscious deliberation, thus enabling the therapist to sample the client's mental life. The therapist's primary task is to listen to the client's thoughts, understand the client's mental life and behavior, and communicate this understanding to the client in the form of interpretations, or comments that increase the client's self-knowledge.

The client will naturally talk about many things, including his or her problems, current interpersonal relationships, relationships with family members, childhood memories, and dreams. Over time, the therapist will become increasingly familiar with the client's mental life. The client's communications enable the therapist to empathize, to form a picture of the client's subjective experience. Although the client may report every aspect of his or her thoughts and conduct faithfully and without reserve, the client cannot intentionally report the unconscious aspects of mental life. This is due to the fact that self-awareness is restricted by the operation of defenses. These unconscious aspects, especially the wishes, unpleasures, and defenses that constitute the client's pathogenic psychic conflicts, can be discovered only over time, through the application of the psychoanalytic method.

Freud employed an archaeological metaphor to describe the psychoanalytic process. The archaeologist observes a particular terrain, studies it carefully, and begins to excavate at selected sites. The process of excavation is conducted in a methodical fashion, starting at the geological surface and proceeding layer by layer to an uncovering of artifacts and objects at successively lower levels. Although psychoanalytic treatment is not archaeology, the metaphor highlights certain meaningful parallels. Like an archaeological dig, a psychoanalytic investigation proceeds from the surface to the depth—from facts and feelings that are on the surface to those aspects of mental life that are hidden and can be observed only when they are uncovered. Although analysts vary somewhat in their usage of the term, most writers use the term *surface* to characterize the observable or manifest aspects of the client's mental life (Freud, 1905a; Levy & Inderbitzen, 1990; Paniagua, 1985, 1991; Poland, 1992).

A therapy session is composed of innumerable surfaces, some of which are allowed to pass by without particular attention, while others become focal points for exploration. The surfaces selected for "excavation" may be determined by the client, whose attention is drawn to those life events and experiences that are emotionally meaningful in one way or another. Some surfaces are selected by the therapist, who notices loaded comments, pregnant pauses, incongruent gestures, or various discontinuities in the client's thought and brings them to the client's attention. Since the process of psychoanalytic therapy is a collaborative venture, the selection of any surface for exploration should be consensual (Poland, 1992). Any selected surface is progressively uncovered as the client verbalizes the thoughts that come to mind in connection with it. These associations reveal the network of feelings and thoughts within which the particular experience is embedded. They provide clues to the emotional meanings of the manifest experience. When the client follows these associated thoughts and feelings, they often link up with other trains of thought that help explain the meaning of an experience by connecting the surface to deeper and deeper motivational roots.

In an archaeological site of any size, excavation proceeds at a number of specific areas simultaneously. The process of digging begins more or less simultaneously at each of these selected surfaces, with new surfaces selected for excavation as the dig proceeds. As selected areas are unearthed and their contents identified, the archaeologist's understanding of the other areas under excavation is enhanced. Similarly, psychoanalytic exploration entails the concurrent investigation of an expanding number of surfaces. As each individual surface is explored, the therapist comes to understand the specific conflicts responsible for the manifest phenomena comprising that particular surface. As numerous surfaces are explored, the therapist will discover that similar conflicts determine multiple different surfaces. These conflicts are called *core conflicts* because they lie at the core of many different features in the client's mental life. A familiarity with the client's core conflicts can come about only when they are discovered over and over again as numerous individual surfaces are explored. The unique power of psychoanalytic therapy derives from the fact that the exposure and progressive mastery of core conflicts permit the client to alter a very wide range of problematic behaviors.

Freud's archaeological metaphor also provides a model for the therapeutic action of insight. The buried relics that archaeologists discover are often in states of remarkable preservation. As a result of being buried, these artifacts were protected from the destructive effects of exposure to the elements. Buried, they existed in a timeless universe, unaffected by the passage of the years. The tragic aspect of archaeology lies in the fact that the process of discovery is inherently destructive. When these precious artifacts are uncovered, they are once again exposed to the corrosive effects of the elements and thus returned to the realm of passing time. Freud discovered that unconscious wishes and fears are similarly protected from the effects of time. Because they are unconscious, they do not partake in developmental processes. They are not transformed by learning or by the individual's developing capacities for judgment and reality testing. Freud characterized the unconscious sector of the mind as timeless because unconscious contents, like buried relics, are isolated from the effects of passing time. When "buried" wishes and fears are uncovered in psychoanalytic therapy, however, they are exposed to the "psychic elements"—the impact of the client's own mature mental functions (Freud, 1909; see also Loewald, 1971).

Although the archaeological metaphor is useful, it should not be taken too far. Psychoanalytic treatment does not follow a simple course of progressive uncovering as the archaeological metaphor might appear to suggest. The client is a living person, not an archaeological site. The therapist cannot simply dig through the client's psyche, shoveling through the layers of the client's mental life as though the client were an inanimate field. Unconscious wishes, thoughts, feelings, and memories are not merely buried by the psychic debris of passing time. They were intentionally buried because, when experienced, they were painful. As these contents are revealed, the client feels these old and forgotten pains anew, and the old defensive methods, by which the painful contents were buried in the first place, are once again set in motion. The client inevitably comes to see the therapy as a hazard and the therapist as a menacing figure who imperils the client's precarious stability and well-being. The therapeutic process and the collaborative relationship between the therapist and the client is thus inexorably complicated by the client's suffering and defensiveness. This inner turbulence gives rise to resistance.

Resistance may be defined as the client's paradoxical opposition to the process of psychoanalytic therapy. Resistance is a manifestation of the client's defensive functioning as it is mobilized in the context of psychoanalytic therapy. It reflects the client's feeling of being endangered by therapy and gives rise to efforts, large and small, to retard or disrupt the treatment. Resistance is evident in curious discontinuities of thought, abrupt shifts of content, odd circumlocutions, ellipses, non sequiturs, unproductive silences, and other such signs of a derailed train of thought. Sometimes the client's resistance will manifest as a feeling of resignation about the treatment, doubts about its efficacy, latenesses and missed appointments, problems in paying or scheduling, and other disruptive actions. In more extreme cases, the client may attempt to abandon treatment entirely, sometimes through a determined effort to "get it together" and a concomitant improvement in mood, which the client mistakes for a cure (the so-called *flight into health*). More destructive clients may unconsciously seek to derail the treatment by "proving" its worthlessness: by getting worse, by engaging in self-destructive activity, by adopting a combative attitude, or by trying to seduce the therapist into a sexual or criminal partnership.

Resistance is an inevitable feature of every psychoanalytic therapy, from the very beginning of treatment to the very end. The success of therapy depends in large part on the therapist's capacity to deal productively with the client's resistance. Psychoanalytic technique aims to modify the client's resistance by exposing and exploring it, so that the client may understand the unsettling feelings that motivate it. As the client recognizes and grapples with these painful feelings, they are gradually reduced, and defenses relax. As a result, previously warded-off contents can emerge and be assimilated into the client's conscious mental life (Weiss, 1971, 1993; Weiss & Sampson, 1986). This process continues throughout the course of treatment. It is the basic method by which unconscious contents are uncovered (Brenner, 1976; Busch, 1995; Gray, 1994).

The process of psychoanalytic therapy differs from archaeology in another profound way. Archaeological artifacts do not arise from their place of burial on their own accord. The same cannot be said of buried wishes, fears, grief, or memories. When buried feelings are stirred up, they return to life, like the mummies of old horror films. Repressed contents spontaneously arise because they are buoyed up by unconscious wishes seeking gratification. This tendency to return is facilitated whenever resistance is reduced. This is why the interpretation of resistance promotes the process of uncovering. The mobilization of archaic wishes can be a source of great emotional turbulence. In some instances, for example, the client may be unable to tolerate the arousal of these wishes without also taking some actions to gratify them. In other instances, the arousal of repressed wishes is so threatening that the client is driven to take desperate defensive measures. Depending on the nature of the wishes and defenses involved and depending on the strength of the client's capacity to exercise judgment and restraint, these urges can give rise to very destructive behavior. This is sometimes loosely referred to as *acting out*.

Unconscious wishes are aroused by temptations—enticing prospects for the fulfillment of longings and desires. The therapist, who listens empathically and attentively for many hours, who provides acceptance, support, and understanding, and makes no demands for reciprocation, often comes to represent such a temptation. Because the therapist does not divulge personal information or engage the client socially, the client has no clear picture of the therapist's personality or life circumstances. As a result, the client's perception of the therapist will, to a large extent, come to reflect the influence of the client's fantasy life. This phenomenon is called *transference.* Transference is fueled by unconscious wishes and the unpleasures and defenses with which they are associated. Because these conflicts derive from childhood relationships with parents and other significant figures, the transference tends to replicate aspects of these childhood relationships.

Transference presents the psychoanalytic therapist with a major challenge as well as an unparalleled opportunity. Because transference is a distortion, the presence of transference is an inevitable source of confusion for the client. Sometimes the client will be very pleased by the appearance of transference feelings, as occurs, for example, in cases where the client feels the therapist to be very loving, nurturing, or protective. Sometimes the client will be frightened or upset by transference experiences, as when the client feels the therapist is dismissive, angry, or condemning. In both cases, the client is likely to experience the therapist as *really* loving or *really* hostile. These experiences are of potentially great value because they bring aspects of the client's emotional life to the light in a manner that both therapist and client can observe together. On the other hand, if transference feelings are too intense or too readily taken for reality, they can derail the therapy entirely. Where the client is intent on gratifying transference wishes, the demand for gratification can supplant the goal of understanding. Where the client feels endangered by the therapist, this fear may engender a total disruption of treatment. Transference presents a challenge that the psychoanalytic therapist attempts to manage interpretively. The therapist maintains a therapeutic attitude of interest toward the client's transference feelings and attempts to engage the client in a collaborative effort to explore them. This process helps the client recognize the transference as an expression of his or her own psychology rather than as a veridical perception of reality.

Resistance and transference are closely related. Resistance is often triggered by fears that are aroused within the transference. At the same time, transference may be utilized as a means of resisting the process of treatment by changing the agenda from the understanding of conflicts to the pursuit of gratifications. At the beginning of his career, Freud saw both transference and resistance as unfortunate impediments to the exploration of the client's mental life. It is a credit to Freud's genius that he discovered a means to exploit these phenomena for therapeutic purposes, turning them from mere obstacles into unique opportunities. In a famous passage, Freud (1914b) defined psychoanalysis as the therapeutic method that takes the facts of transference and resistance as its starting point. Many of the procedures of psychoanalytic therapy, in fact, may be best understood as techniques designed to protect the treatment from the disruptive effects of transference and resistance and to ensure that they will be exploited to their fullest potential.

THE TECHNIQUE OF PSYCHOANALYTIC THERAPY

The goal of psychoanalytic therapy is the promotion of the client's self-knowledge or insight. Psychoanalytic technique is the method by which this is accomplished. This technique is best understood if the practitioner has a clear appreciation of what is meant by insight or self-knowledge. The philosopher Bertrand Russell differentiated between *knowledge by description* and *knowledge by acquaintance*. Knowledge by description refers to information about phenomena that have not personally been experienced. Knowledge by description is composed of ideas without any actual experiential referents. As a result, such knowledge lacks the personal and compelling quality of knowledge that derives from actual experience. Knowledge by acquaintance, on the other hand, is information acquired by the individual through direct contact with the phenomena in question. The goal of psychoanalytic therapy is self-knowledge of this personal and authentic kind. In a classic essay, Richfield (1954), citing Russell, introduced the term *ostensive insight* to describe insights that are subjectively meaningful because they "incorporate the actual, conscious experience of their referents" (p. 404).

Ostensive insight can be achieved only through a conjoining of actual experience, on the one hand, and observation, on the other. Accordingly, a fundamental aim of psychoanalytic technique is to promote both the client's experience of mental life as well as his or her observation of this experience. To experience mental life is to encounter directly the urges, desires, emotions, images, and other events comprising mental life as specific realities with perceptible qualities and intensities. To observe mental life is to apprehend and describe the particularities of what is experienced and to reflect thoughtfully on these observed particularities from the perspective of one's mature sensibility and with the participation of one's best judgment and highest mental faculties. Without experiencing the events of mental life, the client has nothing to observe or reflect on. Without observation and reflection, nothing can be learned from experience. Accordingly, the technique of psychoanalytic psychotherapy is designed to promote an expanding experience of mental life in the context of ongoing self-observation and reflection. In a seminal essay, the psychoanalyst Richard Sterba wrote that psychoanalytic treatment must facilitate a "therapeutic split" in the client's mind, thus enabling the client to take his or her own experience as the object of observation. In order to acquire insight, he reasoned, the client must be able to "oscillate" between the "experiencing" and "observing" sectors of his or her mind (Sterba, 1934). These ideas are still central to contemporary psychoanalytic technique.

The technique of psychoanalytic therapy may be understood as a complex system of interdependent parts, which function in concert to promote insight by facilitating the expansion of inner experience in conjunction with self-observation and reflection. Writers differ in the way they conceptualize the elements of psychoanalytic technique. In my view, psychoanalytic technique features the creation of a *therapeutic situation* within which a *therapeutic relationship* and a *therapeutic dialogue* can be initiated. The *therapeutic situation* is the basic set-up of the treatment, which includes the working agreements and ground rules by which the treatment is conducted, and the interpersonal conditions created by the therapist's attitude of acceptance, respect, and dedication to the goal of understanding. The *therapeutic relationship* is a unique human relationship, intentionally structured to permit the unfolding of intimate longings in an interpersonal context in which they will be studied rather than gratified. The *therapeutic dialogue* refers to the communications through which the client reveals his or her inner life to the therapist and to the therapist's efforts to understand the client's experience and to communicate this understanding to the client in a timely and sensitive manner. Together, the three components of technique create a safe and permissive interpersonal context for the mobilization of unconscious wishes and associated affects, while simultaneously establishing controlled conditions for these experiences to be communicated, studied, and understood.

The Therapeutic Situation

The therapeutic situation is initiated when the therapist and the client each agree to work together in a specified manner toward the achievement of specified goals, according to the terms of an explicit *therapeutic contract* (Menninger, 1958). The therapeutic contract is the indispensable basis for the formation of the therapeutic situation. It is a rational agreement between equal adults, designed to serve the needs of both parties. The terms of the contract are the basis for the working relationship between the client and the therapist. The therapeutic contract includes an explicit explanation of the roles and responsibilities of each party, the frequency and duration of therapy sessions, and the basic ground rules of the treatment, including arrangements regarding the fee, missed sessions, vacations, and so on. These structures constitute the *frame* of the therapy, a metaphor suggesting boundaries that contain the therapeutic process (Langs, 1973, 1974).

Psychoanalytic therapy can proceed only within the context of fixed and stable arrangements. These ensure the continuity of the therapeutic process and the intelligibility of the client's responses to it. Fixed routines are a baseline from which potentially meaningful deviations are discernible. Lateness in attending sessions or paying bills, for example, cannot be observed if the scheduled times for appointments and for paying bills are overly vague. An anxious client will often feel the urge to avoid or cancel therapy sessions. If the schedule is overly flexible, the client will feel freer to act on this impulse than if the schedule were fixed. Such "acting out" permits the client to avoid dealing with the distressing affects that have been aroused. The therapist can address such problems only if he or she can recognize them. The frame helps to ensure that the client's emotional reactions are recognized and addressed within the context of the therapy.

The fixed arrangements of the therapy always include regular times for therapy sessions. A minimum of at least one session per week is generally required, and more frequent sessions are often preferable. Sessions should be scheduled for a fixed length of time, usually forty-five or fifty minutes. The relationship between the therapist and the client is strictly limited to verbal interactions within the context of scheduled appointments (except for emergencies, of course). Beyond attendance and payment for services, the client's principal responsibility is to observe and express, as openly as possible, the feelings, thoughts, and ideas that pass through his or her mind during the course of the session and, at times, to reflect on the therapist's communications. The therapist's principal responsibilities are to listen attentively, to help the client speak freely through the investigation of resistances, to form conjectures about significant aspects of the client's mental life, and, at appropriate times, to communicate this understanding to the client.

The therapeutic situation is also shaped by the therapist's professional manner and attitude toward the client. The therapist should be professional and courteous in manner, empathic, reasonable, and consistent in routines and habits. (Of course, this applies to all therapists.) The psychoanalytic therapist also strives to maintain a specialized "analytic attitude" (Brenner, 1976; Schafer, 1983). The analytic attitude is a natural expression of the therapist's basic intent to help the client by understanding his or her psychic conflicts. It is an attitude of acceptance, empathy, respect, and benevolent curiosity about all the client's experiences. Brenner observes that the analytic therapist should behave "naturally" with the client. For the psychoanalytic therapist, "naturally" means in a manner that is in accord with the therapist's intent to understand psychic conflicts. It is "natural" for the psychoanalytic therapist to be curious about the client's fantasy life, to listen for latent content, or to restrict social chitchat with clients. It would be just as "natural" for therapists of another stripe to hug their clients, socialize with them, and so on. These forms of interaction would be quite unnatural for the analytic therapist, who is intent on helping through understanding (Brenner, 1976).

The analytic attitude is one of profound respect for the client's individuality and autonomy. This respect is often conveyed by the term *neutrality*. Neutrality is manifested in many forms. The therapist's respect for the client's individuality manifests as neutrality in regard to the client's life decisions. The psychoanalytic therapist imposes no private ideals on the client and refrains from the use of personal influence or authority to shape the client's attitudes or to direct the client's life. As Freud wrote: "We refused most emphatically to turn a client who puts himself in our hands in search of help into our private property, to decide his fate for him, to force our own ideals upon him, and with the pride of a Creator to form him in our own image and to see that it is good" (Freud, 1919, p. 164). The therapist's neutrality is manifested in the therapy as an attitude of impartial and nonjudgmental receptivity to all the client's communications. This is operationally reflected in the dictum that the client determines the content of the hour. In regard to the client's psychic conflicts, the therapist's respect for the client's individuality is manifested by neutrality in relation to all sides of the conflict. Anna Freud (1936) characterized this as a position of "equidistance" from each side. Neutrality should not be confused with personal indifference, unfriendliness, or disinterest with regard to the client's welfare. Neutrality is not an attitude of uncaring. On the contrary, it is the analytic therapist's way of caring (Dorpat, 1977; Hoffer, 1985; Gitelson, 1952; Kris, 1982; Poland, 1984; Shapiro, 1984; Wallerstein, 1965). True neutrality should be differentiated from a "pseudo-neutral" disregard for the client's welfare, especially in the context of dangerous acting out (Poland, 1984; Dorpat, 1977; Menninger, 1958).

Abstinence and *anonymity* are principles that derive from the attitude of neutrality and serve to ensure that the therapeutic "process proceeds on the basis of what the client brings to it" (Gitelson, 1952). The *principle of anonymity* directs the therapist to refrain from self-disclosures—from expressing personal points of view, life experiences, suggestions, values, and so on. It protects the treatment from intrusions of the therapist's personality, which may "confound the discovery process" (Shapiro, 1984). Self-disclosure may suggest to the client that cure can be achieved through intimacy, love, or "lessons" from the life of the therapist rather than through self-understanding. Equally important, self-disclosures introduce personal facts, which may complicate the transference. It should be emphasized that anonymity is appropriate only in the context of a treatment designed to promote the uncovering of unconscious fantasies and psychic conflict. It would make no sense in a therapy whose curative properties were unrelated to the therapeutic relationship, or whose therapeutic action resulted from experiences of intimacy or identification with the therapist (see Goldstein, 1994).

The *principle of abstinence* directs the therapist to conduct the treatment in a manner that does not gratify the client's demands for emotional relief through any means that might undermine the goal of understanding. Abstinence entails "the inhibition of short-term helpfulness" to promote "substantial long-term analytic goals" (Poland, 1984), even when the client explicitly requests such help. The abstinent therapist will not try to help the client through advice, guidance, reassurance, sympathy, love, or any form of special affection that may relieve emotional pain without illuminating its meaning. The abstinent therapist also declines to gratify wishes extraneous to the treatment contract or to take on special roles that the client consciously or unconsciously strives to impose or induce. Most important, abstinence provides a vital measure of safety by assuring the client that, no matter what he or she wishes and no matter how he or she strives to induce, seduce, or provoke the therapist into gratifying those wishes, the therapist's attitude and conduct will be predictably and routinely geared toward the expansion of understanding.

The structure of the therapeutic situation, the consistency of the frame, and the reliability of the therapist's benign and disciplined responsiveness provide a context of safety, within which the client may express himself or herself freely without being rejected, criticized, or exploited. Of course, every client will experience the basic structures of the therapeutic situation according to his or her unique psychology. Many clients will experience the therapeutic situation as a source of security or as a "holding environment" (Modell, 1976). Sometimes the client will experience the therapeutic situation as a source of frustration, danger, or injury. However the client perceives it, the consistent and unchanging features of the therapeutic situation will provide an optimal backdrop for the exploration of the client's mental life and psychic conflicts.

The Therapeutic Relationship

The therapeutic relationship is the interpersonal context for the activities comprising the therapeutic process. In all forms of therapy, as in all forms of social work treatment, the social worker approaches the client with an attitude of respect, acceptance, and human understanding. The affirmative qualities of this relationship facilitate the client's participation in the treatment and generally promote a sense of safety and well-being. It is generally recognized that any therapist's positive attitude toward a client engenders therapeutic effects that are independent of those produced by the therapist's specific techniques. Carl Rogers and his associates, for example, identified the therapist's empathy, genuineness, and unconditional positive regard as independent curative agents in psychotherapy (Rogers, 1957, 1961; Truax, 1963; Truax & Carkhuff, 1967). Within psychoanalytic circles, it has long been recognized that the therapist's benevolent attitudes toward the client may soften the client's harsh self-criticism (Alexander, 1925; Strachey, 1934; Kris, 1982, 1995). Alexander and French (1948) held that the therapist's conduct, if different from that of the pathogenic parent, provides a "corrective emotional experience," which disrupts the client's expectations of hurtful responsiveness. Kohut and other self-psychologically oriented therapists have cited empathy as an essential curative feature in psychotherapy (Kohut, 1984; Rowe & MacIsaac, 1993; Wolf, 1988).

Traditional psychoanalytic therapists affirm the importance of the therapeutic relationship without regarding relational factors as primary agents of therapeutic change. Most analysts distinguish between the curative effects of insight and those of relational factors (e.g., Oremland, 1991). Self-knowledge and the capacity for continuing self-inquiry, which develop in the course of psychoanalytic therapy, are qualitatively different, at least conceptually, from alterations that accrue as a result of identifications with another person or internalizations of another's positive regard for oneself. This is not to elevate the former at the expense of the latter. There is good evidence that supportive therapeutic relationships have enduring positive influence (Wallerstein, 1986). But a naive reliance on relational factors to alleviate complicated psychological problems may be superficial. Most clients, for instance, suffer from low self-esteem as a result of their psychic conflicts and maladaptive compromise formations. Recall, for example, that Mr. A was intensely self-critical in regard to his stage fright and that Ms. B always felt "inadequate." In most instances, the client's feelings of self-doubt, inadequacy, shame, or guilt will be alleviated to some degree by the therapist's positive regard (e.g., Rogers, 1957, 1961; Truax, 1963; Truax & Carkhuff, 1967). If the client internalizes the relationship with the therapist, the therapist's positive attitudes can become an inner source of positive regard that counteracts the client's self-doubts after treatment is ended. This improvement in self-esteem may enable the client to enjoy life more, establish better relationships, take new risks, and tolerate disappointments. These are very positive results, but they are not quite the same as the results attained through a psychoanalytic exploration of the client's problems. One may imaginatively compare the actual outcomes in the cases of Mr. A and Ms. B with the results that might have been achieved had they been treated by a warm and empathic therapist who did not uncover their psychic conflicts. This contrast may be observed in the following case:

> Mr. C. *was a twenty-eight-year-old social worker who sought therapy because he was unable to approach women he found attractive. These women were invariably of a "classy" type, and he felt sure they would reject him. He felt painfully inadequate and inferior in relation to other men and was particularly ashamed of his penis, which he felt was too small. He had been successfully treated for this problem for three years while in college. His therapist was a "humanistic" social worker, an older man whose attitude of "support" and "friendship" had boosted his confidence sufficiently to enable him to begin dating.*

Mr. C hoped I would help him, as his former therapist had, by providing him with encouragement and support. I articulated my understanding of Mr. C's wish, adding my own suggestion that we try to discover why he feels so badly about himself. Mr. C was skeptical (he had read that psychoanalytic therapy was "obsolete") but he agreed to give it a try, and we contracted for twice-weekly therapy. We soon discovered that Mr. C was reluctant to describe his romantic yearnings to me unless I explicitly assured him of my "support." Further exploration of his need for my "support" revealed that Mr. C feared I would disapprove of his sexual desires for "classy" women, that we were rivals for the love of the same woman, and that I would humiliate him for daring to poach on my turf.

Mr. C's emotional problems were the consequence of persistent oedipal conflicts. His feelings of inadequacy and low self-esteem represented, in a condensed and disguised form, his feelings of being small and inferior in relation to his father, especially regarding the size of his penis; misery about his inability to become his mother's exclusive love object; guilt over trying to displace his father in his mother's affections; and a defensively motivated stance of self-effacement and self-criticism, employed to ward off his father's punishment ("I am so inadequate and my penis is so small that I am no threat to you; I suffer so greatly already that no further punishment is needed").

Mr. C sought a nurturing, supportive therapeutic relationship in order to counteract his feelings of guilt and fear of punishment. Had I attempted to help him by providing him with "support," as his former therapist had done, he might have been sufficiently emboldened to begin dating "classy" women again, as he had after his first therapy. Such help would not, however, have enabled him to understand why he desired "classy" women or why he felt so "inadequate" when he tried to woo them. In all probability, his problems with women would have recurred, as they had after his first treatment. The use of the therapeutic relationship to reduce Mr. C's guilt and anxiety would have fostered his reliance on my support as a defense, an outcome that would promote his dependency on me and might inspire otherwise unnecessary identifications with me. While such identifications may be therapeutic in some ways, they may also complicate the client's life. Mr. C had gone to college to study journalism, a field in which he majored and in which he excelled. His decision to become a social worker was an identification, motivated by his dependence on his therapist's "support." The therapeutic relationship had enabled Mr. C to date "classy" women but saddled him with a career to which he had never aspired.

To summarize, the therapeutic relationship is central to the conduct of psychoanalytic therapy. While the therapeutic relationship may produce beneficial effects, the aim of psychoanalytic psychotherapy is the attainment of self-knowledge, not merely the improvement of attitudes, feelings, or behavior (Eissler, 1963). Psychoanalytic therapists traditionally regard the therapeutic relationship as the interpersonal context for all therapeutic procedures. As such, it serves two essential functions. As in any other form of psychotherapy, the therapeutic relationship is a safe and supportive interpersonal context for the specialized activities comprising the therapeutic method. In psychoanalytic treatment, the therapeutic relationship also serves as an interpersonal medium for the emergence and expression of the client's psychic conflicts. This specialized use of the therapeutic relationship as a vehicle for the study of the client's mental life is unique to psychoanalytic treatment. These two dimensions of the therapeutic relationship are referred to as *the helping alliance* and *the transference*.

The Helping Alliance

Psychoanalytic therapy is a collaborative process that requires the client and therapist to cooperate, as partners in the therapeutic enterprise. This partnership is predicated on a shared understanding of the aims and methods of the treatment. The introduction and explanation of the therapeutic contract inaugurates this partnership. The therapist's conduct, including the therapist's attitude of concern and empathy, the therapist's recognizable intent to understand rather than to change or manipulate the client, the therapist's attitude of neutrality and respect for the client, and the therapist's abstinence and anonymity all contribute to the formation of a sound partnership.

If a reasonable partnership has been established, the client's cooperation will be motivated by rational considerations as well as diverse unconscious motivations, such as wishes for love, protection, nurturance, and so on. In large part, the client's cooperation will depend on the client's perception of the therapist as caring, well intentioned, and professionally competent. In a classic paper, Zetzel (1956) emphasized the importance of the client's experience of the therapist as a benevolent figure on whom he or she can safely depend for emotional nurture and support as well as therapeutic help. Zetzel characterized this aspect of the client's relationship to the therapist as the therapeutic alliance. In her view, the promotion of the therapeutic alliance is a critical priority in working with clients whose relationships are vulnerable to disruption as a result of their emotional problems. In such cases, a robust therapeutic alliance may stabilize an otherwise stormy or tenuous therapeutic relationship. Zetzel believed that the therapeutic alliance is promoted by the therapist's nurturing attitude and fueled by the revival of the client's love for the nurturing figures of childhood. Some years later, Greenson (1965) introduced the concept of the working alliance. Like Zetzel, Greenson believed that it was important to promote a productive working partnership with the client, especially where the client's capacities to cooperate were in question or prone to disruption. In contrast to Zetzel's thinking, however, Greenson envisioned the working alliance as a rational partnership, motivated by a reasonable desire to achieve realistic goals. Luborsky (1976), employing empirical research methods, discovered the existence of two kinds of alliances, which he characterized as helping alliances. Type 1 alliances are based on the client's experience of the therapist as "supportive and helpful with himself as the recipient." Type 2 alliances are based on a sense of "working together in joint struggle against what is impeding the patient" and are characterized by a feeling of shared responsibility for the therapeutic process and a sense of "we-ness" in relation to the therapist (p. 94). Both types of alliance coexist, with a shift to the second type typically occurring as treatment progresses (Luborsky, 1984). Luborsky's type 1 and type 2 alliances correspond closely to those described by Zetzel and Greenson, respectively.

The client's capacity to form a helping alliance is a reliable predictor of success in psychotherapy (Luborsky et al., 1988; Luborsky, 1994). While the emergence of a helping alliance is a good prognostic sign, difficulty in establishing an alliance in the early phases of treatment is not predictive. The client who attends sessions usually has some hope of getting help, and the client's capacity to trust the therapist or the therapeutic process often grows as a result of good treatment. Where the client's attitude toward the therapy and the therapist is negative or stormy, the therapist has a choice of therapeutic measures. The therapist may invite the client to participate in a joint effort to examine the attitudes, feelings, or concerns that deter the client from a more productive engagement in the therapy. This invitation signals the therapist's interest, emphasizes the importance of collaboration, and keeps the treatment on course by enabling the therapist to employ the instruments of analytic helping (i.e., listening and understanding) to the client's problems as they show themselves in the therapy. To whatever extent the client participates in this exploration and to whatever degree this exploration reveals the cause of its disruption, the alliance and the treatment are both promoted.

Sometimes, often with more disturbed clients, the helping alliance is better promoted by noninterpretive methods. Luborsky (1984) recommends specific techniques to promote both type 1 and type 2 alliances. To encourage a type 1 alliance, he suggests the therapist "develop a liking" for the client, convey understanding and acceptance of the client as a person, communicate support for the client's desire to achieve therapeutic goals, express a realistically hopeful attitude about attaining those goals, and provide recognition for any progress the client has achieved. He also recommends providing direct support for the client's defenses and psychosocial functioning. To promote type 2 alliances, Luborsky suggests that the therapist encourage a "we bond," convey respect for the client, recognize the client's growing ability to "use the basic tools of treatment," and refer to the experiences that the therapist and client have already been through together.

The Transference

While the helping alliance is the central and enduring basis of the client's relationship to the therapist, the client's attitudes toward the therapist will take on progressive complexity as therapy proceeds. In fact, the client normally develops multiple concurrent relationships with the therapist. Each reflects a different organization of motivations and mental representations of the self and of the therapist, and each is manifested by different patterns of interpersonal behavior. Mr. A, for example, began to view me as a dismissive authority whom he wished to hurt. This was manifested in the treatment situation by enthusiastic reports of his theatrical triumphs and by his occasional remarks about my ignorance about theatrical events or about my inability to help or understand him (e.g., "It's too bad you can't know what it's like to receive a standing ovation so that you could understand my feelings"). Ms. B grew to fear me as a sexual predator who would use my great powers of persuasion to seduce her. This fantasy first showed itself by expressions of anxiety about my emotional power over her. Later she expressed concern that I might suggest that we have a session over dinner, in which case she would "have" to invite me to her home for cocktails, after which she would be powerless to resist my sexual intentions. Mr. C feared that I wished to punish him for sexually approaching "classy" women and thereby "poaching" on my turf.

In these examples, the client's view of the therapist did not fit the objective reality of the relationship actually existing between them. When asked, "What is it that gives you the feeling that I am dismissive toward you?" Mr. A angrily noted that I never attend his plays or admire his success. In response to a similar inquiry, Ms. B protested that I am too empathic, a sure sign of my sexual designs. Mr. C complained that I offer no explicit endorsement for his desires to date "classy" women, evidence of my opposition to his romantic wishes. Although these clients accurately perceived certain objective features of my behavior, they interpreted these features in a highly unrealistic way. The meanings they ascribed to my behavior reflected their own particular hopes and fears. Put simply, these clients confused me with fantasy figures, persons with whom they interact in their imaginations. This fascinating phenomenon is called *transference.*

The concept of transference was introduced by Freud when he discovered that clients often confuse the therapist with the significant figures of childhood, unconsciously attributing to the therapist various characteristics that belonged to those childhood figures. As a result of this confusion, Freud observed, the client reexperiences feelings and attitudes that originated in his or her childhood relationships as if they were aspects of the current relationship with the therapist. These feelings and attitudes are unconsciously *transferred* from the mental representations of childhood figures to the representation of the therapist. In an early paper, Freud characterized transference as a "new edition of an old object relationship," forged under the pressure of drives seeking gratification (Freud, 1912a). Transference relationships, he observed, are highly stereotypical because each new transference relationship is modeled on the same "stereotype plate" or "template." In a more recent contribution, Greenson (1967) defined transference as the "experiencing of feelings, drives, attitudes, fantasies, and defenses toward a person in the present which do not befit that person but are a repetition of reactions originating in regard to significant persons of early childhood, unconsciously displaced onto figures in the present. The two outstanding characteristics of a transference reaction are: it is a repetition and it is inappropriate" (Greenson, 1967, p. 155).

These definitions correctly emphasize the confusion of past and present relationships. Transferences, however, need not reproduce the actual interpersonal relationships of childhood. These relationships, construed through the eyes of the child, are inevitably distorted as a result of the child's immature mental functioning. An important aspect of the child's relationship to parents and other significant caretakers are the fantasies he or she elaborates about them. These include sexual fantasies, such as Ms. B's oedipal desires for her father, as well as aggressive fantasies, such as Mr. A's fantasy of humiliating his father. Transference is best viewed as "a revival in current object relationships, especially to the analyst, of thought, feeling, and behavior derived from repressed fantasies originating in significant conflictual childhood relationships" (Curtis, 1973).

Although transference was discovered in the context of the therapeutic relationship, it is actually a feature of all our interpersonal relationships (Freud, 1912a; Bird,

1972; Brenner, 1976, 1982). Whenever we encounter new people, we approach them with our own unique interpersonal agendas. Although we have realistic wishes, goals, or concerns that are appropriate to current lives, our feelings about the new person are also determined by unconscious wishes and fears of childhood origin. Even as adults we remain unconsciously attached to the love objects of childhood and unconsciously seek to relive these relationships. This is most evident in the sphere of romantic love. In romantic love, the lover's image of the beloved is formed by merging realistic perceptions of the beloved with preexisting mental representations of childhood love objects or fantasied versions of such persons. Freud (1905b) described the experience of falling in love as a process of "refinding" childhood love objects in the persons of adulthood. Transference effects this "refinding," permitting us to experience feelings of intense intimacy and familiarity with people who are actually newcomers in our lives. The exhilaration of romance is due, in part, to the unexpected joy of "refinding" these lost love objects, just as the pain of romantic disillusionment or loss is often profound grief at the "relosing" of them. This effort to refind childhood love objects explains Ms. B's love for "enchanting" men and Mr. C's fascination with "classy" women (as well as the conflicts each experienced in connection with these wishes). As illustrated in the case of Mr. A, transference may also be driven by hostile wishes, such as the wish to avenge injuries inflicted in childhood by a powerful aggressor.

Transference is sometimes conceptualized as a cognitive distortion that occurs when new persons or situations are classified according to existing categories or prototypes formed during the course of development. While this view is accurate, it does not explain the driving power of transference. Transferences are not merely automatic assumptions that are operative until proven otherwise. Transferences may have extraordinary power over the individual's mental functioning. It is often observed, for instance, that "love is blind," that lovers often idealize the objects of their romantic passion in flagrant disregard of the beloved's realistic attributes. This is not simply a result of cognitive error, but a motivated distortion, fueled by unconscious motivations, such as longings for reunion with the love objects of childhood. All transferences may be understood as attempts to gratify unconscious fantasies in the context of real life. Transference reflects the operation of the pleasure principle, which seeks to transform fantasies into actualities, to experience fantasied relationships as real interpersonal events.

Analysts have traditionally categorized transferences to the therapist as either *positive* or *negative*. Positive transferences are characterized by warm, friendly, or loving feelings. *Negative transferences* are characterized by hostile, rivalrous, or sadistic feelings. Anna Freud (1936) introduced the concept of the *transference of defense* to refer to the tendency to treat others defensively, as though they were potentially hurtful. It is also common to classify transferences according to the primary object in relation to whom the transference feelings originated (e.g., *mother transference, father transference*) or according to the developmental level at which the transferred feelings originated (e.g., *preoedipal transference, oedipal transference*). These classifications are a useful shorthand for describing the prominent features of any given transference, but they fail to convey the actual complexity of transference phenomena. No transference is purely positive or purely negative, although it may appear that way at any given moment. All transferences, like all relationships, are ultimately ambivalent. They are constituted by complex configurations of wishes, anxieties, depressive affects, and defenses, forged in the process of development in relation to the significant figures of childhood. Transferences, in other words, are compromise formations (Brenner, 1982).

This is also illustrated by the phenomenon of romantic love. The capacity for feelings of romance originates with the Oedipus complex. Most children develop a feeling of romantic love for one or both parents during the oedipal years (see Chapter 3 in this book). This love is normally doomed to defeat. Under normal circumstances, the child is dissuaded from his romantic quest by his inability to "win" exclusive possession of the desired parent and by feelings of guilt and fear of retaliation from the rival parent. This is a very bitter defeat for some children, leaving emotional scars such as feelings of inferiority, fear of rejection, fear of hostile or dangerous rivals, and so on. When love is aroused in adult life, it is associated with these affects of unpleasure, along with the psychological defenses habitually employed to ward them off. The adult experience of falling in love, then, cannot be described as a transference of love alone but, rather, as a transference of a whole configuration of emotional forces (Bergmann, 1987). Ms. B's love for "enchanting" men, which represented her oedipal wish for a tryst with her father, aroused feelings of anxiety, guilt, and revulsion, which she managed in adult life, as she did in childhood, by suppressing genital feelings. Mr. C's love of "classy" women, which represented an oedipal love of his mother, triggered guilt and fears of punishment, which he warded off in adult life, much as he did in childhood, by restricting his sexual desires, and by adopting a placating and subordinate stance to father figures in order to elicit their pity and protection.

From the clinical perspective, the most significant distinctions to be drawn in regard to the classification of transferences pertain to the subjective context in which they are experienced and understood by the client. Tarachow (1963) introduced the useful distinction between transferences that are apprehended as *real* and those that are experienced *as if* they were real. *As-if* transferences are relational experiences of great affective power and immediacy, but they are bounded or framed within a realistic perspective. The client recognizes the transference feelings as inappropriate to the actual character of the therapeutic relationship and thus experiences them with an attitude of reflection and curiosity. When the client experiences the transference *as if* it were real while retaining a realistic perspective, the "experiencing" and "observing" parts of the client's personality are in a state of balance and cooperation. This is optimal for therapeutic exploration and insight.

When transference is consistently mistaken for reality, however, it is may be disruptive to the therapeutic relationship, and refractory to the therapist's efforts to interpret it. When a transference is experienced as a taken-for-granted reality, the client can experience the therapist only from within the transferential frame of reference. Such a transference is called unanalyzable or, in extreme cases, a transference psychosis. If Mr. A had been convinced that I really was contemptuous of him, or if Ms. B had been certain that I really intended to seduce her, it might have been impossible for me to help them. The occurrence of an intractable and unanalyzable transference may indicate that the client requires a more supportive and reality-oriented form of therapy. Sometimes, however, an unanalyzable transference crystallizes as a consequence of subtle or unconscious aspects of the client-therapist interaction. An unanalyzable transference may be provoked or reinforced by the therapist's eccentric, inconsistent, or irrational responsiveness to the client. This may occur when the therapist is overwhelmed by the client's trasnference, or when the therapist is caught up in his own transference to the client. This phenomenon is called *countertransference*. When the therapist's functioning is impaired by his or her emotional reactions to the client, an improvement in the therapist's understanding through supervision or therapy may restore the prospects for a better outcome. Sometimes, however, it is in the client's best interest to refer the client to another therapist for continued treatment.

To summarize, the helping alliance and the transference coexist as aspects of the therapeutic relationship. It is optimal for the transference to be nested within the realistic context of the helping alliance. The transference is a potentially invaluable vehicle for the communication of inner life, but it can disrupt the therapeutic enterprise if it becomes a dominant reality.

The Therapeutic Dialogue

The therapeutic dialogue is a unique form of discourse, structured to promote the exploration of the client's mental life and the discovery of the psychic conflicts that cause his or her problems. In brief, the client is invited to express, as freely as possible, all the thoughts that pass through his or her mind in the course of the session, thus giving voice to his or her stream of consciousness. This process is known as *free association*. The therapist, in turn, listens to the client's associations and forms hypotheses, or conjectures, about the psychological conflicts they reveal. When he or she has understood something that may help the client, the therapist communicates this understanding in a statement or a series of statements, sometimes referred to as interpretations. Once the therapist has spoken, the therapist returns to listening, now with a special ear for the client's response to the interpretation. The client's reactions help the therapist to judge the accuracy of the interpretation and to refine it in accordance with accumulating evidence.

Once the therapeutic situation has been initiated, the therapeutic dialogue assumes a characteristic form, determined by the aims of exploration and discovery. A basic principle is that the therapy hour "belongs" to the client. As a rule, the therapist does not open the session by selecting or suggesting a topic or in any other way influencing the client's first communications. The client begins the hour with whatever thoughts or feelings are passing through his or her mind at that particular moment. The therapist gives the client room to settle into his or her musings, to shift from topic to topic as his or her attention is spontaneously drawn from one mental content to another. The therapist listens to the client's associations in a state of open receptivity, tuning in to the client's feelings and thoughts, as well as to his or her own reactions and intuitions.

In keeping with the goal of discovery, the therapist will not interfere with the unfolding of the client's thoughts by encouraging the client to talk about one thing at a time, or trying to "help" the client stay focused on the main point, or in any other fashion that might be natural in another context. Most therapists listen quietly for long stretches of time, intervening only when the client encounters obstacles to the free flow of his or her thoughts or when the client is attempting to clarify the feelings or reactions that have already been produced. Although the therapeutic dialogue entails multiple exchanges between the client and the therapist, they do not occur in the same manner or rhythm as social interactions. The therapeutic interaction is not less "natural" than social dialogue. It is a "natural" expression of the unique aims of psychoanalytic therapy.

For the purpose of clear exposition, I will discuss the client's communications first, followed by a description and explanation of the therapist's communicative tasks. Although I discuss the communications of each party separately for the purposes of presentation, it should be recognized that I am actually describing a dialogue, albeit a most unusual one (see Kaplan, 1968).

The Client's Communications

In psychoanalytic psychotherapy, the client is invited to participate in an unusual procedure called free association. Free association is a method for the exploration of mental life. Although psychoanalytic therapists differ in the way they introduce and explain the task of free association (Lichtenberg & Galler, 1987), most therapists instruct or, preferably, invite the client "to say whatever comes to mind, to speak freely and without regard to any purpose or agenda, to hold nothing back, to make no judgement as to what should or should not be spoken." Free association is not merely an exhortation to extreme honesty. It is a method for promoting an altered state of mind in which the client's attention may shift quite freely, without the organizing influence of realistic concerns or agendas. The mental activity involved in free association is characterized by the flow of thoughts from one idea to the next, and resembles the apparently aimless thought that naturally occurs when one is daydreaming.

Free association is employed as an investigative tool because it facilitates the expression of unconscious activity. Free association reduces the organizing influence of purposeful thought and suspends the rules of normal conversation. Purposeful thought concentrates attention on a limited number of focal concerns. When purposeful thought is suspended, this concentration of attention is relaxed, and mental contents that were previously marginal or disregarded may attract notice. A second characteristic of free association is the verbalization of thoughts while they are forming. In everyday life, we think before we speak. We normally edit our thoughts for coherence, relevance, consistency, and social desirability before we communicate them. As a result, our spoken words do not readily reveal the multiple or conflicting trains of thought from which they are derived. In free association, however, the client speaks while he or she thinks. Free association thus reveals much of the raw material typically edited out in the fashioning of our normal discourse. Free association permits the client to verbalize the "inner dialogue" that occurs between the different sides of his or her personality. Citing Freud's structural model, Bergmann (1968) characterized free association as a "trialogue" in which the voices of the id, ego, and superego may be heard.

The rationale for the technique of free association derives from the discovery that mental life is regulated by the tendency to seek pleasure and to avoid unpleasure. Unconscious wishes exert a more or less continuous pressure on all mental activity. Unconscious wishes prompt us to recall and relive past experiences of gratification and to imagine new scenes in which our wishes are satisfied. Mr. A, for instance, frequently thought about being a star, Ms. B about "enchanting" men, Mr. C about "classy" women. If free association simply facilitated the unfettered expression of wishes, however, psychoanalysts would never have learned about psychic conflicts. The fact is that many of the client's wishes do not emerge in comfort, but in the context of unpleasurable affects. When Mr. A reported his fantasies about being a star, he was often quite anxious. When Ms. B talked about her sexual feelings toward "enchanting" men, she felt nauseated and often, for no apparent reason, also talked about women whom she felt were hostile to her. When Mr. C described his wish to date "classy" women, he felt "inadequate" and fearful of my criticism. These recurring, patterned associations between wishes and unpleasures reveal the influence of psychic conflict. Of course, the meaning of these recurring associations is rarely apparent at the outset of the treatment. Mr. A's wish to be a star was not explicitly expressed as a wish to humiliate his father, and his anxiety initially had no recognizable meaning as a fear of retribution. Ms. B's excitement about "enchanting" men, her nausea, and her concerns about the enmities of various women friends had no overtly meaningful relationship. The same may be said about Mr. C's idealized view of "classy" women, his manifest feelings of "inadequacy," and his fear of my criticism. When wishes and unpleasures repeatedly occur in the same trains of thought, however, it may be assumed that they are both aspects of an unconscious psychic conflict.

Free association, as Loewenstein, (1963), Eissler (1963), and others have emphasized, is a most difficult challenge precisely because it facilitates the experience of psychic conflict. The arousal of the client's repressed wishes inevitably triggers feelings of unpleasure, which engage the client's defenses. No client can speak without restraint or inhibition, especially at the outset of treatment. Even the prospect of free association typically stirs up feelings of embarrassment, shame, guilt, exposure, suspicion, and so on. These feelings are usually connected with the client's central conflicts. The exploration of these feelings is thus not merely preparatory to the therapeutic process; it is an essential aspect of it. It is therefore important to introduce the technique of free association in a manner that will encourage the client to discuss his or her feelings and questions about it. I generally invite the client to free-associate (rather than instruct the client). I also explain to the client that free association is naturally difficult and discomforting, and that it is just as important for us to work together to understand these discomforts as it is for us to understand anything else that free association may enable him or her to express (Lowenstein, 1963; Gray, 1986; Busch, 1994). (With clients who are unusually threatened or psychologically vulnerable, I suggest that they speak as freely as they wish. This contributes to a feeling of safety and control and enables them to cooperate with a level of openness they can handle.)

As the client expresses the various concerns and hesitations that the invitation to free-associate stirs up, the therapeutic dialogue usually gets under way. Most clients eventually try to associate as freely as they can, observing and discussing feelings of reluctance that crop up along the way. As their discomforts are reduced, their associations become freer and freer. Even when the client speaks with minimal reluctance and restraint, however, the "freedom" of the client's associations is restricted by unconscious defenses. The technique of free association is intended to suspend, or at least reduce, the client's conscious reluctance, but free association is never totally free because the expression of warded-off wishes (itself a signal of increased associative freedom) arouses associated unpleasures, which mobilize defenses that curtail or disrupt the client's ongoing associations. This sequence of wish, unpleasure, and defense may sometimes be quite obvious, as when a client expresses a wishful fancy or musing, becomes visibly agitated or uncomfortable, and then issues another statement that undoes or modifies the meaning of the wishful communication. An obsessional client, for example, will often make a snide or hostile remark ("He's such a pain in the neck"), express discomfort ("Please don't get me wrong"), and then retract it ("He's really a good guy; he's just doing his job"). Some overt behaviors may also be recognized as serving defensive purposes. When he expressed fantasies of stardom, Mr. A not only became anxious; he also became self-critical, often severely so. For a time, Ms. B became so upset by her nausea that she had to stop speaking. Mr. C insisted on hearing expressions of support. Such sequences of mental activity are meaningful expressions of the client's psychic conflicts.

This sequence of wish, unpleasure, and defense is not always readily recognizable. Defenses are often automatically engaged with such remarkable rapidity that no recognizable trace of the briefly aroused wish and associated unpleasure is evident in the client's communications. Fortunately, however, free association is a sensitive instrument for the detection of such defensive functioning. When defenses have eliminated or disguised distressing contents, the associative process often betrays subtle effects of defensive tampering. This is evident as discontinuities in the flow, pauses, shifts of posture or facial expression, subtle shifts of attention to other material or environmental distractions, abrupt transitions to "more important" matters, curious non sequiturs or illogical conclusions expressed with blithe conviction, vague references or omissions in a story that may leave the therapist feeling as though he or she "missed something," and so on. The meaning of such discontinuities can often be discerned through attention to the associative context in which it occurs. An associative context is the network of associations within which a particular thought, affect, or other event occurs. It may be defined as the thoughts that precede and follow a particular event. Discontinuities often occur regularly in the same associative contexts, that is, when the client's associations reflect a particular theme, such as rivalry with powerful men or dependency on uncaring authorities. In such instances, the discontinuities probably reflect defensive functioning mobilized by wishes and unpleasures connected with that theme.

To summarize, unconscious wishes exert a continuous pressure on mental life. As a result, the client's associations are shaped, in part, by the influence of his or her unconscious wishes. Unconscious wishes, however, are conflictually entangled in affects of unpleasure. This entanglement is also reflected in the client's associations. When unconscious wishes are aroused, they emerge in association with specific affect of unpleasure. These affects habitually mobilize specific defensive operations that reduce this unpleasure. Free association reveals that specific wishes, specific unpleasures, and specific defensive operations cluster together in the same associative contexts. By systematically charting these recurring clusters of wish, pleasure, and defense in the client's free associations, the client and therapist are able to discern the unconscious conflicts that underlie the client's pathology.

We turn now to a discussion of the natural flow of a client's thoughts during the course of an hour. The client's free associations naturally begin at the surface of his or her thoughts and proceed, metaphorically, in both "vertical" and "horizontal" directions. Horizontal associations are thoughts about other surfaces that are, in one way or another, connected with the first. Vertical associations expose progressively deeper aspects of an event or experience. This is illustrated by the following example, drawn from the treatment of Ms. D.

Ms. D was a depressed forty-four-year-old woman, a computer programmer, who was emotionally inhibited and frustrated in all her relationships. Although she had a few good women friends, her romances were all unfulfilling and painful, due to the egocentrism of the "macho" men she chose and to her own "mousiness" with them. Ms. D *opened one session in the first year of her therapy by describing a dream in which she could not get a taxi in a snowstorm. With no further thoughts about the dream, she went on to describe a recurring plumbing problem that her landlord would not fix, an incident in which her boyfriend Mark arrived late for a dinner date, and finally, a childhood incident in which her father did not pick her up from school. The dream, the landlord, Mark's lateness, and the childhood memory all evoke a similar feeling of being neglected. The data suggest that a feeling of neglect has organized the constellation of the client's associations.* Ms. D *continued: "I am still bugged about the dream. It's the same feeling. The cab drivers don't care. I'm standing out there in the cold and no one cares.* That's *the feeling:* no one cares. *It's so painful, really, to feel so unimportant. I've felt this way so much. Other people are just so into their own things. I get so angry. You have to be a squeaky wheel to get oiled in this world . . . but you can't get too squeaky or people think you're a crank. You always have to be nice about every damned thing. Do you know, my toilet's been leaking for four months, and I leave a million mousy little messages on the landlord's machine.* I'm *afraid to piss* him *off! I should have him thrown in jail! I'm also sick and tired of being so mousy around Mark. I'm sick of this* Minnie Mouse *and* Macho Mark *shit."*

In this sequence, Ms. D's *associations revealed a good deal more about her state of mind and psychic conflicts. She expressed wishes to be cared for, feelings of frustration and helplessness, aggressive wishes to fight back, anxieties about being ignored or dismissed if she does fight back, and descriptions of the "mousy" attitude with which she reduces her acute feeling of endangerment. Where the first series of associations was largely horizontal in character, these latter associations also took a vertical direction. They add to our depth of understanding. They also continued in a horizontal direction, as Ms. D linked the various episodes at deeper levels. Her anger and mousiness in relation to her landlord, for example, prompted an association with Mark. In later sessions, similar feelings emerged in connection to her father and toward the therapist. As it turned out, unspoken transference feelings were the organizing impetus behind the whole sequence of Ms. D's thoughts in this session.*

The client's free associations often take the form of stories or "narratives" about significant relationships and situations. This reflects the centrality of interpersonal relationships in human life. Our sexual and aggressive wishes always engage us with other people. This is true even when anxieties and depressive affects disrupt relationships in extreme ways, as occurs in schizoid characters or schizophrenics. Even among those very sick individuals in whom outward relatedness is dramatically interrupted, fantasy life reflects a continuing, albeit imaginary, involvement with other people (Arlow & Brenner, 1964). Our relationships with other people may be seen as compromise formations, formed to gratify our wishes despite our unpleasures. Of course, each of our actual interpersonal relationships is unique because each of our partners brings a different personality to the encounter. Even so, certain relatively invariant relationship patterns are usually evident in all the significant relationships of any individual (see Luborsky & Crits-Christoph, 1990). Where the individual suffers from emotional conflicts, these will generally be apparent in their relationships. It is not surprising that relationship problems are the most common complaint of clients seeking psychotherapy.

The client's stories about his or her relationships are important surfaces to be explored. They permit the therapist to identify the client's maladaptive patterns of living and to explore the psychic conflicts that shape them. In describing any one interpersonal episode, the client will typically be reminded of others in which a similar conflict or feeling is present. These associated episodes will come to include a growing number of childhood memories in which the client recalls significant experiences with parents and other childhood figures. The client's associations will also come to reflect the client's experience of the therapist. If the client is engaged in the treatment, the therapist will naturally become a person of growing importance to the client. The client may see the therapist as a person who might fulfill abandoned hopes or as one who might repeat past hurts and injuries. As the client's psychic conflicts influence his or her experience of the therapist, the transferential dimension of the therapeutic relationship will become increasingly salient.

Transference typically begins to develop unconsciously and initially appears to the client as an aspect of reality. The therapist's yawn is taken as an "obvious" sign of boredom, his beard as a "self-evident" sign of religiosity, a cough as a "clear" expression of irritation. As the transference is forming, the client's free associations begin to reflect the client's emerging experience of the therapist, often in the form of indirect allusions, such as references to other figures toward whom the client harbors a similar feeling (e.g., authority figures like teachers or coaches, service providers like the taxi driver in Ms. D's dream, and so on; see Gill & Hoffman, 1982), or as expressions of interest about the therapist's life or professional activities. The client's first expressions of transference may seem trivial. On one occasion, early in his treatment Mr. A interrupted his enthusiastic description of a theatrical "triumph" to ask if I took notes. He was "just curious," he said, brushing off my inquiry about what prompted the question. He returned to his narrative, and again, as he described the audience's thunderous ovation, he paused to ask if I took notes. In a state of mounting anxiety (much like his stage fright) he expressed a fear that I might envy his "triumphs," feel humiliated to be a mere therapist while he is a "star," and that I might sell my notes about him in order to disgrace him in the eyes of his admirers. His "confession" was offered amid a flurry of self-recriminations and apologies. This intense and most revealing transference first manifested as a "simple" question—ostensibly nothing more than idle curiosity. Mr. A's deepening associations, however, provided our first glimpse of the conflict that had given rise to his stage fright: aggressive wishes to cause me (his father) to suffer from feelings of envy, coupled with fears of retribution, and a defensive attitude of self-criticism and self-denigration. Over time, the same wish, unpleasure, and defense appeared repeatedly in relation to his father, in relation to other men, in relation to the audience, as well as elsewhere.

To recapitulate, the client's associations expand horizontally and vertically. Horizontal associations link interpersonal episodes or life situations that share subjectively significant characteristics. Vertical associations expose the psychic conflicts that are significant in those situations. Most of the client's narratives will pertain to the client's current or recent relationships, to the client's childhood relationship with parents and caretakers, and to the client's ongoing relationship with the therapist. Each of these domains offers numerous surfaces for the exploration of psychic conflict.

I close this discussion with a few observations about the role of the client's nonverbal material in the therapeutic dialogue. These include *paraverbal communications*, *enactments*, and *symptoms*. Although communication in psychoanalytic therapy is predominantly verbal, the client's associations are always accompanied by paraverbal features, including the pitch, tempo, and tone of the client's voice, various facial expressions and bodily postures, and small movements of the hands or feet. These behaviors often express aspects of subjective experience of which the client is unaware or is unable to express. Paraverbal behavior often expresses unverbalized affects associated with the client's thoughts. Affects always accompany subjectively meaningful trains of thought. They can be metaphorically described as the music that accompanies the client's words. Expressions of affect are particularly notable when the words and the music do not go together. A client may announce his great joy about finally getting his divorce, while looking sad and wringing his or her hands. Another may dolefully report the same event while smiling or tapping out a tune with his fingers. When affects are incongruent with the client's manifest thoughts, they are usually appropriate to latent trains of thought. The appearance of the affect in such instances reflects the fact that affects are often harder to ward off than thoughts. These latent thoughts may be discovered by "following the affective track," that is, by asking the client to note the feeling and listening for the client's associations.

Transference is sometimes expressed through enactments. In the preceding discussion, transference has been described as an aspect of fantasy life that becomes manifest in the client's free associations. Because transference is driven by unconscious wishes, the client is motivated to confuse transference fantasy with social reality so that transference wishes may be actualized in the relationship with the therapist. As a result, transference is sometimes expressed as social behaviors, often very subtle, intended to induce the therapist to adopt the role he or she plays in the client's fantasy life (Boesky, 1982, 1989; Jacobs, 1991; McLaughlin, 1987, 1991; Sandler, 1976). Enactments may be regarded as expressions of the client's efforts to live out the transference with the therapist rather than to achieve insight into it (Freud, 1914a). For a period of time, Mr. A made a series of curious requests. He asked me to get him a glass of water, to pass him the tissues when he was no farther from the box of tissues than I was, to jot down a few key comments I had made so that he could refer to them later, and to save a review of his play, which he knew would appear in the particular newspaper I read. Over time, we recognized that he wished me to assume the role of a subordinate assistant, a derivative of his wish to "tower over me." The following incident, taken from the case of Ms. B, is a more dramatic example of enactment.

On one occasion, Ms. B arrived at my office with her grocery shopping. While waiting for her session to begin, she put the groceries in the refrigerator of a private kitchen, located behind a closed door in the waiting room. I learned of this when she thanked me at the end of the session for having a refrigerator handy. Having been thanked, the impulse was naturally to say, "You're welcome," a comment that would have signaled participation in the intimate arrangement Ms. B had engineered. Fortunately, I refrained from such reciprocation. In the next session, I suggested to Ms. B that we examine the thoughts that prompted her to use my refrigerator. After initially protesting that the kitchen is no more private than the bathroom, she acknowledged having viewed the kitchen as "our" kitchen, a thought that spontaneously reminded her of a recent dream in which she was living with me in the office suite. She had had no recognition of the fact that she was acting inappropriately when she blithely entered my closed-off kitchen.

These examples demonstrate that enactments have important potential communicative value. If the therapist can recognize an enactment and understand it as the behavioral expression of transference desires, he or she can help the client to verbalize and explore its emotional meaning. Enactments may thus augment the client's associations as communications of inner life.

Finally, I turn to a most fascinating phenomenon that has important communicative potential, although it is not an intentional communication. One of the most interesting events that occurs in psychotherapy is the spontaneous appearance of a symptom during a session. This is by no means rare. Mr. A often became acutely anxious during his sessions, Ms. B sometimes experienced nausea, and Ms. D frequently felt intense waves of depressive affect. Symptoms crystallize when psychic conflicts become too intense to be managed by ordinary means. The conflicts determining the symptom may be discovered by reconstructing the thoughts and feelings with which the client was struggling at the time the symptom emerged. When a symptom crystallizes during a therapy session, the therapist has an unusual opportunity to observe the thoughts that preceded and followed the onset of the symptom, that is, to study the associative context in which it has appeared. When symptoms occur frequently enough in therapy sessions, the psychic conflicts that determine them may be discerned by identifying the invariant aspects of the associative contexts in which they repeatedly occur. The study of associative contexts is a most valuable method by which a great many recurrent phenomena, including symptoms, mysterious affects, and defensive disruptions of thought (as described earlier), may be investigated (see Luborsky & Auerbach, 1969). This is illustrated by the following example:

Ms. E was a forty-one-year-old woman, a child of Holocaust survivors, who entered therapy to overcome anxieties about marrying her boyfriend of long standing. Shortly after her wedding, she developed a mysterious dermatitis, which flared up only in the company of her mother-in-law. Although prone to allergies as a child, she had never suffered from them as an adult. At first, she thought she was allergic to something in her mother-in-law's house, but she soon discovered that the worst bouts occurred when the mother-in-law visited at Ms. E's home. Neither Ms. E nor her doctor could identify the responsible allergen. Ms. E concluded that she must be allergic to something her mother-in-law wears, perhaps her perfume.

In succeeding weeks, Ms. E rarely talked about her mother-in-law and showed no interest in doing so. The subject was raised again, however, when she suffered a particularly miserable dermatitis during an impromptu weekend visit by her mother-in-law. It seemed her mother-in-law was taking over her life, prying into her personal business, reorganizing the kitchen, and insinuating herself into private aspects of her marital life. As she spoke, Ms. E felt a mounting rage that she tried to control, saying that she did not want to hurt her mother-in-law's feelings. "But she's constantly getting under my skin," she muttered, scratching her arms and face. To my astonishment, her skin had broken out in large red splotches! The associative context of this and several later episodes revealed that the "allergen" was a state of mind in which she felt "invaded" and unable to maintain social boundaries. Although she wished to assert herself, she felt guilty about hurting a needy parent. Over time, we discovered that this dilemma recapitulated a conflict she experienced with both her parents and which had caused her anxiety about forming intimate relationships.

While psychoanalytic therapy is a method of treatment that is primarily verbal, paraverbal communications, enactments, and symptoms are important expressions of the client's inner life. Their value, however, depends on the elucidation of their meaning through the free association method. Just as the value of the transference depends on its containment within the subjective context of the therapeutic alliance, the communicative potential of nonverbal behavior is fulfilled only when its meaning is illuminated by client's verbalized associations.

Therapeutic Listening

The psychoanalytic therapist listens to the client's free associations in order to understand the client's mental life. The client's conscious thoughts are referred to as the *manifest content,* or, metaphorically, as the surface of the client's mental life. The unconscious undercurrents are referred to as *latent contents* and are metaphorically located at some depth below the surface. The therapist's goal when listening to the client's associations is to "hear" or infer the latent contents of the client's communications. The listening process by which the therapist apprehends the latent content is highly complex and differs from therapist to therapist. Freud (1912b) suggested a listening attitude of unfocused receptivity in which all conscious puzzle solving is suspended. He termed this listening stance "evenly hovering attention" and likened it to the client's free association. By suspending the therapist's inclination to conscious "figuring," evenly hovering attention diminishes the therapist's propensity to focus on contents that fit preconceived expectations or ideas about what is important. Evenly hovering attention thus enables the therapist to hear unanticipated themes and patterns in the client's associations, much as it would enable a music lover to recognize subtle themes in a complex musical composition.

Freud discovered that the client's associations elicit emotional reactions in the therapist, which provide clues to latent aspects of the client's mental state. These include resonating affects or memories from the therapist's own mental life, as well as complementary reactions to the interpersonal pressures the client is exerting in the therapeutic relationship (sometimes called the *induced countertransference*). The therapist's own associations to the client's material will often illuminate important connections by recalling the contents of previous sessions, experiences with other patients, literary themes or figures, and so on (Freud, 1912b; Arlow, 1980). These reactions in the therapist do not reveal the client's unconscious, but they may alert the therapist to unnoticed aspects of the client's communications or enable the therapist to recognize subtle connections, patterns, or parallels between one set of observations and another.

Many analytic thinkers place special emphasis on empathy as a method for understanding the client's mental life (Fliess, 1942; Fromm-Reichmann, 1950; Greenson, 1960; Kohut, 1959; 1984; Rowe & MacIsaac, 1993; Schafer, 1959; Schwaber, 1995). Empathy is an aspect of evenly hovering attention. It may be described as an imaginative process of putting oneself in the client's shoes through "transient trial identifications" (Fleiss, 1942). The therapist imagines what it is like to be the client and then examines this empathically constructed experience to understand the client, a process characterized as "vicarious introspection" (Kohut, 1959). Through repeated empathic experiences, the therapist builds up a "working model" (Greenson, 1960) of the client's mental life, a model that is accessed and refined with each successive therapeutic encounter.

While evenly hovering attention and empathic listening prompt the therapist to form numerous impressions of the client's mental life, these processes are not sufficient to guide the therapist's interpretive activity. The therapist's impressions must be tested and refined through systematic observations of repetitive patterns in the client's thought and behavior, and they must be logically organized to form coherent conjectures about the client's mental functioning and psychic conflicts. These logical activities augment the unfocused receptivity and empathic attunement described above. In practice, then, the therapist "oscillates" between alternative states of mind, shifting back and forth between unfocused receptivity and empathy, on the one hand, and objective observation and logical analysis of the data, on the other (Arlow, 1980; Fenichel, 1941; Ferenczi, 1919; Spencer & Balter, 1990). This shifting of perspectives parallels the client's oscillation between experiencing and observing (Sterba, 1934).

Conjectures. Conjectures are the therapist's hypotheses about the client's mental life (Brenner, 1976). They are formed through the various modes of therapeutic listening and reflect the therapist's efforts to understand the client and the client's problems. The formation and refinement of conjectures is preliminary to the activity of interpretation. Conjectures vary in regard to their depth and their breadth, in accordance with the stage of the treatment and the extent of the therapist's understanding. Some conjectures pertain to the particularities of a specific moment, such as the client's reaction to a particular event, while others pertain to wider patterns of thought and behavior. Some conjectures pertain to contents that are relatively accessible to the introspection, such as a lurking feeling of sadness or a passing thought about the therapist's appearance. Others pertain to the deeper unconscious determinants of such feelings and thoughts.

Although therapists vary in the ways they arrive at conjectures, once conjectures are formed, they must be tested empirically. The therapist's formulations should correspond to the actual facts. They should accord with the contents of the client's associations, paraverbal communications, enactments, and so on. The therapist can often test the validity of a conjecture by using it to predict future behavior or associations. A school teacher, Mr. F, described an episode in which his girlfriend acted in an obviously careless and selfish manner. After only the briefest pause, he went on to speak about her kindness and decency with unusual softness and gratitude. I conjectured that Mr. E was warding off angry feelings by adopting attitudes of a contrary character. Some moments later he became quite agitated about the selfishness of a school secretary who simply refuses to take telephone messages because "she's too damned busy doing her nails!" This outburst provided initial confirmation, since the feelings expressed toward the secretary corresponded to those I imagined he might feel in relation to his girlfriend. I tested my conjecture further by predicting that Mr. F would again express especially loving attitudes in situations where his girlfriend behaves in a hurtful way. The repetition of the predicted pattern over a course of several months further confirmed the conjecture.

The Interpretive Process

Interpretations are statements a therapist makes to the client, by which he or she communicates an understanding of the client's mental life. The therapist may schematically organize the interpretive task by reference to Malan's two triangles, the triangle of conflict and the triangle of persons (Malan, 1979). Malan represents psychic conflict as an inverted triangle. The three points of the triangle represent the three components of conflict: a conflictual wish, an associated unpleasure, and a defense. The wish is represented at the bottom of the pyramid to indicate that it lies at the metaphoric root of the conflictual configuration, and the unpleasure and defense are located at the upper corners. To interpret a symptom, character trait, or any other compromise formation, the therapist must illuminate the wishes, unpleasures, and defenses that give rise to that compromise formation and elucidate the way these components are functionally connected. Such interpretations are called dynamic because they illuminate the dynamic forces (wishes, unpleasures, and defenses) that determine any given expression of mental activity.

Dynamic interpretations, or interpretations of the triangle of conflict, always link an observable surface, that is, a conscious aspect of mental life or behavior, with its unconscious roots. Dynamic interpretations can only be made, then, from a manifest point of departure. This is another way of saying that interpretation can only lead to ostensive insight when the client is in direct contact with the phenomenon being explored. It follows that psychic conflict should be interpreted when the client is struggling with some real manifestation of it, such as a problem or relationship, during the therapy session. Any important psychic conflict will be discernible in three separate spheres of the client's life: the client's current social relationships, the history of a client's childhood relationships with parents and caretakers, and the client's transference to the therapist. These three spheres may be represented by another inverted triangle, which Malan calls the triangle of persons. Childhood relationships are represented at the bottom, with current relationships and transference at the upper corners, to signify that childhood relationships influence the shape of later relationships, including the client's current relationships and the transference. A complete interpretation of any significant psychic conflict is achieved when it has been interpreted in all three spheres. Malan describes the linking of the three corners of the triangle of conflict and the three corners of the triangle of persons and the completion of these two triangles. The completion of the triangles enables the client to recognize madadaptive patterns of living as they occur in his life, to understand the psychic conflicts that fuel them, and to understand their origin in the significant relationships of childhood.

The interpretive process unfolds in a natural and systematic manner, normally proceeding in "installments" (Loewenstein, 1951) over the course of many interactions. Because interpretations are intended to connect manifest aspects of mental life with their latent determinants, effective interpretations begin with a surface that the client can directly experience. This surface, a particular state of mind, let us say, serves as a point of departure for the client's continuing associations. As the client mulls the manifest experience, its marginal and shadowy features come into better focus. The therapist's interventions help the client attend to these aspects or to elucidate them. As the details of experience become salient, associated contents, such as fleeting thoughts that the client had previously ignored or brushed aside, now draw the client's attention and become new focal points of experience. These previously dismissed thoughts are themselves now manifest contents and serve as points of departure for further clarification and elucidation. The client's deepening associations provide a continuing source of new surfaces for exploration and interpretation. The interpretive proceeds in a step-by-step advance, from one newly emergent set of contents to the next.

Of course, the associative process does not proceed in complete freedom. The client's associations inevitably arouse feelings of unpleasure and defensiveness. As a result, resistances repeatedly impede the flow of the client's associations. Whenever this occurs, the resistance itself becomes an important surface for interpretive work.

The successful interpretation of resistance permits the resumption of the flow. Interpretations may be schematically classified as *interpretations of content*, intended to illuminate warded-off or latent contents, such as hidden feelings or impulses, or *interpretations of resistance*, intended to illuminate the interference of the client's defenses in the associative process, as well as the unpleasures that motivate it.

Greenson (1967) described the interpretive process as a natural progression in which four different types of interventions are employed:

1. *Confrontations* (I prefer the word *observations*), comments intended to draw the client's attention to a particular "surface." They may be as subtle as the thoughtful repetition of a phrase the client has spoken, or they may be more explicit requests to focus on the phenomenon in question. Once a phenomenon is in focus, it must be clarified.
2. *Clarifications,* which bring out the details of a particular experience. Confrontations and clarifications help the client to apprehend experience better, but they do not expose its unconscious aspects.
3. *Interpretations,* which are communications intended to illuminate unconscious contents, such as unconscious wishes, affects, or defensive activities. Although all interventions that enhance the intelligibility of mental life may be called interpretations, some authors, like Greenson, employ this term more restrictively, to denote only interventions that "make the unconscious conscious." (According to this convention, confrontations and clarifications are classified as interventions preparatory to interpretation.)
4. *Working through,* the continuing repetition of interpretations of a conflict as it appears over and over again in the client's history, in the client's current life outside the treatment, and in the transference (Freud, 1914b; Luborsky, 1984; Menninger, 1958; Greenson, 1967; Malan, 1979).

The course of any therapy session presents the therapist with an extraordinary array of potential surfaces to explore. The therapist must decide what to interpret, when to interpret, at what level to interpret, and how to interpret. Therapists differ in their preferences for various types of surface. Some therapists prefer to interpret transference material, others prefer to begin with discontinuities in the associative process, and so on (see Levy & Inderbitzen, 1990). The choice of surface may be inconsequential since the same core conflicts lie beneath many different surfaces. What is most important, however, is the process by which the client's conflicts are explored and interpreted. The therapist's choices should be guided by a few basic principles:

1. The interpretive process always begins at the surface with a manifest content to which both the therapist and the client can attend.
2. Interpret at the point of urgency. The surface selected for interpretive work should be affectively charged, experientially immediate, and important to the client. The importance of transference interpretations derives, in part, from the affective immediacy of the transference. (Of course, transference is not always the point of urgency.)

3. Resistance should always be interpreted before warded-off contents. Any given content is warded off because it arouses intolerable unpleasures. To interpret a content that arouses intolerable unpleasures is overwhelming, perhaps even traumatizing to the client. Imagine if Ms. B were told early in treatment that her nausea is a symptom of her conflict over her desire to have sexual relations with her father. In vulnerable individuals, such "wild" or premature interpretations may produce pathological states of disorganization or trigger crises in the therapeutic alliance. Even where no such crisis occurs, premature interpretations of warded-off contents usually instigate further defensiveness, which retards the therapeutic process. The timely interpretation of resistance helps the client process the unpleasure aroused by the warded-off content in manageable doses, and thus prepares the client to manage the unpleasure stimulated by the later interpretation of the warded-off content itself.
4. Interpretations should always be in the neighborhood of the client's thoughts, so that the client can readily connect the therapist's communications with his or her own immediate thoughts and feelings (Busch, 1995; Freud, 1910). Interpretations should be formulated at a depth consistent with the client's subjective experience. Interpretations of warded-off contents should be offered only when those contents are sufficiently close to the client's awareness that they may be recognized when the therapist interprets them.

In general, negative transference or other potential disruptions of the therapeutic alliance should be an interpretive priority. Many therapists, in fact, caution that the interpretation of distressing contents should be offered only in the context of a reliable helping alliance. While this seems desirable, it is often impossible. In fact, the interpretation of distressing contents (after the interpretation of resistance, of course) often serves to enhance the alliance. On one occasion, a very disgruntled client first experienced a feeling of alliance when I, in a state of exasperation, offered a relatively "deep" interpretation that, in his words, "lanced the boil" of his confusion.

A few additional comments about the form and delivery of interpretations may be helpful. Interpretations should always be offered in the spirit of collaboration. They should always be somewhat tentative, since the therapist can never be absolutely certain of their accuracy. Incorrect interpretations are unlikely to be harmful when the client feels free to reject them. They may even prompt the client to offer a more accurate interpretation of his own. Interpretations should usually be short and simple, so that the client may hear them without losing contact with the subjective experiences being examined. If the client is drawn into protracted listening or intellectual processing, the experiential aspect of the process is disrupted. (Excellent discussions of these and other clinical rules of thumb may be found in Brenner, 1976; Greenson, 1967; Lasky, 1993; Levy, 1984; Loewenstein, 1951; and many other basic texts.)

I turn now to a more detailed discussion of interpretation of transference and resistance, the two hallmarks of the psychoanalytic approach (Freud, 1914b).

Interpretation of Transference. The interpretation of transference, like all other interpretive activity, begins at the surface with communications or behaviors that indicate transference. Transference manifestations may be subtle, fleeting, and disguised, especially when the transference is disagreeable or distressing. Transference is often expressed by paraverbal behaviors, enactments, and indirect allusions to other individuals (e.g., "My accountant is so irritating. I give him all the figures, and he gives me gobbledygook that I can't understand!"). When transference is unacknowledged, gentle confrontations may draw the client's attention to surface phenomena that suggest its existence. Depending on the client's response, the therapist can comment that the client seems to be experiencing the therapist in a particular way (e.g., "I sense that you may be feeling a bit irritated with me"). The therapist might explain that feelings about other persons might come to mind during the session because they pertain to the therapist. ("Perhaps your comments about your accountant could also pertain to me. Is it possible that you might be feeling irritated at *me* for taking your thoughts and giving you back gobbledygook you can't use?") Sometimes the client will not recognize any such feeling toward the therapist or will aggressively disavow any such feeling even though the evidence for it is strong. These reactions suggest that the client is warding off the transference feelings because they are discomforting (Gill, 1979). In such cases, the therapist should address the client's resistance.

Once the client acknowledges the transference, it can be explored. All the attitudes, perceptions, and strands of feeling that constitute the transference should be followed and carefully clarified, so that the details of the transference experience may be accurately perceived and felt. The therapist should maintain a consistent analytic attitude during this process. The therapist should be curious and empathic, without becoming reactive or overly responsive in any unusual way (e.g., to Mr. A: "It seems you are very uneasy talking about your exciting reviews with me because you worry that while I *seem* okay, I am wounded and crying inside, because I am not having as great a life as you are"). The therapist should not "correct" the client's transference by emphasizing how he or she *really* feels or behaves ("I understand how you feel, but let me assure you, I feel really fine. Let's get back to the therapy now."). Similarly, the therapist should not inform the client that his or her transference feelings really pertain to someone else ("I think this anger really belongs with your father"). Such comments prematurely dispel the transference, thus precluding its exploration. "Realistic" corrections, moreover, may strike the client as defensive, and may thus complicate the interpretive exploration of the transference.

It is often helpful to inquire about the actual experiences on which the client bases his or her transference feelings. The client may point to specific aspects of the therapist's manner or conduct. While these perceptions are often accurate, the client's interpretation of them will reflect the influence of his or her fantasies. Transference is always connected to current reality. The fact that the client accurately perceives certain aspects of the therapist's personality does not mean that his or her reactions are not transferential. A client who feared that I might be as crazy as his psychotic mother panicked on one occasion when he saw that I was somewhat on edge. This perception of the therapist's edginess may be accurate. The client did not know the intensity or meaning of my tension, although he was quite certain that he did. When the "missing data" were unwittingly supplied by the client's fantasy life, he "observed" that I was "having a nervous breakdown."

Some clients need the therapist to acknowledge the facts to which the transference is connected in order to proceed without feeling that they are "crazy" or that their therapist is "lying" to them. This acknowledgment often enables the client to relax enough to realize that the facts do not speak for themselves, and that other interpretations of the therapist's behavior are possible. The client's ensuing capacity to disentangle realistic perceptions from their transferential elaboration helps protect the client's reality testing, and thus enables transference to be experienced and explored *as if* it were real. The client's understanding that transference feelings may be safely communicated and jointly studied with the therapist is also promoted by the unflappable consistency of the therapist's manner and analytic attitude.

The client's experience and understanding of the transference may be furthered whenever transference feelings are explored. While this is often difficult for the client (and often for the therapist), the affective immediacy of the experience makes it a most productive undertaking. The intensity of the client's transference feelings often enables them to emerge with unusual lucidity. As the client is able to describe his or her transference feelings with progressive freedom, depth, and detail, the therapist will be able to interpret specific unconscious aspects of the transference. As a result, psychic conflicts are often first illuminated in the context of transference. In Malan's (1976) terminology, the triangle of conflict is often completed in relation to the therapist before it is completed in relation to the other spheres. As transference is understood, this knowledge helps illuminate the unconscious conflicts that have shaped the client's other relationships, including those of childhood.

Transference interpretation, then, is central to analytic treatment. Transference is a richly textured experience, formed of multiple developmentally stratified layers of psychic conflict and compromise formation. Because transference experience is often vivid and immediate, it offers an unusually productive surface. There is another aspect of transference, however, that makes its interpretation uniquely mutative (Strachey, 1934). Transference is a psychic reality that is subjectively immediate. It pertains to a social reality that is objectively immediate. When transference is explored in the context of the therapeutic interaction, psychic reality and social reality meet. This is uniquely mutative because it enables the client to experience the therapist as fantasied, while perceiving the therapist as he or she actually behaves. The immediacy of this contrast helps the client to appreciate the distorting effect of transference on the experience of the therapist and prompts the client to consider the possibility of distortions in other relationships. Many therapists believe that the collaborative study of the transference is the most powerful technical procedure of psychoanalytic treatment (Strachey, 1934; Gill, 1979; Malan, 1976, 1979).

Interpretation of Resistance. Psychoanalytic psychotherapy is painful because it stirs up affects of unpleasure. The arousal of these feelings mobilizes resistance. This process is largely involuntary and unconscious, and results in an infinite variety of obstacles to the progress of the treatment. Resistance is a manifestation of defenses in the context of psychoanalytic therapy. The appearance of resistance signals the client's active engagement in a psychic conflict. Resistance is thus a most promising surface for exploration. The skillful interpretation of resistance enables the client to understand and reconsider the motives for his or her defensiveness. This deepens the therapeutic process by permitting the expression of previously warded-off contents. The psychoanalytic approach to resistance is purely interpretive. The interpretation of resistance may be conceptualized as a series of steps. Schematically rendered, the therapist must demonstrate to the client *that* he or she is resisting, *how* he or she is resisting, *why* he or she is resisting, and *against what* he or she is resisting. This is a natural sequence, which begins at the the surface and proceeds, in stepwise fashion, to illuminate deeper determinants. In any given instance, this process may extend over numerous sessions or may be completed by a few terse comments.

Like all other interpretive processes, the interpretation of resistance begins with confrontations that direct the client's attention to the most recognizable manifestations of the resistance. The demonstration to the client that he or she is resisting reorients the client's attitude toward the manifestations of resistance. It alerts the client that these aspects of his or her functioning thwart the treatment and communicates to the client that this paradoxical functioning is meaningful and subject to exploration. A confrontation of resistance should be offered in the spirit of analytic inquiry, with the clear intent to engage the client's curiosity and self-observation. A confrontation of resistance should never be accusatory, indignant, or critical. Such attitudes communicate that the therapist thinks that the resistance is conscious, that it is willful, and that it is not allowed. Naturally such communications are utterly antithetical to psychoanalytic therapy.

The exploration of how the client resists reveals the character of the client's defenses, especially in the context of therapy. This is valuable information, because it equips the client to recognize defensive behavior and eventually to control it. A client who subjects the therapist's comments to insistent, incessant, and pointless intellectual dissection whenever the therapist's utterances strike a vulnerable nerve will be able to participate more productively when he understands that this habit is his means of disrupting the treatment. A client who gets "sleepy" whenever certain distressing thoughts arise in therapy sessions may learn to recognize this "sleepiness" as a resistance and to bring it to the therapist's attention so that they may work in partnership to discover the source of the client's uneasiness.

When the client recognizes that how he or she thwarts the treatment, the therapist can invite the client to explore why he or she thwarts the treatment. If the client does not spontaneously address his or her discomforts, the therapist may note the evidence of the client's distress. This facilitates progressive clarification of the specific affects of unpleasure that appear in the associative context of the resistance. As these unpleasures are addressed, they usually become more tolerable. This is in part due to the influence of the client's mature judgment and reality testing, the supportive presence of the therapist, and the general ambience of safety existing in the therapeutic situation. Feelings that could not be endured in childhood, such as grief or guilt at the death of a sibling, or fears of castration by an angry parent, may be tolerated when re-experienced in adult life, especially in the context of therapy. The uncovering of these painful affects thus reduces the client's defensiveness. As defenses are relaxed, the mental contents against which they had previously been deployed become accessible to exploration (Weiss, 1971).

When previously warded-off contents are recognizable to the therapist and believed to be sufficiently close to the client's awareness to be recognizable, the therapist can interpret the mental content against which the client has been resisting. Although these contents will still trigger affects of unpleasure, these affects are now tolerable, and although they may still stimulate habitual defensive activity, this activity can now be inhibited because it is recognizable (the client knows how he or she resisted) and because it is no longer needed (the client knows why he or she resisted and no longer needs to). When the interpretation of resistance permits the disclosure of the contents which the client has been resisting, it becomes synonymous with interpretation of warded-off contents.

The manifestations of resistance are often rather dramatic, as in the case of clients who attempt to overturn the whole therapeutic endeavor by "proving" that the therapist is an incompetent, or by trying to engage the therapist in criminal activity (one client suggested that we sell illicit drugs together), or by attempting to seduce the therapist sexually. More common signs of resistance are latenesses or missed appointments, rigid routines, monotonous or affectless speech, repetitive material, perseveration about trivia, avoidance of particular topics, expressions of boredom with the treatment, silences, and subtle discontinuities of associative flow. The therapist's basic approach to resistance is the same in every case. It is always interpretive, starting with a manifest surface, and proceeding in the manner described above. Let us return to Ms. D, the emotionally inhibited computer programmer.

One day during the third year of her therapy, Ms. D made an uncharacteristically affectionate comment to me. The following week, she "forgot" her therapy appointment. Recalling her unusual expression of affection, I conjectured that the "forgotten" appointment was a manifestation of resistance triggered by her affectionate feelings. In the absence of confirmatory associations by the client in her next session, I waited and tested my conjecture by predicting that future expressions of affection would be followed by similar behavior or by associations suggesting discomfort and a desire to withdraw.

Ms. D was rather cool in the weeks after the missed appointment, but gradually warmed up again after a while. Two months later, she made another affectionate comment, and again, she "forgot" the next appointment. As the resistance was now demonstrable, I drew Ms. D's attention to the missed appointments and asked for her thoughts about it. She acknowledged that it was indeed curious. On reflection, she noted that she had felt vaguely uncomfortable after the previous session. As she mulled this experience, she recalled having been confused about the schedule. She had had a fleeting thought that I had cancelled the appointment due to vacation plans (in fact, I had cancelled a session for the following month). She'd also thought of cutting back to one session every other week.

"Well," I said, "let's think this over together. You felt uncomfortable in the last session. Then during the week you had the idea that I'd cancelled, and then you thought about cutting back, and then you actually did sort of cut back." I was prepared to suggest that she might be trying to get away from therapy because something upset her, when she shook her head in bewilderment. "I don't know how this happened. I mean, I guess I was more upset than I realize. I don't know, but I guess I somehow avoided the session."

"Yes, somehow," I mulled aloud, inviting her to explore how she had arranged to "forget" the session. "I remember thinking, 'Don't forget your appointment, tonight' and then . . . Actually, I called Mark—do you remember him? Macho Mark? My 'ex.' Anyway I called him that evening and we got into a big fight about why it never worked out, about why he was always so cold to me. It just riled me so. You know, that's funny. The last time I forgot an appointment, it was the same thing. I'd had another fight with Mark."

I noted that she had twice avoided the therapy session by picking a fight with Mark. "Could this all have something to do with how you were feeling after the last session? You said you were uncomfortable. Can you get back to that feeling?" Here Ms. D became irritated, and said she preferred to talk about Mark. She lambasted him for his coldness, for leading her on, for taking advantage of her sexually, and finally for humiliating her. At the end of a long tirade, she commented, "I'm so stupid. I should have seen it coming."

In the ensuing sessions, she spoke about Mark, about how hurt she had been by him, and how she wished she had protected herself by holding herself back from loving him. Since these feelings had come up as we tried to make sense of two "forgotten" sessions, each preceded by sessions in which she expressed affection for me, and each "forgotten" by means of a telephone call and fight with Mark, it seemed reasonable to make the following interpretation: "You've been very agitated about Mark lately, and I've been wondering what brought that up. We were trying to figure out what caused you to 'forget' those two appointments, and since then, you've been thinking a lot about Mark and how much he hurt you, and how you should have pulled back. I wonder if all this might be your way of answering the question about what prompted the 'forgotten' appointment?"

"I don't understand," she said, looking a bit frightened.

"Perhaps you are afraid of being hurt by me, too?" I said softly.

As her tears began to fall, she admitted, "I'm terrified of . . . terrified of becoming attached to you."

It is most useful to interpret resistance as it is occurring, so that the client may observe the rising affects of unpleasure and the defensive activities employed to dispel them. Paul Gray and his associates have developed a method for interpreting resistance as it manifests in the client's associations, called *close process monitoring* (Gray, 1994; Busch, 1995; Pray, 1994; Goldberger, 1996). Gray has likened close process monitoring to the work of an apple picker watching a conveyor belt for bad apples. The therapist listens to the flow of the client's material with an ear to discontinuities suggesting that the flow has been blocked by resistance. Such discontinuities may be blatant, as a massive derailment of the narrative, accompanied by paraverbal signals of distress and followed by a change of topic, or it may be quite subtle—a fleeting pause, shift of posture, and change in the affective tone with which a narrative is reported. Gray characterizes these moments as "breaking points" (Gray, 1986). Breaking points indicate that the client has encountered a conflict. Most important, a breaking point is an accessible manifestation of resistance that can be brought to the client's awareness.

The therapist who monitors the process with an eye to such discontinuities will listen for the moment when a resistance is evident and then draw the client's attention to it (a familiar confrontation). Gray regards as an "optimum surface for interpretive interventions a selection of those elements in the material that may successfully illustrate [for the clients] that when they were speaking, they encountered a conflict over something being revealed, which caused them involuntarily and unknowingly to react in identifiable ways" (Gray, 1986, p. 253). In Gray's view, resistance is usually prompted by feelings of guilt, which derive from the internalization of parental criticism and which the client reexternalizes onto the therapist. In his discussion of Gray's work, Busch (1995) adds that a wider range of unpleasure may stimulate resistance in the session. Busch's perspective is thus more in line with the views presented in this chapter, which in large measure derive from Brenner (1982).

Close process monitoring is a particularly useful approach to the exploration and interpretation of resistances because the breaking point is an immediate experience of conflict to which the client usually has access. Close process monitoring enables the client to participate actively in the therapeutic work. This strengthens the client's sense of ownership and responsibility for the treatment and promotes a robust helping alliance (a type II alliance). It also provides the client with the means to observe his or her own mental life independently. The client who becomes familiar with the defensive disruptions of his or her thought will be able to take note of these experiences as they occur in life. The client need not rely on the therapist's unconscious processes, or intuition, or empathy. Put simply, close process monitoring is a rational procedure, based on an empirical method, which can be practiced by any trained observer.

The Validation of Interpretations

The client's response to the therapist's communications provides an important source of data by which the therapist can assess the accuracy of his or her understanding. The therapist's interpretations may (or may not) have some impact on the client, and the client's responses may be employed to study the character of that impact. An interpretation to the client may be viewed as an experiment whose outcome may help confirm or disconfirm the understanding on which it is based. For example, if a therapist suggests that the client may fear a particular calamity, the client's response may help the therapist determine if the interpretation is true. On one occasion, I was treating a very profoundly disturbed individual, who suffered from an itch in his perineum. The itch was particularly tormenting because he believed that scratching it would cause his legs to fall off. After listening to his thoughts for many weeks, I formed the opinion that this symptom represented a conflict over masturbation, which featured a prominent fear that his penis would be harmed. At an appropriate moment in his associations, I suggested that he might be worried about his penis falling off. "No," he said thoughtfully. "I don't worry about that at all. But I *do* worry that someone will come and chop it off."

Such a response to an interpretation is very convincing because it included the spontaneous expression of the inferred content that I had only begun to approach interpretively. The interpretation about his penis falling off was in the neighborhood of the client's fears, and this prompted a series of private thoughts that enabled the client to recognize and express his fear more accurately. Clients are often able to recognize a content about which they have been "reminded" before being able to evoke that content independently (Kris, 1956). In the case reported above, the client's capacity to experience and verbalize the warded-off fear was prepared by numerous preceding interactions that reduced the client's anxiety and heightened his feeling of safety with me, including similar episodes about other terrifying fears.

In general, the client's response to the therapist's interpretation favors the confirmation of the interpretation when it includes the expression of new material congruent with the interpretation. Other typical confirmatory responses are the spontaneous recall of forgotten events or dreams, a subjective sense that an interpretation clicks, feelings of recognition or familiarity about the contents of the interpretation, or an emotional reaction such as laughter, crying, or anger, which suggests the release of a pent-up feeling. All these reactions suggest that the interpretation has altered the balance of psychic forces, so that warded-off contents can emerge with progressive freedom from the disguises and encumbrances imposed by defenses. A single verbalization of an interpretation does not constitute a valid test of its accuracy, since no single interpretation is likely to alter this balance of forces appreciably (Brenner, 1976).

The client's assent to an interpretation is not necessarily confirmatory, since assent by itself may be motivated by numerous possible factors, such as a need to comply, or relief that the therapist is off the mark, and so on. By the same token, symptomatic improvement does not confirm an interpretation. Symptoms improve for many reasons, including the relational factors described earlier, intercurrent events in the client's life, and so on. Symptoms also improve in response to "inexact interpretations" that provide a soothing and palatable explanation for the client's anxieties or problems (Glover, 1931). However, if a particular interpretation is repeated many times and in many different contexts with no discernible impact on the client's symptoms or problems, this *does* suggests that the interpretation may be inaccurate (Brenner, 1976). (Further discussions of the "validating process" in psychoanalytic therapy—Langs, 1974—will be found in most good textbooks, including Brenner, 1976; Fenichel, 1941; Greenson, 1967; and Langs, 1974, 1977, to name but a few.)

PSYCHOANALYTIC THERAPY AND ITS MODIFICATIONS

Psychoanalytic psychotherapy is a difficult undertaking. It is intended to mobilize fantasies, feelings, and states of mind that are ordinarily painful, disruptive, and confusing. Naturally, this process is productive only if the client can tolerate these disturbing contents and turbulent emotional states and reflect on them with the most mature part of his or her personality. Psychoanalytic therapy may be damaging if the client is overwhelmed by experiences that he or she cannot psychologically digest. It follows that psychoanalytic therapy is not for everyone and that the therapist must assess the client's capacity to benefit from this form of treatment before recommending it.

In brief, psychoanalytic therapy requires that the client possess adequate ego strength to benefit from the process of uncovering without suffering severe disorganization or decompensation and without dangerous acting out. The client must be able to tolerate some measure of anxiety and depressive affect, and manage disruptive impulses safely. Moreover, since the curative process ultimately rests with the client's ability to view his or her mental life from a mature perspective, the treatment will falter unless the client has at least some capacity for mature judgment and reality testing. Participation in psychoanalytic therapy is enhanced by psychological mindedness, a capacity for sustained and cooperative interpersonal relations, and adequate motivation for this form of therapy. Psychological mindedness refers to the client's "ability to see relationships among thoughts, feelings and actions with the goal of learning the meanings and causes of his experience and behavior" (Appelbaum, 1973). To engage productively in treatment, the client must also be able to sustain a therapeutic relationship, even during periods of negative transference, frustration, or disappointment. The client will also need to be sufficiently motivated by long-term goals to tolerate the gradual character of therapeutic change.

For clients who do not possess these attributes, the technique of psychoanalytic therapy may be modified. Where the client lacks sufficient motivation for a sustained course of psychoanalytic therapy, for example, short-term treatments based on psychoanalytic theory may provide adequate relief, while in no way discouraging the client from pursuing a more open-ended therapy at a later time. I have found that "time limited dynamic psychotherapy" (Strupp and Binder, 1984) is a most serviceable, flexible, and theoretically congenial approach, which permits conversion to longer-term therapy if this is later indicated. In my experience, however, many very disturbed clients do quite well in psychoanalytic therapy if the treatment is sensitively conducted and modified to provide an adequate level of psychological support. This may include a greater degree of personal engagement with the client (Tarachow, 1963; Dewald, 1964) as well as increased attention to the therapeutic relationship, including heightened attention to subtle fluctuations in the client's experience of the therapist, more rapid interpretation of the negative transference, and the occasional use of noninterpretive means to strengthen the helping alliance (Luborsky, 1984). It should be emphasized that the therapeutic process must proceed very gingerly with more disturbed clients, whose capacity to tolerate disruptive affects is limited. In a paper that is rapidly becoming a classic, Pine (1984) introduced a series of modifications designed to improve the efficacy of interpretations by protecting the client's capacity to assimilate them without excessive distress, loss of ego functions, or disruptions in the client's relationship to the therapist. He suggests, for example, that interpretations of disturbing contents be offered when those contents are not immediate ("strike while the iron is cold"). Sometimes the therapist may reduce anxiety by assuring the client that he or she is *not* expected to respond to an interpretation at the time it is offered. The therapist can prepare fragile clients for upsetting interpretations by alerting them that they may be upset by what the therapist is about to say. (A brief compendium of modifications for work with more disturbed clients will be found in McWilliams, 1994.)

Some clients who lack the needed ego stengths, motivation, psychological mindedness, and capacity for sustained object relations do better in suppressive or supportive therapy rather than in expressive, uncovering forms of therapy. Supportive therapies are also informed by analytic theory. These therapies, however, employ nonanalytic methods to achieve goals other than insight. Supportive therapies were created to treat clients who reacted adversely to uncovering therapies due to impaired or inadequate ego functioning. Accordingly, supportive therapy entails procedures that provide direct or indirect support to ego functioning. Supportive interventions are intended to suppress disruptive impulses and painful affects, to redirect the client's attention from the inner world to reality, to focus the client's attention on environmental challenges, and to improve adaptive functioning. The specific techniques of supportive therapy are diverse and have accumulated over the course of many years (Alexander, 1961; Bibring, 1954; Dewald, 1964; Gill, 1951, 1954; Glover, 1931; Knight, 1954; Tarachow, 1963). Standard supportive techniques include suggestion to induce adaptive attitudes; abreaction to relieve emotional tension; reassurance to relieve anxieties; advice and guidance to help foster adequate functioning and decision making; praise and encouragement for adaptive functioning; and confrontation and discouragement of maladaptive functioning. The use of these and other supportive techniques has recently been receiving more systematic attention. Two textbooks have been devoted to this form of treatment (Rockland, 1989; Werman, 1984). Rockland's volume on *psychodynamically oriented supportive therapy (POST)* provides a comprehensive exposition of the principles and practices of this form of treatment. In a promising series of papers, De Jonghe and associates (De Jonghe et al., 1991, 1992, 1994) have introduced *psychoanalytic supportive psychotherapy (PSP)*, a sophisticated supportive treatment. While PSP employs traditional supportive techniques, the emphasis is on the creation of a primary therapeutic relationship to promote emotional growth and the development of healthy psychic structures.

A CONCLUDING INVITATION

The client who consults a social worker for help with his or her problems often anticipates that the social worker will prescribe solutions in the form of things to do or ways to think. If the client has consulted a social worker who is a behavioral therapist, a cognitive therapist, or a problem-solving therapist, the client may receive a form of therapy that is more or less in keeping with those expectations. If the client has consulted a psychoanalytic therapist, however, he or she is likely to hear the most astonishing response. If the social worker has decided that a course of psychoanalytic therapy is indicated, he or she will inform the client that there is far more to be understood about the client's problems than can be learned in a single discussion or even in a single series of discussions. The client will probably be surprised to hear from the social worker that the best way to overcome his or her problems is to understand himself or herself as a person, as an individual with a unique life story.

The psychoanalytic therapist extends to the client a remarkable invitation to explore the innermost realms of his or her private self for the sole purpose of self-understanding in the service of a freer and more authentic selfhood. It is probably unlike any other invitation the client has ever received. It is certainly unlike anything the client had in mind when he or she first consulted the therapist. The client who accepts this invitation may encounter many surprises about his or her own inner life. Many of these discoveries are disturbing, especially at first. Over time, other discoveries may occasion joy, often an indescribable joy, as when the client conquers a fear, recognizes a self-defeating habit and masters it, or rediscovers a capacity to love, laugh, or think independently. Psychoanalytic therapy is an extraordinary experience for many clients. But it is rarely what they expected.

The reader of this chapter may similarly discover that psychoanalytic therapy is not like any other form of treatment that he or she has studied before. To be sure, psychoanalytic therapy is not a simple form of treatment for the alteration of specific or delimited problems. It is not a method of modifying the client's behavior or social functioning in any particular direction. It is a treatment for the "psyche," a therapy for the soul. To the reader who finds these ideas intriguing, who would like to help disturbed clients in a profound and private way, this chapter is an invitation to explore the universe of psychoanalytic ideas.

REFERENCES

Alexander, F. (1925). A metapsychological description of the process of cure. *International Journal of Psychoanalysis, 6*, 13–34.

Alexander, F. (1954). Psychoanalysis and psychotherapy. *Journal of the American Psychoanalytic Association, 2*, 722–733.

Alexander, F. (1961). *The scope of psychoanalysis.* New York: Basic Books.

Alexander, F., & French, T. M. (1948). *Psychoanalytic therapy: Principles and applications.* New York: Ronald Press.

Appelbaum, S. A. (1973). Psychological mindedness: Word, concept and essence. *International Journal of Psychoanalysis, 54*, 35–46.

Arlow, J. (1980). The genesis of interpretation. In H. Blum (Ed.), *Psychoanalytic explorations in technique: Discourse on the theory of therapy* (pp. 193–206). New York: International Universities Press.

Arlow, J., & Brenner, C. (1964). *Psychoanalytic concepts and the structural theory.* New York: International Universities Press.

Bergmann, M. (1968). Free association and the interpretation of dreams. In J. E. Hammer (Ed.), *The use of interpretation in treatment* (pp. 270–279). New York: Grune and Stratton.

Bergmann, M. (1987). *The anatomy of loving: The story of man's quest to know what love is.* New York: Columbia University Press.

Bibring, E. (1954). Psychoanalysis and the dynamic therapies. *Journal of the American Psychoanalytic Association, 2,* 745–770.

Bird, B. (1972). Notes on transference: Universal phenomenon and the hardest part of analysis. *Journal of the American Psychoanalytic Association, 20,* 267–301.

Boesky, D. (1982). Acting out: A reconsideration of the concept. *International Journal of Psychoanalysis, 63,* 39–55.

Boesky, D. (1989). *Enactments, acting out, and considerations of reality.* Paper presented on Panel on Enactments, Meeting of the American Psychoanalytic Association. Reported in Panel on Enactments in psychoanalysis, M. Johan (reporter). *Journal of the American Psychoanalytic Association, 40,* 827–841.

Brenner, C. (1976). *Psychic conflict and psychoanalytic technique.* New York: International Universities Press.

Brenner, C. (1982). *The mind in conflict.* New York: International Universities Press.

Brenner, C. (1994). The mind as conflict and compromise formation. *Journal of Clinical Psychoanalysis, 3,* 473–488.

Busch, F. (1994). Some ambiguities in the method of free association and their implications for technique. *Journal of the American Psychoanalytic Association, 42,* 363–384.

Busch, F. (1995). *The ego at the center.* Northvale, NJ: Jason Aronson.

Curtis, H. (1973, May). *Toward a metapsychology of transference.* Paper presented to the annual meeting of the American Psychoanalytic Association, New York.

Dewald, P. (1964). *Psychotherapy: A dynamic approach.* New York: Basic Books.

Dorpat, T. (1977). On neutrality. *International Journal of Psychoanalytic Psychotherapy, 6,* 39–64.

Dowling, S. (Ed.). (1991). *Conflict and compromise: Therapeutic implications.* New York: International Universities Press.

Eissler, K. (1958). Notes on problems of technique in the psychoanalytic treatment of adolescents with some remarks on perversions. *Psychoanalytic Study of the Child, 113,* 223–254.

Eissler, K. (1963). Notes on the psychoanalytic concept of cure. *Psychoanalytic Study of the Child, 18,* 424–463.

Fenichel, O. (1941). *Problems of psychoanalytic technique.* New York: Psychoanalytic Quarterly.

Ferenczi, S. (1919). On the technique of psychoanalysis. In *Further contributions to the theory and technique of psychoanalysis.* London: Hogarth Press, 1951.

Fliess, R. (1942). The metapsychology of the analyst. *Psychoanalytic Quarterly, 11,* 211–227.

Franklin, G. (1990). The multiple meanings of neutrality. *Journal of the American Psychoanalytic Association, 38,* 195–220.

Freud, A. (1936). *The ego and the mechanisms of defense.* New York: International Universities Press.

Freud, S. (1905a). Fragment of an analysis of a case of hysteria: prefatory remarks. *Standard Edition, 7,* 3–122.

Freud, S. (1905b). Three essays on the theory of sexuality. *Standard Edition, 7,* 125–243.

Freud, S. (1909). Notes upon a case of obsessional neurosis. *Standard Edition, 10,* 153–318.

Freud, S. (1910). "Wild" psycho-analysis. *Standard Edition, 11,* 219–230.

Freud, S. (1912a). The dynamics of the transference. *Standard Edition, 12,* 97–108.

Freud, S. (1912b). Recommendations to physicians practicing psycho-analysis. *Standard Edition, 12,* 109–120.

Freud, S. (1914a). Remembering, repeating and working through. *Standard Edition, 12,* 145–156.

Freud, S. (1914b). On the history of the psychoanalytic movement. *Standard Edition, 14,* 7–66

Freud, S. (1919). Lines of advance in psycho-analytic therapy. *Standard Edition, 17,* 157–168.

Fromm-Reichman, F. (1950). *Principles of intensive psychotherapy.* Chicago: University of Chicago Press.

Gill, M. M. (1951). Ego psychology and psychotherapy. *Psychoanalytic Quarterly, 20,* 62–71.

Gill, M. M. (1954). Psychoanalysis and exploratory psychotherapy. *Journal of the American Psychoanalytic Association, 2,* 771–797.

Gill, M. M. (1979). The analysis of transference. *Journal of the American Psychoanalytic Association (Supplement), 27,* 263–289.

Gill, M. M., & Hoffman, I. Z. (1982). A method for studying the analysis of aspects of the patient's experience of the relationship in psychotherapy and psychoanalysis. *Journal of the American Psychoanalytic Association, 30,* 137–167.

Gitelson, M. (1952). The emotional position of the analyst in the psychoanalytic situation. *International Journal of Psychoanalysis, 33,* 1–10.

Glover, E. (1931). The therapeutic effect of inexact interpretations: A contribution to the theory of suggestion. *International Journal of Psychoanalysis, 12,* 397–411.

Goldberger, M. (Ed.). (1996). *Danger and defense: The technique of close process attention.* Northvale NJ: Jason Aronson.

Goldstein, E. (1994). Self-disclosure in treatment: What therapists do and don't talk about. *Clinical Social Work Journal, 22,* 417–433.

Gray, P. (1982). "Developmental lag" in the evolution of technique for psychoanalysis of neurotic conflict. *Journal of the American Psychoanalytic Association, 30,* 621–655.

Gray, P. (1986). On helping analysands to observe intrapsychic activity. In A. B. Richards & M. S. Willick (Eds.). *Psychoanalysis: A science of mental conflict.* Hillsdale, NJ: Analytic Press, 1986.

Gray, P. (1994). *The ego and the analysis of defense.* Northvale, NJ: Jason Aronson.

Greenson, R. R. (1965). The working alliance and the transference neurosis. *PQ, 34,* 158–181.

Greenson, R. R. (1967). *The technique of psychoanalysis.* New York: International Universities Press.

Greenson, R. R. (1960). Empathy and its vicissitudes. *International Journal of Psychoanalysis, 41,* 418–424.

Hoffer, A. (1985). Toward a definition of psychoanalytic neutrality. *Journal of the American Psychoanalytic Association, 33,* 771–796.

Jacobs, T. (1991). *The use of the self: Countertransference and communication in the analytic situation.* Madison, CT: International Universities Press.

Jonghe, F. De, Rijnierse, P., & Janssen, R. (1991). Aspects of the analytic relationship. *International Journal of Psychoanalysis, 72,* 693–707.

Jonghe, F. De, Rijnierse, P., & Janssen, R. (1992). The role of support in psychoanalysis. *Journal of the American Psychoanalytic Association, 40,* 475–500.

Jonghe, F. De, Rijnierse, P., and Janssen, R. (1994). Psychoanalytic supportive psychotherapy. *Journal of the American Psychoanalytic Association, 42,* 421–446.

Kaplan, D. (1968). Dialogue in classical psychoanalysis. In E. Hammer (Ed.), *Use of interpretation in treatment* (pp. 129–140). New York: Grune and Stratton.

Knight, R. P. (1954). Evaluation of psychotherapeutic techniques. In R. P. Knight & C. R. Friedman (Eds.), *Psychoanalytic psychiatry and psychology.* New York: International Universities Press.

Kohut, H. (1959). Introspection, empathy, and psychoanalysis. *Journal of the American Psychoanalytic Association, 7,* 459–483.

Kohut, H. (1984). *How does analysis cure?* Chicago: University of Chicago Press.

Kris, A. (1982). *Free association: Method and process.* New Haven, CT: Yale University Press.

Kris, A. (1995). Support and psychic structural change. In M. J. Horowitz, O. F. Kernberg, & E. J. Weinshel (Eds.), *Psychic structure and psychic change: Essays in honor of Robert Wallerstein* (pp. 95–115). Madison, CT: International Universities Press.

Kris, E. (1956). The recovery of childhood memories in psychoanalysis. In *The selected papers of Ernst Kris*. New Haven, CT: Yale University Press, 1975.

Langs, R. (1973). *The technique of psychoanalytic psychotherapy* (Vol. 1). New York: Jason Aronson.

Langs, R. (1974). *The technique of psychoanalytic psychotherapy* (Vol. 2). New York: Jason Aronson.

Langs, R. (1977). *The therapeutic interaction: A synthesis*. New York: Jason Aronson.

Lasky, R. (1993). *The development and dynamics of the psychoanalytic process*. Northvale, NJ: Jason Aronson.

Levy, S. T. (1984). *Principles of interpretation*. New York: Jason Aronson.

Levy, S. T. (1985). Empathy and psychoanalytic technique. *Journal of the American Psychoanalytic Association, 33*, 353–378.

Levy, S. T., & Inderbitzen, C. B. (1990). The analytic surface and the theory of technique. *Journal of the American Psychoanalytic Association, 38*, 371–392.

Lichtenberg, J. D., & Galler, F. (1987). The fundamental rule: A study of current usage. *Journal of the American Psychoanalytic Association, 35*, 47–76.

Loewald, H. (1971). Some considerations on repetition and the repetition compulsion. *International Journal of Psychoanalysis, 52*, 59–66.

Loewenstein, R. (1951). The problem of interpretation. *Psychoanalytic Quarterly, 20*, 1–14.

Loewenstein, R. (1963). Some considerations on free association. *Journal of the American Psychoanalytic Association, 11*, 451–473.

Luborsky, L. (1976). Helping alliances in psychotherapy: The groundwork for a study of their relationship to outcome. In J. L. Claghorn (Ed.), *Successful psychotherapy* (pp. 92–116). New York: Brunner/Mazel, 1976.

Luborsky, L. (1984). *Principles of psychoanalytic psychotherapy: A manual for supportive-expressive treatment*. New York: Basic Books.

Luborsky, L. (1994). Therapeutic alliances as predictors of psychotherapy outcomes: Factors explaining the predictive success. In A. Horvath & L. Greenberg (Eds.), *The working alliance: Therapy, research and practice* (pp. 38–50). New York: Wiley.

Luborsky, L., & Auerbach, A. H. (1969). The symptom-context method: Quantitative studies of symptom formation in psychotherapy. *Journal of the American Psychoanalytic Association, 17*, 68–99.

Luborsky, L., & Crits-Christoph, P. (1990). *Understanding transference: The CCRT method*. New York: Basic Books.

Luborsky, L., Crits-Christoph, P., Mintz, J., & Auerbach, A. (1988). *Who will benefit from psychotherapy? Predicting therapeutic outcomes*. New York: Basic Books.

Malan, D. (1976). *Toward the validation of dynamic psychotherapy*. New York: Plenum.

Malan, D. (1979). *Individual psychotherapy and the science of psychodynamics*. London: Butterworths.

McDevitt, J. (1996). The continuity of conflict and compromise formation: A 25 year follow-up. *Journal of the American Psychoanalytic Association* (in press).

McLaughlin, J. T. (1987). The play of transference: Some reflections on enactment in the psychoanalytic situation. *Journal of the American Psychoanalytic Association, 35*, 557–582.

McLaughlin, J. T. (1991). Clinical and theoretical aspects of enactment. *Journal of the American Psychoanalytic Association, 39*, 595–614.

McWilliams, N. (1994). *Psychoanalytic diagnosis: Understanding personality structure in the clinical process*. New York: Guilford.

Menninger, K. (1958). *The theory of psychoanalytic technique*. New York: Basic Books.

Modell, A. (1976). "The holding environment" and the therapeutic action of psychoanalysis. *Journal of the American Psychoanalytic Association, 4*, 285–307.

Oremland, J. (1991). *Interpretation and interaction: Psychoanalysis or psychotherapy.* Hillsdale, NJ: Analytic Press.

Orr, D. (1954). Transference and countertransference. *Journal of the American Psychoanalytic Association, 2,* 621–670.

Paniagua, C. (1985). A methodological approach to surface material. *International Review of Psychoanalysis, 12,* 311–325.

Paniagua, C. (1991). Patient's surface, clinical surface and workable surface. *Journal of the American Psychoanalytic Association, 39,* 669–685.

Pine, F. (1984). The interpretive moment. *Bulletin of the Menninger Clinic, 48,* 54–71.

Poland, W. (1984). On the analyst's neutrality. *Journal of the American Psychoanalytic Association, 32,* 283–299.

Poland, W. (1992). From analytic surface to analytic space. *Journal of the American Psychoanalytic Association, 40,* 349–380.

Pray, M. (1994). Analyzing defenses: Two different methods. *Journal of Clinical Psychoanalysis, 3,* 87–126.

Rapaport, D. (1960). *The structure of psychoanalytic theory: A systematizing attempt.* New York: International Universities Press.

Richfield, J. (1954). An analysis of the concept of insight. *Psychoanalytic Quarterly, 23,* 390–408.

Rockland, L. (1989). *Supportive therapy: A psychoanalytic approach.* New York: Basic Books.

Rogers, C. (1957). The necessary and sufficient conditions of therapeutic personality change. *Journal of Consulting Psychology, 21,* 95–103.

Rogers, C. (1961). *On becoming a person.* Boston: Houghton Mifflin.

Rowe, C., & MacIsaac, D. (1993). *Empathic attunement: The technique of self-psychology.* New York: Jason Aronson.

Sandler, J. (1976). Countertransference and role-responsiveness. *International Review of Psychoanalysis, 3,* 43–47.

Schafer, R. (1959). Generative empathy in the treatment situation. *Psychoanalytic Quarterly, 28,* 342–373.

Schafer, R. (1983). *The analytic attitude.* New York: Basic Books.

Schwaber, E. A. (1995). The psychoanalyst's mind: From listening to interpretation—a clinical report. *International Journal of Psychoanalysis, 76,* 271–281.

Shapiro, T. (1984). On neutrality. *Journal of the American Psychoanalytic Association, 32,* 269–282.

Spencer, J. & Balter, L. (1990). Psychoanalytic observation. *Journal of the American Psychoanalytic Association, 38,* 393–421.

Sterba, R. (1934). The fate of the ego in psychoanalytic therapy. *International Journal of Psychoanalysis, 15,* 117–126.

Strachey, J. (1934). The therapeutic action of psychoanalysis. *International Journal of Psychoanalysis, 15,* 127–159.

Strupp, H., & Binder, J. (1984). *Psychotherapy in a new key: A guide to time limited dynamic psychotherapy.* New York: Basic Books.

Sullivan, H. S. (1956). *Clinical studies in psychiatry.* New York: Norton.

Tarachow, S. (1963). *An introduction to psychotherapy.* New York: International Universities Press.

Truax, C. B. (1963). Effective ingredients in psychotherapy: An approach to unraveling the patient-therapist interaction. *Journal of Counseling Psychology, 19,* 256–263.

Truax, C. B., & Carkhuff, R. (1967). *Toward effective counseling and psychotherapy: Training and practice.* Chicago: Aldine.

Wallerstein, R. S. (1965). The goals of psychoanalysis: A survey of analytic viewpoints. *Journal of the American Psychoanalytic Association, 13,* 748–770.

Wallerstein, R. S. (1986). *Forty-two lives in treatment: A study of psychoanalysis and psychotherapy*. New York: Guilford.

Weiss, J. (1971). The emergence of new themes: A contribution to the psychoanalytic theory of therapy. *International Journal of Psychoanalysis, 52*, 459–467.

Weiss, J. (1993). Empirical studies of the psychoanalytic process. *Journal of the American Psychoanalytic Association, 41* (Supplement), 7–29.

Weiss, J., & Sampson, H. (1986). *The psychoanalytic process: Theory, clinical observation and empirical research.* New York: Guilford.

Werman, D. S. (1984). *The practice of supportive psychotherapy*. New York: Brunner/Mazel.

Wolf, E. (1988). *Treating the self*. New York: Guilford.

Zetzel, E. (1956). Current concepts of transference. *International Journal of Psychoanalysis, 37*, 369–376.

9

Couples Therapy

Karen Kayser

For many decades, the profession of social work has recognized the importance of close relationships to individuals and to the stability of families. The long history of helping couples to repair their relationships began with the pioneering work of Mary Richmond in the early 1900s. The importance of working with couples was revealed in many of her papers, including "Concern of the Community with Marriage" (Richmond, 1928). In 1911, enough social work agencies had begun to specialize in the treatment of marriages and families that the Family Service Associations of America was formed. In 1943 it produced the first volume entirely devoted to marriage counseling, *Report of the FSAA Committee on Marriage Counseling*. This was a substantial handbook for training social workers in counseling with couples. Both psychoanalytic and sociological concepts were used in providing practice guidelines for clinicians (Broderick & Schrader, 1991). Hence, marriage counseling originated as a subspecialty within the broader field of social casework. Despite this notable history and foresight, social work has not taken a lead in generating knowledge and training in couples therapy. Furthermore, this is quite remarkable given that social work provides a substantial part of the professionals who actually see couples (Broderick & Schrader, 1991).

Working with a couple requires the practitioner to attend to several levels of analysis simultaneously. While assessing the personalities of two individuals, the couples therapist must also be analyzing the interaction of the dyad and attending to both content and process; that is, what is being communicated between the partners and how it is being communicated. On a broader level, the clinician is also taking into account the extradyadic factors that are influencing the couple.

In addition to these levels of systems, it can be confusing to the clinician when there are two very different perceptions of their relationship or the same event. Often the marital therapist is trying to sort out who has the more accurate view of things or what really happened. Both individuals can be quite convincing when telling their story about a particular event. Perhaps a better question for the clinician to be asking is, "Why are their perspectives so different?"

Work with couples is clearly an important skill to acquire because many settings of social work at one time or another require the clinician to see a dyad—for example, two spouses in a marriage, two roommates, a same-sex couple, a parent and child, or two siblings. The assessment strategies and interventions covered in this chapter are applicable to many types of dyads. Although most of them were designed for work with heterosexual couples, they can be utilized with same-sex couples. However, there will be at least two issues concerning these couples that the clinician needs to aware of: the impact of the same gender-role socialization on the relationship and cultural oppression in the forms of homophobia and heterosexism (Brown, 1995). The therapist must understand the strengths and deficits of each gender role as they affect relationship functioning. Also, a therapist who ignores the cultural oppression may overlook issues pertinent to the problems in the relationship.

CONDUCTING AN ASSESSMENT IN COUPLES THERAPY

The assessment phase of couples therapy needs to be well structured, otherwise some clients will talk endlessly about the ills of their relationship and provide a litany of complaints about the partner. Unless the clinician actively structures and directs the assessment interviews, he or she may obtain much irrelevant information or neglect to get necessary information. No clinical assessment is entirely devoid of a theoretical emphasis, but there are specific topics and questions that must be examined during the initial interview, regardless of theoretical approach to therapy.

The first issue deals with the decision to have individual or conjoint interviews in the first meetings. Typically the assessment phase consists of meeting with partners both individually and together. The individual interview deals with obtaining each partner's own perspective of the relationship and its problems. It is also an opportunity to assess if there are individual problems (for example, anger or depression) that might interfere with the couple's therapy (O'Leary & Arias, 1987). The couple is told that even after treatment begins, the therapist may want to meet with each partner individually, if therapy is not moving or there is perhaps important information that the therapist requires. At times one partner may request an individual session. In these cases, the clinician needs to ensure that both partners are given the same opportunity to meet individually.

There are two ways of handling the issue of confidentiality when seeing partners individually. First, the therapist can promise not to share any information that is disclosed in the individual session with the partner. The problem here is that the therapist may not always remember what was said in the individual interview or the conjoint interview and may inadvertently bring up a piece of information disclosed by only one partner. Or perhaps the therapist wants to discuss something with the couple but doing so would violate the confidentiality of one of the partners. Technically it could not be brought up in the conjoint interview. Hence, such a promise can limit the therapist in what can then be discussed jointly.

Another way of handling this issue is to tell the couple that anything discussed in the individual session may be brought up during the conjoint session, unless they specifically ask the therapist not to do so. In other words, the clinician is guaranteeing confidentiality of anything told that the person would not like the partner to know about (LoPiccolo & Daiss, 1987). In presenting this to the partners, the clinician can normalize the situation by stating that even in the best relationships, there are some thoughts, fantasies, aspects of one's background, and so forth that one is not entirely comfortable in sharing with one's partner (LoPiccolo & Daiss, 1987). If something that a client says in confidence is crucial for the partner to know for therapy to progress, the therapist can discuss this in a separate session.

Some clinicians deal with the issue of confidentiality by never seeing the partners alone. However, the clinician can lose out on some important information (for example, a partner's infidelity) that may be shared in an individual session. Even so, these clinicians would argue that the clinician is colluding with one partner if he or she is aware of information (such as an extramarital affair) and keeping it from the other partner. The trade-off in making this decision is whether to have knowledge about all aspects of the couple and risk the possibility of collusion or possibly be deprived of information that is important to the treatment process in order to avoid collusion. There is no definitive answer to this dilemma; it depends on the therapist's particular style and practice. However, the important points are to maintain confidentiality when it is promised and to be aware of the trade-off with each position.

The individual interview also allows for rapport building. Like individual therapy, this plays an important role throughout the assessment and treatment phases. Some clinicians find it easier to build rapport with each spouse when they have had an opportunity to meet with them individually. Like any other treatment modality, the core ingredients of establishing a relationship involve empathy, warmth, and genuineness. Besides these basic elements of a helping relationship, it is important to convey an expectation of hope to the client (O'Leary & Arias, 1987). Often couples call after experiencing an extensive history of distress or in the midst of an immediate crisis. Taking the difficult step to ask for help and the desire to change should be reinforced. Attention to the positive aspects of the relationship and communicating these to the partners may also promote a sense of hope.

Content of the Individual Interview

Presenting Problem

During the initial individual interview, the clinician obtains a detailed description of the presenting problem. Some questions to ask include: How long has the problem existed? What have you done to try to solve the problem? What seems to work? What does not work? What do you feel you bring to the relationship that is detrimental? This last question is aimed at assessing any individual problems that might interfere with couples therapy. It also helps the partners to look at the contribution of their own behavior instead of a continual focus and blame on the other person. The following may be helpful in introducing the subject: "All individuals have some styles that would interfere in some way with a partner, e.g., working long hours, having a short temper, being prone to depression. What style or problems do you feel you bring to this relationship or possibly to any relationship?" (O'Leary & Arias, 1987, p. 301). This discourse gently encourages disclosures and insights on personal problems, which later can be used productively in therapy.

The individual interview also includes questions about how conflicts are resolved and how the partners usually communicate with each other. The therapist may ask: How do you make decisions about handling money? Is one person designated to make the final decision on major purchases? How much can each of you spend without asking the other? Ineffective conflict resolution and destructive communication patterns are common sources of relationship distress for most couples seeking therapy.

History of the Relationship

During the individual interview, the clinician will want to obtain a sense of the development of the relationship. Questions include: "What attracted you to your partner? How long did you know each other before getting married (or living together)? Did you have any other serious relationships or marriages before this one? If so, what happened in these previous relationships? Who initiated the break-up and why? What kind of social life did the two of you have at the beginning of this relationship? Who initiated it? How were decisions arrived at in regard to what you would do?" (Hiebert & Gillespie, 1984).

Other questions about the history of the relationship focus on developmental transitions such as changes in employment and occupations, births of children, child rearing, children leaving home, caring for aging parents, and retirement. Besides these normative developmental changes, there may be additional stressors during the history of their relationship such as a chronic or life-threatening illness, death, financial crisis, legal problems, or work stressors. Again, the therapist is not only noting whether these events occurred in the relationship but how the couple handled them. For example, how did they go about deciding whether to have children? What were their different attitudes and ideas about it? What kinds of changes took place in the relationship after the child was born? How did each spouse react to the adjustments of having children?

Social History

During the initial interview the clinician can begin obtaining information about the client's family of origin. At this point in the assessment process, the purpose is to collect basic information about the structure and relationships of the family of origin. The clinician will likely continue to obtain more detailed information over the course of therapy. The framework of a genogram is helpful in organizing this information. Areas to cover include the members of the family—their ages, education level, and occupations—and the family's ethnicity. Besides these demographic characteristics, the therapist asks about the nature of the relationships between family members; that is, are they close, distant, conflictual, estranged, or cut off? Specific problems such as substance abuse, mental illness, divorce, or separations should also be noted. *Genograms in Family Assessment* (McGoldrick & Gerson, 1985) is an excellent source for information on constructing genograms. A genogram can also become a therapeutic tool by promoting insight, understanding, and acceptance between both partners.

Screening for Special Problems

The individual interview offers the opportunity to screen for specific individual problems that may affect the couple's relationship. The clinician should ask about alcohol and drug use and abuse, extramarital affairs, severe individual psychopathology (for example, depression, schizophrenia, a history of mental illness), and physical or psychological abuse. These problems are often not mentioned as a presenting problem and require probing. Interview questions pertaining to these areas can be directly asked. However, since clients may consider them to be socially undesirable, the clinician may want to introduce them by stating that the following problems are frequent among couples seeking couples therapy and then ask if they have experienced any of them.

Standardized instruments may also be helpful in screening for special problems. There are several brief depression inventories like the Zung (1965) Self-Rating Depression Scale and the Beck Depression Inventory (Beck, Ward, Mendelson, Mock, & Erbaugh, 1961). The Conflict Tactics Scale (Straus, 1979, 1990) is excellent for identifying abusive relationships. Screening for ongoing physical abuse is critical. In some states, it is illegal for therapists to treat a couple in conjoint therapy if physical abuse is occurring.

Physical Health

A general question about both clients' physical health should be asked. Chronic health problems or illnesses are likely to challenge the couple's relationship in many respects. For example, certain medical conditions, such as neurological diseases, diabetes, renal disease, and high blood pressure, and certain medications can have negative effects on sexual desire and functioning. The clinician needs to have sufficient knowledge of these conditions to determine when a physical or medical examination is warranted.

Sexual Functioning

The distress that a couple experiences in their relationship will likely affect their sexual functioning to some degree. However, when the couple is not coming for treatment of a specific sexual complaint, the clinician may feel somewhat uncomfortable broaching this subject with them. Moreover, if a sexual dysfunction is detected, the couples therapist may not feel competent in treating the problem. Most couples therapists are not trained in sex therapy, yet they must at least be able to assess the presence of a dysfunction and know when a referral to a trained sex therapist is warranted.

The topic of sexual functioning is usually raised after building rapport and asked relatively late in the interview. The therapist may acknowledge that sex is a sensitive and difficult area to discuss with the following comments, "It's a little uncomfortable to talk about something as personal as your sexual relationship. But physical affection and sexual expression is often a problem for many couples having difficulties such as yours. I'm wondering how you are doing in regard to your sex life" (LoPiccolo & Daiss, 1987). The therapist then begins with general questions such as, "Are you sexually active?" and "What impact, if any, have the problems in your relationship had on your sexual functioning?" If problems are mentioned, then the clinician can ask more specific questions regarding a potential dysfunction, such as, "Are you becoming physically aroused when you engage in sex? Is your arousal different during specific sexual activities? During intercourse, how long is the interval between insertion to ejaculation? Is the time interval satisfactory to you?"

The Couple Interview

After interviewing each partner individually, the therapist meets with the partners together. The clinician's attention now shifts to how the partners interact with each other. The challenge is not only to listen to the content—*what* is being told—but the process—*how* it is being told. The following are some aspects to observe:

1. *Affect.* What are the feelings between the partners? Is there a feeling of anger or hostility? Does one partner feel inhibited and perhaps intimidated by the other?
2. *Communication.* Does one partner dominate by interrupting and lecturing? Can each express feelings, positive and negative? Is there a sense of humor and joking between them?
3. *Closeness and intimacy.* Do partners self-disclose feelings? Do they spend time together and enjoy being with each other? Can they provide each other with emotional support? Are there distancing behaviors? Is there a pattern of distancer and pursuer?
4. *Mutuality.* Is there a sense of reciprocity and equity, that is, an equal attention to each other's needs? Does one partner's needs predominate? Are the partners empathic to each other?
5. *Decision making and problem solving.* How does the couple make decisions? Can they talk about decisions? Does one always accommodate to the other? Is there collaboration and compromising?

To facilitate observing their interaction, the therapist may ask the couple to discuss a particular question or issue. For example, they are instructed to spend the next ten minutes discussing the changes they would like to see in their relationship and decide on what the most significant change would be.

Special attention needs to be paid to the less motivated partner. Questions about the decision to seek couples therapy may help determine who might be more invested. Often as early as the initial telephone call or the individual session, the clinician may have an idea of who is more motivated. In these situations, the clinician may mention in the individual interview with the more invested partner that because of differences in motivation, some special attention to their partner (for example, more questioning or empathy) may be necessary to promote changes in therapy (O'Leary & Arias, 1987).

At the end of the couple interview, it is important for the therapist to give the couple some feedback on what he or she has learned and possible goals for therapy. The goals may be not only those that the partners mentioned but additional ones based on the therapist's observation. The partners are asked then if they are interested in pursuing these goals.

The couple will need to be assessed for their appropriateness for couples therapy. As long as both partners are interested in improving the relationship or making a decision about the course of the relationship, then couples therapy is appropriate. However, if one partner has decided to leave the relationship or maintain it in its current form, couples treatment is not appropriate (Margolin, 1987). In these cases, individual therapy may be a better choice, especially for the partner who wants to improve the marriage.

After giving feedback on their relationship, the therapist may want to explain to the couple the treatment approach that will be used. It is not necessary to go into a detailed explanation of the theory but should include items such as giving homework assignments, monitoring their progress with measurement tools, length of sessions, activity level of therapist, use of individual sessions, and so on.

Standardized Instruments

As part of the assessment, the therapist may routinely want to include a battery of standardized instruments. These help with an overall assessment of the couple and can be useful for ongoing monitoring of the couple's progress in therapy, especially pertinent in the current era of accountability and managed care demands. Obviously the clients should not be overwhelmed with numerous scales to fill out. Which instruments the therapist chooses will depend largely on how they will be used. For example, if the purpose of the scale is for ongoing evaluation of a couple's progress, it would be appropriate to use a very short scale of relationships satisfaction, such as the seven-item Abbreviated Dyadic Adjustment Scale (Sharpley & Rogers, 1984) and a scale that measures the particular goal of therapy for the couple, such as communication or intimacy. Table 9.1 contains a list of self-report instruments. The list provides commonly used measures that have established validity and reliability.

When using self-report instruments, the clinician needs to assess the client's truthfulness in answering the questions. Some of the scales contain a social desirability subscale. Clients who strongly agree to items in this subscale are usually trying to present a socially desirable and idealized picture of their relationship. There are scales that have been developed specifically to measure this factor. The Marriage Defensiveness Scale and Sex Defensiveness Scale (Jemail, 1977) were designed to determine the extent to which partners "fake good" when responding to questions

TABLE 9.1
Self-Report Measures for Assessment in Couples Therapy

Aspect of Relationship	*Measures for Assessment*
Commitment	Commitment Scale (Dean & Spanier, 1974)
	Self-rating of commitment (one item) (Broderick & O'Leary, 1986)
	Self-rating of commitment (three items) (Blumstein & Schwartz, 1983)
Communication	Primary Communication Inventory (Navran, 1967)
	Verbal Problem Checklist (Haynes, Chavez, & Samuel, 1984)
	Marital Communication Inventory (Bienvenu, 1970)
	Problem-solving and Affective Communication Scales of the Marital Satisfaction Inventory (Snyder, 1979)
	ENRICH Communication Scale (Olson, Fournier, & Druckman, 1985)
Marital satisfaction	Dyadic Adjustment Scale (Spanier, 1976)
	Marital Adjustment Text (Locke & Wallace, 1959)
	Marital Satisfaction Inventory (Snyder, 1979)
	Index of Marital Satisfaction (Hudson, 1982)
Physical aggression	Conflict Tactics Scale (Straus, 1979)
Intimacy	PAIR Inventory (Schaefer & Olson, 1981)
	Waring Intimacy Questionnaire (Waring & Reddon, 1983)
	Marital Intimacy Questionnaire (Van den Broucke, Vertommen, & Vendereycken, 1995)
Feelings toward partner	Positive Feelings Questionnaire (O'Leary, Fincham, & Turkewitz, 1983)
	Marital Disaffection Scale (Kayser, 1993)
	Disaffection Scale of the Marital Satisfaction Inventory (Snyder & Regts, 1982)
Sexual functioning	Brief Sexual Inventory (Heiman, Gladue, Roberts, & LoPiccolo, 1986)
	Derogatis Sexual Functioning Inventory (Derogatis, 1975)
	Sexual Interaction Inventory (LoPiccolo & Steger, 1974)

regarding their relationship. High scores on these scales should inform the therapist that relationship problems may be understated and that the clients may be defensive in therapy, especially resistant to the use of confrontation.

There are also several standardized observational coding systems that can be used to measure a couple's interactions. The typical format is to ask the couple to respond to some task or question in the clinical setting. Their interaction is audiotaped or videotaped and then coded by the therapist or trained raters. Examples of these coding systems are the Verbal Interaction Task (Guerney, 1977), Marital Interaction Coding Systems (Hops, Wills, Patterson, & Weiss, 1972), Couples Interaction Coding Systems (Gottman, 1979), Coding System for Interpersonal Conflict (Raush, Barry, Hertel, & Swain, 1974), Marital and Family Interaction Coding System (Olson & Ryder, 1977), and Dyadic Interaction Scoring Code (Filsinger, 1981).

THE OBJECT RELATIONS APPROACH TO COUPLES THERAPY

Object relations theory represents one of the psychoanalytic psychologies (the others are drive theory, ego psychology, and self-psychology). These four psychologies are all based on an individual model that emphasizes the unconscious, as well as the conscious, and the relationship between the client and therapist as the vehicle for change. But unlike classical psychoanalysis, which emphasizes drives and instincts as motivating forces in human development, object relations theory emphasizes the individual's need for relationship. In particular, it is based on the idea that adult relationships incorporate some of the characteristics of the infant-mother relationship. An individual's first relationship—between the mother or primary caregiver and child—is critical in affecting the patterns of later adult relationships. The mental images of the early relationships affect choices and behaviors in current close relationships.

Here we will consider how the psychotherapists Fairbairn (1952), Dicks (1967), and, more recently, Scharff and Scharff (1991) have applied object relations theory to a model of marital interaction and therapy. Before describing the techniques of therapy and assessment, let us look at the basic tenets of object relations theory as it relates to couples:

1. *Conscious and unconscious intrapsychic factors influence the choice of mates.* When two individuals enter a relationship, they are not just making a conscious choice based on common interests, sexual attraction, and love, but they are choosing a mate who unconsciously complements their personality traits. A British theorist, Dicks (1967), conducted studies of spouses in therapy and noted that spouses perceived their partner to complement them and fulfill some inadequacy they saw in themselves. Dicks (1967) explains that a spouse perceives the partner as fulfilling a lost aspect of a primary relationship with mother or caregiver.

2. *Unconscious intrapsychic conflicts are the cause of relationship dysfunction* (Baruth & Huber, 1984). The relationship begins to break down when the conscious and especially unconscious needs of both partners are not being met. The dysfunction arises from intrapsychic conflicts that both partners bring into the relationship. These conflicts are largely unconscious and stem from family-of-origin issues, mainly around attachment experiences with the primary caregiver. Each person tends to use defenses to deal with anxiety generated from these conflicts. The conflicts often

deal with wanting something from the partner yet simultaneously being afraid of getting it. (Baruth & Huber, 1984).

3. *Intrapsychic processes are manifested in relationships through the phenomenon of projective identification.* The concept of "projective identification" bridges the intrapsychic and the interpersonal (Scharff, 1995). Individuals have mental images of significant early relationships that influence their behavior in current relationships. The process of projective identification begins when a person experiences the partner as he or she unconsciously experienced a significant person, such as a parent or caregiver, early in life. The mental image of this person in early life is projected onto the current partner. In other words, the individual unconsciously perceives the partner to be similar to the person in the early relationship. The projection typically involves a characteristic that has been a source of conflict for the individual. In addition, the individual is excluding or overlooking the partner's personality traits that are not consistent with this image.

The process becomes interpersonal when the partner is pressured to become a participant in this projection (Ogden, 1990). The partner engages in the identification by also unconsciously viewing himself or herself as the person in the mental image and behaving according to this image. For example, a woman has a mental image of her father as being intimidating and domineering. She projects this image onto her husband by viewing him as controlling. To avoid feelings of intimidation and humiliation, which she experienced with her father, she attempts to make decisions unilaterally and is verbally aggressive toward her husband. To protect himself, her husband responds by his own aggressive behaviors that consequently confirm her projection of control and domination. The woman's conflictual relationship with a domineering father, her interpersonal behaviors with her husband, and the husband's response together make up projective identification.

4. *Change occurs through making the unconscious conscious.* This is possible by creating a therapeutic environment in which the couple's defenses can be displayed, identified, and analyzed and the underlying fears and needs can be experienced and processed together. Current psychic processes of which an individual is unaware and forgotten memories are made conscious. However, this is not a totally intellectual exercise. In order for change to occur, some kind of emotional experience must accompany the intellectual insight. Not only must the individual identify the unconscious desire or idea but must also feel the emotions that accompany it (Baruth & Huber, 1984).

Object Relations Assessment

An object relations perspective requires an assessment of the couple to take a particular focus; that is, more emphasis is placed on early relationship experiences and the development of the couple's relationship. The therapist will be more interested in the history of the individual and the relationship than therapists of other persuasions. Since the goal of therapy is making the unconscious conscious, the therapist will attempt to establish a therapeutic setting in which feelings, thoughts, and desires can be expressed openly. There is very little structure to the interview. The therapist does minimal directing of the clients' communication, allowing the story of the relationship to unfold spontaneously by the couple.

Individual Histories

To obtain a picture of the partners' experiences with early relationships, the therapist may inquire about the person's earliest memories, later childhood and adolescent memories, and recurrent dreams and fantasies. Earliest memories provide a window into the mental images or mental representations that individuals hold of themselves and family members. The emotions that these memories evoke provide additional understanding of the meaning of these relationships to the individual's perceptions of self and others (Baruth & Huber, 1984). Following the earliest memories, the therapist asks questions for more detailed information regarding any childhood difficulties (illnesses, accidents, losses) and their accompanying emotions. Information about family history, history of their parents' marriage, school, peer group relations, dating, and sexual experiences may shed light on the dynamics of the couple's relationship. Scharff (1995) discourages the use of a genogram for taking a family history because it tends to structure the session and not allow for the spontaneous expression of thoughts and emotions that accompanies the telling of the history of family relationships.

The clinician may also be interested in the clients' dreams because they can reveal unconscious information about the dynamics of the marital relationship and the individual's desires and anxieties. According to psychoanalytic theory, when defenses are lowered during sleep, repressed feelings can surface (Baruth & Huber, 1984). In addition to dreams, ongoing fantasies and daydreams about one's partner or the relationship can be enlightening. Although these are typically conscious materials, they may lead to insight about intrapsychic conflicts.

History of Couple's Relationship

According to object relations theory, the reasons for choosing a partner are critical to the understanding of the dynamics of the relationship and its dysfunction. The particular reasons that partners give for choosing each other enable the therapist to uncover the needs that the partner was expecting to be fulfilled but were not. Sager (1981) had originally developed the concept of the marriage contract to describe partners' beliefs about their obligation within the relationship, as well as the benefits they expect from the relationship. Conflicts arise when expectations are not met or partners have conflicting expectations. The therapist needs to help partners first become aware of these expectations and beliefs, which are often unconscious. Then the therapist will need to help partners to express their expectations and beliefs to each other. The following assessment questions can assist the couple in pinpointing these expectations:

- What qualities and characteristics of your partner were most important to you when you became a couple, and why?
- Are they still important to you?

- Are there other aspects of your partner that have become important to you since you became a couple?
- What parts of your life experience influenced your desiring certain qualities and characteristics in a partner? Have your life experiences since then changed your desires?
- How reasonable did your desires and expectations seem to you before the relationship? Do they seem as reasonable to you now?
- Do you want to change any expectations you have for your partner? Do you want to change his or her expectations of you? Of him- or herself? (Martin, 1976, quoted in Baruth & Huber, 1984).

The following case vignette illustrates some of the concepts of the object relations perspective to assessing a couple:

Sally, age twenty-eight, and Ted, age thirty-two, had been living together for four years when they came to therapy for help in making a decision about continuing the relationship. Both partners expressed dissatisfaction with the relationship but were afraid to leave one another. Sally complained that Ted worked too much and Ted complained about Sally's intrusiveness in his life and her overdependence on him.

In taking a history of the relationship, the therapist discovered that Sally was initially attracted to Ted because he appeared to be a very stable and trustworthy person—someone she could rely on emotionally. Ted seemed to fit the image of a person with self-confidence since he had a very successful law career and was motivated to achieve in his law practice. Her relationship with Ted was perceived by Sally as quite different from her early family relationships, which involved a mother who abused drugs and was emotionally unavailable to Sally and a father who was a workaholic and was physically unavailable.

Ted was attracted to Sally's warm and caring personality and her ability to socialize easily with other people. Coming from a family that held very high standards for achievement for him, he felt a level of acceptance from Sally for who he was as a person. He looked to her for the intimacy and warmth that was lacking from his family of origin.

Object Relations Therapy Interventions

A critical task when using the object relations model is creating a therapeutic environment in which partners can trust the therapist, display their defenses, explore inner thoughts and feelings, and process their anxieties. In object relations terms, the therapist develops a holding capacity, that is, "the capacity to bear the anxiety of the emergence of unconscious material and affect" (Scharff & Scharff, 1991, p. 108). Again, the general attitude of the therapist is to avoid doing too much so that themes and issues can emerge on their own. Once the couple's experience takes shape, then the therapist shares the experience and puts it into words (Scharff, 1995). In addition, the therapist takes a neutral position with no preference of one partner over the other as to values or lifestyle (Scharff & Scharff, 1991).

While carefully attending to the clients' feelings, the clinician experiences those feelings in relation to himself or herself and interprets this personal experience to the couple. This is where the therapist's use of self plays a key role in the therapy. Self-knowledge, including understanding of one's own family history and object relations, is necessary in order to use oneself as a diagnostic and therapeutic tool (Scharff & Scharff, 1991). In object relations terms, the therapist serves as an "observing ego" who helps the couple to better understand their conflicts and functioning of the relationship (Baruth & Huber, 1984). To make progress in therapy, the couple needs to identify with the observations and logic of the therapist.

The therapist's listening to the unconscious is a major intervention in helping the couple gain insight into their underlying anxieties, motivations, and conflicts. The therapist must be a keen observer of themes that emerge, silences that occur, and nonverbal language that is communicated. Listening to fantasy and dreams can provide a window to unconscious fears and desires. This task of the therapist is to uncover the hidden and symbolic meaning of the dream, often by analyzing the dream in the context of concerns and experiences of the partners during therapy (Baruth & Huber, 1984). This type of dream analysis differs from the model used in individual psychoanalysis and psychoanalytic psychotherapy, which emphasize the latent content of dreams.

Analyzing and interpreting transference and countertransference are also major tasks of the object relations therapist. Transference occurs not only with the relationship between client and therapist but between the partners as well. Transference occurs when partners experience each other or the therapist as he or she has unconsciously experienced a significant person in the past. It can take one of two forms: the person could project the image of the significant other onto the therapist (or partner), or a characteristic of one's self could be projected onto the other person (Ogden, 1990). Transference puts pressure on the therapist (or partner) to engage in such an identification by reacting in a way consistent with the projected mental image. However, the therapist may not identify with this projection and avoids becoming a participant in the person's projection (Ogden, 1990).

The therapist's task is to interpret these transferences by helping partners to see if they are responding to each other based on reality or a distorted view coming from early relationship experiences. The interpretation enables partners to gain insight into their individual intrapsychic conflicts and provides an understanding of how mental images of significant others influence their current functioning in relationships (Baruth & Huber, 1984). In addition, this insight gives a reasonable rationale for behavior in the relationship, which may alleviate some of the blaming that occurs between partners.

Countertransference for this discussion is defined as the reaction of the partner or therapist onto whom the transference was directed. The object relations therapist is continually mindful of his or her own countertransference reaction to the partners and guards against biases and distortions from past experiences that can interfere with the ability to view the couple objectively. Professional consultation or supervision may help the therapist become aware of such reactions. Some therapists may go to therapy to work on any issue that could be interfering with the effectiveness of treatment (Baruth & Huber, 1984).

Part of the interpretive work of object relations therapy deals with confronting basic anxieties that may seem too intolerable for partners to deal with consciously. According to Scharff & Scharff (1991), when these are labeled, faced, and adapted to, the couple can proceed to the next developmental phase of the couple's life cycle. The term *working through* refers to the continual dealing with the couple's defenses and conflicts. As the therapist peels away layers of repression, more resistance to change is likely to occur, and the therapist must continue to work away at this resistance and conflict until the partners have found more mature forms of gratification within the relationship (Scharff & Scharff, 1991).

As Ted and Sally began to feel comfortable in the therapeutic setting, they disclosed their fears and anxieties about the relationship and each other. Sally expressed a great deal of hurt and anger over Ted's apparent disinterest in the relationship as demonstrated by his spending long hours at work. She even accused him of being unfaithful to her. Sally had recurring dreams of being abandoned by Ted.

Ted expressed his disappointment in Sally's negative feelings toward him and her wanting to "change him." He could not understand her complaints since he was doing the best he could to provide financially for them. Her accusations of being unfaithful gave him an excuse to distance himself further from her.

Through exploration of their family backgrounds, the couple was able to gain insight into the underlying fears and anxieties that were preventing them from making a commitment to each other and obtaining the intimacy that they desired. It was discovered that Sally's relationship with her mother was characterized by a great deal of ambivalence since her mother's drug abuse made her mood and behavior quite unpredictable. At the same time, she felt her father had abandoned the family by spending too much time away from home. Through the therapist's exploration with her, she realized that she projected her own ambivalence onto her relationship with Ted. Even though she wanted to be close to Ted, she feared closeness because of the disappointments she had in her early relationships when she tried to be close to her parents. This helped to explain her behavior of pressuring Ted for more intimacy and then accusing him of being untrustworthy and unfaithful, which created distance in the relationship. In examining their current situation, there was no reason to mistrust him and to expect that he would disappoint her. This insight allowed Sally to not pressure Ted, which made Ted feel more comfortable to be open to intimacy with her.

In exploring Ted's family background, it became apparent that his needs for closeness and intimacy were not met by his successful and overachieving parents. He realized that he was totally dependent on Sally to satisfy all of his emotional needs without providing for hers in return. Part of the problem was that he did not know how to be emotionally supportive and empathic. His family of origin was not very feeling oriented. He realized over time that his overworking was a defense against dealing with her on a more emotional level. By helping him to process his feelings and realize that disclosure of feelings did not make him less of a person (or man), Ted was able to become more emotionally intimate with Sally. Gaining gratification from his relationship, he spent less time at work, which helped Sally in rebuilding her trust.

Toward the end of therapy, the couple announced to the therapist that they had decided to get married. By gaining insight into the dynamics underlying their interaction, they were able to change their behavior and move to the next developmental phase of their relationship: a long-term commitment.

In sum, the object relations approach relies heavily on nondirective listening for unconscious content to emerge, following the couple's emotional responses, analyzing dreams and fantasies, and exploring family history as it relates to the current couple relationship. There is a continual exploration of unconscious forces that could be explaining the recurring patterns of the couple's interaction. As the therapist builds trust with the couple, they are more likely to expose their anxieties that lie underneath their defenses. Through interpretations of resistance, defenses, and conflict, partners are able to face and overcome the power of these anxieties in their relationship. The insight enables them to see how much of their anxieties are based on relationships with significant others in the past and not related to the reality of the current relationship.

The object relations perspective is appropriate for couples who share the therapeutic goal of insight. Since the therapist is somewhat passive, allowing the couple to take an active role in therapy, it may not be appropriate for highly volatile couples who need more active intervention by the therapist.

Object relations couple therapy has undergone the fewest empirical investigations compared to the other two major approaches described in this chapter. One notable study, conducted by Snyder and Wills (1989), found roughly the same effectiveness when comparing insight-oriented treatment with behavioral treatment. In a four-year follow-up study (Snyder, Wills, & Grady-Fletcher, 1991), the researchers found the effects of the insight-oriented treatment were significantly more durable than the behavioral marital treatment. For example, 38 percent of the couples receiving behavioral marital therapy had divorced compared to only 3 percent of the insight-oriented couples. However, Jacobson (1991) has criticized the study for having a preponderance of behavioral techniques in the insight-oriented treatment manual, which resulted in the implementation of a therapy that was not purely insight oriented.

COGNITIVE COUPLES THERAPY

The application of cognitive therapy to work with couples is a fairly recent development and one that is gaining in popularity, especially among behavior therapists. Its popularity may be partly due to the limited effectiveness of a strictly behavioral approach, which pays little attention to couples' internal processes. Furthermore, there has been a growing amount of social psychological research in the area of cognitions, especially in attribution theory. This research supports the role of partners' cognitions in marital distress (Vanzetti, Notarius, & NeeSmith, 1992; Fincham, 1985; Fincham & Beach, 1988; Jacobson, McDonald, Follette, & Berley, 1985), marital dissolution (Fletcher, 1983; Harvey, Wells, & Alveraz, 1978), marital conflict (Howe, 1987), marital violence (Andrews & Brewin, 1990), and postdivorce adaptation (Newman, 1981). Hence, changing how partners think about each other and the relationship can affect their level of satisfaction and their behavior in the relationship.

Postulates of Cognitive Theory

1. *An individual's perception and interpretation of the partner's actions are more important in influencing feelings than the partner's action in itself* (Beck, 1988). How a person feels about the partner often results from how the person interprets the partner's behavior. For example, if a husband buys his wife some flowers, his wife may perceive the behavior as affectionate and thoughtful, with the resulting feelings of love and fondness for him. With a different couple, the same act may be interpreted by the wife as manipulative and controlling with the resulting feelings of anger and suspicion.

2. *By misinterpreting behavior of a partner, an individual often brings about what he or she most wants to avoid* (Beck, 1988). Ironically, a partner whose behavior is continually misperceived may end up actually behaving in the expected way. A wife may misread her husband's behavior as his being angry. In response to this misinterpretation, she withdraws and gives him the silent treatment, which ultimately provokes him to anger—the feeling that she had erroneously interpreted in the beginning.

3. *Partners develop their own interpersonal belief systems about their relationship that consists of attributions, expectancies, assumptions, and standards* (Baucom, Epstein, Sayers, & Sher, 1989; Baucom, Epstein, & Rankin, 1995). *Cognition* is a broad term that can be broken down into several different types of thoughts that influence relationship satisfaction and interactions in a relationship. *Attributions* are an individual's cognitive explanations of the partner's behavior. Based on these explanations, individuals make decisions about how to react toward the partner. They can also have a strong effect on one's feelings toward the partner. Whereas attributions are thoughts about the partner's past or current behavior, *expectancies* focus on the future. These thoughts are predictions about the future of the relationship. Individuals also enter a relationship with preexisting beliefs about the way relationships work, roles for males and females, and other aspects of intimate relations. These are known as *assumptions* (Baucom et al., 1995). They are often based on early experiences. Assumptions influence standards, another type of cognition. Relationship *standards* involve values about the way the relationship should appear and how each partner should behave in it.

4. *Distressed couples often use cognitive distortions similar to those of persons with a psychological disorder* (Beck, 1988). The difference is that the cognitive distortions that occur in distressed relationships are related to the other person, whereas with a psychological problem like depression, the distortion often relates to oneself. Some of the common distortions used in distressed relationships, which have been identified by Beck (1988), are listed in table 9.2.

5. *In distressed relationships individuals often attach negative labels to the same qualities of their partner that they had previously described positively* (Beck, 1988). During the beginning of a relationship, individuals perceive their partner in a way they want them to be and perhaps not the way they really are. If the relationship begins to deteriorate, the positive image of the partner changes to be negative. Negative labels are now attached to the same behaviors that were previously viewed as positive. The

TABLE 9.2
Common Cognitive Distortions in Distressed Relationships

Type of Distortion	*Definition*
Tunnel vision	Viewing the partner or the relationship in a very narrow way, ignoring or minimizing other significant aspects; usually the focus is on what fits their attitude or state of mind; prevents distressed couples from seeing or remembering the good aspects of their relationship.
Arbitrary inference	Making an unfavorable judgment about the partner's behavior when there is no evidence for it. Example: husband assumes that his wife's silence means that she is angry with him when she is really feeling exhausted from a long day's work.
Overgeneralization	When partners are thinking in absolute terms using words like *never* or *always*. "She always blames me for our problems" or "He never listens to me" are examples if in reality these occur infrequently.
Polarized thinking	All-or-nothing types of thoughts; for example, a wife may think that she either must totally give in to her husband's wants or leave the marriage; when partners are unable to see the gray areas and other choices or options to take; their mind frame is either-or, black or white, good or bad; there is no middle ground.
Personalization	When an individual interprets the partner's behavior in a personal way, as though his or her actions were directed at the other personally. Example: a husband interprets his wife's mowing the lawn as, "She's trying to make me feel guilty for spending the day fishing with my friends." He does not entertain other reasons that had nothing to do with him personally.
Mind reading	Belief that one knows what the other is thinking. Because they have known each other for a long time, some spouses insist that they always know what their partner is thinking. However, this may not always be true; acting on erroneous thinking may lead to further problems in the relationship.

partner who was viewed as "laid-back" is now labeled "uncaring," the "spontaneous" partner is called "hysterical," and the "strong, confident" partner is viewed as "rigid" and "controlling." In reality, what has changed is not the partner but the person's perception.

Cognitive Assessment of Couples

The primary goal of a cognitive approach is to learn what and how partners are currently thinking, that is, how they are processing information about the relationship and partner. Unlike the object relations approach that encourages very little structure to the assessment interview, the cognitive therapist asks specific questions to uncover partners' beliefs and assumptions and the cognitive processing that occurs between partners.

Like other theoretical approaches, the cognitive therapist will begin the assessment with a description of the problem areas. The cognitive therapist not only asks about the problems but asks the partners why they think the problem exists and how they think the partner or relationship should be.

The therapist obtains a history of the couple's relationship: how they met, what attracted them, how they made the decision to form the relationship, and significant events in the relationship. During the history taking, the therapist again is assessing each partner's perceptions about these events (Baucom et al., 1995). For example, partners may attend to only negative events, they may attribute negative events to the other person, or they may describe an aspect of their relationship that does not live up to one of their standards. Basically, the clinician is listening with attention to all the types of cognitions—attributions, expectancies, assumptions, standards—and begins to make hypotheses about the clients' belief systems.

During the assessment phase, the cognitive therapist also attends to the more positive aspects of the relationship and each partner. By the time they seek counseling, distressed couples often have a history of attending to the negative events and their partner's flaws. Therefore, extra effort needs to be made in helping them to refocus their attention on the positive. Not only will focusing on the positive instill hope in the therapy, but it is the beginning of modifying cognitive distortions such as tunnel vision or overgeneralization.

Assessment using a cognitive approach is ongoing in that the clinician is continuing throughout the therapy process to assess the cognitive processing of each partner. Also, preexisting relationship beliefs, namely, assumptions and standards, are not always evident in the beginning and require extensive work and time to uncover.

The cognitive therapist relies mainly on the interview with the couple to gain information for an assessment. However, self-report instruments relating to cognitions and beliefs can be administered prior to the couple's first interview in order to identify cognitive distortions or at other times during the assessment phase in order to substantiate certain cognitions that may be troublesome. Table 9.3 presents examples of several standardized instruments. These instruments can assist the clinician in pinpointing problematic areas and flaws in thinking that need further examination with the couple. Obviously it would be too cumbersome to use all the cognitive inventories with a couple, and the clinician will need to select the one(s) that would be most helpful in assessing the couple and planning the treatment.

Similar to the object relations approach, the cognitive therapist develops a therapeutic relationship that is empathic and supportive. This is critical to the task of eliciting the thoughts and beliefs that underlie the couple's feelings. Partners are less likely to make disclosures if the therapist does not communicate sensitivity, warmth, and emotional support.

In contrast to the object relations approach, cognitive therapy with couples is a

TABLE 9.3
Self-Report Measures of Relationship Cognitions

Type of Cognition	*Measures*
Attributions	Dyadic Attributional Inventory (Baucom, Sayers, & Duhe, 1987)
	Relationship Attribution Questionnaire (Baucom, Epstein, Daiuto, & Carels, 1991)
	Attribution Questionnaire (Fincham & O'Leary, 1983)
Expectancies	The Marital Agendas Protocol (Notarius & Vanzetti, 1983)
Standards	The Inventory of General Relationship Standards and Inventory of Specific Relationship Standards (Baucom, Epstein, Rankin, & Burnett, 1990)
	Relationship Belief Inventory (Eidelson & Epstein, 1982)

relatively structured approach with an outline of activities for each session. Within the structure of the therapy, the clinician actively promotes collaboration between the partners. For example, the clinician would ensure that one partner does not dominate the conversation or attack the other partner.

> This might be accomplished by modeling a more appropriate expression of anger, asking the relentless partner to focus on his or her own behaviors (self-focus), or simply by interrupting the pattern and initiating a discussion of ways to alter this destructive cycle.
>
> In all cases the therapist should be supportive but quite firm in his or her expectations and reasons for cutting off one spouse's speaking. After the first interruption, the therapist should share responsibility for monitoring the pattern with the husband or wife by interrupting in this manner: "Hold on, I'm going to interrupt you right there. OK, why am I stopping you?" (Schmaling, Fruzzetti, & Jacobson, 1989, p. 349)

Tom, age twenty-five, and Jane, age twenty-three, had been married for six years. They had two children, ages three and six years old. They were referred for couples therapy following Tom's inpatient treatment for substance abuse. Tom had been laid off from his factory job for the past year and was informed that the company would not rehire him. Jane was a secretary at a local community college. Since Tom no longer received unemployment, the family depended totally on Jane's salary. During the assessment, the couple focused on their inability to resolve conflicts, usually dealing with child-rearing issues and their financial situation. They described a pattern of interaction in which Jane would bring up problems with the expectations of a thorough discussion and Tom in response would stomp out of the room and yell at the children. Jane was especially concerned about Tom's maintaining his sobriety and the effects of his verbal abuse on the children.

The therapist started by teaching them conflict resolution skills. But after repeated incidences of noncompliance with homework assignments, the therapist decided to explore their beliefs about the conflicts they were experiencing in their relationships.

Tom disclosed that he came from a family in which his parents had a traditional marriage—his father was the breadwinner and his mother was a full-time homemaker. There were never any conflicts between his parents because his mother "knew her place" and always agreed with his father. Jane's family of origin consisted of a father who had a drinking problem and a mother who suffered from chronic depression. Jane was the oldest of five children and was often expected to take care of her younger siblings, as well as her parents. She felt that it was her duty to keep her father from drinking.

Cognitive Interventions with Couples

Cognitive interventions are usually implemented in connection with behavioral interventions. Hence, there is a shifting back and forth between a focus on behaviors and cognitions. In reality, it is difficult to deal with one aspect of the relationship without attending to another. As Baucom et al. (1995, p. 77) describe, "At times cognitive interventions are a primary focus of marital therapy with certain couples, and on other occasions cognitive interventions help to buttress behavioral and affective interventions."

The first step in a cognitive approach is to help the couple to identify dysfunctional thoughts when they occur. To introduce this task, the clinician needs to provide a brief explanation and rationale for a cognitive approach. Basically, the goal is to communicate the idea that feelings toward a partner are dependent on the person's thoughts about the partner's behavior and the meaning attached to it, rather than the behavior itself (Schmaling et al., 1989). When individuals are in distressed relationships, they are more likely to misinterpret their partners' behavior and their intent. Therefore, it is important to clarify and check out one's perceptions and thoughts for accuracy rather than merely assuming they are correct. Negative thoughts may not always be distorted, but partners need to determine what aspects of their relationship are distressing because of the particular views they have (Baucom et al., 1995).

A critical task of the therapist is to listen for dysfunctional thoughts and beliefs and to help the partners identify them. In teaching the couple this skill, it may be useful to ask them to begin with identifying an unpleasant emotional reaction, then relate the emotion to the particular situation in which it was experienced. The next step is determining the automatic thought that links the event to the emotional reaction. Self-monitoring forms such as the Automatic Thought Record (Beck, 1988) can be used to assist clients in the process of identifying dysfunctional thinking. The form consists of three columns; the individual partners record a description of a situation or event, the particular emotional states associated with it, and the automatic thought.

When the partners can identify their automatic thoughts, the therapist introduces them to common types of dysfunctional thinking, such as all-or-nothing thinking, tunnel vision, or arbitrary inference and others listed in table 9.2. They use this typology of thinking to identify the errors they are making in their automatic thoughts. When the errors in thinking are identified and labeled, the clinician can help the partners in challenging the reasonableness and validity of the thoughts.

This is the heart of the cognitive approach: that is, developing clients' skills at examining the validity or appropriateness of their cognitions in a systematic manner (Baucom et al., 1995). It must be emphasized that the therapist is not solely responsible for challenging the thoughts but teaches the clients to challenge their own thinking. This is accomplished through a series of questions such as those proposed by Beck (1988):

> What is the evidence in *favor* of my interpretation?
>
> What evidence is there *contrary* to my interpretation?
>
> Does it *logically follow* from my spouse's actions that my spouse has the motive that I assign to him or her?
>
> Is there an *alternative* explanation for his or her behavior? (p. 204)

The final step in modification of cognitive distortions involves replacing the distorted thought with a more rational response. Here the clients may need help thinking of alternative responses that are more reasonable than the distorted thinking. For example, instead of thinking, "My husband is always messy," the wife can think of the times that he has picked up after himself and change the thought to, "He's messy 50 percent of the time." Or she thinks of other explanations for his behavior, for example, "He lets things get messy only when he is working overtime." The goal is for the partners to become their own cognitive therapists and through an inner dialogue be able to arrive at more reasonable thoughts. This type of cognitive restructuring is most effective for modifying attributions and expectancies.

Another intervention for modifying unreasonable thinking is by setting up planned behavioral experiments (Baucom & Epstein, 1990). This intervention involves gathering evidence based on future interaction rather than evidence from the past, as was described in the verbal challenging technique. The couple is instructed to interact in a preconceived manner and then to monitor the results. For example, one wife complained that whenever she disclosed personal feelings to her husband, he would discount them and get angry. The therapist knew from interactions during their conjoint sessions that the husband had the ability to listen with empathy and could respond appropriately to her feelings. Therefore, the therapist had set up an experiment in which daily the wife would disclose a feeling and then would make a note of her husband's reaction. During the next session, the results were discussed and the wife discovered that there was very little evidence to support this perception of her husband. If the planned experiment "fails," the discussion can focus on the reason for its failure and perhaps the need for some behavioral intervention, such as communication training.

When modifying attributions, the therapist can use a strategy of reattribution developed by Baucom and Epstein (1990). Often the problem with attributions is that an individual is predominantly attributing problems in the relationship to the partner without consideration of any alternative explanations. The first step is to make this tendency more explicit so that the interpretations that are made can be assessed for their appropriateness. The clinician asks the couple to discuss the causes and explanations for a problem in their relationship and to think of alternative explanations for the situation. The therapist acknowledges that the original attribution is a possible explanation for the event but emphasizes that it is important to determine whether this is the most accurate or reasonable explanation. The couple is asked how each of the following factors has contributed to the problem: environmental or outside circumstances, each person's behavior, each person's interpretation of the other partner's behavior, and the partner's emotional reactions. This process broadens both partners' views of causality in their relationship. As the therapist guides the couple in testing the relative validity of the various alternatives, the couple may come up with another explanation based on more logical grounds (Baucom & Epstein, 1990).

So far the interventions presented target unrealistic or distorted attributions and expectancies. These are thoughts that occur during an individual's daily processing of information about the partner or the relationship. Standards and assumptions that are long-standing beliefs based on early life experiences are other types of cognitions to modify, and these tend to be more difficult to change. According to Epstein and Baucom (1990), new experiences in a relationship have the potential to change these beliefs, but additional interventions may be needed in modifying these belief systems. These types of beliefs may be identified through the Relationship Belief Inventory. Another way to identify them is through an awareness of a particular theme that emerges when discussing the individual's distorted thoughts. For example, a client may convey numerous distorted thoughts dealing with the fear of abandonment, which is a theme related to an assumption based on earlier experiences of losses of significant persons in his or her life. The process of changing these belief systems involves a discussion about the advantages and disadvantages of the assumptions and standards. In particular, there is an examination of how these cognitions contribute to the couple's relationship distress and conflicts. By carefully examining the advantages and disadvantages, which may include writing them down, partners can recognize the drawbacks and the therapist can help them to "rewrite" the belief in less extreme terms (Baucom et al., 1995). Sometimes partners can hold different assumptions that conflict with each other, or they may have the same assumptions that can lead to distress. In either case, the clinician will need to examine both partners' sets of beliefs.

After explaining a cognitive approach to therapy, the therapist assisted Tom and Jane in identifying their feelings and thoughts during incidents of conflict. Each spouse filled out an Automatic Thought Record when a conflict arose. Tom listed the emotional reactions of anger and shame. When Jane complained about their financial situation, it was interpreted by Tom as a personal attack ("She's blaming me for our money problems"). He identified this error in thinking as personalization. His automatic thoughts also included the belief that his self-worth was based on his ability to provide for his family and act as the head of the household. During conflicts Jane's emotional responses were frustration, anger, and hurt. A frequent thought was, "His leaving during a conflict means he doesn't love me" (mind reading). She also thought that she was responsible for Tom's sobriety, which she identified as a belief based on her experience with her father.

Each thought was examined regarding the evidence for and against it, and more realistic thoughts were cited. Tom learned that discussing conflicts was an opportunity to work things out so that each could get what they wanted. He was jumping to conclusions by thinking that Jane was blaming him for financial problems. Also, he began to realize that his self-worth was not dependent on his role as a breadwinner and that there were many other ways in which he could be supporting his family. Jane learned that she could not automatically assume that Tom did not love her but that his leaving the situation was a learned response to deal with his anxiety about conflict. This alternative explanation allowed Jane to be more patient and understanding, which made Tom feel more comfortable about the situation. Through some planned experiments around Tom's taking responsibility for his sobriety, Jane learned to modify her assumption that she was totally responsible for his sobriety. After these cognitive interventions, the couple was more amenable to the therapist's teaching of conflict resolution skills.

Helping partners to identify and change faulty thinking is not an easy task. A key to implementing cognitive interventions effectively is establishing a therapeutic relationship that communicates respect for and understanding of each partner's belief systems, while teaching them alternative ways of thinking about the partner and the relationship that will strengthen the relationship. Also, it is helpful to reassure the partners that while their cognitive changes may feel uncomfortable on an emotional level, their feelings will also change with practice and repeated discussions (Baucom et al., 1995).

There are at least eight published outcome studies examining the effectiveness of cognitive couples therapy. Five studies have looked at the effectiveness of cognitive restructuring as an addition to traditional behavioral marital therapy (Margolin & Weiss, 1978; Baucom & Lester, 1986; Baucom, Sayers, & Sher, 1990; Behrens, Sanders, & Halford, 1990; Halford, Sanders, & Behrens, 1993). Three examined the effectiveness of cognitive restructuring alone compared to behavioral marital therapy (Emmelkamp, VanLinden van den Heuval, Ruphan, Sanderman, Scholing, & Stroink, 1988). Overall the studies show that cognitive restructuring produces some significant cognitive changes for couples, and it is effective in increasing marital adjustment (Baucom et al., 1995). The combination of cognitive restructuring and behavioral therapy is equally effective in improving marital adjustment compared to behavioral therapy alone. Furthermore, these studies indicate that cognitive therapy is useful in altering expectancies, standards, and assumptions.

BEHAVIORAL COUPLES THERAPY

The application of behavior therapy to couples began in the 1960s when Richard Stuart, a social worker and researcher, published the first study applying behavior therapy to marital problems. Since then the interest in behavioral marital therapy has escalated, and it is the approach with the most empirical research. Behavioral couples therapy relies extensively on the principles of operant conditioning, social exchange, and social learning. More recently the idea of "acceptance" has been incorporated into the behavioral approach resulting in an "integrative behavioral couple therapy (IBCT)" (Christensen, Jacobson, & Babcock, 1995). The integrative behavioral approach emphasizes both behavioral change and acceptance of a partner's behavior that is not amenable to change.

Postulates of Behavior Couples Therapy

1. *Partners mutually influence each other's behaviors through reinforcement, punishment, and extinction* (Stuart, 1980; Holtzworth-Munroe & Jacobson, 1991). This principle of operant conditioning suggests that each partner's behaviors serve as both antecedents to and consequences of the other person's behavior. Therefore, the key to shaping, strengthening, or weakening behavior involves changing the environmental contingencies—in couples therapy, the other partner's behavior (Holtzworth-Munroe & Jacobson, 1991).

2. *Relationship satisfaction often is determined by the reward-cost ratio of the relationship for each partner* (Holtzworth-Munroe & Jacobson, 1991). According to social exchange theory, individuals are motivated to seek rewards and reduce costs. They will attempt to maintain relationships in which the rewards outweigh the costs. Furthermore, according to the norm of reciprocity, the rate of reinforcements received from the partner will determine the rate of rewards given in return to the partner.

3. *In distressed relationships, the negative exchanges outweigh positive exchanges.* Just as the norm of reciprocity applies to positive behaviors, it can also apply to negative behaviors. Especially among distressed relationships, negative behaviors such as blaming, putdowns, and accusations tend to be reciprocal. Nondistressed couples may also experience some negative exchanges, but the positive exchanges occur more frequently. Also, there is a tendency for nondistressed partners not to reciprocate a partner's punishing behavior.

4. *Maladaptive behavior, having been learned, can be extinguished (that is, unlearned) and replaced by new learned behavior patterns.* Again, it is within the context of the couple's relationship that partners learn new behaviors and unlearn the old.

5. *The behavioral approach concentrates on here-and-now problems rather than uncovering or attempting to reconstruct the past.* Since behavior therapists cannot modify historical factors but can influence factors in the current environment of each partner, the focus is on the present and what is happening in the current situation. This focus is pragmatic and not meant to devalue historical events in shaping behavior (Holtzworth-Munroe & Jacobson, 1991). An individual's learning history is important in determining if the person has a "skill" or "performance" deficit because the behavior was never learned.

The Behavioral Assessment

A central task of the behavioral assessment of couples is the functional analysis of the relationship. This requires assessing the interactional sequences of the couple's behaviors in order to pinpoint the ways in which partners act toward each other and their level of relationship satisfaction (Holtzworth-Munroe & Jacobson, 1991). According to Christensen et al. (1995), "Functional analysis examines the variables that control a given behavior by manipulating conditions that are antecedent to that behavior and consequent to that behavior. By observing how the behavior fluctuates in response to those changes, one determines the conditions that control the behavior" (p. 35). The clinician is continuously assessing how partners reward or punish each other's behaviors. Also a number of performance areas or skills are evaluated, such as the ability to discuss problems, skill in identifying reinforcers in their relationship, and their competencies in areas of communication, sex, child rearing, and financial management.

There are several steps in conducting a behavioral assessment. First, the therapist and the couple identify the problem behaviors and the conditions that are maintaining them. In order to delineate the problem areas and controlling influences, the practitioner trains the couple in self-monitoring techniques in which the partners keep records of the occurrence of behaviors and antecedents and consequences. These records enable the therapist and clients to determine what behaviors are infrequent and need to increase and what behaviors are too frequent and need to decrease.

After identifying behavioral excesses or deficits, the therapist distinguishes performance deficits from skill deficits. When an individual is not demonstrating a specific behavior, is the problem that the person does not know how or prefers not to demonstrate it with the partner? For example, a husband does not express his feelings to his wife but expresses them openly to his neighbor or friends at his workplace. This is an important distinction to make in order to plan the interventions.

Behavior assessments emphasize definition and specification of problems and behaviors. However, Christensen et al. (1995) caution clinicians in becoming myopic in these specifications and recommend that they look for linkages among the problems and themes that run through the array of complaints. For example, a wife may ask for more freedom to pursue her own interests, more support, and consideration when making decisions. The theme may be related to her feeling that the relationship is not egalitarian but one in which her husband controls her and is insensitive to her needs.

Several self-report instruments help to identify behavioral changes. The Areas of Change Questionnaire (Margolin, Talovic, and Weinstein, 1983) contains a list of typical changes that couples desire in their relationship. Each respondent reports the change wanted of the partner and changes the partner wants of the other. The Marital Comparison Level Index (Sabatelli, 1984) identifies specific problem areas, and the respondent rates each area in how it compares with his or her expectations. More recently, Douglass and Douglass (1995) developed the Marital Problems Questionnaire, which provides behavioral information about overall marital adjustment, specific conflict areas, and divorce risk.

Patricia, age twenty-eight and Ellen, age thirty-three, entered couples therapy on the verge of dissolving their four-year relationship. The relationship began to break down when they moved from the West Coast to the East in order for Ellen to make a career advancement. Pat had to quit her job and had not found another one during the six months they had been living in their new place. Both Pat and Ellen had been active in a group of lesbian couples where they previously lived but had not found a similar group of mutual friends to replace the old group.

While Ellen had developed new friendships at work, Pat complained that she was quite lonely and depressed. She had noticed that Ellen did not do a lot of the intimate and caring things that she previously did prior to her new job. She also felt taken advantage of by Ellen's expectations that she do all the housework and meal preparation since she was not "working."

Ellen also felt that the relationship had deteriorated and it had become quite mundane and boring. She complained that Pat was constantly making sarcastic comments regarding her new friends and her job, and it was difficult being around her when she acted depressed.

Behavioral Interventions with Couples

Behavioral interventions with couples typically fall into two areas: increasing positive exchanges and relationship skills training. Recently, Christensen, Jacobson, and Babcock (1995) developed a group of interventions that assist an individual in accepting his or her partner's behavior.

Increasing Positive Exchanges

When couples enter therapy, there typically has been a long history of negative and hurtful exchanges between the partners. The relationship may have deteriorated to the point where partners are skeptical that change is even possible. Hence, it is critical for partners to see some immediate positive changes. Behavior exchange interventions are meant to provide some rewards to each partner and instill hope that change can occur in the relationship. These interventions are techniques for building a sense of commitment in the relationship (Stuart, 1980) and to put the couple in a better position for dealing with other areas of conflict that they may have to face during later phases of therapy (Christensen et al., 1995).

There are a variety of behavioral exchange strategies, but they all have two common elements: identifying the positive behaviors that are rewarding to each partner and increasing the frequency of those behaviors by using positive reinforcement. Stuart's (1980) "Caring Days" is one example of a behavioral exchange intervention. Each partner is asked to compile a list of small specific behaviors that convey a feeling of being cared for by the other. After discussing and agreeing on the caring behaviors, the couple is asked to carry out the behaviors. During the week, each partner records on the list of caring behaviors the date on which he or she received the caring act. In addition to change on a behavioral level, keeping track of positive behaviors can produce perceptual changes as partners acknowledge positive aspects of the partner that were previously overlooked or discounted.

When introducing this intervention, the clinician should emphasize two principles. First, the "as-if" principle should be encouraged: the partners act "as if" they cared for the other. Sometimes partners want to wait until they have the feelings first before making changes in their behaviors, but feelings of love and caring often do not grow unless the actions are present and loving actions from one partner will stimulate loving actions from the other (Stuart, 1980). The second principle is the "change-first" principle: each person is expected to change before the partner rather than waiting for the partner to change first (Stuart, 1980). Other similar behavior exchange interventions are described by Jacobson and Margolin (1979) and Weiss and Birchler (1978).

Communication and Conflict Resolution Training

Depending on the interpersonal skills of the partners, behavioral therapists can spend a good deal of time systematically teaching communication and problem-solving skills. The clinician follows a typical skills training approach in which the skill is described and modeled by the therapist, practiced by the couple, and then the therapist gives feedback. As the couple begins to learn and demonstrate the skill, the therapist employs fading; that is, he or she becomes less active and tapers off specific instructions.

An example of this training approach can be shown when teaching couples empathic responding. A detailed description of empathy is given to the couple, and the therapist provides specific examples. Next the therapist sets up a practice exercise in which one partner is the speaker and the other is the listener. The speaker is given five minutes to share feelings about a particular issue or event. After the five minutes, the listener is given a chance to respond with an empathic statement. The speaker provides feedback to the listener regarding the accuracy of the empathic response. After the therapist gives feedback on their performance, the partners change roles, allowing the speaker to be the listener. The couple continues to practice this exercise at home and discusses the results with the therapist at the subsequent therapy session. The therapist may also ask the couple to audiotape their practice sessions at home so he or she can more carefully observe their learning of empathic responding. Eventually practice sessions are no longer assigned to the couple, but periodically the therapist checks with the couple to determine if the behavior change has been maintained.

Promoting Emotional Acceptance between Partners

Integrative behavioral couples therapy (IBCT) uses several strategies to facilitate acceptance when behavior change does not occur. (A more detailed description can be found in Christensen, Jacobson, & Babcock, 1995.)

The first strategy encourages acceptance through empathic joining around the problem (Christensen, Jacobson, & Babcock, 1995). The therapist "reformulates the problem and the partner's behavior in terms of common differences between people, and understandable emotional reactions to those differences" (p. 54). Part of the reformulation involves pointing out the pain that each partner experiences and the efforts that each makes to accommodate the other. For example, when a wife discovered that her husband's lack of self-disclosure was partly the result of his ethnic background and upbringing, she began to understand that his lack of disclosure did not mean that he no longer loved her, a feeling that she had experienced for a long time.

A second strategy is emotional acceptance through detachment from the problem (Christensen, Jacobson, & Babcock, 1995). This is an intellectual analysis of the problem in which the couple discusses the sequence of conflict between them. In particular, they talk about what elicits their reactions and how specific incidents are interconnected. During the discussion, the emphasis is on a detached description of the problematic sequence without the placement of blame or responsibility for change on one person.

A third strategy is acceptance through greater tolerance of the partner's aversive actions (Christensen, Jacobson, & Babcock, 1995). The key to increasing one's tolerance is to give up the struggle to change the partner and accept the behavior. One way to accomplish this is through pointing out the positive features of the partner's negative behavior. This is similar to positive connotation, except that the therapist continues to acknowledge the negative features while pointing out the positive features.

A final strategy for promoting acceptance involves increasing the ability to take care of oneself when confronted with the partner's aversive actions (Christensen, Jacobson, & Babcock, 1995). This may involve a discussion of alternative means to satisfy needs other than with the partner. Christensen, Jacobson, & Babcock (1995) caution that this discussion should not relieve the partner of responsibility for meeting the person's needs. It focuses on what the other person can do only in situations in which the partner is unable to satisfy the needs. They offer specific suggestions for self-care when the negative behaviors are occurring, such as leaving the situation, seeking solace from others, assertively altering the situation, and defining the situation differently.

As these interventions are implemented, the language of acceptance is encouraged by suggesting that the partners describe their own experience rather than talking about the other partner's thoughts, feelings, or actions (Christensen, Jacobson, & Babcock, 1995). To facilitate this language, the therapist prompts the partners with statements such as, "John, you are describing how you think Michelle felt during that incident. Would you talk about what you were feeling at the time?"

Certainly these strategies for promoting acceptance are somewhat provocative and need to be implemented carefully, especially because they have not been empirically evaluated yet. There needs to be a careful assessment of the behavior that is being accepted. For example, physical violence in a relationship should not be tolerated. One of the ironies to the interventions of emotional acceptance is that by giving up on change strategies, behavior change often occurs (Christensen, Jacobson, & Babcock, 1995).

Patricia and Ellen's therapist observed that there had been a decrease of rewarding behaviors and an increase of punishing behaviors in their relationship. She recognized that immediate changes needed to occur in order for this relationship to survive. Therefore, she started by implementing a behavior exchange intervention in which the couple began to exchange small caring acts on a daily basis.

When the partners were beginning to receive more rewards from the relationship, the therapist focused on their ability to communicate constructively and helped them to learn more appropriate ways to express their anger and desires to each other.

As their commitment to the relationship was reestablished and their level of satisfaction increased, the therapist also employed some strategies of acceptance. In particular, she helped Patricia to accept Ellen's socializing with her colleagues by taking care of her own needs. Patricia did this by joining an AIDS activist group and developing some friendships with members of the group.

Behavioral couples therapy has received more empirical investigation than the other two approaches described in this chapter. There have been dozens of outcome studies using control or comparison groups. According to Holtzworth-Munroe and Jacobson (1991, p. 126), "more high-quality research has been done on BMT than all other approaches to marital therapy combined. . . . BMT is the only approach to marital therapy whose efficacy has been clearly established." Despite its extensive empirical background and the optimism of these comments, the approach still does not significantly improve marital satisfaction for one-third of the couples who receive it, and when it works, the gains are at times only temporary. Two-thirds of couples receiving behavioral marital therapy improve substantially, and half recover to the point where they are in the happily married range on measures of marital satisfaction (Jacobson, 1984; Jacobson & Follette, 1985; Jacobson, 1989). Based on the empirical studies of BMT, either behavior exchange or communication and problem-solving training is sufficient by itself to produce the same short-term outcomes as treatment that combines both components (Holtzworth-Munroe & Jacobson, 1991). However, for outcomes that are maintained over time, it appears that the combination of interventions produces better results than either component alone. To my knowledge, there are no published outcome studies evaluating the effectiveness of integrative behavioral couple therapy.

FUTURE DIRECTIONS

In the research on the effectiveness of couples therapy, no single theoretical approach stands out as superior to the others. With only two exceptions (Johnson & Greenberg, 1985; Snyder, Wills, & Grady-Fletcher, 1991), all the approaches are found to be equally effective in helping distressed couples (Baucom & Epstein, 1990). In reality, most couples therapists recognize the limitation of working within only one theoretical framework and incorporate interventions from all three approaches into their work with couples. However, no model has yet been developed that clearly integrates these approaches in a way that permits the clinician to know when and with whom a particular intervention should be used. Further research will need to specify the approaches that may be the most effective given the problems identified and the couple presenting them.

While social workers are encouraged to look to the empirical research for informing their practice, they should be reminded of some of the limitations of this research. For example, all the research studies on couples therapy use samples composed primarily of white heterosexual couples. Obviously, this limits the generalization of results to practice with same-sex couples or couples from different ethnic and racial backgrounds.

Finally, in an era of managed care, clinicians need to be adept at applying brief treatment models to couples therapy. To a certain extent, couples therapy has always required clinicians to intervene quickly since many couples initiate counseling at a time of crisis in the relationship. But with limited financial resources, the practitioner needs to be especially skillful at implementing effective and brief interventions in a systematic way. I encourage readers to become familiar with the application of the problem-focused and solution-focused brief therapy models to couples (cf. Shoham, Rohrbaugh, & Patterson, 1995).

REFERENCES

Andrews, B., & Brewin, C. R. (1990). Attributions of blame for marital violence: A study of antecedents and consequences. *Journal of Marriage and the Family, 52,* 757–767.

Baruth, L. G., & Huber, C. H. (1984). *An introduction to marital theory and therapy.* Prospect Heights, IL: Waveland Press.

Baucom, D. H., & Epstein, N. (1990). *Cognitive-behavioral marital therapy.* New York: Brunner/Mazel.

Baucom, D. H., Epstein, N., Daiuto, A., & Carels, R. A. (1991, November). *The Relationship Attribution Questionnaire: A new instrument for assessing relationship attributions and their impact.* Paper presented at the 25th Annual Convention of the Association for Advancement of Behavior Therapy, New York.

Baucom, D. H., Epstein, N., & Rankin, L. A. (1995). Cognitive aspects of cognitive-behavioral marital therapy. In N. S. Jacobson & A. S. Gurman (Eds.), *Clinical handbook of couple therapy* (pp. 65–90). New York: Guilford.

Baucom, D. H., Epstein, N., Rankin, L. A., & Burnett, C. K. (1990, November). *New measures for assessing couples' standards.* Paper presented at the 24th Annual Convention of the Association for Advancement of Behavior Therapy, San Francisco.

Baucom, D. H., Epstein, N., Sayers, S., & Sher, T. G. (1989). The role of cognitions in marital relationships: Definitional, methodological, and conceptual issues. *Journal of Consulting and Clinical Psychology, 57,* 31–38.

Baucom, D. H., & Lester, G. W. (1986). The usefulness of cognitive restructuring as an adjunct to behavioral marital therapy. *Behavior Therapy, 17,* 385–403.

Baucom, D. H., Sayers, S. L., & Duhe, A. D. (1987, November). *Attributional style and attributional pattern among married couples.* Paper presented at the 21st Annual Convention of the Association for Advancement of Behavior Therapy, Boston.

Baucom, D. H., Sayers, S. L., & Sher, T. G. (1990). Supplementing behavioral marital therapy with cognitive restructuring and emotional expressiveness training: An outcome investigation. *Journal of Consulting and Clinical Psychology, 58,* 636–645.

Beck, A. T. (1988). *Love is never enough.* New York: Harper & Row.

Beck, A. T., Ward, C. H., Mendelson, M., Mock, J., & Erbaugh, J. (1961). An inventory for measuring depression. *Archives of General Psychiatry, 4,* 561–571.

Behrens, B. C., Sanders, M. R., & Halford, W. K. (1990). Behavioral marital therapy: An evaluation of treatment effects across high and low risk settings. *Behavior Therapy, 21,* 423–434.

Bienvenu, M. J. (1970). Measurement of marital communication. *Family Coordinator, 19,* 26–31.

Blumstein, P., & Schwartz, P. (1983). *American couples.* New York: Morrow.

Broderick, J. E., & O'Leary, K. D. (1986). Contributions of affect, attitude, and behavior to marital satisfaction. *Journal of Consulting and Clinical Psychology, 54,* 514–517.

Broderick, C. B., & Schrader, S. S. (1991). The history of professional marriage and family therapy. In A. S. Gurman & D. P. Kniskern (Eds.), *Handbook of family therapy* (Vol. 2, pp. 3–40). New York: Brunner/Mazel.

Brown, L. S. (1995). Therapy with same-sex couples: An introduction. In N. S. Jacobson &

A. S. Gurman (Eds.), *Clinical handbook of couple therapy* (pp. 274–291). New York: Guilford.

Christensen, A., Jacobson, N. S., & Babcock, J. C. (1995). Integrative behavioral couple therapy. In N. S. Jacobson & A. S. Gurman (Eds.), *Clinical handbook of couple therapy* (pp. 31–64). New York: Guilford.

Dean, P. G., & Spanier, G. B. (1974). Commitment: An overlooked variable in marital adjustment? *Sociological Focus, 7,* 113–118.

Derogatis, L. R. (1975). Derogatis Sexual Functioning Inventory. *Clinical Psychometrics Research.* Baltimore.

Dicks, H. V. (1967). *Marital tensions: Clinical studies towards a psychoanalytic theory of interaction.* London: Routledge and Kegan Paul.

Douglass, F. M., & Douglass, R. (1995). The Marital Problems Questionnaire (MPQ): A short screening instrument for marital therapy. *Family Relations, 44,* 238–244.

Eidelson, R. J., & Epstein, N. (1982). Cognition and relationship maladjustment: Development of a measure of dysfunctional relationship beliefs. *Journal of Consulting and Clinical Psychology, 50,* 715–720.

Emmelkamp, P. M. G., Van Linden van den Heuvel, C., Ruphan, M., Sanderman, R., Scholing, A., & Stroink, F. (1988). Cognitive and behavioral interventions: A comparative evaluation with clinically distressed couples. *Journal of Family Psychology, 4,* 365–377.

Fairbairn, W. R. D. (1952). *Psychoanalytic studies of the personality.* London: Routledge and Kegan Paul. Also published as *An object relations theory of the personality.* New York: Basic Books.

Filsinger, E. E. (1981). The dyadic interaction scoring code. In E. E. Filsinger & R. A. Lewis (Eds.), *Assessing marriage: New behavioral approaches.* Beverly Hills, CA: Sage Publications.

Fincham, F. D. (1985). Attribution processes in distressed and nondistressed couples: 2. Responsibility for marital problems. *Journal of Abnormal Psychology, 94,* 183–190.

Fincham, F. D., & Beach, S. R. (1988). Attribution processes in distressed and nondistressed couples: 5. Real versus hypothetical events. *Cognitive Therapy and Research, 12,* 505–514.

Fincham, F. D., & O'Leary, K. D. (1983). Causal inferences for spouse behavior in maritally distressed and nondistressed couples. *Journal of Social and Clinical Psychology, 1,* 42–57.

Fletcher, G. (1983). The analysis of verbal explanation for marital separation: Implications for attribution theory. *Journal of Applied Social Psychology, 13,* 245–258.

Gottman, J. M. (1979). *Marital interaction: Experimental investigations.* New York: Academic Press.

Guerney, B. G. (1977). *Relationship enhancement.* San Francisco: Jossey-Bass.

Halford, W. K., Sanders, M. R., & Behrens, B. C. (1993). A comparison of the generalization of behavioral marital therapy and enhanced behavioral marital therapy. *Journal of Consulting and Clinical Psychology, 61,* 51–60.

Harvey, J. H., Wells, G. L., & Alvarez, M. D. (1978). Attribution in the context of conflict and separation in close relationships. In J. H. Harvey, W. Ickes, & R. F. Kidd (Eds.), *New directions in attribution research* (Vol. 2, pp. 235–260). Hillsdale, NJ: Erlbaum.

Haynes, S. N., Chavez, R. E., & Samuel, V. (1984). Assessment of marital communication and distress. *Behavioral Assessment, 6,* 315–322.

Heiman, J., Gladue, B. A., Roberts, C., & LoPiccolo, J. (1986). Historical and current factors discriminating sexually dysfunctional married couples. *Journal of Marital and Family Therapy, 12,* 163–174.

Hiebert, W. J., & Gillespie, J. P. (1984). The initial interview. In R. F. Stahmann & W. J. Hiebert (Eds.), *Counseling in marital and sexual problems: A clinician's handbook* (pp. 17–34). Lexington, MA: Lexington Books.

Holtzworth-Munroe, A., & Jacobson, N. S. (1991). Behavioral marital therapy. In A. S. Gurman & D. P. Kniskern, (Eds.), *Handbook of family therapy* (Vol. 2, pp. 96–133). New York: Brunner/Mazel.

Hops, J., Wills, T. A., Patterson, G. R., & Wiess, R. L. (1972). *Marital interaction coding system.* Eugene: University of Oregon and Oregon Research Institute.

Howe, G. W. (1987). Attributions of complex cause and the perception of marital conflict. *Journal of Personality and Social Psychology, 53,* 1119–1128.

Hudson, W. W. (1982). *The clinical measurement package: A field manual.* Chicago: Dorsey Press.

Jacobson, N. S. (1984). A component analysis of behavioral marital therapy: The relative effectiveness of behavior exchange and problem solving training. *Journal of Consulting and Clinical Psychology, 52,* 295–305.

Jacobson, N. S. (1989). The maintenance of treatment gains following social learning–based marital therapy. *Behavior Therapy, 20,* 325–336.

Jacobson, N. S. (1991). Toward enhancing the efficacy of marital therapy and marital therapy research. *Journal of Family Psychology, 4,* 373–393.

Jacobson, N. S., & Follette, W. C. (1985). Clinical significance of improvement resulting from two behavioral marital therapy components. *Behavior Therapy, 16,* 249–262.

Jacobson, N. S., & Margolin, G. (1979). *Marital therapy: Strategies based on social learning and behavior exchange principles.* New York: Brunner/Mazel.

Jacobson, N. S., McDonald, D. W., Follette, W. C., & Berley, R. A. (1985). Attribution processes in distressed and nondistressed married couples. *Cognitive Therapy and Research, 9,* 35–50.

Jemail, J. A. (1977). *Response bias in the assessment of marital and sexual adjustment.* Unpublished doctoral dissertation, State University of New York at Stony Brook, New York.

Johnson, S. M., & Greenberg, L. S. (1985). Differential effects of experiential and problem-solving interventions in resolving marital conflicts. *Journal of Consulting and Clinical Psychology, 53,* 175–184.

Kayser, K. (1993). *When love dies: The process of marital disaffection.* New York: Guilford Press.

Locke, H. J., & Wallace, K. M. (1959). Short marital adjustment and prediction tests: Their reliability and validity. *Marriage and Family Living, 21,* 251–255.

LoPiccolo, J., & Daiss, S. (1987). Assessment of sexual dysfunction. In K. D. O'Leary (Ed.), *Assessment of marital discord: An integration for research and clinical practice* (pp. 183–221). Hillsdale, NJ: Erlbaum.

LoPiccolo, J., & Steger, J. (1974). The Sexual Interaction Inventory: A new instrument for assessment of sexual dysfunction. *Archives of Sexual Behavior, 3,* 585–595.

Margolin, G. (1987). Marital therapy: A cognitive-behavioral-affective approach. In N. S. Jacobson (Ed.), *Psychotherapists in clinical practice: Cognitive and behavioral perspectives* (pp. 232–285). New York: Guilford.

Margolin, G., Talovic, S., & Weinstein, C. D. (1983). Areas of Change Questionnaire: A practical approach to marital assessment. *Journal of Consulting and Clinical Psychology, 51,* 920–931.

Margolin, G., & Weiss, R. L. (1978). Comparative evaluation of therapeutic components associated with behavioral marital treatments. *Journal of Consulting and Clinical Psychology, 46,* 1476–1486.

Martin, P. A. (1976). *A marital therapy manual.* New York: Brunner/Mazel.

McGoldrick, M., & Gerson, R. (1985). *Genograms in family assessment.* New York: Norton.

Navran, L. (1967). Communication and adjustment in marriage. *Family Process, 6,* 173–184.

Newman, H. (1981). Communication within ongoing intimate relationships: An attributional perspective. *Personality and Social Psychology Bulletin, 7,* 59–70.

Notarius, C., & Vanzetti, N. (1983). The Marital Agendas Protocol. In L. Filsinger (Ed.), *A sourcebook of marital and family assessment.* Beverly Hills, CA: Sage Publications.

O'Leary, K. D., & Arias, I. (1987). Marital assessment in clinical practice. In K. D. O'Leary (Ed.), *Assessment of marital discord: An integration for research and clinical practice* (pp. 287–308). Hillsdale, NJ: Erlbaum.

O'Leary, K. D., Fincham, F., & Turkewitz, H. (1983). Assessment of positive feelings toward spouse. *Journal of Consulting and Clinical Psychology, 51*, 949–951.

Olson, D. H., Fournier, D. G., & Druckman, J. M. (1985). ENRICH Marital Communication Scale. In D. H. Olson et al., (Eds.), *Family inventories*. Minneapolis: University of Minnesota.

Olson, D. H., & Ryder, R. G. (1977). *Marital and family interaction coding system (MFICS)*. Unpublished manuscript, University of Minnesota.

Raush, H. L., Barry, W. A., Hertel, R. K., & Swain, M. A. (1974). *Communication, conflict and marriage*. San Francisco: Jossey-Bass.

Richmond, M. E. (1928). Concern of the community with marriage. In M. E. Rich (Ed.), *Family life today: Papers presented at the Fiftieth Anniversary of Family Social Casework in America*. Boston: Houghton Mifflin.

Sabatelli, R. M. (1984). The Marital Comparison Level Index: A measure for assessing outcomes relative to expectations. *Journal of Marriage and the Family, 46*, 651–662.

Sager, C. J. (1981). Couple therapy and marriage contacts. In A. S. Gurman & D. P. Kniskern (Eds.), *Handbook of family therapy* (pp. 85–130). New York: Brunner/Mazel.

Schaefer, M. T., & Olson, D. H. (1981). Assessing intimacy: The PAIR inventory. *Journal of Marital and Family Therapy, 7*, 47–60.

Scharff, J. S. (1995). Psychoanalytic marital therapy. In N. S. Jacobson & A. S. Gurman (Eds.), *Clinical handbook of couple therapy* (pp. 164–193). New York: Guilford.

Scharff, D. E., & Scharff, J. S. (1991). *Object relations couple therapy*. Northvale, NJ: Jason Aronson.

Schmaling, K. B., Fruzzetti, A. E., & Jacobson, N. (1989). Marital problems. In K. Hawton, P. M., Salkovskis, J. Kirk, & D. M. Clark (Eds.). *Cognitive behaviour therapy for psychiatric problems: A practical guide* (pp. 339–369). Oxford: Oxford University Press.

Sharpley, C. F., & Rogers, H. J. (1984). Preliminary validation of the Abbreviated Spanier Dyadic Adjustment Scale: Some psychometric data regarding a screening test of marital adjustment. *Educational and Psychological Measurement, 44*, 1045–1049.

Shoham, V., Rohrbaugh, M., & Patterson, J. (1995). Problem- and solution-focused couple therapies: The MRI and Milwaukee Models. In N. S. Jacobson & A. S. Gurman (Eds.), *Clinical handbook of couple therapy* (pp. 142–163). New York: Guilford.

Snyder, D. K. (1979). *Marital satisfaction inventory*. Los Angeles: Western Psychological Services.

Snyder, D. K., & Regts, J. M. (1982). Factor scales for assessing marital disharmony and disaffection. *Journal of Consulting and Clinical Psychology, 50*, 736–743.

Snyder, D. K., & Wills, R. M. (1989). Behavioral versus insight-oriented marital therapy: Effects on individual and interspousal functioning. *Journal of Consulting and Clinical Psychology, 57*, 39–46.

Snyder, D. K., Wills, R. M., & Grady-Fletcher, A. (1991). Long-term effectiveness of behavioral versus insight-oriented marital therapy. *Journal of Consulting and Clinical Psychology*, 59, 138–141.

Spanier, G. B. (1976). Measuring dyadic adjustment: New scales for assessing the quality of marriage and similar dyads. *Journal of Marriage and the Family, 38*, 15–28.

Straus, M. A. (1979). Measuring intrafamily conflict and violence: The Conflict Tactics Scales. *Journal of Marriage and the Family, 41*, 75–88.

Straus, M. A. (1990). The Conflict Tactics Scale and its critics: An evaluation and new data on validity and reliability. In M. A. Straus & R. J. Gelles (Eds.), *Physical violence in Amer-*

ican families: Risk factors and adaptations to violence in 8,145 families. New Brunswick, NJ: Transaction Publishers.

Stuart, R. B. (1980). *Helping couples change: A social learning approach to marital therapy*. New York: Guilford.

Van den Broucke, S., Vertommen, H., & Vandereycken, W. (1995). Construction and validation of a marital intimacy questionnaire. *Family Relations, 44*, 285–290.

Vanzetti, N. A., Notarius, C. I., & NeeSmith, D. (1992). Specific and generalized expectancies in marital interaction. *Journal of Family Psychology*, 6, 171–183.

Waring, E. M., & Reddon, J. R. (1983). The measurement of intimacy in marriage: The Waring Intimacy Questionnaire. *Journal of Clinical Psychology, 39*, 53–57.

Weiss, R. L., & Bircher, G. R. (1978). Adults with marital dysfunction. In M. Hersen & A. S. Bellack (Eds.), *Behavior therapy in the psychiatric setting*. Baltimore: Williams & Wilkins.

Zung, W. K. (1965). A self-rating depression scale. *Archives of General Psychiatry, 12*, 63–70.

10

Children's Treatment Groups:

General Principles and Their Application to Group Treatment with Cumulatively Traumatized Children

Kay Martel Connors, Gerald Schamess, and Frederick H. Strieder

Without any encouragement from parents, teachers, or other adults, children spontaneously and eagerly gather to play together in groups. Group play provides opportunities for latency-age children and adolescents to establish meaningful friendships outside the family; to compete and/or cooperate with age-mates; to learn the rules that govern games, sports, and academic learning; to test out, abide by, or defy social expectations and discover the consequences; to work industriously toward achieving personal as well as externally defined, socially sanctioned goals; and to collaborate with other children in creating mutually compelling fantasies that symbolically express wishes, fears, and family dramas that represent the deepest levels of psychological experience. Potentially, group play and group relationships can markedly advance psychosexual and social development, promote self-cohesion, enhance ego functioning, modify internalized self and object representations, and create opportunities to initiate new relationships in the real world. Although most hierarchical developmental theories do not fully recognize the importance of group play and group relationships, the fact is that many crucial developmental tasks that children must master during latency and adolescence can be mastered only in groups.

The importance, complexity, and subtlety of group play, as well as the ambivalent response it frequently evokes in adults, are well illustrated in the following vignette.

One spring during recess, a fourth-grade class of girls and boys (ages ten and eleven) began to play in and around a storm drain through which a constant stream of water flowed. With notable concentration, the children worked cooperatively over several weeks to dam the water, create tributaries and ponds, build bridges, tunnels, and ships, float various cargos downstream, and create periodic floods that swept away everything they had built as a prelude to building something new.

The teachers who were watching at a distance recognized that the children were having a wonderful time and began to plan how this newly discovered interest in "hydraulics" might be incorporated into the class science curriculum. Their delight ended abruptly, however, when accidentally (or perhaps not so accidentally, since under ordinary circumstances children are quite expert at concealing their group fantasies from adults), they overheard that the project was named "Jessie's asshole." That chance remark made it clear that at a covert level, the play expressed the children's dislike of a particular classmate and was intended, in part, to remind him of his devalued status. Moreover, having confronted the latent content, the teachers realized that the play symbolically incorporated a great many anal and urethral fantasies.

The teachers responded, as teachers often do, first by banning the water play and then by moving recess to a new location where the children no longer had access to the storm drain. Had the teachers been better attuned to the language of children's group play, they might have recognized that the play, in one of its many meanings, symbolically expressed a number of phase-specific developmental themes that fourth graders return to again and again as they work toward sublimating anal and urethral drive derivatives. Moreover, cruel as the scatological reference to Jessie was, it also conveyed an important message about his provocative behavior in class.

Some months later, the teachers requested a psychological evaluation, having decided that Jessie's provocative behavior was as intolerable to them as it had previously been to his peers. At that time, the school social worker advised them that Jessie's provocativeness and his unpopularity reflected an obsession with anality in general, and with anal sexuality (masochism) in particular, issues that had aroused considerable unconscious anxiety in the other class members.

What makes the vignette both fascinating and informative is that the teachers had been at least partially right in viewing the children's play as an expression of "cognitive" interest in "hydraulics." The laboratory-like group-as-a-whole study they were conducting incorporated intellectual interests, the desire to scapegoat Jessie, their own anxieties about Jessie's provocative behavior, and a mutually enjoyable initiative directed toward ego integration—sublimation, mastery, learning, and self-control. Although this particular example of group play occurred in a nonclinical setting, it nonetheless serves as a good starting point for examining the characteristics of children's groups and the potential for therapeutic change inherent in group process.

PRACTICE MODELS

Early Principles and Models

Fifty or more years ago, Slavson (1943) and Axline (1947) devised ways of using group play to treat emotional disturbances in children. By current standards their methods seem remarkably permissive and quite radical. They equipped their group rooms with a wide array of arts and crafts or symbolic play equipment for the group members to use as they wished, expressively, regressively, and/or progressively. The therapist did not plan or introduce specific activities of any kind except for a snack toward the end of each group session. The group members were free to play alone, in subgroups, or together as a total group, pretty much however and whenever they wished. Regression was accepted within very broad limits, and the therapist's fundamental role was to provide a physically safe, emotionally gratifying environment in which the members could interact with one another while expressing their emotional needs, wishes, fears, and family dynamics with a minimum of adult interference. The arts and crafts or play therapy equipment that were put out became a medium of expressive communication, which structured the specific ways in which the group members expressed themselves.

In activity group therapy (Slavson, 1943; Schiffer, 1969), the therapist's role was carefully designed so she or he became a consistent, gratifying, accepting, competent adult with whom the children could positively identify. In nondirective play groups (Axline, 1947; Ginott, 1961), the therapist verbally mirrored what children said and did both as individuals and in their play together, in accord with Carl Rogers's (1942) recommendations about therapeutic technique. At this time and for many years after, children's group therapists did not ask questions, did not confront problematic behavior, rarely set limits, and did not interpret. Therapists quickly discovered that what they did in groups was notably different from what they did while treating children individually and that they could learn a great deal about the dynamics of group play by listening and observing group play without intervening. They also discovered that group play within the structures outlined above could promote marked changes in ego functioning, self representation, and object relations.

Much to their credit, Slavson, Axline, and the other early innovators had discovered the therapeutic action of a carefully constructed holding environment that promoted corrective peer interaction. The groups they developed were structured to provide a safe physical environment, as well as a carefully balanced combination of gratification and developmental challenge. The gratifications included adult acceptance, food, and free access to pleasurable play activities that provided acceptable channels for affective expression. The challenges included the need to preserve the group as a whole even when individual members were in conflict with each other, finding acceptable ways of using play materials to communicate problematic wishes and fears, and developing competencies that were congruent with individual interests and abilities and would be recognized and valued by the other group members. This carefully constructed balance between gratification and the challenges inherent in group life made it possible to activate and planfully use group interaction as the central medium for change.

In activity and nondirective play groups, safety, reasonable limits, and reintegration after regression were ensured by balancing the group's composition, that is, selecting children with different emotional problems and a range of different coping styles. As a result, children without internalized limits or reliable superego structures found it necessary to interact with other children who were threatened by their acting-out behavior and who told them they should stop what they were doing because it was "bad," or they would get *everyone* into trouble. Inhibited, anxious children who constantly struggled with internalized feelings of guilt discovered that other children could play happily and freely, with few internal or external restraints. At times, they learned, it was even possible to defy adult authority without serious consequences. And finally, withdrawn children who were terrified of peer interaction and spent much of their time lost in private fantasies could learn about the pleasures of group play by watching other group members for extended periods of time from the periphery, before tentatively deciding whether they wanted to join an activity.

Startling though the degree of permissiveness, the acceptance of regression, and the therapist's noninterpretative role are to most contemporary practitioners, these groups provide extremely effective treatment for many children with intermediate levels of character pathology: children with conduct disorders (mild and moderate), avoidant disorders, oppositional disorders, gender identity disorders, and dependent personality disorders (Ginott 1961; Schiffer, 1969; Schamess, 1986). The therapeutic context provided by safety, reasonable, unobtrusive limits, the availability of an accepting, gratifying adult, and opportunities for controlled regression constitute a growth-promoting holding environment for these children. By a "holding environment" we mean the supportive continuity provided by the therapeutic situation, as well as the underlying empathy, steadiness and reliability of the object, and attunement to developmental processes that contain potentially disruptive and disorganizing early wishes and fears (Winnicott, 1965).

Over time, as practitioners began to treat a wider range of children, it became apparent that the holding environment had to be modified significantly in order for groups to address the specific needs of children at the higher and lower ends of the developmental continuum. The vignette describing the fourth-grade class is informative in regard to the capacities and needs of children whose ego functioning is relatively well integrated. As a group, those children were able to construct their own holding environment and engage in emotionally and cognitively compelling play with no assistance from an adult authority. The class's awareness that a teacher was distantly available, keeping an eye on what they were doing, was sufficient to help them structure and contain their play. There were no problems with limits, interpersonal disputes were settled amicably, and everyone who wished to participate was able to do so. The play itself was developmentally progressive in that it incorporated a good deal of experiential learning and involved the focused attention that is a prerequisite for mastering impulses and developing sublimations. Moreover, once the scapegoating had been revealed, it seems likely that it could have been managed constructively within the group process, if an adult had been willing to ask the children why they thought Jessie needed to provoke them and why they allowed him to do so. For the most part, the vignette illustrates how relatively healthy, ego-intact children regulate their everyday group life and their group relationships.

At a somewhat earlier point along the developmental continuum, we recognize that children with neurotic disturbances can benefit from a group holding environment similar to the environment that is typically established in adult psychotherapy groups. Activity interview groups (Slavson & Schiffer, 1975) and interpretative groups (Sugar, 1974; Kraft, 1983) provide arts and crafts materials or expressive play equipment as props for neurotic children to use while they are talking and to help them deal with silences. During the beginning stage of such groups, the children tend to gossip about school, other children they know, pets, and play activities. During the middle stage, they tentatively and watchfully begin to talk about their own problems, to take comfort in learning they are not alone in being fearful, unhappy, or angry, and to enact some of their emotional problems transferentially with the other members or the therapist. During the later stages they begin to discuss "such topics as sex differences, sex roles, problems of birth and death and fears of calamitous happenings at home (Anthony, 1957, p. 197). Throughout the group process, therapists ask questions and interpret freely with no particular limitations (Kraft, 1967; Sugar, 1974). Schiffer suggests that coeducational therapeutic play groups with male and female cotherapists can be helpful to latency-age children in working through oedipal problems. "The behavior of the therapeutic 'parents' reduces the inordinate pressures of guilt and anxiety which are attendant to the oedipal conflict. The eventual therapeutic outcome is the development of a healthier superego structure and effective sublimations" (Schiffer, 1969, p. 113).

Homogeneous Groups for Children with Significant Deficits in Ego Organization and Self-Cohesion

Constructing helpful therapeutic environments for children whose ego functioning is severely impaired presents a more difficult challenge. An expanded version of Winnicott's concepts about the facilitating environment and the therapeutic role of "holding" are particularly useful in understanding the role that structure plays in constructing therapeutic groups for such children. Winnicott (1989) originally proposed holding as a way of describing the earliest mother-infant relationship: the period when the infant experiences "absolute dependence" on a caregiver, and the mother provides an "auxiliary ego function" for the infant. "The operation of the facilitating environment starts with near 100 percent adaptation, rapidly diminishing according to the growing needs of the baby. These needs include opportunity for object-relating through aggression" (Winnicott, 1989, p. 101). Holding is a concept that describes everything a mother does in caring for her baby: "In giving consideration to these matters it is necessary to postulate a state of the mother . . . [in which] she knows without thinking about it more or less what the baby needs. . . . The 'silent' communication is one of reliability which in fact protects the baby from automatic reactions to impingement from external reality, these reactions breaking the baby's line of life and constituting traumata" (Winnicott, 1989, p. 259.). Babies who have been "let down" (i.e., experienced environmental failure) "know what it is to be in a state of acute confusion or the agony of disintegration. They know what it is like to be dropped, to fall forever, or to become split into psycho-somatic disruption" (Winnicott, 1989, p. 260).

By extending the concept of holding to include whatever degree of adaptation caregivers and therapists must make to encourage psychological growth in children whose functioning is arrested at different points along the psychosexual-psychosocial continuum, therapists can identify the specific group structures and interpersonal experiences that will make treatment possible. In constructing groups for children with serious impairments in ego organization, therapists must begin with a working understanding of the traumas (in Winnicott's terms, the "environmental failures") the children have experienced, of their ego organization, and of the anxieties and impulses (aggressive and sexual) that disorganize them. This understanding makes it possible to create specific holding environments (group structures) that initially approach the "100 percent adaptation" to the members' emotional needs and vulnerabilities that Winnicott describes as the central component of the earliest mother-child relationship. When they have been well devised, these structures also provide opportunities for the members to master developmentally appropriate challenges and to experiment with individual adaptations to a more demanding environment as they become ready to do so. Following Winnicott, in groups constructed to meet the developmental needs of particular populations of children whose ego functioning is seriously compromised, the "100 percent adaptation" built into the group structure diminishes as the "growing needs" of the members change.

Groups for Children with Pervasive Development Disorders

Treatment groups for children who suffer from schizoid disorders, pervasive developmental disorders, or undersocialized conduct disorders are constructed to provide a holding environment that emphasizes maximum containment, physical safety, protection from aggressive assault, predictability, and direct gratification. Scheidlinger (1960, 1965) describes a therapeutic holding environment for ego-damaged children who have experienced family disintegration, severe deprivation, and extreme poverty. In these "modified experiential groups," the physical environment is designed so the members may use craft materials to act out their conflicts or to develop age-appropriate skills. Carefully supervised, corrective peer interaction is emphasized, and specific activities are introduced not only to provide opportunities for affective expression but also to promote mastery of age-appropriate tasks.

In these groups the therapist actively establishes limits, clarifies reality, and makes certain that each child receives a fair share of the food and materials. After an initial stage of "guided gratification" during which purchasing food, preparing a meal, and serving it plays a predominant role, the group goes through a period of controlled regression, followed by a period of "guided upbringing and socialization" (Scheidlinger, 1965) during which the therapist establishes expectations related to frustration tolerance, impulse control, and age-appropriate socialization. The groups are specifically designed to provide corrective object experiences that strengthen the child's capacity for basic trust and object constancy. As the group members internalize the atmosphere of protection, gratification, and consistency, anxiety decreases to a point where they can more reliably distinguish between fantasy and reality and accept the demands of reality.

A group for "primitively fixated," "postsymbiotic" children is described by Trafimow and Pattak (1981, 1982). In this treatment model, the physical environment is conceptualized as an essential part of the holding environment. In addition to a round wooden table and chairs, the room is furnished with large wooden cubes, each having one open side. All the cubes are bulky enough so that two or more children must cooperate in order to move them. The need to collaborate physically encourages interpersonal contact between the members and leads to the development of shared fantasies, which gradually become part of the group process.

The authors identify three major curative elements. The first and most crucial is the presence of other children who offer each other a range of "objectal alternatives" beyond the orbit of parent-child interaction. The emphasis on peer interaction is based on Trafimow and Pattak's observation that postsymbiotic children tend to be less anxious with peers than with adults and are better able to express their developmental needs to peers. Repeated interactions over time promote identification with the more adaptive personality characteristics of other children in the group. The second curative element is the cotherapy team, which actively establishes behavioral limits (through physical restraint if necessary) and confronts, explores, and interprets. The therapists view themselves as "auxiliary group egos" who address individual children as needed but always work to return the process to the group members. The third curative element is the group-as-a-whole, which gradually assumes the functions of the "mother group" (Scheidlinger, 1974) and of a transitional object (Kauff, 1977), thereby holding and protecting the members, while at the same time supporting their attempts to differentiate, distinguishing what is "me" from what is "not me."

What is remarkable about both of these models is the degree to which the therapists planfully use themselves, the furniture, the play materials, selected activities, and carefully managed peer interaction to create a holding environment that reduces anxiety and regression (what Winnicott might describe as "falling forever"). These groups are specifically designed to promote the internalization of nurturing and protective caregiving objects (both the therapist and the group as a whole), to encourage controlled, positive peer interaction, to strengthen self-control and competence, and to support differentiation and autonomous functioning within a group context. Below, we will examine the modifications in group structure necessary to provide a therapeutic holding environment for children with moderate to severe conduct disorders. To varying degrees, such children have deficits in anxiety tolerance, impulse control, affect regulation, judgment, object relations, and self-cohesion.

Groups for Children with Disorders of Conduct and Impulse

Ganter, Yeakel, and Polansky (1967) present a model of group treatment for aggressive, hyperactive children, half of whom had been referred for residential treatment, and all of whom were having serious behavior difficulties at school. The groups, coeducational in composition, met twice weekly for two-hour sessions over a period of six months. Each group had six members, and where possible, male and female cotherapists. The group holding environment was specifically designed to increase each child's capacity for verbal self-expression and self-observation, while also strengthening ego functioning ("organizational unity"), particularly in the areas of impulse control and reality testing.

To achieve these goals, each session was organized to provide a repetitive, containing structure of carefully graded activities that could be successfully completed in the amount of time allotted for them. A typical meeting included regular periods of craft activity, large-muscle physical activity (games), painting, rhythm activity, and a snack. Each activity was set up in advance in one or the other of two adjacent rooms, and the therapists helped the members move back and forth from one room and one activity to the next room and next activity, with minimum disruption. Each activity was planned in advance to fit into a particular time segment during the session. The children were praised for all their accomplishments, and the therapists actively encouraged problem solving by helping individual members establish priorities, focus their attention, and complete projects.

Verbal self-awareness was encouraged through painting and rhythm activities. A therapist, standing next to a child, would talk about colors, visual forms, and rhythmic patterns in terms of the human experiences and emotions that might be associated with them. As the children played, the therapist would use an already established label ("red is anger," "children jump when they are happy") to comment on the child's activity. The therapist's comments frequently encouraged the child to talk about his or her emotional state. Recordings of conversations between children and therapists were made frequently, especially when the child was angry or upset. The recordings were available to children to listen to and were frequently requested.

Even when provoked, the group therapists were careful not to be drawn into any kind of struggle that might, at the level of transference, replicate punitive, critical, or devaluing family interactions. Behavioral limits in the group were clear-cut and for the most part impersonal. When possible, therapists ignored aggressive, provocative, or hyperactive behavior. Children who acted out and could not regain their self-control without assistance were removed from the group room for a brief "life space" interview that focused on how they were feeling and what had upset them. They returned to the group once they had calmed down.

The holding environment established in these groups not only contained anxiety and acting out, but contributed to feelings of competence and self-esteem. As the members learned to express themselves symbolically through crafts and games, their capacity to verbalize feelings and to manage interpersonal conflicts by talking about them increased markedly. Over the course of the planned six-month treatment, the group members showed notable improvement in judgment, impulse control, and reality testing. Their school behavior was much less problematic, their capacity to learn had improved, and their difficulties at home had diminished markedly.

Rosenberg-Hariton, Kernberg, and Chazen (1991) create a rather different holding environment in their treatment of a similar population of children. They report on an integrated activity-interpretive model of group treatment in which the therapists establish the holding environment by (1) thoroughly orienting the members to the reasons they have been referred and what the group will attempt to accomplish, (2) establishing a regular, predictable time frame for group activities, (3) carefully discussing group rules, (4) actively setting both verbal and behavioral limits, and (5) reassuring the members that the therapists will make themselves available to help each individual member as needed. In this model, it is assumed that anxiety produces acting out and that the initial stage of treatment will be dominated by child-to-adult and peer-to-peer conflicts about power and authority.

During the middle stage of treatment, after acting out has been brought under control, the therapists actively work toward facilitating nonconflictual interaction between the group members. The therapists regularly suggest new ways of behaving, and resolving conflicts. They also work toward promoting self-awareness. With this goal in mind, they confront acting out, comment on how the children interact with one another, ask how individual members perceive their own behavior, and encourage both individuals and the group as a whole to talk about how they feel when other members behave problematically. During the final stage, the group progresses along a dimension of increased individuation as well as increased cohesion. Most significant is the capacity of the group members to observe themselves and other members, verbalizing these observations and sharing them with each other for clarification and validation (Rosenberg-Hariton, Kernberg, & Chazen, 1991).

In both models the holding environment is less concerned with providing direct gratification than it is with limiting frustration and containing anxiety. The common underlying assumption is that anxiety precipitates acting out and that acting out is both disorganizing and self-destructive for these children. In both models the therapists actively work toward containing anxiety by establishing rules and setting firm limits. They also provide each of the group members with a considerable amount of individual support and attention directed toward helping them complete projects, use materials constructively, and manage peer interactions with less interpersonal conflict. These active interventions reduce frustration, strengthen feelings of competence, and promote self-esteem.

In the Retrieval from Limbo model (Ganter, Yaekel, & Polansky, 1967), the holding environment is organized to ensure strict adherence to a carefully timed activity schedule. The therapists move the group members through activities briskly, leaving little time for opposition or acting out. The activities offered are carefully selected so the members can complete them successfully in the time period allotted. The underlying assumption is that this holding environment reduces anxiety, supports ego organization, and improves self-esteem.

Both models also emphasize the central importance of increasing the members' capacity to express themselves verbally. In the Retrieval from Limbo model (Ganter, Yaekel, & Polansky, 1967), the therapists take responsibility for encouraging verbalization by naming emotions, associating them with different physical and craft activities, and encouraging the members to talk about what they are doing and how they feel while doing it. The Play Group Psychotherapy model (Rosenberg-Hariton, Kernberg, & Chazen, 1991) establishes a rather different holding environment. During the middle stage of treatment, the therapist(s) begin to ask the members to reflect on their feelings and behavior and to comment on what is happening in the group. Initially the intent is to help the members identify feelings, but over time, as the process progresses, comments and questions are increasingly directed toward helping the members examine their own and each other's motivation. In both models, the initial emphasis is on recognizing, naming, and talking about feelings. Self-reflection and self-awareness develop as a consequence of containing and verbalizing feelings, before or without acting on them.

The principles used to create the ego-enhancing holding environments provide a theoretical framework for planning children's treatment groups. They are particularly relevant in addressing specific deficits in ego organization and object relations.

PSYCHOEDUCATIONAL GROUPS FOR TRAUMATIZED CHILDREN

Over the past decade, children's group therapy practice has changed markedly. The recent literature suggests that most contemporary children's treatment groups are psychoeducational in focus and time limited by plan, lasting on average from six to twenty sessions. By definition, psychoeducational groups are homogeneous in composition since all the participants have experienced a common childhood trauma (e.g., sexual abuse, incest, divorce, living with parents who abuse substances). Although most reports implicitly recognize that the degree of trauma may vary from group member to group member, the underlying assumption is that children who have experienced a common trauma are more alike than different since the sequelae are similar for every traumatized child. Although the children who participate in trauma-focused groups are often quite heterogeneous in terms of clinical diagnosis and ego organization, diagnostic and developmental considerations are rarely discussed in the psychoeducational, trauma group literature. Most reports ignore such considerations, thus implying they are not central to either group process or outcome.

While this viewpoint is problematic from our perspective, much of the recent literature argues persuasively that psychoeducational groups are helpful to traumatized children. They reduce stigmatization and guilt, provide information about the emotional effects of trauma, encourage the participants to retell their trauma stories in a carefully controlled, accepting environment, and actively teach children how they can protect themselves from retraumatization. For example, Gaines (1986) describes a guidance group for children of divorced parents in which each of eight planned sessions is devoted to an activity that focuses attention on a specific topic. In this group the issues discussed included identifying feelings about divorce, solving problems related to divorce, talking with a peer about the nature and effects of the divorce, and developing positive feelings about oneself. Psychoeducational groups are well described by Gaines (1986) and Rice-Smith (1993) among others. Interested readers will benefit from reading their papers and reviewing the references that accompany them.

PSYCHOTHERAPY GROUPS FOR TRAUMATIZED CHILDREN

In this section, we describe time-limited therapeutic groups for cumulatively and repetitively traumatized inner-city children who suffer from significant problems in ego functioning as well as inadequacies in subphase organization (differentiation, practicing, and rapprochement) stemming from arrested development during separation-individuation (Mahler, Pine, & Bergman, 1975). The group model that will be presented is both developmentally oriented and theme (trauma) centered. It is designed to promote recovery from trauma while facilitating progressive subphase development and ego organization. The model should be of particular interest to clinical social workers because it effectively addresses the emotional and developmental needs of a client population that is both underserved and notably difficult to treat.

The work reported here was done at the Kennedy Krieger Family Center, a department of the Kennedy Krieger Institute in Baltimore, Maryland, which serves children with disabilities (children with handicaps, head injuries, brain disorders, complex cognitive deficits, and neurological impairments). In 1984, the Family Center was created through a grant from the Baltimore City Department of Social Services that funded mental health services for children living in foster care and other out-of-home placements. Foster and biological families were also provided with services. When the grant ended, the center continued to treat the children and their families on a fee-for-service basis. Almost without exception, the children treated at the center have been cumulatively and repetitively traumatized.

More than 90 percent of the referrals to the Family Center come from the Baltimore Department of Social Services. In 1992, 75 percent of the children served (Kates & Iams, 1992) were living in substitute care, 54 percent with nonrelated families, 29 percent with relatives, 9 percent with biological parents, and 8 percent in adoptive homes, special treatment centers, or shelters. On average, these children had spent a quarter of their lives (two or more years) in foster care or some other out-of-home placement. Multiple placements were the rule.

Kates and Iams (1992) found that 86 percent of the children being treated were African Americans living in desperately poor inner-city environments. All had been seriously neglected or physically abused or both. Fifty percent had been sexually abused. Before they were placed in substitute care, they had lived in unpredictable and chaotic home environments. Hunger, inadequate medical care, unsafe and unclean housing, and lack of adult supervision were their "average expectable environment." Parents frequently engaged in drug use, drug trafficking, and prostitution at home, with their children present. Older children regularly took responsibility for obtaining food and clothing for themselves and their siblings. Most had suffered profound losses due to death, illness, the dissolution of family units, or the incarceration of family members.

More than half the parents had long histories of drug and alcohol abuse. Seventeen percent had been incarcerated. Eleven percent had been diagnosed with a major mental illness. Most had been severely and chronically abused or neglected when they were children. Intergenerational patterns of abuse, addiction, and family dysfunction were so severe that even parents who loved their children deeply frequently could not provide adequate care. When parents (typically, single mothers) could not benefit from child welfare services, treatment focused on the termination of parental rights and permanency planning.

Characteristics of Traumatized Children

Children who have been cumulatively and repetitively traumatized typically demonstrate serious problems involving behavior, interpersonal skills, and emotional development. Lenore Terr (1991, p. 11) defines childhood trauma "as the result of one sudden, external blow or a series of blows, rendering the young person temporarily helpless and breaking past ordinary coping and defensive operations. . . . Once the events take place a number of internal changes occur in the child." Cumulatively and repetitively traumatized children have received repeated, severe blows, usually starting at relatively young ages. Terr identifies the following four characteristics commonly seen among severely traumatized children:

1. They strongly visualize or otherwise repeatedly perceive memories related to the abuse.
2. They engage in repetitive behaviors outside their conscious control.
3. They experience trauma-specific fears.
4. Their attitudes about significant people, life events, and future prospects are markedly changed. Traumatized children see their future prospects as very limited. They believe that their communities are unsafe, and their caregivers are unable to protect them.

Terr (1991) also identifies thought suppression, sleep problems, exaggerated startle responses, developmental regressions, fears of the mundane, deliberate avoidances, panic, irritability, and hypervigilance as common characteristics. These symptoms impede the child's ability to decode social cues, regulate affective states and anxiety, manage impulse control, behave in socially appropriate ways, and repress feelings and memories associated with the traumatic events. Chronically and persistently maltreated children are at very high risk for major mental illness (e.g., affective, dissociative, anxiety, and posttraumatic stress disorders).

Given the serious consequences of traumatization, it is important to emphasize that the effect trauma has on development and personality organization is influenced by a number of factors: the child's age, the nature and severity of the trauma(s), their frequency and duration over time, and the degree to which the child's ego organization was intact and age appropriate when the traumatic event(s) occurred. When evaluated according to these criteria, the children treated at the Family Center are in the highest category of risk. In Winnicott's (1989, p. 260) terms, these are children who know what it is to be in a state of "acute confusion," who have experienced "the agony of disintegration," and have been threatened with breaks in their "line of life."

Constructing Treatment Groups: General Considerations

Three principles require consideration in constructing treatment groups for particular populations of child clients: (1) the children's developmental level, especially phase-specific emotional and intellectual capacities and limitations, (2) the nature and causes of the emotional difficulties to be addressed, and (3) the group dynamic principles that determine the kind of structure (holding environment) and process most likely to bring about constructive change. The first of these variables—the developmental capacities and limitations that latency and preteen children bring to treatment—has been thoughtfully discussed by a number of authors, including Ginott (1961), Schamess (1986), and Slavson and Schiffer (1975, Chap. 2).

Group Structure

Schamess (1986) suggests that group structure is a central factor in organizing groups to address the specific developmental and treatment needs of diagnostically diverse populations of children. He defines structure in terms of the size and location of the group therapy room, the furniture and equipment provided, the toys and craft materials available, the length and frequency of meetings, and the extent to which activities are planned and initiated by the therapist. He also includes the degree to which the therapist serves as an auxiliary ego, an object for positive identification, and/or a catalyst who encourages self-awareness by actively exploring, confronting, and interpreting the children's play and what the children say in group sessions. Structure is an essential element in establishing a developmentally appropriate holding environment (Spinner, 1992), since different structural elements can be arranged (within broad limits) to provide whatever degree of adaptation is necessary to address the developmental needs of specific groups of children. In groups for cumulatively traumatized children, careful attention to structure plays an essential role in preventing devastating reenactments of traumatic experiences (Gallagher, Love, & Kimmel, 1993). Once safety has been established, structure creates controlled opportunities for gratification, affective expression, corrective peer interaction, and participation in a constructed, functional, symbolic family system.

The FC Group Therapy Program: Organizational Principles

At any given time, the Family Center offers ten or more different groups that meet weekly for ninety-minute sessions. Groups are composed of six to eight children and are organized around specific traumatic experiences: sexual abuse, familial addiction, grief and loss, adjustment to foster care, adoption, living with parents who are HIV positive or who are sick with AIDS, and others. Social skills, sibling, and problem-solving groups are also conducted. Treatment duration varies from eight to twenty sessions depending on the group theme and the participants' level of ego organization. Generally groups composed of children who are better organized meet for more sessions. The Family Center assumes that children will participate sequentially in two or more groups. Each subsequent group addresses a different traumatic experience relevant to the children's trauma history and is developmentally more demanding of the participants.

Our experience at the Family Center confirms the observation (Rice-Smith, 1993) that when children who have experienced a common trauma are placed in groups together, the groups quickly become cohesive, and the members can be helped to reveal something about the trauma they have experienced, with the result that they feel less stigmatized and less guilty. Although the Family Center groups are also designed to help children recover from trauma, they seek as well to enhance ego organization and ego functioning by helping the members move progressively through the subphases of separation-individuation, while concurrently mastering the challenges inherent in group participation, as the group as a whole evolves through beginning, middle, and ending stages of development.

Both group process mastery, and subphase development are promoted through carefully planned activities designed to help the members (1) feel safe; (2) better understand and empathize with each other; (3) within emotionally tolerable limits, discuss aspects of their common traumas; (4) discuss relevant aspects of their family and living situations; (5) learn to play cooperatively; (6) develop a sense of group identity; (7) deal verbally with interpersonal conflicts; (8) progress toward recognizing and accepting the ways in which each of them is a distinct person, similar to but also different from the others; (9) to the degree they are developmentally ready to do so, individuate and move toward more autonomous functioning; and (10) end the group and say goodbye to each other in an appropriate, affectively meaningful way.

Because all potential group members have been so severely traumatized, referral to group treatment is made after a period of individual treatment during which the children establish (or reestablish) their capacity for positive attachment to a dependable, nontraumatizing, need-gratifying caregiver. In addition to providing opportunities to rework separation-individuation subphase inadequacies and to modify negative self-representations, group treatment also promotes positive attachments to peers, thus laying the groundwork for meaningful friendships outside the group, in foster families, at school, and in the larger community.

The Physical Environment and the Therapist's Role

Although this first principle should be self-evident, it seems prudent to begin by saying that treatment rooms should be designed specifically for children's groups. At the Family Center, the group therapy rooms comfortably accommodate eight or nine children, have one-way mirrors for observers, and are equipped with child-sized chairs and tables. A kitchen area adjoins each group room to facilitate preparing and serving snacks. The therapist is responsible for providing play and craft equipment and for initiating activities. Groups are tightly structured, particularly during the beginning stage of treatment. The therapist actively intervenes both behaviorially and interpretatively to ensure safety, mediate disputes, encourage discussion, and promote cohesion. A senior clinical supervisor is on call during all group meetings. The supervisor supports the therapist, reinforces the group rules, and talks individually with children who have to leave the group temporarily because of anxiety or acting out.

These structures establish some assurance of predictability and safety. They are reinforced in the groups by clearly articulated safety rules that prohibit fighting and verbal abuse and encourage confidentiality and regular attendance. The rules provide fundamental guidelines that are necessary to help members trust each other and the leader(s). They also support the development of more functional interpersonal boundaries. The therapist's active commitment to maintaining rules and other aspects of the group structure assures clients that their aggressive behavior, thoughts, and fantasies will not the destroy the group and will be contained within the process (Pfeifer, 1992).

The Treatment Contract

A formal treatment contract is an essential component of the group structure. By clearly stating the purpose of the group in preaffiliation interviews, as well as at the beginning of each group session, the therapist provides a basis for a group-as-a-whole treatment contract. Since the individual members' contracts interlock with a preestablished group contract, the focus of treatment is clearly articulated for both the therapist and the children. When treatment begins, the therapist's interventions are guided by his or her understanding of each client's personal goals as they relate to the overall group contract. The preaffiliation interview establishes a relationship between the therapist and each child and allows the therapist to anticipate behavior problems and other treatment-destructive resistances (Rosenthal, 1987) that might arise. The preaffiliation interview not only makes it possible to screen individual members in terms of their suitability for a particular group, but also allows the therapist to assess the psychological needs and vulnerabilities each member brings to the group experience.

CLINICAL EXAMPLE 1

A group for preteen girls from addicted families was resistant to talking about themselves during check-in time. However, they adhered to the group contract by writing their concerns on a blackboard. The leader read their concerns, individually acknowledging each member's concerns and encouraging the members to do so as well. Toward the latter part of the middle phase of treatment, the youngest member, Tenesha, wrote on the board, "My mother has AIDS." Initially the members were anxious about discussing the subject, but after the leader encouraged active listening and restated the purpose of the group (to learn and understand the feelings that accompany growing up in a family where a caregiver abuses substances), the other members shared some of their own concerns about caregivers and were able to comfort Tenesha.

In considering this vignette, keep in mind that the female therapist knew from her preaffiliation interviews with each group member that the parents of other children were also HIV positive. Based on that knowledge, she used the group-as-a-whole contract to remind the members that all of them had parents who abused substances and that all of them had agreed in advance to try to understand one another's feelings. By reminding the members of the contract and by recognizing and responding empathetically to the members' anxiety, the therapist reduced the group's anxiety, encouraged self-revelation, and elicited empathy for Tenesha, who initially was at serious risk of being scapegoated. If the therapist had not interviewed every member individually before the group started, she would not have understood the reasons Tenesha's revelation had evoked such an intense response in the other children and would have had no basis for determining how she might intervene helpfully.

Defensive Organization

In psychoeducational groups for traumatized children, anxiety, regression, and transference enactments are usually contained by a structure that emphasizes preplanned group activities and carefully orchestrated group discussions focused on specific themes that the therapist introduces and monitors. Typically behavior in such groups is maintained within reasonable limits in much the way behavior is regulated in emotionally responsive classroom situations. In groups designed to advance ego organization, these structures are not utilized in the same way. In the Family Center groups, we anticipate that problematic patterns of defense, interpersonal conflicts, and transference reenactments will occur and be worked through in some form during the course of treatment. While we give careful thought to limiting the extent and intensity of these phenomena based on what we think the members of a specific group can deal with constructively, we are prepared to recognize and address a wide range of dysfunctional behavior during the course of each time-limited group. From our perspective, working through is the component of the treatment process most likely to produce meaningful changes in ego organization and object relationships. For that reason, it is useful to consider how traumatized children defend themselves and how those defenses are played out in the group process.

Viktor Frankl, the existential analyst, is reported to have said, "An abnormal reaction to an abnormal situation is normal." Faced with repeated, severe neglect and abuse from the very people who are supposed to care for them, traumatized children react in ways that appear to be abnormal until their predicament is understood. In addressing the twin issues of survival and meaningful attachment, traumatized children develop unique coping and defensive strategies that alter the way they view themselves, the world, and their significant objects (Rieker & Carmen, 1986). Typically they employ multiple layers of reality-distorting defenses (Vaillant, 1992). These include but are not limited to splitting, denial, projective identification, somatization, hypervigilance (with paranoid overtones), pathological omnipotence, and dissociation. Because these defenses work by distorting reality, they also undermine judgment, impulse control, and the capacity to modulate affect. Moreover, they affect body image, disrupt progressive cognitive and emotional development, and interfere with object attachments outside the abusive family environment.

In addition to compromising ego functioning, reality-distorting defenses have a profoundly disruptive effect on interpersonal relationships. Their negative impact is particularly apparent in social environments (e.g., school, church, recreational programs) that are not (as) dangerous as the original, traumatizing family environments. The degree to which these defenses are interpersonally problematic can be briefly but effectively illustrated by considering denial and splitting.

At the level of intrapsychic functioning, denial literally wipes out any perception or recognition of danger originating in the external world, thus "protecting" the child from being overwhelmed by anxiety. When enacted interpersonally, the danger the child is defending against tends to surface as anxiety in the object, who feels as if his or her reality testing has been challenged. As a result, adult interactions with children who, for example, having been battered by their parents deny that their parents have done anything to harm them, tend to revolve around what is "true" and what is not, often provoking considerable anxiety and anger in the adult. If the adult cannot tolerate these feelings and does not understand them, he or she may attempt to change the child's view of reality. If this is done forcefully, the child begins to feel emotionally battered. In such interactions, the adult cannot win, and the child inevitably loses, at least emotionally.

At the level of intrapsychic functioning, splitting allows the child to preserve a defensively valued, internalized representation of a good object by projecting anger and other "bad" feelings onto some object in the external world. From an interpersonal perspective, splitting requires that there be a "bad" as well as a "good" object in every interaction. In trying to establish relationships with children who use splitting as a primary defense, helpers have a limited number of choices. At the level of unconscious meaning, they can ally with the child against some persecutory third party, who thereby becomes the "bad object." They can themselves become the "bad object," thereby undermining their attempts to be helpful but allowing the child to maintain a precarious, positive self-representation. Or they can allow themselves to be inducted into the role of "good object," thereby unwittingly supporting the child's view of himself or herself as the "bad" object—a person unworthy of love or care. For children in out-of-home placements, this last variation is commonplace. It preserves the fantasy, no matter how unrealistic, that if they will only behave better, they will be reunited with their biological parents, who will love and care for them.

In treatment groups, therapists must constantly guard against the destructive interpersonal ramifications of reality-distorting defenses when they are enacted as part of the group process. Without citing additional examples, it is sufficient to say that projective identification, dissociation, somatization, and the need to assert omnipotent control all have equally problematic, albeit different, effects on interpersonal relationships, and therefore on the treatment process in groups.

The next example illustrates denial and omnipotent control enacted through a group-as-a-whole fantasy.

CLINICAL EXAMPLE 2

Toward the end of an early session, four group members used mats, chairs, and a table spontaneously to create a "kid's city" where no adults, the leader included, were allowed. The children claimed to be self-sufficient, saying they needed no money and could walk into any toy or food store and simply take what they wanted. Somewhat later in the session, one member suggested that they may need love and care from special grown-ups. Two other members quickly disagreed, insisting they did not need anything from adults.

In this vignette, one member tentatively challenged the denial and assertion of omnipotent control implicit in this shared fantasy. While his challenge had no immediate effect on the other members, as the process progressed, the group members gradually acknowledged that adult caregivers are important to them and that their birth parents and their foster parents had sometimes disappointed them. In this instance, the therapist had been wise not to challenge the members' originally stated view of reality. The therapist had noted that the fantasy was constructed in the context of the care, protection, and supplies she was reliably providing for the group. She realized that the members' denial of need temporarily defended them against the danger implicit in acknowledging that she was becoming a meaningful, need-gratifying object to them, unlike their biological parents. For them to acknowledge their need and her reliability at that stage of the group process would have made it necessary for them to acknowledge their parents' failures and their anger toward their parents.

Repetition Compulsion and Identification with the Aggressor

To complicate the treatment process, cumulatively and repetitively traumatized children also employ repetition compulsion and identification with the aggressor to reinforce their other defenses. As a result, they frequently reenact traumatogenic interactions over and over again, either masochistically by inviting others to scapegoat them or sadistically by victimizing other children as they had themselves been victimized. Since most traumatized children have not achieved a level of ego organization that allows them to make constructive use of interpretation, it is necessary for group therapists to develop interactive, cognitive, and experiential interventions that contain transferential reenactments, modify maladaptive defense mechanisms, and promote progressive emotional development. The following example illustrates repetition compulsion and identification with the aggressor as enacted in the group process. The therapist's role in restoring a sense of safety to both an individual member and to the group as a whole is illustrated.

CLINICAL EXAMPLE 3

John, a nine-year-old boy who had experienced severe neglect, physical abuse, and abandonment, maintained a defensive stance in which he reacted aggressively to peers and adults. His aggression functioned to reduce his fear of being victimized, but led him to misperceive social cues. He regularly interpreted benign acts as threats. In the middle phase of group treatment, John asked another member, Jason, to pass a red marker. When Jason did not respond immediately, John became very angry and began to make provocative statements. A few moments later, Jason pushed the marker across the table, an act that John interpreted as a threat. John said, "You want to fight me." Jason immediately responded by becoming angry, and the leaders had to restrain him physically to avoid a physical fight.

Family Dynamics and Self-Blame

Cumulatively traumatized children, like all other children, need nurturance, care, and protection from reliable adults. This need presents them with an agonizing dilemma. Because they cannot care for themselves emotionally even when they can care for themselves physically, to some degree, they have no choice but to maintain a positive internal representation of a primary caregiver who in their minds loves them, when in actual experience, their biological caregivers have injured them, exploited them, neglected them, or perhaps abandoned them entirely (Weiss, 1993).

For these reasons, cumulative traumatization distorts positive attachments to primary objects and interferes with the development of object constancy. Due to the birth family's inability to support attachment and the child's movement through the subphases of separation-individuation, traumatized children do not develop effective ways of soothing themselves and cannot integrate positive and negative self- and object representations into coherent, whole object representations (Hahn,

1993; Mahler, Pine, & Bergman, 1975). Abusive family environments demand that child victims deny their own needs to accommodate the needs of adult caregivers, "disconfirm" reality as they perceive it, and accept parental judgment and beliefs regarding the reasons for the abuse. Thus, victims are denied an accurate understanding of the abusive experience, their true feelings about the abuse, and the particular meaning the abuse has for them (Rieker & Carmen, 1986). These family dynamics, combined with separation-individuation subphase inadequacies and reliance on reality-distorting defenses, make it difficult for abused children to comprehend who is responsible for their maltreatment. Typically they believe they caused their maltreatment by being "bad," an unconscious attitude that "restores an illusion of control" and reduces feelings of helplessness (Rieker, 1986).

In treatment groups, the holding environment must help these children contain bad feelings about themselves without acting on them. Over time, the group process should also help members verbalize some feelings of hurt, sadness, disappointment, and anger in relation to primary caregivers (see Clinical example 5).

Peer Culture and the Holding Environment

In constructing groups for particular populations of children, the therapist's most essential task is to establish an appropriate holding environment. What is appropriate varies considerably depending on the children's age and the nature of their emotional problems. Cumulatively and repetitively traumatized children not only suffer from deficits in ego organization but enter group treatment assuming that the group will replicate the peer culture they have experienced on the streets (Pfeifer, 1992). Their expectation then is that the group will also be violent, exploitative, depriving, unpredictable, and ruthlessly dominated by its strongest members. This expectation and the life experience that reinforces it make the task of creating a therapeutic holding environment particularly challenging. Effective treatment requires a holding environment organized around nurturance, safety, and carefully controlled opportunities for self-expression. Group structures that contain anxiety, regression, aggression, and acting out are essential. Planned activities should foster attachment and peer interaction while providing opportunities for skill building. Therapists should actively establish the treatment contract, set limits, address the needs of individual members, and organize structured activities that the members will enjoy but do not encourage regression or decompensation.

Once established, the holding environment allows the group members to anticipate that their needs will be met by an attuned and caring adult. In functioning as the group's auxiliary ego, the therapist provides nonjudgmental acceptance, as well as actual and symbolic nurturance. The therapist also facilitates and clarifies communications within the group, actively working toward reinforcing intrapsychic and interpersonal boundaries. When an appropriate holding environment has been established for the group as a whole, the members can begin to feel safe, taken care of, and understood as individuals. The group as a whole can then move toward cohesiveness and its new identity as a constructed, functional, symbolic family.

The following example illustrates the therapists' active role in maintaining the holding environment and in making sure that the group will symbolically represent an inclusive family system that does not scapegoat or expel its members. In this interaction, the therapists affirm that adults protect children. They take responsibility for mediating interpersonal conflicts and address Albert's individual dynamics by emphasizing that it is the grown-ups' job to keep everyone in the group safe. By doing so they take an important step toward correcting the members' transferentially based assumptions about adult caregivers.

CLINICAL EXAMPLE 4

In the first fifteen minutes of the first group meeting, a nine-year-old boy, Albert, successfully replicated his familial role by positioning himself to be the group scapegoat. He quickly provoked everyone in the group, repeatedly disrupting the Name Ball game by intercepting passes to other members. His response to the leaders' limits and his peers' annoyance was to flee from the room. The next week Albert again disrupted the group by interfering with an activity. The members teased and ridiculed him, and again he fled. When he returned to the group, the leaders said they needed to work harder to keep the group a safe place for everyone and that it was the grown-ups' job to help keep everyone's feelings and bodies safe. The members spontaneously apologized for ridiculing Albert, and he visibly relaxed. In subsequent sessions he was much less provocative and more positively connected to the other group members.

The therapists had intervened by interrupting the group's attempt to reenact the victim-aggressor roles members had experienced with primary caregivers. In doing so they made it clear that it was their responsibility to keep the environment safe and that they would adhere to their role as protective caregivers. By insisting that it was their job to keep the group safe, the therapists had taken an important step toward modifying the members' transferential assumption that caregivers blame children for whatever goes wrong, whether in group treatment or in their abusive families.

Cohesion, Therapeutic Culture, and Differentiation

Once structure and the holding environment have been established, the groundwork is set for building group identity and cohesion. Group cohesion offers the members a mutually valued frame of reference (Pfeifer, 1992). In facilitating the development of a positive group identity, the leaders use activities that promote cooperation, mutual problem solving, verbal and symbolic communication, improved impulse control and greater frustration tolerance. As social skills improve, members and therapist(s) together create a new group culture that accepts and encourages individuation. The members gradually recognize and tolerate the ways in which each of them is unique and in which each differs from the others. They begin to accept their differences without feeling that difference in another threatens their own painstakingly constructed sense of self.

A particular benefit of group treatment is the group's ability to meet dependency needs while supporting autonomous functioning. In group therapy, cohesion involves "being on the same wavelength" as the other members, while simultaneously expressing oneself as a unique and distinct individual who is accepted within a "mutually valued frame of reference"—a corrective, symbolic family system (Pfeifer, 1992, p. 361).

CLINICAL EXAMPLE 5

A group of preteen boys comprised of seven African American and two white clients. In the second session, during activity time, the older and bigger of the two white members, John, started scapegoating the only other white client, Bob. The activity was to color a picture of a professional basketball player. Bob correctly colored the player's skin brown, and John said: "What! Just because he's a basketball player you think he's black?" Bob was thrown off guard and stammered, trying to defend himself. John accused Bob of being a "white racist" and stated that he hated people like him. The seven other members, all of whom were African American, initially were thrown off guard by the outburst. After a few moments, however, they began to discuss the importance of getting along regardless of racial differences. The leaders stated their puzzlement about what was happening between the two white members, stating that everyone in the room knew the basketball player was African American. They asked whether the group was really wondering whether they could get along together and care about each other even though they were different. Then John mumbled quietly, "Well, my mother doesn't care about me." Bob said, "My mother doesn't care either." The members stopped making accusatory statements, and the leaders asked if this group could work together and learn to care about each other, even if the guys did not always feel their families cared about them.

As cohesion builds, the nurturing, positive aspects of the group experience are internalized as good object representations. Individual members learn to "rely on characteristics of the group-as-a-whole as a holding self-object through which object constancy can be achieved" (Hahn, 1993, p. 225). Having internalized some aspects of the group holding environment, the members began to modify problematic behavior patterns. As they become better able to tolerate painful affects, the use of reality-distorting defenses decreases. The group holding environment provides a safe, transitional space in which the members can progress toward object constancy, individuation, and a coherent sense of personal identity (Takahashi, 1992).

CLINICAL EXAMPLE 6

A group of preteen boys were talking about how they frequently fight in school. They also stated their belief that the fights started because others picked on them. The therapists asked them how they were able to get along when they were in the group. The internal leader responded: "We are cool with each other." Other members said: "Yeah, we see each other every Tuesday." This interaction happened during the middle phase of treatment. After the group members had confirmed their connectedness, they were able to confront gently the internal leader's regressive and impulsive behaviors in the group by signaling him verbally and nonverbally to "be cool."

Stages of Group Treatment: Separation-Individuation

During the beginning, middle, and ending stages of group treatment, process parallels both the subphases of separation-individuation and the stages of recovery from trauma. Attunement to these parallel processes allows therapists to predict phase-specific behaviors and developmental challenges for both individual members and for the group as a whole. Group therapists attempt to provide the conditions that make it possible for the members to address separation-individuation subphase deficits. The first task is to promote positive attachments among individual members and toward the group as a whole. The second is to contain acting out and prevent retraumatization. The third is to help the members better understand one another's feelings and life situations. And the fourth is to support the members in becoming separate yet connected—individuated but still positively attached to each other, and to the group.

Table 10.1 illustrates how children in group therapy address the subphases of separation-individuation during the beginning, middle, and ending stages of group development. The progression is from thwarted dependency toward individuation in the context of group relatedness.

TABLE 10.1

Stages of Group Treatment: Separation-Individuation Process 1

Beginning	*Middle*	*Ending*
Will my basic needs be met?	Am I unique or special?	Can I care about myself and others?
Can I form attachments?	Will the group contain my feelings and behaviors?	
Will I be protected?	Can I belong to the group even if I have bad thoughts or act out?	Can I exist separately and still belong to the group?

Table 10.2 illustrates the stages of recovery from trauma during the beginning, middle, and ending phases of group development.

TABLE 10.2

Stages of Group Treatment: Recovery from Trauma

Beginning	*Middle*	*Ending*
Am I safe?	Am I intact?	Can I feel okay about myself and still relate to others?
Is the environment predictable?	Can I count on people to listen and follow through when I ask for help?	
I am "bad." Will I be punished, mistreated, or rejected?		Can I learn to trust?
	Will adults maintain their roles?	Can I learn to keep myself safe with help of trusted peers and adults?

The Beginning Stage of Group Development

During the first phase of treatment, trust and consistency are established as emotional needs are gratified. Traumatized children demonstrate extreme caution in relating to peers and therapists. Typically they have difficulty managing anxiety, controlling impulses, and behaving appropriately. Although the great majority want to adhere to rules that ensure safety, repeated interventions are needed to help them manage their behavior and develop attachments to each other, the leader, and the group as a whole. Members often jockey for position and take roles that provide insight into their object relations, family experiences, and how they view the world. In relating to the therapist(s), individual children may be demanding, clingy, oppositional, mistrustful, fearful, aggressive, or some combination, depending on development, family experiences, and intrapsychic organization.

CLINICAL EXAMPLE 7

In the first phase of a latency-age boys' group, one of the members, Mark, was disruptive and sought the leaders' attention in negative ways. The leaders responded by talking about how in this group there was room for everyone to be special and for everyone to be cared about in a special way. Mark reduced his negative attention-seeking behaviors for the remainder of that activity, but needed repeated reassurance about being special and cared for throughout the remainder of that and subsequent sessions. Over time, Mark moved from one-to-one interactions with the leaders, to parallel play with peers, to preliminary explorations of cooperative play.

The Middle Stage

During the middle stage of treatment, group members begin to renegotiate the subphases of separation-individuation. The detrimental impact that trauma has had on their development is manifest in transferential reenactments of problematic relationships. Frightening and overwhelming emotions associated with sexuality, aggression, victimization, and unmet dependency needs surface. The group members typically respond by behaving aggressively or threatening to flee from the group. They may also become oppositional and extremely demanding. Historically these coping strategies have helped them manage overwhelming anxiety and real-life threats. In group, however, the strategies that helped them cope in their families are problematic and at times dangerous.

Therapists are challenged to avoid symbolically or actually reenacting internalized, abusive object relations. If they do not succeed, they perpetuate the child's belief that the world is dangerous and that adults will be unable or unwilling to provide protection. When reenactments take place, the group members become very anxious and are flooded with terrifying memories of abuse (Gallagher et al., 1995). Depending on individual personality organization, intense anxiety will make members dissociate, regress to more primitive stages of development, lose some capacity for reality testing and judgment, flee from the group, or act out aggressively. Because of their vulnerability, group members almost always welcome structured activities and nonpunitive limit setting, even when they complain. Such interventions ameliorate feelings of uncertainty and anxiety that therapists and group members predictably experience during the middle stage of treatment.

CLINICAL EXAMPLE 8

During week 6 of a twelve-week group, Sam, the peer leader of a boys' group, ages eleven to thirteen, fluctuated between regressive and pseudomature behaviors. He persistently teased members by saying they had to buy their food on welfare cards. The leaders adhered to the structured activity that focused on building cooperation. After the activity, Sam led a discussion about relationships with parents and girlfriends, and the group was able to discuss questions they had about sex. The therapists' and the members' refusal to be diverted from the structured activity by Sam's provocative and disruptive behavior provided the ego support necessary for the members to negotiate worrisome feelings related to intimacy and differentiation. Although the manifest process provided no explicit clues, it is interesting to speculate on the unconscious connection between Sam's projections about mothers' buying food on welfare cards and the anxiety about sexuality and intimacy that ultimately emerged in the group discussion.

The Ending Stage

While the middle stage of group development is likely to present leaders with their most difficult clinical challenges, the ending stage often produces the greatest rewards for clients and therapists alike. When the group has successfully moved into the ending stage, a basic level of trust and acceptance has developed. The members are better able to communicate verbally with each other and with the leaders, are more tolerant of each others' differences, and are more respectful of interpersonal boundaries. During this stage of treatment the members themselves are invested in maintaining a safe environment, an important achievement for children who have been severely and persistently abused.

As groups move toward termination, if treatment has been "good enough," the members have internalized the rules and structure of the group, as well as positive representations of the therapist(s), peers, and the group as a whole. They are better able to discuss subjects that had previously been taboo because they provoked so much anxiety and take increased responsibility for participating constructively in group activities. They can also verbalize wishes and needs they previously would have acted on, reflect more thoughtfully about their individual treatment goals, and accept positive reinforcement from therapists for their attempts to act maturely.

In the ending stage, the members no longer equate the pain of separateness with something bad or evil about themselves (Hahn, 1993). They openly express pleasure in being with one another and in playing together. They also have more energy to expend on mastering new social skills and experimenting with more adaptive behaviors. While cumulatively and repetitively traumatized children in group treatment benefit to different degrees, many find that the group experience increases their capacity to look to others as possible helpers and teaches them ways of better protecting themselves from retraumatization. To the degree these psychological changes are internalized (and reasonably well supported by the environments in which they live), reality-distorting defenses become less prominent, learning in group environments (e.g., school, recreational centers) becomes less conflictual, periods of hypervigilance correspond more closely with realistic danger, and sustaining, collaborative relationships with peers and adults become possible. These changes support the group members' gradual, progressive development through the subphases of separation-individuation and encourage realistic feelings of hope for the future.

CONCLUSION

In the first part of this chapter we reviewed a number of children's group therapy models that provide treatment for children with different levels of character pathology. An expanded version of Winnicott's concept of the holding environment was utilized to frame the process of creating specific group structures. Practice reports confirm the hypothesis that group structure is malleable and can therefore be readily adapted to meet the development needs of specific groups of children. For this reason, the structure of any group can be organized to address targeted, problematic deficits in ego functioning. Groups organized according to these principles provide effective compensatory treatment and promote progressive ego development for children at different points along the developmental continuum.

The second part of this chapter describes a model of ego-enhancing group treatment for cumulatively traumatized children from an impoverished, inner-city environment. Although the theory and techniques presented are tailored to a particular population of children, they are generalizable to less severely traumatized populations. The treatment model provides a useful alternative to psychoeducational groups because it is designed to promote recovery from trauma and to strengthen ego functioning. Extensive clinical experience at the Family Center suggests that children assigned sequentially to two or more time-limited groups gradually internalize the gains they have made in ego organization and object relations, and over time, they develop reasonably effective strategies for preventing retraumatization.

This innovative treatment model, although time limited in design, is congruent with the traditional body of long-term, developmentally oriented, experiential children's group therapy. By creating different holding environments and group structures based on the members' level of ego organization and their progress toward recovery, the model provides effective differential treatment focused on repairing ego functioning and promoting ego integration.

REFERENCES

Anthony, E. J. (1971). Group-analytic psychotherapy with children and adolescents. In Foulkes, S. H., and Anthony, E. J., *Group Psychotherapy* (Chapter 8, pp. 186–232).

Axline, V. (1947). *Play therapy*. Boston: Houghton Mifflin.

Gallagher, M., Leavitt, K. S., & Kimmel, H. P. (1995). Mental health treatment of cumulatively traumatized children. *Smith College Studies in Social Work, 65*(3).

Gallagher, M., Love, B., & Kimmel, H. (1993). *Using therapeutic verbalizations to alter the inter-*

nalized world of the traumatized child. Presented at the Tenth Annual International Play Therapy Conference, Atlanta.

Gaines, T. Jr. (1986). Applications of child group psychotherapy. In A. Riester and I. Kraft (Eds.), *Child Group Psychotherapy: Future Tense.* Madison, CT: International Universities Press.

Ganter, Grace, Yeakel, M., & Polansky, N. (1967). *Retrieval from limbo.* New York: Child Welfare League of America.

Garland, J. A. (1992). The establishment of individual and collective competency in children's groups as a prelude to entry into intimacy, disclosure, and bonding. *International Journal of Group Psychotherapy, 42*(3), 395–405.

Ginnott, H. (1961). *Group psychotherapy with children.* New York: McGraw-Hill.

Hahn, W. K. (1993). Developing object constancy in group psychotherapy. *International Journal of Group Psychotherapy, 43*(2), 223–235.

Kates, W., and Iams, R. (1992). *Characteristics of children in treatment at the Family Center (KKFC).* Unpublished paper.

Kauff, P. (1977). The termination process: Its relationship to the separation-individuation phase of development. *International Journal of Group Psychotherapy, 27(1)*, 3–18.

Kraft, I. A. (1967). Children's group therapy. In A. M. Friedman & H. I. Kaplan (Eds.), *The comprehensive textbook of psychiatry* (p. 1463). Baltimore: Williams & Wilkins.

Kraft, I. A. (1983). Personal communication to Gerald Schamess.

Mahler, M. Pine, F., & Bergman, A. (1975). *The psychological birth of the human infant.* New York: Basic Books.

Ogden, T. H. (1982). *Projective identification and psychotherapeutic technique.* New York: Jason Aronson.

Pfeifer, G. (1992). Complementary cultures in children's psychotherapy groups: Conflict, coexistence, and convergence in group development. *International Journal of Group Psychotherapy, 42*(3), 357–367.

Rice-Smith, E. (1993). Group psychotherapy with sexually abused children. In H. I. Kaplan & B. J. Sadock (Eds.), *Comprehensive group therapy* (3rd ed.). Baltimore: Williams & Wilkins.

Rieker, P. P., & Carmen, E. (1986). The victim-to-patient process: The disconfirmation and transformation of abuse. *American Journal of Orthopsychiatry, 56*(3), 360–369.

Rogers, C. (1942). *Counseling and psychotherapy.* Boston: Houghton Mifflin.

Rosenberg-Hariton, J., Kernberg, P. F., & Chazen, S. E. (1991). Play group psychotherapy. In P. F. Kernberg & S. E. Chazen (Eds.), *Children with conduct disorders: A psychotherapy manual.* New York: Basic Books.

Rosenthal, L. (1987). *Resolving resistance in group psychotherapy.* Northvale, NJ: Jason Aronson.

Schamess, G. (1986). Differential diagnosis and group structure in the outpatient treatment of latency age children. In A. E. Riester and I. A. Kraft (Eds.), *Child group psychotherapy: Future tense.* Madison, CT: International Universities Press.

Schamess, G. (1993). *Projective identification and countertransference.* Presented at the Smith College School for Social Work, 75th Anniversary Celebration and Conference, Northampton, MA.

Scheidlinger, S. (1960). Experiential group treatment of severely deprived latency-age children. *American Journal of Orthopsychiatry, 30(3)*, 356–368.

Scheidlinger, S. (1965). Three group approaches with socially deprived latency-age children. *International Journal of Group Psychotherapy, 15(4)*, 434–445.

Scheidlinger, S. (1974). On the concept of the "mother-group." *International Journal of Group Psychotherapy, 24(4)*, 417–428.

Schiffer, M. (1969). *The Therapeutic Play Group.* New York: Grune and Stratton.

Schiffer, M., & Slavson, S. (1984). *Children's group therapy: Methods and case histories.* New York: Free Press.

Slavson, S. R. (1943). *An Introduction to group therapy.* New York: International Universities Press.

Slavson, S. R., & Schiffer, M. (1975). *Group psychotherapies for children.* New York: International Universities Press.

Spinner, D. A. (1992). The evolution of culture and cohesion in the group treatment of ego impaired children. *International Journal of Group Psychotherapy, 42(3),* 369–382.

Sugar, M. (1974). Interpretive group psychotherapy with latency-age children. *Journal of the American Academy of Child Psychiatry, 13,* 648.

Takahashi, T. (1992). *Innovative techniques in object relations group psychotherapy.* Presented at the Fifth Annual Meeting of American Group Psychotherapy Association, New York.

Terr, L. C. (1991). Childhood traumas: An outline and overview. *American Journal of Psychiatry, 148,* 10–20.

Trafimow, E., & Pattak, S. (1981). Group psychotherapy and objectal development in children. *International Journal of Group Psychotherapy, 31(2),* 193–204.

Trafimow, E., & Pattak, S. (1982). Group treatment of primitively fixated children. *International Journal of Group Psychotherapy, 32(4),* 445–452.

Vaillant, G. E. (1992). *Ego mechanisms of defense: A guide for clinicians and researchers.* Washington, DC: American Psychiatric Press.

Weiss, J. (1993). *How therapy works: Process and technique.* New York: Guilford Press.

Winnicott, D. A. (1965). *The Maturational Processes and the Facilitating Environment.* New York: International Universities Press.

Winnicott, D. W. (1951). Transitional objects and transitional phenomena. In *Through pediatrics to psycho-analysis.* New York: Basic Books.

Winnicott, D. W. (1989). *Psychoanalytic explorations.* Ed. C. Winnicott, R. Shepherd, & M. Davis. Cambridge, MA: Harvard University Press.

11

Group Treatment with Adults

Charles D. Garvin

A variety of approaches are currently employed for group treatment of adults by social workers. Some workers have a preferred approach, while others draw on several approaches depending on the purpose of the group. The ways these workers act differ depending on the approach they have chosen, but there are also common elements.

PRACTICE MODELS FOR GROUP TREATMENT WITH ADULTS

Group work in social work did not start out with a variety of such models but rather started when people who were developing practice in certain community institutions in the latter part of the nineteenth and early twentieth centuries began to share their ideas with each other. Examples of these institutions were settlement houses, Jewish Community Centers, and YM/YWCAs, and some of the people were Jane Addams, Grace Coyle, Gertrude Wilson, and Clara Kaiser. The ideas of these group work pioneers related to how to help people, primarily in the inner city, through the processes of mutual aid. These group work pioneers were also interested in helping people learn and use democratic processes in groups to enable them to cope with their circumstances as well as to achieve changes in their environments.

These pioneers did not think of their method as group therapy, but in the 1950s and early 1960s a number of group workers in social work began to test the use of group work method in psychotherapy settings (Konopka, 1949; NASW, 1960). This type of application rapidly spread to other institutions such as prisons, schools, hospitals, family agencies, and child welfare organizations in which social workers offered various forms of treatment. This expansion of the settings in which group work methods were employed was associated with an expansion in the therapeutic approaches *employed.*

The Mediational Model

The creation of this model is usually attributed to William Schwartz (Schwartz, 1994), although it has undergone considerable development by Alex Gitterman and Lawrence Shulman (Gitterman & Shulman, 1994). These authors pay great attention to the processes that occur among members and between members and workers as these people seek to develop authentic and mutually beneficial relationships. Serious attention is paid to the feelings members and workers experience in this process. This approach seeks to be systemic in that the various relevant systems are taken into consideration by the worker who acts as a mediator between these systems. As Schwartz states:

> We would suggest that the general assignment for the social work profession is to mediate the process through which the individual and his society reach out for each other through a mutual need for self-fulfillment. This presupposes a relationship between the individual and his nurturing group which we would describe as "symbiotic"—each needing the other for its own life and growth, and each reaching out to the other with all the strength it can command at a given moment. The social worker's field of intervention lies at the point where two forces meet: the individual's impetus toward health, growth, and belonging; and the organized efforts of society to integrate its parts into a productive and dynamic whole. (Schwartz, 1994, pp. 263–264).

The Remedial Model

This model developed out of the work of Robert Vinter and his colleagues at the University of Michigan. The collection of articles edited by Sundel, Glasser, Sarri, and Vinter (1985) presents a comprehensive view of this model. The model is directed at situations in which the individual member is the focus of change; the group is described as the "means and context" of such change. This approach sharply contrasts with that of Schwartz in its strong emphasis on the establishment of individual treatment goals with each member. These goals are to be precise and operational by design, and the worker helps the members to utilize group processes most likely to help them achieve these goals.

This model also requires that workers seek evidence of effectiveness of the interventions they utilize through a search of the research literature, as well as through an examination of their own practice outcomes. In their search for validation of the model, writers have explored phases of group development (Sarri & Galinsky, 1985), the operation of different group processes (Garvin, 1985), the differential use of program activities (Vinter, 1985), and the worker's intervention in the social environment (Garvin et al., 1985).

The Task-Centered Model

This model of social work practice was originally developed by Reid and Epstein (1972), although the group application was first presented by Garvin (1974). Subsequent to this early paper, a number of articles have reported developments in task-centered group work. One of the latest and most detailed of these may be found in Tolson, Reid, and Garvin (1994).

The task-centered approach sees the group as helping members to select and carry out activities to reach their goals. These activities, referred to as tasks, are created by each group member by drawing on other group members for assistance. The group members subsequently help one another to carry out their tasks. This help may be offered in the form of group problem solving to assist members in overcoming barriers to task accomplishment, support to members in accomplishing tasks, and offering members an opportunity to practice their tasks in the group through role plays and other simulations.

Feminist and Other Models for Member Empowerment

The field of social work has recently introduced the goal of empowerment as one that should be considered in all social work practice, including clinical practice. This goal is particularly relevant when the group members are oppressed by social conditions. People of color, women, gay men or lesbians, and people with disabilities are likely to fall into this category. Several group work writers have described models for this kind of practice (Garvin, 1996; Gutierrez, 1990; Lee, 1994).

Empowerment models in group work stress the following:

1. The members must have an opportunity to exercise significant influence on all phases of the group work process. This influence must start with the decision as to the kinds of groups that agencies will offer and who will be recruited as members and workers. Also included are the ways the group will be facilitated, how the group experience will be evaluated, and when the group will end.
2. The members should be helped not only to work to change themselves but to change their oppressive circumstances.
3. Members may have difficulty deciding on group conditions, change goals, and change methods unless they are helped to attain a critical consciousness (Freire, 1973). This means they are helped to understand the forces that maintain their oppressive social circumstances and whether these forces occur in their own situations.

Very recently, work has been done to develop feminist models of group work, and these are relevant to empowerment objectives (Garvin & Reed, 1995). Feminist group work models draw on feminist theories that deal with how societies deny power to women as compared to men, how the needs and views of women are not represented in social work models, and how many concepts are "gendered" in the sense that women are depreciated, often subtly, by theories and terms that are widely employed. Feminist group work models identify ways that members of groups are oppressed because of their gender and how workers and members can help each other to identify and seek to change sources of such oppression.

Group Psychotherapy Models

The group psychotherapy model emphasizes group procedures that facilitate the development of the members' self-understanding. This understanding includes how their behavior is experienced by others as well as how their thoughts and actions are determined by unconscious elements. The members are helped to use this understanding to explore ways of altering the way they behave within as well as outside the group. An important set of such procedures enables the members to examine processes occurring among each other as well as in the group as a whole. The focus in such an examination is on the relationship implications of interactions. An example is the feedback a member received when he offered advice to another member who saw him as seeking to control her.

The member's new self-understanding may be in areas of thought or feeling of which the member was not previously conscious; workers and members may make interpretations to each other of the meaning of behaviors in order to help bring this kind of understanding about. While social workers draw on the classic work of Yalom (1995), a psychiatrist, in their practice of group psychotherapy, there are also social work writers who have contributed to the understanding of group psychotherapy (Levine, 1979).

CHANGE THEORIES RELEVANT TO GROUP TREATMENT OF ADULTS

Group workers draw on one or more theories of change in considering how to engage in group treatment of adults.

Psychodynamic Theory

A number of theorists have written about group phenomena from a psychoanalytic perspective (Ezriel, 1973; Foulkes, 1965; Whitaker & Lieberman, 1965; Bion, 1959). Some of the ideas of these writers are summarized below:

1. Members of groups will identify common ideational and emotional reactions among themselves and direct their discussion to these. These often relate to individual drives and psychological states.
2. Reactions to therapists include both realistic elements and distortions determined by members' past experiences (i.e., transference).
3. Conflicts occur when a desire to fulfill individual needs gives rise to a fear of the consequences of striving to meet these needs, and these are often shared by members. The consensus reached as to the resolution of such conflicts may be compatible with the goals of group therapy or may hinder the resolution of both individual and group problems.

The task of the group worker operating within a psychodynamic framework is to promote an examination of these phenomena. Such an examination should help the worker to offer interpretations that enable the members to overcome barriers to change. These barriers come from the ideational and emotional reactions, transferences, and conflicts.

The work of Bion (1959) deserves special mention because of its widespread influence on psychodynamic group therapy, especially at the Tavistock Institute in London. Bion was psychoanalytically trained and then became interested in groups. One of his central propositions was that groups often avoid "work" through a set of processes he called "basic assumptions." These consist of dependence on the leader, fight-flight reactions, and some members' pairing off. These states and Bion's analysis of how they occur may be useful in determining why groups at times become mired down in unproductive activities.

Cognitive-Behavioral Theory

Behavioral theory seeks to add to our understanding of how external events (referred to as stimuli) create, maintain, or diminish individual behaviors (for a detailed discussion of this theory, see Martin & Pear, 1992). Cognitive-behavioral theory focuses on how thought processes play a role in the association between external events and behaviors. Cognitive-behavioral theorists insist that the validation of their theories should not depend on untested assumptions about people's thoughts and feelings but that these should be carefully identified through observations and measurements of observable phenomena.

Investigators interested in the application of cognitive-behavior theory to group situations, such as Rose and LeCroy (1991), pay attention to how group processes affect behaviors and cognitions. For example, group members imitate each other, and this process can be employed to help members acquire new behaviors. Members can also help each other to identify thoughts that hinder the acquisition of new behaviors, such as the ideas that one can never change or that one can never be liked by others. Members can also reinforce behaviors of others in the group who are trying to learn these behaviors.

Social Psychological and Small Group Theories

Undoubtedly the theories that are most universally drawn on by group workers are theories about how behavior is affected by interaction with others, especially in small groups. The broad behavioral science area into which these theories fall is that of social psychology. An important social psychological field of inquiry is role theory (Garvin, 1991). This field helps us understand how people act in social positions (e.g., student, parent, drug user) in response to the views others hold of such positions. Other important social-psychological theories of relevance to group work are attribution theory, social cognition theory (Nurius & Brower, 1993), and theories of interpersonal influence.

Small group theory itself illuminates many aspects of groups, such as group development, group structures, group processes, leadership, decision making, the evolution of norms in groups, scapegoating, the allocation of power in groups, and the relationship between group tasks and other group processes. Social workers have contributed a great deal to the development of small group theory (Garvin, 1987). Group workers also draw on many excellent texts written by social psychologists such as Forsyth (1990), Napier and Gershenfeld (1987), and Nixon (1979).

Ecological Theories

Group workers, like all other social workers, have largely come to think of their practice as informed by an ecological perspective in which the interdependence of individuals, groups, and larger social systems such as the organization and community is understood as the basis of practice (Germain & Gitterman, 1995). As Germain and Gitterman (1995) state:

> The ecological perspective makes clear the need to view people and environments as a unitary system within a particular cultural and historical context. Both person and environment can be fully understood only in terms of their relationship, in which each continually influences the other within a particular context. Hence, all concepts derived from the ecological metaphor refer not to environment alone or person alone; rather each concept expresses a particular person:environment relationship, whether it is positive, negative, or neutral. (In accord with the unitary view, person:environment relationships are designated by a colon, replacing the traditional hyphen, which visually fractures their connection.) (p. 816)

Therapeutic Factors

An important understanding of how groups benefit members stems from the idea of therapeutic factors—for example, installation of hope, universality (others are in the same boat), guidance from others, altruism (I can help others), learning from interpersonal action, vicarious learning (learning from the experiences of others), insight (learning important things about one's self), acceptance (accepting others in the group and being accepted by them), catharsis (release of emotions in the group), and self-disclosure. These factors have evolved out of the writing of several authors who have used a variety of research tools to ascertain the sources of therapeutic change in groups (Yalom, 1995; Bloch & Crouch, 1985). Elsewhere I have written about these factors as they apply to social work groups (Garvin, 1997).

THE ASSESSMENT PHASE

The term *assessment* rather than *diagnosis* is used because the group worker seeks an understanding of the nature of the client's problems and the conditions that either maintain these problems or that can be drawn on to ameliorate them. The term *diagnosis* is often more narrowly used to categorize the problem using some set of categories such as DSM-IV (American Psychiatric Association, 1995). Social workers with groups sometimes utilize such typologies in composing groups but find that an assessment process is the most useful one for group treatment aims such as the following:

1. To determine whether to recommend group treatment.
2. To determine, if group treatment is appropriate, the type of group to which the person should be referred.
3. To help the practitioner decide how to compose the group.
4. To help the practitioner and member to select appropriate treatment goals.

Whether to Recommend Group Treatment

This would be an easy determination if there was enough research evidence on the effectiveness of group treatment compared to family and individual approaches, but this is not the case (Toseland & Rivas, 1994, p. 19). Nevertheless, there are situations in which groups have advantages so that clients may be helped to realize they are not unique in their problems, to assist clients who wish to experiment with better ways of improving their relationships, for clients who seek to test their views of reality against the views of others, for clients who seek a place to practice behaviors, and for clients who wish to interact with peers in nonverbal ways by participating in activities. Toseland and Rivas (1994, pp. 467–468) sum up circumstances for referring people to groups as follows:

> Combined findings from the clinical and empirical literature suggest that social workers should consider recommending group treatment for individuals who suffer from isolation or who have other difficulties with interpersonal relationships, and individual treatment for those with highly personal psychological problems. Combinations of individual and group treatment appear to be effective for clients with both needs.

I disagree with Toseland and Rivas on the issue of people with highly personal problems since group work with such people has been effective when this is what they desire. Thus a major factor in recommending group treatment is that the individual accepts the idea of working on problems in a group. Groups, moreover, have been useful for individuals with the same range of problems dealt with in individual treatment.

The same view does not apply to family treatment because some family problems stem from current dysfunctional patterns best altered when workers interact with several or all family members simultaneously. Sometimes the other family members are not available. The group can be experienced by the individual in ways that are analogous to how she or he experiences the family. The group consequently becomes a place where family issues are identified and worked on. (It is also possible to form a group composed of some or all of the members of several families.)

Type of Group

There are many types of groups utilized for group treatment, and the worker must determine which is best for the client. However, it is not likely that all these types will be available, so the worker may choose one that is "second best" or even decide that it is not possible to offer group treatment at all.

Short Term (Time Limited) versus Long Term

A group might be scheduled to meet for a specified number of sessions over anywhere from one to four months. Alternatively, the group might meet for one or more years. The time-limited, short-term group usually focuses on a specific skill or problem such as parenting skills, preparing for retirement, planning for discharge from an institution, or learning how to relate to a family member recently diagnosed as suffering from a severe mental illness. The short-term group will often have an assigned topic for each meeting and a structured plan for the session itself. Clients who are not motivated to remain in the group for a long period of time or who see themselves as learning to cope with a specific issue often prefer such a group. In the current managed care environment, insurance companies and other providers often prefer this type of service.

A long-term group may meet for one or more years. Members often seek such an experience when they recognize that their problems in relating to others are deep seated and even obscure, and they wish to have the opportunity for a great deal of self-exploration based on feedback they receive in the group. Another form of long-term group is very different in that it has been designed to provide support to people who are severely disabled by their emotional problems and can remain in the community only when they receive such support. Sometimes such a group is even offered on a self-help basis in which the members themselves are in charge of all or most aspects of the group.

Open versus Closed

In some groups, the members begin and end the group at the same time, and these are referred to as closed groups. In other groups, members may enter and leave at different times, and these are open. A group with a structured program will usually be closed, while a group in which members work on relationship issues through an examination of interpersonal processes may be an open one. Clients who are referred to a closed group must wait until a group begins, and this can be a disadvantage to certain individuals who should have a group made immediately available to them.

Support versus Therapy

A distinction is often made between support groups and therapy groups. In support groups, members with similar issues provide empathy and encouragement to one another, as well as help in problem solving. In therapy groups, members explore thoughts and feelings (which may be beyond their awareness) in order to alter well-established patterns of behavior. A decision as to whether to refer a person to a support or a therapy group is based on the cllient's goals, motivation, capacity for in-depth exploration, and the nature of the problem.

The distinction between support groups and therapy groups may not be as meaningful a one as some writers contend. This is because workers are often unclear themselves as to what they mean when they advertise a group as support or therapy. It is also true that some inexperienced workers may call their groups "support" because they have not been adequately trained to offer group therapy. In addition, there are many examples of therapy in support groups and many elements of support in therapy group.

Assessment Approaches

The assessment of group members typically begins with an individual interview scheduled before the client enters the group. There is now a considerable body of evidence that such an interview will make it more likely that the clients will remain in the group for the designated period of time and will benefit from the group experience (Garvin, 1987, pp. 72–74; Toseland & Rivas, 1995, pp. 163–164). This interview should include information on the value of group treatment, the difficulties groups have in their formation stage, and the need for members to be open with one another. The clients, in turn, express their expectations for the group, their ideas as to how they will use the group, their reasons for joining, their reservations about affiliating, and what they anticipate will be forthcoming from the worker and other members.

In more formally assessing group members, workers may use the same instruments employed in individual treatment. In addition, however, there are assessment tools that make use of the group context itself. One of these is the opportunity the group offers to observe how the member interacts with peers, which in other forms of treatment can be known only through self-report. The following are some of the interactional behaviors that become evident in groups:

1. *How the member initiates or fails to initiate relationships.* The member may approach others in an aggressive fashion or in a submissive and self-effacing manner. The member may be open or closed to efforts made by others to form a relationship.
2. *How the member responds to feedback from others.* The member may give serious consideration to what others say or may find ways of rejecting this type of information without any thought.
3. *How the member responds to the emotions expressed by others.* The member may respond in an empathic and caring way or in a cold and rejecting manner.

Because the group offers such an excellent opportunity to gather information about the member's typical behavior in interpersonal situations, some workers invite the potential member to participate for a session or two in a pregroup experience. This experience can have the twofold purpose of orienting the client to a group experience while giving the worker information that can be used in planning the subsequent, longer-term group.

When it is not possible to observe the client in a group situation, the worker will use self-report to obtain this type of information during a pregroup screening interview. The worker will ask the clients about the groups in which they have participated, how they felt about the group experience and the other members, how they interacted with others in the group, and what benefits or difficulties resulted from being in the group.

Another assessment device used in some groups is to ask the members to tell their life story to each other. A good example was reported by Adolph (1983) in her work with a women's group in a partial hospitalization program. In the beginning of the group, the women told "herstory" of "growing up female." The women who wished to participate in this experience were given the "herstory outline" a week in advance. Following is an example of how a member used this experience:

> Helene, 60 years old, widow . . . Helene had been a professional actress doing monologues throughout the United States during her younger years. She felt depleted, alone, isolated, impoverished, living on Public Aid, when in the past she had been married to a physician and lived in comparative luxury. Helene's "herstory" was an exciting oral document presented as a dramatic musical event like her former theatrical monologues. She was enthusiastically applauded by the group and encouraged to resume her theatrical life by entertaining senior citizen groups. Helene seemed pleased with that suggestion and did follow through following discharge from the Alternative Hospital Program. (p. 126)

When approaches using instruments originally developed for assessment in one-to-one treatment are employed, there may be advantages to bringing these instruments into the group to obtain the reactions of other members. An example is a chart on which a member recorded how often he initiated conversations with other employees at his place of work. At first he had been reluctant to keep the chart, but the interest of other group members encouraged him to do so. He was also able to tell the other members what his feelings were as he contemplated making such social contacts, and this gave him new insights into the nature of his difficulties.

Members should be helped to formulate goals regarding what they would like to see occur as a result of their group participation. These goals are usually expressed in terms of an improvement in the problem for which the individual sought group treatment. The member may have discussed goals during the pregroup interview yet may want to modify these as she or he experiences the reality of the group and listens to the goals of others. The member may decide that she or he is not comfortable working on some goals with these particular people; the opposite may also be true, and the member may be encouraged to work on a problem that she or he was fearful to divulge when others acknowledge similar difficulties.

It is difficult for some people to think in terms of personal goals. The group context is a place where they can be helped through examples provided by the worker or other members to express personal aspirations in clear and realistic ways. In one group, for example, a member stated that her goal was to get along better with her son. Other members asked her what she meant by "get along better." She explained that she could have conversations with him about his efforts to cope with his psychiatric disability, and she would be able without feeling guilty to set limits on him as, for example, what time he had to come home. Members are often very useful to one another in developing specific goals because of the similarities present in their situations.

CREATING GROUPS

At times the worker begins to conduct a group that is already in existence—for example, one composed of adults who live in the same unit of a residential facility. Under other circumstances, the worker secures a list of potential members from colleagues or from advertising the group in the community or agency. Sometimes the worker will receive the names of a small number of potential members and must begin with all (or almost all) of these people or abandon plans for the group.

The question facing the worker who will have little or nothing to say in the selection of members is, "Given this set of people, what purposes might the group accomplish?" When the worker is able to select members from a pool of possible members, the question is, "Given the agency's purpose for the group, which combination of people is mostly likely to achieve the purpose?" In the first circumstance, the implication is not that the worker determines the purpose and foists it on the members, but rather that this is an issue for the worker and members to resolve together.

The process of composing groups is not usually one that the member shares with other clients. It is possible, however, to bring somewhat of an empowerment perspective to this task by asking potential members what attributes they think should be present in people who will be able to work well together in the proposed group. Workers may be surprised to learn that their cherished ideas about group composition are rejected by those who are most affected by the group's composition.

Some workers have been concerned that if group members are too similar to one another, they will be likely to reinforce rather than resolve their problems. In practice, this is rarely, if ever, the case since there are always sufficient differences among the experiences of group members to provide for different perspectives on a situation. The worker also is in a position to challenge too much conformity if this should become a problem.

On the other hand, members must come to care enough for one another to sustain their commitment to the group, to support one another when the going gets rough, and to become the system of mutual aid envisioned by most group workers. This is likely to occur when members see some similarities in one another, even though they may also see glaring differences. Workers are advised to make a list of the attributes that are most likely to matter when the members meet and look each other over (Garvin, 1987, pp. 58–71). The member who sees nothing in common with other members is most likely to discontinue the group, and reciprocally the other members are not likely to act in an accepting manner toward him or her.

An example is a group established to help members deal with their ability to sustain intimate relationships. The worker hypothesized that the most critical attributes affecting the ways these members identified with each other would be age, sex, marital status, ways they had used to develop intimacy, education, and occupation. Rather than seeking members who were alike on all of these attributes, groups were composed so that no member would be different on all of these criteria. It was anticipated that everyone would be similar to other members in at least a few ways. This proved to be the case as the members introduced themselves to the others. Some men were pleased that there were other men present, for example, and others liked the idea that women were in the group. The women felt similarly. A divorced person was pleased to see that he was not the only person in that category.

There are occasions when the purpose of the group requires that all the members be alike on one attribute—for example, men's and women's consciousness-raising and support groups, groups for women who have experienced an assault from a man, groups of assaultive men, groups to enhance ethnic identity or to help people who have experienced loss, and coming-out groups for gay men and lesbians.

An issue that has recently received much attention is the gender and ethnic composition of the group, especially when the latter involves people of color. Garvin and Reed (1983) have written that there is a tendency in many groups for men to dominate the discussion and to compete with other men. They also note that women are likely to be depreciated by men when they assume positions of leadership and that women's groups are likely to have different developmental patterns from men's groups.

The ethnicity of group members is also important to consider in composing groups. Davis (1984), for example, reported instances when black group members had questioned the legitimacy of all black treatment groups, although this concern shortly disappeared. Black members have also questioned the legitimacy of having a white worker assigned to a predominantly black group. Davis (1984) has done pioneering work on how black-white proportions are perceived differently by black and white members and reports:

> Blacks, it appears, prefer groups that are 50 percent black and 50 percent white—numerical equality. Whites, on the other hand, appear to prefer groups that are approximately 20 percent black and 80 percent white, societal ratios of blacks and whites. Needless to say, the preferences of both groups cannot be simultaneously met. The difference in preference for racial balance has the potential to lead to member dissatisfaction, discomfort, and withdrawal. (p. 102)

Chu and Sue (1984) provide information on compositional issues related to Asian American members as follows:

> In a group of very verbose, articulate and aggressive non-Asians, the Asian member may be hesitant to speak up. In a confrontation, which inevitably happens at some point in a long-term group, the Asian may not know what to say, not being used to such interaction. (p. 30)

These are only a few examples from a growing literature on ethnic composition of groups. This type of inquiry must be ongoing in view of the many changes occurring in American and other societies regarding the interactions among various ethnic groups.

GROUP FORMATION

All groups in which the members do not know one another prior to the group (although there may be a few who have previously met) go through a period of formation. Workers should understand this phase because they can be very helpful to the members in accomplishing formation tasks. If these tasks are not undertaken appropriately, the future of the group may be in jeopardy. During formation, the members agree on group purpose and individual goals, establish group norms, develop initial relationships with each other and with the group worker, determine the kinds of activities in which they will engage, deal with their feelings about the group, and decide how the success of the group will be evaluated. These agreements may be thought of as a contract the members have with each other and with the worker, which may be either implicit or in the form of a written document.

Agreement on Group Purpose

The members will have discussed the group purpose with the worker in their pregroup interviews. The worker, however, should discuss group purpose again when the group begins. As members gain first impressions of one another, they may wish to reconsider or modify that statement of purpose. An example was a group of adults who had recently been divorced. The original stated purpose was to help members deal with their feelings about the divorce. As the members told their "divorce stories," however, they discovered how lonely they now were. They insisted that the group purpose include learning ways of dealing with loneliness, especially on weekends and holidays.

Individual Goals

Members may also have considered individual goals during the pregroup interview but should be asked to clarify these for themselves and other group members when the group begins. We recognize that members may reformulate their goals as the group proceeds and their individual situations change. In a treatment group of five men on probation, the following goals were arrived at by the third meeting:

- Ed's goal was to find a job.
- Sam's goal was to enroll in an educational program for people who want to be electricians.
- Phil wanted to find ways to decrease his use of alcohol.
- Rick wanted to reestablish his relationship with his wife who had left him because he verbally abused her.
- Dick wanted to cut off his relationships with others who broke the law and develop a new set of friends.

Establishing Group Norms

During the formation period, norms are established that may help or hinder the group accomplish its purposes. Some of these are explicitly proposed by the group worker, for example, that members will not inform anyone outside the group about other members of the group (confidentiality). Another norm proposed in most treatment groups is that when members meet outside group sessions, they will report on this at the next group meeting. This norm helps to prevent members from hindering the treatment process by forming cliques. A positive consequence of this norm is that content of discussions outside the group can enhance the content of discussions in the group. Another important norm is that when members are experienced as difficult, this will be discussed at a meeting, and members will not attempt to expel a fellow member.

Workers also seek to promote a norm related to the democratic functioning of the group. This is a complex issue in treatment groups since decisions are not normally made by taking votes; nevertheless, the principle should be that workers help groups to develop as great a measure of democratic decision making as is feasible.

Such decision making may be called on, for example, when the group is considering a change in meeting times. The worker will always try to help the members move to a high level of participation in decision making. Examples are group discussions on fees, group size, and composition principles (although not on specific individuals to be included).

Finally, groups should develop norms for attendance and promptness. When these are not explicit and regularly monitored, it is likely that members will begin to come late and fail to notify anyone when they miss a session. Aside from the disorganization that can ensue under such circumstances, these conditions convey to members that they are not valued and that no one cares when or if they come to the group.

Developing Relationships among Members

In order for the group members to invest themselves fully in the group to accomplish their goals, they must develop relationships with each other. These relationships are likely to continue to deepen as long as the group is in existence. Important aspects of such relationships are that members will trust each other, which means that they will assume that others in the group consciously wish to be of help; the members will believe that they are basically liked and accepted by others in the group; when this is not true, members will be committed to working so that obstacles to this state can be removed.

In order to establish relationships during the formation stage, workers should do the following:

- Help members to identify similarities between themselves and other members of the group. For example, if several woman speak of ways they have been harassed by men, the worker points out this commonality.
- Help members to talk with each other rather than addressing their comments to the worker. For example, the worker points out to group members that they asked him questions rather than asking questions of each other (issues about which the members had the most experience).
- Help members to listen to each other. For example, the worker notes that members are ignoring each others' contributions and suggests that for a short period, each member should summarize the previous comment before speaking.
- Help members reduce distortions in their perceptions of each other. For example, members are asked to select a member who reminds them of someone outside the group. The members are then asked to discuss these perceptions with the member to see how far this resemblance went.

Developing Relationships with the Group Worker

The worker should find ways of developing relationships with all group members. This can be done by making eye contact with members when they speak, allowing one's eyes to shift from member to member during the course of the meeting, and responding empathically to members when they express their feelings. The worker should address members by name and be sure to single out each member during the course of the meeting for a comment, a question, or an encouraging remark.

Planning Group Activities

The worker and members should suggest specific activities as the group evolves that help the group accomplish its purposes. These activities cannot all be planned in advance because it is impossible to anticipate all the events that will occur over time. Nevertheless, the members have a right to be told about the worker's approach to helping the group accomplish its purposes as the group begins. Does the worker anticipate that the members will use discussion and verbal problem-solving methods primarily? Does the worker expect the members to analyze processes occurring in the group and their roles in these processes? Does the worker anticipate introducing other types of activities such as role playing, art, guided imagery, or trips? An understanding of the way that the members will be helped in the group and a consensus on this is necessary for the group to enter the middle stages of group development (in which the members are actively at work to attain their goals). The topic of group development is an important one that goes beyond the scope of this chapter. For a detailed discussion of this concept, see Toseland & Rivas (1995, pp. 86–90).

Dealing with Feelings about the Group

Members often have contradictory feelings about the group. Some of these feelings are positive and tied in with the reasons the members have joined the group and the likelihood that their hopes will be realized. Other feelings are negative as members fear that their efforts in the group will come to naught, that other members will be rejecting and unsympathetic, and that they will leave the group worse off than when they entered. The job of the worker is to strengthen the positive feelings and diminish the negative ones by encouraging the members to express their aspirations and fears. The worker can help members to examine their fears in the light of the reality of the group as they perceive it, and bringing these fears into the open will contribute to this goal.

An example of this occurred in a group of parents working on their parenting skills. One father said he was fearful that other members would be very critical of how he was raising his children. Other members expressed similar concerns, and this recognition of commonality was reassuring. Several members reiterated the idea that they were there to help each other, not to make one another miserable. The worker also encouraged the members to tell the group if they felt they were being criticized excessively.

Evaluation

Being an accountable practitioner requires the worker to help the members evaluate the group experience and their individual progress toward attaining their goals. This process aids the worker in her or his growth as a practitioner by providing feedback as to the effects of her or his practice with the group. It also enables the members to know if they have achieved their objectives and further work they may have after they leave the group. The agency too has a right to know whether its expenditure of resources on the group has accomplished agency purposes. Members should be told this when the group begins, and the means the worker and the members agree to use for evaluation should be clarified in the beginning.

The formation period ends when the membership of the group has stabilized, the purposes of the group clarified and agreed to, initial relationships developed both among members and between members and the worker, and norms established.

CHANGE PROCESSES DURING THE MIDDLE PHASE

During the middle phase, group workers have three major focuses. One is to enhance the ways members relate to one another so that their feelings of trust, closeness, and caring are strengthened. The second is to help the members accomplish group purposes such as problem solving, the acquisition of skills, increased self-awareness, and improved ability to cope with feelings. These processes are not consistent. Most theorists of group development note the likelihood that there will be alternative phases—one in which the group members are actively at work on their relationships and their tasks, the other in which conflict emerges among members or between members and the worker.

Such conflicts are likely to result from inevitable differences among members, the competition for leadership that might emerge, and the changing roles that evolve as different group processes are brought into play. Thus, a third worker task is to help sustain the group during periods of tension and conflict. This is done through reassuring the group that conflict is an inevitable consequence of development, albeit a difficult and sometimes painful one. The worker can help mediate between conflicting parties, help members learn the process of negotiation, and help members establish ground rules so that conflict resolution is experienced as manageable and not destructive to any of the parties.

There are a number of approaches workers use in group treatment with adults. Some workers emphasize one or another of these, while others employ them in some combination. In the discussion, these approaches are described and the client populations and group circumstances for which the approach is the best fit are noted.

Problem Solving

A problem-solving process will be used in virtually all treatment groups. Sometimes this process is employed to help individual members determine how they will cope with a situation in their lives outside the group; at other times the group uses problem solving to resolve a group issue such as how to deal with members' low rate of participation in discussion. When the problem relates to the situation of only an individual member, the group should not impose a group solution on that person. On the other hand, when the problem relates to the group as a whole, a solution can be adopted to which the group agrees.

No problem-solving approach should be rigidly followed in a group since circumstances vary widely. Sometimes problem solving occurs as soon as a member becomes aware of alternatives; at other times it occurs when the member develops insight into an emotional barrier that prevents carrying out an action. An example of the latter was a member who asked the group for help in identifying ways she could ask a coworker out on a date with her. Discussion of this issue made it obvious that she knew ways this might be accomplished, but any option she considered led to her fear of rejection. The discussion quickly turned from the skills of starting a relationship to the sources of her fear of rejection and how she might deal with that fear.

At times, the worker will employ a more systematic problem-solving process. The process begins with specifying the problem in detail, such as who does what to whom, under what conditions, and with what response. The frequency with which the problem occurs should also be examined. The next stage is to determine the goals that will be attained as a result of problem solving. The group then seeks information that will help it to generate alternative solutions to the problem. This information might include what actions the member has used in the past, what actions the person would have liked to use but did not, and the reasons.

The group and the member in question generate alternative solutions to the problem. It is useful to propose more than a single solution. Some groups stop with one and devote time to discussing the pros and cons of that solution as if no alternative is possible, a process that can be unnecessarily restrictive. These alternatives are evaluated for their feasibility with respect to the internal and external resources available to the member and the benefits to that member and to others. There may be undesirable consequences also, and these should be considered.

On the basis of this evaluation, the member chooses one alternative with the help of the group. The group must then help the member carry out the action. The activities that may be used for this include rehearsing the action through a role play, dividing the solution into a series of actions or tasks and discussing each separately, or considering ways of removing barriers to implementing the solution.

CASE EXAMPLE

An example of problem solving took place in a group of patients who suffered from severe mental illnesses and were meeting in a community mental health center. One member, Beth, brought up the problem that she could not stand living with her parents any longer. She was twenty-four years old and had become severely depressed while enrolled in a graduate program. The group asked her a number of questions to clarify the situation. She had been living with her parents since leaving the hospital approximately six months earlier. Her parents were worried that she would have a relapse, and they monitored everything she did. She could not even go to the store to purchase a soft drink without their asking her for details such as which store, did she have money, how long would she be gone, and would she come straight home. Such extensive questioning, it appeared, was unnecessary since she had made similar trips several times a week without any problems.

The group members had become well acquainted with Beth and her abilities and limitations, and they agreed she should consider moving away from her parents. She said that she had moved away to live with her sister a few months before, but the sister's house was too crowded and she had to sleep on a sofa in the living room. In discussing alternatives, the group expressed ideas such as moving in with another sister, locating an apartment where the residents were seeking a roommate, taking an apartment by herself, or going to a halfway house.

These alternatives were evaluated. One problem with several of the ideas proposed was that Beth was living on welfare benefits, although she hoped to secure employment as a secretary and was still polishing her secretarial skills. Following the group discussion, she decided to try to live in an apartment with roommates.

The other group members then began to tell her about their own efforts to obtain this kind of housing. She decided to look in the housing advertisements in the local paper that had a section on "roommates wanted." The group members then volunteered to help her rehearse how she would go about interviewing people in order to find suitable roommates. One problem discussed was how she would respond to questions about what she was doing now and where she had been living.

Cognitive-Behavioral Approaches

These approaches are utilized in groups when members wish to learn specific ways of behaving and to acquire ways of thinking that support such actions. Examples of such situations are those in which members wish to act assertively, cope with stress, or handle specific types of interpersonal situations more effectively. The approach is initiated with the member's specifying the problem situation. It is especially important for the member to describe in detail her or his own behavior and the responses of the other person. Members will often ask the individual questions to help in this process.

The group then helps the member to determine the way she or he would like to behave in the situation. When this is accomplished, it is helpful for the member to have the opportunity to observe what it is like to act in this manner. Therefore, another member who has made progress in attaining this skill role plays the desired behavior, together with other members who act as other people in the individual's situation.

The members then have an opportunity to comment on the role play. The individual also may ask questions. Subsequently the individual role plays himself or herself and also receives feedback from the group, especially on the positive aspects of the role play.

At times it is difficult for the individual to act effectively in the role play. One major reason is that she or he may have thoughts that are detrimental, such as, "Nothing I do works" or "No matter what I do, I will not be liked." The worker together with the group helps the member to identify such thoughts and to replace them with more functional ones. Another source of difficulty is that the member may experience overwhelming anxiety in the simulated (as well as real) situation.

The worker, if she or he has not already done so, may have to teach the group members ways of relaxing in situations that normally make them tense. One means of doing this is to employ progressive muscle relaxation (Toseland & Rivas, 1995, pp. 268–269) in which members learn how they may induce relaxation by systematically relaxing each muscle group in the body. When this skill is acquired, the member is often able to relax without going through each step of this procedure. Other means of relaxation are yoga exercises, meditation, and imagining peaceful scenes.

After the role play, the member is asked to discuss when he or she will try out this behavior in the actual life situation. The member is also asked to report back to the group as to how it went. If at the next meeting the member reports some difficulty, the process might begin again at an appropriate point depending on whether the behavior was entirely wrong for the situation or if the member needs more practice or encouragement.

An example of this process took place in a group of adults working on relationship issues. Sue reported that her boyfriend comes over to her apartment each week and insists that she do his laundry as he claims he does not know how. She had been accepting this task but wished to stop doing so and was not sure how to tell her boyfriend. The group first discussed this with her and reassured her that it was not her responsibility to do her boyfriend's laundry. This was difficult for her as she had typically put meeting other people's needs ahead of her own. A scenario was developed with the help of several group members in which she would tell her boyfriend that she wanted to be of help to him in ways that he really needed but that she did not have time to do his laundry and still get her own chores done. She would offer to teach him how to use the washer and dryer.

One group member volunteered to play Sue, while another volunteered to be the boyfriend. During the role play, the "boyfriend" pleaded with Sue and claimed he could never learn to operate the machines. "Sue" remained adamant in her position. Before Sue tried out her skills in the role play, she indicated that she was sure her boyfriend would abandon her if she did not perform this task, and this issue was discussed in the group. In the discussion that took place after Sue role-played herself, she received the feedback from other group members that she had presented her position in a clear manner and had also persisted in it. One member noted that she had not really looked at her "boyfriend," and this might indicate that she was not sure of her position. She role-played part of the situation again and seemed more comfortable looking at the other player.

Process and Process Illumination

This approach seeks to clarify for members the interpersonal meanings attached to communications among them. For example, if one member asks another to move her chair, this can have a variety of meanings to each of the parties (e.g., superiority, caring, or hostility). The improvement of relationships depends in part on knowing how to communicate what one means to say and to know how other people receive the message. The group offers an opportunity to learn about these issues, acquire ways of improving communication, and testing these outside of the group.

Listed below are some statements that can help the members examine processes (Garvin, 1987:161):

"How did you feel when X said that to you?"
"What did you think Y was saying?"
"What did X remind you of when he said that?"
"Why did X attack Y?"
"Why was X attacked when he said that?"
"Why are you not saying anything now?"
"Why did you laugh when X said that?"
"Each time I said something tonight, you disagreed with me."
"Even though you argue with me, you always sit next to me."

The Use of Program

A major contribution to group treatment made by social workers involves the use of activities, usually collectively referred to as *program,* for group treatment purposes. Discussion, of course, is one type of activity, but other types include the use of such media as art, drama, games, trips, and music, which allow members to communicate information to one another that is not conveyed by words alone while opening up new possibilities for creative problem solving as well as expanded levels of awareness of self and others (Wilson and Ryland, 1949; Middleman, 1968).

An important contribution to an understanding of program was made by Vinter (1985), who identified a series of program dimensions. He pointed out that all activities occur in a physical field, which he defined as "the physical space and terrain, and the physical and social objects characteristic of each activity," and all activities consist of *constituent performances,* which are "behaviors that are essential to the activity and thus are required of the participants." The physical field and the constituent performance compose the activity setting, which produces respondent behaviors. These respondent behaviors are essentially the treatment outcomes for that activity.

An example of an analysis utilizing this model was the use a worker made of the program in a group of clients suffering from severe mental illnesses who regularly met in a community mental health center. The members had difficulty experiencing themselves as a group. The worker noted that there was a guitar in the room as well as some other instruments, such as small drums and cymbals (parts of the *physical field*). She knew how to play the guitar and began to play some well-known tunes. She invited the members to make use of the other instruments to keep time with her *(constituent performance)*. After a few songs, some of the less expressive members began to smile, and all of the members pulled their chairs a little closer together, indicating a greater sense of being in a group *(respondent behaviors)*.

Vinter has also provided a way of analyzing the activity setting so that workers can help group members to make modifications in the activity in order to increase the likelihood of desired outcomes. Following are six dimensions of this analysis together with examples of how these might be employed to enhance the musical activity just described:

1. *Prescriptiveness of the pattern of constituent performances.* This is the extent of the rules that guide the activity. The worker implied a rule when she urged the members to try to keep the same rhythm she used in her playing of the guitar.
2. *Institutionalized controls governing participant activity.* This deals with whether behavior is controlled during an activity by some members, the worker, or norms that all of the members have internalized. In the musical activity, some members pointed out to other members when they were not following the rhythm.
3. *Provision for physical movement.* This refers to the degree to which members are required to or permitted to engage in physical movement as part of the activity. In the example, the worker encouraged a restless member to dance to the music if she wished to do so.
4. *Competence required for performance.* This is the least amount of ability required of members in order to participate. In this musical activity, if the worker thought the members were having too much difficulty in keeping the rhythm, she could have asked one of the musically knowledgeable members to "conduct" by standing in front of the group and moving her arms in time to the music.
5. *Provision for participant interactiveness.* This refers to the amount of interaction among members that is permitted or elicited by the activity. In the musical example, if some members had begun to dance with each other, the amount of interaction would have increased.
6. *Reward structure.* This consists of the rewards that are made available during the activity and how these are distributed among the members. In this musical activity, the members all seemed to have fun, and this reward was distributed among everyone. The worker also entertained the group after this event by playing and singing a few popular songs. This was also a source of gratification that was highly associated with the musical activity in which the group members had just participated.

The Use of Structure and Role Assignments

One of the advantages of working with groups is the opportunity for the worker and the members to alter the group structure so that the group can help its members better attain its purposes. Group structure refers to the ways relationships among the members are patterned. I have categorized aspects of the group's structure elsewhere (Garvin, 1987, p. 92) and shall now describe how these various aspects of structure can be modified for treatment purposes.

Communications Structure

This refers to who in the group speaks to whom and about what. In one group, for example, the members had a problem indicating when they wished to say something, and, even then, members frequently interrupted one another. The members acknowledged this problem, and the worker suggested they try a device used in some Native American groups—a "talking stick." A member who wished to speak would ask the member who was speaking for the stick. No one was permitted to interrupt the speaker until the stick was relinquished to him or her.

Sociometric (Affectional) Structure

This refers to the existence of subgroups in which members are closer to each other than to members not a part of the subgroup. In one group the members noted the existence of a few people who gave more support to each other than to others who were not in the subgroup. They also avoided confronting one another, which they freely did to people outside their clique. The worker spent a considerable amount of time helping the group to analyze this condition. It became evident that the members of this subgroup thought they had more education than other group members. Further discussion led to the awareness of these members that they used this fact to avoid facing certain defenses against intimacy that members outside their clique had tried to bring to their attention.

Power Structure

This refers to who in the group influences whom and how this is done. In a group of men and women working on relationship issues, one of the men maintained that his wife was totally to blame for their difficulties. The other men supported him in this view. The worker helped these other men to realize that they feared this member would question whether they were "true men" if they failed to support him.

Leadership Structure

This refers to who contributes most to the determination and accomplishment of group tasks and to enhancing the quality of relationships in the group. In one group, every time a conflict emerged, one member sought to help mediate the conflict, which precluded other members from playing a role in this process. The worker subsequently initiated a discussion of this topic in the group, and the group learned that this member did the same thing in his family, largely owing to his parents' insistence that he play this role in family conflicts.

Role Structure

In treatment groups where formal roles such as chairperson and secretary seldom exist, the important roles are informal ones, for example, "the mediator," "the clown," "the devil's advocate," and "the rebel." In one treatment group, the worker believed that such roles had emerged, and to confirm her thinking, she listed them on a large sheet of paper and then engaged the group in a discussion of who filled each role. The group quickly agreed on who fit which position. This led to an animated discussion that lasted several weeks as to whether members wanted to fill the roles they were in or wished to be in different roles, and how this related to the way the members were cast in their situations outside the group.

The Use of Interpretation

The worker's role in the discussions of process represents one type of interpretation. There are other types as well. For example, the worker notes a pattern in the responses of the individual ("Each time you began to drink, it was after you had been turned down when you asked for a date") or the worker suspects there is an underlying issue of which the member is unaware ("I wonder if your wife at times reminds you of your sister").

Another very important type of interpretation in groups is made to draw the member's attention to transference phenomena occurring in the group. As Yalom (1995) states:

> Every patient, to a greater or lesser degree, perceives the therapist incorrectly because of transference distortions. Few patients are entirely conflict-free in their attitudes towards such issues as parental authority, dependency, God, autonomy, and rebellion—all of which are often personified in the person of the therapist. These distortions are continually at play under the surface of the group discourse. Indeed, hardly a meeting passes without some clear token of the powerful feelings evoked by the therapist. (p. 193)

Transference phenomena also occur in the reactions of members to each other. This can be one of the richest sources of therapeutic gain in groups as members learn about transference phenomena in the group and then apply this learning to create a reality-oriented basis for their relationships outside the group. Workers should also take note of their own countertransference issues, which may be evoked when the worker displaces affects, attitudes, and conflicts that have their origins in the worker's relationships to parents, children, and siblings, onto the group member(s).

Several countertransference manifestations frequently occur in groups. A major one is when the worker needs to remain in a central position in the group and to receive an inordinate amount of attention from group members. An example of this is a worker who responded to virtually all member comments with one of his own, and this precluded members from giving feedback to one another. Another is when workers assume that most member comments, particularly critical comments, represent their transferential reactions and fail to recognize the reality bases of such criticisms. Still another is when workers devalue their own contributions and are unduly passive during group discussions.

TERMINATION

There are a number of occasions when the worker must help the group deal with an ending. One is when the group terminates, and the other is when a member leaves but the group continues.

When the group has reached its final meetings, the worker must help with a series of issues. The order in which these are dealt with is not an arbitrary one but should be determined by the circumstances of the particular group.

Feelings about the Ending

As was true of group beginnings, members experience a variety of feelings, often contradictory ones, about endings. They often feel regret because they are likely to lose contact with the worker and the other members of whom they have become fond. They also may miss the group meetings. Some fear that they will lose the gains they have made through the group experience. On the other hand, they may be happy to have the meeting time free and that they will no longer have to pay fees for the group. Some will still have mixed feelings, or even negative ones, about how much the group has helped them. The members will benefit from a discussion of all of these issues. Such discussions may help free them to pursue new relationships and other opportunities for growth and change.

Maintaining Changes

Members who have accomplished their goals can benefit from help in finding ways of maintaining these changes once the group ends. This can be aided by helping these members identify their gains and plan ways to continue to use their new competencies. One principle that can be employed in this is overlearning, in which members try out new behaviors, especially under a variety of circumstances, before the group ends. They can also be helped to identify others in their lives who will provide them with encouragement and reinforcement.

Seeking Out New Opportunities for Growth and Change

It is important to remind members that learning is a lifelong process and that this is especially true with respect to learning about relationships. Some members will be benefited by utilizing a different kind of treatment group. Others should try out one of the many kinds of self-help groups that now exist. Still others may benefit by joining a social, educational, recreational, or political movement group.

EVALUATION

The worker can utilize almost any assessment measure in the group that has been developed for one-on-one helping. It is often important, however, for the worker to secure feedback after each session to help in planning the next session. Rose (1984) has developed a simple instrument for this purpose. Some of the questions he asks are the following:

- How useful was today's session for you?
- Describe your involvement in today's session.
- Rate the extent that you were able to disclose relevant information about yourself or your problem.
- How important to you were problems or situations you discussed (or that others discussed) in the group today?
- Circle the number on the scale that best describes the interrelationships among group members and workers in the group.
- Circle all the words that best describe you at today's session (excited, bored, depressed, interested, comfortable).
- How satisfied were you with today's session?

An evaluation process should be part of every group's termination. The members should be asked to indicate the progress they made (or failed to make) in accomplishing their goals, the extent to which the group was or was not helpful, and the ways in which the worker was or was not helpful to the group and its members.

RESEARCH ON GROUP TREATMENT

Research on the effectiveness of group treatment is very difficult because of the problems in maintaining an equivalent control condition, monitoring process events that affect outcomes, and ensuring that the treatment plan is implemented in the intended manner. Bednar and Kaul (1994) have been persistent in identifying and reporting good outcome studies. In a summary of their findings they state:

> Accumulated evidence indicates that group treatments have been more effective than no treatment, than placebo or nonspecific treatments, or than other recognized psychological treatments, at least under some circumstances. This evidence has been gathered under a variety of conditions, from a wide range of individuals, and in many different ways. Although it may not be the best question to ask, there is a large body of research that indicates that group treatments "work." This conclusion must be qualified, however, since it is empirically and intuitively obvious that not all groups have had uniformly beneficial results. We have seen nonrejections of the null hypothesis in the research, and evidence of casualties as well. (p. 632)

One recent examination of studies of group treatment in social work settings (Tolman & Molidor, 1994) looked at fifty-four studies, of which thirty-seven reported the outcome of a cognitive-behavioral group intervention. These cognitive-behavioral interventions included groups for parenting, woman abuse, child abuse, depression, and coping with physical disabilities. Two major deficiencies in the research literature were the absence of research on other practice approaches and the paucity of studies on groups whose members' presenting problems were heterogeneous.

Another promising development was the creation of the annual Symposium on the Empirical Foundations of Group Work, a network of group work researchers who are available to each other for consultation. (More information on this symposium may be obtained from the author of this chapter.)

SUMMARY

This chapter begins with a discussion of how group work emerged in social work practice as well as current group work approaches. These approaches are the mediational model, the remedial model, the task-centered model, feminist and empowerment models, and group psychotherapy models. The change theories drawn on by group work writers are also described, and these consist of psychodynamic theory, cognitive-behavioral theory, social psychological and small group theories, ecological theories, and theories that bear on the operation of therapeutic factors in groups.

Presented next were the activities of group workers during each phase of the group work process. The first phase is that of assessment in which the worker and client determine whether a group experience is desirable and, if so, what type of group will be the most appropriate one. Some types that were discussed were open versus closed groups, short-term versus long-term groups, and support versus therapy groups. The worker will also use assessment information to determine how to compose a group; some principles of group composition were then described. Assessments conducted for group work purposes have some features that distinguish those used for other modalities of treatment and these features were noted. An important compositional issue presented is the proportion of men and women in the group as well as of people from different ethnic backgrounds.

The beginning, middle, and termination phases of the group are then described along with appropriate worker activities during each phase. Beginning phase issues include clarifying group purpose, determining member goals, strengthening relationships among members and between members and the worker, establishing group norms, dealing with feelings about the group, and selecting the group's initial activities.

The kinds of processes that occur in the group's middle phases were then detailed. These include problem solving, skill development, process illumination, program utilization, employment of group structures and role assignments, and interpretation. Important issues of transference and countertransference were noted.

The next section of the chapter described the process of termination. Aspects of termination that were described were handling feelings about ending, facilitating the maintenance of member change, and seeking new opportunities for change and growth. The next section of the chapter presented means for evaluating the group work experience. The chapter concluded by describing the current situation with respect to group work research.

REFERENCES

Adolph, M. (1983). The all-women's consciousness raising group as a component of treatment for mental illness. *Social Work with Groups*, 6 117–132.

American Psychiatric Association. (1995). *Diagnostic and statistical manual of mental disorders* (4th ed). Washington, DC: Author.

Bednar, R. L., & Kaul, T. J. (1994). Experiential group research: Can the cannon fire? In A. E. Bergin and S. L. Garfield (Eds.), *Handbook of Psychotherapy and Behavior Change* (4th ed.) (pp. 631–663). New York: Wiley.

Bion, W. (1959). *Experiences in groups and other papers.* New York: Basic Books.

Bloch, S., & Crouch, E, (1985). *Therapeutic factors in group psychotherapy.* New York: Oxford University Press.

Chu, J., & Sue, S. (1984). Asian/Pacific Americans and group practice. *Social Work with Groups, 7,* 23–36.

Davis, L. (1984). Essential components of group work with black Americans. *Social Work with Groups, 7,* 97–109.

Ezriel, H. (1973). Psychoanalytic group therapy. In L. R. Wolberg & E. K. Schwartz (Eds.), *Group Therapy,* (pp. 191–202). New York: Intercontinental Medical Book Corporation.

Forsyth, D. R. (1990). *Group dynamics* (2nd ed.). Pacific Grove, CA: Brooks/Cole.

Foulkes, S. H. (1965). *Therapeutic group analysis.* New York: International Universities Press.

Freire, P. (1973). *Education for critical consciousness.* New York: Seabury Press,

Garvin, C. D. (1974). Task-centered group work. *Social Service Review, 48,* 494–507.

Garvin, C. D. (1985). Group process: Usage and uses in social work practice. In M. Sundel, P. Glasser, R. Sarri, & R. Vinter (Eds.), *Individual change through small groups* (pp. 203–225). New York: Free Press.

Garvin, C. D. (1987). Group theory and research. in A. Minahan (Ed.), *Encyclopedia of social work* (18th ed.). Silver Spring, MD: National Association of Social Workers.

Garvin, C. D. (1991). Social learning and role theories. In R. Greene (Ed.), *Human behavior theory and social work practice.* New York: Aldine de Gruyter.

Garvin, C. D. (1996). Group work with the seriously mentally ill. In P. Ephross & G. Grief (Eds.), *Group work with special populations.* New York: Oxford University Press.

Garvin, C. D. (1997). *Contemporary group work,* 3rd. ed. Boston: Allyn & Bacon.

Garvin, C. D., & Reed, B. G. (1983). *Groupwork with women/Groupwork with men: An overview of gender issues in social groupwork practice.* New York: Haworth.

Garvin, C. D., & Reed, B. G. (1995). Sources and visions for feminist group work: Reflective processes, social justice, diversity, and connection. In *Feminist Practice in the 21st Century.* Washington, DC: NASW.

Garvin, C. D., et al. (1985). Group work intervention in the social environment. In M. Sundel, P. Glasser, R. Sarri, & R. Vinter (Eds.), *Individual change through small groups* (pp. 273–293). New York: Free Press.

Germain, C. B., & Gitterman, A. (1995). Ecological perspective. In R. L. Edwards (Ed.), *Encyclopedia of Social Work* (19th ed.) (pp. 816–824). Washington, DC: NASW Press.

Gitterman, A., & Shulman, L. (eds.) (1994). *Mutual aid groups, vulnerable populations, and the life cycle* (2nd ed.). New York: Columbia University Press.

Gutierrez, L. (1990). Working with women of color: An empowerment perspective. *Social Work, 35,* 149–153.

Konopka, G. (1949). *Therapeutic group work with children.* Minneapolis: University of Minnesota Press.

Lee, J. A. B. (1994). *The empowerment approach to social work practice.* New York: Columbia University Press.

Levine, B. (1979). *Group psychotherapy: Practice and development.* Englewood Cliffs, NJ: Prentice Hall.

Martin, G., & Pear, J. (1992). *Behavior modification: What it is and how to do it.* Englewood Cliffs, NJ: Prentice Hall.

Middleman, R. (1968). *The non-verbal method in working with groups.* New York: Association Press.

Napier, R., & Gershenfeld, M. (1987). *Groups: theory and experience* (3rd ed.). Boston: Houghton Mifflin.

National Association of Social Workers. (1960). *Use of groups in the psychiatric setting.* New York: NASW.

Nixon, H. (1979). *The small group.* Englewood Cliffs, NJ: Prentice Hall.

Nurius, P., & Brower, A. (1993). *Social cognition and individual change: Current theory and counseling guidelines.* Newbury Park, CA: Sage.

Reid, W., & Epstein, L. (1972). *Task-centered casework.* New York: Columbia University Press.

Rose, S. (1984). Use of data in identifying and resolving group problems in goal-oriented treatment groups. *Social Work with Groups 7,* 23–36.

Rose, S., & LeCroy, Charles. (1991). Group treatment methods. In F. Kanfer & A. Goldstein (Eds.), *Helping people change* (4th ed.) (pp. 422–453). New York: Pergamon Press.

Sarri, R., & Galinsky, M. (1985). A conceptual framework for group development. In M. Sundel, P. Glasser, R. Sarri, & R. Vinter (Eds.), *Individual change through small groups* (pp. 70–86). New York: Free Press.

Schwartz, W. (1994). The social worker in the group. In T. Berman-Rossi (Ed.), *Social work: The collected writings of William Schwartz* (pp. 257–276). Itasca, IL: Peacock.

Sundel, M., Glasser, P. Sarri, R., & Vinter, R. (Eds.). (1985). *Individual change through small groups.* New York: Free Press.

Tolson E., Reid, W., & Garvin, C. (1994). *Generalist practice: A task-centered approach.* New York: Columbia University Press.

Tolman, R. M., & Molidor, C. E. (1994). A decade of social group work research: Trends in methodology, theory, and program development. *Research on Social Work Practice, 4,* 142–159.

Toseland, R., & Rivas, R. (1995). *An introduction to group work practice* (2nd ed.). Boston: Allyn & Bacon.

Vinter, R. (1985). Program activities: An analysis of their effects on participant behavior. In M. Sundel, P. Glasser, R. Sarri, & R. Vinter (Eds.), *Individual change through small groups* (pp. 226–236). New York: Free Press.

Whitaker, D. S., & Lieberman, M. A. (1965). *Psychotherapy through the group process.* New York: Atherton Press.

Wilson, G., & Ryland, G. (1949). *Social group work practice.* Boston: Houghton Mifflin.

Yalom, I. (1995). *The theory and practice of group psychotherapy* (4th ed.). New York: Basic Books.

Part III

Specialized Clinical Issues, Themes, and Dilemmas

12

Family Violence and Clinical Practice

Louise R. Kerlin and Jerrold R. Brandell

This chapter provides a framework for clinical work that involves the most common types of dangerous behavior accompanying presenting problems encountered in an ordinary outpatient mental health or family service setting. The chapter focuses on partner battering, child abuse, and child sexual abuse, relating them to suicidal and homicidal threats because of the frequency with which these behaviors are found together. It does not focus on elder abuse, involuntary treatment, or the treatment of violent offenders, nor does it examine the relationship of violence to cultural themes and societal structures. It reviews the literature on clinical work with clients who have violence in their lives and provides a model of relatively comprehensive intervention designed to confront such violence, interrupt it when possible, and remediate its causes and effects.

Because the recognition of violence in intimate settings has become truly widespread only in the past three decades, our language about it carries many meanings that have been noted to contribute to the stigmatization of those who suffer from it. There is only partial consensus on appropriate terms. We use the term *victim* to refer to a person in an abusive situation, *survivor* to refer to one whose situation no longer includes violence, *battering* to refer to partner physical violence, and *abuse* to refer to violent behavior toward children. Some situations between partners include violence by women; however, the greatest number of situations involves males, whose physical and economic power is greater than their female partners (a state of affairs that is held in place by the societal system that contains the family). However, women are capable of violence as well, and therefore our language does not refer only to males as abusers and batterers. The methods we propose recognize the power differential between stronger and weaker and between those who are violent and those who are not.

INCIDENCE OF VIOLENCE IN CLINICAL POPULATIONS

Most new practitioners who practice in typical outpatient mental health settings do not think of themselves as working with individuals and families who have a potential for violence; however, a growing body of statistical evidence indicates a need for readiness to deal with such problems as child abuse, partner battering, sexual abuse, and suicide.

John Briere (1992) exhaustively summarizes the recent literature on incidence of psychological, sexual, and physical abuse. Psychological abuse occurs by itself in 11 to 13 percent of reported abuse cases, but is always a component of the other two types. He identifies rates of physical abuse as between 10 and 20 percent of the general population.

Sexual abuse, defined as "sexual contact, ranging from fondling to intercourse, between a child in mid-adolescence or younger and a person at least five years older," occurs at a rate of 20 to 30 percent among females in the general population and at a rate of 10 to 20 percent among males (Finkelhor, 1979; Finkelhor et al., 1989; Finkelhor, Hotaling, Lewis, & Smith, 1989; Henschel, Briere, Magallanes, & Smiljanich, 1990; Russell, 1986; Wyatt, 1985). In female inpatient and outpatient groups, six studies report an incidence between 36 and 70 percent (Briere & Runtz, 1987; Briere & Zaidi, 1989; Bryer, Nelson, Miller, & Krol, 1987; Carlin & Ward, 1989; Chu & Dill, 1990; Craine, Henson, Colliver, & MacLean, 1988; Goodwin, Attias, McCarty, Chandler, & Romanik, 1982). Between 5 and 16 percent of adolescent males perpetrate sexual abuse, and the average adolescent offender commits 380 sex crimes during his lifetime (Ageton, 1983; Abel et al., 1984). Hansen and Harway (1993) summarize the studies of Gelles and Straus, which indicate that domestic violence occurs to 3.8 percent of all women each year and to 16.7 percent of married women over the course of the relationship. Violence occurs in 22 to 67 percent of dating relationships.

Lesbian relationships report a rate of approximately 25 to 59.8 percent, and in a study that included gay male and lesbian relationships, 47 percent reported using physically aggressive tactics and 3 percent reported violent tactics (Renzetti, 1993).

In a CMHC (Community Mental Health Center) population 38.6 percent were found to have or have had a concern with violent behaviors (Barnhill, et al., 1982). It is easy to see that with rates as high as these, the outpatient clinician will often see clients who either present at intake with dangerous behaviors or who have exhibited them in the past. It is important for social work clinicians to develop skills in recognizing the signs of violence in the home and be able to take appropriate steps to intervene (Harway & Hansen, 1993b).

ASSESSMENT OF VIOLENT BEHAVIOR AT INTAKE

The assessment process begins with the initial telephone call. If depression is mentioned, it is appropriate to ask about suicidal ideation, and when the answer is in the affirmative, to continue with an assessment of plan, means, lethality, and intent. Because suicide is a relatively rare event but suicidal ideation is highly correlated with risk factors for other forms of violence, which are statistically more common, (Gondolf, 1990; Plutchik & van Praag, 1990), it is appropriate to inquire about homicidal ideation and to assess it in the same orderly way. If the prospective client is thinking of suicide or homicide and cannot provide a good no suicide–no homicide commitment until the intake interview, it may be appropriate to refer the person for hospitalization at that time. If marital conflict is mentioned, it is appropriate to ask, "Is there any physical violence involved?" and to explore in detail any that is disclosed (Register, 1993). If the client is in a severe partner-battering situation, the practitioner should be aware of available shelters and make a referral. If the client refuses the referral or is in a less severe situation, other safety options should be offered and then explored further at the intake interview. The therapist should also discuss the best strategy for the intake interview in order to maximize full disclosure of the battering and safety for the victim (Register, 1993). Child abuse is more difficult to address in such a telephone call, but if information is volunteered, it should be explored, confidentiality discussed, and appropriate steps taken to protect the victim(s). If there is any voiced or implied threat of any dangerous behavior to anyone in the course of an intake call and the prospective client is not amenable to referral, consultation should be sought immediately to determine the need for further action. Action will depend on the age of the person in danger, the type of danger, legal mandates, and relevant agency policies about those who are not yet clients.

THE INTAKE INTERVIEW

It is sensible to begin each intake interview with a discussion of confidentiality (Briere, 1989). Most clients have no difficulty with a statement of the three situations in which confidentiality is abrogated. The clinician may simply state: "I want you to know that everything you say here is confidential, except for three kinds of things. If I learn that a child is being abused or neglected, I have to report it to the child welfare authorities, and if I believe that you or one of you is going to hurt yourself or someone else, I have to do everything I can to stop it." Most clients, even those who are potentially violent, agree that these exceptions make sense. It is also good practice to advise the clients at intake that if confidentiality has to be breached, the clinician will always discuss the need for such actions with the client beforehand. The only exception would be situations in which such disclosure might endanger someone. However, as soon as that person's safety can be ensured, the disclosure should be made. Most clients feel a sense of security in knowing the therapist will take charge at such a time, and even if they feel angry when it happens, they tend retrospectively to support the therapist's right to make such a decision.

It is also important to obtain at intake the name of a family member or other person to contact should there be a need to involve others in hospitalizing or protecting a person. Most settings routinely collect this information.

Theresa, a city worker, and Steve, a firefighter, presented as angry and defended when they brought pretty thirteen-year-old Marika to the clinic. Their eighteen-year-old daughter Jessica had left home and did not accompany them, but Marika's six-year-old brother, Stevie, was there. The clinician introduced herself and exchanged a few words with each family member. Marika presented as aloof and disdainful, and refused to participate beyond giving her name.

Social worker: Did you get a chance to read the materials I sent you about the clinic?
Theresa: A little. It's been a busy week, and she . . .
Social worker: (Interrupting) I want you to know about some things before we get into what's wrong here. Do you know about confidentiality?
Steve: You can't give out information.
Social worker: Close. I only can give out information if the adults give permission in writing, except in four situations. I can consult with clinic supervisors to get help in working with you if I need it. There are three other exceptions. If someone is going to hurt himself or someone else, I have to do everything I can to stop it, and if a child is being abused, I have to report it to protective services.

The tension in the room eased slightly, and Steve replied, "I know about that. I've had to make reports, and help get people to the hospital. Sometimes you have to."

The most crucial steps in assessing violent behavior are a willingness to acknowledge the signs that it might be present (Lion, 1987) and to ask about it in ways that maximize the chances that it will be disclosed (Herman, 1988). The therapist who asks in a confident, welcoming, nonjudgmental way and hears the answer calmly has a much greater chance of hearing the truth about dangerous behavior. In order to maintain this presentation consistently, the practitioner needs the support of relatively clear-cut plans of action should dangerous behaviors be revealed and accessible consultation to help in sorting out risk and for taking appropriate action in confusing situations. Gondolf (1990) recommends an orderly protocol of direct questions that address escalating forms of violent behavior in the family, the results of such violent behavior in terms of the injuries sustained, the need for police intervention, and the need for other forms of assistance, including shelter and child welfare intervention. Practitioners should obtain descriptions of the most recent incident, the worst incident, and at least one other incident (Register, 1993; Walker, 1992). Although these recommendations relate specifically to battering, it is good practice to generalize them to other forms of family violence.

The level of violence in battering should be assessed. Mild battering might include pushing, slapping, shoving, holding, verbal abuse, or name calling. Moderate battering might include punching with fists, hitting in the face or head, pulling or dragging by the hair, and kicking. Severe violence often includes the use of weapons, clubbing, choking, or attempts to run over victims with a car (Register, 1993). However, it is important to be aware that pushing a person may cause that person to strike his or her head against a heavy table, resulting in a concussion or even permanent injury to the spinal column; punching and kicking can result in a ruptured spleen or kidneys, broken ribs, and punctured lungs. Death can result from "mild" or "moderate" abuse or battering. Even if past injuries are assessed and are minor, worse injuries could occur next week, tomorrow, or even in the car on the way home from the clinician's office. Battering tends to increase in intensity over time (Harway, 1993). Recent violence and a past history of violence are the most important factors to assess in determining the potential for violence in the near future (Feinstein, 1990).

The therapist combined circular questioning with review of the intake paperwork to explore Marika's difficulties and the accompanying family dysfunction. Both parents sat tensely, with angry expressions on their faces. Theresa was the spokesperson, cataloguing Marika's problems in a helpless tone. Her grades had slipped at the end of seventh grade; she was now failing three classes and seemed not to care; she was arguing with her parents about every issue and spending all her time with her sister and a fifteen-year-old boyfriend. The parents feared she would get pregnant as her sister had at fourteen.

The therapist widened the discussion to ask each family member his or her point of view. Marika hinted at other problems but would not reveal them. Everyone else blamed her and pointed to her behavior. The clinician again widened the discussion to include the parents' experiences as adolescents. This revealed generational alcoholism. In addition, both parents had been the scapegoats in their families of origin. Marika was the current scapegoat in this family; her sister had filled that role before her. The parents began to argue about Marika's behavior.

Steve: You're too soft on her. If you'd show a little backbone, she wouldn't have these problems.

Theresa: Yeah, you think your loud mouth and your belt can fix everything.

Social worker: Is this how it goes? [Both parents looked startled.]

Marika: Yeah. But that's not how it ends.

Social worker: Tell me what happens next.

Stevie: Sometimes Dad pushes Mom.

Social worker: How do you feel when that happens?

Stevie: Scared.

Marika: Mad. It's not my fault they fight.

Social worker: [to parents] Is that what happens next?

Theresa: Sometimes. But usually we just yell.

Social worker: [to Steve] Can you remember the worst thing that happened when you had a fight?

Steve: Not really. I don't see where this has anything to do with Marika's problems.

Social worker: You were talking earlier about how you felt about your parents' fights, how that was part of the reason you had trouble in school.

Theresa: Steve, we should tell her. Maybe this is a chance to change things.

Steve: If that's how you feel, you tell her.

Theresa: I will. He usually just pushes me out of the way, but once he was really mad and pushed me through the wall. I ended up with two black eyes and had to stay home from work for a week.

Social worker: Steve, is that how you remember it?

Steve: I don't think it was a whole week.

Social worker: How did you feel?

Steve: I hated it, okay? Look, I'm not an abuser. I just don't know what to do sometimes. It seems like they don't care what I think. I work hard for them. I risk my life every day on the job for them. Why don't they care?

The clinician explored other family members' feelings about this incident and learned it had occurred about six months ago, just before the school year started. Throughout the interview she encouraged each person to verbalize feelings and thoughts about the family's situation, to diminish the chances they would be acted out later.

Single persons, no matter what their living situations, should be assessed for the possibility of violence in their intimate relationships, both past and present. Lesbian and homosexual relationships should be recognized and battering in them assessed and approximately addressed (Renzetti, 1993). (See Chapter 9 for additional discussion of same-sex couples and domestic violence.)

Clients who present because of violent behavior in the community or homicidal ideation toward someone outside their family, even if they live alone, may also be violent toward sexual partners, ex-partners, or their children. This should be a subject of assessment at intake (Gondolf, 1990). Thoughts of violence are associated with violent behavior. Escalating risk is associated with increasing intensity and specificity, the greatest risk being associated with a strong desire to kill a specific person. In the interview itself, such a person may progress from relative calm to increasingly agitated psychomotor activity, anger verbalized toward the interviewer, and approach-avoidance behaviors, a sequence that may signal imminent violence (Feinstein, 1990). The practitioner should be prepared to decrease the intensity of the interview process and seek consultation about how to handle the situation.

Surprising numbers of children and adults disclose abuse in the course of family sessions and conjoint interviews that include their abusers. When this happens, it is useful to seek confirmation immediately from the person identified as the batterer and others who are present in a matter-of-fact way. Questions should then be asked to help the clinician assess other patterns of abuse. Battering and child abuse have a strong positive correlation, and one is often predictive for the other (Bowker, Arbitel, & McFerron, 1988; Stacy & Shupe, 1983; Stark & Flitcraft, 1988). It is important to interview each vulnerable person alone, if only briefly, to provide that person with an opportunity to tell all that they are willing to tell at that time:

Social worker: You know, it sounds as if there's a lot of anger here, but it also sounds as if you care a lot about each other, and you'd like things to change. We need to be sure that we've talked about all the bad stuff that happens when people get angry. Does anyone else ever get hurt?

Stevie: I get my butt beat.

Social worker: Can anyone tell me what he means?

Discussion clarified that Steve had used his belt to punish Stevie for taking money from his wallet about a month earlier and had threatened Marika but not followed through. The clinician then talked to the children and each parent alone in order not to single out the mother. No new information was revealed about the violence, but Marika disclosed drinking with her boyfriend, and when the clinician screened for symptoms of depression, Marika revealed that she has thoughts of being dead. She had made a suicidal gesture by taking six Tylenol the night she brought home her first-semester report card. No one but her sister knew. The mother had thought of taking pills herself, and Stevie thought of going out without his coat and hiding in the neighbor's garage until he died. Steve had flashbacks of times he had been in danger and said that sometimes he thought he had a "death wish." The clinician got a commitment from each of them not to harm himself or herself in any way, and then told the children that their suicidal thinking and actions would have to be revealed to the parents.

ASSESSING FOR VIOLENCE

History

Violence in the family of origin forms part of the etiology of many common presenting problems, including depression, anxiety, and interpersonal difficulties such as violence in current relationships (Briere, 1989; Jaffe, Wolfe, & Wilson, 1990; Rosenberg, 1984; Stacey & Shupe, 1983). Individuals who witness family violence may themselves become victimizers or victims; they may also respond with greater resiliency, attempting to provide care for parents or younger siblings. The traumagenic quality of the violence is increased by four factors: the age of the child, the severity of the violence, whether the child is a victim of abuse (Berman, 1993), and the characteristic deficits in most abusing families of available soothing and calming (Steele, 1976). Many abusers see themselves as caring and protective, and many victims of battering have incredible resilience that carries them through difficult situations, which they nevertheless may fear to leave.

Those who defend against abuse by identifying with the aggressor decrease their sense of vulnerability by becoming like the more powerful person in the abuse scenario. As adolescents they may commit juvenile offenses. As adults they may become abusing spouses or parents or commit violent behavior in the community (Gondolf, 1993; Steele, 1976a).

Harway (1993) reports histories of violence in the parental homes of battered women. However, there are some indications that the relationship between childhood abuse and later experiences of being battered is less than clear. Feminist practitioners in particular have cited this relationship as a caution against the use of historical evidence to blame the victim for her own abuse and thereby also avoid placing responsibility on the batterer (Stark & Flitcraft, 1988a). According to this research, battered mothers are less likely to come from alcoholic, disorganized, or violent homes than are nonbattered mothers of abused children.

Other types of trauma and loss in childhood, such as the physical absence of the father during the batterer's childhood development (Gondolf, 1993), are sometimes associated with current family violence.

Psychological Indicators

Medical model practitioners tend to view violence as a symptom of underlying difficulties conceptualized as depression, personality disorder, and psychosis (Lewis, 1987; Lion, 1987). "Abuse-focused" practitioners tend to view the underlying difficulty as a history of violence in the family of origin, which serves to destigmatize the effects; furthermore, such practitioners are inclined to understand the sequelae of early exposure to violence within the framework of posttraumatic stress disorder (Briere, 1992; Courtois, 1988; Herman, 1992; Walker, 1992). (See Chapter 13 for a comprehensive discussion of posttraumatic stress disorder.)

In addition to posttraumatic stress symptoms, which also may be characterized as symptoms of mood or anxiety disorders, there may be cognitive distortions. Victims and survivors may profoundly distrust others, devalue themselves, or sexualize relationships. They may under- or overestimate their personal power or overestimate the amount of danger in the world (Briere & Runtz, 1990; Briere, 1992; Courtois, 1988; Finkelhor and Browne, 1985; Herman, 1992; Kempe & Kempe, 1976; Walker, 1992).

Children present with developmental delay that has no neurological explanation (R. Kempe, 1976) and with symptoms of depression and anxiety including insomnia, nightmares, bedwetting, fearfulness, social withdrawal, misbehavior, and somatic problems. Lower abdominal or pelvic pain may indicate sexual abuse (Herman, 1988).

Behavioral Indicators

Because of the pervasive effects on behavior of current and historical violence, adult abuse victims and survivors are often diagnosed with one of several personality disorders. Common designations for women are histrionic, dependent, and borderline (Briere, 1989, 1992; Herman, 1992; Walker, 1992). Common diagnoses for men are antisocial personality disorder (Herman, 1992) and narcissistic personality disorder (Jocque, 1995). Because of angry behaviors, children are often diagnosed with oppositional defiant disorder or conduct disorder.

Personality disorders are associated with character rigidity and poor outcomes in psychotherapy owing to the ego syntonicity of symptoms associated with them. Childhood behavior disorders are much more workable, but both types of diagnoses can be stigmatizing because of the emphasis on problematic behavior.

Diagnosis is essentially a descriptive system (Frances, First, & Pincus, 1995), and it may prove more useful to understand personality disorders and behavior disorders as arising from acute or cumulative traumata of childhood. According to some research studies, there are few differences in the personalities of abused and nonabused women, and whatever differences are found in the clinical literature are artifactual, due to the impact of the abuse itself and the failure of societal structures to respond to abuse victims' distress (Harway, 1993; Stark & Flitcraft, 1988). Most of the behavioral effects of posttraumatic stress disorder are manifested in relationships with others. Caretaking roles are common. Intimacy is disturbed by isolation and withdrawal (Briere, 1992; Herman, 1992), which may be straightforward ("Leave me alone!") or involve the use of mood-altering chemicals, suicidal threats, gestures, and attempts, and compulsive behaviors like bulimia, overeating, spending, self-mutilation, and sexual behaviors (Briere, 1992). Social withdrawal may alternate with intense interactions (Berman, 1993; Briere, 1992; Courtois, 1988; Herman, 1992) involving interpersonal aggressiveness, expectation of aggression, adversariality, and manipulation. These alternatively distancing and intrusive behaviors comprise the roles described as victim, victimizer, and resilient child (Berman, 1993). They express and manage the intolerable feelings generated by reminders of past abuse encountered in intimate relationships (Briere, 1992). These feelings create a depressive state in which the individual loses the ability to play and to experience the healing power of temporary regression (Kempe, 1976).

Children also reenact the sexual behavior they have experienced with other children and sometimes with adults, producing the "seductive" behavior that perpetrators often identify in order to shift responsibility away from themselves. During adolescence, running away, suicide attempts, substance use, hysterical seizures, promiscuity, and early pregnancy may indicate sexual abuse (Herman, 1988).

Family Factors

The behaviors of abuse victims and survivors may also be conceptualized in terms of family structure and process. Boundaries in the family are altered and become either too rigid, especially in the case of partner battering or incest (Herman, 1988; M. E. Traicoff, 1982), or very diffuse. The family may be too isolated or incorporate relative strangers to occupy the roles and status accorded to members. Generational boundaries are blurred. Parents see their children as "hopeful substitute(s) for their own parents" (Kempe & Kempe, 1976; McKinney, 1976). In a rigidly structured family, if one parent is unable to fulfill a role, the other parent does not fill it; instead a child is co-opted to its tasks, a structure frequently accompanying incest (Herman, 1988). There are constant struggles over who is to take care of whom, struggles in which family members manipulate each other to meet personal needs without being consciously aware of the needs or considering whether the other family members are willing or able to meet them (Barnhill, 1982; Justice & Justice, 1976). Daily routines to meet children's needs for food and sleep may be disrupted (Berman, 1993). Despite the frequent struggles and unhappiness inside the family, jealousy between partners is common (Harway, 1993), and fear of abandonment keeps the members from leaving (Herman, 1988; Madden, 1987). In such a chaotic structure, it is not surprising that personal boundaries are unclear and there are toxic emotional triangles that mediate discord in the subsystems. Sibling violence, perhaps the most frequent form of family violence (Power, 1988) and one that is often minimized or denied, occurs in such a context of parental abdication, inconsistent limit setting, and chaotic family structure (Madden, 1982).

Inadequate communication over emotional issues, and at times over simple-day-to-day matters as well, seems to be a function of the intolerably intense feelings that are evoked by previous and intercurrent violent behavior. There may be strong spoken or unspoken family rules, and much of the communication may be indirect. There are important family secrets that obscure the family's daily functioning

(Herman, 1988; Traicoff, 1982). Battering partnerships are characterized by conflicts due to disparities in sex role attitudes, education, socioeconomic status, ethnicity, race, and religion (Harway, 1993), issues that are difficult to resolve even when there is optimal communication.

Family functioning is complicated by cyclical alterations in process that may be related to the violence itself, to substance use, and to other behaviors, which serve to release the tensions associated with current stress and historical trauma. After an episode of the violence, substance use, or other behavior, the whole system reacts with shame and efforts to avoid any recurrence. Family members usually present this phase of family process as the normal state of their family, and the violent or substance-abusing behavior as an aberration. However, as inevitable environmental stresses accumulate, this system lacks the flexibility to adapt to them. Tension builds, leading to another episode of violence or substance use and the repetition of the cycle (Fossum & Mason, 1986).

This daily conflict and unhappiness creates a state of chronic, repetitive loss that recapitulates the losses experienced by the adults when they were children. As a result they are usually very motivated to stay together but have difficulty adjusting to the normal losses presented by the maturation of the children. The entry of the oldest or youngest child to kindergarten or first grade may precipitate a crisis. Adolescence is especially difficult. Parents experience the children's normal drive for independence as a serious threat to the family's cohesiveness, and the inevitable conflicts often escalate into abusive behavior (Herman, 1988). Environmental stressors such as joblessness and poverty add to such a family's vulnerability to abuse incidents of all kinds (Barnhill, 1982; Farrington, 1980; Gelles, 1973; Gil, 1970; Gondolf, 1993; Groth, Hobson, & Gary, 1982; Justice & Justice, 1976; Kempe & Kempe, 1976; Sonkin, Martin & Walker, 1985).

Assessment should include careful attention to the roles, strengths, weaknesses, and interactions of each child in a violent family (Kempe & Kempe, 1976), as well as each parent figure, including absent parents and grandparents. Absent persons may be crucial to the maintenance of current patterns of response to stress.

The Impact of Chemical Dependency

Alcohol and many other drugs, inasmuch as they are associated with behavioral disinhibition, raise the potential for any kind of impulsive behavior and hence the risk of violence as well as suicide, at least in cultures where it is believed they will (Gelles & Cornell, 1990; Shapiro, 1982). Alcohol intoxication has been specifically linked to child sexual, physical, and psychological abuse (Kaplan, Pelcovitz, Salzinger, & Ganeles, 1983; Murphy et al., 1991). Hallucinogens like PCP, inhalants like glue, amphetamines, barbiturates, benzodiazapines like Valium, and cocaine, especially crack cocaine, have all been implicated in violence. Narcotic drugs suppress violence, but addicts may resort to violence in the family context in order to obtain funds for their drug habit (Gelles & Cornell, 1990; Lion, 1987).

It is important not to see the violent behavior as merely a symptom of the addiction (Cooley & Severson, 1993; Herman, 1988; Stark & Flitcraft, 1988a), but it is crucial to assess the use of intoxicants by all family members at intake. The clinician should ask for specific information about patterns of use and not rely on the evaluative statements made by family members. The place of substance use in a particular family's process, especially its relationship to any violent or suicidal behaviors, must be identified. Persons who are intoxicated, are in withdrawal, or are long-term or consistent users are at very high risk for violence (Shapiro, 1982). (See Chapter 23.)

Biological Factors

According to some theorists the symptoms of posttraumatic stress disorder result from the normal responses of the autonomic nervous system (ANS) and the endogenous opioid system, which are interlinked. ANS arousal produces the intrusive and vigilant symptoms, and the endogenous opioid system produces an analgesia, or denial state similar to that produced by externally introduced opioid drugs (van der Kolk, 1988).

In either aggressor or victim, minimum brain dysfunction, a history of brain injury from accident or illness, or tumors of the limbic system and seizure disorders can be contributing factors to family violence. If the client has a history of disease or injury or does not respond to other interventions, a referral for neuropsychological testing or neurological examination may open up other avenues (Elliott, 1982; Feinstein, 1990; Lion, 1987).

A thirty-four-year-old mother brought her two daughters, ages eight and thirteen, for therapy because she was having trouble managing them. She had been raised in an alcoholic family and had left the girls' father three years before because of the battering that had gone on in the marriage. After several months of family sessions, many issues that affected the children's behavior had been addressed, but the mother was still having trouble being consistent with them. She complained of poor coordination and memory lapses, beginning with one battering incident about five years earlier, when she had been hospitalized for a head injury. She was angry about the marriage, her injuries, and her inability to get anyone to take her complaints of coordination and memory problems seriously. The client had a Medicaid managed care plan, and the therapist consulted with the gatekeeper about the problem. She suggested and approved payment for neuropsychological testing, which confirmed the client's report of her problems. Although no medical intervention was recommended, the client was able to focus and work through her anger. She developed motivation to use a variety of organizing tools to help her with her memory loss and through the use of charts and lists was able to become much more consistent.

RATIONALE FOR INTERRUPTION OF VIOLENT BEHAVIOR

Violence, as well as chemical dependency and suicidal ideation, threats, and attempts, can be understood to constitute coping strategies of great power for individuals, albeit inherently maladaptive ones. They operate in family systems as equally powerful homeostatic forces (Shapiro, 1982). Thus it is unlikely that any change the client seeks from therapy can be achieved while these behaviors continue. Rachlin (1990) points out that people are not "helped to grow" by killing or maiming another person. Neither are they helped to grow by being battered or sexually exploited.

Madanes (1990) comments, "To encourage kindness in ourselves and in others is consistent with every model of therapy. The practice of altruism is at the basis of all therapy, since therapy itself is a calling that requires an interest in doing good for others." The *NASW Code of Ethics* (1990) encourages fostering "maximum self-determination on the part of clients." This includes not engaging in "any action that violates or diminishes the civil or legal rights of clients." The social worker's responsibility to society includes acting to "expand choice and opportunity for all persons, with special regard for disadvantaged or oppressed groups and persons." In clinical settings, working directly with clients to end interpersonal violence can be viewed as fulfilling these ethical mandates.

CONFRONTING THE BEHAVIOR AND PROTECTING ITS TARGETS

Once the clinician has heard about an endangering behavior, the most important task is to ensure the safety of the client(s). For this purpose, clients include all family members the clinician has seen, as well as anyone else to whom they may pose a credible threat.

Flexibility is useful. It is easier to focus on the referrals needed if the clinician has anticipated dealing with a disclosure of violent behavior. Intake sessions may require longer than the allotted time, and it may be impossible to complete paperwork in the usual time frame. Consultation may be necessary while the clients are still in the office. It is helpful for clinicians and supervisors to discuss in advance how these issues should be handled in a particular setting.

All dangerous behaviors and disinhibiting factors like chemical dependency must be confronted as soon as they are noticed. Their seriousness is emphasized by the practitioner's calm determination. Once the behaviors have been confronted, steps must be taken to interrupt them (Register, 1993).

If the perpetrators are present, the clinician should ask them to take responsibility for their behavior and stop the abuse, assessing their willingness and ability to do so. If they appear willing and able to give a commitment to stop their behavior, it should be obtained. If there is substance use, the clinicians should request an abstinence commitment. The practitioner should ask about weapons, and if there are any, concrete plans should be made for their safekeeping outside the home.

Voluntary steps may be insufficient to stop the violence, or there may be legally mandated reports that must be made, as in the case of child abuse. If a perpetrator refuses to take responsibility for violent behavior, involuntary hospitalization may be an option if either the family or the therapeutic setting can file for commitment. In addition, domestic violence victims should be referred for legal assistance.

Violence toward children, by statute, is investigated and assessed by child welfare authorities, even if family members have agreed to end it. Since the agreement may have been made in a self-serving way or be impossible for family members to keep, there is considerable risk in failing to make a report in exchange for a no-violence contract. Accurate descriptions of several violent incidents should be sought so that protective services may make accurate decisions about whether to investigate. Families sometimes choose to discontinue treatment when a protective referral is made at intake. It is useful to discuss this issue with the family and offer referrals for treatment elsewhere. This often works in a paradoxical way, thereby allowing the family to decide to return.

In Marika's family the motivation for change was quite high. Both parents saw themselves as successes in other areas. Their older daughter had had significant problems, and they saw Marika and perhaps Stevie going the same way if they did not find a way to stop it. They had standing in the community to maintain.

When the clinician processed the children's suicidal ideation with them, they were horrified, especially when both children confirmed it. When the clinician told them she would have to make a protective services report because of the belt whippings, Steve just put his head in his hands and said, "I knew it." Theresa put up a halfhearted argument. When the clinician reiterated her need to make the report, she offered to give them a referral elsewhere. They looked at each other and decided to continue at the clinic. The clinician explored the presence of weapons in the home. Steve agreed to give his sister his gun, which he spontaneously admitted having thoughts of using. The sister was to call the clinic to confirm the transfer, and Steve gave the clinician her home number. Both parents agreed to a one-week abstinence contract, and Steve agreed to call his old sponsor in Alcoholics Anonymous for support and to go to meetings on the days he was not working. The parents also agreed to suspend any violent behavior or punishments until the next session. The clinician worked out a plan whereby if Steve got very angry, he would go to his sister's house overnight. If he refused, Theresa was to take the two children and go there herself. Both things had actually happened, but in a less planful way, in the past. Much of the intake information was deferred for collection at a later interview, although the clinician got a signature on the billing form. She was not absolutely sure the family would return. However, they seemed drained by all the disclosures, and it appeared unlikely that any violence would occur that night.

SUICIDAL BEHAVIOR, IDEATION, AND THREATS

Since suicidality is so highly associated with violence, it is often part of the picture at intake. Practitioners need to be familiar with techniques for assessing suicidality. If a client cannot give a good no-suicide commitment, hospitalization is appropriate. However, if the suicidal person is a victim of abuse or battering, care should be taken that neither the person nor family members interpret this as evidence of craziness and use it to place responsibility for the violence on the victim.

PARTNER VIOLENCE

Shelter programs provide an immediate method for interrupting violence when the violent partner is unwilling or unable to desist, and they serve as a useful alternative if the battering resumes. The multidimensional treatment that is recommended here over the long term is duplicated by shelters on a more intensive and short-term basis. In addition, most have aftercare services, which can continue to supplement an ongoing relationship with a therapist (Register, 1993). The location of most shelters is secret, but Traicoff (1982) reports good results in a shelter program that encourages visitation and on-site family treatment involving the batterer. If the client is the batterer and refuses to stop the behavior, or if the victim is willing to institute commitment proceedings, involuntary hospitalization of the batterer is an option, though seldom accomplished without great difficulty. However, if a victim does not wish to leave a battering situation, the therapist has no way of compelling her to do so and it is not clinically useful to try. In this situation, further treatment planning should focus on creating as much safety as possible within the situation, thereby allowing the family members to make decisions toward permanent safety (Seskin, 1988). All voluntary intervention should continue to place responsibility for the violence on the perpetrator(s) (Briere, 1989).

DEALING WITH CHEMICAL DEPENDENCY AS A COMPLICATING FACTOR

When violence and chemical dependency are present, both must be addressed at once. The therapist may ask the family members to agree to a rule forbidding the violent behavior, as well as asking for a commitment that the chemical use cease immediately. The user may require a controlled period of mandatory abstinence in an inpatient facility or structured outpatient treatment to assist with the stresses of early recovery. For the protection of all family members, the user's agreement must be obtained before proceeding with treatment planning.

STATUTORY REQUIREMENTS

A series of court cases beginning with *Tarasoff v. Board of Regents* (1976) have established two duties of therapists in cases where clients have a potential to harm a third party. In evaluating this potential, the clinician should take into account the client's apparent hostility, any threats, and the client's history of violent acts. The first duty is to exercise the "care and skill of a reasonable professional" in identifying clients who present a risk of harming others (Dix, 1987). The second is to exercise "reasonable professional care" in protecting others whose safety may become or has already been compromised (Dix, 1987). "Reasonableness" is decided based on what other clinicians in a similar situation might do (Applebaum, 1985b). A protective course of action must be selected, and then implemented (Applebaum, 1985a). This might include relying on current treatment, intensifying the treatment efforts, arranging for the client to give up weapons to others for safekeeping, hospitalizing the client (voluntarily or involuntarily), alerting law enforcement, or warning the intended victim. Since certain of these actions constitute a breach of confidentiality, it is appropriate to discuss the possibility and to advise the client at the time the breach becomes necessary (Beck, 1985b; Dix, 1987). Applebaum (1985a), Beck (1985b), and Rachlin (1990) recommend discussing these various alternatives with the client and also advise against warning intended victims unless all the other remedies have been exhausted. Beck (1985b) underscores the need for consultation before undertaking warning or if the clinician has any doubt at all about the assessment.

Reamer (1994), in evaluating how to balance confidentiality and protection, recommends that the clinician be able to present evidence that the client poses a threat of violence to a third party, that the risk of violence is "significant," that it is "imminent," and that there is evidence identifying a probable victim, either directly or by inference.

When partner battering is not the presenting problem, the clinician has a responsibility to assess for violence, and if it is found, to assess the risk according to the standards. The practitioner has a responsibility to conduct a careful and knowledgeable evaluation of the potential for harm, to address the violence in the treatment plan, and to take appropriate steps to stop the violence. Appropriate actions include the development of a safety plan with the client that may include a list of both legal and appropriate psychosocial community resources. In addition, there is a responsibility to assess for and report child abuse, to make efforts to get treatment for the perpetrator, and to document clearly these elements and the client's response, as well as the rationale for the treatment modalities used (Cervantes, 1993).

Records should reflect the factors considered in evaluating a client's potential for violence and the consultation that was sought, and if a client has made a threat or showed hostility that in the clinician's opinion did not reflect an actual risk, the incident should be documented and the reasons carefully recorded. If there is any uncertainty, consultation should be sought (Applebaum, 1985b; Dix, 1987; Reamer, 1994). Consultation should always be sought immediately in any situation where there is a danger to anyone and protection is not easily arranged.

All situations that might cause a reasonable practitioner to suspect that a child is in danger of psychological, sexual, or physical abuse or neglect or to have been so mistreated should be reported to child welfare authorities in the manner in which the laws of each state require. It is the clinician's responsibility to become familiar with such laws, and when there is uncertainty, for the clinician to obtain information from the state department of human services or social services, or the state office of the National Association of Social Workers. Failure to report may put a clinician at risk for criminal penalties and civil lawsuits, but reporting also may put her or him at risk if the report can be shown to have been made "in bad faith" or maliciously (Reamer, 1994).

The family may put tremendous emotional pressure on the practitioner not to report; however, in addition to the legal mandate to do so, a failure to report is collusive with the forces in the family supporting the violence. Such failures to report also deprive the family members of opportunities to reduce isolation and may tend to disconfirm the victim's reality.

In all these situations, there is a burden on the practitioner to be knowledgeable and up-to-date concerning the law and the resources necessary to follow the law (Cervantes, 1993).

REMEDIATION OF CAUSES AND EFFECTS

Historically, mental health professionals have failed to deal with family violence directly and have collaborated poorly with those community agencies created to deal with it (Gondolf, 1990). Both failures have seriously weakened the quality of service available to members of violent families.

Violence in the family represents a serious failure of basic life tasks and as such requires intensive intervention, from both mental health agencies and other resources. The families are often isolated and have fluid internal boundaries and poor communication. Their interactions with multiple agencies can lead to chaos without firm agency and professional boundaries (Briere, 1989) and good ongoing collaboration between the various professionals involved.

THE USE OF MULTIPLE INTERVENTIONS

Multiple interventions alter the family's routine and provide therapeutic contacts with different sources of change and solution. The literature on battering and child physical and sexual abuse advocates the use of four major therapeutic approaches: individual therapy, group therapy, education and support, and family therapy.

At least part of the rationale for multiple services is the opportunity they provide for family members to interact with a variety of individuals (Beezley, Martin, & Alexander, 1976; Giaretto, 1976; Ounsted & Lynch, 1976; Steele, 1976). Many communities now have a network of specialized services for violent families that can be used in addition to outpatient therapy for intervention.

The goals of intervention are to reduce denial of abusive behavior (past and present) and its impact, to interrupt the behavior, to place the responsibility for change on the perpetrator, and to eliminate the use of violence as a coping mechanism. Other goals are to introduce behavioral alternatives, to reduce shame and isolation, to stimulate internal growth through new interpersonal experiences, to increase the ability to trust, and to encourage the reorganization of the client's worldview and identity so as to promote a positive integration of the abuse experience (Briere, 1989, 1992; Giaretto, 1976; Harway, 1993; Herman, 1988, 1992; Ounsted & Lynch, 1976; Walker, 1992).

Perpetrators of battering and abuse may also be survivors, but they are often more difficult to treat. In effect, their violent behavior gives them power and is therefore difficult to renounce. Another reason is that violent individuals typically have become entrenched in their use of identification with the aggressor; this defense serves as a barrier to the person's own past pain as well as that of others. Such clients rarely come to treatment willingly, and even when they do, they may not be motivated to stop their violent behavior. When there are additional problems, such as chemical dependency, the likelihood of successful treatment is further diminished (Gondolf, 1993).

Marika's family participated in various interventions during the sixteen months they had contact with the clinic. Both parents and Marika took part in chemical dependency information groups, and the parents were referred first for more extensive assessment, then later for individual chemical dependency treatment. Both attended AA, and Marika went with them to AlaTeen. The following fall, the parents were referred for parent education. Family therapy focused on generational patterns of chemical dependency and abuse, the difficulty of adjusting to the children's increasing independence, and finally, the core problems in the marriage. Marika's individual therapy focused on her anger and sense of abandonment by her parents, her fear of being like each parent in different ways, and her own fear of the future. Steve was referred to a batterers' group and attended for the prescribed period. However, at termination, Steve's therapist observed that Steve continued to believe that his behavior was justified under certain circumstances. The clinician never became aware of any further abuse of the children or of any resumption of the battering. Marika's school performance stabilized, and she began to participate in several extracurricular activities. She expressed an interest in law, law enforcement, or firefighting. Her relationships with boys became less consuming.

MEDICAL INTERVENTION

Referrals for medical care are useful first steps in working with violent families (Steele, 1976b). The high level of stress in such families often increases the impact of existing medical problems and may create a greater risk of developing an illness. Not surprisingly, health problems can interfere with clients' ability to regain emotional equilibrium (Walker, 1992).

Health care in such families is often neglected. Clients may have sustained injuries from earlier or current abuse of which they remain unaware (Lewis, 1987) and for which they have had no medical treatment. Other medical conditions such as hypertension, thyroid disease, infections, or anemia can affect clients' behavior, mood, and reality testing. In one situation, a battered adult survivor of physical and sexual abuse experienced several weeks of severe anemia that had gone undetected. Her lowered energy level contributed significantly to an existing depression and precipitated a highly lethal suicide attempt.

Obtaining medical care is an opportunity for clients to focus on improving self-care and to reduce denial of the seriousness of their own situation. The clinician should ask for releases to obtain records of medical evaluations, so health information can then be integrated into the treatment plan.

INDIVIDUAL THERAPY

Individual treatment allows an intensive focus on the needs of a particular client. If the client is an adult in an unsafe situation, individual treatment can focus on empowerment in assisting the client in overcoming helplessness. Furthermore, individual therapy can assist clients in problem solving and provide them with help in dealing with social agencies (Register, 1993). It is an excellent venue for establishing trust and for setting limits to which the client agrees, although the therapist may anticipate that such limits will be tested (Madden, 1987).

Individual therapy is important for the child or adult client whose history includes sexual, physical, or emotional abuse. Most authors now advocate therapy that focuses on the abuse as the cause of the client's difficulties and avoids blaming, stigmatizing, or framing the client's problems as a "sickness." Such therapy respects the survival skills that clients have acquired in an abusive milieu; furthermore, the therapist displays a positive regard for the client rather than regarding that person as "sick." Finally, the ultimate goal of treatment with such clients is psychological growth rather than a cure per se. If the client has impairments in the areas of affect regulation, self-support, and self-definition, these can be addressed first. When some resolution has occurred, the therapist can begin to explore the effects of posttraumatic stress. Roles in current relationships may be explored and connections drawn to victim, aggressor, and caretaking roles that may have been played out in earlier abusive relationships (Brendler, Silver, Haber, & Sargent, 1990; Briere, 1989, 1992; Giaretto, 1976; Harway, 1993; Herman, 1988; Stark & Flitcraft, 1988b).

When the client is a child, cognitive, affective, and social development as well as psychosexual development must be taken into account in treatment planning. The successful completion of such tasks is often severely compromised by exposure to violence and/or victimization (Berman, 1993).

Individual therapy can be flexible enough to allow the clinician to approach clients wholistically, so that there is attention not only to psychological matters but also to physical and spiritual well-being. Desensitization and relaxation exercises can be taught (Briere, 1989). Physical activity and good nutrition can be fostered to help in healing the body and reducing ANS arousal. Clinicians may encourage clients in their efforts to develop their own spiritual frameworks, which may have been stunted or abandoned as irrelevant during a period of abuse (Sargent, 1989). Any healthy humor the client brings to the situation can be nurtured. These more adaptive coping strategies may help to ameliorate conflict and reduce violent behavior in the client's life (Merwin & Smith-Kurtz, 1988).

Cognitive therapy can be useful for adult survivors of sexual abuse as well as for battering victims. In fact, it is an indispensable part of treatment for battering partners and parents. It may help them to reframe the behavior of others, gain some distance, and thereby alter their perspective on their own behavior, which may defuse conflict further (Bedrosian, 1982; Briere, 1989; Twentyman, Rohrbeck, & Amish, 1984).

Individual therapy for violent persons as well as for survivors should include efforts to address the consequences of their behaviors on others. They can also be helped to recognize the physiological signs of an impending loss of control and various alternative behaviors that may prove more adaptive. These techniques might include leaving the scene of the conflict or problem or various relaxation routines. Additional techniques include helping the client substitute more positive ways of thinking about the problem, writing about it, or carrying on an internal conversation about it with the therapist (Briere, 1989).

Individual treatment may be contraindicated for children who must remain in homes where partner violence has not ended. If it is undertaken, it should be only with a clear understanding that certain kinds of adaptive strategies (e.g., assertiveness) may place the child at even greater risk (Berman, 1993).

PSYCHIATRIC CARE

Psychiatric intervention is necessary in order to obtain medication that may be appropriate in helping clients to combat anxiety and depression associated with victimization (Lion, 1987; Madden, 1987; Roth, 1988; van der Kolk, 1988). Psychiatric consultation may be useful in making decisions as to whether violent or suicidal individuals should be hospitalized. If medication or hospitalization is introduced as part of planning for victims, these strategies should be presented and discussed with clients and their families to avoid interpretation by them as evidence of their "craziness."

THE USE OF GROUPS

Groups have been recommended for a variety of problems related to domestic violence. They can be of benefit to adult survivors of physical abuse (Walker, 1992) and sexual abuse (Briere, 1989; Herman, 1981, 1992; Walker, 1992), victims of domestic violence (Seskin, 1988; Stark & Flitcraft, 1988a; Register, 1993; Walker, 1992) and nonoffending parents in sexually abusing families (Giaretto, 1976). They are recommended for children, including child victims of sexual abuse (Sirles, Walsma, Lytle-Barnaby, & Lander, 1988) and traumatized children of abused women (Peled & Edelson, 1995). They are recommended to benefit parents who physically abuse their children (Barnhill, 1982) and are seen by some authors as a treatment of choice for perpetrators of domestic violence (Power, 1988; Nosko & Wallace, 1988; Farley & Magill, 1988) as well as adolescent (O'Brien, 1985) and adult perpetrators of sexual abuse (Giaretto, 1976).

Group participation reduces denial of the violence and its effect on family relationships. Group process has been shown to decrease shame and isolation and also provides a venue in which feelings can be explored and new styles of interaction experienced. An additional advantage of groups is a psychoeducational focus that permits clients to identify and change behaviors that have contributed to the abuse (Madden, 1987).

Most treatment of batterers and perpetrators is conducted in groups, primarily because it is a highly effective mode of treatment for confronting abusive attitudes and behavior. Treatment techniques include anger management, skill building in communication patterns including conflict management and assertiveness training, stress reduction, and cognitive restructuring in areas related to sex roles and attitudes in order to increase accountability. Good treatment should minimize the likelihood of participants' viewing the learning process as a means to obtain a quick fix to satisfy spouses or societal authorities (Gondolf, 1993).

When treatment groups are not available, there is still general value in the use of community support groups as an adjunct to individual and family treatment. Alcoholics Anonymous, Rational Recovery, Narcotics Anonymous, Al-Anon, Nar-anon, Co-Dependents Anonymous, Ala-teen and Ala-Tot, Adult Children of Alcoholics, Survivors of Incest Anonymous, Sex Addicts Anonymous, Parents Anonymous, Parents United, Recovery, Inc., Emotions Anonymous, and Agoraphobics in Motion are examples of the various groups that can be found in many communities. These groups can provide clients with opportunities to decrease their shame and isolation and help them to experience a different type of interaction. They can explore feelings in a more controlled and safer environment, and even develop cognitive structures for the more effective management of violent impulses.

CONJOINT FAMILY STRATEGIES

Conjoint methods of treatment—those that include perpetrators of physical violence or sexual abuse—are not recommended by most specialists until the violent parties are willing and able to stop their violent behavior. Violence creates a source of power and control that effectively prevents change in family interaction. Perpetrators may verbalize compliant stances in sessions while giving subtle nonverbal cues of violent retribution for change, or they may have verbalized threats prior to the sessions. Revictimization can be triggered by interactions in sessions. Victims and nonoffending family members remain vulnerable because of a fear of loss and the need for love and acceptance (Briere, 1989).

The usual methods associated with systems theory avoid assigning responsibility for problems to any individual and encourage all family members to change their attitudes and behavior in order to develop a solution. In violent families, however, such a stance gives power to the violent person and reduces the power of those who are unwilling to be violent or are simply less physically powerful. This effectively prevents meaningful therapeutic change. Not only is it ineffective, but it may be damaging to assign responsibility for the violence to the couple, to the system, and particularly to the provocative behavior of the victim. It is equally problematic to avoid assigning any responsibility. Responsibility should be assigned to the batterers or abusers because they alone can change their behavior. Any other strategy excuses them from doing so.

The social context of abusive behavior consists of attitudes about the relative power of men and women in the family, as well as the rights of parents to control the lives of children. It is virtually impossible to challenge abusive behavior without identifying and confronting the evidence of these attitudes in individual client families (Hansen, 1993). The clinician must never lose sight of the destructive impact of violent behavior on family relationships (Bograd, 1992). If there is any sense on the clinician's part that the batterer or abuser is being superficially compliant, family therapy should either not be employed or should be immediately discontinued.

Behavioral contracts need to be carefully constructed to avoid placing the responsibility for ending the violent encounters on anyone but the violent parties. Such contracts must never explicitly or implicitly promote the idea that a cessation of violence should be linked to increased compliance with the wishes of the abuser (Brendler, Silver, Haber, & Sargent, 1990; Stark & Flitcraft, 1988a). There is one exception to this rule: if the only victim is an adult who is unprepared to leave a battering partner and that partner is not engaged in treatment, family therapy may focus on strategies for creating short-term safety for the victim and planning for the children's security.

If there is no ongoing substance abuse, psychotic process, or other serious psychopathology, and the violence has ended, conjoint and family sessions may be effective for empowering the survivor. If the perpetrator is included, mutually agreed upon rules should be made to protect the survivor from revictimization during or as a result of a session and to assist the batterer in controlling violent behavior. If there is a threat of violence, the session should be ended and the plan to see the couple conjointly reevaluated (Bedrosian, 1982; Berman, 1993; Hansen & Goldenberg, 1993; Papp, 1988; Power, 1988). Saving the relationship or reuniting the family should never be the goal of work with violent families (Berman, 1993).

Despite the dysfunction present in violent families, their ability to come together for treatment and work cooperatively with the therapist generally means they are at less risk for continued violence (Feinstein, 1990). Dyadic sessions, or sessions excluding the perpetrator, may be used to strengthen key relationships prior to sessions including all family members (Briere, 1989; Giaretto, 1976). The goals of family treatment are to create firm but permeable boundaries, clarify family roles, defuse triangles in which one family member mediates conflict between two others, increase positive direct communication, decrease secrecy, normalize developmental change, and decrease the power of compulsive cycles.

Development of personal boundaries begins with the recognition of abusive behaviors and the commitment and planning necessary to stop them. This work may begin with a confrontation of the perpetrators if they are ready to stop the behavior (Hansen & Goldberg, 1993), or it may include only nonoffending family members or survivors, and focus on the creation of safety, privacy, and interpersonal support (Briere, 1989; Giaretto, 1976).

Subsystem boundaries and roles should be clarified (Brendler, Silver, Haber, & Sargent, 1990; Hansen & Goldberg, 1993). Marital and parenting issues should be separated. In marital work, the positive qualities in each partner and the relationship should be examined and supported (Hansen & Goldberg, 1993). The family hierarchy should be corrected so that the parents are in charge of the family. If family members are seen together, the development of conflict resolution skills should be addressed. Interaction should be modified so that only positive behavior is rewarded (Madanes, 1990). Sibling solidarity should be promoted. Any rigid roles that have developed among the children, including scapegoating, should be defused (Bedrosian, 1982; Berman, 1993; Hansen & Goldberg, 1993; Papp, 1988; Power, 1988). If neither parent is able to protect the children, new protectors should be sought from within the extended family (Madanes, 1990).

The external boundaries of the family should be clarified and its isolation from the outside world reduced. If there are triangles that include the parents of a violent couple, such triangles should be confronted and defused (Hansen & Goldberg, 1993). If representatives of other systems such as probation officers, protective service workers, or foster care workers have power in the family hierarchy, it is appropriate to include them in sessions in order to increase communication and clarify their roles (Brendler, Silver, Haber, & Sargent, 1990).

The final task is to decrease the fear of abandonment among family members by increasing the capacity for intimacy. Communication and conflict resolution skills must be strengthened. Work can focus on decreasing the intensity of the emotional interaction and increasing the accuracy of the couple's interpersonal perceptions. The therapist can utilize such techniques as asking the clients to speak to her rather than to each other, reframing communications in a less inflammatory way, supporting the assertive communication of anger and the batterer's ability to take responsibility for the violent behavior (Hansen & Goldberg, 1993; Madanes, 1990). Covert strategies for meeting needs should be exposed. Positive communication should be increased in order to support the sense of being loved and to decrease the anxiety about abandonment (Madanes, 1990). Secrets must be exposed and family members desensitized to the issues they protect, a process that challenges family rules, traditions, and myths (Brendler, Silver, Haber, & Sargent, 1990; Madanes, 1990). Compulsive cycles should be explored, so that as intimacy increases and shame lessens, such cycles may lose their power (Fossum & Mason, 1986). Family developmental tasks should be identified and family members encouraged to develop an understanding of how intimacy can continue in the context of change and growth.

When the family cannot remain together and be safe because the perpetrator is unable to give up the violent behavior, the therapist can help the survivor to relinquish her unilateral efforts to work on the relationship and to refocus instead on her needs and those of the children (Hansen & Goldberg, 1993). If the adult victim of battering is unable to leave, the therapist should clearly identify for the parents the negatives for the children in such a situation (Berman, 1993). (For information about family treatment, refer to Chapter 6.)

THE NEED FOR CONCURRENT CHEMICAL DEPENDENCY TREATMENT

Inpatient treatment may be necessary to help an actively chemically dependent family member take the initial steps toward sobriety. Outpatient chemical dependency treatment may follow an inpatient stay or may in itself provide sufficient structure to help the client achieve consistent abstinence. Twelve-step programs are usually part of treatment, and once sobriety is reliably achieved, such programs may become the most important method of maintaining it (Shapiro, 1982). Sobriety and violence-free living should be valued above keeping families and couples together, and whatever supports both should be encouraged (Cooley & Severson, 1993).

CONTROVERSIES

One major controversy pertains to the recommendation of family treatment for domestic violence. Some therapists, most notably feminist clinicians, have been disinclined to recommend family treatment owing to the possibility that the batterer may gain additional control over the partner and other family members. They advise strongly against the use of contracts that exchange the cessation of violence for increased compliance with batterers' wishes (Stark & Flitcraft, 1988a). Nonfeminist approaches typically avoid assigning responsibility for the violence and attend equally to the behavior of perpetrator and victim(s) even when the latter are children.

Reporting of child abuse and other efforts by practitioners and public agencies to intervene in family violence have been regarded in the past by some as interference in the family and a form of social control. However, as child abuse reporting laws have become universal in the United States, this controversy has lost currency. Some experts believe that media preoccupation with domestic assault, whether the result of positive or negative motives, has contributed to this trend.

Many critics identify the medical model itself as being a barrier in working effectively with a variety of life problems, including family violence, for several reasons: it relies excessively on institutional hierarchical structure, ignores the weight of social and political circumstances, and is implemented by people who may view themselves as being superior to their patients and other helping professionals (Gondolf, 1990).

Largely aligned with the traditional medical model viewpoint is the notion that diagnostic categories underlie violence as well as the responses of its victims. Increasingly mental health professionals accept the idea that violence forms part of the etiology of a variety of diagnostic categories, in addition to being part of the symptomatology. Feminist therapists, however, object to the use of diagnostic categories because they are viewed as a way of stigmatizing victims of interpersonal violence. They note that, when used to guide treatment, such categories are inherently problematic: they deflect the therapist from the violent context of the victim's behavior and the adaptiveness of her behavior within the context of a battering relationship; furthermore, traditional diagnostic categories deny the victim's reality and can cause the therapist to avoid dealing with safety issues (Harway, 1993).

TRANSFERENCE ISSUES

Transference refers to the process by which a client feels and behaves toward the clinician and other figures as though they were important figures from the past; this involves both projection and displacement and in a sense is the client's unconscious effort to re-create such early relationships and the affective milieu in which they existed. Clients who have grown up in abusive environments bring to their relationships an expectation that those in caretaking roles will also behave inconsistently, alternating positive behavior with hostility and destructiveness. Therapeutic relationships are no exception. These feelings and expectations are most intense in connection with power dynamics, trust and abandonment, anger, and, in the case of those who have been sexually abused, sexuality.

Because the client's earliest experiences with authority have been contaminated by terror, the therapist's inherent greater power in the treatment relationship induces a similar dynamic intensity (Herman, 1992). Clients feel helpless and unequal, and much of the work of therapy involves rebalancing the power dynamic, so that they can experience themselves as being in control of their participation in the treatment relationship. Clients may continually feel they have lost control in therapy and test the therapist, using behaviors that were successful in their families of origin (Briere, 1989; Courtois, 1988; Herman, 1992; Walker, 1992). Aversive, angry, or blaming behaviors are easier to identify than placating and caretaking ones (Courtois, 1988). Power dynamics vary with the gender of the therapist and client, and the family dynamics in the client's family of origin (Briere, 1989).

Clients from abusive environments have great difficulty with trust. They perceive themselves negatively and expect to be rejected by others. If they are met with positive regard and consistent respect, they often become frightened and behave in ways designed to create interpersonal distance. It is easier for them to tolerate loss if they themselves create it. Once they allow themselves to open up in treatment, any events that threaten the loss of the therapist, including vacations and planned termination due to good progress, may trigger a return to earlier and more archaic levels of functioning (Briere, 1989; Courtois, 1988; Herman, 1992).

A family of four had been seen for about ten months at a family service agency. The presenting problems consisted of poor supervision, physical abuse (belt whippings) of the ten-year-old daughter who was scapegoated, and battering initiated by the husband but including retaliation by the wife. The parents were both physical abuse survivors who had been together since high school. They were highly motivated and had benefited from prior work on family-of-origin issues, marital communication, and conflict resolution exercises, as well as from their participation in a parenting group. The influence of the grandparents, the source of much conflict, had been defused, and the little girl's behavior and her treatment by the parents had improved. Violence stopped immediately following the first interview.

The clinician had always been clear with them that treatment could not last much longer than six months, but when she reminded them at the beginning of the termination phase that only four more sessions had been approved, they became angry and hostile and accused her of not trying hard enough to get additional sessions for them. They appeared thirty-five minutes late for their next session. When the therapist reminded them that only fifteen minutes would be available for the interview, they reported an angry incident at home immediately before the session. Their five-year-old son had used a forbidden word to his father, who had shoved a full-size bar of soap into his mouth. Traces of blood could still be seen. When the clinician told the family members she would have to make a report to protective services, they stormed out of the office. More sessions were approved for the purpose of processing their feelings about the loss of the therapist, but they refused to return to her. Instead they were assigned to another clinician who attempted to help them work through their loss. Success in that area was difficult to judge, but there were no more reports of abuse before they terminated.

An abrupt shift from positive attachment and idealization to rage at the clinician, as in the preceding case example, is characteristic of abuse survivors in treatment. Clients continually scrutinize the therapist's behavior. Because they have few experiences on which to base a benign view of human motivation, when the clinician inadvertently reminds them of a hostile figure from the past or fails to live up to the idealized image (as she or he inevitably must) they react with fear and rage (Briere, 1989; Herman, 1992). This intense anger is associated with an inability to recognize, at that moment, any of the therapist's positive actions or characteristics. This splitting of the external object is paralleled by the abused client's view of himself or herself as all good or all bad; consequently such clients evince sharp shifts in mood and self-concept. This defensive phenomenon is known as splitting. Splitting is a defensive residue of early life experience in which a child is abused, then treated lovingly, even indulgently, by violent parents. Transference rage, as well as the anxiety and depression that stem from it, is most common when clients are legitimately grieving their past mistreatment but are as yet unable to direct their anger toward its actual objects (Courtois, 1988; Herman, 1992).

Clients who have been sexually abused often repeat portions of the dynamics of the original abuse scenario with the therapist. Their experiences have taught them that the only value they can have in a relationship is a sexual one. They may present themselves as feeling that a sexual relationship is the only convincing evidence of caring (Herman, 1992). This sexualization of the treatment relationship stems not from any actual desire to have a sexual relationship with the therapist but from unconscious assumptions based on the abuse experience. Such assumptions might include ideas about what sort of behaviors might be expected by those with power or the client's belief that the only way to procure support and affiliation is to barter for it by using sex (Briere, 1989).

As the case example shows, seeing clients together as a family does not dilute the transference dynamics. Children who are seen in play therapy may displace transferential material onto the play process, but the therapist inevitably will receive some of it (Maravasti, 1989).

In order to create a therapeutic environment for the client, the clinician should maintain an empathic stance, alert to her or his own responses, and willing to use them in understanding the client. In a therapeutic relationship the clinician is respectful, egalitarian, and realistically trustworthy. He or she does not react to rage with rage or abandonment or to sexualization with seduction or abandonment (Briere, 1989; Courtois, 1988; Herman, 1992; Walker, 1992). However, many countertransference reactions are possible, and the therapist's use of countertransference may provide important clues to the client's experience.

COUNTERTRANSFERENCE ISSUES

We are choosing to adopt a broad modern definition of countertransference to include all of the therapist's emotional reactions to the client and to other persons or entities significant to the therapy. These reactions are regarded as important clues to the process of the therapy (Racker, 1957; Heimann, 1950; Little, 1951, 1957; Wilson & Lindy, 1995b).

Wilson and Lindy (1995b) address the countertransference phenomena encountered in the treatment of posttraumatic stress disorder. Since ongoing violence and suicidality are highly correlated with a history of trauma and since posttraumatic stress disorder is often a diagnosis in situations where there is ongoing violence, an understanding of therapist countertransference may be especially relevant to this clinical population. Lindy and Wilson define countertransference broadly to include "normative" and "personalized" therapist reactions to the material presented by the client and to the client's transference. They postulate that the strain of remaining in empathic contact with persons who have experienced great pain and suffering causes each therapist to react in characteristic ways along a continuum from overidentification to avoidance. Normative reactions, which anyone might experience, consist of empathic disequilibrium and empathic withdrawal. Empathic disequilibrium occurs when the clinician experiences discomfort from overidentification with the client but does not withdraw. Empathic withdrawal describes an avoidance of the client's pain. The personalized reactions, which result from the therapist's own unresolved conflicts and traumatic experiences, are described as empathic enmeshment and empathic repression. In empathic enmeshment, the clinician is unable to separate his or her own unresolved issues from the client's. In empathic repression, the clinician loses the ability to "feel with" the client in order to defend against her or his own pain. Wilson and Lindy regard normative reactions as a potentially invaluable tool in understanding and relating to the client's subjective experience. When countertransference reactions, particularly those of the personalized type, are mismanaged, the likelihood of treatment disruption increases significantly (Wilson & Lindy, 1995b). Consistent with the self-psychological treatment model, Wilson, Lindy, & Raphael (1994) emphasize the therapist's reactions and responses, which form part of the "dance of empathy." It is through the therapist's ability to use himself or herself in empathically resonant, attuned ways that the client gradually becomes better able to make better use of the relationship. The therapeutic experience of being soothed and calmed is gradually transmuted and internalized by the client.

Empathic enmeshment may lead the clinician into overidentification, projection, and boundary confusion, perhaps the most prevalent countertransferences (Briere, 1992). Herman (1988) notes that female therapists may overidentify with the sexual abuse victim, male therapists with the offender. Boundary confusion may lead the therapist into such countertherapeutic behaviors and attitudes as premature and intrusive questioning, unrealistic expectations for family change (Mrazek, 1981), and even overt sexual behavior toward the client.

Sexually abused clients may switch roles in therapy frequently. The clinician may respond by switching to a complementary role. Such unrecognized countertransference behavior encourages reenactment of past maladaptive roles rather than meaningful change (Ganzarain & Buchele, 1988).

A twenty-year-old survivor of incest, six months after discharge from inpatient chemical dependency treatment, regularly expressed suicidal thoughts and profound self-blame for both incest and drug use, but at the same time was resistant to attending Narcotics Anonymous meetings to maintain her recovery. The therapist spent much of each session encouraging and reassuring her, while having more and more angry thoughts about her reluctance to give up her depressive thinking. At the end of each encounter, the client would firmly but reluctantly agree not to use substances or commit suicide. The therapist felt uneasy about taking a much delayed and needed vacation despite careful planning for coverage. While he was away, the client relapsed. At her first session after his return, the therapist found himself taking responsibility for the client's use of drugs, although the client reassured him it was not his fault. After the session, following consultation with a colleague, he realized what had happened. As a result he was able to address both the behaviors and feelings with the client in the next session. The work then focused on helping the client identify more clearly her inability to control the incest, as well as her ability to be responsible for her behavior now as a young adult. She began to attend recovery meetings consistently and gradually developed a better capacity for self-comfort.

Clinicians whose own personal histories include experiences of victimization or exposure to domestic assault may be more vulnerable to empathic enmeshment (Friedrich, 1990). A therapist who is a survivor may be able to explore the positive elements in the relationship between the victim and offender but may also impose elements of her or his own experience on the treatment, or even be overwhelmed by an intrusive reexperience of his or her own abuse. Therapists who are themselves survivors need to achieve a thorough resolution of their own trauma. The therapist's disclosure of his or her own victimization to the client should be carefully evaluated for several reasons, not the least of which is to avoid presenting the self as a model to the client (Mrazek, 1981).

In working with battered women, there is a temptation to try to motivate them to leave their abusive partners before they are ready or to become angry (like the assailant might) when they return to a battering relationship. If the clinician has negative attitudes toward female roles that include power, independence, noncompliance, and deliberate failure to nurture the partner, it will be difficult for her or him to support actions that are independent or noncompliant or do not provide nurturance to abusive partners. Conversely, positive clinical attitudes toward these qualities can help the client change her interactions with her batterer or leave him. In addition, the therapist must be willing to discuss violence and to communicate a nonviolent value system without attempting to impose it (Register, 1993). Operationally, this issue can be framed as the need to identify a style of interaction with victims of violence without adopting a passive or controlling stance indigenous to violent systems.

Other reactions have been noted. Therapists may have a need to be with abused children or families because of a compulsion to rework some part of their own experience (Friend, 1972). An insistence on a certain treatment modality, especially if applied globally, may be a signal that the therapist is reworking his or her own family role (Maravasti, 1992).

Examples of empathic withdrawal and repression might include the following: clinicians may fail to recognize the existence and intensity of family violence (Gondolf, 1990), to report suspected child maltreatment (Zelman, 1990), or to recommend hospitalization; or perhaps clinicians may refuse treatment due to the client's noncompliance. They may make innaccurate reports to court personnel or other authorities (Madden, 1987). Such failures can be motivated by guilty identifications with perpetrators, attempts to defend against hostility toward them, a need to please (Maravasti, 1992), realistic or projective fear of verbal or physical retaliation by the family, or feeling the report represents the clinician's failure in helping or controlling the family (Pollak & Levy, 1989). Madden (1987) identifies a danger of using medication to manage violent clients when the clinician grows weary of treating them.

Empathic disequilibrium creates uncertainty, vulnerability, and unmodulated affect (Wilson & Lindy, 1994). Common emotional responses to sexually abusive families include anger, overidentification, helplessness, horrified disbelief, sexual fantasies, guilt, a need to blame, and rescue fantasies (Ganzarain & Buchele, 1988; Mrazek, 1981). McCann and Pearlman (1990) identify the psychological effects of working with victims as "vicarious traumatization." The therapist's worldview becomes insidiously altered as she or he becomes familiarized with clients' trauma.

Physical abuse victims and battering parents evoke strong countertransference reactions based on the dynamics of authority and power. Therapists may use reaction formation to guard against grandiose or authoritarian wishes or experience a euphoria when the client's transference evokes a feeling of power (Maravasti, 1992).

All of these reactions may surprise the inexperienced clinician with their intensity. If ego syntonic, they may seem as intoxicating as falling in love. If ego dystonic, their power to shame may cause secrecy and obsessive rumination. Both types of countertransferential reactions can lead to dysjunctive therapeutic moves or to therapeutic stalemates. However, minimizing the negative impact of countertransference reactions rests on four relatively simple recommendations: self-examination, consultation, supervision, and learning experiences.

Self-examination (Madden, 1987) may occur in solitude, in casual interaction, or in the context of the therapist's own psychotherapy. Briere (1989, 1992, p. 162) recommends the last as an "especially efficient way to address the roots of abuse-related countertransference" and to support the high levels of objectivity and trustworthiness needed in work with child abuse survivors.

Consultation and supervision provide immediate and regular structured opportunities to review clinical work, get feedback, reduce uncertainty, and defuse shame (Briere, 1989, 1992; Lion, 1987; Madden, 1987). Madden (1987) warns that it may be difficult to find a consultant with whom one feels comfortable in discussing feelings evoked by work with violent clients. Supervision implies a greater degree of accountability than consultation and may be the best choice for less experienced practitioners. Lion (1987) notes that countertransference issues may be responsible when clinicians differ significantly in their estimates of the dangerousness of abuse situations.

Learning experiences provide a supportive framework in which to evaluate one's own responses (Briere, 1992; Lion, 1987; Madden, 1987) and help to erode denial of countertransference responses.

Mixed case loads, socializing with nonclinicians, and becoming involved in political action are also recommended as ways to reduce problematic countertransference responses (Briere, 1989).

OUTCOMES

The most desirable outcomes occur when intervention allows abuse victims to receive support and protection while the abuse is intercurrent or has just been disclosed. In incestuous families, a major criterion for termination is the restoration of the mother-daughter relationship or another protective relationship (Herman, 1988; Madanes, 1990). Taking this example as a model for other abusive situations allows the construction of a general rule. In abusive families a positive outcome has been reached when violence can be prevented and victims feel safe even when perpetrators are not cooperative. Positive outcomes for abusers themselves depend largely on the absence of psychosis, personality disorder, and chemical dependency and on the length of time spent in treatment. Progress is difficult, and good progress takes time (Gondolf, 1993).

CONCLUSION

It is painful to recognize the pervasiveness of violent behavior present in clinical populations and impossible to avoid encountering it. Accurate assessment depends on the social worker's willingness to ask questions about violence and a readiness to help clients achieve safety. Because of the emergent nature of dangerous situations and the strong transference and countertransference feelings they engender, clinicians must develop self-awareness and an openness to consultation. Intervention requires knowledge of and willingness to use the law as well as community resources in helping family members achieve safety because no meaningful change is possible while the violent behavior continues.

In order to treat violent families and their members successfully, clinicians need knowledge of the dynamics of these families, knowledge of other treatment resources, and a willingness to share the task of treatment with others. Good professional boundaries, as well as the collegial and supervisory support required to keep them intact, are crucial. Patience and realism are necessary to see these clients through the treatment process to a reasonably successful conclusion.

There is a dual reward for the development of these skills and strengths. The first is the knowledge that every client has been given an opportunity to eliminate violent behavior from his or her life. The second is that as families are helped to become less violent, their children may in turn grow up to lead violence-free lives.

REFERENCES

Ageton, S. (1983). *Sexual assault among adolescents.* Lexington, MA: Lexington Books.

American Humane Association. (1981). *National study on child neglect and reporting.* Denver: Author.

American Humane Association. (1984). *National study on child neglect and reporting.* Denver: Author.

American Psychiatric Association. (1987). *Diagnostic and statistical manual of mental disorders* (3rd ed., rev.). Washington, DC: Author.

American Psychiatric Association. (1994). *Diagnostic and statistical manual of mental disorders* (4th ed.). Washington, DC: Author.

Applebaum, P. S. (1985a). Rethinking the duty to protect. In J. C. Beck, *The potentially violent patient and the Tarasoff decision in psychiatric practice.* Washington, DC: American Psychiatric Press.

Applebaum, P. S. (1985b). Implications of Tarasoff for clinical practice. In J. C. Beck, *The potentially violent patient and the Tarasoff decision in psychiatric practice.* Washington, DC: American Psychiatric Press.

Bedrosian, R. (1982). Using cognitive and systems intervention in the treatment of marital violence. In L. Barnhill (Ed.), *Clinical approaches to family violence.* Rockville, MD: Aspen.

Barnhill, L. (Ed.). (1982). *Clinical approaches to family violence.* Rockville, MD: Aspen.

Barnhill, L., Squires, M., & Gibson, G. (1982). Epidemiology of violence in a CMHC setting. In L. Barnhill (Ed.), *Clinical approaches to family violence.* Rockville, MD: Aspen.

Beck, J. C. (1985a). *The potentially violent patient and the Tarasoff decision in psychiatric practice.* Washington, DC: American Psychiatric Press.

Beck, J. C. (1985b). Overview and conclusions. In J. C. Beck, *The potentially violent patient and the Tarasoff decision in psychiatric practice.* Washington, DC: American Psychiatric Press.

Becker, J. V., & Abel, G. G. (1985). Methodological and ethical issues in evaluating and treating adolescent sexual offenders. In E. M. Otey & G. D. Ryan, *Adolescent sex offenders: Issues in treatment and research.* Rockville, MD: U.S. Department of Health and Human Services.

Beezley, P., Martin, H., & Alexander, H. (1976). Comprehensive family oriented therapy. In R. E. Helfer & C. H. Kempe (Eds.), *Child abuse and neglect: The family and the community.* Cambridge, MA: Ballinger.

Berman, P. S. (1993). Impact of abusive marital relationships on children. In M. Hansen & M. Harway, *Battering and family therapy: A feminist perspective.* Newbury Park, CA: Sage.

Bograd, M. (1992, July). Values in conflict: Challenges to family therapists' thinking. *Journal of Marital and Family Therapy, 18* (3), 245–256.

Bowker, L., Arbitel, M., & McFerron, J. (1988). *On the relationship between wife beating and child abuse.* Newbury Park, CA: Sage.

Brandell, J. R. (Ed.). (1992). *Countertransference in psychotherapy with children and adolescents.* Northvale, NJ: Jason Aronson.

Brassard, M. R., Germain, R., & Hart, S. N. (Eds.). (1987). *Psychological maltreatment of children and youth.* New York: Pergamon.

Brendler, J., Silver, M., Haber, M., & Sargent, J. (1990). *Madness, chaos, and violence: Therapy with families at the brink.* New York: Basic Books.

Briere, J. N. (1989). *Therapy for adults molested as children: Beyond survival.* New York: Springer.

Briere, J. N. (1992). *Child abuse trauma: Theory and treatment of the lasting effects.* Newbury Park, CA: Sage.

Briere, J. N., & Runtz, M. (1987). Post sexual abuse trauma: Data and implications for clinical practice. *Journal of Interpersonal Violence, 2,* 367–379.

Briere, J., & Runtz, M. (1990). Differential adult symptomatology associated with three types of child abuse histories. *Child Abuse and Neglect, 14,* 357–364.

Briere, J., & Zaidi, L. Y. (1989). Sexual abuse histories and sequelae in female psychiatric emergency room patients. *American Journal of Psychiatry, 146,* 1602–1606.

Bryer, J. B., Nelson, B. A., Miller, J. B., & Krol, P. A. (1987). Childhood sexual and physical abuse as factors in adult psychiatric illness. *American Journal of Psychiatry, 144,* 1426–1430.

Carlin, A. S., & Ward, N. G. (1989, August). *Subtypes of psychiatric inpatient women who have been sexually abused.* Paper presented at the annual meeting of the American Psychological Association, New Orleans.

Cervantes, N. (1993). Therapist duty in domestic violence cases: Ethical considerations. In M. Hansen & M. Harway, *Battering and family therapy: A feminist perspective.* Newbury Park, CA: Sage.

Chu, J. A., & Dill, D. L. (1990). Dissociative symptoms in relation to childhood physical and sexual abuse. *American Journal of Psychiatry, 147,* 887–892.

Conte, J. R., & Shore, D. A. (1982). *Social work and child sexual abuse.* New York: Haworth Press.

Cooley, C. S., with Severson, K. (1993). Establishing feminist systemic criteria for viewing violence and alcoholism. In M. Hansen & M. Harway, *Battering and family therapy: A feminist perspective.* Newbury Park, CA: Sage.

Courtois, C. (1988). *Healing the incest wound.* New York: Norton.

Craine, L. S., Henson, C. H., Colliver, J. A., & MacLean, D. G. (1988). Prevalence of a history of sexual abuse among female psychiatric patients in a state hospital system. *Hospital and Community Psychiatry, 39,* pp. 300–304.

Dix, G. E. (1987). Legal and ethical issues in the treatment and handling of violent behavior. In L. Roth (Ed.), *Clinical treatment of the violent person.* New York: Guilford.

Elliott, F. (1982). Biological contributions to family violence. In L. Barnhill (Ed.), *Clinical approaches to family violence.* Rockville, MD: Aspen.

Farley, D., & Magill, J. (1988). An evaluation of a group program for men who batter. In G. Getzel, (Ed.), *Violence: Prevention and treatment in groups.* New York: Haworth Press.

Farrington, K. M. (1980). Stress and family violence. In M. A. Straus & G. T. Hotaling (Eds.), *The social causes of husband-wife violence.* Minneapolis: University of Minnesota Press.

Feinstein, R. E. (1990). Clinical guidelines for the assessment of imminent violence. In H. M. van Praag, R. Plutchik, & A. Apter (Eds.), *Violence and suicidality: Perspectives in clinical and psychobiological research.* New York: Brunner/Mazel.

Finkelhor, D. (1979). *Sexually victimized children.* New York: Free Press.

Finkelhor, D., & Browne, A. (1985). The traumatic impact of child sexual abuse: A conceptualization. *American Journal of Orthopsychiatry, 55,* 530–541.

Finkelhor, D., Hotaling, G., Lewis, I. A., & Smith, C. (1989). Sexual abuse and its relationship to later sexual satisfaction, marital status, religion and attitudes. *Journal of Interpersonal Violence, 4,* 279–399.

Fossum, M. A., & Mason, M. J. (1986). *Facing shame.* New York: Norton.

Frances, A., First, M. B., & Pincus, H. A. (1995). *DSM-IV:* Its value and limitations. *Harvard Mental Health Letter, 11,* 3–6.

Friedrich, W. N. (1990). *Psychotherapy of sexually abused children and their families.* New York: Norton.

Friend, M. R. (1972). Psychoanalysis of adolescents. In B. B. Wolman (Ed.), *Handbook of child psychoanalysis* (pp. 297–363). New York: Van Nostrand Reinhold Co.

Ganzarain, R. C., & Buchele, B. J. (1988). *Fugitives of incest.* Madison, CT: International Universities Press.

Garbarino, J., Gutman, E., & Seeley, J. (1986). *The psychologically battered child: Strategies for identification, assessment, and intervention.* San Francisco: Jossey-Bass.

Gelles, R. J. (1973). Child abuse as psychopathology: A sociological critique and reformulation. *American Journal of Orthopsychiatry, 43,* 611–621.

Gelles, R. J., & Cornell, C. P. (1990). *Intimate violence in families.* Newbury Park, CA: Sage.

Gelles, R. J., & Straus, M. A. (1987). Is violence toward children increasing? A comparison of 1975 and 1985 national survey rates. *Journal of Interpersonal Violence, 2,* 212–222.

Giaretto, H. (1976). Humanistic treatment of father-daughter incest. In R. E. Helfer & C. H. Kempe (Eds.), *Child abuse and neglect: The family and the community.* Cambridge, MA: Ballinger.

Gil, D. G. (1970). *Violence against children* Cambridge, MA: Harvard University Press.

Gondolf, E. W. (1990). *Psychiatric response to family violence: Identifying and confronting neglected danger.* Lexington, MA: Lexington Books.

Gondolf, E. W. (1993). Treating the batterer. In M. Hansen & M. Harway (Eds.), *Battering and family therapy: A feminist perspective.* Newbury Park, CA: Sage.

Goodwin, J., Attias, R., McCarty, T., Chandler, S., & Romanik, R. (1982). Effects on psychiatric inpatients of routine questioning about childhood sexual abuse. Unpublished manuscript.

Graziano, A. M., & Namaste, K. A. (1990). Parental use of physical force in child discipline: A survey of 679 college students. *Journal of Interpersonal Violence, 5,* 449–463.

Groth, A. N., Hobson, W. F., & Gary, T. S. (1982). The child molester: Clinical observations. In J. R. Conte & D. A. Shore (Eds.), *Social work and child sexual abuse.* New York: Haworth Press.

Hansen, M. (1993). Feminism and family therapy: A review of feminist critiques of approaches to family violence. In M. Hansen & M. Harway (Eds.), *Battering and family therapy: A feminist perspective.* Newbury Park, CA: Sage.

Hansen, M., & Goldberg, I. (1993). Conjoint therapy with violent couples: Some valid considerations. In M. Hansen & M. Harway (Eds.), *Battering and family therapy: A feminist perspective.* Newbury Park, CA: Sage.

Hansen, M. & Harway, M. (1993). *Battering and family therapy: A feminist perspective.* Newbury Park, CA: Sage.

Hart, S. N., Germain, R., & Brassard, M. R. (1987). The challenge: To better understand and combat the psychological maltreatment of children and youth. In M. R. Brassard, R. Germain, & S. N. Hart (Eds.), *Psychological maltreatment of children and youth.* New York: Pergamon.

Harway, M. (1993). Battered women: Characteristics and causes. In M. Hansen & M. Harway (Eds.), *Battering and family therapy: A feminist perspective.* Newbury Park, CA: Sage.

Harway, M., & Hansen, M. (1993a). An overview of domestic violence. In M. Hansen & M. Harway (Eds.), *Battering and family therapy: A feminist perspective.* Newbury Park, CA: Sage.

Harway, M., & Hansen, M. (1993b). Therapist perceptions of family violence. In M. Hansen & M. Harway (Eds.), *Battering and family therapy: A feminist perspective.* Newbury Park, CA: Sage.

Heimann, P. (1950). On countertransference. *International Journal of Psychoanalysis, 31,* 81–84.

Helfer, R. E. & Kempe, C. H. (Eds.). (1976). *Child abuse and neglect: The family and the community.* Cambridge, MA: Ballinger.

Henschel, D., Briere, J., Magallanes, M., & Smiljanich, K. (1990, April). *Sexual abuse related attributions: Probing the role of "traumagenic factors."* Paper presented at the annual meeting of the Western Psychological Association, Los Angeles.

Henson, C. H., Colliver, J. A., & MacLean, D. G. (1988). Prevalence of a history of sexual abuse among female psychiatric patients in a state hospital system. *Hospital and Community Psychiatry, 39,* 300–304.

Herman, J. L. (1988). Father-daughter incest. In F. M. Ochberg, *Post-traumatic therapy and victims of violence.* New York: Brunner/Mazel.

Herman, J. L. (1992). *Trauma and recovery.* New York: Basic Books.

Jaffe, P. G., Wolfe, D. A., & Wilson, S. K. (1990). *Children of battered women.* Newbury Park, CA: Sage.

Jocque, J. (1995). Personal communication.

Justice, B., & Justice, R. (1976). *The abusing family.* New York: Human Sciences Press.

Kaplan, S., Pelcovitz, D., Salzinger, S., & Ganeles, D. (1983). Psychopathology of parents of abused and neglected children and adolescents. *Journal of the American Academy of Child Psychiatry, 22,* 238–244.

Kempe, R. (1976). Arresting or freezing the developmental process: Related aspects in child psychiatry. In R. E. Helfer & C. H. Kempe (Eds.), *Child abuse and neglect: The family and the community.* Cambridge, MA: Ballinger.

Kempe, R., & Kempe, C. H. (1976). Assessing family pathology. In R. E. Helfer & C. H. Kempe (Eds.), *Child abuse and neglect: The family and the community.* Cambridge, MA: Ballinger.

Lewis, D. O. (1987). Special diagnostic and treatment issues concerning violent juveniles. In L. Roth (Ed.), *Clinical treatment of the violent person.* New York: Guilford.

Lion, J. R. (1987). Clinical assessment of violent patients. In L. Roth (Ed.), *Clinical treatment of the violent person.* New York: Guilford.

Little, M. (1951). Countertransference and the patient's response to it. *International Journal of Psycho-Analysis 32,* 32–40.

Little, M. (1957). "R"—The analyst's response to his patient's needs. *International Journal of Psycho-Analysis 38,* 240–254.

Madanes, C. (1990). *Sex, love, and violence: Strategies for transformation.* New York: Norton.

Madden, D. J. (1982). Adolescent violence in the family. In L. Barnhill (Ed.), *Clinical approaches to family violence.* Rockville, MD: Aspen.

Madden, D. J. (1987). Psychotherapeutic approaches in the treatment of violent persons. In L. Roth (Ed.), *Clinical treatment of the violent person.* New York: Guilford.

Maravasti, J. A. (1989). Play therapy with sexually abused children. In S. M. Sgroi (Ed.), *Vulnerable populations: Sexual abuse treatment for children, adult survivors, offenders, and persons with mental retardation* (Vol. 2). Lexington, MA: Lexington Books.

Maravasti, J. A. (1992). Psychotherapy with abused children and adolescents. In J. R. Brandell (Ed.), *Countertransference in psychotherapy with children and adolescents.* Northvale, NJ: Jason Aronson.

McCann, I. L., & Pearlman, L. A. (1990, Fall). Vicarious traumatization: The emotional cost of working with survivors. *Advisor, 3.*

McKay, M. M. (1994, January–February). The link between domestic violence and child abuse: Assessment and treatment considerations. *Child Welfare, 73.*

McKinney, J. (1976). Arresting or freezing the developmental process: Related aspects in developmental psychology. In R. E. Helfer & C. H. Kempe (Eds.), *Child abuse and neglect: The family and the community.* Cambridge, MA: Ballinger.

Merwin, M. R., & Smith-Kurtz, B. (1988). Healing of the whole person. In F. M. Ochberg (Ed.), *Post-traumatic therapy and victims of violence.* New York: Brunner/Mazel.

Mrazek, P. B. (1981). Special problems in the treatment of child sexual abuse. In P. B. Mrazek & C. H. Kempe (Eds.), *Sexually abused children and their families.* New York: Pergamon Press.

Murphy, J. M., Jellinek, M., Quin, D. Smith, G., Poitrast, F., & Goshko, M., (1991). Substance abuse and serious child maltreatment: Prevalence, risk, and outcome in a court sample. *Child Abuse and Neglect, 15,* 197–211.

National Association of Social Workers. (1990). *Code of ethics of the national association of social workers.* Washington, DC: Author.

Navarre, E. L. (1987). Psychological maltreatment: The core component of child abuse. In M. R. Brassard, R. Germain, & S. N. Hart (Eds.), *Psychological maltreatment of children and youth.* New York: Pergamon.

Nosko, A., & Wallace, B. (1988). Group work with abusive men: A multidimensional model. In G. Getzel (Ed.), *Violence: Prevention and treatment in groups.* New York: Haworth Press.

O'Brien, M. (1985). Adolescent sexual offenders: An outpatient program's perspective on research directions. In E. M. Otey & G. D. Ryan (Eds.), *Adolescent sex offenders: Issues in treatment and research.* Rockville MD: U.S. Department of Health and Human Services.

Otey, E. M., & Ryan, G. D. (1985). *Adolescent sex offenders: Issues in treatment and research.* Rockville, MD: U.S. Department of Health and Human Services.

Ounsted, C., & Lynch, M. (1976). Family pathology as seen in England. In R. E. Helfer & C. H. Kempe (Eds.), *Child abuse and neglect: The family and the community.* Cambridge, MA: Ballinger.

Papp, P. (1988). Couples. In M. Walters, B. Carter, P. Papp, & O. Silverstein (Eds.), *The invisible web: Gender patterns in family relationships.* New York: Guilford.

Peled, E., & Edleson, J. (1995). Process and outcome in small groups for children of battered women. In E. Peled, P. G. Jaffe, & J. L. Edleson (Eds.), *Ending the cycle of violence: Community responses to children of battered women.* Thousand Oaks, CA: Sage.

Peled, E., Jaffe, P. G., & Edleson, J. L. (1995). *Ending the cycle of violence: Community responses to children of battered women.* Thousand Oaks, CA: Sage.

Plutchik, R., & van Praag, H. M. (1990). Psychosocial correlates of suicide and violence risk. In H. M. van Praag, R. Plutchik, & A. Apter (Eds.), *Violence and suicidality: Perspectives in clinical and psychobiological research.* New York: Brunner/Mazel.

Pollak, J., & Levy, S. (1989). Countertransference and failure to report child abuse and neglect. *Child Abuse and Neglect, 13,* 515–522.

Power, R. (1988). Differential models of social work groups with family violence. In G. Getzel (Ed.), *Violence: Prevention and treatment in groups.* New York: Haworth Press.

Rachlin, S. (1990). Psychiatric liability for patient violence. In H. M. van Praag, R. Plutchik, & A. Apter (Eds.), *Violence and suicidality: Perspectives in clinical and psychobiological research.* New York: Brunner/Mazel.

Racker, H. (1957). The meanings and uses of countertransference. *Psychoanalytic Quarterly 26,* 303–357.

Reamer, F. G. (1994). *Social work practice and liability.* New York: Columbia University Press.

Register, E. (1993). Feminism and recovering from battering: Working with the individual woman. In M. Hansen & M. Harway (Eds.), *Battering and family therapy: A feminist perspective.* Newbury Park, CA: Sage.

Renzetti, C. M. (1993). Violence in lesbian relationships. In M. Hansen & M. Harway (Eds.), *Battering and family therapy: A feminist perspective.* Newbury Park, CA: Sage.

Rosenberg, M. S. (1984). *The impact of witnessing interparental violence on children's behavior, perceived competence, and social problem-solving activities.* Unpublished doctoral dissertation, University of Virginia.

Roth, L. (1987). *Clinical treatment of the violent person.* New York: Guilford.

Roth, W. T. (1988). The role of medication in post-traumatic therapy. In F. M. Ochberg (Ed.), *Post-traumatic therapy and victims of violence.* New York: Brunner/Mazel.

Russell, D. E. H. (1986). *The secret trauma: Incest in the lives of girls and women.* New York: Basic Books.

Sargent, N. M. (1989). Spirituality and adult survivors of sexual abuse. In S. M. Sgroi (Eds.), *Vulnerable populations: Sexual abuse treatment for children, adult survivors, offenders, and persons with mental retardation* (Vol. 2). Lexington, MA: Lexington Books.

Saunders, S., Anderson, A., Hart, C. A., & Rubenstein, G. M. (1984). *Violent individuals and families: A handbook for practitioners.* Springfield, IL: Charles C. Thomas.

Seskin, J. (1988). Sounds of practice II: Group work with Battered women. In G. Getzel (Ed.), *Violence: Prevention and treatment in groups.* New York: Haworth Press.

Sgroi, S. M. (1989). *Vulnerable populations: Sexual abuse treatment for children, adult survivors, offenders, and persons with mental retardation* (Vol. 2). Lexington, MA: Lexington Books.

Shapiro, R. L. (1982). Alcohol and family violence. In L. Barnhill (Ed.), *Clinical approaches to family violence.* Rockville, MD: Aspen.

Sirles, E. A., Walsma, J., Lytle-Barnaby, R., & Lander, L. C. (1988). Group therapy techniques for work with child sexual abuse victims. In G. Getzel (Ed.), *Violence: Prevention and treatment in groups.* New York: Haworth Press.

Sonkin, D. J., Martin, D., & Walker, L. E. A. (1985). *The male batterer: A treatment approach.* New York: Springer.

Stacy, W., & Shupe, A. (1983). *The family secret.* Boston: Beacon Press.

Stark, E., & Flitcraft, A. (1988a). Personal power and institutional victimization: Treating the dual trauma of woman battering. In F. M. Ochberg (Ed.), *Post-traumatic therapy and victims of violence.* New York: Brunner/Mazel.

Stark, E., & Flitcraft, A. (1988b). Women and children at risk: A feminist perspective on child abuse. *International Journal of Health Services, 18,* 97–118.

Steele, B. F. (1976a). Violence within the family. In R. E. Helfer & C. H. Kempe (Eds.), *Child abuse and neglect: The family and the community.* Cambridge, MA: Ballinger.

Steele, B. F. (1976b). Experience with an interdisciplinary concept. In R. E. Helfer. & C. H. Kempe (Eds.), *Child abuse and neglect: The family and the community.* Cambridge, MA: Ballinger.

Straus, M. A., & Hotaling, G. T. (Eds.). (1980). *The social causes of husband-wife violence.* Minneapolis: University of Minnesota Press.

Traicoff, M. E. (1982). Family interventions from women's shelters. In L. Barnhill (Eds.), *Clinical approaches to family violence.* Rockville, MD: Aspen.

Twentyman, C. T., Rohrbeck, C. A., & Amish, P. A. (1984). A cognitive-behavioral approach to child abuse: Implications for treatment. In S. Saunders, A. Anderson, C. A. Hart, & G. M. Rubenstein (Eds.), *Violent individuals and families: A handbook for practitioners.* Springfield, IL: Charles C. Thomas.

van der Kolk, B. (1988). The biological response to psychic trauma. In F. M. Ochberg (Ed.), *Post-traumatic therapy and victims of violence.* New York: Brunner/Mazel.

van Praag, H. M., Plutchik, R., & Apter, A. (1990). *Violence and suicidality: Perspectives in clinical and psychobiological research.* New York: Brunner/Mazel.

Walker, L. (1992). *Abused women and survivor therapy: A practical guide for the psychotherapist.* Washington, DC: American Psychological Association.

Walters, M., Carter, B., Papp, P., & Silverstein, O. (1988). *The invisible web: Gender patterns in family relationships.* New York: Guilford.

Weimers, K. S., & Petretic-Jackson, P. (1991, August). *Defining physical child abuse: Ratings of parental behaviors.* Paper presented at the annual meeting of the American Psychological Association, San Francisco.

Wilson, J. P. & Lindy, J. D. (1995a). *Countertransference in the treatment of PTSD.* New York: Guilford.

Wilson, J. P., & Lindy, J. D. (1995b). Empathic strain and countertransference. In J. P. Wilson & J. D. Lindy (Eds.), *Countertransference in the treatment of PTSD.* New York: Guilford.

Wilson, J. P., Lindy, J. D., & Raphael, B. (1995). Empathic strain and therapist defense: Type I and Type II CTRs. In J. P. Wilson & J. D. Lindy (Eds.), *Countertransference in the treatment of PTSD.* New York: Guilford.

Wyatt, G. E. (1985). The sexual abuse of Afro-American and white American women in childhood. *Child Abuse and Neglect, 9,* 231–240.

Zelman, G. L. (1990). Child abuse reporting and failure to report among mandated reporters. *Journal of Interpersonal Violence, 5,* 3–22.

13

The Challenge of Clinical Work with Survivors of Trauma

Roberta Graziano

Basically, the victim who will not remain silent is challenging society's vision of itself, bearing witness to uncomfortable moral truths and demanding from everyone, including the therapist, a kind of moral accounting: "And where do *you* stand," the victim asks, "not on abstract issues of truth and justice, but on *this* war and *this* violence and *this* brutality, *this* terrible thing that happens every day in *our* world, yours as well as mine?"

—J. Jay (1991)

Psychic trauma has probably existed since the beginning of humankind. Although the term *posttraumatic stress* and its related diagnostic classification, posttraumatic stress disorder, have only recently become a recognizable part of the mental health vocabulary, as well as gaining increasing notice in the media and among the public at large, the concepts underlying the current nomenclature have been observed, described, and studied for many centuries.

Long before there were psychiatrists, there were accounts, both factual and fictional, of catastrophic events and their effects on people. Trimble (1985) traces some of these, from Shakespeare's Hotspur (in *Henry IV*), who, following battle, suffered from sleep disturbance, intrusive memories, startle reactions, and depression, among other symptoms, to Samuel Pepys's description of the aftereffects, on him, of the Great Fire of London in 1666 (which included terror and nightmares), through Dickens's account of a railway accident in which he was involved in 1865 and his subsequent development of a phobia. More widespread scientific interest in the behavioral, physiological, and emotional phenomena engendered by trauma arose, beginning in the mid-nineteenth century, in connection with medicolegal issues surrounding the compensation of victims of railway and industrial accidents and, early in the twentieth century, with the spread of workers' compensation legislation. Interest also arose in the military sphere. Following the Civil War, attention was given to the idea that the emotional stress of wartime experiences could generate a spectrum of symptoms. During World War I and again in World War II, this interest was renewed as ways were sought to treat soldiers exhibiting "shell shock" and "combat fatigue" so that they might rapidly return to service. The women's movement of the 1970s enabled many women to speak for the first time of the traumatic aftereffects of sexual abuse, rape, and domestic violence (Herman, 1992). Over the past century and a half, a variety of terms have been used to describe the symptoms exhibited following various traumatic events, including "railway spine disorder," "hysteria," "compensation neurosis," "[Holocaust] survivor's syndrome," "rape trauma syndrome," "battered wife syndrome," "post-Vietnam syndrome," and "child-abuse syndrome," among many others (Meichenbaum, 1994).

Freud believed at first that many psychiatric difficulties he encountered in his patients, including hysteria, were the result of early trauma (Breuer and Freud, [1893–1895] 1957; Freud, [1896] 1962). However, after he began to theorize, nearly a century ago, that childhood fantasies, rather than actual occurrences, were responsible for his patients' symptoms, there began a marked shift, first in psychoanalysis and then in psychiatry in general, away from a consideration of the role of overwhelming life experiences in the etiology of mental illness. It is only in the past two decades that both those who are a part of the recent move toward a biomedical, genetic model and those who adhere to the more traditional focus on the dynamic and intrapsychic components of mental functioning have begun to accommodate to the idea that a wide variety of traumatic events, at any period in life, can have a crucial impact on people's emotional and physical selves. As more attention has been paid to examining both the spectrum of these experiences and the similarities among their effects, the realization has arisen that "the human response to overwhelming and uncontrollable life events is remarkably consistent" (van der Kolk, 1987).

DEFINITIONS AND THEORY BUILDING

Although the *general* response to overwhelming events may be consistent, there has been debate as to the definition of trauma and other terms, as well as about the cohesiveness of the symptomatology of those who have undergone such experiences. For our purposes, we will compare two definitions of trauma. The first is by Figley (1985): "an emotional state of discomfort and stress resulting from memories of an extraordinary, catastrophic experience which shattered the survivor's sense of invulnerability to harm." This definition emphasizes the extraordinary nature of the *event*. In contrast, Meichenbaum (1994) emphasizes the extraordinary *effort* needed to cope with the event(s): "extreme or severe events that are so powerful, harmful and/or threatening that they demand extraordinary coping efforts. Such traumatic events are neither very rare, nor unusual." These two definitions may reflect a changing outlook on the nature of trauma, to include not only one-time, unusual, shattering occurrences such as natural disasters or hostage situations, but also everyday, ongoing situations such as domestic violence.

Terr (1991) distinguishes between Type I (short-term) and Type II (prolonged) traumatic events. The former are unexpected, single occurrences, surprising and devastating but of limited duration (e.g., rape, car accident). They are likely to lead to symptoms of intrusive ideation, avoidance, and hyperarousal. The latter are stressors associated with sustained and repeated ordeals, more likely to be intentional and of human design (e.g., combat, ongoing abuse). These stressors may eventuate in feelings of helplessness, dissociation, characterological and interpersonal problems, use of self-protective mechanisms such as detachment, constricted affect, and substance abuse, among other symptoms (Meichenbaum, 1994).

Regardless of the ordinary or extraordinary nature of the event or ongoing experience,

> the natural consequent behaviors and emotions of a trauma *during* a catastrophe is the *traumatic stress reaction* and can be defined as *a set of conscious and unconscious actions and emotions associated with dealing with the stressors of the catastrophe and the period immediately afterwards*. . . . Post-traumatic stress reactions are defined as *a set of conscious and unconscious behaviors and emotions associated with dealing with the* memories *of the stressors.* (Figley, 1985)

Those who have followed discussions of trauma and its sequelae have noted with interest first the inclusion of the diagnostic category of posttraumatic stress disorder (PTSD) in DSM-III (American Psychiatric Association, 1980), then the inclusion of the clinical presentation of PTSD in children in DSM-III-R (American Psychiatric Association, 1987), and the struggle over whether to include additional categories, such as complex PTSD (Herman, 1992) and disorders of extreme stress (van der Kolk et al., 1993), in DSM-IV. These efforts, though unsuccessful, may have helped to broaden the original stressor criteria to include, in DSM-IV (American Psychiatric Association, 1994), the concept of vicarious traumatization. In all of this, however, the diagnosis itself remains controversial, as it is virtually the only one in which, as Pynoos (1994) notes, "the diagnostic gateway is the occurrence of a specific personal experience. In a dramatic fashion, PTSD reopened the psychiatric door to the serious vicissitudes of life, and there has been tremendous clinical pressure to push through this opening an enormous backlog of human experience that otherwise seems to have no place in an 'etiologically free' classification system." The same event may have very different effects on different people, and PTSD is by no means the inevitable outcome. "Specific details need to be understood about each experience, including characteristics of the event itself and the perceptions, affects and interpretations on the part of the victim" (Davidson, 1994). Despite the foregoing, however, "although the nature of the trauma, the age of the victim, predisposing personality, and community response all have an important effect on ultimate posttraumatic adaptation, the core features of the posttraumatic syndrome are fairly constant across these variables" (van der Kolk, 1987).

POSTTRAUMATIC STRESS DISORDER

These core features to which van der Kolk refers have been identified in a number of ways, starting with Lindemann (1944), refined by Horowitz (1976), and described by van der Kolk (1987) as "a phasic reliving and denial, with alternating intrusive and numbing responses." Herman (1992), perhaps more poetically, depicts the syndrome as follows: "The conflict between the will to deny horrible events and the will to proclaim them aloud is the central dialectic of psychological trauma." Perhaps the definitive current description is provided in DSM-IV (American Psychiatric Association, 1994). A brief version is presented below:

> The essential feature of Posttraumatic Stress Disorder is the development of characteristic symptoms following exposure to an extreme traumatic stressor involving direct personal experience of an event that involves actual or threatened death or serious injury, or other threat to one's physical integrity; or witnessing [such] an event . . . ; or learning about [such an event] experienced by a family member or other close associate. The person's response . . . must involve intense fear, helplessness, or horror (or in children, the response must involve disorganization or agitated behavior). The characteristic symptoms . . . include persistent reexperiencing of the traumatic event, persistent avoidance of stimuli associated with the trauma and numbing of responsiveness, and persistent symptoms of increased arousal.

The symptoms can include recurrent and intrusive recollections of the event, recurrent dreams in which the event is replayed, dissociation, intense psychological distress, or physiological reactivity in response to triggers that resemble or in some way are symbolic of an aspect of the original event, avoidance of stimuli associated with the trauma, amnesia for an aspect (or aspects) of the event, diminished responsiveness or "psychic numbing," feelings of detachment from others, reduced ability to experience emotions, a sense of a foreshortened future, persistent symptoms of anxiety, sleep disturbances, hypervigilance, exaggerated startle response, irritability or anger outbursts, and/or difficulty concentrating.

A number of questions have been raised as to the prevalence of PTSD. In their survey of studies of the epidemiology of PTSD to see how widespread it is in the general population, Davidson and Fairbank (1993) concluded:

> Lifetime and current prevalence rates of PTSD varied widely according to the diagnostic method. . . . Whatever the diagnostic method used, however, it is clear that PTSD and partial forms of PTSD combined were common in the general population, ranging from 8% to 16%, and were almost an expected and predictable response to combat (e.g., occurring in 53% of Vietnam veterans). PTSD became chronic in more than 50% of all cases and was accompanied by psychiatric comorbidity in the great majority. . . . [A]lthough personal background characteristics played a significant role in PTSD prevalence, exposure to extreme events made a significant contribution to the prevalence of PTSD that was independent of the effects of personal background characteristics. These findings . . . provided support to validate the concept of PTSD as a "stress response" illness.

As to whether the characteristic effects of PTSD occur regardless of ethnicity, culture, or gender, Marsella, Friedman, and Spain (1994), in their review of studies of various ethnocultural groups, victim populations, traumatic events, and clinical topics, suggest that this is the case:

> The results of these studies are generally consistent with the results of existing biological research, which suggests that there is a universal biological response to traumatic events. . . . However, although the response to a traumatic event may share some universal features, especially as the trauma becomes more severe, ethnocultural features may play an important role in the individual's vulnerability to PTSD, the expression of PTSD, and the treatment responsivity to PTSD.

In order to provide the most effective treatment for each individual, then, it is most important for the worker or therapist to develop transcultural competency, to be aware of ethnocentrism, and to be open to learning from the client; otherwise treatment may be more hurtful than helpful:

> Symptoms differ among ethnic groups, as do definitions of a "problem," of mental health and disability, of physical illness, and of psychic pain. Therefore, the clinician needs to comprehend the various cultural accommodations to mental illness characteristic of the ethnic groups in question, and ethnic group members' help-seeking behavior and expectations. (Parson, 1985)

COGNITIVE, AFFECTIVE, AND SOMATIC EFFECTS

Those who have studied trauma have looked at it from varying perspectives, depending on their own backgrounds, orientation, and professional education. Clinical social workers, using a biopsychosocial framework, have long been aware of the need to take a multitude of factors into account in their direct work with individuals, families, groups, and communities and must now be prepared to add concepts of traumatic stress to these elements. There is mounting evidence that traumatic events are associated with the development of various disorders and conditions. This is especially significant when we consider the following statistics and statements (Meichenbaum, 1994):

1. It has been estimated that 40%–60% of psychiatric outpatients and 50% of psychiatric inpatients report histories of early childhood victimization (e.g., physical and sexual abuse) (Herman, 1992).
2. A majority of American women (68.9%) have experienced at least one type of traumatic event during their lifetime (Resnick et al., 1993).
3. There is an association between somatization disorder, dissociation and a history of abuse in female psychiatric patients. This was noted more that a century ago by Janet, and recently supported by Pribor et al. (1993). Women who have chronic pelvic pain are likely to have been sexually assaulted as children (Walker et al., 1992). Somatization disorders are widespread among Holocaust victims, increase over time in rape victims, and there is a strong association between chronic PTSD and physical illness (Barsky et al., 1994; Shalev et al., 1990; White et al., 1989).
4. Of those individuals who have borderline personality disorder, roughly 1/3 fulfill the criteria for PTSD. There are high rates of traumatic childhood experiences, including physical and sexual abuse and exposure to violence, in

adolescent and adult patients with borderline personality disorder (Gunderson & Chu, 1993).

5. 15.2% of all male Vietnam . . . veterans currently have PTSD . . . 21% among African Americans; 28% among Hispanics (Kulka et al., 1990). Further, "The general consensus in the literature is that PTSD currently exists in many World War II and Korean War veterans 4 or 5 decades after their actual combat experiences" (Falk et al., 1994).
6. 1.3 million American women are currently estimated to have rape-related PTSD and approximately 211,000 will develop it each year (Calhoun & Resnick, 1993). Rape victims may constitute the largest single group of PTSD sufferers (Foa et al., 1993).
7. There is a clear link between spouse abuse and familial child abuse. Survivors of physical assault by male partners evidence high levels of depression, suicidal ideation, substance abuse, and PTSD symptoms.

We must also be aware of the coexistence of substance abuse, depression, eating disorders, panic attacks, self-mutilation, and other phenomena that are linked to trauma and to resulting PTSD.

Trauma's lasting effects on the mind and body must be taken into consideration when we try to understand a client's somatic symptoms, behavior, and ways of thinking about the world, the future, and relationships. The age or developmental stage at which the traumatic event occurred; frequency, intensity, and duration of the trauma; gender; and ethnocultural features of the victim are among the variables that can shape responses. So too are such factors as whether the situation was one that affected a large group or community (e.g., a flood, combat) or one in which the victim was alone or isolated (e.g., rape, torture).

In general, one can speculate that the human tendency to construct stories, or narratives, to explain or make sense of experiences is called into action during and after traumatic events. Each individual constructs a unique narrative that may have a crucial influence on subsequent development of posttraumatic symptomatology. For example, those who are able to find meaning in the event, accept their current life or compare themselves with those who are not as fortunate, imagine that things could have been worse, and believe they have learned or grown from the experience may be relatively symptom free. Those who cannot remember anything positive, believe that they will never have control over events, feel that they are to blame for their misfortunes, cannot make sense of their intrusive memories, or continue to dwell on the way life might have been may remain in a state of chronic distress. Moreover, the meaning that the event has for the individual is a determining factor: a child may ascribe very different meaning to being molested by a stranger than to being molested by a trusted family member. To take this example further, a child might develop transient anxiety following the former event, especially when he or she is in or near the location where the incident occurred or sees someone who may have physical characteristics similar to the perpetrator. However, his or her essential sense of self as a relatively good person in a relatively safe and predictable world may not be affected in a lasting fashion. By contrast, a child abused by a parent may find the world turned upside down; those who should be protecting are causing pain; perhaps it is because (the child thinks) I am bad and deserve to be hurt (Briere, 1989); I can't trust anybody anymore; nothing good is going to happen.

Traumatic memories may be imprinted in the mind in vivid, indelible images and sensations. These visual, aural, and bodily encodings of fragments of intolerable happenings may be inaccessible to cognitive and verbal retrieval.

> These unusual features of traumatic memory may be based on alterations in the central nervous system. A wide array of animal experiments show that when high levels of adrenaline and other stress hormones are circulating, memory traces are deeply imprinted. The same traumatic engraving of memory may occur in human beings. . . . Van der Kolk . . . speculates that in states of high sympathetic nervous system arousal, the linguistic encoding of memory is inactivated, and the central nervous system reverts to the sensory and iconic forms of memory that predominate in early life. (Herman, 1992)

The inability to express in words the sensations and images attendant on traumatic memories may develop when

> an individual is confronted with *overwhelming* affects: in other words, his affective responses produce an unbearable psychic state which threatens to disorganize, perhaps even destroy, all psychic functions. . . . The capacity to tolerate emotions becomes diminished. In addition, there is a regression in the affects themselves, both their cognitive and expressive aspects. This regression accounts for the high incidence of psychosomatic disorders, and the disturbance in affectivity and capacity for verbalization . . . called "alexithymia." (Krystal, 1978)

In alexithymia, which literally means "without words for feelings," emotional arousal is responded to by a denial not of "the reality of the triggering event but a denial of the emotions aroused by it" (Jones, 1991). This avowal severs the connection between incident and affect.

What all this might mean is that the narrative constructed following a traumatic experience may not be told in words. Instead, it may be expressed in actions or somatic symptoms.

> *Yvette, a young professional woman, was successful at work and had good relationships with her friends. She prided herself on her ability to remain calm and behave rationally under pressure. One evening during a therapy session, the sound of an airplane flying quite low produced visible anxiety and fidgetiness, behavior she had not exhibited before. Gentle questioning uncovered a memory from her childhood in a Third World country. She was in the schoolyard at recess, when suddenly a plane appeared, flying quite low, and began shooting. The other children and teachers fled, but Yvette was unable to move, and a classmate pulled her to safety. Yvette connected this to the reality that a political uprising was going on at that time but was puzzled at remembering that she felt she was not permitted to move and had to stand still in a situation where immobility could have meant her death. She thought that this was illogical and very unlike her. When I pursued this with her, she recalled having had to stand still while being beaten by her father, a regular occurrence. Her delivery was factual and unemotional; when I*

asked how she had felt during the physical abuse, she said she just knew she had to get through it, and if she had tried to run away, she would have been abused even more severely. I made a connection between her immobility in the schoolyard and having to stand still while being beaten under threat of even worse pain, and Yvette acknowledged, for the first time, that perhaps there was some validity to the idea that things that had happened earlier in her life could explain behavior that had seemed irrational.

Traumatic memories may also appear in the form of flashbacks, triggered by any reminder of the original situation or experience. These flashbacks, which are vivid mental or sensory images of a fragment or moment during the overwhelming, terrifying event, may set off verbal or physical reactions or reenactments that are inexplicable in terms of the present but quite understandable in the light of what has gone before.

Joan was married to a man who, she felt, was very unlike her father, who had been abusive and terrifying. She had great difficulty when they had sex, to the point where her husband, Roger, a gentle and considerate man, was becoming confused and exasperated because Joan would suddenly push him away or freeze during intercourse. In a couples session, Joan was helped to make the connection between certain ways that Roger touched her sexually and flashbacks to being touched by her father. Joan said, "It's like the minute Roger does that, my father is right back in the room."

Somatic symptoms may be manifestations of the biochemical and neurophysiological accompaniments to traumatic stress that have been discovered during recent research, where it has been found that "extreme threat to the organism, whether a laboratory animal or an individual exposed to extreme stress, may result in long-term changes in behavior and neurobiological systems" (Bremner et al., 1994; see also Krystal et al., 1989). The brain's capacity to activate systems that facilitate selective attention, a function that would be beneficial in a life-threatening situation, may also result in

> a strengthening of memories acquired during stress. These strengthened memories may be ultimately adaptive in dealing with subsequent threats. However, this may result in troubling memories that are intrusive and do not fade away long after the potential danger has been removed. . . . Acute neurobiological responses to trauma, such as release of norepinephrine, may facilitate the encoding of traumatic memories. (Bremner et al., 1994)

Similarly, van der Kolk and Greenberg (1987) note that while activation of the autonomic nervous system is necessary to cope with major stress, many traumatized people "continue to to respond even to minor stimuli with an intensity appropriate only to emergency situations. . . . Autonomic arousal, no longer a preparation to meet external threat, becomes itself a precipitant of fear and emergency responses."

Meichenbaum (1994), in an excellent summary of responses displayed by patients with PTSD, includes the following:

1. Greater sympathetic nervous system arousal, including abnormal startle response, and difficulty in getting used to repeated presentations of stimuli; hyperresponsiveness to reminders of original traumatic event; changes in the

functioning of the hypothalamic-pituitary-adrenocortical axis, the endogenous opioid system (lowering of the pain threshold, inability to feel pain), and the physiology of sleep and dreaming (difficulty falling asleep; restless sleep; frequent awakening; decreased sleep time; traumatic nightmares, which are different than other kinds of nightmares in that they are usually "playbacks" of actual traumatic experiences).

2. Neuroendocrine disturbances, such as cardiac reactivity, long-lasting elevations in blood pressure, changes in immune and digestive system functioning, and elevations in various physiological and chemical components of the urinary, adrenal and circulatory systems. [Thus, as Davidson and Foa (1993) note, "There is also an increased risk of associated chronic medical disorders such as hypertension, bronchial asthma, and peptic ulcer."]
3. As a result of the above physiological changes, hypersensitivity and vulnerability may be heightened due to the phenomenon of "kindling," repeated intermittent stimulation of the brain ". . . produced by repeated traumatization, as in child abuse, or by one trauma followed by intrusive experiences. Kindling may also account for the frequency of neurological abnormalities in trauma victims." (van der Kolk and Greenberg, 1987)

Thus, we find that those who have suffered a traumatic experience often display reminders of the original event in the form of "body memories," which replicate or reenact the original injury or physical disorder, or they may exhibit somatic symptoms triggered by reminders of the original trauma.

Ella reported considerable physical and emotional abuse by child care workers and religious personnel in the orphanage where she had spent many years of her childhood. As an adult, she suffered from frequent headaches, ear infections, and sinus problems, which would arise during times of interpersonal stress. Many of these physical symptoms seemed to have no organic basis. When Ella returned to school in midlife to earn a college degree, her headaches and earaches intensified, and she experienced recurrent panic attacks as well. Several flashbacks during therapy sessions led to Ella's realization that the physical abuse of her childhood had often occurred in the classroom, where Ella had been hit in the face, had her ears boxed, and had her head banged against the blackboard. This discovery was a turning point in both the diminution of the symptoms and the improvement of Ella's academic performance.

Of course, many survivors of trauma do not "remember" at all; instead, they utilize amnesia, disavowal, and dissociation to defend against unspeakable memories and protect them from experiencing intolerable feelings. Both client and worker may then be astonished at the various ways in which these memories surface, and may indeed be unable to connect the various symptoms (somatic, emotional, etc.) with earlier occurrences, which, because of their dangerous or life-threatening content, had to be "forgotten," at the time, in order for the individual to continue to function.

Zita's older sister, Annie, had been sexually abused by their father from early childhood until she left home as an adolescent. Zita, however, insisted that this had never happened to her. After several months in treatment, she mentioned that she had had an "image" of herself, age four, and Annie, both being treated with an ointment on their genitals, administered by their mother. On hearing this, Annie told Zita that this treatment had been for a venereal disease. Zita continued to have no memory of being sexually molested in any way.

Dissociation is described in DSM-IV (American Psychiatric Association, 1994) as "a disruption in the usually integrated functions of consciousness, memory, identity, or perception of the environment." Amnesia ("inability to recall important personal information, usually of a traumatic or stressful nature"), fugue (suddenly traveling away from home or work, with an inability to remember one's past and confusion about one's identity or assumption of a new identity), multiple personality disorder, and depersonalization ("feeling of being detached from one's mental processes or body") are all aspects of dissociation. But just what is disrupted or detached, and from what?

"To a degree, the self is separated from its own experience. Aspects of the self are segregated, and realms of experience are relegated to a 'not-me' domain. . . . When life experience is abhorrent, self-construction comes to a grinding halt. Bridges are not built; moats abound" (Allen, 1995). Recent studies indicate that dissociation is strongly linked to trauma and that different kinds of traumatic experiences may be linked to varying symptoms or syndromes along the dissociative continuum. Awareness of the potential for dissociation in one or more forms should be an integral ingredient in the assessment and treatment of trauma:

> Dissociation is more likely to happen during and in the aftermath of physical trauma. Depersonalization, derealization, and psychogenic amnesia are common symptoms during natural disasters, combats, and other forms of physical trauma. In turn, a history of trauma has been found to be an almost universal etiology of such extreme chronic dissociative disorders as multiple personality disorder. In these cases the failure of integration of memory and identity serves a defensive purpose—against painful affect, recognition of physical helplessness, and physical pain. While such defenses can be quite adaptive, they carry with them a risk of failure to work through traumatic events, leading to chronic and severe posttraumatic dissociative symptoms in some instances. (Spiegel, 1993)

Thus, whereas some individuals will communicate via words, others through somatic phenomena, and still others through flashbacks, those who dissociate tell their "stories," paradoxically, through creating gaps in the continuity of their personal narrative.

ASSESSMENT AND TREATMENT STRATEGIES IN CLINICAL SOCIAL WORK

Although the array of features described may seem daunting when considering the assessment and treatment of survivors of trauma, the experience itself can be exhilarating as well as challenging. The most liberating feature of trauma work for me is the opportunity to "depathologize" the client and to view treatment as a way of helping a person (or people) to emerge from the aftereffects of real incidents that would have been painful, terrifying, or overwhelming to almost anyone. Once the existence of traumatic events in the past (and/or present) has been established, both client and worker (or therapist) can trace the connection between the original occurrences and current symptoms or behavior, and collaborate on strategies for change. (That is not to say, however, that establishing the existence of the trauma, tracing the connection, and/or collaboration are necessarily simple processes.)

Until recently, the average assessment or clinical interview did not target trauma factors, and often no information regarding traumatic experiences was elicited. Alternatively, clients would mention events that, if one were using a trauma framework, had been clearly traumatic, but these references were either overlooked, ignored, misunderstood, or misinterpreted by the interviewer. Many clients, of course, seek (or are referred or mandated to) treatment because of events or situations that may be, at least on the surface (or in the client's or the clinician's mind), a far cry from overwhelming, catastrophic events, but during the course of therapy, treatment, or recovery, trauma-related issues may surface, often with disturbing results. Still other clients, even if asked, may deny the existence of any traumatic events in their past, yet their behavior, symptoms, or ways of thinking or relating may point to the possibility of trauma as an etiological factor. In any assessment, both symptoms and experiences must be weighed to determine whether there exists a basis for trauma or PTSD as the principal factor, whether the person suffers from PTSD (or a related disorder) in conjunction with another psychological disorder, or whether trauma should be ruled out altogether. What this implies is that questions or strategies for appraising trauma need to be included in an assessment as a matter of course. An open-ended clinical interview in any setting can be supplemented with specific questions; a self-report scale can be added to the assessment process; measures of comorbidity (that is, the occurrence of PTSD or a related disorder along with another diagnosis, such as schizophrenia, substance abuse, or a personality disorder) can be an additional feature of the assessment; or an assessment can be structured so as to include both an interview and a number of questionnaires and rating scales that measure PTSD symptoms, adjustment, cognitive skills, strengths, and comorbidity, among other factors (Meichenbaum, 1994). The most important elements are the manner in which questions are asked, and asking the right questions—questions tailored to clients who know at the outset that they have had traumatic experiences or those who do not raise the issue of trauma initially but whose awareness of having been victimized or having survived a traumatic experiences surfaces later in treatment. Meichenbaum (1994) provides an excellent review of ways in which to ask questions so as to give clients control, elicit information, enlist the client in a collaborative process, analyze the problem or situation, establish goals, assess coping efforts, and develop strategies for moving ahead. He points out that, in general, "'why' questions tend to be unanswerable and lead to self-doubt, further self-preoccupation, intrusive ideation and poorer adjustment. Instead . . . clinicians can focus on 'what' and 'how' questions." These might include, for example, "What would you be doing differently to be on track?" or "How will you let someone else know that?" Another tactic is to ask clients to put the story of their victimization-trauma on a time line, which also includes positive events, as well as to visualize a future time line. Encouraging clients to offer suggestions as to what can be done (in the present or the future) may result in better follow-through than suggestions made by the clinician.

What must also be added, in considering both assessment and treatment approaches, is the likelihood that once the issue of having lived through events that may have been catastrophic, terrifying, and/or life threatening has been raised, the affective, cognitive, behavioral, and somatic baggage that accompanied the original event will resurface during the assessment process as well as in the treatment relationship. Therefore, from the very beginning, it is essential to have on hand, in addition to a working knowledge of the various manifestations of posttraumatic distress, a philosophy of treatment and a repertoire of techniques or interventions that can serve to diminish anxiety and help the client regain his or her equilibrium.

The establishment of an environment where the client will begin to feel comfortable and safe is a cardinal rule in any therapeutic situation. However, when working with individuals whose basic assumptions about safety and security have been shattered, who may believe that there is no predictability in life, that events occur at random, and that they have no control over anything (Janoff-Bulman, 1985, 1992; McCann & Pearlman, 1990b; McCann et al., 1985), the maintenance of a safe place is even more important. Whenever possible, interviews or sessions should take place in an environment that allows for privacy, has a minimum of interruptions, and is reasonably free of outside distractions. (At the same time, this kind of setting may, for some clients, actually raise anxiety, especially if the traumatic events for them were related to child sexual abuse or a situation where they were isolated or trapped. It is important to check with the client periodically as to whether anything about the location, or about the worker's appearance or manner, is causing discomfort.) From the beginning, the emphasis must be on the client's ability to stop a particular line of questioning or discussion at any time he or she begins to feel unsafe. The client and worker may devise their own code, whether it is a word or a gesture, to signify "no more." A confrontational approach on the part of the worker, which might prove successful in other settings or with other client populations, may well retraumatize the client with PTSD or related issues.

> Therapist and survivor together explore and work through defenses and fears which impede the remembering process. Some defenses are resolved in a rather simple and straightforward process while others need more extensive assessment and interpretation. Abandonment fears as well as fears of being disbelieved, blamed, further shamed, or rejected by the therapist are especially salient concerns which require direct discussion and reassurance. Real losses and abandonments in the past support these fears. . . . Disparate, fragmented evidence often must be pieced together, much like completing a giant jigsaw puzzle (a useful metaphor for the memory retrieval process). . . . [The therapist] must remain cognizant that traumatic material is being evoked and that remembering may be terrifying and even life-threatening. (Courtois, 1988, 1992)

The issue of trust is a difficult one for survivors of trauma. If their early lives were secure, their previous assumptions about an "average expectable environment" or "good-enough" world have now been splintered, and they may fear ever trusting again. If they grew up in an atmosphere that disregarded or could not fulfill their needs for security and nurturance (e.g., child abuse, wartime, famine) they may not only not trust others but may also disregard their own perceptions, needs, and wishes, and instead become overly responsive to the needs of the "other" (including the therapist or worker). The latter phenomena have been noted not only by those studying trauma, but by psychodynamic investigators such as Khan (1963), Winnicott (1960b), Kohut (1971, 1977, 1984), and Ferenczi (1933). Consequently, clients may utilize defenses and ways of relating, even in treatment, that were originally designed to protect themselves against further traumatization. These include compliance, denial, and dissociation.

The therapist needs to establish enough trust to engage in a working relationship, which will then entail the client's verbalizing or experiencing feelings that may be perceived internally as deadly. Yet the therapist must also serve the crucial function of bearing witness to the unspeakable experiences clients have undergone, which are always struggling to be expressed. Therapists may have to make provisions for listening that are somewhat different from the usual ones, including letting a person stay longer in a session (if a particularly distressing flashback has just occurred, or the client is extremely anxious, or self-control is tenuous). They may need to be available by telephone between appointments, to help deal with intrusive thoughts, flashbacks, or panic attacks that may result from material uncovered or discussed in a session. They may need to help get a client "out" of a flashback, or reground him or her in reality, when overwhelming feelings or memories threaten to destroy from within. They may need to provide a physical environment that offers a choice of closeness or distance (more than one client chair, in different parts of the room) and that can be altered or talked about if any element seems to arouse distress (Graziano, 1992).

Sara came into a session with a criticism of my choice of music on the waiting room radio. I explained that the radio was on to ensure privacy and that she could choose whatever station she liked while she was sitting there. Sara went on to say that the music I played reminded her of her foster father; she thought of it as "old people's music." She added that it was the radio as background noise that she really objected to. In tracing the concept of background noise and what that meant to her, Sara mentioned that it was noise that seemed to go on endlessly, like a washing machine. I asked her where the washing machine had been located in her foster home. She became increasingly uncomfortable and began to dissociate, but we were able to establish, by collaborating on drawing a floor plan, that the washing machine had been in the basement, where her foster brother had his room, and it was next to the bathroom where he had sexually abused her over a period of many years. She had thought as a child that the abuse, like the noise of the washing machine, would go on forever. Sara came out of the flashback visibly relieved and can now either reassure herself in situations where background noise exists or take steps to eliminate it.

Sometimes spoken words will not come, and a client will need to be encouraged to use nonverbal means, such as drawing, poetry, journals, photographs, movement, body work, or music, to express parts of the story that cannot yet be talked about aloud. (Joan, for example, produced two videotapes on incest and child abuse that told her story through her drawings, writings, and poetry. These were shown on local cable television and won awards. Ella has revealed, in journals and poems brought to her sessions, previously unspeakable memories; she has also been able to use guided imagery to escape from horrifying flashbacks.) From time to time, the worker too will need to make connections through actions or symbolic gestures rather than verbally. "In this way, we may address experiences which are either unavailable in the verbal realm or too 'dangerous' to be spoken aloud. Understanding the 'meanings' may have to wait. Once the connections become clearer, however, the symptoms may not need to be relied upon, as we and our clients find more effective ways to construct the story of their reality" (Graziano, 1996).

Rachel entered treatment in her early forties, several years after she had developed Graves' disease, a disorder of the thyroid. She was suffering from severe panic attacks, could hardly go out of her house or ride the bus, and had physical sensations of "worms inside her arms," in addition to migraines and asthma. She attributed her anxiety and distress to the Graves' disease; her symptoms persisted despite high doses of Synthroid and antianxiety medication. Rachel reported that she had been helped very much by a therapist, Joe, whom she had seen some fifteen years previously for "primal therapy," which she described as "lying on the floor curled up and uttering the primal scream." A few months after we began treatment, Rachel developed a perforated intestine and underwent emergency surgery, including a colostomy. I visited her in the hospital, where her anxiety was maximal, and later at home, where she reported that not only did she have no pain but she was already (one week postsurgery) walking two miles a day, something she had not done even before she became ill. The same pattern recurred when she had further surgery to reverse the colostomy; she felt no pain and immediately engaged in strenuous physical activity. I was disconcerted by her seeming inability to feel pain, but Rachel dismissed my concerns. Later, she asked me to accompany her on a visit to Joe: she needed a letter from him to support her application for supplementary security income. When we arrived, Rachel was clearly shocked at Joe's appearance and functioning, though she had already known that Joe, now elderly, had been quite ill.

On the way home, she denied any distress, but in our next session, she brought in poetry that she had written during the time she was in therapy with Joe. She also began to show me poetry she had written since she had started treatment with me. I remarked that the poetry appeared to be written in a variety of voices; this precipitated a period of severe fragmentation and anxiety of nearly psychotic proportions and led to the uncovering of numerous other "people" behind the voices and a tentative diagnosis of multiple personality disorder. During this period, Rachel was frequently unable to talk coherently in our sessions but, at my suggestion, kept a journal, wrote poetry, drew pictures, and spoke into a tape recorder; she then brought the journal, poems, drawings, and tapes to our sessions. What they all revealed was a childhood of constant physical abuse by her father, emotional distance and verbal abuse by her mother, and sadistic emotional, verbal, and physical abuse by her older sister. Specific elements included her father repeatedly throwing her on the floor and kicking her in the stomach, and her sister sitting on her chest and punching her in the nose. To survive in this milieu, Rachel had created a world of others that protected her from physical and emotional pain. Some were older females who were tough and self-reliant; one had the specific job of absorbing pain; at least one was a boy (a strong and valued figure in Rachel's culture). Their purpose was to shield the vulnerable "young one" from the terrifying anguish of emotional abandonment and physical suffering.

Once we had identified many of the others and their functions and discussed them within a framework of trauma and its effects on children, Rachel's symptoms began to abate, the others receded into the background, and Rachel was better able to deal with the reality of her current physical condition. This included tracing the connections between her father's abuse and the feelings aroused by her stomach surgery and her sister's physical attacks and her asthma. Eventually she was able to reduce her antianxiety medications, discontinue attendance at a group for psychiatric patients with chronic medical conditions (where she was consistently the highest-functioning member), seek better medical care, and enter a college program.

The others have now receded, a majority of the panic attacks and physical symptoms of anxiety have disappeared, and Rachel is working toward her bachelor's degree. Without the traumatic stress framework, I would have assessed and treated Rachel as a person with a chronic psychiatric disorder, as had the other mental health personnel she had encountered (except for Joe). Working with Rachel necessitated my educating both Rachel and myself, as well as many medical and mental health professionals, about trauma, posttraumatic stress, and dissociation. As a result, she has received more appropriate treatment all around.

Many clients function normally for years before an event or trigger reveals the existence of a single, earlier trauma; others will have experienced many different kinds of trauma over the years, starting with their early lives. Working with a client who has had a multitude of traumatic experiences, beginning in childhood, can present special problems because of the difficulty of determining the meaning (or layers of meaning) of a particular symptom, trigger, or reenactment. Even if the individual has not developed a dissociative disorder such as multiple personality disorder, there may be instances of inexplicable behavior that can be understood only within the context of an early need for self-protection, which may have been compounded or intensified by later experiences.

Heidi grew up in eastern Germany in the 1930s. Her mother was verbally and physically cruel, and Heidi had been very afraid of her. On one occasion, her mother had locked her in her room after a severe beating, and Heidi had been so terrified that, rather than ask to be let out to go to the bathroom, she defecated on the floor and threw her feces out the window. Heidi's father was more affectionate. She enjoyed various activities with him, especially attending the local Protestant church, taking walks in the woods, and going to opera performances. When Heidi was twelve (which corresponded with the time that Hitler became extremely powerful), she experienced a great change at school: her teachers began to be mean and punitive, and she was forbidden to join the school youth group. When she asked why, she was told it was because her mother was Jewish. This was astonishing to Heidi; she had not known it before. Heidi was sent to a nearby city at age sixteen, to be a companion to an elderly woman, who eventually de-

nounced her to the Gestapo on learning that she was half-Jewish. Heidi was placed in a slave labor camp, where she was raped by a fellow inmate. When the Russians invaded Germany, Heidi was able to escape from the camp, to find her mother and sister, and, after surviving for several weeks in the woods by eating berries and roots, to find refuge on an isolated farm, where she managed to fight off a sexual assault by two American soldiers. She fled the farm and made her way to a large city, where she narrowly escaped death in an Allied bombing attack.

After the war, Heidi came to the United States, where she married an older Jewish man, who was verbally and physically abusive. His family called her a "Nazi" because she considered herself Christian and spoke German. By the time Heidi sought treatment for "depression," she was about fifty years old. She had migraines, terrifying anxiety attacks, and claustrophobia; smoked and drank to excess; had few friends and was socially phobic; and was working in a menial job where her boss was verbally demeaning.

Shortly after beginning therapy, Heidi talked about her frequent episodes of leaving home: she would pack a suitcase and take a bus or train, not having a destination; would disembark in a strange town and stay for a few days, feeling frightened and lonely; and would return home, where her husband would be angry and abusive. She was also deeply distressed about the fact that whenever she attended the opera (her only recreation), she would develop a headache and feelings of suffocation and would have to run out of the theater.

After a few months in treatment, Heidi (who had already demonstrated her tendency to leave home—and therapy—abruptly) announced that she was going back to Europe to revisit her home town, which she had left some thirty-five years previously. She had no advance plans; she just intended to arrive there and stay for an unspecified amount of time. She seemed unconcerned (even after I verified with her that her home town was now in fact part of Czechoslovakia instead of Germany) as to how she would manage in a country whose language and customs she did not know and which, at the time, was still firmly under Soviet domination. I presented Heidi with a map, and together we located the town where she had lived and the city where she had worked (both now renamed). I asked her to keep track of her journey on the map and assured her that I would be thinking about her while she was gone; I would want to know about her trip and would be waiting for her when she got back.

Heidi returned angry and confused: nothing was the same; her home town had been resettled by Czechs, and nobody spoke German; and even the Protestant church had been reconsecrated as a Catholic church. Mindful of her German heritage, I said that it seemed to make her very sad that her fatherland (a term Germans use for their native country) no longer existed as she had known it. Later she was able to tell me, with considerable shame, of sexual abuse by her father, beginning when she was five or six years old. This was a very different picture than she had given initially. Eventually Heidi was also able to connect her trips to the opera with her father, and the betrayal by the old woman (a retired singer), to her physical symptoms and claustrophobia. In addition, she began to piece together the many connections between abuse, betrayal, imprisonment (or being "locked up"), and fear of death, which were the components of her need to "run away." She also spent a long time struggling with the issues around her father's warmth and supportiveness of her versus his using her sexually, and the links between these items and her enjoyment of various activities (church, opera, hiking) and distress around sex. Heidi became increasingly aware of the fact that she had received both life-sustaining and destructive things from him. Had it not been for the outdoor skills she had learned from him, she would not have been able to survive in the woods; her aesthetic and spiritual life was rooted in experiences she had first had with him; her difficulties around sex and fear of betrayal in relationships were strongly tied to his sexual molestation of her and his failure to protect her from her abusive mother. Many of these themes resonated even more strongly because of her later experiences of betrayal, rejection, sexual assault, abuse, and narrow escapes from death, both during the war and afterward with her husband, his family, and her employer.

In addition to the work of making connections between the various pieces of Heidi's puzzle, therapy included such elements as helping her to find a German-language Protestant church, where she enjoyed both religious and social activities; supporting her in taking well-planned vacations, where her destination, length of time away, and accommodations were set ahead of time; encouraging her to learn to drive, especially after her husband became ill, so that she could more easily get to the places she planned to go, and working out with her, after his death, ways in which she could overcome her phobia of highway driving; including her in a support group for survivors of child abuse so as to minimize her feelings of isolation, shame, and guilt; sustaining her efforts to find a better job and helping her to find ways to assert herself at work; and, finally, after many years where our contact was only of the sporadic, touching-base variety, wishing Heidi well as she moved to another region after retirement and reassuring her that we could continue to stay in touch.

TREATMENT MODALITIES

Successfully treating trauma victims requires breaking out of the security of standard therapeutic techniques. Since the effects of trauma cannot disappear from the history of the victim, the therapist must help the victim learn how to live that history in the present with others.

—J. Jay (1991)

Most of the discussion so far has focused on individual casework with trauma victims and survivors. This treatment includes the establishment of a supportive relationship; careful detective work to create meaning out of what may appear to be a fragmented experience of a shattered self; a psychoeducational component, which provides information about trauma and its aftereffects on mind, emotions, and body and serves to normalize and legitimize the client's feelings and beliefs about self, others, and experiences; empathic listening; nurturing hope and supporting the client's efforts at healing; providing constancy and containment in the face of the client's flashbacks, terror, and other reactions; and a solid understanding of the dynamics underlying the symptoms, affects, and various behavioral manifestations of the survivor's trauma.

In addition to individual treatment, family therapy, group, and other adjunctive approaches (such as psychopharmacology) are often extremely helpful. Family work can assist the survivor's significant others to understand the workings and aftereffects of trauma and its impact on their family member, as well as the impact on the family, both over time and in the present. Survivor, worker, and family members can collaborate on issues such as decreasing retraumatization in everyday life, reducing blame when the survivor is experiencing symptoms of PTSD, eliciting support and (if necessary) containment, and establishing trust. It must also be remembered that traumatization, in the form of spousal battering and child abuse, can begin in the family and that patterns of family violence can be transmitted across many generations. Thus, the family is a critical component of the survivor's vulnerability, resilience, and recovery, and the whole family can suffer when one or more members are affected by overwhelming events (Krugman, 1987). Family work can play a crucial role in prevention of trauma as well as in alleviating some of its effects.

Group approaches that have proved helpful include self-help support groups, such as those that use a twelve-step approach (e.g., Survivors of Incest Anonymous), as well as support groups facilitated by a worker or therapist, psychoeducational groups, and a variety of structured, time-limited groups designed specifically for survivors of a particular kind of trauma, as well as groups composed of family members or significant others of survivors. These groups may emphasize a variety of approaches: cognitive-behavioral, crisis intervention, task-oriented, psychodrama, and others. (Scurfield, 1985; Scurfield et al., 1984; Herman & Schatzow, 1984; McCann et al., 1988; Mennen & Meadow, 1992; Danieli, 1988; Getzel & Masters, 1983; van der Kolk, 1987; Solomon, 1992).

> The group process helps to combat the sense of isolation and uniqueness, stigmatization, feelings of shame, guilt, and self-blame that many PTSD clients experience. The resolution of traumatic experience is facilitated by *the presence of survivors with the same, or a similar, set of traumatic events.* Clients working together with people who have had similar experience provides a common bond, "normalizes" experiences, reduces a sense of alienation, fosters identification of common issues, provides an opportunity to share common coping techniques. (Meichenbaum, 1994).

Groups can develop healing rituals, ceremonies, and other activities in order to symbolize or celebrate the transformation of "victims" into survivors, or demonstrate the emergence into a fuller and healthier life. "Ceremonies compartmentalize the review of the trauma, provide symbolic enactments of transformation of previously shattered relationships, and reestablish connections among family and with society in general. . . . Ritual and ceremony are highly efficient vehicles for accessing and containing intense emotions evoked by traumatic experience" (Johnson et al., 1995).

> *A social work student working in a Veterans Administration hospital noticed that many of the veterans of World War II who attended the mental health clinic were former prisoners of war. They were exhibiting various symptoms of PTSD. On inquiry, she discovered that each felt ashamed of his nightmares and anxiety attacks, but none of them had ever talked to other World War II veterans, even other ex–prisoners of war, about their reactions. She formed a support group, which she co-led with her supervisor. After an initial period of distrust, the men were able, often with great distress, to talk about their experiences in Japanese or German prison camps. They shared their feelings of guilt over*

having survived and been taken prisoner when so many of their buddies had been killed, as well as their shame at returning home after the war and being ignored by the public at large, not being "heroes." They had always had to hide their stories, as they felt (sometimes correctly) that their friends and families would be turned off, alarmed, or disgusted by the details. After several months, the group, which named themselves the Ex-POWS, staged a fund-raising event. They used some of the profits to buy a flag and other materials, which were used in a ceremony they developed that became part of each meeting, and donated the rest of the proceeds to a fund for use by other former prisoners of war. Most of the group members, who were in their late sixties and seventies, reported that their symptoms had abated considerably and that they now felt that they too should be accorded the same respect (by society and by the armed forces) that their non-POW comrades had received.

The issue of medication for clients with PTSD is a matter of ongoing debate. It appears that different kinds of medication may be effective for different aspects or symptoms of PTSD with different clients, that outcomes may be contradictory or inconsistent, and it may take a longer time for any medication to be effective with this population than with those in other diagnostic categories (Kudler & Davidson, 1994). In general, those considering the use of medication for PTSD have concluded that pharmacotherapy in and of itself rarely provides complete remission of PTSD but can be helpful in controlling or ameliorating such symptoms as insomnia, flashbacks, trouble concentrating, physiological hyperreactivity, depressed mood, and explosiveness, among others. Further, therapy alone may not suffice for some: "Psychotherapy alone may not be effective for reducing avoidance symptoms in PTSD patients with alexithymia. . . . medications may therefore have a particularly critical role, in agreement with previous studies of alexithymic psychosomatic patients, who do not respond to psychodynamic therapy and benefit from antidepressants" (Kosten et al., 1992). However, the quality of the relationship of doctor and patient, and the necessity for the doctor to emphasize that the medication might alleviate symptoms, will not cure the PTSD but may help the person to think more clearly and be more receptive to therapy, are paramount (Meichenbaum, 1994). Collaboration between psychopharmacologist, worker, and client is most important, and explanations and information will both assist the client in understanding the purpose of the medication and its effects and facilitate client cooperation.

Regardless of treatment modality and therapist orientation, however, the matter of therapist reactions to clients' traumatization will surface, with attendant countertransference reactions. It is essential that the worker not contribute to or mirror the denial, avoidance, rejection, shaming, blaming, reification of theory, and self-deception prevalent not only in society at large but in the mental health professions. Though "this denial which has been observed in many settings stems from a fundamental human difficulty in comprehending and acknowledging our own vulnerability" (Solomon, 1995), professionals must do everything possible to combat these difficulties, so as to provide the kind of help that clients who have suffered overpowering and life-threatening experiences so urgently need. Consultation, education, and support (particularly in the form of peer support from others also engaged in trauma work, whether it be formal or informal, structured or open-ended) are necessities in order to do the work well and responsibly.

Four therapists, who also were survivors of childhood sexual abuse, met as a result of a professional conference on incest. They formed a peer support group and met regularly for several years. They used this forum to discuss the ways in which their own experiences affected the therapy they did with incest survivors (a major part of their professional work), as well as a place where they could safely discuss personal issues related to their own traumatization. They made a presentation at a conference on child sexual abuse that was instrumental in the formation of other peer support groups. They also established what became a large network of mental health professionals (social workers, psychologists, psychiatrists, psychiatric nurses, art and activities therapists, etc.) who were working with survivors of child sexual abuse. Meetings of the network featured presentations by members on innovative aspects of their work, as well as workshops and lectures on topics such as psychopharmacology, movement therapy, and multiple personality. Most of the members of the network had never had an opportunity to meet with other professionals who were doing trauma work and felt that their skills, knowledge base, and personal ability to deal with issues of trauma had been enhanced by the information, support, and networking opportunities provided by the group.

SUMMARY

This chapter has explored basic concepts of trauma and provided definitions of traumatic stress and posttraumatic stress disorder. The effects of trauma on mind, body, and memory have been discussed, and treatment strategies and modalities have been outlined. An attempt has been made to link the discussion of treatment to the theoretical constructs in such a way as to illustrate the main ideas with appropriate clinical vignettes. Since the study of trauma and approaches to its treatment are both new territory (despite their historical antecedents) and since, in some ways, utilizing a trauma framework is so different from more traditional psychodynamic approaches, there is much room for innovation in working with the varied populations that can be thought of as survivors of trauma.

In many ways, the treatment of survivors of trauma is demanding and difficult. If the worker is not cognizant of the theories underlying the concept of traumatic stress and is not alert to the various workings and manifestations of trauma in the somatic, affective, cognitive, and behavioral realms, the work can also become bewildering and frustrating. However, once a framework for understanding trauma is established and basic principles of treatment are understood, a new realm unfolds, in which some of the more pathology-oriented approaches may have to be put on the sidelines, but where the potential exists for helping a client struggle free from the nightmarish captivity of past events.

Among the most important features in the therapist throughout assessment and treatment are an understanding of concepts of trauma, including PTSD; a willingness to hear what the client is trying to say, although the presentation may not be in words; an ability to tolerate descriptions, images, and reenactments of truly horrifying, and often hardly imaginable, events; capacity for empathy without overidentification; a belief in the resilience of the human spirit in the face of tremendous odds; and knowledge that therapy can help clients to cope more effectively but cannot erase their pasts. This will mean learning to master one's own impatience at the sometimes achingly slow progress of treatment; advocating for that treatment to take as long as it needs to (a formidable challenge in an era of budget reductions, regulations, limitations, and managed care restrictions); living with uncertainty as to whether one is doing the right thing, especially as it will sometimes appear (because the individual is "feeling" the intense affects that had been dissociated, or the emotional pain that had been somatized) that the client is getting worse instead of better; daring to be creative; understanding and working through one's own traumatic past and its effects, if they exist; and obtaining support and consultation when the transitory exhaustion, despair, and hopelessness that are occasional by-products of doing trauma work threaten to traumatize the helper. In essence, understanding and using the principles underlying the concept of trauma can both return us to and provide a new perspective on our grounding in social work, with its emphasis on the person-in-situation and the biopsychosocial perspective that trauma workers in other disciplines are beginning to discover.

A final word is necessary on the subject of bearing witness. One of social work's core principles is that of client advocacy. In the face of society's (and some professionals') reluctance to allow knowledge of trauma to enter awareness, we must support our clients' efforts to make sure that events such as the Holocaust and phenomena such as the torture of political prisoners are not forgotten.

> The determination to "bear witness" is reflected in a massive outpouring of survivor memories; in public gatherings for commemoration; in initiation and support of programs and institutions that focus on the tragedy. . . . In working with victims of severe, massive trauma, these and other culturally syntonic ways of remembrance and mourning must be understood and integrated into society's consciousness and into our conceptual orientation for clinical practice. These activities help in filling fragments of memory, enhance an understanding of oneself, and facilitate the long-delayed process of grieving. . . . The emotional benefits of these "self-healing" approaches must be understood and integrated into clinical practice. (Graziano and Rosenbloom, 1995)

REFERENCES

Allen, J. G. (1995). Dissociative processes: Theoretical underpinnings of a working model for clinician and patient. In J. G. Allen & W. H. Smith (Eds.), *Diagnosis and treatment of dissociative disorders.* Northvale, NJ: Jason Aronson.

American Psychiatric Association. (1980). *Diagnostic and statistical manual of mental disorders* (3rd ed.). Washington, DC: Author.

American Psychiatric Association. (1987). *Diagnostic and statistical manual of mental disorders* (3rd ed. rev.). Washington, DC: Author.

American Psychiatric Association. (1994). *Diagnostic and statistical manual of mental disorders* (4th ed.). Washington, DC: Author.

Barsky, A. J., Wool, C., Barnett, B. A., & Cleary, P. D. (1994). Histories of childhood trauma in adult hypochondriachal patients. *American Journal of Psychiatry, 151,* 397–401.

Bremner, J. D., Davis, M., Southwick, S. M., Krystal, J. H., & Charney, D. (1994). Neurobiology of posttraumatic stress disorder. In R. Pynoos (Ed.), *Posttraumatic stress disorder: A clinical review.* Lutherville, MD: Sidran Press.

Breuer, J., & Freud, S. (1957). *Studies on hysteria.* New York: Basic Books. (Original work published 1893–1895.)

Briere, J. (1989). *Therapy for adults molested as children: Beyond survival.* New York: Springer.

Calhoun, K. S., & Resick, P. A. (1993). Post-traumatic stress disorder. In D. Barlow (Ed.), *Clinical handbook of psychological disorders.* New York: Guilford.

Courtois, C. A. (1988). *Healing the incest wound: Adult survivors in therapy.* New York: Norton.

Courtois, C. A. (1992). The memory retrieval process in incest survivor therapy. *Journal of Child Sexual Abuse, 1,* 15–31.

Danieli, Y. (1988). Treating survivors and children of survivors of the Nazi Holocaust. In F. M. Ochberg (Ed.), *Post-traumatic therapy and victims of violence.* New York: Brunner/Mazel.

Davidson, J. R. (1994). Issues in the diagnosis of posttraumatic stress disorder. In R. S. Pynoos (Ed.), *Posttraumatic stress disorder: A clinical review.* Lutherville, MD: Sidran Press.

Davidson, J. R., & Fairbank, J. A. (1993). The epidemiology of posttraumatic stress disorder. In J. R. Davidson & E. B. Foa (Eds.), *Posttraumatic stress disorder: DSM-IV and beyond.* Washington, DC: American Psychiatric Press.

Davidson, J. R., & Foa, E. B. (1993). Introduction. In J. R. Davidson & E. B. Foa (Eds.), *Posttraumatic stress disorder: DSM-IV and beyond.* Washington, DC: American Psychiatric Press.

Falk, B., Hersen, K., & Van Hasselt, V. B. (1994). Assessment of post-traumatic stress disorder in older adults: A critical review. *Clinical Psychology Review, 14,* 383–416.

Ferenczi, S. (1955). Confusion of tongues between adults and the child. *The selected papers of Sandor Ferenczi,* vol. 3: *Final contributions to the problems and methods of psychoanalysis.* New York: Basic Books. (Original work published 1933.)

Figley, C. (1985). Introduction. In C. Figley (Ed.), *Trauma and its wake: The study and treatment of post-traumatic stress disorder.* New York: Brunner/Mazel.

Foa, E. B., Rothbaum, B. O., & Steketee, G. S. (1993). Treatment of rape victims. *Journal of Interpersonal Violence, 8,* 256–276.

Freud, S. (1962). The aetiology of hysteria. In J. Strachey (Ed. and Trans.), *The standard edition of the complete psychological works of Sigmund Freud* (Vol. 3). London: Hogarth Press. (Original work published 1896.)

Getzel, G., & Masters, R. (1983). Serving families of homicide victims. *Social Work with Groups,* 6, 81–94.

Graziano, R. (1992). Treating women incest survivors: A bridge between "cumulative trauma" and "post-traumatic stress." *Social Work in Health Care, 17.*

Graziano, R. (1996). The adult survivor of childhood sexual abuse: Linking inner and outer world. In J. Sanville & J. Edward (Eds.), *Fostering healing and growth: A psychoanalytic social work approach.* Northvale, NJ: Jason Aronson.

Graziano, R., & Rosenbloom, M. (1995). Body, mind and trauma: Beyond words. *Proceedings, 34th Annual Conference, International Conference for the Advancement of Private Practice of Clinical Social Work.* Victoria, British Columbia, Canada.

Gunderson, J. G., & Chu, J. A. (1993). Treatment implications of past trauma in borderline personality disorder. *Harvard Review of Psychiatry, 1,* 75–81.

Herman, J. L. (1992). *Trauma and recovery.* New York: Basic Books.

Herman, J. L., & Schatzow, E. (1984). Time-limited group therapy for women with a history of incest. *International Journal of Group Psychotherapy, 34,* 605–616.

Horowitz, M. J. (1976). *Stress-response syndromes.* Northvale, NJ: Jason Aronson.

Janoff-Bulman, R. (1985). The aftermath of victimization: Rebuilding shattered assumptions. In C. R. Figley (Ed.), *Trauma and its wake.* New York: Brunner/Mazel.

Janoff-Bulman, R. (1992). *Shattered assumptions: Towards a new psychology of trauma.* New York: Free Press.

Jay, J. (1991, November–December). Terrible knowledge. *Family Therapy Networker,* pp. 18–29.

Johnson, D. R., Feldman, S. C., Lubin, H., & Southwick, S. M. (1995). The therapeutic use of ritual and ceremony in the treatment of post-traumatic stress disorder. *Journal of Traumatic Stress, 8,* 283–298.

Jones, D. M. (1991). Alexithymia: Inner speech and linkage impairment. *Clinical Social Work Journal, 19:* 237–249.

Jones, R. T., & Ribbe, D. P. (1991). Child, adolescent and adult victims of residential fire: Psychosocial consequences. *Behavior Modification, 15,* 560–580.

Khan, M. M. (1963). The concept of cumulative trauma. In *The privacy of the self.* New York: International Universities Press.

Kohut, H. (1971). *The analysis of the self.* New York: International Universities Press.

Kohut, H. (1977). *The restoration of the self.* New York: International Universities Press.

Kohut, H. (1984). *How does analysis cure?* A. Goldberg & P. Stepansky (Eds.). Chicago: University of Chicago Press.

Kosten, T. R., Krystal, J. H., Giller, E. R., Jr., Frank, J., & Dan, E. (1992). Alexithymia as a predictor of treatment response in post-traumatic stress disorder. *Journal of Traumatic Stress, 5,* 563–573.

Krugman, S. (1987). Trauma in the family: Perspectives on the intergenerational transmission of violence. In B. A. van der Kolk (Ed.), *Psychological trauma.* Washington, DC: American Psychiatric Press.

Krystal, H. (1978). Trauma and affects. *Psychoanalytic Study of the Child, 33,* 81–116.

Krystal, J. H., et al. (1989). Neurobiological aspects of PTSD: Review of clinical and preclinical studies. *Behavior Therapy, 20,* 177–198.

Kudler, H., & Davidson, J. R. (1994). General principles of biological intervention following trauma. In J. R. Freedy & S. E. Hobfoll (Eds.), *Traumatic stress: From theory to practice.* New York: Plenum.

Kulka, R. A., et al. (1990). *Trauma and the Vietnam generation: Findings from the National Vietnam Veterans readjustment study.* New York: Brunner/Mazel.

Lindemann, E. (1944). Symptomatology and management of acute grief. *American Journal of Psychiatry, 101,* 141–148.

Marsella, A. J., Friedman, M. J., & Spain, E. H. (1994). Ethnocultural aspects of posttraumatic stress disorder. In R. S. Pynoos (Ed.), *Posttraumatic stress disorder: A clinical review.* Lutherville, MD: Sidran Press.

McCann, I. L., Pearlman, L. A., Sakheim, D. K., & Abrahamson, D. J. (1985). Assessment and treatment of the adult survivor of childhood sexual abuse within a schema framework. In S. M. Sgroi (Ed.), *Vulnerable populations* (Vol. 1). Lexington, MA: Lexington Books.

McCann, I. L., & Pearlman, L. A. (1990b). *Psychological trauma and the adult survivor: Theory, therapy and transformation.* New York: Brunner/Mazel.

McCann, I. L., Sakheim, D. K., & Abrahamson, D. J. (1988). Trauma and victimization: A model of psychological adaptation. *Counseling Psychologist, 16,* 531–594.

Meichenbaum, D. (1994). *A clinical handbook/practical therapist manual for assessing and treating adults with post-traumatic stress disorder (PTSD).* Waterloo, Ontario, Canada: Institute Press.

Mennen, F. E., & Meadow, D. (1992). Process to recovery: In support of long-term groups for sexual abuse survivors. *International Journal of Group Psychotherapy, 42,* 29–44.

Parson, E. R. (1985). Ethnicity and traumatic stress: The intersecting point in psychotherapy. In C. R. Figley (Ed.), *Trauma and its wake.* New York: Brunner/Mazel.

Pribor, E. F., Yutzy, S. H., Dean, J. T., & Wetzel, R. D. (1993). Briquet's syndrome, dissociation and abuse. *American Journal of Psychiatry, 150,* 1507–1511.

Pynoos, R. S. (1994). Introduction. In R. S. Pynoos (Ed.), *Posttraumatic stress disorder: A clinical review.* Lutherville, MD: Sidran Press.

Resnick, H. S., Kilpatrick, D. G., Dansky, B. S., Saunders, B. E., & Best, C. L. (1993). Prevalence of civilian trauma and posttraumatic stress disorder in a representative sample of women. *Journal of Consulting and Clinical Psychology, 61,* 984–991.

Scurfield, R. M. (1985). Post-trauma stress assessment and treatment: Overview and formulations. In C. R. Figley (Ed.), *Trauma and its wake.* New York: Brunner/Mazel.

Scurfield, R. M., Corker, T. M., & Gongla, P. A. (1984). Three post-Vietnam "rap therapy" groups: An analysis. *Group, 8,* 3–21.

Shalev, A. Y., Bleich, A., & Ursano, R. J. (1990). Posttraumatic stress disorder: Somatic comorbidity and effort tolerance. *Psychosomatics, 31,* 197–203.

Solomon, S. D. (1992). Mobilizing social support networks in times of disaster. In C. R. Figley (Ed.), *Trauma and its wake, II.* New York: Brunner/Mazel.

Solomon, Z. (1995). Oscillating between denial and recognition of PTSD: Why are lessons learned and forgotten? *Journal of Traumatic Stress, 8,* 271–282.

Spiegel, D. (1993). Afterword. In D. Spiegel (Ed.), *Dissociative disorders: A clinical review.* Lutherville, MD: Sidran Press.

Terr, L. (1991). Childhood trauma: An outline and overview. *American Journal of Psychiatry, 148,* 10–20.

Trimble, M. R. (1985). Post-traumatic stress disorder: History of a concept. In C. R. Figley (Ed.), *Trauma and its wake.* New York: Brunner/Mazel.

van der Kolk, B. A. (1987). The psychological consequences of overwhelming life experiences. In B. A. van der Kolk (Ed.), *Psychological trauma.* Washington, DC: American Psychiatric Press.

van der Kolk, B. A. & Greenberg, M. S. (1987). The psychobiology of the trauma response: Hyperarousal, constriction, and addiction to traumatic reexposure. In B. A. van der Kolk (Ed.), *Psychological trauma.* Washington, DC: American Psychiatric Press.

van der Kolk, B. A., Roth, S., Pelcovitz, D., & Mandel, F. A. (1993). *Complex post traumatic stress disorder. Results from the DSM IV field trial of PTSD.* Unpublished manuscript, Harvard Medical School.

Walker, E. A., Katon, W. J., Nerras, K., Jemelka, R. P., & Massoth, D. (1992). Dissociation in women with chronic pelvic pain. *American Journal of Psychiatry, 149,* 534–537.

White, P., & Faustman, W. (1989). Coexisting physical conditions among inpatients with posttraumatic stress disorder. *Military Medicine, 154,* 66–71.

Winnicott, D. W. (1960b). Ego distortion in terms of true and false self. *The maturational processes and the facilitating environment.* New York: International Universities Press, 1965.

14

Clinical Social Work in the Context of Managed Care

Sidney H. Grossberg and Jerrold R. Brandell

Managed care comes very close to defining the practice climate of the 1990s. The transformative changes that have occurred in the mental health delivery system are dramatic and have had far-reaching ramifications: employers and consumers rather than service providers are now making decisions as to which services will be offered; length of stay for inpatient services in both mental health and substance abuse facilities has been drastically reduced, concomitant with an emphasis on providing clients with the least restrictive method of care; and increasingly, providers are expected to use practice approaches that minimize treatment duration and intensity.

THE CHANGING SCENE

To see why managed care has made such inroads in the delivery of mental health and substance abuse services, it may be instructive to use a real-life example. A large California-based corporation, GTE, spent $11.3 million in 1986 on mental health and substance abuse services, which, based on their predictions, was projected to rise to $13.3 million in 1987. Instead it hired a managed care company and actually lowered the 1987 costs to $9.3 million, $2 million less than the previous year and $4 million less than projected costs. Costs continued to decline in 1988, when expenses were $7.5 million; there were further reductions in 1989 (total cost $5.5 million) and in 1990 (total cost $4.9 million). Other statistics are even more striking: over this four-year period at GTE, there was a 40 percent increase in the number of people using mental health and substance abuse services and an equally dramatic change in the kind of care. In 1986, the ratio of inpatient to outpatient services was 90 percent to 10 percent, for a total cost of $11.3 million. Two years later, it had changed to fifty-fifty, with actual costs at $7.5 million. By 1990, inpatient services were only 30 percent of the total; at 70 percent, outpatient services represented the balance. Total costs now were $4.9 million. Despite the millions of dollars in savings to GTE over this five-year period, the actual number of employees using mental health or substance abuse services *increased by 40 percent.*

According to one national survey, fee-for-service payments to providers constituted 96 percent of their practice in 1984. Within several years, however, unmanaged fee-for-service reimbursement was only 28 percent, while health maintenance organizations, preferred provider organizations, and managed fee-for-service payments to providers constituted 72 percent of payments.

Some managed care companies have marketed their services to employers specifically for substance abuse and mental health services. These large managed care companies are given an amount of money, computed on either a monthly or annual basis, based on the number of enrollees in the plan (also referred to as a capitated or per head basis); they then provide a limited number of sessions to enrollees while being at risk for profit or loss. In effect, if too many people require hospitalization or other services, the managed care company loses money. If the managed care company is able both to promote less costly inpatient services and a larger proportion of outpatient services, considerable profits may be realized.

Insurance companies may develop their own managed care division, selling products on an HMO capitated risk basis and/or lowering fees to providers. Other insurance companies have hired managed care companies to take over the reimbursement of providers on a capitated at-risk type of arrangement or by using a preferred provider panel. If present trends continue, it is quite probable that in the very near future, all reimbursement by insurance companies will be paid through managed care rather than through direct, unmanaged fee-for-service arrangements.

Managed care companies, while aggressively marketing their services to major employers throughout the country, have also begun to sell to smaller employers within regional markets. In consequence, referrals themselves, not simply payments, are coming through the managed care companies and through those insurance companies with managed care contracts. In effect, an employee who wants to use mental health or substance abuse benefits must go to particular providers selected either by the employer or the managed care company that has negotiated a contractual arrangement with the employer's medical reimbursement system. Consequently, both the amount of payments and number of referrals made to providers have risen dramatically in the past decade.

Some providers have questioned the claim that managed care, though cost-efficient, can provide services of high quality. However, how managed care defines quality may differ markedly from a provider's use of this term. The term *quality* for the clinician likely evokes the image of a seasoned practitioner who has an understanding of therapeutic methods and techniques, of transference and countertransference, and who is able to identify and to provide long-term or short-term treatment based on the client's needs, and so on. On the other hand, when the administrator in a managed care company talks about "quality of service," she or he may be referring to the difference between an inpatient unit that houses children and adults on the same floor and one that is exclusively designed for adult admissions (the latter representing a higher quality of service). Whereas the clinician tends to use this term with a microscopic focus, the managed care administrator is more inclined to conceive of quality with a broader lens, and in more universal terms.

One managed care company was able to identify how it had enhanced the quality of services to a large national corporation. Prior to its involvement, some corporate employees were receiving mental health care at unapproved treatment facilities. Although this large company required that its employees be treated in interdisciplinary settings with psychiatrists, psychologists, and social workers, the insurance company was being billed for psychotherapy services by family practitioners, internists, and gynecologists, most with no training in mental health. The managed care company ended this practice by requiring that employees be treated only by mental health practitioners, a move that raised the quality of services. It also discovered a number of other problems: some providers were fraudulently billing the insurance company at higher rates than were justified; other providers were failing to visit hospitalized patients on a daily basis; multiple psychotropic medications were being prescribed to patients by physicians who were not knowledgeable about drug interaction effects; and a small number of providers actually had prior felony convictions. Furthermore, certain hospital programs used by this corporation in the treatment of its employees had very limited mental health presence. In several of these psychiatric inpatient units, adolescents and children were not segregated from adult patients. By such systematic efforts, the managed care company did improve the quality of services and could make that claim to employers and employees. However, the term *quality* when used in this sense appears to have a somewhat more universal or global meaning than the practitioner's use of this term.

There is a crisis in this country in the delivery of mental health services. We have an overabundance of practitioners who treat nearly everything in the psychological realm, yet there is not enough money to pay for unlimited mental health and substance abuse services for all. Managed care is attempting to deliver an acceptable level of services with finite dollar resources. Many practitioners believe that every client is entitled to receive an optimal level of care, although this may no longer be a realistic objective. Clinicians are being asked to deliver care that may help restore a person's functioning to premorbid levels, though they are no longer encouraged to attempt more extensive structural or personality changes.

The key to clinical social work under managed care will be how the therapist deals with specific functional impairments of the client: adaptations to work, in important interpersonal relationships, and in aspects of intrapersonal functioning. Managed care companies want to know which symptoms, specifically behavioral symptoms, indicate that a person is not functioning at home, at work, or socially. Goals are then established to restore a client to his or her previous level of functioning. Insurance companies and managed care companies will no longer be willing to pay for abstract goals, such as to make the client feel better or become self-actualized or better adjusted.

It is critical to understand that the managed care or insurance company is not responsible for this change in focus; it is, rather, employers purchasing medical benefits for their employees who are now stipulating a "restoration to functioning" criterion rather than just providing unlimited reimbursement for the treatment of an employee who is, for example, chronically unhappy or depressed. For many companies, such as some of the large aircraft companies in the northwestern United States, the choice may be either managed care or no mental health and substance abuse care at all. Such companies have been losing money, and in order to compete around the world with other manufacturers, they can spend only a finite amount of funds to pay for medical benefits. The same is true of automobile manufacturers, refrigerator makers, and others where production costs have gone up, but not as precipitately as health care costs. These companies are willing to cut mental health benefits to lower the costs of medical care. They are giving managed care companies a last chance to bring these benefits under control, knowing that failure to do so brings the possibility of no benefits at all.

It is of some interest that in employee surveys taken by both managed care companies and employers, the consumer satisfaction level given to managed care companies is often very high, frequently in the 90 percent range. Employees like feeling that they are being referred to selected, qualified providers and that they are being given the least amount of treatment needed to restore their functioning to wherever it was prior to the onset of their problem.

In reality there are high-quality managed care companies and poor-quality managed care companies. Some companies are cost oriented and are concerned only with saving the employer money, while others are more principled, making a determined effort to provide truly quality services. However, it is also sometimes true that good elements can be found in an otherwise poor-quality company, or that a company that is in most respects well managed and ethical in its operations may not be consistently so. Like most other complex issues, one really cannot discuss this topic from the position that managed care is either all good or all bad.

CLINICIAN AND CLIENT REACTION TO MANAGED CARE

Some of the changes wrought by managed care have had a discernibly negative impact on clinical social work providers. Providers are now being paid less; clinicians are spending more time with paperwork and telephone calls simply to receive authorization for interviews; there has been a gradual shift from long-term treatment toward shorter-term treatment, and a corresponding bias toward the use of medications; behaviorally oriented symptoms must now be documented in records, with a goal of symptom amelioration rather than insight into the conflicts that may be causing the behavioral symptoms. Because the managed care company wishes to save money, an adversarial relationship may develop between the provider and the case manager. Managed care has introduced not just a third party, the insurance company, to the patient-clinician relationship, but also a fourth party: the managed care case manager. Furthermore, until recently, protocols or guidelines used by managed care firms were not typically given to providers.

With the knowledge that there is a very real potential for abuse of clinical records, clinicians for a number of years put the most benign and nondescript material in their case records. With the rise of managed care, many clinicians have been inclined to exaggerate the client's symptoms to increase the likelihood of the managed care company's authorizing treatment or additional sessions. Neither method, of course, is honest or legally defensible. It seems that we may be entering yet another era, one of greater honesty in record keeping, driven in part by the increased demand for documentation of treatment compliance and outcome effectiveness.

Issues of confidentiality are raised when clinical material must be given over the telephone, by fax, or in writing to case managers so that treatment or additional sessions may be authorized. Providers and patients are understandably concerned about who will have access to the data once this material goes into a managed care company's computers.

If a therapist is unable to obtain additional sessions from the managed care company, certain transferences, countertransferences, and reality reactions occur in the therapist-client relationship. The first question that arises is: where is the failure? Is the failure due to the client's not having been "good enough" or because she or he does not have serious enough symptoms to warrant further sessions? Has the therapist been inadequate in his or her ability to obtain more sessions or to communicate the need of the client? Will the client experience the therapist as an abandoning parent? Following is an example derived from clinical supervision (conducted by the first author) that illustrates some of the dilemmas that may occur.

One of my supervisees, John, called the managed care company and received four sessions allotted to treat his client. Although the client was only moderately depressed, when he was evaluated on the GAF (Global Assessment of Functioning), as required by the client's managed care company, he received a very low score. The therapist subsequently diagnosed the client as suffering from a major depression. The case manager called John, and John returned the call from his home, as he had taken the case manager's message home with him that evening. Unfortunately, John had neither the form that he filled out for the managed care company nor the client's record with him. When the case manager asked John if his client was "really that bad off," John replied that he was. The case manager then requested psychological testing and medication review since the client had been diagnosed with a major depression. John said that his client would not want this and asked me as his supervisor what he should do when the case manager called back. My suggestion was for John to be honest and tell the case manager that once he was able to review the GAF score, it was higher than he had remembered, and that he did not have access to the case record when he spoke earlier with the case manager. I also said that John must be direct and honest with his client if the two of them decided that medication or testing was not desirable and to tell the client that if the case manager insists that these are necessary for the client to access his benefits, then the client should be given the choice as to whether to go through with psychological testing and medication review in order to utilize this benefit.

The example illustrates how managed care has changed the clinician's and client's decision as to what is best for the therapy. In effect, both are now forced to tolerate the added dimension of having another person intervening or adding parameters to the treatment.

TRANSFERENCE AND COUNTERTRANSFERENCE ISSUES

As an independent variable in psychotherapeutic treatment, managed care can exacerbate transference and countertransference issues. For example, since the provider has been chosen by the managed care company and given a "preferred" status, transference from the client to the therapist as *the* authority figure may be more intensive than if the client had independently arranged for treatment with the therapist. Countertransference reactions and the potential for disjunctive countertransference responses increase significantly since the therapist realizes that referrals will come from the managed care company; loyalty may therefore be more closely tied to the company than to the appropriate treatment needs of the client. The therapist's judgment about the nature and length of treatment given may be compromised owing to the therapist's concerns about the managed care company's evaluation. The therapist may become especially invested in the client's ability to demonstrate functional improvement (as required by the managed care organization) in order to justify the referral from the managed care company.

Countertransference reactions and responses are more likely to occur when the clinician is forced to serve two masters: the client and the managed care organization. Before the advent of managed care, the therapist's principal, if not exclusive, concern was the best interests of the client. Managed care companies contend that they help the therapist do the best, most efficient job and that the client's best interests are synchronous with that of the managed care company. Economic motives, however, may bring such a contention into question.

One of the key issues in transference and transference management has to do with splitting, a defense in which persons, the self, or situations are experienced as *all* good or *all* bad. Therapists can unintentionally provoke such defensive splitting in clients, so that the managed care company is regarded as *all* bad and the therapist, who is simply working in behalf of the client's best interests, is perceived as *all* good. Such an attitude is clearly disadvantageous for clients inasmuch as a major goal of therapy is to help the client to stop viewing people as being all good or all bad; rather, clients should be helped to see that there are advantages and disadvantages, good and bad, in each of us. It is appropriate for clients to experience ambivalent or mixed feelings, but the clinician may inadvertently promote or collude with the client's tendency to split self and object experience into all good or all bad in situations where managed care is involved in the service delivery equation. (For a somewhat different view of how transference may be shaped by managed care, see Shechter, 1994.)

Therapists may also become angry due to their burden of paperwork and telephone calls, sometimes displacing this anger onto the client. Therapists too may project responsibility onto clients for their own failure to fulfill the managed care criteria for success; furthermore, the therapist's failure to procure additional sessions may lead to a feeling of impotence. Therapists must be especially cautious that such frustrations and reactive anger are not enacted countertransferentially in the treatment relationship.

The following case example, also derived from a case supervised by the first author, illustrates some of these problems.

> *A client's insurance changed from private fee-for-service to managed care, but neither client nor therapist was aware of this since the employer did not make this clear to the client. Consequently, the client continued paying the fee, for which he was reimbursed. The client then discovered that he did in fact have to request service through his managed care company; subsequently, the therapist called the company and was forced to refund the client what he had paid from the date the managed care arrangement had become effective. The managed care company then gave the therapist retroactive authorization for the interviews that had already been completed with the client, though at a lower fee. In general, the therapist had no problem getting authorization for sessions, although she was angry because of the numerous telephone calls she was required to make.*
>
> *At one point in the case, the therapist encountered a case manager, Joan, who gave her a great deal of difficulty. Joan asked the therapist a number of complicated clinical questions in a telephone conversation that took place at the end of what had been an exhausting day. She was unprepared to answer these questions in part because on previous occasions when she had requested prior authorization, the pattern had been one of very brief questions (how many sessions were needed, what the therapist intended to do in those sessions, etc.). As a result, she was not fully prepared to respond, and Joan authorized fewer sessions than the twenty sessions previously received when the therapist had called for prior authorization. After these few additional sessions had elapsed, she called Joan again, requesting additional sessions. Joan questioned the length of time this therapist had been seeing his client (almost two years). She refused to give authorization for more appointments and referred her instead to the psychiatric director of the managed care company. After explaining the case history to the psychiatric director, twenty additional visits were authorized. However, when he referred the therapist back to Joan to complete the paperwork, she stated that the twenty interviews were contingent on a psychiatric evaluation. The therapist was then forced to request a full psychiatric evaluation from the clinic psychiatrist in order to justify her request.*
>
> *At this time, the client was informed that the therapist would not be able to accept his managed care insurance the following year owing to the excessive time that had been required in order to telephone for repeated reauthorizations. The client went to his workplace, and his employer told him that they did have a selection of insurance plans; they suggested, however, that before switching to a different plan, he call the managed care company to find out what the nature of the difficulty had been. At this point, the managed care company's account representative for the client's employer called the clinic di-*

rector to ask why therapists had complained to their employees about the managed care company. The account manager asked the director whether the clinic wanted to maintain a contract with the managed care company, to continue to receive referrals, and so on, indicating that they would not be able to do this if the therapists continued to complain about them.

The therapist called the account representative to apologize. She seemed to have calmed down. The next time she called for prior authorization, she learned that Joan, the original case manager, had been switched to another department.

From the example of supervision, it seems relatively clear that the therapist's behavior would be likely to promote splitting in the client: the therapist is a hard-working "good" professional who is trying to do right by her client, and the all-bad managed care company is obstructionist and unreasonable, causing a great deal of difficulty and requiring the therapist to make unnecessary telephone calls. The therapist's anger at the managed care company had spilled out into the therapy, causing the client a great deal of abandonment anxiety when he learned that the therapist was altogether unwilling to accept his insurance in the coming year. The therapist's reaction further jeopardized a large contract with the managed care company due to her anger at the reduction in fees and other annoyances.

THREE CLINICAL FACES OF MANAGED CARE

Treatment of the following three cases was conducted under a managed care arrangement at a large psychiatric outpatient clinic. The first is of a woman with panic attacks and anxiety, the second involves treatment of a depressed client, and the third is of a neurotic seven-year-old girl.

The client sought treatment for panic attacks, describing rapid heartbeat and feelings of being overcome by an unfocused fear several times a week. This condition had begun several months before initial contact; she stated that the panic attacks had never occurred while she was at work. She was prompted to make an appointment when she realized she was becoming so fearful of an attack that she was beginning to restrict her activities. She was already being evaluated by a cardiologist, the second one whose opinion she had sought. The first examination had revealed no pathology, and there were no other health problems.

The client was a young adult white woman of middle-class background, a college graduate, who had been working for several years in a health-related field. She presented in a very engaging, conversational manner, stating somewhat perfunctorily that there had been no trauma in childhood. She reported that her spouse was emotionally restrained though supportive, happy and successful in his career, and that they had a comfortable home. She was puzzled by the panic attacks since she believed everything in her life was very good.

She revealed that she felt vulnerable and fearful at the prospect of asserting herself. She seemed at intake to have the capacity to think and reflect on her own feelings and relationships.

Initially six individual psychotherapy sessions were authorized over a two-month pe-

riod, then three appointments for a one-month span, and finally twelve sessions over a four-month time frame. In total, twenty-one sessions were authorized. Goals were accomplished in twenty appointments.

At intake a plan was made for a psychiatric consultation in order to assess medical factors and the need for medication. Xanax (5 mg) was prescribed. The client found that her symptoms were relieved when she used it, though she was reluctant to do so. She did indicate that it was reassuring to have it available, and during the span of the treatment she used it four or five times.

Diagnostic impressions were of a person who was dismissive of her own feelings and seemed to wish to assure herself of her own adequacy by achieving certain goals. An early, brief marriage had ended in divorce, and her career, about which she expressed some disappointment, had been suggested to her by her father when she was a teenager.

During the first sessions, the client observed that her panic attacks seemed to occur when she felt bored. As this area was explored in greater depth, her love of learning and her ambition were more fully revealed. Such an ambition was troubling to her since she was very fearful of change. She was then able to discuss her true dissatisfaction with the career she had settled for, which lacked any possibility for advancement and was more routine than scientific. As treatment progressed, she was able to use the relationship to increase her tolerance for ambiguity and to consider possibilities for greater fulfillment in a more rewarding career. Ultimately, she made the decision to return to graduate school.

During this process she began to experience her spouse differently. She gradually was able to see that she had projected feelings onto him that "belonged" to her family of origin, whom she experienced as rigid, judgmental, and incapable of dealing with uncertainty. She felt that they had offered no support for her efforts to explore ideas and were similarly unsupportive of her psychosocial development and feelings.

As she began exploring graduate schools, her panic attacks ceased, and she became more aware of a long-standing anxiety dating back to childhood. There were opportunities to examine this in connection with some unanticipated frustrations in the graduate school application process. Her impulse was to retreat and become passive. As she became increasingly aware of this as a pattern throughout her life, she began to assert herself in innovative and effective ways.

In the last part of the treatment, she became involved with her husband in more creative and rewarding social activities, became more discerning in friendships, and began to appreciate her ability as a leader.

As her symptoms diminished, sessions were scheduled on alternate weeks. At termination there was acceptance of her individuality and a renewed ability to pursue her own growth.

This client progressed very well in treatment and there were no conflicts regarding authorizations from the managed care company.

The next clinical example might also be considered rather typical of those cases now treated under the aegis of managed care.

The client is a thirty-year-old white divorced woman who entered once-weekly individual psychotherapy approximately one year ago. The therapist had strongly recom-

mended a two-times weekly treatment, but the client did not feel she could adjust her work schedule. As the therapeutic relationship unfolded, it also seemed that she wished to avoid making a deeper attachment to the therapist.

The client resides in a rental home with her three small children, maintains full-time employment, and attends college courses paid for by a grant she was awarded. She is financially independent and supports her three children, although her income is very modest. Her ex-husband previously lived with the family for a period of time and had assumed all responsibility for the children's daily care. At that time, the client felt incapable of providing nurturance to her children and was easily irritated by their dependency on her.

The client was given up for adoption by her biological parents at age twelve. Her father was described as critical and emotionally abusive to her, while her mother was very passive and needy. The client's father had insisted that her mother put her in a foster care home, where she remained for three years. At the age of fifteen she was adopted by a couple who offered her security but whom she never thought of as her parents.

When the client came into treatment last year, she had complained of feelings of rejection in a two-year relationship with her black boyfriend. She appeared vulnerable and passive, and characterized this relationship as one involving chronic victimization. The critical and rejecting nature of this relationship seemed to be a repetition of the rejection she had experienced with her biological parents years earlier. The client was tearful and described symptoms of fatigue and appetite loss. She disclosed intense feelings of self-blame and a strong sense that she was unlovable. Her self-defeating behaviors in this relationship were numerous and illuminated conflicts over dependency, anticipation of abandonment, and the underlying belief that she deserved to be punished.

An initial authorization of ten sessions was obtained, which covered the first two and one-half months of treatment. Ten additional sessions were approved for the remainder of that calendar year. Two more authorizations for additional treatment sessions were approved, although the case manager was initially reluctant to honor the therapist's third request for additional sessions. On this occasion, the case manager questioned the client's progress and the anticipated length of treatment. As justification, the therapist emphasized three important dynamic factors that had been revealed in this client's therapy: (1) the client was struggling with severe conflicts related to early abandonment, (2) her attachments were perceived as tenuous, and (3) she exhibited intense self-hatred, with clear potential for suicidal ideation, and possible suicidal behavior should there not be sufficient opportunity for these issues to be addressed. The case manager consented to ten additional sessions.

This brings us to the current situation. The client has now made considerable progress; her depression is diminished, and she has ended her relationship with her boyfriend; she has also developed a few meaningful and supportive relationships. She has gained a great deal of insight into her personality dynamics, including her unconscious tendency to replay early rejections in her contemporary adult relationships. In addition, she now feels less threatened by her children's dependency on her and has gained awareness of her tendency to project her own dependency and intimacy conflicts.

The future length of treatment remains somewhat uncertain, although this issue has been addressed. The client is aware of insurance limitations and of the fact that she has been approved for only six more sessions. She has indicated an interest in continuing with the same copayment arrangement but expresses doubt that she can pay the full fee. It seems likely that the managed care company will grant her one last brief extension so that her progress will not be jeopardized by a premature termination. However, she has begun preparing for his possibility. She is now able to discuss openly her feelings of attachment to the therapist and can acknowledge that the issue of termination evokes a recrudescence of the parental abandonment during her early adolescence. For this reason, termination will be a critical phase of her treatment, requiring sensitive management.

In summary, this case has progressed exceptionally well, and authorizations have been easily and consistently obtained. It is important to highlight that this case involves only once-weekly treatment and that the client's depression was never life threatening at any point during the treatment. If the client had been seen with greater frequency (say, two or three times weekly) or if the depression had presented greater risk to her, the insurance restrictions could have become an impediment to her progress.

In the case example that follows, the clinical work did not unfold smoothly. This vignette is highlighted by the clinician's own description of the nature of the difficulty and the relationship that it had to the managed care process.

Dayna was a seven-year-old white girl in the first grade, referred by her pediatrician following his discussion with Ms. T, Dayna's mother, about her attention problems at school. Presenting complaints included restlessness at home and at school; distractability and sadness in class; incomplete schoolwork (scribbling over her work and deliberately giving wrong answers); bedwetting since age five; occasional nightmares, with fears of monsters and spiders; sleepiness, fatigue, and boredom; and concrete and scattered thinking.

Dayna lived with her mother. Her father had been completely absent since her birth but abruptly moved in with her and Ms. T when Dayna was about five and a half years old; subsequently, he left again, and until age seven Dayna saw him only one or two times.

Ms. T worked Monday through Saturday from 3 to 11 P.M.*, and Dayna had been left in the care of eight different sitters in the preceding two years. Typically the sitter would pick her up from school, and Dayna would go to bed at the sitter's home. Her mother would arrive at the conclusion of her workday (about 11:30* P.M.*), awaken Dayna, and take her home. One month into the therapy, Dayna's father consented to sit for Dayna after school under a similar arrangement. However, the father's motives were mixed inasmuch as he later used this arrangement as a rationale for stopping child support payments to Ms. T.*

The initial diagnosis was neurotic depression and enuresis, with anxiety disorder to rule out. The initial diagnostic information was shared by telephone with a case manager, along with the following goals: to decrease the extent of depressive symptoms, eliminate Dayna's enuresis, and improve her attention span.

Dayna's symptoms seemed to be related to her desire to spend more time with her mother. She experienced considerable guilt over related aggressive fantasies in connection with this and over being bounced between various sitters. Coupled with her confusion about her peripatetic father, this led to fears (about her own "monstrous" feelings), depressive affect, enuresis (a regressive-angry wish to be "babied"), and regressive tendencies in class (the wish to be sent home). Dayna needed a chance to explore and work through her feelings about her parents' absences in play, thought, and in words, so that her symptomatic expression might thereby be diminished.

The case manager initially approved payment for eight sessions. My recommendation to Ms. T was for twice-weekly individual treatment, given the number and severity of Dayna's symptoms, the level of disorganization, and the need for structure and continuity. Unfortunately, scheduling problems necessitated a once-weekly treatment regimen to start, in conjunction with twice-monthly parent conferences with Ms. T. Given the short-term insurance benefit (thirty-five sessions yearly), I explained to Ms. T the chance that Dayna's needs could require psychotherapy beyond the limits of her benefit, and we discussed the nature of private-fee arrangements in the light of this possibility.

Dayna's enuresis disappeared shortly into the therapy. Prevalent themes in her talking and play included "mean" people and animals and how she became frightened by spiders in her toy box at home. The latter seemed related to an initial play inhibition in therapy. Typically, she would sit in her chair complaining of boredom, wishing she could play, despite the fact that the toy box was next to her chair. She made reference to adults angered over various matters concerning children. Interventions during this phase addressed her worries that playing with my toys would make her think scary thoughts, her fear of angering me, her confusion about her parents' arguments, and her worry that she herself might have some "scary-mean" feelings. Only gradually was Dayna able to bring in a few of her own toys and then subsequently begin exploration of my toy box.

After the initial authorized sessions had elapsed, I asked the case manager for reauthorization. I explained that although Dayna was no longer neurotic and had begun to express her sadness and disappointment over her mother's schedule and the various changes in her life, she was still quite distracted, disorganized, and anxious. I also mentioned that we had recently agreed to intensify the frequency of therapy to twice weekly. I requested authorization for psychological testing because of Dayna's difficulty in comprehending basic questions and ideas and her related academic problems that indicated the possibility of a learning disability or intellectual deficiency, or both.

The case manager was annoyed, mentioning that twice-weekly therapy required preapproval and that in any event he saw no justification for an increase in frequency. He insisted that I arrange a psychiatric evaluation to confirm the need for increased frequency and for psychological testing. Reluctantly, I consented and explained that I was unaware that an increase in frequency required preapproval. The case manager also took issue with the fact that I had discussed with Ms. T at the outset of treatment the possibility of her daughter's need for therapy beyond the insurance benefit. I explained that I viewed such a discussion of the realistic possibilities of length of therapy as an issue of professional integrity and informed consent. The case manager claimed that I, as well as others at my clinic, were "obviously" not interested in working together with case management and that he would need to speak to the clinic director. I assured him that I had every intention of working closely with case management but that he certainly had the right to contact the clinic director.

The case manager and I agreed that I would discuss the need for a psychiatric evaluation with Ms. T (if she wished to continue to utilize the mental health benefit) and that I contact the case manager again as soon as I had obtained the results and recommendations of the evaluation. He implored me not to discuss the issue of psychological testing with Ms. T before he had an opportunity to discuss this further with me. I explained that although I certainly would not refer Dayna for testing before authorization was granted, I could not possibly abstain from discussing such important clinical matters with Ms. T solely on the basis of the case manager's administrative needs.

The supervising case manager subsequently contacted the clinic director, who then discussed the issues with me in a concerned but supportive manner. He empathized with my position but was also worried that his predicament could place the clinic's contract with the managed care company at risk. With that in mind, he asked if I could describe for him my interaction with the case manager, and I agreed. The director and I then examined the reality needs of my role as therapist and that of the case manager, who was obliged to adhere to his company's policies.

The senior case manager telephoned me the next day, and I described my interactions with the case manager. The senior case manager explained that preapproval was not required for an increase in session frequency, but that case management did require post hoc demonstration of medical necessity for such a change. He added that although he did not expect me to check with case management prior to every clinical decision, there was an expectation that I would work closely with managed care (he expressed particular concern that any potential conflicts between the insurer and Ms. T's labor union be avoided, an issue that had emerged earlier in my discussion with Ms. T in regard to the mental health benefits to which she and Dayna were entitled). He was receptive to my depiction of the case manager as adversarial and antagonistic and promised to speak with him.

A few days later, Dayna had a psychiatric evaluation. The psychiatrist concurred with my recommendations for an increase in session frequency and for psychological testing. I then reported these conclusions to the case manager, who said he would contact me again after consulting with his medical director. Instead, the managed care company's senior case manager returned the call and stated that their medical director was unwilling to authorize either psychological testing or twice-weekly therapy. Furthermore, the medical director would now authorize only family therapy, although the senior case manager was unable to provide any explanation for this sudden shift. He empathized with my point that individual therapy had already proceeded successfully for about three months without complaints from case management and that interpersonal conflicts between Dayna and her mother were not a primary source of the problems. I also explained that I did not have expertise in family therapy.

The senior case manager suggested that Dayna be transferred to a family therapist. I said that while I would present this option to Ms. T, I also felt obligated to advise her that such a change would likely add to Dayna's confusion and anxiety; further, such a move seemed particularly ill advised inasmuch as a solid treatment alliance had been established and there had been significant therapeutic progress. I also believed an abrupt shift would recapitulate the pattern of unsettling changes in caregivers that Dayna had previously endured. The senior case manager and I agreed that the entire situation was hopelessly complicated.

To compound the complexity of this case, the medical director at my clinic contacted the medical director at case management. The latter was unyielding in her position that only family therapy would be authorized but was unable to offer any specific reason as to why she had not previously taken exception to the handling of the case.

I then met with Ms. T and presented the results of the psychiatric evaluation, the position of case management, and my own clinical judgment as to the potential hazards for Dayna of an abrupt change in either treatment modality or therapist. Ms. T stated emphatically that she wanted me to continue to work with Dayna and expressed both puzzlement and anger with case management. We agreed to continue the therapy at my private office under a private-fee arrangement (which the clinic director had recommended in the event Ms. T chose to continue with me, to avoid any further conflict between case management and the clinic).

The transition to my private office was uneventful. Dayna was offered the explanation that since the new office would be closer to her home, it would be easier for her mother to bring her in for her appointments. (I felt strongly that Dayna should not be burdened by yet another contentious situation involving adults that she might be likely to misinterpret.) Ironically, Ms. T's financial circumstances precluded twice-weekly treatment for Dayna (even at a very reduced fee), so therapy was conducted on a once-weekly basis. I continued seeing the mother twice monthly, and Dayna's school agreed to provide psychoeducational testing.

Most case managers maintain boundaries and are respectful of the clinician's judgment, so that there is little basis for conflict. This seems particularly true when case management standards are clearly written and unambiguous. In this situation, however, there was ambiguity about clinical standards within the case management system (the need for preapproval for increased frequency), complicated by the case manager, who became both anxious and adversarial in response to my suggestions and recommendations. An additional factor was my own irritation when I began to feel that someone was attempting to prescribe my clinical behavior. Perhaps not too surprisingly, a chaotic and disagreeable scenario quickly developed.

In retrospect, it is probably wise to apprise case management of certain clinical decisions that are under consideration before they are actually made. In this way, conflicts may be avoided, and the occasional insecure case manager can feel a greater modicum of control over the case. At the same time, the therapist and client can remind themselves that ultimately they reserve final judgment as to how best to proceed. If the decision is for treatment in the context of case management, case management directives and limitations should be clear to both client and therapist. However, it should be equally clear that when the client and/or therapist find themselves at clinical odds with case management, they always have the right to choose an alternative path outside the boundaries of insurance.

This case has reminded me that it is almost always better to avoid debating clinical judgments with case management. For example, when the senior case manager suggested a shift to family therapy I might have said, "Fine. I'll discuss this with Ms. T and get back with you." Then, behind closed doors I could have discussed the issues honestly with Ms. T (as I would do regardless), while avoiding further contentious discussion with case management. In effect, it served no useful purpose to debate the matter with the senior case manager (other than perhaps to register my irritation). Some conflicts, of course, are unavoidable: for example, a therapist and case manager, both armed with sound clinical reasoning to support their respective viewpoints, may simply disagree about a client's clinical needs. However, in this situation, it was not so much a disagreement over conflicting though well-reasoned clinical positions as it was a battle for control, to see who was in charge.

In this case, I became ensnared in an impossible conflict. Ideally, I wanted to "do right" by case management by following their dictates—to preserve my own business relationship as well as the contract that my clinic maintained with them—and yet I knew that to do so would have compromised both my client's clinical needs and my own professional judgment and ethics. Although Ms. T ultimately made an autonomous decision as to how she wished to proceed (which is as it should be), I also knew that my candor with her had risked my future relationship with this particular case management company.

CASE RECORDING AND THE DIALOGUE BETWEEN THERAPIST AND CASE MANAGER

From the viewpoint of the case manager and insurance company, a case must show medical necessity to qualify for treatment and to avoid rejection for session authorization. In this instance, medical necessity requires a sufficient degree of psychopathology to warrant a medical diagnosis (e.g., neurotic depression, anxiety neurosis, or oppositional disorder) for which units of psychotherapy can then be applied to ameliorate the condition. Most insurance companies will not pay for marriage counseling, legal issues, or educational issues.

It is also important for the clinician to *behaviorize* his or her use of clinical language. Rather than stating that the client is anxious or depressed and that therapy is intended to alleviate the anxiety and depression, the behavioral components of depression are emphasized: changes in appetite; refusal to eat; feeling sad, hopeless, or low; talking about being fatigued or tired; having no energy to do anything; having mood swings; talking about worthlessness, guilt, or inadequacy; and pacing or wringing of hands are examples of useful symptom specificity. If a client says, "I am depressed," the therapist would want to know specifically what depression or suicidal feelings mean to that particular person inasmuch as feelings can mean different things to different people. Depressed behaviors might include hopelessness, helplessness, fatigue, sadness, lowering of self-esteem, emptiness, feeling hemmed in and incapable, decreased interest in personal appearance, lack of communication, decreased interest in sex, sleep disturbances, slumped shoulders, furrowed brow, blue spells, neglect of responsibilities, self-accusations, feelings of loss, shame, and disappointment, feelings of unworthiness, and other behaviorally specific symptoms. "Feelings of anxiety," for example, may be described as a sense of dread, tension, nervousness, apprehension, sense of loss, insecurity, hypersensitivity to noise, restlessness, increased muscular tension, tightness in the throat, a feeling of being smothered, trembling, sweating, and many other such behavioral examples.

In writing a report for a managed care company, it is useful to include relevant history, the presenting problem(s), symptom(s) and behavior(s), treatment objectives (which should be articulated with respect to short-term and long-term goals), and treatment strategies to achieve these various goals.

Representative goals for insomnia might be for the client's demonstrated ability to sleep for longer periods of time. For low energy, a reasonable goal might be for the client to feel more vigor, as reflected by increased participation in athletic activities. For a client whose presenting complaint has been decreased effectiveness or productivity at work or school, a higher job performance evaluation or improved grades would signify measurable progress. For social withdrawal, a typical goal would be for the client to demonstrate increased participation in social activities (e.g., based on actual attendance at social functions). Such specific goals and symptoms appeal to managed care case managers, who generally require the use of behavior-specific language in treatment reports.

While it is always desirable to be able to demonstrate treatment progress, insurance and managed care companies realize that therapy, in a manner analogous to a person's day-to-day life, is also subject to certain vicissitudes and unanticipated developments. So long as the clinician makes an attempt to explain the basis of therapeutic stalemates or failures, such problems should not pose a significant problem for managed care. When it is feasible, managed care firms tend to encourage therapists to refer their clients to outside support groups such as Alcoholics Anonymous, the Secular Organization for Sobriety, and others that will continue to provide support to the client once therapy has been concluded. Case managers also seem to appreciate the therapist's initiative in requesting and facilitating medical evaluations whenever these are deemed necessary.

Case management poses unique and often daunting challenges for the case manager, whose responsibilities include fielding requests for assistance from clients, matching clients up with providers, performing follow-up on more serious cases, and handling complaints from providers, clients, and employee representatives, all of which must be done with a high degree of efficiency. In general, it behooves the clinician to recognize that such competing demands make this work complex and inherently stressful; such awareness may minimize the potential for an adversarial discourse between the clinician and case manager, a development that rarely benefits anyone, least of all the client.

The American Psychiatric Association's *Diagnostic and Statistical Manual* (DSM-IV, 1994) is an indispensable guide for clinicians who must dialogue with case management. DSM-IV, which is intended to be atheoretical, contains current psychiatric diagnoses and associated symptomatology, a "global assessment of functioning" scale, and a severity of psychosocial stressors scale. Because DSM-IV clinical diagnoses are behavior specific, this manual provides a simple framework for identifying discrete symptoms that may be the target of interventions in the treatment plan. The clinician must be able to identify clearly those symptoms or problems that require resolution, whether there is a need for medical consultation, and how various symptoms are related to the clinical diagnosis. Later he or she will be expected to assess the client's progress in achieving resolution of conflicts or amelioration of symptoms, or to specify goals for any subsequent sessions that the case manager is asked to authorize.

MANAGING THE PRACTICE

A therapist who wishes to be listed on a managed care panel must first determine which insurance and managed care companies are used by the largest employers in the area. Although membership on certain panels may be closed, persistent and attractive applications ultimately will be acted on favorably as panels are opened to accommodate new business contracts. Special skills, such as experience working with substance abuse, eating disorders, and victims of domestic violence, or proficiency in a foreign language, will augment the appeal of an application.

Agencies that train their therapists to understand concepts of medical necessity, to behaviorize their clinical language, and to be flexible in the use of short-term versus long-term therapy will be more successful in their relationships with managed care companies. Clients in most cases can continue therapy even after their managed care or insurance benefits have been exhausted, if they are willing to pay the therapist or the agency privately or at a reduced fee. The duration of treatment is thus not necessarily controlled by managed care's preference for time-sensitive therapy. Even prior to the arrival of managed care, clients and therapists were often compelled to develop creative solutions when therapy could not be brought to a natural termination before insurance benefits ran out.

Clinicians are now constantly monitored by managed care companies and case managers. Some companies have instituted formal procedures in which therapists are asked to provide case examples or other written case material so that they can be rated on "managed care–friendly" factors. Other companies assign a numerical rating to the provider's "cooperativeness" at the conclusion of each telephone contact between case manager and provider. Still other companies send out the criteria on which they rate providers; one such company rates providers on a scale from one to six in such areas as quality of care and cooperativeness.

Once a provider has been listed on a managed care panel, reappointment or recredentialing is often based on a series of performance indicators—for example, member complaints, results of satisfaction surveys, utilization statistics, readmissions, accuracy of paperwork, and results of internal quality management studies.

LEGAL ISSUES

Clinical social work practice in the context of managed care throws certain legal issues into high relief, among these confidentiality and client abandonment.

Since the therapist is required to share various kinds of clinical information with the case manager, the client is routinely asked to sign a release-of-information form. Some companies, however, have begun to ask providers to fax them case material. The dilemma here is all too obvious: if a wrong number is inadvertently used, the possibility arises that information of a highly confidential and potentially damaging nature will be read by someone other than for whom it was intended. It therefore becomes important to apprise the client of the possibility, as part of the release and authorization process, that material may be faxed and that the client agree not to hold the therapist liable should the material be sent accidentally to a wrong number.

"Abandonment" used in this particular context refers to the forced termination of a case when no managed care benefits remain. In order to avoid such an undesirable state of affairs, there must be a continuity-of-care plan. Such a plan typically gives a client two weeks' notice that therapy cannot continue because benefits have run out and/or refers the client to an agency that will be able to provide continuing treatment. Such actions should be well documented in the case record and in a formal letter to the client. Legalities aside, it is probably professionally and ethically more responsible to continue seeing a client with whatever creative fee arrangements can be arranged, even if benefits do run out.

If a client cannot continue for financial reasons and additional sessions were denied by a case manager, the therapist must document that (1) the case has been discussed with both a supervising case manager and the medical director of the managed care company and (2) the case has gone through an official appeals process. These steps are necessary when, in the therapist's opinion, denial of further treatment places the client in jeopardy. If the client is not truly in jeopardy but wishes to continue treatment in a search for truth, insight, or global well-being, such an appeal process is not easily justified. A *client who is truly in crisis cannot be abandoned. Such a client must be treated for no fee until an adequate continuity-of-care plan is devised,* such as a referral to a community-based agency or other alternative care.

Managed care and the law are evolving as more cases have come before state courts. Some courts have found that the provider has ultimate responsibility for not abandoning a client; other courts have ruled that a managed care company can be held liable should something happen to a client due to their negligence. At present, the laws are very inconsistent from state to state, and many decisions are being appealed; for the time being, there is no standard set of legal guidelines. For this reason, it may be best to err on the side of caution by having an attorney examine any contract before signing with a company. Some managed care companies have put "hold-harmless" clauses into their contracts, which stipulates that should a mistake be made by either the therapist or the managed care company, the managed care company will not be liable and the therapist must provide all legal expenses for the defense. It is best not to sign such a contract without legal safeguards.

TRENDS

Most managed care companies prefer to contract with group practices to enhance the likelihood of locating a therapist with specific attributes (e.g., an African American man, a Spanish-speaking woman) who may be matched with a particular client from the managed care company's large pool of clients.

Managed care companies have begun to use capitation to provide group practices with a fixed amount of money for all potential clients in a certain geographic area. In this instance, the group practice itself assumes the managed care role, deciding which clients receive a greater or lesser number of sessions.

Managed care will also be especially interested in practices that offer a continuum of services. From the perspective of a managed care company, the best group practice is one that has the capability of providing a client with whatever kinds of service may be required, thus relieving the company of a significant administrative burden. For example, a group practice that can provide not only outpatient treatment but also partial hospitalization, day care services, and even inpatient hospitalization will be preferable to one that is able to offer only outpatient services.

It also seems inevitable that practitioners who do not offer managed care–friendly, cost-efficient, quality treatment will eventually cease to receive referrals from managed care. Managed care will continue to reward providers who are able to show positive behavioral outcomes and good patient satisfaction response to surveys. Payment to providers will be based on both market competition and the number of clients a managed care company is able to refer to the practitioner. Case managers are less likely to feel the need to micromanage therapists they deem to be managed care–friendly; such clinicians will also receive more client referrals. Clinicians whose profiles fail to show positive behavioral outcomes and high levels of consumer satisfaction, or are otherwise viewed by managed care as "unfriendly," are more likely to be closely monitored.

Another significant development with interesting ramifications for clinicians and agencies is the rediscovery of research on outcome effectiveness in the domain of managed care. Although research models for evaluating clinical outcomes have existed for many years, there has been little motivation to use these in most clinical settings. Managed care companies, however, are especially interested in using treatment models with proven "effectiveness" and are likely to provide a sustained impetus for practical research investigations of therapeutic outcome effectiveness and consumer satisfaction.

Electronic billing and computer-to-computer billing via modem between group practices and managed care companies will become commonplace. And finally, larger managed care companies will continue to purchase smaller managed care and employee assistance companies. The resulting pattern may yield a limited number of very large managed care companies that refer to an increasingly select number of service providers.

REFERENCES

American Psychiatric Association. (1994). *Diagnostic and statistical manual of mental disorders* (4th ed.), Washington, DC: American Psychiatric Association Press.

Shechter, R. (1994). Managed care and psychoanalytically-oriented psychotherapy: The influence of professional culture-clash on transference. *Journal of Analytic Social Work, 2,* 47–59.

15

Psychopharmacology and Clinical Social Work Practice

Barbara Halin Willinger

Psychopharmacology historically has been the domain of psychiatry, and it remains so to this day. However, inasmuch as social workers intervene with clients in a variety of settings, ranging from hospitals to family and child agencies to private practice, they are in a unique position to recognize and assess the need for medication, initiate the referral to a psychopharmacologist, and participate in monitoring the effects of the medication. Social work psychotherapists have become aware of the adjunctive and effective use of psychotropic drugs and increasingly collaborate with psychopharmacologists who may already be medicating their patients or with whom they have forged a professional relationship. Unquestionably, social work plays a significant role in psychopharmacology. Given this involvement, it is a conundrum that so little direct attention is accorded this vital piece of training by either graduate schools or the profession itself.

In general, social workers have not been well educated about medications, their effects, and their myriad symbolic meanings. This may be attributable in part to the emphasis that social work theory has historically placed on sociological and psychological determinants of behavior rather than the contribution of biological factors. "Social workers must realize that major emotional illness results not only from unconscious conflicts, as emphasized by psychoanalytic theory, but may also result from an alteration in body chemistry or other physical factors" (Matorin & De Chillo, 1984, p. 580).

The numbers of patients concurrently treated by a nonmedical psychotherapist and a psychiatrist-psychopharmacologist has continued to climb since 1984, when there were 210,000 such patients nationwide (Beitman, Chiles, & Carlin, 1984). These numbers do not include patients prescribed psychotropic medications by internists, family practitioners, or other nonpsychiatric physicians. With the popularization of drug information by television, magazines, and newspapers, clients are more likely to ask about the use and effectiveness of medications. It is therefore imperative that social workers be knowledgeable, whether it is to correct their distortions or to support cooperation in their medication regime.

There was an explosion in the use of psychotropic medications in the 1950s with the introduction of Thorazine, a drug used to treat the symptoms of psychosis: thought-disordered thinking, delusions, and hallucinations (visual, auditory, olfactory, and tactile). Other antipsychotic drugs followed, and recently there has been a proliferation of medications for treating a variety of psychiatric disorders.

Freud in 1940 alluded to the use of medication concomitant with existing verbal therapy:

> The future may teach us to exercise a direct influence, by means of particular chemical substances, on the amounts of energy and their distribution in the mental apparatus. It may be that there are other still undreamt-of possibilities of therapy. (Gutheil, 1982, p. 321)

Freud did not envision medication as superseding the power and effectiveness of the personal therapeutic relationship. However, the structure and economics of our current health care system may be eroding the clinical autonomy held by mental health professionals and moving treatment in the direction of short-term, seemingly cost-effective methods. It is critical that social work clinicians be educated and remain flexible about psychiatric medications, not as a substitute for the therapeutic relationship but as an appropriate component of the treatment when indicated.

REVIEW OF THE LITERATURE

Beginning in the 1960s the establishment of community health centers and outpatient psychiatric clinics was juxtaposed with the deinstitutionalization of psychiatric patients (Matorin & De Chillo, 1984; Miller, Wiedeman, & Linn, 1980). The universality of psychotropic medication for mental illness was accepted, and social work assumed greater responsibility for direct primary care, thereby necessitating a new level of collaboration with psychiatrists. As early as 1968, Hankoff and Galvin observed that "the greatly extended treatment of the severely mentally ill patient in the community setting has increased the need for social workers to integrate knowledge about the psychopharmacological agents" (p. 41).

Social work literature that focused on psychopharmacology from the 1970s through 1992 was written primarily by educators and practitioners in either hospitals or mental health clinic settings. These articles include an overview of various psychotropic medications; indications for use and limitations; the nature and extent of social work responsibility in the monitoring of medication; psychodynamics of the interplay between patient, therapist, and psychiatrist; and a validation of and plea for ongoing educational training in psychopharmacology (Bentley & Reeves, 1992;

Berg & Wallace, 1987; Davidson & Jamison, 1983; Gerhart & Brooks, 1983; Levine & Dang, 1977; Matorin & De Chillo, 1984; Miller et al., 1980).

Hospitals and clinic settings have historically required staff to become conversant about medications, since good patient care is reinforced through cooperation among the multiple disciplines represented on the treatment team. Social work's role is often defined as one of

> "physicians' helper" and "consultant-collaborator." . . . Both presume that social workers will perform such activities as encouraging compliance with medication schedules, monitoring for the side effects associated with a variety of psychotropic drugs, and working with families and significant others on matters that relate to medication. (Berg & Wallace, 1987, p. 144)

A study of second-year social work students found an alarming practice involving some students actually writing prescriptions for the psychiatrist to sign, and counting or placing pills in containers for patients (Miller et al., 1980). Although monitoring is not uncommon, the authors raised concern about such responsibility being undertaken by students who lack adequate training and knowledge. Over half the students who participated in the study found their classroom instruction inadequate to meet the perceived needs in their settings. The authors concluded that schools of social work and psychiatric institutions should jointly determine psychopharmacology course content.

Whereas beginning clinicians experience a gap between their education and real-life role expectations, this division apparently diminishes after two years of employment in a psychiatric setting. Staff can then recognize side effects, incorporate adequate information about appropriate dosage levels, and differentiate medications according to target symptoms (Berg & Wallace, 1987).

Clinical social work, of course, is not limited to the treatment of psychiatric patients or those in psychiatric settings. The educational training needs of clinical populations (e.g., with medically ill patients, adolescents, and incest survivors) are of equal importance since these clinicians are also called on to evaluate patients' need for psychotropic medication. They too must understand when to refer a client for consultation and believe in the efficacy of medication. Yet despite the acknowledged need by professionals, a report issued by the Council of Social Work Education (1990) found that inclusion of psychopharmacology material is "sparse, elective, and probably dependent on the interest of particular instructors" (p. 2). In an informal 1995 survey of New York City graduate schools of social work, I found only one school offering a required three-hour workshop for second-year students that was exclusively centered on psychopharmacology.

An additional concern is the paucity of written material by private practitioners regarding the incorporation of psychotropics with psychotherapy. Many clinicians are aware of the dynamic issues that arise in therapy, particularly transferential manifestations related to splitting and oedipal dynamics. However, the dynamics surrounding the use of medications continue to be viewed as the province of the psychiatrist.

To understand more clearly the role of medication in therapy apart from its use with severely disturbed clients, one must look to psychiatry for elucidation. It is of some interest that clinical psychiatry has had to work through its own conflicts and ambivalence regarding the use of medication. In 1962, Mortimer Ostow became a psychiatric pioneer in the use of combined medication and therapy. He felt strongly that "drugs should not be used in psychoanalysis or psychotherapy unless they are essential to protect the patient or protect treatment. If treatment can be successfully conducted without drugs, none should be given" (Kahn, 1993, p. 226). The underlying fear in prescribing medication was that the client's motivations for change would be disrupted, and, with the alleviation of symptoms, the patient would discontinue treatment (Klerman, 1983; Hausner, 1993). This has not proved to be the case.

It is not the purpose of this chapter to delve into current research regarding the efficacy of medication; however, there is general consensus that psychotropics are invaluable with both psychotic manifestations and also with particular target symptoms. A recent informal study by Consumer Reports (*Mental Health*, November 1995) concluded that "40% of readers who sought professional help received psychiatric drugs" (p. 738).

Both social work practitioners and students will benefit from formalized training in psychopharmacology. There is no doubt that such training needs to become a formal component in the graduate social work curriculum before the social work profession can realistically move toward obtaining prescription privileges (Abroms & Greenfield, 1973; Cohen, 1988; Dziegielewski, in press).

PSYCHOTROPIC DRUGS

In order to maximize therapeutic effectiveness with clients on medication, it is essential for clinicians to have a basic knowledge of drug actions and their effects, the most common psychotropic medications, their dosage range, and the most common side effects.

"A drug acts by producing a quantitative alteration, either an increase or reduction, in a normal body function or process" (Wise, 1986, p. 36). Each drug has a minimal level of efficacy. When the level of active drug in the body exceeds the level of efficacy, toxicity occurs.

Each drug must reach its site of action, wherever in the body that may be, in order to elicit an effect. This is accomplished through absorption and distribution. In the process of absorption, the drug moves from its site of administration into the bloodstream. Once in the bloodstream, the drug must then disperse into the tissue to reach its site of action (referred to as the *process of distribution;* Wise, 1986).

The absorption and distribution of a given drug occur simultaneously with its excretion. All oral medications are absorbed in the stomach and ultimately released through the kidneys and bladder. Since metabolic breakdown varies from person to person, medications need to be individualized and monitored until either a therapeutic dosage is achieved or another similar drug replaces the one being tried. The biological half-life of a drug is the time it takes for the body to eliminate half of the drug molecules from the bloodstream. For example, some drugs, like Xanax, Serax,

Restoril, Halcion, and Ativan, are short acting (i.e., quickly eliminated), while other benzodiazepines, or anxiolytics, like Valium, Dalmane, Klonopin, and Librium are long acting.

Most psychotropic drugs act on the neurotransmitters, the chemical messengers that relay communication from one nerve cell to another in the brain. The neurotransmitters most often referred to are serotonin, dopamine, and norepinephrine. One of the functions of the neurotransmitters is to help speed up a drug's reaction, or turn it on or off, thus influencing physiological or psychological behavior (Radcliffe et al., 1985; Schatzberg, 1991; Wise, 1986; Yudofsky, Hales, & Ferguson, 1991; B. McGreal, personal communication, October 1995).

Antidepressants

These medications are especially useful in alleviating symptoms of a major depressive episode, dysthymic disorders, the depressed phase of a bipolar disorder, panic disorders, and sometimes anxiety. The serotonin-reuptake inhibitors, or atypical drugs as they are sometimes called, are the newest group of medications, frequently prescribed because of markedly diminished anticholinergic effects (dry mouth, constipation, urinary retention, and gastrointestinal upset.) In addition, their overdose potential is lower than that of other antidepressant drugs.

Selective Serotonin Reuptake Inhibitors (SSRIs)

These drugs are among the newest medications and appear to have the fewest side effects. They are used primarily for the treatment of depression but have also been prescribed for obsessive-compulsive disorders, obesity, and bulimia. (See Table 15.1; for atypical agents, see Table 15.2.)

TABLE 15.1

Selective Serotonin Reuptake Inhibitors

Medication	*Dosage Range*	*Common Side Effects*
Zoloft (sertraline)	50–200 mg	Nausea and vomiting Insomnia Headache Temporary weight loss Ejaculatory and erectile disturbance Anorgasmia
Prozac (fluoxetine)	20–80 mg	
Paxil (paroxetine)	20–50 mg	
Luvox (fluvoxamine)	100–300 mg	

Tricyclics

This class of antidepressants is now referred to as heterocyclics. Most require approximately two weeks for initial patient response and up to four weeks for positive therapeutic results. A major drawback is the risk of suicide or unintentional overdose. (See Table 15.3.)

TABLE 15.2
Atypical Agents

Medication	*Dosage Range*	*Common Side Effects*
Trazodone (desyrel)	50–600 mg	Most sedating antidepressant; used for insomnia Possible hypotension Some anticholinergic effects In young men, painful erection
Serzone (nefazadone)[a]	200–600 mg	Similar to Trazodone, with fewer sedating effects
Effexor (venlafaxine)[b]	225–375 mg	Possible hypertension
Wellbutrin (bupropion)[a]	100–400 mg	Beneficial for elderly–no significant sedation or cognitive impairment In elevated dosages, increased incidence of seizures

[a] Does not cause sexual dysfunction.
[b] For treating resistant depression.

Monoamine Oxidase Inhibitors (MAOIs)

These medications were developed in the 1950s as the first specific antidepressants. They are no longer prescribed initially because of the need for dietary restrictions and the difficulty in ensuring accurate compliance. They are clinically indicated and utilized when tricyclic therapy has not been effective or for panic attacks. (See Table 15.4.)

TABLE 15.3
Tricyclics

Medication	*Dosage Range*	*Common Side Effects*
Tofranil (imipramine)[a] Elavil (amitriptyline)[a] Pamelor (nortriptyline)[a] Sinequan (doxepin)[a]	150–300 mg 150–300 mg 75–150 mg 150–300 mg	Anticholinergic: dry mouth; constipation; urinary retention; gastrointestinal upset Orthostatic hypotension (sudden drop in blood pressure when standing up) Sexual dysfunction
Norpramin (desipramine)	150–300 mg	Orthostatic hypotension Less anticholinergic Restlessness, insomnia, agitation

[a] The most sedating medications.

TABLE 15.4
Monoamine Oxidase Inhibitors

Medication	*Dosage Range*	*Common Side Effects*
Nardil (phenelzine)	10–90 mg	Orthostatic hypotension
Parnate (tranylcypromine)	10–50 mg	Hypertensive crises from interaction with such foods as aged cheeses or meats, pickled or salted herring; or certain medications in the categories of decongestants or stimulants
Marplan (isocarboxazid)	30–50 mg	Anorgasmia or impotence

Mood Stabilizers

These medications are frequently effective in instances of manic excitement as well as averting recurrences of mania or depression in bipolar patients. However, they require careful monitoring. They are not effective until therapeutic blood levels are reached and are potentially toxic if the levels are exceeded; in the latter case, confusion, delirium, and seizures, among other side effects, may occur. (See Table 15.5.)

TABLE 15.5
Mood Stabilizers

Medication	*Dosage Range*	*Common Side Effects*
Eskalith (lithium)	300–2,400 mg	Tremor Thirst Diarrhea and nausea Hypothyroidism; test thyroid regularly
Tegretol (carbamazepine)	600–1,600 mg	Diarrhea and nausea
Depakote (valproic acid)	750–3,000 mg	Liver dysfunction

Antipsychotics

These medications are efficacious for schizophrenia and management of manic states, psychotic depression, and psychotic reactions to hallucinogens. (See Table 15.6.)

Anxiolytics

These medications are the most commonly used psychotropic drugs worldwide because of their relative safety. They are most effective in treating acute anxiety, generalized anxiety disorder, and insomnia. In order to decrease the risk of either

TABLE 15.6
Antipsychotics

Medication	*Dosage Range*	*Common Side Effects*
Thorazine (chlorpromazine)	25–2,000 mg	Extrapyramidal symptoms/Parkinsonian effects: slowed movements, muscle rigidity ("cogwheeling"), shuffling gait, drooling Akathesia: restlessness Anticholinergic Involuntary movements of limbs; uncoordinated movements of the neck, face, and eyes Early dyskinesias: reversible Tardive dyskinesia: involuntary movements of the tongue and mouth; occurs after long-term use and is not reversible Orthostatic hypotension Sedation
Mellaril (thioridazine)	25–800 mg	
Stelazine (trifluoperazine)	4–40 mg	
Haldol (haloperidol)[a]	1–30 mg	
Prolixin (fluphenazine)[a]	1–30 mg	
Serentil (mezoridazine)	10–100 mg	
Navane (thiothixene)	10–60 mg	
Trilafon (perphenazine)	4–64 mg	
Moban (molindone)	30–225 mg	
Orap (pimozide)	1–30 mg	
Loxitane (loxapine)	20–250 mg	
Risperidone (risperdal)[b]	2–8 mg	Fewer acute and chronic extrapyramidal side effects
Clozaril (clozapine)[b]	100–600 mg	Potential blood abnormality (agranulocytosis) requiring weekly blood tests Lower potential for extrapyramidal side effects

[a] Available in Decanoate.
[b] Also effective in treating negative symptoms of psychosis: blunted affect, social withdrawal, and poor motivation.

dependence or withdrawal, benzodiazepines should be given at a low dosage for short periods of time. (See Tables 15.7 and 15.8.)

THE DECISION TO REFER FOR MEDICATION

Community-based agencies and mental health clinics frequently employ social workers as primary therapists or case managers and psychiatrists as consultants, diagnosticians, and psychopharmacologists. In this context and in private practice, primary therapists make decisions to refer clients for medication; the referral is based on recognition of symptoms but not necessarily with the accompanying knowledge of specific drugs.

Psychiatric research has shown that psychotherapy alone is efficacious for mild depressions, adjustment disorders, some anxiety disorders, and personality disorders.

TABLE 15.7
Benzodiazepines

Medication	*Dosage Range*	*Common Side Effects*
Xanax (alprazolam)[a, b]	0.5–8 mg	Drowsiness; Potentiation of the effects of drinking alcohol; Withdrawal symptoms if the drug is abruptly discontinued
Serax (oxazepam)[a]	10–60 mg	
Restoril (temazepam)[a, c]	15–30 mg	
Halcion (triazolam)[a, c]	0.125–0.25 mg	
Ativan (lorazepam)[a, d]	0.5–8 mg	
Valium (diazepam)[e]	15–30 mg	Drowsiness; Potentiation of the effects of drinking alcohol; Withdrawal symptoms if the drug is abruptly discontinued
Klonopin (clonazepam)[e]	0.5–10 mg	
Librium (chlordiazepoxide)[e]	10–100 mg	
Dalmane (flurazepam)[c, e]	15–30 mg	

[a] These medications have a shorter acting half-life.
[b] For anxiety associated with depression.
[c] Also for acute insomnia.
[d] Can be administered intramuscularly for agitated psychotic patients.
[e] Remain active for 30–100 hours; less frequently used than the other benzodiazepines.

However, sometimes a client's symptoms necessitate more immediate action either within the initial session or soon after. These situations may include, but are not limited to, the following:

- Clients whose severe depression or anxiety interferes with daily functioning.
- Psychotically depressed clients.
- Clients who are moving toward or are already in a manic episode.
- Clients with new-onset or recurrent episodes of schizophrenia.
- Clients with obsessive-compulsive disorders.
- Personality-disordered clients whose behavioral problems, "whether from acting out or from primary primitive pathology interrupt the therapeutic relationship or place the patient in imminent danger" (Dewan, 1992, p. 103).
- Clients who express suicidal ideation where hospitalization is believed not to be imperative (Dewan, 1992; McCollum, Margolin, & Lieb, 1978).

TABLE 15.8
Nonbenzodiazepines

Medication	*Dosage Range*	*Common Side Effects*
Buspar (buspirone)[a]	15–35 mg	Does not produce dependence
Ambien (zolpidem)	5–10 mg	Sedation

[a] Maximum effectiveness reached in 4–6 weeks.

Two clinical vignettes follow:

> *Tim, a forty-year-old single man living with his parents, was referred for psychotherapy by his internist because of recurring obsessive thoughts concerning courses he had failed in high school. Tim was employed and enjoyed occasional contact with a few friends but spent most of his time in solitary pursuits, movies, and concerts. Tim's parents, in their seventies, were highly critical of his obsessions as well as many of his "nervous" behaviors. In addition, family dynamics were such that his parents rarely spoke to each other and often criticized each other in private conversations with Tim.*
>
> *Within the first three months Tim requested medication, at the suggestion of his mother; she wanted something to "stop me from repeating the same stories over and over." The therapist attempted to explore Tim's passive-dependent dynamics, but with little gain. At the same time, the therapist consulted a psychopharmacologist, who felt medication would decrease the severity of Tim's ruminations. Tim began and continued Zoloft, and his obsessive thoughts did abate. The meaning of Tim's obsessions is now partially understood, and Tim now feels more in control of them when they do occur.*

While it is generally accepted that psychic pain can provide motivation for a client in the therapeutic process, there is also widespread agreement that medication can be of great value when the client's symptoms become overwhelming or cannot be mastered within the treatment milieu (Dewan, 1992; Goldhamer, 1993; Kahn, 1993; Levine & Dang, 1977; McCollum et al., 1978; Ostow, 1993). The question of when and how to introduce the option of medication rests with the therapist and his or her understanding of the client's psychodynamics. In this departure from psychodynamic technique, the clinician needs to discuss the reason for the medication and describe its function and purpose. This should optimally occur over several sessions in order for the client's reactions to be understood and worked through.

> *Fred, a sixty-two-year-old gay man, had been in treatment for five years once weekly with a hospital-based clinician, when medication became an issue. He began therapy when he discovered his HIV seropositivity status and his AIDS diagnosis based on his T-cell count.*
>
> *Initially Fred worked through his adjustment to the diagnosis, regaining an interest in life and friends. He also came to understand his shame around his homosexuality. Although he understood intellectually that his compliant, affable relationship to his therapist and others was a defense against anger and disappointment with early maternal caregiving figures and a fear of abandonment, he was unable to change his interpersonal relationships significantly.*
>
> *In the fourth year of treatment, Fred developed an erotic transference and attachment to a fellow church member who had made himself available and had shown interest in Fred. The patient's increased attachment was met by Chuck's ambiguity and ambivalence about his own sexuality juxtaposed with Chuck's parentalized attitude and critical demeanor.*
>
> *As therapy continued to explore Fred's wishes and fears about intimacy, attachment, and rejection, he also described symptoms of decreased energy and diminished interest in socializing. Organic issues were ruled out after consultation with his physician. Fred*

soon acknowledged the severe drop in his T-cells several months earlier, resulting in unexpressed fears of deterioration related to feelings of shame and humiliation. Psychotherapy continued along with discussion of medication; medication for Fred signified "weakness" and that he was "crazy." When his symptoms did not remit and in fact, included difficulty concentrating and insomnia, Fred was ready to accept medication. He was prescribed Zoloft 25 mg, but due to some side effects was switched to Paxil 10 mg. His depressive symptoms decreased.

TRANSFERENCE THEMES

Each client brings his or her own unique set of realities and transference reactions to the treatment milieu. For our purposes here, transference will be defined as "the unconscious attachment to others of feelings and attitudes which were originally associated with important figures in one's early life" (American Psychiatric Association, 1957, p. 63). Whenever transference phenomena occur in the interpersonal therapeutic relationship or in the context of medication-related issues, such reactions should be explored and worked through when they prove inimical to the treatment.

Clients who enter treatment requesting medication, who are already on medication from previous therapies, or who seek medication treatment on their own present interesting dynamic dilemmas for the therapist, such as issues of competition and control, fear of dependency, and preoedipal conflicts (Goodman, 1995a). Such dilemmas may, in fact, lead to valuable insights into the patient's internal world and to possible transference issues.

Sharon, a thirty-year-old single female, began therapy due to overwhelming anxiety at work; she was an interior decorator who had been with the same employer for several years. She had also terminated her therapy six months earlier.

Within the first month, Sharon informed her therapist of an appointment she had made with a psychiatrist in another state, who was a well-known author and analyst. An MAOI was prescribed for Sharon, based on the diagnosis of "atypical depression with associated feelings of shame and humiliation."

Sharon was the youngest of three daughters born to a rural fundamentalist couple; Sharon's two sisters were five and ten years older than she. The parents were hard working, emotionally vacuous, and unaffectionate. Sharon recalled her father being "playful" until she began school; her mother became important during puberty. Sharon's identification with her mother included overt negative and humiliating reactions toward the father when he engaged in unacceptable behaviors such as "drinking" and "singing loudly in church."

Sharon described a lonely childhood made bearable by her imagination and fantasy world that included an "imaginary friend" and "forts" (a tree house) to which she retreated. As an adult Sharon treated herself with "happy food," cheese, and yogurt. Although these foods are prohibited with the MAOIs, Sharon originally experienced no difficulty in depriving herself as it suited her masochistic tendencies. As her self-deprivation became understandable during analytic exploration, the therapist suggested Sharon see her psychopharmacologist. Unlike the parents she could not burden with her needs (which prompted her finding the psychiatrist) or the mother of latency age who misun-

derstood her needs, the therapist was appropriately responsive; Sharon was switched to Xanax. Sharon's transferential reenactment of her fear and wish for dependency, along with her identification with moralistic parental principles as a defense against vulnerability and aggression, was already present in the therapeutic space even before the therapist's understanding and interpretation.

COUNTERTRANSFERENCE THEMES

The therapist's countertransference in relation to the question of medication also needs to be understood and considered. Therapists oriented exclusively toward psychotherapy or psychoanalysis may tend to regard the need for medication as evidence of their personal failure with the patient and therefore make fewer suggestions, particularly if they have had little or no experience in settings in which medication has been used to advantage.

In other instances, therapists may raise the issue of medication related perhaps to their need to feel useful and helpful, as a defense against their feeling of helplessness or impotence. Medication can also be a way of creating emotional distance from the patient, a protection against and fear of the client's rage or anger, or expiation of guilt for the therapist's own hostile feelings toward the client (Dewan, 1992; Goodman, 1995b).

Colleen, a thirty-year-old married mother of two children, presented with depression and suicidal ideation: "I want to jump in front of a train and end it all." Her husband's involvement in her treatment and Colleen's avowed belief that "God would not forgive" her if she were to attempt suicide (she was formerly a nun) provided some solace to the therapist when Colleen refused medication. Treatment was tumultuous over the years, and Colleen was ultimately diagnosed with borderline personality disorder.

Colleen was the second of four children; all her siblings suffered some emotional disturbance. Colleen's mother either ignored her or was critical and disdainful, while Colleen's father treated her as "special" and provided love not experienced from her mother.

Although Colleen's external life improved with therapy, the transference remained the area of therapeutic impasse. Colleen would often implore the therapist to hug her and be "more than a therapist." Each refusal was met by Colleen's tremendous rage or hopelessness. The therapist raised the issue of medication during these states, only to be met by Colleen's refusal. In the transference Colleen became the demanding and yet rejecting child who would not be silenced, and she induced in the therapist a sense of helplessness. The therapist eventually realized that she was motivated to discuss medication with Colleen in part because of her wish to refer the client to a psychopharmacologist—a symbolic caring father—thus sparing herself Colleen's rages.

PSYCHODYNAMICS OF PHARMACOTHERAPY

Each individual brings to therapy unique problems, reality perceptions, transference distortions, and interpretations about medications. It is not surprising that the psychodynamics of medication can replicate the psychosexual levels of development. However the emotional meaning to the patient may or may not be conscious, thereby making accessibility for introspection rather variable.

Clients can perceive the recommendation for medication positively, as a symbolic reenactment of receiving nurturing and food as a child, as a response to their dependency needs, and as an empathically attuned validation of their suffering (Goodman, 1995a; Gutheil, 1982; McCollum et al., 1978; Thale, 1973), as the following case examples illustrate.

Katrina, a forty-one-year-old woman, had several failed in vitro fertilization attempts; on the last attempt, she became pregnant but miscarried in two months. She was appropriately depressed and increased the frequency of her sessions. Katrina's father had evidenced narcissistic and manic traits during her childhood; her mother was a depressed alcoholic and "martyr." Katrina's acceptance and love came at the expense of pseudoindependence and perfectionistic performance. Motherhood was one area in which she could not yet succeed. Despite ongoing psychotherapeutic work, Katrina's symptoms of irritability, anhedonia, and insomnia did not remit. When the therapist raised the possibility of medication, Katrina declined, since she was undecided about another attempt at in vitro fertilization, but said, "I know you understand my suffering." She experienced the suggestion as being "fed" as opposed to being "left" in her suffering.

According to Hausner (1993), medication can take on aspects of a transitional object or transitional phenomenon: "Winnicott recognized that transitional objects are 'created by the infant and at the same time provided from the environment.' Transitional objects . . . may be viewed as a defense against anxiety, a 'resting place' in the continuous task of keeping inner and outer realities separate yet related" (p. 89). The client therefore may imbue the medication with qualities so that it becomes a symbolic way of merger with the therapist, or the psychopharmacologist, to perhaps alleviate the reality of separation between visits.

Sharon, referred to earlier, indicated several years later in her therapy that she had run out of medication and was considering renewing it. This occurred when the therapist and she were exploring her fear of competition and her enacted retreat from fulfilling this (she had turned down a promotion). Sharon's paranoia regarding retaliation and punishment increased, and in referring to the medication, she said, "I need to know it's there, just in case." Medication renewal was supported while psychodynamic exploration continued, including her wish and fear of dependency on the therapist.

Debby, a newly appointed college professor, was referred by her psychiatrist who was medicating her with Zoloft and Klonopin. Debby presented with crippling anxiety and obsessive-compulsive rituals revolving around her class performance. The patient, although compliant with medication, viewed it as a negative representation of herself and would continually stress the importance of being medication free. The therapist's goal was for the therapeutic relationship to replace the medications, and in fact Debby discontinued the Klonopin as the treatment alliance strengthened. During the therapist's vacation, which overlapped with the pharmacotherapist's, Debby felt abandoned and enraged, and increased her Zoloft 25 mg, only to experience agitation and inability to concentrate. The medication could not replace the therapist. With the reestablishment of the therapeutic connection and the decrease of the medication, Debby returned to her former baseline and therapy resumed.

An example of the transitional phenomenon can sometimes be found on psychiatric inpatient units or outpatient clinics when the client resists a change of medication or a change in dosage by the new psychiatrist, experiencing the drugs as a symbolic representation of the lost therapist–maternal object (Adelman, 1993).

Conversely, clients may have negative reactions to the suggestion of medication. These may include narcissistic injury or a feeling that the therapist lacks confidence in them. Their idealization of the therapist may be shattered and experienced as an object loss. Some patients may even express rage, recalling early bodily intrusions in the form of forceful feeding, enemas, or incestuous acts (Goodman, 1995b; Gutheil, 1982; McCollum et al., 1978; Ostow, 1993).

A twenty-four-year-old student had been screened by a referral service and given the name of a psychopharmacologist and social work clinician. By the time Mike called the social worker, he had been started on one of the SSRIs; Mike had been diagnosed with a dysthymic disorder and obsessive personality with paranoid traits. He continued in therapy with concomitant medication for one and a half years, when his therapist left for vacation. Rather unexpectedly, Mike regressed, withdrew from friends, dropped out of school, and became increasingly paranoid and obsessive. Significantly he had also discontinued Prozac. This episode, eventually worked through, bore a vital resemblance to earlier traumatic losses. Medication was not resumed.

Four years later Mike experienced the loss of a serious love interest and became hopeless and withdrawn. Shortly after, he was offered a promotion. The therapist decided to discuss medication, since Mike had begun self-medicating with alcohol. His self-medication, plus a history of parental emphasis on achievement, made the current discussion more sensitive. Mike verbalized his fear of the therapist's lack of interest in him, as well as his feeling of being pressured by her to succeed, a pressure similar to that he felt from his parents. The therapist reminded him that earlier he had stopped school while on Prozac, and she had not "pressured him" to resume his education. The referral now was to alleviate his verbalized suffering and withdrawal, and to support his professional functioning. Subsequently, Mike began Prozac since he did want to succeed at work and had accepted the promotion.

Clients can also interpret medication discussion as an attempt by the therapist to control them and their affects, like Colleen, thereby recreating early struggles and memories related to that developmental period. Responses to issues of control, domination, and authority can range from rage and rebelliousness to anxiety and compliance. Clients may feel pushed away or punished for not doing well enough in therapy, as with Mike, but can also perceive themselves as having little or no responsibility for their recovery (Dewan, 1992; Thale, 1973).

Another significant dynamic is a phenomenon referred to as the "transference to the medications themselves." Gutheil (1982) describes this in a schizophrenic patient who refused his medications because he interpreted the letters "M.S.D." as analogous to "LSD." Another patient, a male paranoid schizophrenic, refused to take Moban since it was a "male medication (Mo)" but was less threatened by "Stella-zine" (p. 326). Another dimension of this phenomenon is the "placebo or placebo-related effect—a positive response that is inexplicable either by the actual effects of the medication or by the medication's pharmacokinetics" (Gutheil, 1982, p. 325).

At the moment a pharmacotherapist enters the treatment, triangulation occurs, and this may or may not present transference problems. In the case of Tim, he fantasized his therapist and pharmacotherapist as the caring parental unit he wished for. One might also see the emergence of oedipal dynamics, including guilt, jealousy, desire, and competitiveness. Clients may perceive themselves as torn between the two clinicians, recreating earlier perceptions of having to choose between their parents. Any of these responses can be understood as an outgrowth of the client's characteristic ways of experiencing and responding to emotionally meaningful past and present objects. In this context, any information revealed to the client by one clinician concerning the other or the interactions between the two clinicians assumes a potential transference significance (Goodman, 1995a).

Libby, a client with a history of psychiatric hospitalizations who was already medicated with antidepressants, entered treatment. She asked her social worker to speak to her psychiatrist. Regular contact ensued regarding dosage changes and effectiveness. Not surprisingly, the two clinicians shared some personal information about themselves with each other. At one point in the treatment, Libby told her therapist the information she had learned from the psychiatrist about her. It became clear that Libby felt "too burdened" by this knowledge, experiencing it as a violation of boundaries. Although this helped Libby to understand her own history, she and the analyst agreed that a different pharmacotherapist would be consulted.

Finally, one must be attuned to the potential for countertransferential reactions arising within the context of the triangulation. The psychiatrist's or therapist's feelings of competitiveness, jealousy, inadequacy, aggression, or contempt can undermine the client's positive reaction to medication and its potential usefulness. The therapist may also be subject to anxiety that the patient may leave treatment and feel helpless and narcissistically vulnerable (Goodman, 1995a; Klerman, 1983).

It is within this multidimensional framework that clinicians must be responsible for and attuned to the numerous transference and countertransference possibilities inherent in the concomitant use of psychotropics and psychotherapy.

THE COLLABORATIVE RELATIONSHIP

The clinician's role is influenced by the setting, the role definition, and his or her own knowledge and expertise. Traditionally social work viewed itself as having subordinate status to that of the physician. The doctor's decision about medications went unchallenged; the social worker encouraged and supported the client's compliance with medications. Any discussion of side effects was redirected to the psychiatrist.

Gradually the social work clinician has assumed a more active role as the intermediary between the psychiatrist and the client's family, presenting the family dynamics (which influence heavily the selection of psychotropics), participating in the therapeutic milieu created for the client, and coordinating and implementing the discharge plan. Social workers lead psychoeducational programs and groups geared toward increasing the client's and caretakers' knowledge about medications and side effects. The goal of such groups is to foster increased responsibility for and participation in the management of the illness. The additional activity of advocacy and consultation, in which the social worker utilizes and disseminates knowledge about the law as it pertains to the client's right to self-determination, further defines the role social workers have enacted on inpatient units and in community-based mental health clinics (Gerhart & Brooks, 1983).

A third role of the social worker is that of consultant-collaborator in which the clinician, informed about medications and side effects, makes appropriate referrals, monitors progress, and interfaces with the psychiatrist (Gerhart & Brooks, 1983; McCollum et al., 1987). Even if the clinician cannot always select the consulting psychopharmacologist, it is important to establish an effective alliance, since the goal of the consultation is the mitigation or alleviation of the client's symptoms.

The clinician, whether agency based or in private practice, is responsible for preparing the client and the psychopharmacologist for the consultation. The clinician discusses the reason for the referral and the potential usefulness of the medications and explores all related fantasies, expectations, and transferences. It is also important for the client to understand that the efficacy of the medication may not be instantaneous or "magical," particularly with antidepressants, and that medications are not a substitute for therapy. Nevertheless, some clients will view medication in this way and terminate therapy.

The psychopharmacotherapist needs to be apprised of the reason for the consultation, the client's history, a description of the dynamics of treatment (including transference), previous usage of psychotropics or substances, and any known medical illnesses.

In order to avoid potential conflicts inherent in these triadic situations, it is important that neither psychiatrist nor therapist view each other as a competitor, or fear that one will lure the patient away from the other. These issues can and do arise in the collaborative process. If they are not resolved and continue to interfere with the therapy, a change in psychopharmacologist may be necessary. However, the goal is a collaboration based on mutual trust and respect, which permits each professional the freedom to discuss the therapeutic strategy of the other.

Following the consultation, the professionals should speak with one another. It is also useful to review the client's experience, not only for possible transference implications but to confirm the client's understanding of and knowledge about the medications. We have only to think of our own experience in a physician's office to appreciate the potential for omission and misunderstanding irrespective of our intelligence.

Successful collaboration is maximized when the therapist reports emerging symptomatology to the psychopharmacotherapist that might be missed with monthly or even less frequent pharmacological revisits, as, for example, when a client's obsessive ruminations increase in frequency. Conversely, the psychiatrist may be able to inform the therapist of some transference manifestation of which the therapist may be unaware. In this way, the two practitioners may assist each other in their mutual efforts to guide the client toward greater positive functioning.

SUMMARY

In 1976, Bockar predicted that "non-medical psychotherapists will and should be doing the vast majority of psychotherapy in the near future" (Bockar, 1976, preface). There is little doubt twenty years later that she was correct. Whether the social work clinician is an autonomous practitioner or a collegial team member, there are many instances in which the question of medication arises. The clinician's involvement may begin with the recognition of the need for medication through a biopsychosocial assessment conducted at intake or during the course of long-term counseling or therapy. It may extend to work with the client or family in assisting with monitoring of medications, through education regarding side effects, identification of warning signs of relapse, and supporting the value for medication compliance when appropriate. Medication may become a powerful tool that elicits or uncovers hidden areas of a client's dynamics. At the same time, the value of psychotropics for the amelioration of psychic distress is no longer in doubt.

Pharmacotherapy is a medical procedure. It is within the expected expertise of the psychiatrist to know the specific actions of each medication, its side effects, and its interactions with nonpsychotropic medications that clients may be taking. The social worker's ongoing task is to incorporate into established social work roles an understanding of medications and their impact on and meaning to the client. Clinicians must find their own way to do this, be it on-the-job training, individualized collaboration, or engaging consultants to conduct small group seminars.

Each clinician must continue to be responsible for his or her individual growth and development. However, the time seems ripe for the implementation of the Council on Social Work Education Report (1990) in which recommendations were made to integrate course work pertaining to the area of medications and their dynamics into the social work curriculum. In addition, the National Association of Social Workers, which represents the broad spectrum of the field, should develop workshops and conferences that address psychopharmacology and clinical social work practice.

Social workers cannot ignore the fact that cost constraints now heavily dictate allowable treatment modalities. Although it is unlikely that drug treatment will ever become the only available treatment, it behooves social work practitioners to deepen their knowledge about medications. Only in this way can they begin to develop confidence in their ability to identify which situations call for particular medications, which do not, and the likely consequences and related dynamic issues associated with each possibility.

REFERENCES

Abroms, G. M., & Greenfield, N. S. (1973). Drug-prescribing and the nonmedical therapist. *Clinical Social Work Journal, 1,* 132–134.

Adelman, S. A. (1993). Pills as transitional objects. In M. Schachter (Ed.), *Psychotherapy and medication: A dynamic integration* (pp. 109–120). Northvale, NJ: Jason Aronson.

American Psychiatric Association, Committee on Public Information (1957). A *psychiatric glossary.* Washington, DC.

Beitman, B. D., Chiles, J., & Carlin, A. (1984). The pharmacotherapy-psychotherapy triangle: Psychiatrist, non-medical psychotherapist, and patient. *Journal of Clinical Psychiatry, 45,* 458–459.

Bentley, K. J., & Reeves, J. (1992). Integrating psychopharmacology into social work curriculum. *Journal of Teaching in Social Work,* 6 (2), 41–58.

Bentley, K. J., & Walsh, J. (1996). *The social worker and psychotropic medication.* Pacific Grove, CA: Brooks/Cole.

Berg, W., & Wallace, M. (1987). Effect of treatment setting on social worker's knowledge of psychotropic drugs. *Health and Social Work, 12,* 144–152.

Bockar, J. A. (1976). *Primer for the nonmedical psychotherapist.* New York: Spectrum Publications.

Cohen, D. (1988). Social work and psychotropic drug treatments. *Social Service Review, 62,* 577–599.

Council on Social Work Education (1990). M. F. Libassi (Project director), Contract report. Alexandria, VA: CSWE.

Davidson, M., & Jamison, P. (1983). The clinical social worker and current psychiatric drugs: Some introductory principles. *Clinical Social Work Journal, 11,* 139–150.

Dewan, J. J. (1992). Adding medications to ongoing psychotherapy: Indications and pitfalls. *American Journal of Psychotherapy,* 46 (1), 102–110.

Dziegielewski, S. F. (in press). Should clinical social workers seek psychotropic prescription privileges? In B. A. Thyes (Ed.), *Controversial issues in social work practice.* Boston: Allyn & Bacon.

Gerhart, U., & Brooks, A. (1983). The social work practitioner and antipsychotic medications. *Social Work, 2,* 454–459.

Goldhamer, P. M. (1993). The challenge of integration. In M. Schachter (Ed.), *Psychotherapy and medication: A dynamic integration* (pp. 215–224). Northvale, NJ: Jason Aronson.

Goodman, A. (1995b, October). Recognition of psychodynamics in pharmacotherapy. *Psychiatric Times, 12* (10), 17–21.

Goodman, A. (1995a, November). Psychodynamics in pharmacotherapy: Practical application. *Psychiatric Times, 12* (11), 54–55.

Gorman, J. M. (1995). *The essential guide to psychiatric drugs.* New York: St. Martin's Press.

Gutheil, T. (1982). The psychology of psychopharmacology. *Bulletin of the Menninger Clinic,* 46 (4), 321–330.

Hankoff, L. D., & Galvin, J. W. (1968). Psychopharmacological treatment and its implications for social work. *Social Work, 13,* 40–47.

Hausner, R. (1993). Medication and transitional phenomena. In M. Schachter (Ed.), *Psychotherapy and medication: A dynamic integration* (pp. 87–107). Northvale, NJ: Jason Aronson.

Kahn, D. (1993). Medication consultation and split treatment during psychotherapy. In M. Schachter (Ed.), *Psychotherapy and medication: A dynamic integration* (pp. 225–238). Northvale, NJ: Jason Aronson.

Klerman, G. (1983). Conceptual issues in combined treatment. In M. H. Greenhill & A. Gralnick (Eds.), *Psychopharmacology and psychotherapy* (pp. 13–20). New York: Free Press.

Levine, C., & Dang, J. C. (1977). Psychopharmacology and social work skills. *Social Casework, 58* (3), 153–158.

Libassi, M. F. (1990). *Psychopharmacology in social work education* (Contract No. 89-MF7005390ID). Rockville, MD: National Institute of Mental Health.

Matorin, S., & De Chillo, N. (1984). Psychopharmacology: Guidelines for social workers. *Social Casework, 65* (10), 579–589.

McCollum, A. T., Margolin, C. B., & Lieb, J. (1978). Consultation on psychoactive medication. *Health and Social Work, 3* (4), 72–98.

Mental health: Does therapy help? (1995, November). *Consumer Reports* 60 (11), 734–439.

Miller, R. S., Wiedeman, G. H., & Linn, L. (1980). Prescribing psychotropic drugs: Whose responsibility? *Social Work in Health Care, 5,* 51–61.

Nevins, D. B. (1993). Psychoanalytic perspectives on the use of medication for mental illness. In M. Schachter (Ed.), *Psychotherapy and medication: A dynamic integration* (pp. 239–254). Northvale, NJ: Jason Aronson.

Ostow, M. (1993). How does psychiatric drug therapy work? In M. Schachter (Ed.), *Psychotherapy and medication: A dynamic integration* (pp. 215–224). Northvale, NJ: Jason Aronson.

Radcliff, A. B., Sites, C. F., Rush, A., & Cruse, J. (1985) *The pharmer's almanac.* Denver.

Schatzberg, A. F., & Cole, J. O. (1991). *Manual of clinical psychopharmacology,* (2nd ed.). Washington, DC: American Psychiatric Press.

Thale, T. (1973). Effects of medication on the caseworker-client relationship. *Social Casework, 54,* 27–36.

Wise, M. (1986). Working with medicated clients: A primer for social workers. *Health and Social Work, 11,* 36–41.

Wolski, R. (1994). Psychotropic medications. In S. Austrian (Ed.), *Mental disorders, medications, and clinical social work* (pp. 241–259). New York: Columbia University Press.

Yudofsky, S. C., Hales, R. E., & Ferguson, T. (1991). *What you need to know about psychiatric drugs.* New York: Ballantine Books.

16

Clinical Practice in Urban School Settings

Phyllis I. Vroom, Lenora Stanfield, and Roxanne Barzone

For many African American families, the point of entry into clinical social work services is through "child-focused problems" (Hines & Boyd-Franklin, 1982) identified in the public school. Recognition of the strategic location of schools in the lives of children and youth and their families has led to the placement of social work, mental and physical health services, and other supportive services and programs on site in many urban schools (Children's Aid Society, 1993; Hooper-Briar & Lawson, 1994; U.S. General Accounting Office, 1993; Vroom, Holbert, & Spurlock, 1995). The aims of these services are multifocused: to decrease the likelihood of children's dropping out of school, usually as they move from middle to high school and to support adaptive academic performance and social functioning; to prevent or provide interventions for mental health problems; and to provide a range of concrete, supportive, and therapeutic services to improve and maintain effective functioning of these children and their families (Caple, 1990; Children's Aid Society, 1993; U.S. General Accounting Office, 1993).

Central to site-based services is the concept of contributing to the resilience or strengths of children, youth, and their families by increasing the quantity and qual-

Note: The WSU Collaborative Project is funded by the DeWitt Wallace–Reader's Digest Fund through the National Center for Social Work and Education Collaboration of Fordham University. We give special thanks to Ann Williamson Blake and the student interns placed at the University Public School of Wayne State University and Rolando Shorey and staff of Diversified Youth Services.

ity of "protective factors" (Allen-Meares, 1995) that militate against the risks, or probabilities, of academic failure and lead to students' dropping out of school. Risk is defined as a continuum of probabilities, ranging from minimal to high, of "future negative events" (McWhirter, McWhirter, McWhirter, & McWhirter, 1993, p. 6). Academic failure has been a consistent predictor of dropping out, which in turn is strongly associated with such "future negative events" (McWhirter et al., 1993) as substance abuse, unemployment, unwed teen parenthood, and delinquent and criminal behavior. Allen-Meares posits that

> the concept of risk leads to the notion that if the risk is known for certain children and their families, it may be possible to create and organize buffers to mediate adverse outcomes. These buffers can be identified as factors that act as barriers to prevent or mediate negative outcome. For example, independently of the immediate family, a child may develop coping skills nurtured by others or by an institution such as a school. (1995, p. 37)

This chapter describes two models of clinical practice offered by two different social work programs providing services on site in two urban, public middle schools. The purpose of these programs is to "create and organize buffers" that strengthen the academic and social competence of youths and their families and increase the capacity of schools to serve as a nurturing, supportive environment for each.

THE PROGRAMS

The Collaborative Project Between the School of Social Work and the College of Education of Wayne State University (WSU) is offered in the WSU University Public School (UPS). Fordham University was awarded a grant by the DeWitt Wallace–Reader's Digest Fund to serve as the National Center for Social Work and Education Collaboration. The Wayne State Collaborative Project, one of ten such collaborative projects coordinated by Fordham, endeavors to change the life chances of children with low academic achievement who are judged to be at risk because they come from low-income and/or single-parent families with limited supportive networks, and/or live in poor, high-crime communities (Caple, 1990; McWhirter, McWhirter, McWhirter, & McWhirter, 1993). Project staff consists of a social work faculty–field instructor and ten graduate social work interns and an education faculty–field instructor and fifteen undergraduate and graduate education interns. The social work faculty–field instructor also serves as coordinator of the project.

Within the University Public School, the Collaborative Project coexists with counseling staff, a community mental health agency, a teen health center, and a plethora of tutorial, recreational, and educational enrichment programs. The community mental health agency is staffed by a therapist with an M.A., a case manager with a B.S.W., a parent advocate, and clerical staff. The teen health center is directed by a faculty–field instructor from the College of Nursing; this nurse practitioner coordinates the services of the university's medical doctors, medical students, residents, and nurse interns involved with the UPS. All of these services are coordinated by one of the assistant principals of the school through a coordinating team designated as the CARE team. This team comprises the UPS counselor, project staff, the community mental health agency staff, the nurse practitioner–educator, and the assistant principal in charge of supportive services. Children and families are referred to the CARE team primarily by teachers and counselors.

Diversified Youth Services (DYS) is a community mental health agency in Detroit offering a range of programs, both inpatient and outpatient, for children, youth, and their families. These services include residential treatment, day treatment, a residential school program, and school-based mental health programs, one in the McMichael Middle School and the other in a high school. DYS also provides outreach services to families in the community in which it is located, one characterized by high rates of unemployment, crime and delinquency, substance abuse, and female-headed, single-parent families. DYS-McMichael school staff includes one social worker with an M.S.W., two case managers with a B.S.W., a consulting psychiatrist, a consulting psychologist, and a nurse practitioner, who visits on site once a week. DYS agency services are also available to McMichael pupils and their families. DYS staff works collaboratively with the principal and assistant principal, the counseling staff, and other programs at the middle school.

The two programs examined in this chapter were selected because they represent two trends in site-based school services. The Collaborative Project, funded by a grant with matching funds from the School of Social Work and the College of Education, provides services to children and families through a design for interprofessional collaboration. The DYS school program is funded by the Wayne County Community Mental Health Board to locate preventive and interventive services in public schools.

Both middle schools have three grade levels (sixth, seventh, and eighth grade), and the youth range in age from eleven years to thirteen or fourteen; some are fifteen and sixteen years old because of repeated academic failures to move from one grade level to the next. Both school populations are predominantly African American and low income. The UPS has a population of between 365 and 380 pupils; McMichael's is approximately 430. At the UPS, over half of the school population receives free or reduced lunches; over 60 percent receive such at McMichael.

The UPS is a charter school. By law, charter schools are public schools with special approved missions. The UPS has an extended day, 8 A.M. to 5 P.M., and an extended school year—approximately 210 days compared to 180 for regular school programs. The UPS school population is citywide and selected at random from a pool of applicants. By law, the university holds the charter for the UPS and is its own school district. McMichael, a Detroit public school, is unionized ; the UPS, a university public school, is not.

McMichael is one of five public middle schools involved in a comprehensive program involving a coalition of governmental (state and local) departments (the state departments of commerce, education, and mental health), businesses, community organizations, and social service agencies called Detroit COMPACT. Pupils and their families in COMPACT sign a contract agreeing to meet attendance, behavior, and academic performance requirements. Summer employment and a college or trade school education are guaranteed to pupils who meet contract requirements. COMPACT is a community response to the high dropout rate, particularly in COMPACT school districts. In some instances, the dropout rate is over 50 percent of youth. From an ecological perspective, COMPACT is an attempt to modify environmental resources to provide incentives for these public school students, particularly those of low-income and/or limited opportunities from depressed neighborhoods, to meet the educational expectations and demands of a technological society.

Although the approaches to practice vary between the Collaborative Project and DYS, the two programs address similar clinical problems and share similar experiences. It is not known yet if the outcomes of each program are similar since both programs are relatively new. Evaluative data, not discussed in this chapter, provide a baseline that encompasses descriptions of program processes and quantification of such data as before- and after-intervention grades, attendance, and performance on state and national standardized tests, questionnaire data on family functioning, and self-esteem data. Some of these descriptive data have informed this chapter. However, staff are the key informants through descriptions, observations, and insights in their case records and discussions about service provided to the schools, the children, and their families.

THE WSU/UPS COLLABORATIVE PROJECT

Practice Model

A practice model is characterized by a belief about the behavior of the person and the situations in which people find themselves, the role of the environment in human behaviors, and a belief about the focus of assessment and interventions (Compton & Galaway, 1989). The practice model of the Collaborative Project is informed by an ecological systems perspective and a generalist model that guides the design of services through a problem-solving approach, (Compton & Galaway, 1989; Hoffman & Sallee, 1993; Kirst-Ashman & Hull, 1993; Landon, 1995; Zastrow, 1995). In addition, social learning theory shapes practice with individual youth in the classroom and in group services aimed at preventing academic failure. Usually work with individual youth and supportive work with families, though guided by a generalist practice model, is defined by a problem-solving approach to assessment and appropriate interventions.

Ecological Systems Perspective

The Collaborative Project is guided by the person-in-environment framework of clinical social work practice (see Chapter 1 for a more extensive discussion of person-in-environment and ecological systems concepts). This framework is amplified by an ecological systems perspective as described in the work of Bartlett (1970),

Allen-Meares (1995), Allen-Meares, Washington, and Welsh (1986, 1995), Germain and Gitterman (1980, 1995), and Landon (1995). The situations in which these youths find themselves are viewed transactionally: attention is focused on the character and coping of the youth as they interact with salient elements of their family and school.

More specifically, within the ecosystems perspective, project activities are aimed at multiple factors: the perceived qualities of family and school environments, the coping capacities, self-concept, self-esteem, self-efficacy, and social competencies of these middle school youths; the rules, roles and relationships, emotional climate, expectations and demands, and structures of their nuclear and extended families; and the family's network (or lack) of connections with other social institutions (school, work, recreation, religious, and other social resources systems) as they affect the social functioning of these youths. Within the school, activities are aimed at the resources, rules, structures, emotional climate, roles and relationships, and expectations and demands of peers, teachers, and other school personnel. Other qualities of these youths' impinging environments, or contexts, are also addressed—for example, resources, the organization of the school, and mediating structures between the school, family, and other resources systems.

The social worker is viewed as responsible, in conjunction with the client systems and those for whom interventions are intended, or targeted, for altering either seriatim or simultaneously salient targets in the person-environment complex (Germain & Gitterman, 1995). Targets of intervention may include perceptions and appraisals of stressors and the coping patterns and competencies of persons used to achieve the best fit or match between them (Allen-Meares, 1995; Bartlett, 1970; Folkman, 1984; Germain & Gitterman, 1980, 1995; Lazarus, 1980; Lazarus & Folkman, 1984) and the qualities of their environments. Where possible, project activities (true also of DYS services) may seek to change family and school environments if demands are excessive or inappropriate, if expectations conflict, if there is a lack of resources to meet demands and expectations, or if violence may prove harmful to the physical or psychological well-being of students.

The ecological perspective remains an ideology, a lofty ideal, unless there are true opportunities to operationalize its constructs. Access to pupils with problems is often less of an issue than opportunities to intervene in the school and classroom environments.

Case Illustrations

Parent Career Fair and Workshops

Project staff surveyed parents about their career interests and their need for information about developmental needs and issues facing their adolescents. Simultaneously, unbeknown to project staff, the nurse practitioner had surveyed parents on their concerns about the health and sexuality of UPS pupils. In addition, the community mental health parent advocate, through discussions with parents, had identified parent interests and concerns regarding career opportunities for themselves, adolescent sexuality, and discipline. In the spirit of interprofessional collaboration, project staff proposed that all service providers, parent representatives, and teachers meet to plan activities that would respond to the feedback from parents. The result of these work sessions was a dually focused program: a career fair in which representatives were available from several schools and colleges, the university's Office of Admissions and Financial Aids and the Employment Service, and two local community colleges, to provide information and answer questions regarding access to their programs and services and parent education workshops on substance abuse, teen sexuality, discipline, and a session provided by teachers on "How to Help your Child with Homework." About thirty parents, 10 percent of the families of children enrolled in the school, attended the program, most of them with their children. Most of the parents said they wanted to attend all of the workshops. Presenters accommodated to these wishes, and all moved to a larger room to accommodate workshop participants and presenters.

The underlying theme for the workshops focused on strengthening the trusting relationship and open communication between these adolescents and their parents. Each presenter emphasized content in her area of presentation, such as identifying substance abuse, confronting the adolescent with knowledge of use, and community resources for the treatment and maintenance of sobriety and a drug-free lifestyle. Presenters were able to build rapport and trust with parents by using self-disclosure, giving practice principles illustrated by practical examples, and asking participants to give examples of their own interactions with their children that illustrated the principles. It was one of the teachers who was able to confront, with parental acceptance, a pervasive issue in parental discipline that affects trust: parental remarks that might be perceived by the adolescent and others as disparaging, demeaning, and even violent. The teacher began,

> Now, before I start talking about how you [parents] can help your children with homework, I need to talk about something that has bothered me a lot. You know, I work with your children all day, and sometimes they can make me want to do or say something really violent, but I don't. I mean, sometimes they can get on your last nerve. But if I do say something I would regret later, I risk losing your child. Also, that child might imitate me and do it to somebody else. They may not be able to pay attention to what's going on in class or may not want to do their homework, or work with or for me anymore. Now I really wish some parents would remember that, because more than once, I've heard parents "calling their children out of their name" [a colloquialism referring to calling a child a name using curses or other disparaging epithets]. You know what I mean—words like the "b" word and the "f" word, and other names, too. How do we expect children to respect and trust us if we "call them out of their name"?

Discussion ensued among workshop presenters and parent participants about alternative ways to handle anger with children. Workshop presenters and parents made distinctions between "fussing behavior" and the disparaging, demeaning language used by some parents and their children. The workshops provided the mechanism for open discussion of issues pertinent to a number of the youths receiving individual and group services from project interns and community mental health staff. In addition, the workshops provided information and outreach to parents, many of whom came because of problems in the families. As important, the career fair offered opportunities for parents to link with educational resources that might serve to improve their employment opportunities and other life chances.

The parent advocate and the nurse faculty–field instructor have continued to offer parent education workshops that are primarily centered around the topics of discipline, sexuality, and substance abuse. Parents continue to be interested in sessions on prevention and identification of substance abuse, unwed pregnancy, sexually transmitted diseases, and handling disciplinary issues related to family rules about housework, appropriate ways to disagree with an adult (especially a parent), doing homework, and free time with peers. A recent survey of the UPS pupils by the assistant principal in charge of support services confirmed that these topics were of greatest interest to the adolescents. For these reasons, the collaborative planning group will continue to offer one or two larger schoolwide parent events.

Violence Prevention

Both project staff and school personnel had identified the need for programs addressing violence on several fronts: family, neighborhood, and school. In addition to the teachers' concern about violent language and the tendency of the youths to use violent language and physical violence to settle differences in school, two vignettes illustrate the extent of the problems confronted by all the systems.

The project director and evaluator thanked the project group worker and the boys' group for allowing her and a representative from the National Center for Social Work and Education Collaboration to meet with them. She said that they were interested in some of the things that were on the boys' minds, some of the things that might worry them, or at least that they might be concerned about. She said that it might help the school to know what kinds of services are needed. One seventh-grade boy described how he was in his backyard and had witnessed a family member being shot. Another described how a member of his extended family had been murdered recently and how all of the relatives had attended the funeral. Several of the boys described how they could hear gunshots throughout the night. In response to the question of how safe each of the boys felt in his neighborhood, all responded that they were not safe; they worried about getting shot themselves. The project staff and the boys continued to discuss how each of the boys felt; the boys seemed to need to describe the violent situations and their responses repeatedly. When asked how the school could help, if at all, the boys thought that it was useful to have a group where they could talk about their experiences as well as go on field trips and have fun.

During a regularly scheduled, schoolwide, parent-teacher-child conference day, the parents of a sixth grader were told of the child's classroom behaviors that proved distracting to the teacher and the other pupils. Increasingly, the parents grew angry and began to accuse the teacher of being unfair to the child. Finally, one of the parents threatened the teacher with physical violence in a way that was frightening to all those present at the meeting. One of the other teachers and a pupil left the room and got an assistant principal, who intervened and deescalated the situation.

To counter the incidence and continued potential for violence, parents, teachers, and the school administration decided that they would invoke a dress code and prescribed uniforms, a solution that project staff did not greet with universal enthusiasm. All school participants developed a handbook that included rules and expectations for parents, teachers, support staff, and pupils that were discussed and agreed upon in schoolwide meetings. A hall and lunchroom duty program was instituted with participation of all school personnel, including project staff and interns, the community mental health agency staff, and parents. Parents are required to contribute at least one and a half hours each month of volunteer time at the UPS in a variety of programs staffed by the parent advocate, including hall and lunchroom monitoring and involvement in cocurricular (tutoring, educational enrichment, and recreation) programs. Most important, the school decided also to devote a substantial portion of its budget to a program of tutoring, educational, and enrichment (TREE) activities that occurs for the most part between 3:30 and 5:00 P.M. Individual and group services provided by the project occur during TREE time.

Another outcome of the desire to prevent violence and intervene in violent situations was the establishment of a crisis team and a conflict resolution committee, chaired by the on-site project coordinator (and social work faculty–field instructor). This committee has instituted programs and activities on peaceful ways to handle conflict, including bringing in local experts to train pupils and staff on conflict resolution techniques. The committee has engaged all members in the school in community activities related to peace and peaceful conflict resolution such as a city-wide poster contest on peace.

These illustrations of larger systems issues and interventions exemplify the importance of both individual and larger systems approaches to address both the public issue aspect of private troubles as well as the need of organizations and service providers to develop protective factors in persons and their environments to serve as buffers against risks. These observations embody the ecological systems perspective.

At the micro- (e.g., person) and mezzo- (e.g., family and peer group) end of the "P-E (i.e., person–environment) fit" equation are a group of clinical services offered by the project. These services are designed to alter maladaptive coping patterns of individual adolescents and, to a limited extent, their family members, and groups of adolescents in the classroom; where classroom and family are viewed as context, the goal is to increase their capacities for these systems to nurture and sustain adaptive coping patterns. In schools, two kinds of behavior are flagged as major indicators of adaptive or maladaptive coping: academic performance and citizenship, or the extent to which the child or youth exercises socially responsible behavior skills and patterns (Helper, 1995; Warger & Rutherford, 1993). Often academic performance and the social skills involved in competent classroom performance are integrally related (Warger & Rutherford, 1993). Attainment of effective social skills is viewed as an essential component of mental health at all age levels (Hepler, 1995) and social competence among children and youth (Warger & Rutherford, 1993). Two programs initiated by the project address both academic performance and social skills: the behavioral groups led by social work interns and social skills training of individuals and the class as a group, based on a behavioral model. Social work and education interns colead social skills training in the classroom and jointly provide social skills training to adolescents in the classroom context.

Achievement Groups

Achievement groups are so designated since they are based on a copyrighted model of social group work developed by Charney (1993). The theoretical model is informed by the work of Bandura (1969, 1986). The model of intervention, including the framework for group composition (Bertcher & Maple, 1971; Davis, 1980), draws particularly on the work of Bandura (1969, 1977, 1978, 1986), Garvin (1987, 1991), and Rose (1974, 1989; see also Rose & Edelson, 1987).

Achievement groups are based on the assumption that learning, particularly learning of new behavior, is based on observing and imitating models. These latter processes (modeling and imitation) are facilitated by vicarious reinforcement (Bandura, 1969, 1986; Salkind, 1981) as well as direct teaching and positive reinforcement. In order to facilitate modeling and imitation, four processes are attended to in the group: attention, retention, motor reproduction, and motivation (Salkind, 1981; Charney & Vroom, 1988).

Group Composition. Pregroup work is intended to make the group attractive to members and provide the best climate for work. This work begins with attention to group composition and subsequently involvement of the adolescents, their parent or parents, and teachers in setting and monitoring behavioral goals and agreeing to reward goal attainment. Goal attainment may be rewarded through social reinforcement, such as acknowledgment of achievement of personal and social goals, and through tokens and activities enjoyed by the adolescents. Groups are composed of from eight to ten of the same-gender youths, half of whom have been identified by teachers and counselors as "underachievers"; the other half are identified as "role models."

Determination of underachievement is based on grades and performance on standardized tests. Students who are underachieving must have grades below C, and role models must have grades of B or better. Other group member characteristics are considered carefully: generally, a two-to-one ratio of youth with nonaggressive to aggressive behavioral patterns is maintained; a one-to-one ratio of underachievers' race/ethnicity and that of role models is required; and role models must be credible and attractive to underachievers (they must be perceived as leaders whose coping patterns are viewed as attainable by the underachiever).

Contracting for Grades and Social Skills. After the adolescent and the parent, usually in a home visit, consent to group membership, each underachieving adolescent contracts for grade improvement in one or two subject areas, but by only one grade level to "offset the possibility of failure" (Charney, 1993, p. 114). In addition, the group member contracts for behaviors in the classroom and in the achievement group ("in-group behaviors") that are viewed, usually by the teachers, as instrumental to target grade achievement.

Visits are made to the home of role models and their parents as well. Generally, the underachievers and their parents are gratified to know that they and their child, respectively, are viewed as having potential to perform well academically and behaviorally; role models and their parents are pleased at the perception of social competence and leadership abilities of these youths.

The group member and the social work intern sign a contract for grade and behavioral goals that the pupil intends to achieve. Academic goals are reinforced by a reward of $1.00 for goal achievement at the end of the year. In-class and in-group target behavioral goals are monitored daily by the teacher (the social work intern collects the monitoring sheets weekly) and reinforced with tokens given by the social work intern in group session. These tokens most often are relatively inexpensive toys, school supplies, and sometimes candy and snacks (the most popular backup reinforcers). Target behaviors may include "completing assignments," "getting along with peers," "respecting the teacher," and "paying attention" (Charney, 1993, p. 115).

Group Activity. Group activity revolves around a single topic discussion that initially is focused on target behaviors of group members. Later, other topics may be introduced that relate to vicarious reinforcement (e.g., career choices and what it takes to achieve a desired career). Group members may also be introduced to adult role models who have achieved success by doing "what it takes" (staying in school, doing homework, persisting in spite of obstacles). Role plays and rehearsal of desired behaviors are used. Since group sessions are only one hour, general play activities are not used. Group members have found the discussions, role plays, and role rehearsals, which rivet their attention, all enjoyable and informative (Charney & Vroom, 1988). An excerpt from a social work intern's process recording from one of the project achievement groups (Charney & Vroom, 1988, pp. 5, 6) illustrates the single-topic discussion and involvement of group members around the themes of honesty and cheating. (The designation "UA" means "underachiever" and "RM" is "role model,")

Worker: I'd like to discuss a confidential matter with you today, which means we will not discuss anything that we have revealed outside of this room. Is that a promise?

Group: Yeah.

Worker: What do some students do when they have a test?

Ahmed(UA): They cheat.

John(RM): Yeah, we study, and they cheat.

Worker: How does that make you feel, John?

John: Mad. Sometimes the cheater gets better grades without studying.

James(RM): Yeah, sometimes the good guys come in last.

Worker: Have you ever cheated, James?

James: I did a couple of times and felt real bad.

Tom(UA): I cheated and got caught. I got a big red E on my test.

Ken(UA): When I cheated, my teacher told my mom, and I was grounded for three weeks.

Ray(UA): I was grounded for six weeks.

Worker: How did you feel about it?

Ray: Mad. Some kids cheat all the time and don't get caught, and I get six weeks.

Worker: What about kids who cheat all the time? Do they learn very much?

Alonzo(RM): They learn how to be crooked.

James: They're not learning. They'll never get into college.

Jeff(UA): What does it take to get into college?

James: You gotta have good grades. You gotta pass a test.

Worker: Yes, you have to take the ACT and the SAT.

Jeff: What's that?

Worker: When you're a junior in high school, you'll be tested in different subjects and be compared to kids all over the country.

James: You can't cheat on those tests.

Worker: No, it would be very hard to cheat. You would be watched very closely. It's almost time to go. Let's go over what we discussed. What's the problem with cheating?

Alonzo: You get punished.

James: You don't learn anything.

Jeff: You can't pass the ACS.

Tom: You mean SAT—like "sit," only "sat."

Ray: Then you can't go to college, and you end up on welfare.

Worker: Next week, we'll talk more about why you might want to think about kinds of vocations.

Role plays and role rehearsals are used to reinforce new behaviors and to provide insight to members in the achievement groups. In one group, members discussed, modeled, and rehearsed "how to show respect for the teacher and the class." Members, role models, and underachieving pupils alternately role-played pupils and a teacher who had difficulty with a pupil who talked and left their seat without permission. Subsequently, appropriate classroom behavior was modeled and rehearsed. For the underachievers, the object lesson of experiencing how it felt to teach when a classmate is being disruptive was as compelling as the experience of observing and imitating the role model's appropriate behavior. Charney has developed over thirty-six topics and suggestions for role plays relevant to target behaviors, such as relationship to teachers and parents, intergroup relations, anger, and fear.

The four processes: attention, retention, motor reproduction, and motivation exemplify achievement group sessions. Activities related to these processes include contracting for grade improvement, setting goals for changes in classroom and group behaviors, presenting single-topic discussions in group, using role plays and behavioral rehearsals, using tokens for reinforcers, and using social reinforcement, such as praise and positive comments of student interns, teachers, parents, and group members. Attention to group composition is a critical component underlying achievement group processes; poor group composition can undermine goals for individual members. To date, achievement group members have shown significant improvement in grades and citizenship compared to control groups (Charney, 1993).

Social Skills Training

Social skills training has been described for social work practice (Hepler, 1995) and for education (Warger, n.d; Warger & Rutherford, 1993). Warger (n.d.) defines social skills as "specific, identifiable, learned behaviors performed effectively that produce positive social consequences in social situations" (p. 6). She and her colleagues have specified the model as follows:

Phase 1: Curriculum
- Identify social skill to be taught.
- Define social skill as observable behaviors.
- Determine performance based assessment.

Phase 2: Instruction
- Directly teach the social skill.
- Provide application.

Phase 3: Self Control
- Student [pupil] monitors, evaluates and provides self-reinforcement.
- Evaluate success.

Instructional Strategies
- Direct teaching
- Modeling
- Social Reinforcement
- Practice (Warger, n.d.)

Some examples of classroom social skills are "following directions," "coping with aggression from peers," "listening," and "accepting the answer no."

With teacher permission, a pair of education and social work interns were assigned to sixth-, seventh-, and eighth-grade classrooms to observe pupil and teacher behaviors and classroom climate. Over several class periods, if a student has difficulty with critical classroom skills, the pair meet with the pupil and identify the problematic behaviors. Then the pair model the social skill (e.g., listening: "relax, keep eyes on speaker or face the speaker, keep hands still (in lap), keep feet still (placed on the ground)" [Warger, n.d.]). The student then practices the skill and, with appropriate acknowledgment and praise, returns to the classroom.

Initially the student is observed by the interprofessional pair and the teacher and receives immediate feedback for appropriate and inappropriate behaviors. Appropriate behaviors are reinforced with praise and acknowledgment. Inappropriate behaviors result in immediate feedback, review of skills, practice, and then reapplication in the classroom. Unlike the use of tokens in achievement groups, reinforcement in social skills training is social.

Although the reward systems differ, the goal for both achievement groups and social skills training is for the adolescent to internalize the controls of the authority figures (teacher, interprofessional pair). Social skills training was introduced in the UPS in the 1995 fall term, achievement groups in the 1994 winter term. In addition to intervening with students having problems with social skills, interns taught social skills to classroom groups beginning in fall 1995. Significant improvement in behaviors of targeted students has been observed by teachers, such that some skeptical teachers are now inviting intern pairs into their classrooms for individual and group social skills training.

Work with Parents and Guardians

Through home visits, social work interns (and, where it is possible to overcome scheduling difficulties, interprofessional pairs) provide ongoing feedback to parents or guardians about their child's progress in individual counseling, achievement groups, or social skills training. In some instances, a student has had all three treatments. Discussion with parents or guardians also revolves around social reinforcement of social skills in the home. Interns explore whether a parent or guardian or both parents would like other services or would like to be linked through referral with other resources, including health, financial, or educational. Elsewhere, when staff were professionally trained social workers holding the M.S.W., parents and family were engaged in couple and family treatment (Charney, 1993).

Individual Counseling

The framework for individual counseling is person-in-environment, and the model for assessment and intervention is a generalist model. A problem-solving approach is used to gather data on the problem presented; the history of the child and family related to the problems; child-teacher, child-parent, and child-family interactions; child and family coping and strengths; and family resources, or their absence, to address both the problems and needs they identify. Data for assessment are taken after initial contacts since many youth and their families may be suspicious of the intent of social work staff (Boyd-Franklin, 1989). Intervention and assessment activities may occur simultaneously, since the behavioral problem for work, such as underachievement or inappropriate or puzzling classroom behaviors (e.g., withdrawal from participation), have been identified.

The adolescent, the parent or parents or guardians, and the social work intern mutually agree on the goals and hoped-for outcomes of service related to academic and classroom performance. Initial interventions and interventions subsequent to the assessment are based on agreed-on goals and objectives. Before group or individual services are initiated, parental-guardian permission for service is obtained, and their involvement is determined based on the nature of the problem and mutual agreement for service. At a minimum, ongoing feedback of student progress is maintained with families through home visits and parent or guardian visits in school.

All social work interns are assigned adolescents for individual counseling; their behaviors may be withdrawn or aggressive. One social work intern described her work with a very withdrawn adolescent female. The intern used a combination of activities, discussion, and social skill training to increase the student's interaction with peers and attention in the classroom. The student and intern went on field trips, "did fingernails and hair," talked about school, clothes, and what it might be like to have girlfriends and boyfriends, and practiced and applied "speaking up in class with permission." The intern reported that the student improved her grade by one level at the end of the fall term and, according to her teacher, had increased her listening skills and classroom participation.

Four case situations illustrate the kinds of situations brought to the social work interns, as well as the problems facing the youth they serve. The first interview with Marcus was taped-recorded; later, the recording was edited into a process recording and included in a paper by the intern (Phillips, 1995). Sections of the remaining interviews were process recorded by each of the three student interns.

Marcus, an eighth grader at the UPS, was referred to the project by the school nurse. A juvenile diabetic, Marcus was inadequately monitoring his blood sugar level and eating improperly, including skipping meals or not eating enough when he did eat. Often Marcus did not feel well enough to attend classes or do his homework. At one of their sessions, Marcus told the student intern that he fell asleep in the nurse's office when he had gone there because of a stomachache; later, when he returned because the stomachache had not abated, he fell asleep again. The student intern explored with Marcus whether the stomachache and sleepiness were related to his blood sugar level or "something different."

Marcus: Well, not really, because my stomach was hurting day before yesterday. It wasn't because of my diabetes.
Intern: Okay. Do you think it's something to worry about?
Marcus: Yeah, but I had a dream.
Intern: You had a dream?
Marcus: About (hesitation) . . . I died. And my mom came to my funeral, and everybody came . . . my aunt, my uncle, and everybody except my father.
Intern: Your father who you haven't seen in a long time?
Marcus: No, my stepfather. That's the one I mean.
Intern: Your stepfather didn't come?
Marcus: [Nods head yes]
Intern: You said your aunt was there. Is that your aunt who passed away?
Marcus: I had the dream about her too.
Intern: Can you tell me about the dream?
Marcus: She threw a picture off the wall, but it didn't break. And then all the stuff that my uncle took to the basement that was my aunt's, it came back upstairs in its own place where she had put it.
Intern: By itself?
Marcus: Yes. [Later in the interview, Marcus revealed that his aunt was a diabetic and that he was very angry with his uncle for dating the nurse who cared for his

aunt while the aunt was ill. After exploring Marcus's anger with his uncle, the student intern returned to Marcus's dream.]

Intern: In the dream where you had died, where was this at?

Marcus: At my grandma's, right where my aunt died. But I wasn't in the bed like my aunt. I was in the chair.

Intern: What was it like to be in the chair?

Marcus: After I died, I didn't feel nothing. Then when I was at my funeral, the flowers fell down, and then about five minutes after that, the door on the casket just fell. Nobody had put it down. I'm going to have a bad funeral 'cause my dreams come true.

Intern: So, do you think this dream will come true?

Marcus: Yes.

Intern: What's that like for you to think that your dream might come true?

Marcus: I don't know. I get scared. God said don't be afraid of death because it's just him. But I prefer to die in my sleep. And I want to die before my parents die.

Intern: Can you tell me a little bit more about that?

Marcus: Because I don't want to see my mother cry. Well, I know she's going to cry, but what I'm saying is I didn't really mean it. I didn't want her to cry 'cause I know she's going to cry. But I don't want to cry at her funeral. I don't want to see how she died. [The student intern realized that Marcus did not want to lose any more people he loved. However, the student intern continued to pursue how Marcus felt and what he thought about when he died in the chair. In earlier interviews, Marcus had explained to the student intern that he called his aunt's grave "the little house" as distinguished from the "the big house" in which his aunt, uncle, and cousins had lived and where his uncle and cousins now live.]

Marcus: I was thinking about my aunt that had gone to sleep [died]. Well, she woke up. She had left her little house. I was thinking about her, and I saw somebody pull up in the driveway. And I looked out the window, and there was a funeral car—those hearses. And she came out of it [hearse]. She knocked on the back door, and she said, "Oh, I have my key." She just opened up [the door] and came in.

Intern: And then what happened?

Marcus: And then everyone was happy to see her. And then I went in there, and I was like, "Well who's she," and I saw her and I was like, "Oh my God." And I had to sit down in the chair and that's when I died. Oh my goodness, I know why I died in that dream—because I told my mom if I could die to bring my aunt back, I would. It doesn't matter. I'm just going to die.

Intern: So you think in the dream that was your aunt coming back and the trade-off was that you would have to die?

Marcus: [Silence]

Intern: That's a pretty tough trade-off.

Marcus: I wish her to come back. And then I wouldn't mind dying if she could come back.

The student intern asked Marcus if he thought about dying a lot. Marcus said that it made him mad and that "I wish somebody else would get diabetes." Toward the end of the session, the student intern and Marcus discussed his feelings of grief when his aunt died. As Marcus cried, the student intern, a male, told Marcus that his feelings were to be expected: "Nobody likes to see a loved one pass away, especially somebody who you really cared about a lot like the way you cared about your aunt."

Later toward the end of the interview, the student intern asked Marcus, now crying profusely, "Do you ever get much of a chance to talk about her?" Marcus shook his head no. The student intern inquired, "Would you like to continue talking about her in one of our next sessions?" When Marcus nodded yes, the student intern replied, "We can do that all you want."

In later interviews, the student intern will focus on several of Marcus's themes. One theme of considerable significance is his fear of dying prematurely of a diabetic-related condition like his aunt, who was quite young (he may not be aware that early death because of diabetes is not inevitable). Marcus also needs to be able to mourn his aunt's death and express his anger about his uncle's "replacement" of his aunt. In Marcus's mind, his uncle simply seems to have forgotten all about his aunt, and this constitutes a recurring theme in other portions of the interview. His attachment to and yearning for the aunt are revealed in the interview, as well as his strong connection to other members of his extended family. A home visit with Marcus's parents may reveal that Marcus's mother, and perhaps his stepfather and members of the extended family, are similarly angry at the uncle for dating the aunt's nurse so soon after the aunt's death. One wonders also if Marcus fears that his stepfather will forget him as his uncle (by marriage) appeared to forget his wife, Marcus's aunt. A home visit or parent-family session is a requirement when interns are working with pupils therapeutically, individually or in groups, or when students are working on classroom- and school-related social skills.

Student interns have worked with pupils regarding other losses they have experienced—for example, parental absence that results from mental illness or when parents are emotionally or physically unavailable because of alcohol or drug dependency. In the following case situation, a seventh-grade student, Leah, was referred to project staff because of her shyness and withdrawal from the teacher and her peers. In addition, she was not paying attention in class and was not doing her homework consistently. Her teachers worried most about Leah's isolation.

Leah, a seventh-grade pupil of Puerto Rican national origin, has two sisters and a brother. She and her sisters live with her grandmother, and her brother lives with her mother in another state. During Leah's first interview with the student intern, she said that her grandmother hits her when she asks to live with her godparents, who live in the same neighborhood as Leah and her grandmother. In this initial interview, the student intern and Leah talked about Leah's godparents—how they treat her nicely and do many things with her. Leah said that her grandmother says that her mother does not want her and that her grandmother hits her sisters whenever they ask for anything that the grandmother does not want to give them. Later in this first interview, Leah repeats that she wants to live with her godparents. Leah asks the student intern, "Can a psychiatrist help you get adopted?" In subsequent interviews, Leah returns to this theme. Leah told the student intern that the grandmother had warned Leah not to tell the social work student any family business. After this, for five subsequent interviews, Leah would describe the fun she had with her godparents and would discuss her strong wish to live with them, but she would not discuss anything about the family. After a holiday break, Leah described a visit that she, her sisters, and grandmother had with her mother and brother. She said that her brother had to leave her mother and return with Leah and her sisters to her grandmother's house. The mother was in jail. Leah said that she talked to her mother when she got out of jail. Leah told the student intern that she knew that her mother would be "okay," but she was worried that the brother would end up in foster care as she and her sisters did before they went to live with their grandmother.

In subsequent interviews, Leah continued to tell the student intern about her godparents and the good times she had with them. She also said that the counselor and her grandmother had agreed that Leah should be seen by the community mental health worker at the UPS. Leah had told her grandmother and the counselor that she wanted to keep seeing the student intern too. The student intern told Leah that she was aware that Leah would be seeing the community mental health therapist and was glad that she and Leah would continue seeing each other as well.

Several sessions later, Leah came to her interview with the student intern with a troubled look on her face. Leah had discovered some marijuana in a drawer where the grandmother kept her makeup. Leah brought the marijuana to school and showed it to a counselor, who reported this to the child protective services. Leah asked the student intern if the child protective services worker could help her live with her godparents. The student intern explained that finding the marijuana in her grandmother's house did not guarantee that Leah would be able to live with her godparents. She and Leah agreed to meet in a few days, and the student intern went to speak to the counselor out of her concern about what would happen to Leah when she got home and what the future might portend for this twelve year old.

Leah, through passive-aggressive means, tried to achieve the end that she had asked and wished for repeatedly. Her yearning to be with her mother and her subsequent idealization of her godmother and godfather and demonization of her grandmother have been amply described in the literature on object relations theory and therapy (Cashdan, 1988; St. Clair, 1986). Leah continues to be seen by the therapist at the community mental health agency about her issues of loss, feelings of rejection, anger, and her splitting and its effect on her relationships (Cashdan, 1988). One hopes that there will be an exploration of the most nurturing living arrangements for her and her siblings and that her grandmother and godparents, critical members of the family system, will be brought into the network of treatment (Aponte & Van Deusen, 1981; Boyd-Franklin, 1989; Speck & Attneave, 1973).

The next case example is descriptive of a common reason for which project staff are referred pupils for individual and group counseling: disruptive behavior in the classroom.

Harrison was referred to the project staff because he was disruptive in the classroom. Frequently he left his seat or talked without permission. He seemed unable to remain still for more than three or four minutes. During the previous academic year, two student interns, one an education and the other a social work intern, observed Harrison in a classroom. Later the social work intern described to Harrison the behavior he had observed.

Intern: Remember when I came into Ms. K's class and sat down for a few minutes?
Harrison: Yes.
Intern: I saw you take off your shoes, then take off your socks, then get out of your seat four times in five minutes. This type of activity creates problems in the classroom.
Harrison: Yeah, I know. Well, I'll improve.
Intern: Harrison, when we talk the next session, let's talk about specific ways you can improve.
Harrison: Okay.

Although Harrison and the student intern identified specific behaviors that Harrison would change and role-played how he would behave in the classroom, his gains were very small. Harrison was referred to the in-school community mental health agency for psychiatric examination. He was found to be hyperactive, and Ritalin was prescribed. Harrison and his teachers noted the difference in his attention span when he took the Ritalin. At the beginning of a new academic year, Harrison's classroom behavior was described again by teachers as "out of control" and he was referred to project staff again. In his first interviews with the student intern, Harrison let it be known he would rather be in the gym. However, he told the student intern about his career goals and his interest in chess. After four interviews, Harrison and the worker joked about who would win in their chess game. By the fifth interview, Harrison talked about how he and his brother "hated" their father and told the student intern that "he [the father] drinks a lot."

Intern: Is that why you don't like him?
Harrison: Yes, and other things.
Intern: Would you like to talk about them with me?
Harrison: Not today.
Intern: Okay. Maybe another time.

The student intern then talked to Harrison about completing an assessment form, explaining that the assessment with him and his parents helped her to know what goals they needed to work on. The student intern informed Harrison that she would be making a home visit and explored his feelings about that. Prior to the next interview, Harrison had been suspended from school for a week. The student intern asked Harrison how he and his mother felt about his being suspended. Harrison said his mother was upset.

Intern: How do you know she was upset?
Harrison: She hit me.
Intern: Once?
Harrison: Yes, it didn't hurt. I even laughed.

After continued exploration with Harrison concerning his feelings about being kicked out of school, the student intern asked what he could do to stop it from happening.

Intern: What do you think you can do?
Harrison: I don't know. I have good days and bad days.
Intern: When do you have a good day?
Harrison: I take medicine.
Intern: What's the name of it?
Harrison: I don't know.
Intern: What does it do?
Harrison: It calms me down.
Intern: Is it Ritalin?
Harrison: No. I don't know.
Intern: When do you take it?
Harrison: At night before I go to bed.
Intern: When was the last time you took it?
Harrison: A couple of weeks ago.
Intern: Why don't you take it all the time?
Harrison: I don't like to.
Intern: Why don't you like to?
Harrison: I don't like to think that I'm crazy or out of control.

In her scheduled interview with Harrison's mother, the student intern planned to focus on Harrison's fear that taking medication means he is "crazy or out of control." In addition, she hoped to explore and specify with the parents the ways that the family and school might interpret his hyperactivity in order to help Harrison understand his hyperactivity and his inability to pay attention. She also planned to discuss with him the role that medication plays in helping him to attend, concentrate, and stay in school. While family therapy is beyond the knowledge and skills of this beginning graduate student, it was expected that the various family roles and relationships would be explored with a view to referring the family for treatment, if indicated.

Because of the visibility of the interns in the lunchrooms, through hall monitoring, and in the classrooms, adolescents drop in on project staff (as they do with the community mental health staff and the nurse-practitioner). Drop-ins may visit once to talk to an adult about a crisis or more often to discuss problems that they are unable to resolve. Both the Collaborative Project and DYS program identify a range of drop-in issues: issues of sexual and physical abuse, a perceived threat or actual threat of a fight with another student or students, and verbal or physical altercations with a parent, sibling, or member of the extended family. After time-limited exploration, cases of abuse are reported immediately to the Department of Social Services (DSS). Where there is some doubt of abuse, even if family violence is involved, DSS may request that project or the UPS community mental health agency staff, or DYS staff follow up and work with the adolescent and their family.

DIVERSIFIED YOUTH SERVICES: MCMICHAEL SCHOOL

The Diversified Youth Services (DYS) program at McMichael is guided by an ecological perspective and a generalist approach; however, the focus of practice is primarily at the micro- or mezzo-level with interventions directed predominantly toward individuals, groups, and families. DYS workers conceptualize their practice as generalist; a problem-solving approach is used during the process of assessment, and interventions may be multimethod and directed at multiple systems (Compton & Galaway, 1989; Hoffman & Sallee, 1993; Johnson, 1995; Kirst-Ashman & Hull, 1993; Landon, 1995; Zastrow, 1995). DYS handles individual and schoolwide crises (e.g., if a youth is killed in a violent or accidental encounter or dies in a fire). The crisis intervention model is exemplified by the work of Gilliland and James (1993), who have delineated a six-step model of crisis intervention: (1) defining the problem, (2) ensuring client safety, (3) providing support, (4) examining alternatives, (5) making plans, and (6) obtaining commitments. The authors state, "Our six-step model of crisis intervention emphasizes actively, assertively, intentionally, and continuously assessing, listening, and acting to systematically help the client regain as much of the pre-crisis equilibrium, mobility, and autonomy as possible" (p. 32).

Gilliland and James's (1993) model includes an assessment of client coping capacities and environmental resources that describes both the person-in-environment focus of DYS and their approach of determining the danger of the situation, and the ability of the youth, the family, and the school to cope with the crisis. Many of the drop-in situations are crises calling for immediate action; others require longer-term attention. DYS services are brief (generally no more than eight sessions), although this was not the case in the past. The agency is now adapting its school-funded services to a brief services model.

Similar to the collaborative project and in consonance with Boyd-Franklin's (1989) principles of working with black families, assessment begins after a rapport is established with the family. Initial problem solving and limited, goal-directed interventions may occur early in order to win the child or family's confidence (Boyd-Franklin, 1989). Workers state that history taking in the initial sessions may serve to heighten the family's suspicions (Boyd-Franklin, 1989), as was the case with Leah's family, described earlier in this chapter.

The ecological systems perspective and a generalist approach provide for the workers' differential use of a variety of interventions based on the nature of the problem. DYS workers describe the most frequently used interventions in the schools as crisis intervention, brief work with individuals and families, and educational and behavioral groups with youths and their families. When funding permits, workers' preferred family modality is structural family therapy (Aponte & Van Deusen, 1981; Minuchin, 1974; Minuchin & Fishman, 1981) and Boyd-Franklin's (1989) multisystems approach, which combines elements of structural family therapy, Bowenian, and strategic family systems approach (pp. 121–187) (see also Kerr & Bowen, 1988; Papp, 1981; Stanton, 1981).

As a COMPACT school, DYS collaborates with a broad array of organizations and services that are targeted to support the coping capacities and environments of individuals, families, and the school. Work with parents or guardians or with families usually occurs in the home. However, family interviews can be held in the school. Referral and treatment at DYS's outpatient programs are available for adolescents and families with severe mental health or family problems, including depression and withdrawal, attempted suicide, consistently violent or aggressive behavior, and sexual and physical abuse by parents, guardians, or the living-together partner of the parent.

In addition to services to "drop (or walk)-ins," crisis intervention, and ongoing work with adolescents and their families, DYS provides bimonthly educational groups for adolescents and summer individual and family and group services. Group services in the summer are for educational and cultural enrichment. Some selected illustrations of the diverse practice situations addressed by DYS staff are embodied in the following case situations.

A seventh-grade girl, M, dropped in very upset. Another girl told her that A, another seventh grader who "had a big mouth and was always causing trouble," said that M had sex with several seventh-grade boys. M says that she "doesn't do that" and does not know why A would spread such a lie. M does not want to go to class because everyone will believe this about her. The worker finds out from M what she would like the worker to do: listen to M? meet with A and the other girl? discuss with M how to handle this in school? M and the worker discussed how M would handle the situation for now. Then the worker gave M a pass to class and an appointment for later in the day.

The DYS case records show also that approximately seven to eight students drop-in because of fights with their peers in school or in the neighborhood. The fights usually result from what "she said [that] he said." Many of these crises are viewed as normative crises that may result in outcomes that are harmful to the child and a threat to the school. For example, some of the preadolescent fights, if ignored, may escalate and result in violence involving weapons. Schoolwide interventions have been introduced at general assemblies to role-play how youths might handle threats of violence or walk away from them if possible. Workers encounter situations weekly in which they review with their middle school clients various social skills for handling potentially violent situations, how to avoid them, and how to walk away from a fight, particularly when peers exacerbate the situation by encouraging the adversaries to fight.

J, an eighth-grade boy, dropped in because he was told by L, an eighth-grade acquaintance ("he's not really my friend"), that a group of boys was going to jump him after school. L said that at least one of them might have a gun or maybe could get a gun. After talking for a while about whether J could believe L (was L trying to "get something going"?), the worker and L talked about how he could go about cooling off the situation by taking several steps (make sure not to provoke anyone to anger; keep calm; maybe joke but don't be sarcastic; don't act scared by tone of voice). The worker got J to agree that he would walk away and get a grown-up if he could not avoid a fight. The worker and J agreed that the worker could tell the assistant principal so that he would be alerted to a possible fight. The worker and J agreed that, if necessary, the worker would meet with J and the group of boys who supposedly threatened him. J was given a pass to go to class late and a follow-up appointment for later in the day.

Records show that a number of child and family situations brought to DYS staff members' attention involve the mother's boyfriend. The mother's boyfriend may be a source of emotional and financial support for the family or peripheral to the family's functioning (Boyd-Franklin, 1989). Whatever the boyfriend's role and relationship with the children, his presence as part of the household "has an impact on the family alignments, boundaries, and roles" (Boyd-Franklin, 1989, p. 198). Boyd-Franklin (1989) suggests that once the presence of the boyfriend is acknowledged, the worker should explore including him in the family sessions (p. 198). The boyfriend may have continuous arguments with the child and the mother about the mother's discipline. The child may feel neglected because the boyfriend "gets all of her attention and time." The adolescent in these family situations comes to the worker's attention because of lack of completion of work or apparent sadness or depression; some are self-referred drop-ins who want to talk about their unhappiness with their family life. One preadolescent and his mother were seen by the worker through self-referral by the parent. The worker held a family session that allowed her to see the strengths of the family and the family's high hopes for and disappointment with the client. The session also enhanced communication and rapport among the worker, the adolescent, and the mother.

> *Ms. P came to the school to discuss her son with the social worker. According to the mother, H had been a model student at school and a model child at home, an assertion confirmed by school records. Now H is staying out late, not following the rules, not doing his homework regularly, and getting to school late. Ms. P works but is able to leave the house with H in the morning. Several times H has made her late for work as he "takes his time" getting ready. H, an eight grader, is the youngest and only child now living at home. Ms. P's two older children, both young men, have moved away from home in the last four years. One is married and working and is beginning his family; the other is working and going to school. The worker asked Ms. P to give her some idea about what has caused H to change. Ms. P is proud of the job she has done with her children. She gives their father credit as well. Although they are divorced and his work has been sporadic in recent years, he has been financially and emotionally supportive of all of the boys. The worker asked if Ms. P would consent to a family session and if Mr. P could come. She said that a family session might help them to understand what was going on and how each member could help. The family session was in Ms. P's home and included Ms. P, her former husband, H, and his older brothers. The family members tended to gang up on H, pointing out all of the "bad things" he had done. The older boys said that H had "no excuse for his behavior after all Mama had done." Ms. P explained that she had high expectations for all of the children and could not understand what was causing H to act as he was. The worker congratulated the family for being "there for each other." H did not say much in the family session, even when the worker asked him what he thought the reasons were for his change in behavior. She suggested that there might be ways in which each family member could help and that she would like to see H individually and then meet with the family again. She asked them what were H's strengths, saying that one of the reasons they might be so angry was that he had seemed to be so "good" in the past. Each of the older brothers talked about how good H was in school and that they wished they had his academic ability. One brother said, "We [black men] had to be prepared be-*

cause 'they' [whites] would not give [us] a break." He hates for his little brother to "mess up." Mr. *P said that H was good in school, and he was dependable.*

When the worker saw H individually, she asked him how he thought the family meeting went. H said that he thought it went okay. The worker said that H had been very quiet at the session and wondered what was going on. After some moments of silence, H said that he felt left out. His mother had a new boyfriend, and she no longer had time for him as in the past. He and his mother used to go to the movies, watch videos together, and talk, but now she spent "too much time with him." The worker asked if H could meet with him and his mother and if he could tell her what he had told the worker. When H and Ms. P met with the worker, H haltingly explained to his mother what he told the worker. The three of them talked about how his mother's new boyfriend was good for her and did not have to be bad for H. The mother talked about some of the ways to include H in some of their activities. The worker explored whether Mr. P and H's brothers could do more with H when Ms. P was out on a date and even if she was not out on a date. The next sessions continued to focus on how Ms. P and H could adapt to the new circumstance (Ms. P's boyfriend), reporting on the things that H had done with her and Mr. P, and occasionally with Ms. P and the boyfriend. Ms. P was reluctant to involve the new boyfriend too much because she was not sure about the direction their relationship would take; however, she thought that some activities together were important. Although a total family session has not occurred, both Ms. P and H have expressed satisfaction with their progress to date.

If students are to receive ongoing services from DYS staff, they are required to receive a health evaluation by the DYS nurse and a psychiatric review to determine the diagnosis, both of which are a requirement for community mental health funding. Psychological testing is done at the request of the worker or psychiatrist.

In some instances, the situations confronting the child and family are not clear-cut; the parent or parents with their disengaged or violent behavior border on being neglectful or abusive. Often the workers are aware of both the strengths of the families they serve and some of the maladaptive patterns that they have developed to cope with overwhelming burdens in the face of limited resources. Some single-parent families exemplify this combination of adaptive and maladaptive patterns in the face of limited psychological, social, and material resources (Lindblad-Goldberg & Dukes, 1985; Lindblad-Goldberg, Lasly, & Dukes, 1988). Workers are also aware of the projected rage of some adults who are struggling to manage their lives and give their children opportunities in the face of a society that limits opportunities for themselves and their children. The worker seeks to strike a balance between understanding the circumstances, burdens, and rage of the parent, while asserting the rights of the child and responsibility of the parent for his or her child's safety, protection, and nurturance and for the child to have a chance to grow and develop into a healthy adolescent and adult.

This burden of balancing the potential of family strengths with the actuality of their existing behavior can present the worker with both value dilemmas and practical concerns. For example, when the family's treatment of the adolescent borders on neglect or abuse, the worker confronts the choice of precipitating the upheaval of a family system and removal of the child into a foster care system that may not always serve the best interest of the child. Or the worker confronts the choice of preserving the family when there might be some doubt about the family's ability to function effectively for the child. In the following case examples, workers faced these value and practical dilemmas. Although the DSS did not accept either of the family situations, described later as child protective cases, the DSS and DYS workers both decided that there was enough doubt to warrant DYS intervention.

Two years ago, a sixth-grade boy was referred to DYS because of "immature behavior" in the class room. He whined, clung to the teacher, talked out of turn, and was "provoking" to other students. The sixth grader is the oldest of four siblings in a single-parent home. Much of the care of his siblings and the housework was left to the sixth grader and his sister, who was in the fifth grade. He said that sometimes he and his siblings were hungry because there was not enough food in the home. The social worker found that the mother worked two jobs and out of necessity placed too much of the parental burden on the sixth grader and his sister, they were eleven years and ten years of age, respectively. Through further discussion with the mother, the worker found that the mother felt overwhelmed and overburdened ("tired all of the time," "just running from job to job and home") and did not have a kinship or friendship network that she could depend on for child care. Her arrangements for child care were haphazard now that her great-aunt, because of illness, could no longer care for the children. She depended on her girlfriends, a boyfriend, and a neighbor to provide child care when the two older children were in school. Her own mother worked, and she did not feel that her friend could do a good job of caring for her children; her friend was also overwhelmed and "just trying to make it" herself.

The worker helped the mother to locate an affordable day care program for the younger children. She also helped the mother to identify healthful snacks and quick meals that could be fixed so that the children would not be hungry, especially when the mother felt too tired or overburdened to cook. Because the mother's work schedule was unalterable, the worker worked with the sixth grader individually, focusing on social skills and self-esteem through activities and discussion. The worker helped the sixth grader, as well as the mother, to see that he had been very helpful to his mother, brothers, and sisters, but the job was too big for him.

This student has since graduated from the eighth grade and is attending the nearby high school. The DYS case manager helped the student obtain summer employment. Initially, this student visited the worker regularly, and now he drops by occasionally to say hello. When the youth moved to the seventh grade, the worker began seeing his sister, who is now in the sixth grade and stops by to see the worker. The sister reports that the brother "loves high school" and, ever the caretaker, "constantly pushes" his siblings to stay in school. The sister is doing well in school academically and socially.

One of the DYS workers reports another situation in which the parent's work schedule, expectations, and method of discipline caused her child to be referred to

DYS. With well-functioning single-parent families, roles and boundaries are clear, flexible, and

> children have easy access to the parent. The parent may be working or on public assistance; the children are well cared for and their basic needs are met. Emotionally, both parents and children feel free to give and receive nurturance and communicate their own needs. In some functional single-parent families, there may be a parental child who helps the mother care for younger children. This may be an economic necessity. . . . Once again, it is not the presence of this structure that is dysfunctional. . . . A single-parent family with a parental child can function quite well as long as the parent does not abdicate parental responsibilities or overburden this child in an inappropriate way. (Boyd-Franklin, 1989, pp. 191–192).

Boyd-Franklin describes the "overcentralized mother" who may exercise an "inordinate amount of control" and power in all situations but is usually feeling overwhelmed and overburdened. Recognizing this pattern of power and control in the face of adversity, the worker in the next clinical example was well aware of the underlying rage of the mother but chose to focus instead on her goals for her child and her motivation to maintain order in the face of her difficult challenges as a single working mother.

The sixth grader, CM, came to see the assistant principal because he was angry and depressed about the severe whipping he had received from his mother. There were visible welts on the youth's back, and he appeared very afraid for the assistant principal or DYS staff to contact his mother. The assistant principal filed a protective service report with the DSS, which reviewed the situation and decided it did not require removal of the child from the home. Since DYS was in the school, the DSS worker asked the DYS worker to continue working with the family.

In a morning call, the DYS worker found that the mother, Ms. M, worked a late shift. The sixth grader was responsible for cleaning certain parts of the house. When the mother found that CM had not done his chores, she would wake him up at about 5 A.M., shortly after she arrived home, and beat him with an extension cord. The DYS worker worked with Ms. M to get her to give up the use of the extension cord, and she worked with CM about doing his chores and managing when his mother was at work. The worker expressed her understanding of Ms. M's desire to have a "clean and orderly home" for her child and to teach her son to be disciplined and responsible. The worker pointed out how the mother's desire to raise her son to be responsible might backfire if her son was so upset that he could not do his homework or concentrate in school. The mother and the worker explored alternate ways to discipline the child. They also talked about how normal it was for children to backslide on their chores and responsibilities. The worker pointed out that the important thing was for the consequences to fit the rule that was broken. The worker found that the mother came from a family where every infraction against the rules resulted in a beating. "You couldn't get away with anything" with her mother. She said that she and her brothers and sisters "were afraid to do wrong" because the mother would beat them, and they all turned out okay. The worker said that a lot of families were raised that way, but she knew of families that turned out all right without beatings and did not seem to be so angry and resentful of their parents. The worker asked Ms. M if she had felt some anger or resentment about her whippings. The mother did not say she felt anger or resentment; rather, she said she "didn't like it" and neither did her brothers and sister. But now that she is a grown-up, she understands why her mother disciplined them as she did. The worker also worked supportively with CM. Praising him for being responsible and for being a good student, she observed to him that it must be hard to live up to everyone's expectations for him to do well in school and at home all of the time. Later, CM talked to the worker about peer-related issues; he was teased frequently for being short and thin. This eleven year old reports that the whippings with the extension cord have ended, although he still gets spankings sometimes. His grades and attendance are good.

CONCLUSION

Clinical practice in urban school settings requires a collaborative, multisystems, multimethods approach based on a generalist model and an ecological perspective (Allen-Meares, 1995; Caple, 1990). Interventions may need to be targeted simultaneously to the school environment, the classroom, and the youth's behavior in the classroom, and toward the pupils, both individually and in groups, as well as toward maladaptive patterns in family functioning. Where feasible, broader community interventions may be required (Allen-Meares et al., 1986; Caple, 1990). Often urban youths are beset by threats to their safety from violent families and neighborhoods and violence in schools. Many children are seen in schools by social work and mental health workers because of their experience with the loss of a significant member of their family through illness, death, violence, placement outside the home, or absence of parents because of alcohol and drug abuse (Caple, 1990; McWhirter et al., 1993). These youngsters experience overwhelming anxiety, grief, helplessness, and rage that often cannot be contained. This rage can periodically erupt into crises requiring a range of brief and longer-range interventions to relieve their trauma and its aftermath (Gilliand & James, 1993).

The Collaborative Project and Diversified Youth Services comprehend the broad range and scope of services needed to strengthen families and to intervene in the maladaptive patterns that children and their families develop or to intervene by addressing aspects of the environments that fail to sustain and nurture them (Chestang, 1972). However, limited project and agency resources often constrict the application of the wholistic approach, including multisystem interventions that are based on the ecological perspective and generalist method. Clinical services and integrated approaches with other professionals (Hooper-Briar & Lawson, 1994; Holbert & Vroom, 1995) within and external to school settings are critical to address the complex needs of children and youth, their families, and the schools where they function in many of their major social roles.

Societal investment in services to youth and families in schools may be the sole point of entry into needed social and mental health services for many urban and minority families (Caple, 1993; Hines & Boyd-Franklin, 1982). Such services can make the difference in academic achievement and social skills and, subsequently, the life chances of many of these youth. Their mental health, the well-being of their families, and the responsiveness of their schools depend on it.

REFERENCES

Allen-Meares, P. (1995). *Social work with children and adolescents.* White Plains, NY: Longman.

Allen-Meares, P., Washington, R. O., & Welsh, B. L. (1986). *Social work services in schools.* Englewood Cliffs, NJ: Prentice Hall.

Aponte, H., & Van Deusen, J. (1981). Structural family therapy. In A. Gurman & D. Kniskern (Eds.), *Handbook of family therapy* (pp. 310–360). New York: Brunner/Mazel.

Bandura, A. (1969). *Principles of behavior modification.* New York: Holt, Rinehart and Winston.

Bandura, A. (1977). Self-efficacy: Toward a unifying theory of behavior change. *Psychological Review, 84,* 191–215.

Bandura, A. (1986). *Social foundations of thought and action.* Englewood Cliffs, NJ: Prentice Hall.

Bartlett, H. (1970). *The common base of social work practice.* New York: National Association of Social Workers.

Bertcher, H., & Maple, F. (1971). *Group composition: An instructional program.* Ann Arbor, MI: Campus Publishers.

Boyd-Franklin, N. (1989). *Black families in therapy: A multi-systems approach.* New York: Guilford.

Caple, F. S. (1990). The black family and the school. In S. M. L. Logan, E. M. Freeman, & R. G. McRoy, *Social work practice with black families: A culturally specific perspective* (pp. 115–132). New York: Longman.

Cashdan, S. (1988). *Object relations therapy: Using the relationship.* New York: Norton.

Charney, H. (1993). Project Achievement: A six-year study of a dropout prevention program in bilingual schools. *Social Work in Education, 15* (2), 113–117.

Charney, H., & Vroom, P. I. (1988, October). *Project achievement: A cross-cultural group and family treatment program for underachievers.* Paper presented at the Social Work Annual Program Meeting of NASW, Philadelphia.

Chestang, L. W. (1972, 1980). *Character development in a hostile environment.* In M. Bloom (Ed.), *Life span development* New York: Macmillan.

Children's Aid Society. (1993). *Building a community school: A revolutionary design in public education.* New York: Author.

Compton, B., & Galaway, B. (1989). *Social work processes* (4th ed.). Belmont, CA: Wadsworth.

Davis, L. E. (1980). Racial balance—A psychological issue: A note to group workers. *Social Work with Groups, 3* (2), 75–85.

Folkman, S. (1984). Personal control and stress and coping process: A theoretical analysis. *Journal of Personality and Social Psychology, 46,* 839–852.

Garvin, C. (1987). *Contemporary group work* (2nd ed.). Englewood Cliffs, NJ: Prentice Hall.

Garvin, C. (1991). Social learning theory and role theory. In R. R. Greene & P. H. Ephross (Eds.), *Human behavior theory and social work practice* (pp. 151–176). New York: Aldine.

Germain, C., & Gitterman, A. (1980). *The life model of social work practice.* New York: Columbia University Press.

Germain, C., & Gitterman, A. (1995). Ecological perspective. In *The Encyclopedia of Social Work* (19th ed.) (Vol. 1, pp. 816–822). Washington, DC: NASW Press.

Gilliland, B. E., & James, R. K. (1993). *Crisis intervention strategies* (2nd ed.). Pacific Grove, CA: Brooks/Cole.

Hines, P. M., & Boyd-Franklin, N. (1982). Black families. In M. McGoldrick, J. K. Pearce, & J. Giordano (Eds.), *Ethnicity and family therapy* (pp. 84–107). New York: Guilford.

Hoffman, K., & Sallee, A. (1993). *Social work practice: Bridges to change.* Needham Heights, MA: Allyn & Bacon.

Holbert, J., & Vroom, P. I. (1995, April). *Learning to collaborate—Preparing teachers and social workers for partnership: The Wayne State Experience.* Paper presented at the Annual Program Meeting of the American Educational Research Association, San Francisco.

Hooper-Briar, K., & Lawson, H. A. (1994). *Serving children, youth and families through interprofessional collaboration and service integration: A framework for action.* (Monograph) Oxford, OH: Danforth Foundation and the Institute for Educational Renewal at Miami University.

Johnson, L. C. (1995). *Social work practice: A generalist approach* (4th ed.). Boston: Allyn and Bacon.

Kerr, M. E. & Bowen, M. (1988). *Family Evaluation.* New York: Norton.

Kirst-Ashman, K., & Hull, G. (1993). *Understanding generalist practice.* Chicago: Nelson-Hall.

Landon, P. S. (1995). Generalist and advanced generalist practice. In *The Encyclopedia of Social Work* (19th ed.) (Vol. 2, pp. 1101–1108). Washington, DC: NASW Press.

Lazarus, R. S. (1980). *The stress and coping paradigm.* In L. A. Bond & J. C. Rosen (Eds.), *Competence and coping during adulthood* (pp. 28–74). Hanover, NH: University Press of New England.

Lazarus, R. S., & Folkman, S. (1984). *Stress, appraisal and coping.* New York: Springer.

Lindblad-Goldberg, M., & Dukes, J. (1985). Social support in black, low-income, single-parent families: Normative and dysfunctional patterns. *American Journal of Orthopsychiatry,* 55, 42–58.

Lindblad-Goldberg, M., & Lasley, & Dukes, J. J. (1988). Stress in black, low-income, single-parent families: Normative and dysfunctional patterns. *American Journal of Orthopsychiatry,* 58 (1), 104–120.

McWhirter, J. J., McWhirter, B. T., McWhirter, A. M., & McWhirter, E. H. (1993). *At-risk youth: A comprehensive response.* Pacific Grove, CA: Brooks/Cole.

Minuchin, S. (1974). *Families and family therapy.* Cambridge, MA: Harvard University Press.

Minuchin, S., & Fishman, C. (1981). *Family therapy techniques.* Cambridge, MA: Harvard University Press.

Papp, P. (1981). Paradoxes. In S. Minuchin & C. Fishman (Eds.), *Family therapy techniques* (pp. 244–261), Cambridge, MA: Harvard University Press.

Phillips, J. (1995). *Interview and analysis of interventions with Marcus, a juvenile diabetic.* Paper presented in class at Wayne State University, School of Social Work.

Rose, S. (1972). *Treating children in groups.* San Francisco: Jossey-Bass.

Rose, S. (Ed.). (1980). *A casebook in group therapy: A behavioral-cognitive approach.* Englewood Cliffs, NJ: Prentice Hall.

Salkind, M. J. (1981). *Theories of human development.* New York: D. Van Nostrand.

St. Clair, M. (1986). *Object relations and self-psychology: An introduction.* Monterey, CA: Brooks/Cole.

Speck, R., & Attneave, C. (1973). *Family networks.* New York: Vintage.

Stanton, M. D. (1981). Strategic approaches to family therapy. In A. S. Gurman & D. P. Kniskern, *Handbook of family therapy* (pp. 361–402). New York: Brunner/Mazel.

U.S. General Accounting Office Report. (1993). *School-linked human services: A comprehensive strategy for aiding students at risk of school failure* (GAO/HRD-94-21). Washington, DC: Author.

Vroom, P. I., Holbert, J., & Spurlock, M. (1995, March). *Interprofessional collaboration: Empowering urban children and families in a university public school.* Paper presented at the 41st Annual Program Meeting of the Council on Social Work Education, San Diego, CA.

Warger, C. L. (n.d.). *A collaborative approach to social skills instruction.* Unpublished manuscript available from the Foundation for Exceptional Innovations, 1648 Bennington Hollow Lane, Reston, VA, 22094.

Warger, C. L., & Rutherford, R. B. (1993). Co-teaching to improve social skills. *Preventing School Failure, 37* (4), 21–27.

Zastrow, C. (1995). *The practice of social work* (5th ed.). Pacific Grove, CA: Brooks/Cole.

17

Clinical Practice with the Elderly

Steven Barlam and Harriet Hailparn Soares

In society as a whole, many people feel uncomfortable with issues surrounding aging. This is true of professionals as well. There are some who believe that psychotherapy is impossible with the geriatric population, given the perception that older adults are "too set in their ways" and "lack the necessary capacity for insight." This is not the case. In spite of the fact that many older people may not be familiar with the concept of therapy and that quality geriatric psychotherapy is not easily accessible, there will continue to be many opportunities for clinical work with older adults.

Bette Farber, a sixty-nine-year-old married woman, called a social worker to set up an appointment for psychotherapy at the encouragement of her daughter. She had never before been in therapy and had many mixed feelings about making the initial call. At the first session, she felt quite anxious when she saw that the therapist was nearly half her age. Would the therapist truly understand? She told him that her life had drastically changed in the past few months. After a sudden serious heart attack, her husband was left with irreparable brain damage, recognizing no one and needing total care. Bette had tried to care for him at home but found that it was virtually impossible for her to cope with the level of care that he required. She had planned to celebrate her fiftieth wedding anniversary in the following month, and instead she was forced to place him in a nursing facility that could manage his care. She came to the therapist with hopes of making sense of this devastating situation. She found herself emotionally labile, unable to sleep at night, and pushing away her friends and family.

As the therapeutic relationship progressed, it became clear that there were unresolved issues relating to her relationship with her husband. Whereas initially she had described her marriage in glowing terms, gradually she was able to talk honestly about long-term disappointments. She realized that she did not have the time that she had banked on to work on these issues with her spouse. She had always been fearful of being too close and intimate with her husband, which related to unfinished business with her parents. She had thought that if she did not get too close, she would not be vulnerable. Now that her husband was no longer available to her, she found that this defense had not protected her from unbearable pain.

The therapist helped her through the process of anticipatory grief, during which time she became aware of old patterns that continued to haunt her in other significant relationships. Her husband's unexpected illness had reactivated feelings of abandonment and vulnerability stemming from her childhood. She now became keenly aware how old unresolved feelings and issues affected her relationships with her own children, who were her best source of emotional support, and began to work on strengthening her bonds with them.

This example clearly demonstrates how psychotherapeutic interventions with older adults can help them through the difficulties that may confront them. Geriatric clients bring with them a varied range of life experiences, family histories, and worldviews. It is impossible to make sweeping generalizations about them.

When discussing older populations, cultural variations affecting issues of aging need to be addressed. It would be impossible in a brief chapter to describe specific details as to how different cultures approach aging. When a professional works with an individual from a different background and culture, it is important to be sensitive to one's own cultural bias and to be aware of cultural differences. In the field of aging, there is much written in the area of multicultural issues, available to everyone who does this work.

CLINICAL ISSUES

Finding Meaning in Life

Jacob Greenspan, an upper-level manager in the aerospace industry, retired at age sixty-five, only to start a variety of new activities. He advised minority businessmen and helped them obtain loans. He was a part time marshal for the sheriff's department. As always, he was active in his synagogue, going to synagogue daily to pray and writing a congratulatory letter to every bar mitzvah boy. He and his wife had a loving relationship, and she depended on him to do all of the shopping and to keep everything in the house working properly. His sons came to him for advice, and he had wonderful, close relationships with his grandchildren.

As Mr. Greenspan grew older, his heart condition worsened, he had several heart attacks, and his energy level and mobility decreased drastically. His vision worsened. He gave up driving and could no longer walk more than half a block. His wife also became ill, and they needed in-home help. Although he was forced to give up many of his activi-

ties, he remained actively engaged in life. He wrote a history of the business his father had started and had it published. He continued to fix things around the house. Using a magnifying glass, he read the daily paper, enthusiastically wrote letters to the editor, and saw several published. The letters to bar mitzvah boys continued. He was unable to walk to the synagogue and, except when his sons were able to drive him there, prayed at home daily. Although contacts with friends became restricted and many friends died, his close involvement with his family remained. His enthusiasm for life, people, the news, and all kinds of involvements remained despite his limitations.

Dorfman (1994) speaks of the aspirations the elderly can continue to have and that are necessary to maintain a good quality of life. She talks about a continued need for autonomy, personal growth, opportunities for helping, social ties, and pleasure. Regardless of the degree of dependence that gradually comes with aging, people can retain a sense of control over their environments, engage in meaningful activities, and pursue relationships.

Dorfman also speaks of the need for the older person's characteristics to fit in with the characteristics of the environment as well as "an emphasis on the fit between personal values orientations and environmental supports for the fulfillment of those values (and the aspirations they motivate)" (Dorfman, 1994, p. 135). There are difficulties if the values and aspirations of an older person do not fit in with his or her environment. An older person who values independence can become distressed as he or she becomes more dependent and opportunities for autonomy decrease. For instance, placement in a nursing home can drastically reduce choices and alternatives and be an enormous blow to a patient's sense of autonomy.

Solomon (1992) says that successful aging is related to the qualities of flexibility and adaptability. Mr. Greenspan showed these qualities as his health deteriorated and his activities became more limited. In addition, Mr. Greenspan continued to feel productive and felt he had something to contribute to his family and his community.

The concept of reciprocity is an important one, since people often find meaning is a function of what they have to contribute. As people age, there are fewer opportunities for traditional productivity. The skilled clinician needs to be creative and sensitive in helping people find ways to feel productive in the face of dependency.

Victor Frankl (1963), based on his experiences in the Holocaust, formulated a "will to meaning"—the need of each individual to search for meaning in his or her own life, no matter what the circumstances. He retains an optimism about people's capacity to find meaning in life, even in the face of suffering and loss.

The likelihood of successful aging also depends on the interests and activities a person brings into old age. Mr. Greenspan, with a broad repertoire of interests, was able to enjoy activities despite his limitations and remain involved in life. Individuals whose interests are varied have a better chance of aging successfully. Someone who enjoys playing golf, but cannot after a broken hip, may remain active by pursuing alternative interests that do not depend on physical mobility to keep a person active.

Unsuccessful aging can follow when an individual has a limited repertoire of activities. For instance, a woman whose whole life was devoted to raising children and caring for a husband might have a more difficult time as a widow, with familiar roles no longer available and a paucity of alternatives. A successful and high-powered attorney who spent long hours at work and had no outside interests and few friends was at loose ends when he retired at age seventy-six and became severely depressed.

Developmental Issues

The psychologist Erik Erikson identified eight developmental stages, with the final stage in the life cycle being integrity versus despair. The strength derived from the elderly person's struggle with these two issues becomes wisdom (Erikson, 1950). An older person "learns to convey the integrity of experience, in spite of the decline of bodily and mental functions" (Erikson, Erikson, & Kivnick, 1986, pp. 37–38). During this time, there is an opportunity to integrate all areas of life, including past and present relationships and events. A sense of wholeness and integrity can lead to the retention of a vital involvement in life (Erikson, 1982).

People frequently have unresolved issues from other life stages, which can prevent them from dealing successfully with subsequent life issues. "At every successive developmental stage, the individual is also increasingly engaged in the anticipation of tensions that have yet to become focal, and in reexperiencing those tensions that were inadequately integrated when they were focal; similarly engaged are those whose age-appropriate integration was then, but is no longer, adequate" (Erikson, Erikson, & Kivnick, 1986, p. 39). Did they feel successful in work? Were they able to form an identity successfully during adolescence? Do continued threats to their autonomy that can come with age reactivate old feelings of shame as dependency increases?

Changes and Losses

With aging, there are multiple losses, which become compounded. All areas of a person's life can be affected. Life frequently narrows and becomes more restricted. People ultimately can lose a sense of power over their own lives and face the ultimate loss, which comes with mortality and death. One loss can throw off an individual's equilibrium. Stability becomes more tenuous due to accelerated losses and less resiliency.

The myth of the golden years describes old age as a time of peace, but often it is a time of much stress, with fewer opportunities and resources for restitution and repair. Serious multiple losses can lead to physical illness. A widow is more likely to become physically ill in the months following her spouse's death.

There are many potential losses that can accompany the aging process: retirement from work, loss of social status, death of family and friends, isolation from social contacts, deterioration of physical health and mental acuity, loss of productive and familiar roles, lessened financial security, loss of feelings of control, loss of independence (and increasing dependence on others), loss of privacy, and loss of familiar surroundings resulting from placement or relocation.

The goal of clinicians is to help people achieve a new equilibrium, come to terms with irreversible changes and losses, help them grieve, and set realistic expectations.

Emily Humphrey lived in a nursing home and was bedbound due both to osteoporosis leading to multiple fractures and to heart disease. Compression fractures of the spine caused severe pain. Clearly she had experienced dramatic changes in her life, including deterioration of her physical health, institutionalization, and the loss of independent functioning, which lead to emotional distress. The social worker at the nursing facility encouraged her to reminisce, acknowledged and validated her losses and pain, and helped her to find meaning in her life through new relationships and activities. Always creative, she found new outlets for her talent, felt productive, and thus found new meaning in her life. She sewed beautiful rag dolls and stuffed animals, knit countless baby blankets for family and friends, and made Christmas ornaments. Always looking forward to her next project, she retained her wonderful sense of humor and infectious laugh. She formed new and satisfying relationships with staff and residents in the nursing home, as well as maintaining relationships with her family and some friends from before. Her defenses allowed her to endure and adapt.

Defenses and Coping Styles

People have lifelong styles of dealing with loss in order to cope and survive. Adaptation depends on coming to terms with the losses that have occurred and drawing on remaining resources rather than perpetually grieving. Successful grieving means accepting the mistakes and limitations of the past and realizing that one cannot go back, only forward. "Such losses or events are dealt with by a series of adaptive mechanisms that can either lead to mastery of the new situation or failure accompanied by impairment of functioning" (Beaver & Miller, 1992). People who have been successful throughout their lives in dealing with change and loss are more likely to use the same effective style of dealing with loss in old age. Successful aging comes from the ability to adapt to changing individual and environmental conditions. Mrs. Humphrey showed this adaptability in her remarkable adjustment to the nursing home. People who lack the ability to be flexible, to adapt to loss and change, have more difficulty with aging.

Knight (1986) speaks of various styles of successful aging. He says that some people remain active and engaged with the outside world, while others retreat to a more interior world.

Loss can exacerbate and magnify maladaptive defenses. With the losses that accompany aging, frequently people feel helpless, out of control, and fearful. Defenses such as denial, regression, projection, displacement, splitting, and projection may be used to avoid the emotional pain that accompanies loss.

Denial

In order to ward off the pain caused by loss, some people deny the reality of the loss. Deterioration in independent functioning and threats to a person's self-image cause distress and these may be denied in an attempt to avoid pain and to maintain old patterns of functioning.

John Peterson, a man who saw himself as strong and invincible and had never been able to accept his own weaknesses, denied his vision problems and his slowing reflexes, and adamantly insisted on driving despite the risk involved. To give up his driving would have been narcissistically mortifying to Mr. Peterson, whose use of denial had overcome his ability to reason.

Regression

Regression to a former stage of development may follow a traumatic event.

Anna Sabor, who had always been somewhat dependent on her husband, was widowed. Fearful and feeling alone, she regressed to behaviors similar to those of a child. She called her children several times a day, crying. She could not bear to be alone. Her bills had not been paid (although this had always been her responsibility), and her house went uncleaned. Her children struggled with setting limits in the face of her unconscious attempts to get them to take care of her.

Projection

Projection is a defense whereby painful feelings, conflictual wishes, and unacceptable thoughts are attributed to someone else.

Marianne Collingsworth was a quiet, passive woman who had never felt comfortable expressing anger. When her son moved her into a retirement facility despite her somewhat weakly expressed desire to stay at home, she was understandably very angry. Her anger felt unacceptable to her. Projecting it, she became afraid that her son was angry at her and would stop visiting.

Displacement

Displacement is used as a defense to avoid experiencing unacceptable feelings toward another person.

Sofia Valdez was very upset because she was told by her son that she could not move in with him and his family. Instead of experiencing her anger at him, she became furious at his wife, whom she blamed for the decision. When the expression of anger toward one person is seen as potentially dangerous, the anger may be directed toward someone less threatening.

Splitting

Splitting is used when an individual is unable to cope with ambiguity and imperfection. This defense is used to avoid accepting the realities of a situation.

Agnes Keith, a woman with a borderline personality disorder, maintained her equilibrium throughout adulthood. She had always had difficult relationships with others but lived an independent, though isolated life. She became ill, dependent, and frightened and required a caregiver. Her needy feelings were exacerbated by her frailty, but close rela-

tionships were terrifying. Now she could no longer manage on her own, and caregivers were called in. She was filled with rage about her unmet needs and felt bitter and lonely. In the space of four months, she had eleven different caregivers. Frequently each caregiver was "wonderful" at first, but after some time would be blamed for not satisfying her needs. Her tendency first to idealize and then to devalue gave rise to tumultuous caregiving situations. Splitting, always a defense Miss Keith tended to use, became very problematic when she depended on others to care for her. (Rose, Soares, & Joseph, 1993)

Unfinished Business

The elderly need opportunities to come to terms with the past and find meaning in the present. Some of the issues they must face are unfinished business, loss, and the anticipatory loss of one's own life. Everyone has unfinished business—old issues that people struggle with, flashbacks to old roles, and old scripts. It is impossible for any child growing up to be satisfied all of the time, so that these are issues for everyone: fantasies, wishes, hopes, regrets, and longings. When older people try to come to terms with their lives, these powerful issues are stirred up. Regrets from the past, unresolved conflicts, unmet needs, and expectations can cause stress. These feelings tend to be unconscious, repetitive, and persistent. Even if they become conscious, they may persist. The difficulty with unfinished business is that it remains unfinished, because old feelings of regret and loss can never be completely resolved. These old issues can lead to difficulty in primary relationships with spouse, parents, and children. They also can affect current relationships with extended family, friends, and colleagues.

For older adults, the losses and stress of aging and illness can trigger old issues that may have been dormant. It is difficult to make decisions, set limits, and act rationally when one is unconsciously trying to resolve old issues. Exacerbation of sibling rivalry can occur. Family patterns of scapegoating and old alliances may be reactivated, and old feelings of guilt and ambivalence can resurface.

Freda Reiner was a ninety-two-year-old Holocaust survivor. Born in Hungary, she was intelligent, proud, dramatic, verbal, funny, and engaging,—but also exasperating. She could be paranoid and angry at times, and she struggled with depression. Resourceful and liking to be in control, she became hysterical, demanding, and unreasonable when she was feeling helpless and dependent.

Mrs. Reiner insisted on being home with her beloved cat, despite her limited mobility and activity level owing to serious cardiovascular and respiratory problems. She was wheelchair bound and because of limited in-home care was alone much of the time. She had been in and out of nursing facilities, which she said were "like zoos" and were only for people "already dead." She could not bear being surrounded by demented, very ill patients; being associated with them was a narcissistic blow.

She had one daughter who had her own physical and financial problems and felt helpless to meet her mother's needs and demands; moreover, they had a long-term conflicted relationship. Her daughter at times felt she was "breaking into little pieces" and said her mother was an expert in provoking guilt in her. When Mrs. Reiner fled from

Hungary, she sent her young daughter alone to England, where she was raised in boarding schools. Mrs. Reiner came to the United States and supported herself as a saleswoman. They were reunited only after her daughter was grown. Mrs. Reiner and her daughter have never resolved the issues resulting from this traumatic separation. As a result of Mrs. Reiner's deteriorating health, this family's unfinished business was stirred up. Mrs. Reiner was overwhelmed by feelings of guilt now that she needed care from the daughter she had "abandoned." Her daughter's ambivalence, her anger at being abandoned, and her longing for a close relationship with her mother complicated the situation.

Death and Dying

Although death is inescapable, it can seem inconceivable. (See Chapter 24.) Fear of death is universal. People use denial and magical thinking when faced with the idea of death rather than allowing themselves to feel vulnerable. With aging, the certainty of death comes closer. Social workers can help people come to terms with their lives and prepare for their deaths. In social work practice with the elderly, these issues are essential to deal with, although this painful issue can sometimes cause problems in allowing honest and open interchange (Kubler-Ross, 1969). Dealing with death and bereavement can raise social workers' own anxieties about potential losses and rekindle feelings about past losses. Death is certainly talked about more openly today than previously, but it still is a topic of great discomfort. Professionals who work with the elderly need to be comfortable dealing with the dying person, as well as bereaved family members.

In addressing this difficult issue, it is important to be attuned to and to begin where the client and family are. Differences in beliefs, individual and family styles, and cultural backgrounds affect how people approach death. Social workers first need to examine and understand their own beliefs. Then they need to be sensitive to the issues that the client and family are facing—their cultural background, their individual characteristics, and their willingness to confront the reality of the situation. Generational differences need to be looked at as well.

In a therapeutic group for adult children, the topic of death and dying brought out many differences. A Filipino woman felt that death was a subject never to be discussed with the dying person. A man from Russia felt even more strongly; he thought that the truth would quickly kill the dying person because that person would give up hope. Other participants felt comfortable with the reality of death and wanted to be open to discussing the subject with their family members.

There are similar differences in openness and comfort in dealing with planning for death. Writing a will, or durable power of attorney for health care ("living will"), and making pre-need funeral arrangements means contemplating the end of one's life, which some people find too painful and frightening to contemplate.

Elisabeth Kubler-Ross speaks of five stages in the process of coping with dying. The grieving individual goes through these same stages. The first stage of denial and isolation is one of disbelief, shock, and feelings of unreality. During the second stage, anger, the individual feels rage and resentment at the situation. At the third stage, bargaining, people try to avoid their death (or loss) by looking for ways to stay in control of the situation. Depression, the fourth stage, is a time when grief for what is lost is experienced, and fantasies and hopes for the future are mourned. Finally, the last stage, acceptance, is the time when there is resolution, and peace is made with reality (Kübler-Ross, 1969). People may move back and forth between these stages or get stuck in one. One needs to be respectful of the stage a person has attained rather than imposing an agenda for the individual.

In the field of hospice care, professionals are reexamining the stage theory of coping with dying and grief. Although it may provide some comfort to have a structure, the reality is never as simple and clearly delineated as a stage model would have one believe.

An empathic and compassionate willingness to listen to a dying person in the struggle to deal with approaching death is a major gift that can be offered to that person. Helping a person come to terms with his or her life is a task that can lead to a peaceful acceptance of one's mortality. Distancing reactions are common among people who do not allow the dying person to face the truth. A caregiver who openly deals with death enables the dying person to be honest and say goodbye.

George McGuire, a burly New York truck driver, was never very comfortable in talking about feelings. He was diagnosed as having liver cancer at age seventy-four. The family, to "protect him," did not talk to him about it and insisted that their father did not know he was dying. Their fear of dealing with his reaction to the truth created distance between Mr. McGuire and his family. The hospital social worker encouraged them to discuss his illness openly. Despite many years of a problematic relationship with his father, his first-born older son was chosen by the family to tell him the truth. Mr. McGuire breathed a sigh of relief when his son spoke the truth to him: "I knew it all along." There had been a mutual collusion in which both sides pretended there was nothing seriously wrong. When Mr. McGuire left the hospital, he insisted on going fishing with long-time friends at their mountain cabin and traveled to visit family out of town. He reminisced, watched his grandchildren play, and made a point of expressing his appreciation to his wife, friends, and each son and daughter-in-law. The long-time estrangement from his older son was partially resolved. He flew to Boston to attend a grandchild's second birthday party. Remaining in bed until the last guest left, he was then rushed to the hospital for internal bleeding. It was clear that he would die soon, and he insisted that he wanted to die in New York. When he arrived in New York, he was taken to the hospital where he died early the next morning.

Mr. McGuire died having tied up many of the loose ends in his life. He maintained as much control as possible over his life and his death until the end. Because so frequently the elderly have lost control over so much of their lives, it is important to empower them so that they maintain as much control as possible over their deaths. As Mr. McGuire's death approached, he felt an awareness that the end would come soon. This awareness is not uncommon in the dying and can sometimes be heard in the dreams and symbolic language of the dying person.

Bereavement

There is a Mexican saying: "Sorrow, like the river, must be given vent lest it erode the bank." Unresolved, unexpressed grief can lead to physical illness and psychosomatic damage, continued depression, and an inability to reengage in society, form new relationships, and build a new life. During the first few weeks after a loss, a resistance to treatment may be the mourner's effort to regain some balance after an initial disorientation. For some people, it takes much longer than others to be able to talk about their loss and to mourn openly. After the initial reaction to the bereavement, people may be more open to grief work.

Sometimes unfinished business makes it difficult for people to mourn successfully. Danieli (1994), focusing on Holocaust survivors, speaks of the impact that traumatic life experiences have on how people deal with aging and loss.

Eva Lasky, a Holocaust survivor, was reunited with her husband after the war after seven years in labor camps. The rest of her family had perished. They started life over moving first to Israel and then to the United States, where their two daughters were born. Mrs. Lasky seemed to have come to terms with her past losses, raising her children, operating a small grocery store with her husband, and having many friends. But when her husband died, all of her feelings of loss and isolation were reactivated. Having started one new life after the almost miraculous reunification with her husband, she was unable to start another. She never was able to mourn his death successfully, becoming isolated and remaining depressed, instead.

Families can have unreasonable expectations of an older bereaved person. A daughter called a social worker and said she was concerned because her father was still brooding after the death of his wife. When the social worker asked for additional information, the daughter said that her mother had died two weeks before. A situation like this can be complicated by the fact that adult children of bereaved parents are also dealing with their own feelings of loss in their own way, and perhaps with different styles than their parents are.

Anticipatory Grief

People can begin the mourning process before the death of a loved one. In much the same way as in bereavement, anticipatory grief can lead an individual through the stages of denial, anger, bargaining, depression, and acceptance in an attempt to come to terms with the anticipated loss. At times this process may enable people to grieve and come to terms with a loss before death, but this is not always the case (Sprang & McNeil, 1995).

Walker et al. (1994) discuss anticipatory grief in relation to caregivers of persons with Alzheimer's disease and other chronic illnesses. They emphasize the need to encourage caregivers to remain actively engaged throughout the length of the ultimately terminal but lengthy illness and at the same time to grieve and let go. At times, anticipatory grief can ease postdeath mourning, and at other times it seems to make for more difficulty in successful mourning. Sensitivity to individual differences in the needs of the caregivers and their process of grief is important.

Variables such as social stigma of the illness (e.g., Alzheimer's, other dementias, AIDS) may influence the caregiver's ability to retain a bond with the ill person. Feelings of shame, embarrassment, guilt, and anger impede open mourning, and an attempt at secretiveness can cause difficulties in the relationship between the patient and caregiver, thereby complicating the grieving process. The gradual loss of function that can accompany chronic illness may be experienced as "psychosocial death," an ambiguous state that is very difficult to mourn.

Intergenerational Issues

Because generational and cohort characteristics can lead to differences within families, it is necessary to look back to a client's family of origin, as well as the client's current family constellation. Some practitioners use a genogram to clarify family history and relationships and to plan interventions. A genogram is a diagrammatic description of a family's structure. Ingersoll-Dayton and Arndt (1990) discuss the ways that using genograms can facilitate assessment and interventions in work with families.

Aging leads to crises that can stir up old pain and old unresolved family issues, and can lead to the regressive activation of old conflicts.

Dorothy Stoltz, eighty-two years old, and her unmarried forty-five-year-old daughter had never lived separately. Although they had always had a contentious, difficult relationship, the situation was fairly stable until Mrs. Stoltz became disabled by a stroke. The daughter had never received the approval she craved from her critical mother, who projected all of her life's disappointments onto her. With Mrs. Stoltz's illness, the situation became worse. Mrs. Stoltz became even more critical because of her unhappiness with her disability and by a new dependence on her daughter. The daughter's feelings of low self-esteem were stirred up by her mother's constant berating and humiliating criticisms, and she responded with rage, feeling trapped into caring for a mother who gave her no appreciation.

Family styles as well as individual styles of coping can affect how people deal with loss and stress. The style of the elderly person may not match the coping styles used by other family members in response to the needs of their elderly relative. The histories of the individual and the family affect the way they ask for help and how they are able to use help. Some families are protective and look toward the future, planning ahead. Other times there can be intervention only in a crisis. The clinician often must wait for the situation to deteriorate in order to intervene at a time when family and individual defenses are less rigid.

Marital Issues

Marital problems of elderly couples can be exacerbated by illness, disability, and dependency. Couples who have attained some kind of stability, despite unresolved marital issues, can have that balance collapse with the stress of illness and caregiving.

Antone and Isabelle Furtado came to the United States from Portugal when they were both teenagers. Married young, they had a traditional marriage: Mr. Furtado was the head of the family, and Mrs. Furtado was subservient to him, taking care of the household and the children. When upset, Mr. Furtado frequently took it out on his wife, whom he berated. Although Mrs. Furtado felt belittled by his verbal abuse, she swallowed her anger and maintained her subservient role. When Mr. and Mrs. Furtado were in their eighties, they grew more frail. Despite her physical limitations, Mr. Furtado still expected his wife to care for him and the household and grew angry with her when his needs weren't met. Mrs. Furtado, very unsteady on her feet, fell one morning. Her husband paid no attention and yelled at her because his lunch was late. Mrs. Furtado, feeling frightened and needy and overwhelmed by his anger and his demands, packed a suitcase, called a cab, and moved to her daughter's home.

In other marital situations, a well-functioning balance that met the needs of both members of a couple can be devastated by illness and dependency. Roles are restructured, and a dependent wife becomes more responsible out of necessity as her husband becomes ill.

John and Gertrude Howell had been married for almost sixty years. Mrs. Howell was a sweet, passive, and dependent woman. Her husband made all of the decisions, managed the finances, was very much in control of everything that happened in the family, and enjoyed his wife's dependency on him. Mrs. Howell was perfectly satisfied with this arrangement as well. When he was in his eighties, Mr. Howell's functioning began to deteriorate, his memory was failing, he was forgetting to pay bills, and he was easily confused. Following a medical and psychiatric geriatric evaluation, a diagnosis of early-stage Alzheimer's disease was made. The change in his functioning left the family in a turmoil. Mr. Howell did not easily give up his controlling role and denied his deficits. Although Mrs. Howell knew she had to step in, she felt completely inadequate and was overwhelmed and angry at her increased responsibilities. She also struggled with dealing with Mr. Howell's frustration and denial.

Marital issues for adult children can also affect older family members.

Catherine Williams came to a clinical social worker for direction in providing care for her elderly, recently widowed mother. She seemed to be overly involved, visiting seven days a week, and interfering with her mother's attempts to start a new life. It became clear through the interview that she was experiencing problems in her own marriage. Her involvement with her mother seemed to be quite functional in helping her to avoid her own marital issues.

Adult Child and Aging Parent Issues

Adult children of aging parents struggle with many stresses. They are caught up in the needs of their parents, as well as all of the other multiple, and at times conflicting, demands in their lives. These adult children can become overwhelmed by feelings of guilt, anger, grief, ambivalence, and unrealistic expectations. Their attempts to do the right thing for their parents and struggles to set appropriate limits are complicated by unfinished business and individual limitations and styles.

It is essential to provide adult children with clear direction, information, and help in formulating effective coping strategies. When people feel out of control and overwhelmed, they need information in order to make informed choices, and at the same time they need validation to support them in their struggle with powerful feelings. What are their alternatives? How can they prioritize their parent's needs and at the same time take care of themselves? How can they be helped to accept their limitations and the limitations of what can be done for their parents?

Some adult children may be part of the "sandwich generation," caught between parents who are becoming more and more needy and their own children, who have needs of their own. The sandwich generation is usually middle aged, but these years can be extended. A woman eighty years old struggled to keep her 102-year-old mother, completely disabled by a stroke, out of a nursing home, so she could die at home. At the same time, her fifty-six-year old son lost his job, and she worried about his future as well.

Parental and Adult Child Expectations

Molly Starsky was a widow, who at eighty-six was a very narcissistic and needy woman. Her only child, a daughter, was born when Mrs. Starsky was in her early forties. After she fell and broke a hip, she could no longer live alone. Her expectation was that her divorced daughter, a single mother and successful businesswoman, would send her son to live with his father and move in to care for her. When her daughter, not surprisingly, refused to go along with this plan, her mother was indignant: "After all, the only reason I had you was so that you could care for me in my old age."

Although this is an extreme example, it is not uncommon that aging parents, brought up in a generation when women worked outside the home less frequently and often cared for aging relatives at home, would expect to be cared for in the same way by their children. In a situation like this, parents can be painfully disappointed when other arrangements are made. The following scenario can be true as well.

Hannah Chapin was a feisty, active ninety-year-old woman, weighing eighty-nine pounds. She had lived an independent zestful life, traveling, playing bridge, and volunteering at the local senior center twice a week. She managed quite well until she was in her mid-eighties, when her ambulation became unsteady, her eyesight worsened, and she had trouble taking care of her daily needs. Her relationships with her family were warm and loving. Her eldest daughter and her son-in-law very much wanted her to move in with them; they had an extra room, and she would be loved and cared for. Mrs. Chapin refused, and moved into a board and care home near the senior center, saying that her independence was very important to her and that she would maintain as much of her old lifestyle for as long as possible. She appreciated her daughter's offer but did not want to rely on her family or be "a burden on them."

The discord that can occur when expectations and scripts of parents and children differ can cause ongoing conflict in relationships. The disappointment and anger that result may cause stress for both parties involved.

Sibling Issues

The ties and conflicts between siblings are some of the most powerful experienced, frequently leading to complex and ambivalent relationships. Sibling relationships begun in childhood and continuing into old age may involve bonds of affection and support, but also unresolved conflicts that can be stirred up by changes in family equilibrium. With aging and dependence, old sibling issues are exacerbated for adult children. Sibling disputes about caregiving and living alternatives can make decision making tortuous, and old family roles emerge.

Patrick and Anne Jackson's two daughters have lived independently for years and saw each other rarely. After Mrs. Jackson broke a hip and Mr. Jackson showed symptoms of beginning dementia, a reactivation of old sibling issues occurred. The older daughter said that her unemployed, adopted younger sister was trying to take advantage of their parents, was wasteful, and was not to be trusted. She felt that only she had good judgment around caregiving issues and was careful with conserving her parents' funds. Her younger sister, always feeling the outsider, saw this as a chance to win her parents' approval and love. She felt her older sister was trying to withhold money and care from their parents in order to increase her inheritance.

Variations in sibling styles of conflict resolution, setting priorities, and problem solving lead to difficulties, making family decisions complicated. Rivalries for parental affection and approval, aroused by caregiving needs, complicate matters.

Changes in Roles

There is some controversy about the use of the term *role reversal,* sometimes used to describe the way adult children may eventually take care of their elderly parents. Some see their role as "parenting their parents." Brody (1990), Seltzer (1990), and Gurland (1990) independently agree that it is a phrase that has outlived its usefulness. It is a fairly simplistic way of describing the changes in roles that can occur within a family as older family members age and become more dependent. "It should go the way of other gerontological theories that failed to recognize the rich diversity of elders and their families, even when the range of behaviors and attitudes are constricted by disease" (Gurland, 1990, p. 38). The concept of role reversal seems to underestimate the length, complexity, and depth of the history between adult child and parent, the intricate network of feelings and expectations, the ambivalence, the unfinished business, the power of the long-term relationship. Although a parent may become dependent on an adult child, that parent always remains the parent, at least in memory. The caregiving adult child can be left with powerful feelings of pain, grief, and ambivalence about the parent and the caregiving role.

Issues around Dependency

Issues of illness, disability, and dependency stir up old feelings in the elderly. People are raised to value independence, and its loss has profound implications. "Regardless of age, dependency and the need for services can elicit feelings of resentment, anger and envy" (Soares & Rose, 1994, p. 153). People are frequently ambivalent about depending on others, and despite obvious neediness, sometimes entirely ungrateful.

Motenko and Greenberg (1995) reframe the role of dependence, saying that "it is not a marker of decline and deterioration, but a necessary development for mutual growth and enhancement of late-life family reciprocity. Accepting dependence helps an older person maintain his or her competence, autonomy, and self-esteem" (p. 382). The role of the social worker in helping reframe this for the older adult may be crucial to a positive adjustment and a continued sense of autonomy.

INTERVENTIONS

Assessment

Depression

The losses and isolation that accompany old age often lead to mourning and depression. Frequently older adults who have functioned well throughout their lives may become overwhelmed by these losses, and their previously adequate defenses may no longer be sufficient to enable them to regain equilibrium. Others may never have had adequate defenses and emotional resources to deal with loss.

Yesavage (1993) states that 2 percent of elderly people in the community suffer from major depression. Another 2 percent have dysthymia. Mentally intact residents of acute and long-term care facilities may have a rate of depression of 20 percent. In spite of these numbers, a majority of these individuals are not receiving treatment by mental health professionals (Dorfman et al., 1995; Yesavage, 1993).

Differential Diagnosis of Dementia

Depression in the elderly sometimes shows up with symptoms that are different from those of younger people. Symptoms of dementia can sometimes be caused by depression, and these diagnoses can overlap. Dementia can be caused by drug toxicity, reversible organic illness, nutritional disorders, intercranial masses, infections, and arteriosclerotic complications (Yesavage, 1993). All of these may be reversible. When dealing with the elderly, it is very important to have a thorough medical assessment to screen for reversible organic conditions, substance abuse, and toxic reactions to medications and to differentiate between depression and dementing conditions.

Eleanor Phillips went into a nursing home shortly after her only son died. Although she seemed very depressed, she was also quite confused and forgetful. Although reminded from time to time of her son's death, she never remembered it. How much of her forgetfulness was due to her dementia? How much did her depression cause her forgetfulness? These are sometimes very difficult answers to ascertain given the complicated and intertwined issues.

Psychotherapy

Individual

Are older people amenable to individual counseling, or are they "too set in their ways," too inflexible? Many professionals have the preconception that older people are unable to make use of individual therapy. But Horton (1982) finds little evidence for this presumption and espouses an eclectic approach for working with the elderly. Crises can be a good time to intervene; people are more flexible at times of crisis, more likely to be open to help, and more likely to change. Individual therapy with an older person is not always done in a traditional context, but may take place in a care management relationship, a senior center, and other less traditional settings. Husaini et al. (1994) observe that although many older people with psychiatric symptoms access mental health systems, a large proportion are more comfortable going to family physicians or clergy.

Groups

Different types of groups are frequently used when working with an elderly population. Bereavement groups, support groups for caregivers, assorted self-help groups, day treatment groups, and social support groups are available in most communities.

Groups can be less threatening compared to individual treatment, since they allow a participant to get help without being the sole focus of attention. Groups deal with the universality of the issues that are raised, which can provide much comfort and support.

Support groups are also used to provide help to children of the elderly. Frequently adult children who are caregivers find themselves under a great deal of stress and overwhelmed with powerful feelings. These groups can provide education and support, lessen isolation, help with setting limits, impart knowledge of resources, and help with ambivalent feelings such as guilt and anger.

Solomon and Zinke (1991) write about the use of group psychotherapy with depressed older patients. They feel these groups can help older people with common themes of isolation, loss, and death. Feelings of helplessness, dependency, and loss of autonomy can be addressed in a mutually supportive group. This can be a slow and difficult process, and the therapist must be prepared to deal with much ambivalence and resistance.

Couples

With aging, a former marital equilibrium can become precarious, and old unresolved marital issues can be restimulated. In addition, new issues related to caregiving, illness, and dependency can arise. At times this can give couples an opportunity to resolve old issues. At other times the balance can become so unstable that resolution seems difficult or even impossible. In a marriage with a history of emotional or physical abuse, an abused wife may find caring for her needy, dependent spouse intolerable.

Family Interventions

Aging is a family affair, it affects everyone within the family system. That is why interventions that include the family are desirable in clinical work with the elderly. As older adults become more dependent, it becomes more and more likely that their families will be involved and affected by these changes. Coping with crises and planning for the future necessitate the involvement of the family in order to mobilize available resources and formulate and implement the most appropriate plans. The involved family can include any concerned family members: children, grandchildren, brothers and sisters, nieces and nephews. Supportive family can be instrumental in facilitating effective interventions.

When intervening with the family the clinician must work with old family issues and unfinished business exacerbated by the stress and demands of the current crisis. In multigenerational family work, the older adult's participation in the family meetings is not always essential, although the central issues may be related to aging. Families often need an opportunity to develop a working plan that takes into account all of their feelings. When an elderly individual denies risk, a family's ability to stand together will be more effective than when there is irreconcilable family dissension.

Other Interventions

Care Management

A care manager usually becomes involved with a client around concrete issues. This allows opportunities to develop a relationship with the client and to make therapeutic interventions. Many older people are unlikely to seek help from usual mental health settings or from private therapists. Concrete services offered by a care manager become intertwined with therapy. "Gradually, a different type of relationship often evolves. As issues come up, our clients begin to discuss feelings and to allow us to offer not only support, but interpretations and other psychotherapeutic interventions. We teach them how to be clients—how to use us to deal with intrapsychic and family issues as well as concrete needs and services" (Soares & Rose, 1994). An individual or family crisis most often motivates the request for concrete services. A care manager must be sensitive to the psychological issues that may underlie a request for services. The trusting relationship between client and social worker is the key to effective therapeutic interventions. Morrow-Howell says that "a case manager can not simply arrange services on behalf of a client without attending to the intrapersonal and interpersonal struggles of the people involved" (Morrow-Howell, 1992, p. 127). She feels very strongly that clinical case management is "the service most consistent with the profession's mission and the social service most often needed by elderly clients and their families" (p. 129).

TECHNIQUES AND TOOLS

Clinicians have many tools that can be used. Any one tool cannot address all needs. Clients may suffer from emotional pain and have medical, spiritual, psychological and social needs. Empathy, validation, and support are universal elements in successful work with an elderly population. A compassionate connection to an older person in distress through a therapeutic relationship can help him or her deal with painful losses and come to terms with life. Some of the tools that are commonly used in effectively addressing the needs of older clients are reframing, prioritizing, using empowerment techniques, encouraging reminiscence, and limit setting. With the elderly, brief therapy and crisis intervention are the most frequently used models for clinical intervention.

Reframing

Reframing a situation can help a client look at something from a different perspective, which can free the person to move forward.

Louise Tillaman, a recent widow, worried that she was "becoming cuckoo." When asked what she meant, she described periods where she felt upset and confused by the changes in her life and so overwhelmed that she became immobilized. The social worker pointed out that this reaction was certainly understandable in the light of her losses and major changes in her life, and that except for periodic episodes of feeling overwhelmed, she was dealing with her loss quite well. This new way of looking at the situation relieved her anxiety and enabled her to go on with the task of grieving and moving on with her life.

Prioritizing

Much of the clinical work with the elderly involves crisis intervention and helping people cope with complicated and many-layered situations. Short- and long-term prioritizing can be essential in alleviating client and family anxiety so that effective problem solving can occur. In a crisis, a short-term plan put in place can give clients and families time to work on a more long-range solution.

Following an earthquake, Elizabeth Olsen, a recent widow without a strong support network, found herself immobilized. Her home suffered serious damage, and she needed temporary shelter. In addition, she worried about safeguarding her belongings and tending to needed household repairs. Her therapist worked with her to prioritize a list of things she needed to accomplish and to come up with a plan. This list seemed much more manageable to her than the amorphous, disorganized body of tasks over which she had agonized.

Setting Limits

One important tool for clinicians in work with the elderly is the use of appropriate limits. Clients overwhelmed with feelings related to change and loss need the therapist to help contain these feelings in a safe manner. Appropriate use of limit setting can provide much comfort and relief to clients and families.

Walter Gordon, a seventy-seven-year-old widower, had been in weekly treatment with a social worker for just over one year. He had a dependent personality and had always leaned on his wife. In the course of treatment, the social worker became the object of this dependent transference, and the client began to call him several times a week. The social worker strived to maintain firm boundaries in order to maximize the client's independence.

Empowerment

Empowerment is particularly important when working with an elderly population because so many of the issues with which older adults grapple have to do with loss of control and feelings of helplessness. For those who have suffered losses and a loss of control over many parts of their lives, empowerment comes from looking to their strengths. It consists of exploring ways to compensate for changes and for strategies to put them back in control of their lives. This may mean reinforcing their rights and encouraging them to speak up for themselves in regard to medical care or in other areas where self-advocacy would be useful. If a person feels empowered even in small ways, feelings of helplessness can be ameliorated. For women in particular, Browne (1995) speaks of the need to broaden the definition of empowerment in order to take into account the variety of experiences women have in society and the range of alternatives for empowerment that exists for them. Empowerment can include activities that are group and network oriented, as well as more individually oriented activities. She feels that social workers should "see connections and friendships, as opposed to domination and conflict, as sources of power and strength for older women" (p. 362). The means of empowerment can vary greatly, depending on gender differences, cultural expectations, socioeconomic status, race, and other factors.

Florence Moore, an African American woman of seventy-five, suddenly became the guardian of two young grandchildren when her daughter died. Limited financially, she was poor in concrete resources but rich in emotional support. A network of neighbors and family members provided the backup and emotional connections she needed to continue with the task of raising her grandchildren and lessened her feelings of vulnerability and helplessness.

Histrionic and needy, eighty-two-year-old Eloise Dakowsky had a fight with another customer in the market after an accident with a shopping cart. The store manager evicted her from the store, leaving her feeling humiliated and helpless. Her therapist helped her write a letter to the store management explaining her side of the story.

Edwin Taylor was losing his vision, became unable to manage day-to-day household tasks, and was terrified he would have to move to a retirement facility. A referral to the Braille Institute provided him with the training he needed to work out new ways of managing, as well as devices that enabled him to read his mail, write checks, and take care of other tasks.

Reminiscence

The concept of reminiscence as a therapeutic intervention has grown over the past thirty years. Through reminiscence, older people can be helped to come to better terms with their lives. It becomes an adaptive mechanism that can be encouraged by the professional. In order to pass successfully through Erikson's stage of integrity versus despair and through that integration attain wisdom, people must deal with unfinished business, grieve losses, and relive successes and times of happiness. Kuntz (1991), speaks of the importance of reminiscence and life review in therapeutic interventions with the elderly: "When combined with sound psychotherapy principles and experiences, such activities both demonstrate a cultural interest in valuing elders' experiences, and an ability to understand and interpret older adults' needs from a developmental point of view" (p. 53). Reminiscence helps people to find meaning in their lives and to come to terms with its limitations. In addition, the reminiscing person may have the feeling of being able to contribute through sharing meaningful experiences. Sherman and Peak (1991) discuss the use of reminiscence in groups of the elderly and talk about its benefits to mood and self-esteem.

> *Having lost most of her vision, Madeleine Jardine, a dignified, proud eighty-seven-year-old widow, born in France, lived an isolated life in her small apartment. With her social worker, she reminisced about her husband and the romance and excitement he had brought into her life. She had run away from home and moved to Turkey to marry him, and had been disowned by her family. She called him her* grand amour. *Their relationship was sometimes tumultuous, and life was hard. Although her life was now limited, reminiscing enabled her to remember a time of happiness and come to terms with her regrets.*

Brief Therapy versus Long Term

The current generation of elderly is often not familiar with the concept of therapy. They may feel that therapy is only for "crazy" people. Therefore, clients need to be educated and familiarized with therapy. Although traditional long-term therapy may prove not to be the model of choice, it is possible for the social worker to educate and engage older clients in a therapeutic relationship. Many older adults are more likely to be comfortable with therapeutic interventions at the time of a crisis or in a less formal context. Brief therapy can address many of the difficult situations that the elderly individual faces. Frequently a therapeutic relationship can continue for years, supportive for the most part, with intermittent opportunities for brief therapy of a more intensive nature. Brief therapy may not always pertain to the duration of the relationship, as seen in the following example.

> *When Jacob Greenspan lost his wife, he went through a painful period of mourning. He became ill and increasingly frail. He no longer had energy for his many activities and spent much of his day in bed asleep. In his withdrawal, he seemed to be preparing for his own death, feeling that he had lived a full life and that it was time to go. His social worker, who continued to provide care management, visited him at home. She usually found him curled up in bed with little energy to engage in conversation. One day she arrived on a visit and found him up, sitting in his favorite chair and obviously ready to talk, as in previous, healthier times. He said that he felt terribly guilty because he was glad his wife had died before him. In exploring this, it became clear that he had always worried that his wife, a rather dependent woman, would be left alone and helpless if he died first. He had been relieved that she had predeceased him. Talking about his feelings seemed to comfort him. After this meeting he continued to withdraw and shortly afterward he died.*

Crisis Intervention

Crisis intervention is a particularly appropriate technique to use with a population confronted with acute crises of dysfunction, illness, death, bereavement, and serious loss. The goal of crisis intervention is to mobilize people's strengths in order to reach a new, adaptive equilibrium. At times of crises, people are frequently more open to therapeutic intervention. "A minimal amount of effort at this time can produce a maximal effect; a small amount of help, appropriately focused, can prove more effective than more extensive help at a period of less emotional accessibility" (Golan, 1978, p. 9). One task is to help families and elderly individuals regain stability, but there is also the opportunity to help them develop new, more adaptive ways of functioning.

ISSUES FOR THE CLINICIAN

Countertransference Issues

Work with older clients can reactivate unconscious childhood and family issues for the professional. Clinicians must examine the beliefs and feelings that come from their pasts and can contaminate their current work with clients. "In our work with older people and their families, we come face to face with thoughts, memories, feelings, and unresolved issues from our own lives" (Genavy & Katz, 1990, p. 13). Through supervision and self-examination, clinicians must strive for self-awareness.

In a group supervision setting, a student intern described her work with an elderly client and her family. It became quite apparent that although the focus of the intervention was family based, one daughter of the client was conspicuously left out of the presentation. In discussing this omission, the student laughed and stated, "Oh. I didn't mention this daughter? She is very involved in her mother's life, and in fact I keep meaning to call her to invite her to participate in family meetings, but I guess I've been avoiding her since she said something during the intake that really pushed my buttons." As the supervisor explored this further, the student became aware of how the daughter of her client reminded her of her older sister with whom she had a problematic relationship. Through professional supervision, the student became aware of the countertransference and was able to work more effectively with the family.

Personal Beliefs and Biases About Aging

It is quite common for people to stereotype an aging population. When a doctor describes a physical problem such as incontinence as "just old age" or an elderly man's daughter says that old people cannot be trusted to make their own decisions or a teenager asserts that old people are asexual, they are using stereotypes. The issues of aging can be so painful that stereotyping may be used as a way to distance oneself from suffering. Stereotypes tend to depersonalize a situation in such a way that the need for compassion and empathy is lost.

Loss and Separation

Although everyone deals with losses from the time of birth, issues of loss arise constantly for those working in the field of aging. When professionals look at these issues, they cannot help but go back to their own lives, their own families, their own personal experiences. The universality of the issues that are involved ties them together with those who are suffering. Helping people at a time of loss can be painful because clinicians not only feel the client's pain but are reminded of their own losses as well.

Control

It is not always easy to watch clients make decisions that have a negative impact on their lives. Professionals may experience feelings of lack of control in certain situations that they encounter, which reactivate old issues of vulnerability. Under these circumstances, a social worker can understandably grow frustrated and angry if a client does not fulfill the professional's expectations. This situation may then affect a client's right to self-determination.

Death

Clinicians working with the elderly constantly confront issues surrounding their own mortality and that of those close to them. The fear of death is universal, and feelings of helplessness in the face of death can be expected. Clinicians need to be aware of their own styles of dealing with these difficult issues. Unresolved issues around separation can be stirred up with the ultimate separation that comes with death.

Family-of-Origin Issues and Unfinished Business

A social worker found herself becoming extremely involved with one of her elderly clients, a charming and needy woman whose unending appreciation somehow made it very difficult for the worker to set limits. When examining her feelings, the worker realized that her client was giving her the warmth and appreciation she had always longed for from her own mother, who had been cold and distant.

Older clients may come to symbolize significant people with whom one has unresolved conflicts. This can become problematic. The social worker may see the older client as a needy child or the good or bad mother. Voices from the past, unresolved guilt, anger, love, and nostalgia may arise, becoming obstacles to effective clinical work.

Frailty of Clients

When clients are elderly, frail, and at risk, there may be feelings of urgency to intervene despite resistance from the client or the client's family. Sometimes it may be difficult or impossible to intervene until there is a crisis, and it is necessary for professionals to contain their anxiety in the meantime. There often are external pressures from others who are involved to *do* something, which heightens the anxiety of the social worker.

The anxiety of working with frail, at-risk clients may be so high that at times, unconsciously or consciously, a professional may be tempted to precipitate a crisis in order to get resolution and closure. This response to anxiety is not in the client's best interest, although tolerating one's anxiety can be challenging when working with the elderly.

Rescue Fantasies

This same frailty may lead to rescue fantasies in those who work with the elderly. Despite an older person's desire to remain independent and despite the realities of aging and loss, a worker may try to solve all problems and heal all wounds. An elderly woman was frantic because her rent was very high. She did not want to leave her home of many years, but after paying her rent, she had almost nothing left over for any other expenses. Unfortunately, rent subsidies were unavailable, and other alternatives had already been exhausted. Her social worker found the woman's plight so painful that instead of helping the woman deal to with this dilemma adaptively, she colluded with her and diverted homemaker funds illegally to pay the woman's rent.

Setting limits may be difficult for many reasons: difficulties with being authoritative in the face of neediness, feelings about the limitations and losses inherent in the aging process, or the strong feelings elicited by the demanding client with a personality disorder. The client may have magical or unrealistic expectations of the worker. It may be easier to focus on concrete issues and solutions rather than have to deal with the painful problems we cannot solve.

Assumptions About Sexuality

Frequently people assume that the elderly are nonsexual or, conversely, that they are able to maintain their sexuality as it was when they were younger. Perhaps the assumption that the elderly are nonsexual comes from our difficulty in accepting the sexuality of our parents. The other extreme is the denial of the loss of sexuality or the loss of sexual opportunity. This may be an outgrowth of our own denial that this is a potential loss for us (Rose & Soares, 1993). Although the potential for sexual relationships may continue, the paucity of opportunities for such relationships in the light of an elderly person's health problems or lack of available partners may work against such potential being realized. The clinician must listen for clues that sexuality may be an issue in need of being addressed. This may be another loss the older person is mourning.

Red Flag Issues

Abuse

Elder abuse is much more common than previously believed (Anetzberger et al., 1993). The frail elderly are particularly vulnerable because of their isolation, helplessness, and dependence. Caregivers may have feelings of ambivalence about their caregiving role and also may be under enormous physical, emotional, and financial stress.

It is important for the clinician to be aware of situations that may potentiate the risk of abuse when evaluating families and elderly clients. Mrs. Stoltz, the stroke victim described previously, was cared for by a daughter who felt trapped and full of rage—a situation with a high potential for abuse. The social worker working with the family set a goal of separating the two, because neither had much capacity for insight into the nature of their conflict, and the mother was at substantial risk of being physically abused.

Laws pertaining to elder abuse can put social workers in a difficult situation. Since abuse must be reported, how can this be addressed in a positive way for the client, so that the experience becomes therapeutic? If a client is also the abuser, the situation can be particularly delicate.

Harold and Clara Deutsch, a couple in their eighties, became therapy clients in a family social service agency, wishing to address strains in their relationship. Mrs. Deutsch was tiny and very frail. Her husband was stronger, but he too was unwell and feeling overwhelmed by the task of caring for his wife. They formed an excellent relationship with their social worker, and it soon became apparent that Mr. Deutsch's rage at his situation was spilling over daily and putting his wife at risk. One day, Mrs. Deutsch told their therapist that he had pushed her, and she had fallen. The social worker, knowing that she must report the abuse, worried about what this would do to her relationship with Mr. Deutsch. After informing both of them, she reported the abuse to the authorities. Mr. Deutsch's initial response was anger and the feeling of having been betrayed by the social worker. It was clear that he was frightened and shamed by his loss of control. However, eventually he was able to view her intervention positively. The problem was now in the open to be discussed, and the outside support enabled him to have better control of his impulses.

Medications

As people age, drugs are metabolized differently, and side effects and idiosyncratic reactions can and often do become more common. Combinations of several medications may have serious side effects as well. Elderly individuals often take many different medications. Problems can arise when physicians prescribe medications without being aware of the prescriptions written by other physicians. Doctors not trained in geriatric medicine may not be sensitive to prescription interactions, metabolic differences, and problems with specific medications for the geriatric population. They may prescribe multiple drugs in order to counteract their helplessness in response to their patient's multiple symptoms. The elderly may misuse medications as well, keeping outdated prescriptions, having difficulty in taking correct dosages or forgetting dosages, self-medicating, and cutting amounts to save money or because the side effects are unpleasant. It can be helpful to have clients use one pharmacy and to inform the primary care physician of any medications found that have been prescribed by others. Psychopharmacologists who are familiar with the elderly can be consulted in order to evaluate an individual's regime of medication.

Substance Abuse

Alcoholism in the elderly is not uncommon. Some older alcoholics are at the end of a long road of alcohol addiction; others turn to alcohol after losses and depression associated with such issues as retirement, widowhood, or loss of functioning. The elderly can be more sensitive to alcohol, and symptoms such as unsteadiness and dementia can be exacerbated by alcohol. Abuse of drugs also can be a response to loss and depression. Sensitivity to the possibility of both alcohol and drug abuse is essential when assessing an older person. One eighty-two-year-old man was hospitalized when he suddenly became incontinent, developed slurred speech, and fell several times. An evaluation showed that his long-term alcoholism was complicated by a recent addiction to an antianxiety medication. In addition, there were traces of cocaine in his system. There are substance abuse programs specifically designed to address the needs of the older population. Traditional tools such as twelve-step programs combined with individual therapy have proved to be the most successful.

Suicidality

The elderly have a much higher risk of suicide than the general population, and such suicides tend to be underreported. "Although people [over] 65 years [old] account for only 11% of the population, they commit 17% of all suicides" (Yesavage, 1993, p. 24; (Sprang & McNeill, 1995). Successful suicides are more common in the elderly. Older men commit suicide more often than women (five to one) and than younger men (three to one) (Sprang & McNeill, 1995). Risk of suicide is associated with the high rate of major depression in the elderly. Thus, it becomes important to screen for suicidality when dealing with depressed elderly clients. The clinician is forced to face the ethical dilemma of balancing the responsibility to protect a client from self-harm versus the client's right to self-determination. Clients may feel the need to stay in control of their own lives (and deaths), yet social workers are mandated to report and intervene in response to active suicidality.

Restricted choices and alternatives that can accompany old age lead to increased feelings of helplessness, and thus the risk of suicide increases. Clinicians are divided over the most effective and humane treatments for suicidal depression. Various combinations of medications, psychotherapy, and in some instances electroconvulsive therapy have been recommended.

Ethical Issues

Kane (1993) speaks of ethical issues faced by case managers who work with the elderly. These issues include dealing with risks and with clients who make decisions that jeopardize their health and safety, balancing the often conflicting needs of elderly clients and their families, making decisions around placement, and protecting confidentiality, while still communicating with family and other caregivers.

Self-Determination and Risk

A competent adult may legally decide to refuse treatment. In evaluating the situation, how does a professional interpret a client's ambivalence? Who is competent? Do people have the right to make bad decisions? Social workers are often confronted by difficult issues of independence versus dependence, risk versus safety, and quality of life versus quantity of life. Is it better to live a more independent life, with the risk that it may be shorter, or do everything possible to create a protected environment? At times it is best to let people decide to take a certain amount of risk.

Lena De Salvo was a totally bedbound multiple sclerosis patient, who at seventy-five years of age was mentally sharp but completely dependent on her caregivers, who came only eight hours a day. The rest of the time she was alone. When her social worker first met her, she was able to move one finger, which she used to control the telephone, lights, and television. Gradually she lost the ability to use even this finger. Fiercely independent, she desperately wanted to stay at home and maintain as much control as possible over her life and environment. Her social worker recognized this desire and despite the obvious risks supported it. She was able to find funding for an apparatus that enabled

Mrs. De Salvo to control the phone, lights, medical alert unit, front door lock, and television by blowing into a straw.

The issue of self-determination becomes more problematic when working with people who are not competent or who have poor judgment due to dementia or denial.

Ninety-three-year-old Edith Galloway lived alone in a small apartment over a drugstore. Piles of newspapers and old food containers littered the floor. Five cats roamed around the two little rooms. Mrs. Galloway had always lived an eccentric, isolated existence, and had not seen a doctor in twenty years. She prided herself on being a consumer advocate, wrote to cereal companies with complaints about their cereal, called politicians to protest noisy traffic outside her window, and was quite effective in getting her needs met. She was frail and tiny, but feisty and strong in her determination to remain at home and independent. Her determination to remain home continued despite a decline in health, signs of dementia, serious weight loss, and increased risk. She refused medical treatment and denied the need for more care, leaving the social worker to grapple with ethical dilemmas: Was she gravely disabled? Did Mrs. Galloway have the right to make decisions that might disadvantage her or even jeopardize her well-being? What indeed were the social worker's legal and ethical obligations to this client?

The issue of self-determination becomes especially complex when the possibility of suicide arises. When an individual is terminally ill, contemplating suicide may be an expression of one's desire for self-determination and control over one's death. Such a decision is complicated and extremely controversial. For those who are left, suicide brings grief and pain.

With recent advances in medical technology and treatments, people are living longer with multiple illnesses, decreases in functioning, and increased levels of dependency, all of which often negatively affect the quality of life. When an individual loses what is perceived as a satisfactory quality of life and feels powerless to change the situation, suicide may be viewed as an option that provides a sense of control. A physically dependent individual may need to ask for assistance from family, friends, or professionals with the act of suicide. In recent years, there has been much controversy surrounding the role of the professional in assisted suicides. Social workers are bound to the professional code of ethics that prohibits any actions that are illegal and may bring harm to the client. Clinically, the social worker must strive to understand the meaning behind suicidal thoughts and provide empathetic support.

Conflicting Family Needs

The aging process affects not only the older adult, but also the entire family. When working with an elderly client, the clinician is often confronted with the divergent needs of both the older client and the client's family. Within the family unit itself, oftentimes, there are conflicts of need arising from individual family members' different perceptions, expectations, and history.

Andrew Grady, a former policeman, lived with his wife. Mrs. Grady had severe osteoporosis and cardiovascular disease, and was recovering from a broken hip. She was un-

able to walk safely without assistance, needed help bathing, and could not help with any household chores. Mr. Grady had always been proud and autocratic, and Mrs. Grady had always given in to her husband's wishes. Their roles changed when Mr. Grady became the primary caregiver. Then he had a stroke, leaving him physically unsteady, emotionally labile, and forgetful and confused. His massive denial of his deficits made him angrily refuse all of the social worker's attempts to provide additional home help, since having a caregiver in the home reminded him of his limitations. Under pressure, he would reluctantly agree to have a caregiver and then, in a rage, fire the person when she showed up. Although his wife was at risk and fearful, she continued to defer to him to avoid his rage. Complicating the situation, the couple's son took his father's side in refusing a caregiver, while their daughter supported her mother. Adult protective services became involved, and a psychiatric hospitalization followed. The situation was resolved only when the police were called following an altercation between Mr. Grady and his wife, leading to his long-term placement.

Placement Issues

Self-determination becomes a central issue in regard to placement. Most people prefer to live at home as long as possible. Placement is often seen as a terrifying alternative, and even when an elderly person's functioning deteriorates, there can be a desperate desire to remain home in familiar surroundings as long as possible. Although frequently people come to terms with this dilemma and find a degree of relief and safety when they move to more supportive environments, others stubbornly refuse to be placed, despite serious risks to their health and safety.

At times it is possible to help an elderly client work through pain and ambivalence and become reconciled to a decision for placement. Sometimes a decision is not made until an acute crisis: a broken hip, a stroke, or perhaps a psychiatric hospitalization. Families, spouses, and adult children struggle with ambivalence around this issue.

When working with a client who suffers from senile dementia, placement issues become extremely difficult for involved families. Family members are put in a position of making decisions on behalf of their older relative. There can be a conflict between meeting the needs of the older person and those of the family, with the specter of guilt and remorse looming large if the family feels forced into placing an elderly relative without that person's consent.

Issues of Confidentiality

When working with elderly individuals, the question of who the client is often arises. The social worker must identify the primary client while being sensitive to the needs of the client's family system. The social worker often has to walk a tightrope to maintain confidentiality in the face of client risk, caregiving needs, and the needs of the client system. The primary client holds the privilege of confidentiality. Confidentiality, however, can often be clouded by issues of competency and safety. If a family member is paying for the treatment, often there is an expectation that information will be shared. It is extremely important for the clinician to maintain the confidential relationship with the primary client.

CONCLUSION

Working with the elderly can be extremely rewarding yet challenging. The issues older adults face are unique to this population and can often be emotionally charged due to losses, changes, and the developmentally appropriate task of finding new meaning in life. These issues are often complicated by unfinished business, dysfunctional defenses, and deteriorating physical health. The skilled clinician needs to be sensitive to these issues in order to intervene effectively.

There is a wide range of both traditional and nontraditional settings in which older adults receive mental health services: senior centers, residential facilities, nursing facilities, hospitals, care management programs (both in-home and in-office settings), mental health clinics, and traditional therapeutic office settings. The challenges that will face clinical social workers in the future include working within the managed care system to ensure quality services in an era of cost containment, developing new and innovative programs to address the dilemmas faced by families caring for the increasing population of older adults, balancing safety issues while respecting the client's right to self-determination, and being sensitive to their own feelings about aging and how these can affect clinical work.

REFERENCES

Anetzberger, G. J., Lachs, M. S., O'Brien, J., O'Brien, S., Pillemer, K. A., & Tomita, S. K. (1993). Elder mistreatment: A call for help. *Patient Care, 27*(11), 93–130.

Barlam, S., & Shatkin, P. (1988). The use and misuse of labels in geriatric case management. *GCM Journal, 3*(4), 11, 19.

Beaver, M. L., & Miller, D. A. (1992). *Clinical social work practice with the elderly: Primary, secondary and tertiary intervention* (2nd ed.). Belmont, CA: Wadsworth.

Brody, E. M. (1990). Role reversal: An inaccurate and destructive concept. *Journal of Gerontological Social Work, 15*(1/2), 15–22.

Brown, C. V. (1995). Empowerment in social work practice with older women. *Social Work, 40*(3), 358–364.

Danieli, Y. (1994). As survivors age. *Clinical Quarterly, 4*(1), 2–7.

Dorfman, R. A. (1994). *Aging into the 21st century.* New York: Brunner/Mazel.

Dorfman, R. A., Lubben, J. E., Mayer-Oakes, A., Atchison, K., Schweitzer, S. O., De Jong, F. J., & Matthias, R. E. (1995). Screening for depression among a well elderly population. *Social Work, 40*(3), 295–304.

Erikson, E. (1950, revised 1963). *Childhood and Society.* New York: Norton.

Erikson, E. (1982). *The life cycle completed.* New York: Norton.

Erikson, E., Erikson, J., & Kivnick, H. Q. (1986). *Vital involvement in old age.* New York: Norton.

Freeman, E. M. (1984). Multiple losses in the elderly: An ecological approach. *Social Casework: The Journal of Contemporary Social Work, 65*(5), 287–296.

Frankl, V. E. (1963). *Man's search for meaning.* New York: Pocket Books.

Genevay, B., & Katz, R. S. (Eds.). (1990). *Countertransference and older clients.* Newbury Park, CA: Sage.

Golan, N. (1978). *Treatment in crisis situations*. New York: Free Press.

Gorey, K. M., & Cryns, A. G. (1991). Group work as interventive modality with the older depressed client: A meta-analytic review. *Journal of Gerontological Social Work, 16*(1/2), 137–156.

Gurland, B. (1990). Symposium on roles reversal: A discussant responds. *Journal of Gerontological Social Work, 15*(1/2), 35–38.

Horton, A. M. (1982). *Mental health interventions for the aging*. New York: Bergin.

Husaini, B. A., Moore, S. T., & Cain, V. A. (1994). Psychiatric symptoms and help-seeking behavior among the elderly: An analysis of racial and gender differences. *Journal of Gerontological Social Work, 21*(3/4), 177–195.

Ingersoll-Dayton, B., & Arndt, B. (1990). Uses of the genogram with the elderly and their families. *Journal of Gerontological Social Work, 15*(1/2), 105–120.

Kane, R. A., & Thomas, C. K. (1993). What is case management and why does it raise ethical issues? In R. A. Kane & A. L. Caplan (Eds.), *Ethical conflicts in the management of home care: The Case Manager's Dilemma* (pp. 3–4). New York: Springer.

Keizer, J., & Feins, L. C. (1991). Intervention strategies to use in counseling families of demented patients. *Journal of Gerontological Social Work, 117*(1/2), 201–216.

Knight, B. (1986). *Psychotherapy with the older adult*. Thousand Oaks, CA: Sage Publications.

Kübler-Ross, E. (1969). *On death and dying*. New York: Macmillan.

Kuntz, J. A. (1991). Reminiscence approaches utilized in counseling older adults. *Illness, Crises and Loss, 1*(4), 48–54.

Kunz, J. A. (1991). Counseling approaches for disoriented older adults, illness. *Crises and Loss, 1*(2), 91–96.

Lindemann, E. (1944). Symptomatology and management of acute grief. *American Journal of Psychiatry, 101*(2).

Lund, Dale A. (1989). *Older bereaved spouses*. New York: Hemisphere Publishing Corporation.

Maddox, G. (1991). Aging with a difference. *Generations, 15*(1), 7–10.

Morrow-Howell, N. (1992). Clinical case management: The hallmark of gerontological social work. *Journal of Gerontological Social Work, 18*(3/4), 119–130.

Motenko, A. K., & Greenberg, S. (1995). Reframing dependence in old age: A positive transition for families. *Social Work, 40*(3), 382–390.

O'Connor, D. (1993). The impact of dementia: A self psychological perspective. *Journal of Gerontological Social Work, 20*(3/4), 113–128.

Parad, H. J. (Ed.). (1965). *Crisis intervention: Selected readings*. New York: Family Service Association of America.

Rose, M. K., & Soares, H. H. (1993). Sexual adaptations of the frail elderly: A realistic approach. *Journal of Gerontological Social Work, 19*(3/4), 167–178.

Rose, M. K., Soares, H. H., & Joseph, C. (1993). Frail elderly clients with personality disorders: A challenge for social work. *Journal of Gerontological Social Work, 19*(3/4), 153–165.

Seltzer, M. M. (1990). Role reversal: You don't go home again. *Journal of Gerontological Social Work, 15*(1/2), 5–14.

Sherman, E., & Peak, T. (1991). Patterns of reminiscence and the assessment of late life adjustment. *Journal of Gerontological Social Work, 16*(1/2), 59–74.

Smith, E. D. (1995). Addressing the psychospiritual distress of death as reality: A transpersonal approach. *Social Work, 40*(3), 402–413.

Soares, H. H., & Rose, M. K. (1994). Clinical aspects of case management with the elderly. *Journal of Gerontological Social Work, 22*(3/4), 143–156.

Solomon, K., & Zinke, M. R. (1991). Group therapy with the depressed elderly. *Journal of Gerontological Social Work, 17*(1/2), 47–55.

Solomon, R. (1992). Curriculum for clinical practice. In M. J. Mellor & R. Solomon (Eds.), *Geriatric social work education* (pp. 101–117). Binghamton, NY: Hayworth Press.

Sprang, G., & McNeil, J. (1995). *The many faces of bereavement.* New York: Brunner/Mazel.

Watt, L. M., & Wong, P. T. P. (1991). A taxonomy of reminiscence and therapeutic implications. *Journal of Gerontological Social Work, 16*(1/2), 37–56.

Walker, R. J., Pomeroy, E. C., McNeill, J. S., & Franklin, C. (1994). Anticipatory grief and Alzheimer's disease: Strategies for intervention. *Journal of Gerontological Social Work, 22*(3/4), 21–39.

Yesavage, J. (1993). Differential diagnosis between depression and dementia. *American Journal of Medicine, 94*(5A), 23S–28S.

18

Treatment of Infants and Their Families

Ramona Rukstele

Clinical work with children and their parents is a time-honored tradition in the field of social work. The innovative work of social workers, psychologists, educators, pediatricians, and psychiatrists at the beginning of this century pioneered important social interventions and child-rearing approaches. Like the kindergarten and nursery school movements in Europe, industrialized America transformed its perceptions about childhood and the needs of young children (Peterson, 1987). All of these forces paved the way for what later evolved into the child guidance movement, developmental psychology, and child psychiatry as a medical subspecialty. A parallel development was the emergence of the subspecialty of psychiatric social work as the importance of evaluating the child-in-situation became recognized. Clinical social workers became integral members of multidisciplinary treatment teams in outpatient settings and in children's psychiatric hospitals.

During the first half of this century, the growth in services to children was revolutionary. The juvenile court system, established in 1900, became responsible for dependent and delinquent children, and the number of Societies for the Prevention of Cruelty to Children increased rapidly across the country (McCrea, 1910; Giovannoni, 1993). In 1912, Congress subsidized the opening of the Children's Bureau in the Department of Labor (Shonkoff & Meisels, 1992). Established with a philosophy of prevention, the bureau's primary attention was directed to the problems of working children and the high level of infant mortality (Lesser, 1985). This step on the part of government to take responsibility for the welfare of children was strongly supported by the Social Security Act of 1935, which spelled out a federal mandate for maternal and child health, help for disabled children, and aid to indigent and neglected children (Magee & Pratt, 1985).

As services and interest grew, institutions of higher learning expanded the availability of clinical training. During this period, professional organizations were formed, and standardized developmental assessment tests were devised (Freedman et al., 1976). Because of the significant influence that early childhood education had on early childhood services, attention turned to the improvement of training methods for disabled and disadvantaged children. Services to children and families at risk for abuse, delinquency, and other emotional problems became available, and the principle of prevention was secured within the tapestry of social and educational programs dealing with young children and their families (Shonkoff & Meisels, 1992).

In 1965, the federal government continued its support of children by improving the medical care system for the impoverished. The Early and Periodic Screening Diagnosis and Treatment Program was instituted and emphasized prevention services for poor children through the Medicaid provision of the Social Security Act. That same year, Head Start was established as a time-limited intervention for poor children. The program was designed to include parent involvement and was built on the assumption that the early experiences of poor children are important to their future development (Zigler & Valentine, 1979). Because evidence mounted that early intervention to disabled children could alleviate or even prevent severe delays, Congress in 1968 amended Public Law 94-142, the Education of the Handicapped Act, to include early intervention programs for vulnerable infants and toddlers. This amendment, reauthorized by Congress as P.L. 102-119 and also known as Part H, provides federal grants to state, local, and private agencies to develop a core of "comprehensive, coordinated, multi-disciplinary, and interagency" services (P.L. 99-457, sec. 671). Diagnostic and therapeutic programs are available to infants and toddlers under the age of three with developmental or health conditions that may result in developmental delays, and for three- to five-year-old preschoolers.

Clinical social workers have been involved with children's services and infant mental health since their inception. Clinical social work's interest in human behavior has been strong; it has always participated in the interdisciplinary debates regarding etiology and developmental theory. These theoretical arguments have long revolved around the same recurring issues: nature versus nurture, the importance of culture and context in the formation of character, and the weight of the importance of early childhood experiences and relationships. Yet no one is sure which forces, what combination, and what circumstances absolutely result in risk or resilience. The study of risk factors predates the more current work attempting to identify protective factors. There appears to be consensus in the literature that biology, environment, and experience are the primary ingredients in the recipe for human development.

THE BIOLOGICAL BASE OF EARLY RISK AND RESILIENCE

Early theories of growth and development maintained that biology was destiny. Arnold Gesell, a proponent of the maturational school and a pediatrician and psychologist, believed that infant development is primarily "autogenous," meaning a result of growth and maturation (Gesell, 1925). These early developmental theories cataloged physical and behavioral milestones and discounted the impact of experience on development. Human development was simply viewed as a linear progression.

While the maturationists focused only on biology, behaviorists argued about the overwhelming impact of environment on infant development. Psychologists such as John B. Watson and B. F. Skinner focused exclusively on the importance of external influences as shapers and conditioners of behavior (Watson, 1925; Skinner, 1948). On the other hand, Freud's psychoanalytic theory was highly motivational. He stressed the dynamic interaction among intrapsychic structures, cognitive functions, and social context. According to Freudian theory, it was these forces that determine individual character and personality formation.

With time, it became clear that no one theory was sufficient; neither nature nor nurture alone can explain how we develop into distinct individuals. Although biologic and genetic factors must be taken into consideration, the quest for cause and effect now includes attention to the complex transaction between nature and nurture. Among all of the biological factors, genetics, temperament, prematurity, and maternal substance abuse are most important to clinical social work practice in educational, health care, and family services settings.

Genetics

Research in the field of behavioral and psychiatric genetics, neurochemistry, and biology has increased understanding of brain development and genetically based developmental disorders. There are two categories of genetic causes for syndromes that involve developmental delay: abnormalities that are the result of heredity (malformations) and abnormalities that are caused by some kind of noxious agent or constraint (deformations). Disorders that are hereditary and cause malformations are passed on to infants by virtue of the family's genetic legacy. Genetic counselors can trace disorders such as schizophrenia, cystic fibrosis, and sickle cell disease through a family lineage for multiple generations. Deformations are typically caused by teratogens, substances that cause birth defects. Research and scientific advances have shown that viruses, medications, drugs of abuse, and exposure to occupational toxins can cause serious damage. These substances represent the most common teratogens responsible for developmental deformities. Some of these deformities may be lethal and result in spontaneous abortion or neonatal death (such as anencephaly). Others are not fatal but harm the developing fetus and have lifelong consequences for the child (such as fetal alcohol syndrome, rubella, or syphilis). Several variables determine the harm that a teratogenic agent will cause. The nature of the teratogen, the timing of the exposure, the dosage and duration of the exposure, maternal health status, and fetal susceptibility are the factors affecting how deleterious the effect of exposure to harmful substances will be (Robinson & Linden, 1993). Although knowledge in this area has dramatically increased, many disorders of infancy and early childhood remain unexplained.

Statistics suggest that 1 to 2 percent of infants born in the United States have a

TABLE 18.1
Conditions with a High Probability of Causing Developmental Delay

Chromosome disorders	Neurological disorders
Down's syndrome (trisomy 21)	Spina bifida/neural tube defects
Sex chromosome anomalies	Hydrocephalus
Fragile X syndrome	Epilepsy
Atypical development disorders	Metabolic disease
Autism	Wilson's disease
Failure to thrive	Maple syrup urine disease
Infantile schizophrenia	Sanfilippo syndrome
Fetal alcohol syndrome	Phenylketonuria (PKU)
Neuromotor muscle disorders	Orofacial disorders
Cerebral palsy	Cleft lip
Myasthenia gravis congenita	Cleft palate
Wilson's disease	Robin sequence
Hereditary progressive muscular dystrophy	Treacher Collins syndrome

congenital condition that includes impairment. Infants born with chromosomal anomalies, neurological disorders, metabolic disorders, chronic medical illness, or severe infectious disease have a high probability of manifesting developmental delays (Blackman, 1992). These delays may affect cognitive development, physical development, communication, social and emotional development, or adaptive development (P.L. 102-119, sec. 303). Clinical social workers will encounter children with these problems in hospital, rehabilitative, social service, and educational settings. The early identification of these children is an important key ensuring appropriate intervention. Table 18.1 lists some of the most commonly encountered physical and mental conditions that include a high probability for developmental delay. It is important to note however, that the actual delays are inconsistent and variable (Robinson & Linden, 1993).

Temperament

Temperament is also considered to be a biological contribution to early development. Stella Chess, Alexander Thomas, and Herbert Birch (1965) described nine biologically rooted personality aspects that are present at birth. They proposed that activity level, rhythmicity, approach or withdrawal, adaptability, threshold of responsiveness, quality of mood, intensity of reaction, distractibility, and attention span and persistence are innate qualities that characterize infant behavior in a steady way. This consistency is not absolute however, insofar as it operates within the context of relationships. Chess and her group suggested that temperamental differences interact with parental temperament and psychology and produce a specific response. Four broad categories based on the temperamental features were proposed: difficult babies, slow-to-warm-up babies, easy babies, and a group displaying a various mix of qualities. Babies who have problems in all areas are more likely to be considered "difficult," and it was theorized that troubled interactional patterns will emerge. Chess introduced the controversial concept of "poor fit" to describe the combination of children and parents where temperamental and psychological discordance result in difficult relationships (Chess et al., 1959, 1965).

Many current personality researchers use different dimensions of temperament. They suggest that temperament can be characterized by assessing avoidance of harm, reward dependence, persistence, and novelty seeking. Molecular personality research proposes that these four traits are genetically determined and cause a biological predisposition for the strength or tenacity of the characteristics. Recent work on the genetics of personality has demonstrated a genetic explanation for impulsive, novelty-seeking behavior (Cloninger, 1996). Some twin studies suggest the likelihood of a genetic basis for temperamental differences (Saudino, 1991; Bouchard & McGue, 1990; Rosen, 1987). Whereas most parents will describe their children as having intrinsic temperamental differences, the literature further suggests that a baby's temperament alone will not absolutely predict later personality or relationship style. Research continues to determine the degree of importance of temperamental differences, parental reactions, and mitigating factors such as gender, social support, socioeconomic status, prenatal attitudes, parenting style, parental self-esteem, marital satisfaction, and parental dysfunction (Tirosh et al., 1992; Oberklaid et al., 1993). Each of these factors should be evaluated by social workers when dealing with parents of young children. Parental impressions of temperament are strongly influenced by internal psychological forces (Zeanah et al., 1990; Sameroff et al., 1982; Vaughn et al., 1987).

Prematurity

Premature birth is another biological factor that influences development because it increases the risk of disability. Babies who are born prematurely (before the thirty-seventh week of pregnancy) and require neonatal intensive care are at increased risk for developmental delay or disability. Drugs, alcohol, and nicotine abuse, lack of prenatal care, and poor nutrition are the most common causes of prematurity. Not all prematurity is the result of maternal noncompliance or recklessness; medical complications also cause preterm births. The body of knowledge about the effects of prematurity has increased with the dramatic sophistication of life-saving medical technologies. Stated another way, medical technology has boosted the likelihood of survival for low-birth-weight babies and increased the number of children in this country whose infancy includes a stay in the local neonatal intensive care unit (NICU). These infants and their parents are widely studied in order to understand which factors increase vulnerability to developmental disturbances. (Main & Main, 1991; Rosenberg, 1991; Hayden & Beck, 1982; Als, 1986).

The sophistication of neonatal medical technology is directly responsible for the increased survival rate of physically fragile newborns. These same scientific advances, however, result in prolonged periods of incubation and separation from a consistent, caring adult. Klaus and Kennell's (1976) work drew attention to the influence that routine institutional early separation had on new mothers and babies and helped popularize the notion of bonding in the immediate postpartum period. Ongoing research has set aside a rigid circumscribed sensitive period for bonding to take place but has gone on to describe the contribution of prolonged incubation, noxious environmental overstimulation, and early separation from a consistent caregiver to the development of feeding problems, failure to thrive, and behavior problems (Goodfriend, 1993; Sroufe, 1983; Long & Lucey, 1980; Als, 1986).

The dynamic interaction between nature and nurture is a critical consideration for vulnerable infants. Very low-birth-weight and extremely low-birth-weight babies born to poor families are challenged to overcome greater obstacles than children born to middle-class families. The interaction of social class and complications at birth influences their prognosis for optimal cognitive, academic, and social functioning. The probability of a poor outcome is mediated by the number of risk factors and their combination, and the presence of protective factors (Sameroff & Chandler, 1975). Although we lack precise understanding of the synergism of this interaction, research has made gains in identifying the important elements (Rutter et al., 1979; Sameroff et al., 1987). Table 18.2 lists components that contribute to the ecology of risk. Early identification and attention to families manifesting these qualities cannot be overemphasized. Numerous studies have made a correlation between these same elements of risk and later problems such as child abuse and neglect and child mortality (Elmer & Gregg, 1967; Kempe, 1971; Klein & Stern, 1971).

Serious medical illness and prematurity are a common combination. Babies born prematurely and with a low birth weight (below 1,500 grams) frequently spend many months in the NICU, if they survive. Those who do survive face a greater chance for developmental problems, cognitive disorders, and chronic health concerns. These infants are not only smaller than full-term infants, they are different (Saigal et al., 1991; Klein, Hack & Breslau, 1989). Generally these babies tend to be less alert, less responsive, and difficult to rouse. In addition, they tend to cry differently, have less organization of their sleep and wake activity, and are more likely to be irritable (Field, 1983; Gardner et al., 1984). Given these differences, it is not surprising that many parents of premature children tend to behave differently with their babies when compared to parents of full-term infants. Many researchers have devoted their attention to the study of premature babies and the effect of preterm birth on parent-child interactions (Field, 1977; Frodi et al., 1978; Goldberg, 1978). The long-term effects of these differences seem to be determined by the emotional and environmental resources that compensate for the biological deficits of preterm babies (Plunkett et al., 1988; Goldberg, 1978; Frodi & Thompson, 1985).

Premature babies tend to be fussy. Parents express less satisfaction with these children, who tend to smile less, avert their gaze, and are harder to soothe when distressed. Studies document the absence of genuine affective zest in parent-infant face-to-face interactions. Many parents report feeling out of sync and disconnected from their preterm babies. Studies of their face-to-face interactions confirm what many parents intuitively report. The videotapes demonstrate parents' overcompensating for baby's unresponsiveness, dominating the interaction rather than adjusting

TABLE 18.2
Common Risk Factors

Parental Features	*Neonatal Features*	*Environmental Features*
Single-parent household/ absence of father	Low birth weight	Homelessness
No prenatal care	Respiratory distress	Poverty
Maternal age of less than 15 years	Asphyxia	Family size
Maternal phenylketonuria	Intracranial hemorrhage	Absence of social support
Maternal acquired immune deficiency syndrome	Seizures	Violence
Parental deafness or parental blindness	Evidence of central nervous system abnormality	
Maternal use of anticonvulsants, anti-neoplastics, or anticoagulants	Microcephaly or macrocephaly	
Parental substance abuse	Central nervous system infection	
Parental mental retardation	Suspected hearing impairment	
Parental mental illness	Suspected visual impairment	
Homelessness	Major congenital anomalies	
Lack of parenting education, negative attitudes	Severe chronic illness	
	Failure to thrive and anemia	

to baby's cues, and experiencing less enjoyment and synchrony in their exchanges (Crnic et al., 1983; Field, 1977; Goldberg, 1978).

Barnard et al. (1984) compared parents of full-term and preterm infants at intervals over the first two years of life. They observed that mothers of premature infants wore themselves out attempting to engage babies not capable of responding as expected. Sadly, by the time premature babies became more alert, mothers had adapted a less engaging demeanor. These babies were being understimulated by their caretakers as compared to the control group at the very time they could be most responsive to human interaction. By the time these babies were two years of age, the mothers were less stimulating and less responsive to the baby's interactional cues than mothers in the full-term group. Research continues to examine the long-term effects of these early interactions.

Maternal Substance Abuse

In 1990, at least 4.5 million women of childbearing age were using illegal drugs. Parental substance abuse is the leading known cause of mental retardation; the number of babies born impaired as a result of fetal alcohol syndrome exceeds those born with Down's syndrome or spina bifida. Babies who have fetal alcohol syndrome have skull and facial deformities, joint and limb malformations, and small head size, and they may display a failure to thrive. These children go on to experience various levels of life-long functional disturbance and learning disabilities (Smith, 1979; Van Dyke & Fox, 1990).

Another frequent drug of abuse during pregnancy is cocaine, which can be lethal to babies before their birth (Bingol et al., 1987; Gratacos et al., 1993). According to the Office of the Inspector General, at least 100,000 babies are prenatally exposed to crack each year in the United States. The literature has associated cocaine and crack use with low birth weight, smaller head circumference, fetal strokes, intrauterine growth retardation, central nervous system damage, congenital physical malformations, and intellectual and learning impairment (Bingol et al., 1987; Kantrowitz, 1990; Norris, 1991). Many studies describe these babies as being tremulous, irritable, and generally difficult to console. In addition, these babies manifest muscular rigidity, frantic fist sucking, a high-pitched cry, and disorganized rooting (Chanry et al., 1988). Because of the relative newness of the crack cocaine epidemic, there are few reports from longitudinal developmental studies of these babies. Anecdotal findings report evidence of increased developmental problems such as motor dysfunction, intellectual impairment, speech and language delays, hyperactivity, and emotional and behavioral problems (Schneider et al., 1989; Hawley et al., 1995). Some infant investigations conclude that with the passage of time, these children have no significant physical or neurobehavioral impediments (Mayes et al., 1992). It is difficult to isolate the specific effects of cocaine alone, however, because adverse outcomes are associated with many of the risk factors commonly associated with maternal substance abuse. Once again the ecology of risk (poor nutrition, no prenatal care, environmental deficiencies, limited financial and social support, and single parenthood) is speculated to potentiate the actual degree of developmental and physical disability (Hurt et al., 1995). The postnatal environment of vulnerable infants weighs in heavily in the equation of risk and resilience.

THE ENVIRONMENTAL BASE OF EARLY RISK AND RESILIENCE

Clinical social work education has always stressed rigorous evaluation of a person's interacting systems; the person-in-situation lens has both separated and defined social work's expertise. Infant mental health research supports the understanding of the influence of external factors on development and confirms the richness of the interplay between inner and outer developmental forces.

The American family has undergone dramatic changes in the late twentieth century. Complex social trends and political and economic forces have reconfigured the family constellation and redefined the family unit. According to the Carnegie Institute (1994), there are at least 12 million children under the age of three in the United States. Three million of these children, 25 percent of the total, live in poverty, with a single parent. In turn, these changes have modified the nature of family life. An ever-increasing number of children under the age of three spend long hours in out-of-home care because their mothers must work. Financial stability is increasingly elusive, and many families lack the safety net of social support. Surrounded by violence in turbulent cityscapes or suspended in rural isolation, the contemporary family feels endangered. The threat of a crisis is ever present for overburdened families living precariously on the edge. Poverty, exposure to violence, and trauma will be reviewed as primary elements of external influence.

Poverty

The most recent report from the National Center for Children in Poverty (1990) accounts the highest rate of poverty among children in over twenty-five years. Their impoverishment is characterized as "deep and intense" (Knitzer & Aber, 1995, p. 174) and as it worsens, so does the plight of 4 million children teetering in near poverty. Poverty cuts across both ethnic lines and landscapes; poor infants and children are everywhere, and they come in every color. The following clinical vignette is of a family suffering from some of the effects of poverty.

Victoria Salvez is a single twenty-nine-year-old Latina mother of three children, the youngest just eight weeks old. She has been meeting with a social worker since the second month of her last pregnancy because of numerous problems, including unstable housing and financial struggles and because of intense expressed ambivalence about continuing the pregnancy. Ms. Salvez reportedly scheduled several appointments to terminate the pregnancy because of her financial worries but ultimately kept the baby because she said she wanted the child. During her pregnancy, her sessions typically found her very tearful and afraid, with major themes focusing on her self-doubts about her efficacy as a mother. She was compliant with prenatal care and usually brought her other children along with her to the visits. She frequently commented that Damon, age nine, was a great help to her with his younger brother, Dominic, age three. The children were always observed to be neat and clean, and Damon was observed by staff to be helpful to his little brother. Dominic actively sought out his brother rather than his mother for assistance, a behavior Ms. Salvez made reference to during clinic visits.

Today, two and a half months postpartum, Ms. Salvez expresses relief that the discomfort of pregnancy has ended, but she notes very little enjoyment or joy with the new baby. Damon sits in a chair reading a school book and Dominic sits on the office floor playing with a beeper and stubbornly trying to make it clip to his pants. Baby Anthony snoozes in an infant carrier on the floor. Meanwhile, Ms. Salvez explains that she moved again last night. Her mother's boyfriend sold Damon's snow boots for crack, and so she packed her things and went to stay with her boyfriend. Dominic is busy and intent and seemingly unaware of his mother's conversation until her frustration and sadness break way to tears again. He comes to the desk, snatches tissue from the box, and climbs into his mother's lap to sop up her tears, cooing softly for his mama not to cry.

Ms. Salvez has an enormous number of questions about the baby's development. He has been a difficult feeder, arches his back and stiffens in her arms, and wails through the night. She worries about the seizures he had at birth. She has also been very worried about Baby Anthony's hearing and vision; she seems to think that he may also be more responsive to Damon, but is not convinced that there is not an underlying physical problem.

The social worker is concerned for this family on many levels. The relationship disturbances already amiss with Ms. Salvez's older children point to the need of interactional guidance for intervention. This family's well-being is compromised even more by the stress of a baby with a possible developmental disorder and limited cultural and environmental support. The service plan that resulted for the Salvez family included in-home public health nurse intervention for feeding problems; language-appropriate, bicultural informational materials about child development and the medical aspects of disability; social service intervention and financial education for stabilization of economic and housing tensions; and group support with parents who speak the same language and share cultural traditions, child-rearing patterns, and values. Equally important, Ms. Salvez agrees to the need for interactional guidance, which will address the structure and the style of her interactions with each of her children.

Poverty stacks the deck against infants, multiplies the risks they face, and influences every aspect of their lives. *Undernourishment during pregnancy* increases the chances of low birth weight, infant death, spina bifida, and other birth defects (Gortmaker, 1979; CDC, 1992). *Poor nutrition during infancy* negatively influences normal growth and affects cognitive development, motor coordination, and long-term IQ scores (Pollitt, 1988). *Homelessness* is associated with increased infant mortality, increased exposure to communicable diseases, asthma, delayed immunizations, and family separations (Mihaly, 1991; Wood, 1990). *Substandard housing* is frequently crowded, unsafe, and dangerous due to the increased incidence of lead toxicity. *Inferior child care* is characterized by understimulation and insensitive, restrictive interactions. *Parental distress* is associated with substance abuse, harsh and inconsistent discipline, physical punishment, and development and behavior problems (McLoyd, 1990). *Increased family stress* leads to greater family conflict and depression and increases the chance for maltreatment. *Disrupted relationships* are twice as likely in financially burdened marriages (U.S. Census Bureau, 1992). *Lack of routine medical care* is linked to inadequate prenatal care, lower-quality care, lack of immunizations, or unnecessary repetitive immunizations due to discontinuous care (U.S. General Accounting Office, 1987). *Disability* is more likely to have lifelong effects. The National Health Interview Survey demonstrated that conditions which impair normal daily functioning increase as family income decreases (Ries, 1990). Poor families are far less likely to have access to early childhood special services (Hawkins & Rosenbaum, 1992). *Exposure to violence* is increased in the highest-poverty neighborhoods (NRCP, 1993). *Teenage pregnancy* is far more likely to occur among the poor. As family income increases, the number of teens who become teenage mothers decreases (Children's Defense Fund, 1995).

In summary, poverty is cruel to children and devastating to families, and it presents an overwhelming array of problems for clinical social workers to negotiate. The effects of long-term poverty are so severe and insidious that every resource available must be used to shorten the amount of exposure that infants and young children endure. According to the Children's Defense Fund, every year that a child lives in poverty reduces by two percentage points the likelihood of completing school by nineteen years of age.

Exposure to Violence and Trauma

Unfortunately for many children, growing up involves pernicious versions of trauma that include rape, physical abuse, painful separations, kidnapping, and exposure to brutal violence. In the past, the word *trauma* was a medical term that applied to any serious body injuries. Contemporary life and clinical practice applies the same term to include emotional and psychological injuries. Despite long-standing interest in the study of trauma, it was only in the late 1960s that American legislation mandated child abuse reporting laws, and not until 1974 was the definition of child abuse officially changed to include neglect and emotional damage. The psychiatric community revised its diagnostic manual only in 1987 to recognize children who suffer disturbances following traumatic events (APA, 1987).

Violence is a common occurrence in inner-city neighborhoods across the country. So extreme and pervasive is the carnage that children are frequent victims of violence, and they are "covictimized" by viewing the savagery (Shakoor & Chalmer, 1991). Many children suffer severe symptoms as a result of living in an environment where the threat of danger is ever present. Chronic fear and emotional trauma are frequent consequences for the very young growing up in what Garbarino and his associates have descriptively named "urban war zones" (Garbarino et al., 1992, p. 3). The National Institute of Mental Health's Community Violence Project makes clear that a new public health problem has emerged: children witnessing violence. When community violence is balanced with a considerable level of violence in the home, the NIMH report suggests an extraordinary disadvantage for normal development in children (Richters & Martinez, 1993).

Lenore Terr (1991) defines childhood traumas as "the mental result of one sudden, external blow or a series of blows rendering the young person temporarily helpless and breaking past ordinary coping and defensive operations" (p. 11). Terr maintains that external traumatic events cause internal mental changes, possibly even biological changes, to take place inside the child. The experience of being extremely frightened will leave a psychic wound that will last for years if it is left untreated (Terr, 1991).

Despite even routine exposure to trauma, young children do not build up a resistance to its effects. In fact, increased exposure seems to result in increased vulnerability (Pynoos & Nader, 1988). The transactional effect of repeated exposure and interacting risk factors increases the negative outcomes for young children and has an additive effect (Garbarino, 1992). It is thought that repeated traumas can result in major personality changes (Terr, 1989). It is not surprising, then, that the symptoms of children in violent urban settings are similar to those experienced by children during war. Children have been described as experiencing intrusive thoughts, anxiety, decreased concentration, depression, fear of recurrence, and sleep disturbances. Even infants and toddlers under the age of three have shown symptoms of posttraumatic stress disorder, including disrupted patterns of eating, sleeping difficulties, and difficulty relating (Udwin, 1993). Terr concurs based on her experience with traumatized children, but she proposes four characteristics that are especially important because they endure and seem to affect all victims: reseeing or refeeling the event or elements of the experience, playful reenactments or trauma-related repetitive behaviors, trauma-related specific fears, and depressed and pessimistic attitudes about people, life, and the future (Terr, 1991).

Many of the symptomatic features of traumatized children can resemble the presentation of different disorders; there are many diagnostic categories with similar key features. The presence of a constellation of characteristics alone should not determine diagnosis. Because of this, it is of critical importance that clinicians gather information in a manner that permits relevant data to emerge. The prevalence of violence warrants that every psychosocial assessment include an evaluation of the degree of danger and fear in the lives of children and their parents. Questions about traumatic events, the age of first exposure, the amount of exposure to violence, the number of significant losses, play habits and restrictions, and any fear-ridden experiences are important components in an evaluation. Many children are instructed to hide in bathtubs at the sound of loud noises and are accustomed to riding in cars lying down on the floor of the back seat to avoid stray bullets. Clinical treatment must include the opportunity to express fears, worries, and superstitions. Asking young children about the presence of "good luck charms" can be particularly revealing and a segue to meaningful information.

Clinicians and investigators familiar with young children who grow up in violent environments report that given the opportunity, even very young and preschool children can verbally describe their traumatic experiences (Martini et al., 1990). This is surprising to many and an important consideration when placed alongside findings that teachers and parents of traumatized children consistently underestimate and under-report both the degree of exposure to violence and the amount of distress associated with children's victimization and covictimization (McFarlane, 1987; Belter et al., 1991; Yule, 1990). Although there may be many explanations for this phenomenon, the concern cuts deeply to relationship issues and the glaring fact that violence does not occur in a vacuum. Contemporary violence involves children's relationships with significant others. Sometimes these are other children and adults who share the youngster's lot as victim, and sometimes these are trusted figures who are the perpetrators of the violence.

Physical and Sexual Abuse

Although it is impossible to separate out relationship and attachment themes when examining the physical and sexual abuse of children, these subjects will be initially reviewed here as instances of external trauma and violence against children. According to the Children's Defense Fund, there were more than 1 million cases of confirmed child abuse and neglect in 1993, the most recent year for which data are available. Every day three children die as a result of child-abuse-related assault (CDF, 1995). Child abuse occurs more often among the poor, but it is not limited to any socioeconomic group (Pelton, 1978). Infants and children under the age of three are more likely to be targets of abuse. There is also significant statistical evidence that low-birth-weight infants, premature babies, and children with developmental disabilities or attention-deficit/hyperactivity disorder have a greater chance of being maltreated (Klein & Stern, 1971; Parke, 1977; Zigler, 1980).

Studies of the long-term consequences of child abuse are inconclusive. Many writers associate physical abuse with later emotional problems, subsequent substance abuse, violent behavior, and spousal abuse. One widely held belief is that of the "intergenerational transmission of child abuse," asserting that abusing parents were themselves abused as children and that violence against children begets violence against the next generation of children. Zigler and Hall's extensive review of the literature (1993) strongly disputes this popular conviction. Although it is true that some abused children become abusive parents, these authors cite that this is true for only one in every three cases.

Infant studies of the short-term consequences do report significant differences in both the social and cognitive development of abused infants by their first birthday. Observational studies of toddlers and preschool children describe abused children as being more aggressive to peers and their caretakers, less socially skilled than peers, and prone to avoidant behavior (George & Main, 1979). Furthermore, these children are characterized as responding to distressed peers with aggression rather than empathy or concern. It is speculated that their reactions mimic the response that they have experienced from their abusive parents. There is general agreement that maltreatment has a profound effect on children's feelings of worthiness and results in emotional and/or behavioral dysfunction (Egeland et al., 1983).

There is a positive correlation between physical abuse and sexual abuse, although sexual abuse is more often undisclosed (Junewicz, 1983; Kempe & Kempe, 1978). Finkelhor (1994) studied adult retrospective surveys of child sexual abuse and found figures suggesting that at least 20 percent of American women and 5 to 10 percent of American men experienced abuse as children. There is no societal reason to doubt that these statistics might represent contemporary America.

Survey research of children who have been sexually abused reports family characteristics that are significantly predictive: the absence of a biological parent in the household, unavailability of the mother, marital conflict and violence, and the presence of a stepfather in the household (Finkelhor, 1994). An important consideration that all researchers note, however, is the prerequisite presence and pathology of the individual perpetrating sexual abuse.

Sameroff and Chandler's transactional model (1975) for understanding child development is recommended as a framework for examining the maltreatment of infants and children. Cicchetti (1993) suggests this paradigm in order to appraise judiciously the dynamic interrelationships and interactions between the child, the parent, and the environmental forces that may culminate in cruelty or abuse. This perspective avoids oversimplified and one-dimensional explanations for maltreatment and averts interventions that focus only on a "bad" parent, or a "difficult" child, or a "stressful" environment. The treatment literature confirms that in order to succeed, interventions must address every key component owing to the dynamic transactions among each level.

Resilience

The issue of resilience is an important consideration in any discussion about the long-term effects of exposure to stressors such as poverty and abuse. Although there are fewer studies examining children's ability to persevere despite overwhelming odds, writers have scrutinized these situations. Werner (1989) considered children who had been exposed to poverty, perinatal stress, parental disturbances, and disordered family units. Despite serious impediments, one-third of the sample became competent and caring adults. This result has been described by other investigators who studied children in a variety of situations, including children evacuated during World War II, Lebanese children during the 1982 war in Beirut, Kuwaiti children following the Iraqi invasion, and children living in violent urban settings. These studies tend to divide protective factors that increase the likelihood of resilience into two categories: internal and external variables. Internal, individual features include age and developmental level, temperamental traits, cognitive skills, and positive self-esteem (Werner, 1990; Lösel & Bliesener, 1990). External, environmental characteristics that seem to protect children include family stability, a constructive and affirming relationship with a parent or other significant person, a social network of supportive relationships, and parents who model respectful relationships and coping skills (Werner & Smith, 1982; Lösel & Bliesener, 1990). Parental resilience is a very important factor influencing the development of resiliency in children (Anthony & Cohler, 1987). Parents who are coping well are likely to contribute structure, order, and predictability and create physical and psychological safety within the home.

The application of these findings to clinical practice guides clinical social work interventions. Because it is the interplay of internal and external factors rather than their mere presence or absence that leads to successful or unsuccessful adaptations, it is important to evaluate the unique characteristics of each child and family constellation carefully. The study of protective factors also underscores the importance of not omitting assessment of strengths and repeating the common mistake of focusing on the evaluation of weaknesses and deficits alone.

THE RELATIONSHIP BASE OF EARLY RISK AND RESILIENCE

No one ever accurately anticipates the mantle of parenthood. Because new life and human development begin within the context of parenthood, it is important to understand issues influencing a child's parents. Parental role adjustment, attachment, loss and depression, and adolescent pregnancy will be reviewed because of their significant impact on the relationship base of early development.

Parental Adjustment

Current practice standards warrant that clinical work with any infant or young child include a sensitive understanding of the child's parents and their relationship. This assessment can serve as a beginning intervention and as a way of gathering cogent information. Research suggests that attitudes about the baby-on-the-way and parental psychology during pregnancy influence the relationship that will unfold. Even when these data are collected retrospectively, social workers can gain insight to the inner lives of parents.

All pregnancies represent a turning point that requires internal adjustments on the part of the parents for the optimal development of the child. The power of pregnancy to change a woman's body is but a metaphor for the psychological and emotional adaptations that must occur for both parents to accommodate the transition in self-identity to include parent. These transitions are usually more dramatic during first pregnancies. Because of the dramatic and unfamiliar physical changes, we tend to see the signs of these internal transitions sooner in women than in men. The literature supports the idea that acceptance of pregnancy is the first main challenge. Mothers and fathers begin trying on their impending roles and responsibilities by fantasizing about themselves as parents. These images are influenced by memories of their own childhood, the culture they live in, and current life circumstances (Galinsky, 1987). Most expectant parents are familiar with the personal inventory that transpires when they swear to "never sound like my mother." And because of the power of personal history, most parents are familiar with the seemingly universal discovery that influences from the past tend to revisit the present.

The bond with the baby that begins to develop in utero represents a powerful connection. Brazelton calls this the "prehistory of attachment" (Brazelton & Cramer, 1989, p. 5). Once the baby is born, innate temperament, physical appearance, gender, and the presence of physical problems all combine with parental factors to begin a real, rather than imagined, relationship. Hence, the baby born is never the baby who was expected during the pregnancy. No matter how deeply loved and anticipated, every newborn is not the one envisioned. The interactions that transpire when these expectations clash with the real baby are the subject of intense psychological scrutiny. Zeanah et al. (1990) reported anxious pregnant parents ascribing adverse temperamental qualities to their fetus. Helping parents understand the forces that shape their expectations can assist them in perceiving their child more realistically.

Whether beginning work during pregnancy or after the baby is born, assessment should include an inquiry about prenatal attitudes and feelings. The following questions, which only begin to hint at the deeper level of relatedness, can begin this dialogue and elicit information about the emotional forces that propel parental expectations and shape the beginning relationship with the baby:

- What was your reaction when you found out you were pregnant?
- Was this a planned pregnancy or an accident? Were you seeking to become pregnant?
- How long had you been trying to conceive?
- What was your partner's reaction?
- Does a baby fit your lifestyle?
- Can you tell me about your daydreams during pregnancy?
- Tell me about any plans you made for the baby ahead of time.
- Did you have a nickname for the baby? When did you select the real name?
- What is the significance?

A clinical vignette is presented.

Lisa May was referred for evaluation after being found by a nurse crying in a storage room in the NICU. Mrs. May had delivered her first child, Nancy, six days ago at thirty-two weeks gestational age. Nancy weighed 3 pounds 2 ounces at birth and was born with immature lungs. She required ventilation and intravenous feeding.

Mrs. May is a thirty-one-year-old married woman who worked as an accountant until her unexpected delivery. She and her husband of five years were thrilled about being pregnant and looked forward to becoming parents. She described what she felt to be was a "charmed" married life that had been "ideal" thus far and included a "perfectly" timed pregnancy. During this first contact, Mrs. May was frequently tearful and sat slumped in her chair. Her mood and manner seemed tired, depressed, and overwrought. She spoke candidly about herself, wept openly and without apology, and suggested that mere talking was exhausting at the present time.

When asked about her distress and the episode in the storage room, Mrs. May acknowledged bewilderment. She stated that after the initial shock and surprise of an early delivery, she and her husband had been able to discuss their worries for Nancy, but they did not really believe that the baby would die. Their extended family was also optimistic and supportively helpful to the couple. She reported that the first few days after discharge, she had come to the NICU daily and volunteered that she had impressed the nursing staff with her composure and comfort around the medical machinery. This information was confirmed by the medical staff, who noted how at ease Mrs. May had been in the austere setting, how positive in attitude, and how well she seemed to deal with a situation most parents find initially intimidating. Within a few days, however, Mrs. May began to notice herself becoming more irritable and tearful. Her visits with Nancy became briefer, and she found herself crying for no apparent reason. Mrs. May's previous optimism was replaced with avoidance of Nancy and depression.

As time passed, Nancy improved in the NICU. She gradually showed a steady weight gain until a plateau, which corresponded with her mother's abrupt absence from the NICU because of her depression. Although Mrs. May had recouped her physical strength and was returning to routine activities, her outward image had changed from a meticulously well-groomed and cosmetically adorned woman to a clean but noticeably undecorated, stark appearance. Biweekly sessions focused on her feelings of loss despite Nancy's survival and her disappointment with herself and her daughter. Mrs. May's concerns for the baby were strangely unrealistic and inconsistent with the medical facts of Nancy's condition. With time and exploration, the recurring themes of imperfection and disappointment became prominent, and Mrs. May's anger was a frequent emotion. She described her family and her parents as becoming increasingly less tolerant of her anger toward Nancy. Resentment toward her parents, a feeling Mrs. May was intensely uncomfortable with, began to emerge.

It was the unveiling of resentment that began the uncovering process for Mrs. May. Sessions revealed that Mrs. May was born and raised in a suburban setting to parents who enjoyed an upper-middle-class status and an upwardly mobile mind-set for their daughters. Mrs. May was the second of two siblings, and her sister was six years her senior. Mrs. May was initially uncharacteristically vague about her sister, but with time began to disclose her secrets. Despite her parent's best efforts, her older sister developed from an overly outgoing and rambunctious tomboy as a girl to an out-of-control and belligerent juvenile delinquent. Her fast living was eventually curtailed by tragedy. When Mrs. May was fifteen years old, her sister was the victim of a boating accident that sev-

ered the lower trunk of her body and left her paralyzed, in a wheelchair, and a caustic ever-present resident of the family home.

The pace of treatment accelerated with the realization that for Mrs. May, Nancy represented her sister. Her tiny daughter had come to embody her bitter, angry, manipulative, technology-dependent sister. Mrs. May described her own adolescent burden of trying to help her parents by attending first to her sister's complicated medical care and then by trying to protect them from any other disappointments by being perfect and dutiful. Within a trusting relationship, Mrs. May was able to identify how she continued to feel these obligations to her parents and begin to adjust to the current situation. Preventive intervention for Nancy's relationship with her mother was accompanied by relief and intrapsychic changes for her mother.

Although continued sessions with Mrs. May were necessary to deal with her own adolescent developmental issues, little intervention was needed to facilitate a positive relationship with Nancy. Because her personal development had been nurturing and relatively stable until her sister's shocking dismemberment, Mrs. May brought sensitivity and insight to the clinical work. She had the internal resources to accommodate herself to the misrepresentations she had imposed on her daughter and was available to attune her sensitivities to the baby's needs. Mrs. May's enjoyment with falling in love with Nancy was a marvelous respite. Infant-parent psychotherapy techniques were highly useful for work with Mrs. May in the exploratory work that assisted in the identification of her powerful transference to her daughter.

Attachment

There has been an enormous amount of study into the variable quality of relationships and the forces that compel human beings to affiliate with other human beings in a particular way. Although Freud was probably the first to position a child's mother as the first object of attachment, this theory was replaced by an ethological view. John Bowlby's and Mary Ainsworth's work (Ainsworth & Bowlby, 1991) on attachment theory has redirected and dominated psychological research on the development of social relations. Bowlby (1940) began his work with a keen interest in family relationships and their impact on children. His early work with maladjusted children at the London Child Guidance Clinic linked child symptomatology to maternal deprivation and separation (Bretherton, 1992). Later, his interest in loss and his research into the effect of separation from mother during early childhood challenged the conventional wisdom on the emotional needs of young children (Robertson & Bowlby, 1952). Over time Bowlby concluded that mental health was contingent on a child's experience with a "warm, intimate, and continuous relationship with his mother (or permanent mother substitute) in which both find satisfaction and enjoyment" (Bowlby, 1951, p. 13).

Bowlby equated the need to build strong emotional bonds to others with the other basic instincts. He contended that humans are biologically prewired and programmed for relationships for self-preservation (1958). Infants cry in order to get their needs met. Caregivers respond because of a wired-in desire to stop the crying and to meet the baby's needs. Babies smile and crawl to communicate and interact with their caregivers. Caregivers seem innately predisposed to finding baby's physical characteristics appealing (Alley, 1983). According to Bowlby, all of these are examples of attachment behaviors that result in the establishment of a reciprocal and preferred relationship to a specific caregiver. Attachment is defined as an affectional connection with "some other differentiated and preferred individual who is usually conceived as stronger and/or wiser" (Bowlby, 1977, p. 201).

Normal development proceeds within the context of early preferred relationships. Most infants form specific attachments between the ages of six and eight months, and typically with mother first. "Secure base behavior" refers to the individual balance between being very close to mother and moving away in order to explore the world and returning again for reassurance (Ainsworth et al., 1978). While the early initial interactions between mother and infant establish the affective relationship, the young child's interest in mastery of physical skills and the environment also evolves as maturation and motility progress. Relationships with others in the family network are a strong influence on young children. The entire relationship system that the child internally experiences—security and anxiety, predictability and chaos, and the balance between overstimulation, understimulation, and harmony—ultimately results in the formation of an "internal working model" (Main & Goldwyn, 1984). Despite elasticity, these models also show relative continuity in terms of the baby's core internal representations of self, self-worth, expectations of others, and relationships. The internal model serves as a kind of template for the evolving context of future relationships and interaction styles (Main et al., 1985; Sroufe, 1979).

All attachment relationships that develop are not alike. Mothers who are responsive and affectionate to their baby's needs and alert to the baby's pace during feeding, playing, explorations, and reunions are considered to be sensitive. Ainsworth's evaluation of the range of maternal sensitivity to children led to work describing three different types of infant attachment patterns (Ainsworth, 1963, 1967). Ainsworth's controversial laboratory experiment known as the Strange Situation studied infants' behavior in response to a series of separations and reunions with a stranger and a parent and resulted in a classification system for rating infant attachment (Ainsworth & Wittig, 1969).

The infant and the resultant mother-baby interactional template is highly influenced by maternal internal working models. Zeanah and Anders (1987) suggest that parents have internal working models of their child even before the infant's birth. Other research documents that mothers frequently overestimate the degree of intent and volition on the part of the baby (Fraiberg, 1980; Hinde, 1976; Cramer, 1987). Intent is attributed by mothers onto their children and powerfully shapes their perception of the relationship. These impressions in turn regulate whether a baby is regarded as good, bad, loving, rejecting, headstrong, or lazy. The interactional mirroring back of these perceptions shapes the growing child's internal representations of self and others.

Many of the theoretical concepts used by attachment theorists continue to be investigated. A large body of literature examines the relative continuity of internal working models and their assessment. Studies with expectant mothers have predicted the result of baby's Strange Situation performance on the basis of the mothers' recollections of nurturance in their own childhood (Fonagy et al., 1991). Sroufe et al. have shown that certain aspects of toddler behavior can be predicted from the quality of the baby's attachment during infancy. Research continues and includes important longitudinal studies that will greatly increase knowledge of early development and the longevity of early experience.

The social learning theorists explain attachment differently. They rely on the principles of operant conditioning to explain the interaction between infant and primary caregiver. In their view, a mutually reciprocal interaction develops that produces an attachment between the infant and the mother or other primary caregiver. Despite these differences in theoretical principles, both schools of thought reach agreement on the similar conclusion. Early interactions between infant and primary caretaker comprising mutual stimulation, response, and reciprocal reinforcement result in a relationship of critical importance to normal child development.

Loss and Depression

Attachment themes are extremely important in clinical work that deals with situations of loss. Every year, over half a million women lose a baby. Ironically, the reaction to a loss of a baby is not always correlated to the strength of the desire to be pregnant, and contrary to popular belief, most parents do not find these losses trivial. Ectopic pregnancy, miscarriage, stillbirth, and neonatal death all represent the death of a child and the end to the dreams and fantasies developed during pregnancy. Many parents grieve the loss of an entire lifetime with that child. Research confirms that the loss of the relationship to the deceased baby causes real grief and requires mourning (Leon, 1990; Lietar, 1986). Because of the social pressures exerted on parents to minimize and forget their loss, bereaved mothers and fathers are swiftly encouraged to try again, and many do seek to replace the deceased child quickly. But although they may succeed and have a subsequent pregnancy, many new parents experience a cruel surprise when they find they are still bereaved. Mourning does not magically dissipate because another child has been born. Many clinicians believe that maternal bereavement and depression affect the development of infants and young children.

Whether attributed to loss, life circumstances, or personality adjustment, depression during pregnancy is not unusual and frequently disables mothers. Studies confirm what clinical practice suggests: maternal depression not only affects a mother's relationship with her child but can contribute to the development of other constitutional vulnerabilities. Research has shown maternal depression to be significantly associated with behavior problems in preschool children (Gross et al., 1995). Although both mother and infant contribute to the evolution of an interactional pattern, mothers are far more responsive to intervention. This is especially important when the research literature continues to demonstrate that not only is maternal mood associated with problematic behavior but increasingly likely to reinforce negative behavior patterns in children. Researchers report a vicious cycle of depressive and negative maternal self-assessment, which reinforces negative feelings of attachment in infants

(Milgrom, 1994). These considerations are meaningful not only to mothers who are familiar with depression and whose social networks preclude optimal functioning. They are also relevant to others for whom depression is an unfamiliar experience until unbidden and surprising postpartum depression interrupts normative patterns of mother-infant interactions.

Any kind of depression interferes with the maternal characteristics necessary for optimal mother-infant interactions. Babies need physical stimulation, sensitivity, eye contact, affective engagement, reciprocity, a balance between quiet and stimulation, appropriate responses, and adjustment to their own level of sensitivity. Maternal depression as well as other disorders such as anxiety disorders, obsessive-compulsive disorder, and substance abuse interfere with the likelihood that these qualities will be present. Tronick's work (1989) has exquisitely demonstrated infants' distressed reactions to mothers who are not emotionally available because of problems such as depression.

Adolescent Pregnancy

The developmental, psychological, and social problems involved with teenage pregnancy are well documented. Data released in 1993 for 1991 showed that the birthrate for teenagers rose for the fifth year in a row. The contextual factors associated with premature parenthood frequently make it impossible to prepare adequately for a new baby. Poverty, low socioeconomic status, lack of education, the absence of social support, and interpersonal instability are the grim reality for most teen mothers in the United States, where the birthrate for teens is higher than in most other developed countries (Jones et al., 1985). It is no surprise that the majority of these pregnancies are unplanned and that most teenaged mothers are single (Forrest, 1994).

Young women challenged by a multitude of personal and social problems are often unable to recognize the importance of prenatal care. These same women have the highest rate of prenatal care noncompliance. They are the most likely not to keep recommended appointments or follow through with physician's instructions. As a result their babies are at a higher risk for premature birth, low birth weight, birth defects, and death. Another subpopulation, infants born to adolescents in foster care, is especially vulnerable. These teen mothers have already experienced abuse or neglect, which forced their own out-of-home placement.

A clinical vignette follows.

Brenda is a seventeen-year-old high school student expecting her first child in a few weeks. She was referred for social work evaluation during her eighth month of pregnancy because of chronic complaints about headaches, which her physician believes to be stress related. When asked about her troubles, she thoughtfully and deliberately replies, "My problem is that my mother had me when she was fourteen years old." Alternately sounding like an experienced adult and like the teenager she is, she recounts her struggle to get ahead. Despite her goals and ambitions, Brenda's hunger for the attention and affection her own mother could never seem to give her is a recurring theme.

Brenda describes herself as "bumping around" from family member to family mem-

ber trying to avoid foster placement with a stranger. Most recently the teenager has been living with her grandmother, whose rules she intensely resents. At odds with her elder, out of touch with her boyfriend, Brenda's only wish is for a place of her own, alone with her baby. For the time being, she resolutely believes that having her own place will fix everything. "Just once," she says, "just once, I wish I came first in someone's life."

Her pregnancy has been uneventful, and Brenda has continued to attend school and to perform adequately. Her unremitting wish for independence is a frequent subject of our discussions. She is eager for the baby to be born, not only because she expects the infant to gratify her craving for love but also because the social service system will grant her adult status following delivery. Her fantasy includes a prompt relocation to her own apartment where she and her baby can be alone together. This illusion, despite all of its sad adjustments, provides her the motivation to keep up with prenatal visits and maintain her education. She sees very little past holding her warm newborn in her arms and sidesteps any discussion of the colder realities of single parenthood and child care. In her mind, beneath a thin veneer of adolescent bravado and false maturity, the baby will finally be someone who cares for her.

Initial work with Brenda focused on establishing a relationship that could be sustained after the baby's birth. Environmental concerns were of profound importance: if the teen moved into her own apartment and fulfilled her independent strivings, the risks of solitary single parenting would likely be overwhelming and potentially dangerous to the baby. Before delivery, every effort was made to engage her cooperation to strengthen and extend the network of support available to her. Conjoint sessions with her grandmother, a willing child care provider, were initiated in order to address the conflicts at home. The teen also began to attend group meetings with other teen mothers where mutual trials and tribulations could be discussed.

On an internal level, sessions focused on Brenda's resistance to letting people help her. There were numerous examples in her past of well-meaning teachers and neighbors who were attracted to Brenda's bright and determined disposition. Brenda's position was stubborn: if her mother did not want to help her, why should anyone else bother? This work would take a protracted series of sessions dealing with Brenda's ambivalent attachment to her mother. Furthermore, this work would directly affect Brenda's ability to develop a realistic view of her baby. Treatment needed to prevent Brenda's internal pressures from blinding her to the needs and cues of her baby. The social worker understood that without intervention, no baby could ever live up to Brenda's expectations.

There are many different kinds of intervention programs for teen mothers. Significantly, almost all demonstrate that intervention has a generally positive outcome for adolescent girls and their babies. Studies demonstrate increased positive medical outcomes, increased educational outcomes for mothers, and improvement for the development outcomes for their babies.

SUMMARY

It is fitting to offer one last consideration pertaining to clinical work with infants and their families. Although the subject of resilience has already been examined as a function of protective factors, there is another dimension of strength that warrants final attention. The philosophy of early intervention recognizes the vitality and might of human potential. It rests on an unyielding belief in the ability to intercede in young lives and create new possibilities. The philosophy of early intervention is guided by the knowledge of experience and research. We have joined parents in their determination to overcome tremendous obstacles. We know that early relationships are malleable and that new life can inspire new beginnings. Recent community efforts have challenged public leaders and government to regain their humanity and to put children first. Clinical social workers understand from experience that an ounce of prevention truly can result in a pound of cure in the lives of our youngest children.

REFERENCES

Ainsworth, M. D. S. (1963). The development of infant-mother interaction among the Ganda. In B. M. Foss (Ed.), *Determinants of infant behavior* (pp. 67–104). New York: Wiley.

Ainsworth, M. D. S. (1967). *Infancy in Uganda: Infant care and the growth of love.* Baltimore: Johns Hopkins University Press.

Ainsworth, M. D. S. (1982). Attachment: Retrospect and prospect. In C. M. Parkes & J. Stevenson-Hinde (Eds.), *The place of attachment in human behavior* (pp. 3–30). New York: Basic Books.

Ainsworth, M. D. S., Blehar, M. C., Waters, E., & Wall, S. (1978). *Patterns of attachment: A psychological study of the strange situation.* Hillsdale, NJ: Erlbaum.

Ainsworth, M. D. S., & Bowlby, J. (1991). An ethological approach to personality development. *American Psychologist, 46,* 331–341.

Ainsworth, M. D. S., & Wittg, B. A. (1969). Attachment and the exploratory behaviour of one-year-olds in a strange situation. In B. M. Foss (Ed.), *Determinants of infant behavior* (Vol. 4, pp. 113–136). London: Methuen.

Alley, T. R. (1983). Growth-produced changes in body shape and size as determinants of perceived age and adult caregiving. *Child Development, 54,* 241–248.

Als, H. (1986). A synactive model of neonatal behavioral organization: Framework for the assessment of neurobehavioral development in the premature infant and for support of infants and parents in the neonatal intensive care environment. *Physical and Occupation Therapy in Pediatrics, 6,* 3–55.

American Psychiatric Association. (1987). *Diagnostic and statistical manual of mental disorders* (3rd ed., rev.) Washington, DC: Author.

Anthony, E., & Cohler, B. (Eds.). (1987). *The invulnerable child.* New York: Guilford.

Barnard, K. E., Bee, H. L., & Hammond, M. A., (1984). Developmental changes in maternal interactions with term and preterm infants. *Infant Behavior and Development, 7,* 101–113.

Belter, R. W., Dunn, S. E. E., & Jeney, P. (1991). The psychological impact of Hurricane Hugo on children: A needs assessment. *Advances in Behavior Research and Therapy, 133,* 155–161.

Bingol, N., Fuchs, M., Diaz, V., Stone, R. X., & Gromisch, D. S. (1987). Teratogenicity of cocaine in humans. *Journal of Pediatrics, 100,* 93–96.

Blackman, J. (1992). *Warning signals: Basic criteria for tracking at-risk infants and toddlers.* Arlington VA: Zero to Three/National Center for Clinical Infant Programs.

Bouchard, T. J., & McGue, M. (1990). Genetic and rearing environmental influences on adult personality: An analysis of adopted twins reared apart. *Journal of Personality, 58* (1), 263–292.

Bowlby, J. (1940). The influence of the early environment in the development of neurosis and neurotic character. *International Journal of Psycho-Analysis, 21*, 1–25.

Bowlby, J. (1951). *Maternal care and mental health.* World Health Organization Monograph, Serial No. 2, p. 13.

Bowlby, J. (1958). The nature of the child's tie to his mother. *International Journal of Psycho-Analysis, 49*, 1–23.

Bowlby, J. (1977). The making and breaking of affectional bonds: II. Some principles of psychotherapy. *British Journal of Psychiatry, 130*, 201–210.

Brazelton, T. B., & Cramer, B. (1989). *The earliest relationship.* Reading, MA: Addison-Wesley.

Bretherton, I. (1992). The origins of attachment theory: John Bowlby and Mary Ainsworth. *Developmental Psychology, 28* (5), 759–775.

Carnegie Corporation of New York. (1994). *Starting points: Meeting the needs of our youngest children.* New York: Carnegie Corporation of New York.

Chanry, N. E., Franke, J., & Wadlington, W. B. (1988). Cocaine convulsions in a breast-feeding baby. *Journal of Pediatrics, 112*, 134–135.

Chess, S., Thomas, A., & Birch, J. (1959). Characteristics of the individual child's behavioral responses to the environment. *American Journal of Orthopsychiatry, 29*, 791–802.

Chess, S., Thomas, A., & Birch, H. G. (1965). *Your child is a person.* New York: Viking Press.

Children's Defense Fund. (1992). *Helping children by strengthening families.* Washington, DC: Author.

Children's Defense Fund. (1995). *The state of America's children 1995.* Washington, DC: Author.

Cicchetti, D. (1993). Perspectives from developmental psychopathology. In D. Cicchetti and V. Carlson (Eds.), *Child maltreatment* (pp. 377–431). New York: Cambridge University Press.

Cloninger, R. (1996, January 2). Variant gene is connected to a love of the search for new thrills. *New York Times*, pp. A1, B9.

Cramer, B. (1987). Objective and subjective aspects of parent-infant relations: An attempt at correlation between infant studies and clinical work. In J. Osofsky (Ed.), *Handbook of infant development* (2nd ed.). New York: John Wiley.

Crnic, K. A., Ragozin, A. S., Greenberg, M. T., Robinson, N. M., & Basham, R. B. (1983). Social interaction and developmental competence of preterm and full-term infants during the first year of life. *Child Development, 54*, 1199–1210.

Egeland, B., Sroufe, L. A., & Erickson, M. (1983) The developmental consequence of different patterns of maltreatment. *Child Abuse and Neglect, 7*: 459–469.

Elmer, E., & Gregg, G. S. (1967). *Developmental characteristics of abused children. Pediatrics, 40*, 596–602.

Fenichel, O. (1945). *The psychoanalytic theory of neurosis.* New York: Norton.

Field, T. M. (1977). Effects of early separation, interactive deficits, and experimental manipulations on infant-mother face-to-face interaction. *Child Development, 48*, 763–771.

Field, T. M. (1983). High risk infants "have less fun" during early interactions. *Topics in Early Childhood Special Education, 3*, 77–87.

Finkelhor, D. (1994). Current information on the scope and nature of child sexual abuse. *The Future of Children, 4*(2), 31–53.

Fonagy, P., Steele, H., & Steele, M. (1991). Maternal representations of attachment during pregnancy predict the organization of infant-mother attachment at one year of age. *Child Development, 62*, 891–905.

Forrest, J. D. (1994). Epidemiology of unintended pregnancy and contraceptive use. *American Journal of Obstetrics and Gynecology, 170,* 1485–1489.

Fraiberg, S. (1980). *Clinical studies in infant mental health: The first year of life.* New York: Basic Books.

Freedman, A. M., Kaplan, H. I., & Sadock, B. J. (1976). *Modern synopsis of psychiatry/II.* Baltimore: Williams & Wilkins.

Freud, S. (1953–1966). *Standard edition of the complete psychological works of Sigmund Freud.* London: Hogarth Press.

Frodi, A. M., Lamb, E., Leavitt, L. A., Donovan, W. L., Neff, C., & Sherry, D. (1978). Fathers' and mothers' responses to the faces and cries of normal and premature infants. *Developmental Psychology, 14,* 490–498.

Frodi, A. M., & Thompson, R., (1985). Infants' affective responses in the strange situation: Effects of prematurity and of quality of attachment. *Child Development, 56,* 1280–1291.

Galinsky, E. (1987). *The six stages of parenthood.* Reading, MA: Addison-Wesley.

Garbarino, J., Dubrow, N., Kostelny, K., & Pardo, C. (1992). *Children in danger: Coping with the consequences of community violence.* San Francisco: Jossey-Bass.

Gardner, J. M., Karmel, B. Z., & Dowd, J. M. (1984). Relationship of infant psychobiological development to infant intervention programs. *Journal of Children in Contemporary Society, 17,* 93–108.

George, C., & Main, M. (1979). Social interactions of young abused children: Approach, avoidance and aggression. *Child Development, 50,* 306–318.

Gesell, A. L. (1925). *The mental growth of the preschool child.* New York: Macmillan.

Giovannoni, J. (1993). Definition issues in child maltreatment. In D. Cicchetti & V. Carlson (Eds.), *Child maltreatment* (pp. 3–37). Cambridge: Cambridge University Press.

Goldberg, S. (1978). Prematurity: Effects on parent-infant interaction. *Journal of Pediatric Psychology, 3,* 137–144.

Goodfriend, M. S. (1993). Treatment of attachment disorder of infancy in a neonatal intensive care unit. *Pediatrics, 91* (1), 139–142.

Gortmaker, S. L. (1979). Poverty and infant mortality in the United States. *American Sociological Review, 44,* 280–297.

Gratacos, E., Torres, P. J., & Antolin, E. (1993). Use of cocaine during pregnancy. *New England Journal of Medicine, 329,* 667.

Gross, D., Contad, B., Fogg, L., Willis, L., & Garvey, C., (1995). A longitudinal study of maternal depression and preschool children's mental health. *Nursing Research, 44*(2), 96–101.

Hawkins, D., & Rosenbaum, S. (1992). *Lives in the balance: A national, state and county overview of America's medically underserved.* Washington, DC: National Association of Community Health Centers.

Hawley, T. L., Halle, T. G., Drasin, R. E., & Thomas, N. G. (1995). Children of addicted mothers: effects of the "crack epidemic" on the caregiving environment and the development of preschoolers. *American Journal of Orthopsychiatry, 65* (3), 364–379.

Hayden, A. H., & Beck, G. R. (1982). The epidemiology of high risk and handicapped infants. In C. T. Ramey & P. L. Trohanis (Eds.), *Finding and educating high-risk and handicapped infants* (pp. 19–51). Baltimore: University Park Press.

Hinde, R. (1976). On describing relationships. *Journal of Child Psychology and Psychiatry 17,* 1–19.

Hurt, H., Brodsky, N. L., Betaucourt, L., Brachman, L. E., Malmud, E., & Giannetta, J. (1995). Cocaine exposed children: Follow-up through 30 months. *Journal of Developmental and Behavioral Pediatrics, 16* (1), 29–35.

Jones, E. F., Forrest, J. D. D., & Goldman, N. (1985). Teenage pregnancy in developed countries: Determinants and policy implications. *Family Planning Perspectives, 17,* 53–63.

Junewicz, W. J. (1983). A protective posture toward emotional neglect and abuse. *Child Welfare, 62,* 243–252.

Kantrowitz, B. (1990, February 12). The crack children. *Newsweek,* pp. 62–63.

Kempe, C. H. (1971). Pediatric implications of the battered baby syndrome. *Archives of Disease in Childhood,* 46, 28–37.

Kempe, R., & Kempe, C. H. (1978). *Child abuse.* Cambridge, MA: Harvard University Press.

Klaus, M. H., & Kennell, J. H. (1976). *Maternal-infant bonding.* St. Louis: C. V. Mosby.

Klein, M., & Stern, L. (1971). Low birth weight and the battered child syndrome. *American Journal of the Disabled Child, 122,* 15–18.

Klein, N. K., Hack, M., & Breslau, N. (1989). Children who were very low birth weight: Developmental and academic achievement at nine years of age. *Journal of Developmental and Behavioral Pediatrics, 10,* 32–37.

Knitzer, J., & Aber, J. L. (1995). Young children in poverty: Facing the facts. *American Journal of Orthopsychiatry 65* (2), 174–176.

Leon, I. (1990). *When a baby dies.* New Haven, CT: Yale University Press.

Lesser, A. J. (1985). The origins and development of maternal and child health programs in the United States. *American Journal of Public Health, 75,* 590–598.

Lietar, E. F. (1986). Miscarriage. In T. A. Rando (Ed.), *Parental loss of a child* (pp. 121–127). Champaign, IL: Research Press Company.

Long, J. G., & Lucey, J. F. (1980). "Noise and hypoxemia in the intensive care nursery." *Pediatrics,* 65, 143–145.

Lösel, F., & Bliesener, T. (1990). Resilience in adolescence: A study on the generalizability of protective factors. In K. Hurrelmann & F. Lösel (Eds.), *Health hazards in adolescence.* New York: Walter de Gruyter.

Magee E. M., & Pratt, M. W. (1985). *1935–1985: 50 years of U.S. federal support to promote the health of mothers, children, and handicapped children in America.* Vienna, VA: Information Sciences Research Institute.

Main, M., & Goldwyn, R. (1984). Predicting rejection of her infant from mother's representation of her own experience: Implications for the abused-abusing intergenerational cycle. *Child Abuse and Neglect,* 8 (2), 203–217.

Main, M., Kaplan, N., & Cassidy, J. (1985). Security in infancy, childhood and adulthood: A move to the level of representation. In I. Bretherton & E. Water (Eds.), *Growing points of attachment theory and research.* Monographs of the Society of Research in Child Development 50 (1–2, Serial No. 209).

Main, D. M., & Main, E. K. (1991). Preterm birth. In S. G. Gabbe, J. R. Niebyl, & J. L. Simpson (Eds.), *Obstetrics: Normal and problem pregnancies* (2nd ed.) (pp. 829–880). New York: Churchill Livingstone.

Martini, D. R., Ryan, C., Nakayama, D., & Ramenofsky, M. (1990). Psychiatric sequelae after traumatic injury: The Pittsburgh regatta accident. *Journal of the American Academy of Child and Adolescent Psychiatry, 29,* 70–75.

Mayes, L. C., Granger, R. H., Bornstein, M. H., & Zuckerman, B. (1992). The problem of prenatal cocaine exposure: A rush to judgment. *Journal of the American Medical Association, 276,* 406–408.

McCrea, R. C. (1910). *The humane movement.* New York: Columbia University Press.

McFarlane, A. C. (1987). Family functioning and overprotection following a natural disaster: The longitudinal effects of post-traumatic morbidity. *Australian and New Zealand Journal of Psychiatry, 221,* 210–218.

McLoyd, V. C. (1990). The impact of economic hardship on black families and children: Psychological distress, parenting, and socioemotional development. *Child Development, 61,* 331–346.

Mihaly, L. K. (1991). *Homeless families: Failed policies and young victims.* Washington, DC: Children's Defense Fund.

Milgrom, J. (1994). Mother-infant interactions in postpartum depression: An early intervention program. *Australian Journal of Advanced Nursing, 11*(4), 29–38.

National Center for Children in Poverty. (1990). *Five million children: A statistical profile of our poorest young citizens.* New York: National Center for Children in Poverty, Columbia University School of Public Health.

National Research Council Panel on High Risk Youth. (1993). *Losing generations: Adolescents in high risk settings.* Washington, DC: National Academy Press.

Norris, M. L. (1991, July 7–14). The class of crack's innocent victims: The first wave of drug-disabled children jolts ill-prepared schools. *Washington Post Weekly Edition,* p. 11.

Oberklaid, F., Sanson, A., Pedlow, R., & Prior, M. (1991). Predicting preschool behavior problems from temperament and other variables in infancy. *Pediatrics 91* (1), 113–120.

Office of the Inspector General. Office of Evaluation and Inspections. Department of Health and Human Services. (1990). *Crack babies.* Washington, DC: U.S. Government Printing Office.

Parke, R. (1977). Socialization into child abuse: A social interactional perspective. In J. L. Tapp & J. F. Levine (Eds.), *Law, justice, and the individual in society.* New York: Holt, Rinehart, & Winston.

Pelton, L. (1978). Child abuse and neglect: The myth of classlessness. *American Journal of Orthopsychiatry, 48,* 608–617.

Peterson, N. (1987). *Early intervention for handicapped and at-risk children—An introduction to early childhood—special education.* Denver: Love Publishing.

Plunkett, J. W., Klein, T., & Meisels, S. J. (1988). The relationship of preterm infant-mother attachment to stranger sociability at three years. *Infant Behavior and Development, 11,* 83–96.

Pollitt, E. (1988). Developmental impact of nutrition on pregnancy, infancy, and childhood: Public health issues in the United States. In N. W. Bray (Ed.), *International Review of Research in Mental Retardation, 15,* 39–41.

Pynoos, R., & Nader, K., (1988). Psychological first aid and treatment approach to children exposed to community violence: Research implications. *Journal of Traumatic Stress Studies, 1* (4), 445–473.

Richters, J. E., & Martinez, P. (1993). The NIMH Community Violence Project: I. Children as victims of and witnesses to violence. *Psychiatry 56,* 7–221.

Ries, P. (1990). *Health of black and white Americans, 1985–1987.* Vital and Health Statistics, 10th ser. 171. Hyattville, MD: National Center for Health Statistics, Public Health Service.

Robertson, J., & Bowlby, J. (1952). Responses of young children to separation from their mothers. *Courier of the International Children's Centre, Paris, 2,* 131–140.

Robinson, A., & Linden, M. G. (1993). *Clinical genetics handbook.* Boston: Blackwell Scientific Publications.

Rosen, C. M. (1987, September). The eerie world of reunited twins. *Discover,* pp. 36–46.

Rosenberg, A., (1991). The neonate. In S. G. Gabbe, J. R. Niebyl, & J. L. Simpson, (Eds.), *Obstetrics: Normal and problem pregnancies* (2nd ed.) (pp. 697–752). New York: Churchill Livingstone.

Rutter, M., Maughan, N., Mortimore, P., & Ouston, J. (1979). *Fifteen thousand hours.* Cambridge: Harvard University Press.

Saigal, S., Szatmari, P., Rosenbaum, P., Campbell, D., & King, S. (1991). Cognitive abilities and school performance of extremely low birth weight children and matched term control children at age 8 years: A regional study. *Journal of Pediatrics, 118,* 751–760.

Sameroff, A. J., & Chandler, M. J., (1975). Reproductive risk and the continuum of caretaking casualty. In F. D. Horowitz, M. Hetherington, S. Scarr-Salapatek, & G. Siegel (Eds.), *Review of child development research* (Vol. 4, pp. 187–244). Chicago: University of Chicago Press.

Sameroff, A., Seifer, R., Barocas, R., Zax, M., & Greenspan, S. (1987). "Intelligence quotient scores of 4-year-old children: Social environmental risk factors." *Pediatrics, 79,* 343–350.

Sameroff, A. J., Seifer, R., & Elias, P. K. (1982). Sociocultural variability in infant temperament ratings. *Child Development, 53,* 164–173.

Saudino, K. (1991). Infant temperament and genetics: An objective twin study of motor activity level. *Child Development, 62* (5), 1167–1174.

Schneider, J. W., Griffith, D. R., & Chasnoff, I. J. (1989). Infants exposed to cocaine in utero: Implications for developmental assessment and intervention. *Infant and Young Children, 2* (1), 25–36.

Shakoor, B., & Chalmer, D. (1991). Covictimization of Afro-American children who witness violence and the theoretical implications of its effect on their cognitive, emotional, and behavioral development. *Journal of the National Medical Association, 83,* 233–238.

Shonkoff, J. P., & Meisels, S. J. (1992). Early childhood intervention: The evolution of a concept. In S. J. Meisels & J. P. Shonkoff (Eds.), *Handbook of early childhood intervention* (pp. 3–31). New York: Cambridge University Press.

Skinner, B. F. (1948). *Walden two.* London: Macmillan.

Smith, D. W. (1979). Mothering your unborn baby. In M. Di Bendetto (Ed.), *Prevention of developmental disabilities: A report of a conference on the prevention of developmental disabilities.* Columbus: Nisonger Center, Ohio State University.

Sroufe, L. A. (1979). The coherence of individual development. *American Psychologist, 34,* 834–841.

Sroufe, L. A. (1983). "Infant-caregiver attachment and patterns of adaptation in preschool: The roots of maladaption and competence." In M. Perlmutter (Ed.), The Minnesota symposia on child psychology (vol. 16, pp. 41–84). Hillsdale, NJ: Erlbaum.

Terr, L. (1989, May 17). Consultation advised soon after child's psychic injury. *Clinical Psychiatric Times.*

Terr, L. (1991). Childhood traumas: An outline and overview. *American Journal of Psychiatry, 148,* 1, 10–19.

Tirosh, E., Harel, J., Abadi, J., Berger, A., & Cohen, A. (1992). Relationship between neonatal behavior and subsequent temperament. *Acta Paediatrica, 81* (10), 829–831.

Tronick, E. (1989). Emotions and emotional communication in infants. *American Psychologist, 44*(2), 112–119.

Udwin, O. (1993). Annotation: Children's reactions to traumatic events. *Journal of Child Psychology and Psychiatry, 34* (2), 115–127.

U.S. Census Bureau [Donald J. Hernandes] (1992). When households continue, discontinue, and form. *Current Population Reports,* series P23-179. Washington, DC: Government Printing Office.

U.S. General Accounting Office. (1987). *Prenatal care: Medicaid recipients and uninsured women obtain insufficient care.* Washington, DC: Author.

Van Dyke, D. C., & Fox, A. A. (1990). Fetal drug exposure and its possible implications for learning in the preschool and school-age population. *Journal of Learning Disabilities, 23* (3), 160–163.

Vaughn, B. E., Bradley, C. F., Jaffe, L. S., Seifer, R., & Barglow, P. (1987). Maternal characteristics measured prenatally predict ratings of temperamental difficulty on the Carey infant temperament questionnaire. *Developmental Psychology, 23,* 152–161.

Watson, J. B. (1925). *Behaviorism.* New York: Norton.

Werner, E. (1989). Vulnerability and resilience: A longitudinal perspective. In M. Bambring, F. Losel, & H. Skowronek (Eds.), *Children and risk: Assessment, longitudinal research and intervention* (pp. 157–172). New York: Walter de Gruyter.

Werner, E. (1990). Protective factors and individual resilience. In S. J. Meisels & J. P. Shonkoff (Eds.), *Handbook of early childhood education.* Cambridge: Cambridge University Press.

Werner, E., & Smith, R. S. (1982). *Vulnerable but invincible: A longitudinal study of resilient children and youth.* New York: McGraw-Hill.

Wood, D. L. (1990). Health of homeless children and housed poor children. *Pediatrics, 86* (6), 858–866.

Yule, W., & Williams, R. (1990). Post traumatic stress reactions in children. *Journal of Traumatic Stress, 2,* 279–295.

Zeanah, C. H., & Anders, T. F. (1987). Subjectivity in parent-infant relationships: A discussion of internal working models. *Infant Mental Health Journal, 8* (3), 237–251.

Zeanah, C. H., Carr, S., & Wolk, S. (1990). Fetal movements and the imagined baby of pregnancy: are they related? *Journal of Reproductive and Infant Psychology, 8,* 23–36.

Zigler, E. (1980). Controlling child abuse: Do we have the knowledge and/or the will? In G. Gerbner, C. Ross, & E. Zigler (Eds.), *Child abuse: An agenda for action* (pp. 3–34). New York: Oxford University Press.

Zigler, E., & Hall, N. W. (1993). Physical child abuse in America: Past, present, and future. In D. Cicchetti and V. Carlson (Eds.), *Child maltreatment* (pp. 38–75). New York: Cambridge University Press.

Zigler, E., & Valentine, J. (Eds.). (1979). *Project Head Start: A legacy of the War on Poverty.* New York: Free Press.

19

Time-Sensitive Clinical Social Work Practice

Roberta Ann Shechter

Clinical social work, historically known as casework, is a pragmatic profession. The ideas that underpin this work are not formulated in a vacuum, so that worldly concerns often dictate how casework is practiced. Clinical theories—the abstract assumptions that guide practice—are responsive to the personal opinions, psychosocial needs, and economic limitations of clients. Consequently, short-term therapy is not a new phenomenon. According to Parad, the bulk of casework has always been short term (Parad, 1971, p. 119). The profession's anchor in agency practice has been a formative influence. Rarely explicit, the commitment to a brief treatment focus is a commonplace and a matter of practice setting. For example, time limits are an expected aspect of casework in a school, court, or hospital. Therapeutic contact can last for a school semester, occur immediately before or after a court appearance, or be limited to the duration of a hospital stay. Even in the field of child guidance, where casework is usually thought of as long-term treatment, research has shown that 72 percent of the clients are seen for fewer than five sessions (Parad, 1971, p. 137).

Short-term treatment may be an integral aspect of the social work profession, yet historically we have maintained a negative attitude toward it. In some circles, brief therapy is considered superficial, an effort at abbreviating long-term treatment, and therefore a second-class form of client care (Kogan, Hutn, & Blenkner, 1951, p. 137). This negative attitude emerged gradually. In the early years of the profession, social agencies were concerned with the problems triggered by urban life and industrialization. The goals of casework were tangible and limited in focus, for example, helping a client find a job or better housing or helping the worthy poor raise their quality of life. Emphasis was on the social, "the interrelationship of the individual and the pathology of society" (Cohen, 1958, p. 317). By 1900, present-day fields of practice were emerging: child and family care, health and medical, probation and parole, aid to the traveler and foreign born, and mental hygiene. As early as 1909 there was a call to shift attention from social issues to personal meaning, from symptom to cause and more "intensive long-term cases" (Parad, 1971, p. 142). Slowly social workers became increasingly drawn to the formulations of Sigmund Freud and the ego psychologists who followed him. These psychodynamic ideas remain an important force in clinical social work. The position of the caregiver has moved from that of supplying aid to enabling.

War and other large-scale personal tragedies and sociopolitical events sparked the profession's interest in short-term therapy. Two key factors led to this change: government policy statements that committed federal and state tax dollars to the improvement of the mental health of every citizen in need and publication of clinical research that showed how to assess need and intervene in situations that required quick response. World War II focused attention on the troubles of American soldiers. Psychiatrists in military hospitals developed brief treatment protocols for combat neurosis and the transient personality disorganization that can result from battle exhaustion and injury (Straker, 1980, p. 222). On the civilian front, tragedy struck in Boston in 1942. The celebration following a Boston College–Holy Cross football game ended in disaster. Five hundred people lost their lives and two hundred were seriously injured in a fire that raged through the Coconut Grove Night Club. Hundreds of families were in shock or grieving their losses. Research conducted by Massachusetts General Hospital indicated that a hazardous event, sudden death of a family member or threat of loss immediately induces a crisis (Linderman, 1944). This crisis can be described by a predictable sequence of grief and bereavement behaviors (Davanloo, 1980b, p. 247).

In displaced persons camps following World War II and in the public health arena in the 1950s, Gerald Caplan (1964) expanded on Linderman's work. Caplan refined the concept of time as a factor in crisis. According to Caplan, much happens quickly. A state of personal crisis tends to last no longer than four to six weeks. During these weeks an individual generally goes through four stages of crisis. In the first stage, an emotionally significant event occurs, triggering a sense of personal crisis. The event may be catastrophic or a normal part of daily living that unpredictably unleashes disabling anxiety. Levels of anxiety often rise when there is a sudden change in life structure or a transition in personal development. The change or transition may be positive or negative—the birth of a child or death of a parent, marriage or divorce, the threat of school failure or impending graduation. All of these changes bring the specter of new experience, the unknown that can stir anxiety and require new modes of problem solving. If habitual ways of problem solving do not adequately handle the situation and new ways are not quickly developed, then a sense of internal stress, emotional disequilibrium, and role confusion is the result.

In the second stage of crisis, the struggle to cope continues, and individual anxiety increases. The third stage of crisis begins as the person suffering stress draws on reserves of strength in his or her ego and evolves novel methods of problem solving. These third-stage behaviors are a thrust for mastery. If the new behaviors successfully handle the crisis, the individual enters the fourth stage with an improved level of ego function and growth in problem-solving capacity. If the behaviors of the third stage are inadequate to deal with the crisis, then anxiety continues and disorganization increases. Third-stage behaviors are crucial to the Caplan model of crisis resolution. With these behaviors, a new state of equilibrium is reached, and the capacity to handle a similar type of crisis in the future is ensured.

Caplan's crisis intervention ideas differ in language but nevertheless are synchronous with the ego-plasticity concepts of Spitz and Hartmann (Spitz, 1965, p. 86). In Caplan's view, every individual who undergoes a crisis has the potential for rapid emotional growth and change. Ego psychologists use the dyadic situation of mother and child as their model of change. Therapist, like mother, is a mediator between client and environment, encouraging an ever-expanding capacity for improved personal functioning. These positivistic and egalitarian views of the human condition were reflective of the political climate of that time. Caplan's ideas and those of ego psychology are shared by current practitioners of clinical social work. These ideas typify those that have led to a more positive attitude toward brief therapies.

Community mental health legislation passed by Congress in 1963 promised psychotherapeutic care to all who need it. Federal funds infused social agencies, and community-based psychiatric clinics were established across the nation. Social work schools expanded their enrollments. Hope abounded that ideals were attainable, but need continued. New ways were sought to spread available therapeutic resources, and the interest in short-term modes of therapy increased (Bloom, 1992, p. 7). Preliminary research seemed to indicate that limited contact, between four and six sessions, had a therapeutic effect (Garcia & Irwin, 1962, p. 75). Short-term care appeared to be effective, and many social agencies established brief treatment programs. As the coffers of public funds for mental health dwindled in the 1970s and 1980s, these programs expanded in number. Less agency money meant restrictions on staff time and less direct service time allotted to each client. Those in need must now be helped in fewer treatment hours. A short-term therapy model of service delivery seemed a logical choice and was, in fact, a pragmatic decision. However, most social workers still viewed long-term therapy as the preferred way of dealing with clients. But because value conflict cannot be tolerated indefinitely in the ranks of any profession, these treatment programs, originally introduced as unwelcomed necessities, gradually became more positively regarded.

Social and economic forces continue to influence the profession—how social workers deal with clients and think about their work. Recently the source of economic influence has shifted from the public to the private sector. Government funds are increasingly less available to underwrite the cost of patient care, and business interests have stepped into this void. Clients join health maintenance organizations (HMOs) and preferred provider networks (PPOs). The client's therapy is then subsidized by an insurance company that insists on having a deciding voice in the kind of service provided. Insurance companies are in the business of making money. They employ managed care companies to oversee clinical work, which then becomes subject to regulations that help the insurance company spend less on each client. Short-term therapy is believed to be both cost-contained and cost-effective and is consequently mandated by managed care companies. Social agency programs are now shaped to meet the demands of a new funding source, the business community.

Short-term therapy is an unavoidable reality in the current practice of clinical social work. The demands of managed care challenge professional ethics and authority (Bollas & Sundelson, 1995) as social workers struggle to maintain control of treatment planning. Their therapeutic judgments may be influenced, but should not be solely guided, by the financial interests of an insurance company or the funding concerns of a social agency. Traditionally, client need has determined how clinical social work is practiced. This should continue. Short-term therapy does not suit everyone, but it can help many. The strength of social work authority in today's mental health marketplace will depend on how well social workers understand the theory and techniques of time-sensitive treatment—both when and how to practice it effectively.

TIME AS A FACTOR IN TREATMENT, 1885–PRESENT

Earlier Concepts

Our current ideas about time as a factor in the therapeutic process are rooted in the psychodynamic tradition of Sigmund Freud. In his early years, Freud was an active clinician who shared his ideas quickly and saw patients for brief periods of treatment. He worked closely with people, observed their behaviors, and developed concepts that described the origins of psychopathology. The length of these treatments was not an issue. Katrina (1885), one of his first case studies, had a problem of contemporary interest. She met Freud while he was on vacation in the Austrian Alps. The daughter of a local innkeeper, Katrina joined Freud on his daily walk and poured out her heart. Katrina was suffering from somatic complaints. Freud traced her physical symptoms of dizziness and stomachaches to their traumatic source: sexual abuse at the hands of her stepfather. Sharing the details of her pain and anxiety brought Katrina relief and catharsis. Katrina and Freud met once. Their time together may demonstrate that some symptoms can be quickly relieved if treatment is clearly focused.

As Freud's fame spread, patients often traveled great distances for consultations and could stay in Vienna only briefly. The Czech composer Gustav Mahler was treated by Freud during a four-hour walk in a park (Jones, 1955, pp. 79–80). On this walk Mahler was cured of impotence. The essential ingredients in Freud's speedy and successful treatments were the analytic mind of both patient and therapist, their mutual capacity for deep reflection, and a shared belief in the healing power of understanding. The amount of calendar time allotted to a particular treatment was of no importance to Freud. The psychodynamic meaning of symptoms and what they indicated to him about the structure of the human mind had precedence. For Freud's patients, the central concern was relief from pain.

Freud's initial concept of time was determined by his place in the history of science. Freud was a Victorian, and his ideas about time and space were based on nineteenth-century physics. Freud's view of the universe was Newtonian—a closed system in which each element inevitably determines the other. The human mind, like the universe, was deterministic and closed, and these qualities influenced the nature of the unconscious. In this closed system, the unconscious was timeless. The free association of thoughts could bring ideas from the deepest recesses of the mind to its surface—from the unconscious to consciousness. The forgotten past gave the present its meaning, and present-day symptoms could be understood in the context of early trauma. Since the unconscious was timeless, all was related through time.

Freud's ideas about time broadened in his 1905 monograph on infantile sexuality. Time now had a developmental purpose. The human psyche, through the neutralization of drive, matured with the passage of time. Time was now marked by psychosexual stages—the oral, anal, and genital—and had acquired a biological dimension. During each stage of the libido, sexual and nutritional longings were invested in a particular zone of the human body: the mouth, anus, or genitals. The libidinal needs of a stage must be adequately gratified and its central developmental tasks mastered before a shift in the focus of investment becomes possible and movement into the next stage could occur. Blocks in gratification of libido result in unneutralized energy that is carried forward into the next stage, influencing the nature of behavior in that later time frame. Passage through the psychosexual stages of developmental time is a universal experience. Everyone has done it, some more easily than others, with more or less libidinal gratification along the way. Some deprivation is inescapable. It is a matter of degree.

The work of Ferenczi and Rank, two disciples of Freud, included a number of ideas that have become assumptions in brief treatment. Chief among these are ideas about the nature of time in significant relationships. These early theorists believed that the timelessness of the Freudian unconscious could be harnessed for a purpose. They proposed that a patient need not explore early history in depth in order to make personality changes. The experiential transference, feelings, and thoughts about significant figures of the past, now projected onto the person of the therapist, could be used to promote change. The experiential transference bridged time and played out the past in the present, so that change was fostered by a reparative present-day transference experience (Bauer & Kobos, 1995, p. 19).

Alexander, a more recent psychoanalytic theorist, extended Ferenczi's ideas about time and the healing power of transference with his concept of the "corrective emotional experience" (Alexander & French, 1946). To provide this experience, Alexander manipulated the transference. A patient was helped to relive an earlier traumatic relationship but experience a different outcome. Alexander considered problematic transference inevitable. A corrective emotional experience unfolded when a therapist's reactions to a patient's transference expectations were visibly different from the behavior of an earlier object relation (usually a parent). This behavioral difference helped the patient understand the source of psychic pain, and "in this experience the ego of the patient was given a second chance" (Eisenstein, 1980, p. 29).

Alexander believed that manipulations, within the corrective emotional experience, caused treatment to move at a faster pace. He also believed that every patient had a natural predilection for dependency longings that led to a wish to be treated rather than cured. The experience of treatment could become an end rather than a means. To prevent this from happening, Alexander experimented with the frequency and duration of treatment sessions. Time was manipulated in order to avoid the deepening of dependency.

Current Ideas

Three basic psychodynamic themes guide the practice of time-sensitive clinical social work. These themes, found in the literature between 1970 and 1995, are the source of pathology and symptom, time and ego strength, and central focus of treatment and therapeutic technique.

Source of Pathology and Symptom

Freud's theories about the developmental source of pathology continue to be influential. Time is viewed as a factor in the evolution of the symptoms or maladaptive behaviors that are brought into the clinical situation for repair. Partially motivated by feelings and thoughts that stem from earlier life experience, symptoms give voice to the unconscious. In symptoms, the repressed past is alive in the present. It is this level of psychic life that the short-term therapist addresses explicitly through interpretation and implicitly by ego-supportive techniques. Recent life events have the power to undermine various ego defenses that ward off the memories of past problems. Anxieties in the present uncover fears that are rooted in developmental frustration (Edelstein, 1990, p. 11).

Time and Ego Strength

Two important contributors to recent ideas about the role of time in the promotion of ego strength are James Mann and Daniel Goldman. Mann and Goldman believe that time has many meanings, meanings that can be harnessed for therapeutic gain. They developed a twelve-session treatment model that sets a definite ending date from the outset of therapist-client contact. This ending date makes time a conscious aspect of treatment and brings its unconscious meanings into the therapeutic experience. Personal problems are addressed as difficulties in dealing with time (Mann & Goldman, 1982, p. 21). Freud's view of the unconscious as timeless, and the inevitability of the individual's changing attitude toward time as a function of developmental maturity proceeds, are the two basic concepts that underpin their model. Limiting the time spent in treatment to twelve sessions is seen as a stimulus for higher-level ego function, which occurs as a result of such changing attitudes toward time.

To use the time constraints suggested in the Mann and Goldman model requires an understanding of time's developmental meaning. According to these theorists, the human psyche is structured by two kinds of time. Infancy is marked by the infinite existential timelessness of endless childhood experience. As people mature, they become reality tied, and time seems more limited. Adulthood is governed by the finite categorical time of clock and calendar. Attitudes about time are never pure, so that daily life is a fusion of child and adult time. Adult time dominates in a person with a strong ego. Time awareness in brief treatment confronts a client with the need to problem-solve in the here and now and give up the longings of child time.

Mann and Goldman's ideas about time harmonize with those of an earlier brief treatment theorist, David Malan. Malan connected duration, the time spent in treatment, with treatment focus. He suggested that by limiting treatment to a specific set of issues that were mutually agreed on by client and therapist, therapy time could be shortened to between ten and forty weeks (Malan, 1976; Marmor, 1980). The stronger the patient's ego is, the shorter the treatment. Malan believed that the psychoanalytic techniques of free association and free-floating attention discouraged a readiness to confront and deal with anxiety, and his ideas had a cognitive thrust that was in keeping with the early explorations of Freud and later ego psychologists—that once conflicts are brought into awareness, understanding and change follow. A significant Malan contribution was his emphasis on the connection between specified conflict and treatment time.

Central Focus of Treatment and Therapeutic Technique

The key to successful short-term therapy is setting and maintaining limited goals. These goals must be relevant to the client's presenting problem and focus treatment in a way that engages client curiosity and motivation for change. The strength of this focus is based on the close association between treatment goals and the latent meanings of a presenting problem. The stronger this connection is, the clearer is the focus. Treatment goals are a product of the working alliance of client and therapist. In the working alliance, the client and the therapist jointly select an issue that gives the conflict beneath a client's presenting problem a profound personal meaning. Narrowing the focus of treatment to a limited set of meaningful goals lends hope that change can occur. Maintaining a specific focus propels change.

How treatment goals are conceptualized varies with each clinical theory. Mann and Goldman draw on the ideas of Mahler, Pine, & Bergman (1975) to determine the central focus of care. They view life as a series of developmental crises that are never completely resolved. Repetitive confrontations with the pain of separation and the fears of loss and abandonment undermine self-esteem and promote a negative self-concept. Underlying the client's presenting problem is a wish for repair through reunion with an early pain-inducing object relation, usually a parent. In fact, the client's current object relations are often a repetition of unrequited early longings and infantile conflicts. The short-term nature of treatment forces the client to muster ego strength and move from infantile wishes to more mature ways of relating to other people. Viewing the goals of treatment as the resolution of chronic psychic pain and improved self-concept requires both supportive and insight-oriented ways of working. Interpretations tend to connect current life experiences with early relationships and maintain a positive relationship between client and therapist. The reliving of painful early separations in the experiential transference of the therapeutic relationship is dealt with only if it interferes with treatment progress.

Habib Davanloo (1980a) believes that character analysis is a central task of brief therapy. Since this analysis is done through the interpretation of an experiential transference, promoting the development of transference becomes a central focus of treatment. Working actively in the transference, Davanloo cuts across time; the past comes alive in the present, and dysfunctional behavior patterns are challenged.

Davanloo is an assertive therapist. Assuming that his clients have adequate ego strength and are comfortable with a confrontive therapeutic style, Davanloo aggressively interprets the demands that clients make on him, and the transference unfolds. In his interaction with a client, Davanloo listens for language that reveals libidinal longings. He observes defensive behaviors that bind anxiety. Then he focuses the interpretive work on the transference repetition of the client's relational difficulty as it is expressed in the presenting problem of a client. These interpretations are lent power by the connections made with the client's early history. For example, he might confront a passive-dependent woman with her wish for the therapist's advice and guidance by saying, "You would like me to tell you what to do just as your father once did." In an effort to mobilize her ego into a more active mode of behaving, he might continue, "I wonder what stops you from deciding how to deal with this issue. Why depend on the opinion of another?" Davanloo works persistently with the client's ego by pointing out character armor—the unconscious habitual ways of behaving that promote problems.

Building on the ideas of Malan, Davanloo organizes his clinical observations by using two psychoanalytic constructs: "the triangle of conflict" and "the triangle of person" (Davanloo, 1980a, p. 77). The triangle of conflict is a way of categorizing behavior and explaining the origin of a symptom. Each corner of this triangle holds a variable that gives rise to the symptom: impulse, defense, and anxiety. If the impulse, which strives for expression, is unacceptable, anxiety is stirred, and various defenses are used to restore a state of calm. The triangle of person diagrams the latent connections in a client's object relational world—unconscious with conscious and past with present. Significant people in the client's early life, usually parents, are at one point on the triangle, and the therapist is at a second. The third point represents current life relationships (e.g., spouse or work colleagues). Interpretations are designed to address connections between points on either of these two triangles.

Davanloo applies his way of working to a wide variety of clients. I believe that it is most effective with people who have considerable ego strength and are able to tolerate high levels of anxiety and anger stirred by confrontive transference interpretations. In Davanloo's model, the number of sessions allotted to a patient is proportional to the nature of the pathology. People with neurotic conflicts (of an oedipal nature) have briefer treatments—generally from five to fifteen sessions (Bloom, 1992, p. 62). Those who suffer from severe character problems may be seen for as many as thirty sessions. The greater the difficulty is, the deeper the pathology and the more extensive the treatment. This flexible use of time makes pathology a governing factor in the length of treatment.

Peter Sifneos practices two forms of brief treatment: anxiety-suppressing and anxiety-provoking therapy. Each is short term but with a different central focus. The first he believes works effectively with the hospitalized, a very disturbed population. Goal determines technique. Support, reassurance, environmental manipulation, and medication decrease or eliminate the anxiety that is blocking life decisions required for resuming an existence outside the hospital (Sifneos, 1987, p. 45).

Anxiety-provoking therapy is a twelve- to fifteen-week treatment. Its definite time frame and questioning technique engage the ego of the patient in self-assessment and goal-directed change. Sifneos believes that successful treatment must have a strong cognitive component. The therapist is part teacher and enabler of change. She or he questions the client, and these questions both stimulate anxiety and connect the present problem with the past experiences. Questions activate the client's ego in the working alliance, and treatment goals are defined behaviorally. Change is judged on three fronts: interaction with the therapist should be increasingly less tense over time, symptoms should decrease, and interpersonal relationships should improve. Unlike Mann and Goldman, Sifneos does not set a termination date until some of these treatment goals have been achieved. The latent focus of treatment is oedipal conflict, as revealed by the client's difficulty with issues of competition and intimacy. Anxiety-provoking therapy is also effective with pre-oedipal problems or those that spring from early developmental longings. Unlike Davanloo, Sifneos avoids confrontation with character issues. Although his approach is active and confrontive, Sifneos has a gentler style.

There are two models of cognitive therapy and one of task-oriented treatment that increase the repertoire of useful techniques in time-sensitive clinical social work. The two cognitive models are those of Albert Ellis (Ellis & Abrahams, (1978) and Aaron Beck (Beck et al., 1979). The task-oriented model was developed by William Reid and Laura Epstein (1972). Each of these schools of thought has an impact on the practice of time-sensitive clinical social work, and each makes a contribution that should not be overlooked.

Albert Ellis's rational-emotive therapy is a cognitive behavioral approach to problem solving. It assumes that every person has a number of self-defeating beliefs that underpin dysfunctional behaviors. Its treatment goals are fourfold: the uncovering of self-defeating beliefs, the admission of having these beliefs, the recognition of their irrational qualities, and the replacement of these ideas with reason. Beck's cognitive restructuring therapy was developed to deal specifically with the problems of depression. Depression, according to Beck, is the outcome of cognitive distortion—errors in thinking that spring from both early learning and inferences about the self and about others that are a consequence of life experiences that carry a threat of loss or deprivation. Beck's treatment techniques promote introspection. His goals are the elimination of the unrealistic ideas and distortions in a client's worldview that are a direct cause of pathology. Both cognitive theorists believe that psychopathologies are problems of intellect that can be mastered by understanding (Bloom, 1992, p. 203).

In contrast, psychodynamically informed clinical social work has a developmental view of the origins of pathology. Like the cognitive theorist, the social work clinician mobilizes the autonomous ego functions of intellect, cognition, perception, and synthesis to reality-test ideas and promote change in clients. This similarity in ego-building method may allow the selective incorporation of various cognitive treatment techniques into time-sensitive clinical social work practice. Both Ellis and

Beck assign homework between treatment sessions, a technique that may prove useful in the context of brief treatment. However, the purpose and dynamic of homework should be understood from an ego psychological perspective.

Homework assignments serve both conscious and unconscious purposes. Activities are encouraged that address aspects of the client's presenting problem. Consciously the client's attention is directed to cognitive distortions and irrational beliefs that undermine adaptive behavior. Anxieties that surface in the course of doing an assignment must be mastered to complete it, and the experience of dealing with these anxieties is brought into the therapy session for discussion. Homework assignments also have unconscious meanings and consequences, inasmuch as they are symbolic of the therapist and therapy. Doing the assignment, in effect, represents taking the therapist home and playing out the therapeutic object relation in one's internal world. The completion of the assignment may lead to the internalization of a more benign introject. Negative expectations about an action or result must be overcome and the therapist's definition of how to cope with a problem taken into the self. Achievement of this positive outcome brings pleasure and improved self-esteem.

The task-centered casework ideas of William Reid and Laura Epstein (1972, 1977, 1978) can, with some modification, be incorporated into time-sensitive clinical practice. The focus of treatment is chiefly interpersonal and therefore involves the understanding of others rather than self-reflection. Treatment goals are behavioral: the carrying out of tasks that lead to improved role performance, smoother social transitions, and lowering of reactive emotional distress. Lasting no more than eight sessions, help typically involves the delineation of tasks and suggestions, ego-supportive work that leads to problem resolution while minimizing the exploration of conflict (Reid & Epstein, 1972, p. 25).

The following case illustrates elements of crisis intervention and brief therapy that are commonly integrated in the practice of time-sensitive clinical social work.

Linda, a twenty-five-year-old African American woman, was referred to my practice by her company's employee assistance program (EAP). Our first contact was on the telephone. Although this conversation lasted no more than five minutes, it was telling. It began with my question, "What led you to call me?" In a soft, barely audible voice with the trace of a southern inflection, Linda said, "My supervisor at work thinks that a little therapy would be a good idea. I agree. My EAP has approved six sessions. Why not use them? I need to talk to someone. I have a short fuse lately, a real attitude. I'm just so unhappy, and I feel so trapped. Today I almost walked off my job. Yesterday I stayed at home in bed and watched television all day." When I asked Linda how many days of work she had missed recently, she replied, "Three or four in the last month." Then in a rush of words, she continued, "I'm scheduled to take the Law Standardized Aptitude Test (LSAT) in seven weeks. I can't study. I have no energy. I've canceled the examination before, but I want to take it this time; I don't know what to do." "Calling me was a good beginning," I said. "Let's make an appointment for Wednesday and talk over what is going on."

Session 1. *Linda arrived promptly for our appointment. No more than 5 feet 2 inches in height, she wore a brown coat dress that was only one or two shades darker than her skin color and sported a carefully shaped flattop haircut. She appeared older than her stated age of twenty-five, conservative, a woman hiding from the notice of others. Her deep purple lipstick blended with the earth tones of her dress and skin. Long manicured fingernails painted in bright pink enamel were a stark contrast to the rest of her presentation. They peeked out from the folded hands in her lap as she settled into a chair. Linda had made eye contact for only one moment, then followed me silently from the waiting room into my office. Now she kept her eyes averted, examining book titles on a low shelf near her right shoulder. Viewing her behavior as an effort to contain anxiety and wanting to put her at ease, I said, "Tell me what brought you here today." "Coming here was really my mother's idea," Linda said. "I feel like my life is over. I keep telling my mother that, and she gets angry. She says it doesn't have to be that way. She thinks I'm silly, but that is how I feel, that my life is over."*

I responded, "Your life is over? Tell me what that means and how long you have felt this way."

"I'm not sure," she said. "I think I've felt this way since I broke up with Steven last week. Steven is, or I should say was, my boyfriend. Steven is a scumbag. We'd been going out for three months when I broke up with him. I found out that he lives with a woman and has a child. I thought he lived with his parents. I thought that he was at least five years younger than he really is. I found this out when his 'wife' called me. He's not really married, but he might as well be. He's been with her for seven years; their child is four. When I confronted Steven about his woman and his child, he told me that his child is ill and needs him. There was no question of his leaving his family for me. I exploded when I heard this, and I told him never to try to see me again. I told him this on the bus going to work. We travel together every morning—he's the bus driver. It's an express line that takes me from the Bronx to Manhattan. I told him in the morning that I never wanted to see him again. But that night he came to my house. He actually sat in the kitchen sweet-talking my mother; his tongue is like sugar. I was upstairs trying to study for the LSAT. I didn't even know that Steven was in the house. When I went down to the kitchen and saw him, I exploded again. I threw dishes at him—anything that was at hand. I broke one of my mother's prized platters, and she was furious at me. Even when I told her later about Steven and the details of his life, she was still angry with me, not him. She said that I'm too particular. But all I want is my own man—someone who'll be faithful to me."

Linda's sadness was suddenly replaced by an intense angry energy that seemed to well up from inside her and ignite the air around us. In a louder voice and with less carefully modulated speech, she said, "I get real angry. I fume. I fume whenever I think about the lies that Steven told me. He talked and talked about our future together, the vacations that we would have, our children, what dreams he had. And I joined him in those dreams. Now I feel like such a fool!"

"And now you feel sad and angry," I said.

Linda looked directly at me. Just as her anger had come on suddenly, so too did her grief. Our eyes locked; hers were tear filled, with one tear streaming down her cheek. She was unmindful of it. We were silent together.

I said, "And now you're in mourning."

"Yes," Linda agreed. "I miss Steven. He's a scumbag, but I miss him." Now she cried unrestrained, reached for a tissue, blew her nose, and said, "I guess people cry here. You must be used to this."

I said, "Yes, sadness brings many people into therapy."

"Most of the time I'm more mad than sad," Linda countered.

I said, "Yes, you mentioned being angry a lot of the time. On the telephone you called it an attitude. When do you feel this attitude? In relationships with men or at other times as well?" I asked.

"I've had some fights with boyfriends in the past. There was one guy in high school who drew a knife on me. I fought with him, first to avoid the knife, and then I drew one myself. This happened in my sophomore year. I was fifteen at the time. It happened at home. I was in the kitchen with this boyfriend. He was also a friend of my mother. She really liked him. And he was a devil scumbag. Mother broke up the fight. She says I have to do something about my temper." Linda paused.

"Do you think your mother is right about that?" I asked. "She may be worried about what your temper could lead to. Do you ever worry about that? A temper can be a dangerous thing."

"No, I don't lose my temper often," Linda said. "I have fought, but only one or two times. I might yell at a boyfriend, but I don't do anything beyond that usually."

"On the telephone you told me that sometimes you have an attitude at work. Does your temper get you into trouble there?" I asked.

"At work, I do have an attitude sometimes," Linda said, "but it's short-lived. It happens when people keep me waiting on the phone, or interrupt my work, or make demands of me that I think are unfair."

"Unfair?" I asked.

"Yes. Unfair," she responded. "My job is a dead-end proposition. I was happy to get it after I finished Marshal College. Having a B.A. from Marshal wasn't that helpful in getting a job. My cousin was already working in the accounting firm that employs me, so she helped to get me in. I don't mind the job. It's interesting some of the time, but I wouldn't want to be doing it for the rest of my life. I majored in political science. I want one day to be a criminal lawyer. I've always wanted to be some kind of lawyer."

"When did you finish college?" I asked.

"Three years ago," she said. "I graduated from Stanford High School of Science eight years ago. I was a fairly good student. It wasn't easy to make A's, and I didn't make them regularly. When I graduated I had a scholarship to Harbor College, but I decided not to take it. Now I'm sorry that I didn't." Linda looked at the floor and seemed sad again.

"What made you decide against taking the scholarship?" I asked

"Marshal seemed like the easiest way to go," Linda said. "I had friends going to Marshal—people from the church—and it was close to my home. I found going to Stanford High to be a lot of pressure, and I wanted to have an easier time in college. Also, I wasn't sure I could handle Harbor College and work at the same time. I needed to work part time and partially support myself while I was in college, and, if I look back on it honestly, Harbor College seemed like a snooty school. I changed my mind during junior year at Marshal, and I reapplied for a Harbor College scholarship, but I didn't get one.

I wish now that I had gone to Harbor College. Harbor is such an excellent school that going on to law school from there would have been a natural progression. I should have gone to law school right after college, but it feels as if it's just too late. If I do go to law school, I would like it to be away from New York City, away from my family. But I'm not sure that mother can handle everything on her own. She's getting old; she's sixty-five. When I come home at night, I help her cook; I clean on weekends. If I go away, leave New York, I'm not sure who would take care of her."

Session 2. *Linda began her session with an admission that "last week I didn't tell you something important. I don't tell most people. No one at work knows. I don't want to deal with their reactions. I guess it is really my own reaction that I don't want to deal with, I'm just so angry."*

"My older sister, Mary, has AIDS," Linda continued. "She got AIDS from a boyfriend. She knew that he was an addict, but did not know that he was HIV positive, and he died last year. Mary's very sick, and she makes unreasonable demands on Momma. She's angry all of the time. She makes my Momma's life miserable." Linda's eyes filled with tears. "My sister has a ten-year-old son; his name is Roy. He's a hellion, but I love him dearly. What will become of him when Mary dies?"

I said, "This is so sad. I wonder if there's a connection between your sister's illness, your mother's need to take care of her, worries about your nephew, and your own feeling of being trapped."

"Yes," Linda said, simply. She continued, "I'm not sure I should leave home. I think my sister and nephew need me, and I know my mother needs me. But I want so badly to get into some law school and go away and leave everything behind. My brother, Jerry, did that; he lives in Denver. I talked to him on the telephone last night, and he said that I must get away in order to save myself. I think he's right, but it's just so difficult. I make more money than anyone else in my family. Mary asks me for money all the time. I've even given her my credit card. That was a mistake because now I've got debts that she has piled up."

We explored the meaning of Linda's inability to limit Mary's use of her credit card. I interpreted the need to give Mary money as Linda's way of relieving her survivor guilt. Clarifying the central issue of Linda's treatment, I said, "You want to be helpful to your family, and you want to begin your own life in a planful way. You're not sure if it is possible to do both. You equate moving on in life with abandoning your family. You seem to feel that you need to sacrifice yourself in order to take care of Mary, your mother, and Mary's child. No wonder you feel trapped. I wonder if that perception—your need to be the family caretaker—is accurate?"

Linda looked directly at me. Her eyes were now dry. She said, "My mother tells me I don't need to take care of anyone. Mary has welfare. My father and mother will take care of Roy when Mary dies, and Roy is a sturdy soul. He'll survive—that is, if he can stay away from cocaine himself. My parents tell me all this. They want me to go to law school—in fact, they've encouraged me to apply to USC. I have a cousin in Los Angeles who I could live with, but I'm not sure about the move."

"Linda, you are in the midst of making a life decision that is difficult. You would like to go to law school and live apart from family, but leaving them is not easy. You're con-

cerned that mother will not survive without your help; your sister's illness adds another complication. It may be hard for you to proceed with your life while Mary has very little to look forward to. It may be hard to plan your future while she is dying."

DISCUSSION

The first task in any well-organized psychotherapy is to establish a treatment contract with the client. This contract includes a conceptualization of treatment goals, based on the presenting problems and psychodynamic issues of the client. When the client requests brief treatment, as Linda did, treatment goals must be specific and limited in scope. Many clients begin therapy with a definitive number of sessions allotted by their medical insurance. Linda had six. To formulate clearly focused treatment goals and determine whether brief therapy is the appropriate form of care for a particular client, the therapist reflects on a series of important questions:

- What is this client's most important presenting problem?
- What are the emotionally painful psychodynamic issues that underpin the problem?
- Is the client fully aware of the problem and motivated to change?
- What ego strengths does the client possess that help or hinder change?
- What environmental issues and family and work relationships may be triggering or complicating the presenting problem?

These questions were in my mind while I listened to Linda on the telephone and saw her during our first two sessions. I found it difficult to clarify Linda's presenting problem. On the telephone she spoke of feeling trapped, depressed, and filled with dread over the prospect of taking a scholastic aptitude exam. When she entered our first session, her ideation had shifted. She now focused on the loss of a boyfriend and saw this loss as her reason for needing "to talk to someone." Eventually her associations returned to her fear of taking the aptitude test and then shifted to her worry about applying to law school. These two tasks, taking the exam and applying to law school, were developmentally normal aspects of Linda's young adult strivings that stirred conflict. While the completion of these tasks represented the prospect of a developmental gain and an independent and satisfying adult life, it also meant the abandonment of family. Linda viewed herself as indispensable to her family. She believed that her elderly mother needed her help with daily chores, and her older sister, suffering from AIDS, was financially dependent on her. Linda here seemed to project her own neediness and difficulty about separating from her family into the current problems that each member faced. Although age and illness were important issues, Linda's ambivalence about independence had surfaced in other situations and went back many years.

Linda's intelligence and hard work had led to superior academic performance in high school. At graduation she chose the emotionally safe path by attending a college in her neighborhood rather than accepting a scholarship offered by a more prestigious "snooty school." This appears to have been a developmently regressive choice, which Linda soon regretted. Going to Marshal rather than to Harbor College may have symbolized a retreat into her family. Linda was facing the same challenge once again: remain in her protective family circle and be its valued support or move on with her life. Repetition of this earlier choice seemed to activate the original separation anxiety.

Linda had conflict about other life choices as well. Her fury in our first session seemed connected to both the loss of her boyfriend and her mother's accusation that she was too fussy in her choice of men. This accusation meant to Linda that her mother thought her unworthy of a life partner who would be as reliable as Linda's father. Mother's comment and Linda's disappointment and angry response were based on the dynamics of oedipal competition that occurs frequently in mother-daughter relationships. The dual source of Linda's fury seemed to intensify it. First she felt betrayed by her boyfriend, later by her mother, and then viewed these two as having colluded against her. Linda's history of combative behavior appeared to be associated with similar situations involving oedipal confrontation. So in spite of some indication of problems in the control of aggression, I viewed her flights of temper as isolated events in a person of great ego strength. My understanding of Linda's oedipal fury deepened as sessions progressed.

Combining crisis theory with psychodynamic ideas enriched my comprehension of Linda's presenting problem, the tempo of treatment, and the need to keep it time limited. The pending LSAT exam was a hazardous event, the more so because she had failed to take it on a previously scheduled date. Turning away from the exam a second time might have replicated her experience of having turned down the college scholarship, which had earlier led her to feel a sense of failure and low self-esteem. Linda needed help to meet the challenges of taking the exam and to complete her law school application. The fullness of content and the fluidity of feeling in our first therapy session were the products of Linda's being in a state of crisis. At the end of our second session I limited the focus of Linda's treatment to her conflict over separation from family. I addressed both sides of this conflict: her wish to go to law school and her fear that by doing so she would be alone in the world and abandoning her family in their time of need. Her guilt seemed tied to the intensity of her own neediness. Viewing others as being in need of her was actually a reflection of her need for them. By setting a termination date that limited treatment to the allotted six sessions, separation issues were activated in the therapy relationship. The rationale for this action was to make time a therapeutic tool. The brevity of our relationship played out my belief in Linda's capacity to move on with her life.

Session 3. *Linda entered my office with a definite spring in her step. She settled into her chair smiling but silent. I waited a minute or two, then said, "Did you have any thoughts after our last session?"*

She said, "I'm feeling better lately. Knowing why I've felt stuck helps. If I don't take the LSAT *and apply to law school, life will pass me by, and you are right about it being hard for me to leave my family. I want to. My brother did it, and I know I can. But it would be easier if my parents were a little younger; I feel that they need me. My father is a short-order cook. He has always earned a good living, but times are tough. Last year he borrowed money from me to pay the taxes on our house—it's a brownstone. My father is smart; he bought it for peanuts, and he'll sell it for a pretty penny when he retires next year. My parents will move from the Bronx when he retires. I could wait for that, make my changes when they do. But I shouldn't wait any longer. I'm twenty-five. Now is a good time to go to law school."*

Linda continued to describe the pressure she felt on a daily basis, her sense of being torn between family responsibility and her own life goals. She said, "It's hard for me to go home at night. It's hard to study. Mary's in the living room; her son, Roy, is running in and out of all the rooms. There's never enough quiet. I decided that enrolling in the LSAT preparation course at Kaplan, using those tapes, and studying at Kaplan, would be the best way to go. It would also give me an excuse for not going home."

"An excuse?" I asked.

"I feel that I must go home," she said. "If I have to go to an LSAT preparation class, then there's a reason for not going home."

"So it's your own sense of guilt, a feeling that you're needed at home," I said, "rather than a reality that pulls you there."

"Yes," Linda replied. "I talked it over with my mother. She thinks the LSAT preparation course is a good idea. I enrolled in it before, but I never completed it. That was last year. I've been trying to take this exam for a year-and-a-half. I'm going to do it now: I'm determined."

I wondered if her brother and sister had attended graduate school. Linda said no. She is the first in her family to graduate college, and she will be the first to have a profession. Her brother in Denver has a good job in an engineering firm, but he got his skills through on-the-job training, not in an academic program. I said, "So you will be the first in your family to have extensive education. It is not easy to be the first. Sometimes moving beyond one's family in this way can cause some guilt, too."

"That may be true," Linda said, "but I have felt different from my brother and sister for a long time. They got into so much trouble when they were younger—drugs, alcohol, the works. I've stayed away from all that. I do drink sometimes, when I go out to clubs, but never more than one drink; I don't like the feeling of being out of control."

Session 4. *Linda entered my office and announced, "Yesterday I refused to give Mary my credit card. I thought about what you said about limiting her. I told Mother that we—you and I—had discussed how I give Mary my credit card, and she runs up bills. Mother said that you're a good influence on me. She also told me that I should ask you to help me with my English."*

"Your English?" I asked.

"Yes," Linda laughed. "Mother says that I need to speak more correctly and that you would know about that."

"Helping you with your speech is not what I'm here for," I said, "but I wonder if your talk about language is really a worry about fitting in and feeling comfortable as a student in a predominantly white law school. That worry may have stopped you from taking the LSAT in the past. It might have stopped you from accepting a scholarship to Harbor College."

Linda was startled, then pensive. She said, "I wonder whether you understand the kind of neighborhood I live in. When I go home from work, I don't leave my parents' house. I can't walk on the street comfortably, and I have to watch myself. I can take care of myself, but it isn't comfortable. The family has been talking about moving for a while. We have always lived in our brownstone; it is nice. My room is on the top floor. My parents' bedroom is on the second floor, and so is Mary's and Roy's room. The first floor has the living room where Mary hangs out. If my parents were to sell the house, with the real estate market the way it is, they wouldn't get as much as they'd like to one day; they'd like to hold on to it for a while. Our neighborhood might be gentrifying. Wouldn't that be a kick? Then they could retire to Florida in peace. I guess after Mary dies, they'll take my nephew with them unless I stay in New York and he lives with me."

"These are all very difficult decisions to make," I said, "and thoughts to have. We're really talking about the future, the time after your sister's death."

"Yes," Linda said, "and you know, I don't like Mary much. She can have a sense of humor, but she's caused so much trouble in the family for so long that it's hard to be anything but angry with her right now. She was my parents' only kid to have a hard-core drug problem. She always cut school and hung out with street people. There was a time when my parents didn't know where she was. She just disappeared and lived on the street. I remember my mother's tears. Sometimes Mary and I have good talks, and we go shopping together; it can be good. But she's not the older sister I've always wanted; she never will be. She's not an easy woman to be around, and she's always in a contrary mood. My father says I'm too critical of Mary. He says I'm too critical of everyone, especially myself."

By our third session, Linda was better organized in her problem-solving capacities and somewhat calmer. She had begun the working-through phase of this treatment by centering her attention on feelings about leaving her family. Early in the third session, Linda admitted the importance of the LSAT exam and her law school application: if she did not follow through this time, life might pass her by. She voiced worries about leaving her family. I helped her test the reality of these worries and eventually clarified her dilemma as intrapsychic rather than interpersonal by stating that "her family might need her, but her own feeling about their need was greater than fact." This comment addressed Linda's defenses. In response she explored the history of her law school application efforts. I focused indirectly on her anxiety about achievement, hoping that this tactic would help her to contain her anxiety rather than exacerbate it. When I wondered if she were the first in her family to go on to graduate school and pointed out that to become better educated can stir guilt based on a sense of moving beyond family, my intent was to normalize her fears about achievement. Linda's response to these speculations was to recognize that she was different from both her brother and sister. Both had difficulties with drugs and alcohol; Linda, by contrast, had never abused substances. This reflection bolstered her emerging autonomy from her family, confirmed her sense of impulse control, and strengthened what I believe to be her inherent ego strength.

Linda continued the working-through process in the fourth session. Her identification with me seemed apparent when she withheld her credit card from her sister. Linda's show of strength earned approval both from her mother and me. In her mother's eyes, I seemed to be Linda's bridge to the (white culture) world outside her neighborhood. Linda's evident desire for entry into that world was expressed in a request that I help her with language diction. To do this, however, would not have been therapeutic or respectful of her cultural difference and may well have been ego diminishing. I did view her request as an indication of Linda's anxiety about fitting into a predominantly white law school. In the past, similar anxiety had led her to reject a Harbor College scholarship and avoid the LSAT. Linda's reaction to this clarification was restrained anger. She challenged the extent to which I understood how violent her urban neighborhood really was. Her expression of anger may have been an effort both to underscore and bridge our cultural differences. I gently directed her attention to her difficulty in leaving behind that world, though it had consumed her sister, Mary, through drugs and an expected premature death from AIDS. Linda now gave vent to her anger at Mary and finally seemed able to mourn her.

Session 5. *Linda began the next session talking about her father. The final words in Linda's previous session had been a reference to her father's opinion about her critical attitude toward others and herself. In her eagerness to talk about her father, it was as though time had not passed between this session and the last one. This sense of timelessness seemed to be an indication of Linda's termination anxiety. I waited for an opening to remind her that we had only one more session. In a rush of words, Linda reported, "I have judgments about everyone, but maybe most about my father. He's far from perfect. He's been relatively faithful to my mother, but last week when we went shopping, Mary and I, we saw my father's son again. He has a son by another woman, a son the same age as I am. When my mother was pregnant with me, my father began to wander, and he got involved with a woman in our neighborhood. His son, David, was born a month after me. My father was a fast worker. I didn't know about David until recently; I found out about him on an earlier shopping trip with Mary, about a month ago. We were in the grocery store, standing in the checkout line, when Mary said, 'You see that man over there? He's our father's son.' I felt the room go around. I felt lightheaded, anxious; I didn't know what to say. Mary laughed, and then she said, 'I thought you knew, Linda. He's your age.' Dammit, Mary can be cruel! I didn't know. I talked about it with my father that night. He said that he paid child support for David until four years ago, and he'd never told me about David because he didn't want me to be upset. I wish he had told me."*

"I wonder if you always knew about David yet did not admit that knowledge to yourself," I commented.

"No, I didn't know," Linda said. "I wish I had. I'm not sure why. It would have been easier to know. Maybe because everyone else in the family knew about David. Mary, my cousins, aunts, uncles—everyone knew. No one told me. I'm the only one who wasn't a party to the fact that David existed."

"Do you feel angry with your father for his philandering?" I asked.

"Not anymore," Linda said. "Things can happen. Daddy doesn't need to be perfect. But dammit, if I have a man, he'd better not end up in some other woman's bed. Not my man!" Linda laughed, and I joined her.

She sat in silence, a bit forlorn, for a moment. Then she continued, "My father has done his best by us. We never had to worry about food or the roof over our heads, and he did support David. He is a good father."

"So you would like to find a man at least as good as your father has been to your mother," I said.

"Yes," she said. "I really would like that. I would have like to have known about David, but I'm not angry. It was a long time ago. He didn't desert us, and he didn't desert the other woman. He didn't desert David. That is what a man should be—reliable. Daddy didn't tell me about David because he didn't want to cause me pain; maybe he was right. Maybe it's best that I found out recently. I can understand him now. When I was a kid I would have been just plain angry."

Session 6. *As our last session began, Linda described the steps that she was taking in the direction of law school. "The LSAT is next week, and I've written to my cousin in California. I've asked her to look into the law school at USC, and I've also written for an application. It feels like a very faraway place to go, but it may be easier for me to get into that school than one here in New York City. They seem to be interested in out-of-state students. I'm also going to apply to places closer to home. I don't think I can do well enough on the LSAT to get into Harbor College, although that is what I would like. But I don't think I'll make it. Fordham and Yeshiva would be much easier entry for me. If I apply to USC and I don't get in the first time, I might apply again next year. But I have some hope about doing well on the LSAT. The practice tests at Kaplan last night were easy enough, and I've liked studying at the tape center. Everyone there is doing the same thing. It's much easier to concentrate there than at home."*

"Enrolling in the LSAT class at Kaplan was a good move," I said. "It helped you to focus on your goal more clearly."

Linda agreed. She then looked at me with a twinkle in her eye and said, "I haven't told you about George. I met George five days ago, on the train. The subway can be a good place to meet men. He's a nice guy. He owns a delicatessen in our neighborhood. We've gone out twice this week, and last night he told me that he's looking for a wife. Pretty funny, huh!"

I now reflected, "So there's a new man in your life, and he's looking for a wife. That must be exciting. You, in fact, may be a good catch for him." We both laughed.

"George is picking me up after my class at Kaplan tonight," Linda said. "We're going to go to a club in the Village where we can dance. George had considered going to law school himself at one time."

"So I guess he is supportive of you and your ambitions," I added.

"Yes, he is," Linda agreed.

"That would be in your father's tradition," I said. We laughed again together, and the session was over. Before she left my office I wished Linda good luck on her exam. She said that she would call and tell me how it went. She telephoned the following week to let me know that the exam had gone well.

Our last two contacts were termination sessions. In the first of these, Linda resolved what I believe was her unconscious reason for needing therapy: a sense of betrayal arising from her father's failure to tell her about his out-of-wedlock son. It was easier for Linda to be angry at Mary, the messenger of information, than at her father, the perpetrator of sin. Linda respected her father's willingness to support his son, forgave him his secret, and expressed longing for a similarly reliable man of her own.

In our final session, Linda focused directly on two vital areas of life: work and love. She made law school a reality by sorting through the details of the application process. The study center that was helping her prepare for the LSAT exam constituted a new support and reference group. Linda could now see the road ahead. She had begun to welcome a different kind of man into her life, one who would encourage movement onto this road. My approval of George, and the link that I made between feelings about him and Linda's father, gratified her oedipal longings. At that moment in the transference I was the mother who wanted her to move forward in her work life but also to succeed in developing a loving relationship with a man.

Linda terminated after six sessions, as we had previously planned, although her separation and oedipal conflicts were by no means totally resolved. Such developmental issues require more intensive treatment. However, our brief encounter put her on the path to change. One always wonders how much a client values therapy. Linda's assessment of her treatment was demonstrated four months later when a friend of hers called me and said, "Linda sent me. My problems are like hers, and she said that you were helpful."

Unlike the work of Davanloo, my clinical treatment of Linda did not use transference to confront characterological patterns of behavior. Transference existed as a positive element in the therapeutic alliance, and because it did not block treatment progress, it was not interpreted. The nature of Linda's transference was maternal. I was the enabler, her ego bridge out of family and into the world at large.

SUMMARY

Time-sensitive clinical social work is an effective model of short-term treatment. Building on the ideas of crisis intervention theory and ego psychology, this chapter examined the history of this model, discussed time as an organizing principle in treatment, and concluded with a case example that integrated these ideas into practice. This form of clinical social work practice is rooted in the pragmatic trends of social work's professional history and in ideas that spring from the Freudian psychoanalytic tradition. Ego psychology and crisis intervention theory supply the rationale for its clinical techniques.

The profession of social work has long been committed to acting as a mediator between client and environment: encouraging a capacity for improved personal functioning in the face of undermining social stressors. Economic forces, an element of environment, have always influenced the nature of services rendered to clients. Economics have influenced the current widespread use of brief therapies. Recently the predominant source of much mental health funding has shifted from the public to the private sector, and business interests are increasingly influencing treatment decisions. A client's therapy is often subsidized by insurance payments that are controlled by the policies of a managed care company that considers brief treatment cost-effective and therefore usually the preferred form of care. The current professional struggle is one of maintaining an authoritative voice in treatment planning. Knowledge is a key factor in upholding this authority. Understanding the theoretical base of short-term therapy is essential in knowing when and how to use it as an effective modality of care. (See Chapter 14.)

Viewing time as a factor in the therapeutic process is a basic assumption of the Freudian school of thought. The Freudian concept of a timeless unconscious proposes a connection between past and present: early personal history, current symptoms, and maladaptive behaviors. In addition, time is considered to have a developmental purpose, a direct impact on the psychosexual maturation of the individual. The timeless unconscious gives transference its healing power. Experiential transference bridges time, bringing the past into the present, constructing a corrective emotional experience, and surfacing dysfunctional behavior patterns that can be challenged by a therapist's interpretations.

Recent clinical theorists believe that putting limitations on treatment time can support a client's motivation for therapeutic gain and that well-focused and clearly limited treatment goals propel change. These ideas are in harmony with those of crisis intervention theory. Crisis theory suggests that the energy available for dealing with a crisis is most accessible during the six weeks following a hazardous event. During this time, experiencing a great sense of emotional disequilibrium, the individual's ego strives for mastery over stressors and develops new modes of problem solving, and rapid emotional growth occurs. Clinical theorists vary in the way that they define treatment goals. For example, Caplan views the reestablishment of a sense of inner calmness along with an improved capacity for coping with the recurrence of a similarly hazardous event as a valid outcome of crisis intervention. Mann and Goldman consider the further resolution of separation-individuation conflict as a viable treatment goal. Davanloo believes that character analysis is the central task of brief therapy and self-awareness its goal. Ellis, Beck, Reid, and Epstein all emphasize the importance of cognition and task-centered realities in problem-solving activities that can lead to healthier adaptation.

In the case illustration used, time had a role in both the therapist's assessment of the client's problems and the goals of treatment. Therapy was limited by insurance coverage to six sessions. Information was swiftly gathered and used to formulate rapidly attainable treatment goals. The client's limited time in treatment helped to confront resistances to change, and the avoidance of reflection was overtly challenged. As the connections between wishes and fears springing from early family relationships and current dysfunctional behaviors came into awareness, they were interpreted. These interpretations had both cognitive and learning dimensions that seemed to enhance the client's ego strength. In this clinical situation, transference was an enabling aspect of the therapeutic relationship that supported the resolution of separation conflict by encouraging growth. The client's participation in short-term therapy required preexisting ego strength and motivation for change. These personal attributes enabled the client to maximize her use of limited therapeutic time.

REFERENCES

Alexander, F., & French, T. (1946). *Psychoanalytic therapy.* New York: Ronald Press.

Bauer, G., & Kobos, J. (1995). *Brief therapy.* Northvale, NJ: Jason Aronson.

Beck, A., Rush, A., Shaw, B., & Emery, G. (1979). *Cognitive therapy of depression.* New York: Guilford.

Bloom, B. (1992). *Planned short-term psychotherapy: A clinical handbook.* Boston: Allyn & Bacon.

Bollas, C., & Sundelson, D. (1995). *The new informants.* Northvale, NJ: Jason Aronson.

Caplan, G. (1964). *Principles of preventive psychiatry.* New York: Basic Books.

Cohen, N. (1958). *Social work in the American tradition.* New York: Holt, Rinehart and Winston.

Davanloo, H. (1980a). A method of short-term dynamic therapy. In H. Davanloo (Ed.), *Short-term dynamic psychotherapy* (pp. 43–71). New York: Jason Aronson.

Davanloo, H. (1980b). The technique of crisis evaluation and intervention. In H. Davanloo (Ed.), *Short-term dynamic psychotherapy* (pp. 245–281). New York: Jason Aronson.

Edelstein, M. G. (1990). *Symptom analysis: A method of brief treatment.* New York: Norton.

Eisenstein, S. (1980). The contributions of Franz Alexander. In H. Davanloo (Ed.), *Short-term dynamic psychotherapy* (pp. 25–41). New York: Jason Aronson.

Ellis, A., & Abrahms, E. (1978). *Brief psychotherapy in medical and health practice.* New York: Springer.

Freud, S. (1885). Studies in hysteria. In *Standard Edition* (Vol. 2, pp. 125–134). London: Hogarth Press.

Garcia, R., & Irwin, O. (1962). A family agency with the problem of dropouts. *Social Casework, 43,* 71–75.

Jones, E. (1955). *The life and work of Sigmund Freud* (Vol. 2). New York: Basic Books.

Kogan, L., Hutn, J., & Blenkner, M. (1951). A study of interrelated factors in the initial interview with new clients. *Social Casework, 32,* 23–30.

Linderman, E. (1944). Symptomatology and management of acute grief. *American Journal of Psychiatry, 101,* 141–148.

Mahler, M., Pine, K., & Bergman, A. (1975). *The psychological birth of the human infant.* New York: Basic Books.

Malan, D. (1976). *The frontier of brief psychotherapy.* New York: Plenum.

Mann, J., & Goldman, R. (1982). *A casebook in time-limited psychotherapy.* New York: McGraw-Hill.

Marmor, J. (1980). Historical roots. In H. Davanloo (Ed.), *Short-term dynamic psychotherapy* (pp. 3–12). New York: Jason Aronson.

Parad, L. (1971). Short-term treatment: An overview of historical trends, issues and potentials. *Smith College Studies in Social Work, 41,* 119–146.

Reid, W., & Epstein, L. (1972). *Task-centered casework.* New York: Columbia University Press.

Reid, W., & Epstein, L. (1977). *Task-centered practice.* New York: Columbia University Press.

Reid, W., & Epstein, L. (1978). *The task-centered system.* New York: Columbia University Press.

Sifneos, P. (1987). *Short-term dynamic psychotherapy: Evaluation and techniques.* New York: Plenum.

Spitz, R. (1965). *The first year of life.* New York: International Universities Press.

Straker, M. (1980). Crisis intervention: An overview. In H. Davanloo (Ed.), *Short-term dynamic psychotherapy* (pp. 221–236). New York: Jason Aronson.

20

Social Work Interventions with Alcohol and Other Drug Problems

Maryann Amodeo

Too often when clinicians think of intervening with alcohol and other drug (AOD) problems, they think of chronic alcoholics, heroin addicts, and women with crack cocaine habits. These populations constitute only a fraction of the clients seen in social work settings who have AOD problems. The majority of alcohol- and drug-involved clients have not reached the stage where functioning is dramatically impaired. They are living in families, attending school, holding jobs, and maintaining households.

They often come to human services agencies with presenting problems related to family life, health or employment status, and educational or career goals. Most often they have not recognized that their drinking and drug use either contributes to or is the cause of the problems for which they seek help. Consequently they do not bring up drinking and drug use as an aspect of the presenting problem and, if asked about it, would say that it does not interfere in their lives. Such clients often continue on workers' caseloads for long periods as the AOD problem remains hidden from both worker and client. Unidentified, it undermines the achievement of therapeutic goals. Thus, a major challenge for social work is to acquire the screening and brief intervention skills necessary to identify and motivate these clients to seek help.

RATIONALE FOR SOCIAL WORK INTERVENTION

Of an estimated 18 million Americans with alcohol use problems (to say nothing of those with drug use problems), less than 15 percent receive treatment (U.S. General

Accounting Office, 1991). This may be changing as health care settings, driven by the need for cost containment, implement early screening and brief intervention methods. But AOD problems are currently pandemic in society and in virtually every setting where social workers see clients: family service, health, mental health, child welfare, school, employment, and court and correctional settings.

If AOD problems are not identified in mental health settings, they can masquerade as other diagnoses (e.g., cocaine dependence can create symptoms of depression; alcoholism withdrawal can create symptoms of panic attacks), leading to inappropriate treatment, for example, the prescribing of psychotropic drugs. Thus, clients who use AOD regularly and come to sessions high are unlikely to benefit from the sessions because the chemicals cause distortions in perception, new learning, memory, and affect. When clients have developed tolerance to these drugs, their use may not be discernible to the worker; thus, the worker and client may spend many hours designing and trying to implement a service plan that ultimately comes to nothing.

AOD problems can be life threatening, especially when they have progressed to the chronic stage, but death can also be caused in the earlier stages or with only occasional use by particularly vulnerable individuals such as the elderly, teens and preteens, and those with medical conditions exacerbated by alcohol and other drug use.

Finally, alcoholism and drug dependence are conditions that often involve intergenerational transmission. For many families, if no intervention occurs, intergenerational transmission is almost certain.

POTENTIAL FOR UNIQUE CONTRIBUTIONS BY SOCIAL WORK

Social workers can be found in a variety of settings designed to help healthy populations lead a full and satisfying life: schools, day care centers, youth recreation programs, adoption agencies, and health centers, among others. This access to healthy populations provides the opportunity for unique contributions in the area of prevention of AOD problems. This means that social workers are in an ideal position to facilitate primary prevention (promote health before problems begin) and secondary prevention (screening, identification, and brief intervention when problems are in the early stages and have not progressed into full-blown conditions), as well as tertiary prevention (treatment of the full-blown condition) and rehabilitation (intervention designed to limit the debilitation caused by the chronic condition).

Social work's ecological perspective increases the likelihood that workers will adopt a wholistic approach in assessing and intervening with AOD problems. Rather than assuming that the problem resides only in the individual or only in the environment, the ecological perspective looks at the interaction between them. It is a person-in-environment and environment-in-person perspective (van Wormer, 1995).

Social work training provides specific skills that are needed for effective work with alcohol- and drug-involved clients. Among those skills are family outreach and intervention; working with a range of defenses, including denial, avoidance, and intellectualization; working through loss and grief to resolution and recovery; the ability to use differential approaches to treatment, including cognitive, behavioral, psychodynamic, and family systems; and an appreciation for the role of self-help programs, natural support networks, and indigenous healers in client recovery.

SCOPE OF THE PROBLEM

Consequences of Abuse and Dependence

If a thorough discussion of the scope of AOD problems in the United States were to be undertaken, this chapter would be so long as to preclude attention to any other clinical issue. Thus, only a few aspects of the problem will be highlighted.

Although there has been some decline in per capita alcohol consumption in the United States since the early 1980s, many of the pernicious effects of alcohol consumption continue. Alcohol was a contributing factor in half of all fatal traffic crashes in 1990. Alcohol-related mortality accounted for about 5 percent of all deaths in the United States in 1988. Heavier drinkers die at younger ages, and estimates of years of potential life lost per individual from alcohol-related conditions such as alcoholic liver disease and fatal traffic crashes are substantially higher than those associated with conditions such as cancer and heart disease.

Alcohol was the most frequently used drug among high school seniors in 1990. Despite their underage status, 90 percent of this group had drinking experience, 32 percent drank heavily (five or more drinks at a single sitting) in the two weeks prior to the survey, and 3.7 percent reported drinking daily (*Eighth Special Report to the U.S. Congress on Alcohol and Health,* 1993).

The economic cost of alcohol and drug abuse is more than two and a half times that of all other forms of mental illness combined (Group for the Advancement of Psychiatry, 1991). Medical treatment of alcoholism and drug addiction, combined with the psychiatric consequences of these conditions, is responsible for approximately 40 percent of hospital usage in the United States (Beasley, 1987).

A nationwide household interview survey indicated that in 1988 approximately 15.3 million individuals met the DSM-III-R criteria for the diagnoses of alcohol abuse or dependence, or both. Rates were higher among males than among females and highest in the younger age groups surveyed—those between eighteen and twenty-nine years old (*Eighth Special Report to the U.S. Congress on Alcohol and Health,* 1993).

Either directly or indirectly, 50 percent of the patients seen in emergency rooms are there because of alcohol or other drug abuse (Evans & Sullivan, 1990). Between 30 and 40 percent of homeless Americans are alcohol abusers, and 10 to 15 percent are drug abusers (Caslyn & Morse, 1991; McCarty, Argeriou, Huebner, & Lubran, 1991). Concerning drug abuse only, truancy, school dropout, and absence from the labor force increase with use. Drug-using adolescents tend to leave school earlier, start work earlier in low-paying jobs, and form families earlier. Entry into other forms of criminal activity is more likely (Kail, 1992). Significant health problems are associated with needles that are not sterile, adulterants in the drugs, the drugs themselves, and lifestyle issues associated with drug use.

Intravenous drug abuse has played a major role in the spread of the AIDS epidemic. Intravenous drug abusers comprise the second largest group that has contracted AIDS in the United States. HIV infection is spread among intravenous drug abusers primarily through the sharing of needles, but it can also be spread through sexual contact. The AIDS epidemic is expected to grow for some years. Since most individuals infected with HIV do not yet have symptoms and do not know they are infected, there is a great likelihood of continued spread of the disease.

Drugs of Abuse

Alcohol is the drug most misused in the United States, but there is still much societal resistance to accepting it as a drug. Alcohol's legal status contributes to denial about its characteristics as a drug and its devastating effects. Polydrug use (the same person's regular use of more than one drug) is a common pattern and can include taking drugs with different or opposite physical effects in sequence on the same occasion (Maisto, Galizio, & Connors, 1991). For example, cocaine users may switch off to alcohol and other sedative drugs when they feel too overstimulated. A polydrug pattern is the most common pattern seen among clients in treatment in the United States.

Major categories of drugs of abuse are:

1. Alcohol.
2. Other depressants, including barbiturates (sleeping medications), benzodiazepines (minor tranquilizers), and quaaludes.
3. Stimulants, including cocaine and amphetamines.
4. Marijuana.
5. Hallucinogens, including LSD and mescaline.
6. Opiates, including heroin, codeine, Percodan, Demerol and Darvon.

For a comprehensive discussion of drugs of abuse, the following books are recommended: Doweiko (1993), Maisto, Galizio, and Connors (1991), Palfai and Jankiewicz (1991), Ray and Ksir (1990), and White (1991).

DEFINITIONS AND DIAGNOSTIC ISSUES

Much of the research and writing on alcohol and other drug abuse has focused on alcoholism rather than drug dependence, but many researchers and clinicians believe that explanatory models for alcoholism are applicable to other drug dependencies. Although there are significant differences in the psychoactive qualities of various drugs and their potential for dependence and physical addiction, there are also significant similarities. For the purposes of this chapter, frameworks developed to describe alcoholism are also applied to drug dependence.

DSM-IV Criteria for Abuse and Dependence

The *Diagnostic and Statistical Manual of Mental Disorders*, fourth edition (American Psychiatric Association, 1994) provides criteria for substance abuse and dependence, as well as specific information on various drugs of abuse and their addiction course. The primary feature is a maladaptive pattern of use, occurring within a twelve-month period, leading to failure to meet major role obligations; legal, interpersonal, or social problems; or use in situations that are physically hazardous.

Dependence is characterized by three or more of the following occurring at any time in the same twelve-month period: tolerance, withdrawal, impaired control, restructuring of activities to facilitate drug taking, and continued use despite persistent negative consequences.

An Addiction Continuum

Doweiko (1993) has developed a continuum of degrees of drinking and drug use:

1. Total abstinence from drug use.
2. Rare social use of drugs (using one or more drugs on a social basis).
3. Heavy social use/early problem use (abusing one or more drugs on an episodic basis).
4. Heavy problem use/early addiction (abusing one or more drugs on a continual basis).
5. Clear-cut addiction (p. 12).

Such a continuum is helpful because it allows for the classification of drug use of various intensities and patterns, and it minimizes the tendency to think of alcohol and other drug dependency as an all-or-nothing phenomenon.

Alcoholism and Drug Dependence as Diseases

Alcoholism and drug dependence have been defined as diseases by the American Medical Association (Doweiko, 1993). Like other diseases, they have identifiable signs and symptoms, are chronic, are progressive in the sense that they become worse if untreated, can be fatal if untreated, and result in tissue damage. Although much of the general public understands that alcoholism and drug dependence are treated as diseases, this concept has met with some controversy over the years.

In 1960, *The Disease Concept of Alcoholism* (Jellinek, 1960) was published. Based on a survey of Alcoholics Anonymous members, it described alcoholism in behavioral and psychological terms, with identifiable stages and progressive symptoms, including loss of control or the inability to limit drinking, a pattern of negative consequences, and finally withdrawal symptoms and the psychological and physical devastation that often accompanies chronic alcoholism. This schema made a significant contribution to explaining alcoholism but was based on key concepts that have since been challenged: that progression occurs inevitably, that the progression of symptoms occurs in the order that Jellinek delineated, and that a total lack of control occurs. Vaillant

(1983) found that drinking patterns change over time so that some individuals who have a pattern of abuse are able to move back to social use and that alcoholics are more likely to experience impaired control (Vaillant, 1990) rather than a total loss of control over their drinking.

These and other challenges (Fingarette, 1988; Peele, 1989) notwithstanding, Jellinek's model continues to have utility in identifying the types of symptoms that often appear as individuals move from moderate, nonproblem use, to abuse, to dependence. A benefit of the disease conceptualization is that clients, family members, and the general public can see that addiction has biological and physiological aspects, which make it more than willful acting out. The term conveys that the sufferer did not seek the condition, which can lead to reduced moralism and stigma, facilitating the securing of help. However, a drawback is that this medicalization of addiction emphasizes the biological over the psychological and social. It minimizes the influences of culture and societal forces in the development of AOD problems and can lead to myopia in the choice of intervention approaches.

Alcoholism and Drug Dependence as Multicausal and Multivariant Conditions

Alcoholism and drug dependence can be thought of as biopsychosocial illnesses (Wallace, 1989). They are considered to be multicausal conditions involving a range of factors, including genetic and/or biological (e.g., inherited predisposition to dependence), psychological (e.g., experiences of early trauma or repeated losses, or existence of a preexisting psychiatric disorder), familial (e.g., lack of parental limits on use or parental role modeling of excessive use), and cultural (e.g., cultural norms reinforcing drinking and drug use as a rite of passage or measure of masculinity). (For a comprehensive discussion of theories of etiology of alcoholism and drug dependence, a number of texts and articles are available, among them, Doweiko, 1993; Freeman, 1992; Levin, 1987, 1995; Pattison & Kaufman, 1982; Schuckit, 1986; Tartar & Sugarman, 1976; Wallace, 1989; and Washton, 1989.)

These factors make a differential contribution to the development of AOD problems for various individuals. Alcoholism and drug dependence can also be thought of as multivariate conditions in that they display themselves in diverse patterns of dysfunction (Pattison & Kaufman, 1982). Thus, for some individuals, medical consequences and physical symptoms predominate and result in the diagnosis. For others, it is a persistent pattern of negative social consequences such as employment, relationship, and legal problems that result in the diagnosis. For others, it is the inability to limit or control the amount consumed that results in the diagnosis.

Alcoholism and Drug Dependence as Primary Illnesses

Alcoholism and drug dependence should be viewed as primary illnesses rather than as symptoms of other disorders, the prevalent view in the mental health field twenty-five years ago. While use may begin in response to another disorder or personal problem, these conditions take on lives of their own as a person progresses into alcoholism or drug dependence. Regardless of precipitants, a cycle of dependence has been established that will generate negative consequences of its own.

Alcohol and Drug Abuse and Dependence Among Adolescents

Adolescents deserve special attention as a population at high risk for developing AOD problems and as a group that often experiences AOD problems in ways that differ from the progression described for adults. The challenge for clinicians who work with adolescents is to neither underestimate nor overestimate the severity of the AOD problem for any individual client. The former mistake is common among workers who assume that drinking and drug use is a normal phase of adolescent development and will spontaneously disappear as teens mature and find other interests. The latter mistake is common among workers who assume that the behavior exhibited by teens will invariably persist into later years. Neither assumption is borne out by research (Doweiko, 1993).

McNeece and DiNitto (1994) recommend that the presenting symptoms of a substance-abusing child or adolescent be considered from a developmental framework, that is, how much damage is likely to occur from this behavior based on the individual's age and developmental level. They suggest that clinicians examine the level of medical risk for the child or adolescent, for example, from sexual practices and the risk of human immunodeficiency virus (HIV) infection when using substances. They also recommend an examination of the meaning of the substance use to the child or adolescent. Are substances being used to cope with dysphoric states? Are they exacerbating more serious emotional disorders? (Research suggests that substance abuse may be a causative or contributing factor in conditions such as conduct disorders, affective disorders, attention deficit hyperactivity disorder, and anxiety disorders.)

McNeece and DiNitto (1994) also recommend that clinicians pay close attention to the contexts of the AOD problem, including legal, social, familial, and educational. Because they are minors, children and adolescents must function within these contexts, and ideally, it is within these contexts that incentives for behavior change can be identified. Clinicans would do well to examine the forces within these spheres that act to intensify or diminish the drinking and drug use behaviors, assess the overall severity of the situation, and mobilize individuals and resources to motivate the child or adolescent to get help.

ASSESSMENT AND INTERVIEWING METHODS

Countertransference and Transference

Potent and negative countertransference is often generated in workers facing clients who have AOD problems. In part, this is the consequence of living in a society that has a long history of moralism toward such individuals, viewing them as morally weak, lacking in self-discipline, unwilling to change, and untreatable. In part, this also results from personal experiences many clinicians have had using alcohol and other drugs themselves and interacting with family members and loved ones with AOD problems.

These life experiences can be thought of as filters, or lenses through which clinicians see AOD-troubled clients, and they often intensify workers' difficulties in viewing clients objectively and responding to their needs. For example, a clinician who has used alcohol and other drugs and was able to control the use without trouble, or found it easy to reduce the use when problems began, may be impatient or angry with the compulsive nature of the client's use. The clinician whose own use of alcohol or other drugs is excessive may resist labeling a client's use as abuse or dependence unless it far exceeds the clinician's own pattern and has become debilitating. Growing up in an alcoholic or drug-dependent family provides another filter, which may leave the clinician feeling cynical, overwhelmed, or defeated when faced with clients with AOD problems (Amodeo & Drouilhet, 1992).

In addition to these forms of direct countertransference, indirect countertransference, or the worker's responses to influences outside the worker-client relationship, is common for workers who see AOD-troubled clients, particularly involuntary clients. Referral agencies such as courts, schools, and child welfare organizations often convey the expectation that it is the worker's responsibility to see that the client becomes clean and sober. Responding to the real or perceived pressure of a third party watching over the treatment process, workers often become directive, overcontrolling, and confrontational (Amodeo & Drouilhet, 1992). In response, clients often defend against any acknowledgment that behavior change is necessary. They perceive that the worker is allied with or is an agent of the referring institution, that the worker is engaged in an effort to force them to relinquish something that has become central to their existence (drinking or drug use), and that admission of a problem may result in further losses, such as placement of children in foster care. The clinician's ability to identify his or her countertransference responses and manage them appropriately is key to working effectively with this population.

Identifying Risk Factors and Indirect Indicators

Assessment is the cornerstone of effective prevention and intervention with AOD problems. Since clients often do not correlate their drinking and drug use with the presenting problem, it will be through workers' careful assessments that AOD problems will be identified. Routine screening for AOD problems should occur as part of every psychosocial history. In some settings where alcohol and other drug abuse may affect 80 percent or more of the client population (e.g., child welfare agencies, court clinics, and other forensic settings), workers should assume that clients have AOD problems until such problems have been specifically ruled out.

A number of formats have been recommended for conducting assessments, some using social work frameworks (Freeman & Landesman, 1992; Orlin & Davis, 1993; van Wormer, 1995) and others based on the perspectives of medicine, nursing, and psychology (Clark, 1981; Doweiko, 1993; Estes & Heinemann, 1986; Estes, Smith-Dijulio, & Heinemann, 1980; Liftik, 1995; Metzger, 1988; Washton, 1989). These formats provide guidance for clinicians about the aspects of the client's life to be examined, the order in which the assessment should occur, specific questions to be raised, and methods for determining severity. One of the most useful of these formats has been described by Liftik (1995), who recommends that prior to asking specific questions about drinking and drug use, clinicians should be alert to risk factors in clients' backgrounds and current circumstances that make them particularly vulnerable to developing such problems and indirect or hidden indicators of alcohol or other drug problems in clients' family, educational, employment, health, and relationship history. Risk factors can include parental and extended family attitudes about drinking and drug use, family history of alcoholism and drug dependence, age when drinking and drug use first started, experiences of early trauma, and peer group involvement with AOD.

Risk factors can be discussed with clients in the context of helping them determine whether they are currently at risk for developing a dependence on AOD, and if so, how they can limit current problems and prevent more serious ones. Clients are often familiar with discussions of risk factors from medical settings, where they have heard about their risks for conditions such as heart disease depending on family history and individual status with regard to smoking, cholesterol, or weight gain. Such a discussion can be supportive to clients since it is focused not on demonstrating that clients have problems but on offering assistance in preventing the further development of problems.

Indirect indicators or red flags often consist of the negative consequences of drinking or drug use. They may include behavioral signs, such as personality changes, erratic job performance, unexplained memory lapses, or the smell of alcohol during appointments; medical signs such as gastritis (from drinking), hepatitis (from drugs), or dripping nose (from intranasal cocaine use); or social indicators, such as having a heavy drinking and drug-using peer group or engaging in social activities that revolve around AOD.

Mrs. Kent, a thirty-year-old African American woman, applied to the adoption agency to adopt her cousin's daughter, Gemini, who was three years old. Gemini's mother was cocaine dependent and was unable to care for the child. Mrs. Kent was a single parent who was separated from her husband.

The worker conducting the adoption home study could see that Mrs. Kent cared about Gemini's well-being. She had taught Gemini how to dress herself and fix food for herself when she was hungry. When she had time, Mrs. Kent played with Gemini and read to her.

During home visits, Mrs. Kent often looked haggard and depressed. When the worker mentioned that Mrs. Kent looked fatigued, Mrs. Kent became angry and defensive, saying she often had trouble falling asleep or woke up during the night and could not go back to sleep. She went on to say that if she finally fell asleep, she would not be able to get up until noon or early afternoon. She was vague about how long the pattern had been going on and dismissed the worker's questions with statements that it was "nothing for the worker to worry herself about."

She also seemed to have little energy to clean the apartment or fix meals and delegated these tasks to her two biological children, who were ten and eight. She relied on the children to care for themselves. Even Gemini was in the habit of going by herself to Mrs. Kent's mother's apartment on the top floor of the building. Using the fire escape, Gemini would climb three flights of rickety metal stairs in daylight and darkness, good weather and bad, to see "grandma." Witnessing this and hearing that it happened all the time, the worker was alarmed that Mrs. Kent did not see the danger. Gemini could fall several stories if she lost her foothold; she was out of sight for hours at a time in a building with occupants Mrs. Kent did not know; and the building was in a neighborhood known for its share of violence.

There were a number of red flags that Mrs. Kent had an alcohol or other drug problem. Each of these indicators appearing alone in a case might mean little. It is the accumulation or constellation of factors that should alert the worker to the likely presence of AOD problems.

- Problems sleeping and awakening; appearing haggard and fatigued. AOD use could be involved in various ways. Heavy drinking can lead to interrupted sleep; cocaine users may have trouble falling asleep, then feel fatigued and depleted when they "crash."
- Inconsistent parenting of young children and parentification of older children. AOD-involved individuals often have difficulty with consistent parenting. When drug free, they can be attentive and involved; when high, they tend to be self-involved and preoccupied with drug seeking. Their children learn early in life to care for themselves.
- Defensive responses to innocuous comments or questions. AOD-involved clients are often hyperalert to criticism. Comments that could be seen as covert references to the individual's addiction will be met with defensiveness and hostility.
- Relatives who are AOD dependent. Because heredity plays a role in AOD dependence, having relatives who are AOD dependent may put a person at greater risk. Also, drug-dependent relatives may initiate other family members into drug use, introduce family members to dealers, pressure family members to keep them company in their drug taking, and portray drug taking in a positive light.

The worker would need to do a detailed AOD history here given the number of indirect indicators and risk factors. Such an AOD history requires more time when alcoholism or drug dependence are present due to denial and other defenses common to addictions. A full session or multiple sessions may be needed.

Maintaining the Therapeutic Alliance During Assessment

Clients are often convinced that no drinking or drug problem exists in spite of comments to the contrary from others in their lives. Involuntary clients are particularly determined to prove to the worker that no problem exists and to have this message conveyed back to the referring agency—the court, employer, child welfare agency, school, or similar other organization. Inexperienced workers commonly fall into the trap of prematurely discussing whether there is a drinking or drug problem and what should be done about it. Clients begin these discussions by asserting that changes in their lives are unnecessary. Workers, focusing on why the clients have been sent to treatment, often respond by pointing out that behavior change is necessary to prevent future trouble. They would like to see clients avoid the negative consequences they know are likely, such as arrests, accidents, loss of significant relationships, having children sent to foster care, or disability or death. Workers may also feel pressured by the sense that the referring institution expects the worker to get the client clean and sober quickly.

When workers declare that a problem exists and that clients need to change, they are seen as adversaries. Henceforth, clients withhold important personal information or engage in defensive debate and dismissal of the workers' ideas and concerns. In the following vignette, the worker avoids this trap by refocusing the assessment to provide an opportunity for the development of rapport and trust prior to discussing alcohol and other drug issues.

Kevin was a twenty-two-year-old Irish American male mandated by his company to have an evaluation at a substance abuse clinic. In a random urine screening, Kevin tested positive for marijuana. During the initial session with the worker, Kevin contended that he was only a "social user," smoking marijuana whenever friends came over. He told the worker that she would never convince him otherwise. The worker knew she needed to avoid discussing such a charged issue so soon in the therapeutic relationship since it was likely that they would become polarized over it.

Instead she told Kevin that she needed more background information to help her see his situation as a whole and asked Kevin to describe his educational, family, work, and social life and talk about his goals for himself in counseling and in life in general. She knew that this background information would help her see if there were indirect indicators of a substance abuse problem. Also this approach would be less likely than a direct discussion of drinking and drug use to mobilize the denial, avoidance, and other defenses that would be there if Kevin was indeed in trouble with AOD.

The worker learned that Kevin lived at home with his parents and two brothers. He described his family as close and said his parents were concerned about and involved with their children. His mother still made sure there was a hot meal on the table if Kevin planned to be home for the evening. He had lived in the same neighborhood through his elementary, junior high, and high school years. He enjoyed school because he was able to hang out with friends, but said that in high school he was singled out by teachers as a wise guy. This led to his frequently skipping school.

Kevin said his goal for counseling was to keep his job. He believed his only problem was that he was unfairly singled out due to random drug testing. He believed most of the other employees used AOD in a way similar to him.

Before the first session ended, the worker told Kevin that their task would be to explore the role drinking and drug use played in his life and to determine whether there was anything about his drinking and drug use that he wished to change. The worker stated that a decision about change would be entirely up to Kevin and that the worker was prepared to accept whatever conclusion Kevin came to about this. This was said to underscore the fact that the worker did not intend to force Kevin to give anything up and would not serve in the role of an agent of coercion.

Integrating Drinking and Drug Use Questions into the Psychosocial Assessment

Clients will be less defensive if drinking and drug use are discussed as part of exploration of other aspects of the client's history. This minimizes the possibility that the client will feel singled out or interrogated. Also, clients are generally more able to acknowledge past than current problem behavior. Following are examples of questions about childhood and adolescence in the psychosocial history that can help to bring the client's experiences with AOD to the surface. In parentheses are issues the worker should be thinking about:

- *Extended family:* Did your family have much contact with your extended family—grandparents, aunts, uncles, and cousins? What were these relationships like? (Was there alcoholism, depression, suicide, social isolation, or estrangement in the extended family?) What were family gatherings like? Was there lots of eating, drinking, dancing, and athletics? (Did these occasions end in drunkenness, arguments, brawls?)

- *Parental discipline:* Was it strict or loose? What were the issues: dating, sex, drinking? (Was there permissiveness around drinking and drug use? Was there subtle encouragement of drinking and drug use? Was there neglect of the children so that the parents were unaware of what the children were doing?) What were parental attitudes and rules?

- *Peer group:* How connected were you with peers? What type of kids did you hang around with? Were they into sports, cars, sex, drugs, outdoor activities, good grades, going to college? Where did you fit in? Did you begin experimenting with drinking and drugs with your peer group? At what age? What were those experiences like: exciting, scary? Did you feel out of control? Did you get physically ill? Did you get punished? What types of drugs did you try?

- *School performance:* How did you do in school socially and academically? What were the factors contributing to your performance? If it was poor, did drinking or drug use play any role?

- *Coping methods:* When some things went badly for you at home, in school, or with your friends, how did you deal with it?

Kevin's assessment continues.

> *Having learned that Kevin often skipped school and had been singled out as a wise guy, the worker commented that many teens had experimented with drinking and drug use by this point in their school experience, and she wondered what Kevin's experience had been by the time he got to junior high. Kevin acknowledged that by the time he was twelve or thirteen, he was drinking and had tried drugs, and sometimes he went to school when he was high. The worker then asked what drugs he had used. He said, "Pretty much only alcohol and marijuana." The worker noted that he had said "pretty much," which she interpreted to mean that there were other drugs, but she decided to move away from drinking and drug use questions because Kevin had become tense. She believed that he would become more defensive if she pressed the issue at that point.*

Instead she returned to general questions, asking about his high school experience, including whether teachers continued to see him as a wise guy, whether there were parts of the school experience he enjoyed, and his grade-point average at graduation. He volunteered that as a high school senior, he was using cocaine and selling small amounts to get money to buy his own. Within a year after graduation, he was stopped but not arrested for drunk driving by a police officer who was also a neighbor. Kevin was incredibly relieved because he had cocaine in the car, but the car was never searched. After this close call, he stopped using cocaine. This latter statement he made with pride, as if demonstrating that he was not a person who became dependent on drugs.

In describing his social life, Kevin said that he and his friends often went to a local bar. Still cautious about asking directly about AOD, the worker decided to return to this after learning more about Kevin's social life. Asked to talk about his relationships with women, Kevin said he had had several girlfriends since age sixteen but the relationships ended in conflict. He found that girls tried to control him and were jealous of his close relationships with his buddies.

The worker wondered to herself if Kevin's girlfriends were concerned about his AOD use and were thus seen as "trying to control him." Since Kevin had talked about the local bar as a place where he spent much of his time, the worker asked how often he and his friends gathered at the bar and how long they typically stayed. Kevin said most nights they stopped in at least for a while. The worker then said, "Tell me about your drinking." Kevin said on a typical evening he drank one or two six-packs and had a mixed drink or a shot. In response to the worker's probing, he said that he drank more on some evenings and might return home intoxicated two or three times a week, usually on weekends.

Taking a Focused Drinking and Drug History

Having noted risk factors and indirect indicators, the clinician may need to go on to take a focused drinking and drug history. Liftik (1995) recommends that the clinician avoid mobilizing denial and defensiveness by asking a series of questions about drinking and drug use when the client has already indicated through the more general assessment that these topics are off-limits. He recommends, as do other authors (Amodeo, 1995a; Brown, 1985), that the focus of the interview be shifted at least temporarily to other aspects of the presenting problem. AOD problems are usually so persistent and pervasive that they surface again soon, albeit in disguised form. When issues come up that sound AOD related—for example, panic attacks, intense or extended arguments, verbal abuse, violence, medical emergencies, memory problems, or performance problems at work—the clinician should ask directly, "Were you high when this occurred?" "What role did drinking play in this incident?" "Had you used cocaine in the day or two before this occurred?"

One of the benefits of taking a drinking and drug history is that it gives clients an opportunity to hear themselves report on the role of AOD in their lives. Clients see that what they perceived to be isolated incidents or random drinking and drug-using behavior falls into a pattern. Workers should strive to engage clients in a dialogue that provides a picture of the client's typical pattern and also atypical experiences or one-time events. The following six parameters can be kept in mind by workers as they engage clients in a dialogue: (1) quantity (amount used); (2) frequency (regularity of use); (3) duration (length of time the pattern has continued, in years, months, weeks, or days); (4) precipitants (factors that trigger use, including thoughts, feelings, bodily sensations, interactions, or situations); (5) consequences (effects or results of use); and (6) control (extent to which there have been efforts to limit use by reducing amounts or frequency, or establishing external controls such as asking others to hide the drugs or take charge of money that could be used for drugs).

If clients evidence a pattern of repeated negative consequences, there is a likelihood of substance abuse. If clients evidence both repeated negative consequences and impaired control (i.e., taking the substance in larger amounts or over a longer period than intended), there is a likelihood of substance dependence. The DSM-IV criteria for each should be examined carefully.

Considered together, the parameters are especially helpful in identifying opportunities for prevention and early identification, that is, in identifying patterns where no diagnosis would be made but clients could be warned that their use was heavy or hazardous and could lead to eventual trouble.

The salience of AOD in a person's life should also be considered in an assessment (Babor & Grant, 1992). Salience means prominence, importance, or conspicuousness. Reframed, salience reflects the nature and intensity of a person's relationship with AOD. Salience is the extent to which this relationship dominates the thoughts and actions of the person, affects the person's sense of self-esteem and well-being, and results in the sacrificing of other relationships in preference for this one. The following case illustrates this dynamic.

Saul was a twenty-nine-year-old second-year medical student when he initiated therapy with a social worker in private practice. He was from an upper-middle-class Jewish family. His father was a physician and had exceedingly high expectations of Saul. Saul reported that his problems began when he started medical school one and one half years ago. He became depressed and anxious, fearing that he would not succeed. He spent much of his time alone and had no close friends.

The therapist agreed to work with Saul on his adjustment to medical school, his father's expectations of him, and his own expectations of himself. The worker suggested they meet for eight sessions.

During the fifth session, the therapist noticed the smell of alcohol while meeting with Saul and realized that he had smelled alcohol before. He had not included AOD questions in his assessment so he could not rule out a substance abuse problem. In the next session, when Saul talked about persistent anxiety related to his academic performance, the worker asked Saul if he ever used AOD to manage this anxiety. Saul said he had not used drugs since college, and then he had used only marijuana, but that he generally had a few drinks during the evening when studying. He said he had never associated this with his feelings of anxiety. The worker asked him what types of drinks he preferred and how many he typically had. Saul said he usually had three or four gin and tonics. The worker asked whether Saul usually drank at times when he was not studying. Saul said he would often have a few drinks when watching television, listening to music, or reading.

The worker told Saul that exploring drinking was important because, without Saul's recognizing it, his drinking might have increased to the point where it was having a negative effect. The worker said that it was important to identify any factors that might contribute to Saul's feelings of anxiety, lack of productivity, and poor self-esteem. The worker was aware that alcohol is well known for affecting all three.

The worker then explored whether there were days when Saul drank more than four drinks and the maximum consumed on those days, how long the pattern had continued, whether Saul had experienced memory lapses, and how Saul felt physically and emotionally on days when he did not drink. The worker learned that Saul seldom had more than four drinks per night, but on mornings when he felt especially anxious, he also drank one to three drinks just before leaving for school. Daily drinking had continued for over a year, but there were no blackouts and no withdrawal symptoms.

When the worker asked Saul to picture spending evenings without drinking, Saul said he felt isolated and restless, with nothing to look forward to. The worker pointed out that moderate, nonproblem drinkers do not develop an intense relationship with alcohol and that Saul needed to consider whether his drinking pattern should be changed. Saul was frightened by the idea that he might be psychologically hooked on drinking.

Continued Assessment Using a Reduced Use Experiment

To determine whether clients meet the DSM-IV dependence criterion related to impaired control, workers can suggest that clients engage in a reduced-use experiment or, alternatively, an abstinence experiment: preplanned, time-limited attempts by clients to modify their drinking and drug use patterns. Details are worked out with the clinician to ensure that the experiment is a real test of the criterion. Such experiments work only if clients are receptive to trying them. If clients are pressured into them, especially under circumstances where clients are mandated to attend treatment, there is a high likelihood that clients will convey the idea that the experiments were successful, whether this is true or not.

The worker suggested that treatment be extended to work on the drinking issue. He suggested that Saul try to cut down on his drinking for a two-week period, limiting himself to no more than two per night and none at any other time of the day. Saul tried this for two weeks and was unsuccessful. The worker suggested he try for another several weeks, asking him every session or two about his progress on this goal. At times he reported fairly close adherence to the goal but acknowledged going over the limit about half the time. Within eight weeks, Saul realized he would need to remain abstinent for the long haul since even one or two drinks triggered the desire to keep on drinking.

FRAMEWORKS FOR VIEWING THE TASKS OF TREATMENT

Many theoretical frameworks—cognitive-behavioral, psychodynamic, family systems, and person-in-environment—have been used to view the treatment of AOD problems. Each has made a valuable contribution to understanding the helping process and has a place in intervening with AOD problems. Three frameworks offer guidance to clinicians in structuring and sequencing the work.

Determining Readiness for Change

Prochaska and DiClemente (DiClemente, 1991; Prochaska & DiClemente, 1983) have developed a stages-of-change model that provides a method for assessing clients' readiness to alter addictive behavior. Six stages that mark the individual's progress through the change process are outlined:

1. *Precontemplation.* The individual has never considered changing the addictive behavior because he or she does not believe that the behavior is a problem.
2. *Contemplation.* The individual begins to think about changing the behavior but is not convinced it needs to be changed.
3. *Determination.* The individual recognizes that change is necessary and makes plans to change (e.g., setting a date for the change and announcing to others that the change will occur, or reducing the frequency of the behavior targeted for change).
4. *Action.* The individual stops the addictive behavior.
5. *Maintenance.* The individual continues the action over the long term, integrating the new behavior into the course of daily living.
6. *Relapse.* The individual fails to maintain the behavior change.

Individuals in the relapse stage who do not remain there over the long term will return to contemplation and perhaps progress again through the other stages. Success has often been preceded by movement through the sequence several times.

Miller and Rollnick (1991) have utilized this framework as part of their "motivational interviewing" method based on reflective listening. Client ambivalence is seen as a predictable dynamic, and clinicians are encouraged to validate its presence and assist clients in examining the content and feelings related to it as a necessary step toward action. The choice to change behavior rests with the client. Clinicians are advised to adopt a nondirective stance in negotiating goals and assisting clients with them. This means that abstinence may or may not be the goal.

Bean (1984) outlines eight tasks of recovery that incorporate both cognitive and psychodynamic theory and help clinicians focus on abstinence and recovery in a sequenced way. The worker's role is initially educational. Grief work related to loss of alcohol is seen as a necessary step in achieving and maintaining abstinence. Psychotherapy is helpful in achieving long-term recovery since the addiction process is viewed as one that profoundly changes identity. Understanding alcoholism from three perspectives—medical, psychological, and moral—is seen as essential in the treatment. Workers are encouraged to help clients see the disease aspects of their condition so they will accept medical treatment, the cognitive distortions and self-defeating patterns that have developed so they will accept psychotherapy, and the internalized societal moralism toward alcoholics that they themselves experience so they can begin to forgive themselves for having the condition.

Brown (1985) describes a developmental model of recovery incorporating cognitive, behavioral, psychodynamic, and family systems theory. Like the Prochaska and DiClemente and Bean models, it guides the clinician to work on tasks in a sequenced fashion. The model describes four stages:

1. *Drinking,* when clients come for treatment for other reasons and are unaware of their alcohol or other drug problem.
2. *Transition,* when clients experiment with abstinence but have not yet made a commitment to it.
3. *Early recovery,* marked by a commitment to abstinence, a time when acquiring the tools of abstinence is the central issue, and cognitive methods and twelve-step programs are most essential.
4. *Ongoing recovery,* when identity, intimacy, and examining life goals are the central issues, and psychotherapy can be most useful.

Although the framework explicitly addresses only alcoholism, it is equally applicable to drug-dependent clients. It is based on a perspective that views alcoholism as having profound emotional consequences for the alcohol-dependent drinker. It reminds the clinician to be aware of the emotional vulnerability of the alcoholic and the elaborate defenses erected to cope with the vulnerability.

Finally, the model demonstrates how to integrate psychotherapy and abstinence work, providing guidance on addressing trauma and responding to increases in environmental stresses. Specific methods for working with denial and other defenses during these stages are described by Amodeo (1995a, 1995b) and Zweben (1995).

Following detoxification from heroin and prescription pain medication, Laura, a forty-four-year-old white, divorced woman, began treatment to prevent relapse and deal with symptoms of anxiety and panic, which sometimes made it difficult for her to get out of bed in the morning. She worked as an administrative assistant for an advertising agency. There was considerable pressure on the job. She functioned efficiently on the job through her three-year opiate addiction, but her work began to deteriorate at the point she entered the detoxification program.

The outpatient therapist recommended that Laura attend at least three meetings of Alcoholics Anonymous (AA) or Narcotics Anonymous (NA) each week and find a temporary sponsor until she got to know enough people in the program to choose her own permanent sponsor. Therapy sessions were spent practicing cognitive and behavioral techniques for managing anxiety, and Laura often called AA and NA friends for support during an especially stressful workday. Eventually the worker recommended that Laura take imipramine for her panic symptoms since they continued unabated for some weeks.

Within six months, Laura no longer experienced daily anxiety. Within a year the panic symptoms had diminished almost entirely. She began to consider applying to graduate school. She also began dating Devlin, a man who lived in her apartment building. Therapy focused on Laura's improved self-esteem, her self-image as a woman, and her career goals.

She then became preoccupied with her relationship with Devlin and whether he would make a permanent commitment to her. All discussions returned to this subject. The worker knew that intense emotional involvements could threaten early abstinence.

Although Laura had been drug free for a year, she had periodically experienced impulses to return to drug use. The worker saw Laura as still managing the tasks of early abstinence and was concerned about how Laura would handle rejection. Further, Laura had discovered that drinking was an important activity in Devlin's life. The worker saw Laura as being vulnerable to relapse from spending time with someone whose life was organized around drinking.

The worker suggested that Laura get some distance from the relationship by seeing Devlin less often or taking a break from the relationship. Laura became furious and defensive, saying the worker did not trust Laura's judgment and had not observed her progress. The worker then engaged in "hand wringing" (Bean, 1986), a vivid demonstration of worry and concern on the part of the therapist related to the client's physical and emotional safety and ability to engage in self-care. The worker "worried aloud with Laura" about Laura's preoccupation, spelling out the risks to Laura of being unable to focus on other issues or moderate her involvement. The worker stressed that for many recovering people, spending time with someone who was so often high could lead to relapse—to rationalizations about the power of AOD to restimulate the addiction.

In addition, the worker recommended that Laura increase her attendance at AA and NA and begin attending Al-Anon, for family members and friends concerned about someone's drinking or drug use. Laura attended an initial Al-Anon meeting but was convinced that the program was unnecessary because Devlin would soon give up drinking.

Within a few months, she began getting intense headaches, had her doctor prescribe pain medication, and relapsed to using heroin. She struggled to control her use, then tried to taper off and stop. Over a three-month period, she called frequently to cancel appointments because she was too "dope sick" to come in. The worker offered to arrange detoxification, but Laura declined. Finally, Laura called from a detoxification unit where she had admitted herself. She was getting "clean" and had decided that, following her detoxification stay, she would go to a recovery home until her abstinence was solid.

In retrospect, the worker could see that she had allowed the therapy to "move too far from the alcohol and drug axis" (Brown, 1985) once Laura's anxiety had diminished and she had several months of abstinence. Instead, therapy had focused on the feasibility of graduate school, career goals, and identity issues. When Laura became involved with Devlin, the worker realized that she should have responded to this environmental demand by shifting back to the alcohol and drug focus. She and Laura should have reexamined the tools Laura would use to maintain abstinence, Laura's definition of high-risk situations at this new juncture in her life, and Laura's backup plan for abstinence if her typical coping methods failed and she found herself thinking about the possibility of using drugs again.

TREATMENT METHODS AND THE CONTINUUM OF CARE

Abstinence

In general, abstinence rather than controlled use is the treatment goal. Most treatment agencies in the United States operate on this abstinence model, viewing this as the only path to recovery. Although some individuals, especially young people, may be treated for misuse of AOD and return to moderate, nonproblem use, practice experience supports the need for abstinence as a treatment goal for those who have developed alcoholism or drug dependence (Hester & Miller, 1995). This issue is controversial, however. Research is under way that may someday identify individuals for whom a controlled-use treatment goal is more appropriate.

Treatment Methods

In many communities, a continuum of services developed to treat alcoholism and drug dependence addresses acute and chronic needs and includes elements such as detoxification, inpatient and outpatient, long-term residential, and follow-up services and specialized services for high-risk groups such as pregnant and parenting women, individuals with HIV or AIDS, youth, elderly, dually diagnosed clients, linguistic minorities, and clients of color for whom traditional services may be inappropriate. Treatment services along the continuum vary in intensity and are meant to respond not only to the client's current status but also to the severity of the addiction.

A number of treatment modalities are utilized within this continuum of services, including didactic education about addiction, individual counseling, group therapy, family education and treatment, urine testing, psychotropic medications, exposure to twelve-step programs, and relapse-prevention training (Doweiko, 1993; Levin, 1995; Maisto, Galizio, & Connors, 1991; Washton, 1989). High success rates for these programs are often claimed, but controlled studies of outcome are often lacking (Institute of Medicine, 1989).

Typically clients participate in more than one modality during a single course of treatment. Over time, many clients utilize services at various points along the continuum of care. For example, after completing detoxification, a client might attend a partial hospital program and then move to outpatient status.

When offering treatment options, workers should consider the gender, age, ethnicity, culture, and sexual orientation of the client. These factors influence the client's ability to respond to typical or mainstream treatment methods, which were often designed for middle-aged, white, heterosexual males. Effective treatment methods for some clients may include use of an indigenous community healer rather than appointments with a psychiatrist, joining the neighborhood Pentecostal church rather than attending Alcoholics Anonymous, residing at the local Buddhist temple rather than going to a residential treatment facility, or going to a sweat lodge rather than a detoxification center.

For a comprehensive description of the structure of treatment programs and specific treatment modalities, a number of references are recommended, including Brisbane and Womble (1985), Doweiko (1993), Friedman (1993), Hester and Miller (1995), Kinney (1991), Levin (1995), O'Dwyer (1993), O'Farrell (1993), Pattison and Kaufman (1982), Spiegel (1993), Vanicelli (1992), and Washton (1989).

Twelve-Step Programs

Twelve-step programs such as AA, NA, and Al-Anon are important self-help resources. Workers often suggest that clients attend these programs without preparing clients for what they might find when they arrive and without exploring clients' apprehensions about attending.

To maximize the success of the referral, workers are advised to read literature on the programs and attend meetings themselves (many are open to the public). This will help workers confront their own stereotypes of the program—the most significant barrier to making an effective referral. The client's ideas and concerns about the type of people who attend, the requirements for membership, the philosophy, and what will be expected of the client at meetings and afterward should be thoroughly explored. Meetings in different locations should be suggested so clients can sample the personality of different groups. If clients reject these programs as an option, a power struggle should be avoided. If clients have difficulty initiating or maintaining abstinence by other means, twelve-step programs can be reintroduced later as a resource. The suggestion can be made that clients try again to work on recovery in their own way, but agree to attend a specified number of future AA or NA meetings if their method fails.

Concerning research on twelve-step programs, McCrady & Delaney (1995) point out that although the data on effectiveness are limited and mixed, the vast majority of people who initiate involvement with AA discontinue their involvement in less than a year (AA, 1990). But evaluation studies suggest that there are positive benefits of AA: large numbers of individuals attend, and those who continue attending are likely to remain abstinent. Combining AA and professional treatment probably increases the likelihood of a positive outcome (McCrady, 1995).

Myra is a thirty-two-year-old Latina diagnosed as cocaine dependent. The drug problem was identified by a protective service worker responding to a report of neglect related to Myra's three-year-old daughter, Angelina. The worker referred Myra to an inpatient program. The program, reluctant to accept cocaine-dependent clients unless they had first tried less costly outpatient treatment, accepted Myra because her repeated efforts to quit on her own had been unsuccessful, her apartment building was a mecca for drug deals, and the worker advocated strongly for this service plan. Angelina was placed in foster care.

As a condition for Angelina's return, Myra was mandated to attend outpatient counseling and undergo regular urine screening following discharge. Myra developed a positive relationship with the clinician assigned to her and attended sessions regularly. Myra relapsed several times during her initial months in treatment. Urine screens were helpful in alerting the worker to these relapses, but the worker asked Myra to agree to tell the worker about relapses prior to receipt of the urine test results. This strengthened the therapeutic alliance and kept the worker out of the watchdog role.

After several months of "dirty" urines, Myra established eight months of abstinence. She received badly needed dental care, moved to a safer neighborhood, and began to plan for Angelina's return to live with her. Then Myra's mother died unexpectedly, and the foster family alerted Myra that they suspected Angelina had been sexually abused by a teenager in their neighborhood. Myra's feelings of loss, guilt, and anger about both incidents precipitated a relapse. The worker increased her sessions with Myra to twice per week and referred Myra to a local addictions program for daily acupuncture treatments designed to help clients avoid relapse. Nevertheless, Myra continued to relapse about every five weeks.

In a case review, a program administrator raised the question of whether Myra should continue in the program since she had established little abstinence. The worker was adamant that Myra should remain in the program if she chose since she had made considerable progress in treatment. She had come regularly to sessions, visited regularly with Angelina and managed the visits in a healthy way, established eight months of continuous abstinence in slightly more than eighteen months, notified the worker when relapses occurred, and examined precipitants and ways to avoid them in the future. She had also completed long-needed dental care, moved to a safer neighborhood, and utilized more frequent counseling sessions and acupuncture when they were offered.

While the worker saw abstinence as a crucial measure of recovery, she emphasized that it should not be seen as the sole measure of progress in someone like Myra for whom drug dependence had been a way of life.

Eventually the worker decided to recommend that Myra enter a substance abuse day treatment program where she would be involved in relapse-prevention activities for several hours every day. If Myra resisted, the worker would point out that the current treatment plan seemed to offer insufficient support. Myra could recommend methods she thought would be better—for example, daily AA or NA meetings or getting on a waiting list for a long-term residential program—but some change seemed necessary to reduce relapses. Myra's safety was the agency's primary concern and with such frequent relapses, she was not physically or emotionally safe.

Family Intervention Approaches

Many alcoholics have extensive marital and family problems (O'Farrell & Birchler, 1987). Although there is significant evidence that problem drinking leads to marital and family conflict, it is also likely that marital and family factors play a role in the development and maintenance of alcohol problems (O'Farrell, 1995). Family members of alcoholics and addicts develop their own maladaptive patterns in order to survive, and these include an increased risk for AOD problems themselves, chronic health disorders, depression and anxiety, and difficulties with intimacy (Bepko & Krestan, 1985; Brown, 1995; Dulfano, 1992; Jackson, 1954; Steinglass, 1987).

AOD problems in the family can be viewed from the perspective of the family life cycle, with some types of alcoholic families impaired in their ability to offer a positive legacy to their children (Steinglass, 1987). Family rituals are another area of study for family therapists, with disrupted family rituals more common among transmitter families, in which alcoholism is passed to the next generation (Wolin et al., 1980).

Interventions for families and couples have also been described in terms of stages, with specific therapist tasks intended for each stage. Usher (1991) presents four stages:

1. *Treatment initiation,* when the alcohol is removed and the family accepts the problem and contracts for change.
2. *Learning,* when the family confronts the "emotional desert" of family life.

3. *Reorganization,* when ruptures in relationships are repaired and growth and change occur.
4. *Consolidation* when intimacy develops.

Bepko & Krestan (1985) and Brown & Lewis (1995) offer different schemata but also utilize stages of recovery to guide interventions.

Behavioral interventions focusing on marital interaction have been studied more extensively than family systems and psychodynamic approaches, and they currently have the greatest empirical support. O'Farrell (1995) describes a number of these behavioral interventions within three stages of recovery: (1) initial commitment to change, (2) the change itself, and (3) the long-term maintenance of change. He warns clinicians of typical obstacles encountered during the initial stage, including alcohol-related crises, the potential for violence between the partners, and the dynamic of blaming. Focusing on the change itself, he reviews such methods as behavioral contracting, structuring the spouse's and alcoholic's role in the recovery process, decreasing family members' behaviors that trigger or enable drinking, and dealing with drinking that occurs during treatment. Among the interventions recommended to improve marital and family relationships are planning shared recreational and leisure activities and homework entitled, "Catch Your Partner Doing Something Nice," a technique involving the daily recording of caring behaviors performed by the partner. These methods increase the couple's awareness of benefits from the relationship and increase the frequency with which spouses acknowledge and initiate pleasing or caring behaviors in the relationship. He concludes by pointing out that the most promising marital and family therapy method is a behavioral approach that combines a focus on the drinking and drinking-related interactions with work on more general marital relationship issues.

Matching Clients with Treatment Modalities

In the past fifteen years, more rigorous research designs and more sophisticated statistical procedures have been employed to assess treatment efficacy. Studies have been designed to examine multiple outcome measures (e.g., amount, duration and frequency of drinking; employment, social adjustment, medical services utilization), reinforcing the conclusion that outcome cannot be determined by measuring changes in drinking and drug use alone or by ignoring drinking and drug use and measuring only psychological or social functioning. This has led clinicians and researchers to try to determine reasonable goals and expectations from various types of treatments and types of clients expected to benefit from each (Institute of Medicine, 1989).

Patient characteristics that seem to predict poorer outcomes include lack of social stability, severe psychiatric diagnoses, severe symptoms of alcohol dependence, and presence of antisocial personality disorder. Research is examining the effectiveness of matching clients to particular treatments before treatment begins. This is likely to be especially useful for groups such as adolescents, elderly, dually diagnosed clients, and the homeless.

Most of the studies on treatment matching have included fairly small samples, have considered different outcome variables, and have not yet been replicated in more varied samples of clients with alcohol problems (Allen & Kadden, 1995). The National Institute on Alcohol Abuse and Alcoholism has established a multisite clinical trial to explore client-treatment matching possibilities. Called Project MATCH, this is the largest and probably most complex study of effectiveness ever undertaken in the field of alcoholism treatment (Project MATCH Research Group, 1993). Results are likely to make a significant contribution toward improving treatment outcome by helping programs assign clients to those interventions found most effective for clients with similar profiles (Allen & Kadden, 1995).

RELAPSE AND RECOVERY

A relapse is a return to use after an apparent period of abstinence and recovery. Relapse is a common problem in AOD treatment, and research has focused more intensely in recent years on determining methods for relapse prevention. In general, AOD-involved clients are considered to be at high risk for relapse during the first year of abstinence. Specific relapse-prevention methods have been identified to assist clients in early and ongoing recovery. Such methods include avoiding high-risk situations, developing a drug-free peer group, identifying personal signs of impending relapse (physical, emotional, and cognitive), and utilizing a predesigned plan to avoid acting on relapse impulses. Relapses can serve as opportunities for learning if clients can be helped to reflect on situations that preceded or seemed to trigger the relapse (Daley, 1987; Gorski & Miller, 1986; Marlatt & Gordon, 1985). Cognitive-behavioral methods have been used widely in relapse prevention and have been shown to increase positive treatment outcomes.

One of the most challenging issues for the AOD treatment field is addressing the chronic relapsing behavior of clients with dual disorders. It is common, for example, to find that addicted women in treatment have extensive trauma histories and have been diagnosed with posttraumatic stress disorder (PTSD). For at least some, drinking and drug use seems to have suppressed the trauma memories and provided temporary help with the anxiety, panic, depression, sexual dysfunction, or other symptoms associated with PTSD. Relapse has been common among such clients if the trauma work is done too soon, for example, in the first three months of abstinence. On the other hand, some clients whose memories and emotions are on the surface and need to be addressed may relapse because the trauma work is not done soon enough. A differential assessment is necessary in these cases, and clinical tools and guidelines are still evolving.

Recovery is a developmental process occurring over time and involving certain biopsychosocial benchmarks. Personnel in the addictions field often use the terms *recovering alcoholic* or *recovering addict* to describe individuals in recovery. The term *recovering* emphasizes that although individuals have made a commitment to abstinence and have demonstrated an ability to move in that direction, they continue to be vulnerable to relapse. Since the work of recovery is viewed as never fully done, the past tense of the word, *recovered,* is carefully avoided.

Recovery is also seen by many as involving necessary life changes above and beyond abstinence: repairing relationships damaged through years of drinking and drug use, dealing with shame and self-hatred, addressing experiences of early trauma, and giving up patterns acquired during addiction, including the "addict mentality" and a personality of secretiveness, manipulation, and self-absorption.

CHALLENGES FOR THE PROFESSION

Many challenges face social work in the 1990s and beyond. The emerging system of managed health care will impose a number of constraints on practice as it has been known in the past, as well as offer a number of opportunities for creative work in this area. For example, long-term individual and group therapy, typically the cornerstones of treatment for clients and families, will give way to a heavier reliance on client self-education through reading and client self-monitoring through the use of behavioral tools and other types of homework. Social workers will need to acquire the screening and brief intervention skills necessary to identify and motivate a range of clients—not only those diagnosed with AOD abuse or dependence but also those whose hazardous use could lead to physical, psychological, or social problems. Another challenge, facing the addictions field as a whole, will be to use research findings in designing treatment programs and matching methods to the needs of particular clients. Social work is a profession uniquely suited to meet each of these challenges.

REFERENCES

Alcoholics Anonymous. (1990). *Alcoholics anonymous 1989 membership survey.* New York: Alcoholics Anonymous World Services.

Allen, J. P., & Kadden, R. M. (1995). Matching clients to alcohol treatments. In R. K. Hester and W. R. Miller, *Handbook of alcoholism treatment approaches: Effective alternatives* (2nd ed.) (pp. 278–291). Boston: Allyn & Bacon.

American Psychiatric Association. (1994). *Diagnostic and statistical manual of mental disorders* (4th ed.), Washington, DC: Author.

Amodeo, M. (1995a). The therapist's role in the drinking stage. In S. Brown (Ed.), *Treating alcoholism* (pp. 95–132). San Francisco: Jossey-Bass.

Amodeo, M. (1995b). The therapist's role in the transitional stage. In S. Brown (Ed.), *Treating alcoholism* (pp. 133–162). San Francisco: Jossey-Bass.

Amodeo, M., & Drouilhet, A. (1992). Substance-abusing adolescents. In J. R. Brandell (Ed.) *Countertransference in psychotherapy with children and adolescents* (pp. 285–314). Northvale, NJ: Jason Aronson.

Babor, T. F., & Grant, M. (Eds.) (1992). *Programme on substance abuse: Project on identification and management of alcohol-related problems. Report of Phase II: A randomized clinical trial of brief interventions in primary health care.* Geneva: World Health Organization, chapter 16.

Bean, M. (1982). Identifying and managing alcohol problems of adolescents. *Psychosomatics, 23,* 389–396.

Bean, M. (1984). Clinical implications of models for recovery from alcoholism. *Addictive Behaviors, 3,* 91–104.

Bean, M., & Zinberg, N. (Eds.). (1981). *Dynamic approaches to the understanding and treatment of alcoholism.* New York: Free Press.

Beasley, J. D. (1987). *Wrong diagnosis—wrong treatment: The plight of the alcoholic in America.* New York: Creative Infomatics.

Bepko, C., & Krestan, J. A. (1985). *The responsibility trap.* New York: Free Press.

Brisbane, F. L., & Womble, M. (Eds.). (1985). *Treatment of black alcoholics.* New York: Haworth Press.

Brown, S. (1985). *Treating the alcoholic: A developmental model of recovery.* New York: Wiley.

Brown, S. (Ed.) (1995). *Treating alcoholism.* San Francisco: Jossey-Bass.

Brown, S., & Lewis, V. (1995). The alcoholic family: A developmental model of recovery. In Stephanie Brown (Ed.), *Treating alcoholism.* San Francisco: Jossey-Bass, 279–315.

Caslyn, R. J., & Morse, G. A. (1991). Correlates of problem drinking among homeless men. *Hospital and Community Psychiatry, 42,* 721–724.

Clark, W. (1981). Alcoholism: Blocks to diagnosis and treatment. *American Journal of Medicine, 71,* 275–286.

Daley, D. (1987). Relapse prevention with substance abusers: Clinical issues and myths. *Social Work, 32* (2), 138–142.

DiClemente, C. C. (1991). Motivational interviewing and the stages of change. In W. R. Miller & S. Rollnick (Eds.), *Motivational interviewing* (pp. 191–202). New York: Guilford.

Doweiko, H. (1993). *Concepts of chemical dependency* (2nd ed.) Pacific Grove, CA: Brooks/Cole.

Dulfano, C. (1992). *Families, alcoholism, and recovery.* San Francisco: Jossey-Bass.

Estes, N., & Heinemann, M. E. (Eds.) (1987). *Alcoholism: Development, consequences, and interventions,* St. Louis: C. V. Mosby.

Estes, N., Smith-DiJulio, K., & Heinemann, M. E. (1980). *Nursing diagnosis of the alcoholic person.* St. Louis: C. V. Mosby.

Evans, K., & Sullivan, J. M. (1990). *Dual diagnosis.* New York: Guilford.

Fingarette, H. (1988). *Heavy drinking: The myth of alcoholism as a disease.* Berkeley: University of California Press.

Freeman, E. M. (1992). Addictive behaviors: State-of-the art issues in social work treatment. In E. Freeman (Ed.), *The addiction process: Effective social work approaches* (pp. 1–9). New York: Longman.

Freeman, E. M., & Landesman, T. (1992). Differential diagnosis and the least restrictive treatment. In E. Freeman (Ed.), *The addiction process: Effective social work approaches* (pp. 27–42). New York: Longman.

Friedman, E. G. (1993). Methadone maintenance in the treatment of addiction. In S. L. A. Straussner (Ed.) *Clinical work with substance-abusing clients* (pp. 135–152). New York: Guilford.

Gorski, T., & Miller, H. (1986). *Staying sober: A guide for relapse prevention.* Independence, MO: Independence Press.

Group for the Advancement of Psychiatry. (1991). Substance abuse disorders: A psychiatric priority. *American Journal of Psychiatry, 148,* 1291–1300.

Hester, R. K., & Miller, W. R. (1995). *Handbook of alcoholism treatment approaches: Effective alternatives.* Boston: Allyn & Bacon.

Institute of Medicine. (1989). *Prevention and treatment of alcohol problems: Research opportunities.* Washington, DC: National Academy Press.

Jackson, J. K. (1954). The adjustment of the family to the crisis of alcoholism. *Quarterly Journal of Studies on Alcohol, 15* (4), 562–586.

Jellinek, E. M. (1960). *The disease concept of alcoholism.* New Haven, CT: College and University Press.

Kail, B. L. (1992). Recreational or casual drug use: Opportunities for primary prevention. In E. M. Freeman (Ed.), *The addiction process: Effective social work approaches* (pp. 96–107). New York: Longman.

Kinney, J. (1991). *Clinical manual of substance abuse.* St. Louis: Mosby Year Book.

Levin, J. D. (1987). *Treatment of alcoholism and other addictions: A self-psychology approach.* Northvale, NJ: Jason Aronson.

Levin, J. D. (1995). *Introduction to alcoholism counseling: A bio-psycho-social approach* (2d ed.). New York: Taylor & Francis.

Liftik, J. (1995). Assessment. In S. Brown (Ed.), *Treating alcoholism* (pp. 57–94). San Francisco: Jossey-Bass.

Maisto, S. A., Galizio, M., & Connors, G. J. (1991). *Drug use and misuse.* Fort Worth: Holt, Rinehart and Winston.

Marlatt, G. A., & Gordon, J. R. (1985). *Relapse prevention: Maintenance strategies in the treatment of addictive behaviors.* New York: Guilford.

McCarty, D., Argeriou, M., Huebner, R. B., & Lubran, B. (1991). Alcoholism, drug abuse, and the homeless. *American Psychologist, 46,* 1139–1148.

McCrady, B., & Delaney, S. I. (1995). Self-help groups. In R. K. Hester and W. R. Miller (Eds.), *Handbook of alcoholism treatment approaches: Effective alternatives* (2nd ed.) (pp. 160–175). Boston: Allyn & Bacon.

McNeece, C. A., & DiNitto, D. M. (1994). *Chemical dependency: A systems approach,* Englewood Cliffs, NJ: Prentice Hall.

Metzger, L. (1988). *From denial to recovery: Counseling problem drinkers, alcoholics and their families.* San Francisco: Jossey-Bass.

Miller, W. R., & Rollnick, S. (1991). *Motivational interviewing.* New York: Guilford.

O'Dwyer, P. (1993). Alcoholism treatment facilities. In S. L. A. Straussner (Ed.), *Clinical work with substance-abusing clients* (pp. 119–134). New York: Guilford.

O'Farrell, T. J. (1993). A behavioral marital therapy couples group program for alcoholics and their spouses. In T. J. O'Farrell (Ed.), *Treating alcohol problems: Marital and family interventions.* New York: Guilford.

O'Farrell, T. J. (1995). Marital and family therapy. In R. K. Hester and W. R. Miller (Eds.), *Handbook of alcoholism treatment approaches: Effective alternatives* (2nd ed.) (pp. 160–175). Boston: Allyn & Bacon.

O'Farrell, T. J., & Birchler, G. R. (1987). Marital relationships of alcoholic, conflicted, and nonconflicted couples. *Journal of Marital and Family Therapy, 13,* 259–274.

Orlin, L., & Davis, J. (1993). Assessment and intervention with drug and alcohol abusers in psychiatric settings. In S. L. A. Straussner (Ed.), *Clinical work with substance-abusing clients* (pp. 50–68). New York: Guilford.

Palfai, T., & Jankiewicz, H. (1991). *Drugs and human behavior.* Dubuque, IA: Wm. C. Brown Publishers.

Pattison, E. M. (1982). A systems approach to alcoholism treatment. In E. M. Pattison & E. Kaufman (Eds.), *Encyclopedic handbook of alcoholism* (pp. 1089–1108). New York: Gardner Press.

Pattison, E. M., & Kaufman, E. (1982). The alcoholism syndrome: Definitions and models. In E. M. Pattison & E. Kaufman (Eds.), *Encyclopedic handbook of alcoholism* (pp. 3–26). New York: Gardner Press.

Peele, S. (1989). *Diseasing of America.* Lexington, MA: D. C. Heath.

Prochaska, J. O., & DiClemente, C. C. (1983). Stages and processes of self change of smoking: Toward an integrative model of change. *Journal of Consulting and Clinical Psychology, 51,* 390–395.

Project MATCH Research Group (1993). Project MATCH: Rationale and methods for a multisite clinical trial matching patients to alcoholism treatment. *Alcoholism: Clinical and Experimental Research, 17,* 1130–1145.

Ray, O., & Ksir, C. (1990). *Drugs, society and human behavior* (7th ed.). St. Louis: Times Mirror/Mosby College Publishing.

Schuckit, M. (1986). Etiologic theories on alcoholism. In N. J. Estes & M. E. Heinemann

(Eds.), *Alcoholism: development, consequences, and interventions* (pp. 15–30). St. Louis: C. V. Mosby.

Spiegel, B. R. (1993). 12-step programs as a treatment modality. In S. L. A. Straussner (Ed.), *Clinical work with substance-abusing clients* (pp. 153–170). New York: Guilford.

Steinglass, P. (1987). *The alcoholic family*. New York: Basic Books.

Tartar, R. E., & Sugarman, A. A. (1976). *Alcoholism: Interdisciplinary approaches to an enduring problem*. Reading, MA: Addison-Wesley.

U.S. Department of Health and Human Services, Public Health Service, National Institutes of Health, National Institute on Alcohol Abuse and Alcoholism. (1993). *Eighth special report to the U.S. Congress on alcohol and health*. Washington, DC: Government Printing Office.

U.S. General Accounting Office. (1991). *VA Health Care: Alcoholism Screening Procedures Should Be Improved* (HRD Publication 91-71). Gaithersburg, MD: Author.

Usher, M. L. (1991). From identification to consolidation: A treatment model for couples and families complicated by alcoholism. *Family Dynamics of Addictions Quarterly, 1* (2), 45–58.

Vaillant, G. (1983). *The natural history of alcoholism*. Cambridge, MA: Harvard University Press.

Vaillant, G. (1990). We should retain the disease concept of alcoholism. *Harvard Medical School Mental Health Letter, 9* (6), 4–6.

Vanicelli, M. (1992). *Removing the roadblocks: Group psychotherapy with substance abusers and family members*. New York: Guilford.

van Wormer, K. (1987). Training social work students for practice with substance abusers: An ecological approach. *Journal of Social Work Education, 23* (2), 47–56.

van Wormer, K. (1995). *Alcoholism treatment: A social work perspective*, Chicago: Nelson-Hall.

Wallace, J. (1989, June). A biopsychosocial model of alcoholism. *Social Casework: The Journal of Contemporary Social Work*, 325–332.

Washton, A. (1989). *Cocaine addiction: Treatment, recovery, and relapse prevention*. New York: Norton.

Weinberg, J. (1974). Interview techniques for diagnosing alcoholism. *American Family Physician, 9* (3), 107–115.

White, J. M. (1991). *Drug dependence*. Englewood Cliffs, NJ: Prentice Hall

Wolin, S. J., Bennett, L. A., Noonan, D. L., & Teitelbaum, M. A. (1980). Disrupted family rituals: A factor in the intergenerational transmission of alcoholism. *Journal of Studies on Alcohol, 41* (3), 199–213.

Zweben, J. E. (1995). The therapist's role in early and ongoing recovery. In S. Brown (Ed.), *Treating alcoholism* (pp. 197–229). San Francisco: Jossey-Bass.

21

Clinical Practice with Lesbians

Eda G. Goldstein

In addition to empowering gay men and lesbians, the gay liberation movement that gained momentum in the 1970s drew attention to the widespread nature and debilitating effects of discrimination against homosexuals, advocated for protecting their civil liberties, and worked toward their greater inclusion and acceptance in society. It also led to increasing dissemination of knowledge about the nature and diversity of homosexuality and to changes in attitudes toward and beliefs about gay men and lesbians. The results of several decades of research clearly show that homosexuals cannot be reliably differentiated from heterosexuals in their personality characteristics, family background, gender identity, defenses, ego strengths, object relations, psychopathology, problems in living, and social adjustment (Falco, 1991; Gonsiorek, 1982a, 1982b; Gonsiorek & Weinrich, 1991). A significant advance occurred in 1973 when the American Psychiatric Association decided to remove homosexuality per se from its *Diagnostic and Statistical Manual of Mental Disorders* (APA, 1980), although it created the category ego-dystonic homosexuality (homosexual feelings or behavior about which one is uncomfortable), which also was eliminated in 1988.

Even the psychoanalytic literature, which regarded homosexuality as pathological, began to publish critiques and revisions of traditional views, and more affirmative treatment models for gay men and lesbians have emerged (Burch, 1993a, 1993b; Falco, 1991; Glassgold & Iasenza, 1995; Gonsiorek, 1982a; Isay, 1989; Malyon, 1982; Martin, 1982; O'Connor & Ryan, 1993; Schwartz, 1989; Spaulding, 1993; Weille, 1993). Nevertheless, homophobia among mental health professionals has lingered (DeCrescenzo, 1984; Gonsiorek, 1982b), and case studies of gay and lesbian patients that are presented at professional conferences and in publications still reflect traditional views and practices to a startling degree (Gould, 1995).

Despite these changes, the professional literature paid more attention to male than female homosexuality until recently, so much so that lesbians have been referred to as an "invisible" or "unseen" minority. Among the reasons that might account for this invisibility are that, in comparison to gay men, lesbians are more able to conceal their sexual orientation by passing as heterosexuals, and they do not command as much economic power. Alternatively, some feel that lesbians are deliberately ignored and devalued first as women and then as lesbians (Potter & Darty, 1981) because they are more threatening to a male-dominated patriarchal society than are gay men.

Whatever the underlying reason for their invisibility in society and professional literature, lesbians have been discriminated against in both the gay and straight worlds. It has only been since feminist writers identified the male bias toward women generally that is inherent in most personality theories, professional attitudes, and treatment services, that more gender-sensitive theories and practices have been put forth. Nevertheless, the early literature gave short shrift to lesbianism, perhaps because feminists did not want their cause to be weakened by its association with a stigmatized population. Psychodynamic writings did not fare any better until more recently, for as Glassgold and Iasenza (1995, p. xv) point out, there have been few open lesbian theorists and analysts since lesbians as well as gay men often have been excluded from training institutes in America or have tended to remain closeted if they were accepted due to realistic concerns about professional advancement.

THEORETICAL PERSPECTIVES ON LESBIAN DEVELOPMENT

Traditional and even some revisionist views on lesbianism assume that heterosexuality is the only normal pathway for expressing sexuality, and they equate lesbianism with severe psychopathology. Early writings about homosexuality generally refer to men, and even those that address lesbianism specifically are based on observations of women patients who suffered from serious emotional disturbances.

While expressing tolerance toward homosexuals as a group, Freud did regard homosexuality as a perversion and his views exerted considerable influence on the ways in which mental health professionals diagnosed and treated gay and lesbian patients. Freud (1920) described lesbians either as rejecting heterosexuality due to penis envy or severe disappointment in men or as repudiating their femininity as a result of envy or devaluation of their mothers. He saw female homosexuality as a failure to resolve the normal oedipal stage. Instead, lesbians showed a negative oedipus complex, taking their mothers rather than their fathers as love objects and using their fathers instead of their mothers as objects of identification. Thus a woman who loved other women developed a "masculinity complex," which reflected her rebellion against her own femaleness, her wishes to be a man, her rejection of heterosexuality, and her adoption of masculine traits. Followers of Freud, including Helene Deutsch, a prominent early analyst, subscribed to this view. Deutsch (1932) viewed lesbians as incapable of mature love and as suffering from frustrated heterosexual wishes for the father, resulting in preoedipal fixations on the mother.

As theoretical attention shifted to delineating the nature of ego development and the separation-individuation process, lesbians were seen as suffering from preoedipal pathology or developmental arrests (Deutsch, 1995; Eisenbud, 1982; Magee & Miller, 1992; McDougall, 1980; Prozan, 1992; Siegel, 1988; Socarides, 1988; Suchet, 1995). For example, Socarides (1988) argued that difficulties in negotiating the separation-individuation stages and problems in gender identity lead to female homosexuality. Siegel (1988) viewed her lesbian patients as suffering from serious pathology resulting from incomplete differentiation from the mother and deep feelings of castration and genital loss arising in early separation-individuation stages. McDougall (1980), although more accepting of lesbians' sexual orientation, nevertheless described patients who were severely disturbed and saw their lesbianism as an effort to avoid psychic disintegration or psychosis. Eisenbud (1982) viewed lesbianism as a reparative effort to deal with early deficits.

Early feminist writers challenged Freudian, Eriksonian, and Mahlerian theories of women's development generally and provided the foundation for a new understanding of lesbians. Chodorow (1978) and Gilligan (1982) argue that females have a different individuation process from males because of their primary attachment to a same-sex rather than opposite-sex parent. They describe mothers and daughters as sharing a greater sense of identification and merger with one another, resulting in a more prolonged closeness and a more diffuse individuation process. Further, they observe that female self-development, when compared to male self-development, involves more permeable rather than rigid boundaries, an emphasis on relationships rather than autonomy, and a greater capacity for empathy, caring, and intuition. Similarly, members of the Stone Center for Developmental Services and Studies at Wellesley College in Massachusetts (Jordan, Kaplan, Miller, Stiver, & Surrey, 1991) regard women's self-development as evolving in the context of relatedness and view enhanced connection rather than increased self-object differentiation and separateness as women's major goal. Further, Benjamin (1988) emphasizes the importance of the balance between oneness and separateness, merging and differentiation. In Benjamin's view, true independence involves both self-assertion and mutuality, separateness and sharing; She argues that the individual's inability to reconcile dependence and independence leads to patterns of domination and submission.

Some writers have utilized these newer ideas to propose that lesbianism reflects a more normal developmental outcome of positive mother-daughter attachment and that women's sexuality is more fluid and variable over the life cycle. Citing Chodorow (1978), Suchet (1995) argues that because of the normal nature of the girl's lingering intense tie to her mother, there is a "bisexual relational triangle" during the girl's oedipal phase, the resolution of which leads to more mature and differentiated as well as connected relationships with both their mothers and fathers. Love between women later in life can be based on more mature rather than preoedipal bonds. Weille (1993) speculates that since the little girl normally does not give up her attachment to the mother when she turns to her father but instead maintains this bond, which provides her with continuity and a core sense of self, it is logical that a normative outcome for women is bisexuality. The daughter maintains her libidinal connection to the mother while developing a triadic relational structure. Reiter (1989) further suggests that the girl's primary and continuing attachment results in her acquisition of a firm gender identity as a woman and that women consequently may have the capacity for greater fluidity in their sexual interests without its detracting from their sense of femaleness. This view might help to explain why many lesbians come out later in life, after they have had significant relationships with men, or they move back and forth between men and women in their love relationships, thus showing a long-standing bisexual orientation (Burch, 1993a).

In psychoanalytic theory generally, newer contributions in object relations theories (Greenberg & Mitchell, 1983) and self psychology (Kohut, 1971, 1977) have emphasized attachment behavior, relatedness, and empathic attunement in child-parent relationships and their impact on later development. For example, Kohut clearly identified three main types of early selfobject needs: (1) the need for mirroring that confirms the child's sense of vigor, greatness, and perfection; (2) the need for an idealization of others whose strength and calmness soothe the child; and (3) the need for a twin or alter ego who provides the child with a sense of humanness, likeness to, and partnership with others. Although not all of these selfobject needs may be gratified, rewarding experiences with at least one type of selfobject give the child a chance to develop a cohesive self. In healthy development, these early selfobject needs become transformed and continue in more mature ways all through life. Utilizing this perspective, it seems likely that the gratification of selfobject needs in early relationships contributes to loving bonds between members of the same sex. This may account for the fact that twinship issues, in particular, appear to be common in both lesbian and gay relationships and often are reflected in the transference between therapists and patients (Cornett, 1990; Goldstein, 1994).

Since Kinsey's (1948) famous study of sexual behavior, increasing evidence has challenged some early stereotypes of sexual behavior. For example, many individuals are not purely homosexual or heterosexual and sexual behavior appears to exist on a continuum. There has been greater understanding as well of the origins and nature of gender development as distinct from sexual object choice (Goldner, 1991; Stoller, 1977). For both men and women, an individual's gender identity encompasses a range of identifications with early male and female caretakers, as well as the internalization of attitudes and behavior of others toward the developing child. It is erroneous to equate lesbianism with a rejection of femininity since studies show that lesbians generally have a strong gender identity, that is, a core sense of femaleness, and have moved away from playing out gender roles such as "butch" or "femme" (Falco, 1991, p. 10). Further, they may view their sexual identity—whether they regard themselves as gay, lesbian, or bisexual—in rigid or flexible ways and their actual sexual behavior may vary.

There is not one type of homosexuality, and although gay men and lesbians share some commonalities, there are significant differences between them. For example, in terms of their awareness of their lesbianism, numerous studies show that lesbians reflect at least two distinct patterns: one in which they had a conscious sense of being lesbian at an early age and one in which they identify as lesbians later in life, often after having had relationships with men, and sometimes marrying and having children (Burch, 1993a). For lesbians, like heterosexual women, emotional bonding seems to be more important than sexuality, whereas the reverse tends to be true for men.

Recent research supports the view that for many women, lesbian object relations and self-development arise as a variant of positive developmental experiences in contrast to the traditional belief that they reflect arrested, immature, narcissistic, and undifferentiated object relations. For example, in Spaulding's (1993) study of twenty-four college-educated lesbians who had positive identities and achieved high scores on measures of psychological stability, the women showed "evidence of highly evolved, differentiated and integrated level of object and reality relatedness" (p. 17). Further, their views of their parents did not correspond to common stereotypes in that lesbians saw both their mothers and fathers as strong, positive role models, who were nurturing, successful, and warm (p. 19).

A more affirmative view of female homosexuality underpins the very definition given to the term *lesbianism,* which involves "a special affinity and special feeling" toward other women and represents "a special capacity and need to love and express one's love for people of the same gender in all the meanings of the term" (Woodman & Lenna, 1980, p. 11) rather than an inability to love men or a rejection of femininity. This definition, however, allows for the fact that many lesbians, like heterosexual women, have conflicts surrounding the expression of their sexuality or gender identity confusion that stem from developmental difficulties. The presence of such problems, however, does not imply that their loving and sexual feelings toward other women stem from pathological development.

LESBIAN IDENTITY FORMATION

An important contribution to understanding the special features of lesbian identity formation has been the delineation of the stages of "coming out," that is, the ways in which individuals acknowledge their sexual identity to themselves and others (Cass, 1979; Coleman, 1982; Falco, 1991; Lewis, 1984). It involves integrating one's sexuality into one's self-concept and integrating one's identity into one's life. While the adolescent and young adult periods are extremely important times for lesbian identity formation (Hetrick & Martin, 1988), this process often occurs much later for many women—sometimes after they have attempted a heterosexual adaptation, married, and become parents. While some of those who have been involved with men may have had the awareness of being emotionally and or sexually attracted to other women early in their lives, others experience such feelings later in life. Some women identify themselves as bisexual or live as heterosexuals while having clandestine relationships with women. Some lesbians, even when involved in committed relationships with other women, still may experience sexual feelings toward and fantasies about men.

When lesbians come out during adolescence or young adulthood, they face other developmental tasks simultaneously, including separation from and achieving new types of relations with families of origin, evolving an occupational identity, and developing intimate relationships. Women who come out later in life may already have achieved a life structure that must undergo changes that have complex consequences involving husbands, parents, children, friends, and coworkers.

The stages of the coming-out process are similar whatever the chronological age of the woman. Coleman (1982, p. 32) describes these steps as precoming out, coming out, exploration, first relationships, and identity integration. Each has its own issues and poses crucial tasks that must be mastered. Not all individuals, however, go through each stage, and the process for many persons is more fluid and complex. In the precoming-out period, the individual may be more or less aware of same-sex feelings but feels alienated, alone, and stigmatized. Denial, repression of sexual feelings, or other defensive reactions, low self-esteem, and serious symptoms may result. While the coming-out stage is marked by a great deal of confusion, it begins the task of self-acceptance and tolerance. During this period, individuals tend to seek out validation from the external environment. In the exploration stage, the individual likely experiments with new behaviors and in the first relationship stage looks for a more intimate partner. The integration of a lesbian identity, the final stage, often is a lengthy, evolving, and complex development. It goes beyond acceptance and tolerance to include pride and sometimes community involvement and political activism. Clearly the outcome of all of these stages is affected by the presence or absence of peer, family, and social supports, positive role models, gratifying relationships, and societal attitudes and policies (Hetrick & Martin, 1988).

Being a member of a stigmatized and oppressed group shapes the nature and process of lesbian identity formation. Since women are socialized into a society that views heterosexuality as normal and "compulsory" (Rich, 1980) and homosexuality as undesirable, the bedrock of healthy narcissism and self-acceptance is challenged and seriously compromised for girls who sense that they are different. They lack positive reflections of themselves in family, friends, media images, and society (Buloff & Osterman, 1995). A lesbian's core identity goes "unmirrored," and her "true self" often is hidden away, even if she is loved in other ways by those close to her (Gair, 1995, p. 111). It does not seem surprising that lesbians might utilize certain defenses such as splitting in order to cope with an inner experience of being "bad."

The long-lasting negative effects of these common experiences are compounded when parents and other close relatives are shaming, rejecting, devaluing, and otherwise psychologically as well as physically assaultive. While progress is gradually being made in altering society's condemnation of lesbians, oppressive policies and practices are manifested concretely in discrimination in housing, employment, insurance, inheritance and other forms of legal protection, marital arrangements, child custody, foster care, and adoption proceedings, medical care, and the like. These forms of discrimination create additional stresses. Further, there are daily assaults on lesbians' self-esteem and feelings of safety and acceptance that make it more difficult to achieve and maintain a positive self-concept. These include the continuing risks involved in being viewed as a lesbian by family, friends, coworkers, and employers; exposure to negative portrayals of gays in the media, humiliating jokes, and the hate-filled rhetoric of right-wing and religious groups; the threat of violence; constraints on showing affection or closeness in public; and the ongoing absence of supports such as being able to talk about the significant others in one's life or to celebrate the anniversary of a significant relationship.

At the same time, lesbians, like other women, show positive functioning and achieve considerable satisfaction over the life cycle in their work and personal lives. Many attain considerable education, economic success, and career advancement, sometimes feeling that they have to be especially hard working and skilled in order to be accepted and to advance. The view that lesbians grow old alone without longstanding committed relationships, children, or close ties to parents and siblings has been challenged. Further, some states recognize lesbian marriages or other domestic partnership arrangements and increasingly, single and coupled, lesbians are raising biological, foster, or adopted children, struggling with both similar and unique parenting issues as heterosexuals (Baptiste, 1987). Studies of aging lesbians have shown both commonality with and differences from older heterosexuals in their needs and coping styles (Berger, 1992; Berger & Kelly, 1986; Tully, 1992).

PRINCIPLES AND FOCUSES OF CLINICAL SOCIAL WORK INTERVENTION

In working with lesbian clients, the clinician should consider the following principles and focuses as guidelines (Goldstein, 1995).

Balancing a Focus on Group Membership and Individualization

It is important for the practitioner to be sensitive to the common problems, life experiences, values, characteristics, and strengths of clients by virtue of their group membership. For example, fear of mental health professionals is widespread among lesbians who may suffer from internalized homophobia or who anticipate being judged negatively, labeled inappropriately, and otherwise mistreated by homophobic practitioners who may attempt "to cure" their deviance rather than relate to their human concerns. On the positive side, lesbians, like members of other oppressed groups, have developed certain strengths that have helped them to cope adaptively.

While sensitivity to the commonalities that lesbians show that stem from their group membership is crucial to accurate assessment and all other aspects of the treatment process, the principle of individualization always must be a central concern of the practitioner. Since lesbians do not always share the same experiences or show the same degree of group identification, the practitioner needs to avoid overgeneralizing and stereotyping.

Lesbianism is not a psychiatric illness, nor do lesbians suffer from a disease that needs to be cured or from other forms of psychological maladjustment or personality disorders. Lesbians love other women; they do not by definition hate men. There is no such person as a typical lesbian. They do not all become aware of their loving and sexual feelings toward other women at the same time. Many have had or will have sex with men or have married and have children. Most lesbians do not by definition reject their femininity, feel or look masculine, or wish they were men. Some, although by no means all, of those gay women who adopted more masculine behavior or a "butch" position in previous years did so because of a lack of female role models for women who did not display traditional or acceptable "feminine" behavior. While many lesbians are estranged from their families of origin, others maintain close ties. Like their heterosexual counterparts, some have sexual problems, relationship difficulties, severe emotional disturbances, and bleak histories reflecting physical and sexual abuse, alcoholism, and psychiatric illness.

As a group, women tend to be more economically disadvantaged than men, and a lesbian's stigmatized status may have contributed to her inability to pursue educational or career goals. Further, lesbians often do not receive tax, health, and other types of benefits that are available to married heterosexual women, although this is changing as some private and public employers are recognizing domestic partnership arrangements. As there have been more opportunities for women generally and more lesbians who are educated or financially successful are more visible, it is clear that they have more disposable income and economic resources than has been thought previously.

The problems that lesbians present when they seek help from mental health professionals are diverse. Some of their concerns do relate specifically to their sexual object choice, for example, how to deal with their emerging feelings of attraction to same-sex individuals or whether to disclose their sexual orientation to family, friends, or coworkers. Most lesbians, however, usually come to professionals for help for a range of reasons that have little to do with their sexual orientation or are related to it only indirectly. Like those who are straight, they seek help in dealing with the problems of living, career issues, relationship problems, life crises, depression, anxiety, physical illness, unemployment, parenting concerns, and the like. Nevertheless, in order for a practitioner to be sensitive to the particular needs and concerns of lesbian clients, they must appreciate that the lesbian client's membership in a stigmatized and oppressed group may be playing a role in the presenting problem. For example, a woman's relationship problems with her female partner may stem from her reticence to socialize publicly together and her refusal to include her in family gatherings. This stance may result from her own negative attitudes toward her lesbianism and her fear of others' disapproval. A lesbian's repeated failures in the occupational arena may stem from her fear of socializing with her associates for fear they will learn about her personal life, resulting in her appearing to be aloof and disinterested in being part of the work team. Similarly, a woman's depression and alcoholism may be caused by her attempts to deny recognition of her own wishes and needs to be with other women, leading her to try unsuccessfully to have relationships with men and leaving her with tormenting doubts about her ability to love.

Whether the presenting problem itself is related to the client's sexual orientation, the practitioner who intervenes with lesbians must be well acquainted with the special features of lesbian life, develop expertise in working with this population, and acquire knowledge of community resources. While it is necessary to recognize that there is not one type of lesbian or gay relationship and that there are major differences between gay men and women, it also is important to understand the common attitudes, developmental issues, relationship patterns, and concerns of the lesbian community.

Making Appropriate Use of Diagnostic and Developmental Concepts

One of the concerns that arose as a result of the gay liberation movement related to the indiscriminate use of clinical diagnoses to label homosexual men and women as suffering from mental or personality disorders. An antilabeling stance was present among many in the gay community, while others recognized that there's a place for clinical and developmental diagnoses when they are used properly (Gonsiorek, 1982b). The fact that homosexuality is not a disease does not mean that all lesbians, for example, are free of emotional disorder. Like everyone else, they may show the full range of problems encountered by helping professionals. The practitioner must bear in mind, however, that certain syndromes may be intensified, if not caused, by the awareness of same-sex feelings in a society that views homosexuality so negatively. Likewise, coming out, while liberating for many individuals, may have dramatic and unsettling consequences and lead to an outbreak of symptoms or to ongoing dysfunction, which can be misdiagnosed as reflecting more severe personality pathology.

Early and enduring wounds and a negative self-concept may be present that stem from the lack of mirroring and outright condemnation of same-sex feelings during the developmental process (Gair, 1995). Lesbians themselves may turn on themselves and suffer from internalized homophobia, feeling shame not only of their sexuality but of themselves as people. Research has shown that like other high-stress groups, lesbians may be prone to develop feelings of self-alienation, self-contempt, depression, alcoholism and other types of substance abuse, and suicidal behavior as a consequence of their stigmatized identity and oppressed status (Anderson & Henderson, 1985; Coleman, 1982; Falco, 1991; Hetrick & Martin, 1984). The high incidence of depression, childhood sexual abuse, and rape in the female population generally affects lesbians; lesbians of color have an additional burden as a result of racism.

For all these reasons, the practitioner should refrain from explaining behavior too quickly in pathological terms and from the mechanical application of diagnostic labels and theories based on personal weakness in understanding lesbians. For example, in working with a young lesbian alcoholic who grew up in a religious family in a small midwestern town and who moved away in order to avoid humiliating them and herself as a result of her sexual orientation, the therapist should consider the role that alcohol may play in helping her cope with her feelings of shame and rage at being viewed as a second-class citizen and excluded from family life rather than immediately assuming that the client manifests severe ego deficits and characterologic difficulties. In working with a depressed African American closeted middle-aged lesbian who grew up in the South and who has been a loner with difficulty initiating relationships and who seems to prefer her isolation, a practitioner would be remiss in labeling her a "schizoid personality" and focusing on her pathology. Instead, the clinician should explore the client's fears of rejection and feelings of shame and failure regarding her lesbianism and help her to reflect on the ways in which she has had to adapt to her own culture's and family's expectations of her and to the lack of available options, role models, and safety for her to become intimate with other women.

Exercising Self-Awareness

The therapist's self-awareness of his or her own attitudes and beliefs about lesbians is crucial to the treatment process (Isay, 1989; Martin, 1982; Schwartz, 1989). Practitioners must be sensitive to their own homophobia as well as homophobia in their lesbian clients, refrain from inadvertently reinforcing it through their own biases and stereotypes, and help to empower their clients. For example, when a client expresses her ambivalence about pursuing her interests in other women, the worker needs to consider whether this client is demonstrating characteristic features of the early stage of coming to terms with a stigmatizing identity and continue to help the client to explore and validate the legitimacy of her feelings rather than quickly interpret the client's ambivalence as a sign that she should pursue "straight" life. In working with a lesbian who is fearful of disclosing her sexual identity to her family despite the fact that she is living with a female partner, the worker must help her consider the negative consequences of her continuing to hide and remain invisible in their eyes rather than collude with her staying in the closet.

There is a fallacy, however, to the commonly articulated view that helping professionals who are like their clients in gender or sexual orientation, for example, will be free from negative attitudes and thus be more effective in the helping process than those who are unlike their clients. There are many instances in which the use of workers who share similar characteristics with their clients may be therapeutically indicated, enabling them to feel more easily understood and accepted and providing them with positive role models. Sameness between worker and client, however, is not always a panacea and may lead to mutual blind spots (Schwartz, 1989). For example, although some straight clinicians may have difficulty accepting a lesbian client's interest in other women, it may be equally difficult for a closeted lesbian practitioner who herself suffers from internalized homophobia to help a lesbian client who is demeaning of other lesbians and secretive in disclosing her sexual orientation out of shame and fear. The ability to be empathic and respectful of clients, whether one is similar to or different from them, requires the practitioner to exercise self-scrutiny of his or her own values, attitudes, and biases since these shape all aspects of the intervention process.

Strengthening Self-Esteem

Empowerment is an important goal of intervention. It involves helping clients to increase their sense of personal control over their lives, to feel good about themselves, and to believe that they can have an impact on others and the world around them. In order to help in empowering lesbian clients, it is important for the practitioner to identify and support their strengths. Emphasizing areas of dysfunction or pathology may be experienced by them as blaming or may contribute to their already negative self-concept. Instead, the practitioner must convey respect for the ways in which the lesbian client has attempted to cope with difficult life circumstances, to search out, validate, and enhance the positive features of her functioning, and to identify and combat her own internalized homophobia. Crucial as a strengths perspective is, however, it does not obviate the need to assess inadequate or impaired coping mechanisms. The practitioner must strive to achieve the proper balance between maximizing strengths and modifying dysfunctional behavior and attitudes.

Reshaping the Therapeutic Relationship

In order to empower clients effectively, it may be necessary to ensure that the therapeutic relationship itself is based on collaboration, trust, and the sharing of power rather than on the more usual hierarchical model. Some writers have suggested that it is necessary to demonstrate this equality in concrete ways, such as using first rather than last names, creating a more informal atmosphere, engaging in self-disclosure, and being more real and genuine in communicating to the client. Since clients differ in their needs and problems, expectations of the treatment relationship, fears of exploitation, values with respect to authority, need for clear boundaries, and degree of pathology, a flexible rather than doctrinaire approach to structuring the client-worker relationship is indicated.

The thoughtful and selective use of self-disclosure can facilitate or may be necessary with lesbian clients for many reasons: their own internalized homophobia, shame, and feelings of difference and aloneness; their fear of being judged, misunderstood, and victimized by mental health professionals and their resultant need for concrete evidence that the therapist can appreciate and relate to the client's lifestyle; and their need for role models and validation (Cornett, 1990; Gabriel & Monaco, 1995; Goldstein, 1994; Isay, 1989; Kasoff et al., 1995). At times therapist self-disclosure also helps the client to share or deepen her exploration of highly charged material.

Often lesbian clients may not wish to see a therapist who is heterosexual, although it may be possible for a straight or non-self-disclosing therapist to overcome such feelings if he or she shows attunement to the client's concerns and lifestyle. Other lesbians may seek out straight therapists or not care initially about the sexual orientation of the therapist. Later in the treatment they may request personal information about the therapist's sexual orientation. It is not always a simple matter to determine what the client really wants to know. Although there is a risk that the client will misuse personal information that is disclosed or that a therapist may act out his or her countertransference by revealing personal information, there are risks in not self-disclosing. Depriving the client of one's realness or of information that can help the client to connect to the therapist may be experienced as too rejecting or nonaffirming. Further, it may convey the message that the therapist is ashamed or fearful of revealing her lesbianism. One author (Goldstein, 1994) described the lesbian therapist's dilemma as follows:

> Advocating the use of self-disclosure is fraught not only because of the possibility that it opposes prevailing views about therapeutic technique and potentially invites countertransference acting-out but also because it challenges the usual power arrangements that are reflected in the traditional therapist-patient relationship. Moreover it raises the issues of therapists' right to privacy and of how transparent and real we are willing to be to our patients. . . . We want to help them [clients] to discover and be themselves, to value who they are, to find positive ways of meeting their needs, and to take risks. An important question that each of us needs to ask ourselves is whether we should model that type of individual to our patients. (pp. 431–432)

Facilitating Identity Formation and the Coming-Out Process

A crucial aspect of the intervention process is helping lesbians to cope with their own identity formation, or what is known as the coming-out process. The practitioner who is sensitive and affirmative in work with lesbians needs to understand the different patterns that exist and the psychological, behavioral, and attitudinal features of each of the stages of coming out and gear interventions accordingly. Lack of familiarity with these common characteristics and sequences will result in the practitioner's misinterpreting the lesbian client's reactions and missing opportunities to help the client to move forward in the process of her own identity formation.

Even after coming out to oneself, decisions about whether and how to disclose that one is a lesbian to parents, children, friends, and coworkers usually are fraught with conflict (Falco, 1991; Shernoff, 1995). The therapist must refrain from taking a position with which he or she is comfortable personally but may not be attuned to the client's life situation or needs. It is easy even for a lesbian therapist to collude with a client's fears of the negative consequences of exposure or to support openness on principle before the client is ready. It is important to help clients explore and evaluate the real and imagined negative consequences of coming out in comparison to the destructive effects on personal relationships, the cumulative and sometimes insidious stresses, and the assault to self-esteem that result from remaining silent or trying to conceal one's sexual orientation. Too often lesbians may choose to remain closeted and attempt to lead double lives at the expense of their being able to achieve a more integrated and liberated life. When they do come out, they often learn that the people from whom they were hiding suspected that they were gay. Alternatively, some lesbians have experienced severe rejection, ostracism, violence, and discrimination as a result of their openness. When clients decide to disclose their lesbianism in certain situations, it is useful to help them consider and possibly rehearse the process of sharing with others and to prepare them for possible outcomes.

Lesbians may lack knowledge of available resources and be fearful of and reticent to take risks that seem to threaten their security. Often such individuals have not had access to role models who have led the way with respect to different ways of thinking, feeling, and acting. The client's self-determination may be enhanced rather than violated by the worker's taking an active role in educating her about options, providing a vision for change, and encouraging clients to take constructive actions that are consistent with their needs and abilities. Advocating for the client's right to realize her potential is different from imposing one's own values and opinions on the client indiscriminately. The practitioner must be careful, however, not to make suggestions or encourage solutions that may be too frightening, guilt producing, or alienating. For example, in working with a depressed Irish Catholic lesbian who keeps attempting to force her family of origin to accept her and her female partner and include them in family events despite the family's repeated critical harangues, hurtful attacks on her character, and rejecting attitudes, efforts to help her move away from her family must be undertaken with an appreciation of the strong value placed on family given her cultural background.

A frequent problem that arises as a result of the stigma attached to lesbianism is the relative isolation of many lesbians. Because of their fear of the negative consequences of exposure, their own internalized homophobia, and their lack of knowledge about or reticence in using gay support networks, many gay and lesbian individuals lack connections to the larger gay community. This may be particularly acute for those who are older and have lived a more closeted existence, often in a very long-term relationship that may have ended in death or separation. It also may be very stressful for younger individuals who live with disapproving parents or relatives. The practitioner must provide clients with information about available resources, explore their reluctance to reach out to the lesbian community, and encourage them to develop support systems.

Consciousness-raising, self-help, and discussion groups are useful in clinical work with lesbians. They help to decrease isolation, strengthen group identification, clarify issues of common concern, increase feelings of acceptance and self-esteem, provide validation and support, develop problem-solving skills and new ways of negotiating interpersonal relationships, and acquire experience in collective action.

Both individual and group intervention can empower clients to advocate for themselves more effectively and to contribute to change efforts in the community and society. Not only do such activities help lesbian clients to feel that they can make a difference, but they also are necessary to achieve freedom from oppression and equal access to social resources.

Identifying Health and Legal Issues

As women, lesbians experience numerous health-related issues that warrant special attention throughout their lives. Fearful of being discriminated against, they may not avail themselves of medical help, and when they do often are not treated properly. Some with low self-esteem may not take care of themselves or value their bodies. Partners may not be given information, included in important decisions, allowed to visit or care for their partners, or given needed support during crises. There are legal concerns as well that lesbians have as members of an oppressed and stigmatized group (Shernoff, 1995). Issues related to inheritance, maintaining control over one's assets, obtaining medical and insurance benefits, being able to provide that one's assets and possessions are distributed according to one's wishes after death, child custody arrangements, alimony, adoption proceedings, and estate planning can be problematic. The practitioner must be able to identify the health and legal issues that their clients manifest even when the clients themselves may not be aware of them and help connect clients to appropriate legal resources.

WORKING WITH COUPLES

Lesbian couples often seek help in dealing with their relationship problems. Roth (1985) and others have identified a number of common problems and concerns. She argues that the most significant factors influencing lesbian couples is that they are both socialized as women, they are not a socially sanctioned unit, and their full commitment to one another requires the acceptance of a stigmatized identity. She describes five major issues presented by lesbian couples in therapy: distance regulation and boundary maintenance, sexual expression, unequal access to resources, stage differences in coming out and the management of identity, and problems in ending the relationship.

As women, many lesbian couples form very close and nurturing bonds and seek refuge from society's assaults in their relationship. They may spend a good deal of their leisure time with one another, always socialize together, and sometimes isolate themselves from others. Some practitioners may misunderstand this closeness and view it as pathological. At the same time, their very closeness may militate against the couple's being able to acknowledge and deal with conflict (Kleinberg & Zorn, 1995). In many instances, each member of a couple may submerge her own identity in the couple relationship or show tendencies toward merger, codependence, possessiveness, and jealousy of one another's outside involvements. Other lesbian couples show considerable distance and may live apart or keep their finances and friendships separate and have difficulty communicating. Practitioners must be able to set aside their own biases about the importance of autonomy or intimacy in relationships and individualize the members of the couple. It is important to assess the degree to which the apparent closeness or distance in a couple is adaptive and positive or stifling and dysfunctional.

Often a lesbian couple coming for help will complain of diminished sexual interest and activity. This phenomenon seems to be quite common and seems related to the degree of closeness rather than distance or anger that exists in the relationship. There is not a clear and uniform explanation for this. One factor is that as women, both members of the couple are likely to have been socialized to be passive rather than assertive sexually; each may wait for the other to initiate sexual contact. Further, the degree of emotional intimacy that the couple shares actually may supersede or create a barrier to sexual interest in some instances. When one member of a couple is more bothered by this pattern, it clearly becomes more of an issue. It may be important for the practitioner to distinguish whether the lack of sexual activity is related to more serious underlying relationship problems, difficulties in assertiveness, sexual inhibition, or too much closeness. Before concluding that there is a sexual problem per se, it may be important for the practitioner to help the couple to identify ways in which they can create the conditions that will foster more sexual intimacy.

Unequal access to financial resources can be a problem in lesbian couples and lead to unequal distribution of power in the relationship or to some of the problems associated with traditional roles in traditional straight relationships, including physical abuse, which does exist in lesbian couples despite the fact that both members are women.

The stage of the coming-out process that each member of a couple is in and their degree of comfort with their lesbian identity may create conflict for them. One partner may feel left out of special occasions or holidays that her partner shares with her family of origin from whom she hides her lesbian identity. Similarly she may feel resentful of a partner who has an active social life with straight friends or work colleagues who do not know she is a lesbian. Alternatively, some partners are quite fearful of socializing with or showing too much overt closeness or affection to their partners who are open about their lesbianism. Further, some couples may have difficulty deciding to move in together because of their differing degrees of openness with others.

Lesbians often have very close and nonsexual friendships with other women. Some of these relationships may have previously been more intimate, as many lesbians tend to maintain their former partners in their lives. Although often coexisting with close family ties, these friendships sometimes give lesbians the sense of family and stability that they would not otherwise experience. The practitioner must be sensitive to the significance of these relationships and refrain from too quickly labeling them in negative terms, such as the client's "hanging on to" or not separating from past relationships. At times, however, these friendships pose certain stresses when a woman partners with someone who feels threatened by them. While in certain instances these friendships may be used defensively or reflect some other type of dysfunctional bond, this is not always the case, and the new partner may be too possessive. Because lesbians seek friendships with other women, their relationships outside their partnership may create jealousy. Finally, since lesbians often have difficulty separating from one another when their intimate partnership is over, a couple may need help in ending their relationship.

As more lesbians are entering relationships in which there are children already or into which children are born or adopted, there is a need for help around coparenting and related concerns. Although many of the issues that lesbian couples face around children are similar to those of straight couples, there are some unique concerns that stem from the couple's own attitudes toward the impact of their lesbianism on their children, the couple's ability to decide who the "mother" of the child is and to negotiate other types of division of roles and responsibilities, the feelings that the children have about having lesbian parents, and the degree of support systems and the attitudes of others outside the family. Other issues are emerging for which there is little precedent, such as whether and how to include a male donor in the family in the case of artificial insemination or whether and when to share with a child who the donor is. The practitioner must strive to be aware of his or her own attitudes about child rearing and help couples to make decisions and adopt practices that make sense for them.

Many of the principles and focuses of clinical social work with both individual and couples can be seen in the following case example.

Ms. M, a thirty-five-year-old lesbian of Irish Catholic background, sought treatment because she was tired of living a double life but felt trapped and unable to extricate herself from the situation she had created. While unhappy about the way she was living for many years, she said that her recent thirty-fifth birthday had deepened her depression. Ms. M lived alone in New York City and worked as a nurse but maintained a committed and basically happy although increasingly strained three-year relationship with a thirty-six-year-old woman, Ms. S, who also worked in the health field and lived with her two cats in an apartment in New Jersey, about an hour's commute from the city. The couple spent time together there on weekends, where they also saw a few friends whom Ms. S. brought into the relationship. Ms. M also spent one night a week in New Jersey, and Ms. S spent one night a week in New York. Ms. S had no close family nearby, since she was an only child and her father had died and her mother, who knew she was gay, lived in Florida. Both members of the couple wanted to live together and buy a house in the country. Ms. M reported that she and Ms. S had spoken of having a child, through either artificial insemination or adoption, and were concerned that they were getting too old to implement this plan. Ms. M took responsibility for the fact that it was she who was standing in the way of the couple's realizing their dreams. Ms. M's parents and adult siblings lived on Long Island, and she believed that they did not know that she was a lesbian or that Ms. S even existed. Ms. M always attended family gatherings alone and made up stories about her social life when her parents pressed her for information. She felt upset about not being able to share family gatherings with Ms. S and for the pain she was causing her partner, who increasingly felt left out and deprived of a more normal "married" life. Ms. M also felt weary of not being able to discuss important aspects of her personal life with family members. She felt concerned that Ms. S would end the relationship if she did not act or if she verbalized her resentment toward Ms. S for pushing her to be more open with her family. Further, Ms. M was not open about her lesbianism at the hospital where she worked—not because she feared repercussions on the job but because of her concern that somehow the information would leak to her family. Consequently she did not get close to anyone at work or socialize with colleagues. While interested in painting, she did not have time to pursue any courses because of her fragmented existence.

Ms. M feared that her family, particularly her father and two brothers, would ostracize her if they knew she was a lesbian and that although her mother and sister might accept her that she would be causing them pain and that a rift in the family would inevitably occur because of her father's stubbornness and rigidity. She felt caught in a conflict between her wishes for a more normal life with her partner and her wish to protect her mother and sister. At a deeper level, she feared her father's disapproval of her and as a child and adolescent often accepted his negative judgments of her feeling herself to be a bad person if she displeased him. She went to private Catholic schools as a child and was shy and very pretty. Her mother loved to buy girlish clothes for her and took pleasure in Ms. M's appearance. Ms. M was very attached to her female friends at an early age and never developed a strong attraction to boys. Both her parents and her religious education instilled in her a strong sense of right and wrong and self-sacrifice. She began to feel she was different from her peers in high school, when she felt extremely possessive of her friends, was very sensitive to rejection, and was not interested in boys. She did not consciously label herself a lesbian, although she knew what the term meant and that it represented something to be feared and hated. One of her cousins was a lesbian, but the family rarely talked about or saw her, and a sense of shame and disgust surrounded her. Ms. M did date in order to belong, and she eventually had sex with one older boy with whom she went steady, but she broke off their relationship when she went to college because she did not love him. She continued to live at home while attending college and became a loner. In retrospect she realized she was protecting herself from her lesbianism, although she did not acknowledge this at the time. She had her first homosexual experience with another woman nurse when she was in graduate school and still living at home. She was "blown away" by the experience in that she felt very much in love and sexually excited for the first time in her life. The relationship lasted only several months as the woman moved back to the Midwest upon receiving her degree. While she wanted Ms. M to accompany her, Ms. M could not imagine being able to leave her family. Ms. M grieved for this relationship for many years and felt quite lost. She had no ties to the lesbian community at this time, and despite the intensity of relationship and its aftermath, Ms. M still did not identify herself as a lesbian. When she was thirty, she moved to the city—against her parents' wishes, who believed a girl should leave home only when she married. She felt that she needed to have more of a social life and greater independence. She met Ms. S a few years later at a professional conference.

In our initial session, Ms. M indicated that she had seen two lesbian therapists whom Ms. S had recommended in the preceding two weeks but was put off by their strong advice that she share her lesbianism with her parents. She had come to me because in the hospital library she had seen a book I had written, and two of her social work colleagues had talked highly of me. She said that she thought she would try a straight therapist and hoped that I would understand and not judge her. I asked her why she assumed that I was straight, as she put it. She looked startled and responded that it never occurred to her that someone who was as successful as I was gay. Curiously, she did not ask me directly at this time if I were a lesbian. I remember thinking that it seemed important to her to think I was heterosexual, perhaps because she wanted approval for her lesbianism from a straight woman, or to test out how a straight woman would respond to her being a lesbian, or because she was so homophobic herself that she could only idealize or look for help from someone who was heterosexual or literally could not imagine that a lesbian could be a successful therapist. Ms. M herself commented, however, that she guessed she was more ashamed of her lesbianism than she had thought.

The early part of the year-long therapy consisted of my attempts to empathize with how trapped, torn, and alone Ms. M felt and exploration of her feelings about and her attempts to cope with being a lesbian. An important part of these sessions involved both identification of what made her feel good and bad about herself and how her reactions stemmed from the messages she received during her upbringing and validation for the ways in which she had struggled to make a life for herself.

As Ms. M felt safer in the therapeutic relationship and less alone, she experienced a lessening of her depression and more energy to invest in dealing with her situation. She asked if I would see her and Ms. S together as part of the treatment. She did not think it would bother her to share me with Ms. S. Further, rather than feeling that I was operating solely on Ms. M's behalf, Ms. S felt good about seeing the therapist who also was seeing Ms. M since she felt that I would be able to help both of them as a result of know-

ing the situation. Couples sessions were held every other week for a few months in addition to weekly sessions with Ms. M. One focus of these meetings was on supporting the strengths in the relationship and what it meant to both members of the couple. A second focus was helping the couple air their mutual concerns and frustrations without feeling that the relationship would terminate. Yet a third focus was helping the couple to identify the different places they were at in their own acceptance of their lesbianism and to help them determine what might relieve some of the tension in the relationship on the way to achieving a more integrated lifestyle. Because neither Ms. M nor Ms. S was a part of the lesbian community in either New York or New Jersey and because Ms. M was so isolated, I provided information about local resources and encouraged the couple to join either a discussion group or a lesbian couples group in either location.

In individual sessions, I explored with Ms. M her fears of disclosure, how she might begin to share information about herself, and how she might handle the consequences of coming out to her parents and siblings. It was at this point that she asked me if I was a lesbian, indicating that it would give her a sense of strength to feel that I had shared some similar struggles as she and had survived. I responded that I was and that although my issues were not exactly the same as hers, I certainly understood the dilemmas she was facing. This seemed to lead to Ms. M's willingness to be more experimental with her family. She decided to invite Ms. S to dinner with her sister and rehearsed with Ms. S how she wanted her to behave. The event was quite successful, and later, to Ms. M's surprise, her sister asked if Ms. S was a special friend. Ms. M gulped and responded with a yes. Her sister replied that she was glad that Ms. M was not alone in life. This talk led to Ms. M's confiding her dilemma to her sister and to the latter's giving Ms. M advice about how to approach their mother.

Although Ms. M experienced considerable anxiety during the process of her sharing her lesbianism with her family and the results were not immediately positive, she felt enormous relief and greater closeness with Ms. S. In the therapy she ventilated about each new episode in her saga, and I tried to help her maintain her sense that she was a good person in the face of the emotional upheaval that ensued. Ms. M's mother was thrown off-balance for a time but ultimately was accepting, as she did not want to lose her relationship with Ms. M. Her father refused to speak to her for many months. This was very difficult for the client. Ms. M's mother continued to see her despite her husband's protests and wound up liking Ms. S. Ms. M's brothers also did not abandon her, and the father was alone in his condemnation. In order to pacify his wife and sons, he eventually agreed to allow Ms. M and Ms. S to attend family gatherings, although he remained sullen and noncommunicative.

This change had many reverberations. For the first time in her life, Ms. M felt that she was not hiding. It became clear that so much of her being a loner was related to how much she was containing within herself. She became friendlier and more open at work and learned that many of her male and female colleagues also were gay. The couples group that she and Ms. S attended not only helped them to learn about how other lesbian couples dealt with certain issues but also opened the door to a sense of community that neither had had previously. As treatment ended, Ms. M and Ms. S were moving in together, and although they thought they might have some adjustment issues, they wanted to be on their own, knowing that they could return if the need arose.

About a year later, the couple did ask for some sessions to discuss their plans to buy a house together. They had sought legal advice about how to go about this in terms of protecting themselves and one another but wanted to talk through some of the financial issues that were arising in contemplating this step, which related to the very different ways each approached the handling of money.

CONCLUSION

This chapter has explored positive ways of understanding lesbian development. Practitioners working with lesbians must be sensitive to the special issues that lesbians face as a stigmatized and oppressed group and to both their shared and unique concerns, needs, and problems. In order to be effective in work with lesbian individuals and couples, the practitioner, gay or straight, must be willing to share power appropriately in the therapeutic relationship, exercise self-awareness about his or her own biases and internalized homophobia, and engage in an affirmative and empowering intervention model that integrates the best of clinical theory in an individualized way.

REFERENCES

American Psychiatric Association. (1980). *Diagnostic and statistical manual of mental disorders* (3rd ed.) Washington, DC: Author.

Anderson, S. C., & Henderson, D. C. (1985). Working with lesbian alcoholics. *Social Work, 30*, 518–525.

Baptiste, Jr., D. A. (1987). Psychotherapy with gay/lesbian couples and their children in "stepfamilies": A challenge for marriage and family therapists. *Journal of Homosexuality, 14*, 223–239.

Benjamin, J. (1988). *The bonds of love: Psychoanalysis, feminism, and the problem of domination.* New York: Pantheon.

Berger, R. M. (1992). Research on older gay men: What we know, what we need to know. In N. J. Woodman (Ed.), *Gay and lesbian lifestyles: A guide for counseling and education* (pp. 217–232). New York: Irvington Publishers.

Berger, R. M., & Kelly, J. J. (1986). Working with homosexuals of the older population. *Social Casework: The Journal of Contemporary Social Work, 67*, 203–210.

Buloff, B., & Osterman, M. (1995). Queer reflections: Mirroring and the lesbian experience of self. In J. M. Glassgold & S. Iasenza (Eds.), *Lesbians and psychoanalysis* (pp. 93–106). New York: Free Press.

Burch, B. (1993a). Heterosexuality, bisexuality, and lesbianism: Rethinking psychoanalytic views of women's sexual object choice. *Psychoanalytic Review, 80*, 83–98.

Burch, B. (1993b). *On intimate terms.* Chicago: University of Illinois Press.

Cass, V. C. (1979). Homosexual identity formation: A theoretical model. *Journal of Homosexuality, 3*, 219–235.

Chodorow, N. (1978). *The reproduction of mothering.* Berkeley: University of California Press.

Coleman, E. (1982). Developmental stages of the coming out process. In J. C. Gonsiorek (Ed.), *Homosexuality and psychotherapy: A practitioner's handbook of affirmative models* (pp. 31–44). New York: Haworth Press.

Cornett, C. (1990). The "risky" intervention: Twinship selfobject impasses and therapist self-disclosure in psychodynamic psychotherapy. *Clinical Social Work Journal, 19*, 45–61.

DeCrescenzo, T. A. (1984). Homophobia: A study of attitudes of mental health professionals toward homosexuality. In R. Schoenberg & R. Goldberg with D. Shore (Eds.), *With compassion toward some: Homosexuality and social work in America* (pp. 115–136). New York: Harrington Park Press.

Deutsch, H. (1932). On female homosexuality. In R. Fleiss (Ed.), *The psychoanalytic reader* (pp. 208–230). New York: International Universities Press, 1948.

Deutsch, L. (1995). Out of the closet and onto the couch: A psychoanalytic exploration of lesbian development. In J. M. Glassgold & S. Iasenza (Eds.), *Lesbians and psychoanalysis* (pp. 19–38). New York: Free Press.

Eisenbud, R. J. (1982). Early and later determinants of lesbian choice. *Psychoanalytic Review*, 69, 85–109.

Falco, K. L. (1991). *Psychotherapy with lesbian clients: Theory into practice.* New York: Brunner/Mazel.

Freud, S. (1920). The psychogenesis of a case of homosexuality in a woman. In *Standard Edition* (Vol. 18, pp. 145–172). London: Hogarth Press.

Gabriel, M. A., & Monaco, G. W. (1995). Revisiting the question of self-disclosure: The lesbian therapist's dilemma. In J. M. Glassgold & S. Iasenza (Eds.), *Lesbians and psychoanalysis* (pp. 161–172). New York: Free Press.

Gair, S. R. (1995). The false self, shame, and the challenge of self-cohesion. In J. M. Glassgold & S. Iasenza (Eds.), *Lesbians and psychoanalysis* (pp. 107–124). New York: Free Press.

Gilligan, C. (1982). *In a different voice: Psychological theory and women's development.* Cambridge, MA: Harvard University Press.

Glassgold, J. M., & S., Iasenza. Eds. (1995). *Lesbians and psychoanalysis.* New York: Free Press.

Goldner, V. (1991). Toward a critical relational theory of gender. *Psychoanalytic Dialogues, 1,* 249–272.

Goldstein, E. G. (1994). Self-disclosure in treatment: What therapists do and don't talk about. *Clinical Social Work Journal, 22,* 417–433.

Goldstein, E. G. (1995). *Ego psychology and social work practice* (2nd ed.) New York: Free Press.

Gonsiorek, J. C. (Ed.). (1982a). *Homosexuality and psychotherapy: A practitioner's handbook of affirmative models.* New York: Haworth Press, 1982a.

Gonsiorek, J. C. (1982b). The use of diagnostic concepts in working with gay and lesbian populations. In J. C. Gonsiorek (Ed.), *Homosexuality and psychotherapy: A practitioner's handbook of affirmative models* (pp. 9–20). New York: Haworth Press.

Gonsiorek, J. C., & Weinrich, J. (1991). *Homosexuality: Research implications for public policy.* Newbury Park, CA: Sage.

Gould, D. (1995). A critical examination of the notion of pathology in psychoanalysis. In J. M. Glassgold & S. Iasenza (Eds.), *Lesbians and psychoanalysis* (pp. 3–18). New York: Free Press.

Greenberg, J. R., & Mitchell, S. A. (1983). *Object relations in psychoanalytic theory.* Cambridge, MA: Harvard University Press.

Hetrick, E. S., & Martin, D. A. (1984). Ego-dystonic homosexuality: A developmental view. In E. S. Hetrick & T. S. Stein (Eds.), *Innovations in psychotherapy with homosexuals* (pp. 2–21). Washington, DC: American Psychiatric Press.

Hetrick, E. S., & Martin, D. A. (1988). Developmental issues and their resolution for gay and lesbian adolescents. In E. Coleman (Ed.), *Integrated identity: Gay men and lesbians* (pp. 25–43). New York: Harrington Park Press.

Isay, R. A. (1989). *Being homosexual: Gay men and their development.* New York: Farrar, Strauss, and Giroux.

Jordan, J. V., Kaplan, A. G., Miller, J. B., Stiver, I. P., & Surrey, J. L. (1991). *Women's growth in connection.* New York: Guilford.

Kasoff, B., Boden, R., de Monteflores, C., Hunt, P., & Wahba, R. (1995). Coming out of the frame: Lesbian feminism and psychoanalytic theory. In J. M. Glassgold & S. Iasenza (Eds.), *Lesbians and psychoanalysis* (pp. 229–264). New York: Free Press.

Kinsey, A. (1948). *Sexual behavior in the human male.* London and Philadelphia: Saunders.

Kleinberg, S., & Zorn, P. (1995). Rekindling the flame: A therapeutic approach to strengthening lesbian relationships. In J. M. Glassgold & S. Iasenza (Eds.), *Lesbians and psychoanalysis* (pp. 125–144). New York: Free Press.

Kohut, H. (1971). *The analysis of the self.* New York: International Universities Press.

Kohut, H. (1977). *The restoration of the self.* New York: International Universities Press.

Lewis, L. A. (1984). The coming-out process for lesbians: Integrating a stable identity. *Social Work, 29,* 464–469.

Magee, M., & Miller, D. C. (1992). "She foreswore her womanhood": Psychoanalytic views of female homosexuality. *Clinical Social Work Journal, 20,* 67–87.

Malyon, A. K. (1982b). Psychotherapeutic implications of internalized homophobia in gay men. In J. C. Gonsiorek (Ed.), *Homosexuality and psychotherapy: A practitioner's handbook of affirmative models* (pp. 59–70). New York: Haworth Press.

Martin, A. (1982). Some issues in the treatment of gay and lesbian patients. *Psychotherapy: Theory, Research, and Practice, 19,* 341–348.

McDougall, J. (1980). *Plea for a measure of abnormality.* New York: International Universities Press.

O'Connor, N., & Ryan, J. (1993). *Wild desires and mistaken identities: Lesbianism and psychoanalysis.* New York: Columbia University Press.

Potter, S. J., & Darty, T. E. (1981). Social work and the invisible minority: An exploration of lesbianism. *Social Work, 26,* 187–192.

Prozan, C. K. (1992). *Feminist psychoanalytic psychotherapy.* Northvale, NJ: Jason Aronson.

Reiter, L. (1989). Sexual orientation, sexual identity, and the question of choice. *Clinical Social Work Journal, 17,* 138–150.

Rich, A. (1980). Compulsory heterosexuality and lesbian existence. *Signs, 5,* 631–660.

Roth, S. (1985). Psychotherapy with lesbian couples: Individual issues, female socialization, and the social context. *Journal of Marital and Family Therapy, 11,* 273–286.

Schwartz, R. D. (1989). When the therapist is gay: Personal and clinical reflections. *Journal of Gay and Lesbian Psychotherapy, 1,* 41–53.

Shernoff, M. J. (1995). Family therapy for lesbian and gay clients. In F. J. Turner (Ed.), *Differential diagnosis and treatment* (4th ed.) (pp. 911–918). New York: Free Press.

Siegel, E. (1988). *Female homosexuality: Choice without volition.* New York: Brunner/Mazel.

Socarides, C. (1988). *The preoedipal origin and psychoanalytic therapy of sexual perversions.* Madison, WI: International Universities Press.

Spaulding, E. C. (1993). The inner world of objects and lesbian development. *Journal of Analytic Social Work,* 5–31.

Stoller, R. (1977). Primary femininity. In H. Blum (Ed.), *Female psychology: Contemporary psychoanalytic views* (pp. 59–78). New York: International Universities Press.

Suchet, M. (1995). "Having it both ways": Rethinking female sexuality. In J. M. Glassgold & S. Iasenza (Eds.), *Lesbians and psychoanalysis* (pp. 39–62). New York: Free Press.

Tully, C. (1992). Research on older lesbian women: What is known, what is not known, and how to learn more. In N. J. Woodman (Ed.), *Gay and lesbian lifestyles: A guide for counseling and education* (pp. 235–264). New York: Irvington Publishers.

Weille, K. L. H. (1993). Reworking developmental theory: The case of lesbian identity formation. *Clinical Social Work Journal, 21,* 151–160.

Woodman, N. J., & Lenna, H. R. (1980). *Counseling gay men and women.* San Francisco: Jossey-Bass.

22

Clinical Social Work Practice with Gay Men

Carlton Cornett

Gay men present some unique challenges to and opportunities for clinical social workers. Gay male clients can be understood from a psychodynamic theoretical perspective; however, the greatest challenge facing the clinician is to adapt this perspective to an understanding of the unique aspects of the encounter with the gay man. To be effective in understanding the gay client, the clinician must employ a perspective that takes into account internalized homophobia and the self-alienation that results from it.

ALIENATION FROM THE SELF

Freud proposed that the vast majority of difficulties that impel clients to seek out the services of an analyst or psychotherapist (including clinical social workers) have, at their base, an inadequate resolution of the oedipal transition. During the last decade of the nineteenth century and the first decades of this century, that was probably an adequate etiological explanation for the clinical presentations of most clients deemed appropriate for psychoanalytic treatment. However, most of those clients who were assessed as being potentially amenable to psychoanalytic treatment had neuroses like conversion disorders and so forth. Clients with other than classical neurotic difficulties were often seen as inappropriate for psychoanalysis.

Beginning in the 1940s and 1950s, classical psychodynamic theorists began to

Note: I wish to express appreciation to my lover, DeWayne Fulton, for his editorial advice and creative technical assistance.

attempt application of oedipally related concepts to a wider range of disorders, thereby expanding the clientele who could potentially be helped through psychoanalytic principles. However, during this same period came challenges to the idea that oedipal dynamics form the etiology of most types of psychopathology. Two of the most important of these challenges came from the interpersonal paradigm of Harry Stack Sullivan (1953b) and the more existentially oriented work of Rollo May (1953).

Sullivan (1953a, 1953b) emphasized the importance of interpersonal interactions and the internalization of these into a self-representation that guides the thoughts, feelings, behavior, and, ultimately, perceptions, of the individual: "The self may be said to be made up of reflected appraisals. If these were chiefly derogatory . . . then the self dynamism will itself be chiefly derogatory. It will facilitate hostile, disparaging appraisals of other people and it will entertain disparaging and hostile appraisals of itself" (1953a, p. 22).

Through the "reflected appraisals" of others in her or his environment, the child develops a relatively enduring representation of the self that affects both intrapersonal and interpersonal attitudes and actions. If the reflected appraisals of others are generally and consistently positive, the child develops the capacity to feel confident and proud and to put these feeling states into action through assertive behavior. If these appraisals are generally and consistently negative, the child develops a view of self as inadequate, which then creates much anxiety in interpersonal relations. This anxiety is managed through the use of various defensive operations, the structure and extent of which determine the type of psychopathology.

Like Sullivan, May (1953) was interested in the importance of relationships in the formation of personality. However, whereas Sullivan's work often focused (at least early in his writing) on microrelations (i.e., relational interactions between two people, chiefly the therapist and client), May began to look at personality development from a more macrorelational perspective (the role that culture and society play in shaping positively or negatively the personality). As May examined Western society, he saw people as increasingly behaving like automatons, devoid of any real sense of self and functioning only in ways that would be potentially pleasing to others. He saw people as becoming decreasingly motivated by internal factors (other than the need for approval) and likened most people's functioning to that of an actor in a play:

> It is as though one had always to postpone his judgment until he looked at his audience. The person who is passive, to whom or for whom the act is done, has the power to make the act effective or ineffective, rather than the one who is doing it. Thus we tend to be *performers* in life rather than persons who live and act as selves. (1953, p. 60)

May viewed people as increasingly empty and termed ours the "age of emptiness."

More recently, Kohut (1984) and self psychology theorists have added an important understanding of the intrapsychic structural consequences of the internalization of narcissistically injurious interactions, from both microrelational and macrorelational interactions. Kohut observed that if a child's narcissistic developmental needs are not met, the child will not develop a cohesive and vigorous self.

The child, and later adult, will then be prone to periods of overwhelming anxiety, resulting in experiences of fragmentation (the lack of a clear and coherent sense of who and what one is). Coupled with the propensity for fragmentation experiences also comes a difficulty in maintaining consistent, functional levels of self-esteem. Although Kohut's theoretical paradigm began as an intrapsychic model of human development, it is gradually growing in directions that make it compatible with interpersonal (Galatzer-Levy & Cohler, 1993; Wolf 1988) and existential (Cornett, 1992, 1993a; Gottesfeld, 1984) perspectives.

These perspectives are all useful in understanding the sense of personal alienation that most often seems to bring gay men to consult a clinical social worker. Together, they provide an understanding of the development of internalized homophobia, defined broadly as the internalization of culture's virulent anti-homosexual bias, which accounts for much of this alienation. Although there are differences of opinion as to what age is most important in the development of internalized homophobia—Green (1987) proposes childhood interactions as pivotal, while Friedman and Downey (1995) emphasize late childhood, and Malyon (1993) emphasizes adolescence—there is general agreement that the internalization of society's antihomosexual bias (taking place through both micro- and macrorelational interactions) results in contempt and loathing for the self. This, in turn, results in a pervasive alienation from one's self and a fragmented, inchoate identity. Such alienation can be seen most tangibly in:

- A client's inability to describe his feelings, thoughts, or values.
- A judgmental stance toward himself and the world.
- A decreased capacity for empathy with himself and others.
- A sense that he is "empty" or "incomplete."
- A propensity toward involvement in relational interactions that are physically or emotionally harmful.
- Difficulty tolerating moments of pride or accomplishment.
- Difficulty consistently maintaining a level of self-esteem, which allows facing setbacks without crippling anxiety.
- A general sense of being undeserving of understanding, acceptance, and love.

Chernin (1995) has suggested that the metaphor of the oedipal drama may be more usefully replaced by the Egyptian myth of Isis. It was Isis's task to search the four corners of the earth gathering the pieces of Osiris who had been dismembered by his brother, Seth. When thinking about clinical work with gay men, the myth of Isis is indeed an applicable metaphor.

The structure and function of Western culture is often referred to metaphorically in terms of brotherhood (e.g., "Big Brother," "the brotherhood of man," "my brother's keeper"). In this sense, it is the gay man's brother who dismembers him through the pervasive homophobia that characterizes society. Like Isis, it is the role of the clinician to help the client search for the disavowed, disowned, and split-off pieces of his identity that, if reintegrated, would make his self whole. The manifestations of an alienation from the self can be seen in my first session with Martin, a gay man with whom I worked over eighteen months.

It was a crisp fall afternoon when I invited Martin into my office from the outer waiting room. He had called a few days earlier requesting an appointment, saying only that he "needed to talk to somebody about some things." As he entered the office and greeted me, he grasped my hand firmly (even a little painfully) with a determined nod. I motioned toward the chair opposite mine, and he sat without speaking. As I sat, I became aware that the sense of comfort I had experienced earlier—in smelling the rich fragrance of the fall season's first fires wafting through the beautiful deep red and orange hues of the trees—was being replaced by a vague anxiety.

I am often anxious when meeting a client for the first time. Questions run through my mind. Will this person bring a difficulty with which I can be helpful? Will I be able to understand this person and effectively communicate that understanding? Will it be comfortable working with this person, or will it be an arduous task? My anxiety on this day had other, not readily definable, elements as well. I wondered if it was already a part of Martin beginning to communicate his story to me.

I smiled and asked, "What do you prefer to be called?"

"Martin. Martin's fine," he responded.

"Okay, I'm Carlton," I rejoined.

Many of us who were trained psychodynamically were taught that the whole issue of names, titles, and so forth (e.g., what the client wishes to call the clinician, how this is broached, if he wishes to address the clinician) can be a source of important dynamic information. However, I prefer to make explicit how my client wishes to be addressed and, similarly, how I wish to be addressed at the outset. I do this for two reasons. First, a name is perhaps the most important tangible symbol of identity to a person, and identity is the central issue in clinical work with gay men; communicating directly about identity from the outset sets the stage for this work.

The second reason that I address the issue of names at the beginning of work with a new client is that I wish to invite him into a personal and intimate relationship. I want to be able to address him directly and avoid as much as possible only marginally personal interactions. I prefer to be called by my first name because I believe that this communicates my willingness and availability to be involved as an authentic individual in the emotionally intimate work that transpires between a clinician and client (Strean, 1988).

"Perhaps we can begin with what brings you here today," I offered.

"Okay. Well, I guess that's okay. I mean, I'm not completely sure what's happening right now," he began. He laughed anxiously and continued, "I guess I'm depressed."

"Depressed?" I queried in an effort to get a phenomenological sense of what Martin referred to as depression.

"I feel bad all the time. Nothing makes me happy. I hate everything about my life." Martin's facial expression conveyed a painful anger.

"When you say you feel bad all the time, what do you mean?" I again attempted to understand the phenomenological experience of feeling "bad," a word related to morality that is often employed, especially by gay men, to describe emotional experiences.

"I don't know. Bad. You know, like angry, but also like that's wrong, and also like there's really no point to anything anyway."

"Sort of enraged, but also kind of guilty or even empty?" I asked quietly.

"Yeah!" he exclaimed with clear surprise that anyone could understand him.

CREATING A THERAPEUTIC ENVIRONMENT

Because the internalized homophobia that leads to alienation from the self occurs developmentally in a relational context, the most important aspect of clinical work with gay men is the establishment of a helpful relational context for the encounter. R. D. Laing captures this idea in his description of clinical work as the "*obstinate attempt of two people to recover the wholeness of being human through the relationship between them*" (1967, p. 53, italics in the original). All other forms of "technique" are secondary to the creation of this relational environment, the foundation of which is philosophical and rooted in the clinician's understanding of her or his value system regarding the endeavor (Will, 1981).

Change and the Clinician's Health Values

The clinician must first elaborate for herself or himself the goal of the encounter with the client. What is she or he attempting to do with the client? Will the client be different after their work together? If so, how? Even more broadly, what constitutes an emotionally or psychologically "healthy" person? Answering these questions will give the clinician at least a rudimentary sense of her or his health values. This understanding is crucial because the clinician's health values will guide her or his thinking about work with the client (Isay, 1993; Will, 1981).

A time-honored value regarding clinical work is that its ultimate product should be a change in the client. The client should be somehow different—optimally less distressed—than when he began. His symptomatology should be reduced, and he should "feel better." No matter how well intentioned this philosophy may be pursued, it is generally unhelpful in clinical work with gay men.

First, gay men have generally been appraised as inadequate, wrong, or in need of change throughout their lives. The clinician's belief that the gay client needs to change often communicates, perhaps on a level out of both participants' conscious awareness, that the client is inadequate as he is. The clinician's conscious belief that homosexuality is as viable a sexual identity as heterosexuality does not vitiate this, because the experience of the expectation of change re-creates the narcissistic injuries that have characterized other relational interactions.

Second, whether a client changes as a result of work with the clinician is not under the clinician's control. As clinicians we have no control over whether our clients change. Therefore to pursue change as the goal of clinical work puts both participants at risk—the clinician at risk for narcissistic injury, which then places the client at risk that the clinician will feel compelled to pursue change at a cost to the client.

Obviously, it is impossible to delete the hope for client change, from our philosophical understanding of clinical work entirely. After all else is said, most of us grow to care about our clients and hope that their lives will be more satisfying than when they originally sought our care. Even Laing's description of clinical work proposes that some change is a part of effective clinical work. Therefore, I am not naively or disingenuously suggesting that the hope for improvement in our clients' lives be suppressed, only that it be subordinated to a more realistically attainable goal: creating an environment of empathic understanding that is not dependent on the client's alteration of himself for us. Paradoxically, when such an environment is created, the client often does make significant changes in his life.

Resistance

Resistance traditionally is conceptualized as the client's active, albeit unconscious, attempts to oppose the clinician's efforts to induce change. From this perspective, resistance is composed of the client's attempts to avoid relinquishing the compromise adaptation of his symptomatology.

In considering clinical work with gay men, resistance can be conceptualized as evolving from three primary motivations. Although differentiation is offered regarding the motivations of resistance, it is worth noting that all are intimately, perhaps inseparably, related. All three motivations are derived from threats to the status quo of the client's identity. Kohut offers the most cogent conceptualization of resistance as "activities undertaken in the service of psychological survival, . . . as the patient's attempt to save at least that sector of his nuclear self however small and precariously established it may be" (1984, p. 115).

First, resistance can represent a fear of change. This is not the fear of giving up the so-called secondary gains of symptomatology. Instead, it represents attempts to avoid identity disruption (Castelnuovo-Tedesco, 1989). Although the constant negative appraisals from the larger culture and within other relationships are narcissistically injurious, the client develops an identity, or perhaps pseudoidentity (see the discussions of the false self in Winnicott, 1965, 1989), around these appraisals. He seeks to avoid experiences that threaten this identity and the limited security it provides. Therefore, he often resists the notion that change should be sought as part of the experience with the clinician. It has been my observation that resistance increases in direct proportion to the clinician's belief that change is the goal of the clinical endeavor.

The second motivation for resistance is as a reaction to lapses in the empathy of the clinician (Kohut, 1984). Resistance represents the client's attempts to draw the clinician's attention to a lack of sensitivity in addressing old narcissistic wounds and/or that the client is experiencing a level of anxiety that threatens to result in fragmentation.

Finally, in working with gay men, resistance can represent a fear of hope (Cornett, 1993b, 1995). Because gay men internalize a derisive view of themselves from the larger culture, there is a conviction, of which they are generally only vaguely aware, that their lot is to be one of rejection and contempt. If the clinician is empathically attuned to the client, the experience can be a disjunctive one for the latter. The experience of empathic understanding and responsiveness challenges the client's worldview and thus threatens identity disruption.

In reviewing the motivations for resistance, there is a quality that suggests a double-bind for the clinician: if the clinician is empathic, resistance may result; if she or he is generally unempathic or even demonstrates the inevitable lapses in empathy that are a part of everyone's humanity, resistance also often results. Although for different reasons, this conceptualization confirms Freud's (1912a, 1912b) contention that resistance is ubiquitous to the therapeutic endeavor. It also confirms Freud's contention that responding to resistance is one of the keys to effective clinical work.

Responding to Resistance

Effectively responding to a client's resistance requires that the clinician view resistance as a means of communication and thus an ally rather than opponent to clinical work. It also requires that the clinician be able to identify the motivation for any given expression of resistance. Is the client responding to a fear of identity disruption (being asked to give up or contemplating on his own giving up one view of himself in favor of another)? Is he responding to an unempathic remark or action by the clinician? Has the work activated a sense of hope that must be squelched? The extent to which the clinician can be helpful in the face of resistance depends largely on her or his ability to understand this motivation and communicate this understanding to the client.

During the early weeks of our work together, Martin gradually began to let me become acquainted with him. He described himself as a lonely child and an even lonelier adolescent. Beginning in elementary school he had been teased by peers as a "sissy," "homo," and "faggot." He was intuitively aware from a very early age that he was somehow different and that derogatory names resonated to something in him, although he could not intellectually identify what until he was in high school.

During high school Martin's alienation from his peers increased. Uninterested in the types of activities that captivated schoolmates, such as sports and heterosexual dating, he became increasingly isolated. During these years, he gradually became aware of what homosexuality meant. Although he probably could not have articulated it at the time, he later came to realize that as his understanding of his homosexuality grew, so did his shame in it.

Martin's parents were neither overtly abusive nor very empathically attuned. Both had a career and were preoccupied with success at work. As Martin described them, both were desperate to provide for the financial needs of the family, while believing that the emotional needs would somehow be met automatically. He perceived them as having little time for him (which he attributed, like all the other rejections of his life, to his homosexuality). When either or both spent time with him or acknowledged him in some way, he would become paralyzed. He reported at these times feeling simultaneously enraged at the gesture and undeserving of the kindness it symbolized.

As the first weeks passed into months, Martin continued the phenomenon begun during our first hour. Whenever I effectively communicated that I understood what he was saying, he reacted with surprise. This is often a very subtle manifestation of the fear of hope. Every moment of empathic responsiveness is treated in an isolated way. There is a concentrated effort to avoid the hope that the experience of being understood in a relationship can be sustained. However, as we began to explore this and Martin became aware of the dynamics involved, his resistance took another form.

In the third month of his therapy, sessions with Martin began to take a new turn. From the time he sat down until the hour ended, he talked nonstop, providing no opportunity for me to comment. There was a clear sense of communication being blocked rather than his simply having a great deal to communicate. After a couple of sessions of this, I decided that there was something transpiring between us that was deserving of exploration and in the next session commented on it about halfway through the session. (Martin had paused momentarily to catch a quick breath.)

"Martin," I began, "I wonder if you've noticed that other than greeting you and ending the session, I haven't said anything for our last two appointments."

"Huh. Well, I hadn't really thought about it, but I guess you're right," he responded somewhat distractedly.

"What do you think that might mean?" I prodded.

"I don't know," he said with some consternation. He looked thoughtful for a moment and then continued "Oh, wait, you're saying I'm not letting you talk—huh, okay, so why?"

"That's the $65,000 question." I smiled.

After a few quiet moments Martin offered, "I guess I know what it might mean."

I nodded, encouraging him to go on.

"Well, I don't mean to hurt your feelings, but I guess I just don't believe you—you know, when you're all affirming and supposedly interested. No offense."

"None taken," I replied. "Let me make sure I understand: when it seems like I understand you, part of you doesn't believe it?"

"Part of me?" he queried.

"Well, yeah. After all, you keep coming, so I would imagine that part of you believes that I can understand you, or you would probably have just quit."

Martin looked thoughtful.

I continued, "Perhaps it's uncomfortable, maybe even frightening, to be understandable, so part of you prevents those experiences of feeling understood by not allowing me to communicate understanding to you."

He looked embarrassed and offered meekly, "I like it too much."

"Being understood?" I clarified.

"Yeah, I like the attention. It's selfish; it's not me."

"So, maybe being understandable would make you someone different than you've always thought you were?"

With his confirmation of this, my work with Martin moved back into an interactive mode.

This example demonstrates the complexity of resistance. Initially Martin discounted himself as generally not understandable by feeling surprised whenever he felt understood. However, as this ceased to be effective, he employed a resistance—keeping me silent—which did two things: minimized moments of feeling understood, thus minimizing his hope that he was generally understandable, and protected his identity. He had long believed himself beyond understanding. Being confronted with the possibility that this was not the case, he was forced to entertain the possibility of an identity different from the one to which he had grown accustomed.

The core of clinical work is creating a relational environment conducive to the client's reclaiming those aspects of his identity that have been alienated. Part of this is accomplished through a philosophical understanding of the ultimate goal of the process—as Erikson (1987) put it, the clinician's "way of looking at things." However, the creation of this relational environment is also accomplished through the active construction of the clinical environment.

ANONYMITY, NEUTRALITY, RESPECT, SENSITIVITY, AND COURTESY

Menaker argues that

> The present-day population suffers primarily from a sense of alienation, from a loss of meaningfulness in life, from disillusionment and an absence of faith in themselves and others. . . . The psychological help they require is not in the resolution of conflict but rather in affirmation in a new relationship that will make good an emotional loss or fill a void created in the course of development by lack of emotional sustenance. (1989, pp. 75–76)

This position, argued as well by May (1953) thirty years earlier, is descriptive of the primary difficulties that bring people to the offices of clinical social workers. It is certainly descriptive of the primary difficulty that brings the gay man to a clinician's office.

As Menaker proposes, the heart of clinical work is an affirming relationship. There are multiple ways in which the experience of therapy can be affirming of the client. Five of the most important for the gay male client involve thinking about traditional (and, in some cases, commonsense) concepts in slightly novel ways.

Anonymity

The classical psychodynamic literature has placed the clinician's relative anonymity in an eminent position. Most clinical theorists acknowledge that complete clinician anonymity is impossible and stress that anonymity can be thought of only in relative terms. One's manner of dress, office decor, and so forth all impart information about the values, tastes, and personality of the clinician. However, from this perspective, it is argued that the clinician should maintain the maximum level of anonymity possible. Clinician anonymity fosters an environment that allows the client to project freely onto her or him. The analysis of these transference projections then forms the basis of the clinician's interpretive efforts. Clinician revelations cloud the transference and make interpretive resolution of it more difficult.

In working with gay men, however, the concept of anonymity is best approached with more flexibility. Rather than remain as anonymous as possible to elicit transference material, the clinician is better served by conceptualizing relative anonymity in terms of the client's alienation from himself and his search for an integrated, authentic, and complete identity.

The clinician should ensure that her or his values and preferences—in short, identity—do not overwhelm the client. Overuse of self-disclosure by the clinician does overwhelm the client and puts the clinician's identity at the center of the clinical endeavor. At this level clinician self-disclosure is unempathic and prevents the client's unfettered search for and creation of his own authentic identity. However, there may be times when clinician self-disclosure is facilitative of clinical work. Kohut (1977) identified a universal human need to feel connected to the rest of humanity. He termed this the twinship need. Essentially, one yearning common to all human beings is for experiences in which one feels confirmed as a part of the human community—as a person among persons. For the gay man who has faced rejection from the larger heterosexual culture throughout his life, the yearning for twinship confirmation can be intense. It is in response to such yearnings that clinician self-disclosure can be an affirming interaction with the client.

To be therapeutic, a revelation by the clinician must meet two qualifications. First, it should confirm the shared nature of a perception, thought, and/or emotion between client and clinician. Second, the revelation should not be so personal to the clinician that it actually precludes the client's sharing in it (that it actually alienates the client from the experience of connection to the clinician [Cornett, 1991]).

Goldstein (1994) has argued that clinician self-disclosure can be helpful in work with lesbian clients. Indeed, it appears from both anecdotal and empirical research that self-disclosure by the clinician may be valued by most clients and that, at least from the perspective of the client, it is facilitative of helpful clinical work (see Ramsdell & Ramsdell, 1993, 1994). Certainly with gay men or other groups of clients whose identities are treated as anathema by the larger culture, moments of confirmation by the clinician's limited and careful use of self-revelation can be valuable. Thus, relative anonymity, if employed flexibly, can serve an affirming function for the client by both maintaining his identity and its development as the focus of the clinical endeavor and by furthering that identity through connection to the clinician and through her or him the larger community of humanity.

Neutrality

Neutrality has been defined in various ways in the psychotherapeutic literature. For Schafer (1983), neutrality is the clinician's refusal to side with one intrapsychic agency against another (e.g., in a conflict between superego and ego, the clinician remains equally engaged with, and equally distant from, both sides, avoiding favoring one over the other). This ego psychological view of neutrality places the clinician in a fairly passive role, concentrating on remaining a neutral observer (and, ultimately, interpreter) of the client's internal conflicts.

The interpersonal paradigm has challenged the notion that the clinician can remain completely external to the client's conflicts. Conceiving of all that takes place in the therapeutic relationship as reciprocally influenced, Sullivanian theorists view clinician neutrality in a more active light. Winer, for instance, proposes:

> One definition of neutrality that has made sense to me is that we work to extricate ourselves from repeated countertransference enactments with our patients. . . . Defining neutrality as our effort to work ourself clear means that we need to be as aware as possible of all the things we need to get clear of. (1994, p. 212)

While both the ego psychological and interpersonal perspectives have much merit, neutrality, I believe, begins in Winer's contention that "we need to be as aware as possible." Isay (1989, 1993) proposes another model of neutrality in clinical work with gay men: that neutrality be an active, nonjudgmental curiosity regarding all aspects of a client's life and functioning. It is a consistent wondering about the feelings, thoughts, and motivations that guide all aspects of the client's commerce with himself and the world.

It is important to define neutrality as active, nonjudgmental curiosity because curiosity is an opposite mode of perception from condemnation. Because our culture is so condemning of homosexuality, a part of the homophobia that gay men internalize is a stance toward themselves that emphasizes condemnation and trivializes curiosity. The clinician's ability and willingness to be curious about the client rather than condemning or contemptuous generally gradually awakens a dormant curiosity in the client to understand himself (and, not inconsequentially, others) rather than simply dismiss or condemn. This type of curiosity is directly affirming of the client and forms the therapeutic dyad's greatest ally in discovering and creating the client's authentic identity.

Respect

For clinical work to be successful with a client, it must be founded on a basic respect for that client as a person. For any client, being treated respectfully is affirming. The obverse is also true: being treated disrespectfully is a narcissistic injury to any client. For the gay man, respect is an especially vital component of clinical work due to the repeated narcissistic injuries sustained in commerce with the larger culture.

Beyond this basic conception of respect, another avenue of thinking about the concept is important in clinical work with gay men. Psychotherapeutic respect is the consistent attempt by the clinician to be honest with herself or himself and the client, especially about values, personality characteristics, and so forth, that have an impact on the relationship with the client.

In the heterosexual environment, in which the developing gay man must hide vital aspects of his identity, through either conscious suppression or unconscious denial, honesty becomes a limited and valuable commodity. The very act of concealing one's homosexuality and the need to scan the environment constantly for information as to who knows or does not know, and to the consequences attendant on this knowledge, can lead to complex perceptual anomalies and deficits in one's certainty regarding the acuity and accuracy of perceptions. The clinician's consistent striving for honesty with herself or himself and the client, especially in regard to their shared interactions, is affirming of the client's perceptions (if a client perceives some quality about the therapist or their interaction, it is accurate on some level).

In this description of respect, honesty is not equivalent to respect; the act of striving for complete honesty is the crucial factor. None of us, no matter how much training, supervision, or personal therapy we have had, can always be totally honest with ourselves and others. Because of our humanity, there will always be occasions when our motivations, feelings, and so forth are out of our own awareness. However, the attempt to maintain an overt and honest relationship with oneself and one's client throughout the clinical endeavor is deeply respectful. Will asserts that "the therapist. . . will influence his patient not only by what he does but also by being who he is. To some extent he serves as a model and a source of identity; what he values in life will influence his professional work" (1970, p. 12).

It is critical that the clinician strive to be as aware as possible of those values that influence clinical work and to acknowledge honestly their impact to herself or himself and the client. Some areas of the clinician's value system that may require particular scrutiny include the following:

- Whether homosexuality is pathological or a normal variation of human sexuality.
- How comfortable she or he is hearing about gay sexual behavior (this is crucial because, in this age of AIDS, much contempt for the self and self-hatred are expressed through sexual behavior).
- What she or he believes about monogamy (nonmonogamous relationships are not uncommon among gay male couples) (McWhirter & Mattison, 1984).
- Feelings and values regarding AIDS.

The clinician's constant attempts to be honest with herself or himself and the client about all the areas of both participants' worldviews that affect their relationship will be deeply affirming of the client. However, no less important, such a stance offers the clinician opportunities to grow.

Sensitivity

From its inception, social work as a profession has been concerned with person-in-environment. Clinical social workers have always espoused a concern about how the client fits into a larger cultural context. This concern, if actualized in the clinical relationship, predisposes clinical social workers to the type of sensitivity that facilitates clinical work with gay men.

There has often been a tendency among clinicians to view a client's functioning from the perspective of the clinician's cultural heritage and experience. There are some inherent difficulties in such a stance. First, clinical work is an enterprise that requires symbolic communication. Symbols take on different meanings in different cultural contexts. Language itself, our chief means of symbolic communication, is understandable only in a particular cultural context. To truly understand the nuances of any symbolic communication, the clinician must have some familiarity with its particular context.

It is inherently unhelpful to attempt to understand the gay client through heterosexual cultural assumptions. One of the frequent difficulties I have heard expressed by practitioners beginning work with gay men is a confusion regarding what is "pathological" and what "healthy," especially regarding homosexual relationships. When one attempts to fit a homosexual couple into a heterosexual mold, it does indeed become confusing to understand dynamics specific to that relationship that may be interfering in the partners' satisfaction because the relationship overall may not match the clinician's paradigm of satisfying relationships. Further, to try to understand homosexual individuals or couples using a heterosexual model re-creates the antihomosexual bias that has been internalized and is to some extent at the base of the client's difficulties anyway. Instead, it is much more helpful for a clinician who will be working with gay men to attempt to understand something of the cultural context in which the client lives.

The extreme of this position is the promotion of stereotypes. Obviously, this is not helpful to clinical work in any way. However, to believe that the external realities impinging on the client are inconsequential is equally unhelpful.

One way of understanding the cultural ethos of the gay client's life is reading the writings of gay men—journalism, fiction, political commentary, and so forth. Another is to count among one's peer group gay colleagues and friends who can answer generic questions about the gay subculture. Finally, taking part in activities that interest gay men—gay-themed movies, political discussion groups, gay-oriented lectures, and so forth—can also be a valuable way to gain an empathy regarding the gay client's macrorelational environment, which can complement the empathy derived from immersion in the client's particular internal world.

Courtesy

A final quality necessary to the creation of an environment that will encourage the creation or discovery of the client's authentic identity is courtesy. Typically, we define courtesy as those acts of polite interpersonal commerce that communicate a sense of valuation of another. Like respect, courtesy is directly affirming of a client. Also like respect, courtesy in the clinical context has a specific meaning that enhances its capacity for affirmation.

One of the most important areas in which our culture's antihomosexual bias affects the gay man is enculturation. All the rituals, institutions, and symbolic rites of passage in this culture are heterosexually oriented. There are few, if any, activities of enculturation that can be adapted by the gay man without much effort. It is in these activities of enculturation that the individual's identity is strengthened and confirmed as being a member of the collective community.

Clinical work offers an important, if subtle, opportunity to open this area for exploration and also an opportunity to offer the client an experience of socialization and enculturation that can later be utilized as a model for emulation. That opportunity involves enculturating the client to the special, idiosyncratic relationship at the heart of sound clinical work.

Too often clinicians, especially those of a psychodynamic orientation, neglect this important activity. In an effort to allow all of the client's world to unfold without contamination, clinicians often do not tell the client why and how they see the process as unfolding and achieving an outcome. Sullivan (1954) pointed out that the simple act of explaining the nature of therapy to a client and socializing him to the endeavor greatly increases its effectiveness. This can be as remarkably simple as indicating to a client where to sit, what types of material (e.g., dreams) the clinician believes are important, and why the therapist practices in the manner that she or he does. Such simple acts by the clinician have been borne out by psychotherapy research as critical to its outcome (Luborsky, 1984; Strupp & Binder, 1984).

For the gay man this is particularly important because to neglect the act of socializing him to the therapeutic relationship symbolically repeats other experiences of being excluded from the culture's activities of confirmation. Conversely, to enculturate him to the process of therapy offers a symbolic experience of social confirmation that is affirming of his identity and provides a measure of safety and predictability as he allows the clinician to become deeply acquainted with him.

Anonymity, neutrality, respect, sensitivity, and courtesy set the context of the clinical work and affirm the client's identity, both as it is presented and as it evolves. The final area of the clinical relationship to discuss are those aspects of the relationship between clinician and client that have traditionally been referred to as transference and countertransference.

TRANSFERENCE AND COUNTERTRANSFERENCE

Traditional conceptions of transference and countertransference have focused on these as roughly parallel phenomena, differentiated primarily by whether the client (transference) or clinician (countertransference) is the focus of discussion. From the classical psychodynamic perspective, both involve two key elements. The first is projection of the intrapsychic contents of one participant onto the other. The second is a corresponding distortion of the relationship between the two based on responses to these projections.

There are a number of difficulties associated with conceptualizing transference and countertransference in this manner. One of the most important in terms of the clinical social worker's interest in the client as a part of a larger cultural and social system is that such a view places the clinician in the role of ultimate arbiter of reality. Fromm (1980) likens such a view of transference to a form of social control that inherently places the client in a position of childlike ignorance and helplessness, dependent on the clinician to define reality for her or him. Many of the so-called reparative models of psychotherapy, which strive to replace homosexuality with heterosexuality, have used such conceptions of transference and countertransference to the detriment of many homosexual people.

Self psychology and the interpersonal perspective have offered more useful ways of conceptualizing transference and countertransference, especially in clinical work with gay men. Integrated, they describe transference and countertransference reactions as phenomena with two levels, the compensatory and the narrative. Kohut (1977, 1984) offered a conceptualization of both transference and countertransference as involving use of one participant by the other as a selfobject (an extension and strengthening of the self in a weakened sector). Galatzer-Levy and Cohler (1993) have suggested that the more experience-near term *essential other* replace selfobject. The self psychological model identifies three primary essential other transferences: mirroring, idealizing, and twinship:

• *Mirroring.* Essential other transference phenomena are founded on a deficit in the sector of the self that directly regulates self-esteem. Because the client has not received sufficient unconditional affirmation through parental or societal (generally both) interactions, he requires much direct recognition and acknowledgment of accomplishments to maintain a functional level of self-esteem. Essentially the clinician functions as an empathic audience who acknowledges moments of client pride and accomplishment, the experience of which ultimately leads to the client's internalization of the ability to do so for himself more consistently and reliably.

• *Idealizing.* Essential other transference phenomena are rooted in deficits in that sector of the self that provides for the regulation of anxiety through merger or identification with a larger ideal. The objects of idealization can be people (in optimal development, parents), larger ideas, movements, groups, and so forth. The clinician often becomes an idealized figure in a client's life, and her or his capacity to tolerate this ultimately allows growth to return to this sector of the client's self.

• *Twinship.* Twinship transference phenomena involve the client's need to feel confirmed as a person among persons, as part of the human community. The clinician's function is to serve as that source of confirmation and link.

Together, the mirroring, idealizing, and twinship transference phenomena constitute one level of transference, the compensatory level. The client uses the clinician initially to compensate for deficits in the self until, through the clinical work, the self is strengthened and becomes sufficient in this sphere.

Interpersonal theory offers another extremely important idea about transference (and countertransference as well): the recognition that transference and countertransference reactions are founded on real qualities in the two participants of therapy (Winer, 1994). All of a client's reactions to a clinician are based on real qualities in the clinician, even though those qualities may be out of the clinician's awareness. The same is true of the clinician's reactions to the client. Each of the client's reactions to the clinician is built around some realistic core quality or qualities. These reactions generally then become a dramatic means of describing the genesis of the client's deficits in his self. In this way, the client describes the developmental phenomena that produced his particular compensatory transference reactions. These transference reactions thus tell the story, using real aspects of the clinician's identity, of how his particular self-deficits were formed. This second level of transference is thus the narrative level.

Countertransference is a parallel phenomena (and is universal). It involves the clinician's using the client as an essential other. It can also be based on one particular developmental area (mirroring, idealizing, or twinship) or, more commonly like transference, fluctuate among all three.

Countertransference has often been conceived of as a sign of the clinician's inadequate resolution of her or his own neurotic difficulties. However, this has gradually been changing, although countertransference is still commonly looked on as an undesirable, though unavoidable, part of clinical work. Kohut's (and the interpersonal paradigm's) view of countertransference, however, places it as a source of information about the client and the relationship between client and clinician.

Countertransference can have a positive, negative, or neutral impact on clinical work. For instance, the ability to enjoy being idealized is helpful to the client and serves a mirroring function for the clinician. This is an example of countertransference as having a positive impact on clinical work. An example of a neutral impact is the fee. The fee is a source of valuation and affirmation of the clinician's skill and expertise, thus serving a mirroring function, but neither appreciably adds to or detracts from the client's experience. A more negative impact can be seen in the clinician's use of the client as a mirroring essential other, by requiring that he accept the clinician's values, worldview, and so forth as his own, even if these do not legitimately fit the client's authentic identity. A model of clinical work presuming that the client's transference is a distortion of reality, and that part of the clinician's function is to correct this distortion through interpretation, is particularly vulnerable to this type of negative countertransference (Cornett, 1995).

TRANSFERENCE AND TECHNIQUE

The heart of psychodynamic technique has often been conceived of as the analysis and interpretation of transference phenomena. I prefer to think of the heart of clinical technique with gay men as amplification of transference phenomena rather than interpretation of them. Through amplification of the client's essential other yearnings (the compensatory level of transference) and reconstruction of the events that lead to those yearnings (the narrative level of transference) the client is freed to discover and create his authentic identity. The latter occurs as a natural growth reaction once barriers to it are removed through the overall experience of therapy.

The distinction made between interpretation and amplification is not simply a matter of semantics. Interpretation is founded on the notion that the clinician ultimately has greater knowledge about the client than does the client. This is an inaccurate and narcissistically injurious notion for any client and is particularly fraught with danger for the gay client. Generally interpretation, because it is an activity that supposes to present information to the client that is not available to him, also encourages compliance with the clinician's views rather than authenticity. It is a real danger of interpretive clinical work that the clinician may, instead of assisting the client in discovering and creating his own authentic identity, simply promote a variant inauthentic or false self—one more in keeping with the clinician's identity and health values.

Over the first several months of my work with Martin, he gradually reported a decrease in the symptoms that had originally brought him to my office. Initially compensatory transference phenomena focused on twinship yearnings. He was curious about me—my values, my life outside the office, and so forth. He was most interested in discovering areas of shared interest and experience. I focused on amplifying the intensity of his yearning and, when it seemed appropriate, would confirm his perceptions of what we did in fact have in common.

Although in the first six months of therapy twinship transference phenomena predominated, mirroring and idealizing transference phenomena were interspersed. After approximately six months, idealization became the prominent feature of his transference.

Like many other gay men, Martin's moments of idealization served dual and contradictory functions. The first was to bolster his self-esteem by being connected to me, whom he saw as a figure of confidence and power, through our therapeutic relationship. The second was to compare himself disparagingly to his idealized image of me and confirm himself as inadequate. Initially, his idealization felt heady to me. However, this quickly came to be replaced by a vague anxiety—the same kind of anxiety I had felt on first meeting Martin.

Soon, in response to his idealization, I found myself increasingly critical of my interactions with Martin. On a couple of occasions I noticed myself making disparaging remarks about myself when he would make a comment that I felt overestimated me. In the seventh month of his therapy this pattern reached a point at which it could be clarified. In one session Martin complimented me on what I was wearing. Without thinking it through consciously, I responded that I appreciated the compliment but that I had nothing special on. At that point he confronted me.

"What's that about?" he began.

"What's what about?" I responded, a little stunned but vaguely aware of what he alluded to.

"All the criticism of yourself. [He was obviously responding to the cumulative experience of my self-criticism rather than this one interaction.] Whenever I point out something I like about you, you bash yourself. It's like you don't like it that I like you."

A light came on in my head. "Or, that I don't want you getting close to me."

"Yeah," he said, seeming a little surprised.

"I've been aware of that happening too, but I wasn't sure what to make of it. I'm still not sure what it's all about, but I have the intuition that you've experienced it before."

Martin confirmed that this was indeed a familiar experience for him. Beginning with his father, any man he liked or wanted to be close to would push him away. Martin's transference and my countertransference dovetailed (as is often the case). On the level of the compensatory transference, he needed to idealize me because he had not been allowed to be close to a man in this way (which we ultimately discovered he had believed was due to his homosexuality). My compensatory transference was to use Martin as a mirroring essential other. However, this raised my anxiety and touched some of my own unresolved shame (alas, a vestige of internalized homophobia that is never completely eradicated). I responded by discounting and disparaging myself (also parallel to Martin's reaction), which then offered an opportunity to clarify Martin's narrative transference. Men he had tried to get close to pushed him away. He hypothesized that this was because of his homosexuality; however, my reaction suggested that it was probably related to a sense of inadequacy in these men themselves, a fear of disappointing him, and anxiety or shame about their own homoerotic yearnings brought out by his idealization.

Martin's therapy lasted about eighteen months. Much of our work focused on remnants of his internalized homophobia, which were illuminated by both our reactions to the relationship. By the end of this period, Martin reported a greater sense of satisfaction with his life, was dating steadily, and asserted himself regularly in social and vocational interactions. The last quality is the most convincing sign that a gay man has at least begun to integrate all facets of his identity and is operating from an authentic system of values and feelings.

CONCLUSION

The core difficulty that gay men present involves an alienation from the core feelings and values that comprise the authentic identity. This alienation is in large measure the result of the internalization of our society's antihomosexual bias, popularly termed internalized homophobia. The crucial element in addressing this alienation is the relationship created by clinician and client. The clinician must focus her or his efforts on creating an environment that affirms the client. Clinical social workers, with their interest in the interface between the individual and his social context, are uniquely positioned to work with gay men. The only ingredient necessary for success in this endeavor is the courage to explore ourselves as we aid our clients in exploring themselves.

REFERENCES

Castelnuovo-Tedesco, P. (1989). The fear of change and its consequences in analysis and psychotherapy. *Psychoanalytic Inquiry*, 9, 101–118.

Chernin, K. (1995). *A different kind of listening: My psychoanalysis and its shadow*. New York: HarperCollins.

Cornett, C. (1991). The "risky" intervention: Twinship selfobject impasses and therapist self-disclosure in psychodynamic psychotherapy. *Clinical Social Work Journal, 19*, 49–61.

Cornett, C. (1992). Beyond words: A conception of self psychology. *Clinical Social Work Journal, 20*, 337–341.

Cornett, C. (1993a). Dynamic psychotherapy of gay men: A view from self psychology. In C. Cornett (Ed.), *Affirmative dynamic psychotherapy with gay men* (pp. 45–76). Northvale, NJ: Jason Aronson.

Cornett, C. (1993b). "Resistance" in dynamic psychotherapy with gay men. In C. Cornett (Ed.), *Affirmative dynamic psychotherapy with gay men* (pp. 93–115). Northvale, NJ: Jason Aronson.

Cornett, C. (1995). *Reclaiming the authentic self: Dynamic psychotherapy with gay men*. Northvale, NJ: Jason Aronson.

Erikson, E. H. (1987). *A way of looking at things: Selected papers from 1930 to 1980*. Ed. S. Schlein. New York: W. W. Norton.

Freud, S. (1912a). The dynamics of transference. *Standard Edition* (Vol. 12, pp. 99–108). London: Hogarth Press.

Freud, S. (1912b). Recommendations to physicians practicing psychoanalysis. *Standard Edition* (Vol. 12, pp. 111–120). London: Hogarth Press.

Friedman, R. C., and Downey, J. (1995). Internalized homophobia and the negative therapeutic reaction. *Journal of the American Academy of Psychoanalysis, 23*, 99–113.

Fromm, E. (1980). *Greatness and limitations of Freud's thought*. New York: Mentor.

Galatzer-Levy, R. M., and Cohler, B. J. (1993). *The essential other: A developmental psychology of the self*. New York: Basic Books.

Goldstein, E. G. (1994). Self-disclosure in treatment: What therapists do and don't talk about. *Clinical Social Work Journal, 22*, 417–433.

Gottesfeld, M. L. (1984). The self-psychology of Heinz Kohut: An existential reading. *Clinical Social Work Journal, 12*, 283–287.

Green, R. (1987). *The "sissy boy syndrome" and the development of homosexuality*. New Haven, CT: Yale University Press.

Isay, R. A. (1989). *Being homosexual: Gay men and their development*. New York: Farrar, Straus, Giroux.

Isay, R. A. (1993). On the analytic therapy of homosexual men. In C. Cornett (Ed.), *Affirmative dynamic psychotherapy with gay men* (pp. 23–44). Northvale, NJ: Jason Aronson.

Kohut, H. (1977). *The restoration of the self.* New York: International Universities Press.

Kohut, H. (1984). *How does analysis cure?* Ed. A. Goldberg and P. Stepansky. Chicago: University of Chicago Press.

Laing, R. D. (1967). *The politics of experience.* New York: Pantheon Books.

Luborsky, L. (1984). *Principles of psychoanalytic psychotherapy: A manual for supportive-expressive treatment.* New York: Basic Books.

Malyon, A. K. (1993). Psychotherapeutic implications of internalized homophobia in gay men. In C. Cornett *Affirmative dynamic psychotherapy with gay men* (pp. 77–92). Northvale, NJ: Jason Aronson.

May, R. (1953). *Man's search for himself.* New York: Norton.

McWhirter, D. P., and Mattison, A. M. (1984). *The male couple: How relationships develop.* Englewood Cliffs, NJ: Prentice Hall.

Menaker, E. (1989). Otto Rank and self psychology. In D. W. Detrick and S. P. Detrick (Eds.), *Self psychology: Comparisons and contrasts* (pp. 75–87). Hillsdale, NJ: Analytic Press.

Ramsdell, P. S., and Ramsdell, E. R. (1993). Dual relationships: Client perceptions of the effect of client-counselor relationship on the therapeutic process. *Clinical Social Work Journal, 21,* 195–212.

Ramsdell, P. S., and Ramsdell, E. R. (1994). Counselor and client perceptions of the effect of social and physical contact on the therapeutic process. *Clinical Social Work Journal, 22,* 91–104.

Schafer, R. (1983). *The analytic attitude.* New York: Basic Books.

Strean, H. S., as told to Freeman, L. (1988). *Behind the couch: Revelations of a psychoanalyst.* New York: Wiley.

Strupp, H. H., and Binder, J. L. (1984). *Psychotherapy in a new key: A guide to time-limited dynamic psychotherapy.* New York: Basic Books.

Sullivan, H. S. (1953a). *Conceptions of modern psychiatry.* New York: Norton.

Sullivan, H. S. (1953b). *The interpersonal theory of psychiatry.* New York: Norton.

Sullivan, H. S. (1954). *The psychiatric interview.* New York: Norton.

Winer, R. (1994). *Close encounters: A relational view of the therapeutic process.* Northvale, NJ: Jason Aronson.

Winnicott, D. W. (1965). *The maturational processes and the facilitating environment.* New York: International Universities Press.

Winnicott, D. W. (1989). *Psycho-analytic explorations.* Ed. C. Winnicott, R. Shepherd, and M. Davis. Cambridge, MA: Harvard University Press.

Will, O. A., Jr. (1970). The therapeutic use of self. *Medical Arts and Sciences, 24,* 3–14.

Will, O. A., Jr. (1981). Values and the psychotherapist. *American Journal of Psychoanalysis, 41,* 203–212.

Wolf, E. (1988). *Treating the self: Elements of clinical self psychology.* New York: Guilford.

23

Clinical Social Work in Psychiatric Rehabilitation

David P. Moxley

What is distinctive about clinical social work with people who are identified as seriously mentally ill? While clinical psychiatry increasingly focuses on the illness and impairment dimensions of serious mental illness, adopting a model of practice more akin to internal medicine than to a once widely endorsed psychosocial approach, and addresses the psychological, cognitive, and emotional aspects of individual functioning, clinical social work confronts the social context of this long-standing and apparently intractable social problem. Although serious mental illness is increasingly characterized as a neurobiological disease (Andreasen, 1984), the distinctive mission of social work, compared to the other clinical disciplines, lies in the profession's focus within this problem area. The profession is concerned with addressing the social consequences of serious mental illness, ones that have been documented as profoundly negative (Gallagher, 1987; Gerhart, 1990).

Such a conception of practice is no different from the role of social work in many other health and medical fields. Increasingly the profession responds to the social needs of people who experience a range of biomedical issues. But it is not these issues per se that set the focus of social work intervention. Rather it is the consequences—social and personal—that give clinical intervention by social workers its purpose and meaning. Indeed, successful intervention into these negative consequences can make an impact on the path and outcome of a disease state (Susser, Hopper, & Richman, 1983). By reducing stress, increasing support, helping people to make lifestyle changes, and organizing resources that support coping, clinical social work may contribute to the realization of positive outcomes in problem areas that are increasingly framed by biomedical models. Achievement of these outcomes can contribute profoundly to the improvement of quality of life among people coping with a particular biomedical problem (Institute of Medicine, 1991).

The profession's commitment to a person-in-environment perspective requires social workers to view mental illness as much more than a disease and much more than impairment induced by biological, genetic, or metabolic processes despite significant institutional forces that legitimize biomedical and illness frameworks. Clinical social work's contribution to the well-being of people identified as seriously mentally ill may lie more in the application of its traditional professional tools within this field of practice than in the adoption of the tools of a psychiatry that reflect a narrow biomedical approach. These tools include the formation of a close working alliance with a person based on a belief that serious mental illness does not preclude growth and development, the championing of needs and goals that hold personal importance and value to the person, the creation and activation of supports that are effective in fostering social functioning, the fulfillment of what Towle (1987) refers to as "common human needs," the activation of ego and environmental strengths, and the fostering of skills to overcome environmental barriers that can frustrate the fulfillment of needs and goals.

Clinical social work with people who are seriously mentally ill is consistent with clinical social work practice in other fields. It requires social workers to look beyond diagnosis and symptoms to achieve a rich and situational understanding of the implications of the problem for how people want to lead their lives. It is in this rich understanding of the person in which the meaning of the term *clinical* is found for social work practice with people who are identified as seriously mentally ill.

A person-in-environment construct influences the conception of problem and intervention in clinical social work. And it is the aim of practice to improve a person's functioning, and perhaps the functioning of a person's intimate system as well, in environments that can be quite demanding. This is not to assert that people with mental illness or the members of their intimate systems cause or are responsible for mental illness. An emphasis on functioning in this context recognizes that serious mental illness can have profound implications for people's capacities to navigate daily life and to execute the tasks of daily living. The focus of clinical social work lies in helping people to execute these tasks successfully with the assistance, if necessary, of relevant social and environmental supports. The experience of serious mental illness can be most challenging, and it is the clinical social worker who can be a reliable, available, and understanding companion on this often unpredictable and arduous journey.

PSYCHIATRIC REHABILITATION AS A DOMAIN OF PRACTICE

The traditional tools of the profession are consistent with the transdisciplinary domain of psychiatric rehabilitation. By domain, I refer to the techniques, symbols, and knowledge that compose a field of practice (Gardner, 1993), in this case, psychiatric rehabilitation. Social work and its clinical variant has contributed considerable practice knowledge to this domain. The domain of psychiatric rehabilitation has been informed historically by the innovative practices of social workers who have operationalized key person-in-environment ideas in working with people identified as seriously mentally ill. On the contemporary scene, social workers have contributed important psychiatric rehabilitation practice knowledge like strengths-based practice (Saleeby, 1992), outcome-driven rehabilitation practice, strategies for social skill development, assertive community treatment, advocacy (Rose & Black, 1985), and a diversity of case management approaches (Rothman, 1992; Rapp & Wintersteen, 1989; Rose, 1992).

Nonetheless psychiatric rehabilitation stands as its own domain operating independent of any one discipline (Bennett, 1983). It has amassed relevant empirical knowledge based on its own research and practice (Flexer & Solomon, 1993; Farkas & Anthony, 1989; IAPSRS, 1994; Anthony & Spaniol, 1994). Its knowledge and practice base is an amalgam of contributions by mental health practitioners, rehabilitation-oriented workers, and people with serious mental illness, and their families, who as consumers or ex-patients have formed self-help and consumer-run alternatives (Chamberlin, 1990). What we now refer to as the domain of psychiatric rehabilitation is a product of a broad social movement, emerging just prior to the onset of deinstitutionalization, which gained momentum during the ensuing decades, to establish itself during the 1970s and 1980s as a viable alternative to community mental health and traditional psychiatric practice (Rutman, 1987).

This movement brings together advocates of very different backgrounds who share a common purpose: to improve the life chances of people with serious mental illness and to advance their quality of life. The mission of this domain of practice is to help people with serious mental illness, and related psychiatric disabilities, to be successful in roles and environments of their own choosing. The domain fosters supports, skills, and desired environmental qualities that help individuals overcome both disability and handicap, and realize developmental outcomes consumers see as personally relevant and valuable.

In other words, psychiatric rehabilitation, like clinical social work in the field of serious mental illness, seeks to confront directly the negative social consequences of the problematic status assigned by our society to people with serious mental illness. By this concept, practice seeks to help people to function better using their own criteria in the appraisal of their success. Functioning, however, is seen as a construct influenced greatly by the environment, social forces, and culture that combine to create situational qualities supportive or nonsupportive of an individual's performance, promote or prevent access to life-sustaining and life-enhancing resources, and encourage or discourage the achievement of personal well-being.

This chapter struggles to conceptualize the interface between clinical social work and psychiatric rehabilitation. I invoke the term *struggle* because much work is required to refine what clinical social work means and does within this distinctive domain. This chapter is not the final word on clinical social work in psychiatric rehabilitation but merely a beginning statement. We can conceive of several variations on what clinical social work does to address the social problem of serious mental illness. Indeed, perhaps three salient domains can be identified:

1. Practice in traditional psychiatric settings in which social workers foster the adjustment of people with serious mental illness to treatment settings or help people make the transition from one setting to another, such as in discharge planning. This form of practice often takes place within inpatient settings as well as within halfway houses and group homes.
2. Practice that takes place in community mental health settings in which crisis intervention, brief hospitalization, short-term therapy, day treatment, or group interventions are orchestrated on a private practice or milieu model of treatment.
3. Practice that is framed by a rehabilitative approach in which the improvement of functioning by supporting people to learn, work, and live in situations of their own choosing serves as the principal aim of clinical social work.

This chapter focuses on the third variant.

THE AIM OF PSYCHIATRIC REHABILITATION

A rehabilitative approach is designed to foster the development of people with serious mental illness so they can gain the skills, supports, and capacities to achieve goals and outcomes of their own choosing. Psychiatric rehabilitation is not tied to any particular setting. As a domain it addresses the need to pursue a specific mission in virtually any life context in which people with serious mental illness may function. It is not surprising to see psychiatric rehabilitation practiced within a variety of environments, including housing, employment, recreational, educational, medical, psychiatric, and community mental health settings (Farkas & Anthony, 1989). And through involvement in rehabilitative supports, it is not surprising to see people with serious mental illness successfully pursue roles as workers, students, home owners, and parents.

The pragmatic orientation of psychiatric rehabilitation seeks to promote the success of people with serious mental illness in the mastery of those requirements created by normative life roles that they find personally important and meaningful. A focus on the achievement of quality of life and a decent standard of living are the kinds of positive differences psychiatric rehabilitation seeks to achieve in the life situations of people with serious mental illness (Moxley, 1994).

Clinical social work in psychiatric rehabilitation therefore is infused by the knowledge of psychiatric rehabilitation and also infuses knowledge produced by the profession into psychiatric rehabilitation. Clinical social work in psychiatric rehabilitation also recognizes the distinctiveness of its contribution as a discipline and values the benefits it derives from close collaboration with other disciplines, professions, and stakeholders within a transdisciplinary domain. Clinical social work in psychiatric rehabilitation builds on its own traditions, knowledge, and practices to increase the efficacy of rehabilitation so that the domain is better able to improve the living circumstances and quality of life of people with serious mental illness while remaining cognizant of the need to address the many negative consequences that can counteract the successful achievement of these outcomes. As advocate, the clinical social worker in psychiatric rehabilitation recognizes that people identified as seriously mentally ill must often learn to function in what can be hostile environments (Burt & Pittman, 1985).

SETTING THE BOUNDARIES OF PSYCHIATRIC REHABILITATION AS A DOMAIN

Policy and Programmatic Background

The concepts of serious mental illness and psychiatric disability are important to delimiting the domain of psychiatric rehabilitation. Both require practitioners interested in psychiatric rehabilitation practice to adopt a broader conception of mental illness than that communicated by medical perspectives. This is not to dismiss the importance of accurate diagnosis or the influence of neurobiological processes, but rather to emphasize that practitioners committed to addressing the social consequences or personal implications of mental illness must recognize the role of social factors in sustaining the problem. Diagnoses like schizophrenia or manic-depressive illness may offer a specific framework guiding the efforts of psychiatric professionals who are seeking to treat the symptomatic and biomedical aspects of these disorders, but diagnosis alone is not sufficient to target the interventions and practice of psychiatric rehabilitation. Total reliance on diagnosis to establish the target population of the domain may obscure the broader aspects of functioning, social reaction, and negative social consequences that practitioners of psychiatric rehabilitation must address.

The concept of serious mental illness is a product of work undertaken during the 1970s. This work contributed to the National Plan for the Chronically Mentally Ill (1980), part of a national effort to target mental health resources on a population that has been traditionally neglected or ignored by community mental health and health care systems. Motivated by criticisms from Congress, informed professionals, and consumer advocates that federally funded community mental health centers ignored the plight of people with serious mental illness who were considered very vulnerable to neglect, abuse, diminished quality of life, and poor independent living outcomes, the National Institute of Mental Health initiated reform efforts. The National Plan sought to define a population most in need of rehabilitative, community, and medical support. The National Plan was to inform the Mental Health Systems Act of 1980, a federal policy initiative to make people with serious mental illness a higher priority for services and for the allocation of funds by providers of public mental health care.

The criticisms leveled at the National Institute of Mental Health originated in the early to mid-1970s when Congress recognized the failure of the federally supported and financed community mental health program to respond to the needs of people with serious mental illness who were leaving public psychiatric facilities. These needs were becoming increasingly visible as deinstitutionalization was proceeding, and people with immediate and pressing support needs were appearing in communities in isolated, degraded, and impoverished living situations (Isaac & Armat, 1990). These criticisms resulted in the creation by the National Institute of Mental Health of a grants and demonstration program, the Community Support Program (Turner & TenHoor, 1978). This program seeks to initiate, develop, and improve local systems of community support designed to assist people with serious mental illness to obtain the resources needed to function on a daily basis. This programmatic model calls for the integration of well-managed services designed to foster the quality of life of people with serious mental illness in community settings (NIMH, 1980; Stroul, 1989, 1993), an ideal often unrealized in actual practice (Johnson, 1990).

Although there is some controversy concerning the effectiveness of the Community Support Program, commitment to this approach remains strong among many state and local mental health systems as they seek to expand and improve coordinated systems of support that include case management, rights protection, housing opportunities, vocational development, health and mental health care, support to families, and crisis and emergency services. The Reagan administration's recision of the Mental Health Act of 1980 and the creation of state block grants under the Alcohol, Drug Abuse, and Mental Health Administration enabled state governments to dedicate more federal and state resources to people with serious mental illness and to reduce the priority placed by community mental health centers on services to traditional clients—people often coping with acute mental health problems (Armour, 1989).

Simultaneously, Anthony (1979) created and disseminated models of psychiatric rehabilitation offering a framework of practice and empirical justification for the efficacy of psychiatric rehabilitation (Anthony et al., 1972). Much of Anthony's work paralleled an emerging practice base fostered by innovative social clubs, peer support programs, services founded and run by ex-patients, and clubhouses. These alternatives, which emerged as early as the 1940s, represent grassroots efforts, often forming and surviving on limited budgets and resources. This practice base continued its expansion into the 1960s, 1970s, and 1980s. Grassroots responses to community support and community building for people with serious mental illness continue to this day as families and consumers establish meaningful alternatives designed to promote community, reduce isolation, fight stigma and misunderstanding, and prevent neglect (Chamberlin, Rogers, & Sneed, 1989).

What is referred to as psychiatric rehabilitation in the 1990s is a product of these policy and programmatic forces that brings together under one umbrella the work of community support programs, social clubs, consumers and family members, and practitioners committed to a rehabilitation framework. Together these elements contribute to a distinctive approach to working with people who are identified as seriously mentally ill. Psychiatric rehabilitation stands as both programmatic innovation and social movement committed to the improvement of the quality of life of a specific and focused population of people—individuals who both historically and in contemporary society have felt the brunt of oppression and diminished status.

Essential Criteria of Serious Mental Illness

Psychiatric rehabilitation focuses on serving and supporting people who are characterized as seriously mentally ill. Serious mental illness is defined by the intersection of several different criteria that together focus attention on individuals who have the most severe and enduring problems created by mental illness (Goldman, Gattozzi, & Taube, 1981; Farkas & Anthony, 1989). What is referred to as serious mental illness is formed by the nexus of diagnosis, duration, and severity criteria that are used to focus resources, effort, and professional attention on individuals characterized as severely disabled (Liberman, 1988).

Relevant diagnoses are limited to the most severe and persistent cognitive, affective, and personality or characterological disorders. Diagnosis itself is a necessary criterion for defining the population of people referred to as seriously mentally ill, but diagnosis alone does not fully set the parameters for inclusion. So-called serious diagnoses preclude the inclusion of diagnoses that have less severe implications for functioning and well-being.

The idea of substantial impairment usually is invoked to identify people whose functioning is well below the norms required to perform adequately in community environments. People who are substantially below average in adaptive behavior in spheres such as personal care, self-sufficiency, employment, communication, and socialization are considered to be disabled. However, substantial subaverage functioning may be transient or time limited.

Like diagnosis, moderate to severe deficits in functioning is a necessary but insufficient criterion for the definition of serious mental illness. The temporal dimension of impairment is another criterion. Duration as a criterion requires the problem of mental illness to be persistent, with a duration of a year or more generally accepted as the length of time needed to characterize the problem as one of long standing. Functioning as a criterion focuses attention on whether a person has the ability to execute essential tasks of daily living. Duration focuses attention on the persistent nature of these functional problems.

When diagnosis, duration, and problems in functioning are brought together as criteria, we can speak of serious mental illness (Liberman, 1988). The term itself is fraught with problems, and clinical social workers may be suspect about its usefulness to practice. Practitioners, however, must remember that the concept of serious mental illness was formulated as a policy and programmatic tool to define a group of individuals whose needs are substantial, whose problems of functioning are moderate to severe, who are often ignored or neglected by human service, mental health, and other professionals, and who require a range of ongoing supports designed to help them lead decent, dignified, and productive lives.

The construct of serious mental illness defines a population that can be considered vulnerable and at risk of poor life outcomes. Targeting this population underscores the unique needs of people with serious mental illness. Targeting this population also underscores the serious and often complex problems of functioning resulting from persistent mental illness (Anthony, Cohen, & Farkas, 1990; Anthony, Cohen, & Vitalo, 1978), as well as the social reaction to serious mental illness experienced by members of this population (Farkas & Anthony, 1989; Anthony, 1994).

The size of the population formed by the nexus of these criteria is not trivial. Goldman and Manderscheid (1987) estimate that between 350,000 and 800,000 people have severe emotional problems and another 700,000 people experience moderate disabilities (Lawn & Meyerson, 1993). Goldman, Gattozzi, and Taube (1981) estimate that between 1.7 and 2.4 million people can be considered seriously mentally ill when diagnosis, duration, and problems in functioning are considered together as defining criteria. Many of these individuals reside in psychiatric facilities, community residential programs, nursing homes, and specialized care facilities (Kaplan & Sadock, 1989), although many return to their families for care and support (Minkoff, 1978).

Clinical portrayals of this population typically invoke the diagnoses of schizophrenia, recurrent affective disorders, and senile dementia or other organic problems. Demographically, people identified as seriously mentally ill are more likely to be female, unmarried, and older than people without disabilities (Goldman & Manderscheid, 1987; Lawn & Meyerson, 1993). Violation of social norms resulting in incarceration in jail for petty crimes (Belcher, 1988; Steadman, McCarty, & Morrissey, 1989; Teplin, 1984), involvement in recreational alcohol and drug use (Ridgely, Goldman, & Talbot, 1986; Lehman & Dixon, 1995), homelessness, and health problems can exacerbate problems among people composing this population.

From a biomedical perspective, the problem of serious mental illness is thought to evolve from multifactorial forces involving genetic predisposition, biological and neurological problems, childhood stress, and environmental stressors (Anthony & Liberman, 1986). Stress may be a salient factor triggering symptoms and problems of functioning, and perhaps serious mental illness can be viewed as a state of heightened sensitivity to environmental stress (Anthony & Liberman, 1986). For clinical social work, social factors that reduce quality of life (including negative social reaction, poor community supports, limited or diminished access to basic resources and opportunities, and the absence of proactive systems of rehabilitation) may be more relevant organizers of practice than the conception of this problem emanating out of an illness model (Moxley & Freddolino, 1994). These factors left unaddressed can put people with serious mental illness in untenable, stress-producing situations, environments conducive to the exacerbation of illness and impairment. Media exposés of people living in squalor, isolation, or abusive situations illustrate in dramatic terms the need to address social and situational factors.

Serious Mental Illness as a Social Problem

Negative clinical portrayals of people with serious mental illness sometimes can read like stereotypes devoid of any personal content. They are to be viewed with caution since problems in functioning can be produced by unsupportive and problematic environments. People with serious mental illness are in jeopardy of degraded lives and abuse and neglect within communities (Freddolino & Moxley, 1988; Scallett, 1986;

U.S. Senate, 1985). They are at risk of rights violation to such an extent that the only meaningful piece of mental health legislation passing Congress, and signed into law during the 1980s (Public Law 99-319) authorized the formation of a protection and advocacy system specifically designed to protect the rights of people with serious mental illness who were in institutions. These abuses were thought to be eradicated by the spirited and legalistic mental health advocacy of the 1960s and 1970s, but they seem to reemerge, illustrating their intractability and the negative social dynamics influencing this social problem.

Research on violence shows that people with serious mental illness are more likely to be victims than perpetrators. And recent innovations in disability rights policy highlight the failure of employment, housing, education, communication, and law enforcement systems to meet the needs of citizens with the most severe disabilities.

The dramatic depopulation of state hospitals during a relatively short period (Foley & Sharfstein, 1983) held the promise of higher quality of life as people escaped the horrors of daily life in state facilities (Grob, 1991, 1994). However, the public soon discovered that people with serious mental illness found only mistreatment and rejection in inhospitable communities (Johnson, 1990). Tragically, people left institutions with poor or nonexistent supports, only to take up lives often characterized by despair, degradation, and abuse. In many communities, institutions were replaced by urban ghettos, poverty, homelessness, and substandard rehabilitation and health care (Bell, 1989). Significant rates of homelessness among people with serious mental illness, estimated at some 30 percent of all homeless people (United States General Accounting Office, 1988; Tessler & Dennis, 1989), pale in seriousness when one considers that the rate of unemployment among members of this population is well over 80 percent (Rapp, 1992) despite substantial evidence to demonstrate the benefits of employment and the strong desire to work among many people with serious mental illness.

There are profound inadequacies in the organization of services designed to help people with serious mental illness lead decent lives in the community (Mechanic, 1987). A pattern of frequent readmission to brief hospital care created a systemic syndrome referred to as the "revolving door," testimony to the inadequate nature or the absolute absence of effective community-based systems of support. During the early 1980s readmissions to psychiatric hospitalization in public facilities grew to almost 70 percent of all admissions (Goldman, Adams, & Taube, 1983). Many community mental health systems fail to respond to the needs of this population despite the original intent of Congress to prioritize the access of people with serious mental illness to community services (Armour, 1989). Traditional mental health services are often inadequate for this population and for addressing in a meaningful way the biopsychosocial aspects of the problem of serious mental illness.

A Focus on Disability and Handicap

Clinical social work is committed to advancing the quality of life of oppressed and vulnerable populations, a cornerstone value of the profession (Gitterman, 1991). The very real environmental threats to the well-being of people with serious mental illness make social factors important and relevant elements of a practice framework guiding social work in the domain of psychiatric rehabilitation. The constructs of diagnosis and symptoms alone may wane in relevance to the profession when clinical social work focuses on the dimensions of disability and handicap rather than the dimension of illness.

Disability directs our attention to aspects of social functioning and to those qualities of functioning that are diminished not only by impairment but, perhaps more important for social work than for other mental health disciplines, by environmental and situational stressors or inadequacies (Institute of Medicine, 1991). Handicap is produced by the social reaction to serious mental illness involving societal misunderstanding and negative stereotypes that individually or collectively can create or exacerbate numerous problems for people (Anthony, 1972). If we take seriously the profession's commitment to addressing the needs of people in their environments, we must recognize that functioning is an ecological rather than an individualistic concept and that the qualities of a situation interacting with the qualities of the person produce functioning (Germain & Gitterman, 1980). The functioning of a person can be influenced dramatically by the interplay among settings and environments—ones that are immediately salient and ones that are not quite visible. But together they form a complex situation influencing the way people function (Bronfenbrenner, 1979).

Functioning as an ecological concept has important implications for the manner in which we view and interpret disability. Contemporary conceptions of disability question whether the impact of disability must be serious or profoundly limiting for individuals. Disability may be reduced or prevented when social supports and personal coping resources are increased and readily accessible. The American Association on Mental Retardation (AAMR), in its recent reformulation of its definition of mental retardation, added a third factor to supplement its two-dimensional model composed of intelligence and adaptive behavior by recognizing the pivotal role of social and personal supports in social functioning. When organized within a context of self-determination, choice, and cultural sensitivity, these supports can reduce the extent of disability and increase functioning in critical realms of everyday life (Moxley, 1994). It may be difficult now to talk about disability in dichotomous terms: as if a person is or is not disabled based on absolute criteria.

Disability may be better thought of as distributed along a continuum, with people having lesser or more amounts of this quality. A person's position on this continuum is substantially influenced by the presence or absence of environmental and personal resources that support functioning. Disability policy in the United States may need to recognize that with adequate and appropriate supports, assistive technologies, and opportunities, people who were once identified as disabled can become active participants in mainstream activities (Moxley, 1992).

The buffering role of social and personal support has long been recognized within the domain of psychiatric rehabilitation as an essential factor in preventing or reducing the impact of disability resulting from mental illness. Effective role functioning, according to psychiatric rehabilitation practice, is seen as emanating from a matrix of supports, services, and opportunities that are informed and infused by people's preferences, values, and life aims. By establishing and articulating this personalized matrix of support for each individual, psychiatric rehabilitation frames disability in a situational manner, one that does not have to be an ongoing, lifelong reality.

Thus, the very terms *persistent* and *chronic,* which are at the heart of the contemporary definition of serious mental illness, may be anachronisms. Researchers are questioning whether our entire conception of serious mental illness must be reframed. Psychiatric rehabilitation hypothesizes (and many practitioners of psychiatric rehabilitation may assume) that the organization of this personalized matrix of support can make recovery from serious mental illness possible and can be used to promote effective functioning (Moxley, 1994). As Anthony (1994) suggests, by replacing chronicity with recovery as an overarching concept, we may have a new, positive vision guiding our work.

As a concept of psychiatric rehabilitation, recovery does not mean a return to a premorbid state. According to Anthony (1994), recovery is best viewed as a "deeply personal, unique process of changing one's attitudes, values, feelings, goals, skills, and/or roles" (p. 559). Recovery is grounded in the direct experiences and perspectives of people with serious mental illness. It involves the adoption of new ways of living, as well as the personal creation of meaning and purpose in one's life, aims directly relevant to what clinical social work does best.

THE PURPOSE OF CLINICAL SOCIAL WORK IN PSYCHIATRIC REHABILITATION

Clinical social work in psychiatric rehabilitation can adopt a recovery frame of reference and offer assistance to people with serious mental illness to create their own stories of recovery—ones infused by what is important to them and ones directed by their own life goals. Perhaps these achievements inform the purpose of clinical social work in psychiatric rehabilitation. But clinical social workers cannot necessarily do this work alone or undertake it in a traditional fashion through office-based psychotherapeutic practice. The domain of psychiatric rehabilitation is action oriented, experiential, interactional, milieu and community based, and collaborative, which means that environmental intervention, self-help and mutual support approaches, and skill development opportunities all figure in as relevant aspects of practice in psychiatric rehabilitation. These activities and interventions are often undertaken in the actual environments in which people need to perform and are designed to help people master environmental demands and stressors using the strengths of the person, a situation, and a community (Rapp, 1992).

Clinical social work in psychiatric rehabilitation unfolds in real-life settings, often in the community, such as in people's homes, on street corners, and in employment settings. Pragmatic outcomes are pursued: the attainment of employment (Simmons, Selleck, Steele, & Sepetauc, 1993), enrollment in higher education (Moxley, Mowbray, & Brown, 1993), the enhancement of vocational development (Black, 1988), and the creation of a home (Carling, 1993). All of these outcomes illustrate how discrete achievements can add up to a better life for people with serious mental illness. These outcomes also can become the substance of the practice objectives of clinical social work in the domain of psychiatric rehabilitation.

There are very real threats found in stigma, discrimination, and neglect that can frustrate the realization of these outcomes and the fulfillment of the common human needs they reflect. They require clinical social work in psychiatric rehabilitation to be vigilant in its efforts to combat handicap as part of interpersonal practice (Farkas, Anthony, & Cohen, 1989). The existence of handicap underscores for social work that the problem of serious mental illness is much more than medical in nature. It encompasses issues pertaining to functioning in an ecological context, a context in which social justice, equity, and quality of life must be recognized as important features of practice. This social justice perspective is very compatible and consistent with the espoused values of the social work profession.

What, then, is the purpose of clinical social work in the domain of psychiatric rehabilitation? Clinical social work makes use of its own strengths and capacities in this domain. The traditional tools of social work can make clinical social workers effective collaborators with other stakeholders in the achievement of the mission of psychiatric rehabilitation. The focus of the profession on people in context, and on helping people to craft their own lifestyles, is very relevant to psychiatric rehabilitation, especially when one adopts a recovery framework. The purpose of clinical social work in psychiatric rehabilitation can be framed as the offer of assistance to people identified as seriously mentally ill, the purpose of which is to help them achieve outcomes they see as personally meaningful and valued. This is realized through the organization and implementation of supports and opportunities that help them to achieve success in their daily lives.

The clinical social worker practices as a purposeful agent to support changes in the person and in the person's life space that help to achieve valued outcomes while cognizant of the need to respond to the social and situational forces that stand as barriers preventing the realization of success by the person (Wintersteen, 1986). This purpose—and the commitment to people with serious mental illness it represents—builds on the domain's efforts to promote the growth and development of people in spite of the severity of symptoms or illness. It is a purpose that certainly is compatible with the best traditions of social work as a profession and psychiatric rehabilitation as a domain. And it is a purpose that makes clinical social work relevant to the realization of recovery. The synergy created by the melding of clinical social work and psychiatric rehabilitation offers hope in a social problem area that too often engenders only pessimism among many mental health practitioners.

ADVANCED ORGANIZERS OF CLINICAL SOCIAL WORK IN PSYCHIATRIC REHABILITATION

Clinical social work in psychiatric rehabilitation is informed by advanced organizers that are derived from both the profession of social work and the domain of rehabilitation. By advanced organizers, I mean those ideas and concepts offering clinical social work inspiration, direction , and understanding in its quest to fulfill its purpose within psychiatric rehabilitation. Advanced organizers offer a framework for understanding and implementing action within a field (Stufflebeam & Shinkfield, 1985). In its quest for a coherent approach to practice, clinical social work in psychiatric rehabilitation must make explicit those basic ideas and concepts that give it substance and relevance in this domain. It must also make explicit those ideas and concepts from psychiatric rehabilitation that inform the purpose and practice of clinical social work in this domain.

Advanced Organizers from Clinical Social Work

Person-in-Situation and Social Functioning

One of the foundational ideas derived from social work is the person-in-situation or the person-in-environment. Incorporation of this idea into practice requires clinical social work in psychiatric rehabilitation to move beyond relating behavioral and functional qualities totally to assumed biomedical or intrapersonal causes. Person-in-situation thinking incorporated into clinical social work practice suggests that behavioral forms and their functional expressions are very complex and stand as products of not only people interacting with their environments but also as products of how people perceive their environments. To understand behavior is to understand how people perceive and interact with their environments, a basic aspect of social work practice (Bartlett, 1970) and clinical practice in social work (Strean, 1978; Waldfogel & Rosenblatt, 1983).

Social functioning is another advanced organizer derived from the profession, and it is linked to the person-in-situation construct. People function within situations. It is the qualities of these situations, and the efforts of people to deal with them in an active manner, that influence behavior dramatically. Thus, to understand the behavior of people with serious mental illness and to take effective rehabilitation action requires clinical social workers to understand fully the situational presses, situational supports, and situational demands acting on people, as well as people's efforts to respond to the demands of a situation in a manner they see appropriate or effective.

Clinical social workers must keep at the forefront of their practice in psychiatric rehabilitation the need to understand how people perceive their situations and the implications of these perceptions for how they act. There is always the threat that practitioners may discount people's perceptions since they may assume that serious mental illness and the cognitive, affective, or behavioral challenges it can create render people incapable of serving as good reporters of their desires, wishes, and perceptions. Framing practice using concepts of the person-in-situation, and social functioning, means that clinical social workers in psychiatric rehabilitation are very interested in how people with serious mental illness view their situations and wish to take action in these situations.

Ego Psychology and Strengths-Oriented Practice

Ego psychology stands as another advanced organizer of clinical social work in psychiatric rehabilitation. Ego psychology has informed clinical social work for some time. The ego is the apparatus of adaptation that promotes active coping with one's environment and can promote resilience through self-observation, self-regulation, and self-control (Hartmann, 1939). Ego psychology offers a positive framework guiding clinical practice in social work (Goldstein, 1984).

Vaillant (1993) in his recent work on ego psychology makes the observation that serious mental illness may reduce people's capacities to use defense mechanisms effectively as a strategy for coping with interpersonal interactions, stress-producing situations, and the environmental press of everyday life. At its best, clinical social work in psychiatric rehabilitation helps people learn how to use their the ego as a protective agent and internal ego strategies for acting within an environment in a resilient and adaptive manner. Indeed understanding how people cope is a fundamental aim of ego psychology. Vaillant's own research illustrates the profound implications of the maturation of the ego for positive human development. He shows that people who in early life demonstrate so-called maladaptive behavior can develop into very competent adults and execute their life work and responsibilities in effective ways in spite of their limitations. Despite problems in functioning, many people can and do learn how to cope and function effectively, a tribute to the positive influence of the ego on functioning.

Vaillant's research underscores the importance of taking the possibility of recovery in the field of psychiatric rehabilitation seriously since ego psychology reminds us that people can overcome their limitations—or even use earlier limitations as an advantage in the present. An illness is not necessarily the person's destiny, a hypothesis that is receiving much attention as stories of remarkable recoveries from serious illnesses are increasingly documented.

Ego psychology as an advanced organizer links to strengths-oriented practice, an emergent model guiding social work. Diagnostic systems easily reinforce deficit perspectives of how people function, making it routine practice to inventory the problems people confront in their daily lives and the inadequacies they demonstrate. A strengths approach counters this negative framework and offers a positive frame of reference for understanding the personal, community, and systemic strengths that can be operating in any situation.

As an advanced organizer, a strengths perspective complements the profession's person-in-situation and social functioning frameworks. Together these frameworks can influence how assessment is conducted, rehabilitation planning is undertaken, and intervention is offered and implemented. A strengths orientation requires clinical social workers in psychiatric rehabilitation to ask positive questions about how people cope, meet challenges, and triumph in their daily lives. A strengths orientation can also remind practitioners that a diagnostic perspective has its own limitations and may not offer situationally specific information about how to work with people in innovative and creative ways. A focus on strengths may contribute to the formation of psychosocial interventions that are more robust than ones suggested by diagnosis, assessment of impairment, and the identification of deficits.

Effectance Motivation

Motivational schema tied to ego psychology and to a strengths perspective suggest that people are motivated by what White and others refer to as ego energies: people are motivated to manipulate their environments and by novelty and mastery (White, 1963). The concept of effectance motivation is relevant to clinical social work in psychiatric rehabilitation. According to this concept, people seek to explore and investigate their environment to learn about its challenges and to learn how to master these challenges. Positive support and the reward of these efforts, no matter how small, increases the motivation of people to explore their environments. But these drives can be dampened through punishment, discouragement, neglect, and discrimination—situational contingencies that people with serious mental illness often confront in their personal lives.

Indeed, clinical social workers practicing with people with serious mental illness may witness behaviors that are more a product of the frustration their clients have experienced in their efforts to influence their situations and of the adaptations they have made to what are often negative situations than a product of illness or impairment (Taylor, 1979). The idea of effectance motivation suggests the use of positive developmental drives and the importance of assisting people in learning how to effect the changes they desire in the situations that form the substance of their daily lives (Wine, 1981). This practice guideline derived from the concept of effectance motivation links to the profession's own cardinal value of self-determination.

Milieu

A final idea serving as a relevant advanced organizer is that of milieu, roughly translated to mean environment or surroundings. Most clinical social workers are familiar with this concept through its application to the intentional creation of treatment settings in hospitals, residential settings, day programs, and therapeutic communities. I invoke the idea of milieu as a reminder that clinical social work does not merely take place beyond closed doors when practitioners meet with individual clients or with small groups of clients. Often clinical social work occurs in settings in which relatively large groups of individuals come together in sustained interactions to accomplish a specific purpose. The clinical social worker is a member of this setting. The behaviors of the worker can be very influential in shaping the atmosphere and culture of this setting. A milieu setting is rich in interaction, and so-called treatment actually occurs in the here and now through purposeful interactions in small and large group events and activities.

The idea of milieu is very much a characteristic of clinical social work in psychiatric rehabilitation. Clinical social workers practicing in this domain will likely find themselves in clubhouse settings, vocational development programs, and psychiatric rehabilitation centers. These settings and programs rely on the structuring of activities and the creation of settings that foster a desired kind of culture—one typically characterized by informality, an explicit task structure, nonhierarchical interactions among participants, and self-disclosure by participants. Clinical social workers in these milieus may be on duty all day long and involved in sustained and intensive interactions with members of these settings. The traditional fifty-minute hour will not likely exist. Rehabilitative interactions may unfold in the context of group tasks. And the traditional use of space in which clinical social workers practice in the confines of offices may give way to collective space the boundaries of which are ambiguous or lack a permanent function (Moxley & Taranto, 1994).

These six advanced organizers form a positive framework for guiding practice. The practice emerging from the use of these advanced organizers suggests that clinical social work in psychiatric rehabilitation is situationally oriented with the aim of fostering the social functioning of people with serious mental illness. Despite the targeting of a specific population through the use of diagnostic and impairment criteria, clinical social work uses these as mere starting points of a practice that can unfold in a positive and hopeful manner. The basic tenets of ego psychology and a strengths perspective contribute to this positive frame of reference and to the hope psychiatric rehabilitation can engender.

The idea of effectance motivation focuses the attention of clinical social workers on helping people to improve their functioning through engagement with their environments and through the pursuit of mastery and effective coping (Maluccio, 1981; Wine, 1981). And the idea of milieu underscores a challenge to clinical social workers: to develop an approach to practice in which they become active participants in the process of recovery in partnership with people who are doing the work of rehabilitation in real-life settings. This experiential quality is infused into practice and becomes a distinguishing quality of clinical social work in psychiatric rehabilitation. It is this quality that differentiates clinical social work in psychiatric rehabilitation from clinical social work that uses psychotherapy as a principal means of effecting change.

Clinical social work practice informed and framed by these advanced organizers is not a panacea for rectifying the illness dimension of serious mental illness. But although the psychosocial strategies implied by these advanced organizers cannot cure mental illness, they can contribute to the achievement of a positive impact on the functional expression of the illness and the life circumstances of people, outcomes consistent with the purpose of clinical social work in psychiatric rehabilitation (Wintersteen, 1986). Realization of these outcomes can make a relevant contribution to a person's pursuit of recovery (Moxley, 1994).

Advanced Organizers from Psychiatric Rehabilitation

The Criterion of Ultimate Functioning and the Specificity of Environmental Support

The action and experiential orientations of psychiatric rehabilitation are based on two important ideas that contribute to the practice of teaching people to execute role functions and behaviors in the actual environment in which they are to be performed. The criterion of ultimate functioning requires the practitioner of psychiatric rehabilitation to gain a full understanding of the behavioral setting in which a person will function and to understand the demands and requirements of effective role functioning created by this setting.

This advanced organizer directs the attention of the clinical social worker to the assessment of actual performance situations so that the conditions can be created that support successful functioning of people in these situations. According to this criterion, it is very problematic, for example, to teach a person how to cook or how to maintain a household in a simulated situation based in a day treatment facility and then expect the person to generalize this knowledge and skill to a real-life situation. According to psychiatric rehabilitation practice, it is more productive to help people secure housing and then to support their role performance within their actual housing situation. People who receive active support in learning how to use, clean, and maintain their actual home will more likely become better at maintaining their homes. The practitioner of psychiatric rehabilitation knows full well that people may require support over time in mastering these role demands and understands that when people move to new households, they may need to master role requirements created by novel living environments.

The criterion of ultimate functioning guides rehabilitative practice in any environment in which a person must function. This means that clinical social workers in psychiatric rehabilitation may find themselves working in homes, work settings, educational environments, and various community environments (such as grocery stores) as coaches, teachers, trainers, and mentors. Reports from the literature illustrate how clinical social workers may combine concrete helping with more psychotherapeutic and counseling activities in actual community settings, a form of practice that is referred to as clinical case management (Harris & Bachrach, 1988).

The idea of environmental specificity is consistent with the criterion of ultimate functioning. Environmental specificity requires the practitioner of psychiatric rehabilitation to tailor or otherwise customize a specific support to assist a person in executing an actual role or role function. Environmental specificity may be the psychosocial equivalent of a physical prosthesis, like a prosthetic limb used to restore the function of a lost arm. A person with a serious affective disorder, whose functioning is reduced but nonetheless seeks to be a successful college student, may be assisted by a coach who helps the person rise in the morning, complete hygiene tasks, get dressed, and arrive at class on time. The coach may work with the student to organize course work and complete assignments. And the coach may substitute for the student in class when the student is unable to attend because of a depressive episode. The coach in this example of supported education can be considered an environmentally tailored intervention who functions much as a physical prosthesis does. The coach extends the person's functioning and helps the person to master role requirements created by the person's desire to function as a student pursuing higher education (Moxley, Mowbray, & Brown, 1993). This support operates like an auxiliary ego in which the worker extends the functioning of the client through the extension of his or her own capacities for judgment, appraisal, reasoning, and problem solving to the person receiving support (Goldstein, 1984).

Some social workers may dismiss this coaching merely as enabling, arguing that it only encourages dependency. But practitioners of psychiatric rehabilitation view such personalized and customized support as good practice and as an appropriate response to the disabling and handicapping factors influencing serious mental illness. The resulting dependency of a person on a coach is more likely a natural outcome of two people working closely together to achieve a mutual goal than it is an outcome of enabling. We have many normative examples in which people can become productively dependent on others in anticipation of movement toward more autonomy. Dependency will likely diminish over time as people gain confidence and experience positive outcomes achieved through coping and effective functioning. In other words, environmental specificity links logically to the promotion of effectance motivation and the aim of situational mastery of role demands.

Clinical social workers may or may not operate as the auxiliary ego. Yet it is very likely that the worker uses assessment, intervention planning, and support activities, all of which are designed to put into place a relevant and robust support system. The purpose of this support system is to help people with serious mental illness to master the requirements of daily living, to execute successfully the requirements of roles they choose to fulfill, and to learn and develop from trying new ways of behaving, even with risk of failure. In this form of practice, clinical social workers may find themselves functioning as members of assertive community treatment teams, clinical case managers, staff members of clubhouses, or program supervisors who are responsible for overseeing the organization and arrangement of specific environmental supports.

Consumerism

Consumer involvement is a cardinal idea framing psychiatric rehabilitation practice. It is also an idea consistent with clinical social work and its practice. As emphasized by Strean (1978), "the human potential is always taken as a given by the social worker, and therefore he accepts the client as an interacting partner in a professional relationship that will psychosocially enhance him" (p. 32). Consumers and ex-patients have offered considerable leadership to the field of psychiatric rehabilitation in the formulation of innovative programmatic and community support alternatives designed to help people with serious mental illness to participate in communities of their own choosing and to fulfill both life-sustaining and life-enhancing needs.

As an advanced organizer, consumerism in psychiatric rehabilitation means several different things. It refers to an ideal role relationship between professionals and the people they serve in which the needs, desires, and aims of consumers drive service delivery. Data on expressed needs among consumers typically downplay mental health and psychiatric problems and prioritize critical independent living requirements found in access to housing, income, involvement in employment, participation in training and education, and access to health care (Freddolino, Moxley, & Fleishman, 1988). Consumerism in psychiatric rehabilitation means that professionals listen carefully and sensitively to those needs identified by consumers as important, assist consumers to plan to fulfill them, and help consumers to take action in the social environment to fulfill these needs (Moxley & Freddolino, 1990).

Consumerism also refers to the inclusion of peer support and mutual help into psychiatric rehabilitation as legitimate means of assisting people to function better in community settings. There is considerable variation in the range of peer supports and mutual help alternatives within the field of psychiatric rehabilitation. Self-help systems like Schizophrenics Anonymous and the Manic Depressive Association help people cope with specific illnesses and their medical, behavioral, and social implications. An alternative like Recovery, Inc. is designed to help people to manage the symptoms of their illness through participation in a structured mutual support alternative that embraces a certain ideological perspective, one that endorses a medical model.

People with serious mental illness may come together because they want to address issues pertaining to stigma, social rejection, and discrimination (Chamberlin, 1978, 1990). Many of these individuals see themselves as ex-patients who have been abused or disenfranchised by mental health providers and mental health systems. Ex-patients have been instrumental in the formation of alternative treatment programs, medication-free treatment, crisis intervention services, drop-in centers, peer support alternatives, and programs that support cultural enrichment, community involvement, and employment. In addition, people with serious mental illness, regardless of whether they see themselves as consumers or ex-patients, have sought roles as advocates and have elevated the fulfillment of housing, employment, and income needs as responsibilities of contemporary mental health systems.

Last, consumerism means that personal experience with serious mental illness, and with treatment and rehabilitation systems as a client, is a bona-fide credential that equips people to serve in rehabilitative roles with other people with serious mental illness. Consumer employment is increasingly seen by psychiatric rehabilitation systems ostensibly as a means of fostering more sensitive services and of making services and supports more accessible. Consumers as rehabilitation employees are often willing to undertake tasks and activities that may not fall within the strict and sometimes inflexible role definitions of credentialed professionals and yet are crucial to the well-being of people with serious mental illness (Mowbray et al., 1996). Thus, consumers may be hired to serve in case management, housing support, and job coaching positions, as well as in outreach and crisis intervention roles.

Outcome Orientation

The identification, monitoring, and evaluation of outcomes are important procedures that strengthen the accountability of psychiatric rehabilitation practice. There is some question, however, as to who actually frames the substance and threshold of these outcomes. Ideally, the consumer-driven beliefs of psychiatric rehabilitation demand that outcomes are framed by the desires, wishes, and needs of consumers (Cohen & Anthony, 1988), while in actual practice there is most likely a tension between what a system or organization seeks to produce as outcomes for its funders and what consumers want. As identified by Moxley and Daeschlein (1997), consumer-driven outcomes share some of the following qualities: they

1. are articulated using the voice of consumers and the needs and concerns they identify, describe, and prioritize.
2. are truly linked to what consumers want to achieve, not to what a human service system says it is willing or able to achieve.
3. are relevant to the daily life of consumers and communicate the impact or changes consumers want to achieve in their daily lives.
4. are truly ends statements that communicate a change independent of service provision and service delivery.
5. will bring satisfaction to the consumer when they are accomplished, especially

when evaluated by the extent to which the accomplishment of outcomes improves the quality of life, standard of living, or life satisfaction of the person.

Increasingly clinical social workers in psychiatric rehabilitation will be required to practice in an accountable fashion with explicit outcomes that are relevant to the creation of change. However, whether this change is defined in consumer or system terms resides in the kind of culture of rehabilitation in which clinical social workers execute their roles. System-driven cultures will focus on the benefits accruing to mental health programs or to their funders, while consumer-driven cultures will focus on the benefits accruing to the direct users of rehabilitation alternatives (Moxley, 1997). With the movement to managed rehabilitation and mental health care, the distinction between client and consumer may become more pronounced, with the term *client* reserved for the funder of service and the term *consumer* reserved for the direct user. This distinction may have critical implications for how outcomes are formulated and used in psychiatric rehabilitation.

Team-Based Collaboration

It is unlikely that clinical social workers in psychiatric rehabilitation will practice in isolated situations or in solo practice. Indeed, previous advanced organizers illustrate the intensive character of psychiatric rehabilitation and the likelihood that clinical social work in this domain will unfold in milieu and community situations, the boundaries of which are difficult to control or even to establish. The highly dynamic nature of psychiatric rehabilitation is also influenced by new stakeholders, who will work with clinical social workers as colleagues and collaborators. Interactions between clinical social workers and these new colleagues may be quite novel, as when:

1. A clinical social worker collaborates with members of an organized family group interested in the implementation of an evening outreach program for people who can become quite isolated.
2. A clinical social worker in psychiatric rehabilitation collaborates with consumers who are fulfilling professional rehabilitation roles yet are also receiving clinical or rehabilitation services from the same agency that is employing them.
3. A clinical social worker collaborates with professionals who do not possess typical mental health credentials but nonetheless possess crucial skills and knowledge that are quite relevant to the provision of rehabilitation—for example, people with business and entrepreneurial backgrounds, computer specialists, teachers, performing artists, or visual artists.

The variations in these interactions and in the people who fulfill rehabilitation roles reflect the transdisciplinary character of the domain. It is likely that this character will be expressed through team configurations in which professionals, consumers, and family members work together to put rehabilitation principles and practices into action on behalf of groups of people or on behalf of individuals. Professional education prepares clinical social workers well for team-based interactions and as effective members and leaders within team configurations. Yet the evolution of roles within this domain may create ambiguity and some confusion for clinical social workers who hold tight to rigid role definitions, degree-oriented credentialing, and hierarchical status. These role innovations and their organization into teams may also require clinical social work to examine issues raised by confidentiality, privacy, and ethical practice.

As clubhouses, community treatment teams, outreach teams, community-oriented case management, and other team-oriented service delivery approaches are disseminated as psychiatric rehabilitation alternatives, clinical social workers may find themselves in innovative organizational structures requiring new forms of collaboration. Thus, effective teamwork and the collaboration it demands is a pivotal advanced organizer for framing clinical social work in the domain of psychiatric rehabilitation.

THE RICHNESS OF CLINICAL SOCIAL WORK IN PSYCHIATRIC REHABILITATION

The boundaries, purpose, and advanced organizers of clinical social work in psychiatric rehabilitation reflect the rich, vital, and satisfying character of practice within this domain. Innovations in the domain itself have modified the roles and functions of traditional mental health practitioners, including clinical social workers. Although the term *clinical* still has relevance in this domain, it does not refer to the treatment of people who are ill or to the remediation of deficits. Alternatively the term *clinical* refers to the achievement of an ecologically and situationally rich understanding of people with serious mental illness and how individuals who bear the burden and demands of this label fare in circumstances that can challenge even the most adaptable among us. "Clinical" suggests a new way of taking action: of having the competencies as professionals to tailor and customize support systems for people that help them to develop and to achieve outcomes that exceed what the stereotypic labels of diagnosis and illness may condition practitioners to expect.

Clinical social work in psychiatric rehabilitation may be more about venerating people who find themselves in very tough circumstances. Rather than identifying deficits, clinical social work in psychiatric rehabilitation may be more about identifying supports that help people to succeed in everyday life regardless of an illness that can have profound medical, psychological, and social consequences. The advanced organizers speak to the richness of clinical social work in psychiatric rehabilitation: a form of social work practice that continues inventing and reinventing itself by building on its own traditions, and by adopting new and viable rehabilitation practices, as the domain of psychiatric rehabilitation evolves over time.

THE PROCESS OF CLINICAL SOCIAL WORK IN PSYCHIATRIC REHABILITATION

Basic Attributes of Clinical Social Work in Psychiatric Rehabilitation

The basic attributes of a rehabilitation model stand out when we examine the process of clinical social work in psychiatric rehabilitation. The model itself is informed by a cardinal practice principle of clinical social work: that working with people involves the conscious and purposeful use of the self in interaction with another person who has been labeled as mentally ill. This cardinal principle influences three basic attributes of clinical social work in psychiatric rehabilitation: the importance of self-determination to rehabilitation practice, the achievement of a humanistic understanding of the person with serious mental illness, and the experiential character of rehabilitation practice.

The rehabilitative model possesses a positive practice ethos shaped by the endorsement of self-determination by client and worker. This value is reflected in every step of the rehabilitation process as the clinical social worker focuses on the personal strengths of people with serious mental illness and the situational strengths of the environment in which the person functions. Self-determination is expressed by the infusion of hope: that people do not have to look forward to a future dominated by illness but can formulate a personal vision or story of their own development and their own growth as unique people (Coles, 1989).

More important, practice in psychiatric rehabilitation requires clinical social workers to look beyond the diagnosis and the symptoms, reaching a more informed and deeper understanding of the person. And practice in psychiatric rehabilitation requires clinical social workers to resist prejudging people based on diagnoses and symptoms. The knowledge base of psychiatric rehabilitation is founded on empirical observations that diagnoses and symptoms offer very little explanatory power in predicting whether people can achieve success in independent living, employment, or education (Anthony, 1979; Anthony, Howell, & Danley, 1984; Anthony & Jansen, 1984). The operationalization of self-determination in psychiatric rehabilitation complements a humanistic appreciation of the person, realized in part through sensitive listening and understanding. Psychiatric history is not destiny, and illness is not destiny. Listening to people with serious mental illness means listening closely to what they want for themselves. Self-determination linked to humanistic practice can result in the formulation of a mutual appreciation between worker and client of a future that can be greatly influenced by present decisions, present actions, and effective social supports.

So another value of the rehabilitation model stands out in this process. Clinical social work in psychiatric rehabilitation is oriented to the here and now and uses experiential activities to achieve relevant objectives and goals and to address the barriers operating in situations that can stall or prevent the realization of consumer-defined outcomes. The experiential quality of clinical social work in psychiatric rehabilitation requires client and worker to invest considerable energy in assessing situations, planning action, taking action, and evaluating the consequences of action using the preferences, values, and personal criteria of the person as the standards of success. This assessing-planning-acting-evaluating sequence also is strategic in character. Client and worker look closely at the environment to identify opportunities that will help the person achieve a desired outcome, identify the best set of actions for taking advantage of these opportunities, identify the best set of actions to offset forces that can diminish or prevent success, and identify how to use supports to assist in the achievement of a desired outcome.

Four Basic Processes of Clinical Social Work in Psychiatric Rehabilitation

Clinical social work in psychiatric rehabilitation unfolds in four basic phases, similar to a problem-solving format that underlies professional social work practice. These four processes reflect some of the realities of serious mental illness. It is not a transient issue facing people but one that can continue even though the illness may not follow a standard trajectory for everyone. Second, the social consequences of what is referred to as serious mental illness can create isolating and degrading circumstances that can interfere with the personal realization of community and acceptable support systems. Third, these same consequences, and the medical stereotypes attributable to serious mental illness, can mean that people coping with the many dimensions of this problem are prevented from articulating what they want for themselves, having these ends taken seriously, and receiving support that enables them to reach these outcomes. Thus, the four processes identified here are considered fundamental to the realization of what is referred to in psychiatric rehabilitation as consumer-driven practice.

Achieving an Understanding of the Person as an Empowered Actor

This phase requires the clinical social worker to formulate a unique and distinctive understanding of the person labeled as seriously mentally ill. I underscore the idea of labeling because it is likely that clinical social workers will practice with people who already have received this label, and the label itself may come to define the person. Expectations, stereotypes, and clinical interactions may be driven by this labeling, and it is very easy for programmatic responses to be framed almost exclusively by diagnostic perspectives.

> *George Williams, a thirty-three-year-old man diagnosed with schizophrenia when he was beginning the second year of a premed program at a major university, is preoccupied by the meaning of his diagnosis to him personally. Prior to the onset of his situation, he saw himself as a committed student who was expecting to excel in medical school and to begin a career as a pediatrician. Over the past thirteen years, since the onset of this issue, Mr. Williams has been told by many professionals to lower his sights, lower his expectations, and take on the role as a sick person who will be ill for his entire life. Only recently has he begun to question these expectations and attitudes. Despite some very serious cognitive problems, Mr. Williams wants to return to the university to pursue what he now calls his "unfinished business." Few, if any, treatment professionals will endorse this chosen path, and several have communicated to him that he should only expect elevated stress that he cannot handle.*

But people are more than labels. The achievement of an understanding of the person as an empowered actor is not driven by a diagnostic perspective. Alternatively, the clinical social worker incorporates three principal approaches to assessment that helps the worker to understand the person in context. First, the assessment of strengths and assets enables clinical social workers to gain an appreciation for the personal resources, coping strategies, and environmental and situational assets the person uses in the present and has developed historically (Brown &

Hughson, 1987). These strengths can easily be ignored or even framed as problematic or "pitiful" attempts at trying to cope. A deficit orientation to assessment can result in the impression that the person lacks any assets.

Second, the assessment of strengths and assets can inform the worker about a person's functioning in situations and the situational factors that influence outcome. Functional assessment that focuses on situations turns the social worker's attention away from a preoccupation with the person as an isolated actor and away from a preoccupation with personal characteristics to the consideration of situational factors, elements, and characteristics that can influence the person's attempts at using strengths, assets, and coping strategies. Functional assessment informed by situational analysis can offer clinical social workers in psychiatric rehabilitation some powerful tools for the creation of supportive interventions to help people identified as seriously mentally ill to achieve what they personally value.

Third, the social worker uses sensitive listening to hear the stories and dreams of the person. These can be easily discounted as delusional or as symptomatic of the medical aspects of serious mental illness, but statements like "I want to move into a castle and live like a knight" or "I want to save the world like a Messiah" can cloak deeply felt personal dreams concerning what a person wants to achieve in the realization of a home or residence, or in a job or career.

A clinical social worker experienced in psychiatric rehabilitation met Mr. Williams at the adult foster care facility where he has lived for five years. Mr. Williams engaged the worker in an animated and energetic discussion about higher education. Rather than terminating this discussion, the worker encouraged Mr. Williams to set up a meeting with him at a local clubhouse. At this meeting, the worker encouraged Mr. Williams to share his story about the many frustrations he experienced in trying to get some support to continue his education. This story of despair soon turned into a story of hope. Mr. Williams was able, with the support of the worker, to sketch an exciting vision of his reengagement with the sciences he loved and of returning to campus as a student. Worker and client collaborated in identifying Mr. Williams's strengths involving his motivation, his love of learning, his continuous reading, his successful completion of high school, and his ability to listen and attend when he did not feel under a great deal of stress. Situational assessment revealed that Mr. Williams's motivation was dampened by the low expectations operating within the adult foster care arrangement, his medication level that was not conducive to participation in education, and the absence of support for his dream. Based on this assessment, client and worker established the goal of investigating university programs and of planning new housing, health care, and rehabilitation supports that would promote his success in enrolling as a student in a local university.

Understanding the person as an empowered actor requires the clinical social worker to relinquish a focus on the diagnosis and to embrace a focus on the person. The clinical social worker trying to achieve this sensitive understanding must approach the process of understanding as somewhat of a blank slate, achieving an understanding of strengths, gaining an appreciation of a person's functioning in the context of situations, and listening very closely to what people want to achieve in their lives in spite of the many challenges serious mental illness can create for them. The empowerment process was initiated with Mr. Williams by the worker's accepting what the person was saying as true and as important: he wanted to become a student.

The openness and sincerity of the worker to the achievement of this understanding is a powerful tool in the building and strengthening of the alliance between worker and client. At first, this alliance may be somewhat threatening to both worker and client. Initially they may be somewhat suspicious of each other as they struggle with their stereotypes of one another, but as these stereotypes begin to crumble, they can begin to recognize each other as partners who have formed their own situation that can be compromised by many disabling and handicapping factors. As this process unfolds, the worker is less likely to hide behind formalized interactions, rituals, and procedures and the client is less likely to discount the worker as merely the representative of the system.

An alliance built on strengths can underscore to both the worker and client that the partnership they seek is a proactive one—one that will enable them to accomplish specific goals and to realize specific outcomes. An alliance built on the understanding of situations and the demands created by situations offer a pragmatism to the partnership: worker and client must target specific aspects of situations and the person's coping with these specific aspects and achieve a resolution to the barriers they identify in order to maintain proactivity. And an alliance built on an understanding of the person's worldview infuses clinical social work in psychiatric rehabilitation with a truly personalized character. Thus the first phase of clinical social work in psychiatric rehabilitation puts in place powerful foundations of helping, ones that can support subsequent work because they help worker and client to establish an effective alliance. Proactivity, pragmatism, and personalization are these critical foundations and need to be at the forefront of the worker's mind as basic strategies of effective practice in psychiatric rehabilitation.

Formulating Aims and Outcomes Using the Preferences of the Person

This phase emerges naturally out of the foundations of proactivity, pragmatism, and personalization. Formulating aims and outcomes continue the work of psychiatric rehabilitation designed to help the person identified as seriously mentally ill to become an empowered actor. Aims and outcomes form what Rose (1992) refers to as "direction": a distal vision guiding the work undertaken jointly by client and worker.

Aims and outcomes, however, can be the short-term expression of this distal direction that infuse meaning and perhaps some urgency into the present. People with serious mental illness often confront dramatic issues in their lives, and if these are left unresolved, they can create serious negative outcomes like homelessness, hospitalization, neglect, and abuse. Issues left unaddressed such as the availability of housing, the quality of housing, the availability of adequate work and income, and access to good physical health care can create considerable stress for people, resulting in unwanted and avoidable problems in functioning.

The proactive character of clinical social work in psychiatric rehabilitation requires the client and worker to identify outcomes that may demand immediate attention so that people can achieve momentum toward the direction they have chosen. These outcomes are not identified as discrete statements independent of a context, environment, or situation. Indeed the clinical social worker in psychiatric rehabilitation brings functional and situational thinking to bear here in working with clients in the formulation of outcomes and in the identification of those situational factors that must be addressed in a proactive manner. If an outcome focuses on the achievement of independent living, the worker and client may need to formulate a plan for addressing stress created by neighbors, demands created by landlords, and frustrations created by the absence of convenient transportation. And the worker and client may need to formulate a plan for putting into place supports and helping resources to achieve the desired outcome. Proactivity in this phase underscores the necessity of linking outcome to barrier reduction or management and to the optimization and implementation of situational supports.

Pragmatism in this phase is reflected by the content of the outcomes themselves. It is likely they represent critical areas in daily living and personal development. People will likely want to work on the realization of housing, income, work, vocational development, good health, and social interaction or community involvement. The focus of the work in this phase requires the client and worker to translate expressed needs into specific statements of outcomes and then to operationalize these into specific steps and tasks. The pragmatism of the outcomes suggests that client and worker are guided by life domains and what needs to be achieved within specific life domains in order to realize progress toward the larger aims of quality of life and a good standard of living.

Achieving this pragmatism may be difficult for some clinical social workers. They may want to focus on a person's self-esteem and to improve this personal characteristic before any other work is undertaken. From the perspective of psychiatric rehabilitation, self-esteem is a dependent rather than an independent variable. In traditional clinical practice, changes in self-esteem may be seen as necessary to effect changes in other life domains. For example, a person may need to increase self-esteem before he or she can be successful in work or career. In psychiatric rehabilitation practice, however, improvement of self-esteem is an outcome of the achievement of success in everyday life. Thus, a person who is supported in the achievement of something that is personally valued will experience an improvement in self-esteem. The improvement of self-esteem is dependent on the successful realization of valued outcomes—an observation consistent with the role of effectance motivation in human development.

A pragmatic orientation to outcome likely demands flexibility on the part of clinical social workers. They may need to change their practice as their clients become more active and involved in communities and activities of their own choosing. People who are seeking to increase their involvement in work, employment, or education may need social workers who are very action oriented, willing to modify meeting schedules and the length of meetings, and willing to meet in alternative locations in the community. A project designed to help people to achieve employment outcomes, for example, resulted in staff members meeting with clients for initial interviews in restaurants and then subsequently in various community locations during their clients' breaks from work or during lunch hours in order to troubleshoot immediate problems or issues emerging during that day on the job. But since many of the workers were involved in second-shift or even third-shift work, this required clinical social workers to modify their own workday. Role flexibility on the part of clinical social workers will be needed as people identified as seriously mentally ill become more involved in the achievement of pragmatic outcomes that influence their use of time, physical availability and location, and involvement in new situations.

Personalization in this phase will likely influence the substantive character of the outcomes formulated by client and worker. Personalized outcomes will be informed by the understanding achieved in the first phase and by the understanding of the purpose of psychiatric rehabilitation shared by client and worker. Personalization may influence the kind of housing a person seeks. It may influence people's conceptions of vocational development and their ideas about what constitutes satisfying careers.

Mental health programs may set limits on this personalization and actually depersonalize the outcomes that can be pursued. Mental health programs, for example, that establish a range of residential options may offer this set of resources as the only legitimate option. Commitment to personalization in psychiatric rehabilitation requires programs to respond to what people want. It does not mean limiting the options available to people. Personalization of outcomes can place considerable stress on psychiatric rehabilitation programs and amplify some of the contradictions and even hypocrisies that may be operating in programs. Personalization will probably require clinical social workers to operationalize vigorously the profession's ethical commitments to fostering resource development and programmatic innovations informed and influenced by the personal perspectives and expressed needs of consumers.

Formulating aims and outcomes offers the basis of an action plan, which gives substance and meaning to clinical social work in psychiatric rehabilitation. Personalization means that the action plan is linked to what people want to achieve in their lives and that this plan is designed to achieve in the here and now something of importance to the personal lives of people identified as seriously mentally ill (Kisthardt, 1992). Pragmatism means that something tangible is achieved that contributes to the quality of life and standard of living of people served. And proactivity means that the plan contributes to the achievement of a long-term direction and that the barriers and supports needed to achieve this desired direction are identified and addressed so success can be realized through the client and worker's taking action collaboratively.

The collaborative character of the alliance is reflected by the content of the action plan. Specific roles are identified for the achievement of desired aims and outcomes. These roles identify the contributions made by the client, the worker, the client and worker together, and third parties to the achievement of each aim and outcome. Specific tasks are generated that give to the plan the character of a working document useful to guiding client and worker toward the ends that are to be achieved now and in the long run.

Mr. Williams's case manager contacted the clinical social worker a week following the setting of the client's rehabilitation goal to report that the worker had "pushed the guy over the edge." The clinical social worker took this at face value and shared with the case manager that the decision Mr. Williams made about his involvement in higher education was an enormous one with great personal consequences. The clinical social worker met with Mr. Williams and the case manager to discuss the situation. Mr. Williams was indeed in crisis over this decision, and he emphasized how much change this would mean to him. During the course of the meeting, the clinical social worker collaborated with Mr. Williams and the case manager in breaking down the goals into feasible objectives, and specific supports were identified for each objective. For example, one objective was for Mr. Williams to get "reacclimated to the campus," and a clubhouse member who attended the university was identified as a potential mentor for Mr. Williams. Important needs were translated into specific objectives and supports, such as finding a new place to live near the campus (with the help of the case manager), appraising his academic and career interests (with the help of the clinical social worker), and identifying a support system on campus (with the help of other clubhouse members attending the university). Mr. Williams left feeling that his dream was intact, but he did tell both the clinical social worker and the case manager that he "could go over the edge again." However, he wanted them to help him to identify the sources of stress, resolve these, and get back on track. Mr. Williams wanted to be a student.

Taking Action to Achieve Outcomes

The nature of the rehabilitation plan calls for action, another aspect of the pragmatism of psychiatric rehabilitation. The value of the rehabilitation plan lies in whether it directs the actions of the worker, client, and other parties. The form of action required by effective psychiatric rehabilitation practice is very similar to task-oriented practice in professional social work (Epstein, 1988). Client and worker embellish and operationalize the plan through the specification of tasks. The problem-solving features of taking action in psychiatric rehabilitation are reflected by the content of the encounters between clients and workers. These encounters focus on the discussion of the tasks that form action, the execution of these tasks by responsible parties, the identification of barriers and challenges, and the implementation of tasks relating to the formation of needed supports.

Proactivity in this phase is found in the extent to which tasks are relevant to the achievement of specific outcomes, the extent to which tasks are executed, and the extent to which tasks are valid—that is, their execution leads to desired progress toward outcomes. Serious mental illness can be an immobilizing situation. It can result in a reluctance to take risks by the person identified as seriously mentally ill. Attempts to achieve specific tasks may not be made because the person holds the perception that failure will ensue.

Mr. Williams's support system was broadened through the identification of the rehabilitation plan. Joining the case manager and the clinical social worker as part of this support system were several clubhouse members pursuing higher education and a university academic counselor who helped Mr. Williams to evaluate his academic skills. However, many of the tasks that needed to be achieved were the responsibility of Mr. Williams, who increasingly felt the "stress and pressure" created by his goal and the dream it represented. By the time Mr. Williams officially matriculated as a student, he was feeling considerable stress. He had found a new place to live, was seeing a new psychiatrist who was willing to balance his medication with his educational work, and joined an on-campus support group organized by the case manager and the clinical social worker for people with serious mental illness seeking success as students. During the third week of the term, Mr. Williams decided to drop out of school because he was convinced that he had failed the classes. The clinical social worker saw this response as a stress reaction and helped Mr. Williams and his support system to troubleshoot the issues that were seen as barriers. In the meantime, the case manager and clinical social worker worked with faculty and another student to keep Mr. Williams enrolled. A very caring student kept notes and met with Mr. Williams several times over two weeks to review the content of his two courses. This helped Mr. Williams to stay involved as he was troubleshooting his concerns. A product of this incident was the development of a personal stress management plan designed to help prevent Mr. Williams from experiencing overwhelming stress and to help him address issues before they resulted in crisis situations.

The clinical social worker in psychiatric rehabilitation is very sensitive to the possibility of learned helplessness and to the reluctance of people to undertake tasks in the face of what they perceive to be overwhelming odds. Learned helplessness may account for many of the behaviors we refer to as symptoms because it is difficult to discern those problems that emerge out of illness and those that emerge out of the environmental response to illness. Nonetheless, the clinical social worker uses the alliance, the desired outcomes, and the necessary actions and tasks to form a supportive situation in which people can attempt action, learn from their action, and celebrate the effects they make on their situations.

A strategy countering learned helplessness useful in the action phase lies in the articulation of social work practice using effectance motivation. The clinical social worker is cognizant of the importance of framing tasks in a feasible manner. Modeling, rehearsal, and practice are used as social learning approaches supporting successful accomplishment of the tasks at hand. People are prepared with success in mind and with the vision of what successful task accomplishment can produce. Early in the psychiatric rehabilitation process, tasks can serve as targets directing a collaboration in which worker and client work together closely to achieve something tangible and valued. Efforts on the part of the person are recognized and rewarded even though this may occur in a low-key way. And the worker and client reflect together to understand how task accomplishment fits into a bigger picture, one informed by the direction a consumer wishes to take. Later in the process, consumers will undertake tasks on their own, using encounters with the clinical social worker more for review, planning, and evaluation.

Mr. Williams successfully completed his first semester. He was thrilled, and so were the members of his support system. The group as a whole decided to make a special meal at the clubhouse to celebrate their accomplishments and Mr. Williams's successful academic experience. It was great to see new friends come from the university (such as the student who served as a mentor as well as Mr. Williams's sociology instructor). Everyone at the dinner engaged in talking about their own academic experiences, including the ups and downs of student life. Mr. Williams learned some informal but important lessons: many people find higher education challenging, and during this time it is not unusual for people to change their minds about courses, drop courses, and seek special assistance.

Outcomes and direction are complex entities composed of many different tasks. Finding a job that pleases a person is very complex, especially when an illness has created a substantial lapse in time in which one has not been employed or in which one has not been involved in education. Learning about what different work opportunities are available, learning about what work situations are found to be personally valued, and identifying one's work assets and strengths are complex tasks that need to be broken down and undertaken in a way that increases the probability of successful execution.

Involvement in task completion is not merely something the worker or client undertakes alone. There is ample opportunity for team-based collaboration in which different people work to accomplish a range of tasks relating to the achievement of a successful outcome. And there is ample opportunity to infuse consumerism and peer support into the completion of tasks. Task-oriented practice in the action phase can be implemented within the context of a support system. This support system is personalized and pragmatic: it seeks to execute the tasks necessary to the successful achievement of outcome. Execution of the tasks can be undertaken in a manner that decreases the stress experienced by the person identified as seriously mentally ill.

Thus, the use of the client-worker alliance, and the creation of personalized support systems, constitute two important strategies for taking action in psychiatric rehabilitation. For the clinical social worker, these two strategies mean that the worker often practices at the interface of a complex system created by the provision of direct support to the consumer, case management activities, environmental modification, and liaison to alternative providers of support such as peers who offer self-help and mutual support opportunities (Moxley, 1989).

Ongoing evaluation plays a significant role in the action phase of psychiatric rehabilitation. The form of evaluation most consistent with the aim of helping people identified as seriously mentally ill to become empowered actors can be characterized as satisfaction driven. Too often people without power are asked to defer to the judgment of people who are perceived to be in more powerful roles, a situation that can reinforce learned helplessness and the loss of motivation. Evaluation that empowers requires people to reflect on their satisfaction and those qualities and standards that influence whether the rehabilitation process holds personal value for them. This approach to evaluation reflects another strategy for supporting the personalization of psychiatric rehabilitation. Such evaluation can contribute to the enhancement of assertiveness, personal control, and personal efficacy as people reflect on whether they are satisfied with what is happening and as they see things change in the rehabilitation process in response to their appraisal and critique (Moxley & Freddolino, 1990).

This form of evaluation can be easily incorporated into psychiatric rehabilitation practice. The worker can periodically encourage the client to reflect on what is happening, what is being achieved, how the work of rehabilitation is being undertaken, and to identify whether this work is satisfying to the client. At first, a person may be reluctant to engage in this form of criticism for fear of reprisal. But as people witness the sincere interest of workers in whether they are satisfied with the rehabilitation process and its outcomes and as they see actual changes in the process and direction of rehabilitation, then it is more likely that evaluation will become an established feature of the action phase. More important, encouragement of a critical and reflective posture on the part of consumers can contribute to their empowerment within the rehabilitation process, an outcome that may generalize to other situations in their daily lives.

The clinical social worker was very interested in Mr. Williams's evaluation of the adequacy and effectiveness of the supports he received for participation in higher education. Through this evaluation process, which took five to ten minutes during each encounter, the worker learned that Mr. Williams liked on-campus support and was very pleased with having another student who could help him on campus. This student mentor became a pivotal person in his life and was instrumental in helping Mr. Williams to keep on track in his studies. However, the evaluation process also identified a serious weakness in Mr. Williams's housing situation. He had moved from the adult foster care situation to an apartment near campus. He was very frustrated by the partying that occurred over the weekends and the excessive noise that disturbed his studying. By the end of the semester Mr. Williams identified the need to move to a new location, and his support system helped him to bring this to a successful outcome. According to Mr. Williams, his new living situation needed to be conducive to someone who wanted to be a serious student.

Following Along in the Spirit of Support

Clinical social work in psychiatric rehabilitation is not conceptualized as a time-limited activity with an identifiable end point. The idea of termination with its notion of finality may not be appropriate to thinking about the ending or winding down phase of this form of clinical social work practice. Following along as a distinctive phase in the rehabilitation process communicates that psychiatric rehabilitation does not (or does not have to) possess a point at which all work is completed, and the work comes to a close. The concept of recovery recognizes serious mental illness not exclusively as a disease but as a life process in which people find themselves in extraordinary circumstances, and these circumstances serve to redefine a person's life and life space dramatically. Following along gives credence to the high probability that people's experience with serious mental illness has its own trajectory, and they may be involved for some time in the search for personal meaning in this experience and in trying different avenues of coping and living with this experience and the meaning they attribute to it.

Following along as a set of practice procedures means that people may find a time when they feel their work has been completed, and they want to move out of the alliance and disengage from the process of psychiatric rehabilitation. Following along means that the door does not close and that the person can easily reactivate involvement in rehabilitation and in the alliance with the clinical social worker. The client and worker may establish various milestones when they will meet for friendly visiting and for discussions about what is occurring in the person's life. Friendly visiting offers opportunities to review previous work and accomplishments, look at and address present circumstances and events, and consider the future and appraise new directions. The plan for client and worker to meet every three months merely to check in can serve as one strategy for implementing follow-along procedures.

Alternatively client and worker may identify certain transition points or events that can trigger contact and the rejoining of the two parties. These transition points may be anticipated events that arise within employment, education, or family life. A person participating in higher education, for example, may want to get together prior to final exams to organize a support system to navigate what can be a stressful period. Or specific events like the end of a romantic relationship may be identified as a triggering event calling for a need to get together.

Mr. Williams and his support system became quite sensitive to the break points occurring each semester. He used the term break points *to emphasize that these events could "make or break his academic performance." Certainly midterm examinations and final examinations created situations in which support needed to be intensified, and even crisis resources needed to be in place. Although these situations were quite stressful, the most stressful situation came at the beginning of the term when Mr. Williams learned about the requirements for each of his courses. Once these were known, Mr. Williams met with his support system to plan appropriate supports. Mr. Williams became so adept at planning around his break points that he was able to formulate advanced directives that guided the support system's actions and decisions in case his functioning was reduced. By his third semester in the university, his academic adviser became a part of this support system, and this person knew what actions were to be taken to ensure that Mr. Williams would be successful. The adviser, in conjunction with the case manager and clinical social worker, were all involved in following along with Mr. Williams during each semester to help him troubleshoot academic, income, housing, and mental health issues. This follow-along continued throughout Mr. Williams's undergraduate education, which he finally completed in the field of biology. His work in the sciences continues to this day. As a graduate student, he is working on a doctorate in biology while still using a support system that helps him to negotiate those transitions and issues that can potentially throw him off his new life course.*

A commitment to self-determination on the part of the worker will most likely lead to the creation of follow-along procedures that are under as much control of the person as possible. Thus, people are helped to formulate a personal plan for self-monitoring. This means that it is up to the person to trigger reentry into the rehabilitation process or the activation of specific kinds of supports. This does not necessarily mean that the worker refuses to engage in appropriate and ethical outreach. Workers may periodically initiate their own contacts out of personal and professional concern for the person. But the attention and the subsequent offer of assistance are not forced on the person. The contact is identified as a friendly visit—an overture that can be accepted or declined by the person. These overtures may be made when a worker learns that a person may have lost a job, entered the hospital, or become homeless. The respectful and friendly offer of assistance is another reflection of the commitment of clinical social workers practicing in psychiatric rehabilitation to making available pragmatic and personalized supports to people. Offering follow-along assistance to people based on their preferences is another strategy for respecting the person as an empowered actor within the psychiatric rehabilitation process.

CONTEXTS OF PRACTICE

The process of clinical social work can be applied within the wide range of contexts operating in the domain of psychiatric rehabilitation. One of the many interesting aspects of psychiatric rehabilitation is found in the domain's numerous auspices that can serve as hosts to the form of practice described earlier. From my own experience as clinician, clinical administrator, and consultant, I have seen the ideas, principles, and practices of psychiatric rehabilitation applied successfully in a diversity of contexts, including social development organizations like YMCAs, general or psychiatric hospitals, public interest law offices, mental health centers, community colleges and universities, public housing alternatives, and shopping centers. This diversity demonstrates that psychiatric rehabilitation does not have to take place in any specific context but rather can be implemented in a range of locations, organizations, and auspices. A strength of the domain is its diversity and the variation that exists among psychiatric rehabilitation programs and services (Freddolino, Moxley, & Fleishman, 1989). The domain's integrity is found in its focus on serious mental illness, its distinctive mission of improving the quality of life and life circumstances of people, and its consumer-driven approach to practice.

Two programmatic contexts illustrate how clinical social work in psychiatric rehabilitation can unfold and the types of tasks and activities clinical social workers can undertake in these contexts. They are the clubhouse and the psychiatric rehabilitation center. I identify these programmatic alternatives simply as illustrative examples of practice contexts. They do not document the complete programmatic variation that characterizes psychiatric rehabilitation.

The Clubhouse

The clubhouse model has emerged in many local communities to stand as a distinctive programmatic form in psychiatric rehabilitation. Fountain House, a New York City–based program, was the initial clubhouse and served as the prototype on which many clubhouse programs have been modeled. Initially founded as a peer support program, Fountain House served as a refuge for people who found only isolation and the absence of fellowship in the city. Fountain House expanded dramatically over the approximately five decades of its existence to model and disseminate the clubhouse-based principles and practices. It offers a range of pragmatic daily living supports for people with serious mental illness in a personalized manner. These supports are designed to assist people to achieve success in their daily lives and to promote the spirit and outcomes indicative of recovery by helping people to live, work, and learn in their communities.

The prototype of the clubhouse developed and disseminated by Fountain House contributed to the emergence of a movement to expand clubhouses nationally and globally. The clubhouse model has been translated into specific standards that are revised periodically by members of these organizations who come together to expand and refine these standards (Propst, 1992b). The practice of clinical social workers who serve as staff members in the context of a clubhouse will be framed and influenced by these standards since they have been broadly disseminated and embraced by programs that are seeking integrity as clubhouse programs. Clinical social workers practicing in this context will:

1. Share membership in the clubhouse with people who have serious mental illness. People are viewed as members, not as patients. Patienthood implies a passivity that is foreign to the clubhouse setting. The idea of membership communicates a person who actively contributes to the formation, development, and continuation of the clubhouse. It also speaks to the voluntary nature of the club (Glickman, 1992a). People get and stay involved because they want to, not because they are required by a therapeutic stipulation. Membership is lifelong, without performance requirements created by artificial rules relating to compliance or conformity.

2. Work with people individually and in small and large groups on the pragmatic tasks of operating the clubhouse. The club itself does not offer mental health services or therapy, although it can create therapeutic outcomes like improved self-concept, increased self-esteem, and skill development. The clubhouse cannot operate without an active membership that attends daily to undertake the duties and responsibilities of operating a facility, organizing and communicating with other members, preparing meals, and offering supportive programs and activities.

3. Work with people to create a milieu driven by the values of attentiveness, kindness, caring, and informality. Within good clubhouses, it is difficult to tell the difference between professional staff and club members. Dress is informal and unpretentious. Communication is nonhierarchical, people interact as peers, and the pace may be rather laid back. A good clubhouse achieves this ambience of informality and radiates support and warmth in recognition of the importance of creating a place where people "feel needed, wanted and accepted because of who they were and what they had to contribute, not because they suffered from the harrowing effects of mental illness" (Propst, 1992a, p. 3).

4. Work with people to become participants in the clubhouse while creating supports for people to become participants in their communities and in the greater society through housing, employment, education, recreation, and cultural enrichment. The clubhouse is not insulated from its community but rather seeks to become an

active contributor to community life, at the same time that clubhouse members seek to become active citizens who take advantage of the opportunities, rights, benefits, and resources a community offers to all of its citizens.

Clinical social workers practicing in clubhouse settings may find themselves breaking out of traditional paradigms governing clinical interaction (Glickman, 1992b). They will find themselves working within a milieu whose purpose is found in the activation of contributions by all members. In this milieu, clinical social workers will likely find themselves practicing as mentors, coaches, educators, and facilitators. Group work will likely become more salient than individual work. And clinical social workers will likely find themselves interacting with more traditional psychiatric programs (such as inpatient units, outpatient programs) in collaboration with clubhouse members who are the principal providers of outreach, membership recruitment, education to professionals, and social marketing.

The Comprehensive Psychiatric Rehabilitation Center

This context finds its distinctiveness through its focus on the provision of skill development and tangible supports to people with serious mental illness. Unlike the clubhouse, the psychiatric rehabilitation center will most likely adopt a skill development, education, and support approach that is integrated with the provision of accessible mental health and psychiatric services (Brown & Hughson, 1987). However, mental health and psychiatric services are probably secondary and ancillary to a center's mission of helping people to gain the skills and supports necessary to the achievement of independent functioning within their communities. Compared to the milieu, informal, and interactional approach adopted by clubhouses, the psychiatric rehabilitation center adopts a more explicit and formal classroom and group approach to skill development. The provision of support is more likely undertaken by professional rehabilitation staff rather than by peers (Brown & Hughson, 1989).

Psychiatric rehabilitation centers are often organized around the provision of pragmatic resources and supports that focus on specific life domains. Comprehensiveness is found in the coverage of these domains by the center, and therefore it is not unusual for a psychiatric rehabilitation center to offer housing assistance, employment opportunities, recreational activities, health care access, linkage to entitlements, and vocational development, all colocated and integrated in an accessible fashion. The coordination of this comprehensiveness is the function of a case management component.

Progressive psychiatric rehabilitation centers are moving away from the provision of these activities and opportunities based exclusively on a facility model. Embracing the philosophy of normalization (Wolfensberger, 1972), progressive centers implement these activities within regular community settings. They adopt practice arrangements that place rehabilitation personnel in support roles with the purpose of supporting people's functioning and performance in a community setting. Over the past ten years, many psychiatric rehabilitation centers have moved from the operation of group homes, halfway houses, sheltered employment programs, and day programs to the operation of supported housing, supported employment, and supported education options.

A support model means that rehabilitation personnel work with people to identify a personally valued goal, to make choices about their lifestyle and living circumstances (e.g., where they want to live), to assist people to make their choices a reality, and then to organize, implement, and sustain the supports that are critical to helping people to achieve success in their goal area. This model of "choose, get, and keep" reflects the foundational principles of psychiatric rehabilitation, and the practicality of the model reflects its usefulness in helping people to achieve success in any life domain.

Clinical social workers practicing in psychiatric rehabilitation centers will find themselves in roles framed by the aims of skill development and functional support. And it is likely that their practice will be framed by a "choose, get, and keep" model. Rehabilitation within these centers is increasingly characterized by a team-based and strengths-oriented process. Thus, clinical social workers in this context:

1. Work in team contexts to conduct functional analyses of the strengths of consumers within the context of real-world situations or settings. Thus, for example, the Center of Vocational Alternatives in Columbus, Ohio, an agency committed to the enhancement of work and employment for people identified as seriously mentally ill, increasingly conducts the assessment of people within real work settings that are tailored to the preferences of consumers. Community vocational assessment is similar to how many psychiatric rehabilitation centers assess and evaluate people in situations rather than in simulated or controlled environments that is typical of sheltered workshops, psychometric testing situations, and transitional housing programs. Situational assessment enables consumers and workers to understand how people function in the light of the demands and supports created by specific environments. Strengths and assets that may not come to light in deficit-oriented testing situations can be made quite visible by in vivo assessment situations. In addition, this approach to assessment offers consumers and rehabilitation personnel opportunities to gain an understanding of those supports, assistive technologies, and environmental modifications needed by the person to increase the probability of successful performance. More important, the assessment situation itself offers consumers information and knowledge to evaluate whether they find a specific environment or context acceptable and satisfying.

2. Work closely with consumers in crafting rehabilitation aims and outcomes that are consistent with their desires, wishes, and preferences. These aims and outcomes in conjunction with situationally specific assessment data offer psychiatric rehabilitation centers opportunities to design personalized and pragmatic rehabilitation plans. These plans translate consumer preferences into tangible strategies for offering support, reducing barriers, and promoting the achievement of valued outcomes.

3. Practice in real-life situations within actual communities with the aim of providing environmental supports to people who are working in competitive situations,

living in their own homes, using the amenities of the community, and fulfilling their daily living needs through shopping and commerce. Clinical social workers in this context become experts in the creation and improvement of environmental support systems that are effective in producing the outcomes valued and prioritized by consumers. As experts in the provision of these consumer-driven environmental supports, clinical social workers understand how support can be used to counteract the negative social consequences created by serious mental illness.

4. Position the psychiatric rehabilitation center within networks of community resources and organizations that can be partners in the process of community support even though their specific missions probably do not prioritize the support of people with serious mental illness. Clinical social workers extend supports into communities formed, for example, by higher education, housing, or business so that people with serious mental illness can take advantage of the resources and opportunities mediated by these communities. This aspect of practice will be informed by the idea of recovery as psychiatric rehabilitation centers look at strategies for helping people to become less preoccupied by illness and more focused on human and community development.

CONCLUSION: ADOPTING A BEST PRACTICE PERSPECTIVE

Over the past twenty years, the psychiatric rehabilitation community has learned a great deal about effective practice with people identified as seriously mentally ill. There has been considerable effort by public and nonprofit mental health systems to identify best practices suggested by the domain of psychiatric rehabilitation and to adopt these as foundational qualities of progressive systems of rehabilitation and community support. The work has been arduous, especially as serious mental illness is framed as a disease and an illness, and not as a social problem that negatively affects the lives of millions of our citizens. I am constantly reminded of the considerable work the profession of social work and the domain of psychiatric rehabilitation must undertake to improve substantially the life chances of people identified as seriously mentally ill. Scenarios for the next twenty years do not suggest that our society will find a cure for serious mental illness, nor does it appear that neurobiological interventions will emerge to extinguish this problem forever.

Clinical social work has considerable relevance in this very complex area of practice. It has a distinctive role to play in the transdisciplinary matrix created by the domain. But progress in this domain may ebb and flow. I am reminded of a graduate social work student who came to see me as his adviser to discuss his field placement in a traditional day treatment program for people with "chronic mental illness." He related to me stories of mental health staff who characterized program participants as "chrons" and how he was taught only after two weeks as an intern to lower his expectations of people enrolled in the program.

He underscored the purpose of the program: to give people a low-demand environment in which they could be monitored and in which medication compliance could be ensured. I found disturbing his response to my inquiry about whether he agreed with this approach. He stressed that the participants simply did not have the neurobiological capacity to cope with anything demanding or stress producing. I then inquired into what our own professional code of ethics, philosophy, and core practice principles suggest to him about working with people identified as seriously mentally ill. He was not sure about whether a connection existed.

I related to this student an incident that I experienced some twelve years before when as a mental health administrator I was called by a day treatment supervisor who alerted me to the fact that persistent cigarette smoking among program participants finally resulted in what could have been a serious fire. It seems one of three gentlemen with diagnoses of schizophrenia, and who were most likely overmedicated, dropped his lighted cigarette into the sofa on which the men would spend their mornings sitting passively without moving. Alarmed by the smoke filling the room and seeing a staff member panic, the three men took control of the situation, organized the participants to evacuate the facility safely, returned to extinguish the fire, moved the sofa outside, and then called the fire department. The supervisor called me after he regained his composure. I entered the program one hour after the incident. What did I see? The three men found another sofa to sit on! I found them inert, staring silently into space.

The student appeared to be motivated either by my story or by my challenge to his professional sense of purpose and mission. It was at this point I introduced him to clinical social work in psychiatric rehabilitation. We spent the remainder of the semester in weekly discussions about what constitutes best practice and what can be used to guide professional social work in this domain. I shared with him the five best practices I have personally abstracted to guide my own practice in this domain, and I integrated these with the foundations of professional practice in social work:

1. *Understanding how people with serious mental illness experience environmental and situational factors and the influence of these factors on their behavior.* Best practice in clinical social work calls for a sensitivity to the environment in which people with serious mental illness function. We cannot attribute what we see as diminished functioning exclusively to the illness or impairment created by serious mental illness. We must look for factors operating in a situation and in an environment and need to understand people's appraisal of or reaction to these factors.

2. *Listening to people's stories and to subjective experiences concerning their situations.* Deficits are too easy to identify and are accentuated by many mental health systems and practices prevalent in the field of psychiatry. Few of us fare well when others focus on what is wrong with us. It takes time, creativity, and professional competence to understand people's strengths. Stories and storytelling may be the best strategies to unearth strengths. Part of this storytelling lies in the openness of workers to hearing people's subjective understanding of their own illness and of the consequences of their illness. Another part lies in hearing where people want to go with their lives.

3. *Achieving a dialogue among two equal but different parties.* Understanding peo-

ple's visions of themselves as purposeful actors may be crucial to human development. Too often practice can degrade into meaningless exchanges about symptoms and problems. Dialogue requires each party to develop and present a perspective. Dialogue concerning how people see themselves and what direction they want to take may be one of the most powerful tools a social worker can use to help people develop. Dialogue can personalize and empower. Indeed, establishing dialogue between the social worker and the consumer may be essential to putting self-determination as a value into action.

4. *Forming an alliance between worker and consumer, the purpose of which is to identify, address, and conquer barriers.* Challenging barriers that can obstruct the achievement of a desired direction is essential to proactive practice. The story about my student's internship is a story about illness. It communicates assumptions about illness and their translation into lowered expectations, negative attitudes, and ultimately diminished status of people with serious mental illness. These stories illustrate how expectations and attitudes can crystalize into potent environmental barriers that can frustrate human development.

5. *Recognizing that supports are effective tools of rehabilitation. Their targeting and use require social workers to adopt creative intervention roles that shift practice from the office to the environment of ultimate functioning so pragmatic and personalized outcomes can be achieved in a proactive manner.* Appreciating and using the richness of support can sensitize clinical social workers to the many different ways barriers can be resolved and strengths employed to help people with serious mental illness to be successful as they define it. Support can come internally, from within, and the clinical social worker can be instrumental in helping people to appreciate and to understand their internal resources and capacities. Support can come from the organization of tangible environmental resources that can be employed to troubleshoot situations, extend a person's performance, or solve immediate problems that can upset an otherwise good living situation. Targeting support on a specific problem in a specific environmental setting may be the most effective way of orchestrating clinical intervention. To paraphrase the psychoanalyst Winnicott, these supports can be the basis of strategies for helping people to function "in a good enough manner."

The student described above incorporated these best practice guidelines into his own work as a clinical social worker committed to the mission of psychiatric rehabilitation. Unfortunately he was not able to overcome the programmatic culture of his field placement, but he is now a senior rehabilitation specialist in a progressive psychiatric rehabilitation center. He has made a sustained effort to integrate clinical social work into the domain of psychiatric rehabilitation. This effort has been successful. It is visible in his practice. Through his efforts, people get and keep employment, they select and maintain housing, they navigate symptomatic flare-ups while they keep active in their communities, and they pursue career development and advanced education. These are the outcomes that make psychiatric rehabilitation distinctive as a domain, and they illustrate how clinical social work can make a fundamental difference in helping people with serious mental illness plan and execute their own journey of recovery.

REFERENCES

Andreasen, N. (1984). *The broken brain.* New York: Harper & Row.

Anthony, W. A. (1972). Societal rehabilitation: Changing society's attitudes toward the physically and mentally disabled. *Rehabilitation Psychology, 19,* 117–126.

Anthony, W. A. (1979). *The principles of psychiatric rehabilitation.* Amherst, MA: Human Resource Development Press.

Anthony, W. A. (1994). Recovery from mental illness: The guiding vision of the mental health system in the 1990s. In International Association of Psychosocial Rehabilitation Services, *An introduction to psychiatric rehabilitation* (pp. 556–567). Boston: Author.

Anthony, W. A., & Jansen, (1984). Predicting the vocational capacity of the chronically mentally ill: Research and policy implications. *American Psychologist, 39,* 537–544.

Anthony, W. A., & Liberman, R. P. (1986). The practice of psychiatric rehabilitation: Historical, conceptual, and research base. *Schizophrenia Bulletin, 12*(4), 542–559.

Anthony, W., & Spaniol, L. (Eds.). (1994). *Readings in psychiatric rehabilitation.* Boston: Boston University Center for Psychiatric Rehabilitation.

Anthony, W. A., et al. (1972). Efficacy of psychiatric rehabilitation. *Psychological Bulletin, 78,* 447–456.

Anthony, W., Cohen, M., & Farkas, M. (1990). *Psychiatric rehabilitation.* Boston: Center for Psychiatric Rehabilitation.

Anthony, W. A., Cohen, M. R., & Vitalo, R. (1978). The measurement of rehabilitation outcome. *Schizophrenia Bulletin, 4,* 365–383.

Anthony, W. A., Howell, J., & Danley, K. (1984). The vocational rehabilitation model of the psychiatrically disabled. In M. Mirabi (Ed.). *The chronically mentally ill: Research and services.* Jamaica, NY: SP Medical and Scientific Books.

Armour, P. K. (1989). Mental health policymaking in the United States: Patterns, process, and structures. In D. Rochefort (Ed.), *Handbook on mental health policy in the United States* (pp. 173–192). Westport, CT: Greenwood.

Bartlett, H. M. (1970). *The common base of social work practice.* Washington, DC: National Association of Social Workers.

Black, B. J. (1988). *Work and mental illness: Transitions to employment.* Baltimore: Johns Hopkins University Press.

Belcher, J. R. (1988). Are jails replacing the mental health system for the homeless mentally ill? *Community Mental Health Journal, 24,* 185–195.

Bell, L. V. (1989). From the asylum to the community in U.S. mental health care: An historical overview. In D. A. Rochefort (Ed.), *Handbook on mental health policy in the United States* (pp. 89–120). Westport, CT: Greenwood.

Bennett, D. H. (1983). The historical development of rehabilitation services. In F. N. Watts and D. H. Bennett (Eds.), *Theory and practice of psychiatric rehabilitation.* New York: Wiley.

Bronfenbrenner, U. (1979). *The ecology of human development: Experiments by nature and design.* Cambridge, MA: Harvard University Press.

Brown, R. I., & Hughson, E. A. (1987). *Behavioral and social rehabilitation and training.* New York: Wiley.

Burt, M. R., & Pittman, K. J. (1985). *Testing the social safety net: The impact of changes in support programs during the Reagan administration.* Washington, DC: Urban Institute Press.

Carling, P. J. (1993). Supports and rehabilitation for housing and community living. In R. W. Flexer and P. Solomon (Eds.), *Psychiatric rehabilitation in practice* (pp. 99–118). Boston: Andover.

Chamberlin, J. (1978). *On our own: Patient-controlled alternatives to the mental health system.* New York: McGraw-Hill.

Chamberlin, J. (1990). The ex-patients' movement: Where we've been and where we're going. *Journal of Mind and Behavior, 11*(3, 4). 323–336.

Chamberlin, J., Rogers, J., & Sneed, C. (1989). Consumers, families, and community support systems. *Psychosocial Rehabilitation Journal, 12*(3), 93–106.

Cohen, M., & Anthony, W. A. (1988). A commentary on planning a service system for persons who are severely mentally ill: Avoiding the pitfalls of the past. *Psychosocial Rehabilitation Journal, 12*(1), 69–72.

Coles, R. (1989). *The call of stories: Teaching and the moral imagination.* Boston: Houghton Mifflin.

Epstein, L. (1988). *Helping people: The task-centered approach.* Columbus, OH: Merrill.

Farkas, M. D., & Anthony, W. A. (Eds.). (1989). *Psychiatric rehabilitation programs: Putting theory into practice.* Baltimore: Johns Hopkins University Press.

Farkas, M. D., Anthony, W. A., & Cohen, M. A. (1989). Psychiatric rehabilitation: The approach and its programs. In M. D. Farkas & W. A. Anthony (Eds.), *Psychiatric rehabilitation programs: Putting theory into practice* (pp. 1–27). Baltimore: Johns Hopkins University Press.

Flexer, R. W., & Solomon, P. L. (1993). (Eds.). *Psychiatric rehabilitation in practice.* Boston: Andover.

Foley, H. A., & Sharfstein, S. S. (1983). *Madness and government: Who cares for the mentally ill?* Washington, DC: American Psychiatric Press.

Freddolino, P. P., & Moxley, D. P. (1988). The states' role in fine tuning the new federal mandate for rights protection and advocacy for people labelled mentally ill. *New England Journal of Human* Services, 13(2), 27–33.

Freddolino, P. P., Moxley, D. P., & Fleishman, J. (1988). Daily living needs at time of discharge: Implications for advocacy. *Psychosocial Rehabilitation Journal, 11*(4), 33–46.

Freddolino, P. P., Moxley, D. P., & Fleishman, J. (1989). An advocacy model for people with long-term psychiatric disabilities. *Hospital and Community Psychiatry,* 40(11), 1169–1174.

Gallagher, B. J. (1987). *The sociology of mental illness.* Englewood Cliffs, NJ: Prentice Hall.

Gardner, H. (1993). *Creating minds: An anatomy of creativity seen through the lives of Freud, Einstein, Picasso, Stravinsky, Eliot, Graham, and Gandhi.* New York: Basic Books.

Germain, C. B., & Gitterman, A. (1980). *The life model of social work practice.* New York: Columbia University Press.

Gerhart, U. C. (1990). *Caring for the chronic mentally ill.* Itasca, IL: Peacock.

Gitterman, A. (Ed.). (1991). *Handbook of social work practice with vulnerable populations.* New York: Columbia University Press.

Glickman, M. (1992a). The voluntary nature of the clubhouse. *Psychosocial Rehabilitation Journal, 16*(2), 39–40.

Glickman, M. (1992b). "What if nobody wants to make lunch?" Bottom line responsibility in the clubhouse. *Psychosocial Rehabilitation Journal, 16*(2), 55–59.

Goldman, H. H., & Manderscheid, R. (1987). The epidemiology of psychiatric disability. In A. T. Meyerson & T. Fine (Eds.), *Psychiatric disability: Clinical, legal and administrative dimensions* (pp. 13–21). Washington, DC: American Psychiatric Press.

Goldman, H. H., Adams, N. H., & Taube, C. A. (1983). Deinstitutionalization: The data demythologized. *Hospital and Community Psychiatry, 34*(2), 129–134.

Goldman, H. H., Gattozzi, A., & Taube, C. A. (1981). Defining and counting the chronically mentally ill. *Hospital and Community Psychiatry, 32*(1), 21–27.

Goldstein, E. G. (1984). *Ego psychology and social work practice.* New York: Free Press.

Grob, G. N. (1991). *From asylum to community: Mental health policy in modern America.* Princeton, NJ: Princeton University Press.

Grob, G. N. (1994). *The mad among us: A history of the care of America's mentally ill.* New York: Free Press.

Harris, M., & Bachrach, L. (1988). *Clinical case management.* San Francisco: Jossey-Bass.

Hartmann, H. (1939). *Ego psychology and the problem of adaptation.* New York: International Universities Press.

Institute of Medicine. (1991). *Disability in America.* Washington, DC: National Academy Press.

International Association of Psychosocial Rehabilitation Services (1994). *An introduction to psychiatric rehabilitation.* Washington, DC: Author.

Isaac, R. J., & Armat, V. C. (1990). *Madness in the streets.* New York: Free Press.

Johnson, A. (1990). *Out of Bedlam: The truth about deinstitutionalization.* New York: Basic Books.

Kaplan, H. I., & Sadock, B. J. (1989). *Comprehensive textbook of psychiatry* (5th ed.). Baltimore: Williams and Wilkins.

Kisthardt, W. E. (1992). A strengths model of case management: The principles and functions of a helping partnership with persons with persistent mental illness. In D. Saleeby (Ed.), *The strengths perspective in social work* (pp. 59–83). New York: Longman.

Lawn, B., & Meyerson, A. T. (1993). A modern perspective on psychiatry in rehabilitation. In R. W. Flexer & P. Solomon (Eds.), *Psychiatric rehabilitation in practice* (pp. 31–44). Boston: Andover.

Lehman, A. F., & Dixon, L. B. (1995). *Double jeopardy: Chronic mental illness and substance use disorders.* New York: Harwood Academic.

Liberman, R. P. (1988). *Psychiatric rehabilitation of chronic mental patients.* Washington, DC: American Psychiatric Press.

Maluccio, A. (1981). *Promoting competence in clients.* New York: Free Press.

Mechanic, D. (1987). Correcting misconceptions in mental health policy: Strategies for improved care of the seriously mentally ill. *Milbank Quarterly, 65*(2), 203–230.

Minkoff, K. (1978). A map of the chronic mental patient. In J. Talbot (Ed.), *The chronic mental patient.* Washington, DC: American Psychiatric Press.

Mowbray, C., Moxley, D., Thrasher, S., & associates. (1996). Consumers as community support providers: Issues created by role innovation. *Community Mental Health Journal, 32,* 47–67.

Moxley, D. P. (1989). *The practice of case management.* Newbury Park, CA: Sage.

Moxley, D. P. (1992). Disability policy and social work practice. *Health and Social Work, 17*(2), 99–103.

Moxley, D. P. (1994). *Serious mental illness and the concept of recovery: Implications for social work practice in psychiatric rehabilitation.* Boston: Boston University Center for Psychiatric Rehabilitation.

Moxley, D. P. (1995). *Case management by design: Reflections on principles and practices.* Chicago: Nelson-Hall.

Moxley, D. P., & Daeschlein, M. (1997). Properties of consumer-driven case management. In D. P. Moxley, *Case management by design: Reflections on principles and practices.* Chicago: Nelson-Hall.

Moxley, D. P., & Freddolino, P. P. (1990). A model of advocacy for promoting client self-determination in psychosocial rehabilitation. *Psychosocial Rehabilitation Journal, 14*(2), 69–82.

Moxley, D. P., & Freddolino, P. P. (1994). Client-driven advocacy and psychiatric disability: A model for social work practice. *Journal of Sociology and Social Welfare, 21*(2), 91–108.

Moxley, D., & Tarnato, S. (1994). Changing programmatic models: Issues in the transition from community mental health practice to community support and rehabilitation. Manuscript submitted for publication.

Moxley, D., Mowbray, C., & Brown, K. (1993). Supported education. In R. Flexer and P. Solomon (Eds.). *Psychiatric rehabilitation in practice* (pp. 137–153). Boston: Andover.

National Institute of Mental Health. (1980). *Guidelines for community support programs.* Washington, DC: Author.

Propst, R. (1992a). Introduction. Special issue on the clubhouse model. *Psychosocial Rehabilitation Journal, 16*(2), 3–4.

Propst, R. (1992b). Standards for clubhouse programs: Why and how they were developed. *Psychosocial Rehabilitation Journal, 16*(2), 25–30.

Rapp, C. A. (1992). The strengths perspective of case management with persons suffering from severe mental illness. In D. Saleeby (Ed.), *The strengths perspective in social work* (pp. 45–58). New York: Longman.

Rapp, C. A., & Wintersteen, R. (1989). The strengths model of case management: Results from twelve demonstrations. *Psychosocial Rehabilitation Journal, 13*(1), 23–32.

Ridgely, S., Goldman, H., & Talbot, J. (1986). *Chronically mentally ill young adults with substance abuse problems: A review of relevant literature and creation of a research agenda.* Baltimore: University of Maryland Mental Health Policy Center.

Rose, S. (Ed.). (1992). *Case management and social work practice.* New York: Longman.

Rose, S., & Black, B. (1985). *Advocacy and empowerment: Mental health care in the community.* Boston: Routledge & Kegan Paul.

Rothman, J. (1992). *Guidelines for case management: Putting research to professional use.* Itasca, IL: Peacock.

Rutman, I. (1987). The psychosocial rehabilitation movement in the United States. In A. Meyerson & T. Fine (Eds.), *Psychiatric disability: Clinical, legal, and administrative dimensions.* Washington, DC: American Psychiatric Press.

Saleeby, D. (Ed.). (1992). *The strengths perspective in social work practice.* New York: Longman.

Scallet, L. J. (1986). *Protection and advocacy systems for people receiving mental health services.* Washington, DC: Policy Resources.

Simmons, T. J., Selleck, V., Steele, R. B., & Sepetauc, F. (1993). Supports and rehabilitation for employment. In R. W. Flexer & P. Solomon (Eds.), *Psychiatric rehabilitation in practice* (pp. 119–136). Boston: Andover.

Steadman, H., McCarty, D., & Morrissey, J. (1989). *The mentally ill in jail: Planning for essential services.* New York: Guilford.

Strean, H. S. (1978). *Clinical social work: Theory and practice.* New York: Free Press.

Stroul, B. A. (1989). Community support systems for persons with long-term mental illness: A conceptual framework. *Psychosocial Rehabilitation Journal, 8*(1), 35–43.

Stroul, B. A. (1993). Rehabilitation in community support systems. In R. W. Flexer & P. L. Solomon (Eds.), *Psychiatric rehabilitation in practice* (pp. 45–61). Boston: Andover.

Stufflebeam, D. L., & Shinkfield, A. J. (1985). *Systematic evaluation.* Boston: Kluwer-Nijhoff.

Susser, M., Hopper, K., & Richman, J. (1983). Society, culture, and health. In D. Mechanic (Ed.), *Handbook of health, health care, and the health professions.* New York: Free Press.

Taylor, S. E. (1979). Hospital patient behavior: Reactance, helplessness, or control? *Journal of Social Issues, 35,* 156–183.

Teplin, L. (1984). Criminalizing mental disorder: The comparative arrest rate of the mentally ill. *American Psychologist, 39*(7), 794–803.

Tessler, R. C., & Dennis, D. L. (1989). *A synthesis of NIMH funded research concerning persons who are homeless and mentally ill.* Amherst, MA: Social and Demographic Research Institute, University of Massachusetts, and Delmare, NY: Policy Research Associates.

Towle, C. (1987). *Common human needs* (Rev. ed.). Silver Spring, MD: National Association of Social Workers.

Turner, J. C., & TenHoor, W. J. (1978). The NIMH Community Support Program: Pilot approach to a needed social reform. *Schizophrenia Bulletin, 4*(3), 319–348.

U.S. Department of Health, Education, and Welfare. (1980). *National plan for the chronically mentally ill.* Washington, DC: U.S. Government Printing Office.

U.S. General Accounting Office. (1988). *Homeless mentally ill: Problems and options in estimating numbers and trends.* Washington, DC: Author.

U.S. Senate Committee on Labor and Human Resources, and Committee on Appropriations (1985). *Care of institutionalized mentally disabled persons* (Senate Hearings 99-50, Parts 1 and 2). Washington, DC: U.S. Government Printing Office.

Vaillant, G. E. (1993). *The wisdom of the ego.* Cambridge, MA: Harvard University Press.

Waldfogel, D., & Rosenblatt, A. (1983). *Handbook of clinical social work.* San Francisco: Jossey-Bass.

White, R. W. (1963). *Ego and reality in psychoanalytic theory.* New York: International Universities Press.

Wine, J. D. (1981). From defect to competence models. In J. D. Wine and M. D. Smye (Eds.), *Social competence* (pp. 3–35). New York: Guilford.

Wintersteen, R. T. (1986). Rehabilitating the chronically mentally ill: Social work's claim to leadership. *Social Work, 31*(5), 332–337.

Wolfensberger, W. (1972). *Normalization: The principle of normalization in human services.* Toronto: National Institute on Mental Retardation.

24

Mourning and Loss: A Life Cycle Perspective

Margaret O'Kane Brunhofer

Loss and mourning are universal human experiences, integral to the human condition. Movement through the life cycle naturally involves substantial change and separation, loss of what was and adaptation to what is. Individuals and families are continually confronted with new life experiences, developmental tasks, and life cycle alterations that require adjustment to loss. Sometimes the loss is through death or loss of health, while others losses involve change in role, status, or life circumstance. All transitions over the life cycle pose some degree of loss, either real or symbolic. Children lose the illusions of childhood as they develop and grow into adolescence. Young adults lose the security of their family of origin as they move toward increased reliance on themselves. Young couples experiencing parenthood lose the personal freedom they enjoyed during their single years. Midlife adults lose the family unit, as they once knew it, as their children grow and leave the family home. Later-life adults lose their mate, their occupational role, and ultimately their health. Indeed, the longer we live, the greater the number of losses we sustain and the more we must mourn.

We are not usually aware of the loss and mourning dynamics associated with life transitions. Typically we conceive of loss and mourning as reactions to death, a taboo subject in U.S. society. Neimeyer (1988) used the term *death anxiety* to describe the typical reactions to the issues of death and dying in our society. He suggests that death anxiety is the fear of one's own death and of others and that this anxiety inhibits our ability to cope with the final phase of life. Kamerman (1988) noted our characteristic responses to death as indexes of death anxiety. In our culture, we seclude the dying, allowing most of them to die in hospitals, away from family and friends. We employ professionals, funeral directors, to make the corpse appear lifelike. Our death rituals commence immediately, so we can dispose of the body quickly. If we talk about death, we typically use euphemisms, saying one has "passed away" or "gone to a better place." This allows us to avoid the reality of death.

We frequently deny the dying person the opportunity to acknowledge the awareness of their own death. We also avoid discussion of their reactions to the dying process. As for those left behind, the bereaved, we discourage the outward expression of their emotion and equate a good reaction to the loss as a composed, stoic one. The mourner is expected to manage a brief transition period between the death ritual and daily routine. Finally, the mourner is not expected to dwell on the death or to mention the loss.

Individuals and families must confront loss and mourning experiences within a death-denying ecological context. Since we have difficulty acknowledging loss through death, other types of losses are often not acknowledged. Recognition of the loss by those who provide support and comfort is necessary to resolve and adapt to loss. Otherwise mourners may have significant difficulty grieving and resolving their loss.

Mourning, the period following loss, is characterized by varying degrees of painful grieving and a range of intense emotions: feelings of shock, panic, anxiety, sadness, and anger, among others. Working through these feelings is the task of the mourning process. The mourner must accept and resolve the loss and adapt to a changed life.

Social workers invariably work with clients coping with loss. Some losses are identified by clients, while others are unarticulated and unresolved. All loss experiences influence the psychosocial functioning of the individual and the family. For effective practice, social workers need an awareness of the range of experiences across the life cycle that involve a loss. Practitioners also need to understand the characteristics of the mourning process and methods for facilitating the grief reactions of individuals and families.

ATTACHMENT AND LOSS

The Concept of Attachment

Attachment theory provides a useful framework for understanding the concept of loss. Bowlby (1980), a British psychiatrist and psychoanalyst, is well known for his research and writings on attachment theory. Bowlby studied human separation and loss and developed a theory of attachment. He believed attachment resulted from our human need for safety and security, both required to support our physical and psychological development. Bowlby noted the enduring affectional bonds associated with significant relationships. Motivation to maintain proximity to those who show concern for us is characteristic of these "affectional relations." When the attachments are threatened or lost, intense feelings of distress result. Bowlby (1973) identified universal responses to the loss of or disruption to the focus of our attachment. Anger, protest, depression, anxiety, and eventual detachment are the emotions typically associated with separation. The resolution of a loss can occur once the subject is able to modify his or her internal world, concede that the external world has changed, and redirect attachment behavior to others in the environment.

The Concept of Loss

Loss is experienced at all stages of the individual and family life cycles. It is understood and resolved in differing ways, dependent on many factors. Personality, age and life stage, social support, previous loss experiences, and circumstances related to the loss will influence the mourner's experience. The nature of the loss, its symbolic meaning to the mourner, whether it is expected or unexpected, normative or nonnormative, are important factors contributing to the loss experience (Walsh & McGoldrick, 1991).

Rando (1984, 1993) categorized loss as comprising physical losses and psychosocial losses. Physical losses are tangible losses, including persons or objects evident to others—for example, the death of a loved one or cherished belongings. Psychosocial losses are symbolic, intangible losses not necessarily evident to others—for examples, one's child leaving home or immigration to a new country. Positive life events may also involve a symbolic loss. Chemically dependent individuals, new to recovery programs, must confront the loss of their former lifestyle and the chemical that formerly played a significant role in their everyday life.

Physical losses are more frequently acknowledged by others, whereas symbolic losses are less often understood. As a result, they may not be viewed by others as legitimate loss experiences. Mourners coping with these kinds of losses may gain little support or understanding from others.

The timing of the loss in the life cycle and the opportunity to prepare for a loss are significant factors affecting the experience. An expected, normative loss is the death of one's parents, inasmuch as children generally outlive their parents. The normative timing of such a loss is thought to be during one's adult years. If the death occurs earlier in the life cycle, it is viewed as a nonnormative loss because it occurs unexpectedly relative to time. An example of an unexpected loss would be the diagnosis of a chronic illness during the young adult years, a period when one expects to enjoy good health. This type of loss is viewed as nonnormative as well. Each of these experiences results in a loss and mourning reaction.

Every loss causes a degree of disruption and pain in our lives, but the more profound the loss is, the more intense are the disruption and the affective reaction. O'Connor (1984) proposed a "circle of loss" as a model to outline the relationship of the threat of the loss to oneself. Factors that contribute to the significance of the loss are the intensity of emotional pain and the upheaval associated with the loss. The most painful losses are those associated with our own physical status, and these are represented in the model as the core of the circle. Losses of health or a body part are the most significant and are associated with the most intense mourning reactions. Social workers can expect that individuals who have been informed of a terminal illness or a chronic health condition will confront an acute loss of self and experience severe anguish. The next ring in the circle of loss is loss associated with the separation from significant others, such as abandonment by an important person, the loss of a parent, the death of a spouse, or marital dissolution. Clients confronting abandonment, widowhood, parental death, or divorce experience a significant grief response.

Life experiences that require adjustment to our ways of living are included in the third ring. Examples are the loss of special acquaintances and retirement. When working with clients who have recently relocated to a new city or who leave the workforce, social workers should appreciate the losses and grief work clients need to address.

The fourth and outer ring of the circle involves the loss of desired opportunities, lost objects, and changes in one's social network. An individual dealing with a rejection from a desired school program or the emotional sequelae of a home burglary are examples. O'Connor (1984) suggests that every significant loss is experienced as a loss of oneself and as an end. As a result, loss threatens our sense of survival, always causing some disruption in our lives.

DYNAMICS OF MOURNING AND GRIEF

Mourning and Grief in Individuals

An understanding of loss and its impact on psychological functioning has been provided by Freud in his classic paper, "Mourning and Melancholia" (1917, 1957). Freud described the psychological dynamics of object loss, the loss of a loved one. Mourning results from this loss and is characterized by distinct differences in one's usual behavior and psychological functioning. The mourner experiences considerable psychic pain, in varying degrees, throughout the bereavement period and must expend considerable time and energy to incorporate the reality of the loss. Typical reactions to loss result in dejection, withdrawal, and disinterest in one's world for a period following the loss. In the classic psychoanalytic perspective, the work of mourning is completed "bit by bit," and resolution of the loss occurs only after the bereaved individual successfully withdraws the libidinal energy attached to the loved object. Freud noted that denial of the loss may result in a "hallucinatory wish psychosis," a form of incomplete mourning whereby object decathexis is unresolved. Freud's observations have been developed by others (e.g., Abraham) who have studied individuals coping with loss.

Lindemann (1944) was one of the first researchers to investigate grief reactions. He studied the reactions of victims of the Coconut Grove fire in Boston. From his research, he identified the typical and atypical physical and psychological reactions to loss. He described the process of grief and mourning reactions and proposed that the grief response comprises a definite syndrome. Lindemann (1944) proposed three important tasks that must be addressed to resolve the loss successfully. Initially, one must detach oneself from the loved one or the loss. This involves emancipating oneself from the attachment to the loss. While not expected to forget the loved one, one must divest the emotional energy that is bound up in the attachment. The next task of grief requires a readjustment and environmental accommodation to loss. For a recent widow, this typically requires a redefinition of identity. The widow or widower must begin to experience himself or herself as a "me" rather than a "we." Developing new relationships is the focus of the third task. Bereaved individuals must now invest their energies into other important relationships and develop a means for incorporating the memory of the loss into their current lives.

Intense feelings of distress and painful emotions are associated with the mourning period. Somatic symptoms (e.g., gastric distress), respiratory disturbances (sighing), fatigue, and mental distress are all experienced. One may have difficulty eating and sleeping, and may speak of having a "heavy heart" and of feeling mental anguish. Shock and disbelief are common reactions. Grieving individuals may report they cannot believe the loss has occurred. Feelings of guilt are present, with the bereaved examining their behavior to decide if through commission or omission they somehow contributed to the occurrence of the loss. Irritability and anger are characteristic, along with difficulties in expressing warmth and appreciation to those who attempt to provide comfort to the bereaved.

Normal Grief and Mourning Reactions

Due to the range and intensity of emotions experienced by the bereaved, grief reactions are both physically and psychologically taxing. Rando (1984) suggests "grief is work," with physical and emotional strain. She described the psychological reactions to grief and proposed three phases: avoidance, confrontation, and reestablishment. Rando stressed that grief responses do not progress in stages in an orderly, linear fashion, but may be seen in varying intensity over the course of the mourning period.

Mourners in the avoidance phase experience shock and numbness as they attempt to acknowledge that a significant loss has occurred. Individuals usually respond with disbelief, experiencing confusion and an inability to act. They may seem dazed and deny the significance of the loss. One client reported a sense of disbelief, that "this cannot be happening" when informed by doctors that her child had been diagnosed with a progressive muscle disease that usually resulted in death during the teenage years. These feelings of disbelief may be present for days or weeks following the loss and are often prominent during the period when the bereaved's support network initially offers emotional support and comfort. The numbness may be mistaken for "doing well" in accepting the loss or "holding up." In reality, these emotions comprise the initial psychological reaction to the trauma that the bereaved are not yet able to incorporate.

The confrontation phase is characterized by intense and painful emotions. Panic and extreme anxiety are felt as the numbness wears off and restlessness and irritability are often experienced. Mourners may report anguish and despair. As the reality of the loss is incorporated, depressive affect is common, with characteristic feelings of hopelessness, helplessness, and sadness. A profound yearning and pining for the deceased may be felt, sometimes followed by frantic efforts to search for and recover the deceased. Anger may be present and may be displaced onto others. In a death, the caregivers to the deceased or the deceased himself or herself may be the focus of the anger. Pollock (1961) noted mourners may express hostility toward the professionals (e.g., medical staff, funeral personnel, clergy) who attend to the deceased. In one treatment session, a recently widowed woman reported to the social worker that she was feeling intense anger toward her recently deceased husband. She felt that he had abandoned her at a very difficult time in their lives, leaving her to cope with the difficulties their children had been presenting to them. Guilt reactions may also be present, often triggered by the disagreements and ambivalent feelings the bereaved may recall having for the departed one.

During this phase, mourners have difficulty concentrating and are distractible due to the emotional and physical energy that is bound up in the grief work. Behavioral manifestations of grief may include decreased energy and extreme fatigue. Mourners may have sleep difficulties and experience vivid dreams of the deceased. Changes in normal eating patterns, difficulty experiencing pleasure in daily activities, and periods of intense crying and sobbing may also be reported.

Rando (1993) describes the subsequent, temporary upsurges of grief (STUG) responses that mourners often experience. These are sudden, brief episodes of intense emotional reactions mourners may feel as they attempt to manage their daily activities. A client described an experience in the grocery store when she came across her recently deceased husband's favorite cereal on the grocery shelf. She began to cry uncontrollably, fleeing the store and feeling confused and embarrassed. Another client who had delivered a stillborn infant five years earlier described the anguish she felt when her neighbor, pregnant at the same time, described her own daughter's first day at kindergarten. The client was reminded of her own dead infant and her unrealized hopes and dreams for the child. These reactions are examples of STUG responses.

Mourners often have difficulty initiating social activity and requesting emotional support from significant others while experiencing these emotions. Their social withdrawal should not be interpreted as a desire to be left alone. They need the attention and comfort of others to cope successfully with their emotional distress. The bereaved often feel they lack control and are confused and frightened by the range and intensity of the emotions that surface during the mourning period.

The reestablishment phase, the third and final phase, is characterized by the gradual return to one's interests and social involvements. Psychological distress is less intense and less frequent. The mourner is now able to invest energy and interest in new relationships and experiences. Acceptance of the loss occurs, culminating in the establishment of a satisfactory method for remembering the deceased and the gradual adaptation to the changes that the loss has effected.

Many factors influence grief reactions. The expected or sudden nature of the loss has an impact on the mourner's experience. Expected losses are often accompanied by some anticipatory grieving. While such individuals do have the opportunity to prepare psychologically for the loss, their grief reactions are nonetheless painful since the actual loss must still be mourned. When a loss is expected, individuals have the opportunity to address unresolved issues in the relationship and to say goodbye. This provides for some degree of closure and the resolution of unresolved aspects of the relationship.

Sudden losses are often followed by an intense experience of shock and disbelief. The mourner must cope with an unanticipated loss and feels considerable confusion and denial. The avoidance phase is often longer and replete with intense emotions and disorganization. Since there has not been an opportunity to prepare for the loss and consider needed adaptations in one's life, mourners initially require more support. A client whose husband abruptly left her and her three children reported her difficulty believing her husband was not returning home. She continued to prepare the family dinner, setting a table for five family members for several months, until she could acknowledge that her husband was gone and that she would have to alter her usual daily routine.

Dynamics of Grief and Mourning in Families

Loss in families, particularly loss through death, is experienced uniquely by each family member. Factors such as age, gender, and role function in the family will affect an individual's response. Family members often differ in the range and intensity of emotional responses. The length of time needed to accept and resolve the loss is also related to one's coping methods and the survivor's unique relationship with the deceased (Walsh & McGoldrick, 1991).

A major family task following a loss is for the family to give permission to its members to mourn openly. Bowen (1976) has stressed the importance of family communication following a loss. Families that allow for open, reciprocal communication and the freedom to express their thoughts and feelings are better able to grieve. Bowen suggests that closed or fused family systems—those that block communication—are vulnerable to long-term dysfunction following a death. Fused family systems often experience an "emotional shock wave" or ". . . a network of underground 'after shocks' of serious life events that can occur anywhere in the extended family system in the months and years following serious emotional events in the family" (Bowen, 1976, p. 339). These long-term sequelae often hamper role functioning and interpersonal relations in and outside the family system, and influence relationships across generations.

While communication patterns and tolerance for differences in the mourning process support healthy adaptation to loss, other factors also influence the family's response and adjustment to loss. Death in the family represents the loss of important relationships. The nature of the family's grief reaction to this loss is influenced by how and when the family relationship was lost. The expected or sudden occurrence of death in the family is a significant factor to consider. The role held by the deceased family member also has an important impact on the survivors (Worden, 1991).

The nature of death, whether expected or unexpected, has ramifications for the family. Expected deaths that follow terminal illness can cause emotional and financial strain on the family. Anticipatory grief responses, or grieving before the death, may result in emotional distancing from the terminally ill family member. To protect one another from painful emotions, family members may become detached and remote. Expected deaths do allow the family to prepare for the loss and provide time to discuss unresolved relationship issues, along with an opportunity to say goodbye. Conversely, sudden death in the family does not allow for any preparation or for time to finish unfinished business, and it is characterized by intense emotional distress. It is not unusual to see long-term negative effects following sudden deaths in families (Herz, 1980). If violence was associated with the death, the grief response can be exacerbated (Walsh & McGoldrick, 1991).

Certain illnesses (e.g., AIDS) can influence the family's mourning. The stigma associated with the cause of death may reinforce feelings of shame and guilt in family members and result in abbreviated death rituals and mourning responses. Death from suicide may cause overwhelming, intense reactions in family members; bewilderment and disbelief, along with anger and guilt, are often paramount as families try to search for clues to the death. Blame and scapegoating of family members may result. Families may not receive adequate support as friends and acquaintances may feel significant discomfort in acknowledging the loss. It is not unusual for chronic anxiety and a sense of insecurity to follow sudden death as families learn that a catastrophe can occur without warning (Rando, 1984).

Just as the timing of a loss affects the individual's mourning experience, the expected or untimely loss of a family member also has implications for future family functioning. Death is usually associated with and expected during the later stages of the family life cycle, and a lesser degree of family stress is related to such deaths. Death at early life stages is considered nonnormative because the life cycle has been interrupted. Prolonged mourning responses may follow untimely death at which survivor guilt may frequently be present (Walsh & McGoldrick, 1991).

The role status of the deceased family member is another important dynamic in family adaption to the loss. The more pivotal the role of the deceased family member within the family unit, the more difficulty the surviving family members will experience following the death. Both the functions of the deceased member's role in the family and the level of emotional dependence on that family member will influence the reactions to the loss (Herz, 1980). If the roles assigned to the deceased were pivotal to the family's functioning (e.g., wage earner) reorganization of the family system will be more difficult. Vess, Moreland, and Schwebel (1985, 1986) suggest that "child-present" families will experience more stress than "child-absent" families because child-rearing demands and economic issues will tax the family system.

Unresolved Loss and Grief

Social workers frequently work with individuals and families who are having difficulty coping with loss. Many losses are unacknowledged and unresolved, never grieved by the mourner. Social and psychological factors can contribute to such losses, resulting, at times, in complicated grief reactions.

Lindemann (1944) described pathological grief reactions as those that distorted the normal grief response. Delayed grief reactions are those characterized by no apparent emotional response to the loss.

> *A fifteen-year-old girl was brought for treatment by her mother who was concerned with serious parent-child conflict in the home. The girl reported that her father had been killed six months earlier in a car crash. When the social worker asked the fifteen year old about the death, the girl reported the details of her father's accident, expressing little*

emotion. She said that her friends seemed to feel more sadness about her father's death than she did. During treatment, she was able to acknowledge that she felt the need to take care of her mother during the months following her father's death. She believed her mother was devastated by the loss and required her support and therefore denied the expression of her own feelings and reactions in order to protect her mother from additional strain.

In this case, the daughter had not been able to express her own grief over the loss of her father. Later, when her mother was better able to manage her own grief, the daughter was finally able to grieve her father's death, a response that she had suppressed for some time.

Distorted grief can include exaggerated grief responses where the mourner's excessive reactions may begin to interfere significantly with daily functioning (Rando, 1993). Such individuals may experience disabling panic attacks or profound despair.

A forty-two-year-old client reported to her social worker that she could barely leave her bed in the morning since her divorce five months earlier. Most days she arrived at her job several hours late. On the weekends, she stayed in bed all day and through the night. While family and friends were calling her and encouraging her to spend time with them, she consistently refused their support and became quite angry with them. She cried for hours each day, ate little, and had ruminative thoughts of her former spouse.

This client's behavior suggests a distorted grief response. The client was unable to manage her life activities and expressed hopelessness and deep despair. After assessing the degree of her depression, the social worker referred her for a psychiatric evaluation. Once the client began to take the prescribed antidepressant medication and became more functional, treatment focused on discussing the loss and the pain the client had experienced with the failure of her marriage.

Chronic grief reactions are marked by a prolonged mourning period. Grief is experienced for a lengthy period without a lessening of the intensity and range of emotions seen during the initial months following the loss (Rando, 1993). Parents coping with a child with disabilities or an adult child with chronic mental illness often experience chronic grief as they arrive at the realization that their hopes and dreams for their child will never be fulfilled.

Facilitating Grief

Facilitating grief reactions and helping individuals cope with loss requires an active involvement with the bereaved. The clinician must be a nonjudgmental listener and be able to appreciate that the client will express intense, painful affects. Genuine concern for the bereaved should be expressed, acknowledging the significance of the loss to them. Social workers should not minimize the importance of the loss or suggest that the loss is minor compared to what others have experienced. At times, clients try to minimize their own losses as a way to escape the pain associated with loss. As with all other clinical situations, social workers should attempt to remain empathically attuned to the client, always endeavoring to understand the client's unique perspective of the loss. Practitioners should never propose their own philosophical or religious understandings as methods to resolve the loss (Rando, 1993). Respect for the mourner's philosophical or belief system and his or her beliefs regarding life after death, future reunions, and so on can provide the mourner with a sense of peace and inner comfort.

Worden (1991) proposed ten principles to guide treatment with the bereaved. These principles provide a broad framework for social workers engaged in grief therapy and include interventions focused on education, habilitation, rehabilitation, and maintenance of social functioning. In the beginning stages of treatment, the social worker should emphasize that the loss actually happened. Discussion of the loss with the bereaved helps to actualize this reality. Educating the bereaved and the bereaved's support network about the grief process early in the treatment is useful and may need to be repeated at other points in the therapy. The range and intensity of feelings experienced by grievers are often confusing and overwhelming. Mourners often report they "feel crazy," are flooded with thoughts and feelings about the loss, and feel unable to cope with daily life as they had prior to the loss. Mourners profit from learning that the grief process is characterized by many intense emotions and with preoccupation over the loss, factors that can undermine their usual coping capacities. Learning that these feelings will diminish in intensity and range over the course of the mourning period can assuage the mourner's anxiety about loss of control and ineffective coping.

The clinician must also acknowledge the likelihood of differences in grieving styles. Individuals cope with their grief in varying ways. These differences are especially true for men and women (Rando, 1986). The clinician's respect for these differences and acknowledgment of their normality is important.

> *The mother of a recently deceased eight-month-old infant described her frustration with her husband. He seemed to have resolved his feelings within several months of the infant's sudden death. The wife, however, believed that her husband should have been as preoccupied and despairing as she continued to feel. Discussion of gender differences helped her to accept the differences between her husband's and her own style of grieving. She noted her husband's tendency to spend considerable time at his basement work bench, fixing broken appliances and toys, as his unique method for dealing with his feelings of loss. She came to understand this behavior as representing his efforts to "make things right for the family."*

Bereaved individuals need the involvement of a supportive network. They require others to listen to them verbalize their thoughts and feelings about their loss. Clinicians should help the bereaved to clarify their thoughts and feelings and allow for the ventilation of ambivalence, anger, and guilt associated with the deceased. Particular attention should be given to the individual's anxiety and sense of helplessness. The bereaved often require assistance to manage life without the deceased. Feelings of sadness and despair must also be discussed and related to the meaning of what has been lost.

The social worker should support the coping capacities of the bereaved to further the management of their daily lives and help mourners to clarify how the roles and responsibilities assumed by the deceased can now be managed. Because bereaved individuals are experiencing considerable emotional distress, they can benefit from assistance in problem solving. They may require help with certain decisions, which is most usefully approached by clarifying issues that require resolution.

The provision of active, ongoing support to the bereaved is a critical aspect of the treatment. This is particularly important during the first year following the loss. Holiday times, special family occasions, and the anniversary of the loss are critical times to contact the bereaved and to offer comfort to them. Throughout the treatment process, the social worker should clarify both adaptive and nonadaptive coping patterns. The use of alcohol and drugs during the mourning period can interfere significantly with grieving, since these substances numb feelings and provide an escape from the pain of the loss. Assessment of the mourner's use of alcohol and drugs should be done routinely. Along with this, behavior that complicates the normal process of mourning and potentially leads to pathological grief reactions should be identified and assessed. Clinicians should clarify earlier losses that the mourner has experienced and the methods used to resolve these prior losses.

A critical aspect of grief resolution requires the bereaved to divest the emotional energy focused on the deceased and begin to invest in new relationships. This constitutes the major therapeutic goal of the treatment. Bereaved individuals need the freedom to engage in other relationships, without feeling disloyal to the deceased loved one, a process that takes considerable time. The social worker must also appreciate the griever's need to have sufficient time to mourn a loss and identify ways to commemorate the loss. For some individuals, depending on the nature of their loss, grief resolution may require up to two, three, or more years before resolution has been achieved.

These principles provide a broad overview of the factors that social workers engaged in grief counseling should consider in their work. Offering some understanding of the behavior of significant others can also be therapeutic. Mourners report a range of reactions from their support network, from consistent concern and interest to a pretense that nothing significant has occurred. Family and friends who are silent about the loss rarely appreciate the message the mourner may infer from their silence. Mourners may feel that others are insensitive to their feelings and needs or are unwilling to extend themselves. Hearing that others are often unaware of the needs of the bereaved or are uncomfortable expressing their own feelings of loss can assist the bereaved to understand the behavior of others better.

Social workers should be particularly sensitive to the feelings of mourners during the termination phase of treatment. Termination represents loss of the therapist and the therapeutic relationship and involves further grief work. Since this additional loss may be difficult for the mourner to manage, termination should be well planned and openly discussed.

Transference and Countertransference Considerations

Clinical work with mourners is demanding and may be stressful. Since clinicians often see themselves as helpers and gain gratification from this role, they may have difficulty dealing with their own powerlessness in helping mourners. Therapists experience a range of intense, painful affects in mourners. They cannot alter the mourner's circumstances or assuage the mourner's painful feelings. Indeed, such efforts can be detrimental in that they can undermine the therapeutic work.

Rando (1993) refers to the changes that may occur in the therapists' "assumptive world" as she or he witnesses the trauma of mourners. The death and loss experience of mourners can arouse significant anxiety in therapists and heighten their own sense of vulnerability. Clinicians may also be reminded of their own losses when engaged in grief therapy. Those who have unresolved losses or who experience concurrent loss may experience difficulty in helping mourners.

The management of transference and countertransference reactions may be difficult for clinicians engaged in grief therapy. The clinician may experience intense emotional reactions to the content, the affect, and the process of the mourner's therapeutic work. Mourners may express a range of intense emotions during the confrontation phase of grief work. Therapists may feel frustration, anger, and hopelessness in reaction to the mourner's feelings and to the repetitive nature of the material discussed by the mourner. They may attempt to thwart the expression of the mourner's feelings or minimize the significance of the loss to guard against the mourner's grief reactions. Clinicians should monitor and examine their reactions to the mourner to further the therapeutic process. Clinical supervision and peer support can provide good opportunities for this examination.

Grief Therapy with Families

Families might not enter treatment with unresolved mourning as their presenting concern, but it may be uncovered during the diagnostic process as one dynamic impeding healthy family functioning. Once uncovered, the major focus of the initial therapeutic work should be sanctioning the grief of the family. Fulmer (1983) suggested that therapists should support enactment of the grief feelings and provide education about the mourning process to help normalize the feelings of the family members. The social worker should be active in the sessions, clarifying whether family interactions are meant to support or suppress the expression of grief.

Stierlin, Rucker-Emblen, Weitzel, and Winsching (1980) and Worden (1991) suggest that therapists should note dates and causes of death in the multigenerational family system during the early phases of treatment. The use of a genogram (see Chapter 1) facilitates this process (Walsh & McGoldrick, 1991). Other significant events in the family (e.g., births, relocation) should be noted since they can directly influence the family's movement through the mourning process (Walsh, 1978). These connections should be examined once the therapeutic alliance has been developed. Clarification of the roles played by the deceased family member and how they are currently being filled should also be included in the assessment process. Renegotiation of role assignment may be one aspect of the therapeutic work. Alliances and triangles in the family system should also be examined. At times one family member may be the focus of the unresolved feelings the family carries for the deceased member (Worden, 1991).

To uncover unresolved family issues related to the death, the therapist must engage the family in a direct and open discussion of the deceased, exploring miscommunications and misperceptions. The therapist must be comfortable with the subject of death and assume a calm, nonreactive posture. Hare-Mustin (1979) and Bowen (1976) suggested that the therapist must not collude with the family by avoiding the painful topic of death or by using euphemisms that reinforce the taboo of death. In family meetings, the therapist should raise the family's awareness of communication patterns and relationship strains that have resulted from the death. Dysfunctional patterns of behavior can be reframed as methods that family members use to protect one another from their pain (Fulmer, 1983). The therapist should expect frequent resistance to opening the channels of communication but should nevertheless persist with open discussion.

Paul and Grasser (1991) proposed that treatment should provide a "corrective mourning experience" (p. 96). They suggested that therapists should ask direct questions about the loss. This approach can activate mourning by encouraging family members to reminisce, express feelings, and empathize with one another. Such a therapeutic approach can also influence the disequilibrium in the family and result in better understanding, communication, and a new level of emotional closeness.

When working with families who have young children, the use of family drawings can also be a valuable tool in treatment (Schumacher, 1984). Asking the family to draw a picture of the family before and following the death may enhance an understanding of the impact of the death on the family unit. This technique can be particularly useful for children since their drawings often communicate alliances and feelings among family members. Herz (1980) suggests that therapists be sensitive to "side shows," or behavior that is symptomatic of unresolved loss. Separate sessions with parents may allow the unfolding of toxic issues and lessen the frequency of side shows. Such opportunities may also help the therapist to gain an understanding of the parents' perception of the children's adaptation to the loss and the degree of shame and guilt that the parents may themselves be experiencing. Normalizing such feelings of guilt for the parents can be useful, since they often view it as pathological (Miles & Demi, 1991–1992). Separate sessions with the children can provide an opportunity to explore feelings and issues openly that children fear may upset their parents. In a case where a child has died, it is important to allow siblings the opportunity to explore guilt they may experience in surviving the sibling's death. Attention to fantasies about causing the sibling's death and fears about their own mortality should be carefully explored. Using therapeutic play activities for children under age eleven can permit the child to enact and ultimately to resolve ambivalent feelings experienced toward the deceased family member (Baker, Sedney, & Gross, 1992).

Prescribing rituals can be another useful and powerful therapeutic tool in family treatment (Imber-Black, 1991). Rituals give the family a shared activity where open emotional expression and support are encouraged, permitting the family to acknowledge their loss publicly. Such rituals are particularly useful on holidays and anniversaries of the death or birth of the deceased family member. "Besides helping to resolve contradictions, face anxiety, and strong emotions, rituals support transitions" (Imber-Black, Roberts, & Whiting, 1988, p. 19).

If rituals were not held at the time of death, the therapist can help the family in structuring a farewell ritual. This can allow the family to acknowledge their loss, reminisce, and move on. Therapists can assist families to create their own unique rituals by emphasizing the need for innovation and flexibility (Imber-Black, 1991). Looking at a family picture or visiting the grave site as a family unit may have meaning for the family and support grief resolution (Fulmer, 1983).

Hare-Mustin (1979) has issued a warning to therapists who take on family grief work. She suggests that therapists need to resolve their own unfinished business, their unresolved mourning experiences. In other words, to be effective, therapists must deal with their own death anxiety and the multiple losses they have experienced during their lifetimes.

Grief Therapy with Groups

Various forms of group treatment can be useful for certain mourners. For individuals with limited support networks, groups offer the opportunity to share feelings and concerns with other grievers and identify methods for resolving the loss. Videka-Sherman (1982) studied the role of support group membership for bereaved parents. Her findings supported the value of self-help groups for parents coping with a child's death. Involvement with bereavement support groups, available in many communities, may provide grievers with an important adjunct to individual or family grief counseling.

As with all treatment groups, it is essential to screen members to determine their appropriateness for group intervention. Groups composed of grievers who have sustained similar losses are most beneficial (Piper, McCallum, & Hassan, 1992). Group cohesion and therapeutic progression result from the sense of "universality" members experience in a group (Yalom, 1985).

The timing of the griever's involvement in a group is another factor to consider. Group membership is useful during the confrontation phase when grievers have acknowledged that a loss has occurred and are more able to cope with their distress.

OVERVIEW OF LIFE CYCLE LOSSES

Loss, both tangible and psychosocial, occurs throughout the life cycle. When the loss involves the death of a family member early in the life cycle, it can be more difficult to resolve. We consider such early deaths unnatural, denying individuals their expected long lives (Walsh & McGoldrick, 1991). Loss in the later years is considered normative; indeed, anyone who lives long enough confronts many substantial losses.

Childhood Losses

Loss experiences are understood and resolved differently, depending in part on one's age and life stage. Children have differing capacities to understand and to cope with loss compared to adults, and they are more dependent on adults to grieve their losses. Children's loss experiences are less understood and are frequently unacknowledged (Doka, 1989). However, children must cope with a range of losses beginning in their early years. As they develop and are expected to behave in more adult ways, children are confronted with tangible losses, such as their favorite blanket or other transitional object. They may have to cope with the death of a pet, or a move to a new home and the concomitant loss of neighborhood friends and the security of their school and teachers. The death of a parent or grandparent, or separation from a parent following a parental divorce is a significant, tangible loss that children increasingly encounter. Entering the foster care system represents substantial loss to children as they cope with the loss of their parents and, sometimes, of their siblings, and much else that was familiar to them in their daily lives. Even with normal life events, such as the birth of a sibling, children confront the loss of parental time and attention as these important commodities come to be shared with the newborn.

When working with children who are coping with loss, social workers can begin by acknowledging the loss and the feelings associated with it, both to the child and the child's parents. Parents may have a limited appreciation of the child's experience of the loss and the underlying dynamics the loss represents. Educating parents about the child's capacity to understand the concept of loss is an essential part of the treatment. In her study of childhood bereavement, Furman (1974) noted the value of parental discussions with the child about death and loss. Such acknowledgment and responsiveness to the children's feelings about the loss were believed to help them grieve their current loss as well as significant losses that occurred in their later years.

Children's age and level of cognitive functioning will influence their understanding and response to loss (Waas & Stillion, 1988). Infants and toddlers are incapable of a cognitive understanding of the concepts of death and loss, yet they may have acute awareness of separation from important adults in their lives and respond with distress when these adults are unavailable. From ages three to five, children are unable to comprehend the finality of death, viewing it as a reversible event, like sleep or being away on a trip. For these reasons, phrases such as "final rest" or "gone to a better place" are of little use when explaining death to young children and can actually be damaging. The child may begin to develop a fear of going to sleep or being separated even briefly from parents. Providing the child with honest, concrete details of the death and reassurance of continued parental support in dealing with the loss are useful interventions. Around ages five to nine, children are better able to understand the finality of death but will have difficulty relating it to themselves and to important people in their lives. At this age, they are also better able to understand causative factors contributing to death and have an awareness that serious illness or old age increases the likelihood of death.

Along with their differing cognitive capacities for understanding death and loss, children's grief responses also differ. Children frequently manifest their grief through behavioral expression rather than through verbal discussion. Physical aggression, overactivity, clinging behavior, and detachment from previously enjoyed activities may serve as expressions of grief. Frequent crying, sleep difficulties, and nightmares may also be noted. School-age children may develop academic difficulties when, in consequence of their grief, they become distracted and less able to concentrate on their school work.

An eleven-year-old girl had recently been hospitalized on the pediatric unit, complaining of severe stomach pain. Extensive medical testing could not identify a physiological basis for her complaints. The psychosocial assessment completed by the hospital social worker identified the recent death of her aunt as a precipitant to her physical complaints. Medical staff determined that her condition was psychosomatic and referred her to the social worker. After completing a comprehensive assessment of the girl with her mother, other symptoms of the child's grief were noted. She was having difficulty sleeping and had frequent nightmares. She was clinging to her mother and often attempted to stay home from school. Her parents were particularly worried about their daughter's condition. They had been planning a special weekend away from home in several months, and they believed their daughter might have considerable difficulty coping with their absence.

The death of this child's maternal aunt was the first significant loss she had experienced. She was particularly close to her aunt and had spent considerable time with her. The aunt was several years younger than the child's mother and had been ill for a brief time before her death. The eleven year old had not been included in the family's death rituals, and they had provided little explanation to her about the specifics of her aunt's condition, either before or following the death. The hospital social worker believed that the aunt's death had triggered the girl's fears of losing her own parents.

Treatment focused on work with this child and her parents. The parents were advised to begin to discuss the details of the aunt's death with their daughter, allowing her to ask whatever questions she might have regarding her aunt's condition. They were also advised to reminisce about the times their child had spent with her aunt and to share their own feelings of loss with their daughter. The social worker recommended that the child visit her aunt's grave site. Children's books about death and loss were suggested as another vehicle to permit the child to acknowledge the loss and feelings natural to the grief process. Individual play sessions augmented by discussion helped the child to express her confusion about the loss. The therapist also encouraged the child to express her conflictive feelings about separation from her parents and further encouraged her to talk with her parents about their planned trip. Over a twelve-week period, the child's stomach cramps remitted, she reported that she was sleeping better, and she planned where she would spend the weekend while her parents were away from home. She stayed overnight at a girlfriend's house and reported that she had enjoyed the experience. A final session with the child following her parents' trip revealed she had tolerated their absence well, enjoying the time she spent with a schoolmate's family.

Once the child's grief reaction and fears were acknowledged and addressed, she was able to mourn her aunt's death with the assistance of her parents. The parent's sensitivity to their daughter's separation fears and the comfort that they were then able to provide permitted her to mourn the loss of her aunt and gradually resume her normal activities.

Rando (1984) offers several useful suggestions for adults involved with bereaved children, some of which may also be appropriate for children who must cope with other types of losses. She suggests that adults be open and honest with the child regarding the circumstances of the loss, since this can reduce the child's tendency toward magical thinking. Young children may believe that their thoughts and behavior somehow have contributed to a loss. Providing rational, truthful explanations can dispel these beliefs.

Children should be informed of the reality of the loss soon after it occurs. This lessens the chances of their learning of the loss from someone else. Considerable reassurance and attention from adults will be necessary to assuage the child's sadness and anxiety. The child should also be reassured that his or her needs will continue to be met.

In the case of loss through death, it is important to involve children in memorial services and funeral rituals. Children learn about grief and mourning from the significant adults in their lives. Exclusion from grief rituals is confusing to children and denies them opportunities to receive comfort for their own grief. They are also deprived of the opportunity for ritual closure that such ceremonies offer older family members. Of course, it is important that children be prepared for what they may see at a funeral or memorial service. This allows the child the opportunity to decide if he or she wishes to be involved in the ritual. It is also important that children be provided with ways to remember the deceased, whether through pictures or special objects that can facilitate the process of grief resolution.

Grief reactions in children frequently follow parental divorce. When the custodial parent becomes preoccupied with his or her own grief and new role responsibilities, that parent's ability to attend to the child's needs and to understand the child's behavior may also be diminished.

A four-year-old boy was brought for treatment by his mother, who had recently separated from her husband. The mother expressed concern about the child's increasingly aggressive and oppositional behavior. He was destroying his toys, hitting his younger sibling, and refusing to accept parental limits. Over the four months of play therapy sessions, this child typically focused on the doll house and family figures. He provided a story about the doll family, often re-creating conflicts between the mother and father figures. The social worker offered interpretations of these stories, acknowledging the fear and confusion a child feels when his parents separate. During parent guidance sessions, his mother was helped to understand her son's behavior as an expression of his sadness, confusion, and anger over the separation and approaching divorce. His mother began to talk with the child about his feelings, allowing him to verbalize a range of emotions and to ask questions about what family life would be like following the divorce. The child's father was also seen for several individual sessions. Visitation plans were discussed and explanations for his son's behavior were provided during these sessions. The importance of regular visitation with the father was stressed and both parents were able to develop an amicable plan for visitation. His parents purchased several books about family divorce and frequently read these to their son. The child's behavior began to change as both parents were increasingly able to acknowledge his feelings of loss. His parents provided him a number of opportunities to ask about the changes in family life, and were able to reassure him of their ongoing involvement in his life. Frequent, regular visitation with the father then began and both parents reported improved family interactions.

The loss of daily contact with a parent is a significant loss indeed for a child. Young children often fear abandonment by their custodial parent after a divorce. It is critical that they receive substantial reassurance that the adults in their lives will continue to be available to them (Wallerstein & Kelly, 1980).

Therapeutic work with child grievers should always include work with the parents or significant adults in the child's life. Providing guidance and resources to the parents will help the therapeutic efforts with the child. Many children's books dealing with the themes of death and loss are available (Goldman, 1994).

Clinical work with the child who has lost a sibling presents a significant challenge to the therapist. The death of a child in the family is considered almost universally to be the most devastating loss. In such tragedies, parents lose the hopes and dreams they held for their child, as well as a part of themselves. Hare-Mustin (1979) has noted the sense of emptiness and profound grief reactions that parents experience. Guilt is a common response in parents and may constitute one of the most prominent, intense reactions (Rando, 1986). Parents may feel their behavior, whether through commission or omission, was responsible for the child's death. Parents also experience "recovery guilt" as they begin to work through the mourning process and experience some renewed enjoyment in their lives. Any pleasure may be experienced as a sign of unfaithfulness to the deceased child. One mother whose first baby had died from sudden infant death syndrome noted the guilt she felt upon the birth of her second child. She was ecstatic caring for her newborn, yet felt her feelings reflected a lack of love for her deceased child.

Grief reactions following a child's death are prolonged and complicated for both the parents and the surviving children. The surviving children are often overlooked and their needs unmet as their parents are consumed with their own grief. Surviving children gain a new status, that of a survivor, which can impose a significant hardship for them. Krell and Rabkin (1979) noted a number of maladaptive reactions seen in families following a child's death. A surviving child may try to replace the dead sibling, taking on special attributes of the deceased. "The absent child thus remains in some sense alive, a misbegotten restoration protecting the family from having to fully face their loss" (Krell & Rabkin, 1979, p. 473). This can impede the child's own sense of identity as she or he tries to represent not one but two children to the parents. Such children may become "precious children," bound to the parents who have become vigilant and overprotective. Or they may be "haunted children," who collude in the family's conspiracy of silence, where little is ever said about the deceased child. Family members may suppress details of their child's death and their feelings about the loss when significant guilt and shame are present. These family interaction patterns impede the psychosocial development of the surviving children and the mourning experience for the entire family.

Marital relations are also affected and strained following a child's death. Each partner has had a different relationship with the child, and most likely their methods for coping with the loss will also differ. Gender differences appear to account for the typically greater emotional expressiveness shown by mothers than by fathers over the loss of a child (Bohannon, 1990; Rando, 1986). Miles and Demi (1991–1992) and Rando (1986) suggest that spouses are out of sync with one another, often unable to support the needs of their partner. Over time, however, most couples are able to resume satisfactory marital relations (Bohannon, 1990).

Adolescent Loss

Both tangible and psychosocial losses are experienced during the adolescent period. Tangible losses might include rejection by a romantic interest, exclusion from membership on a desired team or squad, or lack of acceptance by a preferred peer group. Teenagers may lose friends to death, through suicide or homicide. Many psychosocial and symbolic losses are also experienced during this stage. Adolescents are expected to give up their dependencies on their families and take on increased responsibility for themselves. Biological growth results in body image changes, and therefore the loss of the former image of oneself; identity issues require the loss of one's former vision of oneself and an adaptation to a complex, altered understanding of self.

Cognitive development occurring during this period equips adolescents to discern death from other kinds of losses. Death is now conceived of as a final, irreversible event that affects everyone. As a result, when death occurs, adolescents have a heightened awareness of their own mortality. Gender differences in grief work may now be clearly seen, as compared with younger children (Crenshaw, 1990). Social workers should be aware that adolescent males may engage in increased aggressive behaviors and are more likely to use alcohol or drugs to cope with their loss. Females are usually more verbal about their feelings, soliciting attention and consolation from others.

The separation-individuation process may complicate grief reactions for adolescents (Rosen, 1991). Ambivalent feelings experienced toward one another by both adolescents and their parents may result in complicated grief reactions for both the adolescent and the parent. When a death occurs in the family, adolescents may respond in ways that undermine their own developmental needs and tasks. The teenager may adopt a family role as the "perfect child," failing to engage in the challenging and questioning of authority that is so typical of adolescent behavior. Mishne (1992) observes that adolescents often feel rage when a parental death occurs, displacing their rage onto the surviving parent and idealizing the dead parent.

A seventeen-year-old girl complained of significant anxiety and depression. She explained that she lived with her mother who was widowed two years earlier. This teenager had adopted the role of "mother's companion." She rarely engaged in social activities with her peers and instead worked diligently on her academics. She reflected on the pride her father would have felt over her school performance since he had valued education and had saved for her college tuition. When confronted with the sacrifices she had made in her social life, the teenager acknowledged she felt lonely and isolated. Treatment focused on increasing her awareness of her own needs and feelings. Over the course of the treatment, she could acknowledge the anger she felt for her mother, who relied on her for support and companionship. The daughter became better able to disagree with her mother on meaningful issues and increasingly was able to schedule time with friends. She came to recognize the rage she felt with her father for leaving her without his support and for the increased responsibility she had been feeling for her mother since his death.

Adolescent suicide has dramatically increased over the past two decades. Bolton (1986) describes the reaction that parents often experience when a teenage child takes his or her own life. They feel they have failed their child, and this sense of parental failure is magnified further if the suicide is experienced as a rejection or punishment of the parent. These are painful emotions that parents must cope with during the mourning process, and resolution of their grief is generally a long, slow process. Parents must be able to forgive themselves for not being perfect parents, which, in turn, will lessen their guilt feelings. If they can gain a better understanding of the factors that contributed to the hopelessness and despair of their child, then parents may be better able to resolve their own grief. Finally, parents should be encouraged to be open with others about their loss. This openness can help decrease the stigma associated with death by suicide and signal to family and friends the intense grief the parents are experiencing.

Fearing a contagion effect, adults sometimes disregard the adolescent's grief. Social workers should encourage the adults involved with grieving adolescents to discuss these tragedies and to mourn their loss.

A group of seven tenth- and eleventh-grade teenage girls were assessed as high risk for self-destructive behavior following the deaths of two classmates, one a suicide and the other a homicide. The school social worker offered an eight-week grief resolution group to the survivors to support their mourning and reduce the potential for self-destructive sequelae. During the first session, the girls were quiet and listened to the social worker briefly describe the mourning process, acknowledging that the girls were mourning two significant losses. The girls were initially passive, but then became hostile toward the social worker, confronting her with the fact that they believed their families and school personnel were insensitive in refusing to discuss the deaths. In following sessions, the teenagers began to describe their confusion and sadness about their deceased friends and their own feelings of vulnerability. They reminisced about their friends and expressed a range of feelings about their deaths. One session was used to write farewell letters to both friends. A meeting with the girls' parents was scheduled to provide the parents with an understanding of the mourning process, but few parents responded. The social worker admitted to the girls the difficulty that adults often have in dealing with death, particularly when it is violent death. At the last session, the girls expressed their appreciation for having had their feelings acknowledged and for the opportunity to deal with their grief.

Young Adult Losses

Leaving home, choosing an occupational role and a life partner, and becoming a parent are the major normative tasks of young adulthood. In adapting to an adult role and its attendant responsibilities, young adults sustain many real and symbolic losses. Gould (1978) identifies the illusions and false assumptions that must be resolved during the adult years, foremost among which is the symbolic loss of one's parents as providers of safety and security. Young adults are expected to leave the financial security and emotional comfort of their families and to develop increased autonomy and an adult identity. Parents are no longer perceived and experienced as caretakers and rescuers, and childhood dependencies and beliefs regarding parental omnipotence are given up.

Choosing a life partner often entails involvement with several potential love interests. The resulting disappointments and rejections, which are universal, are experienced as both real and symbolic losses. Young adults coping with estranged relationships grieve the loss of their potential companion and the life they had anticipated sharing with their partner. Marriage results in the loss of one's prior identity and requires that self-interest and self-concern be expanded and augmented to include an other. Parenthood demands the individual's adaptation to significant time constraints as well as other major changes in daily activities. Couples confronted with miscarriage, stillbirth, or neonatal death must mourn their lost infant. Those coping with infertility issues must grieve the loss of the ability to conceive a child of their own. Certain chronic illnesses, such as diabetes or rheumatoid arthritis, are initially diagnosed during the young adult years. Young adults so diagnosed must cope with the loss of function, often debilitating, and then begin to make life adjustments to accommodate to a chronic health problem.

It is not infrequent that the unexpected death of a parent or parental divorce occurs during this stage. Multiple changes in family roles, responsibilities, and activities may result from such losses.

A thirty-year-old married woman initiated treatment following the sudden death of her recently divorced mother. She was having difficulty grieving the loss of her mother's death and adapting to her new responsibilities for a disabled sibling, previously cared for by her mother. She reported overwhelming sadness over the loss of her mother, with whom she had a warm and loving relationship. She longed for her mother's companionship and for the guidance and assistance her mother had provided her in raising her own children. Over the course of the treatment, she expressed anger toward her deceased mother, both for leaving her too early and for the increased responsibility that she had inherited for her disabled sibling. The treatment facilitated the expression of these thoughts and feelings and helped her to identify the symbolic losses that had also resulted from her mother's death. Therapy also enabled her to clarify her responsibilities for her sibling and to develop methods for managing these responsibilities. She was eventually able to find a meaningful way of commemorating her mother and to reminisce about her with her own children.

This client had sustained multiple losses when her mother died. Not only had she lost an important relationship, but she also lost her mother's presence in the lives of her own children. With new responsibilities for her sibling, she lost both time and flexibility to attend to her own children's needs.

Couples coping with the death of an infant through miscarriage, stillbirth, or neonatal death often receive minimal support and recognition while mourning their loss (Nichols, 1990). Loss of a child, whatever the age of the child, always represents a loss of self, of one's hopes and dreams for one's offspring. Yet this loss is frequently misunderstood and may be minimized by the couple's support network. When a significant loss is negated by others, complicated mourning may be the result. Couples require an adequate explanation of medical factors that contributed to the loss, acknowledgment of the loss, and support and comfort from family and friends (DeFrain, 1991).

Midlife Losses

During the middle adulthood years, children leave home, causing alterations in family life and in role functioning for midlife parents. Women who have primarily invested their energies in a maternal role lose their primary role identification and may experience this separation from their children as a major calamity. Midlife adults may have limited involvement with their children if these relationships become strained. During this period, midlife couples are faced with more time together so that partners begin to refocus on each other. Divorce sometimes results when couples are unable to negotiate satisfying relations, the result being the loss of one's long-term partner and companion.

Another loss associated with this period is related to time. Midlife adults experience time differently, with more awareness of the finite nature of time, of "time left" (Neugarten, 1976), leading to a heightened awareness of one's mortality. Women face menopause, signifying the end of their childbearing capacities. Disappointments with one's work status and prior expectations for occupational success are often confronted during the middle years (Levinson, 1978). Role loss and identity changes may be the result of forced early retirement or job loss for some midlife workers.

A normal decline in physical stamina and abilities occurs during this period, with some midlife adults experiencing the onset of significant health problems that may require adjustments in lifestyle and lead to changes in the individual's self-image. Frail elderly parents may require care by their midlife children, resulting in the loss of time and freedom. Adaptation to new, more demanding daily routines may be the result, particularly for midlife women.

All of these life changes involve some degree of grief and mourning, as illustrated by the following example.

A forty-three-year-old divorced father of two entered treatment. He had been feeling sad, had little energy, and reported experiencing little enjoyment in his daily life. He could not identify any recent events that triggered his depression. In discussing his situation, he said that he had tense relations with his two young adult children. He had no hope for more frequent and gratifying contact with his children but deeply wanted a more significant role in their lives. He reported experiencing intense feelings of guilt over his decision to divorce the children's mother during their early adolescence. The initial phase of treatment focused on helping him identify his losses and provided clarification and validation of his feelings about them. Once he was able to mourn the loss of expectations for a warm family, this client was able to understand and begin to deal with his feelings. As he worked through his grief, he was able to begin problem solving to reestablish his relationship with his children.

Other losses surfaced during the treatment, particularly those related to his occupational standing and intimate relationships. This client's occupational goals had never been realized. He felt angry and bitter about his work status, often ruminating about his situation. Gradually it became possible for him to discuss his unrealized dreams and mourn his lost expectations. He was also experiencing dissatisfaction in his third marriage yet desperately wanted to preserve it. He was assisted in understanding the strains in this marriage, as well as his contribution to these problems. Subsequently, he decided to seek marital therapy with his wife to resolve these marital difficulties.

Social work treatment with this client involved the identification and resolution of both current and past losses that he had not been able to mourn. His depression was the result of these unresolved losses.

Complicated mourning may occur when grief reactions are delayed or absent. When life events involving loss are not acknowledged, the mourner is at much greater risk for experiencing depression.

A forty-seven-year-old woman reported a long history of personal dissatisfaction and unhappiness. She had recently engaged in several incidents of hitting and punching herself and became alarmed when her husband threatened to leave her if she did not seek treatment. Fearing the loss of her spouse, she reluctantly scheduled an appointment with a social worker. In discussing her past experience, she mentioned she had given up her only child for adoption over twenty-five years earlier when she was a single woman. Only one of her siblings and a close friend were aware of her pregnancy and the adoption, neither of whom had ever again mentioned this event. The woman felt sadness in never having had the opportunity to be a parent and in not knowing her child. She poignantly described the anger and jealousy she felt when seeing families together, enjoying one another's company. She began to recognize that her long-standing depression reflected this loss that she had sustained and never had any opportunity to mourn. Treatment focused on helping her to grieve the loss of her child. She revealed the guilt and anguish that she had felt for so many years and was able to recognize that her inability to talk about the adoption and her fantasies of the child she never knew had been a principal cause of her despair and anger.

Chronic depression or dysthymic conditions often result when significant losses are never mourned. When a loss is discounted, the mourner is unable to express associated painful thoughts and affects and remains incapable of completing the grief work.

Later-Life Losses

Older adults sustain many losses of a physical, social, and psychological nature. (See Chapter 17.) While such losses are normative and expected, they are nonetheless painful, and can result in significant mourning experiences.

Retirement represents the permanent leave from the occupational world. The retiree often experiences substantial loss with this transition. One loses the occupational role, which is a source of identity. The daily rhythms of life revolve around work and define one's time schedule. Work also provides a social network with coworkers, with whom the worker often spends more time with than family members and friends. In our society, occupational standing provides a source of prestige, and those who do not participate in the workforce are often viewed as having lesser social status.

While retirement is generally regarded as a reward for one's life of labor, leaving the workforce requires a significant adaptation to loss, which is inherent in this experience. If older adults are unable to compensate adequately for such losses by developing new daily rhythms, furthering their interests and their social contacts, they may have significant difficulty with this transition. Cox (1988) refers to the concept of "retirement syndrome" as an experience that male retirees in particular may face if unable to compensate for such losses.

As older adults lose their physical vigor, relocating from the family home to smaller living quarters may become necessary. Such a move may allow for continued independence and self-sufficiency, but it also represents a significant loss. The family home and neighborhood are important ties to one's family history, and neighborhood surroundings are reminders of life events involving children, friendships, and daily life patterns.

At times, older adults who are faced with debilitating health conditions must move to nursing homes, a placement that symbolizes a major loss. Decline in health, inevitable in the later years, represents one of the most difficult losses to sustain (O'Connor, 1984). A loss of autonomy often accompanies this decline in health status.

Married couples inevitably lose their life partner, often considered the most significant life loss for the surviving spouse (Lopata, 1972). Social and emotional needs formerly met by the spouse must be met through relationships with others. Living patterns, reflecting the long-term relationship, are altered and significant adjustments are required by the widow or widower to cope with these major life changes.

> *A sixty-eight-year-old retired carpenter seemed unable to develop a satisfying daily schedule since leaving his employment eight months earlier. His wife noticed her husband's sadness and apparent boredom. She had become concerned about his increased drinking, irritability, and excessive sleeping. She told the social worker at the senior citizens' center of her concerns. The social worker encouraged her to bring her husband with her to a weekly lunch at the center, where the social worker could meet with them. When the couple came, the social worker encouraged the man's wife to verbalize her concerns to him and to express her worry about his limited daily activity and alcohol intake. The husband became tearful, acknowledging the difficulty he was having with his retirement and the depression he was experiencing. The social worker helped the husband identify activities that might interest him, as well as provide structure for his day. Over several sessions, the husband had identified various activities, both at home and in the community, which he would initiate. He discussed his former work and how gratifying it had been for him. He then decided to contact his fellow retirees once he was able to acknowledge that he missed their companionship.*

The focus of treatment for this client addressed the losses associated with his retirement. He was assisted in identifying substitute activities. Efforts to increase his self-esteem and to help him expand his social network were major treatment goals.

CONCLUSION

Individuals experience a multiplicity of losses as they move through the life cycle. Although all loss experiences are characterized by some degree of pain, these experiences can also result in opportunities for growth. Following resolution of their loss, mourners often report a heightened sensitivity to others and an increased appreciation for life and human relationships. They may more readily acknowledge others' losses and offer needed support and compassion to mourners. Pollock (1989) suggests that the outcome for some mourners may be the "ability to feel joy, satisfaction, and a sense of accomplishment" (p. 28). Clinicians who work with mourners may also develop new understandings and sensitivities toward individuals and the human experience.

REFERENCES

Baker, J., Sedney, M., & Gross, E. (1992). Psychological tasks for bereaved children. *American Journal of Orthopsychiatry, 68(11)*, 105–116.

Bolton, I. (1986). Death of a child by suicide. In T. Rando (Ed.), *Parental loss of a child* (pp. 201–212). Champagne, IL: Research Press.

Bohannon, J. (1990). Grief responses of spouses following the death of a child: A longitudinal study. *Omega, 22*, 109–121.

Bowen, M. (1976). Family reaction to death. In P. Guerin (Ed.), *Family therapy: Theory and practice* (pp. 335–348). New York: Gardner Press.

Bowlby, J. (1973). *Attachment and loss, Vol. 2: Separation, anxiety, and anger.* New York: Basic Books.

Bowlby, J. (1980). *Attachment and loss, Vol. 3: Loss, sadness, and depression.* New York: Basic Books.

Crenshaw, D. A. (1990). *Bereavement: Counseling the grieving through the life cycle.* New York: Continuum.

Cox, H. G. (1988). *Later life: The realities of aging.* Englewood Cliffs, NJ: Prentice Hall.

DeFrain, J. (1991). Learning about grief from normal families: SIDS, stillbirth, and miscarriage. *Journal of Marital and Family Therapy, 17 (8)*, 215–232.

Doka, K. J. (Ed.). (1989). *Disenfranchised grief: Recognizing hidden sorrow.* Lexington, MA: Lexington Books.

Freud, S. (1917/1957). Mourning and melancholia. In J. Strackey (Ed.), *The standard edition of the complete works of Sigmund Freud* (Vol. 14, pp. 243–258). London: Hogarth Press.

Fulmer, R. H. (1983). A structural approach to unresolved mourning in single parent family systems. *Journal of Marital and Family Therapy. 5*, 51–58.

Furman, E. (1974). *A child's parent dies: Studies in childhood bereavement.* New York: Yale University Press.

Goldman, L. (1994). *Life and loss: A guide to help grieving children.* Muncie, IN: Accelerated Development.

Gould, R. L. (1978). *Transformations: Growth and change in adult life.* New York: Simon & Schuster.

Hare-Mustin, R. (1979). Family therapy following the death of a child. *Journal of Marital and Family Therapy, 5,* 51–58.

Herz, F. (1980). The impact of death and serious illness on the family life cycle. In M. McGoldrick & E. Carter (Eds.), *The family life cycle: A framework for family therapy* (pp. 223–240). New York: Gardner Press.

Imber-Black, E., Roberts, J., & Whiting, R. (1988). *Rituals in families and family therapy.* New York: Norton.

Imber-Black, E. (1991). Rituals and the healing process. In F. Walsh & M. McGoldrick (Eds.), *Living beyond loss: Death in the family* (pp. 207–223). New York: Norton.

Kamerman, J. B. (1988). *Death in the midst of life.* Englewood Cliffs, NJ: Prentice Hall.

Krell, R., & Rabkin, L. (1979). The effects of sibling death on the surviving child: A family perspective. *Family Process, 10,* 471–479.

Levinson, D. J. (1978). *The seasons of a man's life.* New York: Ballantine Books.

Lindemann, E. (1944). Symptomatology and management of acute grief. *American Journal of Orthopsychiatry, 101,* 141–148.

Lopata, H. Z. (1972). *Widowhood in an American city.* Cambridge, MA.: Schenkman.

McGoldrick, M. & Walsh, F. (1991). A time to mourn: Death and the life cycle. In F. Walsh & M. McGoldrick (Eds.), *Living beyond loss: death in the family* (pp. 30–49). New York: Norton.

Miles, M. S., & Demi, A. S. (1991–1992). A comparison of guilt in bereaved parents whose children died by suicide, accident or chronic illness. *Omega, 24(3),* 203–215.

Mishne, J. (1992). The grieving child: Manifest and hidden losses in childhood and adolescence. *Child and Adolescent Social Work Journal, 9(6),* 471–490.

Neimeyer, R. A. (1988). Death anxiety. In H. Waas, F. Berardo, & R. A. Neimeyer (Eds.), *Dying: Facing the facts* (pp. 97–136). Washington, DC: Hemisphere Publishing Co.

Neugarten, B. L. (1976). Adaption and the life course. *Counseling Psychologist, 6(1),* 16–20.

Nichols, J. A. (1990). Perinatal grief: Bereavement issues. In J. A. Nichols (Ed.), *Unrecognized and unsanctioned grief: The nature and counseling of unacknowledged loss* (pp. 19–29). Springfield, IL: Charles C. Thomas Pub.

O'Connor, N. (1984). *Letting go with love: The grieving process.* Apache Junction, AZ: La Mariposa Press.

Paul, N. (1967). The role of mourning and empathy in conjoint marital therapy. In G. Zuk & I. Boszormenyi (Eds.), *Family therapy and disturbed families* (pp. 186–205). Palo Alto: Science and Behavioral Books.

Piper, W., McCallum, M., & Hassan, F. (1992). *Adaptation to loss through short-term group therapy.* New York: Guilford.

Pollock, G. H. (1961). Mourning and adaption. *International Journal of Psycho-Analysis, 42,* 341–361.

Pollock, G. H. (1989). The mourning process, the creative process, and the creation. In D. Deitrich & P. C. Sabad (Eds.), *The problem of loss and mourning: Psychoanalytic perspectives* (pp. 27–60). Madison, WI: International Universities Press.

Rando, T. (1984). *Grief, dying and death: Clinical interventions for caregivers.* Champaign, IL: Research Press.

Rando, T. (1986). *Parental loss of a child.* Champaign, IL: Research Press.

Rando, T. (1993). *Treatment of complicated mourning.* Champaign, IL: Research Press.

Rosen, H. (1991). Child and adolescent bereavement. *Child and Adolescent Social Work Journal, 8(1),* 5–16.

Schumacher, J. (1984). Helping children cope with a sibling's death. In J. Hansen (Ed.), *Death and grief in the family* (pp. 82–94). Rockville, MD: Aspen.

Stierlin, H. Rucker-Emblen, I., Weitzel, N., & Winching, M. (1980). *The first interview with the family.* New York: Brunner/Mazel.

Vess, J., Moreland, J., & Schwebel, A. (1985, 1986). Understanding family role reallocation following a death: A theoretical framework. *Omega, 19* (2), 116–127.

Videka-Sherman, L. (1982). Coping with the death of a child: A study over time. *American Journal of Orthopsychiatry, 52*, 688–698.

Waas, H., & Stillion, J. M. (1988). Death in the lives of children and adolescents. In H. Waas, F. Berardo, & R. A. Neimeyer (Eds.), *Dying: Facing the facts* (pp. 201–229). Washington, DC: Hemisphere Publishing Co.

Wallerstein, J. S., & Kelly, J. B. (1980). *Surviving the breakup: How children and parents cope with divorce.* New York: Basic Books.

Walsh, F. (1978). Concurrent grandparent death and birth of a schizophrenic offspring: An intriguing finding, *Family Process, 17*, 457–463.

Walsh, F., & McGoldrick, M. (1991). Loss and the family: A systemic perspective. In F. Walsh & M. McGoldrick (Eds.), *Living beyond loss: Death in the family* (pp. 1–29). New York: Norton.

Worden, J. (1991). *Grief counseling and grief therapy* (2nd ed.). New York: Springer Publishing Co.

Yalom, I. D. (1985). *The theory and practice of group psychotherapy.* New York: Basic Books.

Index